HISTORY OF MODERN EUROPE SINCE 1789

For Students of B.A., M.A. and Aspirants of Competitive Examinations

V D MAHAJAN
MA (Hons.), LLB, PhD
Formerly Professor
History and Political Science
Punjab University, Lahore
and
Faculty of Law
University of Delhi

S. CHAND PUBLISHING

S Chand And Company Limited

(ISO 9001 Certified Company)

S Chand And Company Limited

(ISO 9001 Certified Company)

Head Office: D-92, Sector–2, Noida – 201301, U.P. (India), Ph. 91-120-4682700

Registered Office: A-27, 2nd Floor, Mohan Co-operative Industrial Estate, New Delhi – 110 044, Phone: 011-49731800

www.**schandpublishing.com**; e-mail: **info@schandpublishing.com**

S. CHAND PUBLISHING

Marketing Offices:

Chennai	:	Ph: 23632120; chennai@schandpublishing.com
Guwahati	:	Ph: 2738811, 2735640; guwahati@schandpublishing.com
Hyderabad	:	Ph: 40186018; hyderabad@schandpublishing.com
Jalandhar	:	Ph: 4645630; jalandhar@schandpublishing.com
Kolkata	:	Ph: 23357458, 23353914; kolkata@schandpublishing.com
Lucknow	:	Ph: 4003633; lucknow@schandpublishing.com
Mumbai	:	Ph: 25000297; mumbai@schandpublishing.com
Patna	:	Ph: 2260011; patna@schandpublishing.com

First Edition 1959
Subsequent Editions and Reprints 1978, 81, 83, 85, 86, 88, 89, 91, 92, 95, 97, 98, 2007, 2008, 2009, 2011, 2012
Revised Edition 2013
Reprints 2014, 2015, 2018, 2021 (Twice), 2022 (Twice)

Reprint 2023 (Twice)

ISBN: 978-81-219-0338-7 **Product Code:** H5MEU41HIST10ENAN13O

PRINTED IN INDIA

By Vikas Publishing House Private Limited, Plot 20/4, Site-IV, Industrial Area Sahibabad, Ghaziabad – 201 010 and Published by S Chand And Company Limited, A-27, 2nd Floor, Mohan Co-operative Industrial Estate, New Delhi – 110 044.

Dedicated
to
Prof. J. F. Bruce
Who Taught me
European History

Preface To The Fourteenth Revised Edition

The Fourteenth Revised Edition of "**History of Modern Europe Since 1789**" is a boon for the students.

There were The Great Personalities of the Revolution before the rise of Napoleon. The first in the list is the name of Mirabeau. There was The Vienna Settlement of 1815 which was based on the three principles like restoration, legitimacy and compensation. There was independence of Belgium which came after the fall of Napolean, the ruler of Holland were restored and given a new constitution of the people. The rest of the errors have been rectified. The modified maps have been placed in the proper place. The study of this book will give the view that Europe was an extremely strong nation.

It is our earnest hope that students and teachers will find the revised edition very much beneficial. At last the precious suggestions and critical comments for the improvement in the subsequent edition by the readers are very much welcome. The book is reformatted and published in bigger size.

AUTHOR

Preface To The Thirteenth Edition

I have great pleasure in placing the fourteenth edition of the book in the hands of the readers. In this edition I have rewritten the chapter on "The Cold War" and added a new Chapter on "German Revolution and the Weimer Republic (1918-1933)." I have no doubt that these additions have added to the utility of the book.

I have always held the view that a study of the history of Modern Europe is very essential for the people of my country. The reason is that revolutionary changes took place in Europe during the period covered by this book and those changes affected profoundly the whole of the world. There was the unification of Germany and Italy during the nineteenth century. There was the Industrial Revolution in Europe which changed the face of the whole world. There was the expansion of Europe in all parts of the world. There was the disintegration of the Turkish Empire and the emergence of the Balkan States as independent entities. There was also the disintegration of the once great Empire of Austria-Hungary which should serve as a warning and lesson to the leaders and people of India who are wasting all their energy and time in wresting power from one another. A study of the History of Modern Europe is both instructive and inspiring.

A study of this history shows that both individuals and nations had to make tremendous sacrifices to achieve their goals. They worked very hard to achieve what they can rightly be proud of. We can learn a lesson from Europe that no country can safeguard its territorial integrity unless it puts great emphasis on her defence. Defence preparedness is essential in the modern world and that is not possible without industrialising our country. It has been found from experience that industrialisation and defence-preparedness go together. There is a race going on in the world and each nation is inventing its own weapons and we in this country cannot and must not rely upon the weapons bought or got from other countries. It is rightly pointed out that the Northern States succeeded against the Southern States in the Civil War (1861-65) in the United States as the Northern States were industrialised while the Southern States were not.

We must not forget that it is only a strong nation which is respected in the world and can have a say in the affairs of the world. All this is possible only if the people of India work very hard and produce surplus wealth which can be used for military preparedness. We must subordinate our individual interests to those of the country. We must always remember that nobody will die if India lives.

I thank once again all those who have patronised this book. This gives me the satisfaction that my labours have been appreciated.

D-805, New Friends Colony,
New Delhi-65
November 1, 1985

VIDYA DHAR MAHAJAN

CONTENTS

CHAPTER

1 EUROPE ON THE EVE OF FRENCH REVOLUTION

Condition of Europe in General

With the outbreak of the French Revolution, "European, history merges into the history of one nation, one event and one man; the nation is **France, the event is the French Revolution and the man is Napoleon."** However, before we deal with the French Revolution itself, it is desirable to refer to the condition of Europe on the eve of that great event in European history.

Generally speaking, Europe was organised aristocratically. This was true not only in the case of monarchies but also in the case of Republics. The Republic of Venice was governed by an oligarchy and the same was the case with Switzerland. Even in England where Parliament was strong, the power rested not with the people but with the landed aristocracy. Parliament itself was controlled by big landlords. The man in the street still did not count. If this was true of England, the same was the case in other European countries like Austria-Hungary, Prussia, Russia, France, Spain, Poland, etc. In most of the European countries, the rulers were despots although during the 18th century they were called enlightened despots. The people had no hand in the administration of the country. They did not enjoy any personal liberty and everything depended upon the whims of the rulers. Serfdom prevailed almost everywhere in Europe.

European rulers at that time were dishonest and unprincipled. International morality reached its lowest ebb during the 18th century. A man like Frederick, the Great, did not hesitate to annex Silesia in spite of his promises to Charles VI, the father of Maria Theresa. Russia, Prussia, and Austria conspired among themselves to put an end to the very existence of Poland. There was a general craze for territorial expansion at the expense of the weaker neighbours. "No consideration was paid to race limits or national boundaries." In the words of Prof. Holland Rose, "That respect of dynastic rights and treaty obligations which generally held sway when Christendom was more than a name, now gave place to a state policy which avowedly aimed at little else but gain of territory or markets." Prof. Hazen says, "The old regime in Europe was disloyal to the very principles on which it rested" and those principles were respect for the established order and regard for regality and engagements.

All over Europe there were privileged classes which were completely or partially exempted from taxation and the burden of taxation fell on the unprivileged classes. The rich paid less to the state and the main burden fell on the poor. European society was organised on a feudal basis and the landlords acted like petty sovereigns in the localities. The serfs were attached to the land and most of the proceeds from land went into the pockets of the landlords. The condition of the serfs was miserable. To quote, "The great sub-structure of European society was an unhappy, unfree, unprotected, undeveloped mass of human beings, to whom an opportunity for growth and improvement was closed on every side." While a few enjoyed privileges, the others suffered. Inequality in every field weakened the very foundations of the social system. There was hardly any awakening among the masses of Europe and thus the system continued.

As regards the religious condition of Europe, Western and Central Europe were roughly divided between a Protestant North and a Roman Catholic South. In the Centre, people of Switzerland and

Savoy were Protestants. The people of Ireland and Poland were Catholics. In Eastern Europe, the Orthodox or Greek Church held sway over Russia and the Balkans. The Jews were found all over Europe. In some places, they were tolerated, while at others persecuted.

Europe was not free from religious strife but religious toleration was making headway. It was felt that persons of different faiths could be the loyal subjects of the state. The growth of humanitarianism also played its part. The spread of the spirit of scientific inquiry made for tolerance. There was the decline of dogmatic religion.

The Roman Catholic Church was attacked and its position was weakened. In 1763 was published a book entitled **On the Present State of the Church and the Lawful Authority of the Roman Pontiff**. This was written by a Roman Catholic bishop. It denied the authority of the Pope over the bishops. Joseph II was influenced by this book and he made the Church subordinate to his authority. The Pope was forced to modify the famous Bill of 1713 against the Janenists in France. In 1759, the Jesuits were turned out from Portugal. In 1764, their Order was suppressed in France. In 1767, they were expelled from Spain, Sicily and Parma. In 1773, the Pope abolished the Order of the Jesuits. The Jesuits got protection only in Russia and Prussia.

Germany. As regards the political condition of Europe, there were a large number of states which were struggling for expansion and supremacy. Germany was disunited and weak. There were more than 360 sovereign states and their only bond of union was their inclusion in the Holy Roman Empire. The Holy Roman Emperor came from Austria-Hungary for the last many centuries. There was an Imperial Diet to regulate the internal affairs of the Holy Roman Empire, but it was not strong enough to accomplish anything. Voltaire pointed out that the Holy Roman Empire was neither **Holy** nor **Roman** nor an **Empire.** The affairs of Germany were controlled by Austria and Prussia and both of them were deadly enemies of each other.

Prussia. As regards Prussia, its prestige had been raised very high during the reign of Frederick, the Great, who ruled from 1740 to 1786. It was he who annexed Silesia and in spite of the efforts of Maria Theresa during the War of Austrian Succession and the Seven Years' War to get back the same, Frederick was able to retain it notwithstanding heavy odds against him. Although Catherine, the Great, wanted to annex the whole of Poland herself, Frederick persuaded Austria to join hands with him to force Russia to give them a part of the spoils. The result was that when the first partition of Poland took place in 1772, Frederick was able to get West Prussia as a part of his share. With the help of West Prussia, Frederick was able to link up East Prussia with the rest of his territories and thereby establish the territorial continuity of Prussia. Frederick also prevented Austria from acquiring Bavaria by exchanging it with the Austrian Netherlands or Belgium. He also formed the Frustenband or the League of German Princes with a view to putting a check on the power of Austria in Germany. Frederick was absolutely unscrupulous in his dealings with other countries. He followed a policy of expediency which was explained by him in these words: "Take what you can, you are never wrong unless you are obliged to give back." "If there is anything to be gained by being honest, honest we will be; and if it is necessary to deceive, let us be scoundrels." Regarding the conquest of Silesia, he observed: "My soldiers were ready, my purse was full." Again, "Silesia was that part which was most useful to the House of Brandenberg."

As regards his home policy, he promoted the material resources of the country. He improved agriculture by draining marshes. He constructed new canals. He encouraged industries by giving subsidies. He worked day and night to bring about the material prosperity of his country. He followed a policy of religious toleration and was prepared to allow even the Turks to come to Prussia, if they could add to the prosperity of his country.

When Frederick died at the age of 74, he left behind him a kingdom which was nearly double in size with a population more than doubled. He considered himself as the first servant of the state.

However, he always thought more of Prussia and not of Germany. He considered the German language as a "Jargon devoid of every grace." In spite of that he was regarded throughout Germany as a great national hero and he captured the imagination of the people of Germany in the same way as Luther had done before.

Frederick did not rule Europe of the whole world, but he was the most celebrated king of his time. His principles and methods of "enlightened despotism" were admired and copied by half the rulers of his day. When he died, a peasant pronounced his epitaph in these words: **"Who is now** to rule the world ?"

After the death of Frederick, the Great, in 1786, Frederick William II came to the throne. He was a man of feeble intellect and vacillating nature. He was opposed to both Austria and Russia. When the French Revolution broke out in 1789, Prussia was interested more in the affairs of Poland than those of France.

Austria-Hungary. The Habsburgs ruled in Austria-Hungary. Their Emperor was also the Emperor of the Holy Roman Empire. However, this state was not very strong because the territories were scattered and there were people of many nationalities within the Empire. There was no solidarity on account of their racial, religious and linguistic differences. The bond of union between the Bohemians, Hungarians, Netherlanders, Milanese and Austrians was a very weak one.

Maria Theresa was the ruler of Austria from 1740 to 1780. She was a woman of lofty character and high spirits. She was one of the greatest women rulers of modern times, comparable to Queen Victoria of England. Her husband was the Emperor but she was the real ruler. She was kind, generous and beautiful. She was loved by Germans, Magyars, and Slavs. All of her subjects thronged to kiss her hand at the palace on New Year's Day. She was an able ruler and vigorous reformer. It was she who made the Austrian army march in step for the first time. Even Frederick, the Great, admitted that her measures were worthy of a man. It is true that she lost Silesia to Prussia but she left no stone unturned to recover the same. She had her share of the partitioning of Poland.

She was succeeded by **Joseph II** who became the Holy Roman Emperor in 1765 after the death of his father. He inherited the dominions of the House of Austria in 1780 on the death of his mother. He was a typical enlightened despot. He was industrious and conscientious. He worked day and night for the improvement of his people. His object was to unite all the dominions of the House of Austria by abolishing all differences of race, language and religion. He aimed at welding together the various races of his Empire into one Austrian Nation. He abolished the old territorial divisions and redivided the whole of his Empire into 13 provinces. Each province was put under a military commander. Provinces were divided into districts and towns and a uniform system of government was set up in all of them. German was declared to be the official language all over the Empire. The judicial system was overhauled. A uniform code of law was prescribed for the whole country and the people were guaranteed equality before law, freedom of press and religious toleration. He founded a large number of schools. He abolished all privileges of the nobles and the clergymen and everyone was required to pay a tax of 13 per cent on his land. He tried to bring the Church under the control of the state and lessen the control of the Pope. The control of the clergymen in educational field was lessened. He practically abolished serfdom within his Empire.

However, his reforms were carried out in a hurry, unmindful of the sentiments and traditions of the people. The people were not ready for chose reforms. Joseph II boasted that he had made **philosophy the architect of his Empire,** but by doing so he committed a blunder. He ought to have known that philosophical ideas rarely find a place in the practical life of the people. It was impossible to force the people to rise to the high ideals which were set for them by the genius of Joseph II. The result was that all his reforms failed. His attempt to consolidate his Empire almost brought about its dissolution. The Empire of Austria-Hungary was a polyglot Empire and it was impossible to create out of it a homogeneous state. Joseph II was trying to do the impossible, and no wonder he failed. However, he had the courage to cancel all his reforms before his death. To quote, "In the most courageous act of the reformer's career, he decreed the revocation of his entire work."

It is said about Joseph II that "he does not know how to eat or drink or amuse himself or to read anything but official reports." In spite of that he failed because, as Frederick said, "he took the second step before he took the first." Joseph himself suggested the following for his epitaph, "Here lies a prince who, with the best of intentions, failed in all he attempted."

A reference may be made to the foreign policy of Joseph II. The main object of his foreign policy was to re-establish the supremacy of the Habsburgs in Germany and also to readjust the boundaries of his Empire. Joseph II co-operated with Prussia in the first partition of Poland to prevent Russia from annexing the whole of Poland. Along with Russia, and Prussia, Joseph II got a share of the spoils. He was also able to get Bukovina from the Turks. He forced Holland to give up the barrier fortresses which were allowed to be garrisoned by her by the Treaty of Utrecht of 1713. He unsuccessfully tried to throw open the river Scheldt. He entered into an alliance with Russia to check the growing influence of Prussia. He tried to exchange the Austrian Netherlands with Bavaria but failed to do so on account of the opposition of Prussia. He also declared war against the Turks with a view to dismembering Turkey. However, he did not succeed in his mission on account of the hostile attitude of Prussia. Prussia, England and Holland entered in a Triple Alliance to help the Turks and in 1791, Leopold II, who came to the throne of Austria in 1790, retired from the war.

The Austrian Empire was in a state of intense ferment on the eve of the French Revolution. She was not only interested in the affairs of France but was also concerned over the intrigues of Russia and Prussia in Poland. This divided attention was in the interests of the cause of the French Revolution.

Russia. Catherine, the Great, was the ruler of Russia from 1762 to 1796. She was a very clever and crooked woman and she followed in the footsteps of Peter, the Great. She was an enlightened despot. She took pleasure in the company of the learned persons of Europe and patronised literary persons like Diderot. She set up a very efficient system of administration but otherwise did not care much for the lot of the people. No freedom was given to the people in any field and her word was law in every sphere.

Her foreign policy was directed against Poland and Turkey. The war between Russia and Turkey started in 1768. The Turks were defeated and forced to evacuate Moldavia and Wallachia. The war was ended by the Treaty of Kutchuk-Kainardji in 1774. By this treaty, Russia got Azoff and a number of other places which gave her control over the northern shore of the Black Sea and also over the Sea of Azoff. The Black Sea was opened to Russian navigation. The independence of the Crimea was recognised. Russia was to have her Consuls in Turkey. Russian subjects were to be allowed to visit the holy places in Palestine. Russia was given the right to interfere in the internal affairs of Turkey to protect the Greek Christian subjects of Turkey. Peace between Turkey and Russia did not last long and war was renewed in 1787. At this time, Catherine joined hands with Joseph II to Austria to dismember Turkey. Austria was forced to withdraw from the war in 1791 on account of the Triple Alliance between England, Prussia and Holland. However, Russia carried on the war alone which was ended in 1792 by the Treaty of Jassy. By this treaty Turkey recognized the Russian annexation of Crimea. Thus she lost her control over the northern coast of the Black Sea up to the river Dniester.

Catherine, the Great, played the most important part in the three partitions of Poland in 1772, 1793 and 1795. Her original idea was to annex the whole of Poland but both Prussia and Austria joined hands to force her to give them a part of the spoils in 1772. As regards the partition of 1793, Austria got no share but Prussia got something. In the third partition of Poland in 1795, Russia got the lion's share, although both Prussia and Austria also got their shares. It cannot be denied that Catherine, the Great, raised the prestige of Russia in Europe. Her achievements can be summed up in her own words thus: **"I came to Russia as a poor girl; Russia has dowered me richly, but I have paid her back with Azov, the Crimea and the Ukraine."**

Great Britain. The Hanoverians ruled England. In accordance with the provisions of the Act of Settlement, George I ascended the throne of England in 1714 after the death of Queen Anne. He was succeeded in 1727 by his son George II who ruled up to 1760. It was during the reign of George I and George II that the Whig oligarchy ruled in England. It was during that period that the cabinet system was put on a stable basis. The office of Prime Minister came into existence under Walpole. England had to fight the Jenkin's Ear War, the War of Austrian Succession and the Seven Years' War. The Seven Years' War was still in progress when George III came to the throne in 1760. He ruled up to 1820. He differed from his father and grandfather in many respects. He was born and brought up in England and glorified in that fact. From the very beginning, he was determined to set up his personal rule. Pitt, the Elder, resigned in 1761 and Lord Bute, King's own tutor, acted as Prime Minister from 1761 to 1763. From 1760 to 1770, George III followed the policy of creating dissensions among the Whigs and also giving training to his own friends whom he could trust. Having accomplished this by 1770, he appointed Lord North as his Prime Minister and the latter occupied that position up to 1782. It was during this period that the dispute with English colonies in North America took a serious turn and the War of American Independence started. England was defeated and she had to recognise the independence of the American colonies by the Treaty of Versailles of 1783. In December 1783, Pitt, the Younger, was appointed Prime Minister and he held that office up to 1806 with some break. When the French Revolution broke out in 1789, Pitt, the Younger, was at the helm of affairs in England. The Industrial Revolution and the Agrarian Revolution were making a lot of progress in England and as a result England was leading Europe in the field of agriculture and industrial production. France was destined to get the greatest amount of opposition from England.

Poland. Poland was a very powerful State during the 16th and 17th centuries and she was responsible for saving Vienna which was besieged by the Turks in 1683. She saved not only Germany but the whole of Europe from the danger of Turkish domination. However, she began to decline from the 18th century and her very name was removed from the map of Europe towards the end of the century. That was due to many causes.

Polish monarchy was elective and the result was that after the death of every king, there were intrigues and the neighbouring countries got an opportunity to interfere in the internal affairs of Poland. The Great Powers had their own groups in Poland which backed their interests. Those groups owed their allegiance to their foreign patrons and were prepared to subordinate the interests of their own country to those of their patrons. At the time of the election of a Polish king, the nobles of Poland managed to get a large number of concessions and this process was repeated on the occasion of the election of every king. The nobles managed to get a large number of privileges and concessions and consequently the position of the king became very weak. As a matter of fact, real power was in the hands of the nobles. Moreover, the election of foreign princes as the kings of Poland added to her difficulties. Those princes brought their own dominions along with them when they became kings of Poland and consequently Poland was unnecessarily dragged into European politics.

Another unfortunate institution of Poland was the **Liberum Veto** by which even one member of the Polish Diet had the power to veto any bill in Parliament. The result was that no legislation could be passed unless there was unanimity in the Diet. This was impossible to secure because the other Powers which were interested in the fall of Poland, could easily manage to win over a few nobles to oppose the progressive legislation in the country. The Liberum Veto was the most absurd thing and proved to be fatal. This gentlemen's agreement was the most stupid political instrument which could not be found in any sane country. The nobles insisted on it on account of their vanity and pride, unmindful of its consequences.

There was too much inequality in Poland. While on the one side the nobles had all their privileges, the condition of the peasants was simply deplorable. The result was too much bitterness in the society. Under the circumstances, there was no solidarity in Polish society and that considerably weakened the strength of the country. Religious differences added to the difficulties of Polish patriots. The Polish Protestants were cruelly persecuted by the Catholics. Racial differences also were responsible for the lack of homogeneity in Polish society. There were many elements in Poland who looked up to foreign countries for help and support for their independence. Unluckily, Poland had no geographical unity and the various parts of the Polish kingdom did not consider themselves as the parts of a single organism. Poland had no natural boundaries of rivers or mountains and consequently it was difficult for her to defend herself from foreigners. It was unlucky for Poland that during the second half of the 18th century some very unscrupulous persons were the rulers of the neighbouring states. Both Catherine, the Great, and Frederick, the Great, were absolutely unscrupulous in their dealings, and no wonder Poland met her doom at their hands.

Both Catherine, the Great, and Frederick, the Great, had their eyes on Poland. To begin with, they tried to exclude the House of Saxony from the throne of Poland. They got their opportunity in 1763 when Augustus III, King of Poland, died. Both Russia and Prussia put pressure on the Polish nobles and got their nominee elected. The new King of Poland was Stanislaus Poniatowsky who was a great favourite of Catherine. Having put their nominee on the throne of Poland, preparations were made for the partition of the country. The patriots of Poland resented the influence of Russia and formed a League to resist the same. War started between Russia and Poland and Russia was able to break the resistance of the Poles. Frederick proposed the partition of Poland but the proposal was rejected by Catherine who wanted to have the whole of Poland for herself. However, the opportunity of Frederick came when war started between Russia and Turkey. When Austria and Prussia joined hands, Russia agreed to the partition of Poland. The first partition took place in 1772. By this partition, Russia got Livonia and a part of Lithuania and thus advanced up to the Duna and Dnieper. Prussia got West Prussia and Austria got Zips and Red Russia (Galicia). On the attitude of Maria Theresa, the cynical remark of Frederick, the Great, was that **"she weeps but takes all the same."**

After the first partition of 1772, Poland became dependent on Russia and for some time the patriots of Poland could do nothing on account of an alliance between Russia and Prussia. Things improved after 1781 on account of an alliance between Prussia and Austria which was more friendly to Poland than Prussia. In 1787, there started a war between Russia and Turkey. In 1788 was formed the Triple Alliance which aimed at checking the ambitions of Russia and Austria. The Polish Diet met in 1788 and decided to carry out certain reforms. Unfortunately, the work ol reforms was delayed because the King of Poland was afraid of Russia and also because the Polish nobles were not in favour of reforms. Opposition came from Prussia also. According to the reforms of 1791, Kingship was to be hereditary in the family of the Elector of Saxony. The Polish king was to control the army and the executive. The Liberum Veto was to be abolished. Religious toleration was to be given to all. Russia resented these reforms and decided to take action against Poland. She also encouraged Austria and Prussia to take interest in the French Revolution so that she might be able to have her own way in Poland. Prussia also gave up her friendly attitude towards Poland and no wonder the Poles resented this change of attitude. The attitude of Austria was friendly. It was in this atmosphere that Russia attacked Poland and defeated the Poles. The latter were forced to cancel the new reforms. They got no help either from Austria or Prussia and all their resistance collapsed. **Poland** was partitioned for the second time in 1793. Austria got nothing. **Russia** got Eastern Poland including Minsk, Podolia, Volhynia and Little Russia and Prussia got Danzig, Thorn, Rosen, Genezen and Kalisch. Russia got four times as much territory and twice as many new subjects as Prussia. The partition revealed the shameless selfishness of the Powers and their utter distrust of one another. Austria strongly resented the partition which was made without her approval and which brought the Russian territory into touch with the Austrian dominions. The relations between Austria and Prussia were strained.

Russia strengthened her position in Poland and the king of Poland became a mere agent of the Russian Minister at Warsaw. The Poles resented the partition and secret societies were set up to regain their independence and carry out the necessary reforms. In 1794, Russia demanded the disbandment of the Polish troops, but that demand was rejected. There were revolts and the Russians were turned out from many places in Poland. Russia attacked Poland and defeated her. All opposition was crushed. It was then that the **third partition of Poland took place in 1795.** According to it, Russia got the land between Galicia and the Lower Duna covering about 2,000 sq. miles of territory. Austria got Cracow and the rest of Galicia and her share included about 1,000 sq. miles of territory in all. Prussia received Warsaw and the land between Bug and the Dnieper, about 700 sq. miles of territory in all. By a treaty of January 1797, Russia, Prussia and Austria asserted "the necessity of abolishing everything which may recall the memory of the existence of the kingdom of Poland."

Guedalla says that the partitioning of Poland was the most shameless and barren act of European diplomacy. It was shameless because it was against the canons of international morality and justice. It was barren because it brought no strength to those countries which received their shares of spoils. The Poles never reconciled themselves to the partition of their country and continued their struggle relentlessly till they got their freedom in the 20th century. The Polish territories in the possession of Russia, Prussia and Austria remained free undigested fragments in three stomachs. The partition of Poland was "a vast national crime". However, the interference of the Great Powers in the affairs of Poland helped the cause of the French Revolution. France was able to maintain her independence because her enemies were divided on the question of Poland and consequently could not take any concerted action against her.

Italy. Italy at that time was merely a geographical expression and was divided into a large number of states. In the north, there was the kingdom of Savoy with Sardinia, the two republics of Geneva and Venice and four duchies of Milan, Parma, Modena and Lucca. In the south were the duchy of Tuscany, the Papal States including Rome and Naples along with Sicily. Corsica went to France in 1769.

After the War of Spanish Succession, Austria succeeded Spain as the dominating power in Italy. Austria had Milan in direct sovereignty. The house of Emperor Francis held Tuscany. Austria exercised a measure of control over Parma, Modena and Lucca. She also cast her hungry eyes on Venice.

It is true that the states of Italy were independent but that did not mean much. The glories of Genoa and Venice were over. The Papal States were the worst governed States in Europe. Naples was very backward. However, Tuscany was the best governed State in Europe. In 1737, Francis, Husband of Maria Theresa, succeeded to the throne of Tuscany. His work was continued by his son, Leopold (1765—90). Serfdom was ended and feudal rights were limited. The Inquisition was abolished. The powers of the Clerical Courts were reduced. Torture was abolished. The annual budget was published. Thus, Tuscany became a model to Italy and Europe.

The most promising feature of the situation in Italy was the steady growth of the house of Savoy. It is true that Savoy (or Sardinia) was not prepared at that time to take the lead in any Italian movement but she developed considerable ability in exploiting her strategic position. She joined sometimes one power and sometimes another and at times was in danger of being crushed. However, she was able to enlarge and consolidate her territories in a manner pregnant for the future.

"Italy (said a French observer about this time) has seven or eight centres of civilization. The simplest action is performed in an entirely different way in Turin and Venice, Milan or Genoa, Bologna or Florence, Rome or Naples. Venice is gay and frank whilst Turin is surely aristocratic, Milanese good humour is as familiar as Genoese meanness. The Bolognese are full of fire, passion, generosity, and sometimes imprudence. As for the Neapolitan, he is the servant of the whim of the moment".

Spain. Spain was a great country during the 16th century under Charles V and Philip II. She became a second-rate power during the course of the 17th century. Reactionary forces directed the destiny of the country. After the War of Spanish Succession, the grandson of Louis XIV of France was recognised the ruler of Spain. In 1761, Spain entered the Seven Years' War on the side of France.

A series of reforms were carried out by ministers like Albernoi and Patino. In the time of Charles III, further reforms were carried out by which the legal system was reformed, brigandage was suppressed, the severity of the Inquisition was lessened, the Jesuits were turned out from the country, and the economic development of the country progressed. An impetus was given to the intellectual life of the country also. The new king, Charles IV, was a weak and unsteady person.

Portugal. Under Pombal, the minister of Joseph I, a large number of reforms were carried out by which industry was expanded, education was encouraged and secularized, the power of the Pope was reduced and the jurisdiction of the Inquisition was curtailed.

SUGGESTED READINGS

Bourne, H.C. : **The Revolutionary Period in Europe, 1763–1815.**

Bruun, G. : **The Enlightened Despots.**

Fisher, H.A.L. : **A History of Europe.**

Gooch, G.P. : **Louis XV: The Monarchy in Decline, 1956.**

Gottschalk, L.R. : **The Era of the French Revolution, 1715–1815.**

Gottschalk, Louis and Lach, Donald : **Europe and the Modern World, 1962.**

Goldsmith, M. : **Frederick, the Great.**

Grant and Temperley : **Europe in the Nineenth and Twentieth Centuries.**

Hayes, G.J.H. : **A Political and Cultural History of Modern Europe & Vols. I & II.**

Johnson, A.: **The Age of the Enlightened Despots.**

Ketelbey, C.D.M.: **A History of Modern Times.**

Lowell: **Eve of the French Revolution.**

Macaulay (Lord) : **Essay on Frederick, the Great.**

Marriott, J.A.R. & Robertson, C.G.: **The Evolution of Prussia.**

Phillips, W.A. : **Modern Europe.**

Robinson & Beard : **Readings in Modern European History.**

CHAPTER

2 CAUSES OF THE FRENCH REVOLUTION

The French Revolution was a great event in the history not only of France and Europe but also of mankind. It gave to humanity new ideas of liberty, equality and fraternity which have found their way in every nook and corner of the world. It was as much a war of bayonets as that of ideas[1] and it seems desirable to refer to some of its important causes[2].

(1) **Social cause.** The most important cause of the French Revolution was the social cause. **"The Revolution of 1789 was much less a rebellion against despotism, than a rebellion against inequality."** There was too much of inequality in French society on the eve of the French Revolution. French society was divided into two parts: the privileged and the unprivileged. The privileged part consisted of the nobility and the clergy. Both of them formed a small minority of the total population of the country. In the total population of 24 millions, there were 150,000 nobles and 130,000 clergymen. Roughly, their combined strength was about one per cent. In spite of their smallness in size they excelled all others in the matter of rank, possessions and privileges. A noble was addressed as "My Lord", "Your Grace", etc. The man in the street was required to salute him as his superior. Ordinarily, his coach was decorated with an ancestral coat of arms. The best seats were reserved for him both in the church and in the theatre. He was not expected to marry below his class. He had a monopoly of practically all the jobs in the army and the Church. Every noble left to his son either a castle or a mansion and also a lot of territory from which he could collect taxes. Montesquieu, a nobleman himself, wrote thus: **"A great noble is a man who sees the king, speaks to his minister and who possesses ancestors, debts and pensions."**

Lafayette has given a vivid picture of the young nobles of France in these words: "We are scornful critics of the old customs, of the feudal pride of our fathers and of their severe etiquette, and everything that was old seemed annoying and ridiculous to us....Voltaire attracted our intellect and Rousseau touched our hearts. We took secret pleasure in seeing them attack the old framework, which appeared antiquated and ridiculous to us... We enjoyed, at the same time, the advantages of the patriciate and the amenities of a plebeian philosophy." The nobility of France was destined for destruction. Their internal strifes destroyed their solemnity. As they were disunited, they fell before the superior strength of the commoners. Enlightened public opinion condemned the wasteful parasitic existence of the nobility. The peasants denied the legitimacy of the entire manorial system. The middle

---

1. According to Kropotkin, "The Great Revolution, that set all Europe astir, that overthrew everything, and began the task of universal reconstruction in the course of a few years, was like the working of cosmic forces dissolving and re-creating a world."

2. According to Kropotkin, "Two great currents prepared and made the Great French Revolution. One of them, the current of ideas, concerning the political reorganisation of States, came from the middle classes; the other, the current of action, came from the people, both peasants and workers in towns, who wanted to obtain immediate and definite improvements in their economic condition. And when these two currents met and joined in the endeavour to realise an aim which for some time was common to both, when they had helped each other for a certain time, the result was the Revolution." **(The Great French Revolution, p. I).**

classes denounced the social discrimination, the fiscal immunities and the innumerable privileges of the nobility which kept capital out of circulation, shackled trade and crippled industry.

Like the nobles, the clergymen also occupied a privileged position. They competed with worldly men in the field of riches, lands and luxuries. The clergymen had castles, cathedrals, palaces, invaluable pictures, golden chalices, rich vestments and rentals from land in the form of tithes. The Cardinal of Rohan had income of 25 million livres.

The Archbishop of Strasbourg had an income of 300,000 dollars a year. He held a court in a splendid palace and entertained 200 guests at a time. Even the sauce-pans of his kitchens were made of silver. There were 180 horses in his stables for the pleasure of his guests.

The Roman Catholic Church in France was a state within the state. It was an intolerable despotism. It was discredited by the quarrels between the Jansenists and Jesuits. It was dishonoured by the worldliness and corruption. It was sapped by wealth, privileges and monopoly. It was undermined from within and without by scepticism and atheism. There was little in common between the wealthy clergy and the parish priests except common sin. Most of the income of the Church went to the higher clergy, *i.e.*, 134 bishops and archbishops, and a small number of abbots, canons and other dignitaries. The total number did not exceed five or six thousands. There was so much of extravagance among the clergymen that the moral sense of the nation was shocked and the people felt indignant. While rejecting the candidature of Brienne, Archbishop of Toulouse, Louis XVI is said to have observed: "Let us at least have an Archbishop of Paris who believes in God."

The condition of the lower clergy was most wretched. They were treated as plebiens. They managed to keep their body and soul together with difficulty. They were discontented and indignant against their superiors who neglected and exploited them. However, it is the lower clergy notably those of the towns, who were alive to the reforming movement of the day. They subscribed to the Encyclopaedia. They read Plutarch and Rousseau. It is when the priests joined the representatives of the people in June 1789 that the Church fell like the Renaissance Papacy for ever.

Prof. Salvemini says, "The lower clergy grew exasperated at so insolent and scandalous a display of luxury and canons, abbots, friars, bishops and archbishops were all detested by the humble parish priests. This dissension between the higher and lower ranks of the clergy was one of the most potent causes leading to the early victory of the Revolution " **(The French Revolution, p. 45).**

It is estimated that the clergy and nobility owned about one-fifth each of property in France. Thus about one per cent of people owned about 40 per cent of property in the country. While they enjoyed privileges, they were exempted from taxes. There was a French maxim that **"the nobles fight, the clergy pray, the people pay".**

If such was the enviable lot of the privileged classes, the condition of the unprivileged classes was not at all satisfactory. The lot of the peasants was particularly unhappy. A peasant had to work on the land of his landlord from sunrise to sunset. Sometimes, the landlord sold his dues to a money-lender and the latter harassed him a great deal. The peasant could not plant according to his best judgment. On account of the absence of rotation of crops, the yield from the land was very low. The landlord kept large flocks of pigeons, deer and game and all of them were fed on the crops of the peasant. Fencing was not allowed and consequently all his crops might be eaten away, but the peasant could not drive away the game on account of the fear of the landlord. He was bound to grind his corn at the mill of the landlord and as the mill was situated at a great distance, he was put to a lot of inconvenience. He was punished if he tried to grind the corn himself with stones. The lord tried the cases of the peasants and whatever fine he imposed and collected, went straight into his pocket. Heavy punishments were inflicted on the peasants by the lords.

The peasant owed a large number of **dues to the lord, the Church and the King.** Ordinarily he had to work three days a week on the land of the lord. During the harvest days he had to work five days a week. Double rent was to be paid on the death of the peasant. If the farm was sold, one-fifth of the price went to the landlord. The peasant paid tithe[3] to the Church which usually amounted annually to one-twelfth or one-fifteenth part of the gross produce of the peasant's land. His dues to the king excelled all others. The **Taille** or land tax was the most important of all the dues. Its amount was not fixed but was considered to be proportionate to the value of the land and dwelling of the peasant. As a matter of fact, the tax collectors managed to take as much as they could lay their hands on. The system of farming taxes multiplied the worries of the peasants. The right of collection was given to the highest bidder and the collectors paid the fixed amount to the Government and tried to enrich themselves as much as they could at the cost of the peasants. The peasants were virtually fleeced. The burden fell especially on the peasants because the nobility and the clergymen paid nothing. Another tax paid by the peasant was **Vingtieme** or income-tax. This amounted to about 5 per cent of all incomes. The nobles paid only a part and the clergymen were completely exempted. Another tax was **Gabelle** or salt tax. This was the most regressive of all the taxes. The Government had a monopoly of salt and everybody above the age of seven had to buy a certain quantity of salt every year (approximately seven pounds) from the Government. The price of salt was about ten times its real value. Nobody was allowed to drink water at salt springs or cook his food with seawater. The price of salt was not uniform and varied from place to place and thereby added to the hardships of the people. Another tax was the Corvee or road tax. Road-making was the duty of the peasants and they had to spend many weeks in a year on the construction and maintenance of roads in their neighbourhood.

It has been estimated that after paying all the dues, the French peasant was left with only about 20% of his total produce. In a few districts of France, the peasants were able to pay their taxes and still live comfortably, but in the rest of France, their conditions was most miserable and can be better felt than described. With the best of harvests they found themselves unable to make their both ends meet. A dry summer or a long winter completely finished them. Starving peasants tried to satisfy their hunger with roots and herbs and thousands of them died of starvation. No one seemed to bother about them. It is rightly pointed out that **"in France, nine-tenths of the population died to hunger, and the tenth of indigestion."**

There was great distress among the peasants. The feudal system of land tenure in France was oppressive and the peasants opposed all movements which deprived them of their common rights. They opposed the enclosure movement and the division of the village commons as the large proprietors gained at their expense. They also suffered on account of the rise in prices during the 18th century. The average general prices of consumers' goods were higher between 1785 and 1789 than they had been between 1726 and 1741. The rise in the cost of living abversely affected those who were nearest the subsistence level. The cereals eaten by the peasants rose more in price than wheat eaten by the well-to-do.

The view of Leo Gershoy is that three principal causes determined the steady decline in the fortunes of the French peasantry and those were a sharp and continuous growth in population, a marked upward movement of prices without a corresponding increase in the real wages and the influence of the Physiocrats in stimulating aggrarian reforms. The population of France grew steadily in the 18th century and this not only accentuated the hardships of the petty peasant proprietor to support a large family from his already meagre lands, but also increased the number of landless peasantry who were

3. The tithe or dime levied upon the crops by the clergy brought them about 120 million livres a year. Its origin lay in the Middle Ages when the clergy saw to the building and repair of roads and helped to maintain public order, administered justice in the ecclesiastical courts and were responsible for education and for care of the poor and sick. In other words, the clergy carried out many functions which civil authorities were incapable of doing. However, in the 18th century, the lay bureaucracy took over most of those functions. The result was that the payment of the tithe to the rich and indolent clergy was considered to be a totally unjustifiable burden. No wonder, everybody tried to evade or reduce the payment of tithe. Although it had dropped to a twelfth, a twentieth or a, fortieth pan of the produce of the land at many places, it was a source of great bitterness.

driven into the ranks of beggars and vagrants. The steady rise in food prices was not counter-balanced by the smaller increase in wages. The increase in prices brought wealth to the moneyed interests and economic distress to the rest of the population. The lot of the average peasant was so bad that more than 20 per cent of the rural peasantry was indigent in times of plenty. Poverty was most acute in the newly industrialised regions of the north and in the provinces of the east where the manorial system was most strongly entrenched. At times of crisis when harvests were poor or epidemics raged, the number of indigents increased considerably. The reports of the intendants, the memorials of the Parish priests and the writings of other contemporaries all attest to the appalling misery of the peasantry on such occasions. The result was that they joined the ranks of the beggars and vagrants who over-ran the roads, pillaging the hamlets and terrorizing the inhabitants, Private relief was important, ecclesiastical relief was inadequate and governmental alms and charity were hopelessly meagre. The condition in hospitals, prisons and workshops and workhouses was indescribably bad.

The bourgeoisie or the middle-class also belonged to the unprivileged part of French society. To this class belonged the professors, lawyers, physicians, bankers and merchants. This class was all powerful in the field of finance, trade and industry. From this class came ministers of state, judges, magistrate, tax-collectors, intendants, etc. They had both brains and money.[4] They were the people who visited the various parts of the world and consequently were wide awake in every possible way. They were profoundly influenced by the French philosophers and consequently were not in a mood to put up with the inferior status which the **Ancien Regime** assigned to them. It is the members of this class who became the leaders of the people of France in their revolt against the **Ancient Regime.**

Prof. Salvemini says, "In the second half of the eighteenth century, therefore, French society might be said to resemble an ancient city, grow up in past times without design or order, built of diverse materials and according to the methods of different ages; with old and out-of-date buildings huddled together amongst new and solid structures. Almost all the inhabitants—working-class, middle-classes and even a large part of the privileged orders—were ill at ease and discontented, amidst the discordant claims of old and new."

"The state officials had become the instruments of a corrupt and reactionary system against which the nation needs must revolt, if it were not to relapse into feudal darkness. The privileged classes plundered the Exchequer, disrupted the administration and paralysed the country's economic life. They had reached the very brink of the abyss without perceiving it, and continued to wrangle with one another, when all were about to be engulfed.

"The commons, forced to choose between their own ruin and the destruction of every vestige of feudalism, had hoped that the King might return to the traditional anti-feudal policy that had been the glory of his dynasty in times past. In the end, tired of waiting in vain, they overthrew what was left of feudalism together with the monarchy that intervened in its support, freed themselves by their own efforts from their last remaining fetters, and set the new seal of the Republic upon modern society." (**The French Revolution,** pp. 45-46).

J.C. Herold says, "The French Revolution was a general mass movement of the nation against the privileged classes. The French nobility, like that of all Europe, dates from the barbarian invasions which broke up the Roman Empire. In France, the nobles represented the ancient Franks and Burgundians; the rest of the nation, the Gauls. The introduction of the feudal system established the principle that every landed property had a lord. All political rights were exercised by the priests and the nobles. The peasants were enslaved, partly by binding them to the soil.

"The progress of civilisation and knowledge liberated the people. This new state of affairs caused the prosperity of industry and trade. In the eighteenth century, the larger part of the land, of wealth,

4. According to Voltaire, "The middle-class has enriched itself through industry and commercial profits have increased; there is less luxory among nobility than formerly and more in middle-class life, so that the contrast between them is not so marked."

and of the fruits of civilization belonged to the people. The noble however, still formed a privileged class: they controlled the upper and intermediate courts, they held feudal rights under a great variety of names and forms, they were exempt from contributing to any of the taxes imposed by society and they had exclusive access to the most honourable employments.

"All these abuses stirred the citizens to protest. The chief aim of the Revolution was to destroy all privileges; to abolish manorial courts, justice being an inalienable, attribute of the sovereign authority; to suppress all feudal rights as remnants of the people's former slavery; to subject all citizens and all property without distinction to taxation by the State. Finally, the Revolution proclaimed the equality of rights. All citizens could fill the employments, subject only to their talents and the vicissitudes of chance. (The Mind of Napoleon, p. 65).

(2) **Rotten administrative systems.** Another cause of the French Revolution was the rottenness of the French administrative system. The King was the head of the state and he acted in an arbitrary manner. According to Louis XIV. "The sovereign authority is vested in my person, the legislative powers exist in myself alone....My people are one only with me; national rights and national interests are necessarily combined with my own and only rest in my hands." Such a system could not be efficient and no wonder the people suffered. The King did not go on tours to visit the various parts of the country and consequently lost his personal touch with the people. He had no knowledge of the sufferings and aspirations of the people. He centred all his attention at the capital where the nobles assembled from all over the country to participate in the frivolities of the royal court. In the time of Louis XV, his mistresses influenced the politics of the country. In the time of Louis XVI, his Queen, Maric Antoinette, interfered in State affairs. It was pointed out that **"the Court is the tomb of the nation."**

The court of Versailles was composed of 18,000 persons out of which 16,000 were attached to the personal service of the king and his family. The rest of the 2,000 persons were courtiers' who were busy in a perpetual round of pleasures and were always busy in feathering their own nests by begging favours from the king. There was luxury on all sides. The occupants of the palace considered themselves to be the darlings of the gods. The king, the queen, the royal children and the brothers, sisters and aunts of the king had their separate establishments. It is stated that the queen alone had more than 500 servants. There were more than 1,900 horses and 200 carriages in the royal stables which cost more than 4 million dollars a year. The table of the king cost more than a million and a half dollars. On the eve of the French Revolution, all this enormous waste amounted to more than 208 million dollars a year.

The administrative system of the country was hopelessly unsatisfactory. Various units of the administration possessed ill-defined and overlapping jurisdictions. At different times, France had been divided into districts under bailiffs and seneschals whose offices were purely ornamental. It had also been divided into provinces under governors. It had been divided into intendancies (under intendants), judicial districts, educational districts and ecclesiastical districts. The conflict of jurisdictions added

5. According to Prof. Salvemini, "Many of them knew neither what their incomes were nor where their estates lay: a great lord would have thought it beneath his dignity to discuss such matters as fertilizers or the housing of his peasants. It was the business of the bailiffs and attorneys to keep his accounts, and his to spend the money. 'My lord Archbishop', said Louis XVI to Monseigneur Dillon, 'it is said that you have a great many debts.' 'Sir', replied the prelate ironically, 'I will inquire of my intendant, and shall have the honour of rendering an account of them to Your Majesty.'

"Naturally, they were riddled with debt. The Due de Lauzun, at twenty-six years of age, had squandered the whole capital of his 100,000 crowns' income and was in debt to the sum of two millions; the Prince de Conti, with 600,000 livres a year, had a horde of creditors at his heels; the Comte de Clermont, Abbot of Saint-Germain des Pres, went bankrupt twice in succession; the millions of the Comte d'Artois and the Cardinal de Rohan went to pay the interest on their debts; the Due de Choisseul had property worth 14 millions and debts amounting to 10 millions; while the Due d'Orleans had creditors claiming 74 millions." **The French Revolution,** pp. 20-21).

to the difficulties and troubles of the people.

The legal system of the country was full of confusion. There was no uniform law for the whole of the country. Different laws were in force in different parts of the country. While at one place German law prevailed, at another place the Roman law was in force. It is estimated that there were about 400 different systems of law in the country. The laws were written in Latin and consequently were not within the comprehension of the people. The laws were cruel and unjust and very severe punishments were prescribed for ordinary offences. Torture was a common feature. The punishments of breaking one's bone on a wheel or cutting off the hands or ears were also imposed. There was no regular criminal procedure. Anybody could be imprisoned on the whim of an inuuential person. All that was required to be done was the issuing of a **letter de cachet** and the person concerned could be kept in prison for an indefinite period without any trial. There was no provision for a writ of **Habeas Corpus.** Men like Voltaire and Mirabeau were imprisoned like many others. There was confusion not only in the field of laws but also in the field of law-courts. There were royal courts, military courts, church courts and courts of finance. Their overlapping jurisdictions added to confusion and injustice. A peculiar institution in France was the **Noblesse de la robe** or nobility of the robe. These persons were judges in perpetuity or for life. Their offices were bought and sold. As these persons bought their offices, they tried to impose as heavy fines as they could to fill their pockets. Their number was in the neighbourhood of 50,000. Such a class must have been a curse to society. That was the negation of all judicial principles.

De Tocqueville wrote thus: "People often complain that Frenchmen despise the law; alas, where could they have learned to respect it? We may say that among the men of the ancien regime, the place which the law ought to occupy in the human mind was vacant, Every suitor demands a departure from the established rule with as much insistence as if he were demanding its observance; in fact, the rule is hardly ever upheld against him, save when it is desired to evade his request."

On the eve of the French Revolution, the French army consisted of 35,000 officers (of whom 1,171 were generals) and 135,000 men. The officers were maintained at a cost of 46 millions a year, although only 3,500 were on active list. The maintenance of the rank and file amounted to 44 millions in all.

Weights and measures had different names and different values in different provinces. Sometimes this difference was witnessed as a person moved from one village to another.

The French **Parlements** were high courts of justice of great antiquity. They reviewed judgments given in the inferior courts of the **bailliwicks, sanechausses** and **prevotes** into which the country was divided for judicial purposes. Towards the end of the 18th century, there were 13 such **Parlements** in France. Each **Parlement** consisted of a close corporation of rich magistrates whose offices had become hereditary in course of time.

Parlements claimed and exercised certain political powers. They had acquired the right of registering royal edicts and ordinances. They could defer the registration and thereby bring pressure on the king. A strong king could deal with them effectively but unfortunately there were no strong kings in France after Louis XIV. In 1771, **Parlements** were abolished by Louis XV but those were revived in 1774 by Louis XVI. The **Parlements** thus revived were in a position to harass royal ministers and circumvent financial reform while posing as champions of popular rights and liberties.

In some parts of France, there were **provincial estates** or local representative assemblies which met periodically. They shared responsibility for local administration with the agent of the Central Government or **Intendant.** They had certain fiscal privileges which they successfully defended against reforming finance ministers. They had the option of making fixed annual grants or **abonnements** in the case of new taxes which enabled them to evade full liability. The assessment and collection of State taxation was also left to the fiscal agents of the estates. Special local taxes were voted in the estates to meet local expenditure. These estates were controlled by the lay or clerical aristocracy and tended to be reactionary and conservative. They were reluctant to any reform designed to weaken or destroy their privileges.

The method of collection of taxes was hopelessly faulty. Taxes were not collected by the state through its own agency; the right of collecting taxes was given to the highest bidder. The result was that while the contractors paid a specific amount of money to the state, they tried to get as much as they could from the people. While the people were exploited, the Government did not benefit in any way. The system of framing of taxes was the most objectionable. It resulted in a lot of oppression and tyranny. As taxes were not paid by the clergymen and nobles, the burden fell on the unprivileged class and this fact was resented bitterly. The whole of the administrative system of France required a thorough overhauling.

De Tocqueville says, "The Government seldom undertakes and soon abandons the most necessary reforms which demand a persevering energy but it constantly changes particular regulations. In the sphere which it inhabits nothing remains an instant in repose. Now rule succeed one another with a rapidity so strange that the agents of the State do not know how they are to obey. Municipal officers complain to the Controller-General himself. The variation of the financial regulations alone, they say, is such as not to allow an officer, were he irremovable, to do anything else but study the new regulations as they appear."

(3) **Successors of Louis XIV.** Another cause of the revolution was the incapacity of the successors of Louis XIV. The Grand Monarch left a legacy of financial bankruptcy for his successors. While on death-bed, he is stated to have advised Louis XV, his great grandson, in these words: "My child,.... endeavour to live at peace with your neighbours, do not imitate my fondness for war, nor the exorbitant expenditure which I have incurred.....Endeavour to relieve the people at the earliest possible moment and thus accomplish what unfortunately, I am unable to do myself." It is well-known that this advice fell on deaf ears and instead of giving any relief to the people, he added to their miseries by his wars and frivolities. He used to say: "After me, the deluge."

About Louis XV's rule, Comte de Mercy, the Austrian Ambassador at Paris, wrote thus to Empress Maria Theresa: "At Court, there is nothing but confusion, scandals and injustice. No attempt has been made to carry out good principles of Government; everything has been left to chance; the shameful state of the nation's affairs has caused unspeakable disgust and discouragement, while the intrigues of those who oemain on the scene only increase the disorder. Sacreo duties have been left undone, and infamous behaviour tolerated."

Dr G. P. Gooch says, "The legacy of Louis XV to his countrymen was an ill-governed, discontented, frustrated France. Viewed from a distance, the ancien regime appeared as solid as the Bastille, but its walls were crumbling for lack of repairs and the foundations showed signs of giving way. The Aboslute Monarchy, the privileged Noblesse, the intolerant Church, the close corporation **Parlements,** had all become unpopular, and the army once the glory of France, was tarnished by the rout of Rossbach. Though there was little thought of republicanism, the **mystique** of monarchy had almost evaporated." **(Louis XV, the Monarchy in Decline,** p. 244)

Louis XVI (1774—93) became king at the age of 20. His helplessness to manage the state of affairs can be judged from the following statements made by him: "It seems as if the universe is falling on me." Again, "God, what a burden is mine and they have taught me nothing." He was awkward and too shy to preside over the meetings of the council. He was lazy and stupid. His hobby was lock-making and shooting deer from the palace window. He might have been a good citizen but he was a failure as a king when the country was confronted with serious difficulties. According to a contemporary, "No one trusts him, for he has no will of his own." He did not seem to be interested in the art of governing and this is clear from his following remark to Malesherbes on the latter's resignation: "How fortunate you are. I wish I could resign too."

Marie Antoinette (1755—93). Marie Antoinette was the daughter of Maria Theresa, Empress of Austria-Hungary. The object of her marriage to Louis XVI was to unite Austria and France into a bond of friendship. She was beautiful, gracious and vivacious. She had a strong will, a power of rapid decision and a spirit of initiative. However, she was lacking in wisdom and breadth of judgment. She did not understand the temperament of the French people and the spirit of the times. Born in a royal family, she could not understand the point of view of the unprivileged. She was extravagant, proud, wilful, impatient of restraint and fond of pleasure. She committed a large number of mistakes and was hated by the people of France. She was the living symbol of French humiliation in the Seven Years' War. She was the centre of a group of greedy persons, who were opposed to all reforms.

This is what Emperor Joseph II, her real brother, wrote about Marie Antoinette: "Let me, my dearest sister, address you with a frankness justified by my affection for you and my interest in your welfare. From what I hear, you are becoming involved in a great many matters that are no concern of yours, and of which you know nothing, led on by intrigue and flattery that excite in you not only self-conceit and a desire to shine but jealousy and ill-feeling. This conduct may well impair your happiness and sooner or later must provoke serious trouble between you and the King, which will detract from his affection and esteem for you, and cause you to fall into disfavour with the public..... Why should you, my dear sister, employ yourself in removing ministers from their posts, in banishing one and giving office to another, in seeing that some friend of yours wins his law-suit or in creating a new and expensive court appointment, in brief, in discussing affairs in a manner that is little suited to your position? Have you ever asked yourself what right you have to meddle in the affairs of the French Government or monarchy? What studies have you made, what knowledge have you acquired, that you believe your opinion of value, particularly in matters calling for such wide experience. You, a charming young woman who think only of frivolity, of your **toilette,** of your amusements; who do not read books or listen to serious talk for more than ten minutes in a month; who never stop to reflect, or to give a thought to the consequences of what you say or do. You simply act on the spur of the moment, prompted by the favourites in whom you believe..........Listen to the advice of a friend, give up all these intrigues, have nothing whatever to do with public affairs and think only of deserving the King's affection and confidence..........For the rest, do some reading, improve your mind. After all, that is the role of every woman in her own home."

(4) **French Philosophers.** Another cause of the French Revolution was the effect of the preachings of the French philosophers. Montesquieu, Voltaire and Rousseau were the three intellectual giants of the age, **Montesquieu** (1689-1755) was a polished and eminent lawyer, well versed in history, serious, acute, a profound student of human institutions and master of a terse and pointed style. On the whole, his writings were not the flights of fancy but the result of systematized and careful thought; weighty, luminous, moderate in tone and scientifically sane. He initiated a philosophic movement and unmasked the batteries of criticism and satire which were to strike at the foundations of the Ancien **Regime** in France. He stood for a constitutional form of government and believed in the supremacy of law. His view was that liberty was impossible without the separation of powers. The legislative, judicial and executive powers must be put in different organs and then alone could there be liberty of the people. The combination of any two powers or all the three in one organ was bound to result in tyranny. Montesquieu analysed the laws which regulate government and custom and thereby destroyed the mysterious prestige which was attached to the institutions of France.

Montesquieu had neither the views nor the attitude of a revolutionary. He was both a Catholic and a monarchist. However, in a moderate way, he criticised the abuses of the Church and the despotism of the state. He compared despotism to cutting down a tree to get at the fruit. He criticised by satire the French manners and customs. He suggested by comparison with England the need for liberty and equality. He exposed by implication the institutions of France.

The Spirit of Laws, his great work, which was the product of 20 years of labour, was published in 1748. It is stated that 22 editions of this book were printed in 18 months. It was a study of political philosophy, an analysis of various forms of governments and their merits and demerits. Setting aside the claim of divinity for the institutions, he examined them with the detachment of a botanist.

According to Prof. Salvemini, "The Spirit of Laws awakened in cultivated persons a taste for juridical and political studies, brought the social sciences into the field of literature, and helped more than any other work to create that atmosphere of sociological and philosophic dilettantism which enabled eighteenth century revolutionary theories to prosper." (**The French Revolution,** p. 64).

Another giant was **Voltaire** (1694-1778). In verse, in prose, in history in drama, and in romance, Voltaire attacked traditions, beliefs and abuses. He exposed their shortcomings mercilessly. He laughed at their absurdities. "Voltaire's rare and verstile wit, his light touch, his unabashed scepticism, his brilliant commonsense appealed irresistibly to the minds of his countrymen. He made the philosophic movement popular. He was identified with many errors and with the gravest faults of taste. But with it all he taught men to despise many follies and to impeach many wrongs." The Church in France was the main target of his attack. He called it the infamous thing. He was a deist and he attacked Christian bigotry and fanaticism and stood for religious toleration. "Since we are all steeped in error and folly, we must forgive each other for our follies." "Worship God and be a good man." On account of their literary merit, Voltaire's writings were widely read and he commanded tremendous influence on his age.

For 25 years, he flooded France with "plays, poems, philosophical tales, satires, burlesques, histories, essays, diatribes, deistic sermons and antibiblical pamphlets, and won for himself, the reputation of the intellectual ruler of his age." He was not an atheist. His view was that "If God did not exist, it would be necessary to create Him." What he attacked was the particular dogmas, the accretions of theology, the complex mysteries and contradictory ceremonials of Christianity that through the ages had engendered fanaticism, persecution and bloodshed, suppressed reason and persecuted free thought. He was not a democrat. The attack on the altar was ultimately to undermine the throne which rested on it, but Voltaire never explicitly aimed at the monarchy and was fully aware of the dangers of popular government. Duc de Choiseul addressed to the new philosophers in 1764 in these words: "Why do you not stop where Voltaire did? Him we can comprehend. Amidst all his satires, he respected authority."

Voltaire was one of the master minds of European history whose name has become the name of an era. We speak of the age of Valtaire in the same way as we speak of the Age of Luther or Erasmus. He was called by the name of King Voltaire. World renowned, he melted into world history. He was a warrior all his life. He was a pillar of cloud by day and of fire by night. He was never tiresome. He was always interesting and generally instructive. He could not tolerate tyranny in any shape or form. He was always ready to take up the cause of the oppressed. He stood for a benevolent despotism and had no love for democracy. He is said to have remarked that he would prefer to be ruled by one lion than by a hundred rats.

The French philosopher whose influence was the most prominent was **Rousseau** (1712—78). He did not like the study and analysis of the past. He did not care for the spread of knowledge and art. It appeared to him that study, knowledge and cultivation degraded man. All societies were artificial. All accepted forms of political organizations were tyranny and abuses. Man was born free but he was everywhere in chains. The surroundings of society destroyed the natural simplicity of man, tainted his virtues and were responsible for his sufferings and sins. Rousseau appealed to the people in these words: **"Sweep away, therefore, all the false fabric of society, the world of ugly want and insolent riches miscalled civilization, the oppression miscalled order, the error miscalled knowledge. Level its inequalities, repudiate its learnings, break its functions, shatter its chains.** Let men return to the simplicity of ancient days, to the idyllic state, when uncorrupted instinct only ruled them, and then once again, innocent and ignorant, as nature made them, and guided only by the 'Immortal and Celestial voices, of reasons, seek the high paths of felicity of life."

Again, "Are not all advantages in our society reserved for the rich and powerful? Are not all lucrative employments held by them alone? Are not the public authorities entirely at their service?

If an influential man defrauds his creditors or commits other villainies, can he not count on impunity before the law? If he is guilty of violence or murder, is not everything hushed up and after six months no longer referred to? But if this same man is robbed, the whole police is at once set in motion, and woe betide the innocent upon whom suspicion falls! Should this rich man have to pass through a dangerous place, he is provided with a large escort. If the axle of his carriage breaks, all fly to assist him. If there is a noise at his door, a word from him and all is silence. If the crowd incommodes him, a sign and all are scattered. If he finds a carter in his way, his servants rain blows upon him. All these conveniences cost him nothing, since the rich are entitled to enjoy them without expending their own wealth on such trifles. But how different is the spectacle of the poor man! The more compassion society owes him the less he receives. All doors are closed to him, even when he has a right to have them opened. Should he, once in a way, obtain justice, he has to labour more for it than others for a favour. If a **corvee** is called for, or a military levy made, he is the first to be taken. He bears not only his own burdens but those his neighbours has managed to shift on to his back. At the least accident that befalls him, all leave him to his fate. If his cart overturns, he is unlikely to escape insults from the duke's servants who hurry by. All gratuitous aid is refused him in his need, precisely because he has no way of paying for it. And woe betide him if he has the misfortune to possess an honest soul, a beautiful daughter or a powerful neighbour. He is lost. Let us, then, sum up in a few words the social compact between the two classes: 'You have need of me, because I am rich and you are poor; let us make an agreement, therefore, between ourselves; I will allow you the honour of serving me, provided that you give me what little you still possess, in return for my trouble in giving you orders.' "

Rousseau gave his own conception of the state of nature in which people were virtuous, equal and free. He also explained how by means of "social contract" the State was created and the state of nature was ended. He propounded the idea of the sovereignty of the people. Every individual was a part of that sovereign. The laws of the country were merely the expression of the general will of the sovereign. As sovereignty rested with the people no government or king could snatch away that from them." The people had the right to revolt against the government. Rousseau condemned all the existing institutions and thereby destroyed their foundations. His writings created a profound impression upon the people. He also created enthusiasm for liberty. The **Social Contract** supplied the text and lit the fire of revolution. It became the gospel of the Jacobin Party and Robespierre became its high priest.

The political influence of Rousseau was incalculable not only in France, but all over Europe. He preached "revolt in the name of nature, against the vicious and artificial social system of his time." His theory of social contract may be historically untenable, but it was another way of saying that those who govern must recognise their responsibilities. The people of France were suffering because the interests of the Crown were divorced from those of the state, because the nobles no longer fought and the clergy no longer prayed and all of them broke the social contract. Rousseau's logic may be faulty, but he appealed to the people who were split and tormented by the pressure of society. Rousseau explained his philosophy with such force and imagination and buttressed it with such arguments that the aggrieved and frustrated could catch fire from its fervour, find encouragement in its protest, hope in its promise and weapons in its armoury. His philosophy sounded the common chord. Rousseau became "the immortal seducer of unquiet souls, the oracle of whoever feels himself misunderstood and disinherited." He became the hot-gospeller of temporal salvation and the prophet of secular society.

Lord Morley assessed the influence of Rousseau in these words: "In the first place, he spoke words that can never be unspoken and kindled a hope that can never be extinguished; he first inflamed man with righteous conviction with the evils of the existing order of things, reduced civilisation to a nullity for the great majority of mankind....second by the fervid eloquence and the burning convictions which he kindled in the hearts of great number of men, he inspired energy enough in France to awaken her from the torpor as of death which was stealing so rapidly over her." The view of Prof. Salvemini is that Rousseau was not a real revolutionary. If he had lived till the Revolution, he would have died either on the scaflold or of heart trouble at the way in which his teaching was being applied. However in that oppressive, decaying society where all were discontented and innumerable arguments could be found to justify revolt, it was natural Rousseau's advice in favour of caution should pass unnoticed and his longing for better world, his vehement protests against the privileges of wealth and birth and his poignant and paradoxical pages full of indignation and injustice and love for equality, should be greatly admired. As men lost faith in their traditional institutions and the citizens prepared for an inevitable struggle against the King and the privileged classes, Rousseau's dogma of popular sovereignty became the battle-cry of the Revolution. (**The French Revolution,** pp. 78-79.)

In addition to the three giants, there were writers of small stature and it is desirable to make a reference to their writings as they also influenced the thoughts of the people. Diderot was the editor of the Encyclopaedia to which many writers made their contributions. He was original, ingentous, reckless in expression and most intense and imaginative in thought. He possessed a magnetic power of conversation and indomitable perseverance. He had an ardent desire for the improvement of mankind.

Helvetius propounded the doctrine that self-interest dictates both the conduct and the views of men, and the attainment of pleasure is their final aim.

Holbach indicated the vices of kings and the slavery of men. He stood for a revolution. To him, atheism and materialism were the only two philosophies of life. To quote him, **"Religious and political errors have changed the universe into a valley of tears."**

The Economists or Physiocrats had great contemporary influence. They were much influenced by the writings of Adam Smith. Their chief representatives in France were Mirabeau, the father of the well-known statesman of the French Revolution, Say and Quesnay. Quesnay (1694—1744) was the real thinker of the movement. His "Tableau Economique" was hailed by some of them as an infallible remedy for the troubles of France. The physiocrats cared little for the abstract speculations of the nine. They believed in certain fundamental doctrine. According to them, all wealth came from the application of labour to land and workmen were the most truly productive, perhaps the only productive class. The action of the Government should be reduced to the minimum. Complete free trade and a universal system of education were the immediate necessities of the state. All taxation should be reduced to a single land tax. The view of Mirabeau was that those principles were sufficient to "set everything right and renew the age of Solomon." Turgot was a disciple of the Economists. His character and writing had already made him well-known and he had acquired valuable experience as an intendant of the province of Limousin. He was appointed the Controller-General of Finance and he was in office for about 20 months and what he did had little permanent effect. But people looked back to his tenure of office as the time when there was a chance to reform to avert the catastrophe of the French Revolution. He wanted to introduce honesty and efficiency into public services. He wanted to check the power of the church. He stood for a juster method of taxation. He wanted to establish freedom of trade within and beyond France. He did not recognise the necessity of taking the people into partnership by summoning any national assembly. However, he worked at his schemes with a passionate zeal for justice and humanity. As was to be expected, his proposals were disliked by the privileged classes and he was replaced by Necker.

The **great contribution of the Encyclopaedists** was that they hated unjust things, condemned slavery, inequality of taxation, corruption of justice and wastefulness of war. They had dreams of social progress and sympathy with the rising empire of industry.

Mallet observes. "The seed sown by these remarkable writers fell upon fruitful soil. The orders which immediately preceded the outbreak of the Revolution in France were orders of vague but widespread agitation. An enthusiasm for the natural greatness of man and a boundless contempt for the age of society in which he lived pervaded the thought of the time. In almost every European country, observers noticed the same presentiment of impending change—a change which, on behalf of humanity, most people were prepared to welcome. Thinkers and talkers alike were full of illusions, full of curiosity, full of unselfishness, full of hope." **(The French Revolution).** According to Kropolkin, "The eighteenth-century philosophers had long been sapping the foundations of the law-and-order societies of that period, wherein political power, as well as an immense share of the wealth, belonged to the aristocracy and the clergy, whilst the mass of the people were nothing but beasts of burden to the ruling classes. By proclaiming the sovereignty of reason, by preaching trust in human nature-corrupted they declared, by the institutions that had reduced man to servitude, but nevertheless, certain to regain all its qualities when it had reconquered liberty—they had opened up new vistas to mankind. By proclaiming equality among men, without distinction of birth, by demanding from every citizen, whether king or peasant, obedience to the law, supposed to express the will of the nation when it has been made by the representatives of the people; finally, by demanding freedom of contract between free men, and the abolition of feudal taxes and services—by putting forward all these claims, linked together with the system and method characteristic of French thought, the philosophers had undoubtedly prepared, at least in men's minds, the downfall of the old regime." **(The Great French Revolution,** pp. 1-2).

The view of David Thomson is that the connection between the ideas of the French philosophers and "the outbreak of revolution in 1789 is somewhat **remote** and **indirect.** They did not preach revolution, and were usually ready enough to lend support to any absolute monarch who was prepared to patronize them and adopt their teachings. Nor were most of their readers inspired to want, or to work for revolution; they were mostly themselves aristocrats, lawyers, business people and local dignitaries, whose lot in the existing order was far from unhappy. The doctrines of the **philosophes** came to be used later on, during the course of the revolution in France often to justify measures that the philosophes themselves would have opposed. Their teachings became more important later; if they had any influence at all on the outbreak and the initial stages of the great revolution, it was only to the extent that they had fostered a critical and irreverent attitude towards all existing institutions. They made men more ready, when the need arose, to question the whole foundation of the old order. What mattered in 1789—and what made men revolutionary almost in spite of themselves—was the whole 'revolutionary situation'; and in producing that situation the work of the **philosophes** played no very important role." **(Europe Since Napoleon,** pp. 4-5).

(5) **Financial Condition.** Another cause of the French Revolution was the condition of the finances of the French Government. It has rightly been pointed out that **"The Revolution was precipitated by the economic factor and the train which had been laid by philosophy was fixed by finance." "The fiscal causes lay at the root of the Revolution."** The wars of the Louis XIV had upset the finances of France. The financial condition of the country was deplorable when the Grand Monarch died. Although he advised Louis XV to improve the finances and desist from wars, the latter did not care for the advice. He rot only wasted a lot of money on palaces and mistresses, but also had the audacity to take part in many wars. He took part in the War of Polish Succession. He participated in the War of Austrian Succession. The Seven Years' War also cost a good deal. France was on the verge of bankruptcy when Louis XVI ascended the throne, but in spite of that France joined the War of American Independence. It is true that France had the satisfaction of having her revenge against England for her humiliation in the Seven Years' War, but French participation in the War of American Independence completely upset the finances of the country. It cannot be denied that it was the French participation in the War of American Independence which precipitated the financial crisis which led to the French Revolution.

The financial system of France was deplorable. The nobility and the clergymen who owned about 40% of the total wealth of the country did not make any contribution towards the State exchequer. No wonder, the burden of taxation fell on the unprivileged classes. That in itself created bitterness. The national debt had increased tremendously and is estimated to have reached the figure of 4,467,478,000 livres. Out of the nominal revenues of 472,415,549 in 1788, the State got 211,708,977 livres and it had to pay 236,999,999 livres as annual interest.

It has been estimated that at the end of the **Ancien Regime** over three-fourths of the annual State expenditure was being incurred on defence and the service of public debt which was in itself mainly the result of previous wars. It was practically impossible to reduce these heavy items of national expenditure without undermining public credit and national security. Financial retrenchment could be made only in the field of civil expenditure which represented 23% of the total expenditure in 1788. Even economy in royal expense costing about 6% could not help matters. Some radical remedy alone could improve matters.

In 1774, Louis XVI appointed Turgot as the Controller of Finance. The latter had been an intendant of a poor province of France. He had made that province prosperous by applying the principles of the most advanced economists. He realised that if the annual deficit of the Central Government was allowed to continue, it was bound to result ultimately in bankruptcy. He outlined his programme in these words: "No bankruptcy, no increase of taxation, no more borrowing." He hoped to tackle the problem of finance by effecting economies and by developing public wealth. The latter could be done by introducing the regime of liberty into agriculture, industry and commerce. As a matter of fact, Turgot succeeded in saving many millions by stopping useless expenditure. However, by doing so, he annoyed all those who were gaining from that useless expenditure. They all joined hands with Marie Antoinette to put pressure on the king to dismiss Turgot. Although the king declared that **"M. Turgot and I are the only persons who love the people,"** he dismissed the Controller of Finance in 1776 and thereby brought trouble for himself.

Necker, a banker of Geneva, was appointed in 1776 as the successor of Turgot. Necker had risen from poverty to power. He had to face a lot of opposition while effecting economies. He was the first person to publish a financial report which showed the annual income and expenditure of the State. Formerly, the whole thing was kept as a secret. There was a lot of indignation in the court circles as the report showed how much money was annually spent on pensions and free gifts to the countries. Necker was dismissed in 1781.

He was succeeded by Calonne. He was an agreeable person. His only purpose was to please all. The members of the court had merely to say what they wanted and the same was granted by Calonne. Calonne had a wonderful philosophy of borrowing. To quote him, "A man who wishes to borrow must appear to be rich, and to appear rich he must dazzle by spending freely." The result of his philosophy was that money flowed like water. In three years, he was able to borrow about 300 million dollars. But the net result of all his acts of commission and omission was that by August 1786, the royal treasury was completely empty and there were no more fools willing to lend to the State. When Calonne proposed a general tax which was to be paid both by the privileged and the unprivileged classes, he was removed from office. The king tried another treasurer but also failed to help him in straightening the finances.

With a view to tackling the financial problem Louis XVI summoned in 1787 an Assembly of the Notables in the hope that they would consent to the taxation of the privileged classes. However, the nobles were not prepared to oblige the king and consequently they were sent home. The king tried new loans but the **Parlement** of Paris refused to register further loans or taxes. The latter drafted a Declaration, of Rights and contended that subsidies could constitutionally be granted only by the Estates-General. The Government took action against the **parlement** of Paris and abolished the same. There was a lot of hue and cry and the soldiers refused to arrest the judges. Crowds demanded the convocation of the Estates-General.

It was under these circumstances that the king was forced to give way and he ordered elections to the Estates-General after a lapse of 175 years (1614-1789). That led to the French Revolution of 1789.

According to Prof. Goodwin, "The immediate causes of French Revolution of 1789 must be sought, not in the economic grievances of the peasants, nor in the political discontent of the middle class, but in the reactionary aspirations of the French aristocracy. Though the revolution established the political power and consolidated the economic position of the middle class, it was set in motion by the aristocracy in the years 1787 and 1788 in the attempts to defend its own fiscal and political privileges, which were threatened by the reforming policy of the Bourbon monarchy. The decision of Louis XVI, in July 1788, to summon the Estates-General, or national representative assembly, which had not met since 1614 marked the Crown's capitulation to the concerted pressure of the lay, ecclesiastical, and judicial aristocracy. These privileged classes expected that the adoption of the traditional method of voting in the Estates-General—by order and not by head—would enable them, not only to prevent radical reform, but also to consolidate their victory over the Crown by a similar subjugation of the third estate. This gross miscalculation rendered inevitable a revolution which might well have been avoided by the nobility's acceptance of the consequences of political and fiscal equality."

Real makers of the French Revolution. While it is admitted that the French Revolution originated with the Third Estate, there is difference of opinion as to whether the peasantry or the middle classes took the initiative in bringing about the Revolution. It is pointed out by some writers that the oppressed peasantry of France, goaded by the extremity of their sufferings, was driven to Revolution. However, this view is not accepted by Prof. Hearnshaw. According to him, condition of the peasants of France was better than those of Germany, Spain, Russia and Poland. Their main grievance was not their exclusion from political power but the weight of the taxes they had to pay. They had neither the brains nor the capacity to precipitate the revolution. It is the enlightened middle-classes which led the way and the peasants merely followed them. The middle-classes had brains. They had money and influence. They were the persons who were deeply influenced by the philosophies of the French philosophers. No wonder, the middle classes were the real makers of the French Revolution.

Why Revolution broke out in France? It is pointed out that monarchical absolutism and oppression of the peasantry existed in most of the countries of Western Europe. There was nothing exceptional in the grievances of the people of France. In spite of that, the revolution started in France and not in any other country of Western Europe. There are many reasons for this. In other countries there were feudal privileges and duties. The feudal lords not only enjoyed certain exemptions from taxes but also performed certain duties. They served in the army of the kings and were responsible for maintaining law and order within their locality. However, in the case of France, the feudal system had become worn out. While the nobles still retained their exemptions and privileges, they were deprived of all their powers and duties by the king. The result was that while in other countries the feudal system was a reality, it had lost all its vitality in France. No wonder, the privileges of the nobles in France were irritating to the people of France. The whole system had become an anachronism and consequently it was condemned. The discontentment against the nobility burst out in the form of the Revolution of 1789.

Another reason was that there existed in France an enlightened middle class which was not to be found in other parts of Europe. The members of this class were well-to-do persons, but they still belonged to the unprivileged class. They had wealth and brains and consequently were not in a mood to put up with the inequality which the **Ancien Regime** imposed on them. They were profoundly influenced by the philosophy of Rousseau, Voltaire and Montesquieu. After having assimilated thoroughly the philosophy of the above intellectual giants, the middle-classes were not prepared to put up with their deplorable position. They could not find any justification for their humiliating condition. **The Social Contract** of Rausseau became the Bible of the Revolution. The writings of the French philosophers put before the Frenchmen an idealism for which they were prepared to make any sacrifices. No such atmosphere existed in other countries of Europe. No wonder, although the unprivileged classes in other countries of Europe also suffered, they had neither any idealism nor any leaders among them who were prepared to challenge the existing order and hence no revolution broke out there.

There was another reason why the Revolution started in France and not in any other country of Europe. It is rightly pointed out that the Revolution was precipitated by the economic factor, and the train which had been laid by philosophy was fired by finance. The annual income of the State was less than the interest it had to pay on the national debt. It was impossible to carry on government under the circumstances. The Estates-General had to be summoned to get the money and that led to the French Revolution. There were no such circumstances in other parts of Europe and although the people had their grievances, they kept on suffering but had not the courage to revolt.

According to Prof. Salvemini, "France was, in fact—however paradoxical the statement may seem at firm—better off than the rest. It was precisely because of the more favourable conditions prevailing in the social life of France that the revolutionary crisis broke out there rather than elsewhere in Europe. The French middle-classes—richer, more educated, in closer contact with the higher ranks of society, than were those of other European nations, and divided from the nobility by less marked differences in their way of life—were more acutely conscious of the injustice that excluded them from political influence and honours; and being possessed of moral and material strength that others lacked as yet, they were first to win that place in public life to which they felt entitled. Furthermore, in other countries, as for instance in Russia, Germany, Denmark, or Hungary, the peasants, utterly ground down by feudal serfdom, were too wretched to grasp such ideas as those of civil equality and liberty. In France, on the contrary, every peasant proprietor felt himself a free man on the piece of ground he had won by the sweat of his brow; and it was to defend himself from what remained of feudal tyranny, and his property from ruthless taxation, that he had recourse to revolution. In no other country, moreover, had the lay and ecclesiastical nobles as in France, deserted the provinces and flocked round the central authority in a scramble for favours; and there was nowhere so deep an abyss between the different social classes as that which the French monarchy, with its centralized State control, had created by removing local administration from the nobility's hands. Elsewhere, the nobles, brutal and semi-barbarous, lived on their fiefs, carried out their political functions, administered justice and provided for the common weal. If the peasants were oppressed, they also felt themselves protected by the rough rule of their lord; and the noble's duties were some justification for his privileges. Finally, in France alone had the capital city acquired such importance as to become the centre of the nation's entire political and administrative life; so that, when the revolutionary forces had gained mastery over Paris, the whole country too succumbed to them. In other nations, administrative centralization was as yet rudimentary or entirely lacking, and provincial life remained more or less autonomous; unrest that arose in one area did not necessarily disturb the rest, and disorder in the principal centre had little effect on the provinces, where those who carried on the administration were not forced to wait for all orders, assistance reproofs and payment to come from the capital. In France, widespread trouble in the provinces had an almost paralysing effect on the capital; while disorder in Paris was a mortal blow to the whole political organism and had repercussions throughout the country." (**The French Revolution,** pp. 188-89). **Again,** "The most dangerous city was Paris, with its more than half a million inhabitants. With the growth of a centralized administration, the capital had attracted to itself a crowd of fortune-seekers both rich and poor. To satisfy the diverse needs of all these people new houses and factories were built, which absorbed a stream of workers and peasants from the provinces. The Government, disturbed yet gratified at such an increase in population—embarrassed at having so large a city to administer, but thankful for additional sources of revenue—wavered between distributing favours and privileges, and imposing absurd restriction, in an effort to stem the flood. But the colossus went on growing with or without the King's permission; rearing up within itself an army of rebels that was to become a most efficacious weapon for destroying old France. On the eve of the Revolution, employers in Paris were complaining that 'the workers were dictating to the Government and making leagues of resistance; what with insolent speeches and insulting letters, they seemed to think that anything was permissible." (**Ibid.,** p. 37).

French Revolution compared with English Revolutions. The French Revolution may be compared with the Puritan Revolution of 1642-49 and the Glorious Revolution of 1688 in England. It is to be observed that the aims of the English revolutions were mainly political. Their object was to put a check on the arbitrary powers of the king and give all the powers to the British Parliament which was considered to be representative of the people. On the other hand, the main motive force of the French Revolution was social and not political. It is true that the people of France had their political disabilities but they do not seem to have cared much for them. The people of France were accustomed to authoritarian traditions for centuries and accordingly they did not seem to have bothered much about the evils of centralised despotism. The people suffered most on account of social inequality. No wonder, the French Revolution was aimed mainly against inequality and that also was its chief achievement.

The English Revolution of 1688 was defensive and conservative in character. There was nothing new in the Bill of Rights which the people got after the Glorious Revolution. There was no violent breach with the past. The king was merely forced to act according to the laws of the country and not to act according to his whim. On the other hand, the French Revolution was revolutionary and destructive. It destroyed the **Ancien Regime** root and branch.

According to Kropotkin, "The insurrection of the peasants for the abolition of the feudal rights and the recovery of the communal lands which had been taken away from the village communes since the seventeenth century by the lords, lay and ecclesiastical, is the very essence, the foundation of the great Revolution. Upon it the struggle of the middle class for their political rights was developed. Without it the Revolution would never have been so thorough as it was in France. The great rising of the rural districts which began after the January of 1789, even in 1788, and lasted five years, was what enabled the Revolution to accomplish, the immense work of demolition which we owe to it. It was this that impelled the Revolution to set up the first landmarks of a system of equality, to develop in France the republican spirit, which since then nothing has been able to suppress, to proclaim the great principles of agrarian communism, that we shall see emerging in 1793. This rising, in fact, is what gives the true character to the French Revolution, and distinguishes it radically from the Revolution of 1648-1657 in England.

"There, too, in the course of those nine years, the middle classes broke down the absolute power of royalty and the political privileges of the Court party. But beyond that, the distinctive feature of the English revolution was the struggle for the right of each individual to profess whatever religion be pleased, to interpret the Bible according to his personnel conception of it, to choose his own pastors—in a word, the right of the individual to the intellectual and religious development best suited to him. Further, it claimed the right of each parish, and, as a consequence, of the townships, to autonomy. But the peasant risings in England did not aim so generally, as in France, at the abolishing of feudal dues and tithes, or the recovery of the communal lands. And if Cromwell's hosts demolished a certain number of castles which represented true strongholds of feudalism, those hosts unfortunately did not attack either the feudal pretensions of the lords over the land, or even the right of feudal justice, which the lords exercised over their tenants. What the English revolution did was to conquer some precious rights for the individual, but it did not destroy the feudal power of the lord, it merely modified it whilst preserving his rights over the land, rights which persist to this day.

"The English revolution undoubtedly established the political power of the middle classes, but this power was only obtained by sharing it with the landed aristocracy. And if the revolution gave the English middle classes a prosperous era for their trade and commerce, this prosperity was obtained on the condition that the middle classes should not profit by it to attack the landed privileges of the nobility. On the contrary, the middle classes helped to increase these privileges, at least in value. They helped the nobility to take legal possession of the communal lands by means of the Enclosure Acts, which reduced the agricultural population to misery, placed them at the mercy of the landowners, and forced a great number of them to migrate to the towns, whereas proletarians, they were delivered over to the mercy of the middle-class manufacturers. The English middle classes also helped the nobility to make of their immense landed estates sources, not only of revenue often fabulous, but also of political and local juridical power, by re-establishing under the new forms the right of manorial justice. They helped also to increase their revenues ten-fold by allowing them through the land laws, which hamper the sale of estates, to monopolise the land, the need of which was making itself felt more and more among a population whose trade and commerce were steadily increasing.

"We now know that the French middle classes, especially the upper middle classes engaged in manufactures and commerce, wished to imitate the English middle classes in their revolution. They, too, would have willingly entered into a compact with both royalty and nobility in order to attain power. But they did not succeed in this, because **the basis of the French Revolution was fortunately much broader than of the revolution in England.** In **France**, the movement was not merely an insurrection to win religious liberty, or even commercial and industrial liberty for the individual, or yet to constitute municipal authority in the hands of a few middle-class men. It was above all **a peasant** insurrection, a movement of the people to regain possession of the land and to free it from the feudal obligations which burdened it, and while there was all through it a powerful individualist element—the desire to possess land individually—there was also the communist element, the right of the whole nation to the land; a right which we shall see proclaimed loudly by the poorer classes in 1793." (**The Great French Revolution,** pp. 95-7).

SUGGESTED READINGS

Acton : **Lectures on the French Revolution.**

Aldington : **Voltaire.**

Aûlard, A. : **Political History of the French Revolution, 1910.**

Belloc, H : **The French Revolution.**

Brinton, C.C. : **A Decade of Revolution, 1789-99.**

Cobban, A : **The Debate on the French Revolution (1789-99), 1945.**

Cobban, A. : **Rousseau and the Modern State, 1934.**

Dickens, Charles : **A Tale of Two Cities.**

Ducros, L. : **French Society in the Eighteenth Century.**

Goodwin : **The French Revolution, 1953.**

Gooch, G.P. : **Maria Theresa and Other Studies, 1951.**

Gottschalk, Louis : **The Era of the French Revolution, 1929.**

Kropotkin : **The Great French Revolution, 1909.**

Lefebvre, G. : **The French Revolution.**

Lowell, E.J. : **The Eve of French Revolution.**

Madelin : **The French Revolution.**

Matthews : **The French Revolution.**

Mathiez, A. : **The French Revolution, 1928.**

Salvemini, G. : **The French Revolution, 1954.**

Shackleton, Robert : **Montesquieu.**

CHAPTER

3 WORK OF THE NATIONAL ASSEMBLY (1789-91)

When Louis XVI (1774-93) could not tackle the problem of French finance, he decided to summon the Estates-General. Elections were held in the winter of 1789 and, in accordance with the old custom and royal request, the electors drafted reports on the condition of their localities and recommendations for their representatives and the government. Those reports and recommendations were called Cahiers and there were many of them. A study of those Cahiers shows that they were not revolutionary in wording. They expressed, loyalty and fidelity to the King. There was no threat of violence even in one Cahier. In spirit, most of the Cahiers reflected the radical political philosophy of the age and demanded thorough-going reforms in the government and society. Many of the Cahiers of the Third Estate were particularly insistent upon the removal of social inequalities prevailing in the country. There was an emphasis on the necessity of establishing national unity and solidarity.

The Estates-General consisted of **three Estates.** The First Estate represented the nobility, the Second represented the clergymen and the Third Estate represented the unprivileged classes consisting of the middle class, the artisans and the peasantry. Formerly, the three Estate met separately and each of them had an equal number of delegates. However, in 1789, the Third Estate was given as many members as those of the nobles and the clergymen put together. This fact emphasised the important part the Third Estate was to play in the future.

The mood of the Third Estate was expressed in a pamphlet written by Abb Sieyes which was circulated in large numbers on the eve of the French Revolution.

"What is the Third Estate?" asked Sieyes.

"Everything."

"What has been in politics up to now?"

"Nothing."

"What does it desire?"

"To become something."

The Estates-General met on 5 May 1789, and the three Estates had their sittings separately. However, the members of the Third Estate maintained that the Estates-General of 1789 was not a feudal assembly but represented the people of France. They demanded that all the three Estates should sit together and there should be voting not by "Order" but by **"Head".** Both the clergymen and the nobles were opposed to this demand and consequently there was a deadlock. On 17 June 1789, the Third Estate declared itself the National Assembly.

On 20 June 1789, the members of the Third Estate went to their usual meeting place, but they found that their entrance was blocked by soldiers. On enquiry, they were informed that there was going to be a special royal session in the hall and the same had been closed for making the necessary arrangements. For a moment, the members did not know what to do. However, after some time, they went to a neighbouring building which served as a Tennis Court and held a memorable session there. Under the Presidentship of Bailly, they took the famous Tennis Court Oath. All the deputies present with one exception voted **"never to separate, and to reassemble wherever circumstances shall require, until the constitution of the kingdom shall be established."**

On 23 June 1789, the special royal session was held. The king declared the recent acts of the Third Estate as illegal and unconstitutional. He also ordered that the three Estates should meet separately. The king, the nobility and the clergy left the hall in a spirit of victory. However, the members of the Third Estate remained in the hall and did not leave. The Master of the Ceremonies addressed them thus: "You have heard the king's order. His Majesty requests the Deputies of the Third Estate to withdraw." Soldiers were also seen at the gate. It was intended to drive out the members of the Third Estate from the hall. At this time, Mirabeau, one of the members of the Third Estate, went straight to the Master of the Ceremonies and thundered thus: **"Go tell your Master that we are here by the will of the people and that we shall not leave except at the point of bayonet."** On a motion of Mirabeau, it was voted that all persons who should lay violent hands on any member of the National Assembly would be "infamous traitors to the nation and guilty of capital crime." De Breze reported all this to Louis XVI. The king did not know what to do. At last, he observed thus: "They wish to remain, do they? Well, let them." Referring to the manner in which the king first refused and then gave way, Mirabeau observed: "This is how kings go to the scaffold."

On 25 June 1789, a majority of the clergymen and a minority of the nobility went over to the National Assembly. On 27 June 1789, Louis XVI ordered all the three Estates to sit as one body. Thus was solved a matter which could have been solved earlier without unpleasantness.

It appears, that the king had not taken his defeat happily. He was determined to intimidate or suppress the National Assembly and regain the ground lost by him. A large number of soldiers were brought to Versailles and Paris and on 11 July 1789 Necker and his colleagues who were in favour of reforms were dismissed. Necker was also ordered to leave the country immediately.

The people of Paris did not approve of the dismissal of Necker, their popular minister. It was feared that the king was determined to use force to suppress the National Assembly. Under these circumstances, there was a riot and the Bastille, which was considered to be the symbol of the **Ancien Regime,** was stormed. It was captured on 14 July 1789 and razed to the ground. **The fall of the Bastille** was considered to be the triumph of liberty in the country. According to Goodwin, "No other single event in the revolution had so many-sided or far-reaching results as the fall of the Bastille. It marked the end of the royal despotism in France, completed the transfer of political authority to the national legislature, and by encouraging the peasants to revolt, paved the way for the fall of feudalism. It freed the country from the restraints of press censorship and thus led to the rise of popular journalism, the political effect of which was amply demonstrated in the preparation of the next revolutionary **journee** in the following October. It was accompanied by an important revolution in the municipal administration of Paris and was quickly followed by an almost complete decentralization of government. It provoked the first emigration of the reactionary nobility, led by the **Cound d'Artois,** and set in train the forces that led, in time, to foreign intervention and war with Europe. For the moment, however, the impression made by the news from Paris in foreign countries was wholly favourable. The popular vengeance taken on de Launay and de Flesselles was condoned, the heroism of the mob loudly proclaimed and the absence of any private plundering generally admired. The fall of the fortress was widely acclaimed as heralding a new birth of liberty, not only in France but throughout the world." Prof. Salvemini says that the capture of the Bastille aroused great enthusiasm among the liberal-minded people throughout the world. The gloomy fortress with its eight towers—where so many political prisoners had languished and from which a resolute government could suppress any attempt at rebellion by the citizens of Paris—seemed the very symbol of the old absolutist France. All who hated the past saw in its fall the now inevitable triumph of liberty. (**The French Revolution,** p. 129).

Although the King removed the troops, reinstated Necker and recognised the National Guard, the people were not contented. National Guards were organized in all the towns. On the countryside, the peasants revolted, plundered the castles of the nobles and took special pains to destroy all the documents of titles of the nobles. Nobles were killed and their castles were razed to the ground. Early in October 1789, rumours reached Paris from Versailles that a banquet was given to some of the crack regiments which had been summoned there. On that occasion the tricolour was stamped upon. Threats were held out against the National Assembly. The queen, by her presence there, sanctioned those outrages. The women of Paris marched to Versailles drawing cannon with them and brought the King, the queen and their child shouting on the way: **"We have the baker and the baker's wife and the little cookboy—now we shall have bread."** It was in this tense atmosphere of storm and stress that the National Assembly or the Constituent Assembly performed its work from 1789 to 1791.

Work of the National Assembly. (1) The most important work of the National Assembly was the abolition of feudalism, serfdom and class privileges. On 4 August 1789, one of the nobles, who was a relative of Lafayette, stated in the Assembly that one of the reasons of the attack of the peasants on the nobility and their property was the prevalence of inequality based on injustice. He maintained that the remedy was not to repress the peasants but to end inequality which was the root cause of the trouble. A resolution was moved and passed that there should be equality of taxes. Then nobles competed with nobles and clergymen with clergymen in giving up their rights and privileges. It was in this atmosphere that the game laws were repealed, manorial courts were suppressed and serfdom was abolished. The clergymen gave up the tithes and other privileges. Sale of offices was to be discontinued. In short, all the special privileges of classes, cities and provinces were swept away. All this happened throughout the night of 4 August 1789. All the separate measures were consolidated and thus the feudal system was abolished in the country. What could not be done by Turgot and Necker was accomplished by the National Assembly. Critics point out that the privileged classes did not show any spirit of sacrifice while giving up their privileges. The people had already helped themselves by destroying all documents of title of the nobles. The privileged classes had already lost their privileges as a result of the action of the peasants themselves. On the suggestion of Archbishop of Paris, Louis XVI was officially proclaimed by the National Assembly as **'Restorer of French Liberty.'**

According to Kropotkin, "The night of August 4 is one of the great dates of the Revolution. Like July 14 and October 15, 1789, June 21, 1791, August 10, 1792, and May 31, 1793, it marked one of the great stages in the revolutionary movement, and it determined the character of the period which follows it." Again, "It would not be fair to try to diminish the importance of that night. Enthusiasm of this kind is needed to push on events. It will be needed again when a Social Revolution comes. In a revolution enthusiasm must be provoked, and words which make heart vibrate must be pronounced. The fact that the nobility, the clergy and the privileged persons of every kind had recognised during that night's sitting the progress of the Revolution, that they decided to submit to it instead of taking up arms against it—this fact by itself was already a conquest of the human mind. It was all the greater as the renunciation was made with enthusiasm. It is true that it was done in the light of the burning chateaux, but how many times had that same light merely provoked in the privileged classes an obstinate resistance, and led to hatred and massacre! That night in August those distant flames inspired other words—words of sympathy for the rebels and other acts—acts of conciliation.

"Ever since July 14, the spirit of the Revolution, born of the ferment which was working through the whole of France, was hovering over everything that lived and felt, and this spirit, created by millions of wills, gave the inspiration that we lack in ordinary times.

"But having pointed out the effects of the enthusiasm which only a revolution could inspire, the historian must also consider calmly how far all this enthusiasm did actually go, and what was the limit it dared not pass; he must point out what it gave the people and what it refused to grant them.

Well, that limit can be indicated in very few words. The Assembly only sanctioned in principle and extended to France altogether what the people had accomplished themselves in certain localities. It went no further." (**The Great French Revolution,** pp. 124-5).

Goodwin says, "The surrender of their feudal rights and fiscal immunities by the aristocracy and clergy on the night of 4th August was not, therefore, the product of spontaneous generosity. Fear, calculation and suspicion inspired the action of many deputies and the famous session was a parliamentary manoeuvre planned by a radical 'cave' in the Breton club on the previous day. The plot was that the partial surrender of feudal privileges should be proposed by members of the liberal nobility at an evening meeting, at which, it was hoped, opponents of the measure would not be present. The initiative was left to the duke d' Aiguillon, whose example as one of the largest landed proprietors in the country would, it was thought, sway the attitude of the more conservative provincial nobility. In fact, d' Aiguillon's motion was anticipated by the viscount de Noailles, who proposed that the Assembly should decree complete fiscal equality and the redemption of all feudal dues, except those involving personal servitude. The latter, he suggested, should be abolished outright. This motion and not d' Aiguillon's passed the Assembly and set the tone of the unprecedented sacrifices which followed. In a mounting spirit of patriotic enthusiasm the representatives of privilege came forward to propose the admission of all citizens to public office and the abolition of feudal jurisdictions, exclusive hunting rights and the purchase of judicial and other offices. Even more impressive and dramatic, according to Dumont, who was an eye-witness of the scene, was the surrender of all municipal, corporate and provincial privileges, proposed by the representatives from Dauphine. The proceedings closed with a loyal address to the King, conferring on him the title of **'Restorer of French Liberty.'**

"In their enthusiasm, however, the members of the National Assembly had overshot the mark, and cooler reflection on the part of the nobility prompted them later to restrict and even to contest some of these sacrifices. The result was that when the decisions of principle were cast in legislative form between 5th and 11th August, middle-class conservatism and legal caution preserved many features of the feudal regime, which had been over-hastily condemned on the night of 4th August. In this way, the 'St. Bartholomew of privilege' came to be a misnomer. Though the **ancien regime** had been dismantled, the declaration of the Assembly that 'the feudal regime had been entirely destroyed' was misleading. In the final draft, ecclesiastical tithes ware abolished, but the most onerous of the feudal dues—those of a contractual nature—were made subject to redemption. Until they were redeemed, on terms which were left for settlement at a later stage, they were to be levied as before. The disillusionment of the peasants was complete and when the king refused his sanction to this limited social revolution the Assembly found itself in a quandary."

(2) The second great work of the National Assembly was the Declaration of the Rights of Man on 27 August. This document reflected the spirit of Rousseau's philosophy and incorporated some of the provisions from the constitutional laws of England and the U.S.A. It became the platform of the French Revolution and influenced the political thought during the 19th and 20th centuries. It states that "the representatives of the French people, constituted as a National Assembly, believing that ignorance, forgetfulness or contempt of the rights of man are the only causes of public misfortunes and of the corruption of governments, have resolved to set forth in a solemn declaration, the natural, inalienable and sacred rights of man; in order that this declaration being constantly before all members of the social body may always recall to them their rights and their duties; in order that the acts of the legislative and executive powers being constantly capable of comparison with the objects of all political institutions may on that account be the most respected; in order that the demands of citizens being founded henceforth on simple and incontestable principles may be always directed to the maintenance of the constitution and the happiness of all."

The following Rights of Man and the Citizen were declared by the National Assembly :—

(*i*) Men are born and remain free and equal in rights. Social distinction can only be founded on public utility.

(*ii*) The aim of every political association is the reservation of the natural and imprescriptible rights of man. These rights are liberty, property, security and resistance to oppression.

(*iii*) Liberty consists in being allowed to do whatever does not injure other people.

(*iv*) The free communication of thought and opinion is one of the most precious rights of man.

(*v*) No person shall be accused, arrested, or imprisoned except in the cases and according to the forms prescribed by law.

(*vi*) Since private property is an invaluable and sacred right, no one shall be deprived thereof except where public necessity, legally determined, clearly demanded, and then only on condition than the owner shall have been previously and equitably indemnified.

(*vii*) Law is the expression of the general will. All citizens have the right to take part personally or through their representatives in its formation.

(*viii*) Sovereignty resides in the nation and no body or individual can exercise authority if it does not take its origin from the nation.

(*ix*) The people have the right to control the finances of the country.

(*x*) All officials of the State are responsible to the people.

The view of Lord Acton was that the Declaration of Rights of Man was "stronger than all the armies of Napoleon." For a quarter of a century, it was the watch-word and the charter of all the reformers and revolutionaries of Europe. While the British Parliament in its Declaration of Right enunciated simply the historic and legal rights of Englishmen against the Crown, France based her action on universal principles and in her declaration made herself the spokesman of the human race. While the English Revolution appeared to foreigners simply a business-like and successful re-arrangement of the constitution, the French Revolution gave a new starting point for the hopes and efforts of all races and nations. However, it cannot be denied that several of its theoretical provisions were ignored or revised in the constitutional legislation of the National Assembly. It did not explicitly formulate all the fundamental opinions of the Deputies. It made no reference to economic theories. A number of its provisions were more concerned with practical realities than with absolute theoretical rights. The latent promise of its basic articles enlisted innumerable recruits and adherents to the revolutionary cause from all ranks of the commoners. The declaration was the death certificate of the old regime and contained the promise of a new life for France. It represented a thorough indictment of the old order and a statement of the general principles upon which the new was to be built.

According to David Thomson, "It was, first, **a Declaration**—a manifesto and a statement of the general principles on which the National Assembly hoped to reform the French system of government. It was, secondly, a Declaration of **Rights**—not a Declaration of Duties. It was an assertion of the new claims and a statement of the political, constitutional, and social rights that its framers held to be essential for making a better regime. It was, thirdly, a Declaration of the **Rights of Man**—a statement intended to have a universal application and which certainly had very far-reaching implications. It was drawn up not for France alone, but for the benefit of men everywhere who wanted to be free and to rid themselves of comparable burdens of absolutist monarchy and feudal privileges. The universalism of the original French Revolution was to be of great importance. It was, finally and fully, a Declaration of the Rights of Man and of the Citizen, and although the last three words of its title are often omitted they are among its most important. It was careful to specify those civil rights that most concretely expressed the immediate aims of the middle classes which now predominated in the Assembly; equality of all before the law, eligibility of all citizens for all public offices, personal freedom from arbitrary arrest or punishment, freedom of speech and the Press, and above all an equitable distribution of the burdens of national taxation and the inviolability of private property. These claims it founded on the two general doctrines that 'the principle of all sovereignty rests essentially in the nation,' and that 'law is the expression of the general will.' These doctrines—intended to be universal in application—would clearly, if accepted, destroy the very foundations of the old order of society and disrupt the State everywhere in Europe. This was the inherent challenge of events in France to every one of her neighbours, including Britain. One French historian has called the Declaration 'the death certificate of the old regime.' It certainly remained a charter of liberalism throughout the nineteenth century.

"Even so, the Declaration is less abstract and most realistic than it might appear at first. Its omissions, as a manifesto of liberalism, are significant. It made no mention of freedom of economic enterprise or of trade, so dear to its bourgeois makers because the older order had already in recent years suppressed the guilds and removed controls on the grain trade; it said nothing of rights of assembly and association, nor of education or social security, although many were aware of how important these were, for these matters were less relevant to the immediate tasks of destroying the old regime. Although it tried to be universal it did not set out to be comprehensive. It deliberately omitted any Declaration of Duties, an omission not remedied until 1795. Its most liberal principles were stated cautiously. Exercise of natural rights is limited by the need to assure enjoyment of the same rights for others. 'Law may rightfully prohibit only those actions that are injurious to society.' Freedom of opinion is limited by the proviso that it must not trouble public order as established by law, and that it must not be abused. Even the sanctity of property is subject to an 'obvious requirement of public necessity'." (**Europe Since Napoleon,** pp. 10-11).

The Declaration has been described as "the most remarkable fact in the history of the growth of democratic and republican ideas" in France, "the gospel of modern times."

According to Prof. Salvemini, "If, by a metaphysical work we mean one wholly confined to theory and out of touch with reality, then none could be found less metaphysical than the Declaration of Rights, to which the history of France and Europe has subsequently given ever wider application. The Rights of 1789 are certainly not 'natural' in a sense implying that all human society not in conformity with them must be considered 'unnatural': but they are 'natural' to us, moderns in the sense that without them our own civilization could not exist, and we ourselves could not live. Every government in France from 1789 onwards has had to give fuller recognition and guarantees to the principles of the Declaration. It was the inspiration of all those peoples who in the nineteenth century rose against despotism and set up their own constitutional governments. All our civil and penal legislation is descended from the Rights of 1789. Oppressed nations, in gaining independence, have found in them moral justification for their efforts. Today the masses still invoke the same principles of equality and freedom, which, having served as weapons in the struggle that put an end to feudalism, have passed now into other hands and have become an instrument of yet wider change.

"It must not be thought that the social conflicts of today have been produced by the Declaration of 1789. Many other factors have contributed to them: the great factories and workshops where the proletariat learns, through the close contacts of common work, to be aware of its own social function and its numerical strength; the complexity and delicacy of our modern economic structure, which causes a crisis at one point to dislocate all the rest; education and the press, both of which spread the ferment of thought into ever wider fields; and the franchise, through which the unpropertied classes can control their governments—all these have created a lack of equilibrium in modern life, prompting men to react against the traditional system of private ownership. But the proletariat is assisted in its struggle today by the same principles that upheld the bourgeoisie of 1789 and which they asserted to be primitive, absolute and common to all men; and the bourgeoisie can never now set them aside unless it wishes to bring the functioning of the social order to a standstill; unless, in fear of death, it wants to commit suicide. The class war, as Faguet rightly observes, had existed even before the

Revolution; but at that time the commons had not had, at their service, 'a general ideal, a kind of dogma, that justified and consecrated the struggle, which was one of strength against strength, of attempts on the part of the weak to support one another against the strong.' Today this is no longer. 'The Revolution' by proclaiming the dogma of equality, has given the class struggle not so much a reason for existing, as a reason for proclaiming that it exists by right, and a reason for appearing to have right on its side.'

"The same may be said of all the other great national, constitutional and legislative achievements of the nineteenth century; they have not sprung directly from the Declaration of Rights, for they are a necessary product of the modern social order. But in the Rights of 1789 they have found their theoretic justification; they have found a time-honoured system of ideas within which they themselves could be incorporated. If this is metaphysics, then all history is metaphysics." (**The French Revolution,** pp. 147-148).

(3) The National Assembly set up a uniform system of administration all over the country. The old provinces, governments, intendancies, **pays d'etat, pays d'election, parlements and bailliages** were abolished. The country was divided afresh into 83 departments. These departments were uniform in size and population and were named after natural features such as rivers or mountains. Each department was divided into cantons and communes. The heads of the local divisions were to be elected by the people and not nominated by the executive. Provision was made for local councils which were to be elected by the people. A new system of courts was provided for the country. The judges of these courts were to be elected by the people. Attempts were also made to simplify and unify the legal system of the country but the work could not be accomplished till the time of Napoleon as first Consul.

(4) The National Assembly also tried to tackle the problem of finance. The State treasury was practically empty and no wonder the Assembly resorted to extreme measures to meet the situation. In November 1789, the Church property in France was confiscated. That property was valued at many hundred million dollars. With Church property as security the National Assembly issued paper currency known as Assignats. Paper money works well so long as too much use of the printing press is not permitted. The paper currency must be kept within reasonable limits. However, the natural temptation of printing more paper currency and thereby adding to the revenue of the State could not be checked by he National Assembly and consequently by 1791, inflation was already well under way. This process was continued in the succeeding years and consequently the whole of the paper currency had to be cancelled during the Directory. It is true that the issuing of **Assignats** tackled the financial problem for the time being, but otherwise the issuing of **Assignats** was one of the sorriest chapters of the French Revolution. Prof. Salvemini says, "Of all the Assembly measures; the issue of the assignats was one that most contributed towards consolidating the new regime and preventing any form of counter-revolution. The assignats were, in fact, a paper currency based not on gold but on the security of Church lands. Should a counter-revolution enable the clergy to recover their possession, the assignats would lose their guarantee, therefore their fate depended upon that of the Revolution. Whoever accepted an assignat—and everyone had to accept them, since they were legal tender—was committed to the revolutionary cause, if he did not want his money to become worthless through a return to feudal and ecclesiastical rule." (**The French Revolution,** p. 169).

(5) The National Assembly dealt with the Church in France. Church property was confiscated in November 1789. In February 1790, the monasteries and other religious communities were suppressed. In April 1790, absolute religious toleration was proclaimed. In July 1790, the **Civil Constitution of the Clergy** was enacted. The number of bishops and priests was reduced and they were made a civil body. They were to be elected by the people and paid by the State. Their association with the Pope was to be merely nominal. In December 1790, a decree was passed by which all Catholic clergymen were required to take a solemn oath of allegiance to the Civil Constitution. As was to be expected, the Pope condemned the Civil Constitution and asked the clergymen in France not to take the oath

to the Civil Constitution. The result was that the clergymen in France were divided into two groups. Those who took the oath were called the **juring clergy** and those who did not take necessary oath were called the **non-juring clergy.** Up to that time, a large number of clergymen belonging to the lower strata had sympathized with the course of the French Revolution, but after that they became opposed to it. It was only a small minority of clergymen who took the oath of allegiance to the Civil Constitution.

The seeds of division were sown throughout the country and they produced an actual civil war before long. The king who had accepted the revolution with hesitation now found himself in a decided opposition to it. The religious fibre in his nature was very strong. He gave his signatures, to the church laws on account of the fear of the storm of opposition which his veto might have created, but the denunciation by the Pope made him profoundly uneasy. He wrote thus, "I ask God to accept my profound repentance for having affixed my name, though against my will, to acts which are in conflict with the discipline and the belief of the Catholic Church". The church legislation was one of the important causes which impelled the king to run away from Paris with all the disastrous consequences.

(6) The National Assembly framed, a new constitution for France and that is why it is also known as the Constituent Assembly. This constitution was completed in 1791 and after the signatures of the king became the law of the country. It was the first written constitution of France. It was based on the principle of separation of powers which was propounded by Montesquieu and embodied in the American Constitution of 1787. The legislature, judiciary and executive were separated from one another and separate departments were set up for each one of them. The legislative authority was vested in one Chamber called the Legislative Assembly. Its members numbering 745 were to be chosen by a system of indirect election for 2 years. The right of voting was to be exercised only by "active" citizens, *i.e.*, those citizens who paid taxes. Only those persons were to be elected as members of the Legislative Assembly who had a certain amount of property. The prescribing of the property qualification showed that the National Assembly was dominated by the bourgeoisie or the middle-class.

Nominally, the executive authority in the State was to vest in the king whose office was to be hereditary. The king was given the power of suspensive veto by which he could postpone the execution of an Act of the legislature. However, he was deprived of all the control over local government, the clergy, the navy and the army. His ministers were not to sit in the **Legislative Assembly.**

The judicial system was completely revolutionized. Formerly, the judges used to buy their positions which carried with them titles and privileges. They had also the right to pass on those positions to their sons. All that was abolished. In future, all judges were to be elected. Their terms of office were to vary from 2 to 4 years. July system was introduced in criminal cases.

Prof. Hazen says, "The Constitution of 1791 represented an improvement in French government; yet it did not work well and did not last long. As a first experiment in the art of self-government it had its value, but it revealed inexperience and poor judgment in several points which prepared trouble for the future. The executive and the legislature were so sharply separated that communication between them was difficult and suspension was consequently easily fostered. The king might not select his ministers from the legislature; he might not, in case of a difference of opinion with the legislature, dissolve the latter, as the English king could do, thus allowing the voters to decide between them. The king's veto was not a weapon strong enough to protect him from the attacks of the legislature yet it was enough to irritate the legislature, if used. The distinction between active and passive citizens was in plain and flagrant defiance of the Declaration of the Rights of Man and inevitably created a discontented class. The administrative decentralization was so complete that the efficiency of the national government was gone. France was split up into eighty-three fragments and the co-ordination of all these units, their direction towards great national ends in response to the will of the nation as a whole, was rendered extremely difficult, and in certain cases impossible."

Estimate of its Work. A survey of the work of the National Assembly shows that it destroyed the pillars of the **Ancien Regime.** It destroyed feudalism. It destroyed the old forms of government. It destroyed the old financial system. It destroyed the old judicial system. It made revolutionary changes in the Church of the country. However, in addition to all this destruction, attempts were made to give France a simple system of administration in which the people had a hand. All this was achieved not only by the efforts of the National Assembly but also by the efforts of all those peasants who revolted on the country-side, destroyed the villas and documents of title of the nobles, killed the nobles and clergymen and thereby struck terror into the hearts of the privileged classes and completely demoralised them.

Critics point out that the National Assembly opened the way to mob rule. It put forward dangerous theories. It created a division in the country on the question of religion. It made the mistake of separating the legislature from the executive. It foolishly passed a law by which the members of the National Assembly were debarred from election to the new legislature under the new constitution. No wonder, much of its work was undone later on. However, some of it remained permanent and became the source of inspiration for the people of the Europe and the world.

The Constituent Assembly secured the unity of France. It set up a new political structure. It let loose the energy of the people and made an honest attempt to inaugurate a common system of laws and an equitable division of burdens. It created a civil and social revolution. It established in the will of the people a new criterion of public policy. It proclaimed a new gospel of the personal dignity of the common man for the whole world.

Kropotkin says, "The work done by the Constituent Assembly was undoubtedly middle-class work. But to introduce into the customs of the nation the principle of political equality, to abolish the relics of the rights of one man over the person of another, to awaken the sentiment of equality and the spirit of revolt against inequalities, was nevertheless an immense work. Only it must be remembered, as Louis Blanc has remarked, that to maintain and to kindle that fiery spirit in the Assembly, 'the wind that was blowing from the street was necessary.' 'Even rioting,' he adds, 'in those unparalleled days, produced from its tumult many wise inspirations! **Every rising was so full of thoughts!'** In other words, it was the street, the man in the street, that each time forced the Assembly to go forward with its work of reconstruction. Even a revolutionary Assembly, or one at least that forced itself upon monarchy in a revolutionary way, as the Constituent Assembly did, would have done nothing if the masses of the people had not impelled it to march forward, and if they had not crushed, by their insurrections, the anti-revolutionary resistance." (**The Great French Revolution,** p. 173).

It is interesting to note that although the laws passed by the Constituent Assembly appear to be purely domestic in character, they actually affected the foreign relations of France. The abolition of feudalism took away the feudal dues from the German subjects who possessed landed properties within the French frontiers. The religious legislation of the Assembly deprived the Bishops of Cologne and Mainz of tithes which they had hitherto received from French subjects. The reorganisation of the Bishoprics of France took from their obedience parishes and districts which had long been theirs. These questions created friction between France and her German subjects and the Empire championed the claims of the Germans who considered themselves to be aggrieved.

Flight of the King (September 1791). Before the National Assembly finished its work on 30 September, 1791, a very important event had taken place in France and that was the attempted flight of the king from the country. Louis XVI had been dragged from Versailles to Paris by the mob. He was living in the Tuileries in retirement and it was only on certain occasions that he was asked to appear by the National Assembly. The king felt that he was practically a prisoner in the hands of the Parisian mob. After the death of Mirabeau, he lost all support. The new constitution framed by the National Assembly deprived him practically of all powers. He felt that it was impossible for him to continue in that unbearable position. He is stated to have remarked: **"I would rather be king of Metz than**

remain King of France in such a position, but this will end soon." A plan was made for running away from France to Austria. The members of the royal family disguised themselves and left their residence in secret. If the royal party had been cautious and also made a determined effort to reach the frontier as quickly as possible unmindful of the inconvenience, there was every possibility of their escape. However, the royal party was captured when it was still 20 miles away from the frontier. It was brought back to Paris under very humiliating circumstances. The unsuccessful flight of the king had very serious consequences. It clearly showed that the king did not approve of the revolution from his heart and was also an enemy of the constitution. Men like Robespierre and Danton demanded that kingship should be abolished and a republic established in its place. However, the constitutional monarchists still had their majority in the National Assembly and consequently no action was taken against the king. The king took an oath to support the constitution and the matter rested there. It was under these circumstances that the National Assembly dissolved itself on 30 September, 1791.

SUGGESTED READINGS

Acton, Lord : **Lectures on the French Revolution.**

Bourne: **The Revolutionary Period in Europe.**

Brinton, C. : **A Decade of Revolution (1789-1799), New York, 1934.**

Lowell : **The Eve of the French Revolution.**

MacLehos : **From the Monarchy to the Republic.**

Mathews : **The French Revolution.**

Robinson & Beard : **Readings in Modern European History.**

Thompson, E. : **Popular Sovereignty and the French Constituent Assembly (1789-1791), 1952.**

Thomson, David : **Europe Since Napoleon.**

CHAPTER 4

THE LEGISLATIVE ASSEMBLY AND NATIONAL CONVENTION

The Legislative Assembly (1791-1792). Elections were held under the constitution framed by the National Assembly in 1791 and the Legislative Assembly met on 1 October, 1791. The Assembly consisted of 745 members, but unfortunately all of them were new to their job. Foolishly, the National Assembly had passed a self-denying law by which its members were debarred from being elected to the Legislative Assembly under the new constitution. This was most unfortunate and the country was to suffer on that account. Most of the members of the Legislative Assembly held extreme views and that could give an indication of the trouble ahead.

Clubs in France. At that time, certain political clubs came into existence and the most important of them were the **Jacobin Club** and the **Cordelier Club.** As regards the Jacobin Club, it was moderate at the outset but it grew more and more radical with the passage of time. This happened particularly after Mirabeau and Lafayette left the Club. The result was that Robespierre, a radical democrat, came to the front. Under his leadership, the radical opinion in the country was mobilised and a large number of branches were established all over the country. After some time, the Jacobin Club became a rival of the Legislative Assembly itself. The Cordelier Club was led by Danton and was radical from the very beginning. Its members were recruited from the lower strata of society and republicanism was strong from the very beginning. These clubs exercised a tremendous influence on the public in the country.

Political Groups in the Assembly. A reference may also be made to the political groups in the Legislative Assembly. **The Constitutionalists** were the supporters of the Constitution of 1791 and consequently stood for a constitutional form of government in the country. They were prepared to accept the king with his limited powers. The Republicans were divided into two main groups, **the Girondists** and **the Jacobins.** The Jacobins were also known as the Mountain on account of their raised seats in the Assembly premises. The Girondists were moderates but they stood for establishing a republican form of government. They were not practical in their approach. Their outlook was more academic than practical. They were very particular about legal forms and processes and were opposed to brute force. According to Prof. Hazen, "The Girondists have enjoyed a poetic immortality ever since imaginative histories of the Revolution issued from the pensive pen of the poet Lamartine, who portrayed them as pure and high-minded patriots caught in the swirl of a wicked world. The description was inaccurate. They were not disinterested martyrs in the cause of good government. They were a group of politicians whose discretion was not as conspicuous as their ambition. They paid for that vaulting emotion the price which it frequently exacts. They knew how to make their tragic exit from life bravely and heroically. They did not know, what is more difficult, how to make their lives wise and profitable to the world. They were a group of eloquent young men, led by a romantic young woman. For the real head of this group that had its hour upon the stage and then was heard no more in the deafening clamour of the later Revolution was Madame Roland, their bright particular star. Theirs was a bookish outlook upon the world. They fed upon Plutarch, and boundless was their admiration for the ancient Greeks and Romans. They were republicans because those glorious figures of the earlier time had been republicans; also because they imagined that, in a republic, they would themselves find a better chance to shine and to irradiate the world. Dazzled by these prototypes they burned with the spirit of emulation." The Jacobins were Republicans of the extreme type. They were prepared to adopt all kinds of means for the establishment and safety of a republican form of government in the country. It is true that the Girondists had a majority in the Legislative Assembly at the beginning, but the influence of the Jacobins was growing every day on account of the backing of the Jacobin Club.

Laws vetoed by King. The Legislative Assembly passed two laws. By the first law all priests were required to act according to the Civil Constitution of the Clergy. It was provided that those clergymen who did not accept the Civil Constitution by a particular date, were to be deprived of their pensions and were also to be considered as suspects. They were liable to be removed from their districts in case of any trouble. The second law dealt with those Frenchmen who had left their country and were persuading foreign powers to intervene on their behalf to crush the French Revolution. They were called the **Emigres.** The law required them to return to France by a fixed date. In the event of their failure to do so, their properties were to be confiscated and they were liable to be punished with death. Louis XVI did not approve of these laws and consequently vetoed both of them. The law against the non-juring clergymen pricked his own conscience and the king himself seemed to be in sympathy with the Emigres. The people of Paris were not prepared to accept such an attitude on the part of the king and consequently they attacked the residence of the king on 20 June 1792. They found the king in one room and the queen and young Dauphin in another. For hours, the king was jostled, insulted and stared at. When the mob left, one of them observed: "We will come back again, and we will get what we want." This was a dangerous precedent.

They came back again. At midnight or 9 August 1792, the tocsin sounded in the capital and the regular government of Paris was superseded by a violent body with Danton as the leader. The National Guards around the palace were removed or melted away. Their commander was murdered. The threat became so serious that at about eight in the morning, the royal family left the palace and with great difficulty took refuge in the building of the Assembly. As he entered Louis XVI observed: "I have come to prevent a great crime." There was a bloody battle between Swiss guards of the palace and the mob. About 600 of them were killed and the palace was captured and looted by the mob. The royal family remained in the building of the Assembly for three days and after that they were imprisoned in one of the gloomy prison-like towers of the temple where they remained till their death.

The object of the rising was achieved. The king was suspended. A provisional government was set up with Danton as Minister of Justice. However, the real power was in the hands of the new Commune of Paris and the Jacobin Club.

Factors leading to War. France was drifting towards war and that was due to many causes. The revolutionaries of France were not contented with the spread of their ideas only in their own country. They seemed to be determined to propagate their ideas in other countries of Europe. Naturally, the rulers of other States were opposed to these activities of the Frenchmen and bitterness was being created. The Emigres were carrying on propaganda against France in other countries of Europe and there was every possibility of their attack on France with foreign help. France had abolished all the feudal dues and tithes. That applied to Alsace and other border provinces which once belonged to the German Empire. The Peace of Westphalia of 1648 had guaranteed certain rights and privileges to the German princes and they seem to have been hit by the action of the French Government. It is true that the French Government offered to compensate the German princes for the loss of their rights, but the princes rejected the offer and appealed to the German Diet. France also annexed Avignon which had been under the Pope from 14th century. This was considered to be a breach of international law. The French were particularly against Austria because she had not dispersed the French Emigres from the German soil. Austria was suspected of helping them. On 27th August 1791, both Austria and Prussia issued the Declaration of Pillnitz. It was declared that the cause of the French Government was the cause of the kings of Europe and both Austria and Prussia were prepared to intervene in France if the rulers of other countries joined hands with them. The threat of foreign intervention was resented by the people of France and that strengthened the hands of Girondists who were in favour of declaring war and thereby getting an opportunity to end the monarchy in France. The French Government gave an ultimatum to Austria and war was declared in April 1792.

Although the Girondists were clamouring for war and started it, they could not prosecute it successfully. These people were impractical politicians and no wonder the French were defeated on all fronts. Their attack on Belgium failed. They were defeated by the combined armies of Austria and Prussia. The Frenchmen attributed their defeats not to their own lack of preparation but to the activities of the king. It was stated that the military secrets of France were passed on to the enemies by the royal family and consequently, the French were defeated. The French king was dubbed as the cause of the French defeats. When the king was being condemned from all quarters, the Duke of Brunswick, who was the Commander-in-Chief of the Allied Forces, issued in July 1792 a manifesto to the French people in which he declared his intention to restore in France the Bourbons to their legitimate position in the State. The French reply to the manifesto was a revolt in Paris in August 1792. The outcome of the revolt was the establishment of the dictatorship of Danton. On 10 August, 1792, the king was suspended and elections were ordered for a National Convention to prepare a new constitution for the country.

The policy of Danton can be summed up in his own words thus: **"In my opinion, the way to stop the enemy is to terrify the royalists. Audacity, more audacity and always greater audacity."** The result of his policy was the wholesale massacre of the royalists in Paris. Men, women and children, nobles and the magistrates, priests and bishops and others suspected of having sympathy with the royalist cause were murdered in cold blood. As the Allies were advancing into France, fear deepened into panic. Supreme control passed into the hands of Danton and his colleagues. On 20 September 1792, the Allies were defeated in the Battle of Valmy and their advance was checked. France was saved from the immediate danger. The victory gave self-confidence to the French troops and after that they won victory after victory. It was under these circumstances that the National Convention met on 21 September 1792.

The National Convention (1792-95). According to Prof. Hayes, "Perhaps no legislative body in history has been called upon to solve such knotty problems as those which confronted the National Convention at the beginning of its session." Something had to be done with the deposed king. The country had to be saved from foreign invasion. Internal insurrection had to be suppressed. A government had to be established. Social reforms had to be completed and consolidated. A new constitution had to be framed for the country. It goes to the credit of the National Convention that it accomplished all these tasks successfully.

The deposed king was put up for trial and was found unanimously guilty of treason. By a small majority, his immediate death was voted upon. While the Girondists pleaded for leniency, the Jacobins demanded his immediate execution. Ultimately, the king was guillotined on Sunday, January 21, 1793. His last words were: **"Gentlemen, I am innocent of that of which I am accused. May my blood assure the happiness of the French."**

Louis XVI was the victim of his errors and his weaknesses and those of his royal predecessors. His tragic death placed a halo around him. His long martyrdom in prison which he bore with patience and resignation, his kindliness and manly courage and his composure in the face of death, served to palliate a personal mediocrity.

Foreign Policy. The work of the National Convention may be discussed under two heads: foreign policy and internal policy. As regards foreign policy, a very difficult situation had to be handled. In

December 1792, the National Convention issued the following decree: "The French nation declares that it will treat as enemies every people who, refusing liberty and equality or renouncing them, may wish to maintain, recall, or treat with a prince, and the privileged classes..." In January 1793, Louis XVI was executed on the ground that he had bribed the members of the National or Constituent Assembly and also written letters to his fellow-monarchs urging them to come to his assistance. Both on account of the French declaration of war against all the monarchs of Europe and the execution of Louis XVI, Austria, Prussia, Great Britain, Holland, Spain and Sardinia joined hands to crush the revolution in France. It was not an easy task for the French revolutionaries to meet the danger from outside. The Convention met the situation with a firm hand. Under the leadership and supervision of Carnot, a spirit of militarism was infused among Frenchmen. On January 31, 1793, Danton declared: "The limits of the republic are set by nature herself and those limits we will attain to the four corners of the horizon, to the Rhine, the Alps, the Pyrenees and the Ocean. These must be boundaries of our republic, and no power on earth shall prevent our reaching them." In February 1793, a compulsory levy of half a million men was ordered. It was enacted in August 1793 that every Frenchman between the ages of 18 and 25 was to render military service. Carnot drafted men, silenced complaints, got extra volunteers, drilled the troops and hurried them to the frontiers of France to check the invasion. He prepared plans of campaigns, appointed trusted officers and infused in them a new spirit of fighting for the cause of the French Revolution. By the end of 1793, he had 770,000 men under arms and most of them were fanatically attached to the cause of the Revolution. Bourgeois citizens, artisans and peasants backed the action of the Government. They sang the Marseillaise and waved the banner of liberty, equality and fraternity.

The militarism of France was based on the principle of **"the nation in arms".** Soon the country was not only cleared of foreign troops, but the war was pressed on into the Netherlands, along the Rhine, in Savoy and across the Pyrenees. The French armies were so much successful that Carnot, who had formerly been given the title of **"Organizer of Defence",** came to be called by the name of **"Organizer of Victory".** It is impossible to do justice to the amazing campaigns of 1794 and 1795. All that need be said is that when the National Convention ended in 1795, the First Coalition against France had been completely smashed. Spain had to humble herself by entering into an alliance with Republican France. By the Treaty of Basle of 1795, the King of Prussia gave France a free hand on the left bank of the Rhine. William V of Holland was deposed and his territory was transformed into the Republic of Batavia which entered into an alliance with France. French troops got possession of the Austrian Netherlands and the territories of the Rhine. Only Great Britain, Austria and Sardinia remained in arms against the French Republic.

Home Policy. As regards the home policy of the National Convention, the latter had to face a very difficult situation. A militant spirit had been created among the people and consequently there were riots at many places, *e.g.*, Lyons, Marseilles and Bordeaux. The peasants in La Vendee revolted with a view to restoring monarchy and re-establishing the Catholic Church. However, all these revolts were crushed with a heavy hand and no dissent was tolerated.

(1) In 1793, the National Convention entrusted the supreme executive authority of France to the Committee of Public Safety. This Committee included important personalities like Robespierre, Carnot and St. Just. From 1793 to 1794, there was a virtual Reign of Terror in France. The chief agencies of the Committee of Public Safety were the Committee of General Security and the Revolutionary Tribunal. By the Law of Suspects, any person who was of noble birth or who had held office before the Revolution or had any relation with an emigre, or who could not produce assigned certificate of citizenship, was liable to be hanged. During this period the guillotine played a very important part. It is estimated that about 5,000 persons were executed in Paris alone during the Reign of Terror. Among those executed were Marie Antoinette and Madame Rolland Although the terror started in Paris, it also spread to the countryside. Local tribunals were established everywhere to search out and

condemn suspected persons. Hundreds of persons were put to death at Lyons. At Nantes, Carrier took the victims into the Loire and drowned them. It is estimated that about 15,000 persons perished in the provinces. The militant spirit took a toll of not only innocent persons, but even the perpetrators of the crimes were not spared. The Reign of Terror ended with the death of Danton, St. Just and Robespierre.

(2) One of the greatest achievements of the National Convention was that it preached the gospel of nationalism to the people. With a view to creating a truly nationalist army, a decree was issued in 1794 by which compulsory military service was prescribed for all able-bodied Frenchmen. The decree stated: "The young men shall go to the battle; the married men shall forge arms and transport provisions; the women shall make tents and clothing, and shall serve in the hospitals, the children shall turn linen into lint: the aged shall betake themselves to the public places in order to rouse the courage of the warriors and preach hatred of the Government and the unity of the Republic." This was the real beginning of militarism on a large scale in Europe.

(3) The National Convention also provided that French was to be the only language for purposes of national instruction throughout the country.

(4) The work of codification of the national laws of the country was also taken in hand and much progress was made in that direction. It was provided that there was to be no imprisonment for debt. There was to be no slavery in French colonies. Women were to have their right to property. The law of primogeniture by which the eldest son got everything and the others nothing, was ended. All children were to have equal shares of the property. A new and uniform system of weights and measures, called the Metric System, was established.

(5) Certain experiments were made in the field of religion also. The National Convention showed hostility towards the traditional form of Christianity. Clergymen were considered to be suspected persons. Attempts were made to de-Christianise France. Churches were transformed into temples of reasons. Several Catholic bishops and priests gave up Christianity. Under the auspices of the Paris Commune, the atheistic "religion of reason" was inaugurated in the Cathedral of Notre Dame in November 1793. The deistic cult of the Supreme Being was also introduced. However, after the fall of Robespierre in July 1794, the National Convention took up the attitude that religion was a private affair and it was not the business of the State either to establish or to maintain an official religion. The result was that religious toleration was given to all and many church buildings were restored for Christian worship in 1795.

(6) The National Convention also made changes in the calendar. The year was divided in 12 months and each month was to consist of three weeks of 10 days each. Every tenth day was declared a holiday. The five or six days left over at the end of the year, were to be observed as National Holidays. The names of the months[1] were changed and the year was to start from 22 September, 1792.

(7) The National Convention also made some experiments in the socialist field. The property of the emigres was confiscated. Persons of wealth, clergymen and nobles were all treated as suspects. Large landed estates were broken up and offered for sale in small parcels on easy terms so that the ordinary people may be able to own land. Thus a large number of peasant-proprietors were created. No compensation was to be given to those who were deprived of their lands. The view of Marat was that **"the rich have *so* long sucked out the marrow of the people that they are now visited with a crushing retribution."** Attempts were made to collect money by means of forced loans with a view to keeping down the cost of living. "The laws of the maximum" were passed which fixed the

1. The names of the months from September to August were Vendemiaire. Brumaire, Frimaire, Nivose, Pluviose, Ventose, Germinal, Floreal, Prairial, Messidor, Thermidor and Fructidor. The contemporary English translation of those names was Wheezy, Sneezy, Freezy, Slippy, Drippy, Nippy, Showery, Flowery, Bowery, Wheaty, Heaty and Sweety.

prices of grains and other necessaries of life and rates of wages. It was also provided that everybody was to be addressed as "citizen". There was to be no gradation in society.

(8) After the fall of Robespierre in July 1794, the laws against the suspects and the laws of the maximum were repealed. The Revolutionary Tribunal was suppressed. By 1795, France was definitely committed to republican form of Government. The constitution which had been drawn up by the Girondists in 1791, was set aside and a new one was prepared in 1795. According to the new constitution, France was to have two chambers: a lower house consisting of 500 members and a Council of Ancients consisting of 250 members to examine and enact the laws. The executive authority in the State was entrusted to a Committee of five Directors known as the Directory. The Directors were to be elected by the legislature and they were to appoint the ministers of the State who were to supervise the enforcement of the laws.

(9) The National Convention was most successful in its organisation of higher education. Only two war-time establishments, the Ecole de Mars, which was a revolutionary military academy and the Ecole Normale, a training school, ended with the Revolution. The other scientific schools were permanent. The School of Public Works later on called the Polytechnic School was established in 1794 to train civil and military engineers. A School of Oriental Languages was set up to keep a close contact with the East. In 1793, the Jardin due roi was reorganised and enlarged into the Museum of Natural History. Its collection was enriched. The most distinguished scientists of France were given subsidies to carry on their researches in its laboratories. Later on, public lectures were given by these savants. A National Conservatory of Arts and Industries was organised as "a museum and a school for industry." Three schools of medicine were founded in 1794 and they gave theoretical and practical instruction to students who were chosen on a competitive basis. In place of the old universities and academies, the National Convention set up a National Institute on 25 October 1795. It was divided into three classes: physical and mathematical sciences, moral and political sciences and literature and fine arts. More than 100 distinguished savants were summoned by the Government to make the National Institute **"the representative body of the republic of letters."**

Reign of Terror (1793-94). It seems desirable to write in detail about the Reign of Terror which began officially with the institution of the Revolutionary Tribunal on 9 March 1793, and ended with the guillotining of Robespierre on 29 July, 1794. To some persons, the Reign of Terror seemed to be aimlessly bloody, disgusting and unnecessary. To others, it appeared to be altogether essential. It is stated that **"stern discipline can manufacture collective heroism."** After the misgovernment of the Girondists, France was badly in need of stern discipline. There were thousands of Frenchmen who were disloyal and cowardly and the Reign of Terror was considered to be essential for them. In order to save France from internal troubles and the danger from foreign invaders, it was considered necessary to turn France into an armed camp. The need was urgent and consequently the measures had to be both stern and speedy.

The Reign of Terror has been described as martial law gone mad. Popular fear, mingled with fury against the counter revolutionaries, took the form of a military organisation. The exigency of the circumstances demanded that something should be done to make the Frenchmen march to the front to fight the enemies and that was made possible by the Reign of Terror which enabled Danton, Carnot and St. Just to meet the situation. Danton was neither blood-thirsty nor corrupt. He was driven by a patriotism which aimed at the salvation of France. He devoted his giant body and voice to the service of the country. Carnot was a born administrator, soldier and strategist. He was thorough in everything he did. It is pointed out that he forged Napoleon's thunderbolts and without him the terror would have been simply disgusting. He organised 13 armies and provided them with all they wanted and thus led them 10 victory. St. Just made his name terrible to the inefficient and the slack. He possessed a fighting patriotism and he moved to and fro between Paris and the headquarters of the armies with a view to putting vigour into the whole show.

By a decree of 1794 compulsory military service was prescribed for all able-bodied Frenchmen. The Committee of Public Security was given police power in order to maintain law and order throughout the length and breadth of the country. The Revolutionary Tribunal was empowered to condemn any person suspected of disloyalty to the Republic. The Law of Suspects enabled the government to arrest and hang any person.

It cannot be denied that the Reign of Terror succeeded in its objective. The French armies were victorious in the Netherlands. They passed from defence to victory. In December 1793, they recovered Toulon and crushed La Vendee. They were in control of the Alps and the Pyrenees. The Allies were pushed back. They were forced to raise the sieges of Dunkirk, Maubeuge, Tourcoing and Fleurus. The discipline was so stern that every commander and soldier was required to do his very best. The commander of Maubeuge was told that his head should answer for the fortress. Although Houchard drove back the besiegers of Dunkirk, he was guillotined because he did not turn the **retreat** into a **rout.**

The success of the French armies was partly due to the unity of command, their fanaticism for their cause and stern discipline. It was also partly due to the weakness of the Allies. There was no unity of command or plan among them. Every ally was busy in his own way. Austria, Prussia and Russia were busy in planning the partition of Poland and dividing their shares and consequently could not concentrate on the war with France. It is true that Pitt, the Younger, tried to concentrate his forces in the Netherlands, but he also indulged in side-shows. The Duke of York, who was the British Commander in the Netherlands, was absolutely inefficient and that is clear from the following :—

The good old Duke of York.
He had ten thousand men.
He marched them up to the top of the hill.
Then he marched them down again.

There were two alternatives which the Allies could follow. They could smash the French armies and the fortresses on the way while advancing to Paris. The other alternative was to attack and conquer all the French fortresses and then proceed to Paris. The second alternative was actually followed by the Allies. Their belief was that the time spent in reducing one by one the "barrier fortresses" would allow anarchy to develop in Paris and if an immediate advance was made against Paris, all the Frenchmen might combine together to defend their country. What actually happened was that the Allies lost valuable time in capturing the barrier fortresses and France got time to prepare her armies to meet them and defeat them.

It cannot be denied that the military machine which saved France was oiled with blood. Everything in France was controlled from the Centre. The representatives of the Committee of Public safety were put in charge of districts and no sign of slackness was tolerated in any shape or form. The city of Lyons had taken up the cause of the Girondists. It took 4-1|2 months to subdue it. When that was done, the National Convention passed the following decree: "The city of Lyons is to be destroyed. Every house which was inhabited by the rich shall be demolished. There will remain only the homes of the poor, of patriots, and buildings especially employed for industries, and those edifices dedicated to humanity and to education." The very name of the city was to be obliterated. It was in future to be known as the **Liberated City (Commune affranchie).** More than 3,500 persons were arrested and nearly half of them were executed. The person in charge of the executions remarked thus: **"What a sight worthy of Liberty, what a delicious moment!"**

The district of Vendee had revolted against the Republic. The people had not approved of the laws against the priests. They had refused to fight in the Republican armies. The Government was perfectly justified in putting down the rebellion but while doing so, it perpetrated atrocities which were not warranted by the circumstances. Carrier, who had been deputed by the National Convention set up a record for barbarity. He considered the method of the Revolutionary Tribunal as slow and ordered the prisoners to be shot in squads. He got the prisoners bound down, put in the boats and the latter sunk in the river Loire. Even the Committee of Public Safety was shocked and asked for an explanation. The reply of Carrier was: "Is it my fault that the boats did not reach the destination ?". The number of dead bodies in the river was so large that water got poisoned. Carrier was removed from his post but no action was taken against him.

Prisons were crowded and constantly men and women were brought before the Revolutionary Tribunal. Acquittals were rare and guillotine was the universal penalty. In October 1793, Marie Antoinette was executed. A large number of the Girondists were executed. On 6 November, Philippe, Duke of Orleans, who had championed the cause of the Revolution voted for the king's death and given his palace to the agitators, was put to death. On 10 November, Madame Roland was executed. When she mounted the scaffold, she exclaimed: **"Liberty! what crimes are committed in thy name!"** On 12 November, Bailly, first President of the National Assembly, met his death. Generals like Custine and Biron were guillotined, charged either with treason or slackness in the pursuit of the enemy.

By the spring of 1794, it was felt that there was no justification for continuing the Reign of Terror because the Allies had already been beaten back. There was general desire to end the horror of tribunals, guillotines, drownings and fusillades. Danton expressed this desire in April 1794 and he had to pay with his life. Robespierre was determined to continue his dictatorship. His ambition was to play the part of Rousseau's dictator. He wanted to interfere with the private beliefs and morals of the people. He wanted to purge France of all that was hostile to his idea of virtue. He guillotined the leading members of the Commune for their atheistic ideas. It is pointed out that heads would have continued to fall like slates if an end had not been put to the life of Robespierre. The latter tried to usurp all the powers into his own hands. Fouche worked behind the scenes upon the fear of the National Convention and thereby helped them to have the courage to oppose Robespierre. Robespierre was publicly accused of subverting liberty. He was outlawed and his arrest was ordered. He put up resistance at the Hotel of Ville. He tried to set the Commune against the National Convention However, all his efforts failed. He was captured and guillotined on 28th July, 1794. With his death, the Reign of Terror ended.

According to Gottschalk and Lach, "Under the Terror the Revolution had assumed somewhat the character of a cult. Patriotism was officially exalted and the government tried to make patriotic celebrations resemble religious rites, the painter David lending his art to enhance their pageantry. The republican, whatever his social standing, wore sans-culottes (the long, loose trouser of the working man), a shirt open at the neck, a red 'liberty cap,' and wooden shoes (leather being badly needed by the army). Women affected the simple, loose, flowing robes of classical times. Wigs, breeches, and buckles became dangerous aristocratic anachronisms. The stately minute of the old days was eschewed in favour of simple and lively folk dances like the 'camagnole'. Theatre and press were strictly controlled, confined to pro-republican propaganda. Mirabeau, Voltaire, Marat, and Rousseau were made into 'revolutionary saints' by being translated to the Pantheon with elaborate pomp." **(Europe and the Modern World Vol. I,** pp. 669-70).

Grant and Temperley observe, "The fall of Robespierre might perhaps have been simply one incident among many in the Reign of Terror; it might have led up to the rule of some fiercer and less scrupulous terrorist; but, as a matter of historic fact, from the moment of the fall of Robespierre, the Reign of Terror began rapidly to pass away. The reasons for this are many. The situation was essentially unstable. The rule of the guillotine could not have been made permanent in eighteenth century France, and public opinion in Paris was turning clearly and violently against it; but there are two reasons more important than any other which rendered the disappearance of the Reign of Terror at this moment inevitable. The first is that the foreign danger was now rapidly disappearing. After the battle of Fleurus, France was herself an aggressive power, and that the assault upon her frontiers, north and east and south, had proved an entire failure. There was rising up in the country a feeling of military confidence and pride that made the Revolutionary Tribunal and the constant batches of victims for the guillotine seem both criminal and absurd. The Reign of Terror was primarily a military measure, and as the military danger passed away the Reign of Terror passed away with it. And then, though less important, whatever else the fall of Rebespierre meant, it meant the victory of the Convention. There had been a direct conflict between the forces of the Convention and the forces of the Commune, between the body that represented France and the body that represented Paris. It was the Convention, it was France that had won. For the first time in the history of the Revolution an attempt to crush by popular force the elected representatives of France had ended in failure and defeat. The Convention felt itself far more confident than before, and it took measures to secure the power that it had won with such difficulty."

According to David Thomson, "The Reign of Terror became possible because of the overthrow of all familiar established forms of government and the double menace of counter-revolution at home and invasion from abroad. That it went so far and lasted so long was due to other causes; above all, to the power of **enrages** and **sansculottes,** the **bross-nus** and the **canaille**—in short of proletarian violence and of criminal extremism exploiting the excitement and savagery of the urban mob. The Terror was directed not just against recalcitrant nobility and clergy or treacherous bourgeoisie, but even more against the mass of ordinary French men and women who were unfortunate enough to fall victim to the twists and tuns of party strife. Many were denounced because the chief anxiety was to save yourself by condemning other. The Terror was not an instrument of class war, and 70 per cent of its victims belonged to the peasantry and labouring classes, mostly in rebellion against the State. The Revolutionary Tribunal of Paris condemned to death 2,639 people; revolutionary courts condemned in all about 17,100. The rest of the Terror's 40,000 victims mostly died in summary mass executions in places such as Vendere and Lyons where there was open rebellion against the Convention. Atrocious though it was, by the test of atrocities committed by more modern dictatorships, the Terror was mild and relatively discriminating." (**Europe Since Napoleon,** p. 21).

It cannot be denied that to some extent the Reign of Terror was a necessity. Perhaps there was no other way to deal with the traitors and cowards. However, the Reign of Terror involved a lot of unnecessary bloodshed, some of which could have been avoided if Robespierre had listened to the advice of Danton and stopped the carnage.

SUGGESTED READINGS

Acton, Lord : **Lectures on the French Revolution.**

Bourne : **The Revolutionary Period in Europe.**

Carlyle : **The French Revolution.**

Clapham, J.H. : **The Causes of the War of 1792.**

Fyffe, C.H. : **History of Modern Europe.**

Gardiner, B.M. : **The French Revolution.**

Greer, D. : **The Incidence of the Terror, 1935.**

Mathews : **The French Revolution.**

Stephens : **The French Revolution.**

Thomson, David : **Europe Since Napoleon.**

CHAPTER 5

THE GIRONDISTS AND THE JACOBINS

The Girondists. It has already been pointed out that the two parties which were prominent in the Legislative Assembly in 1791 were the Girondists and the Jacobins. The Girondists had the majority and the Jacobins were in a minority. The Girondists were so-called from the district of Gironde from which many of their leaders came. On the whole, they were men of high intellectual calibre, education and refinement. They were honest and decent. Their intentions were pure. They were not unscrupulous in their methods. They were moderates. They had a sense of restraint and loved order. They were not prepared to compromise with the past and hoped to establish a Utopia of their own in France. They stood for a Republican form of government. Their view was that if a war was declared there was every possibility of monarchy being discredited and a republic set up in the country. It was partly on account of their zeal that France declared war against Austria in April 1792. As they were impractical idealists, France did not do well in the war. The French armies were defeated everywhere. Instead of setting their house in order and fighting the enemies, attempts were made to put the responsibility of failures at the door of the king. The net result of this condemnation was that his residence was attacked, his Swiss Guards were murdered and he himself had to take shelter in the Legislative Assembly premises. The mob of Paris was supreme. It was under these circumstances that the National Convention met in September 1792.

As soon as the National Convention opened, a republic was proclaimed in France and a struggle for supremacy between the Girondists and Jacobins started. To begin with, the Girondists were stronger and they seemed to be determined to use their power to suppress and punish the leaders of the Paris Commune. They succeeded in dissolving the Commune. However, in other respects the Girondists were not successful. Their proposal for the formation of a guard for National Convention was not accepted. Their demand for the punishment of those who were responsible for the September massacres was rejected. Their attacks on Robespierre, Marat and others created mutual bitterness. Their monopoly of power was threatened by the Jacobins. In October 1792, Pache, the Minister of War, left the Girondists and joined the ranks of the Jacobins. The War Office became the meeting place of the Jacobins and Pache also put his wealth and influence at the disposal of the Jacobins.

The Girondists were also weakened by the trial and execution of the king in January 1793. While the Jacobins had demanded the execution of the king, the Girondists were prepared to compromise with him if only he was prepared to give up the exercise of his discretionary power and act as a constitutional head. The resolution for the execution of the king was carried through by a process of wholesale intimidation.

From the beginning of 1793, the Girondists began to lose ground. Roland, who was a very active member of the Girondist party, resigned his office in January 1793. Garat was put in charge of the Ministry of the Interior. He was a man of moderate views and good intentions but was absolutely unfit for his job. He lacked both vigour and decision. He did not safeguard the interests of his party because although he got information regarding the preparations of the Jacobins to overthrow the Girondists, he did not inform his own party and also did not take any action himself. Foolishly, he did not attach importance to them.

When Pache joined the Jacobin party, he was removed from the War Office but he was elected the Mayor of Paris and thus the Jacobins secured control over the Commune of Paris. At that time, the Girondists' proposals for a new constitution were published. Those proposals were unpractical in their nature and pleased none. The Jacobins got an opportunity to attack the Girondists on the ground that the latter wanted to give more powers to the provinces and thereby weaken the influence of Paris and break the unity of the republic. The Girondists declared a kind of war on the Paris Commune. They condemned the disorders which had been created by the mobs of Paris. They foolishly boasted that the provinces were loyal to them while the Paris Commune was not. They threatened to punish all those who intimidated them but actually took no steps to achieve that objective. Danton tried to bring about a reconciliation but he was condemned by them. He was the only man who had influence and ability to save them. Danton remarked thus: "You know not how to forgive!".

The financial position of the government began to deteriorate and it had to resort to fresh issue of Assignats. As a result of inflation, the value of Assignats fell and prices of commodities went up. The people were hard hit and for all these the Girondists were condemned.

Some of the Girondists protested against the money grants spent in providing cheap bread for Paris. This added to the unpopularity of their party in Paris and a demand for their punishment and removal. On 10 March 1793, it was planned to get rid of the Girondists by force. The Jacobin leaders did not approve of it and consequently the attempt failed.

While the Girondists were wavering and steadily losing ground, the Jacobins were preparing for battle with them. They had behind them all power and priority of the Paris Commune, the prestige of the Jacobin leaders and the backing of Jacobin Clubs all over the country. They also possessed military power. The National Guard was also separately organised. While their opponents were preparing for a battle royal, the Girondists did nothing to save themselves. They could not depend on the Paris Commune whom they had alienated by their speeches and action. It was they who had demanded that Paris be reduced to her eighty-third share of influence in the country. It was they who had said that Paris be reduced to ashes so that posterity might ask on which side of the Seine she stood. The Girondists could not depend upon the National Guard to defend them as it was under the control of the Jacobins. They had no organization of their own which could take up arms on their behalf. They were not considered to be their leaders either by the middle class or by the aristocracy. They had eloquence and parliamentary battalions but that could not save them from the physical forces of the Jacobins.

In April 1793, the Girondists attacked Marat who was responsible for the September massacres of 1792. However, he was acquitted by the Revolutionary Tribunal. The Girondists condemned the plots in the various parts of Paris, but in spite of their condemnation, those plots continued. Instead of compromising, they decided to appeal to the country against Paris. They proposed to shift the National Convention from Paris to Versailles. They talked of dissolving the Paris Commune. In May 1793, they carried a motion appointing an extraordinary commission to enquire into the conspiracies against the National Convention. The Commission ordered the arrest of Herbert, who was the leader of the plotters. This precipitated matters. The Jacobins and the Paris Commune decided to take action against the Girondists. On 31 May, 1793, the Commission was cancelled, but on 2 June, 1793, the National Convention was intimidated to order the arrest of 22 leaders of the Girondist party. They were arrested and hanged. While they were being hanged they went on chanting the Marseillaise until death stilled their voices. Madame Roland uttered the following words: **"Liberty! what crimes are committed in thy name!"** The tragic end of the Griondist leaders created a stir in the country. Lyons, Marseilles, Toulon and Bordeaux declared against the French Government in Paris. Many departments of France prepared themselves to raise the standard of revolt. The Allies were marching on France from many directions. The English fleet was blockading the French ports. Some of the Girondists escaped from Paris and began to organize resistance in the North. However, the Jacobins handled the situation with a firm hand. The revolts were crushed and the Allies were beaten back. The country was saved both from internal troubles and danger.

The Girondists fell, but it cannot be denied that their ideals will always command sympathy and their eloquent hopes and their courage will always win respect. But they will always be considered as incompetent statesmen.

The Jacobins.[1] As compared with the Girondists, the Jacobins were men of rougher stamp, occasionally ill-educated, coarse and unscrupulous. In some cases, they were cruel. In many cases, they were corrupt. However, they were practical and alert politicians who were prepared to run great risks. They were merciless to their enemies, but were prepared to suffer themselves if they were defeated.

According to the Jacobins, all powers and rights resided in the people and the law and government must give way before them. It was the business of the people to watch their rulers, supervise their conduct zealously and always remind them that they were only their agents. It was the duty of the government to obey the people, no matter what its commands were. Popular movements were the highest expression of the law. Even if there was violence and murder, they were still the action of the sovereign. Those who obstructed the will of the people were traitors and those who punished them were guilty of crimes.

The result of such a philosophy was that every man began to assert himself as if he were a part of the sovereign. He began to dictate to the government. Centrifugal tendencies began to take root in the country. Even small municipalities began to assert their independence and refused to listen to any higher authority. It is stated that the priest of a little town established his own dictatorship at the place, issued a complete code for the government, imposed taxes, imprisoned his opponents, confiscated property and exercised all the powers of a sovereign. If the people were sovereign, it followed that any proportion of them were also sovereign. Such a philosophy was bound to result in lawlessness.

The labouring classes also began to assert themselves. They refused to pay rents, tithes, taxes and money claims. The peasants acted likewise. They refused to pay the new taxes imposed on them. They tried to help themselves by taking illegal possession of the property of the State. Trees were cut from the public lands. Even Church property was not spared. Army associations were formed to check the collection of taxes. Customs houses were attacked and clerks were turned out.

It is clear from the above that the Jacobins' philosophy resulted in anarchy in the country. There were riots, murders and acts of pillage everywhere. There was a kind of civil war in the country. Law and order broke down. Anyone could kill anyone with impunity. Mob leaders became the law-givers. The opponents were shown no mercy and were killed everywhere. Wherever law is paralysed, the most violent are the most powerful. It was in this atmosphere that the Jacobin party came to the front and took full advantage of the existing state of affairs to drive out the Girondists from power.

A reference may be made to the party organisation of the Jacobins. It is pointed out that the Jacobin party was the first modern example of what organisation could accomplish in politics. The number of genuine Jacobins was never very large. Probably, when the Jacobins were at the height of their power, their number in Paris did not exceed ten or eleven thousands. Their total number in the country was estimated at three or four lakhs. Jacobin leaders belonged mostly to the middle class. There were lawyers, professional men, clerks, journalists, etc. The important leaders of the Jacobins were Danton, Robespierre, St. Just, Desmoulins, Freron, Robert, Chaumette, Marat, Collot, Gregoire, etc. There were philosophers, visionaries, priests, actors, etc.

The Jacobin party had its headquarters in Paris. However, it had a large number of branches all over the country. By the end of 1790, it had more than 120 clubs all over the country. By the end of 1791, their number was 400. By June 1792, the number rose to 1,200. In August 1792, there were

1. According to Napoleon, "The Jacobins are lunatics and they have no commonsense."

26,000 Jacobin clubs in France. It was through these clubs that the Jacobins were able to dominate the politics of France. These clubs became the centres of revolution. Their members had faith, enthusiasm, recklessness and ambition.

The Jacobins were able to add to their strength by capturing the Paris Commune. By doing so they came to have control over the National Guard. The resources of the capital also came into their hands. The Jacobins controlled the Paris Commune, the Paris Commune controlled the politics of Paris and the politics of Paris controlled France.

By their superior resources, by their better organisation, by their fanaticism for their acts and their unscrupulousness, the Jacobins were able to oust the Girondists. After that, they established the Reign of Terror in the country. However, when the object of the terror was achieved and the foreign invaders were driven out of the country and dissent was suppressed, differences arose among the Jacobin leaders. To begin with, the extreme section of the Mountain, called the Herbertists, was got rid of. After that came the turn of followers of Danton. He and his followers were disposed of by Robespierre. On 28 July, 1794 Robespierre himself and his friend St. Just were guillotined. After the ending of the Reign of Terror peace was restored within the country by stages. The Paris Commune was dissolved. The Revolutionary Tribunal was ended. Restrictions were imposed on the powers of the Committee of Public Safety and the Jacobin clubs were also closed. It was under these circumstances that the Jacobins disappeared from the scene after doing a lot of destruction but at the same time saving the country from the foreign invaders and establishing her prestige.

Kropotkin says, "Most historians, paying a tribute to their authoritarian training, represent the Jacobin Club as the initiator and the head of all the revolutionary movements in Paris and the provinces, and for two generations every one believed this. But now we know that such was not the case. The initiative of June 20 and August 10 did not come from Jacobins. On the contrary, for a whole year they were opposed, even the most revolutionary of them, to appealing again to the people. Only when they saw themselves outflanked by the popular movement, they decided, and again only a section of them, to follow it.

"But with what timidity! They wished to see the people out in the street, combating the royalists, but they dared not with for the consequences. What if the people were not satisfied with overthrowing the royal power? If popular wrath should turn against the rich, the powerful, the cunning ones, who saw in the Revolution nothing but a means of enriching themselves? If the people should sweep away the Legislative Assembly, after the Tuileries? If the Commune of Paris, the extremists the "anarchists"—those whom Robespierre himself freely loaded with his invectives— those republicans who preached 'the equality of conditions'—what if they should get the upper hand?

"This is why, in all the conferences which took place before June 20, we see so much hesitation on the part of the prominent revolutionists. This is why the Jacobins were so reluctant to approve the necessity of another popular rising. It was only in July, when the people, setting aside the constitutional laws, proclaimed the 'permanence' of the sections, ordered the general armament, and forced the Assembly to declare 'the country in danger'—it was only then that the Robespierres, the Dantons and, at the very last moment, the Girondists decided to follow the people's lead and declared themselves more or less at one with the insurrection." (**The Great French Revolution,** pp. 257-58).

SUGGESTED READINGS

Brinton, C. : **The Jacobins, 1930.**

Goodwin, A. : **The French Revolution.**

CHAPTER

6 GREAT PERSONALITIES OF THE REVOLUTION

Mirabeau. It is desirable to refer to the important personalities of the French Revolution before the rise of Napoleon, and the first in the list is the name of Mirabeau. The son of a cruel father, he died at the age of 42 after many ups and downs in his life. He was a man of "instincts and insights". He had "a brain and heart of fire". He was eccentric, violent, ambitious, unscrupulous and cynical. He was ugly, but it is stated that his "very ugliness was a power." He fought duels. His father sent him to prison. He was full of vices and suffered from diseases. However, he was a practical, clear-headed and far-sighted statesman. He was not a theorist. He was the greatest man of the French Revolution. He has been called the "adventurer of genius in a dissolving society". It was he who shook old France to its basis and as if with a single hand held it toppling there, still unfallen. It is stated that when he died in 1791, the funeral procession was three leagues long and the representatives of the king and the prominent members of Jacobin club followed his procession. There was mourning for three days in Paris. That gives an idea of his personality.

Mirabeau had travelled a lot in his youth and thereby acquired a lot of experience. Carlyle refers to this fact in these words: "In these strange wayfarings, what has he not seen and tried? From drill sergeants to Prime Minister, to foreign and domestic booksellers, all manners of men he has seen." Mirabeau visited England and was impressed by the working of the parliamentary system of that country by which the king and responsible ministers worked in co-operation.

Although Mirabeau belonged to the nobility, he was elected to the Third Estate when elections for the Estates-General were held in 1789. His great personality enabled him to come to the front very soon. When the question arose as to whether the three Estates were to meet separately or together, Mirabeau led the Third Estate and demanded that all the three Estates must meet at one place. When the members of the Third Estate met in the Tennis Court to take the oath, it was Mirabeau who declared that he and his followers would not disperse unless and until their demand was accepted. It was under these circumstances that Louis XVI had to give way and agree to the transformation of the Estates-General into the National Assembly. Mirabeau was the leader of the National Assembly and its president.

Mirabeau was a moderate and he did not agree with the extreme views of the Jacobins and consequently left the Jacobin party. He wanted to follow the English parliamentary form of government in France. With that object in view, he wanted the king to become a constitutional head and he asked the National Assembly to co-operate with the king. His scheme failed because both parties refused to play their respective roles. Mirabeau's view regarding the constitutional framework for France may be explained in these words: "Let the king accept the advice of the Assembly, which was most anxious to co-operate with him, and let the leader of the Assembly, Mirabeau himself, become the Prime Minister. Then Louis XVI, Mirabeau, and the National Assembly would reproduce on the French side of the Channel, the admirable partnership of George III, Pitt and the House of Commons."

The National Assembly refused to accept the proposal of Mirabeau because it suspected him. The Jacobins condemned him as "the traitor". The Assembly did not approve of Mirabeau working hand in glove with the king. It refused to play into the hands of reactionary relations and friends of Louis XVI. No wonder, it passed a decree that its members were not to be the members of the king's ministry. In this way, the National Assembly summarily rejected the constitutional scheme of Mirabeau. If this was the attitude of the National Assembly, Mirabeau did not get any better treatment at the hands of the king. Although outwardly the king welcomed his proposals and gave him a lot of money, he did not support him sincerely. He was not prepared to play the role which Mirabeau wanted him to. He hated the very idea of a constitutional head. Mirabeau advised the king to remove the court to Rouen and appeal to the people against the mob-rule of Paris. The king refused to do so, partly because he was afraid of a civil war and partly because of his own habitual lethargy. The queen also did not like the proposal and preferred to get the help of Austria rather than move out of Paris. Both the king and queen did not trust Mirabeau from their inner hearts. They never forgot that it was Mirabeau who was responsible for all the opposition at the beginning. The result was that they did not give their wholehearted co-operation to Mirabeau and were always willing to discredit him in the eyes of the public by showing that he had been accepting their money. They forgot that Mirabeau was the only person who was sincerely working for the cause of monarchy and he alone had the strength to save it. By not giving him their effective support, they were destroying their own cause.

Professor Holland Rose points out that the compromise formula of Mirabeau could not succeed in the atmosphere prevailing in the country. The National Assembly was jealous and the king himself was lethargic. Compromise was possible only when all other alternatives had been tried and failed. To quote him. "Not till political experiments had been tried and failed was a compromise between authority and democracy likely to succeed." Mirabeau was so much upset over the non-cooperation of the king and the Assembly that he is stated to have remarked: **"It is clear that we are perishing royalty, authority, the whole nation. The Assembly is killing itself and us with it.** He died on 2 April, 1791, brokenhearted but he made the following prophecy: **"I carry in my heart the death-dirge of the monarchy, the dead remains of it will now be the spoil of the factions."** New France lost a pilot. It is pointed out that "with him perished the greatest man of the revolutionary epoch and the last hope of the French monarchy." Had he lived, France might have avoided the terrible destruction which it faced after his death. He was the only man who could have brought about a compromise between "the wild asses" of the National Assembly and "the royal cattle" of the court. According to Madame de Campan, **"Mirabeau thought himself an Atlas".** No wonder, after his death there was no other person to shoulder his responsibilities and lead both the people and the king. The regret of Mirabeau was: "I am overwhelmed by the thought that all I have done has been to help on a huge destruction." Had he not died at the age of 42, he could have avoided the anarchy in the country.

When Mirabeau became a member of the Estates-General, he was heavily in debt. He accepted a large sum of money from the king to pay his debts. He got a monthly salary of £240. If Mirabeau had kept all that a secret, he might have been able to carry the National Assembly with him. However, his childish love of display revealed the secret and consequently the National Assembly lost all faith in him. Events might have taken a different turn if Mirabeau had used more restraint in life.

Mirabeau's reputation had already been formed before 1789, but that reputation did not inspire the trust of his fellow deputies. They admired him but did not respect him. In spite of his notorious immorality and venality, he set out to win their confidence and with that object in view took part in every debate whether it was on social reform, finances, foreign policy, the church or the constitution. He had no time or inclination to prepare himself for those debates, but he inspired his collaborators and lieutenants to prepare for him. He was never ill-informed. His words always rang with authority. As a debater, he was not surpassed by anybody. He had the capacity to turn a hostile demonstration into a personal ovation. Whether he read his speech prepared for him by someone or improvised one of his brilliant flights, he commanded silence and attention. He was perhaps the only deputy in the beginning who ventured to speak without a prepared manuscript. Up to the time of his death, the whole course of the Constituent Assembly could be traced through his speeches. It is true that he was opposed to royal despotism, but he stood for a strong monarchy. He described himself as "the defender of a monarchy limited by law and the apostle of liberty guaranteed by a monarchy". Ketelbey points out that Mirabeau was a man of "instincts and insights", of duels, storms, prisons, debts, diseases and vices. He died at the age of 42 worn out by his activities and passions. He was not a theorist. He was not the slave of a formula. He was not the leader of a regular party. However, he was a practical, clear-sighted, far-seeing man, with a "brain and heart of fire." "He it was who shook old France to its basis and as if with his single hand held it toppling there, still unfallen." When he died, there was mourning for three days. The deputies wept. The representatives of the king walked side by side with those from the Jacobin Club in his funeral procession which was three leagues long. It is pointed out that old France was buried with him.

Prof. Salvemini writes, "What would have become if Mirabeau—confronted, as he was, by suspicion and accusations, the shameful truth of which none knew better than himself—if his exasperation, his frenzied and consuming work, and the brutish pleasures in which he tried to drown his agony and discouragement had not struck him down in the prime of the stormy life: if he had lived, for instance, till the flight of the royal family from Paris had revealed the gulf between his ideas and the King's? Induced by the immorality of his private life to abandon the high road of politics, he had lost his way in the devious paths of intrigue; what, then, would have been his position, between the Court, which had pretended to use him without understanding him, and the revolutionaries who had followed him unaware of his real purpose? The brief and violent malady that carried him off on the morning of April 2nd, 1791, ended all the conflicts and dangers in which step by step he had become involved. He disappeared in the tragic last throes of a world that would not let itself be saved, after a life compounded of brilliance and baseness, glory and dishonour." (**The French Revolution,** p. 187).

Marat (1742-1793). If Marat had not taken interest in politics, he might have been known in history as a scientist and a man of letters. He was a physician and he was so skilful in his profession that he had received an honorary degree from St. Andrews University in Scotland. For a time, he was in the service of the Count of Artois.

However, his attention was diverted to politics after summoning of the Estates-General in 1789. There was a feeling in France that Frenchmen should copy the constitutional pattern of Great Britain. This was opposed by Marat whose knowledge of Great Britain convinced him that Great Britain was ruled not by the people but an aristocratic oligarchy. He himself stood for a real reform in which the people of France would have a say and would also be benefited. From 1789 to 1792, he edited a newspaper called Ami Du Peuple or the Friend of the People. In that newspaper, he attacked the court, the clergy, the nobles and even the National Assembly. He was attached to no party and he sacrificed almost everything for his mission. No poverty, misery or persecution could keep him quiet. He was forced to hide in cellars and sewers and he contracted a loathsome skin disease.

Marat loved the people and the people loved him. For the cause of the people, he was prepared to make any sacrifice. He was ready for bloodshed if that could help the cause of the people. He was responsible for the revolt of May 31, 1793 and the expulsion of the Girondist members from the Assembly and their ultimate execution. He was the man who was feared and hated by the authorities but loved and venerated by the masses of the capital. He was assassinated in July, 1793 by Charlotte Corday, a young woman who was fanatically attached to the Girondist faction.

In the death of Marat, people lost their most devoted friend. It is true that Girondins represented him as a blood-thirsty madman who did not even know what he wanted. However, it cannot be denied that when in 1790 and 1791 all the heroism of the people was not able to break the royal power, Marat came to the conclusion that a few thousand aristocratic heads should be sacrificed to make the Revolution a success. Whatever he did was done only with a view to bringing about the victory of the Revolution. It is pointed out that with his love of the people to guide him, Marat was the only revolutionary leader who had a real understanding of events and power of grasping them as a whole, in their intricate bearings on one another. He foresaw what was to come, far better than any of his contemporaries.

Despite his keen intelligence, his sterling honesty and sympathetic advocacy of the poor, Marat was hated and feared. His violent words calling for a dictatorship and mass extermination, his theatrical gestures and his repulsive physical appearance made him one of the most thoroughly loathed of all the deputies. The Girondists made a mistake in attacking him and linking him with Danton and Robespierre.

Danton (1759-94). Danton was the son of a farmer. He studied law and became a lawyer. Before the outbreak of the French Revolution, he acquired reputation as a brilliant young lawyer and a man of liberal tastes. He was fond of books and happy in his domestic life. He possessed a powerful physique and a stentorian voice. He was a skilful debater and a convincing orator. Unlike Mirabeau, he himself remained calm and self-possessed while his audiences were carried away by the enthusiasm. Like Mirabeau, he was interested in the welfare of the class below him. What the nobleman Mirabeau was to the bourgeoisie, the bourgeois Danton was to the Parisian proletariat.

Danton came to the front in the early days of the French Revolution through the favour of Mirabeau. He showed his worth within a very short time. In co-operation with Marat and Desmoulins, Danton founded the Cordelier Club in 1790 and he directed the activities of that club in 1791 and 1792 against the royal family. He was an influential member of the Paris Commune and was largely responsible for the swing of the pendulum in the favour of Republicanism. It is true that Danton was rough and courageous but he was not blood-thirsty. He was a practical statesman who was prepared to adjust his actions according to the need of the situation.

When the Allies surrounded France on all sides in 1792 and the Duke of Brunkswick issued a proclamation asking the people of France to surrender and threatening them with dire consequences if they injured in any way the royal family, there was a revolt in Paris and Danton became the leader. The royal palace was attacked, its guards were murdered and kingship itself was suspended. It was under the dictatorship of Danton that it was decided to strike terror into the hearts of internal and external enemies. On that occasion. Danton summed up his policy in these words : **"In my opinion, the way to stop the enemy is to terrify royalists. Audacity, more audacity and always greater audacity."** The result of that policy was that thousands of men, women and children were put to death. Even magistrates, priests and bishops who were suspected to have royalist sympathies were murdered in cold blood. Danton infused a new life and spirit into the French armies. It is these arimes that were able to push back the Allies from the French borders and regain their lost possessions. He co-operated with Robespierre during the Reign of Terror. However, he felt in the beginning of 1794 that there was not necessity for the continuation of the Reign of Terror and consequently advised a policy of moderation. That was not liked by persons like Robespierre and St. Just and consequently he and his friend Desmoulins were guillotined. And "with his fall, France lost a statesman who could possibly have dominated the course of events."

Like a true statesman Danton tried to remove the differences between the Jacobins and the Girondists with a view to keeping all the Republicans working together for the welfare of France. However, he failed to do so on account of the attitude of the Girondists and Danton was very unhappy over his failure. The only result of that was that the Girondists were liquidated.

According to Grant and Temperley, "The figure of Danton is a somewhat strange one in history of the Revolution. He was often regarded as one of the most blood-stained of the Jacobins. He had advocated in the crisis of August 1792, 'Audacity, Audacity, and always Audacity.' Yet the more his career is scrutinised the more clearly do we see that, though he was capable of violent action when occasion seemed to call for it, his constant effort was to prevent the Revolution from falling into the abyss of anarchy and bloodshed which we know awaited it. He desired to return in many ways to ancient methods; he advocated, at a time when it was dangerous to do so, mercy, authority, and respect for government. Jacobin though he was, it was his aim at first to co-operate with the Girondist party, and he made overtures to them for that end." According to Flenley, Danton and Robespierre were men so different in every way that it was impossible they should work together, save to destroy an enemy or in a crisis. Though both were men of the middle-class, both lawyers, republicans, Jacobins, regicides, there all resemblance ended between the big, generous, careless, jovial Danton, with the voice of thunder, and the small, precise, jealous, severe Robespierre, whose speeches might move the head, but scarcely the heart. Danton had more in common with Mirabeau, or with Gambetta of a later date, with the wide sympathy and the overwhelming oratory of the former, and the fiery patriotism of the latter. Like Mirabeau, too, he had his faults: he has been accused of corruption, and he perhaps gave his friendship too easily. Further, his career was stained by the violence, of August and September 1792. Despite his great influence, during 1793 he seemed to lose interest in politics save in the great question of national defence. Now, he wished to assuage party passions: 'I have no use for hatred,' he said. His wife died and he married again; and withdrew to the quiet of his native town of Arois-sur-Aube, to reappear only at intervals. This was not safe, for Robespierre was jealous of power, and seeds of suspicion grew into great trees overnight and that poisoned air. 'Better be guillotined than guillotine', was all the answer the changed Danton would vouchsafe. He was attacked, arrested, and roused, too late, to defend himself so vehemently before the tribunal that the very walls of the court seemed to quake with the blast of his thunder. The trial had to be stopped, a fresh conspiracy was invented to secure a sentence, and at sunset on 5th April 1794, the greatest of the Jacobins, together with a dozen others, made his last journey through the streets he knew so well."

It is contended that Danton was not a conspirator against the Revolution as alleged by Robespierre at the time of his trial. He was sick of the cruelty and abuses of the Reign of Terror. He regretted his inability to save the Queen from the scaffold. He wept at the execution of the Girondins. Danton was a hand-shaking politician who was courageous and loud and coarse in his speech. He detested men who were wedded to principles, and particularly those principles which threatened his own security. Danton had amassed a fairly large fortune during the Revolution. He owned considerable property near Paris. His new interests as a property owner were threatened by the new policy of the Government. He was appealing more and more to men of means in the National Convention. He was a close friend of the corrupt deputies. He desired peace because he was an opportunist and wanted to save his own property. Peace could bring prestige and power not only to him but also to his friends. He was sincerely conciliator by nature but conciliation towards the factions would have ended the revolutionary regime and inaugurated a middle class republic which the revolutionaries were not prepared to welcome and hence the death of Danton.

Robespierre (1758-94). Robespierre was born in a middle class family and was a classmate of Desmoulins in the law school of the University of Paris. He practised with some success in his native town of Arras. Although he was appointed a criminal judge, he resigned his post because he could not put up with the idea of inflicting the penalty of death on the accused. He acquired a reputation as a writer and speaker. Robespierre was never a demagogue in the correct sense of the word. He was essentially a man of culture. He was both sincere and truthful. He was a keen student of Rousseau and liked to translate his philosophy into action. While doing so, he was unmindful of the sufferings of the people. Although he worked hard for the good of the proletariat, he did not adopt their taste. It is stated that to the last day of his life, he continued to use the knee breeches and silk stockings of the old society and wore his hair powdered.

He was elected to the Third Estate in 1789. He took his place among the extreme radicals whom Mirabeau contemptuously called "The Thirty Voices." As the number of his followers in the National Assembly was small and as Mirabeau dominated the scene, Robespierre could not make much headway in the National Assembly. Under the circumstances, he decided to win over the support of the people of Paris. He was already a member of the Jacobin Club and he became its leader after the withdrawal of its moderate members. After that, he used the Jacobin Club as an instrument for promoting social democracy and he himself became the oracle whom everybody listened.

He co-operated with Danton during the period of the Reign of Terror and when the power of Danton began to decline, he became supreme. He was the leader of the Jacobins and had a lot of influence over the National Convention, the Paris Commune and the Committee of Public Safety. He put an end to the worship of Reason and substituted in its place the worship of the Supreme Being and himself became its high priest. A festival was held to inaugurate the new faith. There was a procession of the members of the National Convention under the leadership of Robespierre and a large number of images were burnt in the garden of the Tuileries. The celebrations ended with a number of speeches. The new faith was not in harmony with the wishes of the people of France and consequently ended with the death of Robespierre.

On 10 June 1794, a law was passed by which the procedure of the Revolutionary Tribunal was changed and made more quick. The people of France were asked to denounce the traitors of the country and even the members of the National Convention were not to be exempted from arrest. No strict procedure was to be followed by the Revolutionary Tribunal and consequently 1,376 persons were put to death between 10 June and 27 July in Paris alone. In this way, Robespierre gave a direct challenge to his opponents. He was himself determined to become the dictator of France. He was supported in his actions by St. Just.

On 26 July 1794, Robespierre made a speech in the National Convention in which he defended his own action and condemned the attitude of his opponents. He did not name his opponents but merely referred to them in vague terms. It is pointed out that if on that day Robespierre had submitted to the National Convention a list of the persons whom he wanted to be arrested, the National Convention would have agreed to that. However, he lost on account of the vagueness of his attack. The vagueness created feelings of uneasiness among the members of the National Convention and everyone of them found himself in danger of his life. It was under these circumstances that the members of the National Convention took up courage to disapprove of his speech. They were also encouraged in their action by Fouche who was working behind the scenes. Robespierre was not prepared for this rebuff. He was so indignant that he went to the Jacobin Club and repeated the same speech which was applauded from all quarters. Thus encouraged he decided to strike again. On 27 July, 1794, he went to the National Convention and tried to address its members. His opponents created so much of noise that he was unable to address. There was a lot of confusion, passion and violence. Ultimately, it was moved and carried that Robespierre, St. Just and his immediate followers should be arrested. They were arrested and handed over to the officers of the Convention to be taken to prison. However, the prison of Paris were conlarge, it decided to use violence and passed a decree declaring Robespierre and his friends. The result was that Robespierre and his followers were released by the Paris Commune and they were brought to the Town Hall. When the National Convention came to know that its enemies were at large, it decided to use violence and passed a decree declaring Robespierre an outlaw. On 27 July, 1794, military preparations were made on both sides. The Hotel de Ville where Robespierre and his friends were taking shelter was besieged and after some time its defences were broken. When Robespierre was captured, he was found with a shattered jaw and it is probable that he might have inflicted that wound himself. He was lying on a table in that condition. As he had already been declared an outlaw, there was no necessity of any trial and consequently on 28 July, 1794, he was guillotined.

Although Robespierre was not the author of the Reign of Terror, he was undoubtedly its most active promoter. He resorted to the Reign of Terror not for its own sake but for the sake of achieving his ideas. His great ambition was to establish the Reign of Virtue and his feeling was that that could be done only by a Reign of Terror.[1] In his pursuit of the Utopia, he was "the anaemic embodiment" of the ideals of Rousseau.

There are different views about Robespierre. The masses admired him without measure. Most of his colleagues respected him and some detested and feared him with deep passion. Some historians consider him as a great humanitarian and an apostle of social justice. There are others who consider him an owlish and scheming intriguer, ambitious and unscrupulous. He was undoubtedly an ambitious person. He sincerely believed that all his actions were for the good of humanity. He was fanatically sincere. In his private life, he was austere and simple to the point of asceticism. He was aloof in his personal contacts. He described himself as "one of the most suspicious and melancholy of patriots." To begin with, he was diffident but later on learnt to talk extempore with eloquence and appeal. If Robespierre was not personally responsible for the butcheries, he did nothing to prevent them. He was considered by the people the personification of the Reign of Terror and no wonder with his death the Reign of Terror ended.

According to Grant and Temperley, "Robespierre was without question an extremely popular figure in Paris, supported by a large number of admiring and devoted friends. It was the tragedy of his life and the cause of his failure that the attempts which he made for the reconstitution and regeneration of France had to be made in an atmosphere of war and of violence. Their failure was probably in any case certain; it was under the circumstances rapid and almost immediate and fatal to himself. He had, as we shall see, a short hour of triumph, and then immediately came his overthrow. His good qualities must not blind us to his obvious defects; he was a man essentially timid and like many timid men easily induced to adopt measures of cruelty. He was vain, and his vanity was increased by the admiration of his friends. Thus it comes to pass that the period during which this prophet of humanity and disciple of Rousseau dominated France is also the period when the Reign of Terror was seen at its worst and most destructive."

According to David Thomson, "Of all the great French revolutionary personalities, Robespierre remains somehow the most memorable and the most symbolic; more than Mirabeau, who was a better orator and a greater statesman; more than Lafayette, whose statecraft failed to measure up to his inflated reputation; more even than Danton, an infinitely more attractive figure and the generous inspiration of national resistance to invasion and reaction. It is strange that so tumultuous and heroic an event as the French Revolution should remain personified in the slight, bespectacled, and unglamorous figure of this fastidious little provincial attorney. Is it that he in some sense represented the precise mixture of social and ideological impulses which triumphed in the Revolution? Socially, he was the archetype of the provincial lawyer, who predominated in the revolutionary assemblies, the feline party intriguer and critic, fluent in the idealistic phrases that so constantly rang through those inexperienced parliamentary bodies. He was the little man of humble origin made great by the upheaval of revolution. In purpose and principle he stood for all that Jacobinism stands for in modern history : a doctrinaire idealism, exalting the principle of the sovereignty of the people, the liberty, equality, and fraternity of all men, the national republic 'one and indivisible'. In his own experience and career, he personified the Jacobin revolutionary impulses." **(Europe Since Napoleon,** p. 18).

According to Kropotkin, "Robespierre has been often mentioned as a dictator; his enemies in the Convention called him 'the tyrant,' and it is true that as the Revolution drew to a close Robespierre acquired so much influence that he came to be regarded both in France and abroad as the most imporant person in the Republic.

1. To quote Robespierre, "The mainspring of government in times of peace is virtue; in times of revolution it is virtue and intimidation — virtue, without which intimidation is disastrous, and intimidation, without which virtue is impotent."

"It would, however, be incorrect to represent Robespierre as a dictator, though certainly many of his admirers desired a dictatorship for him. We know, indeed, that Cambon exercised considerable authority within his special domain, the Committee of Finance, and that Carnot wielded extensive powers in matters concerning the war, despite the ill-will borne him by Robespierre and St. Just. But the Committee of Public Safety was too jealous of its controlling power not to have opposed a dictatorship, and, besides, some of its members detested Robespierre. Moreover, even if there were in the Convention a certain number who were not actually averse to Robespierre's preponderating influence, these would have been nonetheless unwilling to submit to the dictatorship of a Montagnard so rigorous as he in his principles. Nevertheless, Robespierre's power was really immense. Nearly every one of his enemies as well as his admirers felt that the disappearance of his party from the political arena would mean, as indeed it proved, the triumph of reaction.

"How then is the power of Robespierre and his group to be explained ? First of all, Robespierre had been incorruptible in the midst of a host of men who readily yielded to the seductions of riches and power, and this is a very important trait in time of revolution. While the majority of the middle-class men about him shared in the spoils of the national estates when they were put up for sale by the Revolution, and took part in the stock-jobbery; while thousands of Jacobins secured posts under Government for themselves, Robespierre remained an upright judge, steadfastly reminding them of the higher principles of republicanism and threatening those keenest after spoil with the guillotine.

"In all he said and did during those five troubled years of revolution, we feel even now, and his contemporaries must have felt it still more, that he was one of the very few politicians of that time who never wavered in their revolutionary faith nor in their love for the democratic republic. In this respect Robespierre was a real force, and if the communists had been able to oppose him with another force equal to his own in strength of will and intelligence, they would undoubtedly have succeeded in leaving a far deeper impress of their ideas on the Great Revolution.

"These qualities, however, which even his enemies acknowledge in Robespierre, would not suffice alone to explain the immense power he possessed towards the end of the Revolution. The fact is, his fanaticism, which sprang from the purity of his intention, kept him incorruptible in the midst of a widespread corruption. At the same time, he was striving to establish his authority over men's minds, and to accomplish this he was ready, if necessary, to pass over the dead bodies of his opponents. In the work of establishing his authority he was powerfully seconded by the growing middle classes as soon as they recognised in him the 'happy mean'—equally removed from the extremists and the moderates—the man who offered them the best guarantee against the 'excesses' of the people.

"The bourgeoisie felt that here was a man who by the respect he inspired in the people, the moderate scope of his aims and his itch for power, was just the right man to establish a strong government, and thus put an end to the revolutionary period. So long, therefore, as the middle classes had anything to fear from the advanced parties, so long did they refrain from interfering with Robespierre's work of establishing the authority of the Committee of Public Welfare and of his group in the Convention. But when Robespierre had helped them to crush those parties, they crushed him in his turn, in order that middle-class Girondins should be restored to power in the Convention, after which the Therm idorean reaction was developed to its fullest extent." (**The Great French Revolution,** pp. 550-52).

St. Just. St. Just was a friend and collaborator of Robespierre and was also guillotined along with him on the same day. He played a very important part during the Reign of Terror. If Carnot is called the organiser of victory, the contribution of St. Just was second to none. He was the person who inspired the people of France with the fanaticism to die for the principles of liberty, equality and fraternity. He moved from the headquarters to the borders of the country and encouraged the troops to fight valiantly for the cause of their country. He encouraged the patriots and terrified the traitors and the cowards. He was partly responsible for transforming France into a nation in arms.

Carnot (1753-1823). Carnot was one of the most important personalities during the period of the National Convention. It was under his determined leadership that the National Convention inaugurated a system of militarism which was unique in the history of the world. In February 1793, a compulsory levy of half a million men was decreed. In August 1793, it was decreed that every Frenchman between the ages of 18 and 25 was liable to military service. Carnot worked day and night to make these laws effective. He drafted men, silenced complaints, secured volunteers, drilled the troops and sent them to the frontiers. He prepared plans of campaigns and not only appointed trusted officers to take the command but also infused energy and faith in them. It is stated that as a result of his efforts, France had about 770,000 men under arms by the end of 1793. Most of those troops were fanatics for their cause and were prepared to lay down their lives for the sake of their country. Even the bourgeoisie supported his military measures. Artisans and peasants joined the army in large numbers and went to the front displaying the banner of liberty, equality and fraternity and singing the Marseillais.

Carnot carried out a large number of reforms in the army. He created the division as a military unit. He improved the machinery of supply and thereby made his troops more mobile than those of the enemies. He sent the members of the Government as "deputies on mission" with a view to watching the activities of the generals and soldiers. If there was a complaint against any person, he was liable to be guillotined without any explanation.

The militarism of Carnot was based on the revolutionary principles of **"the nation in arms!"** The soldiers were to work not as mercenaries but as missionaries for their cause. No wonder, the invaders were driven out from the soil of France and the war was pressed into the Netherlands, along the Rhine, in Savoy and across the Pyrenees. Carnot was so much successful in his work that his popular title of "Organiser of Defence" was changed into that of "Organiser of Victory".

SUGGESTED READINGS

Beesly : **Life of Danton.**

Belloc, H. : **Life of Robespierre.**

Belloc : **Danton : A Study.**

Bradly, E.D. : **A Short History of the French Revolution.**

Carlyle, Thomas : **The French Revolution.**

Chevallier, J.J. : **Mirabeau, 1947.**

Madelin, L : **Danton.**

Mme. Roland : **Memoirs.**

Stern, A. : **Mirabeau.**

Thompson, J.M. : **Leaders of the French Revolution, 1932.**

Thompson, J.M. : **Robespierre, 1935.**

Welch, O.J.G. : **Mirabeau, 1951.**

CHAPTER

7 THE DIRECTORY (1795-99)

The Constitution of 1795 framed by the National Convention vested the executive authority in France in a committee of five Directors known as the Directory. The Directory was in power in France for four years (1795-99) when it was overthrown by General Napoleon. The Directors were men of mediocre talents and did not hesitate to practise bribery and corruption. They failed to rise to the occasion and could not tackle the problems facing the country.

The first Directors were Carnot, the organiser of victory, Letourneur, an engineer, Larevelliere Lepeaux, a Girondist, Rewbell, a Jacobin and Barras. Barras hailed from the South. In 1789, he was elected to the Third Estate. In course of time, he became a good Jacobin. He took courage to attack Robespierre. He saved the National Convention by employing Napoleon Bonaparte in 1795. Consequently, he was made one of the five Directors. He was a clever politician, a cynic, entirely unscrupulous, immoral who "loved the throne for its velvet," and was always in debt. He had an imposing appearance and fine manners. He was the leader of the Parisian society.

Plots and Intrigues. The period of the Directory was one of plots and intrigues in the country. The royalists and the reactionaries were elected to the legislature in large numbers and they did not hesitate to use fair or foul means to sabotage the government. They were kept, in check only by the use of force by the government.

A reference may be made to the Babeuf Plot of 1796. A political club called the **Society of the Pantheon** was started in October 1795. It attracted a large number of former Jacobins and held meetings by torchlight. It published a newspaper known as the Tribun which was edited by Babeuf who was a young, fanatical agitator. The Directory took action against the Society in February 1796 when General Bonaparte personally closed the meeting place and dissolved the Society. However, the members hit back by setting up a Secret Directory of six members and started making preparations for a revolt. Their object was to revive the Jacobin Constitution of 1793 which had been approved but not enforced. They also aimed at restoring the revolutionary movement to its original purity of idealism and sincerity of purpose. They proposed to proclaim a "Republic of Equals" in which the gulf between the rich and the poor was to be avoided. The programme was to penetrate the units of the army, police and administration by means of revolutionary agents. Thorough preparations were made for the revolt. Arms and ammunition were collected. It was decided that citizens from each district of Paris should march behind banners to support the mutineers of the army. After capturing power, the Secret Directory was to exercise power till fully democratic institutions started working in the country. However, the police had their agents in the movement from the very beginning. The result was that on the eve of the revolt, all the leaders were arrested and the people were dispersed by the use of force. The conspirators were tried in 1797 by a special court. The trial lasted for 3 months and on that occasion Babeuf condemned the administration of the Directory in the strongest possible terms, Babeuf was executed. He won the admiration of all by his sincerity of purpose. It is pointed out that modern communism owes a lot to the ideals of Babeuf.

Finances of France. The finances of France began to deteriorate during the regime of the Directory. There was corruption all around. There was enormous waste in public expenditure. A lot of money was required to support an army of a million men. The population of Paris had to be fed at the cost of the nation. The position of Assignats issued by the National Assembly was already not satisfactory. It was made worse by a policy of further inflation. There was so great a use of the printing press that the value of the Assignats fell. The condition became so hopeless that as many as 300 livres in Assignats were required to get one livre in cash. In 1797, the Government was forced to declare partial bankruptcy. Payment of interest on the national debt was suspended and ultimately the Assignats had to be repudiated altogether. Obviously, such a state of affairs could not be expected to bring any credit to the Government and so the Directory was condemned by the people who were really in great distress on account of the failure of the Directory to tackle the financial problem.

There was no harmony between the Directors and the two legislative chambers. One-third of the Assemblies and one out of the five Directors retired every year. The Directory was not in sympathy with either the Assemblies or the constituencies.

The religious problem demanded attention. The Constitutional Church set up by the Revolution had almost disappeared. A new religious movement called **"Theophilanthropy"** had no real following. The Roman Catholic Church was still strong and popular with the people.

There were more than three hundred thousand emigres. Their property had been confiscated. Many persons were declared emigres so that their property might be captured. No wonder, their relatives protested against those acts of injustice and that created unrest.

In March 1797, elections took place to fill the place of one-third members of the Assemblies. The results showed great gains for the Moderates and anti-Jacobin party. The Directors were not prepared to yield. They appealed to Hoche but he declined. They asked Napoleon to do the needful. He sent his officer, Augereau, to carry out his instructions. The show of force was enough. Carnot was deposed from the Directory. A number of Deputies were arrested, including Pichegrus. After that, the results of 154 electors were cancelled.

Foreign Policy. When the Directory assumed office, France was still at war with Austria, Sardinia and Great Britain. The general plan of the campaign was to advance one French army across the Rhine through Germany and from there into the Austrian dominion and to send another army across the Alps through Northern Italy to Vienna. As regards the army of the Rhine, such great Generals as Moreau, Jourdan and Pichegrus were to be in charge. As regards the army to be sent to Italy, Napoleon Bonaparte was appointed the commander. While the French troops sent to the Rhine did not accomplish much, Napoleon worked wonders. With lightning speed and great personal bravery, Napoleon was able to cross the Alps. Within a year, he was able, to dispose of five Austrian armies and he occupied every fort in Northern Italy. The Sardinians were defeated and forced to give Nice and Savoy to France. Austria made peace with Napoleon by signing the **Treaty of Campo Formio in 1797.** By that treaty, France got from Austria the Austrian Netherlands or Belgium and the Ionian Islands. Austria was given the republic of Venice and she agreed not to interfere in other parts of Italy. It was agreed that a conference was to meet to rearrange the map of the Holy Roman Empire with a view to compensating those German princes whose lands on the left of the Rhine had been appropriated by France. One of the immediate effects of the victory of Napoleon in Italy was the dissolution of the first Coalition. Both Austria and Sardinia left the Coalition and Great Britain was left alone. Another effect of the victory was the sudden rise of Napoleon to fame. He became the talk of the people of France and while the people applauded him, the Government feared him but outwardly flattered him.

In a proclamation issued to the people of France, the Directory boasted: "You will learn with pleasure that several millions of people have been restored to freedom and that the French nation is the benefactor of humanity. The peace of the continent will soon be set on an indestructible base. It remains only now to punish the perfidy of London. There the ills of Europe have sprung; there they must be ended."

In 1797, Napoleon was appointed the General of the Army of England which was formed in France to invade England. In the beginning of 1798 he inspected the coastline and came to the conclusion that it was impossible to cross the English Channel so long as France had not a strong navy. However, he decided to attack the British Empire on some other point. He fixed the Mediterranean open to him and consequently he managed to take a French army to Egypt in 1798. His intention was to side-track the attention of the British navy in the Mediterranean and, after getting the opportunity, to attack England by crossing the English Channel. He also hoped to proceed from Egypt to India and thereby put an end to the British Empire in India with the help of the Marathas and Sultan Tipu. There was also the possibility of his attacking the Ottoman Empire from Egypt and smashing the same. Unfortunately for Napoleon, all his schemes fell through. Admiral Nelson pursued him to Egypt and defeated him in the naval Battle of the Nile (1798). The people of Egypt also revolted against him. His army was small and he felt himself isolated. However, Napoleon managed to escape from Egypt and reached France. From the place of landing all the way up to Paris, he was applauded by the crowds. The people compared the achievements of Napoleon with those of the Directory and condemned the latter.

Overthrow of the Directory. On his arrival in Paris, Napoleon appeared in the role of the modest and studious civilian. At one time, he read a paper before the Institute on Egyptian Archaeology and at another he moved about in the streets of Paris as an ordinary citizen. His object was to advertise himself not at a gambler in empires but a person eager for knowledge and well-versed in the arts of peace. For many weeks, Napoleon contented himself with merely studying minutely the political currents in the country, especially Paris. While doing so, he did not commit himself to any group.

After a lot of deliberation, he decided to enter into a conspiracy with Abbe Sieyes to overthrow the Directory. The two conspirators were poles as under in their ideas. Napoleon Bonaparte was a man of action and believed in the autocracy of the sword and Abbe Sieyes was a philosopher who believed in a policy of checks and balances. However, both of them were agreed so far as the question of the overthrow of the Directory was concerned. It was certainly a difficult task because republicanism was a strong political force in the country. It was the creed of Generals like Jourdan and Moreau and of two of the five Directors. A great majority of the members of the legislature also believed in republicanism. Any revolution which aimed at setting aside the republican form of government, had very little chance of success. It is true that the odds were heavy but Napoleon was determined to carry out his own scheme. The plan was duly executed on 9 and 10 November, 1799. The Council of Ancients passed a decree on 9 November to transfer the legislature to St. Cloud on the pretext of a conspiracy and Napoleon rode to the Tuileries at the head of a brilliant cavalcade and took oath to preserve the republic. Afterwards he spoke the following words to a Secretary of the Directory who came to meet him in the gardens: **"What have you done with this France which I left so brilliant? I left you peace, I find war. I left you victories, I find defeats. I left you the millions of Italy, I find losses of spoliation and miseries."** These words of Napoleon resounded throughout the length and breadth of the country.

On 10 November, the legislators met in the palace of St. Cloud. They found themselves trapped in the midst of a hostile army. When Napoleon appeared in the Lower House, there was a storm of passion against him and he was carried fainting from the hall. However, his life was saved by Lucien, his brother, who was presiding over the session of the Lower House. The soldiers surrounded the legislature and the members fled. A small committee of both Chambers decreed a provisional government consisting of Bonaparte, Sieyes and Ducos. The constitution which was framed a month later placed the supreme powers in the hands of Bonaparte as First Consul. Thus, the Directory was overthrown by Napoleon by ruse and violence. To quote him: **"It is the epoch of my life in which I have shown impossible ability."**

David Thomson writes, "The **Coup** succeeded because neither assemblies nor Directory had any popular esteem left, and the population as a whole—even in Paris—accepted the accomplished fact with little resistance." (**Europe Since Napoleon,** p. 28).

SUGGESTED READINGS

Thomson, D. : **The Babeuf Plot: The Making of a Republican Legend, 1947.**
Thomson, D. : **Europe Since Napoleon.**

CHAPTER

8 THE COALITIONS

Although at the outset, the attitude of the British Government and the people of England was sympathetic towards the French Revolution, there was a violent change later on account of the excesses of the revolutionaries. That was particularly so after the execution of Louis XVI and his queen Marie Antoinette. Great Britain organised as many as four Coalitions to defeat France and succeeded in that object in the long run.

The First Coalition (1793-97). The origin of the First Coalition lay in the failure of the policy of neutrality followed by the British Premier, Pitt the Younger, towards France. When France declared war upon England, Pitt entered into treaties of alliance with Prussia, Austria, Russia, Spain, Holland and Sardinia. Thus, the First Coalition came into existence. Pitt's object was to combine the whole of Europe against the common enemy which dared to challenge all the established governments of Europe. His plan was to subsidize the Allies liberally so that they might bear the brunt of the struggle on the Continent while the English navy was to maintain its supremacy over the seas and conquer the French colonies. From the very beginning, the Allies agreed to indemnify themselves of the expense of France. The war was to be a war of conquest and plunder as well as of self-defence.

To begin with, the Allies were victorious on all fronts and the French were badly defeated. In 1793, the military outlook for France was extremely gloomy. France was threatened on all sides and there took place insurrections in many parts of France.

To meet the emergency, the National Convention resorted to extreme measures. The Committee of Public Safety with unlimited powers was set up. A sort of Reign of Terror was established in the country. It is true that in certain cases there was unnecessary bloodshed but the net result of the Reign of Terror was that the counter-revolution was crushed. Under the leadership of Carnot, Danton and St. Just, the whole of the French nation rose up in arms and the fighting was done with so much ferocity, fanaticism and tenacity that the Allies were beaten back. The French were able to get back Belgium and Holland. Prussia and Spain left the Coalition by the Treaty of Basle in 1795. It appeared that the European Powers were interested more in the partition of Poland than in the prosecution of war. Such was the state of affairs when Napoleon Bonaparte was sent to Italy during the regime of the Directory. He crossed the Alps and defeated the Austrians in a series of engagements. He forced the King of Sardinia to leave the Coalition and also compelled Naples and the Papal States to submit. His success had two important effects: Spain entered into an offensive and defensive alliance with France. The Spanish fleet came into the hands of the French. The result was that Great Britain was forced to evacuate the Mediterranean and the French became its masters. Pitt made offers of peace but those were rejected by the Directory. The year 1797 was very critical for England. Three fleets threatened England with an invasion and there was a lot of dissatisfaction and unrest. However the situation was saved by two naval victories won by England. In the battle of Cape St. Vincent, the Spanish fleet was defeated. The Dutch fleet was defeated at Comperdown.

When Austria was defeated by Napoleon in a series of battles and the very safety of Vienna was in danger, Austria signed the Treaty of Campo Formio in 1797. By that treaty, Austria gave the Austrian

Netherlands (Belgium) to France. She also accepted the French claims to the left bank of the Rhine. The Austrian provinces in North Italy were formed into the Cis-Alpine Republic dependent on France. About the same time, Portugal also made peace with France and the First Coalition was practically at an end. France was left without an enemy on the Continent and England was left without an ally in Europe. England was left to face France single-handed and the Directory started making preparations for an invasion of England. Napoleon was put in charge of that invasion but at the beginning of 1798 he came to the conclusion that it was out of the question to cross the English Channel and consequently the scheme of invading England was given up. It was, however, decided to attack the British Empire on some other point and with that idea Napoleon proceeded to Egypt in 1798.

Causes of failure of First Coalition. What were the circumstances responsible for the failure of the First Coalition? It appears strange that a bankrupt France which was distracted by internal divisions, should come out successful against a Coalition of more than half the Powers of Europe. It was nothing short of a marvel of history. However, the causes of the failure of the Coalition are not far to seek. The Coalition Power did not work harmoniously. They had their differences and each power insisted on working independently. Even their objects were different. The main object of the British Government was to expel the French from the Netherlands and make that province secure for Austria. But the object of Austria was to recover the Netherlands and then to exchange it with Bavaria. The British Government was not prepared to agree to such an exchange. Moreover, both Russia and Prussia were more interested in the partition of Poland than in helping Austria in her struggle against France. No wonder, the want of unity of purpose was fatal to the unity of effort. Instead of a joint advance on Paris, every Allied Power wanted to establish its control over the frontier fortresses of France. The British Government wanted to have Dunkirk, and with that object besieged it. The Austrians wanted Alsace and Lorraine as their share, but the Prussians remained on the Rhine with their eyes fixed on Poland. On account of their selfish aims, the Allies failed to realise the danger from France and the nature of the struggle. To them it appeared that France was in the throes of a revolution and consequently it was easy to defeat her. They failed to realise the fact that they were not fighting against the Bourbon monarchy but against a nation in arms which was inspired by fanatical ideas of liberty, equality and fraternity. No wonder, they failed to rise above their selfishness, and mutual jealousies.

Moreover, the Allied Powers were themselves busy in carrying out another revolution in Poland. Poland was partitioned for the second time in 1793 and Russia and Prussia got their shares. In 1795, the rest of Poland was divided by Russia, Prussia and Austria and after that Poland ceased to exist. During all this period, there was going on rivalry among the Powers for the partition of Poland. Each Power was trying to get more than the others. Hence the Allied armies were paralysed and defeated on all fronts.

The military genius of Carnot marshalled the resources of the country. The Reign of Terror crushed all dissent. The cowards were made brave and the traitors were frightened. The result was that the whole of the French nation fought vigorously and defeated the *Allies*. The French commanders were told that they must win victories or they would be put to death.

The British Commander in the Netherlands was the Duke of York who was absolutely a worthless man and no good results could be expected from such a fellow.

The Second Coalition (1798-1801). The Second Coalition was the direct result of the Battle of the Nile (1798) in which Napoleon was defeated by Nelson. The European Powers were upset by the aggressive policy of the Directory and when they got the news that Napoleon was shut up in Egypt, they decided to act. The Second Coalition was formed in 1798 and included England, Russia, Austria, Turkey and Naples. Its object was to crush the Revolutionary Government at Paris and to confine France to her old boundaries. Prussia remained aloof. The war began with the refusal of Austria to turn out Russian soldiers from her territory on the demand of France.

To begin with, the situation seemed to be favourable to the Allies. The Austrian Archduke Charles defeated a French army and drove it across the Rhine. A combined Anstro-Russian army routed the French in two great battles. In the Mediterranean, the Island of Minorea was captured and Malta was blockaded. However the year 1799 ended very badly for the Allies. The French were able to regain their position. The English were defeated and compelled to evacuate Holland France was saved from the ignominy of defeat and foreign occupation.

Napoleon Bonaparte returned from Egypt. He was welcomed by the French with great enthusiasm. He was able to overthrow the Directory and himself became the First Consul in 1799.

The arrival of Napoleon Bonaparte on the scene was a source of great anxiety to the Allies. Russia left the Coalition. Czar Paul was angry with both England and Austria. While he aimed at the restoration of the old order in Europe by crushing France, Austria was more interested in the acquisition of Piedmont. The conduct of Austria annoyed the Czar. He was annoyed with the British Government because the latter supported the Austrian policy. Moreover, he developed a great admiration for Bonaparte and consequently withdrew from the Coalition.

Bonaparte addressed a letter to the King of England expressing his desire for peace. His object was to add to his popularity by an offer of peace because the French were tired of war. The British Government gave a very haughty answer and suggested that the only security of peace was the restoration of the Bourbon dynasty in France. The tone of the letter added to the bitterness of the French people against England and the purpose of Napoleon was amply served. Napoleon sent one army under Moreau against the Austrians and himself proceeded against Austria with another army. Moreau won a splendid victory at Hohenlinden and Napoleon himself defeated the Austrians at the Battle of Marengo. There were also other French victories and Austria was forced to sign the **Treaty of Luneville** in 1801. This treaty confirmed the terms of the Treaty of Campo Formio of 1797. England was left all alone after 1801 and as both England and France were tired of war, a peace was made in 1802. However, the peace of Amiens turned out to be merely a truce. War began between the two countries in 1803.

The Third Coalition (1805). The Third Coalition was formed by Pitt, the Younger, in 1805 and it included Prussia, Austria, Sweden and England. Napoleon was violating the terms of the Treaty of Luneville and was also interfering in the internal affairs of the neighbouring States, *e.g.*, Switzerland. There was a lot of resentment in Europe against Napoleon on account of his kidnapping and then executing the Duke of Eughien. This incident led to the rupture of relations between France and Russia. Prussia refused to join the Coalition as Napoleon dangled before her the temptation of Hanover which belonged to England.

The object of the Third Coalition was the expulsion of the French from North Germany, the independence of Holland and Switzerland and the restoration of Pledmont to the King of Sardinia. As usual England undertook to pay liberal subsidies to the Allies. It was also agreed that after the close of the war, a Congress of European Powers was to define the law of the nations and establish an European Federation. However, the Third Coalition did not aim at changing the form of government in France.

Napoleon was also thinking in terms of attacking England and was making vigorous preparations for the same. A fine army known as "the Army of England" was mobilized for the invasion of England and three fleets were also collected for the same purpose. The English Channel was protected by Nelson and Cornwallis. The successful blockade of Brest by Cornwallis hampered Napoleon's plan. Efforts were made to attack England by avoiding a fight with Nelson. In spite of that, the Battle of Trafalgar took place in 1805 and the French were defeated completely. This victory not only saved England but secured for the British navy undisputed supremacy on the sea.

Although Napoleon was defeated on sea, he took full advantage of his superiority on land. The Austrian general was surrounded and made to surrender at Ulm. He also inflicted a crushing defeat upon the combined armies of Russia and Austria at Austerlitz in December 1805. The result was that Austria left the Coalition and she was forced to sign the Treaty of Pressburg by which she gave back Venetia to the French kingdom of Italy and Tyrol to Bavaria. The Electors of the two States of the Holy Roman Empire were made kings independent of Austria as a reward of their alliance with France. Russia counted upon the help of Prussia but on account of the shifty diplomacy of the King of Prussia, the Czar also left the Coalition. Prussia entered into an offensive and defensive alliance with France and got Hanover as her reward. Thus, the Third Coalition failed. Its author also died on hearing the news of the defeat of Austerlitz.

The Fourth Coalition (1813). The Fourth Coalition was formed in 1813 after the unsuccessful invasion of Russia by Napoleon in 1812 and his disastrous retreat. The important members of the Coalition were Russia, Prussia and England. Later on, Austria also joined. It was financed by Great Britain. Although the Allied armies were defeated at Dresden, they won many other victories. Napoleon was defeated in the Battle of Leipzig in 1813. With the passage of time, the position of Napoleon went on weakening and the Allies became stronger and stronger. The result was that in 1814, he was completely defeated and forced to abdicate. Although he returned in 1815 to France, he was again defeated in the Battle of Waterloo. Thus, the Fourth Coalition was successful in the ultimate overthrow of Napoleon and the restoration of the Bourbons in France.

SUGGESTED READINGS

Kissinger, H.A. : **A World Restored: Metternich, Castlereagh and the Problems of Peace, 1812-1822.**

CHAPTER

9 NAPOLEON BONAPARTE (1769-1821)

Napoleon was one of the greatest generals the world has produced. He dominated his age and even after his death, his name has gone down in history not only of France or Europe but also of the whole world. He was a man of enormous energy, self-confidence, fearlessness and resourcefulness. He was a fatalist in the sense that he believed from his very childhood that some hidden power was guiding him to victory and glory. He had the capacity to inspire confidence in all those who followed him. He loved his soldiers who reciprocated the same. He had a wonderful memory and it is stated that he remembered the names of the regiments and soldiers by heart.

Napoleon is stated to have remarked: **"I was born when my country was dying. Thirty thousand Frenchmen disgorged upon our shores, drowning the throne of liberty in a sea of blood—such was the hateful spectacle that offended my infant eyes."** France purchased from Genoa the island of Corsica[1] in 1769 and Napoleon was born on 15 August in that island at Ajaccio in that year. He got his military training in France and joined the army at the age of 17 as an artillery officer. He was hardly 20 when the French Revolution broke out in 1789. He distinguished himself in December 1793 when by a skilful direction of his artillery, he was able to recapture Toulon and he was promoted to the rank of Brigadier General. On 5 October 1795, he put down the royalist insurrection of Vendemiaire against the National Convention. The result was that he was given the command of the Interior. He married Josephine on 9 March 1796.

When France was faced with a big crisis on account of the First Coalition, Napoleon was appointed to the command of the army of Italy and it is in Italy that he laid the foundation of an imperishable military fame.

Napoleon's campaign of Italy lasted from April 1796 to April 1797. It has been summarised in these words: **"He came, he saw, he conquered,"** Napoleon had to fight against heavy odds. He had to face the armies of Austria and Sardinia. His soldiers were not only small in number but were also very poorly equipped. No wonder, Napoleon decided to fight his enemies separately and not allow them to be united. He penetrated between the Austrians and Sardinians and defeated the former and drove them eastwards. After that, he turned towards the Sardinians and defeated them. It was in this way that he opened the way to Turin, the capital of Sardinia. The Government of Sardinia sued for peace and agreed to hand over Savoy and Nice to France. Napoleon described his achievements in these words to his soldiers: "In fifteen days, you have won six victories, taken twenty-one stands of colours, fifty-five pieces of cannon, and several fortresses, and conquered the richest part of Piedmont. You have taken 1,500 prisoners and killed or wounded 10,000 men......But, soldiers, you have done nothing, since there remains something for you to do. You have still battles to fight, towns to take, rivers to cross."

After the defeat of Sardinia, Napoleon directed his attention towards the Austrians. He crossed the Po river and the Austrian Commander named Beaulieu, withdrew beyond the Adda river. There

1 Rousseau wrote thus in 1762: "I have some presentiment that this small island (Corsica) will one day astonish Europe." It was a lucky hit.

was no way for Napoleon to defeat the Austrian Commander except by crossing the river by the bridge of Lodi. This bridge was 350 feet long and it was practically impossible to cross it on account of the heavy fire from the Austrians. Napoleon ordered his grenadiers to move forward. Before they could cover half the distance, they were mowed down by the Austrian fire and they began to recoil. Napoleon and other generals rushed to the head of the columns. They risked their lives and inspired their men. The result was that they were able to capture the Austrian batteries. Napoleon wrote thus to the Directory: **"Of all the actions in which the soldiers under my command have been engaged, none has equalled the tremendous passage of the bridge of Lodi."** Napoleon came to be called by his soldiers **"The Little Corporal".**

As the Austrians had retreated to the fort of Mantua, Napoleon laid siege to the same. Between June 1796 and January 1797, four attempts were made by the Austrians to send help to the Austrian soldiers besieged in Mantuna. However, all those attempts were foiled by Napoleon. The latter continued to follow the policy of attacking his enemies piecemeal before they could unite. He always acted upon the policy of attacking while the enemy was divided. He accomplished all this by means of forced marches. It was rightly observed by his soldiers that **"it is our legs that win his battles."** He shot his troops back and forth like a shuttle. By his quick movements, he made up for his numerical weaknesses. Even his enemies were also responsible for his success as they did not put all their troops in one battlefield. At Arcola, the battle continued for three days. Here also victory depended upon the control of a bridge. It was the bridge that separated the Austrian divisions. If they could keep the bridge under their control, the Austrian armies could fight together against Napoleon. However, that was not to be. Napoleon seized a flag and rushed upon the bridge, accompanied by his staff. The Austrians opened fire on them. Many French officers were shot down by the Austrians. However, they refused to desert their general and dragged him with them by his arms and clothes. Napoleon fell into a morass and began to sink. The cry of **"Forward to save the General!"** was raised. The result was that the French struck with all their force and drove back the Austrians and rescued their hero. The army of Napoleon was successful and the Austrians retreated. The battle of Arcola was fought from 15 November to 17 November 1796.

Two months afterwards, another Austrian army tried to come to the help of **Mantua** and another desperate battle was fought at Rivoli. On 13-14 January 1797, Napoleon inflicted a crushing defeat upon the Austrians. Two weeks after that defeat, Mantua surrendered. Napoleon marched up to the Alps and the Austrians were driven back. On 7 April 1797, he reached Leoben which is about 100 miles from Vienna. It was at this stage that Austria sued for peace. Napoleon had achieved a lot. He had fought 18 big battles and 65 small ones. No wonder, he declared thus in a bulletin to the army: "You have, besides that, sent 30,000,000 francs from the public treasury to Paris. You have enriched the Museum of Paris with 300 masterpieces of ancient and modern Italy which it has taken thirty ages to produce. You have conquered the most beautiful country of Europe. The French colours float for the first time upon the borders of the Adriatic."

Throughout his Italian compaign, Nepoleon Bonaparte acted as if he were the head of France. Sometimes he followed the advice of the Directory, but very often he ignored the same. During his stay in Italy, Napoleon Bonaparte busied himself not only with military affairs but also with political affairs. He acted as the creator and destroyer of States. Italy at that time was not a united country and the existence of many States enabled Napoleon Bonaparte to do what he pleased. Napoleon Bonaparte changed the Republic of Genoa into the Ligurian Republic and gave it a constitution similar to that of France. The Duke of Parma and Duke of Modena were forced to submit and make heavy payments. Even the Pope was made to submit. Some of the States were taken from him and the rest were left with him on the condition that he paid a lot of money to the conqueror.

Napoleon Bonaparte conquered the Republic of Venice which was one of the oldest and proudest States in Europe. He held it as a pawn in the game of diplomacy. On the overthrow of the Republic of Venice by Napoleon Bonaparte, Wordsworth wrote thus:

"Once did she hold the gorgeous East in fee;
And was the safeguard of the West; the worth
Of Venice did not fall below her birth,
Venice the Eldest Child of Liberty."

Napoleon Bonaparte had made the preliminary peace of Leoben in April 1797. He made the final peace of Campo Formio on 17 October 1797. During all this period, Napoleon Bonaparte lived a splendid life. He received ambassadors, artists and men of letters. He was surrounded by young officers who were enamoured of him and were prepared to do anything for him. There were also Josephine, his brothers, sisters and mother. Napoleon Bonaparte himself began to put on airs. This is what he said about himself: "What I have done so far is nothing. I am but at the beginning of the career I am to run. Do you imagine that I have triumphed in Italy in order to advance the lawyers of the Directory? Let the Directory attempt to deprive me of my command and they will see who is the master. The nation must have a head who is rendered illustrious by glory."

By the Treaty of Campo Formio, Austria recognised the French annexation of the Belgian provinces. She agreed to cede approximately two-thirds of the imperial territory on the left bank of the Rhine to France, from the Swiss frontier down the river to the confluence of the Main with the Rhine provided that this cession was ratified at the Imperial Congress to be held at Rastatt. The German princes thus dispossessed were to receive compensation elsewhere within the empire. It was agreed that if France obtained any additional territory in Germany at the final peace with the empire. Austria was to obtain an equivalent amount. Prussia was not to share in the dismemberment of the Holy Roman Empire as stipulated in the Treaty of Basel of 1795 as Prussian territory on the left bank was to be restored to her by France. For her loss of Lombardy, Austria received Istria and Dalmatia and the Venetian mainland, including Venice itself, as far as the Adige river instead of the Oglio as provided in the peace of Leoben. The rest of Lombardy was added to the Cis-Alpine Republic whose existence Aust 'a formally recognised. France got the Ionian Islands including Corfu, Zante and Cephalonia. The Duchy of Modena was given to the Cis-Alpine Republic and its Duke got the Austrian territory of Breisgau in exchange. Austria's compensation for loss of Breisgau was the rich Bishopric of Salzburg and some Bavarian territory between the city of Salzburg and the mountains of the Tyrol.

As a result of the Treaty of Campo Formio, the hold of Austria over northern Italy was broken. Venetia was at the mercy of the French. This treaty, together with the Treaty of Basel, made the compensation of Austria in Germany precarious. It laid the foundation for the secularization of ecclesiastical territory and the absorption of the small states in southern and western Germany. The position of Austria in the Holy Roman Empire rested on the ecclesiastical rulers and the princes of the small states. This treaty was the decisive step in a policy which gave France not only the Rhine boundary but the dominant position in Germany and Italy. The view of Sieyes was that "this treaty is not peace; it is a call to a new war." It was an imperialistic peace. It gave France her natural frontiers which Louis XIV had failed to secure in spite of his best efforts. The Ionian Islands were to serve as a stepping stone for Egypt. This treaty gave a death blow to the First Coalition. France was left without an enemy and England without an enemy in Europe. England had to struggle single-handed against France. Prof. Markham observes, "It was a brilliant peace for France and for Napoleon, but it laid the seeds of future war. Owing to the prestige of Napoleon's victories and the internal weaknesses of the Directory, the French peace aims had been diverted from the boundaries—the Rhine, the Pyrenees and the Alps—to Italian annexations, which meant further expansion and war." (**Napoleon and the Awakening of Europe**, p. 33).

Napoleon Bonaparte not only conquered Italy but also plundered her. The object of the Italian campaign was not only to defeat the enemy but also to get something more than what it had cost the

French treasury. No wonder, Napoleon Bonaparte demanded and got a lot of money from the princes whom he defeated in Italy. The Pope had to pay 20 million francs, the Republic of Genoa 15 and the Duke of Modena 10. He also got a lot of money from Milan. It was in this way that Napoleon was able to send a lot of money to France after meeting the expenses of the army.

Italy had not only to pay in cash but also in other forms. Italy was deprived of her works of art. The agents of Napoleon Bonaparte ransacked the art galleries in Italy and whatever was considered to be good was taken away to France. The names of some of the important art treasures taken away by Napoleon Bonaparte from Italy were "The Transfiguration" by Raphael, "The Christ" by Titian, the Apollo Belvedere, the Nine Muses, the Laocoon and the Venus by de Medici. During his career, Napoleon Bonaparte enriched the Museum of the Louvre with more than 150 paintings by Raphael, Rembrandt, Titian, Van Dyck, Rubens, etc. After the fall of Napoleon, many of these art treasures had to be restored to their former owners.

After his first Italian campaign, the name of Napoleon became a household word in France and his popularity knew no bounds. He rose head and shoulders above all his rivals and he was in the forefront of public affairs in France. The Directory decided to fight against England and Napoleon was appointed the General of the army which was meant for the invasion of England. In the early part of 1798, Napoleon surveyed the coastline and came to the definite conclusion that it was impossible to cross the English Channel on account of the British naval supremacy. However, he felt that as the British Empire was spread in various parts of the world, a blow could be given to her by attacking some other part of the British Empire. It was under these circumstances that Napoleon decided to attack Egypt. His plan was that after conquering Egypt, he would be able to turn out the English from India with the help of the Marathas and Sultan Tipu. There was every possibility of his conquering Turkey which was on the decline and unfit to stand his attack. There was also the possibility of sidetracking the British fleet into the Mediterranean and attacking England while the British navy was in the Mediterranean.

Napoleon left Toulon and sailed for Egypt in May 1798. He was able to reach Egypt by avoiding the British fleet. He conquered Malta on the way. He won the **Battle of Pyramids** which made him the master of the Nile basin. However, he was defeated by Admiral Nelson in the Battle of the Nile (1798). The French fleet was completely destroyed and Napoleon was cut off from France. He invaded Syria but failed to capture Acre. He somehow managed to reach France in 1799.

It has already been pointed out that the Directors had not managed the affairs of France successfully and there was a lot of resentment against them. Napoleon took advantage of the situation and with the help of Sieyes he was able to overthrow the Directory on 9 November 1799. This is known as the Coup d'etat of VIIIth Brumaire..

Napoleon as First Consul (1799-1804). After the overthrow of the Directory a new constitution was framed for France in 1799. Under that constitution the executive power was put in the hands of three Consuls who were to be elected by the Senate for 10 years. One of the three Consuls was to be the First Consul. The First Consul was given practically absolute powers. He alone could promulgate laws and appoint and dismiss all civil and military officials in every part of the country. Bonaparte was appointed the First Consul and he immediately consolidated his position by dismissing his colleagues Sieyes and Ducos and appointed in their place two other Consuls who were not strong enough to oppose him. The Council of State was given the power to draft laws, draw up public ordinances, interpret statutes and act as a court of appeal. The Tribunate was to consist of 100 members and was given the power to pass or reject but not alter the laws submitted to it by the Government. The Legislative Body of 300 members was "a dumb assembly" which accepted or rejected, without any power of discussion, the laws expounded to it by the members of the Tribunate or the Council of State. The Senate consisted of 80 members who were appointed for life and were irremovable. It appointed the Consuls, the Tribunate and the Legislative Body. It was given the power to cancel any law considered contrary to the principles of the constitution. Theoretically universal suffrage was established in the country but in actual practice, "popular suffrage was rendered completely ineffective." The electors of each Commune selected a tenth of their number to form "communal lists" of voters. The latter elected one-tenth of their number to form a "departmental list". The latter elected one-tenth of their number to form a "national list". The local officials were selected from appropriate local lists and the Senate nominated members of the Tribunate and the Legislative body from the "National List". The Prefects who were the heads of the Departments and the Mayors who were the heads of the Communes, were to be appointed by the First Consul. It is clear that the Constitution of December 1799 was a mere sham. The appearance of a popular Government was maintained merely to deceive the people and all legislative power was concentrated in the hands of the First Consul. A system of highly centralised despotism, both absolute and bureaucratic, was set up in the country. It is stated that when the Constitution was proclaimed, a woman turned to her neighbour and said, "I have not heard a word. What is in the Constitution?" "There is Bonaparte" was the reply.

It was in 1802 that Napoleon was appointed the First Consul for life with the right to nominate his successor. On a proposal of the Tribunate, which was accepted by the Senate, Napoleon became Emperor in 1804. A plebiscite ratified the proposal by a majority of more than three and a half million votes. The Pope came to Paris to invest Napoleon with the sword and sceptre of the Empire on 2 December 1804. However, when the Pope was going to crown him, Napoleon took the crown from his hands and crowned himself!

Work of Napoleon as First Consul. The fame of Napoleon rests primarily on his military achievements, but as First Consul he carried out a large number of reforms which have made his name immortal. It is rightly pointed out: **"If the conquests of Napoleon were ephemeral, his civilian work in France was built upon granite."**

(1) Napoleon Bonaparte centralised the whole of the system of local government in France. In 1800, he made the entire local government subordinate to himself. The powers of the elective bodies of the departments and arrondissements were to be wielded by prefects and sub prefects who were appointed by Napoleon and were also responsible to him. The local councils were allowed to continue but they were required to sit only for a fortnight in the year to deal with the assessment of taxes. They were to act merely as advisory bodies to the prefects and the sub-prefects. The Mayors of small Communes were to be appointed by the prefects while those of big Communes having a population of more than 100,000 were to be appointed directly by the Central Government. The new system of local government assured the prompt, uniform, and unquestioning execution of the law and decrees of the Central Government.

Napoleon developed the Secretariat of the State. He turned this into the Ministry of State under Marat which became a central registry. It enabled Napoleon to supervise the various ministries without allowing them any collective responsibility. A centralised administration was set up for the assessment and collection of taxes. Collectors of taxes were required to make a deposit in advance of a proportion of the estimated yield of the taxes. These reforms were the work of Gaudin, a financial bureaucrat of the Ancien Regime. By 1800, the tax returns were up-to-date.

According to Herold, "The utter fearlessness with which the young and inexperienced general addressed himself to problems seemingly beyond a single man's scope characterizes the heroic element in Napoleon's mind. There is something of a Hercules in it. Consider, for instance, how the thirty year-old First Consul, within a few weeks after taking power, established a civil administration which proved to be the one and only stable political institution France has had in the past century and a half. There are those who see in Napoleon merely the military strong man, the dictator just as Hercules is esteemed for his muscle rather than his brain. Yet exceptional mental powers are needed to devise a scheme as simple and bold as Hercules' method of cleaning out the Augean stables: a graduate of an agricultural college would never have thought of it. Alexander's handling of the Gordian knot may seem crude; Aristotle never taught him such a trick but perhaps he learned it from Diogenes, the great simplifying cynic." (**The Mind of Napoleon**, p. xviii).

(2) Napoleon tried to improve the financial condition of the country. By a careful collection of taxes, he was able to add to the revenues of the State. By rigid economy, by the severe punishment of corrupt officials and by the practice of forcing other States to support the French armies, Napoleon was able to reduce his expenditure. In 1800, he established the Bank of France which was one of the soundest financial institutions of the world.

(3) Napoleon carried out many reforms in the field of education. Primary and elementary schools were to be maintained by every Commune under the general supervision of the prefects or sub-prefects. Secondly, grammar schools were to be provided for special training in French, Latin and elementary science. Whether supported by the Government or run by private enterprise, they were all put under the control of the Central Government. Lycees or high schools were opened in all important towns and instruction was given in them in the higher branches of learning by teachers appointed by the State. Special schools such as technical schools, civil service schools and military schools were brought under State regulation. The University of France was established to maintain uniformity throughout the educational system. Its chief officials were appointed by the First Consul. No one was allowed to open a new school or teach in public unless he was licensed by the University. A Normal School was established at Paris for the purpose of training the teachers. All the schools were required to take as the basis of their teaching the ethical principles of Christianity, loyalty to the head of the State and obedience to the statutes of the University. The following extract from the catechism which was used by the State for children, makes clear what kind of education was given to the youth of the country.

> "**Question.** What are the duties of Christians towards those who govern them and what in particular are our duties towards Napoleon I, our Emperor ?
>
> "**Answer.** Christians owe to the princes who govern them and we in particular owe to Napoleon I, our Emperor, love, respect, obedience, fidelity, military service, and the taxes levied for the preservation and defence of the Empire and of his throne. We also owe him fervent prayers for his safety and for the spiritual and temporal prosperity of the State.
>
> "**Question.** Why are we bound in all these duties towards our Emperor ?
>
> "**Answer.** First because God, who creates Empires and apportions them according to his will, has by accumulating his gifts upon him, set him up as our sovereign, and made him the agent of his power and his image on earth. So to honour and serve our Emperor is to honour and serve God himself. Secondly, because our Saviour Jesus Christ taught us both by example and precept what we owe to our sovereign : for he was born under obedience to Caesar Augustus, he paid the prescribed taxes, and in the same breath as he said 'Render to God what belongs to God,' he said, 'Render to Caesar what belongs to Caesar."
>
> "**Question.** Are there special reasons why we should be more devoted (**plus fortement nous attacher**) to Napoleon I, our Emperor ?
>
> "**Answer.** Yes, there are; for it is he whom God raised up in difficult circumstances to re-establish the public worship of the holy religion of our ancestors, and to be its protector. It is he who restored and preserved public order by his profound and active wisdom; he defends the State by the strength of his arm; he has become the Lord's Anointed by the consecration he received from the Sovereign Pontiff, the head of the Universal Church.
>
> "**Question.** What ought one to think of those who are lacking in their duty towards our Emperor ?
>
> "**Answer.** According to the Apostle Saint Paul they would be resisting the order established by God himself, and rendering themselves worthy of eternal damnation.

"**Question.** Do our obligations towards our Emperor apply equally towards his legitimate successors in the order established by the Imperial constitutions ?

"**Answer.** Yes, undoubtedly; for we read in Holy Scripture that God, by a supreme disposition of his will, and by His Providence, bestows his empires not only upon particular individuals, but also on families."

Napoleon expressed his views on the education of girls in these words, "What are the girls brought up at Ecouen going to be taught? You must begin with religion in all its strictness. Don't allow any compromise on this point. Religion is an all-important matter in a public school for girls. It is the mother's surest safeguard, and the husband's. What we ask of education is not that girls should think, but that they should believe. . . In the Iycees I only prescribed the necessary minimum. At Ecouen things must be entirely different. Nearly all the exact knowledge taught there must be that of the Gospel. I want the place to produce, not women of charm, but women of virtue: they must be attractive because they have high principles and warm heart, not because they are witty or amusing.... Everyday the pupils must have regular prayers, hear mass, and learn the catechism.

"In addition the girls must be taught writing, arithmetic, and elementary French, so that they may know how to spell; and they ought to learn a little history and geography; but care must be taken not to let them see any Latin, or other foreign languages. The elder girls can be taught a little botany, and be taken through an easy course of physics or natural history. But that too has certain embarrassments. The teaching of physics must be limited to what is necessary to prevent gross ignorance and silly superstition, and must confine itself to facts, and not indulge in reasoning which directly or indirectly touches on first causes....

"But the main thing is to keep them all occupied, for three-quarters of the year, working with their hands. They must learn to make stockings, shirts and embroidery, and to do all kinds of women's work...I should like every girl who leaves Ecouen, and finds herself at the head of a small household, to know how to make her own frocks, mend her husband's things, make clothes for her babies, provide her little family with such occasional delicacies as can be afforded by a provincial housekeeper, nurse her husband and children when they are ill, and know in these matters, because she has been taught it beforehand, what invalids have learnt by experience...

"Dancing is necessary for the health of the pupils; but it must be a cheerful sort of dancing, not the kind they indulge in at the opera. They may have music, too, but only singing...

"With the exception of the headmaster, all men must be excluded from the school. No man must ever enter within its walls, under any pretext whatsoever. Even the gardening must be done by women. My intention is that in this respect the establishment should be as strictly ruled at a convent. The headmistress herself must not be allowed to receive men, except in the parlour; and if it is impossible to exclude a girl's relations in cases of serious illness, at least they must only be admitted by special permission of the Grand Chancellor of the Legion of Honour......I need hardly say that the only women employed in the school must be elderly spinsters, or widows without children; that they must be entirely under the control of the headmistress; and that they must never receive men, or go outside the walls of the school. It would no doubt be equally superfluous to remark that nothing is worse than the idea of letting young girls appear on the stage, or stimulating rivalry among them by allowing them to take places in form. Competition should be banned : we don't want to rouse their passions, or to give play to the vanity which is one of the liveliest instincts of their sex."

Again, "I do not think we need bother about the education of young girls; they cannot be better brought up than by their mothers Marriage is their only destination."

The Institute de France had been established in 1795. Napoleon supported it and appreciated its work in physical sciences, fine arts, mathematics, and literature. However, he discouraged the study of moral and political sciences. By a decree of January 1803, Napoleon suppressed the department dealing with those subjects.

(4) Napoleon also carried out a large number of public works in the country, although he did not spend much money on them. That was due to the fact that he was able to employ the prisoners of war for that work. He enormously improved the means of communication and trade within the country. The splendid highways of France are the achievements of Napoleon. In 1811, Napoleon could count 220 broad military roads which he had constructed. Thirty of these roads radiated from Parts to the borders of France. Two trans-Alpine roads brought Paris in touch with Turin, Milan, Rome and Naples. A large number of bridges were constructed. The most important bridges were at Austerlitz and Jena. The former network of canals and waterways was perfected. Marshes were drained. Dikes were strengthened. The important sea-ports were enlarged and fortified for commercial and naval purposes. This was particularly so with regard to Toulon and Cherbourg.

(5) **The Concordat (1802).** The question of the Church settlement was a difficult one. It was a fashion with the intelligentsia to dismiss religion as a foolish lie and see in the Church an organ of oppression, privileges and obscurantism. The priests were considered to be the prey of a decaying superstition, the allies of the foreigners and enemies of the country. That was the reason why the Church property was confiscated by the National Assembly and the Civil Constitution was provided in the country. However, honest and scrupulous Catholics refused to take the oath and consequently there was a lot of persecution. In spite of that, the schism in the Church persisted. The non-juring clergy had their followers in the fields and woods and the juring clergy enjoyed the barren splendour of empty cathedrals. It became difficult for the Government to pay the salaries of the clergymen. The Catholic Church was disestablished and State became neutral in matters of religion.

This was the state of affairs when Napoleon became the First Consul. His own view was that religion was not a decaying power in the world. He found that all the Catholics had faith in saints and miracles. He felt that spiritual forces controlled the lives of the peasants and soldiers and so he decided to influence and control these spiritual forces. Religion was not to be dismissed like a discarded theory in chemistry. It was the mystery of the social order. Napoleon himself tells us that he was influenced by the sound of the church bells of Ruel and he came to the following conclusion: "The people must have a religion and that religion must be in the hands of the Government. People will say that I am a Papist. I am nothing. I was a Mohammedan in Egypt, I shall be a Catholic here for the good of the people. I do not believe in religions...but the idea of a God." Again, "Fifty emigre bishops in English pay are the present leaders of the French' clergy. Their influence must be destroyed, and for this I must have the authority of the Pope." Napoleon regarded himself as the successor of Charlemagne and he wished to restrict the Pope strictly to religious affairs. Negotiations were conducted with Pope at Paris and ultimately in August 1802, the Concordat was concluded. This governed the relations of the Church and the State in France for 103 years.

The preamble of the Concordat was a compromise between the extreme views of both the parties. It runs thus: "The Government of the French Republic recognised that the Roman Church and Apostolic religion is the religion of the great majority of the French citizens. His Holiness likewise recognises that this same religion has derived and in this moment again expects, the greatest benefit and grandeur from the establishment of the Catholic worship in France and from the personal profession of it which the Consuls of this Republic make." By this Concordat the Papacy was protected against the threat of Bonaparte to secularise the State. Bonaparte also succeeded in defeating the desire of the Pope to have Catholicism declared the state religion. The Government agreed to permit the free exercise of the Catholic worship subject to the Police power of the state and engaged itself to place Churches and Chapels at the disposal of the Bishops. The Papacy and the Government were jointly to make a new distribution of the French Episcopal dioceses, to which the new incumbents were to be appointed by the First Consul and canonically instituted by the Pope. The Bishops were then to appoint the Cures. The Government agreed to pay a suitable salary to Bishops and Cures, who, before entering upon their functions, were to take an oath of fidelity to the Government. The Pope gave up the claim to the confiscated but unsold land of the Church. He also recognised the revolutionary land settlement and declared irrevocable the sale of ecclesiastical property. Each Bishop was given the right to open a chapter in the Cathedral and a seminary in his diocese and the parishioners were permitted to establish Church foundations.

In defence of the Concordat, Napoleon Bonaparte maintained that "Society is impossible without inequality, inequality is intolerable without a code of morality and a code of morality is unacceptable without religion." Again, "In religion, I do not see the mystery of the Incarnation, but the mystery of the social order." "Men who do not believe in god—one does not govern them, one shoots them." "The people need a religion; this religion must be in the hands of the Government." "Fifty emigre Bishops in English pay are the present leaders of the French Clergy. Their influence must be destroyed and for this I must have the authority of the Pope."

It cannot be denied that Napoleon Bonaparte obtained the main objects for which he had been striving. The Concordat maintained the revolutionary sale of the ecclesiastical lands. It assured the Government of the submission of the Clergy who became paid civil servants, bound to it by oath and regulated in their acts of worship by its supervisory regulation. During the Ancien regime, the great wealthy prelates, rich in lands and linked by blood and loyalty to the nobility, had often tied the hands of the Government. All that the revolution had destroyed, and the Concordat confirmed the same. Napoleon Bonaparte was able to detach the Church from the Bourbons and take a great stride towards the perpetuation of the Consulate. He was also able to gain the official endorsement of the revolution by the Church, which it once had condemned as "anathema". This endorsement consequently recognised civil marriages and registration of births, marriages, etc.

The Pope also gained from the Concordat. He gained great prestige by handling the schism and restoring the unity of the faith. The absence of any specific provisions concerning the monastic orders, and the re-establishment of religious congregations was a notable victory for the Papal cause. By giving the Pope the right to demand the resignation of all the Bishops, Napoleon Bonaparte rendered illusory his own right to nominate new ones. Never before the French Clergy or the French Government had attributed such sweeping powers to the Pope. By this provision and the virtual incorporation of the Bishops and Priests into the civil service, Napoleon Bonaparte almost made it inevitable that all protests on their part would be addressed to Rome.

About the Concordat Markham observes: "A Concordat with the Pope would drive a wedge between royalism and Catholicism, finally pacify La Vendee and reassure the buyers of Church lands. A settlement based on the schismatic constitutional Church or on Protestantism would bring none of these advantages. Only a comprehensive agreement with the Pope would suffice." General Delmas comments thus on the Concordat: "A fine monkish trick. The only thing missing was the 10,000 men who gave their lives to suppress all that."

The Concordat was not popular with all the sections of the people in France. While it had the enthusiastic support of half the nation, the small minority represented by the intellectuals, the administrative and political personnel and army circles, was bitterly opposed to it. The rest of the country was more or less indifferent. Bonaparte had reserved for himself the right of "providing by regulation against most serious inconveniences that might arise from a literal execution of the Concordate." By this right, he made effective the police regulations given to him by Article I of the Concordat, viz., that the worship of the Catholic religion should be "in conformity with the police regulations which the Government shall deem necessary for the public tranquillity." These regulations not only filled in the omissions of the Concordat but also provided for the state regulation of Protestantism. They came to be known as the Organic Articles. The Concordat and the Organic Articles were combined in one text and issued as a single law on 8 April 1802. However, the Pope was not aware of the Organic Articles until they were passed and he never accepted them as the provisions of the Concordat. These Articles fully elaborated the "rights and prerogatives" of the state in its relation with the Catholic Church in France. They did so in a spirit which violated the terms of the Concordat.' The Organic Articles were an error and Bonaparte had to regret the same.

Some delay was caused by the refusal of several of the constitutional or juring clergy to confess penitence for their sin of schism. Until they agreed to do so, the Papal representative refused to institute them into office. They finally retracted and most of them were received back into the fold of the Church. The ceremony at Notre Dame took place on 18 April 1802.

According to H.A.L. Fisher, "The principle of establishment, then as now, had many enemies but it is difficult to contest the value of an arrangement which soothed the fears of the peasantry, healed the schism in the French Church, and, save for an inconsiderable body of non-jurors, reconciled the Catholic conscience to the Government of the day." However, it is pointed out that the fact that an appeal was possible to the Pope by the clergy against the tyrannical bishops, and by the bishops against the Government, led in France to the dacay of Gallican liberties and the rise of ultra-montanism in France.

In spite of the Concordat, serious differences arose between Napoleon and the Pope. The Pope did not like the restriction of his powers to purely religious affairs and the dependence of the clergymen of France. He also resented the extension to Italy of the Code Napoleon which authorised divorce. He refused the request of Napoleon to divorce Jerome from Paterson and allow him to marry into some royal family of Europe. The continental policy of Napoleon was not compatible with the territorial sovereignty of the Pope. Napoleon refused to return to the Papacy the Legations of Bologna and Ferrara which he had added to the kingdom of Italy. He confiscated Ponte, Corvo and Benevento which belonged to the Papacy. He seized Ancona in 1805 and refused to restore it to the Papacy. The Pope showed a distinct leaning towards the Third Coalition in 1805 and protested against the appointment of Joseph Bonaparte in 1806 as the King of Naples. He refused to obey the demand of Napoleon in 1806 that he should expel from the Papal States all the enemies of France and close the Papal ports against English trade. In October 1806, he refused to institute Napoleon's nominees in Venetian bishoprics. In 1807, the French occupied and incorporated into the kingdom of Italy certain Italian territories. In 1808, Rome was occupied and the Papal States became practically French territory. In May 1809, Napoleon revoked "the donation of Charlemagne, our august predecessor" and formally added Rome to the French Empire. In June 1809, the Pope excommunicated Napoleon and in July 1809, the former was arrested in Rome and put in a prison.

The Pope refused to institute French bishops and Napoleon appointed in November 1809 an Ecclesiastical Commission for France. However, the Commission refused to act according to the wishes of Napoleon and, therefore, it was superseded in January 1810. In February 1810, the Senate decreed that all future Popes at their enthronement and all clergymen within the French Empire must accept the Gallican Articles. Many clergymen were deported to Corsica as they refused to accept the decree. In August 1811, the National Council ordered that seats should remain empty for not more than 12 months. If the Pope failed to institute the bishops within 6 months, the Metropolitan was authorised to do so. The approval of the Pope was declared necessary for the validity of the order and the Pope refused to do so. In June 1812, the Pope was brought to Fontainebleau and in January 1813, he made a new Concordat with Napoleon which authorised the Metropolitan to confirm the bishops whom Napoleon had appointed. The Pope practically abdicated his temporal sovereignty by agreeing to take up his residence at Avignon and receiving an annual revenue of two million francs. However, later on, the Pope protested against this agreement which he declared he had signed as a prisoner and "in error". When in 1814, Napoleon found his position weak, he handed over the Pope to the Austrians who released him. In 1814, the Pope was restored to his former position.

It is clear from above that the steady opposition of the Pope regained for him the Papal States and he managed to maintain his authority over the clergymen in France. Napoleon's quarrel with the Pope cost him the support of many Catholics in France and enabled his enemies to declare him the enemy of religion.

(6) **The Codes (1804-10).** The most durable part of the work of Napoleon was the legal codes. These codes were drawn up by committees appointed by Napoleon and he himself attended many of their meetings. He helped those committees in their work by his "hard common sense" and "legislative vision". It is wrong to say that Napoleon himself was responsible for the preparation of those codes, but it cannot be denied that he was responsible for their consolidation and popularisation. In spite of their faults, the codes were concise, simple and just. They consolidated the work of the Revolution which had established a secular State based upon a class of peasant-proprietors, a civil law emancipated from religious vices, a system of land tenure devised to secure the maximum of equality, and a law of persons which proclaimed that men had equal rights. The provision of a uniform system of laws, quick in procedure and execution, was a great boon to France.

With regard to the work of the lawyers in the preparation of the Codes, Napoleon observed thus: "I first thought that it would be possible to reduce laws to simple geometrical demonstration, so that whoever could read and tie two ideas together would be capable of pronouncing on them; but I almost immediately convinced myself that this was an absurd idea...I often perceived that oversimplicity in legislation was the enemy of precision. It is impossible to make laws extremely simple without cutting the knot oftener than you untie it."

In August 1800, Napoleon appointed a committee of four lawyers to draw up a Civil Code which was done. According to it, the authority of the father over his family was strengthened and the family was placed "absolutely at the disposal of its head." The father was entitled to imprison his children and his assent was necessary for their marriage. He was to receive the income of their property up to their 18th birthday. A wife was to be under the control of her husband and she could not acquire or sell property without his consent. Contrary to the policy of the Roman Catholic Church, the principle of divorce was admitted. Divorce was allowed by mutual consent and for adultery, cruelty and grave criminal offences. Interest was fixed by law. A man could dispose of by will not more than half of his property.

The **Code of Civil Procedure** was also prepared under the orders of Napoleon. It maintained the principle that conciliation must be attempted before recourse is had to law courts. However, the procedure laid down by the Code proved to be slow and costly and subsequently had to be amended. Criminal and penal codes were also enacted. Capital punishment, imprisonment or deportation for life, branding and confiscation of goods were provided. Maximum and minimum penalties were also fixed for various crimes. Itinerant judges and assize courts were established. Jury system was maintained as a means of judgment but not of accusation. Accused persons had to be tried in public. They were entitled to get the assistance of counsel. They were allowed to examine witnesses in their own defence. No provision was made for the release of persons by a Writ of Habeas Corpus. The **Code of Criminal Procedure** was issued in 1808 and the **Penal Code** in 1810. Both of them showed signs of the stern despotism which Napoleon had established to prevent political offences.

The **Commercial Code** dealt with general commerce, maritime, commerce, bankruptcy and commercial matters. This was a very unsatisfactory code.

According to H.A.L. Fisher, "Critics have assailed the Civil Code as a rapid and superficial structure, as pocket note-book indicating some general legal principles, but far from exhausting the casuistry of life or precluding the growth of jungle of case-law. The task to which modern Germans devoted fifteen years of exhausting efforts, Napoleon dared to accomplish in four months. His temerity has been censured. Yet, however imperfect this Civil Code may be, it is better than no code at all;

and had the work not been done when and as it was, France might be codeless to this day. A single law is better than 200 customs, equality is better than privilege. In the compass of a little volume which may be read and understood by every man woman in the country, the Civil Code depicts the outlines of a civilized and democratic society, adjusting the great bodies of revolutionary enactment to the old and inveterate traditions of the races." Again, "Feminists and socialists will, therefore, find little to applaud in the legal work of Napoleon; nor would he have courted their commendation. The Civil Code belongs to the category not of socialist but of liberal documents, and its importance in the history of civilization lies in the fact that it registers and perpetuates the vast social improvements introduced into Europe by the French Revolution." Again, "The codes preserve the essential conquests of the revolutionary spirit—civil equality, religious toleration, the emancipation of land, public trial, the jury of judgment." To Italy and Germany, "they were the earliest message, as well as the most mature embodiment of the new spirit. In a clear and compact shape, they presented to Europe the main rules which should govern a civilised society."

Leo Gershoy maintains that the Code of Napoleon was profoundly national. It maintained the social conquests of the Revolution. It was "a summary and a correction of the Revolution." It gave unity to legislation which France badly stood in need of. It maintained the emancipation of civil law from religious influence. It defended the revolutionary principle of equality by guaranteeing civil liberty and civil equality. It also bore the impression of Napoleon's authoritarian views particularly in the field of family life. The authority of the father was restored "and the despotism of the state repeated in the structure of the family." The Code contained a number of reactionary provisions, such as subjecting the wife to the power of the husband, debarring her from the administration of their common property and requiring the written consent of the husband for her acquisition of property. The right of divorce was recognised when the same was demanded by both the parties. The law of inheritance followed the revolutionary principle that there should be an equal division of property among the heirs. However, compared to the legislation of the Revolution, the Code was reactionary. In comparison with the legislation of the **ancien** regime, it was revolutionary. Its great virtue lay in its admirable brevity and clarity. Everybody could appeal to its general principles and everybody could understand its specific provisions. With all its defects, it was more progressive than any other civil Code that Europe then had. Wherever Napoleon's armies introduced it in the course of their conquests, and in all other countries where it reached, it brought the social and political ideals of the French Revolution. In that sense, it became as universal as Roman Law and a permanent factor in promoting the democratic ideals of 1789. So far as France was concerned, it was an attempt to reconcile old France with new France.

The Code of Napoleon was adopted not only in France but was also introduced in every country conquered by the armies of Napoleon. It is true that many harsh punishments were retained and the position of women was made distinctly inferior to that of men, but, on the whole, the French Codes remained the most convenient and enlightened set of laws in the world. Napoleon was, therefore, hailed as Second Justinian.

The institution of the Legion of Honour was the personal act of Napoleon. The orders and decorations of monarchy had been abolished by the National Convention and occasionally "Civil Crowns" were awarded to individuals by decrees. In 1802 Napoleon put forward a comprehensive scheme for a Legion of Honour. There was a lot of opposition and criticism of the scheme. The implications of the Legion of Honour were pointed out. It was an affront to democratic equality by the elevation of a small number of individuals to a special status. Napoleon defended his scheme by insisting that there was no real violation of the democratic conceptions of the Revolution as nominations to the Legion of Honour were to be made to all men of eminence irrespective of their blood or wealth. Napoleon maintained that he was throwing open careers to talent. Distinctions were essential even in republics. When critics described these decorations as toys, Napoleon replied: "You are pleased to call them toys, well, it is with toys that mankind is governed." The only result of criticism was that Napoleon did not confer any formal decoration until after the establishment of the Empire in 1804. Excluding the members of the Bonaparte family and a few favoured individuals, who held the title of Prince, there were 31 Dukes, some 400 Counts, more than 1,000 barons and about 1,500 knights, towards the end of his reign. It is true that the old nobility was no more, but a kind of new nobility came into existence. It was undoubtedly a reactionary measure and a modification of the social order created by the Revolution.

(7) **Art.** In spite of his many preoccupation, Napoleon found time for the patronage of art. State palaces were not only restored but also enlarged. The city of Paris was beautified. Broad avenues were planned. Paris began to lay claim as the pleasure city of Europe. Its population almost doubled during the era of Napoleon.

(8) **Colonial Empire.** Napoleon decided to found a new Colonial Empire for France and for that object made elaborate preparations. However, all his efforts failed on account of the British naval supremacy. Finding his position weak, Napoleon sold Louisiana to the U.S.A. in 1803.

It is to be observed that Napoleon Bonaparte crushed dissent in the country with a heavy hand. Conspirators were hanged or banished. So great was the censorship of the press that the defeat of Trafalgar in 1805 was not mentioned by any French newspaper till the overthrow of Napoleon.

According to Prof. Markham, "The work of the Consulate was in the main, to achieve the reforms already projected during the Revolution. In the Council of State, which, under the chairmanship of Napoleon, hammered out the legislation of the Consulate, and in his ministers and prefects, Napoleon had able collaborators and experts. Napoleon's contribution was to get things done; for the first time since 1789 (with the possible exception of the great Committee of Public Safety of 1793-4), France felt the impulse of a powerful, unified will. As Napoleon said of the ex-revolutionaries whom he recruited for his government: 'There were good workmen among them; the trouble was that they all wanted to be architects.' And the success of the Consulate was in direct proportion to Napoleon's success in making his government both civilian and national rather than military. Napoleon insisted that 'it is not as a general that I am governing Frence: it is because the nation believes that I possess the civil qualities of a ruler.' He attracted to his government the ablest men, regardless of their past. Former servants of the monarchy, like Gaudin and Portalis, rubbed shoulders with ex-revolutionaries like Merlin de Douai, Treilhard and Thibaudeau. Among the outstanding prefects were Jean Bon St. Andre, former regicide and member of the Committee of Public Safety, and Mounier, leader of the royalist right in the early days of the States-General of 1789." (**Napoleon and the Awakening of Europe,** pp. 54-5).

About the achievements of Napoleon Bonaparte as First Consul, Leo Gershoy observes that during these years, he ended "the romance of the Revolution" and established authority over the country. He imposed his will on France because of his practical intelligence and soaring imagination, boundless confidence and tireless energy and genius for combining a meticulous attention to details with a clear vision of the ultimate object in view. The reorganization of France was his work. He closed the chapter of republican violence and royalist reprisal. He brought peace and stability to the people without restoring the Bourbons or sacrificing the benefits of the Revolution. However, he was hostile to the idea of liberty which had inspired those who brought about the French revolution. For the idea of liberty, he substituted the idea of authority. He retained the essentially democratic society created by the Revolution but restored and perfected the centralised administration of the **ancien** regime. He might have ended his days as the Emperor of the French and perpetuated his dynasty if he had followed a policy of peace but he failed on account of his belief that war was essential to his political purposes. (**The French Revolution and Napoleon,** p. 381).

Foreign Policy. A reference may be made to the foreign policy of the First Consul. His immediate task was to meet the danger of the Second Coalition which had been formed in the absence of Napoleon in Egypt. By cleverness, Napoleon was able to win over the Czar and thereby he secured his withdrawal from the Second Coalition. Thus, only Austria, and England were left in the field. As regards Austria, Napoleon sent Moreau to attack the Austrians from Germany and he himself proceeded towards Italy to attack the Austrians. Napoleon crossed the Great Bernard Pass and advanced towards Alessandria which was the headquarters of the Austrian force. The battle of Marengo was fought on 14 June 1800 in the neighbourhood of Alessandria. This was the first battle fought by Napoleon since his assumption of the title of First Consul and is considered to be one of his great victories. As a matter of fact, it was very nearly defeat. The French army was attacked unexpectedly while it was divided into three parts. It was driven back with considerable loss. The Austrian General retired into Merengo with the confidence that he had won a victory which could be completed by a subordinate. It was at that stage that a French force arrived with dramatic suddenness under Desaix. He had no instructions from Napoleon. He had heard the noise of the guns and marched straight to them. He arrived to find Napoleon defeated but there was a second battle in which the French were completely victorious. The Austrians withdrew and all the results of the Austrians and the Russians since 1798 were undone. Thompson says, "The Marengo campaign has been so overlaid with legends that the historian is almost afraid to credit Bonaparte with his most fortunate victory. It is not true (as Bourrienne says) that he put a pin on the map three months beforehand to mark the place where he would defeat the Austrians. It is not true that he laid his troops on a prancing steed (as David painted him) over the St. Bernard; his mule was several days behind the advance-guard of Bertheir's army. It is not true that he slept by the road-side at Albaredo whilst the troops stole silently by for fear of waking their general....The tactical aim of the campaign of Marengo was to relieve Genoa and to drive the Austrians out of Lombardy. Its strategical aim had been to compel the Emperor to make peace." (**Napoleon Bonaparte: His Rise and Fall,** pp. 162-64.)

Morean won a decisive victory over the Austrians at Hohenlinden and thus the resistance of Austria was broken. War was ended by the Peace of Luneville (1800) which confirmed the provisions of the Treaty of Campo Formid and slightly increased the French gains.

England alone was left in the field. It was difficult to attack her as France had no strong navy and England had no army on the Continent. Likewise, France had no fleets on the sea which could be defeated by England. By cleverness, Napoleon was able to create the Armed Neutrality consisting of Russia, Prussia, Sweden and Denmark. Its object was to prevent England from searching neutral ships for French goods. Great Britain hit hard. Admiral Nelson bombarded Copenhagen and captured the Danish fleet so that it may not fall into the hands of Napoleon. Czar Paul of Russia was assassinated and the Armed Neutrality was broken. The English were successful in Egypt and the French were forced to evacuate Egypt. Both parties were tired of the war which was not ending in the victory of either party. It was under these circumstances that the Peace of Amiens was made in 1802 between England and France. England promised to restore all conquests to France and her Allies except Ceylon and Trinidad. She also promised to evacuate the Island of Malta. France promised to evacuate Naples and the Papal states. Neither party was proud of the Peace of Amiens although both of them welcomed it because it gave them breathing time. However, it turned out to be merely a truce and war broke out between the two countries in 1803.

The responsibility for the rupture of the Peace of Amiens rests securely on Napoleon. He had never considered the Peace of Amiens as more than a truce in his struggle to humble England and destroy her colonial empire and commercial position. He provoked the war in May 1803 by a deliberate policy which made it clear to all that he was determined to expand the power of France in Europe and revive the naval and colonial supremacy of France which she once possessed. The war which was provoked in 1803 was a steady move towards a dearly determined goal. Ambition played a very great part in his thinking. His love of glory and power and thirst for fame which would make his name immortal, were also responsible for the renewal of the war. Napoleon also knew that he was merely a military upstart in the society of ancient European royalty. His position was insecure and depended upon military triumphs and adulation of the French nation. He was convinced that the great powers of Europe would not accept easily the new Government in France as a permanent part of the European system of states. This was responsible for his decision that France must be first or fail completely. The attitude of Napoleon towards weaker neighbours of France was different from that of the other great European powers. Napoleon considered those states as so many props to his military projects and the areas in which he could settle the beneficial revolutionary institutions. He was moved by "the genuine desire of the born administrator to rid the world of the accumulated debris of worn out institutions." However, this attitude was interpreted by England as a new version of the ancient French ambition for military domination in Europe. Napoleon was the prisoner of a fixed idea that unless he succeeded in breaking the colonial and commercial supremacy of England and forced her to modify her maritime code, his own rule in France was not safe. Napoleon was also convinced that the prosperity of England was artificial which rested upon her commerce and which in turn rested upon her colonies. Napoleon provoked the war in 1803 in order to close the Continent to British products and thereby destroy her prosperity.

What awakened British fears of French military hegemony on the Continent were the happenings in Italy, Switzerland and Holland. Between 1801 and 1802, Napoleon revised the provisional administration of the Cis-Alpine Republic, forced his own draft of a constitution upon the people and named himself as the President. With a view to secure the support of the people of Lombardy, he changed the name of the Republic from Cis-Alpine to "Italian". Its object was to flatter the national aspirations of the people. The state of Piedmont was annexed to France in September 1802 after the Peace of Amiens. In June 1802, the port of Genoa which belonged to the Ligurian Republic, fell into French hands. Likewise, Leghorn, the principal port of the Kingdom of Etruria which had been established by the Peace of Luneville, fell under French control. The small island of Elba was annexed to France. The French control over the Republic of Lucca was strengthened. The result of all this was that the whole of Northern Italy with the exception of Venetia came directly or indirectly under the control of France. With a view to cover his approach to northern Italy, Napoleon acquired full control of the Simplon road through the Alps by separating the Canton Valais from Switzerland. Switzerland was essential for the designs of Napoleon and he wanted a strong and friendly Government in that country. With that object in view he transformed the Helvetic Republic into the Swiss Confederation which became a military ally and satellite of France. Holland had been occupied in 1800. A new constitution was forced on that country. In October 1801, the Dutch burghers were forced to pay heavy indeminities.

Another development which aroused the apprehensions of England was the refusal of Napoleon to arrange a commercial treaty with England and his rigorous enforcement of the existing French laws against the products of British origin. The situation in this connection became very serious after the Peace of Amiens. British products were excluded not only from France but also from the European states under the control of Napoleon and the colonies which England had returned to France and its allies. The new tariff law of 28 April 1803 was a clear indication of the policy of the French Government to preserve the home market for the native manufacturers. The British fear was that Napoleon was determined to destroy their industrial prosperity.

Another factor which created apprehensions in England was the project of Napoleon to set up a great colonial empire in the West. The Island of Haiti in the West Indies was to be the nucleus of the new French empire. However, there were two difficulties in his way. Toussaint L'Ouverture was the leader of the natives of that Island. For more than a decade, he had established his personal ascendancy in the Island. He had assured a plentiful supply of Negro labourers for the white planters, established the necessary commercial relations with England and the United States, reformed the administration and established law and order in the Island. Napoleon was not willing to allow autonomy to a French colony or allow it to trade freely in British products. Moreover, Toussaint L'Ouverture was an obstacle in the realization of his colonial project. In February 1802, the French expeditionary forces were sent to the Island of Haiti. Toussaint L'Ouverture fell into the hands of the French who sent him to a French prison where he died within a year. There was a terrific outbreak of epidemic of yellow fever. General Leclerc, the brother-in-law of Napoleon and the leader of the expeditionary force sent to Santo Domingo, fell a victim to the fever and his successor surrendered to the Negroes in 1803. Out of 33,000 men sent in February 1802, 24,000 died and 7,000 lay suffering in military hospitals a year later. It was under these tragic circumstances that Napoleon sold Louisiana to the United States in 1803 for 15 million dollars.

By his aggression in Holland, Napoleon had made the English sea route to India precarious as the Cape of Good Hope was returned to the Dutch by the Peace of Amiens. Now Napoleon controlled the Batavian Republic. In order to maintain her position, England tried to safeguard the overland routes to India from the Mediterranean but there also Napoleon stood in their way. Napoleon had strengthened his hold over Italy. He had told the Czar that the partition of the Turkish empire was imminent. There was a lot of resentment in England against Napoleon and English newspapers were publishing biting attacks upon him. At this stage, Napoleon raised the question of Egypt by publishing the sensational account of a military observer whom he had sent to Egypt. According to that account, the British forces were unpopular in Egypt and they were otherwise weak. The suggestion was that a small French expeditionary force could easily reconquer the country. French agents were fomenting trouble against Turkey in Southern Greece. The Governor of the French East India colonies received instructions to prepare for active military developments in India.

Under these circumstances, sharp protests from England were natural and peace hung by a thread in 1803. There was a long and acrimonious diplomatic controversy in which neither country was prepared to yield. As England refused to evacuate Malta, Napoleon refused to evacuate Holland and restore Genoa and Piedmont. From a strictly legal point of view, it could be said that England was not fulfilling the terms of the Peace of Amiens but if we take into consideration the situation as a whole, there is much to be said in favour of the attitude of England. It was under these circumstances that war started again in May 1803.

England[2] alone was left in the field. It was difficult to attack her as. France had no strong navy and England had no army on the continent. Likewise, France had no fleets on the sea which could be defeated by the English. However, by cleverness, Napoleon was able to create against England the **Armed Neutrality** consisting of Russia, Prussia, Sweden and Denmark. Its object was to prevent England from searching neutral ships for French goods. Great Britain hit hard. Admiral Nelson bombarded Copenhagen and captured the Danish fleet so that it might not fall into the hands of Napoleon. Luckily, Czar Paul of Russia was assassinated and the Armed Neutrality was broken. The English were also successful in Egypt and the French were forced to evacuate Egypt. Both parties were tired of war which was not ending in the victory of either. It was in these circumstances that the Peace of Amiens was made in 1802 between England and France. England promised to restore all conquests from France and her allies except Ceylon and Trinidad. She also promised to evacuate

2. According to Thompson, "Bonaparte saw four advantages in invasion. First, considered in isolation, it was the quickest and most effective way to complete victory. A revolution in Ireland, backed by a French expeditionary force—still better, a revolution in England itself, caused by a surprise landing and a swift march on London, might end the war in a week. Secondly, if for any reason, the invasion failed, the panic caused by the attempt might still force the British government to ask for terms. Thirdly, the continued menace of an invading force only twenty miles from Dover would perpetuate a war of nerves, and this would double the effectiveness of the mean blockade. Fourthly, the threat of invasion would probably draw off the 'blockading,' squadrons in the Mediterranean and the Bay of Biscay." (**Napoleon Bonaparte: His Rise and Fall,** p. 22).

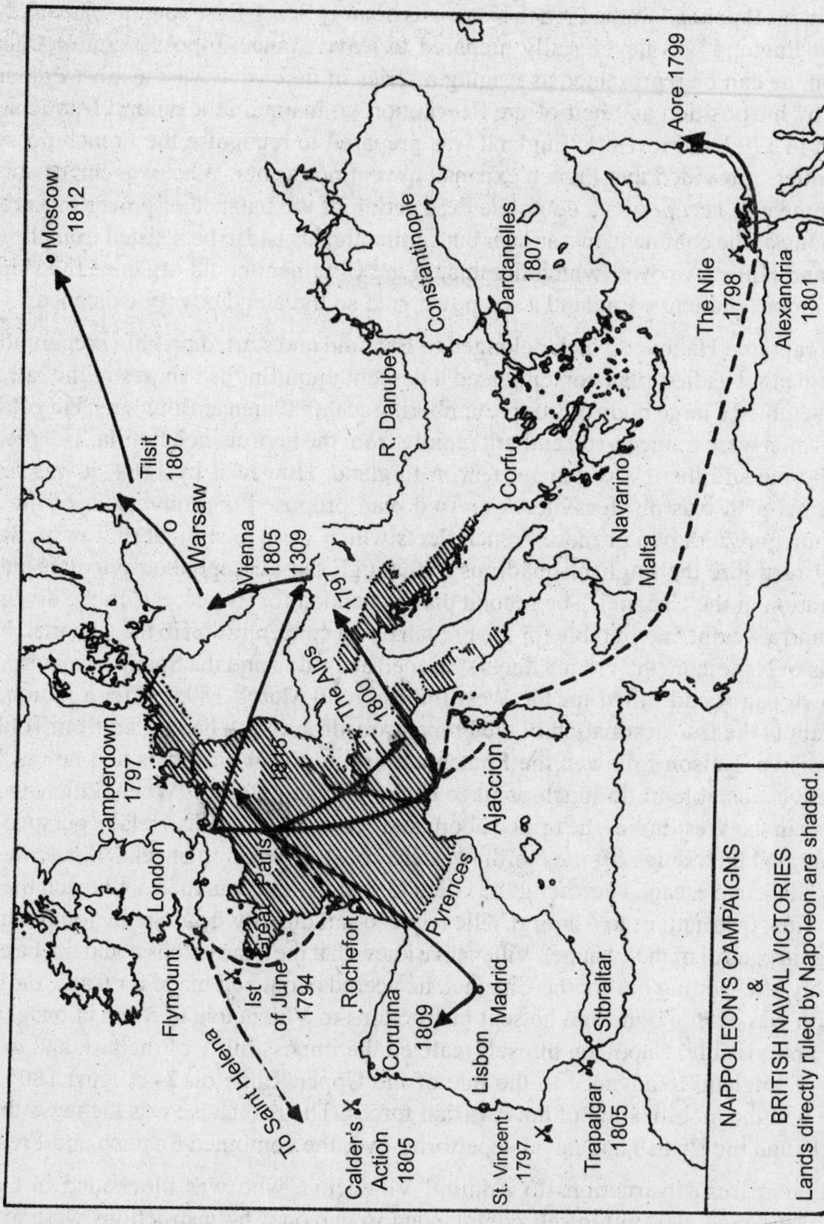

the island of Malta. France promised to evacuate Naples and the Papal States. It is rightly pointed out that neither party was proud of the peace although both of them welcomed it as it gave them breathing time. The Peace of Amiens turned out to be merely a truce and war again broke out between the two countries in 1803. Napoleon had time to consolidate his position at home. He annexed Piedmont. He intervened in the affairs of Switzerland by sending his troops and becoming a mediator. He virtually incorporated Holland into France. He sent a mission to India to stir up the Indian princes against Great Britain. Another mission was sent to Egypt to create the trouble for the English. All these factors were responsible for the renewal of war between the two countries.

According to Markham, "A great deal of ink has flowed on the question of the rupture of the Peace of Amiens. Technically, the English Government was in the wrong and broke the terms of the treaty by refusing to evacuate Malta. From the first, they regarded the Peace as a **'breathing space'** and an **'experimental peace.'** Some French historians notably Sorel, have sought to justify Napoleon by arguing that England was never really prepared to leave France in possession of Belgium; on that assumption, he can be represented as waging a series of defensive wars against England, since he was bound by his position as 'their of the Revolution' to maintain the natural frontiers. But it is clear that, both in 1797 and in 1801, England was prepared to recognise the French possession of the natural frontiers, provided that French expansion went no further. What was impossible for any English government to accept was a complete destruction of the balance of power in Europe and a French, hegemony of the continent, just as later but similar threats had to be resisted from the Germany of William II and Hitler. A power which dominated the Continent could organise the shipbuilding resources of Europe, challenge England's sea-power and so threaten her very existence."

Napoleon captured Hanover which belonged to England and started making preparations for an invasion of England. His first plan contemplated a descent upon English shores in the fall or winter of 1803. He assembled a large body of troops numbering 150,000 men at Boulogne. He got 1,200 flat boats built. His men were trained to disembark rapidly from the unprotected flotilla. The preparations were very elaborate and there was general fear in England. However, by 1804, it was realised by Napoleon that his plan was not feasible. A revised plan proposed the movement of the transport flotilla in conjunction with two or more French fleets which were to slip out of Toulon, Rochefort, El Ferrol and Brest, lure the English squadrons to the high seas, escape their pursuers and effect a rapid concentration in the Channel. The second plan depended for its success on the division of the English fleets and a weather favourable for the French naval concentration in the Channel. Following the instructions of Napoleon, the French fleets stationed at Toulon and the Spanish squadron escaped from the English patrol and sailed for the West Indies on 30 March 1805. After a month, Admiral Nelson learnt about the true destination of the French squadron which had sailed from Toulon under Admiral Villeneuve. Nelson followed the French admiral to the West Indies and he reached there before Villeneuve was able to do much damage to the British colonies. When Villeneuve learned that Nelson was in the West Indies, he turned about and set sail for Europe. Nelson pursued him. The British concentrated their ships off the North-Western coast of Spain to check Villeneuve. It is true that Admiral Villeneuve escaped defeat but he failed to shake off his pursuers and reach the Channel. Napoleon sent final instructions to Admiral Villeneuve to sail directly from Spain, join with the Brest squadron and gain control of the Channel. Villeneuve knew that the instructions could not be carried out and immediately after setting out for the Channel, he veered about and made for Cadiz on 15 August 1805. Napoleon was at Boulogne and he sent instructions to Villeneuve to reach at once. However, the same was not possible. Napoleon himself realized the impossibility of the task and gave orders for the Army of England to advance to the line of the Upper Rhine on 24 August 1805. His plea was that there was the mobilization of the Austrian forces. The real cause was the news that Nelson had come back, and the British had naval superiority over the combined Spanish and French fleets.

Napoleon sent fresh instructions to Admiral Villeneuve who was blockaded in Cadiz by a large British fleet which Nelson himself commanded in person. The instructions were to reach the Mediterranean. These instructions fitted in perfectly with the plans of Nelson. Nelson wanted to draw out of Cadiz the French and Spanish squadrons and give them battle. As his ships had picked up the signal communications of the enemy, he made full preparations. The battle of Trafalgar was fought on 21 October 1805 and that resulted in the naval victory of England. After six hours of ship to ship action, more than half of the combined French and Spanish fleet of 33 ships was destroyed or captured. Four ships were captured later on. The British fleet lost only one ship. However, the biggest loss of Britain was the death of Nelson. It is pointed out that so far as the actual invasion of England was concerned, the victory of Trafalgar had no effect on it because the invasion had already been given up definitely two months earlier.

Regarding Napoleon's projected invasion of England, Prof. Markham observes: "It has often been said that Napoleon's preparations for the invasion of England between 1803 and 1805 were a blind to enable him to assemble and train the Grand Army, which was really intended for the overthrow of the Continental powers. Napoleon himself was the first to produce this explanation, to cover up the failure of the invasion. He is reported to have said in the Council of State as early as January 1805 that the Boulogne camp was a ruse to deceive the continental powers. But it is impossible to read his correspondence for this period, with its constant and almost frenzied attention to the problem of invasion in all its details, without being convinced that he really meant to invade, at any rate, in 1805. One may doubt whether he would ever have attempted a crossing of the Channel in barges unescorted by warships. The assembling of the barge flotilla had been begun before the Peace of Amiens, and it was then regarded by Napoleon as a means of menacing England, rather than as a feasible means of invasion. The flotilla was immensely expanded in 1803-04, and at its peak the project envisaged 2,000 boats of all kinds, to transport barely 100,000 men and their equipment. There is little doubt that once landed, they could have captured London, as there were barely 1,000,000 regular troops in the whole of Britain, and the militia forces raised by Pitt would have had little military value against Napoleon's veterans. But it is possible that Napoleon never intended the flotilla to cross by itself, and that he maintained it as a potential threat, pending the time when his naval forces could make a serious attempt to secure command of the Channel for an escorted crossing.

Napoleon as Emperor (1804-14). In 1802, Napoleon managed to transform the Consulate for 10 years to one for life, with the right to name his successor. In 1804, the Senate approved of a new Constitution which declared him Emperor of the French. Napoleon himself observed: **"I found the crown of France lying on the ground and I picked it up with my sword."** He remained Emperor up to 1814 when he was forced to abdicate after the battle of Leipzig and retired to the island of Elba. After his return from Elba, he remained the Emperor of France for one hundred days and was again defeated in the Battle of Waterloo in 1815. After that, he retired to Paris but was forced to surrender himself to the British. He was sent to the island of St. Helena where he died in 1821 after six years of exile. His will was: "My wish is to be buried on the banks of the Seine in the midst of the French people whom I have loved so well."

Napoleon recognised the gravity of the situation created by the formation of the Third Coalition in 1805 and he decided to meet the same. Not waiting for the Russians, the Austrians sent an army of 80,000 men under General Mack up the Danube into Bavaria. Mack took up his position at Ulm hoping that Napoleon would come through the passes of the Black Forest which were the most direct and usual way for a French army invading Southern Germany. It is true that Napoleon sent some troops to the Black Forest in order to confirm the expectation of Mack that the French army was attacking from that direction, but he also transferred his Grand Army from Boulogne and the shores of the English Channel across Germany from north to south, a distance of 500 miles, in 23 days of forced marches. Napoleon threw himself into the rear of the army of Mack and thereby cut off his line of communications. Napoleon proceeded towards Ulm and when Mack found himself overpowered, he surrendered at Ulm on October 20, 1805. After the victory, he wrote thus to Josephine : **"I have accomplished what I set out to do. I have destroyed the Austrian army by means of marches alone."** Napoleon captured 60,000 prisoners of war, 120 guns and more than 30 generals. He himself lost only 1,500 men.

After the surrender of Ulm, Napoleon won the resounding victory of Austerlitz on December 2, 1805 which was the first anniversary of his coronation as Emperor. We are told that there was terrific fighting. The bravery of soldiers on both sides was boundless. However, Napoleon was superior to his opponents in generalship. The result was that the Allies were defeated and they ran away in different directions. They lost nearly all of their artillery and also a large number of their men. After the victory, Napoleon addressed his troops in these words: "Soldiers, I am satisfied with you. In the battle of

Austerlitz, you have justified all my expectations by your intrepidity; you have adorned your eagles with immortal glory." The battle of Austerlitz was so very decisive that it broke the Third Coalition. On hearing the news of the battle of Austerlitz, Pitt the Younger, is stated to have remarked: **"Roll up the map of Europe, it will not be wanted these ten years."**

The Russians did not make peace and withdrew in great disorder. However, the Austrians concluded the humiliating **Treaty of Pressburg.** By this treaty, Austria ceded Venetia to the kingdom of Italy whose king was Napoleon himself. Only the port of Trieste was left in the hands of Austria. Not Austria but France was in future to be the chief Adriatic power. Bavaria and Baden had sided with Napoleon in the war against Austria and consequently Austria was forced to give to each of them some of her valuable possessions in South Germany. Shut out of the Adriatic and shut out of Italy, Austria lost three million subjects. Austria became practically a land-locked country. She was also compelled to submit to other changes that Napoleon had made or was about to make in many countries.

In the early months of 1806, Napoleon created four kings. "In grateful recompense for the attachment they have shown the Emperor", Napoleon raised the duchies of Bavaria and Wutemberg to the rank of kingdoms. As the King of Naples had sided with his enemies. Napoleon removed the Bourbon King of Naples and put his own brother Joseph on the throne of Naples. Napoleon forced the Batavian Republic of Holland to become a monarchy and accept his own brother Louis Napoleon as its king. Napoleon also abolished the Holy Roman Empire in 1806 and established in its place the Confederation of the Rhine.

In 1806 Prussia was defeated in the Battles of Jens and **Aurestapt** and Napoleon entered Berlin in triumph. It was from here that the Berlin decree which inaugurated the Continental System was issued in 1806.

In 1807, Russia was defeated in the battle of Friedland, but in spite of his heavy losses, Czar Alexander could have continued the military struggle against Napoleon if other considerations had not entered his calculations. He feared that a prolonged war with Napoleon might encourage a revolt among the Poles. He resented very much the lukewarm attitude of England and Austria. Moreover, he was anxious to profit from the troubled affairs of Europe. Napoleon also wanted to give rest to his soldiers and utilize his victory for the fulfilment of his vast continental designs. An armistice ended the hostilities on 21 June 1807 and Czar Alexander and Napoleon held the first of their formal conferences on a raft moored in the Nimen river near Tilsit. For three hours, Napoleon and Czar Alexander discussed the terms of their rapprochement while Frederick William, the ruler of Prussia who was an ally of the Czar, rode helplessly up and down the shore. Napoleon had already warned him when he was presented to him of what was in store for him. It was at Tilsit that Czar Alexander is stated to have remarked to Napoleon: "What is Europe? Where is it? If it is not you and I ?"

The treaties of Tilsit (7-9 July 1807) consisted of an open and secret treaty between Russia and France and an open treaty between France and Prussia. Czar Alexander was made to pay a heavy price for the integrity of his state and his alliance with Napoleon "to assure the happiness and tranquillity of the globe". The Czar recognised the great changes brought about by Napoleon in Holland, Germany and Italy. He declared himself ready to accept all the additional changes that may be made by Napoleon. He gave his assent to the dismemberment of Prussia who lost some of her most precious possessions and half of her population. From the Prussian territory west of the Elbe to which were added lands from Hesse Cassel and the Duchy of Brunswick, Napoleon created the Kingdom of Westphalia which he gave to his brother Jerome. The Polish provinces of Prussia in the east, with the exception of the district of Bialystok, went to form the Grand Duchy of Warsaw under the rule of the King of Saxony. The King of Saxony was given the right to use a military road running through Silesia. Frederick William retained only his provinces of East Prussia together with West Prussia and Ermeland, Brandenburg, Silesia and a portion of the Duchy of Magdeburg. By a separate military Convention, the French troops were to occupy various fortresses in these provinces until the payment of war contributions the exact amount of which was not fixed until September 1808. Pending the conclusion of a general peace with England, French garrisons were to occupy the port of Danzig and the ports of the Duchy of Oldenburg and Mecklenburg. Frederick William recognized the Confederation of the Rhine, Louis as the King of Holland and Joseph as the King of Naples. In secret articles, Prussia was required to close her harbours to the English and take common action with France and Russia against England.

In the secret treaty of alliance between Russia and France, the terms of their future joint action were elaborated. Napoleon made a fool of the Czar by making him believe that he threw open to him the East although Napoleon never intended to make such a generous offer. The Czar offered his mediation between France and England. England was to be asked to return by 1 November 1807 all the conquests she had made since 1805 and to grant complete independence upon the seas. If England refused, the Czar was to declare war, close the ports of his country to British products and ask the Baltic states, Austria and Portugal, to follow suit. Napoleon offered his good offices as a mediator to end the war between Russia and Turkey. In case of refusal by Turkey, Napoleon was to make at the end of three months, common cause with Russia against the Porte in liberating the European provinces from the Turkish yoke, with the exception of Roumelia and Constantinople. The Czar was convinced that Napoleon had committed himself to the eventual partition of the Turkish empire and his own share would be Moldavia and Wallachia. Napoleon also prevailed upon the Czar to remove his naval forces from the Mediterranean, surrender Cattaro to the French and recognise French sovereignty over the Ionian Islands.

Both Napoleon and the Czar could congratulate themselves that they had outwitted each other. The Czar lost no territory but gained an alliancet. The Czar was satisfied with the arrangements concerning the Grand Duchy of Warsaw because they were intended to avert the danger of Polish independence. The King of Saxony was made its ruler and the Czar hoped that he would be able to dominate him. However, the King of Saxony was a member of the Confederation of the Rhine and a military dependent of Napoleon. The Czar was sure that Sweden would refuse to join in a war against England and he could get an opportunity to capture Finland. Napoleon also had no cause for regret. He had broken Prussia and gained full control over Germany from one end to the other. In the Kingdom of Westphalia, he had a French outpost in Germany. He saw a similar advantage in the Grand Duchy of Warsaw, Napoleon lost no time in reducing the sovereignty of the King of Saxony to a minimum and in reserving the essentials of power for himself. He misled the Czar to recognise a grand empire that protruded into Poland and Eastern Adriatic. He had played his cards well. By refusing to reconstruct an independent Poland under the guarantee of Russia, he neglected and endangered the final consolidation of his domination in Italy and Germany. By trying to thwart the secular ambitions of Russia in the Turkish Empire, he earned the bitter and determined hostility of the Czar. He had committed a great blunder. He sacrificed the reality of domination in Europe for the shadow of a universal empire.

Germany. After the defeat of Austria and Prussia, the whole of Germany was in the hands of Napoleon. He had no respect for the Holy Roman Empire. He called its Diet "a miserable monkey house". Many schemes were prepared and ultimately the Confederation of the Rhine was set up in July 1806. The general aim of the Confederation was to break up the German lands into three main bodies. Prussia was to rule in the north and Austria in the south and east. In the west was to be set up the new State of the Confederation of the Rhine which was to be independent of both Austria and Prussia but under French protection. The sixteen States forming the Confederation were to be independent and sovereign. A Diet was to sit at Frankfurt and the common interests of the Confederation were to be considered there. However, the Diet never met and the Constitution remained a dead letter. Napoleon was declared to be protector of the Confederation. He was given the right of determining the contingents which each member was to furnish in case of war. The members were declared to be necessary allies in any war that involved either of the parties. On 6 August 1806, Emperor Francis gave up his title and the Holy Roman Empire came to an end.

Rise of Prussia

Prussia had been defeated in the battle of Jena and humiliated by the Treaty of Tilsit. Her defeat is attributed to many factors. It is true that Frederick the Great had created an exceedingly efficient machinery of Government, but the major defect in that was that everything depended upon the personality of the king. He never consulted the people. The result was that there was a decline in the efficiency of that administrative machinery and it was not able to meet the challenge of Napoleon. The same was true of the Prussian army. It was not in any way the embodiment of the spirit of the nation. It was merely a weapon in the hands of the king which could be used as he desired. The officers in the army were mostly from the noble class. Discipline in the army was harsh and brutal. "The peasant was forced by brutal punishments to defend the country which starved him." The soldiers were not inspired by any national spirit. There was no consciousness of any personal interest in the well-being of the state. Such an army was no match for Napoleon and no wonder Prussia lost before him.

The man called to the helm of the Government after the Treaty of Tilsit was Baron Stein. All the progressive people in the kingdom appealed to him to save the situation. Only recently, he had been dismissed by Frederick William and characterized as "a refractory, insolvent, obstinate and disobedient official" but after Tilsit the King of Prussia was forced to call him back. Stein took over as minister on 1 October 1807 and thus ended the rule of the king's private advisers. He was forced to resign in November 1808 on account of the pressure from Napoleon. But for 14 months he enjoyed practically dictatorial powers, both in domestic and foreign affairs. In those 14 months, he instituted and associated himself with a programme of reforms that put new life into Prussia. This was in spite of the fact that an intolerable financial burden was imposed on Prussia by the French army of occupation.

Stein sent Prince William, the brother of Frederick William, to Paris to bargain for more favourable terms from Napoleon. He personally went to Berlin to seek concessions from the French military governor. At the same time, he made drastic economies. He cut down pensions and reduced the salaries of officials and soldiers and officers in the army and whittled down court expenditure. By using the royal domain as collateral security, he succeeded in floating debentures or mortage bonds and raising more than 70 million francs towards payment of the indemnity and costs of occupation. Unfortunately, the interception of a letter written by Stein led to his fall. In that letter, Stein had written that war between Austria and France was a certainty. The interests of Germany would best be served by fanning the growing resentment against the French and the national uprising in Spain was an example for the German patriots to follow. The wrath of Napoleon knew no bounds and he demanded the dismissal of Stein. Stein not only resigned but also ran away to Austria to save his life. Stein later on joined the service of the Czar and continued to work against Napoleon. Napoleon never forgot what Stein had done and when he made the final settlement with Prussia on 8 September 1808, he limited the Prussian army to 42,000 men and fixed the indemnity at 140 million francs.

Although Stein was forced to go, he had already accomplished a lot. His name is associated with a large number of reforms. The first of those reforms dealt with the peasantry and the land. On 9 October 1807, the King of Prussia put his signatures on the Edict of Emancipation which abolished serfdom with its many personal obligations throughout his kingdom. This change was to take effect after the expiry of three years on 8 October 1810. The first two articles of this Edict removed the existing medieval restrictions on the holding of land and the choice of occupation. The transfer of land from one to another was now legalised by royal permission. The only consideration to be kept in mind was that there should be no diminution of peasant property. The classification of labour was also ended. In future, a noble could take up an occupation which was previously restricted only to the middle classes. Likewise, a burgher could now take up a profession which was previously restricted only to the peasantry. This Edict was a tremendous step in the direction of free economic enterprise. It favoured the development of agriculture by attaching capital to land, particularly to the unproductive land of the impoverished noblemen. It removed all social stigma from all those occupations which were previously considered as ignoble. It enabled enterprising men of all classes to develop their economic abilities without fear of reproach. However, the Edict of Emancipation did not free the peasants from their feudal obligations, whether paid in labour, in kind or in money. It also did not end the manorial jurisdiction of the nobles over the peasants. In spite of these limitations, this reform transformed the Prussian peasant into a citizen of the state. By a decree of 4 September 1811, the peasants on private estates were divided into two classes, both of which were "to be freed from dues and labour duties to the land-owner in return for their relinquishment to him of all claims to a certain fraction of the holdings in which they had by custom or law possessory rights." The hereditary peasant proprietors gave up one-third of their holdings and the peasants without hereditary rights and renters of noble land on a lease basis were required to give up one-half of their tenure. The measure was hedged in by many reservations and was opposed by the privileged land-owners. Moreover, the provisions were not observed during the War of Liberation. The Edict of 1816 superseded them and limited their application to the larger holdings. In spite of all this, the change from feudal tenure to freehold had begun and the peasants had their first opportunity to become an economically independent land-owning class. The barons also gained and they were able to build up large estates at the expense of free but landless peasants.

Stein next turned to the townsmen of Prussia who had lived a separate life of their own dominated by the decadent guilds and excluded from service in the army. On 19 November 1808, the great Edict which laid the foundation of local Government in Prussia during the entire 19th century, was signed. This was not a law to guarantee rights of men and the citizen but an attempt to revitalize the state in the interest of national defence. This was accomplished not by increasing the authority of the state over the towns which was already enormous but by entrusting large powers to the local citizens without depriving the state of its general supervision. However, the law did away entirely with the rights of the lords of manors over towns and villages with more than 800 inhabitants. The legal barriers between the towns of Prussia and the rest of the country were broken down. Liberty made an appearance on Prussian soil. However, the country was not favourable to the growth of self-government. Hardenberg in his "Testament" declared in favour of "democratic principles in a monarchical state." Stein also looked in the same direction. Nothing was done except to make a beginning with provincial assemblies.

Stein also projected a thorough reform of the central administration as well as of its agents in the local administrative divisions. There was a lot to do because the well-regulated state of Frederick the Great had degenerated into a cumbersome bureaucracy. The tenure of office of Stein was too short to allow the full realisation of his plan and of reform but he made a start in the right direction. Some of his ideas were carried to completion by his successors. Stein increased the importance of the ministers and gained a degree of real responsibility for them. He also planned the creation of a true royal council. After his retirement, his successors succeeded in establishing only a smaller ministerial council that met under the Presidency of the King. The administration of justice was separated from the executive. The various special treasuries were consolidated into one central treasury.

Great changes were also made in the military system of the country and Scharnhorst, Gneisenau and Clausewitz played an important part in this connection. Scharnhorst was the great organiser of the new army. He dedicated his life to his task. He believed that only a moral regeneration of the people could transform the army. Geneisenau was an idealist who found much to admire in the French Revolution. He is compared with the French Jacobins of 1793. Clausewitz was the great theorist of military tactics. Frederick William gave full support to these three persons to create a truly national army. Many old officers were dismissed. Those who were responsible for the military humiliation of

1806 were severely punished. The King agreed to the demand of Scharnhorst that the use of mercenary troops must be given up. It was in itself a step forward towards enlisting every citizen in the work of national defence. However, the king did not agree with the proposal of Scharnhorst to create a national militia and preferred to reorganise the existing cantonal system of recruiting. In spite of this, the ideas of Scharnhorst prevailed later on. That was due to the fact that Napoleon limited the strength of the active Prussian army to 42,000 and forbade the organisation of a militia. In order to defeat this provision, the reformers devised their famous "shrinkage system" (Krumper system) whereby the ranks of the regiments were periodically filled with recruits who after a brief period of training, passed into the reserves. The change was made secretly but it helped Prussia to have by 1812 a well-trained force of 150,000 men in addition to the nominal total of 42,000 soldiers in the active army. In spite of the reluctance of the king, the whole male population actually received a longer or shorter training in military service. The reforms also did away with the degrading punishments formerly imposed, upon the soldiers. It is true that the highest positions in the army were still occupied by the nobility, but it became possible in the future for the commoners to become officers. Great improvements were made in weapons, uniforms, drill and tactics. Heave baggage trains were given up as well as the supply stations. In times of war, the army was to live by requisitions. In 1814, universal military service was made legal throughout the country but in practice universal service was already in existence. As a result of the military changes, the army became national. Foreigners were excluded. The system of privilege was destroyed. Career was thrown open to talent in the army. A new spirit and a new standard of military honour and a new code of ethics were introduced in the Prussian army. Instead of being a school of vice, the Prussian army became a school of honour.

All these changes would not have mattered much if there had not been a corresponding change in the minds of the people of Prussia. Intellectually, Prussia was as awake as France before the Revolution. Appeals were made to the nation by Scleiermacher and Fichte. The patriotic poetry of writers like Arndt played its part in awakening the people. The Tugendbund or League of Virtue was founded at Konigsberg in 1808 and it strengthened the feelings of patriotism and idealism among the people. The Gymnastic Society of F.L. John stirred the public opinion. Halle had hitherto been the chief university in Prussia but it was now under the influence of Napoleon. Hence, it was decided to set up the University of Berlin. There was opposition on the ground that the life of a great capital was not suitable for study, but ultimately the University of Berlin was started. From the very beginning, it attracted men of outstanding distinction and was housed in a palace and given an adequate grant by the state. It played an important part in the awakening of the country.

The Continental System. England was the very soul of every coalition that was made against France. Napoleon tried hard to bring England to knees but failed in the battle of Trafalgar in 1805. England, being a nation of shopkeepers, could be attacked through her trade and since Napoleon, had defeated Austria in the Battle of Austerlitz (December 1805), Prussia in the Battle of Jena (1806) and Russia in the Battle of Friedland (1807), he felt that he was in a position to attack England at a point where she was most vulnerable. Such an advice had been given to Napoleon in 1805 by Montgaillard in a memorial presented by him to the French Emperor. That memorial is claimed to be the basis of the Continental System. To quote Montgaillard, **"It is through her commerce that England must be attacked; to leave her of her gains in Europe, Asia and America is to leave her of her arms, to render conflicts and was eternal. To destroy British commerce is to strike England to the heart."**

Thompson puts the ideas of Napoleon in these words: "First, he argued, France is a self-sufficient country, living upon its own produce, and that of its overseas possessions, as a cottage lives upon the produce of his field and of his garden; it does not derive its wealth from outside sources, except in the form of forced contributions from countries it has recently conquered. But Britain is a manufacturing and trading country, producing a surplus of goods which it carries and sells overseas, mainly on the continent of Europe; and like other traders, it 'makes money' in the form of cash paid for those goods, and for their carriage. If it can be prevented from carrying on this trade, its supply of cash will dry up; it will go bankrupt; and it will be unable to pay for the continuance of the war, either by itself or its allies.

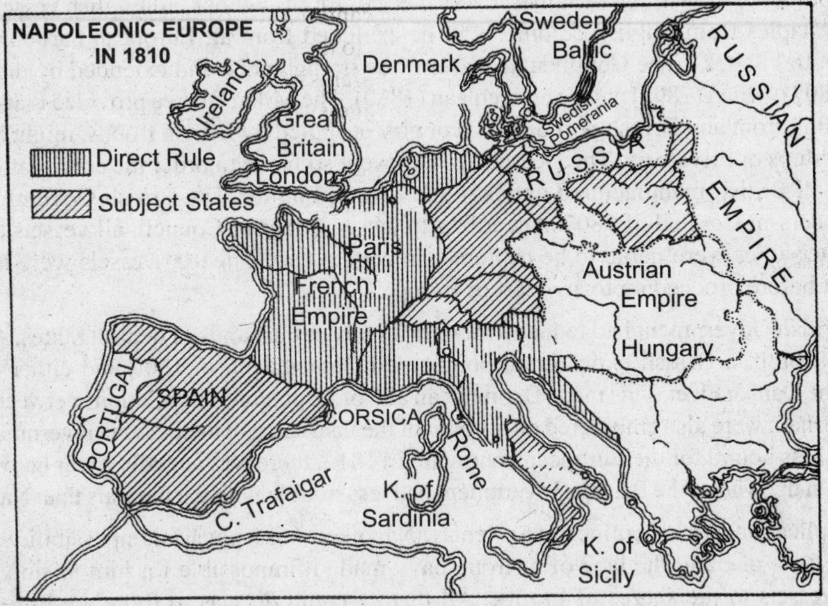

"Secondly, England must accumulate cash (in the form of gold) to pay interest on the enormous national debt, it is incurring, and to back the inflated paper currency with which it is financing its daily affairs. This debt in fact amounted in 1802 to £507 million, only £80 million less than it was on the outbreak of war in 1914, and the interest payable on it averaged £18 million a year. The gold reserves at the Bank of England had sunk almost as low as £1 million in 1797, and might be reduced to danger-point again, if, instead of exporting goods for cash, England could be prevented from exporting or forced to pay out cash for goods imported.

"Thirdly (Bonaparte argued), France since the Revolution, had assimilated its social classes and unified its government upon the basis of agriculture, citizenship, and a First Consul who knew what the country wanted, and controlled all the means of achieving it. But in Britain political power was still disputed between the monarchy, the aristocracy, and the farmers and shopkeepers; the country was torn by the rival interests of the landlords and the city of London and still liable to commercial bankruptcy, labour troubles, and dangerous fluctuations of food prices—all the symptoms which had preceded the revolution of 1789; and these difficulties were supposed to be aggravated by the recent expansion of cheap manufactures beyond the country's needs. In such a situation the closing of foreign markets might well produce commercial bankruptcy, unemployment, and political unrest enough to force the government to sue for peace." (**Napoleon Bonaparte: His Rise and Fall,** pp. 224-25).

Napoleon was convinced in his mind that it was impossible for him to attack England by crossing the English Channel. To quote him, it was **"easier to send troops from Paris to Delhi than from Boulogne to Folkestone."** The British Navy was a great hurdle for him. British prosperity depended primarily upon trade and if that could be destroyed, Great Britain could be brought to her knees. The plan he hit upon was a dangerous gamble, but. Napoleon was prepared to risk it as he was determined to humble England. The plan adopted by him is known as the Continental System which involved the economic blocake of England.

The plan was announced by Napoleon in 1806 in the famous Berlin Decree. It declared: "The British islands are henceforth blockaded. All commerce with them is prohibited; letters and packages with an English address will be confiscated as also every store of English goods on the Continent within the border of France and her allies; every piece of English goods, all English vessels, and those laden with staples from English colonies will be excluded from all European harbours, including those of neutral States." The Continental System was strengthened and extended by the Decrees of Warsaw (1807), Milan (1807) and Fontainebleau (1810). The Milan Decree provided that even neutral vessels sailing from any British port or from country occupied by British troops, might be seized by French warships or privateers. The Decree of 1810 went so far as to order the confiscation or public burning of all British-manufactured goods in the French Empire. The British Government also hit back by Orders-in-Council of 1807. According to these Orders-in-Council, all vessels trading with France or her allies were liable to be captured. In certain cases, neutral vessels were to touch at a British port before proceeding to any part of Europe.

The British Government had to face a lot of difficulty at the hands of neutral States. As Denmark refused to submit, a British expendition bombarded Copenhagen in 1807 and either captured or destroyed the Danish Fleet. This made Denmark an ally of Napoleon. The relations between the U.S.A. and Great Britain were also embittered on account of the insistence of the British Government to search American ships bound for the European continent. In 1812, there was actually a war between the two countries. On the whole, the British Government had less trouble with the neutrals than Napoleon had.

The application of the Continental System by Napoleon was a physical impossibility. His Empire was a very wide one and the lack of a strong navy made it impossible for him to stop the coming of British vessels to the shores of Europe. All that he could do was to force the European States to refuse to trade with England. However, that also was impossible. Europe was dependent upon England and could not live without her and no wonder the people of Europe were prepared to defy Napoleon rather than submit to the Continental System. It has rightly been pointed out that Great Britain could get on very well without silks and other luxuries produced in France, substituting for them woollen and cotton goods, but English warships made almost impossible the importation into Europe not only of all colonial necessities but also of the raw materials necessary for indispensable manufactures. By the system of licences alone it was possible to maintain the French army. Cloth and leather for Napoleon's soldiers were brought from England in defiance of the Continental System. On one occasion, 50,000 overcoats for the French army were purchased from England. Great Britain held the monopoly of coffee, tea and sugar without which the Germans of the Rhine Confederation could not live. Napoleon could not dare to cut off these things entirely even from the French and the Italians. It is pointed out that increasing quantities of British goods made their way into the continent, through Spain and Portugal, up the Danube, under cover of special permits. Devices of all kinds were adopted for smuggling. There was a great increase in the number of funerals until it was found that the hearses were filled with sugar. The enhanced prices of sugar, tobacco, coffee, cotton and other commodities added to the sufferings of the people of Europe without in any way harming the people of England. The only real danger for England was the starvation of her population, but that was avoided because Napoleon allowed the export of French wheat through special permits.

Although Napoleon had to face many difficulties he persisted in his policy of economic boycott of Great Britain. By the Treaty of Tilsit (1807), Napoleon got a promise from the Czar of Russia that he would exclude British goods from his dominions. The King of Prussia also gave a similar promise. Napoleon himself undertook to enforce the Decrees within the French Empire, the Kingdom of Italy, the Confederation of the Rhine and the Grand Duchy of Warsaw. His brother Joseph carried out his will in Naples, Jerome in Westphalia, Elise in Tuscany and Louis in Holland. The outcome of the war with Sweden in 1808 was the completion of the closure of all Scandinavian ports to the British ships. It was Napoleon's determination to enforce the Decrees in the Papal States that compelled him to turn out the Pope from Rome and annex the Papal States in 1809. In 1810, Louis Bonaparte gave clear signs of his intention to side with the Dutch people against Napoleon as he found that the enforcement of the Continental System was suicidal to the people of Holland. He was deposed and Holland was annexed to the French Empire.

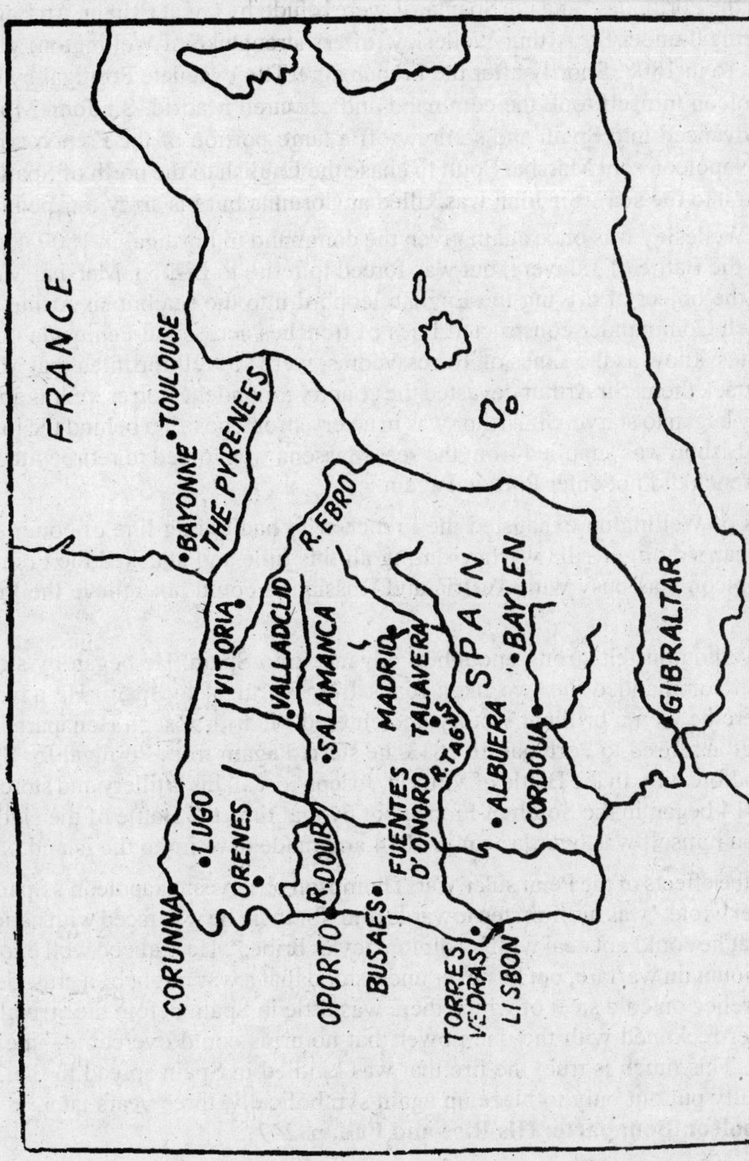

THE PENINSULAR WAR

It was with the object of enforcing the Continental System that Napoleon was forced to interfere in Portugal and Spain. He demanded of Portugal that she should stop all trade with Britain and seize all British subjects and their property in Portugal. Prince John, the Regent, hesitated for some time and finally refused. The result was that French armies made their way through Spain into Portugal. Napoleon's efforts to capture the royal family failed. The British came to the help of Portugal and the Peninsular War started.

The people of Spain did not approve of the passage of French troops through their country to Portugal. They blamed their king for his weakness and there were riots. On the pretext of mediating between the rival factions in the Bourbon Court, Napoleon lured the king and his son to a place on the French frontier and by threats and cajolery persuaded the king and his son to resign all claims to the Spanish throne. In 1808 Joseph Bonaparte was proclaimed the King of Spain. Napoleon's intervention in Portugal and Spain roused forthwith a lot of opposition from the people of both the countries. Both the Portuguese and the Spaniards were helped by Great Britain. An English expedition was sent to Portugal under Sir Arthur Wellesley (afterwards Duke of Wellington) who defeated the French at Vimiero in 1808. Shortly after the French agreed to evacuate Portugal by the Convention of Cintra, Napoleon himself took the command and captured Madrid. Sir John Moore, the British Commander, advanced into Spain and so drew off a large portion of the French army and thereby saved Lisbon. Napoleon sent Marshal Soult to chase the English to the north of Spain and "drive the English leopard into the sea". Sir John was killed at Corunna but his army escaped (1809).

Sir Arthur Wellesley was once again given the command in Fortugal in 1809. He advanced into Spain and won the Battle of Talavera, but was forced to retire to Lisbon. Marshal Massena took the offensive with the object of driving the English leopord into the sea but sir Arthur's tactics foiled him. The English Commander constructed lines of trenches across the Peninsula on which Lisbon stood. These lines, know as the Lines of Torres Vedras, were so well fortifiled that Massena found it impossible to attack them. Sir Arthur devasted the country around the Torres Vedras and consequently the French army began to starve. Sir Arthur was in a very strong position behind the lines with Lisbon as his base and Lisbon was supplied from the sea. Massena was forced to retire with heavy losses in 1811 and the French did not enter Portugal again.

The tactics of Wellington exhausted the French who had a long line of communications. The Spaniards also carried on guerilla warfare during all this time and attacked the French troops at all places. As Napoleon was busy with Austria and Russia, he could not relieve the French troops in the Peninsula.

In 1812, Wellington felt strong enough to advance into Spain. He began by storming the two fortresses which commanded the two main roads from Portugal to Spain. He advanced as far as Salamanca where he won a brilliant victory and entered Madrid. Joseph Bonaparte fled. After this victory, Wellington retired to Portugal. In 1813, he started again from Portugal for Spain and drove out the French before him. In the Battle of Vittoria, Joseph lost all his artillery and stores. Wellington's campaign of 1814 began in the South of France but by that time the Battle of the Nations was going on and Napoleon himself was overthrown in 1814 and made to retire to the Island of Elba.

Regarding the effects of the Peninsular War, Thompson observes: 'Napoleon's Spanish enterprise,' Madame de Stael wrote, 'was his first step towards ruin; for there he was faced with national resistance, the only kind that he could not deal with by diplomacy or bribes'. He realized well enough the danger of village and mountain warfare, but he never understood that a war might be a crusade **(la puissance de l' ame).** He relied on cold steel of which there was little in Spain before the arrival of the English armies. He never reckoned with the one power that no arms could overcome—the enthusiasm of a whole people. This much is true; the fire that was kindled in Spain spread to the Tyrol, where it was with difficulty put out only to blaze up again symbolically, three years later, in the burning of Moscow." (**Napoleon Bonaparte: His Rise and Fall,** p. 247).

In 1812, Lord Liverpool became the Prime Minister of England with Lord Castlereagh as the Foreign Secretary. Castlereagh arranged the Fourth Coalition consisting of Britain, Russia and Prussia and later on Austria. The War of Liberation started. Napoleon was defeated in the Battle of the Nations at Leipzig in 1814.

In 1814, Wellington defeated the French at Toulouse. The Russians, Germans and the Austrians advanced into France. When Napoleon found himself helpless, he abdicated in 1814. Although he came back to France from the Island of Elba, the Allies were determined to finish him. That led to the Battle of Waterloo (1815) in which Napoleon's army was completely routed. In this battle, the Duke of Wellington played the most important part.

Napoleon's invasion of Russia in 1812 proved to be fatal for him. Czar Alexander had come to the conclusion that it was impossible for him to act according to the wishes of Napoleon because they conflicted with the interests of his subjects. He refused to abide by the provisions of the Continental System. Napoleon who had staked his all on the Continental System, undertook the Russian campaign in the spirit of a welcome adventure. To quote him, **"Moscow is the half-way house to India."** He prepared a huge army of more than six lakhs and started the invasion. The Russians followed a policy of retreat and destroyed practically everything on the way. Even the city of Moscow was set on fire by them. Circumstances forced Napoleon to retreat from Moscow and his retreat was one of the most horrible episodes in history. About half a million lives were lost in Russia. The myth of Napoleon's invincibility was exploded. Napoleon's failure to enforce the Continental System in Russia finished the system itself.

About his Moscow campaign, Napoleon stated: "Perhaps I made a mistake in going to Moscow, perhaps I should not have stayed there long; but there is only a step from the sublime to the ridiculous, and it is up to posterity to judge."

As regards the consequences of the Continental System, English exports were not adversely affected by it although the British shippers suffered as trade fell into the hands of the neutrals. However, Englishmen found new markets for their goods, especially for calicoes and prints in South America and the West Indies. During the same period, France tried to find out substitutes for the various things which she used to get previously from outside. Chicory was cultivated to replace coffee. The people were encouraged to use more and more of potatoes and a variety of French-grown tobacco. In 1811, a satisfactory substitute for imported cane-sugar was found in the domestic sugar extracted from beetroot. French indigo took the place of the indigo which was previously imported from English colonies. French industries also gained from the policy of economic imperialism followed by Napoleon. The silk industry of Lyons expanded by leaps, and bounds. The other industries which gained were cotton and woollen industries.

However, after 1810 both sides suffered. The English speculative boom collapsed suddenly in the summer of 1810 and that resulted in heavy unemployment and depreciation of British currency. Trade with the continent fell on account of the fiscal measures adopted by Napoleon in 1810. The situation improved after 1812. During the crucial year 1810, in order to increase the revenue of the French Government, Napoleon permitted the export of huge shipments of grains from Europe to England. The system of Napoleon inflicted temporary hardships upon Great Britain but had no permanent effects. It did not hinder in any way the rapid rate of industrial development in Great Britain. The public credit system of Britain was scarcely affected. The subsidies of Britain to her allies on the continent did not stop. In France, the new economic policy of 1810 increased the prices of colonial products to such an extent that many dealers of Paris were ruined. The loss of the Spanish market made many of them bankrupt. The continental allies of France closed their markets to French goods which were produced especially for them. The artificial prosperity of the new agricultural cultivations and manufacturing industries disappeared. The banks curtailed their loans and credits were strained. The discounts of the Bank of France fell from 715 million francs in 1810 to 319 million in 1811. Business failures in Germany and Holland, involving French manufacturers, precipitated the debacle. Two successive years of inadequate harvests in 1810 and 1811 and the steadily increasing demands of the armies created food shortage. Soaring prices, unemployment and a general economic paralysis was the state of affairs in France. Foreign trade had reached 933 million francs in 1806 but it fell to 605 million in 1813. In the allied and vassal states, the suffering and exasperation caused by the Continental System stiffened the opposition of the patriots to the control of Napoleon. By putting pressure upon the Czar to end the neutral and smuggling trade in the southern Baltic, Napoleon increased tension between himself and the Czar.

Regarding the effects of the Continental System on England, Thompson writes, "From 1803 to 1810 the embargo that Napoleon enforced in the French and Dutch ports, at the mouths of the Ems and Elbe, and, after 1806, in the German Baltic ports, did not seriously hamper British trade.

The total exports of home-produced goods were valued at £41 million in 1805, £44 million in 1806, £40½ million in 1807, £40¾ million in 1808, £50¼ million in 1809, and nearly £50 million in 1810. The value of 'colonial' goods re-exported from England during the same years was, in 1805, £10 million, in 1806 nearly £10 million, in 1807 exactly £10 million, in 1808 £9 million, in 1809 £15¾ million and in 1810 £12¾ million. If then England lived on her export trade, Napoleon's attempt to destroy it was remarkably unsuccessful. It might be said that this was because, during the years in which the continental ports were increasingly shut against her ships, she was able to develop new markets overseas. To a great extent this was so and it was a point which Bonaparte had overlooked in his calculations. Nevertheless the figures, when analysed, show that the proportion of our exports to Europe remained at a consistently high level. In 1805, 37.8 per cent of British-made goods went to Europe, in 1806, 30.9 per cent, in 1807, 25.5 per cent, in 1808, 25.7 per cent, in 1809, 35.4 per cent, and in 1810, 42 per cent, whilst of foreign and colonial goods re-exported from England 78.7 per cent went to Europe in 1805, 72.9 per cent in 1806; 80 per cent in 1807; 71.1 per cent in 1808, 83.1 per cent in 1809 and 76.9 per cent in 1810. In its main endeavour, therefore, the Continental Blockade was, up to 1810, a complete failure,' (**Napoleon Bonaparte: His Rise and Fall,** pp. 235-36).

According to Markham, "Napoleon had not only roused the people of Europe against the Empire by this Continental System, he also lost the confidence of the French middle class, the main beneficiaries of the Revolution and the class which had put him into power. The prolonged economic depression which hit France in 1810-11 was ascribed by them to the Continental System; and from this period dates their indifference to the fate of the regime and the dynasty which was strikingly apparent in 1814. The middle classes had shared his protectionist views and continued obstinately to hold them through the nineteenth century, but they abandoned Napoleon when he ceased to gain them profits. Napoleon was extremely perturbed by the Malet conspiracy in December 1812, during the retreat, from Moscow. Malet, a mad Republican general, announced that Napoleon was dead and proclaimed the Republic. His coup d'etat made some headway before he was arrested; and the significant point about the episode was the fact that none of the officials who had been deceived by Malet thought of proclaiming the accession of Napoleon II."

It cannot be denied that the efforts of Napoleon to enforce the Continental System crippled the resources of France and alienated the sympathy of many States towards him. Great Britain was embittered to the point of desperation. The Continental System, was a grand economic endurance test and Great Britain won it.

Napoleon's Finances

In the matter of finance, Napoleon reintroduced the system of indirect taxation which had been abolished by the Revolution. In the words of Napoleon, "My financial system consists in creating a great number of indirect taxes whose lowly level could be raised in proportion to my needs." In course of time, his needs increased on account of more and more wars and consequently, the burden of indirect taxes also increased. The result was that in 1813 about 40 per cent of the income of the State was derived from taxes on tobacco, salt and liquors. Napoleon never increased the direct taxes. He also did not issue paper currency. All the state expenditures were carefully got audited and France enjoyed the monetary stability throughout the entire Empire. As a matter of fact, Napoleon, was able to balance his budget during most of the period of his reign by adopting such methods as the sale of national property and imposition of indemnities upon the enemy and subject states. A large number of war indemnities, revenues from dependent countries and the proceeds from the sale of confiscated British goods and the customs duties on colonial goods, went to a Special Fund ultimately known as "Extraordinary Domain". Napoleon made it a point by his policy to throw the financial burden of his wars upon the non-French states of his Empire. From the latter he extorted what he needed in specie as well as in manpower and requisitions. So long as he was victorious, the enemy paid the cost of his operations and contributed to the maintenance of his troops, but once he was defeated the weakness of his financial system was exposed. The result was that towards the end of his reign, his financial difficulties were as great as that of the Bourbons in 1789.

Intellectual repression

Although Napoleon brought glory to his country for some time, he deprived the people of their political liberty and personal liberty. It is true that civil liberty was guaranteed by the civil courts, but that guarantee was a hollow one. Napoleon left no stone unturned to suppress the liberty of thought and expression among the people. His view was that liberty was not for the common people. The police adopted various methods to interfere constantly with the private lives of the people. The police could visit the houses of the people at any time. The provision for habeas corpus was suspended and there was very little justice. Anybody could be arrested on suspicion and lodged in jail. Hundreds of police agents and spies were busy in watching the activities of the people and any adverse report from them could put a person in jail. It is estimated that in 1814 the number of political prisoners in France was 2,500.

In order to keep printing under control, the number of printers in Paris was limited to 60 and each one of them was required to take an oath of obedience to the Government. Liberty of the press completely disappeared. There were as many as 70 newspapers in Paris alone in 1800 and by 1810, their number fell to four. More than 100 important provincial journals were suppressed. In their place, an official bulletin was issued by the Government from each Department. The French press became a branch of the Government and only that matter was printed which was inspired by the Government.

The attitude of Napoleon towards theatre and men of letters was the same. The number of theatres was fixed by Government by a Government regulation. Both old and new plays were rigidly censored. The administration of the theatres was handed over to Government agents. No writer could publish his work without getting the approval of the censor. The result was that there was a decline both in the quantity and quality of literature in the French language. There were only two outstanding writers of the Napoleonic age, viz., Madame de Stael and Chateau Briand and both of them were driven into exile. It is maintained that no Jacobin fanatic of 1793-4 could have more effectively organised the domination of the state over the individual than was done by Napoleon. The individual became helpless. No criticism was tolerated. It was feared that if criticism was allowed that might lead ultimately to disloyalty towards Napoleon.

The educational policy of Napoleon did not encourage the free development of the moral and mental faculties of the people. Napoleon stood for an educational system which would teach people to think loyally and uniformly on the problems of religion, politics and social organisation. His educational system was a division of the political organisation. To quote Napoleon, "The system that we propose is not only moral; it is also a political system. Its purpose is to rally behind the government both the new and the old generation, the old through their children and the children through their parents, to establish a sort of public fatherhood." The Imperial University was given a monopoly over public instruction in France. The object of his educational policy was explained by Napoleon himself in these words: "There will never be a fixed political state of things in this country until we have a body of teachers instructed on established principles. So long as the people are not taught from their earliest years, whether they are to be republicans or royalists, Christians or infidels, the state cannot properly be called a nation."

Causes of Napoleon's Failure. Napoleon attained the height of his power in 1808[3] and after

3. Compare the following observations of Thompson : "A military historian, looking for a point at which victory gave place to defeat, might find it between Jena (or perhaps Wagram) and Moscow. A naval historian might prefer Trafalgar. A political historian, looking at the balance of power on the continent, might find the turning point at Tilsit. A historian who envisaged the Napoleonic period as a struggle between France and Great Britain for the control of European and overseas trade would prefer to take the moment when the challenge was thrown down and taken up at the breach of the Peace of Amiens. A Frenchman asking himself at what point Bonaparte's system of government ceased to secure the blessings of the Revolution and began to return to the practices of the Bourbon monarchy, might choose the moment at which the First Consul crowned himself Emperor of the French. But he would be as likely to argue that this act had been implicit in the assumption of Life Consulship two years before, and that it made little difference to the character of the government, or to the working out of the laws and institutions which had been inaugurated at Brumaire.

that his decline began. Many factors were responsible for the rapid fall of the man who had brought nearly the whole of Europe under his control.

(1) One important cause was the limitations of individual genius. It is true that Napoleon was a genius but it is also true that he was a human being. It was impossible for him to do everything himself and since he had too many irons in the fire, it is no wonder that he failed in most of them.

(2) There is always a limit to human energy and after a certain age a person starts feeling the effect of fatigue and exhaustion. In the words of Dr. Sloane, "The causes of his decline may be summed up in a single word, **exhaustion.** There exists no record of human activities more complete than is that of Napoleon Bonaparte's life. In its beginning we can see the worshipper of power stimulating his immature abilities in vain until, with reckless desperation, he closed the period of training and made his scandalous bargain with Bartras; then, grown suddenly, inexplicably rich, becoming with better clothing, food, and lodging, physically more vigorous, he seems mercilessly to drive the rowels into his own flanks until initiative, ingenuity and ruthlessness are displayed with apparently superhuman dimensions. The period of achievement is short but glorious in politics; the age of domination is long and exciting. Throughout both there is the same wanton physical excess and intellectual dissipation. Then comes the turn. Every human age has in it the germs of the next; we begin to due at birth and the characteristic qualities and powers of one period diminish as those of the next increase. So it was with Napoleon. He compressed so much, both as regards the number and importance of events, into so short a space that his times are like those wrinkled Japanese pictures which are made by shrivelling a large print into a small compass—intense and deep but unreal. To change the metaphor, he found the ship of state dashing onward, with her helm lashed and no one daring to take the steersman in hand. He cut the lashings and laid hold. His unassisted efforts as a pilot gave the vessel a new course; but he had not steam or other mechanical power, no **deus ex machina** to aid him; and, as the storm increased, exhaustion followed; he seemed to be steering when, in reality, his actions were under the compulsion of events, he was not controlling and thus continued until the wreck."

However, this point of view is not accepted by Prof. Holland Rose and the same was the view of President Thiers of France. It is pointed out that Napoleon's activity, both before and after Waterloo, was that of a man in good health. It was his judgment that degenerated and proved to be the cause of his failure. It is rightly pointed out that his victories in successive battles made him proud and haughty. His egotism became a mania and consequently he refused to listen to the advice of others. Even persons like Talleyrand and Fouche were not taken into confidence Napoleon started feeling

"The concurrence of these lines of argument points to the year 1802 as the turning point—the year of the Treaty of Amiens, of the Concordat, and of the Consulship for life. Each was a climax, a settlement: of the war in Europe, of the crucial issue of the Revolution of Bonaparte's own rise to power. Each enclosed germs of decay; a treaty which was only a truce, a pacification which inaugurated a new struggle, the climbing of a mountain shoulder which revealed the true summit at least within reach. If an exact moment is needed, let it then be that of the Elevation in the mass of Easter Day, April 18th, 1802, when the material might of the Napoleonic republic did homage to the central circle of the Catholic faith.

"The historian who finds the turning point of Bonarte's career in 1802 need not prove that there were no respects in which he grew more admirable, or France more prosperous, in the years that followed. Such a thesis would be absurd. What he means is that in the long verdict of history, plans begun then, institutions founded, tendencies encouraged already held in them the germs of failure; and that before the rise was ended the fall had begun. (**Napoleon Bonaparte : His Rise and Fall,** pp. 183-84).

According to Grant and Temperley, the year 1807 marks the zenith of Napoleon's power. "Had he died in that year, his career would have seemed the most miraculous in the military annals of Europe and perhaps of the world. He had succeeded in every task, overthrown every enemy. He had rearranged Europe according to his liking. He had no military rival and he was in apparent close and friendly alliance with the Czar of Russia. The French Revolution was left far behind now. It was no France but Napoleon who commanded in Europe. And he had carried with him his family to wealth and fame and power."

that he had the best brain and consequently his judgment, was also the best. No wonder, his decisions sometimes ignored certain facts which could easily have been pointed out to him if he had taken the advice. His calculations became defective and ultimately ended in his fall.

(3) Another cause of his failure was his policy of militarism. Napoleon recruited large armies, trained them and hastened them to the battlefields and was able to defeat one by one all the Great Powers of Europe except England. However, his wars began to take more and more toll of human life and he was forced to recruit even young men of tender age into his army. Such a process could not continue for long and was bound to result in disaster. The militarism which enabled Napoleon to conquer Europe, also proved to be his undoing. French militarism led to militarism in other countries and this was particularly so in Prussia, Russia and Austria. It was the combined militarism of other countries that brought about the fall of Napoleon. Napoleon used to say that "God marches with the biggest battalions," and when the armies of the enemies became bigger than his own, God was bound to march along with them and that was to result in their victories. Moreover, as time passed, Napoleon was forced to recruit more and more of the Poles, Germans, Italians, Dutch, Spaniards and the Danes. The Grand Army of Napoleon became more and more heterogeneous and consequently lost its fighting effectiveness. Napoleon also followed a policy of quartering the French troops upon the lands of his enemies or allies. Undoubtedly, he was able to make some saving in expenditure but this policy created a lot of bitterness. French troops were hated by the people on whom they were imposed and that hatred proved to be the undoing of Napoleon.

(4) Another cause of his failure was the Continental System. Napoleon regarded England as Enemy No. 1 and was determined to humble her. His view was that the prosperity and strength of England were dependent upon her commerce and consequently he decided to exclude British goods from Europe. He issued the famous decrees and did all that he could to deal a blow to British commerce. He failed to realise that the real strength of England lay in her manufactured goods. On account of the lack of a strong navy and the export of wheat to England, Napoleon failed to bring England to her knees. The enforcement of the Continental System compelled him to interfere in many countries and thereby aroused national resentment. The Continental System acted as a boomerang and destroyed its author.

(5) Napoleon himself admitted that it was the Spanish 'ulcer' that ruined him. It was his determination to exclude English goods and nationals from Portugal and Spain that forced him to interfere in these countries. The resistance was stiff and continuous. The physical features of the country and the constant flow of help from England by sea, enabled the people of Portugal and Spain to beat back the French troops from the Peninsula. The victories of the Duke of Wellington exploded the myth of Napoleon's invincibility on land.

(6) Napoleon's invasion of Russia in 1812 was a blunder. His Grand Army was completely destroyed and along with that his prestige. It was his retreat from Moscow in a helpless condition that encouraged his enemies to join hands and bring about his fall.

(7) His kind treatment of his relatives was also partly responsible for his failure. He was kind to his relatives, but most of them were ungrateful to him. Caroline and Jerome were to some extent responsible for the collapse of his power in Italy and Germany. Others, except Pauline, took pleasure in thwarting his will on the occasion of some great crisis. It has been remarked that Napoleon tried to make all his brothers eagles, but they remained ordinary fowls, intent on strutting and crowing before their harems. Napoleon was most unhappy regarding the attitude of his brothers. He would have been a better ruler if he had been a worse brother. He complained to Metternich in 1810 in these words: "My relatives have done more harm, than I have done them good."

(8) Napoleon began to depend more and more on trickery and deceit. One example of his trickery was the manner, in which he removed the King of Spain from his throne. It is claimed that the final cause of his downfall in 1814 was the interception of a letter which proved his lack of sincerity during

the negotiations for peace. He was determined to use all means, fair or foul, to win. He is stated to have remarked: **"I know when to exchange the lion's skin for that of the fox."** No wonder, the Allies refused to have any faith in his declarations and pledges and decided to remove him altogether from the European scene. A policy of deceit does not always pay.

(9) Prof. Holland Rose contends that the hardening of Napoleon's brain was responsible for his failure. That once splendid organizer who acted as a perfect lens, a true balance of alternatives, and a swift framer of resolves, retained the past qualities even in an exaggerated form, but he distorted events so as to fit in with desires and registered fancies as facts. This deterioration has happened to several great warriors and it grew on Napoleon rapidly after Tilsit, still more so after the Austrian campaign of 1809. The increase of his Empire in 1810 was a sign of megalomania which both enlarged his responsibilities and impaired his faculties for meeting them in the right manner.

(10) In the later part of his life. Napoleon became desperate in his actions and that was hardly conducive to his success. Metternich urged Napoleon at Dresden to accept his terms and give peace to Europe. But Napoleon asked: "What is it you wish of me? That I should dishonour myself? Never, I shall know how to die but never yield an inch of territory. Your sovereigns who were born on the thrones may get beaten twenty times and yet return to their capitals. I cannot, for I rose to power through the camp." Metternich asked what he would do when his army of conscripts had perished. The reply of Napoleon was in these words: "You are not a soldier. You do not know what happens in the heart of a soldier. I have grown up on battlefields and a man such as I care little for the lives of a million men."

(11) Napoleon could not tolerate the idea of compromise. It is true that he realized that the Confederation of the Rhine was "a bad calculation," the Continental System "a chimera" and the Grand Empire a lost splendour never to be recovered, but he was not prepared to accept that position. He addressed the members of the Council of States in these words: "Do you wish to descend from the height to which I have raised France, to become a simple monarchy again instead of a proud Empire?" It was too much for Napoleon even to think that he was to leave France weaker than he had made or found her. The very idea of the defection of his allies sent him into a rage and he vowed revenge. He cried out: "Munich must burn, and burn it shall." So long as there was the least chance of success, Napoleon was not prepared to come to terms with his enemies and as hope did not leave him till the end, there was no possibility of a compromise and peace. To the end, Napoleon believed that he would be able to take advantage of the military errors of his enemies and win victory for himself. That was partly due to the inflexibility of his mind and partly to the excess of good fortune during the time of ripening manhood. His victories at the beginning were his greatest misfortune and they steeled him against counsel. He continued to believe to the end that he was "The Man of Destiny". Had Napoleon decided to come to a compromise when his misfortunes started, his parents-in-law would have helped him to retain the French throne.

(12) Napoleon's defeat was also due to the rise of a great strategist in Gneisenau and a great fighting general in Blucher. It was his good fortune that in his early years he did not meet a general worthy of his steel. His contempt for his enemies led to his disaster. He held a very poor opinion of Wellington and Blucher and that cost him his Empire.

(13) Napoleon became boastful and the habit of boasting often leads to the fall of a man. During his intervention in Spain, he wrote the following words: "I may find the pillars of Hercules in Spain, but I shall not find the limits of my power.........1 have seen nothing so cowardly as these Spanish nobles and troops." This was written shortly before the French troops surrendered.

(14) Napoleon lost the support of certain sections of the people through whom he had come to power. As time progressed, he shed off all his Jacobinism and became a great imperialist. In 1793, he was a true hero who had come to liberate France from the clutches of tyranny and invest it with a true republican spirit. However, by 1800, his whole being was changed and he was inclined towards

imperialism. Napoleon himself stated : "The future will discover whether it was not better for the repose of the world that neither Rousseau nor I had ever been born."

(15) Napoleon was always conscious of his own superiority over others and consequently he centralized everything in his own hands and that was the cause of his failure.

(16) His passion for the grandiose overmastered his calculating faculties which in early life had generally held his ambition in leash.

(17) According to Herold, "Though not directly relevant here, the question might be asked with some profit: Why did Napoleon fail? 'Because he bothered God,' said Victor Hugo. That is one answer. Others point to this or that mistake or miscalculation, or declare that Napoleon bit off more than he could chew, or find some basic flaw in his system, or see him succumb to irresistible historic forces, or maintain that his people and allies let him down, or decry in his defeat the triumph of good over evil, or shrug their shoulders and speak of bad luck. Still others maintain that his rise was a historic accident and that his downfall merely cut him down to size. Perhaps, if we accept as a premise the fact that he did fail, then all or any of these reasons may have been decisive." (**The Mind of Napoleon,** pp. xxx-iii).

According to Foch, "He (Napoleon) forget that a man cannot be God; that above the individual is the nation and above mankind the moral law, he forgot that war is not the highest aim, for peace is above war."

About the causes of the failure of Napoleon, Leo Gershoy observes that from 1809 onwards, there was within France itself a mounting tide of discontent and war-weariness which undermined the stability of the Government. Napoleon's repression of political liberty, his despotic organisation of educational and intellectual activities and his unfailing recourse to the police alienated the intellectuals and the old partisans of free parliamentary government. Another cause of grievance was the economic stagnation and economic disorder that ensued from the strict enforcement of the Continental System. This discontent cost him the support of the solid middle class of merchants, manufacturers and bankers. Then there was the increasingly onerous burden of conscription. While rumours of the losses in Spain were in wide circulation, the peasants learnt that Napoleon was contemplating a new war in Russia. Their consternation was universal. Thousands of young men who were eligible for service tried to escape, whether through purchasing exemption or through flight. The Government tried to enforce the conscription law but neither prison penalties nor heavy fines, nor flying squadrons of troops, nor garrisons stationed at the strategic villages prevented the flight from the colours. To illiterate peasant women, Napoleon had become "the Corsican monster". The clergy and the faithful Catholics opposed his rule. If this was the condition in France, the situation was worse outside. The burdens of conscription and the hardships of the Continental System aroused discontent in the allied and vassal states. That discontent was fanned by the spirit of national patriotism. Patriots in Napoleonic Europe bitterly resented the presence of arrogant French officials, army officers and soldiers in their land. Common people were thoroughly disillusioned by the failure of Napoleon to give them the blessings of political liberty. The privileged aristocracy of the conquered states scorned and hated the child of the Revolution. As the events in Spain showed that the armies of Napoleon were not invincible, his enemies took heart and combined together to overthrow him. (**The French Revolution and Napoleon,** pp. 489-90).

Character of Napoleon. Napoleon was a man of the Mediterranean and as such had warm and violent passions and vivid imagination. He was capable of being brutal, caddish and coarse and also gay, considerate and poetic. According to Caulaincourt, "Emperor's feelings were expressed through every pore. When he chose, nobody could be more fascinating." He had charming manners. Very few could compete with him in conversation. He always made a great impression on all those who talked to him.

He had a high sense of humour. He was once told by a lunatic that he was in love with the Empress. His reply was: "You should choose somebody else to confide in." In 1812 when he was returning from Moscow alone with Caulaincourt, he thought of teasing Caulaincourt with the prospect of being captured by the Prussians and exhibited in an iron cage in London. They both drove for miles, yelling with laughter. It is said that on one night at Vienna Napoleon asked for the cold chicken which was always kept ready for him for his supper. When the chicken was brought Napoleon looked at it and observed: "Since when has a chicken been born with one leg and one wing? I see that I am expected to live off the scraps left me by my servants." Napoleon pulled the ears of his servant who had eaten the part of the chicken.

Napoleon was indulgent, familiar and attached by a bond of sentiment to his friends and companions of the youth. His friends like Lannes, Ney, Marmont, Murat, Junot, etc. could say to Napoleon what they pleased. It is stated that Napoleon wept bitterly at the time of death of Lannes and Duroc.

It is wrong to call him a cold-blooded tyrant. He put on a mask in the interests of 'policy'. Napoleon himself said: "There are in me two distinct men: the man of head and the man of heart."

He showered wealth and positions on his brothers and sisters. He made Joseph the King of Naples and then of Spain. He appointed Louis the King of Holland. He made Jerome the King of Westphalia. In spite of that they grumbled. Napoleon complained: "From the way they talk, one would think that I had wasted our parents' estate."

Napoleon had a wonderful memory which helped him to weave plans and dreams in his imagination so that he could, as he said, "live two years in advance". According to Emerson, "He (Napoleon) never blundered into victory, but won his battles in his head, before he won them on the field."

All his intellectual resources were available to him at any time. To quote him, "Different matters are stowed away in my brain as in a chest of drawers. When I wish to interrupt a piece of work, I close that drawer and open another. None of them ever get mixed, never does this inconvenience or fatigue me. When I feel sleepy, I shut all the drawers and go to sleep."

Estimate of Napoleon. Napoleon was one of the greatest conquerors and rulers of the world. He was a genius of a very high order. The large number of volumes written about him testify to his great personality. He will always be remembered as one who laid the foundations of a new social order in Europe. His contribution towards the unification of Italy and Germany cannot be denied. It is difficult to give an accurate estimate of his greatness on account of strong prejudices on the part of those who have written about him. Men like Abbot have tried to praise him as much as they can and others have tried to condemn him. The truth lies between the two extremes. It is too much to say that he was either a robber or a tyrant. He emphasized the idea of equality by abolishing class distinctions and privileges and by throwing, "careers open to talent". The last of the series of benevolent despots, he was at the same time one of the first of great modern statesmen.

Napoleon was a great orator and was successful in appealing to the masses. According to some, he was a great writer. To quote Fisher, "He was the prince of journalists, the father of war-correspondents." He had "an eye for theatrical effect and an incomparable talent for self-advertisement."

It is said that he was very selfish and was prepared to give up everything, even his dearest friends, for the sake of his own interests. No wonder, in the hour of his need, he was deserted by all including his wife. He was prepared to sacrifice the lives of millions of soldiers for the sake of satisfying his own ambition. It is reported that the Battle of Borodino, where the slaughter was the greatest, was regarded by Napoleon as "the finest battle-held I have ever seen." His personality was so great and he hypnotised so much those he met, particularly his soldiers, that they were prepared to sacrifice their lives for him.

"I am not a man like other men," said Napoleon. His view was that religions and moral restrictions did not bind him. Although he professed faith in the Roman Catholic Church in his will, he was probably a materialist without belief in Christ. To quote him, "I was Mohammedan in Egypt; I shall be a Catholic in France."

He was a versatile genius. "He carried human faculty to the farthest point of which we have accurate knowledge. According to Mignet, Napoleon was "the most gigantic being of modern times."

Wellington's view was that Napoleon's presence in the field was worth a force of 40,000 men and his reasons have been summarised thus: "(1) Napoleon was a great homme de guerre, possibly the greatest that ever appeared at the head of a French army.

"(2) He was the sovereign of the country as well as the military chief of the army. The country was constituted upon a military basis. All its institutions were framed for the purpose of forming and maintaining its armies with a view to conquest. All the offices and rewards of the State were reserved in the first instance exclusively for the army. An officer, even a private soldier, of the army might look to the sovereignty of a kingdom as the reward of his services. It is obvious that the presence of the sovereign with an army so constituted must greatly excite their exertions. It was quite certain that all the resources of, the French State, civil, political, financial, as well as military, were turned towards the seat of the operations, which Napoleon himself should direct. Every sovereign in command of an army enjoys advantages against him who exercises only a delegated power, and who acts under orders and responsibilities. But Napoleon enjoyed more advantages of this description than any other sovereign that ever appeared. His presence, as stated by more than one, was likely not only to give to the French army all the advantages above detailed, but to put an end to all the jealousies of the French Marshals and their counter action of each other, whether founded upon bad principles and passions, or their fair differences of opinion. The French army thus had unity of action, (**Napoleon Bonaparte: His Rise and Fall.** p. 285).

Napoleon was a very efficient administrator and organiser. He adapted to the present needs the ideas of the former generations. He was a master of details and methodical in all that he did. By making merit the basis of recruitment, he was able to secure the services of efficient persons. He could himself work 18 hours a day and demanded the maximum amount of work from others. Once he marched 90 miles in three days after the Dresden campaign in 1814. During the four days of the Waterloo campaign, he was on horseback for 37 hours and slept only for 20 hours out of the 96. He could easily see the weak spots in the line of the enemy on account of his wonderful power of observation. His power of striking hard and swiftly at the decisive point was of great value in view of the lack of cohesion among the forces of the Coalitions. He followed up his victories with great vigour. He generally made the most of the opportunity offered to him.

Napoleon rendered great services to France. His victories saved France from foreign enemies. He established a strong and efficient Central Government and thereby saved France from anarchy. "His life and that alone stood between France and civil war." He gave France a sound system of laws. He promoted education and took active measures to improve trade and industry. He relieved the finances of France by compelling other nations to support French armies. He issued no paper money and imposed no income-tax. However, it is pointed out that after the Treaty of Tilsit, he brought misery to France. Had Napoleon died in 1807, France would have been grateful to him. His determination to humble England was at the root of all his troubles.

Critics say that 'Napoleon was the tyrant of Europe. He was not content with the natural frontiers of France. He wanted to extend his authority over other countries of Europe and rule them in a despotic manner. "War and despotism were inseparable and ingrained parts of his nature." "He wished to subdue Europe by France and Britain by means of Europe." The Continental System was an attempt to unite Europe against Great Britain. His bitterness against England is clear from the following words: "Our Government must destroy the English monarchy or it must accept itself to be destroyed by these active Islanders." Napoleon desired to follow in the footsteps of both Alexander, the Great, and Charlemagne. His ambition was not limited to Europe alone and he had a strong desire to go to the East and this is clear from the following words uttered in 1812: "We are going to make an end of Europe, and then to throw ourselves and become masters of India."

According to Emerson, Napoleon was the embodiment of the middle-class qualities then coming to the fore. However, he did not fit into the name of a stock exchange and was the villain of a melodrama. According to Taine, Napoleon was the symbol of the revival of the Italian condottiere. According to Sorel, Napoleon was the champion of great France, the protagonist of her demand for the "natural boundaries". According to Levy, Napoleon was an exemplary bourgeois who was always intent on the preservation of peace, but was driven to war by the successive provocations of all the Powers.

The view of Leo Gershoy is that the rule of Napoleon was neither that of a thwarted Prometheus nor the scourge of an Attila nor the violence of an unchecked Jacobin. His rule was one of mixed blessings. The long period of French ascendancy in the arts and sciences, the universality of the French language and the force of French arms prepared many regions for his domination. The intrinsic strength of revolutionary principles had been alert, intelligent and enterprising bureaucracy that Napoleon built up, helped not a little to popularise those principles in the annexed and occupied territories. There was also the incalculable force of Napoleon's genius, directed towards selecting and driving his assistants, supervising their activity, correcting their weaknesses, elaborating suggestions and gathering into a mighty whole the many divisions of administrative policy. On the debit side must be mentioned his secret police agents, spies, a muzzled press, a rigid censorship and the stifling of all hostile criticism. It shows the suppression of political liberty and introduction of despotism. The continental blockade made French customs agents and inspectors prosperous. Goods were confiscated. The avenues of trade were choked up by a ruinous tariff. Prosperity was destroyed. Brutal administrators, armies of occupation, heavy war indemnities, staggering taxes and the weight of conscription awakened national sentiments against Napoleon. Religious feeling also turned against him when he became the oppressor of the Catholic church. (**The French Revolution and Napoleon,** pp. 469-71).

The view of John Bowle is that Napoleon first mobilized a whole nation for war, exploited the French Revolution and deliberately created for himself a vast popular charisma. Compared by the feats of modern dictators, the devastations of Napoleon were limited. He had no tanks, aircraft or rockets. However, his conscript armies swept over whole countries and in some transformed the social order permanently. After referring to the achievements of Julius Caesar, Constantine, Charlemagne, Charles V, Alexander, the Great, Prophet Muhammed, Chenghis Khan, Timur, Babur, Emperor T ai Tsu of the Ming dynasty of China, Emperor Sheng-Tzu of Manchu dynasty, John Bowle says that no one before Napoleon had mastered peoples who were themselves through superior technology, organization and sea power the potential rulers of the whole world and so glimpsed the prospect of a world empire. It is true that Napoleon failed to subjugate the British, but his conquest of western and central Europe was of world import in a new way. The reason is that what happened in Europe then concerned all mankind leading in our own century to wars fought literally for global domination. Napoleon was the first, as Hitler was the most recent, European dictator to attempt it. Moreover, most previous conquerors had been out more to dominate the world than to change it. Napoleon was an eighteenth century cosmopolitan who wanted to rationalize and reform, sweep away traditional hierarchies and throw career open to talent. He was the first great conqueror who believed in the modern idea of progress. He intended to enhance the lives of his subjects, not just to order and exploit them. While he cynically employed the old religious and dynastic cults to sustain his power, he remained a Voltairean rationalist, watching himself with ironic detachment. Being an outsider and an adventurer he relished his fabulous achievements with an artist or conductor's perception. Unlike most military conquerors, he was an intellectual. He was a born writer and a phrase-maker. He loathed and feared the common people and he lost his will and courage before civilian violence. Like Alexander, Napoleon wanted to construct and in a technologically superior civilization actually to improve. John Bowle concludes by saying that those who take the sword are apt to perish by it. Though briefly a great statesman, he began and ended as a military adventurer. He was a butcher and a colossal egoist, yet a man of great vision, of brilliant and versatile personality and with that flair, force and indefatigable industry which in any sphere of life we call genius, (**Napoleon,** pp. 218-23).

David Thomson says that Napoleon was the supreme opportunist. He was driven by a burning desire for power. He was a masterful opportunist partly because the opportunities before him were so great. The momentum of the revolutionary movement in France had burned itself out and the time was now ripe for a popular soldier with a genius for organisation to take over the authority. The dictatorship of Napoleon was a utilitarian, efficient, industrious and hard-headed Government and its oppressiveness must not be exaggerated. It lacked the fanaticism and passion of the rule of Robespierre and the ruthlessness and brutality of the dictatorship of the 20th century. Although the extreme royalists, fervent Roman Catholics and doctrinaire Jacobins were never reconciled to it, Napoleon managed to win over the support of the great majority of the people of France. From about 1808 onwards, the growing tension within the Empire, the protracted war and the shadow of defeat tarnished his regime, but the people continued to put up with it because there was no satisfactory alternative to it. The memories of revolutionary excesses were still fresh in the minds of the people and there was also the fear of royalist reaction and under the circumstances the rule of Napoleon seemed to be preferable. Another reason was the economic advantages which Napoleon brought to French industrialists, farmers and traders. The continental system was a vast system of economic preferences and protection in favour of France, and against not only Britain but also the rest of Europe. Italy was almost turned into an economic colony of France. It provided raw materials for its industry and a market for French textiles. The economic development of Holland was subordinated to that of France. The introduction of machinery was encouraged in France and discouraged elsewhere. The cotton and sugar-beet industries of France prospered as a result of the policy of protection. In economic terms, the Empire undoubtedly paid handsomely at least for some time.

According to Grant and Temperley, "Napoleon was without question a man of extraordinary force of brain and character, who under all circumstances and in all countries would have won for himself a high position. He had great powers of work and of organisation, rapid insight, courage, a willingness to accept responsibility, resolution in following out a plan once undertaken—all the qualities of the soldier in their highest development; and with all he had the gift of genius which defies analysis. But his rise is much more than story of a capable man winning for himself a high place in the world. It reflects also one of the most general laws that may be observed on the surface of history. We can see constantly how a period of confusion and of revolution ends in the establishment of some strong and often of a personal power. The instances that are usually quoted in comparison with Napoleon's life history are the establishment of the Roman Empire by Julius Caesar after a century of confusion and revolution in Rome, and the personal rule of Oliver Cromwell which followed the Puritan revolution. But these are only the most obvious instances. We may see something of the same sort when the Tudor Monarchy follows the Wars of the Roses; when the strong concentration of the French kings under Charles VII and Louis XI brought to end the long agony and turmoil of the Hundred Years' War in France; or again, when the Thirty Years' War in Germany is followed very generally by the establishment of personal rule."

It has been claimed that Napoleon was equally great as a statesman and as a soldier. The view of Grant and Temperley on this point is that although Napoleon had no chance of developing all his ideas in the midst of hardly interrupted storms of war and his domestic policy was throughout subordinated to military necessities, it cannot be denied that the European situation was largely his own creation. His power in France itself was always intimately bound up with his military prestige and victories. In his social and political schemes, there is very little that is original. For a part of it, the way had been prepared by the Revolution and for the other part, by the old monarchy. The great feature about his statesmanship is not its originality but the immense energy and strength of will and attention to detail with which he carried it out. It was not so novel or so well adapted to the needs of the time. Moreover, in all his work, Napoleon showed no appreciation of the value of political liberty. This great watchword of the Revolution had perhaps at one time appealed to him but his early enthusiasm for it was dead. He now thought of liberty as a disturbing factor that prevented the efficiency of his state. There is no hint in anything that he said or wrote that he thought of it as the great force making for stability, order and efficiency.

According to Dr. Holland Rose, there was only one man who could challenge comparison with Napoleon. The figure of Julius Caesar dominated the Roman world as that of the great Corsican overshadowed the age of the French Revolution. Both men lived in cataclymic periods when the old order was passing away and new ideas called for recognition. In many ways, both Napoleon and Julius Caesar succeeded in linking on the new to the old. Though innovators in youth, they became more and more conservative in manhood. However, Caesar was a greater man than Napoleon. Although he began the serious part of his life late, yet both in war and statecraft, he established an unquestioned supremacy which nothing but murder could end. He led the way both by developing new principles of strategy and by adopting the almost stereotyped polity of Rome to the needs of a fast growing Empire. His clemency and conduct won the affection of the conquered peoples whom he brought under the Roman rule. He left behind him a State both greater and stronger than that before his accession to office. His unparalleled triumphs both at home and abroad neither blinded his vision nor hardened his temper. They were harmonised and humanised by clemency. The same cannot be said of Napoleon. He admitted his failure in the following words which he wrote about Alexander, the Great: "What I like in Alexander is not his campaigns, which we cannot understand, but his political methods. At thirty-three years of age, he leaves a well established Empire which his generals partitioned. He had the art of making himself beloved by the peoples he conquered."

Holland Rose points out that the personality of Napoleon abounds in contradictions. Dowered with the passions of the south, he yet had the cool and calculating instincts characteristic of the northern people. By turns he was mild and stern, placable and unforgiving, generous but egoistic, far-seeing yet far-sighted. On every event and problem, he concentrated a bewildering variety of powers so that in every case we must ask what set of faculties led him to this and not that conclusion. Moreover, at the end of the inquiry we are baffled by the crowning paradox, that he the greatest Emperor and organiser of all time, left France and his enemies stronger than before his appearance in the arena.

Dr. Sloane writes that Napoleon became great because he was the typical man of his day, less the personal mediocrity; the typical burgher in personal character, the typical soldier in war, the typical despot in peace and the typical idealist in politics; capable in all those qualities of analysis; capable consequently of being understood; capable of exhaustion and of being overwhelmed by combinations. The Empire of Napoleon was like a brilliant bubble on the stream of time. Alexander Hellenised the civilisation of his day and prepared the world for Christianity. Charlemagne ploughed, harrowed and sowed the soil of barbaric Europe, making it receptive for the most superb of all secular ideals, that of nationality. Napoleon tore up the system of absolutism by the roots, propagated in the most distant lands of Europe, the modern conception of individual rights, overthrew the rotten structure of the German-Roman Empire, and in spite of himself regenerated the long-abused ideas of nationality and fatherland.

According to Chateaubriand, "Napoleon was a poet in action." He was "the mightiest breath of life whichever animated human clay." According to Leon Bloy, "Napoleon is the Face of God in the darkness."

According to Herold, "The supreme combination of intellect and energy gave Napoleon's mind a magnetic, almost supernatural power—a power that seems to radiate from his pictured features and endows, his very name with magic. If modern times have produced a mythological figure, that figure is Napoleon. Abraham Lincoln is a possible rival, but as a figure of mythology Napoleon has a great advantage; like the Olympians he is beyond good and evil, a true pagan god, eminently classical and Greek. Lincoln, a Christ-like figure from the backwoods, belongs to a different circle.

Few men have expressed the Napoleon mystique so suggestively as Heine in these few sentences: "His countenance, too, was of the complexion we find on the marble heads of Greeks and Romans. The features were as nobly proportioned as those of ancient statues, and on his face was written: "Thou shalt have no other god but me." (Introduction, **The Mind of Napoleon, page XIX).**

According to Talleyrand, "His (Napoleon's) genius was unbelievable. It is the most astonishing career that has been witnessed for the last thousand years. He was certainly the most extraordinary man I ever saw, and in my opinion the most extraordinary men that has lived for many centuries."

Hardy put the following words into the mouth of Napoleon after his defeat at Waterloo:

"I came too late in time
To assume the prophet on the demi-god.
Apart past playing now. My only course
To make good showance to posterity
Was to implant my line upon the throne.
And how shape that if now extinction nears?
Great men are meteors that consume themselves.
To light the earth. This is my burnt-out hour."

The difference between the France of 1799 and 1815 was the work of Napoleon. The former was traditional and chaotic and the latter had respect for person, for contract and for property. The administration was unitary, homogeneous and active. The finances, though not regulated, were restored to vigour. The processes were inaugurated by which the great cities of France became healthy and beautiful. The revolutionary precepts were so modified and assimilated that the efforts of the dynasties failed to change them. It was one of his sayings that "to have the right of using nations, you must begin by serving them alone." The seeds of discontentment were sown by Napoleon among the Christians of Turkey and his emissaries fired their hearts. Serbia was one of those examples and national awakening of the Greeks also began with the hopes similarly aroused.

It is pointed out that indirectly Napoleon made the U.S.A. completely independent of England. Napoleon was responsible for bringing about a war between the U.S.A. and England from which the former emerged with glory and with absolute commercial independence. The purchase of Louisiana from Napoleon revolutionised the American national system both from inside and outside.

Comparison between Napoleon and Hitler. According to Herold, "Certain external and by no means accidental similarities between Napoleons career and that of Hitler have blinded some men to the far more significant contrasts. Unlike Napoleon, Hitler is likely to go down in history as another Attila or Jenghiz Khan. Hitler destroyed the law; Napoleon was a law giver whose code spread across continents. That difference alone should be enough to discourage comparison. Hitler was maniacal crank with an ideology; Napoleon, sane and self-controlled, despised ideologies. Hitler appealed to hatred; Napoleon, to honour. Hitler extolled that dark, instinctual monster which he called the People and which Taine had called the Gorilla; Napoleon had seen that monster in action during the Reign of Terror, and he preferred to perish rather than invoke its power. Napoleon, when he began his career, embodied the hopes of sane and noble minds (not least among them Beethoven's); Hitler began and ended surrounded by a handful of psychopaths. But why insist on the contrast? Perhaps there is no difference between them but the difference between the Age of Reason and the Age of Hatred. It is a substantial difference."

"It is difficult to see how Hitler, as an individual, can be judged as anything but a diseased catalyst of a mass disease. Nothing positive appears on the ledger. Napoleon, on the other hand, in his historic action left positive achievements behind him. Unlike Hitler, he left Europe not in ruins but brought it up-to-date. Even where his genius failed his purpose, its nature was such that it co-operated willy-nilly with the constructive forces of history; the unification of Germany and of Italy, the spread of democratic liberalism might not have been in accord with his intentions, but they most certainly owed much to his action. And as a myth and a symbol he pushed back the limits of human capabilities. It may be a costly process for humanity to produce Napoleons, but if humanity should ever cease to produce them it would be a sign that its energies are exhausted. In order to turn its Napoleons to better enterprises than conquest and war, humanity first would have to turn away from war. To prove Napoleon wrong humanity must change." (**The Mind of Napoleon,** pp. XXXVIII-XXXIX).

Napoleon the child of the French Revolution. Napoleon maintained that he was the child of the Revolution. By abolishing the old political system and paving the way for military despotism, the French Revolution gave Napoleon an opportunity to establish his power. If an extraordinary situation had not been created by the French Revolution, a man like Napoleon would not have got the chance to come to power. After coming to power as First Consul, he got his election as Emperor ratified by the people in 1804. In the Code Napoleon, he embodied the best of the revolutionary principles and laws. He emphasized the principle of equality and recruited his servants and generals on the basis of merit and not status. He gave permanence to the influence of the French Revolution. However, critics point out that although Napoleon was the child of the Revolution, he was the child who killed the mother. He did not care for the principles of liberty and fraternity which were emphasized by the authors of the Revolution. The liberty of the people of France and Europe was crushed in every way and Napoleon tried to impose his own will on the people. He centralised everything in his own hands and thereby destroyed the initiative of the people. His own view was that what the people wanted was not liberty but equality and with that conviction he did not allow people to give expression to their views. Complete censorship was imposed on the press and dissent in any shape or form was crushed. He tried to impose a military discipline on the people. The absolute Government which Napoleon established was the very negation of the idea of a "sovereign people". "He was the last and greatest of the autocratic legislators who worked in an unfree age."

According to Grant and Temperley, "Napoleon was the child of the Revolution, but, in many ways he reversed the aims and principles of the movement from which he sprang. And this was particularly true of the codes. The Revolution had not only swept away what remained of feudalism and ecclesiastical control of the State, but it had attacked the cherished traditions of the lawyers of France. It had striven, above all things, for equality. It had insisted that the inheritance should be divided in equal shares among the children; it had limited very strictly the power of testamentary bequest; it had offended Catholic sentiment by introducing divorce; it had removed all control over question arising out of births, deaths, and marriages from the Church. There was much in all this of which Napoleon in his new mood did not approve. He made friends with the Church. He valued authority. He had little love for equality. He would therefore not merely present the legislation of the Revolution in a short and logical form; he would desire to alter it in important particulars."

According to Flenley, "He was the child and heir of the French Revolution, who if he completed the destruction of liberty, yet preserved equality and built it into the enduring laws he gave to France. **'I closed the chasm of anarchy; I cleansed the revolution,'** he claimed."

According to Prof. Markham, "The reforms of the Consulate, considered as a whole look both ways. From one aspect, they are a continuation of the Revolution; from another, a surreptitious return to the institutions of the Bourbon monarchy. They confirmed and secured the national gains of the Revolution in equality, legal and administrative unity, the career open to talents. In this sense,

Napoleon's claim to represent the revolution is justified. For him and for the mass of the French workers and peasants, the social and administrative aims of the Revolution were far more important than the bourgeois aim of political liberty. The Revolution of 1789 had been, not one but three simultaneous revolutions, social, administrative and political. In 1800, the French people were prepared to abandon the political revolution in order to consolidate the other two.

"Moreover, Napoleon, like Mirabeau in 1790, did not regard the revolution as incompatible with monarchy. Mirabeau, in his secret correspondence with the court, had urged the king to continue the work of Richelieu, and lead the Revolution, by completing the destruction of feudalism and modernising the State. In Napoleon's opinion, the fall of the throne had been due to the 'vanity' of the bourgeoisie and the feebleness of Louis XVI. There were certain features of the Bourbon monarchy which he admired. In the early days of the Consulate, he described the 'old administration' as 'the most perfect that ever existed... while conserving every useful innovation produced by the Revolution, he would not reject the good institutions which it wrongly destroyed.' In 1809, he was to say: 'From Clovis to the Committee of the Public Safety, I embrace it all.' The Bourbon dynasty had failed to rise to the occasion; it was open to Napoleon 'to pick a crown out of the gutter'. He saw no reason why a 'fourth dynasty of France' should not establish itself, based on the changes brought by the Revolution."

According to Gottschalk and Lach, "Although Bonaparte has frequently been reviled as an unscrupulous dictator and conqueror, his regime may also be looked upon as an effort to provide a synthesis of the old and the new for the war-weary and revolution-weary Europe of his day. When he became master of France in 1799, his new charge had undergone a decade of social, economic, and political turmoil in the course of which it had helped to impart to Europe a widely held conviction that 'the source of all authority resides essentially in the nation' (as the French Declaration of Rights of 1789 had stated) and that 'Liberty, Equality, and Fraternity' were objectives for which one should fight, bleed and die. But in the course of that decade France had also imparted, along with notions of popular sovereignty and the hope of a freer and better world, an atmosphere of uncertainty, instability, and fear such as Europe had not known since the close of the religious wars in 1648. The initial success of Bonaparte's triumphs at home and abroad derived not alone from his undeniable personal qualities, his carefully nurtured reputation, and the strength of his following, but just as much from the inability of his rivals and enemies to prescribe better remedies for the patent social, economic, and political illnesses of the times. Though Napoleon was ultimately to forget his principles, as even those who are not conquerors often do, and to act rather out of considerations of expediency, he forced both peoples and rulers of Europe either to adhere to his system or else, in order to survive his onslaughts, to modify the old order and make place for the aspirations embodied in the principles of 1789, whether they liked those principles or not." (**Transformation of Europe,** pp. 32-3).

Sayings of Napoleon. It is difficult to resist the temptation to refer to some of the sayings of Napoleon. According to him, (1) love of one's country is the first virtue of a civilized man. (2) The true wisdom of nations is experience. (3) The heart of a statesman should be in his head. (4) Be clear and all the rest will follow. (5) Love is the occupation of the idle man, the distraction of the warrior and the stumbling block of the sovereign. (6) Unity of command is the first necessity of war. (7) The first quality of a Commander-in-Chief is a cool head. (8) I regard myself as probably the most daring man in war who has ever existed. (9) An army is a people that obeys. (10) Never attack a position in front which may be taken by turning. (11) At the commencement of a campaign, thought should be expended as to whether an advance should be made or not; but when once the offensive has been assumed it should be maintained to the last extremity. (12) Men must be led by an iron hand in a velvet glove. (13) Courage is like love; it feeds on hope. (14) In war all is mental; and the mind and opinion make up more than the half of the actual. (15) Work is my element. I am born and built for work. I have known the limits of my legs. I have known the limits of my eyes. I have never known the limits of my work. (16) The first quality of a soldier is fortitude in enduring fatigue and hardship; bravery is the second. Poverty, hardship and misery are the school of the good soldier. (17) A great captain ought to say to himself several times a day: "If the enemy appears on my front, my right or my left, what should I do?" If he finds himself embarrassed, he is ill-posted. (18) I had the taste for foundation, not taste for property. My property consisted in glory and celebrity. (19) All the ills and curses which can afflict mankind come from London. (20) All my life, I have sacrificed everything—comfort, self-interest, happiness, to my destiny. (21) I have made all the calculations: fate will do the rest. (22) Politics is fate. (23) The strong are good; only the weak are wicked. (24) History I conquered rather than studied... I spurned what was of no use (to me), and I seized upon certain conclusions that pleased me. (25) France needs me more than I need France. (26) A revolution can be neither made nor stopped. The only thing that can be done is for one or several of its children to give it a direction. (27) Outside budgets, there is no salvation. (28) Men take their needs into consideration—never their abilities. (29) Men are moved by two levers only: fear and self-interest. (30) The masses gladly take revenge for the honours they render us. (31) When the fatherland is no more, the patriot must die. If in order to free my countrymen all I had to do was to destroy one man, I should set out this instant and plunge into the tyrant's breast the avenging sword of fatherland and law. (32) He who fears to lose his reputation, is sure to lose it. (33) There is only one thing to do in this world and that is to keep acquiring more and more money and power. All the rest is chimeral. (34) Serving the fatherland is a religion. (35) Government keep their promises only when they are forced or when it is to their advantage to do so. (36) Between meditating and action and carrying it out, you must put an interval of three years. (37) If you wage war, do it energetically and with severity. This is the only way to make it shorter and consequently less inhuman. (38) From triumph to fall, there is but one step. (39) The love of glory is like the bridge that Satan built across chaos to pass from Hell to Paradise; glory links the past with the future across a bottomless abyss. (40) I had taste for founding, not for owning. (41) Men must be very bad, to be as bad as I think they are. (42) My mistress is power, but it is as an artist that I love power. I love it as a musician loves his violin. (43) Conquest has made me what I am and conquest alone can maintain me. (44) I fear insurrections caused by shortage of bread. I would fear them more than a battle of 200,000 men.

Josephine. No account of Napoleon can be complete without a reference to Josephine. He married her in 1796. At that time, she was six years older than Napoleon. Her previous husband had been guillotined a few days before the fall of Robespierre. She had two children from her previous marriage and she had practically no means. However she did not lose heart.

She was very much impressed by the vehemence of Napoleon's passion and the intensity of his glance. She at once agreed to marry him. She was impressed by the self-confidence of Napoleon. Napoleon had addressed her in these words: "Do they (Directors) think that I need their protection in order to rise? They will be glad enough some day if I grant them mine. My sword is at my side and with it I can go far." Josephine has written thus about her inner feelings: "This preposterous assurance affects me to such a degree that I can believe everything may be possible to this man and, with his imagination, who can tell what he may be tempted to undertake ?

Napoleon had his happiest time with Josephine. As a matter of fact, she was the only woman for whom he really cared. Even Madame Walewska who gave him a son, never took her place. It is rightly said that Napoleon conquered Europe and put it at the feet of Josephine. Had there been no Josephine, there would have been no Napoleon. It was she who inspired him. She could amuse him by her indignation and move him by her tears. She was his only refuge from his own family. She was the one person in the world to whom he could say what was really in his mind. He could be his natural-self with her alone.

Unfortunately, all the members of Napoleon's family were against her. Napoleon also foolishly thought of marrying a princess and having a son from her to succeed him. That created trouble and ultimately Josephine was divorced in December 1809. Soon after that, she left the Tuileries and began to live alone at Malmaison. It is there that she died alone. After the battle of Waterloo in 1815 when Napoleon left Paris for the last time, he went to Malmaison to see the ghost of Josephine.

It has rightly been said that Napoleon committed a blunder of his life when he divorced Josephine. When he divorced her, he cut his life in half and threw away the better half of it.

Results of the French Revolution. (1) The French Revolution was not a local event. It influenced profoundly not only the people of France but also those of Europe and the world. The French Revolution stood for certain principles and those were Liberty, Equality, and Fraternity. The example of France became the inspiration of Europe and from there of the whole world. These ideas dominated the Europeon politics throughout the 19th century and after.

(2) The Declaration of Rights of Man by the National Assembly emphasized the fact that sovereignty resides in the people and law is the expression of the general will. The machinery of the State was to be worked in such a way as to bring the greatest good to the people. It cannot be denied that even the benevolent despots like Catherine the Great of Russia, Frederick the Great of Prussia, and Joseph II of Austria recognised the necessity of improving the condition of the people even before the French Revolution, but that was not the generally accepted view of the Governments of Europe. The French Revolution asserted that the people should rule themselves and the government should be not only "for the people" but also "by the people". It was recognized that sovereignty was not a property of which the owner enjoyed the profits, but a magistracy established for the performance of certain duties. It is true that there was at reaction against this principle for some time but ultimately the principle was firmly established in all the States of Europe. The period of reaction lasted particularly from 1815 to 1848 when Metternich was at the helm of affairs in Austria. The middle-class played a very important part in the assertion and establishment of the principle of sovereignty of the people.

(3) The French Revolution asserted that all men were equal before law and there was absolutely no justification for the maintenance of privileges whether based on birth or wealth. The result was that serfdom, feudal restrictions and the limitations imposed by the guilds were abolished. Religious tolerations was assured. The freedom of the press was established and the right of the individual to education was maintained. In the Vindication of the Rights of Woman (1792) Mary Wollstonecraft asserted that women should enjoy equal rights with men.

(4) France became the spokesman of the human race and the idea of liberty became the watchword and charter of all the reformers and revolutionaries. Liberty became a universal creed. Not only personal liberty was secured but efforts were made to achieve political liberty. There was a general demand to have popularly elected legislatures with varying degrees of authorities. In this respect England led the way and France was next to her.

(5) The French Revolution also asserted the principle of nationality. Prior to the French Revolution, the loyalty of the nobles and the love of people for the king had taken the place of patriotism. The French Revolution substituted the idea of the French nation for that of the French kingdom. The flight of the Emperor, Louis XVI, in 1791 showed that the interests of the people and the king were not identical. The declaration of the 11 June 1792 that "the Fatherland is in danger" led to an outburst of national feeling which inspired France to resist her enemies. The aggression of France in other countries of Europe provoked the feeling of nationality among them. This was so in Italy, Portugal, Spain, Prussia, Russia, and Austria. It was the growth of a national feeling among the Spaniards and the Portuguese which enabled them to drive out the Napoleonic armies from the Peninsula. It was the same spirit which enabled the Russians to follow a "scorched earth" policy in 1812. The same feeling

of nationality helped the revival of Prussia. Spain proved that "a whole people is more powerful than disciplined armies." It was the same sentiment of nationalism that enabled the Frenchmen to beat back the Allies during the days of the National Convention. The idea of "the nation in arms" was a great contribution to the world.

(6) It is true that after the Congress of Vienna (1815) there was a reaction against the idea of nationality and an attempt was made to crush it by means of the Protocol of Troppau, but ultimately the principle of nationality triumphed all over Europe. It was this principle that enabled the people of Italy and Germany to achieve their unification and independence. The same was the case with Belgium, Serbia, Greece, Rumania and Bulgaria. The same principle gave a lot of headache to Russia on account of the unsuccessful efforts of the Poles to achieve their independence. The revolt of Hungary in 1848-49 under the leadership of Kossuth was also due to the force of nationalism.

(7) The French Revolution also gave a stimulus to humanitarianism. Efforts were made to abolish slavery and improve the condition of the prisons. Legislation was passed in many countries to improve the conditions of the people in general.

(8) The French Revolution also helped the revival of romanticism by the assertion of individualism, the defiance" of tradition, and the "establishment of human life on a basis of pure feeling." The influence of the French Revolution can be seen in Victor Hugo's Les Miserable, Southey's **Joan of Arc,** Wordsworth's **Prelude,** Shelley's **Mask of Anarchy,** Goethe's **Faust** and in the early works of Coleridge.

(9) On account of the patience with which the Pope put up with the humiliations which were heaped on him by Napoleon, the influence of the Roman Catholic Church was strengthened. Chateaubriand asserted the cause of Christianity against atheism and Maister vindicated the authority of the Pope.

(10) There was another effect of the French Revolution. Not only the attacks but also the confiscation of property by the government weakened the idea of the sanctity of property. The result was that socialism ceased to be merely a speculative doctrine and became a political programme. It is clear that the ideas of the French Revolution have spread in every nook and corner of the world and they are being universally recognized. One can see its effect on the minds of those who drafted the Preamble of the new Constitution of India which came into force on 26 January 1950.

(11) The view of Kropotkin is that the French Revolution made France stronger and prosperous. Formerly, there was scarcity in many parts of France, but as a result of the Revolution, France began to produce much more of the necessaries of life of every kind than in 1789. Never was there in France such an energetic ploughing as in 1792 when the peasants ploughed the lands they had taken back from the lords, the convents and the churches. They goaded their oxen with the cry of **"Allons Prusse! Allons Autriche".** Never had there been so much, clearing of lands as during those years of Revolution. The first good harvest in 1794 brought relief to two-thirds of France—at least in the villages, for all this time the towns were threatened with scarcity of food. A new France was born during those four years of the Revolution. For the first time in centuries, the peasant ate his fill, straightened his back and dared to speak out. A new nation was born. It was owing to this new birth that France was able to maintain her wars under the Republic and Napoleon had to carry the principles of the Great Revolution into Switzerland, Italy, Spain, Belgium, Holland, Germany and even to the borders of Russia. When after all those wars, people expected France in 1815 to be reduced to misery and her land laid waste, what was actually found was that there was more prosperity in France than in the time of Louis XVI. The energy regenerated by the Revolution was so great that in a few years France became a country of well-to-do peasants. Her enemies found that in spite of all the blood she had shed and the losses she had sustained, France, in respect of her productivity, was the richest country in Europe. Her wealth was not drawn from the Indies or from her foreign commerce. It came from her own soil, from the love of the soil and from her own skill and industry.

Kropotkin also points out that the French Revolution brought about the abolition of serfdom and absolutism. Personal liberties were conferred upon individuals, undreamt of by the serf of the lord and the subject of the absolute king. These two achievements represent the principal work of the 19th century, begun in France in 1789 and slowly spread over Europe in the course of a century. The work of enfranchisement begun by the French peasants in 1789, was continued in Spain, Italy, Switzerland, Germany and Austria by the armies of Napoleon. The abolition of serfdom in Europe would have been completed within the first half of the 19th century if the French bourgeoisie, coming into power in 1794 over the dead bodies of Anarchists, Cordiliers and Jacobins, had not checked the Revolutionary impulse, restored monarchy and handed over France to Napoleon. Napoleon began to prop up aristocracy but in spite of that, the institution of serfdom had already received a mortal blow. It was abolished in Spain and Italy in spite of a temporary triumph of reaction. It was closely pressed in Germany after 1811 and disappeared in that country definitely in 1848. In 1861, Russia was compelled to emancipate her serfs and the war of 1878 put an end to serfdom in the Balkan Peninsula. The abolition of absolute power took a little over 100 years to make a tour of Europe. Attacked in England in 1648 and vanquished in France in 1789, the royal authority based on divine right disappeared from all parts of Europe. Equality before law and representative governments were set up in almost all parts of Europe.

Kropotkin further points out that the French Revolution left a legacy on the principles of communism. Throughout the French Revolution, the communist idea kept coming to the front. After the fall of the Girondins, numerous attempts were made in that direction. Fourierism descended in direct line from L'Ange on one side and Chalier on the other. Babeuf was the direct descendant of ideas which stirred the masses to enthusiasm in 1793. There is a direct link between the Enrages of 1793 and the Babeuf conspiracy of 1795 on the one hand and the International Working Men's Association of 1866-78. The popular communism of the first two years of the Republic went much deeper in its analysis than modern socialism. There was communism in the consumption of the necessaries of life and not in production only. It was the communalisation and nationalisation of what is known as consumption. Robespierre declared that only the superfluity of foodstuffs was to become the articles of commerce and what was necessary belonged to all. The communism of 1793 with its affirmation of the right of all to sustenance and to the land for its production, its denial of the right of any one to hold more land than he and his family could cultivate and its attempt to communalise all trade and industry, went straighter to the hearts of things than all the minimum programmes of our own time or even all the maximum preambles of such programmes. As a matter of fact, the French Revolution was the source and origin of all the present communist, anarchist and socialist conceptions. (**The Great French Revolution,** pp. 573-581).

Prof. Goodwin, says that, "In our time the French Revolution of 1789 has been overshadowed by the Russian Revolution of 1917 and its ideals were temporarily dimmed or distorted by the Fascist and Nazi revolutions. Critics inside France have spurned its emphasis upon the primacy of the individual in relation to society and the State, while foreign observers have asked whether it was, after all, 'a mistake' and whether the price which France had to pay for its conquest of liberty and equality was too great. Historians are more disposed to bring the Revolution of 1789 into focus by comparative studies of other eighteenth-century revolutions, of which there were many, and by emphasizing that its essential contribution to the evolution of modern democracy was that it enunciated the principle and worked out the implications of popular sovereignty. Only in a limited sense can the French Revolution be regarded as the source of modern totalitarianism, for the Jacobin dictatorship and the 'revolutionary government' of 1793 were merely the provisional and abnormal forms to which France submitted, in time of civil and foreign war, the defence of its national security and its essentially liberal ideas."

SUGGESTED READINGS

Bowle, John: **Napoleon, London, 1973.**

Butterfield, H.: **The Peace Tactics of Napoleon (1806-8), 1929.**

Fisher, H.A.L.: **Napoleon, 1956.**

Fisher, H.A.L.: **Bonapartism.**

Seeley, J.R.: **Life and Times of Stein.**

Fournier: **Napoleon.**

Geyl, P.: **Napoleon—For and Against, 1949.**

Gooch, G.P.: **Germany and French Revolution, 1948.**

Hales, E.E.Y.: **Napoleon and the Pope.**

Hassall: **Life of Napoleon.**

Hazen: **The French Revolution and Napoleon.**

Hackshor, E.F.: **The Continental System: An Economic Interpretation, 1922.**

Herold, J.C.: **The Mind of Napoleon, 1955.**

Johnston, R.M.: **The Corsican.**

Langsam, W.C.: **The Napoleonic Wars and German Nationalism in Austria, 1930.**

Ludwig, E.: **Napoleon.**

Markham, F.M.H.: **Napoleon and the Awakening of Europe, 1954.**

Rose, J.H.: **The Personality of Napoleon, 1912.**

Rose, J.H.: **Life of Napoleon.**

Rose, J.H.: **Napoleonic Studies.**

Rosebery, Lord: **Napoleon, the Last Phase.**

Seeley, J.R.: **Napoleon.**

Sloane: **Napoleon Bonaparte.**

Thomson, Oavid: **Europe Since Napoleon.**

CHAPTER

10 THE VIENNA SETTLEMENT (1815)

Napoleon had badly mutilated the political map of Europe. He had torn away territories from some States and added them to other States to suit his convenience. However, when he was overthrown in 1814 and sent to the Island of Elba, the problem before the European statesmen was how the map of Europe was to be redrawn. As Metternich had played the most important part in the overthrow of Napoleon, Vienna was chosen as the venue of negotiations and the settlement of Europe. Many emperors, foreign ministers and statesmen assembled at Vienna and carried on deliberations during the winter of 1814-15. There was a lot of controversy among the victors regarding the fate of Poland and Saxony. Prussia desired to annex the whole of Saxony in exchange for the large amount of Polish territory she was surrendering to Russia and Czar Alexander "backed up" Prussia to the limit. Metternich refused to allow Prussia so large an extension of the territory contiguous to Austria and Castlereagh and Talleyrand (of France) stood with him. The difference went right up to the brink of war. At the beginning of 1815, France, Austria and England formed a defensive alliance to resist the claims of Russia and Prussia. This extreme step produced the desired results. The Czar was convinced that the other side would fight rather than give way. The result was that he gave way on some points and Prussia followed suit. Ultimately, Prussia secured only about half of Saxony. The part of Talleyrand has been exaggerated to some extent. It is wrong to say that he created differences between the allies. All that he was able to do was that he inflamed and exploited the differences between the allies to the advantage of France. The result was that all matters were already adjusted when the news came that Napoleon had run away from the Island of Elba and Louis XVIII had left France. The work of the Congress was completed after the overthrow of Napoleon at Waterloo in 1815.

(1) The Vienna Settlement was based on three principles, viz., restoration, legitimacy[1] and compensation. As regards the principle of restoration, it was decided to restore, as far as possible, the boundaries and reigning families of the several European countries as they were before the French Revolution and the rise of Napoleon. The principle of restoration was consistent with that of legitimacy which the French statesman Talleyrand was exploiting in order to save France from further territorial spoliation and to enable his defeated country to play an important part in the deliberations of Europe. The Vienna Settlement restored the Bourbons in Spain, Naples and Sicily. The House of Orange was restored in Holland. The House of Savoy was restored in Piedmont and Sardinia. The Pope was also restored with all his possessions in Italy. The various German princes whose territories had been included by Napoleon in the Confederation of the Rhine were also restored to their territories. The Swiss Confederation was also restored. The Tyrol was restored to Austria. The right of Austria to the Austrian Netherlands was recognised but she was allowed to exchange it for some other territory.

---

1. About the principle of legitimacy, Talleyrand, wrote: "We showed that the principle of legitimacy must be held sacred in the interest of the people themselves, because legitimate Governments can alone be strong and durable, whereas illegitimate Governments, relying upon force only, fall to pieces the moment that support fails them, and then the people are delivered over to a succession of revolutions of which no one was can foresee the end."

(2) During the Napoleonic wars, Great Britain had captured the important Dutch colonies of Ceylon, Cape Colony, South Africa and Guiana. Those colonies were confirmed to her. However, with a view to compensating Holland and also to creating a strong State on the northern frontier of France, the Austrian Netherlands were given over to Holland. The King of Holland was made the King of the United Netherlands. Austria was compensated for her loss of the Austrian Netherlands and shot got Lombardy and Venetia in Italy. The members of the Hapsburg family were put on the thrones of Tuscany, Parma and Modena. Finland and Swedish Pomerania were taken away from Sweden and given to Russia and Prussia respectively. Sweden was compensated in the form of Norway which was taken away from Denmark. Denmark was punished on account of her alliance with Napoleon for a long time.

(3) Prussia also gained a great deal. She got back all the German territories which had been taken away from her by Napoleon. She was also given Swedish Pomerania, two-fifths of Saxony, the whole of Westphalia and most of the Rhineland. One of the reasons why Prussia was given these territories was that it was intended to make Prussia a bulwark against France. However, the result of these acquisitions was that Prussia became the leader of Germany. These concessions added to her mineral resources and helped her to become a great industrialised country. Prussia also became a purely German State by the surrender of her Polish territory to Russia.

(4) With the object of maintaining the balance of power and creating a ring round France, it was decided to enlarge and strengthen the kingdom of Sardinia. To that kingdom, Savoy and Piedmont were restored and Genoa was added.

(5) As regards the settlement of Germany, it was decided not to restore all the petty States which existed before the French Revolution. The Holy Roman Empire had been abolished by Napoleon in 1806 and no attempt was made to revive it. It is true that men like Stein advocated the unification of Germany under the supremacy of a single Power, but Frederick William III did not show any keenness to become the leader of Germany and Metternich had also given a promise to the Princes of South Germany that their sovereign rights would be protected. Neither Prussia nor Austria nor the Princes of the small German States showed any enthusiasm for a unified Germany and so the opportunity to create a united Germany was lost. A loose German Confederation of 38 States was established. There was to be a Diet at Frankfurt which was to consist of Delegates from the various sovereign States of Germany. The Diet was to be presided over by the Chancellor of Austria. Austria was given the right to send six Delegates to the Diet. All the States were not given representation in it. The members were forbidden to enter into an alliance with a foreign Power either against the Confederation as a whole or against a fellow-member. Although the German Confederation was nominally guaranteed by all the European Powers, in actual practice, Austria dominated her politics.

(6) Russia was allowed to retain Finland which she had conquered from Sweden. She was also given Bessarabia which she had captured from the Turks. She also got most of the Grand Duchy of Warsaw.

England occupied Heligoland in the North Sea, Malta and the Ionian Islands in the Mediterranean, Cape Colony in South Africa, Ceylon and other islands.

Austria-Hungary recovered her Polish possessions. As compensation for the Austrian Netherlands given to Holland, she got Lombardy and Venetia. She also got the Illyrian provinces along the eastern coast of the Adriatic. Duchy of Parma was given to Maria Louise, wife of Napoleon and an Austrian Princess. Princes connected with the Austrian imperial family were restored to the throne of Modena and Tuscany.

In the name of legitimacy France was restored but she was hemmed in by the Netherlands, Prussia and Sardinia. The leadership of Europe passed to Austria from France. The Austrian acquisition made her a great power in Europe. She dominated both Germany and Italy. She became more German than before. Although the Austrian Emperor lost the title of the Holy Roman Emperor yet the control of Austria over Germany was complete.

Criticism. The view of Prof. Fyffe is that **"Standing on the boundary line between two ages, the legislation of Vienna forms a landmark in history."** It cannot be denied that the Vienna Settlement of 1815 was not so bad as the Paris settlement of 1919-20. On account of the influence of Castlereagh, the settlement of 1815 was not one of revenue. He rightly told the statesmen present at Vienna that they had assembled not to distribute the trophies of war but to make such a settlement as would give peace to the people of Europe. The principle of compromise was applied wherever possible and consequently there was no thrashing or flogging of France. In 1919, Germany was held responsible for all the acts of omission and commission of William II and was deprived of her territories, colonies, investments, etc., and was made to pay a huge war indemnity amounting to billions of dollars which was not within her competence to pay. It cannot be denied that Napoleon was responsible for acts of wanton aggression and had disturbed Europe in a very bad way, but France was not held guilty for all his misdeeds. Even when Napoleon was defeated for the second time in 1815 at Waterloo, a very mild treaty was imposed on France. Her frontiers were restricted to those of 1791 and not even those of 1789 when the French Revolution actually started. France was required to restore her treasures of arts which Napoleon had plundered from other countries. She was merely asked to pay a war-indemnity of 700,000,000 francs. The period of Allied occupation was cut short in 1818 when France paid off the war indemnity. The result of this kind treatment to France was that there was no general conflagration in Europe for 99 years (1815-1914).

Seaman says, "Nevertheless the Vienna Settlement must not be regarded as having of itself prevented European war for a century. It is possible to say instead that it contained in none of its provisions the seeds of a future war between the great powers, and must thus be rated a better peace than either Utrecht or Versailles. Utrecht rankled in the hearts of the Hapsburgs, and its colonial and commercial clauses were an encouragement to the British to embark in due course on new wars against France and Spain. Versailles humiliated, or appeared to humiliate the Germans; created new democratic States whose democracy had no roots and whose independent sovereignty was illusory; abolished old minority problems only to create new ones; disappointed the Italians and inflated the French; and by appealing to the irrational forces of the mass mind bred a chaos contrasting tragically with the orderliness that Vienna achieved by ignoring the masses altogether. For the disregard of Liberalism and Nationalism at Vienna (in so far as they were disregarded) did not cause war. They were right in thinking in 1815 that before revolutions can make wars, there must first be the wars that encourage the revolutions. They saw that the issues of peace and war are decided by the great powers and by them alone. Hence, the simple fact that the Vienna Settlement contained no clause that offered any of the great powers a pretext for war is its complete and sufficient justification." (**From Vienna to Versailles,** pp. 8-9).

About the Congress of Vienna, Gentz, its Secretary, wrote, "The fine phrases about the 'reconstruction of the social order', 'the regeneration of the political system of Europe", and an enduring peace founded on 'a just redistribution of forces', etc., were intended only to tranquilize the people and give to the solemn reunion an air of dignity and grandeur; the real object of the Congress was to divide among the conquerors the spoils of the conquered." However, Ketelbey does not agree with this view. According to him, it was inevitable that the victorious powers should seek to protect their own interests, but their treatment of the defeated enemy was marked by reasonableness and even generosity. It is true that the victorious powers got their profit, but not so much at the cost of France but as that of other countries such as Poland. It is true that the victorious powers talked of the "rights, freedom, and independence of all nations", they did not mean to draw political frontiers round every group of articulate nationalists. They were determined to prevent another European war and provide safeguards against the same. They had seen the destruction caused even by the people's war and hence, they repudiated the influence and example of revolutionary French democracy in the same way as the United Nations repudiated German Nazism or Italian Fascism after the World War II. It must not be forgotten that the victorious powers had already made peace with France before the Congress of Vienna and they had allowed the representatives of France to go to Vienna on equal terms. What the Congress embodied in its Final Act had already been agreed upon among the powers. The fates of Finland, Norway and Belgium and the states bordering France had already been settled. The major work left to the Congress was to settle the political pattern of the German, Swiss and Italian states and the Polish-Saxon question. The Congress of Vienna restored wherever restoration was possible. It tried to protect Europe against a revival of French imperialism. It provided a guarantee order and initiated a policy for settling future disputes. It built broadly on the principle of a balanced European society of five major powers. The result was that there was no major war for about forty years. Russia gained immensely out of the arrangements made at the Congress of Vienna and it started taking an active part in the affairs of Western Europe and continued to do so till her defeat in the Crimean War. The victors of 1815 acknowledged the disappearance of the Holy Roman Empire, the withdrawal of Sweden into a comparative Scandinavian isolation and the abandonment of her trans-Baltic ambitions. The number of the states in Germany was reduced and that helped the cause of German unification. The newly strengthened kingdoms of Russia and Sardinia were to help the unification of Germany and Italy. It is true that the Congress of Vienna failed to satisfy the aspirations of Poland and it ignored the population of Belgium and yoked Norway to Denmark, but it showed both moderation and political wisdom. It provided a real foundation on which later Europe was to build and it preserved international stability for forty years.

(1) However, it cannot be maintained that the Vienna Settlement was an ideal one and many drawbacks of it can be pointed out. According to Prof. Hayes, "In all these territorial readjustments, there was little that was permanent and much that was temporary. The union of Holland and Belgium lasted but 15 years. The Italian and German settlement survived but 50 years and the Polish barely a century." Napoleon had annexed Holland in 1811 on account of the refusal of Louis to enforce strictly the Continental System. However, there was no justification to group Belgium with Holland. Holland was democratic, Protestant and Teutonic. Belgium was conservative, Catholic and the majority of her people spoke the French language. The people of Belgium did not like the headship of Holland and no wonder they revolted in 1830 and won their independence. It may be noted that England was responsible for, this unnatural union. Her fear was that without Holland, Belgium alone would not be able to resist French pressure and consequently it was necessary to unite her with Holland so that France might not be able to gobble up Belgium in one mouthful. The union of Russia and Finland was dissolved in 1917 and that of Sweden and Norway in 1905. The German Confederation with all its paraphernalia was destroyed by Bismarck. The settlement of Italy was completely upset by Cavour.

(2) Another defect of the settlement was that it ignored altogether the nationalist movement that had stirred the Poles, the Spaniards, the Italians, and the Germans. The Polish nationalist leader Czartorysky attached himself to Czar Alexander I with a view to securing independence for his country but he failed in his efforts. Poland was put under the control of Russia and it was to be ruled as a separate territory. The Poles had to exert themselves throughout the 19th century to achieve their independence and suffered terribly while doing so. They were crushed under the tyrannical regime of Russia. Likewise, the dream of Stein to create a unified German State was not realised. A loose German confederation was created. Austria is blamed for not giving out many, unity and constitutional government. However, it is pointed out that even one hegemony of Britain was considered undesirable. The Congress of Vienna did not overlook Germanic constitutionalism, but the trouble arose on account of the reactionary policies followed afterwards by Metternich in Germany. As regards Italy, it was pointed out that a timely devolution of government from Vienna might have given Italy good government by Italians. The Vienna Congress had no authority to force Austria to

give Italy Home Rule. The Congress united the kingdom of Savoy and Piedmont with republics of Genoa and Nice. The union appeared to be temporary and there was a lot of bitterness in Genoa and Nice. In spite of this, the union of these small Italian States led indirectly to the unification of Italy. Mazzini, the apostle of Italian liberation, was a native of Genoa. Garibaldi, the sword-arm of Italy, was born in Nice. It was from Genoa that the famous "Thousand" Red Shirts sailed in 1860 under the leadership of Garibaldi to liberate Sicily. In 1859, Cavour bought the help of Napoleon III to turn out the Austrians from Venetia and Lombardy by giving him Nice and Savoy.

(3) The hopes of the liberals were frustrated. Rulers who were restored by the Vienna Settlement set up reactionary regimes in their countries and there was repression everywhere. This was particularly so in Spain and Naples where the Bourbons were restored. Metternich himself tried to police Europe. Wherever liberalism raised its head, it was crushed. Liberal ideas were regarded as daggers. The Protocol of Troppau helped the European States to interfere in the internal affairs of other States. Metternich's own view was that "what the European people want is not liberty but peace."

(4) According to Prof. Hayes, the Vienna Settlement was defective in so far as the people were regarded as so many pawns in the game of dynastic aggrandizement.

(5) According to Cruttwell, "It was mean and hyprocritical not to extend the doctrine of legitimacy of Republics. Both Venice and Genoa had a longer and more glorious life of independence than many monarchs, but both were extinguished without a murmur in the supposed interests of securing North Italy against France."

(6) According to Grant and Temperley, "It has been customary to denounce the peace-makers of Vienna as reactionary and illiberal in the extreme. It is indeed true that they represented the old regime and were, to a large extent, untouched by the new ideas. But they represented the best and not the worst of the old regime, and their settlement averted any major war in Europe for forty years. According to their lights the settlement was a fair one. France was treated with leniency, and the adjustments of the Balance of Power and territory were carried out with the scrupulous nicety of a grocer weighing out his wares, or of a banker balancing his accounts. Russia alone gained more than her fair share, and this was because she had an undue proportion of armed forces. The settlement disregarded national claims, forced unnatural unions on Norway and Sweden, and Belgium and Holland. But in each case the ally and the stronger partner (Sweden and Holland) demanded it, and the Allies did not see their way to resist the demand. A more serious criticism, was the disrespect paid to the views of smaller Powers. Though the settlement was supposed to be in favour of the older and existing rights, the smaller States were ruthlessly sacrificed for the benefit of the larger. For this side of the activities of the peace-makers there is little excuse, and it is the gravest criticism of their actions."

(7) Critics point out that the Congress of Vienna did not provide a satisfactory solution of the Eastern question. However, it was impossible for the Vienna Congress to tackle that question successfully. That question was not solved in spite of the efforts made by the European statesmen throughout the 19th century. "The sick man of Europe" was a great puzzle. All the European Powers wanted to have Constantinople and it was impossible to arrive at any settlement. Moreover, Russian treaties with Turkey, particularly that of Bucharest of 1812, added to the difficulties of the problem.

According to Hazen, "The Congress of Vienna was a Congress of aristocrats, to whom the ideas of nationality and democracy as proclaimed by the French Revolution were incomprehensible or loathsome. The rulers rearranged Europe according to their desires, disposing of it as if it were their own personal property, ignoring the sentiment of nationality, which had lately been so wonderfully aroused, indifferent to the wishes of the people. There could be no 'sentiment' because they ignored the factors that alone would make the settlement permanent. The history of Europe after 1815 was destined to witness repeated, and often successful, attempts to rectify this cardinal error of the Congress of Vienna."

According to H.A. Kissinger, "The statesmen at Vienna were not interested in transforming humanity, because in their eyes this effort had led to the tragedy of a quarter-century of struggle. To transform humanity by an act of will, to transcend French nationalism in the name of that of Germany, would have seemed to them to make peace by revolution, to seek stability in the unknown, to admit that a myth once shattered cannot be regained. The issue at Vienna, then, was not reform against reaction—that is the interpretation of posterity. Instead, the problem was to create an order in which change could be brought about through a sense of obligation, instead of through an assertion of power." (**A World Restored,** p. 172). Again, "Whatever one may think of the moral content of their solution, it excluded no major power from the European continent and therefore testified to the absence of unbridgeable schisms. The settlement did not rest on mere good faith, which would have put too great a strain on self-limitation; nor on the efficacy of a pure evolution of power, which would have made calculation too indeterminate. Rather, there was created a structure in which the forces were sufficiently balanced, so that self-restraint could appear as something more than self-abnegation, but which took account of the historical claims of its components, so that its existence could be translated into acceptance. There existed within, the new international order no power so dissatisfied that it did not prefer to seek its remedy without the framework of the Vienna Settlement rather than in overturning it. Since the political order did not contain a 'Revolutionary' power, its relations became increasingly spontaneous, based on the growing certainty that a catastrophic upheaval was unlikely.

"That the Vienna Settlement came to be so generally accepted was not a fortunate accident. Throughout the war Castlereagh and Metternich had insisted that theirs was an effort for stability, not revenge, justified, not by crushing the enemy, but by his recognition of limits. If we compare the outline of the Vienna Settlement with the Pitt plan and its legitimization with that of the instructions to Schwarzenberg, we find that luck, in politics as in other activities, is but the residue of design. This is not to say that the settlement revealed a prescience that made all events conform to a certain vision. Castlereagh, in giving up his conviction of the mechanical equilibrium for that of an historical balance, maintained through confidential intercourse among its members, increasingly separated himself from the spirit of his own country. Metternich, by attempting to maintain predominance in both Italy and Germany, was forced into a policy beyond his resources. His increasingly inflexible struggle for legitimacy revealed a growing consciousness of the insufficiency of Austria's material base for the European task he had set for her. If a policy for pure power is suicidal for an Empire located in the centre of a continent, reliance on unsupported legitimacy is demoralizing and leads to stagnation. Finesse can substitute for strength when the goals are determinate, but it is no substitute for conception when the challenges have become internal. And Prussia, with misgivings and hesitations, with a feeling of national humiliation and grudging surrender, was forced into a German mission in spite of itself. Extending now from the Vistuala to the Rhine, it symbolized the quest for German unity. Scattered in enclaves across Central Europe, its need for security, if not its conception of a national mission, forced it into becoming, albeit reluctantly, the agent of a German policy. Situated athwart the major waterways and land routes, Prussia came to dominate Germany economically before it unified it physically. The defeat in Saxony, so bitterly resented, became the instrument of Prussia's final victory over Austria". (**Ibid.,** pp. 173-74).

The Holy Alliance (1815). It seems desirable to refer to the Holy Alliance of 1815 which was the creation of Czar Alexander I who was a visionary, a mystic, a man of moods and unstable imagination. Such a scheme had been put forward earlier by Sully, the Minister of Henry IV of France, in his Grand Design. The object of the Grand Design was "to deliver them for ever from the fear of bloody catastrophes, so common in Europe; to secure for them an unalterable repose so that all the princes might henceforth live together as brothers." It was intended to set up a General Council or Senate consisting of 66 delegates from the different countries whose duty was to settle disputes and maintain the peace of Europe. However, nothing came out of it on account of the premature death of Henry of Navarre in 1610.

Czar Alexander I was encouraged to put forward his scheme of the Holy Alliance on account of his preponderant influence in Europe after the overthrow of Napoleon. He also had liberal views on account of the influence of his Swiss tutor. What Alexander I wanted was that the rulers of the European States should apply the principles of Christianity in their dealings with one another. They were also to regard their subjects as their children. He intended to spiritualise politics. To quote Alexander, "The present act has no other object than to publish, in the face of the whole world, their fixed resolution, both in the administration of their respective States and in their political relations with every other government, to take for their sole guide the precepts of their Holy religion, namely, the precepts of Justice, Christianity, Charity and Peace, which, far from being applicable only to private concerns, must have an immediate influence on the counsels of princes and guide all their subjects, as being the only means of consolidating human institutions, and remedying their imperfections."

It is to be noted that the Holy Alliance was honoured more in its breach than observance. It is true that Russia, Austria and Prussia made the required declaration but the declaration was not observed in actual practice. The Holy Alliance was an attempt to apply the principles of morality in the field of international diplomacy and to create the political conscience of Europe but it failed in its objective. The Czar did not succeed in providing **"the transparent soul of the Holy Alliance with the body"** and the scheme remained still-born.

Great Britain refused to subscribe to the principle of the Holy Alliance. According to Castlereagh, the Holy Alliance was "a piece of sublime mysticism and non-sense." Metternich looked upon it as "a loud-sounding nothing" or "moral demonstration." To quote Metternich, "The Holy Alliance was merely a philanthropic aspiration clothed in a religious garb." "It was not an institution to keep down the right of the people, to promote absolutism or any other tyranny. It was only the overflow of the pietistic feeling and the Emperor Alexander's application of Christian principles to politics."

The practical importance of the Holy Alliance was negligible. Its principles were never put into practice. However, the people of Europe confused the Holy Alliance with the Quadruple Alliance and as the Quadruple Alliance was used for the purpose of suppressing nationalism and liberalism everywhere in Europe, the Holy Alliance was also condemned and was regarded as a symbol of reaction, a league of princes against their peoples and a conspiracy against liberalism. However, the attitude of the various Powers towards the Holy Alliance showed that there was no unanimity of purpose among the Powers and there was every possibility of their falling out if circumstances so required.

Seaman says that the Holy Alliance "was an important preservative of peace in Europe. For so long as it kept Austria, Russia and Prussia together, peace was almost certain, and war, when it came, only partial. The fact that the Holy Alliance had existed helped to prevent Prussia and Austria from fighting against Russia in the Crimean War, and thus kept the conflict outside the main European area, confining it to the Crimea, where nothing vital could be destroyed and no essential changes be effected. Its collapse after 1856 was the prelude to the destruction of the 1815 Settlement in Italy and Germany; for only because Austria was isolated from an aggrieved Russia could Napoleon III and Bismarck create the new Italy and the new Germany (and indirectly an autonomous Hungary) at Austria's expense. Moreover, Bismarck's first concern after 1871 was to create the Alliance from whose years of eclipse he had profited. The Three Emperors League of 1872 was alleged, like the Protocol of Troppau, to be based on a common resistance to republicanism; and all Bismark's subsequent ingenuity in foreign affairs was directed to the same end at the policy of Metternich, that of preventing Austrians and Russians from fighting over the Eastern Question. For only when that happened would a general European war be inevitable."

SUGGESTED READINGS

Fyffe : **History of Modern Europe.**

Kissinger, H.A.: **A World Restored.**

Lipson: **Europe in the Nineteenth Century.**

Nicholson, Sir Harold: **The Congress of Vienna, 1945**

Phillips: **Modern Europe.**

Seaman : **From Vienna to Versailles.**

Seignobos : **Political History of Europe Since 1814.**

Thomson, David: **Europe Napoleon, 1957.**

Webster, C.K.: **The Congress of Vienna, 1934.**

Webster, C.K.: **The European Alliance.**

Ferrero, G.: **The Reconstruction of Europe, 1941.**

Cresson, W.P.: **The Holy Alliance, 1922.**

Gottschalk and Lach : **The Transformation of Modern Europe, Vol. II.**

CHAPTER

11 CASTLEREAGH AND CANNING

Castlereagh (1812-22). Castlereagh belongs to the category of those statesmen who were called upon to face a very critical situation and who performed their function in a masterly manner. He was helped in his task by his calm, quiet, passionless and unruffled temperament.

Castlereagh was born in 1769 and died in 1822. He was Secretary for Ireland when the union of England and Ireland took place and he was partly instrumental in bribing the Irishmen to support the Union. He was in favour of showing religious toleration to the Catholics. He also worked as Colonial and War Secretary. In 1807, he was responsible for the re-organisation of the army. He made the old militia the basis of the military establishment of the country. He resigned his office in 1809 and fought a duel with Canning. He became Foreign Secretary in 1812 and held that office till 1822 when he committed suicide. According to Lord Brougham, "Castlereagh possessed a fund of plain sense, not to be misled by any refinement of speculation or clouded by any fanciful notions. He went straight to his point. He was brave, politically as well as personally."

When he became the Foreign Secretary in 1812, the condition of European States vis-a-vis Napoleon was not strong. Every State had its own axe to grind and the result was that no effective action could be taken against Napoleon. In these circumstances, Castlereagh went over to the Continent and brought the Allies together. Thus, it was that the war of the Nations started which ended in the overthrow of Napoleon in 1814. Great Britain in 1814 held the same position in the Council of Europe as the United States held in 1919. She alone had the power, the resources and the will to continue war. England was the arbiter of Europe and the credit for that achievement goes to Castlereagh who combined in himself high ideals, sound commonsense and great diplomatic gifts. He not only retained the confidence of the British Parliament and his colleagues in the Cabinet but was also to win the trust and good opinion of the continental statesmen.

Castlereagh had gone to Europe and travelled to the allied headquarters with the definite object of welding the Four Powers into a solid alliance against Napoleon. He also aimed at creating an international organisation to decide the problems which might confront the European statesmen. According to Castlereagh, "in an habitual confidential and free intercourse between the ministers of the Great Powers as a body" lay the best means of removing differences of policy and ensuring a united front for victory and peace. The idea of **"diplomacy by conference"** seems to be a familiar one in the 20th century, but in the time of Castlereagh it was nothing of a revolution. By this one plan alone Castlereagh was stamped as one of the great peace-makers of history.

Castlereagh had gone to Europe to bring the Four Powers nearer one another and the Treaty of Chaumont of March 1814 was his crowning achievement within two months. By this treaty, the Four Powers pledged themselves to continue war until France accepted peace. Each was to provide arms and Great Britain was to give an additional subsidy of £5 millions a year. The alliance was to remain effective for 20 years and the Allies were to defend Europe against any attempt by France to upset the terms of the peace settlement. The signing of the Treaty of Chaumont was followed within a month by the abdication of Napoleon and peace negotiations were started in Paris. The first stage of the peace settlement was arranged at Paris and the rest at Vienna. The final treaty was made in November, 1815.

In the peace settlement Castlereagh played an important part. He was helped in his task by the Duke of Wellington, Metternich and Alexander I. Both Castlereagh and Alexander I were determined to see that France was not treated harshly. To quote Castlereagh, **"It is not our business to collect trophies but to bring back the world to peaceful habits."** Castlereagh was strongly opposed to snatching from France any territory which one day France might attempt to recover by force. He wrote to Lord Liverpool thus: "The more I reflect upon it, the more I deprecate the system of scratching such a Power. We may hold her down and pare her nails so that many years shall pass before she can again wound us, but this system of being pledged to a continental war for objects that France may any day reclaim from the particular State that hold them, without pushing her demands beyond what she would contend was due to her own honour, is, I am sure, a bad British policy."

It was because the European statesmen, under the guidance of Castlereagh, followed a lenient and just policy towards France that the latter settled down under the Vienna Settlement. In spite of the fact that France had troubled Europe for almost two decades, she was treated with amazing moderation. Most of her conquests were taken away, but she was allowed to retain some slight extensions of her Northern and Eastern frontiers. Louis XVIII was restored to the French throne. In spite of the defeat of Napoleon in the Battle of Waterloo in 1815, the terms of peace were not made very harsh. Territorial concessions were withdrawn and she was asked to pay a small war indemnity. She was required to return the captured art treasures. An army of occupation was to stay on the French soil till the payment of war indemnity. By meting out such a lenient treatment, Castlereagh showed that he was a greater statesman then Lloyd George who imposed upon the world a Second World War within a period of twenty years. The Settlement of Castlereagh lasted for about a century (1815-1914).

Throughout the long and complicated negotiations which took place at Paris and Vienna, Castlereagh did not lose sight of his ideal of international co-operation. He got an opportunity to put into practice his ideal when Article 6 of the Treaty of November 1815 was being discussed. In its original form, the Article provided that statesmen of Europe should meet at intervals to discuss the affairs of France. Castlereagh did not approve of the wording and substance and widened the scope of the Article by substituting the following words: "To facilitate and to secure the execution of the present Treaty and to consolidate the connections which at the present moment so closely unite the four sovereigns for the happiness of the world the High Contracting Parties have agreed to renew their meetings at fixed periods, either under the immediate auspices of the sovereigns themselves, or by their respective ministers for the purpose of consulting upon their common interests, and for the consideration of the measures which at each of those periods shall be considered the most salutary, for the purpose and prosperity of the nations and for the maintenance of peace of Europe."

This was Castlereagh's great contribution to European peace. One can find in it the first draft of the Covenant of the League of Nations or the Charter of the United Nations. It was the basis of the so-called Concert of Europe. Castlereagh hoped that all the problems affecting the peace of Europe would be discussed as they arose at the conferences summoned under Article 6 and peace would be maintained because no critical situation would be allowed to develop. Castlereagh's scheme was bound to fail because his contemporaries failed to understand the value of "diplomacy by conference". England herself did not come forward to maintain peace when it was threatened.

It has been contended that Castlereagh **"tied England to the tail of the Holy Alliance."** This assertion is merely a distortion of facts. It is true that Castlereagh believed in the co-operation of European statesmen to settle the problems that might arise from time to time and it was with that object in view that the Four Congresses met at Aix-la-Chapelle (1818), Troppau (1820), Laibach (1821) and Verona (1822). Castlereagh was, no doubt, anxious to settle the problems by means of mutual exchange of thoughts. He had strong faith in mutual exchange of views but it is wrong to say that he in any way approved of the policy of the Holy Alliance which in its practical application became an instrument in the hands of Russia, Prussia and Austria-Hungary to stamp out all liberal ideas and movements in Europe. It is true that England was a member of the Quadruple Alliance and she was ready to co-operate with other powers to settle the problems which might confront the European statesmen. It is also true that Castlereagh was ready to allow Austria a free hand in Italy. He approved of a secret treaty between Austria-Hungary and Ferdinand IV of Naples to maintain absolutism in Naples and Sicily. It is for that reason that Castlereagh regarded the revolt of the Italian Risorgimento as "a sectarian conspiracy and military revolt against a mild and paternal Government." Castlereagh was a "good European" and "a friend of peace." He wished periodic Congresses to dispose of international disputes and thereby avoid cause of war, but he did not wish those meetings to be made the instruments of interference in the internal affairs of States. Castlereagh was opposed to the international policing of Europe which was the main object of Russia, Austria and Prussia. It is for this reason that he objected strongly to the Protocol of Troppau which authorised the powers of the Holy Alliance to interfere with the internal policies of the States.

In 1820, Castlereagh embodied his views in a great State Paper which was afterwards used by Canning as the basis of his own policy. The occasion for the paper was the outbreak of a military revolution in Spain against the tyranny of Ferdinand VII of Spain. In that paper Castlereagh outlined a policy of "non-intervention" in the internal politics of the States. He pointed out that "the Spanish nation is, of all the European people, that which will least brook interference from abroad." This information was based on the views of Wellington. However, this was not the only ground on which Castlereagh stressed the necessity of non-intervention. The Holy Alliance Powers wished to intervene in Spain to restore Ferdinand VII's authority and Castlereagh tried to deter them by recalling the origins of the Four Powers Alliance which had been established by Article 6 of the Treaty of 1815. That Alliance had been intended to serve as a protection for the peace settlement not "as a union of the Governments of the World for the superintendence of internal affairs of other States" and "nothing", Castlereagh declared, "is more likely to impair or even to destroy its utility than any attempt to push its duties and obligations beyond the sphere which its original conception and understood principles will warrant." This was a criticism of the Holy Alliance's misuse of Article 6. As for British policy, Castlereagh stated that Britain could not agree to foreign intervention on behalf of a king who had behaved so badly. To quote Castlereagh, "We shall be found in our place when actual danger menaces the system of Europe. But this country cannot, and will not act upon abstract and speculative principles of precaution." While Britain would defend the peace of Europe against any real danger, she would not follow her Allies against any imaginary menace or when their motive was the defence of tyranny and not of peace.

By his firm statement of policy, Castlereagh did not intend to leave the Quadruple Alliance. However he was definitely determined to see that European Powers did not make intervention a principle guiding their regular actions. Just before his death, Castlereagh was preparing to attend the Congress of Verona where the Spanish question was to be discussed. He had already made up his mind to check the intervention of the European powers to reinstate Ferdinand to his former position. Although he committed suicide on the eve of the Conference, his work was carried on by Canning. Wellington who went to attend the Congress of Verona acted on the same principles as were laid down by Castlereagh. Woodward has rightly pointed out that Canning agreed with the decisions of Castlereagh although he differed from him in his methods. While Castlereagh believed on the policy of holding conferences with a view to solve the difficulties, Canning was opposed to that method. His view was summed up in his own statement: "We shall have no more Congresses, thank God." It was as a result of this policy that the era of Congresses ended.

It was wrong to say that Castlereagh tied England to the tail of the Holy Alliance. He was definitely opposed to the principles of Holy Alliance which enabled the European powers to interfere with the domestic affairs of other States. As a matter of fact, Castlereagh was deadly opposed to the Holy Alliance. He characterised the Holy Alliance as "a piece of sublime mysticism and nonsense." He frankly told Lord Liverpool that the mind of the Czar which entertained or conceived the idea of the Holy Alliance was not "completely sound." He disliked the use of the Holy Alliance as a crusade against liberalism. Castlereagh himself had no sympathy with liberalism, but he detested the idea of intervention in the domestic affairs of another country. The reason why Castlereagh was accused of having tied England to the tail of the Holy Alliance was because the people did not make a distinction between the Holy Alliance and the Quadruple Alliance. His dose association with foreign enemies of liberalism must have strengthened this belief in the minds of the people. Castlereagh was not a good speaker. He had neither the capacity nor the desire to convince public opinion that he was an opponent of the Holy Alliance. It is only modern historical research that has revealed the distinction between the Quadruple Alliance and the Holy Alliance. It is this distinction which has revealed the greatness of Castlereagh. His contemporaries who did not make the distinction, dubber him as one in league with Mettornich, another conservative and reactionary statesman of Europe. It was on account of this ignorance that Shelley summed up the extreme opinion in these lines in his **Masque of Anarchy** (1817) :—

> "I met Murder on the way;
> He had a Mask like Castlereagh:
> Very smooth he looked, yet grim.
> Seven blood-hounds followed him.
> All were fat and well they might
> Be in admirable plight,
> For one by one and two by two
> He tossed them human hearts to chew."

The greatness of Castlereagh has begun to be realised in modern times. It is true that he failed in his ideal of making the European States co-operate among themselves to settle their disputes which might endanger peace, but he was the pioneer who made the suggestion which was embodied in the Covenant of the League of Nations and later on in the Charter of the United Nations. Best tributes to his memory have been paid by those historians who have mastered the details of his work. In his **"The Foreign Policy of Castlereagh,"** Webster describes Castlereagh as "the best European Foreign Minister in (Britain's) history." Seton-Watson describes him as "one of the very greatest and most constructive of British Foreign Secretaries." According to Webster, "Castlereagh had learnt the great lesson that if he wished to avoid war, he must prepare for peace."

According to H.A. Kissinger, "Yet it was this man, more than any other, who forged against European connection for Britain, who maintained the Coalition, and negotiated the settlement which in its main outlines was to last for over fifty years. Psychologists may well ponder how this Irish peer, whose career had given no indication of profound conceptions, should become the most European of British statesmen. No man more different from his great protagonist, Metternich could be imagined. Metternich was elegant, facile, rationalist; Castlereagh, solid, ponderous, pragmatic; the former was witty and eloquent, if somewhat pedantic; the latter cumbersome in expression, although effective in debate; Metternich was doctrinaire and devious; Castlereagh, matter-of-fact and direct. Few individuals have left behind them such a paucity of personal reminiscences. Icy and reserved, Castlereagh walked his solitary path, as humanly unapproachable as his policy came to be incomprehensible to the majority of his countrymen. It was said of him that he was like a splendid summit of polished frost, icy, beautiful, aloof, of a stature that nobody could reach and few would care to. It was not until his tragic death that the world was to learn the price of solitude." (**A World Restored,** p. 30).

George Canning (1822-27). George Canning was born in 1770. Although a man of humble origin, he rose to eminence through his good education at Eton and Oxford. He was a brilliant man. He was the Foreign Secretary of England from 1807 to 1809. There was a gap between 1809 and 1816. In 1816, he became President of the Board of Control. In 1821, he resigned on the issue of the treatment, meted out to Queen Caroline. When he was making preparation to come to India as Governor-General, he was made the Foreign Secretary of England on account of the sudden death of Castlereagh. He was Foreign Minister from 1822 to 1827. He was witty, a skilled debater and a brilliant speaker. He was the leader of the House of Commons.

Like Castlereagh, Canning was a friend and a pupil of Pitt, the Younger,' but the two became rivals of each other. In outlook, one was the antithesis of the other. Castlereagh was an aristocrat and cool and practical in his judgment. He was swayed by a desire to protect Britain's interests by drawing his country with other powers into a close international understanding. However, his policy depended to a large extent on his personality and on his remarkable influence over the statesmen of the Continent. Canning also believed in the necessity for peace, but he did not believe that it could be achieved through co-operation. His view was that Britain should not concern herself with Europe except in times of serious crises when her intervention was necessary as much for the defence of her own interests as for the restraint of aggression. Then she should intervene forcefully and decisively. In the normal times, Britain should abstain from interference in European politics. His policy was more nationalist than that of Castlereagh. On taking office, Canning is stated to have declared : **"For Europe, I shall be desirous now and then to read England."** He summed up his creed in the motto: **"Every nation for itself and God for us all."** Seton-Watson has added to it a corollary in these words: "Devil take the hindmost."

Canning was more in accord with the spirit of his age than Castlereagh. The nineteenth century was an age of nationalism and Castlereagh's internationalism was not in keeping with it. An elector addressed himself to Gladstone in 1831 in these words, **"Damn all foreign countries What has England to do with foreign countries?"** This sums up the British attitude towards Europe. Canning himself summed up the feelings of the Englishmen in these words: **"Let us not in the foolish spirit of romance, suppose that we alone could regenerate Europe."**

Woodward has rightly remarked that Canning differed from Castlereagh, not in his object, but in his methods. Their objective was the same, although their methods differed. Canning acted upon the same policy which had been laid down by Castlereagh in his State Paper of 1822. On taking office, Canning made that State Paper the basis of his policy, although he gave it a characteristic twist. He accepted the breach between Great Britain and her Allies and did not attempt to remedy it. "We shall have no more Congresses, thank God", was his remark. Castlereagh's vision of co-operation disappeared. Canning hated to co-operate with the Holy Alliance Powers on the ground that he was fond of his country's institutions and believed that other countries would benefit by the introduction of institutions on the British model. He wished English institutions to serve as the models for Europe.

Spain. Canning had first to deal with Spain. At the Congress of Verona, France was appointed the executor to restore the reactionary regime in Spain. Conning protested against this intervention and England left the Congress under protest. He was opposed to the general principle of intervention or the policing of Europe by the reactionary Powers. In spite of Britain's protest, the Duke of Angouleme was sent to Spain to restore Ferdinand VII. After his restoration, Ferdinand tried to go to extremes in his reactionary policies. Canning was indignant at this intervention. However, he found himself helpless to oppose the French without an open war with all the European Powers. He had to content himself with a strong protest. When Ferdinand began to think of establishing his control over the

Spanish colonies in South America, Canning made up his mind to check it. He adopted a high tone in his speeches. To quote Canning, **"I resolved that if France had Spain, it should not be Spain with the Indies."** Canning recognised the independence of the Spanish Colonies in South America. With one stroke, British commerce was protected, and, the revolting colonies were freed from the danger of a French attack and the principles of the Holy Alliance were flouted. He boasted in the House of Commons in these words: "I have called a New World into existence to redress the balance of the old". His claim was justified. Although the Spanish colonies had won their own independence, it was the British sea power which protected them from interference. In the face of naval action by Britain, the French did not dare to carry their arms beyond Spain itself. All this was done by Canning by merely a threat. Canning was also assisted by President Munro who enunciated at this time his famous Munro Doctrine in a message to Congress.

Portugal. In the case of Portugal, Canning had to take a strong line of action. He made it clear that England would not tolerate the spread of reactionary forces in Portugal. He extorted from France the declaration that she would not extend to Portugal her support of reaction in Spain. He persuaded the King of Portugal to recognise the independence of Brazil. In 1826, the King of Portugal died and Don Pedro, not wishing to leave Brazil, presented the Portuguese with a constitution. Ferdinand VII of Spain began to intrigue in Portugal in favour of reaction. The Portuguese Government appealed to Great Britain for assistance. Canning sent British troops within four days of the receipt of the appeal and thus the Portuguese constitution was protected by the British bayonets. When Canning announced this step in Parliament, he made a remarkable speech in which he made the following declaration : **"We go to Portugal, not to rule, not to dictate, not to prescribe constitution, but to defend and to preserve the independence of an ally.** We go to plant the standard of England on the well-known heights of Lisbon. Where that standard is planted, foreign domination shall not come."

Greek War of Independence. Canning adopted a strong line of action in the case of Greek War of Independence. He was not prepared to allow Turkey to go on oppressing the Greeks. By his intervention he not only secured a strong and independent position for Great Britain, but was also able to break the Holy Alliance. With a view to protect the British trade with the Levant from an attack, he recognised, in 1823, the Greeks as belligerents. In 1827, he entered into the Treaty of London with Russia and France. The object of that treaty was to secure the independence of Greece. The Treaty of London was a master-stroke. It isolated Austria and split the Holy Alliance. By attaching Russia to Britain, Canning put a check on Russian ambitions in the Eastern Mediterranean. The establishment of a new Greek State promised advantages to British trade. In his Greek policy, Canning got much support from the pro-Greek agitation in France and Great Britain. It is true that Wellington, his successor, tried to undo his work by joining hands with Turkey and making a truce with her, yet the Treaty of London secured Greek independence. Soon after his death, the combined fleets of Russia, France and Great Britain destroyed the Turkish and Egyptian fleets in the Battle of Navarino in October 1827. Although Russia alone reaped the harvest, Canning's policy of recognising Greek independence was successful.

Within five years of his assuming office, Canning set Britain upon the path which she followed for 50 years. He protected British interests and encouraged liberal and constitutional movements abroad. He prevented any general interference by the reactionary powers with the development of liberty and national freedom in Europe and overseas. International co-operation on a wide scale was gone. Canning took pride in the fact that he was responsible for disrupting the Holy Alliance. Under his guidance, Great Britain regained her freedom of action. She could intervene in European affairs where, when and how she pleased without any danger of being used by continental states for the furtherance of their own selfish ends. In this policy, Canning had the support of public opinion. He realised the necessity of national unity in matters of foreign policy and wished to have his countrymen behind him so that foreign governments may understand that he spoke for Britain as a whole and spoke with all her force and all her resources at his command. His frank speeches and the publication of despatches initiated the policy of putting before the electors the means of forming their opinion of foreign policy. According to Temperley: "In Canning's view, it was essential that future foreign policy should be both intelligible and popular." However, Canning did not allow the public to dictate his policy. **He "made foreign policy popular without ceasing to make it effective."** He disclosed only enough information to secure public support because she had no leanings towards democracy. In spite of this, this innovation was regarded to be a revolutionary tendency in the reactionary countries.

According to Cecil, Canning's political philosophy was a well-defined compact of opinion. It can be gathered up into a bundle of phrases. At the root of his ideas lay the thought of the nation as the unit of statesmanship. He saw so far clearly and scarcely troubled to look beyond. We find him abandoning the conceptions of Castlereagh, contending not only against the Holy Alliance, but against a Concert of Europe, foreswearing Congresses, refusing conferences and asking every nation to look to itself and leave the rest to God. He made the notion of a balance of power prominent in his speeches. He accepted as a matter of course the conflict of interests, groups and principles as the basis of his foreign policy. To quote Castlereagh, "Some years ago, I stated that the position of this country in the present state of the world was one of neutrality, not only between contending nations but between conflicting principles; and that it was by neutrality alone that we could maintain that balance, the preservation of which I believe to be essential to the welfare of mankind." Canning admitted that it was "much better and more convenient for us to have neighbours whose institutions cannot be compared with ours in point of freedom." Canning was not immoral. He believed in treaties and the maintenance of treaties. He believed in peace and justice. He had no clear sense of the unseen foundations of society. He had no regard for that common will towards a common welfare which is the basis of international civilization.

Canning's sympathies were with a grade of society which is the backbone of the country. He had the practical efficiency, the strong assurance, and the material outlook that were to make the middle period of Victoria's reign what it became in politics and trade. He lacked the high international courtesy, the sense of European solidarity and the spirit of peace. Combative, competitive and insular, Canning broadened a path for British policy where Palmerston was presently to strut crowing with crest erect. According to Lord Acton, **"No Foreign Secretary has equalled Canning."** However, there are others who do not give him that high praise but still admire him for his qualities of head and heart and his achievements in various fields.

SUGGESTED READINGS

Kissinger, H.A.: **A World Restored.**

Temperley, H.W.V.: **The Foreign Policy of Canning (1822-27), 1925.**

Temperley and Penson: **Foundations of British Foreign Policy.**

Webster, C.K.: **The Foreign Policy of Castlereagh.**

Stewart: **Memoirs of Castlereagh.**

Marriott: **Castlereagh.**

Hill, F.H.: **George Canning.**

CHAPTER

12 CONCERT OF EUROPE (1815-22)

The idea of a Concert of Europe was suggested by the Austrian Chancellor, Kaunitz, in 1971 and it found expression in the Treaty of Chaumont which was made in March 1814, by Great Britain, Russia, Prussia and Austria. The same four Powers tried at the Congress of Vienna to effect "a regeneration of the political system of Europe." The Congress of Vienna sealed the triumph of reaction and restored the pre-revolutionary conditions as far as possible. However, the fear of revolution was so great that the European Powers could not rest contented until they had devised some means to secure the permanence of Vienna Settlement. With that object in view, Great Britain, Austria, Prussia, and Russia entered on 20 November 1815 into the Quadruple Alliance for the maintenance of the treaties with France and for the consolidation "of the intimate relations now uniting the four sovereigns for the welfare of the world." The Powers also agreed to hold periodical meetings "either under the immediate auspices of sovereigns or through their ministers." Those meetings were to be "devoted to the grand interests they have in common, and to the discussion of measures which shall be judged to be most salutary for the repose and prosperity of the nations and for the maintenance of peace of Europe." It was in this way that the Concert of Europe was formed. This system of diplomacy by conferences was one of the most interesting experiments of 19th century. The period that followed the Quadruple Alliance is known as the Era of Congresses. On many occasions, the members of the European Concert met at different places to discuss questions that needed collective deliberations. In these Congresses, the dominating personality was the Austrian Chancellor, Metternich Under his leadership and guidance, the Quadruple Alliance practically established a dictatorship of the Powers. However, the Concert of Europe broke up in 1823 after holding four conferences at Aix-la-Chapelle in 1818, at Troppau in 1820, at Laibach in 1821, and at Verona in 1822.

Congress of Aix-la-Chapelle (1818). The first Congress meet in 1818 at Aix-la-Chapelle where Napoleon had once put forward his own scheme for the welfare of Europe. Regarding this Congress, Metternich is said to have remarked that he had "never seen a prettier little Congress." This Congress marked the zenith of the system by which the Allied Powers endeavoured to establish a joint control over the affairs of all continental States. The Congress was recognized as the Supreme Council of Europe and accordingly it entertained appeals in all kinds of cases.

The most important question before the Congress was that of France and happily a compromise was arrived at on that point. As France had paid off the whole of war indemnity, it was decided to withdraw the Allied Army of Occupation from the French soil and to admit France into the Concert of Europe. It was in this way that the Quadruple Alliance was transformed into the Quintuple Alliance which was called by Metternich as "moral pentarchy." There was a difference of opinion between Russia on the one hand and England and Austria on the other regarding the basis on which France was to be admitted into the Quadruple Alliance. Russia proposed to follow the principles as embodied in the Holy Alliance. However, the view of England and Austria was that France should be admitted by means of a treaty alliance with the four Powers and that was done. The Quadruple Alliance was renewed separately with a view to meeting any danger that might arise from France. However, to please Czar Alexander, a high-sounding statement was issued regarding the aims and objects of the moral pentarchy. It was intended to observe strictly the rights of the people, protect the arts of peace, increase the prosperity of State, awaken sentiments of religion and morality and set an example of justice and concord.

The Congress also called upon the King of Sweden to explain why he had ignored the treaty rights with regard to Norway and Denmark. The ruler of Monaco was ordered to improve the administrative system of his country. The Elector of Hesse petitioned to the Congress that he be allowed to take up the title of king, but it was refused. The Congress also dealt with the question of the disputed succession to the Duchy of Baden. The position of the Jewish citizens in Austria and Russia was also discussed.

In spite of the above achievements of the Congress of Aix-la-Chapelle certain differences arose among the Powers and those differences increased with the passage of time. Those were due to the divergent interests and mutual jealousy of the Powers concerned.

As regards the question of the rebellious colonies of Spain in South America, there was going on a lot of trade between England and those colonies from the time of the French Revolution. As Great Britain had invested a lot of money in those colonies, Castlereagh, the British Foreign Minister, refused to agree to any proposal either to bring them back under Spain or even to mediate between them and Spain unless British interests in those colonies were safeguarded beforehand.

In order to suppress slave trade, Great Britain suggested that the European States should exercise a mutual right of search for slaves. However, the suggestion was not accepted on account of the jealousy of the naval strength of Great Britain. No country was prepared to tolerate British interference with her commerce. The result was that no effective, action could be taken against slavery.

With a view to checking the menace of the Barbary Pirates in the Mediterranean, Russia suggested that an international fleet, representing the various powers, should be stationed in the Mediterranean. However, Great Britain rejected the proposal. She was not prepared to allow a Russian fleet to be stationed in the Mediterranean. Her interests were secure because the Barbary Pirates respected the Union Jack. The result was that the menace of the Barbary Pirates continued.

It has been claimed that the real significance of the Congress of Aix-la-Chapelle lies deeper. It was for the first time that Great Britain came to know of the real intentions of those who had set up the Concert of Europe. On this occasion, Czar Alexander proposed that a declaration should be signed by all the Powers guaranteeing the existing territorial boundaries and also the rights of sovereign princes. As this proposal was in accordance with the views of Metternich, it was accepted by Austria. Prussia also followed suit. It is maintained that a universal guarantee of the status quo would have resulted in the systematic suppression of nationalism, liberalism and constitutionalism in Europe. The declaration would have acted as a crusade against the progressive forces of Europe and thereby proved fatal to her supremacy in the world. There would have been no unification of Italy and Germany. It would have been impossible to separate Belgium from Holland in spite of the grievances of the former. Norway and Sweden would have continued to remain united. Greece, Rumania, Bulgaria and Serbia would have not have got their independence. Poland would have remained under foreign yoke for an indefinite period. Peace would have been secured in Europe at the price of liberty and independence.

However, the credit for the failure of the scheme must go to Great Britain who opposed tooth and nail the move of Russia, Austria, and Prussia. The question was whether the Powers had any right to intervene in the internal affairs of a State merely on the ground that the **status quo** had been upset in a particular country. Whatever the ostensible object of the Concert of Europe, its real object was to control the external and internal affairs of the European States. Great Britain was opposed to such a policy and counteracted the new move of the other Powers. The British stand was that she was not prepared to accept the general principle of international control. However, she was prepared to consider separately the question of intervention whenever an emergency arose in any country. Great Britain rejected the idea that the collective force of the Allies was "to be prostituted to support the established order without any consideration of the extent to which it was abused." According to Castlereagh, "The Alliance was never intended as a union for the governments of the world, or for the superintendence of the internal affairs of other States." Its purpose was not to suppress revolutionary movements in every nook and corner of Europe irrespective of their merits.

The principle of intervention in the internal affairs of other states was, however, accepted in 1820 by the Congress of Troppau in spite of the protests of Great Britain. It was the application of this principle which enabled Austria to suppress revolts in Naples and Piedmont in 1821. France also interfered in Spain in 1823.

Kissinger points out that although at the Congress of Aix-la-Chappelle, there appeared to be outward harmony, "the incompatibility of the various motivations was becoming manifest. With France integrated into the concert of powers, the political contest was finally over and with it disappeared the only motive which could make British participation in Continental affairs acceptable domestically. As Britain increasingly hedged its commitments, a vicious circle was set in motion: the stronger Britain's isolationist tendencies, the more Metternich, aware of Austria's material weakness, came to rely on his most effective weapon of restraining the Tsar: the appeal to Alexander's moral fervour. But the more Metternich flattered the Tsar's exaltation, the more difficult it became for Castlereagh to engage in any joint action. As the Congress of Aix-la-Chapelle ended, both were eager to obscure this, however Metternich, because his bargaining position towards Russia depended on the illusion of his British option; Castlereagh, because of his European vision, which he still hoped he could make prevail against the obtuseness of his Cabinet and, to him, the petty quest for safety of his Allies. Yet he must have sensed that the time for illusions was coming to an end. For, at this moment Metternich engaged in act which left little doubt that the next battle would be fought on a plane where Castlereagh could not follow, whatever his personal sympathies. He submitted two memoranda of the King of Prussia advising him on the administrative structure of his State and urging the impossibility of fulfilling the promise, made during the passionate days of 1813, of granting a constitution to his subjects. The precise arguments used by Metternich are less interesting than this first step which indicated Metternich's intention to function as the conservative conscience of Europe." (**A World Restored,** pp. 230-231).

Congress of Troppau (1820). The second Congress met at Troppau in 1820. Revolutions had broken out in Naples, Spain and Portugal and the people had forced their kings to give them liberal constitutions. The great Powers condemned the revolutions but they differed with regard to the steps to be taken to meet the situation. Russia offered armed assistance to the Spanish king to suppress the revolt. However, Metternich held her back because his hatred of revolution was balanced by his fear of Russian aggrandisement. Naples was considered to be a more urgent problem than others and consequently it was this revolt that occupied the statesmen assembled at Troppau. It was recognized by all the Powers that Austria had a special interest in Italy and consequently she should be allowed to suppress the revolt in Naples. According to Castlereagh, Austria could interfere in Naples on two grounds. She had great interests at stake in Italy. The stability of Lombardy and Venetia was endangered by the revolt and these were within the Austrian Empire itself. The same was the case with Parma, Modena and Tusoany which, were ruled by the members of the Hapsburg family. Moreover, there was a treaty between the King of Naples and Austria by which the latter was bound to come to the assistance of Naples.

However, Metternich was not satisfied with the mere recognition of Austria's right to interfere in the internal affairs of Italy. In addition to a narrow legal justification, he also wanted a moral justification for such interference. Castlereagh, the British Foreign Minister, was not prepared for that. His view was that no State was justified in interfering in the internal affairs of any other State except on the ground of a treaty between the two countries. Moreover, the revolt at Naples was outside the orbit of Great Britain, and consequently there was no justification for Great Britain to interfere in that territory. Castlereagh was not prepared to say that all popular insurrections or revolutions originating from below, were illegitimate and against the public law of Europe.

However, Metternich was backed by Prussia and Russia. At the Congress of Troppau. Czar Alexander declared himself to be a convert of Metternich. Formerly, Metternich was always afraid of Russian designs because Russian agents had spread all over Europe to encourage revolutionary movements. The conversion of Alexander, therefore, brought great relief to Metternich. The change in Alexander was due to the murder of Kotzebue and the mutiny of the Imperial Guards at Petrograd. Czar Alexander declared his conversion to Metternich in these words: "So we are at one, Prince, and it is to you that we owe it. You have correctly judged the state of affairs. I deplore the waste of time which we must try to repair. I am here without any fixed ideas, without any plan; but I bring you a firm and unalterable resolution. It is for your emperor to use it as he wills. Tell me what you desire, and what you wish me to do, and I will do it." The result was that the Quintuple Alliance was divided into two parts. On the one side were the reactionary governments of Russia, Austria and Prussia and on the other were Great Britain and France.

The Congress also passed the famous **Protocol of Troppau** which justified the intervention of one State in the internal affairs of other States. The Protocol provided : "States which have undergone a change of government due to revolution the results of which threaten other States, **ipso facto** cease to be members of the European Alliance, and remain excluded from it until their situation gives guarantee for legal order and stability. If, owing to such alterations, immediate danger threatens other States, the Powers bind themselves, by peaceful means, or if need be by arms, to bring back the guilty States into the bosom of the Great Alliance."

Great Britain, however, refused to be a party to the above declaration. Castlereagh objected to the attempt "to reduce to an abstract rule of conduct possible cases of interference in the internal affairs of independent States." His contention was that the Protocol was bound to be considered as a league of sovereigns against their subjects and there was every possibility of the revolutionary tendencies getting an impetus on account of it. To quote him, "Would the great Powers of Europe be prepared to admit the principle that their territories were to be thrown open to each other's approach upon cases of assumed necessity or expediency of which not the party receiving, but the party administering it, was to be the judge!" The British Government did not join in the police system which was bound to "lead to the creating of a species of general government in Europe, with a superintending Directory destructive of all correct notions of internal sovereign authority."

According to Kissinger, "The Congress of Troppau marks the high point of Metternich's diplomatic skill. Unwilling or unable to adapt Austria to the predominant trends of the period, confronted by the prospect of a battle against nationalism and liberalism, he succeeded in making it a European rather than an Austrian contest and thus avoided symbolizing the incongruity of Austria's domestic structure. Faced with the danger of a resurgent France restoring its Italian position by means of a family compact and an appeal to constitutionalism, he managed to isolate France and to reduce her to impotence. The role of the French representatives at Troppau could not have been more miserable. By appearing as the most conciliatory of the plenipotentiaries, Metternich lured them into one trap after another." **(A World Restored, pp. 266-267).**

Congress of Laibach (1821). The third Congress was held at Laibach. Austria was allowed to send her troops to Naples to suppress the revolt there. This was easily done by the Austrian troops. There had also occurred a revolt in Piedmont in the north of Italy. That revolt was also put down by the Austrian troops on their way back home.

Congress of Verona (1822). The fourth and last Congress was held at Verona in 1822. There were two questions before the Congress, one of which was solved. The Greeks revolted against Turkey and thus the Greek question came up for consideration before the Congress of Verona. Czar

Alexander wanted to take isolated action in the same way as Austria had done in the case of Naples and Piedmont. However, Austria was Russia's rival in the Balkans and Metternich was determined to prevent Russian intervention in Greek affairs. Metternich was also supported by Great Britain who was opposed to Russian interference in the Balkans. Under these circumstances the Greek question was not taken up by the Congress of Verona and the Spanish question alone remained before it.

There was a revolt in Spain in 1820 and the King of Spain, Ferdinand VII, was forced to abolish the Inquisition and proclaim a constitution. However, from the very beginning, he acted in a clever way and appealed to the King of France for help against his subjects. This appeal of one Bourbon to another Bourbon looked like the revival of the old Bourbon family pact and no wonder England felt uneasy. At the Congress of Verona, France announced her intention to intervene in Spain and asked for the moral support of the Powers. Austria Russia and Prussia backed France but Great Britain opposed the proposal. The Duke of Wellington, the British representative at Verona, was instructed by Canning to insist upon "a rigid abstinence from any interference in the internal affairs of Spain." The result was that when the British point of view regarding non-intervention was not accepted, Great Britain withdrew from the Congress and thus the era of Congress ended. Canning, the new Foreign Minister of England, was happy at the idea of the break-up of the Concert of Europe. He said: "The issue of Verona split the one and indivisible Alliance into three parts as distinct as the constitutions of England, France and Muscovy." Again, "Things are getting back to a wholesome state again. Every nation for itself and God for us all. The time for Aeroepagus, and the like of that is gone by."

Causes of failure. The failure of the Concert of Europe was due to many causes. The principle of intervention in the internal affairs of the States divided the Powers into two camps. Great Britain opposed this principle in 1818. But in spite of that the Protocol of Troppau was made in 1820. Again in 1822, Great Britain opposed the intervention of France in Spain and despite her protests France had her way and she did intervene in Spain. Her action was backed by Russia, Prussia and Austria. Great Britain could not put up with this attitude of the other Powers and she withdrew from the Congress of Verona. The era of Congresses collapsed with the withdrawal of Great Britain. The attitude of the British Government can be understood from the following extract from a letter written by Canning to the British Ambassador to Verona in 1823 : "England is under no obligation to interfere or to assist in interfering in the internal affairs of independent nations. The specific engagement to interfere in France is an exception so studiously particularized as to prove the rule. The rule I take to be is that our engagements have reference wholly to the state of territorial possession settled at the Peace, to the state of affairs between nation and nation; not (with the single exception above stated) to the affairs of any nation within itself." Again, "What is the influence we have had in the counsels of Alliance? We protested at Laibach, we remonstrated at Verona; our protest was treated as waste paper; our remonstrances mingled with the air. Our influence, if it is to be maintained abroad, must be secure in the sources of strength at home; and the sources of that strength are in the sympathy between the people and the government; in the union of the public sentiment with the public counsels; in the reciprocal confidence and co-operation of the House of Commons and the Crown."

Autocracy and constitutionalism cannot go together. No wonder, England with her parliamentary institutions found herself unable to pull on with the autocratic Powers of Europe. The Concert of Europe degenerated into a clique for the preservation of autocracy and the suppression of democracy and nationalism in every shape and form.

Mutual jealousies arose among the Powers from the very beginning. In the Congress of Aix-la-chapelle, the Powers disagreed on the question of slave trade and the suppression of the Barbary Pirates. They also disagreed in 1820 on the question of intervention. There was no internal harmony among the Powers. Merely an outward show of co-operation was maintained for some time. However, such a state of affairs could not last long and the matters were precipitated by the intervention of France in Spain.

It was also stated that the Concert of Europe was a product of the Napoleonic Wars and its object was to provide against a common enemy—France. However, when the French danger was over, the unity among the Allies was gone and every Power decided to deal individually with her diplomacy.

The view of Ketelbey is that the era of Congresses went to pieces on many rocks, chiefly on Britain's withdrawal and the mutual jealousies of the Great Powers. The British assertion of the principle of non-intervention was partly a return to a policy of isolation and partly a claim for national independence which was not possible to reconcile with a policy of concerted action. It was a protest against the autocracy of the Eastern Powers and a stand against the potential dictatorship of the Mediterranean system. It is doubtful whether England ever held herself committed to the idea of a common European policy. Her statesmen had not foreseen the logical implications of it as contained in the Protocol of Troppau. The Quadruple Alliance was to Castlereagh only the renewal of the Treaty of Chaumont directed against France. The concert of Europe broke up on the divergent interests of the powers, the irreconcilable differences of constitutional outlook and the absence of any agreed principles of political faith. The powers were agreed that peace must be maintained but they were not agreed on the point what threatened peace. They were ready to defend common interests, but they had none else except the fear of France. They could not decide whether it was better to submerge their individual interests in collective action or to indulge them on the basis of separate spheres of influence. The result was that the concert of Europe for the preservation of peace dwindled to a clique of the Three Gentlemen of Verona for the preservation of Autocracy and collective action was given up for the older principle of national interest and ad hoc alliance.

It was good that the Concert of Europe collapsed. Had that continued, the nationalist and liberal forces in Europe would have got a severe setback. Great Britain rendered a great service to the cause of nationalism and constitutionalism by first protesting and later leaving the Concert.

According to David Thomson, "In so far as the Congress system meant that the Great Powers of Europe could usually meet together from time to time to resolve disputes among them and to preserve a certain balance of power in the continent, it met with the partial success and help to keep the peace. At successive Congresses, such questions as the abolition of slavery, navigation of the Danube, and arbitration of disputes were considered. But in so far as it came to serve the purposes of the Holy Alliance and of at least some partners of the Quadruple Alliance, it was a disturbing force in Europe. The principle of joint intervention, generally accepted in reference to the ex-enemy State of France, became an excuse for a universal meddlesomeness that chimed with the real interests neither of Metternich nor of Britain. Each Power in turn was prompted to intervene : Austria in Piedmont and Naples, France in Spain and Greece, Britain in Portugal and Greece, Russia in Greece. Britain's alarmed by the interventions of reactionary monarchs and by the ambiguous aims of Russia in Turkey, found herself committed to the paradoxical policy of 'intervening to prevent intervention.' Even the long and tense achievement of 'holding the ring' during the Greek revolution broke down in the end, and meanwhile brought terrible losses to the Greeks. The protest of the Monroe Doctrine against the practice of intervention for or against existing regimes helped to force upon public attention this fundamental issue of international relationships. Neither the forces of conservatism nor those of nationalism and liberalism derived unmitigated benefits from it. Intervention favoured monarchs in Spain and Naples, liberal rebels in Portugal and Greece; but neither dynastic monarchy nor national independence stood to gain in the long run from accepting the doctrine that external powers might properly intervene in the internal affairs of States. It was discovered by experience that the Congress system could mean generalizing, and so magnifying every dispute; it meant altering governments everywhere whenever there was an insurrection anywhere. By making peace indivisible, it made peace more fragile for the rival interests of the major Powers were implicated in each revolutionary crisis. The 'Concert of Europe' viewed by the conservative powers as a dam against revolution, was thought of by Britain rather as a sluice gate, allowing for a measured flow of national and liberal powers." (**Europe Since Napoleon,** pp. 119-20).

According to Grant and Temperley, "It is not fair, however, to dismiss this first serious experiment in international government without pointing out some of its merits. The idea of personal conference and mutual confidence between rulers was excellent. Castlereagh was sincere in promoting the reunions, and so was Metternich, up to a point. But Alexander went too far and too fast for both. After 1820 the Congress system became in effect a trade union of kings for suppressing the liberties of peoples. To the continuance of that system, parliamentary England could not consent and parliamentary France only shared in it with reluctance. The smaller Powers, who did not share in it at all, were naturally opposed to it. In the thirties there were European Congresses again which did much good. But, though the Great Powers still took the lead, there was no collective attempt to revive the doctrines of absolutism, to condemn revolution as such, or to proclaim a general policy of intervention by force. Parliamentary England and parliamentary France were, therefore, able to enter freely into conference with the three despotic monarchies of East Europe. The Congress which settled the independence of Belgium is a good example of how Great Powers can meet without embarrassment and effect lasting good, because each respected the institutions and difficulties of the other."

Canning. A reference may be made to the following remarks of Canning : **"I have called a new world into existence to redress the balance of the old."** This was his reply to the French invasion of Spain which he could not check. England was opposed to the general principle of intervention in the internal affairs of other European States. She opposed the move of Russia, Austria and Prussia in 1818 to enforce this principle in European politics. However, in spite of the protests of England, the Protocol of Troppau was adopted in 1820. By this, the European States were allowed to interfere in the internal affairs of their neighbours if there was a revolt in them and that revolt threatened their own security. It was in pursuance of that policy that Austria intervened in Naples and Piedmont in 1821. At the Congress of Verona in 1822, Great Britain opposed the intervention of any country in Spain, but the French troops entered Spain and restored its king to absolute powers. It was evident that England had failed so far as intervention in Spain was concerned. When this happened, Canning made it clear that he would not allow the reconquest of the Spanish colonies in South America, and thereby make up the balance in America for the loss in Europe.

The policy of Canning to create a new world to redress the balance of the old was not the result of any sudden inspiration. It was a deliberate policy which was long contemplated and tenaciously followed. In 1790, Pitt had told Miranda that the emancipation of Spanish America was a matter which would engage the attention of every Minister of England. In 1808, the separation of the Spanish colonies in South America under British protection was an idea present to the minds of both Canning and Castlereagh. This very thought engaged the attention of Canning from his first day at the Foreign Office until it was accomplished. In 1822, Canning wrote thus to Duke of Wellington who represented Great Britain in the Congress of Verona: "Every day convinces me more and more that in the present state of the Peninsula, and in the present state of this country, the American questions are out of all proportion more important to us than the European ones and that, if we do not seize and turn them to our advantage in time, we shall rue the loss of an opportunity never to be recovered."

It cannot be denied that Spain had found great difficulty in governing her American colonies. In 1817, Spain sold to the U.S.A. the territory of Florida for 5 million dollars. Things did not improve even after that. These was anarchy in South America and consequently Englishmen suffered a great deal on account of attacks on their ships. England failed to get any compensation for these. In 1823, Canning appointed Consuls to the Spanish colonies for the protection of British trade. The British Government made it clear to France that she would not allow the reconquest of the Spanish colonies by a Power other than Spain, and she knew that Spain alone could not reconquer them. On the 1 January 1825, the Powers were informed that Great Britain had recognised the independence of Buenos Aires, Colombia and Mexico. The Powers protested against this action of Great Britain but they could do practically nothing. Canning continued his policy in spite of the annoyance of the Great Powers of Europe.

Canning found a powerful ally in the U.S.A. In December 1823, President Monroe enunciated his famous Monroe Doctrine. He declared that "any interference on the part of the Great Powers of Europe for the purpose of oppressing or controlling the destiny of the Spanish American States which had declared their independence would be dangerous to the peace and safety of the United States, and would be considered as the manifestation of the unfriendly disposition towards them." Canning wrote thus in 1824 : "I have very little doubt that the President was encouraged to make his declaration about the South American States by his knowledge of our sentiments. The effect of the ultra-liberalism of our Yankee co-operators on the ultra-despotism of our Aix-la-Chapelle laws gives us just the balance that I wanted." Again, he wrote thus next year: "The thing is done....An act which will make a change in the face of the world almost as great as of the discovery of the Continent now set free. The Allies will fret; but they will venture no serious remonstrance. France will forget; but it will be with a view to hastening after our example as regards South America." The action of Great Britain and United States was decisive. By 1830, the Spanish empire in South America had ceased to exist and consequently the following independent republics came into existence: Mexico, Guatemala, Colombia, Peru, Chile, Bolivia, Paraguay and Rio de la Plata or Buenos Aires.

It is evident from the above that while Canning failed in Europe, he succeeded in America. He could not stop the intervention of France in Spain, but he was able to stop the intervention of Spain or any other Power in Spanish America and thereby establish the independence of the Spanish colonies in America. Canning was right in saying that he had brought a new world into existence in South America and thereby redressed the balance which had been upset on account of the combination of Austria, Russia, Prussia and France.

SUGGESTED READINGS

Fyffe: **History of Modern Europe.**

Phillips, W.A.: **The Confederation of Europe: A Study of the European Alliance (1813-23), 1920.**

Phillips: **Modern Europe.**

Schenk, H.G.: **The Aftermath of the Napoleonic Wars: the Concert of Europe—an Experiment, 1947.**

Seignobos: **Political History of Europe Since 1814.**

Thomson, David: **Europe Since Napoleon.**

Kissinger, H.A.: **A World Restored.**

Ward, Sir A.W.: **The Period of the Congresses 1919.**

CHAPTER

13 LOUIS XVIII TO NAPOLEON III

Louis XVIII (1814-24). After the abdication of Napoleon in 1814 and his departure for the Island of Elba, Louis XVIII was put on the throne of France. He was the brother of Louis XVI. At the time of his succession to the throne, he was 59. He was corpulent and gouty and was unable to sit on horse-back. Both intellectually and by character, he was well qualified to be a king. He had a lot of commonsense and realised the fact from the very beginning that it was impossible to put the hands of the clock back. Like Charles II of England he was not prepared to go on his travels again and he stood for a policy of compromise and reconciliation. He wrote in 1818: "The system which I have adopted and that which my ministers are perseveringly pursuing, is based upon the maxim that it will never do to be the King of two peoples; and to their ultimate fusion—for their distinction is only too real—all the efforts of my government are directed."

The Charter of 1814. On 4 June 1814, Louis XVIII issued a liberal charter. That was partly due to the influence of Czar Alexander I. This Charter embodied the constitution of France up to 1848. Its Preamble ran : "It is our duty according to the example of the kings, our predecessors, to appreciate the results of the constantly increasing progress of enlightenment, the new relations that this progress has introduced into society, the direction impressed upon opinion for half a century, and the important alterations which have ensued; we have recognised that the wish of our subjects for a constitutional Charter was the expression of a real need, but in yielding to this wish we have taken every precaution that this Charter should be worthy of us and of the people whom we have to rule."

The king was to be head of the State and he was given the power of making all appointments, issuing ordinances, declaring war, making treaties of peace, alliance and commerce, commanding the army and navy and initiating and sanctioning laws. Provision was made for a legislature of two houses, viz., a Chamber of Peers and a Chamber of Deputies. The Chamber of Peers was to have a number of members who were to be nominated by the king either for life or as hereditary members. It was to sit in secret and also act as a High Court of Justice. It was to try impeachments of the ministers. The Chamber of Deputies was to be elected by those persons who paid 300 francs annually as direct taxes. Its tenure was five years and one-fifth of its members were to retire every year. It was to meet once a year. It could request the king to introduce legislation on a particular subject.

The Roman Catholic Church was established but religious freedom was given to others also. Both the nobility of Napoleon and that of the **Ancien Regime** were restored on an equal footing. Liberty of the press was guaranteed. Provision was made for trial by jury. Every citizen of France was entitled to have employment under the State. Persons in possession of confiscated property were assured that it would not be taken away from them.

The importance of the Charter lies in the fact that it accepted the work of the French Revolution and the Napoleonic regime. This is clear from the recognition of personal equality; eligibility for office, religious toleration, the Code Napoleon, the Concordat, etc. The Charter was also not inconsistent with the principle of Divine Right of Kings. It was not imposed by the people on the king. On the other hand, it was given by the king to the people as a matter of grace. According to Chateaubriand, "The Charter is a treaty of peace between the two parties into which France has been divided, a treaty by which both parties yield some of their pretensions in order to work together for the glory of their country."

Talleyrand. Talleyrand was one of the cleverest men produced by France. He acted in various capacities throughout the French Revolution, under Napoleon and after the Restoration. He played many roles in life. He belonged to the nobility. He was a member of the church. He was employed by Napoleon in very many difficult tasks. He was clever and cunning. He knew how to play the fox and change sides as circumstances of demanded. Napoleon consulted him on all difficult matters. In spite of that, Talleyrand deserted him towards the end and joined hands with the Austrians. It was through his cleverness that he played an important part in the deliberations of the Congress of Vienna. He coined the doctrine of legitimacy and thereby saved his country. Although France was defeated, it was through his influence that she was not deprived of her territories.

Talleyrand was not an attractive personality. Napoleon once described him as "a mass of filth in a silk stocking." Again, "You are a devil of a man. I cannot help telling you of my affairs or prevent myself liking you."

Parties. There were two parties in France and those were the Moderates who were the upholders of the Charter of 1814 and the Ultra-Royalists. The Ultra-Royalists stood for absolutism and privileges. They wanted an alliance between the altar and the throne. They wanted the church to control education. They stood for censorship of the press and the restoration of the confiscated property of the nobles. Louis XVIII followed a policy of moderation and consequently did not pay any heed to the demands of the Ultra Royalists. He also failed to win over the peasants and the army. According to Wellington, "A king of France is no king without the army." The result of the alienation of the peasantry and the army was that when Napoleon returned from Elba, he was joined by the army and the people. However, Louis XVIII was restored after the Hundred Days.

White Terror. As soon as the news of the defeat of Napoleon in the Battle of Waterloo reached France, the Ultra-Royalists created a reign of terror in the country. The Royalist mobs attacked the Bonapartists. The Protestants were attacked by the Catholics. There were outrages and murders everywhere, and the movement was called by the name of "The White Terror" It was in this atmosphere of intimidation and violence that elections were held and no wonder the Royalists were able to sweep the polls. Talleyrand and Fouche were dismissed. Richelieu was made the head of the new ministry and his chief lieutenant was Decazes. The newly-elected Chamber of Deputies showed itself "more royalist than the king," and came to be known as the **Chambre Introuvable** (1815-16). Although the king, his ministers and the Chamber of Peers stood for a policy of moderation, the Chamber of Deputies under the leadership of the Count of Artois, the brother of Louis XVIII, who became king of France in 1824, demanded revenge against the enemies. Marshal Ney, "the bravest of the brave," was shot as a traitor. Thousands of Bonapartists were either imprisoned or exiled. Some of them were executed and many of them were dismissed from their posts. In September 1816, the **Chambre Introuvable** was dissolved.

Moderates in Power. New elections were held in 1816 and the Moderates were returned in a majority in the Chamber of Deputies. They remained in power up to 1820. In 1818, the Congress of Aix-la-Chapelle decided to withdraw the Allied Army of Occupation from the French soil as France had paid the whole of war indemnity. In 1817, a new electoral law in favour of the Moderates was passed. In 1819, a new press law was passed by which censorship was abolished and press offences were allowed to be tried by the juries.

In February 1820, the Duc de Berri was assassinated by a fanatic named Louvel. The duke was the son of the Count of Artois and was considered to be the hope of the Bourbons. Although the murder was the work of an isolated fanatic, the Ultra-Royalists attributed it to the policy of moderation of the king. Different motives were attributed to the murder. According to one, "I saw the dagger that pierced the Duc de Berri; it was a liberal idea." According to another, "Either Decazes must retired before the reigning dynasty or the race of our king must retreat before him." Decazes himself remarked: "We have been killed with the duke." Decazes was dismissed and the Ultra-Royalists came to power.

Richelieu was once again made the head of the ministry in 1820 and he continued up to 1821. The era of reaction started during his regime. The censorship of the press was restored. The electoral law was changed. The secret ballot was abolished, franchise was narrowed. Double vote was given to the landed interests.

Richelieu was succeeded by Villele who was an able and cautious statesman but a pronounced reactionary. He held office up to 1827. In 1822, the censorship of the press was made more rigorous. The church was given control over education for religious and monarchical propaganda. High tariffs were imposed on imports to favour the landed proprietors and manufacturers. In 1823, French troops were sent to Spain to restore the Bourbons to absolute power. New peers were created to overthrow the liberal majority in the Chamber of Peers. By means of the Septennial Act, the life of the Chamber of Deputies was extended to seven years instead of five.

About Louis XVIII, Grant and Temperley observe that although he consented to give a charter to the people of France, he tried to retain as much power as he could. He was wiser than his ministers but incurably indolent. Hence, the policy of the Clerical and Absolutist ministers (usually called the Ultras) tended to prevail. He showed unwisdom in all directions. They cut down the army. They gagged or bribed or intimidated the press. They committed all sorts of mistakes. They abolished the tricolour. The worst of all they shot Marshal Ney after the defeat of Napoleon at Waterloo. The people were indignant that a man who was a heroic soldier and not a politician, should have been condemned by dubious methods and shot under circumstances of peculiar atrocity. It was openly said with some truth that he was executed at the dictation of the Allies. Some have said that the bourbons owed their fall to the execution of "the bravest of the brave."

Charles X (1824-30). After the death of Louis XVIII in 1824, Charles X became the King of France. At the Court of Artois, he had acted as the leader of the Emigres. During the reign of Louis XVIII, he was the leader of the Ultra-Royalists. He was a man of prejudices and convictions. It was said about him that he "had learnt nothing and forgotten nothing." He took pride in the fact that both he and Lafayette had not changed at all in spite of the change of times. He stood for the supremacy of the church and was prepared to sacrifice even his throne for the sake of the church. According to Wellington, he set up "a government by priests through priests and for priests." He has rightly been compared with Philip II of Spain.

France gained some prestige by a vigorous foreign policy, Algiers was conquered and France joined hands with the British who helped the Greeks against the Turks. When the Turkish fleet was destroyed in the Battle of Navarino in 1827, the French fleet also took part in it. Although France withdrew from the Greek War of Independence, she cooperated with England to lessen the influence of Russia in the Balkans.

Villele. Villele continued to be the head of ministry up to 1827. As the press was opposed to the church policy of the king, it was decided to make the press a creature of the executive. No newspaper was to appear without the sanction of the king. The contents of the newspapers were to be censured by the government. The writer of any article or the designer of any illustration which outraged or turned into ridicule the religion of the State or which excited contempt or hatred of any class was to be punished with a heavy fine of imprisonment for seven years. An attempt was made in 1827 to pass a new law by which the liberty of the press was to be completely ended. Although there was opposition from all quarters, the Chamber of Deputies passed the law but the Government was forced to rescind it on account of the opposition from the Chamber of Peers.

In 1825, a law was passed to indemnify the Emigres for the loss of their lands during the days of the French Revolution. This was done by lowering the rate of interest on the public debt 5 per cent to 4 per cent. It must have annoyed the middle classes because they suffered on account of the lowering of the interest. Religious communities for women were re-established under certain restrictions. An attempt was made to revive the law of primogeniture, but it failed due to the opposition of the Chamber of Peers. A law of sacrilege was proposed which would have punished by death theft of sacred vessels from a church. Those who were guilty of the offence of desecration of the Host were also liable to get their hands cut off. The law was passed with certain amendments, but was never enforced on account of opposition.

In 1827, the National Guard was disbanded. That was due to the fact that while returning from a review held by the king, the members of the National Guard shouted the slogans of "Down with the Ministers" and "Down with the Jesuits." The people of Paris were offended by the disbandment of National Guard and its result was fatal.

Martignac. Villele was succeeded by Martignac who remained in power from January 1828 to July 1829. He was a man of ability, moderation, and experience and he followed a policy of compromise. The Jesuits were deprived of their control over education. The censorship of the press was stopped. Franchise was extended in the provincial assemblies. A large measure of local self-government was proposed. The reactionaries were furious and Martignac resigned.

Polignac. The view of Charles X was that **"concessions ruined Louis XVI"** and therefore he decided not to give any concession. To quote him, "There is no way of dealing with these people: it is time to call a halt." Prince Polignac, a fanatical reactionary and an Emigre, was made the head of the ministry. He did not possess any majority in the Chamber of Deputies. There was a lot of criticism of the government all over the country. However, Charles X addressed the Chamber of Deputies in March 1830 in these words: "The Charter has placed the liberties of France under the guarantee of the rights of the Crown. These rights are sacred and it is my duty to hand them over intact to my successor. I do not doubt that you will help me to realize my good intention; that you will repel shameful insinuations which malevolence has sought to spread abroad. Should conspiracies admit to impede my government, such as I do not wish to anticipate, I will find the means to remove the obstacles, firm in my own determination to maintain the public peace, in just confidence in the people of France, and in their avowed love for their King." This speech of the king was considered to be a challenge to the people. Men like Thiers came forward to resist the reactionary politics of the king. The Polignac ministry was defeated. To begin with, the king prorogued the Chamber of Deputies and later on dissolved it. New elections were held in June and July 1830, but their only result was that the opposition was strengthened.

On 25 July 1830, Charles X issued four ordinances and attached to them the following explanation. "A turbulent democracy is endeavouring to supplant the legal authorities. It dominates the elections by means of newspapers and associations; it endeavours to fetter the rights of the Crown and to dissolve the Chamber. A government that has not the right to take measures for the safety of the State cannot exist. That right, older than the laws, exists in the nature of things. An imperative necessity demands its application; the moment has come to take measures which, if they overstep the ordinary methods of legislation, are undoubtedly in accord with the Charter." By means of four ordinances, Charles X suspended the freedom of the press, dissolved the newly-elected Chamber of Deputies, reduced the life of the legislature from seven years to five years and ordered new elections under a restricted franchise.

The ordinances were a challenge to the people and it was accepted by them. Barricades were constructed in the streets but they were demolished by the government. However, the National Guard and the regular troops joined the people who became the masters of Paris on 29 July 1830. Thiers,

Guizot and Talleyrand offered the throne to Louis Philippe, Duke of Orleans and the offer was accepted by him. Charles X abdicated in favour of his grandson, Henry, Duke of Bordeaux, better known as Count of Chambord. However, nobody bothered about him and consequently Charles X and his family left for England. It was in these circumstances that the July Revolution took place in France in 1830.

Importance of July Revolution. The July Revolution of 1830 was of great importance in the history of France. It brought about a change in the ruling dynasty. The Bourbons were replaced by the Orleanists. The monarchical system was continued in spite of the protests of the Republicans. Minor changes were made in the constitution of France which were embodied in the Charter of 1814. The king was deprived of his power of making ordinances in times of emergency or otherwise. The Chambers were given the power to initiate laws. Catholicism was to be the official religion of France. The freedom of the press was restored. The franchise was extended. It was on the basis of one out of 280 although promise was given for universal suffrage. The Charter was "accepted" but not "granted." The king was to rule by the will of the people and not by Divine Right. He was to be known as the "King of the French." The principle of legitimacy which had played an important part in 1815 was rejected and that is why the Bourbons were replaced by the Orleanists. The Ultra-Royalist party, with its programme, disappeared with the Bourbons from the French scene. The revolution of 1830 was the complement of the Revolution of 1789. It granted equality, liberty, secularisation of property, etc. The Charter of 1814 became the right of the nation and not the free gift of the king who was forced to do so. Those tax-payers who could pay for their uniforms were to form the National Guard which was to maintain the Charter.

The view of Grant and Temperley is that the July Revolution was largely due to Lafayette and Talleyrand. Their plan was a constitutional monarchy of the British type with Louis Philippe as a good solid bourgeois and constitutional king. With comparatively little difficulty, the public was persuaded to try the experiment. The choice of Louis Philippe was not a bad one and the event impressed Europe a good deal. The Revolution in France was bloodless and it set up a solid constitutional monarchy. It seemed to hail the approach of the millennium when all nations would have their parliaments and carry the Magna Carta written on their hearts.

Louis Philippe (1830-48). Louis Philippe was the son of the "Egalite" Orleans who played not a mean part in the Revolution of 1789. As a young man, he fought with the forces of the French Republic at Valmy. After that, he ran away from France and visited various parts of the world including Southern Europe, Sicily, the United States, England and Switzerland. He worked as a tutor in Switzerland. After the Restoration of 1814-15, he came back to France and recovered the family estates and entered the Chamber of Peers. He associated himself with the middle classes and the workers of Paris. Although he was prosperous yet he was genial and accessible. The result was that the people came to believe in his professions of democratic and republican principles. During the crisis of July 1830, Charles X began to realise slowly that the crisis "was not a revolt but a revolution." He then withdrew the ordinances and dismissed Polignac, but the concession came too late and Louis Philippe was put on the throne of France.

Louis Philippe ruled for 18 years and the middle class remained supreme during his regime. He was called the "citizen" king. He was to "reign but not to rule." He gave up the symbols of the ancient monarchy. The crown and the sceptre were set aside. He began to use a white and hat and green umbrella. He sent his children to the ordinary schools and went to the streets to do the shopping himself. He gave up the side of "King of France and Navarre" and took up the title of "King of the French." The qualifying phrase "by the grace of God" was supplemented with the words "and by the will of the nation." The tricolour was restored as the national flag. Titled aristocrats were removed from public offices and their places were taken by commoners. The government was proclaimed parliamentary and representative.

According to De Tocqueville, "He (Louis Philippe) had most of the qualities and defects which belong more particularly to the subaltern orders of society. He had regular habits and wanted those around him to have them too. He was orderly in his conduct, simple in his habits, his tastes were tempered; he was a born friend of the law, an enemy of all excesses, sober in his ways except in his desires. He was human without being sentimental, greedy and soft. He had no flaming passions, no ruinous weakness, no striking vices, and only one kingly virtue : courage. He was extremely polite, but without discrimination or greatness, the politeness of a merchant rather than of a prince. He hardly appreciated literature or art, but he passionately loved industry. His memory was prodigious and capable of retaining the most minute detail. His conversation was prolific, diffuse, original and trivial, anecdotal, full of small facts, of salt and significance....He was enlightened, subtle, flexible: because he was open only to what was useful, he was full of proud disdain for the truth, and he believed so little in virtue that his sight was darkened....He was an unbeliever in religion like the eighteenth century, and sceptical in politics like the nineteenth; having no belief in himself, he had none in the belief of others."

The view of Grant and Temperley is that Louis Philippe was a shrewd man though not very much scrupulous. He was fully conscious of the fact that he was merely a constitutional king. He was tolerant in religious matters although his predecessors were not. Ha did not believe in the divine right of kings. He sent his sons to the ordinary schools. He walked about the streets with an umbrella under his arm. He was anxious to represent himself as the heir of all the historic tendencies of France. As a Bourbon, he claimed to embody the historic past. As the son of Egalite and the soldier of Jemmappes, he claimed to have shared in the glories of the Revolution. He restored the tricolour and the National Guard. He did not refuse to recognise Napoleon and it was during his reign that the body of Napoleon was brought from St. Helena by a son of the Royal house and laid in the most magnificent of resting places at the Invalides.

In the beginning of the regime of Louis Philippe, the industrial capitalists and economic liberals like Laffitte and Casimir-Perier were in power and no wonder that his government was liberal and bourgeois. The French Government was similar to the government established in England after the First Reform Act of 1832. **Casimir-Perier** defined his policy as that of the just mean. He followed a policy of evolution. He aimed at the development of the foreign trade of the country and the establishment of friendly relations with other States. After his death, Guizot and Thiers held office at different times. Both of them belonged to the middle class and were ambitious, aggressive and were great writers. Guizot was a Huguenot and was the Minister of Public Instruction from 1832 to 1839 and Chief Minister from 1840 to 1848. He believed in a policy of peace at any price. He was prepared to go to any length to maintain peace. He was corrupt to the extreme and it was through his corrupt methods that he was able to manage the legislature for eight years. Thiers was a free thinker and an opportunist. He got a lot of money by marriage and was trained in politics by Talleyrand. Although he had risen from the masses, he distrusted them. He was, however, attached to the liberal philosophy of the 18th century and opposed the arbitrary rule of Louis Philippe. He was a great writer and was one of the persons responsible for the overthrow of Charles X. He believed in a vigorous foreign policy and was the leading minister from 1832 to 1836 and Prime Minister in 1840. He was dismissed in that year because he insisted on helping Mehmet Ali even at the risk of a war with England.

The regime of Louis Philippe was bourgeois in action, in purpose and in personnel. Industries were encouraged. Machinery was imported from England and factories were set up in France. A large number of railways were planned and some of them were actually constructed. Private companies were encouraged to execute works of public utility. He did not do anything which could be called "socialistic." He stood for private initiative and individual thrift. Like a good middle-class person, the king invested the income of his family in stocks and shares.

Agitation was carried on for the establishment of free trade in the country. However, it was realised that the infant industries of France were not in a position to compete with British industries and consequently the policy of protection was continued. No legislation similar to that of the repeal of the Corn Laws in England was enacted in France. However, Bastiat, a merchant and economist, organised a Free Trade Association in France in 1846.

As a result of the growth of Industrial Revolution in the country the condition of the workers became very unsatisfactory but, with one minor exception, no labour legislation was enacted. In 1841 was passed a Factory Act which prohibited the employment of children under eight years of age, limited the working days of children under 16 years to 12 hours and prescribed a minimum of schooling for children under 12. This Act had practically no effect as no provision was made for its enforcement.

Under the guidance of Guizot, a law was passed in 1833, concerning education. The Church was left free to conduct elementary schools. However, the control of the government over secondary and higher schools was strengthened. All educational institutions were required to teach "internal and social duties." Although the number of schools was increased, attendance was not made compulsory.

In matters of religion, the government tried to follow a policy of neutrality. The Concordat with the Pope was continued and the government continued to nominate the bishops and pay the salaries of the Catholic clergy. The Government treated all religions alike and in 1831 it put Judaism on an equal footing with Christianity. It began to pay the salaries of the Jewish rabbis in the same way as it paid the Protestant pastors and Catholic priests.

This reign was the great age of Romanticism in France. In 1830, Victor Hugo's play **Hernani** was first produced. Chateaubriand and Mme de Stael led the way for the new movement which Lamartime, Victor Hugo, Alfred de Vigny, and Alfred de Musset revealed in verse and Balzac, George Sand and Dumas revealed in romance proper. There was a struggle between classical and romantic art and we have the natural and colourful painting of Gericault and Delacroix. The "School of 1830", was the great school of paysagistes led by Corot, Dupre and Theodore Rousseau. In sculpture, the reign saw the greatest work of Rude, notably that of the Arc de l' Etoile, one of the greatest achievements of French sculpture. It was also the great age of French historical writing which owed a lot to the inspiration from Chateaubriand. Best examples of historical writings are those of Thierry, Michelet, Guizot Mignet and Thiers. Thus, this reign saw the appearance of a large number of masterpieces of French literature and art.

The Revolutionary Tradition. The first five years of the reign of Louis Philippe were marked by revolts, strikes and demonstrations. These were largely due to the feeling among the Republicans that they had been cheated in 1830. At Lyons, wages were very low and there had been experiments in collective bargaining with the employers for minimum wage scales. In November 1831, the silk workers at Lyons broke out into open insurrection and the immediate cause for it was that 104 out of 1,400 manufacturers in the area refused to observe the agreements with their workers and threatened to close down. The Government was afraid that the revolt may not spread and consequently had stepped in and not only crushed the rising but also declared collective bargaining illegal. The result was that the working class lost faith in the Government and began to look to the secret Republican societies for help. There were a large number of such societies and they ranged from fairly open associations like the Society of the Rights of Man to the traditional type of conspiracy such as the "Families" or the "Seasons." Even the Rights of Man aimed at a Republic in which economic inequalities would be less. The societies influenced by Philippe Buonarroti or Auguste Blanqui were more frankly and thoroughly socialistic or communistic in their aims.

Auguste Blanqui was one of the most outstanding of the professional revolutionaries who haunted Paris under the July Monarchy. He inherited the role and many of the ideas of Buonarroti who died in 1837. Blanqui was the son of a Napoleonic official and was born in 1805. He joined the Carbonari as a student. He was awarded a medal by the new Government for his part in the rising of 1830. He spent nearly half of his long life in 15 different prisons and much of that time was spent in solitary confinement. In April 1834, the Government passed a law restricting the right of association. There were protests against the new law and there was bitter fighting for 6 days. Another rising was planned by the Society of the Rights of Man in the eastern districts of Paris. The rising was suppressed by Adolphe Thiers. Thiers was hated by the Republicans for what came to be known as the "massacre of the Rue Transnonian." Blanqui set up a new secret society which was powerful enough to secure political ends but secret enough to evade police espionage. The result was the Society of Families which was modelled on the principles of the Carbonari. Its immediate object was military action. A unit of 6 members was called a family. Five or six families under one chief, constituted a Section. Two or three Sections made up a Quarter. It was so organised that its leaders would remain unknown until the moment came for action and orders were issued by a Central Committee of unknown membership. By 1836, it numbered some 1,200 people. It had infiltrated into regiments of the garrison for Paris. It owned dumps of arms and a factory for making gunpowder. It had to be dissolved to avoid the police. Immediately another organisation called the Society of the Seasons was set up. Each group of six of this society was known as a week and was commanded by Sunday. Four weeks formed a month under the orders of July. Three months formed a season and were led by Spring. Four seasons formed a year and were directed by a special agent of the Central Committee. This society was led by Blanqui, Martin Bernard and Armand Barbes. The spring of 1839 was fixed for the rising. The Society published secret newspapers and organised working class support in Paris, Lyons and Carcassonne. On account of economic distress, the membership of the society increased. On Sunday mornings, its members marched in formation but were not observed by the police because they mingled skilfully with the Sunday crowds. However, they were "reviewed" by Blanqui from some secluded spot. On 12 May 1839, they were summoned to action stations. It was hoped that the police would be busy in controlling the crowds at the races at the Champs de Mars. The forces of the conspirators concentrated themselves around the gunsmiths' shops and stores in the Paris districts of Saint Denis and Saint Martin. The stores were raided and barricades were thrown up. The Palais de Justice and the Hotel de Ville were occupied and the republic was proclaimed. The mob shouted the Marseillaise. A few soldiers were killed. The National and Municipal Guards were called out. The military garrisons stood to arms. The insurgents were driven back behind the barricades in the working class districts. By nightfall, they were completely routed and most of their leaders were captured. Blanqui himself was caught after 5 months of living in cellars, attics and sewers and was sent to prison for the next eight and a half years. It was the revolution of 1848 that made him free again. The conspirators failed because they had relied upon the readiness of the mass of the people of Paris to support them once the revolt was started. This discredited the men and methods of the secret societies. The result was that the Government became free from the standing threat of insurrections. This does not mean that the revolutionaries did nothing in their prisons. That was due to the fact that all kinds of people were put in jails and prison life became one of the main breeding grounds for republican propaganda and socialist ideas. However, as the working classes were without leaders working with them for long periods, there was no touch between them and their leaders.

Foreign Policy. On the whole, Louis Philippe followed a policy of peace in foreign affairs, although he could not ignore altogether the French desire for La Glorie. He was on very good terms with Queen Victoria, although that was not true of Palmerston. Efforts were made to follow a policy which was in harmony with that of England. Although he desired to have a hand in the affairs of Belgium when the latter revolted against Holland, he later on agreed to follow in the footsteps of England in allowing the people of Belgium to have their independence and their own king. He helped the new State of Greece to find a liberal monarch. He was not prepared to allow Russia to increase her influence in the Balkans.

There stood for a vigorous foreign policy independent of England. In 1836, he was in favour of sending a French army to Spain to suppress an insurrection against Queen Isabella II but he was dismissed from office by the king. In 1840, there was a possibility of war between England and France. That was due to the fact that Thiers, who was the Prime Minister at that time, was determined to help Mehmet Ali, the Pasha of Egypt. Palmerston, the Foreign Minister of England, was determined to crush the growing power of Mehmet Ali and help Turkey against him. Great Britain was supported by Russia and Austria. If Louis Philippe had allowed Thiers to have his way, a war with England was a certainty. At that time, Thiers was dismissed and thus the war was avoided. Guizot was appointed in his place as the Prime Minister and he also believed in a policy of peace. The result was that Mehmet Ali had to surrender Adana and Syria and he was accepted as the "hereditary governor" of Egypt.

In the time of Charles X, the city of Algiers had been occupied by the French troops and its Dey or the ruler was exiled. For many years, Louis Philippe could not make up his mind as to the policy to be followed by him with regard to Algeria. There were three alternatives before the government, viz., to conquer the whole country, occupy only a part of the country or to evacuate the country altogether. The Liberals were in favour of complete withdrawal. Between 1834 and 1939, the French Government continued its occupation of Algiers and a few coastal towns. However, the king gradually allowed penetration into the interior of the country. The things changed in 1839 when Abd-el-Kader declared a Jehad or Holy War against the French. The king was forced to send General Bugeaud with an army of one lakh of men to crush Abd-el-Kader and conquer the whole of Algeria. The struggle was a long one and involved a lot of destruction. However in 1847, Abd-el-Kader was captured and Algeria was pacified. About 40,000 French colonists settled in the country. This was the beginning of the French colonial empire.

Louis Philippe was very keen to further the interests of his family. One of his daughters was married to King Leopold I of Belgium and another to the King of Wurtemberg. In 1846, he married one of his sons to the sisters of Queen Isabella II of Spain.

Towards Revolution. By 1846, however, the middle-class monarchy of Louis Philippe became very unpopular with all sections of the people. The Legitimists regarded Louis Philippe as a usurper because in their eyes, the Count of Chambord, the grandson of Charles X, had a better title to the throne than he himself had. They also considered his government as revolutionary and bourgeois. The **Republicans** aimed at the overthrow of the monarchy and the establishment of a republican government in the country. They stood for universal manhood suffrage and were completely dissatisfied with the bourgeois monarchy of Louis Philippe.

The **Socialists** also condemned the bourgeois government of Louis Philippe. The lot of the working men was unsatisfactory and the government had done practically nothing to improve it. As a matter of fact, it had used force to crush meetings of workers and passed laws to stop the formation of their organizations. The important French socialists were Saint-Simon, Fourier, Cabet, Louis Blanc and Proudhon. Saint-Simon stood for a co-operative State directed by scientists and engineers. His disciples established a socialist humanitarian cult near Paris and were a source of nuisance to the government during the 1830s. Fourier was in favour of the establishment of co-operative communities called Phalanxes. He had some following in France during the 1830s and 1840s. Louis Blanc was a popular agitator who demanded that the State must guarantee a living wage to all workers. To quote him, "To the able-bodied citizens the State owes work; to the aged and infirm it owes aid and protection. This result cannot be obtained except through a democratic power. A democratic power is that which has the sovereignty of the people for its principle, universal suffrage for its origin and for its goal the realization of the formula : Liberty, Equality, Fraternity." Proudhon was a radical revolutionary. He stood for the destruction of private property and authoritarian government and the establishment of a new order on the basis of voluntary co-operation. The followers of Proudhon were small in number but they were determined to destroy rather than to construct anything. The socialist propaganda did a lot to add to the discontentment of the people.

The **Catholics** of France were not happy with the corrupt politics of Guizot who was a Huguenos. They also did not approve of the liberal policy of the government in matters of religion. They condemned the undemocratic nature of July monarchy and demanded legislation in the interests of the working class. The **Patriots** condemned the submissive foreign policy of Louis Philippe. They were not prepared to subordinate their foreign policy to that of England. They stood for national honour and national glory. They condemned the king for dismissing Thiers who stood for the honour of the country. Thiers became the leader of the Patriots against the Guizot administration.

The Patriots were helped by the growth of the **Napoleonic Legend** during the regime of Louis Philippe. While the shortcomings of Napoleon were forgotten, his achievements were glorified. He was considered to be the personification of national glory. He was regarded as a hero and regenerator of society. Louis Philippe completed the Napoleonic Arch of Triumph which commemorated the achievements of Napoleon Bonaparte. He allowed streets to be named after the battles of Napoleon. He persuaded the British Government to allow the dead body of Napoleon to be brought from St. Helena to Paris where it was buried with great ceremony. The Napoleonic Legend also gained in popularity on account of the writings of Louis Napoleon who was the nephew of Napoleon Bonaparte. The result of the Napoleonic legend was that the government of Louis Philippe became all the more unpopular with the people who compared his achievements with those of Napoleon Bonaparte and found practically nothing.

The **Reformers** also condemned the government of Louis Philippe. That was because in spite of their moderate demands for reforms like the broadening of franchise and the eradication of corruption, Guizot and Luois Philippe refused to move in the matter and continued to follow a policy of "do nothing." They depended upon the use of the police, censorship of the press, and the banning of meetings.

In 1847, the liberal reformers began to arrange banquets in which questions of reforms were discussed and efforts were made to mobilize the public opinion. On some occasions, glasses were raised "to the amelioration of the lot of the working classes." On one occasion, Lamartine predicted the fall of monarchy. The Reformers fixed "a monster banquet" for 22 February 1848, but the government banned the same and that precipitated matters. On the appointed day, workers and students assembled and shouted for reforms. The Marseillaise was sung and bonfires were lighted in the streets. On 23 February 1848, the National Guards were ordered to restore order, but instead of doing so they joined the people. The people shouted "Down with Guizot" and the king asked Guizot to resign. The affairs might not have taken a serious turn had not a detachment of soldiers guarding the residence of Guizot fired on the demonstrators and 23 of them were killed and 30 were injured. The demonstrators put the dead bodies on a wagon and displayed the same to the people of Paris in the glaring torch-lights. The result was a revolution. Barricades were put up in the streets of Paris and placards with the following contents were fixed up in all parts of the city, **"Louis Philippe massacres us as did Charles X, let him go to join Charles X."** Louis Philippe tried to handle the situation but failed. Ultimately he abdicated in favour of his grandson, the Count of Paris, and left for England as Mr. Smith.

The manner in which the Revolution of 1848 took place has been described thus : "I had not yet completed my fourth year when one morning my mother took me out of bed, and my dear Father, who had put on his National Guards' uniform, embraced me tenderly. He had on his shako, with a golden cock and a red tuft. The call to arms sounded from the street and the gallop of horses echoed from the pavement. Now and then we heard the sound of shouting, and, in the distance, of the crackle of musketry. My father went out. My mother went to the window, lifted the muslin curtains, and burst into tears. It was the revolution." (**Anatole France, Le Petit Pierre**).

Louis Philippe fell because he failed to win over all the sections of the country. He merely depended upon the support of the middle class which was very small in number and which had no moral or historical right to control the government which was hated by the aristocracy and the masses. If Louis Philippe had made reforms in the social and political fields, there is every reason to believe that he would have been able to win over the support of the people, but he did not do so. He could have appealed to the patriotism of the French people by following a vigorous foreign policy, but even that was not done by him. The result was the fall of the July monarchy.

COMPARISON OF REVOLUTION OF 1830 AND 1848

The Revolution of 1830 was essentially a middle-class revolution. The bourgeoisie were hit hard by the policy of Charles X and it is they who brought about the July Revolution. In 1825, an indemnification bill was passed by means of which the Emigres, whose lands had been confiscated during the French Revolution, were to be given as compensation. Unfortunately, the compensation was given at the cost of the middle-class by lowering the rate of interest on the national debt from 5 per cent to 4 per cent. The people also resented the Sacrilege law that prescribed barbarous punishments in modern times. The character of Charles X also alienated the middle-class. He was a staunch Catholic and believed in the propagation of his faith. According to Prof. Hayes, "The principles he had and cherished were : union of the altar and throne; revival of the institutions of the old regime, political, religious, social and intellectual, detestation of revolutionary doctrines." To quote Charles X himself, "It is only Lafayette and I who have not changed since 1789." Such a person was not fit to rule the people of France who were profoundly influenced by the ideas of liberty, equality and fraternity. No wonder, there was a stiff opposition to his measures. The people were not prepared to allow the Jesuits to be in charge of education in the country. They wanted to give secular education to their children. The censorship of the press was resented. Nothing could be published without the approval of the king. The government of Charles X raised the property qualifications of the voters and consequently the control of the middle-class over the government was lessened. The secret ballot was abolished and the double vote was given to the landed interests in France. In 1827, the National Guard was disbanded. This was resented by the middle-class because they dominated the National Guard. In short, the acts of omission and commission of Charles X resulted in the opposition of the middle class and ultimately to his overthrow in 1830.

The Revolution of 1830 was essentially a **middle-class revolution** but that of 1848 was essentially a **socialist revolution.** The socialists played the most important part in its overthrow. The progress of the Industrial Revolution in France had led lo the creation of a class-conscious proletariat. As the government refused to do anything to improve the lot of the workers, the socialist leaders got an opportunity to exploit the situation to their advantage. The philosophy of St. Simon, Fourier, Proudhon and Louis Blanc created a stir among the workers and there was a demand for social and political reforms. The workers shouted: **Bread or lead.** As the government of Louis Philippe refused to move in the matter in spite of the protests of the people, the discontentment began to grow and ultimately led to the February Revolution.

The immediate causes of the two **revolutions** differed. In the case of 1830, the immediate cause was the issuing of four ordinances by Charles X, but in the case of 1848, the immediate cause was the banquet of 22 February and the shooting of the demonstrators.

If the uncompromising character of Charles X was responsible for the July Revolution, the unpopularity of Louis Philippe was responsible for his overthrow. There was none to raise his finger in his defence. The dismissal of Thiers and the corrupt regime of Guizot from 1840 to 1848 alienated all sections of the people. According to Prof. Hearnshaw, **"No one had wanted him : few respected him; only a small middle-class minority continued to support him."**

In both cases, the people of France wanted the government to follow a vigorous foreign policy and the refusal of the government to do so was partly responsible for the failure. In the case of Charles X, Algiers was conquered in 1830 but the news of its fall did not come in time to save him. The people of France were sick of the policy of inaction followed by Louis Philippe. In his own words, he was determined to "to crush twelve Chambers rather than make war." He directed his foreign policy more in the interests of his own family than that of his country. He did not help the people of Northern Italy or of Poland. When Thiers wanted to help Mehmet Ali against the Sultan of Turkey, Louis Philippe dismissed him and came to terms with Palmerston. Guizot consistently followed a pacific policy. His ideal was: **"Preservation of peace in all places, at all times."** Lamartine retorted that "a stone post could carry out this policy." A member of the French Parliament enquired thus in 1847: **"What have they done in seven years? Nothing, nothing, nothing."**

While the July Revolution was due to the pro-Catholic policy of Charles X, the February Revolution was due to the anti-clerical policy of Guizot. The Huguenot Prime Minister showed favour to the anti-clerical university. He also gave religious toleration, but that was resented by the Catholics.

While the July Revolution put another bourgeois king on the throne, that of 1848 established a republic. In 1830, the grant of universal suffrage was promised, but in 1848 it was actually given. The Revolution of 1830 did not upset the social order and the disturbances caused by the July Revolution were short-lived. Order was restored with the placing of Louis Philippe on the throne. However, in the case of February Revolution, France had to face the bloody massacre of June 1848. The Revolution of 1830 overthrew the Divine-right monarchy, but that of 1848 uprooted the middle class limited monarchy and set up a republic which lasted for four years.

According to Prof. Hayes, "The February Revolution of 1848 was not basically different from the July Revolution of 1830. Both the revolutions were chiefly Parisian affairs, both were essentially political and only incidentally social, both were primarily 'liberal.' One, it is true, set up a monarchy, with a restricted franchise, while the other established a republic, with universal manhood suffrage. But both recognized the principle of popular sovereignty, both employed the Tricolour and the Marseillaise, and, much more significant, both eventuated in the triumph of property-owners and the adoption of policies which reflected the wishes of property owners."

The Provisional Government. After the overthrow of Louis Philippe the second Republic was proclaimed on 26 February 1848. To quote Lamartine, "Royalty is abolished. The Republic is proclaimed. The people will exercise their political rights." Again, "National workshops are opened for those who are without work." The provisional government consisted of Lamartine, a Liberal Catholic leader, Ledru Rollin, a Jacobin republican, Louis Blanc, the Socialist leader and Albert, a working man.

Lamartine regarded the republic as an end in itself but Louis Blanc considered it as a mean to an end. A decree drafted by Louis Blanc provided : "The provisional government engaged themselves to guarantee the existence of the workmen by means of labour. They engaged themselves to guarantee labour to every citizen." A decree of 27 February 1848 provided that "the provisional government decrees the establishment of national workshops. The Minister of Public Works is charged with the execution of the present decree."

Louis Blanc was appointed the president of a commission whose function was "to examine the claims of labour and to ensure the well-being of the working-class." He was installed at the Palace of the Luxembourg. Louis Blanc at the Luxembourg became a serious rival to the authority of the provisional government and more than once an attempt was made to supersede the provincial government and to establish a committee of public safety. The four demands of the Luxembourg Commission were a ten-hour working day, prohibition of sub-contracting, abolition of piece-work and legal minimum wage. A large number of schemes were discussed by the Luxembourg Commission but there is only one achievement which stands to the credit of the commission or its president and that was the impulse given to the idea of co-operative production. It is stated that about one hundred co-operative societies were set up by tailors, saddlers, spinners and other craftsmen.

The provisional government had to face a great danger from the violence of the Paris mob. On three occasions, viz., 17 March, 16 April, and 15 May, attempts were made to overthrow the provisional government which was suffering from internal dissensions. One group was led by Lamartine and the other by Louis Blanc and Albert.

The general elections took place on 23 and 24 April 1848, and the National Assembly met on 4 May 1848. It was elected on the basis of manhood suffrage but the extremists were eliminated altogether. An overwhelming majority of the elected members were Moderates. The provisional government resigned all its authority into the hands of the National Assembly and the latter elected an executive committee on which neither Louis Blanc nor Albert found a place. They were not appointed to the ministry.

The National Assembly had to tackle the problem of national workshops. The provisional government had accepted the principle of national workshops on 25 February 1848, and a decree of 27 February had ordered their immediate establishment. There were no workshops as such and only a few thousand persons were given jobs. The number of those who demanded work went on increasing and the result was that the government was forced to pay without work. Not only the people of Paris demanded work but all kinds of persons from the countryside came to Paris to demand work. The number became so large that there was a serious danger to public order and the National Assembly did not know what to do. It was in these circumstances that Emile Thomas was appointed the director of the national workshops. Although Thomas could not give work to all the unemployed, yet he was able to create order out of chaos. He set up a labour exchange. He centralized the distribution of doles and gave some sort of training to the unemployed. The chances of fraud and disorder were lessened. It is stated that on 16 April 1848, the number of persons enrolled was 66,000 and before the end of May, the figure had risen to 1,20,000.

On 15 May, a mob of about one lakh of persons rushed to the National Assembly and set up a new provisional government. However, Lamartine and Ledru-Rollin were equal to the task. With the help of the army, they were able to defeat and disperse the mob and arrest the rebel leaders. Preparations were made to deal with the menace created by the national workshops. General Cavaignac was appointed the Minister of War and a large number of troops were recruited. The government made radical changes in the national workshops. It was decreed that all workmen, who could not prove that they had resided in Paris for at least six months, were to be sent away from the capital under a passport. Task work was to be substituted for day work. Registration offices were to be opened for employers who wanted workmen. All workmen who refused to work under private employers and all unmarried workmen between the ages of 18 and 25 who refused to enlist in the army, were to be immediately dismissed from the workshops. The government tried to enforce the decrees on 22 June 1848, and that brought forth opposition from the workers. The cry was raised: "Down with the Executive Commission." On 23 June, there was a serious trouble in the whole of the city. Barricades were set up in the streets. General Cavaignac was put in charge of the troops to deal with the situation. From 24 to 26 June 1848, there was bitter street fighting in Paris. There was much bloodshed and about 4,000 rebels were sent to penal colonies overseas. Socialism as an organized movement was stamped out. Louis Blanc was threatened with prosecution and he escaped to England. Proudhon was imprisoned. However, by destroying socialism, the provisional government destroyed itself.

Although General Cavaignac surrendered the dictatorial powers given to him, the National Assembly elected him as the President of the Council. Till the election of the President of the Republic in December 1848, he was virtually the ruler of France. However, he was loyal to the Republic and tried to save it from the Bonapartists, Legitimists and the Communists. The national workshops were abolished. The mischievous clubs were closed down. Some journals were suppressed. The command of the National Guard was given to Changarnier.

After a lot of discussion, the National Assembly was able to frame a republican constitution in October 1848. A provision was made for a single legislative chamber consisting of 750 paid members who were to be elected by departments and colonies on the basis of universal suffrage. The voting was to be direct. It was to be dissolved after three years. Provision was also made for a Council of State to be elected by the Assembly for the drafting of bills. France was to have a President who was to be elected directly by the people on the basis of universal franchise. He was to appoint his own Ministers although the latter were to be responsible to the Legislature. Both the President and the Ministers were to be answerable to the High Court of Justice. The President was to have a suspensive veto on legislation. He was to be elected for four years and a bar was put on his re-election. M. Grevy opposed the provisions with regard to the President is these words: "Are you sure that an ambitious man raised to the throne of the Presidency will not be tempted to perpetuate his power ? And if this man is a scion of one of those families which have reigned over France....will you ensure that this man, this man of ambition, will not end by overthrowing the Republic?" In spite of the opposition of Grevy, the French Constituent Assembly accepted the proposal and thereby gave a death blow to the Republic.

Elections were held under the new constitution and Louis Napoleon was elected the President. He got 5,434,226 votes, Cavaignac got 1,448,107 and Lamartine got only 17,910. With the coming of Louis Napoleon, a new chapter started in the history of France.

Louis Napoleon. Louis Napoleon Bonaparte was born in 1808 in Paris. He was the son of Louis Bonaparte, the brother of Napoleon I, and the King of Holland and of Hortense Beauharnais, daughter of Josephine from her first marriage and the step-daughter of Napoleon I. No wonder, Napoleon I inscribed his name in the family register of the Bonapartes at the time of baptism. When the Allies occupied Paris in 1814, King Frederick William of Prussia brought his children to play with the children of Hortense and that was the first meeting of Louis Napoleon and the future German Emperor. After the Battle of Waterloo, Hortense and her children took refuge in Switzerland. At the time of the Revolution of 1830, the young princes were in Rome and they joined the **Carbonari.** The elder brother of Louis Napoleon died in Italy and in July 1832 "Napoleon II", the son of Napoleon I from the Austrian Princess, also died. After that, Louis Napoleon was considered to be the heir to the claims of the Bonapartists.

In 1836, Louis Napoleon asserted his claim for the first time. He appeared at Strasburg, which was garrisoned by the most strong Bonapartist regiment in the French army and asked them to help him to reestablish the Napoleonic empire. However, he was, arrested in less than three hours but instead of taking action against him, Louis Philippe merely sent him to the United States. In 1840, he landed at Boulogne and declared that the bones of Napoleon I should rest only in a "regenerated France." However, he was arrested, sentenced and shut up in the fortress of Ham. Even in prison, Louis Napoleon continued his agitation. By 1839 he had written a book called **Napoleonic Ideas** in which he propounded his own political views. According to him, "The Napoleonic empire was the perfect realization of the principles of 1789. It rested upon the foundations of national sovereignty. It employed universal manhood suffrage to determine its chief policy. In the field of foreign affairs, it aimed at a confederation of the national state. It was solidified, directed and rendered glorious by its Caesarism." While still in prison he wrote in 1841 **Fragments Historiques** to refute the parallel drawn by Guizot between the English Revolution of 1688 and July Revolution of 1830 in France. In 1844, he wrote **The Extension of Pauperism** in which he put forward a plan for the relief of unemployment, and the material prosperity of France. He maintained that it would be his business to assist capitalists opening up new fields of industrial enterprise and to help peasants by encouraging agriculture. Everybody was to be provided under the national democratic empire and poverty was to disappear altogether. To quote him, "The triumph of Christianity abolished slavery; the triumph of the French Revolution abolished serfdom; the triumph of democracy will abolish Pauperism." In 1845, he wrote **History of Artillery.** In May 1846, Louis Napoleon managed to escape from the fortress of Ham and reached England where he stayed for two years.

When there was a revolution in France in February 1848, Louis Napoleon went to Paris and offered his sword and services to the second Republic. However, both of them were rejected and he was ordered to leave France within 24 hours. When the elections to the National Assembly took place in April 1848, he did not stand for election. However, his supporters carried on propaganda in his favour continuously. When by-elections took place in June 1848, he was elected in his absence from four departments. Louis Napoleon wrote thus to the National Assembly from London : ""My name is the symbol of order, nationality and glory and it would be a great grief to me to see that it is used to increase the troubles which are rending our country." However, he added, "Should the people impose duties on me, I should know how to fulfil them." The National Assembly was upset but Louis Napoleon resigned his seat and the matter ended there. During the bloody days of June 1848, Napoleon was away from the scene and consequently his name was not associated with the massacres. In September, he was re-elected from five constituencies and he took his seat in the National Assembly on 26 September 1848. When the elections for the Presidency took place in December 1848, he was elected by an overwhelming majority.

Napoleon as President (1848-52). As the President of the Second Republic of France from 1848 to 1852, Louis Napoleon followed a policy which aimed at adding to his personal popularity with the people of France. He praised the workers in the factories. He prevailed upon the Assembly to pass in 1850 a law which provided for a scheme of voluntary old age insurance. He tried to please the Catholics and the bourgeoisie. He also tried to encourage the industries of France. A French military expedition was sent to Rome in 1849 to restore the Pope. The Falloux Law of 1850 restored the privileges which the Catholic clergymen exercised in the time of Charles X over the education of French children.

The Assembly which was elected in 1849 had only a handful of Bonapartists. Out of 750 members, 500 were Monarchists. The Republicans were in a minority. There was no party as such in the Assembly and that proved to be advantageous to Louis Napoleon. By following a reactionary policy, the Assembly played into his hands. Public meetings were prohibited and censorship was imposed on the press. Members of the Assembly were to be paid. A law was passed in 1850 by which no one was allowed to vote who had not lived and paid taxes for three years in one and the same district. The result of this law was that the workers who had to move from one place to another in search of employment, were disfranchised completely. Out of the total of 9 million voters, 3 million were removed by the law. Against this there were protests from the cities particularly from Paris. Louis Napoleon took advantage of this position and declared that as the elected representative of the people, he was entitled to prevent the Assembly from disfranchising Frenchmen. The conflict between the President and the Assembly continued for more than a year. When the Assembly declared open war upon him, he dismissed General Changarnier, who was the Commander of the National Guard and the Paris Garrison in January 1851. The dismissal of Changarnier precipitated a crisis. The prestige of the Republic was sinking in the country and that of Napoleon was increasing. There were many persons in France who started thinking in terms of setting up a monarchy or a dictatorship. To quote one, "If there could be anything absolutely new under the sun, it would be the spectacle which France offers to the world today. It is filled with Monarchists who cannot establish a monarchy and who groan under the weight of a Republic which has no Republicans to defend it. In the midst of this confusion only two personages remain standing, Louis Napoleon and the Mountain, two things only are possible, a new revolution or a dictatorship. It is evident to me that force must bring about a solution."

The Assembly passed a vote of no-confidence against the Ministry and forced it to resign. However, the President refused to appoint another. Instead, he reappointed the Ministry which had been censured by the Assembly. The Assembly refused to increase the allowances of the President. A revision of the Constitution was proposed and carried by a large majority but the majority was not such as was required by law to amend the Constitution. However, as time passed, the demand for the amendment of the Constitution began to increase.

In November 1851, Louis Napoleon gave to the Assembly an ultimatum that it must re-establish universal suffrage at once and when the Assembly refused to do so, the President decided to act. His secret was shared by Saint Arnaud, Maupas, Morny, Persigny, Flahaut and Mocquard. On the midnight of December 1-2, 1851, the opponents of the government were arrested in their beds and when the people of Paris woke up in the morning, they found the walls of the city covered with placards which contained two proclamations addressed to the people and the army and the decree. The decree declared that the Assembly was dissolved, universal suffrage was restored and a promise was made that the people should be given an opportunity to express by plebiscite their approval or disapproval. Troops were posted at all the important points and all opposition was put down. The **coup d' etat** of 1851 was a success. There was no serious disorder in the country and the people seemed to have submitted. With popular leaders like Thiers, Cavaignac and Changarnier out of the picture, the plebiscite, took place on 20 December 1851, and the President was empowered to prepare a new Constitution for the Second Republic.

New Constitution (1852). On 14 January 1852, the President promulgated a new Constitution. The life of the President was extended to ten years. He was given the power of sanctioning all laws and decrees. The Ministers were to be responsible to him alone. A Council of State was to be nominated by him and it was to draft laws on the initiative of the President. The Legislature was to consist of two Houses. The Senate was to consist of the Marshals, Admirals and Cardinals **ex-officio,** and 150 other members nominated by the President. The **Corps Legislatif** was to consist of 261 members. The **Corps Legislatif** was given the power of veto but it was not to have the power to initiate or amend legislative projects. The new Constitution was commended to the people as "the only Constitution adapted to the social and administrative institutions of modern France and calculated to secure the liberties of France and the maintenance of Napoleonic principles." Universal manhood suffrage was also provided.

During the year 1852, France was on the way to the empire. Although nominally Louis Napoleon was the President, he put his own effigy on the national coins. He restored to the army and national buildings the gilt eagles. He made a tour of the country and made speeches with a view to winning over all sections of the people. In November 1852, a plebiscite was held by which the people approved the transformation of the Presidency into an hereditary empire. On 2 December 1852, Louis Napoleon was proclaimed emperor as Napoleon III. He ruled France as emperor from 1852 to 1870.

Napoleon III as Emperor (1852-70). The two aspects of the reign of Napoleon III are his home policy and foreign policy. He had already outlined his programme in his Bordeaux address of October 1852. He said, "There is a fear to which I ought to reply. **In a spirit of suspicion some people say : the Empire is war. I say, the Empire is peace....**yet I confess that I, like the Emperor, have many conquests to make. I wish, like him, to conquer, the irreconcilable warring factions and to turn back again into the great popular river the angry side-currents which are likely to lose themselves without profit to anybody. I wish to conquer to religion, to morality, to prosperity, that part of the population still so large, which in the midst of a country of faith and belief, are scarcely acquainted with the precepts of Christ, which, in the bosom of the most fertile country in the world, can scarcely procure for themselves the bare necessaries of life. We have immense tracts of waste lands to bring into cultivation, roads to open, harbours to deepen, canals to complete, rivers to render navigable, a network of railways to link up. Facing us, opposite Marseilles, we have a vast reality to assimilate to France. We have all our great ports of the West to bring near to France by developing the rapid means of communication which are still lacking. On all sides we have ruins to restore, false gods to overthrow, truths to make triumphant. This is how I should understand the Empire, if the Empire is, indeed, to be restored. Such are the Conquests I contemplate, and all you who surround me, who desire, like myself, the welfare of our country, you are my soldiers."

Home Policy. Napoleon III tried to fulfil the promises made to the people. The forces of anarchy were suppressed. Social order was restored. Industry was encouraged. Means of communication were improved. Roads, canals and harbours, were constructed. The railway system of France was completed from north to south and from west to east. Credit was provided for agriculture, industry and commerce. Two great central banks known as the **Credit Foncier,** and the **Credit Mobilier** were established. Land banks were set up in Paris and in the provinces. The improvement of the means of transport added to the prosperity of the peasants. The government took keen interest in the vineyards and wheat fields of the peasants. The number of agricultural societies was increased. Encouragement was given to the breeding of horses. Marshes were drained and land was brought under cultivation.

Paris was rebuilt and made more spacious, more sanitary, more splendid, and more defensible. Broad boulevards and magnificent public buildings were constructed in Paris. Under the supervision of Baron Haussmann, an attempt was made to make Paris the most beautiful and most attractive city in the world.

Napoleon III tried to impress upon the workers that he was one of them. He went about in engine cabs with locomotive engineers. He talked on the roads with artisans and labourers. He drank to the health of the masons, carpenters and plumbers. Subsidies were given to their organisations. Subsidies were given to the inkeepers to guarantee cheap bread to the labourers. Holidays were given to them. Schemes were promoted for the provision of dwellings to the workers, and their insurance against accidents and old age. Labour associations were legalized. A law of 1863 allowed the labourers to form co-operative societies for collective buying and selling. The right of the workers to strike was recognized by a law of 1864. A law provided for voluntary insurance of the workers against death and industrial accidents.

The government followed a liberal policy in the industrial field. The control of the government over private business was gradually lessened. Facilities were provided for the introduction of machinery and the organisation of industrial corporations. Savings banks were established. Tariffs were gradually lowered. In 1860, France entered into a commercial treaty with England by which trade between the two countries was facilitated. In 1855, a Grand International Exhibition was held in Paris and its object was to impress the people with the material progress and prosperity of the country.

Napoleon III consistently followed a policy of keeping the Catholics in good humour. In 1849, he sent the French troops to Rome to restore the Pope. He strengthened the hold of the clergymen upon the universities and public schools in France. One of the reasons why Napoleon stopped in the middle of his Italian campaign in 1859 was the fear of the opposition of the Catholics of France. The Empress Eugenie gave a lot of charity to the Catholic Church. Napoleon III intervened in the Crimean War to support the cause of the Catholic monks in Palestine. He posed as the champion of Catholicism in the world.

At least up to 1860 Napoleon III was practically a dictator of France. He exercised all control in the country. The press was rigorously controlled. The secret police were employed to watch and check the activities of the people. He controlled the legislature by paying the expenses of the 'official candidates' from the national exchequer while the other candidates had to meet their own expenses. The electoral machinery was practically in the hands of the emperor. An Act of 1858 provided that every candidate was to take an oath of fidelity to the emperor. Another law of the same year allowed the government to intern political offenders in France or Algeria or to exile them without any formality of a trial.

This state of affairs continued up to 1860 when the Constitution was revised and the government was liberalized. The Senate and the Legislative Body were allowed to debate and vote an annual address in reply to the speech from the throne. Verbatim reports of parliamentary debates were to be published. The executive was required to keep the legislature informed of its activities.

In spite of these concessions, the Republicans swept Paris in the general elections of 1863. Jules Simon, Thiers, Ferry and Gambetta were returned. Although the government got a majority on account of the influence of the prefects, the opposition was strong enough to give headache to Napoleon III.

In 1866, Olivier founded a party to support the idea of a liberal empire. In 1867, the emperor announced "the crowning of the edifice created by the will of the nation." The press censorship was relaxed. A limited right of public meetings was allowed. The Ministers were to sit in the Legislature to answer questions and take part in the debates.

After the general elections of 1869, Olivier was asked to form the Ministry. The new Ministry was liberal in complexion and responsible to Parliament. The Legislature was given complete freedom of debate, to control public finance and legislate without any restriction. To quote Ollivier, it was "the most truly liberal Constitution which France has enjoyed since 1789."

In his speech from the throne on 29 November 1869, Napoleon III referred to the attacks on the empire and pointed out to the solidarity of the French empire which was based on universal suffrage. He declared that France "evidently desires liberty but liberty united with order." "I will answer for order; assist me, gentlemen, to save liberty." The emperor outlined a further programme of reforms. Authority was to be decentralized. Mayors were to be selected from the councils of the communes. The councils were to be elected by the people. Cantons were also to have their councils too. Free primary education was to be improved. Child labour in factories was to be regulated. Savings banks were to be set up on the countryside for the good of the people. These reforms were submitted to the people and were approved of by them by a great majority. However, Napoleon III was defeated in the Battle of Sedan in 1870 and surrendered. That led to the abolition of the second empire and the proclamation of the Third Republic in France in September 1870.

Foreign Policy of Napoleon III. Both as the President of the French Republic and Emperor of France, Louis Napoleon professed to stand for peace, but actually he followed a vigorous foreign policy which involved France in many wars. His aggressive foreign policy was due to many causes. Louis Napoleon was a nationalist and he sympathised with the people of Italy, Germany and Poland who were fighting for their freedom and unification. It was his nationalism which attracted the French masses to him. It was the name of Napoleon that was responsible for his election as President in 1848 and also his popularity later on. He could justify that name only by following in the footsteps of his uncle which meant war. Napoleon also felt that he could carry with him all the people of France by following a vigorous foreign policy as the people of France yearned for glory. He was also the centre of intrigues and the object of constant appeals for active help to the oppressed nationalities of Europe. The Patriots of Europe looked up to him for assistance. Napoleon himself hoped to get compensation in the form of territories and thereby add to the national pride and prestige.

In the colonial field, Napoleon annexed the whole of Algeria to France and it became a great prosperous dependency. He joined hands with England in a military demonstration against China and many Chinese ports were opened for trade to the Europeans. In 1851, he sent punitive expeditions to Annam and Cochin-China. In 1863, he established a French protectorate over Cambodia.

Rome. In 1849, Louis Napoleon sent French troops to Rome to overthrow the republican regime and thereby restore the Pope. The republic was defeated and the Pope was restored. The French troops remained in Rome from 1849 to 1870. He intervened in Rome with the object of winning over the goodwill of the Catholics of France who wanted the Pope to be restored to his former position.

Crimean War. Napoleon III intervened in the Crimean War in 1854. The relations between Napoleon and Czar Nicholas I were very bitter. The Czar considered Napoleon III as an upstart and Napoleon III Would like to have revenge for the French humiliation of 1812. Businessmen, Liberals and Catholics of France hated Russia on various grounds. There arose certain quarrels between the Catholic and Orthodox monks in Palestine. Czar Nicholas I asked Turkey to recognise the right of Russia to protect the Christians of the Turkish empire. Napoleon III asked the Sultan to resist the Russian "aggression". The Sultan of Turkey did as he was asked to do and war was declared between Turkey and Russia. Both France and England joined hands to preserve the territorial integrity of the Turkish empire. Both the French and the English did not do well in the beginning and their troops suffered terribly. However, things changed for the better after the death of Nicholas I and on Palmerston's becoming Prime Minister of England in 1855. Russia was defeated and peace was made by the Treaty of Paris of 1856. Napoleon satisfied his vanity by presiding over the Congress of Paris. That also raised his prestige.

Italy. Napoleon interfered in the affairs of Italy to help the cause of the unification of the country. He himself had been in his youth a member of the Carbonari which was a secret society working for the expulsion of Austria from Italy and unification of the country. The Bonapartes had Italian blood in their veins. A war with Austria for Italian unification was likely to be popular with the Liberals of France. There was also the possibility of Napoleon getting some compensation. In spite of these factors, Napoleon hesitated to intervene in Italy. He felt that a war with Austria was a risky affair on account of the strength of Austria and her prestige in Italy. A united Italy might become a serious rival of France in the Mediterranean. The Catholics of France were bound to oppose French intervention to help Italian unification on account of the peculiar position of the Pope in Italy. No wonder Napoleon was on the horns of a dilemma. However, his indecision was ended when an attempt was made on his life in 1858 by Orsini, an Italian patriot. Napoleon decided to remove the grievances of the potential Italian assassins and cater to the liberal patriots of France. He decided to risk the reproaches of the Pope and the French Catholics.

It was agreed between Napoleon III and Cavour at **Plombieres** in 1858 that Napoleon III was to help Piedmont to drive out the Austrians from Lombardy and Venetia. He was to get Nice and Savoy as his reward. In April 1859, the Austrian Government gave an ultimatum to Sardinia demanding immediate demobilization. As that was refused, Austria declared war against Sardinia-Piedmont. As Austria was the aggressor, Napoleon III came to the help of Sardinia-Piedmont and their combined armies won the battles of Magenta and Solferino. After the battle of Solferino, Napoleon III stopped the war all of a sudden and made an armistice with Austria which was ratified by the Treaty of Zurich. When the Austrian troops evacuated Lombardy according to the Treaty of Zurich, the people of Parma, Modena and Tuscany revolted and turned out their kings. They also voted their union with the Sardinia-Piedmont. By the Treaty of Turin, Napoleon III recognized the annexation of Tuscany, Parma, Modena and Lombardy by Piedmont and he himself got Nice and Savoy.

According to Taylor, "The annexation of Savoy was a turning point in the history of the second empire. Until then it had been plausible to argue that Napoleon was seeking glory by liberating others, not by the direct aggrandizement of France; now he had taken up the revolutionary policy of the natural frontiers, which seemed to lead directly to a French hegemony of Europe. The British Government could not oppose by war a course of events that was helping in the unification of Italy; but they never recovered the faith in Napoleon III which they lost in March 1860." (**The Struggle for Mastery in Europe,** p. 118).

Although Napoleon III got Nice and Savoy, he was not a gainer on the whole. Russia was already an enemy and he added Austria to that list. The nationalists of Italy did not forgive him on account of the betrayal of their cause at the most crucial stage. Great Britain began to suspect the designs of Napoleon III. Napoleon III found himself isolated and earned for himself a reputation for dishonesty. The Italian intervention split up the Nationalist Party of France. The French Catholics blamed Napoleon for going too far and the French Liberals condemned him for not going far enough. The differences between the two began to widen and Napoleon III failed to keep them together. He had to liberalize his government in 1860 to win over the Liberals.

Many reasons have been given for the sudden stoppage of war by Napoleon III after his victory at Solferino. It is pointed out that Napoleon III was a coward at heart and he could not tolerate the sight of bloodshed which he saw at Solferino. He was also suffering from kidney trouble and his health could not stand further strain. He also felt that if the whole of Italy became one, there would be no place for the Pope in Italy and he had not bargained for such an eventuality. If he had allowed the Pope to be driven out by the Italian nationalists, he would have found himself in a difficult position on account of the Catholic criticism in France. The Austrian armies were firmly established in Venetia and there was every possibility of the French troops being defeated there. There was also the possibility of a danger from Prussia which was mobilizing her forces along the Rhine river.

Rumania. Napoleon III gained some prestige by championing the cause of Rumania. In 1856, Moldavia and Wallachia were given autonomy in their affairs. Two years after, Napoleon secured for them the right to have their own princes and Parliaments. Three years later, he prevailed upon the Powers to allow the two provinces to he united under one Prince. In this way, he helped the cause of Rumanian unification.

The Poles. Napoleon III had the united support of the French people to help the Poles in their efforts to liberate themselves from the subjection of Russia. The Liberals of France stood for Polish independence. The French Catholics wanted Napoleon to help the Poles because the Poles were Catholics. However, when the Poles actually revolted in 1863, Napoleon III did not help them because he was afraid that Prussia and Austria would help Russia and in that case a war with Russia was bound to be suicidal for France. The result was that the Poles were ruthlessly crushed and consequently both the liberals and Catholics of France were disappointed.

Mexico. Mexico became independent in 1823 but she was unfortunate in not having any stable government. In 1861, Juarez became the President of Mexico. Mexico owed money to the creditors of many nationalities, particularly of France, Spain and England. In 1861, Juarez suspended the payment of interest to the creditors for two years. The creditors appealed to their Governments for help. The United States was involved in the civil war and she could not be expected to invoke the Monre Doctrine against the outsiders. Napoleon III decided to exploit the situation in Mexico. He thought of establishing in Mexico a state under the control of some European Power which would act as a bulwark against the Anglo-Saxons, 'this aggressive people which, if it be not stopped, will cover all America and then the whole world. Even if this state were not in French hands, it might be used to win valuable alliances for France. A new chapter in the history of the world might open.' The result was that a joint French, Spanish and British expedition sailed for Veracruz, hoping to exercise pressure which would produce the payment of the required interest on the Mexican debt. Later on, it was found that it would be necessary to conquer the country. On one ground or the other, Great Britain and Spain withdrew and France was left all alone. The work of conquest proved to be a difficult one. The people of Mexico offered successful resistance to the invaders and it was with great difficulty that the city of Mexico was captured in the summer of 1863. In 1864, Napoleon III made Maximilian, the brother of the Austrian Emperor, Francis Joseph, the ruler of Mexico. Maximilian was a traveller and a scientist of distinction and was believed to hold liberal views on politics. Napoleon hoped to get from this move the friendship and perhaps the alliance of Austria. Maximilian accepted the offer after some delay and against the advice of Francis Joseph and of Great Britain. He was supported by the French General Forey and an army of 23,000 men. He was received with an appearance of enthusiasm in the city of Mexico. Unfortunately, his supporters were divided and his opponents were determined. The United States kept quiet so long as the civil war was going on but as soon as the war was over, she applied the Monre Doctorine and asked France to quit Mexico. Napoleon III was now weary of the project. It was bringing constant disappointment and expense. Under these circumstances, Napoleon decided to withdraw the French forces in February 1867. Napoleon hoped that Maximilian would also retire but he refused. He decided to fight against his enemies. The result was that in June 1867 he was forced to surrender to native forces at Queretaro and was shot in the courtyard of that town.

It is obvious that the Mexican enterprise proved to be an utter failure. It acted like a boomerang against Napoleon III. The death of Maximilian alienated Austria. On account of the absence of the French troops in Mexico, Napoleon III was not able to intervene effectively in the Austro-Prussian war of 1866.

According to Hazen, "A most expensive enterprise for the French emperor, it had prevented his playing a part in decisive events occurring in Central Europe in 1864-66, in the Danish war, and the Austro-Prussian war, the outcome of which was to alter so seriously the importance of France in Europe by the exaltation of an ambitious, aggressive, and powerful military State, Prussia. It had damaged him morally before Europe by the desertion of his Protegest to an appealing fate before the threats of the United States. It had lessened his prestige at home."

Austro-Prussian War (1866). There was a war between Austria and Prussia in 1866 which lasted for only seven weeks. The Austrian forces were defeated in the Battle of Sadowa and Austria made peace with Prussia. The rapidity and completeness of the Prussian victory upset all the calculations of Napoleon III. His expectation was that a war between Austria and Prussia would be a long one and he would be in a position to intervene effectively in the war. Napoleon III also thought that Prussia would be defeated and Germany would become hopelessly weak. However, the Austrian defeat at Sadowa completely upset everything. It was the traditional policy of France to keep Germany divided and weak, but the victory of Prussia and the unification of Germany created a great danger for France. The military success of Prussia was considered to be a challenge to France and even a threat to her security. It was rightly pointed out that **it was France that was defeated at Sadowa.** Napoleon III would like to have revenge for his diplomatic defeat. War between France and Prussia became inevitable.

Franco-Prussian War (1870-71). In 1865, Napoleon III had an interview with Bismarck at Biarritz. On that occasion, Bismarck gave an undertaking to Napoleon III that the latter could have compensation towards the Rhine-perhaps Belgium or Rhineland. After the war of 1866, Napoleon III tried to get compensation for France. He asked for Belgium but in vain. He also failed to get the Rhinish Palatinate. Then he tried to buy Luxemburg. The King of Holland was willing to sell, but Bismarck objected. As Napoleon III was not prepared for war, the matter had to be referred to a conference of the powers who had signed the treaties of 1815. The settlement was made in London in 1867 and Luxemburg was made an independent State, neutralised and guaranteed by all the Great Powers. Anyhow, Napoleon failed to get Luxemburg also.

The people of France were getting fed up with the policies of Napoleon III. After 1867, many Frenchmen began to think in terms of restoring the Bourbons or the Orleanists. Many middle-class liberals including businessmen and professional men, began to think of setting up a republic in France. The growth of the royalist and republican tendencies in France must have weakened the position of Napoleon III. The parliamentary elections of 1869 returned 50 royalists and 40 republicans. Napoleon III felt that concession must be given to maintain his position. Consequently, he reduced the rigour of press censorship. He promised to give up the practice of paying the election expenses of official candidates for the legislature. The ministers were to be responsible to the legislature and not to the emperor. He appointed Olivier, a liberal royalist, as his prime minister. A new liberal constitution was drafted for the second empire in 1870. It contained all the concessions given by Napoleon III in 1869. In addition to that, provision was made for a second chamber which was not to be under the influence of the emperor. These reforms might have conciliated partially the liberal royalists, but they did not satisfy the legitimists or the republicans.

In France, there was a lot of anti-Prussian feeling. The liberals of France detested Prussia as a reactionary State. The Catholics of France disliked Prussia as an intolerant Protestant State. The patriots of France hated Prussia because that was a source of danger to their country. The French would like to have revenge for the diplomatic defeat of 1866. Undoubtedly, a war against Prussia would have been popular. However, Napoleon III had no stomach for a war with Prussia. He was already broken in health. Russia had not forgotten the part which France had played in the Crimean War against her and no wonder she was pro-Prussian and anti-French. The Emperor of Austria also had not forgotten the humiliation in Italy at the hands of Napoleon III. The people of Italy had no love for France as Napoleon III had betrayed them at the most crucial stage in their war of liberation. The stationing of French troops in Rome annoyed the Indian patriots as without Rome unification of their country could not be completed. The British statesmen and public opinion suspected the designs of Napoleon III. The southern States of Germany had been won over by Bismarck by a policy of conciliation. No wonder, Napoleon III felt that under the circumstances, a war with Prussia was suicidal. In spite of it, Napoleon III decided to fight against Prussia because there was no other alternative. In the event of a war, there was every possibility of combining all the Frenchmen and also gain some prestige.

Bismarck also believed that a war with France was inevitable because unification of Germany could be completed only after the defeat of France. No wonder, he worked for such a war day and night. A stage came when he was ready to give a blow to France. All that wanted was an excuse to start the war and that was given by the question of the Spanish Succession. The Spanish throne had already been offered twice to Leopold, a Hohenzollern prince related to the royal family of Prussia, but had been rejected. On the intervention of Bismarck, the throne was once again offered to Prince Leopold and Bismarck tried to make the best of the new invitation. There was a lot of criticism in France of the new move which was described as a threat to the very existence of France which was between Spain and Prussia. Napoleon III sent protests to Prussia and Spain and it was announced in Spain that the prince had cancelled his acceptance of the throne. The matter might have ended there, but the French emperor was pressed by his advisers to utilize the occasion to administer an open diplomatic rebuff to Prussia. The French ambassador in Berlin Benedetti, was instructed to obtain from the king of Prussia a solemn public promise that he would never allow a Hohenzollern to become a candidate for the throne of Spain. The interview of Benedetti with the Prussian king at Ems was indecisive. It is stated that Benedetti got instructions from France "to obtain from the king revocation of the acceptance of the prince of Hohenzollern....otherwise it is war." William I, the Prussian king, was friendly, reasonable and favourable to a peaceful solution. Benedetti got urgent messages to demand a definite and speedy answer. William I wired to Spain and France that the acceptance had been withdrawn but Gramont and the French military party who stood for war, were not satisfied. A draft letter of apology to be got from the Prussian king was also forwarded to the French ambassador. Benedetti pressed for pledges that the throne would never be offered again but the king of Prussia put an end to the interview.

Bismarck was not happy at the prospects of peace on account of the withdrawal of the acceptance of the Spanish throne. However, he got an opportunity when he got the Ems' telegram regarding the interview between Benedetti and the Prussian king. He decided to publish the telegram in a shortened form to the press. To quote Bismarck, **"If I do this, it will have the effect of red rag upon the Gallic bull."** Bismarck, Roon and Moltke were happy at the prospect of war. To quote, Roon, **"Our God of old lives still, and will not let us perish in disgrace."** To quote Moltke, **"If I may live to lead our army in such a war, then the devil may come directly afterward and fetch away the old carcass."**

The telegram was shortened in such a way that to the French it appeared that their ambassador had been insulted and to the Prussians appeared that their king had been insulted.

As regards France, there was a general demand for a war against Prussia. Three Cabinet meetings were held to decide the issue of war or peace. Gramont insisted that, "If you mention a Congress again, I shall throw my resignation at your feet." The result was that France declared war against Prussia. To quote Gramont, **"Guarantees we cannot bring you, but we bring you war."**

The war was welcomed in both the countries. France was considered to be the aggressor. The southern States of Germany joined Prussia against France. Everywhere in Germany, the songs of the war of liberation were revived and united Germany marched to the front to the strains of **Die Wacht Am Rhein.** While the Germans shouted **"Nach Paris !"** the Parisians cried out **"A Berlin !"** The Marseillaise was sung again. Marshal Le Boeuf proclaimed "that the soldiers of Jena are ready to the last gaiterbutton." However, the French troops had not even the most necessary articles. They had no artillery or baggage, ambulance or magazines. Their training was deficient. Their officers were inefficient and insufficient. Railway accommodation was inadequate and intelligence service was poor. The French had more maps of Germany which they were going to invade than those of France which they were forced to defend. France did not get help from any quarter. Bismarck had already won over Russia by allowing that country to violate the Black Sea clauses of the Treaty of Paris of 1856. Italy was friendly towards Prussia because the latter had helped her to get Venetia in 1866 and Italy also expected to occupy Rome only if France was defeated in the war. Great Britain under Gladstone followed a policy of neutrality.

The Germans started the offensive and defeated the French in the **Battles of Weissenburg, Spicheren, Worth, Gravelotte** and **Sedan.** The victory of Sedan was a decisive one and after that the French army surrendered and Napoleon III was made a prisoner. This led to the fall of the second empire in France and the proclamation of the Third Republic in September 1870. Bismarck was not satisfied with this and he pressed on to Paris which put up a stiff resistance but after a long siege the city surrendered. The war was ended by the Treaty of Frankfurt of 1871.

It is clear from above that the foreign policy of Napoleon III, after a striking beginning, proved to be an utter failure. Success was essential to keep hold over France after 1860 and success evaded him. He could not out-manoeuvre the enemy, nor hold firm the ally. Neither the Danish nor the Polish nor the Austrian Question brought him credit. The attempt to find a Latin Catholic Empire in Mexico, in which he wasted good years of the sixties while Prussia was going strong, ended in disastrous failure. The strong Anglo-French Alliance of the Crimean War dwindled away by 1864. The rapprochement with Russia which Napoleon III cultivated after the Congress of Paris was destroyed by his sympathies with the Polish revolt of 1863. When Bismarck performed a service, he secured a friend. Napoleon III gave great gifts to Italy, but forfeited her gratitude. The annexation of Savoy wiped out Magenta. The support of the Papacy lost to him the alliance of Piedmont-Sardinia. In 1866, he alienated Prussia without winning Austria to his side. However, his policy was not as self-seeking as of many other statesmen of Europe of his time. He stood for international peace. He sympathised with national aspirations although those were accompanied by an innkeeper's bill. He puzzled rather than guided Europe and consequently was neither understood nor trusted. His policy was inconsistent and unreliable. To quote him, "I never form distant plans; I am governed by the exigencies of the moment." It has rightly been paid that **"Napoleon le Petit" had not the genius of "Napoleon le Grand."**

About Napoleon III, David Thompson says that he was always a dreamer and intriguer rather than a practical statesman. He combined a nostalgic faith in the destinies of his family with a genuine concern for the welfare of the poor and of the French people as a whole. Napoleon III has been called "Saint Simon on horseback" and there is no reason to doubt either the sincerity of his desire to improve material conditions or the reality of the benefits his rule conferred. Politically, his policy vacillated as he sought to appease now the Catholics, now the Liberals, now the Socialists and always the demands of the populace as a whole. His efforts to govern with the masses led to a series of disasters in foreign policy because he believed that the masses wanted glory and were intensely nationalistic. However, his failures should not obscure the more positive material gains that France derived from his rule. Victor Hugo dubbed him as "Half-pint Napoleon". Judged in terms of military glory or original achievement, the second Empire in France under Napoleon III was merely a pale shadow of the First, but it has considerable importance for the material development of France and the shaping of modern Europe.

About Napoleon III A.J.P. Taylor says that he was neither a revolutionary nor a war-monger. He wanted to accomplish a revolutionary foreign policy without calling on the spirit of revolution and to remodel Europe without a war. His favourite dream was a "general congress of the great Powers of Europe" which should settle every question in dispute by peaceful agreement. He was a mixture of the idealist and the conspirator. He was consistent only in one thing and that was he could never resist the temptation to speculate. He plunged in politics in the same way as contemporary capitalists plunged in railway ventures. It is true that he hated war and feared its risks but in the last resort he always came down on the side of action. His feeling was that while doing so he was interpreting the French sentiment, but that was merely the urge within himself. Napoleon III is stated to have told Hubner, the Austrian minister, "there is an urge for expansion in France which must be reckoned with."

According to Seaman, "One of the most interesting exercises in what might be termed comparative biography is to study the similarities and dissimilarities between Louis Napoleon and Adolf Hitler. In many respects their careers run on parallel lines and a study of it either helps to illuminate one's understanding of the other. They rose to power in a remarkably similar defiance of the laws of probability. The performance, the same function of first restoring and then destroying the power of the countries of their adoption, and each destroyed the international foundation on which the Europe of their time was built. In lesser things as in important ones, they are strangely alike. Both were strangers to the people they chose to lead. Hitler spoke German with an Austrian accent. Louis Napoleon spoke French with a German accent. Each had his abortive putsch and consequent imprisonment. Strasbourg and Boulongne were to Louis Napoleon what the Munich rising of 1923 was to Hitler. And if Landsberg meant much less to Hitler than Ham did to Louis Napoleon. **The Extinction of Pauperism** combined with the Memoirs of the first Napoleon bore much the same relation to the origin of the second empire as **Mein Kempf** did to the rise of the Third Reich. They were both essentially speedy characters and proclaimed it by their looks. Hitler's unkept hair and his belted raincoat produced an inescapable effect of back-street vulgarity, and nothing can prevent Louis Napoleon from looking, in some of the less flattering photographs of him, like a shady Italian waiter recently dismissed from service in a fourth rate hotel. And if the eyes of Louis Napoleon were rarely visible and those of Hitler inescapable, Louis Napoleon's eyes seem while remaining half-shut, to have hypnotized the men of his generation almost as effectively as did those of Hitler which were almost always wide open.

"Both had a gang. Both manoeuvred into power with the connivance of politicians who under-estimated their abilities. Both sought to divert the gaze of the masses from politics by a concentration on material prosperity and by a calculated encouragement of public pageantry. The early propaganda of both reveals an adroit use of the device of stealing the slogans of the rival political forces of their day and pretending that they had found the secret of reconciling what the politicians had made irreconcilable. Thus, Hitler stole the nationalist label from his dupes and the socialist lebel from his enemies and persuaded both sides he was their ally. Louis Napoleon likewise offered France both 'democracy' and 'order', both social welfare and social discipline. He came promising universal suffrage to the masses, imperial glory to the army, Catholic liberties to the clericals, and an open field for profitable investment to the businessmen; just as Hitler simultaneously claimed to be liberating

Germany from the monopolistic multiple stores while making it safe for the Ruhr industialists. Finally one might observe that it was for not dissimilar reasons that the one built boulevards and railways and the other built autobahnen.

"Yet there is an essential difference between Louis Napoleon and most other dictators and usurpers, Hitler included, which it clearly understood, provides the key to his character. Most men of this sort combine great ruthlessness with a daemonic possession. This was not true of Louis Napoleon. He had none of that fire in the belly that makes a man of action such as Napoleon I or Hitler, or even a Mussolini. He had neither drive nor organising ability, nor the gift of steady application to routine administration such as characterised his uncle, or Frederick the Great, or Louis XIV; and has lack of the ability to come to a clear-cut decision about anything is the most pronounced feature of his character. Whenever decision was at last grudgingly and uncertainly wrung from him he could only with difficulty be persuaded from going back on it. The **coup d'etat,** the entry into the Crimean War and into the Italian war, the decision to take no action in 1866, and to take action in 1870–he regretted them all as soon as they were made, and endeavoured to go back on all of them, except for the decision of 1870, which proved fatal."

SUGGESTED READINGS

Arnaud, R.: **The Second Republic and Napoleon III, 1930.**

Aubry, O.: **The Second Empire, 1940.**

Dickinson, G. Lowes: **Revolution & Reaction in Modern France, 1927.**

Elton, G. : **The Revolutionary Idea in France (1789-1871), 1923.**

Fisher, H.A.L.: **Bonapartism.**

Fisher, H.A.L.: **The Republic Tradition in Europe.**

Forbes, A.: **A Life of Napoleon, the Third.**

Guedulla, P.: **The Second Empire.**

Guerard, H.: **Napoleon III, 1943.**

Huddleston, S.: **France.**

Marriott, Sir J.A.R.: **The French Revolution of 1848 in its Economic Aspect, 1913.**

Mckay, D.C.: **The National Workshops: A Study in the French Revolution of 1848, 1933.**

Plamenatz, J.: **The Revolutionary Movements in France (1815-1861), 1952.**

Portgate, R.: **Story of a Year : 1848.**

Schapiro, J.S.: **Liberalism and the Challenge of Fascism : Social Forces in England and France (1815-1870), 1949.**

Seignobos, C.: **A History of the French People.**

Simpson, F.A.: **The Rise of Louis Napoleon, 1950.**

Simpson, F.A. : **Louis Napoleon and the Recovery of France (1848-1856), 1923.**

Taylor : **The Struggle for Mastery of Europe.**

Thompson, J.M.: **Louis Napoleon and Second Empire, 1954.**

Whitridge, A. : **Men in Crisis: The Revolutions of 1848.**

CHAPTER

14

INDEPENDENCE OF BELGIUM

Union of Holland and Belgium. In the time of Charles V (1519-55) the Netherlands consisting of 17 provinces was under Spain. However, there was a revolt in the time of Philip II (1555-98) of Spain, and ultimately the seven northern provinces won their independence and came to be known as the United Provinces of Holland and the rest of the 10 provinces remained a part of Spain. The Treaty of Utrecht of 1713 which ended the War of Spanish Succession gave the 10 provinces of Belgium to Austria and the same came to be known as the Austrian Netherlands. During the French Revolutionary War, the Austrian Netherlands were conquered by the French and they remained a part of France for 20 years. Holland was also conquered by France and for many years continued to be a part of France.

After the fall of Napoleon in 1814, the ruler of Holland was restored and he gave a new constitution to the people. The Congress of Vienna decided to set up a strong barrier State on the north-east of France and consequently united the Austrian Netherlands or Belgium with Holland.

Difficulties. It was the realisation of Pitt's most cherished schemes. However, the statesmen assembled at Vienna ignored certain realities. National and religious differences separated the two halves. For centuries, the two parts had been separated and consequently there was not much in common between the two countries. The people of Holland were Protestants and those of Belgium Catholics. They also differed in the matter of language. The French language was not only the language of the literature of the Belgians, but also the spoken language of the upper classes. Though the Flemish portion of the population was related to the Dutch, Dutch element had not developed itself with distinctness.

According to Prof. Fyffe, the antagonism between Belgium and Holland, though not insuperable, was sufficiently great to make a harmonious union between the two countries a work of great difficulty and the government at The Hague did not take the right course to conciliate its opponents. A commission was appointed to draw up a constitution for the United Kingdom and in spite of the protests of the people of Belgium, both Holland and Belgium were given equal representation in the States-General unmindful of the fact that the population of Belgium was much more than that of Holland. Although the people of Belgium rejected the constitution, yet the game was enforced. During the next 15 years, the people of Belgium were excluded from official posts which, in most cases, were given to the people of Holland. No wonder, these foreigners were not welcomed in Belgium. The States-General invariably met in the Dutch territory and never in Belgium. This also was considered to be a grievance. The Dutch language was made the official language for the whole kingdom and this was resented by the people of Belgium. The financial policy of the Dutch government was considered to be unjust to the people of Belgium. Taxes which the people of Belgium disliked were imposed but resisted. Heavy punishments were, inflicted on journalists found guilty of seditious writings. The debt burden of the two countries was not equal and Holland owed more debts than Belgium. As taxation to meet the debt charges was levied uniformly over the United Kingdom, the people of Belgium protested. The imposition of new taxes on flour and meat in 1821 added to the trouble. The religious differences separated the two parts completely. At the time of the union, the

Catholic bishops of Belgium protested against the grant of religious toleration to the Protestants. The Church in Belgium was determined to retain its control over education, but the government tried to transfer the same into secular hands. The one really irreconcilable enemy of Holland was the Church in Belgium. The Clerical Party in Belgium made an alliance with the political opposition to drive out the Dutch from Belgium.

Revolt. For some months before the July Revolution of France in 1830, the antagonism between the Belgians and their government was so violent that no great shock from outside was necessary to produce an out break. The July Revolution gave the necessary spark. The performance of a revolutionary opera gave the signal for the beginning of the revolt. The revolt was deliberately planned by Polignao and stirred up the foreign agitators, most of whom were Frenchmen. The French felt sympathy with the Belgian rebels because they weakened the barrier State and created an opportunity for the annexation of Belgium. The revolt spread from the cities to the countryside.

The king of Holland agreed to set up a separate State for Belgium but that did not satisfy the people of Belgium. The appearance of the Dutch troops at Brussels destroyed all hopes of peace. There was some inconclusive fighting. On the withdrawal of the troops, a provisional government was set up which declared the independence of Belgium. There was a possibility of the crown prince of Holland being accepted as the head of the newly-created State. However, the violence of the revolt, the activity of French emissaries and volunteers and the bombardment of Antwerp by the Dutch soldiers destroyed all hopes of a peaceful settlement.

There was a danger of all the European Powers being involved in the trouble. The independence of Belgium and the separation from Holland was a violation of the Peace Settlement of 1815 which the European Powers had pledged themselves to maintain. However, there was one relieving factor. Most of the European States had recognised Louis Philippe as the king of France and were inclined to support him on the question of Belgium. The interests of Louis Philippe demanded the maintenance of peace and he knew that he could not succeed against a combination of all the European Powers if he followed the advice of the revolutionaries and there was a possibility of his losing the throne and his life as well. He was ably assisted by Talleyrand who believed that the crying need of France was to win some ally and thereby end her isolation. With that object in view, Talleyrand went to London as French ambassador. He interviewed Wellington and William IV and assured them that France was not going to use the Belgian revolt for the purpose of adding to her power. He propounded his doctrine of non-intervention as one which ought to govern the policy of governments of Europe. So complete an understanding was established between France and England that all talk of the European Powers going to war against France on the question of Belgium ended. The regulation of the affairs of Belgium was submitted to a conference at London. Hostilities were stopped. The independence of Belgium was recognised in principle by the conference before the end of 1830. A protocol defining the frontiers was signed by the powers in January 1831.

However, the matter was far from being finally settled. The problem of providing Belgium with a king had still to be settled. The Governments of Holland and Belgium had still to give their consent to the territorial arrangements drawn up for them. The people of Belgium were inclined to elect the second son of Louis Philippe as their king. Although Louis Philippe outwardly declared his opposition to it, he secretly encouraged the proposal. The result was that his son, Duc de Nemours, was elected king in February 1831. This was something which the powers were not prepared to accept and consequently Louis Philippe refused the crown for his son. The final settlement between England and France was that Leopold of Saxe-Coburg be offered the throne and he should marry a daughter of Louis Philippe. Leopold accepted the crown on the condition that some alterations would be made in the frontiers in favour of Belgium.

The difficulty of arranging the frontier of Belgium arose mainly from the position of the Grand Duchy of Luxemburg. In 1814, this Duchy was given to the Government of Holland. In 1830, the people of this Duchy joined hands with the people of Belgium in their revolt and with the exception of the fortress, the whole of the territory passed into the hands of Belgium. The London conference had declared Luxemburg a part of Holland. However, when on the request of Leopold they declared that the question of Luxemburg will be discussed at some other future time, the Government of Holland took up arms and sent 50,000 soldiers to Belgium. Leopold appealed to France for help and a French army immediately crossed the frontiers. The Dutch withdrew and the French troops were also recalled. The London conference took up the question once again and recommended the division of Luxemburg between Holland and Belgium. This was accepted by Belgium but rejected by Holland. The result was that a treaty was made between Leopold and the powers. By the beginning of 1832, the kingdom of Belgium was recognised by all the powers and Palmerston refused to allow France to have any territory from Belgium.

Although the kingdom of Belgium was set up, the problem of overcoming the resistance of the king of Holland had still to be faced. The Dutch king held the fort of Antwerp and refused to listen either to reason or to authority. A French army besieged the fort and the English fleet blockaded the Scheldt river. After a severe bombardment, the fort fell and hostilities ended. Negotiations for peace began once again. The Belgians were not in a hurry to make peace because they had got what they desired. The king of Holland hesitated through sheer obstinacy. This state of affairs continued for years. However, by the Treaty of London, 1839, the independence and neutrality of the kingdom of Belgium was solemnly recognised and guaranteed by all the powers including Holland. It was the violation of this guarantee by Germany in 1914 that was the immediate cause of Britain's entry into the war.

It is to be observed that the attitude of Palmerston during the years of the crisis was one of patience and wisdom. He showed infinite patience in dealing with the obstinacy of the Dutch and the irritating intransigence of the Belgians. He had the wisdom to admit that the Settlement of 1814-5 had failed and some other arrangement had to be made in its place.

SUGGESTED READINGS

Cambridge Modern History, Vol. X.

Ensor: **Belgium.**

Fyffe : **History of Modern Europe.**

Phillips, W.A.: **Modern Europe.**

CHAPTER

15 AUSTRIA-HUNGARY FROM 1815 TO 1918

Austria-Hungary played a prominent part in the overthrow of Napoleon and no wonder Vienna was chosen as the place of deliberations for the resettlement of the map of Europe. Metternich, the Chancellor of Austria, gave to Austrian policy that "vigorous and certain direction which enabled him afterwards to boast himself as the conqueror of Napoleon." Between 1815 and 1918, Austria-Hungary was ruled by Francis I (1792-1835), Ferdinand I (1835-48) and Francis Joseph I (1848-1918).

Metternich. Prince Metternich was born in 1773 and he died in 1859. He was born with a silver spoon in his mouth and entered the diplomatic service of Austria at a very young age. He was able to acquire a lot of diplomatic experience within a short time as he was transferred from one capital to another. When he was hardly 36, he was appointed the Chancellor of Austria and he occupied that position for nearly 40 years when he had to run away from Vienna to England.

Metternich was the central figure not only in Austrian and German politics but also in European diplomacy. He was the most famous statesman produced by Austria in the 19th century. He was the prince of diplomats and was thoroughly at ease in the intrigues of the European politics. His vanity knew no bounds. He felt that the world was resting on his shoulders. To quote him, "My position has this peculiarity that all eyes, all expectations are directed to precisely that point where I happen to be." Again, "Why among so many million men, must I be the one to think when others do not think, to act when others do not act, and to write because others know not how ?" He felt that his death Would leave behind a void.

Metternich was the enemy of the French Revolution and all that it stood for. He described it as "the disease which must be cured, the volcano which must be extinguished, the gangrene which must be burnt out with the hot iron, the hydra with jaws open to swallow up the social order." According to him, democracy could "change daylight into darkest night."

To begin with, he had to play a very difficult role. Napoleon was connected with the royal family of Austria and consequently it was difficult to take action against him. Likewise, Metternich did not want complete collapse of Russia as that was liable to upset completely the balance of power in Europe. No wonder, between 1810 and 1813, Metternich followed the policy of playing off Napoleon and the Czar against each other. When Napoleon attacked Russia in 1812, Metternich promised him help, but at the same time assured Russia that the Austrian troops would not be used against her. The intervention of Austria in the Battle of Nations in 1813 and in the campaign of 1814, brought about the collapse of Napoleon and made Austria the dominant power among the victorious Allies.

At the Congress of Vienna (1814-15). Metternich was given the greatest amount of attention and under him the leadership of Europe passed from France to Austria. He was able to secure as much as could possibly be got for Austria. In exchange for the distant Austrian Netherlands, he got Lombardy and Venetia in Italy. He was able to put the members of the Habsburg royal family on the thrones of Parma, Modena and Tuscany. In this way, he secured effective control over Italy. Likewise, he secured for his country a dominant position in the affairs of Germany. Austria was to be the controller of the

German Diet and without her approval nothing could be done. He was able to create a strong barrier on the frontiers of France so that she might not be able to create any trouble in the future.

Metternich stood for the maintenance of the **status quo** in Europe. He wanted to make the Vienna Settlement permanent and for that purpose he entered into the quadruple alliance with Prussia, Russia and Great Britain. It was decided among the Great Powers to meet from time to time "with a view to discuss the problems facing them and thereby maintain the peace of Europe." In 1818 was held the first Congress at Aix-la-Chapelle. An attempt was made to guarantee the territorial **status quo** as established by the Congress of Vienna but the attempt was unsuccessful on account of the opposition of Great Britain. However, in 1820, the protocol of Troppau was adopted in spite of the opposition of Great Britain. According to that protocol, the European powers were given the right to interfere in the internal affairs of those States where revolutions took place and those revolutions endangered

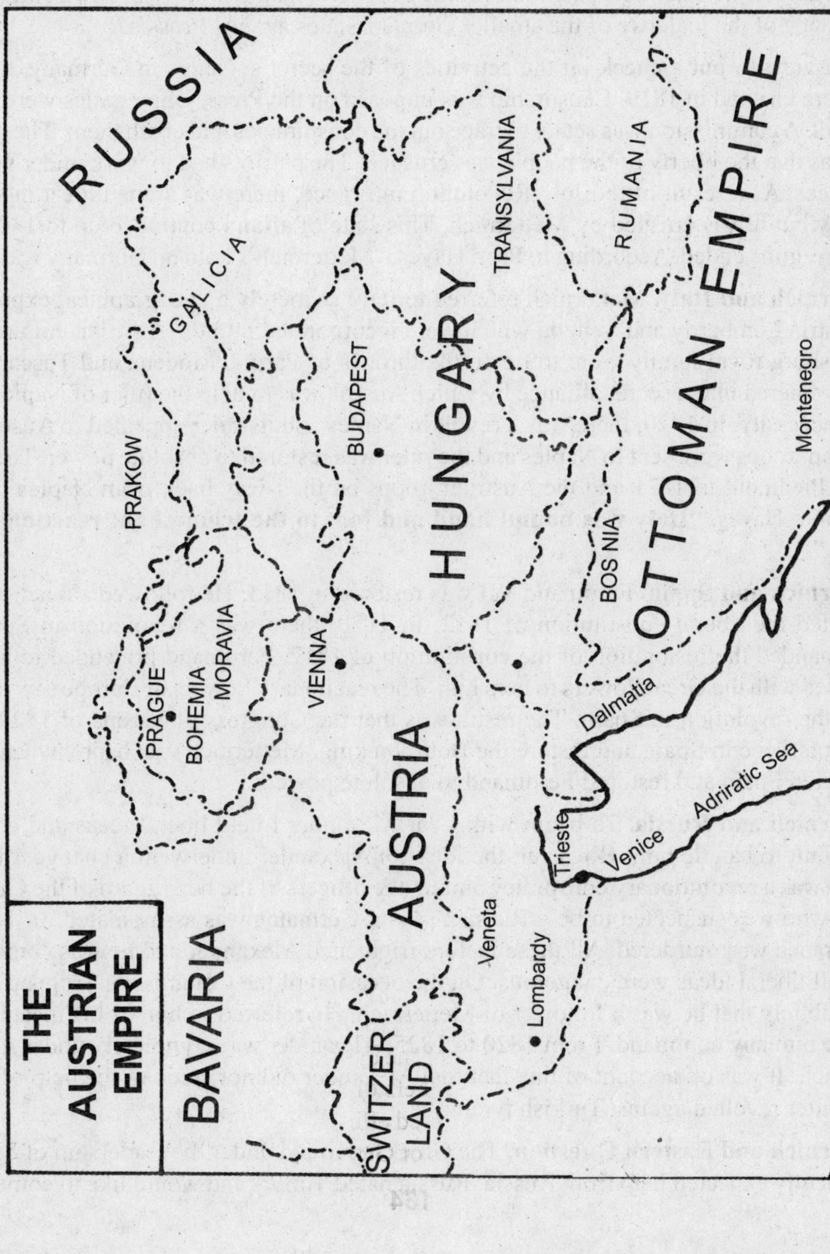

the safety of other States. The protocol enabled Metternich to police the whole of Europe and crush liberalism and nationalism wherever it raised its head. It was in pursuance of this policy that Austrit was able to crush the revolts in Naples and Piedmont. Likewise, France was given the mandate to interfere in Spain and restore the Spanish king to absolute power. The era of Congresses ended in 1822 after the Congress of Verona when Great Britain left the Congress on the question of Spain and her American colonies. However, Metternich had secured what he wanted. Thousands of persons were imprisoned, exiled or executed. Arbitrary government of the worst type was established. Metternich himself was satisfied with the results. He is said to have observed : **"I see the dawn of a better day. Heaven seems to will it that the world should not be lost."**

Metternich and Germany. In spite of the wishes and efforts of the German patriots a loose confederation was created in Germany as that was the only thing in the interests of Austria. The 39 sovereign States of German Confederation could be used by Austria to serve her own ends. Metternich took advantage of the jealousy of the smaller German States against Prussia.

With a view to put a check on the activities of the secret societies in Germany, the Carlsbad Decrees were enacted in 1819. Censorship was imposed on the Press. Universities were to be under State control. A commission was set up to trace out the conspiracies and crush them. The result of this measure was that the liberty of the people was crushed. The patriots had to work under very difficult circumstances. As a result of the July Revolution in France, there was some unrest in some States of Germany but it was crushed by Metternich. This state of affairs continued up to 1848 when the Metternich regime ended. According to Prof. Hayes, "Metternich's hold on Germany was complete."

Metternich and Italy. Metternich referred to Italy as merely a "geographical expression." He got for Austria Lombardy and Venetia which were incorporated into the Austrian empire. Members of the Habsburg royal family were to be on the thrones of Parma, Modena and Tuscany. In 1815, Metternich entered into a secret alliance by which Austria was to help the ruler of Naples and Sicily in case of necessity. In 1820, there was a revolt in Naples and its ruler appealed to Austria for help. The Austrian troops were sent to Naples and the ruler was restored to absolute power. There was also a revolt in Piedmont in 1821 and the Austrian troops on their way back from Naples crushed that also. To quote Hayes, **"Italy was bound hand and foot to the triumphant reactionary chariot of Austria."**

Metternich and Spain. Ferdinand VII was restored in 1815. He followed a reactionary policy and cancelled the liberal constitution of 1812. In 1820, there was a revolution in Spain and the people demanded the restoration of the constitution of 1812. Ferdinand pretended to agree but he corresponded with the Great Powers to help him. The reactionary Powers of Europe saw the haunting spectre of the revolution in Spain. The result was that the Congress of Verona of 1822 authorised France to intervene in Spain and restore the Bourbon king. Metternich was happy when the French armies entered Spain and restored Ferdinand to absolute power.

Metternich and Russia. To begin with Czar Alexander I held liberal ideas and consequently it was difficult to handle him. However, the ideas of Alexander underwent a change after 1815. In 1815, there was a revolutionary conspiracy among the officers of the bodyguard of the Czar. In 1819, Kotzebue, who was suspected to be a Russian spy in Germany, was assassinated. In 1820 Duc de Berry of France was murdered. All these factors frightened Alexander and he was converted to the view that all liberal ideas were dangerous. On the occasion of the Congress of Troppau of 1820, he declared publicly that he was a follower of Metternich. He referred to him as his master and asked him to give him any command. From 1820 to 1825, Alexander was completely under the influence of Metternich. It was on account of this fact that Alexander did not come to the help of the Greeks when the latter revolted against Turkish tyranny.

Metternich and Eastern Question. The Greeks revolted under the leadership of Ypsilanti and they confidently expected help from Russia. Russia hated Turkey and would like to come to the help of the Greeks who professed the same religion as she did. In spite of the community of interests, Alexander was prevailed upon by Metternich to disown Ypsilanti. The result was that the revolt was put down by the Turks and Metternich had the pleasure of imprisoning Ypsilanti in Austria for seven years. The Greeks also revolted in the Morea and the Aegean Islands in 1821. Once again, Alexander was prevailed upon by Metternich not to help them. Metternich cynically remarked that the revolt should be allowed "to burn itself out beyond the pale of civilization."

Metternich and France. After having brought about the fall of Napoleon Metternich tried to encircle France in an "iron ring". With that object in view, Belgium and Holland were combined, the Rhineland was given to Prussia and Genoa was given to Piedmont. Metternich was also not unaware of the fact that the revolutionary ideas had issued from France which could be a source of trouble once again. However, when France paid off the war indemnity in 1818, it was decided to withdraw the allied army of occupation. France was accepted as a member of the Quadruple Alliance which was transformed into the Quintuple Alliance. Metternich was on his guard when a revolution took place in France in 1830.

Metternich and Great Britain. Metternich co-operated with Great Britain in the common task of the overthrow of Napoleon. When that was accomplished, Metternich and Castlereagh co-operated in the Congress of Vienna. Great Britain joined the Quadruple Alliance with Austria and other countries for the purpose of maintaining the **status quo.** However, differences arose between the two countries on the question of the right of one country to interfere in the internal affairs of other countries. The difference of views was visible in the Congress of Aix-la-Chapelle in 1818. In 1820, Castlereagh opposed the Protocol of Troppau. Although Castlereagh committed suicide on the eve of the Congress of Verona, Great Britain opposed French intervention in Spain and left the Congress. That led to the break-up of the Congress system. Canning also opposed the Spanish move to re-establish her hold over her colonies in South America. He was assisted by the American Government which enunciated the famous Monroe Doctrine.

Metternich and Austria. Metternich followed a reactionary policy in Austria-Hungary. He did all that he could to crush liberalism and nationalism within the country. His conviction was that that was the only policy which was demanded by the circumstances of the Austrian Empire. His was a negative policy and he did not seem to like the role which he was called upon to play. To quote him, **"I have come into the world either too early or too late. Earlier I should have enjoyed the age; later I should have helped to reconstruct it. Today I have to give my life to propping up mouldering institutions."** Prevention was the keynote of his internal administration. **"Govern and change nothing"** was the beginning and the end of his programme. To quote him again, **"We follow a system of prevention in order that we may not be compelled to follow one of repression.** We are firmly convinced that any concession a government may be induced to make, strikes at the basis of its existence. Concessions properly so called can only have to do with the rights of sovereignty... they can only be made by a sovereign at the expense of the capital of his own existence." Metternich summed up his own policy in these words: "As for policy, Austria has none....Our policy is exclusively confined to the maintenance of treaties and of public response." Francis II, the Austrian Emperor, referred to the policy of his government in these words: "I also have my Estates; I have maintained their constitution and do not worry them, but if they go too far, I snap my fingers at them and send them home." Again, "He who serves me, much teach what I command".

To achieve his objective, Metternich established the censorship of the press. An elaborate system of esphonage was maintained throughout the country. The universities were put under the strict control of the government. Foreign travel was discouraged and every effort was made to segregate Austria from the rest of Europe. Education was at a low level and neither industry nor commerce developed. According to Karl Marx, "All around frontier wherever the Austrian State touched upon the civilized country, a cordon of literary censors was established in connection with the cordon of custom house officials, preventing any foreign book or newspaper from passing into Austria before its contents had been twice or three times thoroughly shift and founded pure of even the slightest contamination of the malignant spirit of the age."

In spite of his strict measures, Metternich had to admit in 1820 that "Public opinion is absolutely diseased. At Vienna, as at Paris, Berlin and London, in the whole of Germany and Italy as well as in Russia and America, our triumphs are rated as so many crimes, our conquests as so many errors, and our projects as so many follies."

Although Austria seemed to follow "the Chinese principle of immobility," there was a slow underground movement going on which baffled Metternich's efforts. "The wealth and the influence of the manufacturing and trading middle-class increased. The introduction of machinery and steam power in manufactures upsets in Austria, as it had done everywhere else, the old relations and vital conditions of whole classes of society; it changed serfs into freemen, small farmers into manufacturing operatives; it determined the old feudal trade corporations and destroyed the means of existence of many of them. The new manufacturing and commercial population came everywhere into collision with the old feudal institutions. The middle-classes, more and more induced by their business to travel abroad, introduced some mythical knowledge of the civilized countries situated beyond the imperial line of customs; the introduction of railways, finally accelerated both the industrial and intellectual movements. There was a dangerous part in the Austrian States establishments, viz., the Hungarian feudal constitution, with its parliamentary proceedings and its struggles of the impoverished and oppositional mass of the nobility against the government and its allies, the magnates. Pressburg, the city of the Hungarian Diet, was at the gates of Vienna. All the elements contributed to create among the middle-class of the towns of a spirit, not exactly of opposition, for opposition was as yet impossible, but of discontent. A general wish was for reforms, more of an administrative than of a constitutional nature ....The reform plans before the stamp of an innocuousness almost amounting to political virginity. A constitution and a free press for Austria were things considered unattainable; administrative reforms, extension of the rights of the Provincial Diets, admission of foreign books and papers and a less severe censorship—the loyal and humble desires of these good Austrians hardly go any further." **(Karl Marx).**

When the February Revolution took place in France in 1848, the reins of power were in very feeble hands in Austria. The Emperor was semi-imbecile. Metternich was aged. The counsellors were timid and ignorant. No one was ready to lead to make generous concessions. There was hesitation and timidity on all sides. During the first fortnight of March 1848, the struggle was over. Students and professors led a demonstration to the Emperor on 12 March 1848 and on 13th March, there was a conflict between the mob and the troops. Ultimately, the troops joined the revolutionaries. Metternich resigned and ran away from the country declaring that a deluge would follow him. The flight of Metternich was of great importance. It marked the era of the revolution's glory. The strongest symbol of reaction had fallen so quickly. The man who for 30 years had gagged the press, cowed or destroyed the parliaments and imprisoned the revolutionaries of Central Europe, was hunted from his capital and the Continent amid the scorn and execration of the world. The fall and flight of Metternich meant that a tide was sweeping over Europe and kings were running before it in terror.

Estimate of Metternich. Metternich dominated the politics of Europe from 1815 to 1848 and no wonder we talk of the Metternich era. For a long time, he decided as to how events were to shape themselves in Europe. In 1824, he stated that "they look for me as Messiah." However, Metternich had had to admit that he was fighting for a lost cause. According to Gruttwell, Metternich fought a losing game. According to Hayes, in spite of the efforts of Metternich the old regime was doomed and could not be saved. According to Prof. Alison Phillips, "For a tired and timid generation, he was a necessary man; and it was his misfortune that he survived his usefulness and failed to recognize that while he himself was growing old and feeble, the world was renewing its youth."

According to Prof. H.A.L. Fisher, the Metternich system "has secured for the Austrian statesman the plaudits of a generation which has recent knowledge of the tribulations of war. Metternich had many attributes of a great political leader, a brilliant and engaging presence, a cool head, a vast comprehension of affairs, a firm and patriotic will. His prestige as a liberator of his country and as the principle artificer of the ned Europe was immense; the confidence reposed in him throughout the German-speaking world almost unbounded. In the counsels of the autocrats, his was the directing mind so that the period between 1815 and 1848 has not unjustly been called the Age of Metternich. Yet this accomplished aristocrat, whose morals were so loose, whose principles were so strict, and whose influence was so wide, laboured under one of the greatest intellectual disabilities which can vitiate the judgment of a statesman. He saw no mean between revolution and autocracy, and since revolution was odious, he set himself to repress that which is the soul of humane life in society, the very spirit of liberty."

According to Henry A. Kissinger, "It was Austria's destiny that in its years of crisis it was guided by a man who epitomised its very essence; it was its destiny and not its good fortune, for as in Greek tragedy, the success of Clemens Von Metternich made inevitable the ultimate collapse of the State he had fought so long to preserve. Like the State he represented, Metternich was a product of an age in the process of being transcended. He was born in the eighteenth century of which Talleyrand was to say that nobody who lived after the French Revolution would ever know how sweet and gentle life could be. And the certitude of the time of his youth never left Metternich. Contemporaries might sneer at his invocation of the maxims of sound reason, at his facile philosophizing and polished epigrams. They did not understand that it was an accident of history which projected Metternich into a revolutionary struggle so foreign to his temperament. For like the century that formed him, his style was adapted better to the manipulation of factors treated as given than to a contest of will better to achievement through proportion than through scale. He was a Rococo figure, complex, finely carved, all surface, like an intricately cut prism. His face was delicate but without depth, his conversation brilliant but without ultimate seriousness. Equally at home in the saloon and in the Cabinet, graceful and facile, he was the beau ideal of the eighteenth century aristocracy which justified itself not by its truth but by existence. And if he never came to terms with the new age it was not because he failed to understand its seriousness but because he disdained it. Therein too his fate was the fate of Austria." Again, "The reaction against Metternich's smug self-satisfaction and rigid conservation has tended for over a century now to take the form of denying the reality of his accomplishments. But a man who came to dominate every coalition in which he participated, who was considered by two foreign monarchs as more trustworthy than their own ministers, who for three years was in effect Prime Minister of Europe, such a man could not be of mean consequence. To be sure, the successes he liked to ascribe to the moral superiority of his maxims were more often due to the extraordinary skill of his diplomacy. His genius was instrumental, not creative: he excelled at manipulation, not construction. Trained in the school of eighteenth century cabinet diplomacy, he preferred the subtle manoeuvre to the frontal attack, while his rationalism frequently made him mistake a well-phrased manifesto for an accomplished action. Napoleon said of him that he confused policy with intrigue, and Hardenberg, the envoy of Hanover at Vienna, wrote the following analysis of Metternich's diplomatic methods at the height of the crisis of 1812 : 'Endowed with a high opinion of the superiority of his ability...he loves finesse in politics and considers it essential. Since he does not have sufficient energy to mobilize the resources of his country...he attempts to substitute cunning for strength and character...It would suit him best if a fortunate accident—the death of Napoleon or great successes of Russia—were to create a situation where he could let Austria play an important role. Friedrich von Gentz, for long Metternich's closest associate, has left probably the best capsule description of Metternich's methods and personality: "Not a man of strong passions and of bold measures; not a genius but great talent; cool, calm, imperturbable and calculator **par excellence." (A World Restored,** pp. 11-12).

About Metternich, Ketelbey says that his personal charm and social gifts, his diplomatic experience and powers, his insight into men, his flair for the niceties of intrigue and the ease with which he handled intricate questions gave him an ascendancy at the Congress of Vienna and later a "moral dictatorship" over Central Europe. He "could swim like a fish in the sparkling whirl-pool" of Vienna, "no one knew so well as he how to carry through a political intrigue between dinner and a masked ball" or to envelop a difficult situation in a golden mist of fine phrases. Metternich has been attacked on the ground that he was merely an intriguer, an opportunist as "polished dust." Czar Alexander called him a liar, while liberals and democrats then and since have charged him with obscurantism and reactionaries and hostility to the desires and aspirations of the people. The view of Ketelbey is that Metternich was an Austrian Minister and it was the Austrian interests that determined his policy. He fully realised that the Austrian Empire consisted of an incoherent congeries of states and dominions accumulated by hereditary bequests of marriage dowry, as the fruit of war or diplomacy, in the interests of the balance of power or as a bulwark of Christendom against Turkey. It was held together by no consistent principle except common obedience to a single law and Metternich fully realised that its equilibrium would be upset by popular or nationalist agitation. Ketelbey says that behind the opportunism and apparent obscurantism of Metternich lay a radical, defensible principle and an authentic historical vision and that was the preservation of the Austrian Empire. With a clear vision of the new perils, Metternich set himself to suppress the nationalist and democratic movements of Germany and Italy, to counter the aspirations of the people of the Balkans for independence and to check the Czar. At the same time, he tried to build up a five-power equilibrium to sustain the European system against the increased weight of Russia and the diminished weight of France. The aim of Metternich was not so obvious and self-explanatory in peace as in war. It seemed too negative, piecemeal and opportunist and in the end repressive. Metternich knew full well that democracy and nationalism were not likely to succeed as an integrating policy. Therefore, he sought to base Austrian stability on a balanced European society, a general observation of the **status quo** and an international alliance of like-minded rulers. Metternich was in a real sense the victim or the prisoner of his age. A thorough cosmopolitan, he saw both the Austrian and European problem in terms of an equilibrium of traditional, historic units. In the international world, his vision was statesmanlike and realist. However, in the Austrian Empire, in Germany and in Italy, such a policy became stultifying and repressive. It chocked the only proper outlet for the vitality of the people. That seems the real charge against Metternich. Ketelbey concludes by saying that the Europe which condemned him enjoyed 40 years of peace that was largely of his making.

About Metternich Professor Alison Phillips says, "At the crisis of Austria's fortunes, during the final struggle with imperial France when everyone was wavering the sparing or trying to find a way out of a sorry tangle, it was he who had given the Austrian policy the vigorous and certain direction which enabled him afterwards to boast himself the conqueror of Napoleon." Again, "For a timid and tired generation, he was a necessary man; and it was his misfortune that he survived his usefulness and failed to recognise that while he himself was growing old and feeble, the world was renewing its youth."

Revolutions of 1848-49. The February Revolution in France profoundly affected the fortunes of Hungary. When the news of the French revolution reached Hungary. Kossuth (1802-94) proposed to address to the Austrian Emperor a demand not only for a responsible ministry but for the "fraternisation of the Austrian peoples" under the leadership of Hungary. In his speech of March 3, 1848, Kossuth observed: "The suffocating vapour of a heavy curse hangs over us, and out of Charnel house of Cabinet of Vienna a pestilential wind sweeps by, benumbing our senses and exercising a deadening effect on our national spirit. The future of Hungary can never be secured while in other provinces (specially in Vienna) there exist a system of government directly opposed to every constitutional principle. It is our task to establish a happier future on the brotherhood of all the Austrian races, and to substitute for the union enforced by bayonets the enduring bond of a free constitution." The speech was printed and sold in thousands in Hungary and Austria. The result was that there were demonstration in Vienna in March 1848 and Metternich ran away. After making many concessions, the Austrian Emperor also ran away from Vienna to Innsbrock.

As soon as the news reached Italy of a revolution in Vienna and the flight of Metternich, there was a revolt in Milan and the Austrian Viceroy ran away. The Austrian troops under Radetzky also withdrew from Lombardy. A Republican Government was set up in Venice. The rulers of Parma and Modena also ran away. Charles Albert, the ruler of Piedmont, declared war against Austria in March 1848. There was a great enthusiasm all over Italy to turn out the Austrians from the country. Contingents came from all over Italy to fight against the Austrians. It appeared that all was lost in Italy.

Austria had her hold over Germany since 1815. In March 1848, there was a revolt in Berlin and the king of Prussia put himself at the head of the rebels. The Frankfurt Parliament consisting of representatives from all over Germany met in 1848 to draft a constitution for a united Germany. There was great enthusiasm all over the country and the Austrian control over Germany collapsed.

As regards Hungary, Kossuth, the Hungarian leader, demanded a separate parliamentary government for Hungary and the Austrian Emperor granted the same. Hungary passed the famous March laws which abolished feudalism, serfdom and aristocratic privileges.

There was also a revolt in Bohemia. The Czechs had resented the domination of the Germans and after the revolt in Vienna they presented their demands to the Austrian Emperor, but those demands were not conceded by the Austrian Emperor. The Czechs called a meeting at Prague which was attended by the representatives of the Czechs, Silesians, Poles, Ruthenians, Serbs and Croats. The Czechs of Prague revolted and attacked the palace of the Austrian Military Commander and killed his wife. Peace was purchased by conceding the demands.

There was also another revolutionary movement with its headquarters at Agram. Its object was to unite the Croats, Slovenes and Serbs.

Under these circumstances, the condition of Austria-Hungary was very critical and everything seemed to have been lost. However, partly through his own efforts and partly on account of the mistakes of others, Austria was able to re-establish herself.

As regards Italy, Charles Albert was defeated in the Battle of Custozza in July 1848 and thus Lombardy and Venetia were brought under the control of Austria. In March 1849, Charles Albert again declared war against Austria but was again defeated in the Battle of Novara. The Republic of Rome was crushed by the French troops and the Republic of Venice was also defeated by the Austrian troops. Thus, Italy was once again brought under Austrian control.

As regards Germany, the members of the Frankfurt Parliament wasted a lot of their valuable time in academic discussions with regard to the fundamental rights of the people and the boundaries of the new German State After a lot of waste of time, it was decided to offer the throne of Germany to the King of Prussia but the latter refused to accept the same on account of the fear of Austria which had already recovered herself from the shock. Thus, the movement for the unification of Germany on a democratic basis collapsed in 1850. After refusing the throne offered to him by the Frankfurt Parliament, the King of Prussia persuaded the four kingdoms of Hanover, Saxony, Wurtemberg and Bavaria to form a union with Prussia. Austria opposed the union and ultimately Prussia had to surrender before Austria in 1850 by the Convention of Olmutz.

As regards Hungary, the problem was a difficult one. There Kossuth had become a popular hero not only within Hungary but also throughout Europe. Under his influence during the 1840's, Magyar had replaced Latin as the exclusive language used in Hungary for laws, Government business and public education. Magyar language became the double protection for the gentry against German imperial officials and Slav nationalists. This group backed the ideal of Kossuth to make Hungary a Magyar national state although the Magyars were actually in a minority in total population of Hungary. The "March Laws" passed through the Diet by Kossuth provided for Hungarian rule under the nominal kingship of the Habsburgs, with a separate parliament at Budapest elected on a restricted suffrage. The nobility lost their exemption from taxation. The towns were given representation in Parliament. The new assembly met on 4 July 1848. Within 8 hours of its meeting, Kossuth had to proclaim "the country in danger." That was due to the fact that the Slav races, encouraged by the Austrians, had revolted in Croatia and Serbia. Kossuth appealed for and was granted the power to raise an army of 200,000 men to enable Hungary to defend herself. 40,000 of these soldiers were sent to support Austria on the condition that they were not to be used "against the freedom of the Italian nation." By the end of August, General Radetzky had defeated Charles Albert at Custozza and taken Milan and all Lombardy. Windischgratz had crushed Prague. The Austrian Government found itself strong enough to crush Hungary and revoke the "March Laws." On 11 September the imperial army from Croatia invaded Hungary. Kossuth appealed to the Constituent Assembly of Vienna for help. However, in that Assembly, the German and Slav sentiment combined against Magyar claims and gave the Government a majority. There was a second mass rising in Vienna in October 1848 with the object of creating a national Germany and a national Hungary. However, the democrats of Vienna were crushed by Windischgratz. In November, Felix Schwarzenberg, the brother-in-law of Windischgratz, was made the Prime Minister of Austria. He had been an adviser of Radetzky in Italy. He was a man of violence and his chief aim was to accumulate power and use the same to restore order and central authority in the Austrian Empire. In December 1848, Emperor Ferdinand abdicated and Francis Joseph became the Emperor. The new Emperor also stood for the preservation of the prestige and military power of the monarchy. By the end of 1848, the Habsburgs were back in the saddle and the Magyar nationalist movement was doomed.

Faced with anti-Magyar risings of the Slovaks in the North, the Serbs in the South, the Rumanians and Germans in the East and the Croats on the South-West, Kossuth whipped up the Magyar national feeling to a frenzy by the end of 1848. Although Windischgratz, in the winter of 1848, advanced into Hungary and even occupied Budapest, he was compelled to withdraw again by April 1849. On 14 April 1849, the Hungarian Parliament deposed the Habsburgs and elected Kossuth as the Governor. He issued a declaration of Hungarian independence and on 6 June 1849, entered Budapest in triumph. It is maintained that the declaration of independence was a great blunder on the part of Kossuth. He ought not to have openly flouted the authority of Austria. Hungary gained nothing by the declaration of independence but that enabled Austria to ask for the help of Nicholas I, the Czar of Russia Nicholas I and Francis Joseph met at Warsaw on 21 May 1849 and there settled upon the plan of campaign.

The motives of the Czar to intervene in Hungary have been much debated, but they seem to be very simple. A large number of Poles had fought in the Hungarian army and many of them were eminent as generals at the head of it. In March, the Russian troops had entered Transylvania and been expelled by the Hungarian forces. A Hungarian division had been stationed near the Galician frontier expressly to encourage the Poles to revolt against Austria. The Czar was particularly sensitive about the Poles. His view was that all the sovereigns must unite against the revolutionaries. Czar Nicholas I intervened in Hungary partly to suppress the Polish revolt in the bud and partly to help a brother ruler against the revolutionaries.

Hungary was invaded from three sides. It was invaded by Haynau, the new Austrian commander, from Vienna side. It was invaded by Jellacic from Zagreb. Field Marshal Paskievic crossed the Carpathians and attacked the Hungarians in the rear. Gorgei who had been appointed in December 1848 the commander of the Magyar army, found himself in a very bad position. He was hopelessly outnumbered and hampered by the political necessity of defending Budapest and Komarom. Though he met with reverses, Jellacic managed to join hands with Haynau by 14 July 1849. On 18 July, the combined Austrian army entered Budapest. The operations were then transferred to the Theiss (Tisza). Gorgei managed to avoid contact with the Russians under Field Mershal Paskievic, but Haynau caught up with the Southern Hungarian army and utterly routed it at Temesvar on 9 August 1849.

Gorgei had anticipated defeat and informed Kossuth at Arad on 10 August that he would surrender if Haynau were victorious at Temesvar. The reply of Kossuth was that if that happened, he would himself commit suicide. On 11 August, the news of the disaster at Temesvar arrived and Gorgei prepared to surrender and asked Kossuth to abdicate in order to relieve the political head of the responsibility for surrender. There is a lot of controversy on the question of surrender. Kossuth accused Gorgei of deliberately betraying Hungary to the enemy. The charge seems to be absurd and probably it was put forward as a popular explanation of the defeat of Hungary. There is no doubt that both Kossuth and Gorgei knew that resistance was impossible. Even if Georgei had demanded the autonomy of Hungary, neither Haynau nor Paskievic would have accepted any terms except unconditiontal surrender on a military basis. On 13 August 1849, Gorgei led over 23,000 troops to the Russians at Vilagos and laid down his arms. Gorgei was the most remarkable of the revolutionary leaders produced by the upheavals of 1848.

It is true that Paskievic wrote to the Czar that "Hungary lies at the feet of your Majesty", but as a matter of fact, Gorgei's army and the settlement of Hungary were both handed over to Haynau. It is true that the life of Gorgei was spared as a result of the intervention of the Czar, but 13 of his generals known as "the martyrs of Arad" were shot or hanged. About 400 officers were imprisoned. Bathyany, who had been Prime Minister of Hungary, and over 100 politicians, were executed. Kassuth himself, Count Julius Andrassy and 74 others were hanged in effigy. All kinds of cruelties were done. The atrocities of the Slav and Ruman guerrillas passed wholly unpunished. Haynau earned the nickname of "Hyena" for his atrocities.

Kossuth had not committed suicide when surrender came. On 17 August 1849, he buried the Hungarian crown near the border town of Orsova and fled to Turkey from Hungary which he never saw again. He became an eloquent voice in the wilderness. He possessed a marvellous gift of exciting human emotions in favour of Hungary in the United States and England and that made him first man in Hungary. He lived for nearly 50 years and remained irreconcilably anti-Hapsburg. When Haynau visited England, he was mobbed and severely handled by the draymen of Barclay and Perkins Breweries. Lord Palmerston, the Foreign Minister of England, sympathized with the workmen. It is true that on account of the anger of Queen Victoria, Palmerston offered a perfunctory apology for the rough treatment of Haynau, but extended a very friendly welcome to Kossuth. That shows the esteem in which Kossuth was held in foreign countries. After his death, the bones of Kossuth were brought back to Hungary in 1902 in the midst of scenes of emotion such as Hungary had never seen. Undoubtedly, he exercised a volcanic and incalculable power. Without Kossuth, there would have been no revolution in Hungary as the conservative forces there were very strong.

Austria and Italy. Reference may be made to the war between Austria on the one hand and France and Piedmont on the other in 1850. Cavour was convinced that this country could be liberated from the Austrian yoke only with the help of a foreign Power whose military strength was as great as that of Austria. It was with that object in view that he entered into a deal with Napoleon III at Plombieres in July 1858. It was agreed between the parties that while Napoleon III was to help Piedmont to liberate Lombardy and Venetia from Austrian yokes, he would get Nice and Savoy as his compensation. It was in accordance with that agreement that Napoleon III joined Piedmont in the war against Austria in 1859. The Austrians were defeated in the battles of Magenta and Solferino. However, in July 1859, Napoleon III made the Armistice of Villafranca with Austria. Its terms were ratified by the Treaty of Zurich. Piedmont got Lombardy from Austria and Napoleon did not press his claim for Nice and Savoy. After the withdrawal of the Austrian troops from Lambardy, the people of Tuscany, Parma and Modena revolted and turned out their rulers. Ultimately, by the Treaty of Turin

(March 1860), France recognised the incorporation of Tuscany, Parma and Modena into Piedmont and got Nice and Savoy as promised in 1858.

In 1866, Italy entered into an alliance with Prussia and fought on the side of Prussia in the Austro-Prussian War of 1866. Although the Italians were defeated in the Battle of Custozza by Austria, yet they got Venetia after the war as their partner smashed the Austrian resistance.

Ausgleich or Compromise of 1867. Reference may be made at this stage to the Compromise of 1867 between Austria and Hungary. It has already been pointed out that the Hungarians were crushed in 1849 by the combined forces of Austria and Russia. After that, a policy of centralisation and absolutism was followed with regard to Hungary. It was officially announced that "the former constitution of Hungary is annulled by the revolution." The system of local government was superseded and administrative and judicial posts were filled by Austrian officials. German was substituted for Magyar as the State language. Hungary was made a vassal State of Austria.

However, such a state of affairs could not continue long. The war of Italian liberation of 1859-60 proved that Austria was not strong enough to maintain the integrity of her Empire. Many Hungarians joined the enemies of Austria and there was the possibility of a revolt in Hungary. It was realised that a State which was being attacked by outsiders could not afford to fight with its own subjects and consequently the necessity of an understanding with Hungary was felt by Austrian statesmen.

There were differences of opinion with regard to the solution of the difficulty. The German Liberals advocated the maintenance of a unitary and centralised government set up by Schwarzenberg. There were others who stood for a federal form of government. Under these circumstances, many trials were made before a solution acceptable to the parties was arrived at.

The October Charter or Diploma of 1860 restored Hungary to the pre-1848 condition. The five administrative districts were abolished. The Hungarian Diet was restored. The system of local government was also renewed in Hungary. Hungarion officials were appointed in their country. Undoubtedly, the Charter of 1860 paved the way for the reconciliation of Hungary.

However, the Magyars of Hungary were not satisfied with the mere restoration of pre-1848 conditions and institutions. They demanded the enforcement of the March Laws of 1848. On account of the uncompromising attitude of the parties, there was again trouble. The Ministry of Schmerling aimed at centralisation and the maintenance of the territorial integrity of the Austrian Empire and issued in 1861 the February Patent. The Constitution was framed for the whole of the Austrian Empire and Hungary was reduced to the status of a mere province. No wonder, the Patent was rejected by the Hungarian Diet. Hungary refused to send Deputies to the Reichsrath at Vienna. The watchword of Deak, the Hungarian leader, was "the recognition of the laws of 1848." The Hungarians maintained that they had been a separate nation for a long time. They were united with Austria by merely a personal union. The Emperor of Austria became the King of Hungary only when he took an oath to support the fundamental laws of Hungary and was crowned in Hungary with the iron crown of St. Stephen. The fundamental laws of Hungary were centuries old and were merely affirmed by the March Laws of 1848. No change could be made in those laws without the approval of Hungary. They could not be set aside by a unilateral act on the part of the Austrian Emperor. Hungary was a historic State with definite boundaries which could not be altered by the Austrian Emperor at will.

The deadlock continued from 1861 to 1865. In 1865, negotiations were started to resolve the same. Those were interrupted on account of the Austro-Prussian War of 1866 but were resumed in 1867 and result was the Compromise of same year. It is stated that after the Austrian defeat of 1866, Deak was asked what Hungary demanded. His reply was: **"Hungary asks no more after Konnigratz than she asked before it."** The compromising attitude of Deak was helpful to expedite the compromise. Moreover, Austria was turned out from Germany by the Austro-Prussian war and she must find support in some other quarter so that she may be able to stand against Prussia. That was possible only if Hungary was reconciled. The compromise was accepted by Francis Joseph, the Austrian Emperor, and the Parliaments of both the Countries Francis. Francis Joseph was also crowned as the King of Hungary.

The Compromise of 1867 created a curious type of State which was neither federal nor unitary. It set up the dual monarchy of Austria-Hungary, Austria-Hungary was to consist of two distinct and independent States each of which was equal to the other. They were to have the same flag and the same ruler. However, the latter was to be known as Emperor in Austria and King in Hungary. Both Austria and Hungary were to have their separate Parliaments, ministries and administrations. Each was to be completely independent in matters of internal administration. However, provision was made for a joint ministry of three departments viz., foreign affairs, war and finance. There was no common Parliament for the two countries but provision was made for a system of **Delegations.** Parliament of each country was to select a delegation of 60 members and these delegations were required to meet alternately in Vienna and Budapest. These delegations were really committees of the two Parliaments. They sat and deliberated separately. Each of them used its own language and communicated to the other in writing. Provision was made for a joint session only in the case of a difference of opinion between the two delegations and the matter was to be decided by a majority vote. Such matters as tariffs and currency system were not put under the control of the joint ministry or the delegations. They were required to be regulated by agreements concluded between the two Parliaments for periods of 10 years and that resulted in a lot of unnecessary tension after every 10 years.

The dual monarchy of Austria-Hungary was the only possible solution under the circumstances. Francis Joseph, the Austrian Emperor, was not prepared to make any radical change. The compromise was in keeping with the precedents of the past and was intended to maintain the supremacy of the Emperor. Although many concessions were made to Magyar nationalism, the compromise had its own advantages. It preserved the unity of military and diplomatic services in which the Austrian Emperor was most interested. It guaranteed the supreme direction of those affairs by the Emperor himself. It prevented both Austria and Hungary from becoming separate national States. The administrations in Austria and Hungary were dominated by the nobility and the upper middle classes. The Emperor was allowed to exercise an absolute veto over all proposed legislation. He was empowered to retain ministries even when they had not the support of the majority in Parliament.

After 1867, certain differences arose between Austria and Hungary-Austria was progressively industrialised and consequently the manufacturing, commercial and banking interests became very important and competed with the agricultural interests. On the other hand, Hungary remained overwhelmingly agricultural and consequently the industrial interests did not became strong. However, as a result of the economic disparity between the two parts, there was constant haggling between the two over the proportional contribution which was to be made by each country towards the joint expenses of the empire. The tariff policy of Austria conflicted with that of Hungary and vice versa. Austria was in favour of giving protection to industries and establishing free trade in the matter of agricultural products. On the other hand, Hungary was in favour of establishing protection for agriculture and free trade in manufactured goods. Alternately, a compromise was arrived at by which protection was given both to industry and agriculture.

The military reforms of 1868 created bitterness between the two countries. The Hungarian government insisted that the Hungarian troops should be officered exclusively by Magyars and command should be addressed to them only in the Magyar language. Austria did not accept the Hungarian demands and in 1897 Hungary refused to renew the military agreement with Austria. The Emperor was able to maintain the joint army by means of annual decrees. The German language was continued as the official language of command. In 1907, Hungary renewed the military agreement with Austria on account of the dangerous international situation.

Another source of friction was provided by the establishment of a centralised Austro-Hungarian bank at Vienna in 1878. The Hungarians demanded the establishment of separate national banks and were prepared to put up only with a common superintendence. It was agreed that after 1917, every commercial treaty of the dual monarchy with a foreign nation was to be signed, not merely by the joint ministry of foreign affairs, but also by the separate representatives of the Austrian and Hungarian governments.

In spite of its shortcomings, the compromise of 1867 brought certain advantages to both the countries. It was felt that if combined, they could count in the international politics. Their prestige was great and the same was true of their material resources. The joint fiscal arrangements created a wide market for Austrian and Hungarian goods. Thus, Austrian industry got a privileged market in Hungary and Hungarian agricultural products got a privileged market in Austria. Their joint military forces served to maintain the position and reputation of the Habsburg as a great power. Both Austria and Hungary were afraid of Russia and no wonder they co-operated in supporting a big military establishment.

David Thomson says that the Compromise of 1867 rested on an ingenious effort to evade the principles of national unification and independence. It was a synthetic substitute for nationalisation, not an implementation of it. It consecrated political division and national disunity. From the point of view of the Habsburg Empire, it was a masterpiece of conciliatory statecraft devised to perpetuate the Empire as a power unit in European politics, to postpone indefinitely the separatist hopes of subject peoples for independence and consolidate the joint predominance of the Germans and Magyars over the dual kingdom. It represented the principle not of unification, but of partition. It was a partition of territory between the Germans and the Magyars. It accepted and reaffirmed the view that the Austrian Empire was incapable of national unification in the sense in which Italy and Germany were being unified. It may be condemned as leaving to the 20th century a tangle of unresolved problems, as merely papering over the cracks. However it lasted for half a century and it gave Austria-Hungary a period of relative stability at a time when the rest of Central and Eastern Europe was seething with unrest. It was realistic in the sense that it accepted the undeniable fact that the economic and social development of this area could not support a homogenous nation state. Deak and Beust, who were responsible for the Compromise of 1867, showed a spirit of realism worthy of Cavour or Bismarck, but their services were rendered to an ancient dynastic state and not to the cause of integral nationalism.

Watson says: "While it is true to describe the Ausgleich as the logical outcome of the Pragmatic Sanction (1723), subsequent events have nonetheless shown it to rest upon a far more cynical basis than that of a historic evolution. The real motive force which underlies the Dual System is a league between the two strongest races, the Germans and the Magyars, who divided the monarchy between them, and by the grant of autonomy to the two next strongest races, the Poles and Croats; made them their accomplices in holding down the remaining eight." The Slavs were in favour of a federal form of government instead of the Dual Monarchy. They stood for the autonomy of all nationalities within the Austrian Empire which could lay claim to "historic rights." Bohemia was particularly bitter as she left that she was entitled to a better treatment. Thus, it was that the Compromise of 1867 contained within itself the seeds of future discord. The situation in Hungary itself got complicated after 1867. It is true that Deak acted as a statesman and tried to reconcile the non-Magyar elements in Hungary. He offered the famous 'blank sheet' to the Croats and asked them to fill in as they pleased. Croatia was given "complete autonomy in all matters of administration, justice, religion and education, and Croatian is everywhere the language of the legislature and the executive." Foreign affairs alone remained with the Hungarian Diet to which Croatia was permitted to send 40 members. She was allowed to have her own Diet at Agram.

The law of Nationalities of 1866 attempted to solve the problems of the non-Magyar races in Hungary. While Magyar was made the official language of Hungary in legislature and administration, the use of other languages was allowed in schools, courts of law and establishments. It satisfied "the lawful national claims" of the different races in Hungary. However, the Law of Nationalities remained a dead letter from the very beginning. No effort was made to implement its provisions. On the other hand, no stone was left unturned to Magyarise the non-Magyars in Hungary. That was bound to result in bitterness and the ultimate break-up of Hungary itself.

The compromise of 1867 was not the real solution of the problems facing Austria-Hungary. The other minorities in Austria-Hungary were jealous of the concessions given to Hungary in 1867. No effort was made to reconcile them after 1867. The result was that discontentment continued to grow among them and ultimately brought about the complete disintegration of the Austrian Empire after 1918.

Austria-Hungary and the Balkans. The Balkans were of great importance to the Dual Monarchy of Austria-Hungary. That was due to the geographical position of Austria in Europe. She was a land-locked country and stood in need of an outlet to the sea. The Danube river could give Austria access to the sea, but with Constantinople in hostile hands, the advantages of that access were liable to be nullified. Trieste was the Liverpool of the Dual Monarchy and Pola was its Portsmouth. If Trieste went to Italy and Istria and Fiume went to Italy or Serbia (or Jugoslavia), the naval and commercial position of Austria-Hungary was liable to become desperate. Her position on the Adriatic was exceedingly precarious. Secure in the possession or Brindisi and Valona, Italy had no difficulty in barring the access of Austria-Hungary to the Mediterranean. Montenegro and Serbia were also the rival of Austria-Hungary in the Balkans. Montenegrom had already gained access to the Adriatic Sea although her coast-line was less than 30 miles in extent. If the dreams of a Jugoslav Empire were realised even partially, the importance of Trieste, Fiume and Pola was bound to be neutralised. These factors were responsible for Austria taking keen interest in the Balkans. Even if she was denied an access to the Adriatic Sea and the Black Sea, she thought of finding an outlet to the Aegean Sea. No wonder, there was rivalry and hostility between Austria on the one hand and Russia and Serbia on the other.

Austria-Hungary began to take keener interest in the Balkans after her expulsion from Germany and Italy in 1866. By the Treaty of Berlin of 1878, Austria-Hungary got Bosnia, Herzegovina and the Sanjak of Novi-Bazzar. Novi-Bazzar not only formed a wedge between the Slavs of Serbia and those of Montenegro, but seemed to invite Austria-Hungary towards the Vardar Valley and so on to Salonica.

Up to 1903, the ruling family of Serbia was subservient to Austria-Hungary. However, in that year King Alexander and his queen were murdered in cold blood and the Obrenovic dynasty to which he belonged, was completely extinguished. The Karageorgevic family came to power. The new family was virile and opposed to Austria-Hungary. The result was that tension between Austria-Hungary and Serbia began to increase. It resulted in the "Pig-War" of 1905-6. This convinced the Serbians that there could be no economic development of their country so long as they did not get a coast-line either on the Adriatic or on the Aegean Sea. Access to the Aegean Sea was out of the question and as regards the Adriatic Sea, access was possible only if she got Bosnia and Herzegovina or some of the harbours of Dalmatia.

The Serbs felt that they could get Bosnia and Herzegovina, but they were completely disappointed when in 1908, Austria-Hungary which had been given the right of merely occupying and administering them by the Treaty of Berlin annexed them. This action of Austria was like a declaration of war and there was every possibility of such a war between Austria-Hungary and Serbia. Military preparations were made in Serbia but she was persuaded by Russia not to precipitate a crisis as Russia was not in a position to fight against Austria and Germany. Germany also declared her determination to stand by the side of her ally. Serbia asked for compensation in the Sanjak of Novi-Bazzar but she got nothing. On the other hand, she was forced to eat the humble pie and declared that she had no claims to Bosnia and Herzegovina and that she accepted their annexation by Austria. Turkey got some money from Austria-Hungary as compensation and accepted their annexation by Austria. Bulgaria got £50,000,000 from Austria. It was in this way that the Bosnian crisis of 1908-9 was averted. However, that left bitter memories among the Serbians who felt that they had been deprived of their chances of getting Bosnia and Herzegovina.

During the Balkan Wars of 1912-13, Serbia was able to add to her territory and prestige. She was able to strengthen the barrier between Austria-Hungary and Salonica. The Serbian victories during the Balkan wars gave them more of self-confidence and also made them ambitious. Austria could not tolerate the enormous increase in the strength of Serbia and there was every possibility of a clash in 1913. However, that was averted. But on 28 June 1914, the Serbians murdered Archduke Francis Ferdinand of Austria in the Bosnian capital of Serajevo. Austria gave an ultimatum to Serbia and after the expiry of the stipulated period, Austria declared war on Serbia. Austria was supported by Germany and Serbia was supported by Russia, France and Great Britain. Thus, the World War I broke out in 1914. Austria Hungary was defeated during the war and she was broken up by the Treaty of St. Germain and the Treaty of Trianon.

SUGGESTED READINGS

Cecil, A.: **Metternich, 1933.**

Drage: **Austria-Hungary.**

Flenley, R.: **Makers of the Nineteenth Century: Metternich.**

Herman, A.: **Metternich.**

Kissinger, H.A.: **A World Restored, 1957.**

Auernheimer: **Metternich, Statesman and Lover, 1940.**

Malleson, C.B.: **Life of Prince Metternich.**

Sandemans: **Metternich, 1911.**

Woodward : **Three Studies in European Conservatism, 1929.**

Mahaffy: **Francis Joseph.**

Pribram, A.F.: **The Secret Treaties of Austria-Hungary.**

Redlich, J.: **Francis Joseph of Austria.**

Rumbold : **Francis Joseph and His Times.**

Seton-Watson : **The Future of the Hungarian Nation.**

Steed, H. Wickham: **The Habsburg Monarchy.**

Taylor, A.J.P.: **The Habsburg Monarchy.**

Thayer, W.R.: **Throne-Makers.**

CHAPTER

16 UNIFICATION OF ITALY

Settlement of 1815. The Vienna Settlement of 1815 failed to unify Italy. As a matter of fact, it was divided into a large number of States under different rulers. Ferdinand I was restored to Sicily and Naples, the Pope was restored to Rome and the Papal States, and Parma, Modena and Tuscany were given to the members of the Habsburg family. Lombardy and Venetia were annexed to the Austrian Empire and Sardinia and Genoa were added to the kingdom of Piedmont. It was on account of the division of Italy into many independent parts that Metternich referred to Italy as a **geographical expression.** Mazzini described the condition of Italy in these words: "Country, liberty, brotherhood, all are wrested from them; their faculties are mutilated, curbed, chained within a narrow circle traced for them by men who are strangers to their tendencies, to their wants, their wishes; their tradition is broken under the care of an Austrian corporal; their immortal soul feudatory to the stupid caprices of a man seated on a throne at Vienna."

The restorations of 1815 were followed generally by reactionary or demoralising administrations. Ferdinand I restored the hated police system, the press censorship and the authority of the clergy. He persecuted liberal opinion, gave preference to Royalists and offended the people of Sicily by abolishing the autonomous constitution of that Island. In the case of the Papal States, the Inquisition, the Index and all the paraphernalia of medieval church government were restored. A corrupt and inefficient administration created a lot of discontentment. There was social anarchy in the country. There was a tyrannical government in Modena. In the case of Venetia and Lombardy, a deliberate attempt was made to "Austrianize" the political life of the people. In the case of Piedmont and Sardinia, Genoa smarted under the humiliation of subjection to Piedmont. On the whole, there was excessive provincialism in Italy and everything was dominated by Austria.

The Napoleonic regime had infused new life into Italy[1] and given an impulse to union which had been strengthened on many a battlefield. As the restored princes followed a policy a reaction, the democratic and nationalist ideas began to work among the people like leaven. Patriots were roused to a sense of their country's humiliation and democrats inspired to resist oppression as Italians and

1. As a result of Napoleon's rule of Italy, the northern area was well-governed. The kingdom of Naples was under Murat who conceived the bold scheme of uniting all Italy under his rule. During 1814-15, he put his plan into practice and proclaimed the Union of Italy. He was defeated and shot but the ideal that he proclaimed did not die. Murat is still regarded as the earliest modern champion of Italian independence and union. According to Markham, "In Italy, the administrative unification under Napoleon, partial and inconsistent as it was, the introduction of the Code and conscription, hastened the development of the Risorgimento, signs of which had already appeared before Napoleon's first invasion of Italy. Under Napoleon Italian troops fought well in their own units, and suffered about 80,000 casualties: their officers returned from the wars imbued with national sentiment. A few writers like Alfieri and Foscolo, forerunners of the Risorgimento, were anti-Napoleon in feeling because he had betrayed their hopes of national unity. From 1811 onwards, Murat inclined towards the Italian party which resented the predominance of French officials, and Napoleon threatened him with deposition. In 1815, during the Hundred Days, Murat declared war against Austria, and issued a proclamation calling on all Italians to fight for national unity and independence."

not as Sicilians, etc. Secret societies began to spread all over Italy and the **Carbonari** was the most important. It had its mystic rites and symbols, but it concealed and fostered a determined political purpose which was the expulsion of the foreigner and the achievement of constitutional freedom. All classes joined it whether they were nobles, military officers, peasants or priests. However, the liberal and democratic ideas had taken the deepest roots among the gentry, and the bourgeoisie. The Carbonari spread beyond Italy and the black, red and blue of the Carbonari became the flag of the revolution.

Revolt in Naples (1820). Under the impetus of secret societies, a revolution began in 1820 and was not exhausted for 30 years. The first revolt broke out in Naples. Ferdinand I had pledged himself solemnly to respect the liberal constitution of Sicily at the time of his restoration to the throne in 1815. However, in 1816, he cancelled that constitution so that it may not serve as a model for other States of Italy. The excitement created by the Spanish revolution of 1820 spread to the Italian dominions of the Spanish Bourbons. The people of Naples, supported by the army, demanded a constitution on the model of Spain. Ferdinand granted the demands of the rebels with eagerness. He thanked God that He had given him an opportunity to confer that blessing upon his people. He also ratified the concession in a solemn manner. In the presence of the court and ministers, he proceeded to the altar and took the following oath: "Omnipotent God who with infinite penetration lookest into the past and into the future, if I lie, or if I have had in mind to break the oath do Thou at this instant hurl on my head the lightning of Thy vengeance." The king kissed the Bible, the oath was repeated by his sons and the new constitution was publicly proclaimed.

However, Ferdinand I sent a secret message to the sovereigns assembled at Troppau informing them of his intention "to leave his kingdom and with the help of Austrian troops to resume absolute power." In December 1820, he left for Laibach. As soon as he was safe in Austrian territory, he asked for the help of the sovereigns to restore him to absolutism. The result was that an Austrian army was sent to Naples. The troops of Naples ran away. Ferdinand was restored. The constitution was torn up. The rebel leaders were put in prisons or hanged.

Revolt in Piedmont (1821). The revolutionary movement was not confined to Naples alone. The whole of Italy at that time was honeycombed with secret societies. The Government of Victor Emmanuel in Piedmont was weak and reactionary and in March 1821, an insurrection broke out there. However, there was no hostility to the House of Savoy. The slogans of the people were the following: "Our hearts are faithful to our king, but we wish to deliver him from perfidious counsels. War against Austria; at home a constitution; such are the wishes of the people." When the Austrian armies marched to Naples, the Liberals of Piedmont decided to attack the Austrian troops from the rear. However, the movement was badly led and the plans hopelessly failed. Victor Emmanuel resigned his crown in favour of his brother Charles Felix. There were people who wanted the throne to go to Charles Albert. In the midst of divided counsels, the movement collapsed.

Lombardy. In the case of Lombardy, the Austrian yoke was reimposed with great vigour. The rebel leaders were taken to Austria where they had to spend their lives in prisons. The youngmen were conscripted for the Austrian armies. The jails of Lombardy were full of political prisoners. All the subjects were thoroughly watched. Torture was employed to get confessions.

1830. The July Revolution of 1830 in France also affected the Italian politics. The Papal States were very badly affected. From the Papal States, the movement spread to Piedmont, Parma and Modena. However, the rising were everywhere successful. Pope Gregory XVI asked for the help of Austria. Metternich sent the Austrian armies into Italy and the Papal States were occupied by the White coats. Order was restored and the authority of the Pope was re-established. Francis IV was restored to his throne in Modena and Marie Lousie in Parma. However, as soon as the Austrian troops left Italy, fresh revolts broke out and they had to return once again. At this time, France also sent an army to occupy Ancona (1832) and for 6 years Austrian and French troops continued to confront each other in the Papal States.

The insurrections failed because the democratic efforts were disunited and not systematic. The people were not ripe for revolution. Unity was the cry of only a few leaders and not the creed of the masses. However, one thing was clear and that was the weakness of the reactionary States in Italy. They were saved only by the intervention of Austria.

Risorgimento. There were many revolts in Italy against the existing conditions and thousands of persons were sent to prisons or in exile. They stimulated the deep and wide movement of thought and feeling which became so important in Italian history that they were given the title of **II Risorgimento,** the revival or resurrection.

The Risorgimento movement was at bottom a moral one. It was based on the ideal of a free and united Italy. It got strength from the Romantic movement. It reminded the Italians of their greatness in the past. Politically, the revival was patriotic and national. It was a protest against Austrian domination and a demand for unity. It was liberal and democratic. There was a demand for parliamentary form of government, freedom of press, reduction of powers of the church, and the establishment of a republic. It presented the aspirations of the middle classes of Italy to develop themselves economically. It was linked up with the growth of knowledge and science. Such a broad movement could not be incorporated in one single programme. The views and efforts of persons like Mazzini came within its scope.

Mazzini (1805-72). Giuseppe Mazzini was the son of a doctor and professor of anatomy in Genoa. From his childhood, he was influenced by the nationalist movement in Italy. When he was hardly 10, Genoa was put under Piedmont in 1815. This act was very much resented by the people. During the 1820's Mazzini studied the writings of the romantic writers of Italy, France, Great Britain and Germany. His favourite writers were Dante, Shakespeare, Byron, Goethe, Schiller, Scott, Hugo, etc. Even when young, he was impressed by the misery of his country. To quote him, "In the midst of the noisy, tumultuous life of the students around me I was sombre, and absorbed and appeared like suddenly grown old. I childishly determined to dress always in black, fancying myself in mourning for my country,"

He had a bent of mind for literary life. "A thousand visions of historical dramas and romances floated before my mental eyes." But he gave up that idea for the sake of fighting for his country. He called this as his "first great sacrifice."

He joined the Carbonari not because he approved of its methods but because it was at least a revolutionary organisation. He was arrested in 1830 and imprisoned in the fortress of Savona. He was released after six months. The Governor of Genoa told Mazzini's father that his son was "gifted with some talent" but he was "to fond of walking by himself at night absorbed in thought. What on earth has he at his age to think about? We don't like young people thinking without our knowing the subject of their thoughts."

His vast experience helped him to found in 1831 a new organisation known as **"Young Italy".** This society superseded the Carbonari as the centre of nationalist agitation. Its motto was: **"God and the People."** A member had to take an oath. "To dedicate myself wholly and for ever to the task of constituting a free, independent and republican Italy."

Mazzini believed that the young men of Italy could bring about the unification of Italy if they had faith in their mission. To quote him **"Place youth at the head of the insurgent multitude; you know not the secret of the power hidden in those youthful hearts nor the magic influence exercised on the masses by the voice of youth. You will find among the young a host of apostles of the new religion."** Mazzini appealed for martyrs to the Indian cause. He reminded the Italians that they had no citizenship, no country and no national flag. The cries of Young Italy were God, people and Italy. Its methods were education, literary propaganda and revolts.

Mazzini believed that Young Italy must not merely be a body of conspirators. Its main object was to create among the Italians the spirit of self-sacrifice to die for the sake of their country.

Mazzini considered the liberation and unification of Italy as a religion. He was prepared to live and die for it. He was a dauntless leader. He was a man of imagination, poetry, and audacity. He was the master of a persuasive literary style. He had a burning enthusiasm in his heart. All these qualities of Mazzini helped the cause of Italian unification.

Mazzini believed that Austria must be driven out of Italy and the sooner that was done the better. He was not in favour of any foreign help to drive out the Austrians from Italy. To quote him, **"The only thing wanting to twenty million of Italians, desirous of emancipating themselves, is not power, but faith.**

The great contribution of Mazzini lay in the fact that at a time when the people of Italy considered the liberation and unification of Italy as an impossible dream, he made the same a practical ideal. He was able to create a faith among the people for the holy task. He was able to convert a large number of persons who were fired with the same missionary spirit which he himself possessed for the cause of Italian unification.

High hopes were raised in Italy when Pious IX became the Pope in 1846. He followed a liberal policy and it was felt that he might become the leader of the nationalist and democratic forces in the country. The shouts of **Viva Pio Nono** were heard from democratic lips. Metternich was upset. To quote him, "We are prepared for anything except a liberal Pope. Now we have got one. There is no telling what may happen." Austrian troops occupied Ferrara. Charles Albert of Piedmont was indignant and Great Britain protested. However, the zeal of the Pope slackened very soon. He refused to move forward. In spite of this, in every State in Italy, a new spirit was to be found. The movement was almost universal.

Browning's account of Italy represents the feelings of the common man. He makes the Italian in England say the following:

"However, if I pleased to spend
Real wishes on myself—say three—
I know at least what should be.
I would grasp Metternich until
I felt his red, wet throat distil
In blood through these two hands."

1848-49. The year 1848 opened with many problems, popular agitation was increasing in Naples and Sicily for reforms. The democratic parties in the Papal States, Tuscany and Piedmont were demanding a new constitution which transferred real power into the hands of the people. In the case of Lombardy and Venetia, the Austrian yoke was becoming intolerable. The movements of 1848-49 were democratic and nationalist.

In January 1848, a revolution broke out in Palermo which demanded reform, Sicilian autonomy and the constitution of 1812. The demands were granted after some resistance. There were demonstrations in Naples and they also got a new constitution. The result was that there were popular demonstrations in favour of a constitution in Piedmont, Tuscany and the Papal States. In March 1848, Piedmont and Tuscany got liberal constitutions which established constitutional governments in those States.

The same month news came that there was a revolt in Vienna and Budapest and Metternich had run away to London. The revolution broke out in Milan, the Viceroy ran away and the Austrian troops under Radetzky withdrew. A republic was proclaimed in Venice. The rulers of Modena and Parma also ran away. There was a demand for war to end the Austrian domination in Italy. Cavour appealed in these words: "The supreme hour of the Sardinian monarchy has sounded. There is only one path open to the government, the nation, the king—immediate war." Charles Albert declared war against Austria. Tuscany, Naples and the Papal States sent their contingents. However, after some time they were all withdrawn. Charles Albert was defeated in the Battle of Custozza in July 1848. Lombardy and Venetia came under the control of **Austria.** The result of Custozza was that the Moderates were discredited and the Extremists under Mazzini same to the front. **"The war of the princes was finished, that of the peoples begun."**

A republic was proclaimed in Rome under the headship of Mazzini. The authority of the Pope was abolished and the Pope ran away to Naples and appealed to the Powers for help. In March 1849, Charles Albert renewed the war against Austria but he was again defeated in the Battle of Novara. He abdicated and his son Victor Emmanuel II made peace with Austria. After Novara, reaction started in Italy. Sicily was reconquered by Naples. The ruler of Tuscany was restored. Louis Napoleon, the French President, sent an expedition to Rome. Garibaldi was defeated and the Pope was restored. Venice was also captured by the Austrians in August 1849. Absolutism and reaction triumphed everywhere in Italy except Piedmont which did not cancel the liberal constitution given in 1848. Although the movement of 1848-49 had failed, something had been gained. Those who stood for a republican government for Italy or a government under the Pope, were discredited and things were cleared for the unification of Italy under the monarchy of Piedmont. Moreover, during this movement, the people from all over Italy participated unmindful of the fact whether they belonged to one part of Italy or the other. The people of Italy became conscious of themselves. The movement gave the Italian cause "a dynasty to represent it and a people to defend it."

The failure of the revolts in Italy before the rise of Cavour was due to many causes. Austrian position was very strong in Italy and it was not possible to oust her without foreign help. However, the motto of the Italian patriots was that they would be able to achieve their independence and unification without any outside help. That was impossible. It is true that as a result of the Carbonari and Young Italy of Mazzini, ideas of nationalism were spreading all over Italy, but still there was provincialism and selfishness among the people. Very few people thought in terms of Italy as a whole. There was no collaboration among the princes of Italy for Italian unification. As a matter of fact, excepting Piedmont, all others were opposed to it. Austria, Lombardy and Venetia were opposed to Italian unification. The same was the case with the Austrian rulers of Parma, Modena and Tuscany. The Pope was the greatest enemy of Italian unification, because the unification of Italy was bound to deprive him of his territory, capital, income and prestige and he was helped by France and others in his efforts to keep Italy disunited. The Italian patriots had different objectives. Some stood for a Republican Government, others for the leadership of the Pope and still others that of Piedmont. The lack of unity weakened the cause. The patriots pulled in different directions and consequently their divided forces could not achieve much. This was the condition when Cavour came to the front. However, it must be remembered that the failure of the above revolts facilitated the work of Cavour. The cause of Republicanism and that of the headship of the Pope was discredited and thus all the people of Italy could work together for the unification of Italy under the House of Piedmont. Moreover, during these revolts, Piedmont proved herself to be the leader of the people of Italy.

Until his death in 1861, the most important man in Italian politics was Cavour. As a youngman, he had travelled widely in England, France and Switzerland. He was a keen student of advanced Western methods in agriculture, industry and parliamentary government and was fascinated by them. It became a mission of his life to westernize Piedmont and eventually the whole of Italy. He was convinced that railways, factories, banks, milk and business enterprises as working in France and Britain were the only road to economic prosperity in Italy. In October 1850, he was appointed Minister of Agriculture, Commerce and Marine of Piedmont. He made a series of commercial treaties with England, Frânce and Belgium and thereby linked Piedmont to the free trade countries of western Europe. As a Minister of Finance, he raised capital by internal loans for immediate needs and an external loan from England. A part of it was spent on the construction of rail-roads. In November 1852, he formed his own Ministry. In his new capacity, he started in right earnest the improvement of the roads, rail-roads, docks and ports of Piedmont. He expanded her commerce and strengthened her finances. As a young engineer in the army, Cavour had acquired the outlook and aptitude of a technician. He approached the problems of politics with a systematic well-informed and logical mind. He was always prepared to analyse them patiently and carefully in order to find out a solution. By 1854, he had succeeded in running Piedmont on sounder business-like lines. Keeping England and France as his models, he passed the necessary legislation to modernise the structure of business corporations, banks and credit institutions, co-operative societies, the civil administration and the army. After the end of the Crimean War in 1856, Cavour took further a more intensive programme of economic development. He tried to acquire more military and economic strength for his country. The railways of greatest strategic importance were expanded. The Mont Cenis Tunnel was planned to pierce the Alaps and link up the territory of Piedmont with France. Genoa was changed from a naval base into a great commercial port with new docks and leading facilities. Piedmont was linked very closely with the West by rail and steamship. By the time Cavour died in 1861, he had created by diplomatic alliances and wars, a new kingdom of Italy with Piedmont as its core, but still excluding Venetia and Rome.

Before Cavour came on the scene of Italian politics, the boast of the Italian was **"Italia fara de se"** (Italy will act by itself). However, the conviction of Cavour was that Italy herself was not so strong militarily as to fight against Austria. This had been proved by the defeats of Custozza and Novara. Italian unification was possible only with foreign help. Cavour would have preferred British help and Britain was generally sympathetic to the cause of liberal nationalism in Italy and had no immediate demands to make from Italy in return. However, the British Government had made it clear on many occasions that it would not help the people of Italy by military support. Palmerston believed that the survival of the Austrian Empire was necessary for the maintenance of balance of power between Russia and France in Europe. When in 1857, the Archduke Maximilian became the Viceroy of Lombardy, his policy of leniency and conciliation was warmly approved by British diplomats at Vienna and Turin. At the most, Cavour could expect benevolent neutrality from Britain. Britain was determined to avoid any involvement in a general war.

Cavour joined the Crimean War in 1855 on behalf of England, France and Turkey and against Russia. It is true that Piedmont had no interest in the Eastern Question, but he got an opportunity to raise the status of Piedmont. It was a master-stroke of his policy. When the Italian troops complained of mud in the Crimea, Cavour wrote back thus: "Out of this mud, Italy will be made." After victory over Russia, the Congress of Paris was held in 1856. It was before that Congress that Cavour was able to condemn the Austrian rule in Italy and raise the Italian question from the level of a local question to that of an international question. Moreover, he wanted the sympathy of Europe for his cause, particularly that of Napoleon III.

Napoleon III himself had sympathy for the cause of Italian unification. He had once been a member of the Carbonari. The Liberals of France also encouraged him to help the people of Italy. Napoleon III was always ready to embark on foreign adventures in order to gain fresh prestige for his regime. He had tasted the fruits of popularity and prestige from the Crimean War. He favoured the idea of north Italian kingdom coming into existence with French help. The people of France would like the idea of acquiring Nice and Savoy. Napoleon III also felt that by helping Italy, he will be doing what Napoleon I had done in his own time. He will be completing the work started by Napoleon Bonaparte.

In January 1858, bombs were thrown on Napoleon III and the Empress when they were going to the opera. It is true that both of them escaped unhurt, but many persons were killed and wounded. Many Italians were arrested and it was found that Orsini was the chief agent in the plot. Orsini declared that what he had done had sprung from his belief that Napoleon had betroyed the cause of Italy. From his prison, he wrote two letters to Napoleon III appealing to him to free Italy. To quote Orsini, "So long as Italy is not independent, the tranquillity of Europe no less than that of Your Majesty, is a concrete chimera. Deliver my country and the blessings of twenty-five million citizens will follow you in posterity." On the scaffold of the guillotine, the last words of Orsini were "Vive Italie" (Long Live Italy!). Victor Emmanuel had sent General Della Rocca to congratulate Napoleon III on his escape. However, the protests of the French Minister were so hostile that they evoked separate replies from both Victor Emmanuel and Cavour. These replies along with the courage shown by Orsini at the time of his death, confirmed Napoleon III in his resolve to help the cause of Italian unification. Napoleon III is stated to have observed, "Now that is what I call courage." He also published Orsini's last letter appealing to him to support the cause of Italian unification. He took the really decisive step in June 1858.

Napoleon III sent a message to Cavour through a private source that he was going to spend the summer in Plombieres and he would be glad to see him there. Cavour met the Emperor on 21-22 July 1858 at Plombieres and had a long discussion with him, first at his residence and then on a long drive round the town while Napoleon himself held the reins. An agreement was arrived at between Cavour and Napoleon III. France promised to support Piedmont in a war with Austria on the condition that Cavour provided a pretext which would justify the action of France in the eyes of the people of Europe. The Austrians were to be driven out of Italy. The North was to form a kingdom of Italy under Victor Emmanuel II. The whole of Italy was to be united in a federation under the Presidency of the Pope. Victor Emmanuel was to marry his 16-year-old daughter to Prince Napoleon, the cousin of Napoleon. France was to get Savoy and Nice although Savoy was the cradle of the royal house and of the state of Piedmont and Nice was the birthplace of Garibaldi.

The first step in the fulfilment of the Pact of Plombieres was the marriage of the daughter of Victor Emmanuel with the cousin of Napoleon III. In September 1858, little Clotilde agreed to meet Prince Jerome and promised "if he is not actually repulsive to me, I have decided to marry him." Jerome was found to be not repulsive and the marriage was solemnised. In January 1859, the Pact which was so far verbal, was embodied in a formal treaty between the two Governments. It was provided in the secret treaty that in case of war, France was to provide 200,000 men and Austria was to be driven out of Italy. Cavour wrote, "We have Austria in a cleft stick and she cannot get out of it without firing the cannon." The people of Northern Italy were excited. They cheered Victor Emmanuel and the kingdom of Italy. They cried, "Long live the war !".

In March 1859, Russia was won over by a treaty whereby Napoleon III agreed to support a revision of the Treaty of Paris of 1856 in return for Russia's approval of the changes in the settlement of 1815 in so far as it affected Italy. This ensured against Russian intervention. There was no danger of intervention from Britain because popular sympathies in Britain were with the people of Italy. Prussia was expected to follow Britain in seeking mediation and she was not averse to seeking Austria humiliated.

Piedmont and Austria began to mobilise as tension began to increase. Cavour had only one aim in view and that was to force Austria to issue an ultimatum at the right moment and thereby put herself in the wrong. Mobilization in Piedmont dislocated everything. It was more than a precautionary measure. It nearly amounted to a declaration of war. Under pressure from different quarters, Napoleon III began to show signs of backing down. By 18 April 1859, it appeared that the concert of Europe was reviving to prevent an outbreak of war. Great Britain, and to a lesser extent Russia, urged the possibility of settling trouble by means of a European Congress. That was also one of the ideas of Napoleon III and he could not refuse to consider it. His will was so unstable that Cavour was in despair. For a moment, peace seemed to be certain. Cavour is said to have remarked, "Nothing remains for me but to put a bullet through my head." Then came an incident which has not been fully explained. It is possible that Austria was tired of the long delays. It is also possible that he was encouraged by the assurances of loyalty from the different parts of the Empire. Austria despatched to Turin an ultimatum demanding disarmament "within three days" and sent her troops into Piedmont on 19 April 1859. Nobody welcomed the war more than Cavour did. On that occasion, Cavour is said to have observed, "The die is cast and history is made." The Austrian Emperor declared that he was fighting for "the rights of all people and states and for the most sacred blessings of mankind." The general feeling was that Austria had broken the peace. Victor Emmanuel was declared Dictator by the Parliament of Piedmont and the war began.

Every great Power in Europe seemed to be interested in the Italian war and there was much talk of intervention. The attitude of Great Britain and Russia did not matter much, but the action of Germany and Prussia was really the most critical question. Austria was primarily a German power and she was at the head of the Germanic Confederation. Despite her grievances against Austria, Prussia could not be expected to remain unconcerned when Austria was being defeated by the armies of France and Italy. The federal army and the Prussian army were both put on a war footing. The diplomacy of Austria could not induce them to go further than that. However, the fear of German or Prussian intervention was always in the mind of Napoleon III and was partly responsible for stopping the war after the battle of Solferino.

In spite of all this, the armies of Austria had to bear the attacks of their enemies without any allies. Although General Benedek won high reputation for his management of the campaign and the Austrian soldiers displayed great bravery in the battlefield, Austria was defeated. The different national elements in the Austrian army had no interest in the issue of the campaign and no wonder they could not give their very best. Moreover, the higher ranks in the Austrian armies were confined to the nobles alone and these too were great handicaps. The situation in Italy was highly favourable to the national cause. There were spontaneous risings all over the North of Italy. There were risings in Modena. Parma expelled its ruler. There were movements of utmost importance in Tuscany, particularly its capital, Florence. There were great popular meetings in Florence which cheered for "War, independence and Victor Emmanuel." The King of Piedmont was asked to undertake the military dictatorship of Tuscany. These demonstrations in Tuscany were against the desire of Nopoleon III who wanted to make Prince Jerome somehow the ruler of Tuscany. In the Romagna and the Legations, the Papal troops were driven out and the popular cry was for union with Italy and Victor Emmanuel. There was no hope that Pope Pius IX would join the national cause. An effort was made to bring in the kingdom of Naples. Ferdinand II, the ruler of Naples, had just died and he was succeeded by his son Francis II who was married to the sister of the Austrian Empress. No wonder, an attempt to win him over to the national cause failed.

As regards the actual war, the Austrians were undecided. Their troops came in slowly. Count Gyulai held the supreme command and was thought to have owed his promotion over the heads of others on account of his influence at the court. On the Italian side, great reliance was placed on "Hunters of the Alps" who were a body of irregular troops collected from the most enthusiastic elements among the patriots of Italy and commanded by Garibaldi who was considered by the people as the incarnation of the romance of daring and the poetry of the national cause. As the Allied forces advanced into Milan, Garibaldi acted on the left flank along the foothills of the Alps. However, the main brunt of the fighting fell on the French troops. It is conceded that without the support of the armies of France, the national armies were doomed. The Austrians would have fared better if they had remained on the defensive under cover of the fortresses of the "Quadrilateral", but they decided to defend Milan. The issue was decided in two great battles. The battle of Magenta was fought on 4 June 1859 and after heavy fighting the Austrians were defeated. They were defeated but not crushed and hence they retreated towards the "Quadrilateral." The battle of Solferino was fought on 24 June 1859. It was a long drawnout and murderous battle. In the centre and on the right, the French and the Italians won a complete victory. Although the Austrians under Benedek held their ground on their right, the battle was lost in other parts of the field. The losses on both sides were very heavy. The battle of Solferino was a crushing defeat for Austria although it was not decisive of the whole campaign. However, through the action of Napoleon III, the whole campaign ended.

A question has been asked why Napoleon III stopped after having won the battle of Solferino. It is true that Napoleon III was the victor in the field. He had crushed Austria and called a free Italy into existence. When he entered Milan after the battle of Hagenta, he was given a rousing reception which very few conquerors have received. He was called "Our liberator, our saviour, our benefactor." His way was strewn with flowers by the women of Milan. He told the people of Italy that he will do nothing to force his will on them. "Use the good fortune that presents itself to you. Your dream of independence will be realised if you show yourself worthy of it. Unite in one great effort for the liberation of the country."

The cordiality between Napoleon III and the people of Italy did not last long. The slaughter at Solferino profoundly affected the mind of Napoleon III and he would not like to go further in the war. The Italians also did not show themselves easily manageable as expected by Napoleon. The scheme of Napoleon III to put Prince Jerome on the throne of Tuscany completely failed on account of opposition from the people of Tuscany. Although his name was Napoleon, he was not a soldier. He was an expert more in diplomatic combinations and appeals to the imagination of the people than in the art of fighting. Napoleon III also found danger from the side of Prussia whose army had already been placed on a war footing. Prussia now prepared her whole forces and proposed that she should be given the command of the army of Germany. She proposed to Great Britain and Russia to join her in an offer of mediation to both the parties. There was a fear that the French forces may not be compelled to protect the Rhine frontier.

It was under these circumstances that Napoleon decided to stop the war without consulting Piedmont. While doing so, he acted more as a conspirator than a statesman. Napoleon III sent General Fleury on a private mission to the headquarters of Francis Joseph, the Emperor of Austria with an offer of an armistice. The Austrian Emperor was wiling to meet half way. He knew his own critical position. His armies had been defeated in two battles. Hungary was threatening revolt and troops were wanted to suppress it. Austria was not favourably inclined towards Prussian help as in that case she will have to make concessions to Prussia in Germany and she was not willing to do the same. It was under these circumstances that Francis Joseph met Napoleon III at Villafranca and the preliminaries of peace were arranged. Lombardy was to be handed over to Napoleon III who was to transfer the same to Victor Emmanuel. Both France and Austria were to support the formation of an Italian Confederation under the titular Presidency of the Pope. Venetia was to remain with Austria but was to form a part of the Italian Confederation. The rulers of Modena, Parma and Tuscany were to be restored. The Pope was to be urged to introduce reforms in his stale. A meeting of the representatives of all the states concerned was to he held to ratify the terms of the Peace of Villafranca.

It is worthy of notice that the armistice of Villafranca was signed by Napoleon III without consulting Piedmont. The result was that to many Italians and particularly to Cavour, it seemed treason to their cause. Cavour was disappointed. He is said to have remarked, "Nothing can come out of this peace. I will turn the conspirator and revolutionary, but this treaty shall not be carried out." After a violent interview with Victor Emmanuel, he resigned his post as Prime Minister, but later on came back to his post again.

It was found that the people of Tuscany, Modena, Parma and the Romagna were not prepared to allow the Emperors of France and Austria to hand them back to their old rulers. Farini had kept the national standard flying in Modena and in Parma. A similar part was played by Ricasoli in Tuscany. A representative Assembly in Florence declared unanimously in August 1859 that Tuscany desired to become a part of the strong Italy under the constitutional rule of Victor Emmanuel. Victor Emmanuel himself praised the wonderful example of moderation and unity shown by the people of Tuscany and he gave an assurance that he would represent the claims of Tuscany in the coming congress. The people of Parma, Modena and Bologna also demanded union with the kingdom of Victor Emmanuel.

It was found difficult to carry into effect the terms of the peace of Villafranca. The representatives of France, Austria and Sardinia met together at Zurich. Lombardy was annexed to Sardinia, but the Pope did not show any inclination in the creation of an Italian Confederation. The central Italian states refused to submit. It was proposed to refer the matter to a further congress which was to meet at Paris. However, the congress never met. The Pope refused to participate as it had been made clear to him directly or indirectly that the territories of the Papacy were to be reduced to a minimum. Austria was also hostile to the idea of a new congress and hence the same had to be given up.

Cavour who had taken over as Prime Minister again in January 1860 decided to settle the Italian question by direct secret negotiations. Cavour employed Napoleon's favourite method of plebiscites in Italy. An enormous majority in Tuscany and an almost unanimous vote in other places declared for a union with the Kingdom of Victor Emmanuel. Savoy by 1,30,538 votes to 235 and Nice by

24,448 to 160 votes declared for union with France. Thus, Napoleon III was given Nice and Savoy and he was to agree to the union of Tuscany, Parma, Modena, etc., with Piedmont. When Napoleon III accepted Nice and Savoy, Cavour observed, "Now we are accomplices."

In the words of Cavour, "They have stopped me from making Italy by diplomacy from the North, I will make it by revolution from the South." With great caution and skill, he embarked upon one of the most amazing enterprises in the history of the Italian union. The mass of the people of Sicily and Naples were uneducated and illiterate and they took little interest in the political revolution in the country. There were a large number of secret societies working there. There was a section of the people who were full of enthusiasm for Italy. However, it was not certain whether the people of Sicil and Naples would be willing to merge their independence in the kingdom of Piedmont or not, even if it assumed the name of Italy. There was a strong party that desired some form of autonomy. King Francis II was planning to give reforms to his people to satisfy the sentiments of his people but before he had done that, Garibaldi, had landed in Sicily, Garibaldi was a great hero. He was known for his courage. He was the leader of irregular forces. He was devoted to the cause of Italian unity. The annexation of Naples and Sicily depended as much on Garibaldi as on Cavour. Although Cavour and Garibaldi did not see eye to eye with each other, they had to work in cooperation for the sake of Italian unification. On 5 May 1860, Garibaldi left the port of Genoa with two vessels and 1,136 volunteers to whom were distributed red shirts on the way. They landed at Marsala on 11 May 1860. The force at the disposal of Garibaldi could not have overcome the resistance of the troops of Sicily and Naples. However, much depended upon the impression which Garibaldi could produce on the mind of the people of Sicily. Garibaldi possessed reckless courage and that stood him in good stead. He advanced on Palermo and won a wonderful victory outside Palermo and later on captured the city itself. This first victory decided the fate of the campaign in Sicily. King Francis had no supporters in Sicily outside the fortress of Messina. The nationalists of Naples appealed to Garibadi for help, Victor Emmanuel forbade him to pass the Straits and at the same time suggested to him the language in which he should refuse the command. Garibaldi landed at the extreme south of Italy and marched on Naples. There was no resistance. King Francis was betrayed by many of his ministers and soldiers and he left Naples for Gaeta on 6 September 1860. Garibaldi entered Naples and he was welcomed by the people. The triumph of Garibaldi was amazing.

Cavour was happy that King Francis of Naples and Sicily had been overthrown but he was anxious to know what was to take its place. Garibaldi had always declared that he was acting in the name of Italy and Victor Emmanuel but it was not certain as to what he might do in actual practice. The future was uncertain. Mazzini and his followers were working for a republic. There was a strong party which wanted to give to Naples and Sicily a separate and independent status in a free and united Italy. The possibility of the restoration of King Francis could not be ruled out because he was still holding out at Gaeta. It appeared to Cavour that time had come when he and his master must act in order to save the situation. He had no confidence in the intellectual capacity of Garibaldi to deal with the same. He also saw an opportunity of not only completing the settlement of Naples but also adding the Papal lands to Italy.

There were revolts in the Marches and in Umbria. It was difficult to attack the Papal territory as the Pope was recognised as a part of the state system of Europe. However, Cavour declared in a despatch to Pope Pius IX that the King of Sardinia felt himself bound "in the cause of humanity" to prevent the Papal troops from suppressing with violence the popular movements in Umbria. On this pretext, the Italian army entered the Papal states and defeated the Papal army at Castelfidardo. The forces of Victor Emmanuel then pushed on into Naples and took over the authority which had been exercised so far by Garibaldi as a dictator. To begin with, Garibaldi declared that he had no confidence in Cavour and he would not declare annexation to the kingdom of Victor Emmanuel until Rome was conquered. There was some danger of a clash between the Red shirts of Garibaldi and the troops of Victor Emmanuel. However, the danger passed away. King Francis was forced to leave Gaeta and he retired to Rome. Garibaldi met Victor Emmanuel who thanked him for the great services rendered by him to the cause of the country. However, Garibaldi refused to accept any reward for his services and retired to his Island home Caprera. Plebiscites were held in Naples, Sicily and the Papal states and by overwhelming majorities, the people declared for immediate annexation to "the constitutional monarchy of Victor Emmanuel."

The first Italian Parliament met in Turin in February 1861. In March a new constitutional decree containing a single article was promulgated. "Victor Emmanuel II assumes for himself and his successors the title of King of Italy." Cavour died soon after, but it cannot be denied that he was the real creator of Italy as a nation. In the words of Phillips, "Italy as a nation is the legacy, the life-work of Cavour. Others have been devoted to the national liberation, he knew how to bring it into the sphere of possibilities; he kept it pure of any factious spirit; he led it away from barren Utopias; kept it clear of reckless conspiracies; steered straight between rebels and reactions and gave it an organised force, a flag, a government and foreign allies." Another writer says, "If there had been no Cavour to win the confidence, sympathy and support of Europe, if he had not been recognised as one whose sense was just in all emergencies, Mazzini's efforts would have run to waste unquestionable insurrections, and Garibaldi's feat of arms must have added one chapter more to the history of unproductive patriotism." The last words of Cavour at the time of his death were: **"Italy is made, all is safe."** Cavour created **"Italy of the Italians."**

According to Lord Palmerston, **"Cavour left a name, 'to point a moral and adorn a tale.'"** The moral was that a man of transcendent talent, indomitable industry, inextinguishable patriotism, could overcome difficulties which seemed insurmountable, and confer the greatest, the most inestimable benefits on his country. The tale with which his memory would be associated was the most extraordinary, the most romantic in the annals of the world. A people which had seemed dead had arisen to new and vigorous life, breaking the spell which bound it and showing itself worthy of a new and splendid destiny."

Garibaldi (1807-82). Garibaldi was born in 1807 at Nice, then an Italian town. His father was a skipper. He was two years younger to Mazzini. He did not take advantage of the education which his father tried to give him in spite of his scanty means. He acquired "just enough book learning to feed his naturally freedom-loving, romantic and poetical disposition, but not enough to chasen it or to train his mind to wide understanding and deep reflection." He acquired good experience of the Mediterranean by working in coasting trade for ten years. Thrice he was captured by pirates. He was inspired by Italian patriots and exiles to fight for Italian freedom. "He believed in Italy as the Saints believed in God." He was introduced to Mazzini and he joined "Young Italy" of Mazzini. "When I was a youth and had only aspirations towards good, I sought for one able to act as the guide and counsellor of my youthful years. I sought such a guide as one who is athirst and seeks the water-spring. I found this man. He alone watched when all around slept; he alone kept and fed the sacred flame." In 1833, Garibaldi joined in one of the many conspiracies of Mazzini. His part was to enter the Sardinian Navy and win over the sailors to the plot. The conspiracy failed and Garibaldi was prosecuted. He managed to run away, but he was condemned to death by the Government of Sardinia.

The years between 1836 and 1845 were spent by Garibaldi in South America. There he lived a wild and roving life. He took part in the local wars. "He looked upon battles as a pleasure and the hardship of camp-life as a pastime." He acquired the experience of guerilla warfare which was to be of great use to him later on.

In 1847, Garibaldi offered his services to the Pope who at that time was considered to be the hope of the Italian patriots who wanted unification of their country. In 1848, he came back to Italy and placed his services at the disposal of Charles Albert of Sardinia who had declared war against Austria. Thousands of persons flocked to the standard of "hero of Montevideo" to fight against Austria. As the campaign failed, he went in 1849 to fight in defence of the republican regime in Rome. His was a heroic defence but after the fall of that city, he managed to escape with 4,000 troops. He was pursued by the Austrians who did not give him rest anywhere. The pursuit was undertaken both in forests and mountains as if he was some sort of a game. Most of his followers lost their lives. Even his heroic wife, Anita, was killed. Garibaldi himself escaped to Tuscany and from there to Piedmont and ultimately to America. His exploits full of heroism, chivalry and romance moved the Italians to enthusiasm and admiration.

In 1854, Garibaldi came back to Italy with a little money with which he bought a small island of Caprera, near Sardinia. There he built a house in which he lived with the simplicity of a crafter and the status of a King. There he filled his soul with "the breath of liberty, the utter release from crowds and courts and officials and the whole scheme of modern life, to which he was always in mind and heart a stranger; and this liberty would have sufficed him to the end of his days. As he gazed over the unbroken surface of the sea, had he not in his mind's eye seen beyond the eastern horizon those still enslaved shores."

In 1856, Garibaldi met Cavour and in 1857 he announced his conversion to the cause of the Sardinian monarchy. It was a very important happening because it was necessary to heal the breach between the republicans and the monarchists and to combine them against the common enemy. At heart, Garibaldi continued to be a republican but he remained loyal to Victor Emmanuel to the end. There continued to exist a mutual understanding between Garibaldi and the king although at times the relations between Garibaldi and Cavour were strained to the breaking point.

In 1859, he came out of his retirement and collected a large number of volunteers to fight against the Austrians. He was the idol of soldiers from one end to the other end of the country. There were thousands who were prepared and were ready to follow him blindly. He took part in the war in which Napoleon III himself fought. He was very unhappy when after the battle of Solferino, Napoleon III signed the armistice of Villafranca.

As early as the autumn of 1859, the conspirators in Sicily began to appeal to Garibaldi for help. His presence alone could give them success. He hesitated for some time, but ultimately agreed to help them on the condition that the revolt took place in the name of Italy and Victor Emmanuel and it was started by the people of Sicily themselves. His supporters also approached Cavour who understood the political potentialities of a revolt conducted in the name of Victor Emmanuel. Outwardly, Cavour maintained an attitude of strict neutrality but he encouraged the conspirators to revolt. The followers of Garibaldi who had fought in 1859 were stirred and were spoiling for fresh encounters.

On 4 April 1860, the Revolution broke out near Messina in Sicily. When Garibaldi heard of its initial success, he agreed to help the rebels of Sicily and himself appealed to Cavour and Victor Emmanuel for authorisation and help. Cavour found himself in a very difficult position. It was impossible to give an official encouragement. At the same time, it was not possible to evade. There was a popular cry for war. The name of Garibaldi was on the lips of everyone and it was difficult to oppose him. Under the circumstances, Cavour played a double game. He told the ambassadors of the Great Powers that he was completely ignorant of what was happening. At the same time, preparations were allowed to be continued. Volunteers were collected by Garibaldi. The only condition imposed by Victor Emmanuel was that the officers of the Sardinian army should not be enlisted as volunteers. Arms were collected from the arsenals of the national society. The harbour authorities of Genoa connived at the embarkation of the expedition. Admiral Persano of the Sardinian Navy was instructed "to keep between Garibaldi's ships and the Neapolitan fleet."

On 11 May 1860, Garibaldi appeared off Massala on the west coast of Sicily and disembarked his troops. This he did practically under the protection of a small British naval squadron. This was a very friendly gesture on the part of the British Government because without that help, Garibaldi might have faced difficulties. A few days later, Lord John Russell declared in the House of Commons, "We had once a great filibuster who landed in England in 1688." From Massala, Garibaldi advanced to Palermo. There were only a thousand men at his disposal, but the number of Neapolitan troops opposing him was 20,000. On 15 May 1860, the first battle took place. There was hardly any fighting and towards the end of the day, Neapolitan troops ran away. After a fortnight, Garibaldi entered Palermo and proclaimed himself the dictator of Sicily. By the end of July 1860, the whole of the island of Sicily except the fortress of Messina and one or two minor ports was in his hands. The name of Garibaldi had worked miracles. The revolutionaries were encouraged and they rallied to his side.

The success of Garibaldi in Sicily put Cavour and Victor Emmanuel in a difficult position. It was certain that Garibaldi would cross to the mainland and ultimately advance towards the Papal states and even to Rome. Garibaldi had become more and more independent and more and more impatient and distrustful of Cavour and his cautious and diplomatic methods. He was more sympathetic to Crispi and the extreme republicans among his followers. Mazzini himself was in Italy and preparations were being made to invade the Papal states. Cavour was afraid of the intervention of France and Austria if Rome was attacked. However, the diplomatic situation was favourable to the cause of Italian unification. England was friendly, Napoleon III on the whole was sympathetic and was not willing to move without England. Austria was not prepared to act alone as there was the danger of a revolt in Hungary.

Cavour tried to persuade Garibaldi to agree to the immediate annexation of Sicily but failed. After that he decided to play his own game against Garibaldi. He tried to create in Sicily and Naples a strong public opinion against Garibaldi. The agents of Cavour started their intrigues in Naples. Efforts were made to win over the people to the side of Sardinian monarchy. Admiral Persano was sent to win over the Neapolitan fleet.

In the second week of August 1860, Garibaldi crossed the Strait and landed in Calabria. Napoleon III had suggested that an Anglo-French squadron should blockade the Strait of Messina in order to keep Garibaldi in Sicily. But Great Britain did not approve of the proposal. The result was that Garibaldi was able to cross to the mainland of Italy. On 31 August 1860, Garibaldi captured Reggio and began to advance towards Naples. The progress of Garibaldi, became a simple triumphal march. He was received by the people as "a second Christ." On 6 September 1860, the King of Naples left for Gaeta and on 7 September Garibaldi entered the capital by train from Salerno alone ahead of his army. He did not show that he was leading a hostile force. The only obstruction he met was from an excited mob which surrounded his train. As he left the station for the centre of the city, his carriage passed through the troops of Naples who could have killed him without any difficulty. Garibaldi stood up folded his arms and looked straight in the face of the Neapolitan troops. Some of them gave him the salute, but no one fired a shot. It is true that they were acting according to the orders of the King, but anybody could have disobeyed the order and killed him. Garibaldi proclaimed him the dictator of the Kingdom. He appointed Bertani, a follower of Mazzini, as Secretary of State. As a proof of his loyalty to Victor Emmanuel, he handed over the Neapolitan fleet to Admiral Persano of Sardinia. Garibaldi made no secret of his future plans. After Naples, he was to go to Venice and Rome. He was not prepared to listen to the appeals of Victor Emmanuel and Cavour. He rejected their "hypocritical but terrible pretext of necessity; the necessity of being cowards; the necessity of grovelling in the mud before an image of transitory power." The revolution infection had spread to the Papal states. The troops of the People were getting ready to put down the revolt.

It was under these circumstances that Cavour decided to act to save the situation. He declared, "Italy must be saved from foreigners, evil principles and mad men." He decided to anticipate Garibaldi and attack the Papal states with the Sardinian troops and defend Rome from Garibaldi. It was a strange situation. Efforts were made to find out the attitude of Napoleon III if a Sardinian army occupied Umbria and the Marches. The reply of Napoleon III was "Do it quickly." That was all which Cavour wanted. On 11 September 1860, he ordered the invasion of the Papal states. On 18 September, the Papal army was defeated at Castelfidardo. On 29 September, Ancona fell. Thus, the whole of Umbria and the Marches came in the hands of the Kingdom of Piedmont. There had been a race between Garibaldi and the troops of Piedmont. Cavour had correctly stated, "If we do not reach the Volturno before Garibaldi: reaches La Cattolica, the monarchy is lost, and Italy will remain in the prison-house of the revolution." Garibaldi was delayed on account of resistance put up by the people of Capua and thus Cavour won.

After the occupation of the Papal states, plebiscites were held in Sicily and Naples and those were in favour of joining the kingdom of Sardinia. That strengthened the hands of Cavour. Garibaldi also found that without the assistance of the Sardinian troops, he could not conquer the fortresses of Gaeta and Capua. It was under these circumstances that Victor Emmanuel entered the territory of Naples at the head of his army. On 27 October 1860, Garibaldi surrendered his power and his army to Victor Emmanuel. After that action was taken against Capua and Gaeta. Capua was captured in November 1860 and Gaeta in February 1861.

On 9 November 1860, there was an imposing ceremony in the Palace of Naples where Victor Emmanuel was declared the King of Sicil and Naples. Garibaldi formally resigned his dictatorship and asked the people to forget their differences and obey the king. On 10 November 1860, with a bag of seed-corn for his farm, Garibaldi returned to his Island of Caprera and there spent the rest of his life in peace and retirement. On many occasions, he appeared in national and international affairs. He joined the war in 1866 against Austria. He was a volunteer in French service in 1870. It is said that when Cavour agreed to give Nice to France as the price of French help against Austria, Garibaldi burst into tears as Nice was his birthplace and its handing over to France was to result in his becoming a foreigner in Italy.

It is difficult to find a more selfless patriot in the history of the world. If all politicians in the world were to act in the manner in which Garibaldi acted, the face of the world will be completely changed. There will be a competition to serve and the world as a whole will gain.

Victor Emmanuel was a soldier and a man of action. He was not a dreamer like his father. In spite of his authoritarian character, he maintained the constitution granted by his father. He even favoured the Liberals of Sardinia. He was a realist. He pursued revolutionary aims while seeking to avoid revolutionary means.

Venetia (1866). Italy entered into an alliance with Prussia in 1866 with a view to secure Venetia from Austria. When the war started between Austria and Prussia, the Italians also entered the field. However, they were defeated by the Austrian troops, but their entry into the war facilitated the task of Bismarck as Austria was forced to fight on two fronts. No wonder, the Austrians were defeated in the Battle of Sadowa and surrendered. Bismarck did not make any demand on vanquished Austria but merely asked the latter to give Venetia to Italy and the same was done.

Rome (1870). The unification of Italy was completed in 1870 when Napoleon III was forced to withdraw the French troops from Rome which were stationed there since 1849. That was due to the fact that Napoleon had to fight against Prussia and it was necessary to collect troops from everywhere.

It was in this way that the unification of Italy was completed in 1870 as a result of the efforts of the Italian patriots, foreign help and the force of circumstances.

According to A.J.P. Taylor, "The unification of Italy completed what the Crimean War had begun; the destruction of European order. Metternich system depended on Russia's guarantee; once that was withdrawn, the system could be overthrown. Napoleon supposed that a new system, his own, was taking its place. This was to misunderstand the events of 1859 to 1681. Certainly, Italy owed most to French armies and to British moral approval, but these could not have been effective without two other factors-Russian resentment against the Treaty of Paris, and Prussian resentment against the Austrian hegemony in Germany. If Russia had followed a policy less consistently hostile to Austria, if Prussia had carried the war to the Rhine in 1859, Italy could not have been made. After 1861 Russia still aimed at the overthrow of the settlement of 1856; Prussia still aimed at equality, if not hegemony, in Germany. Both continued to work against Austria; this was no guarantee that they would continue to work in favour of France. And, in fact, the leadership of Europe which Napoleon seemed to have gained from the Italian affair was lost within two years over the question of Poland." **The Struggle for Mastery in Europe,** pp. 124-125.

SUGGESTED READINGS

Flenley, R.: **Makers of Nineteenth Century Europe.**

Garibaldi: **Autobiography.**

Holland: **Builders of United Italy.**

Johnston, R.M.: **The Napoleon Empire in Southern Italy and the Rise of the Secret Societies, 1904.**

King, Bolton : **Mazzini.**

King: **History of Italian Unity.**

Marriott: **Makers of Modern Italy.**

Martinengo-Cesaresco.: **The Liberation of Italy, 1815-70.**

Mowrer: **Immortal Italy.**

Murdock: **Reconstruction of Modern Europe.**

Orsi, P.: **Cavour.**

Orsi, P.: **Modern Italy.**

Smith, B. Mack : **Cavour and Garibaldi.**

Taylor, A.J.P.: **The Italian Problem in the European Diplomacy (1847-49), 1934.**

Thayer: **Life and Times of Cavour.**

Thayer: **Dawn of Italian Independence.**

Trevelyan, G.M.: **Garibaldi and the Making of Italy.**

Trevelyan, G.M.: **Garibaldi and the Thousand.**

Trevelyan, G.M.: **Manin and the Venetian Revolution of 1848.**

Trevelyan (Mrs.) **: A Short History of Italy.**

Zimmern : **Italy of the Italians.**

CHAPTER

17 UNIFICATION OF GERMANY

The Vienna Settlement with regard to Germany was hopelessly disappointing from the point of view of German Liberals and patriots. They had been hoping for a unified Germany but instead they got a German Confederation of 39 States. Provision was made for a Federal Diet which was to be presided over by Austria. The ruler of every state was sovereign within his territory and no wonder the sense of self-preservation forced him to oppose the unification of the country and all those liberal movements which were liable to help the cause of German unification. In addition to Austria, there were other non-German elements in the Federal Diet. Hanover, which was under England, was included in the German Confederation and given representation. The Duchy of Holstein which was under the King of Denmark, was also included in the German Confederation and likewise given representation. These foreign elements could not be expected to throw in their weight in the cause of German unity. The Federal Diet was practically given no power over the various States constituting the German Confederation. Austria was the arbiter of the fate of Germany. It was provided in the Federal Act of 1815 that a representative constitution should be framed in every State, but the promise was not fulfilled. Complete reaction set in Germany after 1815. Frederick William III (1797-1840), King of Prussia, could have been expected to lead the patriotic and liberal forces in Germany, but even he fell under the influence of Metternich and consequently joined hands with him to suppress all signs of nationalism and liberalism in the country.

When such was the state of affairs in Germany, the initiative was taken by the universities in that country. Jena became the centre of German liberalism and the university students started a movement which went on growing year after year. The highest ideals of sobriety, chastity and German unity were put before the people. According to Sybel, "The young heroes returning from the war filled the universities with their patriotic indignation, and by the founding of societies of students (Burschenschaften), representing all the universities, they sought to fill all the educated youth of Germany with their enthusiasm for unity, justice and freedom. These societies, for the most part, cherished ambitions which were thoroughly ideal. They did not look to the overthrow of present conditions, but relied upon the training to rising generation. By moral elevation and patriotic inspirations, they hoped to lead the state of the future, to the great goal of national unity. To be sure, their notions of this future state were generally indefinite and were mere unpractical fancies; indeed this enthusiasm rose in some groups to the pitch of wild fanaticism, so that they were even ready to seize sword and dagger for Tyrannicide. Yet such enthusiasts never succeeded in securing in the societies at large any great following for their projects." (**Foundation of the German Empire,** Vol. I, p. 67).

The students' associations began to spread from Jena and within two years, 16 universities came under their control. In 1817, the students decided to celebrate tercentenary of the Protestant Reformation and the anniversary of the Battle of Leipzig. At Wartburg, in addition to the common programmes followed by the students at other places, many kinds of things were burnt and some of them were the emblems of militarism, a copy of the Code of Napoleon, a book by Kotzebue, and many other documents. Metternich attached the greatest importance to the celebration. According to him, the proceedings were merely a symbol of the revolutionary unrest prevailing among the

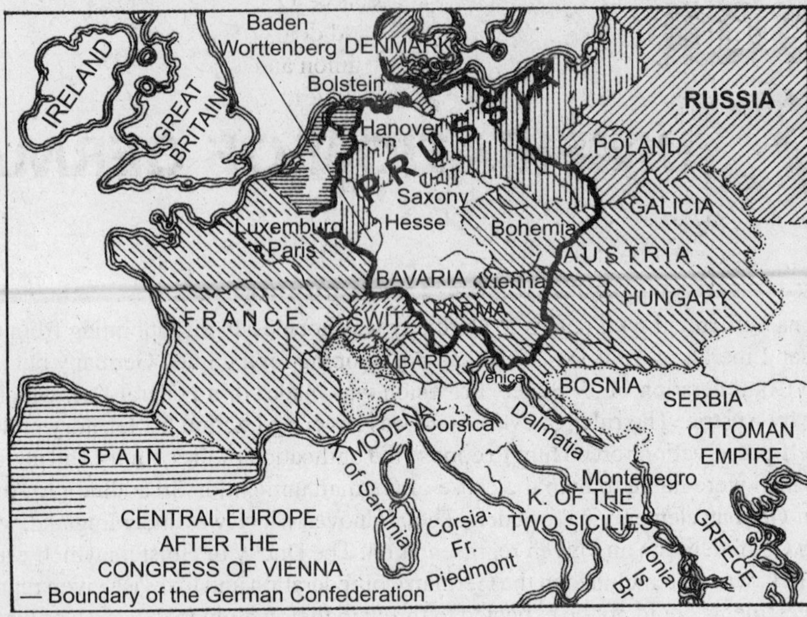

CENTRAL EUROPE AFTER THE CONGRESS OF VIENNA
— Boundary of the German Confederation

people in Germany. When the Congress of Aix-la-Chapelle met in 1818, he tried to impress upon the rulers the dangers that lay ahead. Events—that took place after 1817 strengthened the hands of Metternich. Off and on, there were revolt in various parts of Germany. In March, 1813, Kotzebue, who was considered to be a Russian spy, was murdered by Karl Sand. Metternich decided to take full advantage of the circumstances. With the approval of the King of Prussia, he called a meeting of the ministers of the important States of Germany at Carlsbad in August 1819. Certain resolutions were passed and those were submitted to the Federal Diet which gave its approval.

Carlsbad Decrees (1819). According to the Carlsbad decrees, a special representative of the ruler of the State was to be appointed for each university. He was to reside in the place where the university was situated and he was to exercise a large number of powers under the instructions of the ruler. The agent was to see to the strictest enforcement of the existing laws and disciplinary regulations. He was to observe carefully the spirit which was shown by the teachers in the universities in their lectures and report to the government if there were any signs of disloyalty or rebellion. It was the duty of the ruler to remove from the universities or other educational institutions all those teachers who were considered to be abusing their legitimate influence over the students or who spread among the students harmful doctrines hostile to public order or subversive of the existing governmental institutions. Such a teacher was not to be employed in any other university or educational institution. The laws against secret and unauthorized societies in the universities were to be strictly enforced. Those laws applied especially to the University Students' Union **(Allgemeine Burschenschaft).** Those persons who were considered to be members of the secret or unauthorized societies were not to be admitted to any public office. The students who were expelled from one university were not to be admitted into another. No publication which appeared in the form of daily issue or as a serial not exceeding 20 sheets of printed matter, was to go to the press without the previous knowledge and approval of the State officials. The Federal Diet was to have the right to suppress by its own authority such writings as were inimical to the honour of the union, the safety of the individual State or the maintenance of peace and quite in Germany. There was to be no appeal from such decisions and the governments involved were bound to see that they were enforced. When a newspaper or periodical was suppressed by a decision of the Diet, the editor was not to be allowed to edit another similar publication for five years. Provision was made for a central commission of investigation consisting of seven members. Its function was to have a thorough investigation of the facts relating to the origin and manifold ramification of the revolutionary plots and demagogical associations directed against the existing constitution and the internal peace of the union and the individual States. It was also to investigate into the existence of the plots. The Central Investigation Commission was to furnish the Diet from time to time with a report of the results of its investigations.

By the Carlsbad Decrees, the Emperor of Austria became "the head of an all-powerful German police system." Metternich might have gone still further, but his enthusiasm was cooled by the opposition from certain German States. The ruler of Wurtemburg took up the challenge and gave further reforms to his people and put himself at the head of "a purely Germanic league" to resist Austria and Prussia. The result was that the Final Act of Vienna represented a compromise. The independence of the small States was guaranteed. In 1824, the Carlsbad Decrees were made permanent.

Zollverein. When such was the state of affairs in Germany, certain forces helped indirectly the unification of the country. A reference may be made in this connection to the Zollverein or the Customs' Union. Before 1818, each district in Prussia had its own customs and there were as many as 67 tariff areas in Prussia alone. These areas stood in the way of trade and unity and consequently Prussia could not compete with Great Britain. On account of the long line of customs houses, there was a lot of smuggling. In 1818, the Tariff Reforms Law was passed. By that Act, all raw materials were to be imported free. A duty of 10 per cent was to be levied on manufactured goods and 20 per cent on "colonial" goods. All internal custom duties were abolished. Heavy transit duties on tariff goods passing through Prussia were imposed with a view to compel other States to join Prussia. The result of the reform of 1818 was that Prussia became a free trade area. Internal trade increased and the revenue of the State also showed a rise.

The law of 1818 applied to Prussia alone, but in course of time many other German States joined Prussia. In 1819, Schwarzburg-Sondershausen joined the Union. In 1822, Weimar, Gotha, Merchlenburg-Schwerin, Schaumburg-Lippe, Rudolstadt and Hamburg also joined.

However, there was opposition to the Customs' Union from some German States. In 1828, a Customs' Union was set up in the South under the leadership of Bavaria and Wurtemburg. In the same year, another Customs' Union of the middle States was formed. It consisted of Saxony, Hesse-Cassel, Hanover, Brunswick and the free cities of Hamburg, Bremen and Frankfurt.

However, in 1831, Hesse-Cassel joined the Zollverein and the union of the middle States was broken up. In 1834, Bavaria joined the Zollverein for 8 years. The terms of the Union were that the meetings were to be held at Berlin and other places. Bavarian goods were to be given special treatment. In the same year, Saxony also joined. By 1837, most of the States had joined the Zollverein. Whenever the treaties expired they were renewed. Only Hanover, Oldenburg, Mecklenburg and the Hanse towns remained outside the Zollverein. The main terms of entry into the Zollverein were complete free trade between State and State, uniform tariff on all frontiers and net proceeds to be divided in proportion to population of the States concerned.

To begin with, Austria was completely indifferent to the Zollverein. Metternich did not attach any importance to commerce and consequently ignored the activities of the Zollverein. However, after the overthrow of Metternich in 1848, Austria made a determined effort to join the Zollverein. Prussia resisted the same and was successful. In 1853, a treaty was entered into between the Zollverein and Austria by which certain concessions were given mutually.

The importance of the Zollverein cannot be minimised. According to Marriot and Robertson, "For the first time, Germany became a fiscal and commercial unit. The Zollverein united the German States in bonds of mutual economic interest; it united them under the leadership of Prussia; and it accustomed them to the exclusion of Austria from the Germanic body." According to Fyffe, "The semblance of political union was carefully avoided, but the germs of political union were nevertheless present in the growing community of material interests." Again, "Patient, sagacious and even liberal in its negotiations with its weaker neighbours, Prussia silently connected with itself through the ties of financial union States which had hitherto looked to Austria as their natural head." The reputation of the Prussian Government no less than the welfare of the Prussian people was advanced by each successive step in the extension of the Zollverein.

According to Dr. Bowring, "The Zollverein has brought the sentiment of the German nationality out of the regions of hope and fancy into those of positive and material interests. The general feeling in Germany towards the Zollverein is that it is the first step towards what is called the Germanization. It has broken down some of the strongest holds of alienation and hostility. By a community of interests on commercial and trading questions, it has prepared the way for a political nationality."

July Revolution and Germany. The July Revolution of 1830 in France had also its effects on Germany. There were demands for the grant of liberal constitutions and the same were conceded by the rulers of Nassau, Brunswick, Hanover, Saxony and Hesse-Cassel. The rulers of Bavaria, Wurtemburg, etc., confirmed the liberal constitutions which they had given after 1815. The net result was that while Prussia remained unchanged, the smaller States got liberal constitutions. However, Metternich was able once again to establish his hold over Germany and the Carlsbad Decrees were reconfirmed. The conference was held at Vienna and it was decided to take action against the liberal tendencies of the press and the universities. Provision was made for the establishment of a court to settle the disputes between the rulers and the people of the German States.

Frederick William IV (1840-61). During the long reign of Frederick William III (1797-1840), much could not be expected from Prussia. However, he was succeeded by Frederick William IV in 1840. The new King possessed a strong will and intellect. However, his judgment was not as good as his intellectual capacity. To begin with, he released a large number of political prisoners. Mr. Arndt was reappointed as Professor at Bonn and Dahlmann was also given a chair in the same university. The provincial estates were allowed to meet regularly and discuss their affairs freely. The freedom of the press was restored but he refused to grant a parliamentary constitution. Frederick William IV called a meeting of all the provincial estates in Berlin and it came to be known as the united Provincial Diet or States-General. However, the United Diet was dismissed after some time although it attracted a lot of attention.

From 1830 to 1848, there was going on persistent agitation in the smallest States of Germany. The object of the agitation was two-fold, viz., the unification of Germany and the establishment of constitutional and liberal governments in the States. In 1847, a meeting was held and a liberal programme was adopted. Agitation was to be carried on for the cancellation of the Carlsbad Decrees. Religious toleration, freedom of the press and trial by jury were to be guaranteed. Representative Assemblies were to be set up in every State. Social privileges were to be abolished. A representative assembly was to be provided for the whole of Germany. The standing army was to be substituted by the militia of the people. The army was to take the oath of allegiance to the Constitution and not to the ruler. In the same year, another conference was held. There was a demand for a parliament for the whole of the country.

When the news of the February Revolution reached Germany, the ruler of Baden gave a new constitution to the people and his example was followed by Wurtemburg, Nassau, Brunswick, Weimar, Darmstadt and Hesse-Cassel. The ruler of Bavaria was forced to abdicate and Hanover and Saxony also got liberal constitutions.

So far as Prussia was concerned, there was some trouble in Berlin in March and the King gave a liberal constitution. There was a dash between the people and the troops and ultimately the King of Prussia had to remove the troops from the capital. He also promised to become the leader "of a free and new-born German nation." It was also decided to call a national parliament to frame a constitution.

Heinrich Von Gagern proposed the setting up of a provisional government for the whole of Germany. On 5 March 1848, 50 leaders met at Heidelberg and invitations were issued to the members of the various State legislatures in Germany. On 31 March 1848, about 600 persons attended the meeting at Frankfurt. It was decided at that meeting to set up a legislature of two houses and one executive head of the Federal Government of Germany. The details were to be filled up by a Constituent Assembly of Germany to which representatives were to come from all over the country on the basis of one member for 50,000 of the population. This was done and the popular assembly met at Frankfurt.

The Frankfurt Parliament consisted of about 300 members at the beginning but later on, its membership rose to about 550. Heinrich Von Gagern was elected its president. It was dominated by professors and journalists and no wonder a lot of time was wasted on the discussion of abstract principles. The only work done by the Frankfurt Parliament within the first six months was the appointment of a central executive. Archduke John was selected the Imperial Vicar of the provisional government. By the Christmas of 1848, the fundamental rights of the people of Germany were agreed upon. Some of those rights were civil and religious equality, freedom of the press, trial by jury, abolition of special privileges, etc.

There were two schools of thought with regard to the inclusion or exclusion of Austria from Germany. The "little Germans" insisted on excluding Austria but the "great German" were in favour of the inclusion of Austria. Ultimately, the former won and Austria was excluded. Provision was made for a hereditary king and a German Confederation. The throne of Germany was offered by the Frankfurt Parliament to Frederick William IV of Prussia on 28 March 1849 but the same was rejected on 3 April 1849. Many factors were responsible for his decision. He was temperamentally conservative and was not in sympathy with the aspirations of the Frankfurt Parliament. He was not prepared to be "a serf of the revolution". He believed in the Divine Right of Kings and was not prepared to accept the constitution framed by the Frankfurt Parliament. He might have accepted the throne if the same had been offered to him by the princes, but he refused to accept the same from the people. He was not prepared to accept **"the crown of shame"** out of the **"gutter".** Probably, the real reason was that the King of Prussia was not prepared to fight against Austria. By this time, Austria had recovered herself and if the King of Prussia had accepted the throne offered to him by the Frankfurt Parliament, he would certainly have come into conflict with Austria. That would have meant war and the King of Prussia felt that he was not equal to the task. It was under these circumstances that the throne was refused and with that the work of the Frankfurt Parliament ended. The people of Germany had tried to frame a constitution, but their efforts failed. They wasted the valuable time in the beginning in academic discussions. If they had acted with speed at the beginning, there were greater chances of their success. The failure of the Frankfurt Parliament convinced the Germans that some other method had to be followed to bring about unification of the country.

According to Hazen, "The Parliament of Frankfurt, on which such hopes had been centred, failed in the end, to some extent because of the mistakes of its members,, but chiefly because of the resolute opposition of the princes of Germany, and, in particular, of Prussia and Austria, the two leading German States, neither of which was willing to make any sacrifices for the common good and each of which was jealous and suspicious of the other. It, however, succeeded in drafting a constitution of many high merits, a constitution nobly planned which guaranteed civil liberty to every German, equality before the law, responsible parliamentary control for the central government and for the government of the separate States."

Although the King of Prussia refused the throne offered by the Frankfurt Parliament, he tried to unite the German States under his leadership in another way. His minister, Radowitz prepared the draft of a constitution which was to be the basis of the union. Prussia was to be the president of a college of princes and Austria was to be excluded from it. In March 1850, a German Parliament met at Erfurt. However, Schwarzenberg, the new Chancellor of Austria, was determined to establish the

Austrian hold over Germany and consequently was not prepared to allow the activities of the King of Prussia to continue. The King of Prussia was forced to surrender by the convention of Olmutz. He agreed to dissolve the "union" and the German Confederation of 1815 was restored. Austria was triumphant and reaction set in Germany. It is rightly observed that the humiliation of Olmutz marked the lowest point of Prussia's timidity and surrender. Prussia appeared to be brought as low in the dust as after Jena and even worse. When Prussia was defeated by Napoleon, she was at least true to the idea of German unity. Now, she had begun by promising to champion that cause, but had betrayed those who supported it and acquiesced in the haughty demands of Austria. Germany seemed as feeble and disunited as never before. Prussia had the chance of being the first power in Germany and her king that of wearing an imperial crown but the humiliation of Olmutz seemed to put the union of Germany at a more distant date than ever and permanently disqualify Prussia as its champion.

Although the movement of 1848-49 was a failure, it taught certain lessons to the people of Germany. There could be no unification of Germany so long as Austria was strong enough to oppose the same. That unity could not be achieved by constitutional means. The liberals were not practical men and they talked more of theories and less of the actual problems facing the country. Austria could be turned out from Germany only if Germany had a stronger force than that of Austria and that force could come only from Prussia. The necessity of having a very strong army was realized by all.

Frederick William IV became insane in 1857 and his brother, William I, became the Regent. On the death of Frederick William IV in 1861, he became the King of Prussia.

About Frederick William IV, A.J.P. Taylor says that his determination was contradictory. He wanted a united Germany with himself as its head but at the same time he wanted it without the agreement of Austria. His impossible dream was that Austria should abdicate voluntarily. One of his reasons for breaking with his liberal ministers in November 1848 was their proposal to support Sardinian claims against Austria in the Conference at Brussels, although in essence Prussia and Sardinia had similar aims. In April 1849, he refused the German crown when it was offered to him by the Frankfurt Parliament but immediately afterwards he tried to obtain it by the free agreement of the German princes and no wonder he failed.

William I (186-188). William I was a man of parts. He believed in the destiny and mission of Prussia. He was a Prussian to the core. He believed in autocracy. He possessed all the qualities of a soldier. He was a judge of men and could make a choice of servants on whom he could rely.

The humiliation of Prussia at the hands of Austria had convinced William I that if Germany was to be liberated, that could be done only if Prussia came to have a very big army. In 1849, he had observed thus: "Whoever wishes to rule Germany, must conquer it and that cannot be done by phrases." It was with that conviction in his mind that he appointed Moltke as the Chief of the General Staff and Roon as the Minister of War. It is these two persons who started reorganising the Prussian Army and they put forward their proposals for its further development. The Prussian Landtag or Legislature voted the supplies in 1861 for one year, but in 1862, rejected the same. While William I insisted on the army reforms, the Liberals who had a majority in the Prussian Landtag stood for constitutional reforms. Under the circumstances, a deadlock was inevitable. It is rightly pointed out that there were three alternatives before the King of Prussia. He could give up the reform of the army. He could abdicate. He could suspend the constitution and send the members of the Landtag home. He was in a fix and did not know what to do. Ultimately, it was decided to invite Bismarck from Paris to handle the situation. It was in these circumstances that Bismarck was appointed the Minister-President of Prussia in 1862. He gave the following assurance to William I: **"I will rather perish with the king than forsake Your Majesty in the contest with parliamentary government."**

Bismarck was a "bully and an absolutist." He had no faith in parliamentary institutions. He believed in autocracy and military force. To quote him, **"Not by speeches and resolutions of the**

majorities are the great questions of the day to be decided, but by blood and iron." He agreed with William I that the re-organisation of the Prussian army was absolutely essential for the unification of the country. He was prepared to oust the Prussian Landtag if the latter refused to vote the supplies for the re-organisation of the army. He did not care for constitutional methods if those stood in his way for the realisation of his aim. No wonder, he had to rule the country in an autocratic manner for 4 years and got the money from the people without the authority of the Landtag. The money having been got, the programme of the army reform was carried out.

In 1868, Austria summoned a Congress of the German princes to consider proposals "for the reform of the German Confederation" Prussia was also invited. If the move of Austria had been successful, the Austrian influence in Germany would have continued. Bismarck prevailed upon the King of Prussia not to attend the conference and the latter ended in failure.

Schleswig-Holstein Question. Reference may be made to the Schleswig-Holstein question which Bismarck exploited to serve his ends Schleswig and Holstein were two Duchies under the King of Denmark. There was a personal union of these Duchies with the King of Denmark. Hie Duchy of Holstein was essentially German in blood and was a member of the German Confederation of 1815. Schleswig was populated both by the Germans and the Danes. The people of Denmark wanted to incorporate these Duchies in their country. The people of Germany wanted to include them in the German Confederation. An attempt was made in 1848 to amalgamate the political institutions of the Duchies into those of Denmark. However, the attempt had to be given up on account of the opposition of the Germans, Prussia and the Duke of Augustenburg who had very strong claims on the Duchies. The situation was serious and there was a possibility of war. However, the Powers intervened and a compromise was arrived at by the Treaty of London (1852). Denmark was forbidden to incorporate the Duchies. The Dulke of Augustenburg sold his claims to the King of Denmark.

In 1863, a new king came on the throne of Denmark and he published a new constitution which organically incorporated Schleswig with Denmark and bound Holstein with closer ties. This was cearly a violation of the terms of the Treaty of London. The Schleswig-Holstein question was re-opened once again. The Duke of Augustenburg revived, his claims. Bismarck decided to make the best of the opportunity in the cause of German unification. He did not want the Duchies to go to Denmark or to the Duke. He wanted to include them in Prussia. He also wanted to try the newly-organised armies of Prussia and a war with Denmark could have given such an opportunity. He entered into an agreement with Austria to take joint action against Denmark so that ultimately there may be possibility of a quarrel with Austria on the question of the division of spoils of war.

With these objects in view an ultimatum was given to the King of Denmark demanding from him the cancellation of the constitution promulgated by him. As he refused to do so, both Austria and Prussia declared war against Denmark. The Danes were no match for the combined armies and by the Treaty of Vienna (1864), the King of Denmark surrendered the Duchies of Schleswig and Holstein of Austria and Prussia.

Having got the Duchies, there arose the question of their division. The suggestion of Austria was that both of them should be handed over to the Duke of Augustenburg but Prussia refused to do so. Ultimately, it was agreed by the Convention of Gastein (1865) that pending a final settlement, Austria was to occupy and administer Holstein and Prussia was to occupy and administer Schleswig. The question of the Duchies was not to be brought before the German Diet. It was pointed out that the Convention of Gastein was a great diplomatic victory for Bismarck. He was able to oust the Duke of Augustenburg altogether and he was also able to create a situation in which there was every possibility of trouble with Austria.

According to Taylor, "The treaty of Gastein, like the treaty of Schonbrunn before it (and the Gablenz proposals of May 1866 after it), has been a subject of endless controversy. Some have seen in it simply a calculated step by Bismarck on the path towards an inevitable war; others have found in it the proof of his desire to re-establish the conservative German partnership of Metternich's days. May be it was neither. Bismark was a diplomatic genius, inexperienced in war and disliking its risks. He may well have hoped to manoeuvre Austria out of the Duchies perhaps even out of the headship of Germany, by diplomatic strokes; marvels of this sort were not beyond him in later life. His diplomacy in this period seems rather calculated to frighten Austria than to prepare for war. The only bait he held out to France was that, if Prussia got the Duchies, she would apply 'the national principle' by restoring northern Schleswig to Denmark; all he asked in return was benevolent neutrality." **(The Struggle for Mastery in Europe,** pp. 157-58).

The Convention of Gastein was not favourable to Austria. She was given control over a territory which was hedged in by Prussian territory on both sides. It is rightly pointed out that the Convention merely "papered over the cracks". It was not a solution of the problem. Austria felt that her position in Holstein was not secure and she began to encourage the claim of the Duke of Augustenburg. She also decided to refer the matter to the Diet of the German Confederation. Evidently, that was a violation of the Convention of Gastein. Bismarck asked Austria to stop propaganda in Holstein in favour of the Duke of Augustenburg. Austria refused and the Prussian troops entered Holstein and turned out the Austrians. Bismarck also proposed the reform of the German Confederation on the basis of universal suffrage, but Austria opposed the same. Austria prevailed upon the Diet of the German Confederation to take action against Prussia. Prussia left the German Confederation and declared war against Austria in 1866.

However, before declaring the war, Bismarck had not only made military preparations but also left no stone unturned to isolate Austria diplomatically. The result was that when the war actually started, Austria had absolutely no ally. Reference may be made in this connection to the relations of Bismarck with Russia, France and Italy.

Isolation of Austria: Russia. Bismarck did all that he could to win over Russia and thereby ensure that in the event of a war with Austria, Russia would not join hands with Austria as she had done in 1849 when Nicholas I came to the help of Austria against Hungary. Bismarck was the Prussian ambassador at Petersburg from 1859 to 1862. It was at that time that he tried to win over Russia to the side of Prussia. The Crimean War had broken the Austro-Russian alliance and thereby paved the way for an agreement between Russia and Prussia. Bismarck cultivated personal friendship with Czar. Alexander II and thereby brought the two countries together. This deliberate pro-Russian policy was pursued by Bismarck when he was appointed Minister-President in 1862.

In 1863, the Poles revolted against the Czar. Napoleon III was friendly towards the Polish cause and the Liberals of Prussia were also enthusiastic for their cause. However, Bismarck informed the Czar that "Prussia would stand shoulder to shoulder with him against the common enemy." Bismarck could not tolerate the creation of a united Poland which was bound to be an enemy and a rival of Prussia. That it why he opposed the Polish revolt. However, there were stronger reasons for his anti-Polish attitude. Bismarck knew that he had to depend upon the support of Russia in a war with Austria in the future. He decided to make the best of the opportunity offered by the Polish revolt. He entered into an agreement with Alexander II by which he agreed to take strong action against those Poles who took refuge in Prussia or tried to have recruits in Prussia or in any way used Prussia as a base for their Operations. Although Bismarck was condemned for his action, he cared only for the friendship of Russia and nothing else. It was in this way that Bismarck was able to win over Russia to his own side and he knew that she would not side with Austria in the event of a war between Prussia and Austria.

France, Bismarck also tried to win over Napoleon III to his own side. While Bismarck was the Prussian ambassador in Paris in 1862, he had tried to cultivate good relations with Napoleon III. The latter came to form a very high opinion of Bismarck. In October 1865, Bismarck had an interview with Napoleon III at **Biarritz.** The interview was confidential and no account of it was maintained. However, as a result of the interview, Napoleon III promised the neutrality of France in the event of a war between Prussia and Austria. He agreed to the annexation of the Elbe Duchies by Prussia in the case of victory. In the case of an alliance between Italy and Prussia, he also approved of the giving of Venetia to Italy. Napoleon did not protest against the reform of the German Confederation and the creation of a new State of Northern Germany under Prussian leadership. The question of compensation to France for her neutrality was raised and Bismarck accepted the possibility of petty rectification of frontiers so long as the same was not at the expense of Prussia or Germany. Bismarck seems to have offered what did not belong to him. He seems to have suggested that France could take Southeastern Belgium. The aim of Bismarck was clear. He wanted to secure the neutrality of France but at the same time he did not want to commit himself in such a way that he may have to face any difficulty with regard to compensation to France. It is pointed out that Napoleon III had sympathy with Bismarck so far as the question of unification of Germany was concerned. He was also in favour of helping Italy to take Venetia. He also thought that if a strong State in North Germany was created, there was every possibility of Austria depending upon France. Napoleon III also thought that there was every possibility of Prussia being defeated and in such a case France would be in a position to establish her hold over the smaller States of Germany. Anyhow, Bismarck had secured the neutrality of France and when the war started with Austria, the latter could expect no help from France.

The view of A.J.P. Taylor is that the meeting between Napoleon III and Bismarck at Biarritz in October 1865 was not a repetition of Cavour's visit to Plombieres in 1858. Cavour at that time was resolved on war with Austria and Napoleon III intended to fight it with him. Each was concerned to tie the other down. Cavour wanted a binding promise of support and Napoleon III wanted to secure Savoy and Nice. However, at Biarritz, both Bismarck and Napoleon III were anxious to avoid commitments with a view to keep the future open. Bismarck wanted to prevent a French alliance with Austria but not to get one for himself. Napoleon disliked any agreement between Prussia and Austria and Bismarck told him that there was no Prussian guarantee of Venetia. In exchange, Napoleon stated that a French alliance with Austria was impossible. Though Bismarck and Napoleon discussed "advantages which might offer themselves unsought" such as Northern Germany for Prussia and Belgium or Luxemburg for France, those were vague speculations of the usual Napoleonic kind. The essential bargain at Biarritz was that both kept dear of commitment to Austria, Bismarck for the sake of Germany and Napoleon III for the sake of Venetia. It was Venetia which determined the shape of future diplomatic events. Napoleon was obsessed with it. He was determined to achieve the unfinished programme of 1859. He believed that if he died with Venetia still in Austrian hands, "his son would have a volcano as a throne." The prospect of acquiring territory towards the Rhine was of secondary importance to him. Those demands were made by him merely to satisfy the public opinion in France in order to keep himself popular. So long as Venetia was in Austrian hands, Napoleon could not be won over for a pro-Austrian or even a pacific policy. It was Venetia which in the last resort gave Prussia the hegemony of Germany. In the autumn of 1865, a conservative Italian nobleman, Malaguzzi, tried to pursuade the Austrian Government to sell Venetia to Italy. Although negotiations continued up to February 1866, nothing came out of them. On 23 February 1866, Nicholas Cuza, the Prince of Rumania, was compelled to abdicate. It occurred to Nigra, the Italian representative at Paris, that Austria might acquire Rumania in exchange for Venetia and Napoleon approved of the idea. However, Napoleon III also believed that the Austrians would never give up Venetia unless driven to it by fear and hence he advised the Italians to prod Austria into surrender by simultaneously negotiating with Prussia for a war alliance. The advice was given at the most opportune time. On 28 February 1866, a Prussian crown council had decided to challenge Austria even at the risk for war and as a first step to conciliate Napoleon III by seeking an alliance with Italy. Bismarck approached La Marmora, the Prime Minister of Italy, just when La Marmora had decided to approach Bismarck. An Italian general was to Berlin, outwardly to negotiate but really to alarm the Austrians. Austria was alarmed and rejected the suggestion to get Rumania instead of Venetia as it was considered to be a device to bring down on Austria the hostility of Russia. Under these circumstances, the Italians and Napoleons III were left with no other alternative except to carry on negotiations with Prussia. The result was that what they had begun as a bluff, they had to pursue in earnest. Though Bismarck agreed that in the event of a war, the Italians should get Venetia, he was not prepared to commit himself to go to war for the sake of Venetia. He demanded that the Italians should bind themselves for three months to go to war against Austria in case Prussia did so, but he kept his hands free. But even this was a gain for the Italians. Although it did not guarantee them a war, it guaranteed them Venetia in the event of a war. Napoleon III advised the Italians, "as a friend without assuming any responsibility", to accept the offer of Bismarck and even promised them to protect them from an Austrian attack in case Prussia left them in the lurch. The treaty between Prussia and Italy was signed on 8 April 1866. For three months, Napoleon III could not offer Italian neutrality to the Austrians even if they were willing to surrender Venetia. Likewise, he could not threaten Prussia even if the Austrians offered him the Rhineland and Bismarck did not. It is often said that Bismarck started the Austro-Prussian war without making any concrete promise to Napoleon. The view of A.J.P. Taylor is that this is not correct. Bismarck won the diplomatic campaign by being the first to pay the only price for which Napoleon cared and that price was Venetia. There was no serious chance of Napoleon asking Bismarck not to go to war if he otherwise was determined to do so.

Italy. Bismarck also tried to win over Italy which was the natural enemy of Austria as there were still Italian-speaking areas under the control of Austria. Italy wanted to get Venetia which she could do only with foreign help. A commercial treaty was arranged between Italy and Prussia but Bismarck wanted to have an offensive alliance. Bismarck realised the importance of attacking Austria on two fronts, one from Italy and the other from Prussia. The difficulty in the way of an alliance was that both countries were full of distrust. Each country thought that the other was going to use the alliance as a lever to get concessions out of Austria. In spite of this, a treaty was signed between Italy and Prussia in April 1866 by which Italy was to attack Austria if Prussia started the war within three months. It is rightly pointed out that it was a treaty of mutual insurance and suspicion." Anyhow, the active support of Italy was ensured against Austria.

The King of Prussia wrote to Napoleon III in March 1866 and Napoleon III replied with a promise of benevolent neutrality. However, he put forward his claim for compensation. French politicians like Thiers were opposed to the policy of neutrality in the event of a war between Austria and Prussia. A proposal for a congress was made but Austria turned down the same. Bismarck was happily at the prospects of war.

Austro-Prussian War (1866). The war between Austria and Prussia was a very short one and that is why it is called the Seven Weeks' War. To begin with, it appeared that Austria would be successful as she had the support of Bavaria, Saxony and the other small States of Germany. However, the Prussian military organisation was so efficient that Austria could not stand it. Moreover, Austria had to fight on two fronts. She had not only to fight against the Prussian attack but also against the Italians who declared war against Austria at the same time as Prussia did. It is true that the Italians were defeated in the Battle of Custozza and also in a naval action off Lissa, but the Italian defeats did not affect the outcome of the war. Austria was defeated by Prussia in the battle of **Sadowa** or Konniggratz in Bohemia. After the victory at Sadowa, the Prussian troops clamoured for a march on Vienna and they were supported by the King. Bismarck was opposed to such a move and ultimately he had his way. He offered very lenient terms to Austria and the same were accepted by the **Treaty of Prague** (1866). By that Treaty, Austria acknowledged the dissolution of "the Germanic Confederation as hitherto constituted." She also consented "to a new organisation of Germany without the participation of the Imperial Austrian State." Venetia was given to Italy. The indemnity imposed was a nominal one. Hanover, Hesse-Cassel, Nassau, the free city of Frankfurt-on-the-Maine and the Duchies of Schleswig and Holstein were annexed to Prussia. The population of the northern districts of Schleswig was to be re-united to Denmark if the people expressed such a wish by a free vote. All the States north of the

Maine were to join the North German Confederation under the leadership of Prussia. The Southern States of Germany were allowed to remain independent.

Effects of the War. The Austro-Prussian war had far-reaching effects. Austria was excluded from Germany and Prussia emerged as the leader of Germany. The military efficiency of Prussia was also recognised in Europe. She also came to be regarded as a great military power. The success of Bismarck discredited the Liberals of Prussia and consequently the cause of liberalism in Germany was lost. The acquisition of Venetia by Italy took her a step further in the process of the unification of the country. Only Rome was left outside united Italy. The war also had its effects on the Austrian Empire. The loss of Venetia in Italy and her exclusion from Germany forced Austria to come to terms with the Magyars of Hungary. The result was the Ausgleich of 1867 between Austria and Hungary. A dual monarchy was set up. Both Austria and Hungary were to be independent in their affairs except in matters of war and diplomacy. Both of them were to have the same ruler who was to be called the Emperor in Austria and King in Hungary. Provision was made for joint delegations of the two countries. The new settlement continued up to 1918.

Franco-Prussian War (1870-71). The unification of Germany was not complete even after defeat of Austria in 1866. The Southern States of Germany had still to be united and it was not possible to do so with the help force. If Bismarck had tried to do so, there was every possibility of their being helped by France and that was not proper. Consequently, Bismarck handled the situation cautiously. Between 1867 and 1870, Bismarck followed a policy of winning over the Southern States by a policy of conciliation and help. He gave them money. He gave them military officers to train their armies, but otherwise did not interfere in their affairs. Efforts were made to impress upon them that Prussia was their friend and they had nothing to fear from her.

Bismarck was convinced that "a war with France lay in the logic of history," and he prepared his country for that eventuality. Military preparations were pushed forward and everything was made perfect. Both Moltke and Roon waited for the day when the war would start with France.

Bismarck also was successful in isolating France diplomatically. Italy was already annoyed with Napoleon III of France as he had betrayed her in 1859. Prussia had helped her in 1866 to get Venetia and no wonder Italy was grateful to Prussia. Moreover, French troops were occupying Rome since 1849 and the unification could be completed only if the French troops withdrew from Rome. That was possible only if France was involved in a war where the military pressure forced her to withdraw them. Consequently, Italy could not he expected to fight on the side of France.

Bismarck was also able to secure the neutrality of Russia. Russia had not forgotten the Crimean War in which France had defeated her. Moreover, Bismarck told the Czar he could repudiate the Black Sea clauses of the Treaty of Paris when he attacked France.

Bismarck had won over Austria in 1866 by giving her very favourable terms. Although the Prussians were victorious he did not allow them to enter the city of Vienna as desired by them. Austria was not forced to pay a huge war-indemnity. Bismarck could count upon the neutrality of Austria in the event of a war with France.

If Bismarck wanted a war to complete the unification of Germany, Nopoleon III also wanted a war with Prussia. It was felt in France that it was not Austria which was defeated in the Battle of Sadowa, but that it was the diplomatic defeat of France. No wonder, France wanted to have revenge for that humiliation. Moreover, opposition to Napoleon III was increasing in France and he felt that the only way to win over the support of all the sections of the people of France was by declaring a war against Prussia. It was under these circumstances that the trap was laid by Bismarck and Napoleon III entered the same.

The throne of Spain had been offered twice to Prince Leopold, but the same had been rejected by him. On the persuasion of Bismarck, the offer was renewed once again. There was a lot of agitation in the French press over the offer. It was pointed out that France would be sandwiched between

Prussia and Spain and thus her very existence would be endangered. Although Leopold withdrew his acceptance of the throne, the agitation continued. Napoleon demanded as assurance from the King of Prussia that he would never in future allow the renewal of the candidature of Leopold. Benedetti, the French ambassador, tried to impose himself on the King of Prussia who was at the watering place of Ems. The Prussian King sent a telegram containing an account of his interview with the French ambassador. Bismarck abridged the telegram in such a way that it appeared to the French that their ambassador was insulted and it appeared to the Prussians that their king was insulted. When the news reached France, there was a demand for war against Prussia, and the same was declared.

The most important battle of the war was that of Sedan in which Napoleon III was defeated and he surrendered. Although a republic was set up in France, Bismarck insisted on entering Paris. As that was not acceptable to the people of France, a siege of Paris started. There was a stiff resistance but ultimately Paris had to surrender. The war was ended by the Treaty of Frankfurt of 1871 by which France ceded Alsace and Lorraine to Germany. She was also to pay a huge war indemnity. A ceremony was held in the famous Hall of Mirrors at Versailles in 1871 where the King of Prussia was declared the Emperor of Germany. The Southern States of Germany also joined the German Confederation. It was in this way that the unification of Germany was completed.

According to Hazen, "The Treaty of Frankfurt remained the open sore of Europe after 1871. France could never forget or forgive the deep humiliation of it. The enormous fine could, with the lapse of time, have been overlooked, but never the seizure of the two provinces by mere force and against the unanimous and passionate protest of the people of Alsace and Lorraine. Moreover, the eastern frontier of France was thus seriously weakened."

However, the Franco-Prussian War had other consequences also. It led to the final completion of the unification of Italy. That was due to the fact that when the war started between France and Prussia, French troops were withdrawn from Rome and the Italian troops entered the same. Russia took advantage of the war and repudiated the Back Sea clauses of the Treaty of Paris. The Empire of Napoleon was overthrown in Franch and a Republic was set up in that country.

About the Franco-Prussian War, Prof. Taylor points out that "though victory over France in 1870 certainly united Germany, the war lacked the deliberation or the war against Austria. Between 1862 and 1866 Bismarck steadily screwed up the pressure, despite occasional and perhaps genuine couples; unless the Austrians accepted his terms, the repeated crises were boded to end in war. There was no such steady march to war between 1861 and 1870; indeed no alarm disturbed Franco-Prussian relations between the Luxembourg affair in 1867 and the outbreak of war more than three years later. Nor did Bismarck suffer in these years from the nightmare of coalitions which dominated him later. He dismissed the rumours of French alliance with Austria-Hungary and Italy as 'conjectural rubbish,' which indeed they turned out to be. He was not perturbed by good relations between France and Russia; since these must be based on the abandonment by France of her Polish sympathies, Prussia could always make a third in the partnership. His own policy was more passive than at any time before or afterwards. Though he kept the solid basis of friendship with Russia, this was confined to a common hostility towards Poland; and he never allowed the Russians to draw him into supporting them in the Near East. Ultimately, he hoped for a conservative alliance with Russia and Austria-Hungary; like all alliances based on principle, this had the advantage of providing security without having to pay a price for it. But he knew that he would have to wait until Habsburg resentment at the defeat of 1866 had died away." (**The Struggle for Mastery in Europe,** p. 201).

There is a considerable controversy over the question whether the master-mind of Bismarck had already conceived a plan of action for the unification of Germany when he came to power in 1862 and carried out the same according to a precise time-table. The hero-worshippers of Bismarck and his liberal critics hold the view that he carried out a programme which he had already decided upon. There is one remarkable piece of evidence in support of this view. Disraeli met Bismarck at a dinner in London in 1862 and a little before Bismarck came to power. Disraeli tells us that Bismarck told him about his whole scheme in the course of half an hour's conversation. Later in the evening Disraeli remarked to Saburov of the Russian Embassy in London, "What an extraordinary man Bismarck is! He meets me for the first time and he tells me all he is going to do. He will attack Denmark in order to get possession of Schleswig-Holstein! He will put Austria out of the German Confederation and then he will attack France—an extraordinary man!" If the story is true and both Saburov and the official biographers of Disraeli have confirmed it, there can be no doubt that at least the broad design was already in the mind of Bismarck when he took office.

However, David Thomson says that it is rare in, history for even the greatest of statesmen to plan successfully 10 years ahead and then to impose their plans on the world. The recent biographers are very sceptic about the truth of what Disraeli is said to have reported. It is contended that Bismarck was not like Metternich or Alexander I, a system-maker. He was a brilliant opportunist whose course of action always remained undecided and flexible until the last moment, and his policy looks more clear-cut and coherent in retrospect than it was at that time. He was first and always a Prussian nationalist who believed that Prussian interests demanded that she should dominate the whole of Germany and exclude Austria from German affairs. His policy towards Denmark. Austria and France was guided by the interests of Prussia and unification of Germany was incidental and a by-product of his never-ending pursuit of Prussian interests. His original plan for unification was only up to the Main. It was extended to the Inn as it was found to be necessary for the successful promotion of war against France. To quote A.J.P. Taylor, "Far from using the war to promote unification, he sought unification in order to continue the war." Bismarck was not favourably inclined towards the southern states of Germany because they were Catholic states and were likely to weaken rather than strengthen the predominance of Protestant Prussia and Germany. He brought the southern states of Bavaria, Baden and Wurtenberg in when it became a military and diplomatic necessity to shorten the war against France and preclude intervention by other powers. The southern states could make a separate peace so long as they remained independent, but once they were included in the Empire, they were bound to stay in the war. Likewise, Bismarck at first had no desire to annex Alsace and Lorraine because the province include so many Frenchmen and they could be a source of trouble for Germany. He agreed to annex them only under pressure from the Generals who demanded the territories on strategic grounds.

Similar views are expressed regarding the achievements of Cavour in Italy. It is contented that Cavour was also a brilliant and ingenious opportunist rather than the framer of long-term plans for a distant future. Neither he, nor Bismarck, believed in future. Both of them were always engrossed with the present. They were supreme practitioners of realpolitik and their success is to be explained more by the profound and imaginative grasp of the immediate realities of international politics than by any alleged control over the long-term course of events. They were masterly statesmen and not masterful supermen.

David Thomson maintains that the two views of Bismarck and Cavour that they were opportunists and planners, are not entirely irreconcilable. Both of them cherished certain aims. Both of them had a minimum programme to which they devoted all their energies to achieve. A united kingdom of northern Italy and a Prussian-controlled North German Federation, seemed practical programmes of policy during the 1850's. Both of them were within the grasp of practical politics if Austria could be driven pack, behind Alaps and Main, and if the great powers did not intervene on the side of Austria. Once the sequence of diplomatic movements and military events had started, the events themselves began to take control. The statesmen of Italy and Germany adjusted their policies to take account of each new situation and exploited them to achieve their own ends.

SUGGESTED READINGS

Clark, C.W.: **Franz Joseph and Bismarck : The Diplomacy of Austria before the War of 1866.**

Dawson, W.H.: **Evolution of Modern Germany.**

Dawson, W.H.: **The German Empire, 1867-1914.**

Ergang, R.E.: **Herder and the Foundation of German Nationalism, 1931.**

Friedjung, H.: **The Struggle for Supremacy in Germany (1859-1866), 1935.**

Gooch, C.P.: **Germany.**

Headlam : **Bismarck and the Foundations of the German Empire.**

Henderson, E.F.: **A Short History of Germany.**

Marriott and Robertson: **The Evolution of Prussia.**

Oncken, H.: **Napoleon III and the Rhine: The Origin of the War of 1870-71, 1892.**

Priest: **Germany Since 1740.**

Taylor, A.J.P.: **The Course of German History.**

Thomson, David: **Europe Since Napoleon.**

Taylor, A.J.P.: **The Struggle for Mastery in Europe.**

Thomson, David: **Europe Since Napoleon.**

Valentin, V.: **1848: Chapters in German History, 1940.**

Willoughby: L.A.: **The Romantic Movement in Germany, 1930.**

CHAPTER 18

BISMARCK (1815-98)

Bismarck was one of the most fascinating personalities in the history of modern Europe. It is true that there were other factors which contributed to the unification of Germany during the 19th century, but the main credit for uniting it must go to Bismarck. In the words of Prof. Fyffe, Bismarck led a reluctant nation to a goal which he had himself fixed for it. There is no doubt that but for him, German unity might have remained only a dream for a long time to come.

Bismarck was born on 1 April 1815. His father was a Junker and he got his good physique from him. His mother was the daughter of a distinguished civil servant and the grand-daughter of a professor and it is stated that he got his brain from his mother. Prince Bismarck was educated at Berlin and Gottingen. He was trained for a diplomatic career. He travelled a lot in France and England. He became a member of the Provincial Diet of Pomerania in 1845. He entered the Imperial Diet of Berlin in 1847. In 1849, he was elected a member of the lower chamber of Prussia. In 1851, he was appointed the envoy of Prussia in the Federal Diet at Frankfurt and he remained there for eight years. His stay at Frankfurt profoundly influenced his views on politics. He wrote thus in 1859 about his experience of Frankfurt: "I have brought away as the result of my experience from the eight years of my official life at Frankfurt the conviction that the present arrangements of the Bund form for Prussia an oppressive and at critical times a perilous tie....I see in our connection in the Bund an infirmity which we shall have to repair sooner or later. **Ferro et egni,** if we do not apply timely remedies to it at a favourable season of the year." During his stay at Frankfurt, Bismarck tried to win over the rulers of the minor States of Germany. He tried to strengthen the economic ties of Prussia with them. He opposed the intervention of Prussia against Russia in the Crimean War. To quote him, "Prussia must never let Russia's friendship wax cold." Again, "We had absolutely no interest in the Eastern Question that could possibly justify a war with Russia....we should without provocation be attacking our hitherto friend either out of fear of France or for the **beaux yeux** of England and Austria."

In 1859, Bismarck was appointed Prussian Ambassador in Russia and be stayed there for three years. During his stay there, he tried to win over Russia to the side of Prussia. In 1862, he was appointed the Prussian Ambassador in France, but he had hardly occupied that position for a few months when he was summoned in September 1862 to Berlin to become the Minister-President. He had to tackle a very difficult situation which had risen on account of the determination of William I, King of Prussia, to increase the Prussian Army and the refusal of the Landtag to vote supplies for the same. It is stated that when his appointment was made in 1862, even King William I was not impressed. He referred to him as a thoroughbred reactionary who smelled of blood. He was given the titles of "a swaggering junker", "a borrow braggart", "a Napoleon-worshipper" and "a town uprooter," However, it was this unimpressive person who performed the Herculean job of German unification. Speaking in the Budget Committee only a few days after his succession to power, Bismarck summed up his policy in these world, **"It is not by speechifying and majorities that the great questions of the time will have to be decided—that was the mistake in 1848 and 1849, but by blood and iron."**

It has already been pointed out that Bismarck brought about the unification of Germany by fighting the Danish War of 1864, the Austro-Prussian War of 1866 and the Franco-Prussian War of

1870-71. He was opposed at the beginning and he had to follow arbitrary methods. However, when his position was vindicated after the defeat of Austria in 1866, the opposition ended and he came to be recognized as a great leader. By 1871, Bismarck could say that Germany was "a saturated State" and his policy after that became one of maintaining peace and avoiding war."

Internal Policy. Between 1871 and 1890, Bismarck was the chief figure in the domestic politics of his country and in the international field. During the first few years, he was able to pass a large number of laws for the purpose of welding together the States and the people of Germany.

The legal system of Germany was transformed. Instead of the different systems of laws for the different States, a uniform code of law for the entire German Empire was adopted. Likewise, a uniform coinage replaced the different currency systems of the various States. An imperial railway bureau was set up in 1873 with a view to unify the different railway systems in the various States. The railways were also linked up with the military, postal and telegraphic organisation of the Empire. The control over banking in the country was put in the hands of the Bundesrat by the Bank Act of 1875. In 1876, the Reichsbank or the Imperial Bank was established.' Compulsory military service was enforced all over Germany. The peace strength of the German army was fixed at 4 lakhs. Bismarck's view was that the expenses for the maintenance of the standing army should be made a permanent charge on the revenues of the State, but the Reichsbank refused to oblige him. Ultimately, a compromise was made by which appropriations for the army were made for 7 years at the beginning and for 5 years afterwards. However, Bismarck was clever enough to get the money for the army by creating a kind of war-scare.

It is true that Bismarck enjoyed the backing of the majority of the legislature consisting of the National Liberal Party and the Free Conservatives, but there were certain elements which were opposed to him. The Progressives were a thorn in Bismarck's side. They were not satisfied with the German Constitution of 1871 and demanded drastic changes in the same on the lines of the British parliamentary system. They were also opposed to the policy of blood and iron of Bismarck. They teased Bismarck by their lengthy speeches in the legislature. A few socialists who were the followers of Karl Marx or of Ferdinand Lassalle, were also opposed to him. The deputies from Hanover known as the "Guells" and led by Ludwig Windthorst, were also opposed to him. They demanded autonomy for their State. One or two Danes from Schleswig were also opposed to him and demanded the giving back of northern Schleswig to Denmark. There were a few Poles from Posen and West Prussia who opposed the anti-Polish policy of Bismarck. The 15 deputies from Alsace-Lorraine consistently opposed Bismarck. Even on the occasion of their first appearance in the Reichstag in 1874 they protested against the incorporation of Alsace-Lorraine into the German Empire. There were certain other groups who stood for the rights of the States and as such were opposed to the centralising tendencies of the Bismarckian regime.

The Kulturkampf. ("Battle for Civilization"). Bismarck took action against the Roman Catholic Church in Germany and that was named by Virchow as the Kulturkampf. Bismarck had his old enmity with the Roman Catholic Church. The Roman Catholics were the supporters of Austria and the opponents of the Protestant dynasty of Prussia. The Pope had openly prayed for the victory of Austria against Prussia in 1866. The Roman Catholic Church was opposed to the new German Empire. The authority of the Pope within Germany was very great and his influence over the lay people was also extensive. The Catholic party was anti-national and opposed to the politics of Bismarck. It was creating difficulties between Germany and the Kingdom of Italy. It was a State within a State. Pope Pius IX issued the "Syllabus of Errors" in 1864. In 1870 was propounded the doctrine of Papal Infallibility. It was solemnly proclaimed as "a dogma divinely willed that His Church should be endowed for defending faith or morals and that therefore such definitions of the Roman pontiff are **per se** immutable and independent of the consent of the Church." According to this doctrine, the Catholics were bound to obey more the Pope than the State and that could not be tolerated by any ruler. To quote Bismarck, "It is the infallibility of the Pope which threatens the State. He arrogates to himself whatever secular rights he pleases....declares our laws null and void, levies taxes....in a word, no one in Prussia is so powerful as this foreigner." Again, "The struggle is purely political and not one between a Protestant dynasty and the Catholic church; it is not one between faith and unbelief; it is only the re-appearance of the conflict—older than the advent of Redeemer of the world, as old as the human race itself, the same contest for power as Agamemnon waged with his seers at Aulis and which cost him his daughter, while preventing the Greeks from selling sail for Troy; the conflict that raged all through the Middle Ages between the Pope and the Kaisers." Bismarck was backed by many sections of the German population. The old Catholics under Doctor Dollinger contested the new Papal claim to infallibility and supported Bismarck. The German Liberals condemned the Papal Syllabus of 1864 and supported Bismarck. Virchow, the atheist scientist, also supported Bismarck. The Progressives also supported Bismarck.

In 1872, the Jesuits were expelled from Germany and diplomatic relations between Prussia and the Vatican were cut off. In May 1873 and in May 1874 laws were passed by the Prussian Landtag against the Roman Catholics. These laws came to be known as the "May laws" as they were passed in the month of May. They were also called the "Falk laws" after the name of the Prussian Minister of Education. These laws required that every official of the Catholic Church in Prussia, whether he was a bishop or a priest, was to be a German citizen, a graduate of a German public school and German university. He was also required to be duly certified and "authorized" by the government. All the schools run by the Roman Catholic Church were to be under the control of the State. All Catholic preparatory schools for the clergy were banned. All religious education was to be given in the German language and not in any other language. When the Catholics of Prussia protested against the laws and refused to obey them, more drastic legislation was enacted. The "authorized" persons were forbidden from performing the religious functions. The rebellious clergymen were liable to lose citizenship of the country and also could be imprisoned or exiled. The financial aid to the church was liable to be suspended in any diocese whose bishop was rebellious. Provision was made for compulsory civil marriage in every case. Public excommunications were forbidden. Provision was made for taking up of appeal against ecclesiastical punishments. The State was to have authority in the appointment and dismissal of the priests. In 1875, all religious orders were dissolved.

The Pope declared the May laws as null and void and asked the Roman Catholics to defy them. Bismarck was also adamant in his attitude. He categorically declared thus: **"We shall not go to Canossa, either in body or in spirit."** This refers to the incident of 1077 when a quarrel took place between Pope Gregory VII and Emperor Henry IV. The latter had to go to the Italian town of Canossa and make a humiliating surrender before the Pope. What Bismarck wanted to say was that he would not surrender before the Pope.

It is pointed out that the laws against the Catholic Church were enforced so strictly that in one year, six Catholic bishops were put in prison and Catholic worship was stopped in 1,300 parishes. By 1877, every German bishop and hundreds of priests were either in prison or in exile. Catholic laymen were also removed from the service of the State.

Catholics of Germany were not discouraged in their opposition to the State by the severity of the legislation against them. Under the leadership of Windthorst, a strong Catholic Party known as the Centre Party, was set up to oppose the government and get the anti-Catholic legislation repealed. Within a short time, the Centre Party gained in strength. In the general elections of 1874, its representation in the Reichstag increased from 60 to 90. Windthorst was able to align himself with all the elements opposed to Bismarck and thereby give a lot of trouble to the government. Ultimately, a section of the Conservatives who were otherwise supporters of Bismarck, began to cooperate with Windthorst. When that happened, Bismarck decided to call a halt to his policy against the Catholic Church. He also found another danger from the Socialists which he considered to be more serious than that of the Catholics. They were anti-monarchical, anti-militarist and men without a country. They were the enemies of family-life and the Empire. Bismarck decided to take action against the Socialists and under the circumstances it was desirable to come to a compromise with the Catholic Church. His work was facilitated by the death of Pope Pius IX and the succession of Pope Leo XIII. The latter was diplomatic and willing to compromise. The new Pope was able to find out grounds of agreement without giving up his theoretical claims. The result was that in 1880, the Prussian Landtag empowered the government to use its discretion in the enforcement of the May laws. 'Diplomatic relations with the Vatican were restored. In 1886, the most oppressive laws against the Catholic Church were repealed. Bismarck had to admit that Kulturkampf was a failure. Although he did not go to Canossa, yet there is no denying the fact that he had to admit defeat in his conflict with the Church. The only result of the struggle was the strengthening of the Catholic Party in Germany.

Action against Socialism. As a result of the Industrial Revolution in Germany, the Socialist propaganda began to spread among the working classes in the country. In the elections of 1874, the Socialists got nine seats in the Reichstag. In 1875, the Social Democratic Party was founded. In the elections of 1877, the number of Socialist deputies increased to 12. Bismarck regarded the Socialist principles as the enemy of the State, the family and civilization. No wonder, he decided to take action against them. His work was facilitated by the unsuccessful attempt made on the life of the Emperor William I in 1878. Bismarck held the Socialists responsible for the murderous attempt. A new legislature was elected to which were returned a majority of the supporters of Bismarck. A law was passed by which the circulation of Socialist books, pamphlets and newspapers was forbidden. The police was given the power to break up the meetings of the Socialists and also suppress their publications. The trial and punishment of the Socialist offenders was removed from the jurisdiction of the ordinary courts to those of the palace. The laws against the Socialists were passed for four years at the beginning but they were re-enacted later on. As a matter of fact, when Bismarck resigned in 1890, the laws against the Socialists were still in force. However, the more the Socialists were oppressed by the government, the stronger they became. Their popularity went on growing as they were considered to be martyrs. Their representation in the Reichstag also went on increasing. It is pointed out that the Social Democratic Party won 12 seats in 1881, 24 in 1884, 11 in 1887 and 35 in 1890. The laws against the Socialists were withdrawn after 1890 and after that they won 44 seats in 1893, 56 in 1898, 81 in 1903, 43 in 1907 and 110 in 1912.

Social Legislation. According to Prof. Hayes, Bismarck was the pioneer among the European statesmen to take action on behalf of the workers. His object was two-fold. He wanted to remove the grievances of the workers and thereby weaken the socialist propaganda. Secondly, he wanted strong recruits for the army and that was possible only if the Government paid attention to the condition of the workers. In 1883, a bill was passed which ensured the workers against sickness. In 1884, the employers were forced to insure their employees against accidents. In 1887, laws were passed which limited the labour of women and children, fixed the minimum number of working hours for employees in various industries and provided for the regulation and supervision of factories and mines by the Government. Sunday was declared a holiday. In 1889, provision was made for the insurance of workers against invalidity and old age. The premium was to be paid partly by the State, partly by the employer and partly by the employee. It is rightly pointed out that this socialist legislation went a long way in making Germany one of the leading countries of the world in the industrial field.

Policy of Protection. Bismarck was probably the first important statesman of the 19th century who set aside the principle of free trade and followed a policy of protection. With this object in view, Bismarck gave up his alliance with the National Liberals and joined the Centre Party. By an Act of 1879, a wall of high tariffs was created against foreign imports to protect the German farm-products and domestic manufactures. High duties were also levied on tobacco and sugar with a view to remove the complaint of the agrarian classes that the Act of 1879 was very much favourable to the urban industries. The result of the policy of protection was that the infant industries of Germany were protected and after the lapse of some time were able not only to stand on their own legs but also compete in every nook and corner of the world. The Government was also to get a lot of money. A great impetus was given to the industrial development of the country. Moreover, the tariffs strengthened the Government and unified the Empire.

Imperialism. At the beginning, Bismarck was opposed to the policy of acquiring colonies and developing the German navy. That was due to the fact that he did not want to come in competition with England. His view was that there could be no war between the two countries so long as Germany remained a land rat and Great Britain a water rat. That was one of the reasons why Bismarck did not accept the French offer in 1871 to take some French colony instead of Alsace and Lorraine. However, he had to change his policy later on. The merchants of Bremen and Hamburg wanted new markets for the surplus goods and a source of supply of raw materials. Missionaries wanted colonies to convert people to Christianity. The patriots demanded colonies to add to the glory of their country. There was also the problem of surplus population of Germany which was migrating to the U.S.A. It was felt that Germany must acquire colonies to find homes for the surplus population of Germany which was otherwise being lost to the nation on account of their migration to independent States. The pressure of these factors was so very great that Bismarck had to adopt the policy of colonial expansion. Merchants and missionaries led the way.

In 1879, a German trading company got some privileges in the Island of Samoa. In 1882, the German Colonial Union was formed. Within a very short time, the commercial companies of Hamburg, Bremen and Lubeck got some concessions and established their trading stations in South West Africa, Togoland, Cameroon, East Africa, the Marshall Islands, a part of New Guinea and the islands named the Bismarck Archipelago. In 1884-85, laws were passed by which protectorates were established over these commercial outposts. In 1886, the Government gave subsidies to the German steamers which were plying between Germany and the protectorates. Before his retirement in 1890, Bismarck took steps to transform the protectorates into Crown colonies. These colonies were administered by the German officials and policed by German troops.

About the colonial policy of Bismarck, Taylor says that although domestic needs pushed Bismarck towards colonial ambitions, it is not correct to say that they were imposed upon him by public opinion. It is true that they were in Germany romantic historians who wanted the Reich to be an empire, trading houses who wanted imperial backing for their African trade and adventurers who wanted to be known as the founders of an empire, but these forces could not affect the rulers of Germany because such a thing was possible only in a parliamentary Government and Germany was a managed autocracy and not a parliamentary state. Bismarck took up the colonial impulses in 1884 and exploited them but threw them over without difficulty the moment they had served his turn and after 1885, colonial considerations did not play any important part in his policy. If it is absurd to suppose that Bismarck allowed a few colonial enthusiasts to divert and injure his foreign policy, it is even more absurd to believe that he himself succumbed to ambitions overseas. Bismarck was never distracted by colonial issues. His colonial gains of 1884 were a move in his European policy. Bismarck thought stolely in continental terms and he is stated to have put his position in these words, "My map of Africa lies in Europe. Here lies Russia and here lies France and we are in the middle. That is my map of Africa."

Policy towards Poles, Danes and Guelfs. Bismarck hated the Poles on account of their Catholic religion. He tried to force upon them the use of the German language. Laws were passed to crush nationalism among them. He also transferred the farms of the Poles to the Germans. A similar action was taken against the Danes of Schleswig. He also took action against the Guelfs of Hanover. He was not prepared to allow the people of Hanover to have their autonomy. A secret fund known as the "reptile fund" was set up to crush conspiracies among the Germans of Hanover and also to harass them.

A similar policy was followed by Bismarck in Alsace-Lorrane. He did all that he could to Germanise that territory. He allowed a large number of Germans to migrate to Alsace and Lorraine and settle there. A lot of money was given to the University of Strassburg with a view to make it the centre of German intellectual life and cultural influence. Bismarck failed in his object as the people of Alsace-Lorraine were not reconciled to the German rule. They always followed a policy of non-co-operation. The Government pressure merely added to their fanaticism and their determination to become independent.

Foreign Policy of Bismarck. By 1870, Bismarck had won for his country national unity by his policy of blood and iron. Germany was a satiated country and Bismarck did not stand for any further extension of its territory. However, he was determined to maintain the **status quo** in Europe. There were certain difficulties in the way of his following such a policy. Unlike his generous policy towards Austria in 1866, Bismarck's attitude towards France was rather stiff. After the French defeat at Seddan in 1870, Bismarck refused to give easy terms to France and after a long siege of Paris, he imposed a very humiliating treaty on France. France was not only forced to pay a huge war-indemnity amounting to five milliard francs, but she was also made to give up Alsace and a part of Lorraine. The annexation of Lorraine was an error of the first magnitude. Lorraine was French in blood, speech and sentiments. Metz could only be held by the bayonet and in the effort to hold it, Europe was transformed into an armed camp. It has rightly been pointed out that after Sedan, the Battle of Marne (1914) lay in the logic of history. The people of France were determined to get back Alsace and Lorraine. The German annexation of those territories was described as the snatching away of children from the breast of the mother, and no wonder the people of France stood for a war of **Revanche** to get back those territories. Bismarck knew full well the sentiments of the Frenchmen and did his utmost to provide against the French danger. No wonder, he tried to quarantine France or put her in cold storage. The main object of Bismarck's Foreign Policy was to isolate France diplomatically so that she may not be able to get an ally with whose help she may try to get back Alsace and Lorraine. For that purpose, Bismarck maintained good relations with Austria, Russia, Italy and England. Bismarck described his own policy in these words: "The Foreign Policy of the German Empire since 1871 has been the maintenance of peace and the prevention of anti-German coalitions, and the pivot of this policy is Russia." He also explained his philosophy of alliance to the Russian ambassador in these words : "You forget the importance of being a party of three on the European chess-board....Nobody wishes to be in a minority. All politics reduce themselves to this formula : try to be **a trois** in a world governed by five powers."

According to Brandenburg, "In spite of the efforts to isolate France, Bismarck's policy towards the latter was in no sense hostile. He wished to prevent France from disturbing the peace and from undoing the terms of the Treaty of Frankfurt, and he endeavoured to establish as friendly relations as possible between Berlin and Paris. He went so far as to assure France of Germany's active support in all questions where their mutual interests did not conflict and to consent to her conquest of Annam and Tonquin. He encouraged France in her occupation of Tunis and repeatedly drew her attention to Morocco as a suitable field for her colonial activity. He hoped that a successful colonial policy would in some measure satisfy the French love of prestige, and that the new colonial empire would in time provide compensation for Alsace-Lorraine, so that possibly in the course of a few decades the thought of revenge might die out. He himself well knew that this was but a slender hope. Nevertheless he intended to leave nothing undone that could tranquillise and conciliate."

The Three Emperors' League. In 1873, Bismarck set up the **Three Emperors' League.** By means of this, he was able to bring together Austria, Russia and Germany. It was not a treaty of alliance but it indicated the cordial relations between the three Great Powers. It emphasized the common interests of the three Emperors. It also implied that Austria had forgotten her humiliation in the Battle of Sadowa and was prepared to accept expulsion from Germany. The Three Emperors'

League was a great achievement of Bismarck but it was difficult to maintain the same. During the war-scare of 1875, Russia told Germany frankly that she should not depend upon her neutrality in the event of a German attack on France. That showed that Bismarck could not depend upon Russia and no wonder he decided to cultivate intimate relations with Austria.

Austro-German Alliance. The Three Emperors' League completely broke down in 1878 after the Congress of Berlin. According to Dr. Gooch, "The outstanding result of the Congress of Berlin in the realm of the high politics was the estrangement of Russia from Germany." The Russian press condemned Bismarck and there was an open demand for an attack on Germany. The sentiments of the Russian people can be judged from the following statement of a Russian: "The Congress (of Berlin) is a conspiracy against the Russian people in which the Russian representatives have taken part. The diplomacy of St. Petersburg is more dangerous than Nihilism. It is a disgraceful treachery to the historic mission of Russia and has lost for ever the respect and affection of the Slavs. Russia has been crucified by her own statesmen. A fool's cap and bells have been set upon her head." Bismarck did not like his criticism in the Russian press and decided to enter into an alliance with Austria, whom he had obliged in 1866. Bismarck had to meet a lot of opposition from William I, the German Emperor, but ultimately he succeeded in entering into an alliance with Austria. The famous Austro-German Alliance was signed in 1879 and the secret alliance brought the two countries together in their common opposition to Russia. The alliance was renewed again and again and was still in existence in 1914 when the World War I started.

Dreikaiserbund. It cannot be maintained that Bismarck's choice of Austria in preference to Russia in 1879 was final and the wire between Berlin and St. Petersburg was permanently broken. Bismarck was never a man of one line of argument. Although "the public telegraph between Berlin and St. Petersburg might be broken", the "private wire" could be restored and no wonder he was able in 1881 to restore the **Dreikaiserbund** or the Three Emperors' League.

According to Prof. Taylor, "The new League had little in common with the League of 1873. That had been a last gesture of conservative resistance. But Metternichian fear of upheaval was no longer enough to bring rulers together. After all, it was ninety years since the execution of Louis XVI, more than sixty since the defeat of Napoleon. The memories of 1848 were fading—they counted for something with William I and Fracis Joseph, for nothing with Alexander III. Even Marx's International, fear of which had played some part in the League of 1873, was dissolved. There was social and political unrest in plenty; but its consequences were different. Both Napoleon III and Bismarck had used foreign war to distract attention from domestic opposition. Formerly only a strong government could risk war; soon there would come a time when only a secure government could remain resolutely at peace. Bismarck regarded the League of the Three Emperors as a triumph for conservatism, but he was alone in this view; for the Russians and Austrians alike it was a move in foreign policy. Metternich had been able to tide over the differences between Austria and Russia for more than thirty years merely by playing on the fear of revolution; Bismarck had to offer them both concrete advantages.

"The treaty of 1881 was therefore a practical agreement about the Near East, without even a monarchical flourish. Its only general principle was a pact of neutrality if one of the three empires was involved in war with a fourth Power. Since there was no immediate likelihood of a war between Germany and France, this was straight gain for Russia; it was a promise that Germany and still more, Austria-Hungary, would not join England. The only limitation was in regard to Turkey: there neutrality would apply only if there had been agreement beforehand. This was an unnecessary precaution : the Russians had no intention of going to war with Turkey. Further, the three Powers recognized the European and mutually obligatory character of the rule of the Straits and would insist that Turkey enforce it. This was the essential security against a British expedition to the Black Sea which the Russians had been seeking all along: it was the one thing that mattered to them. Since a Russian garrison at the Straits was impossible, this was the next best thing. The Russians gained still more. The Austrians promised not to oppose the union of the two Bulgarias and thus cut themselves off from England, for whom division of Bulgaria had been the essential achievement of 1887. In return the Russians recognized Austria-Hungary's right to annex Bosnia and Herzegovina, a concession that they had been ready to make ever since 1876.

"The League was a victory for the Russians and perhaps for Bismarck. Germany was freed from having to choose between Russia and Austria-Hungary in the Balkans. Russia got security in the Black Sea in exchange for a promise of peaceful behaviour which her internal weakness compelled her to keep in any case. It was not so easy to see the advantage for Austria-Hungary, as Haymerle insisted. By supporting the Russian interpretation of the rule of the Straits, she committed herself to an eventual breach with England; yet she owed her Balkan position to the co-operation with England in 1878. She got in exchange merely Russian promises which she regarded as worthless. Andrassy and Haymerle had made the alliance with Bismarck in order to secure German backing against the Russians; instead Bismarck had used the alliance to force Haymerle into an unwelcome agreement with them. He was indeed hard put to it to discover practical arguments with which to persuade Haymerle; and a curious result followed. To justify the League, Bismarck had to invent Italy as a Great Power; and then had to take his own pretence seriously. In February 1880 when Haymerle had argued that England should be brought into the Austro-German alliance in order to keep Itaty quiet, Bismarck had answered that Italy was of no importance. A year later he was arguing that the great use of the League of the Three Emperors was to prevent an alliance between Italy and Russia. When the League had been made, Haymerle continued to press for greater security against Russia; Bismarck would not give this. As a substitute, he had to offer Austria-Hungary security on her Italian frontier; this theoretically would free Austrian troops for the defence of Galicia. Thus, the League of the Three Emperors, which was a pact of friendship with Russia, led in a roundabout way to the Triple Alliance, which was implicitly a pact against her. Again, "The League of the Three Emperors, like the Holy Alliance before it, was a fair-weather system. Though designed to prevent an Austro-Russian conflict in the Balkans, in fact it worked only so long as there was no conflict. It gave Europe an impressive semblance of stability between 1881 and 1885; and was perhaps open of some real use to Russia during the dispute with Great Britain over Penjdeh. But it could not survive the strain of new Balkan troubles. (**The Struggle for Master in Europe,** pp. 270-72 and p. 304).

The League broke down during the Bulgarian crisis when the interests of Austria and Russia clashed. On the occasion of that crisis, Bismarck declared, "In Bulgaria, I am Russian," He took up the cause of Russia and refused to support Prince Alexander of Bulgaria.

In 1887, he made the Reinsurance Treaty with Russia. According to this treaty, if one Power found itself at war with a fourth Power, the others were to observe benevolent neutrality and try to localise the war. In agreement with Germany, Russia declared her firm resolution to respect the interests of Austria arising out of the Treaty of Berlin. Any modification in the territorial **status quo** of Turkey in Europe was to be accomplished, only by virtue of a common agreement. It has rightly been pointed out that "the new friendship of a Germany and Russia prevented an Austro-Russian was and a Franco-Russian coalition."

Triple Alliance. In 1882, Bismarck entered into the **Triple Alliance** with Italy and Austria. The formation of the Triple Alliance is usually attributed to Bismarck. It is pointed out that Bismarck encouraged France to capture Tunis which was desired by Italy. The object was to create one more enemy for France and also to win over Italy. When France established her protectorate over Tunis in 1881, Italy decided to join the Austro-German alliance. However, this view is not accepted by Prof. Fay. According to him, Bismarck encouraged France to **"pluck the ripe Tunisian fruit"** and also encouraged her in other colonial adventures with a view to win over her friendship and also to help her to forget the defeat of 1871. According to Dr. G.P. Gooch, the Triple Alliance originated with

Italy. Earlier in 1882, Italy asked for a treaty of alliance with Austria. She wanted to strengthen her position and gain support for future ambitions. Bismarck was not very eager about an alliance with Italy as she was an untrustworthy ally and her resources were also not large. However, Bismarck gradually agreed to admit Italy into an alliance on account of certain advantages. The danger of Italy joining France would be avoided. There will be no necessity for Austria to maintain troops on the Italian frontier in the event of a war with Russia. France would be forced to keep her troops on the Italian frontier in the event of war with Germany. In May 1882, the Triple Alliance Treaty was signed. This treaty was to last for five years and certain changes were made in 1887. However, it was renewed many a time after 1887 and the Triple Alliance existed even in 1914 although by that time Italy had practically gone to the opposite camp. The Triple Alliance was essentially defensive in character and was primarily intended to preserve the peace of Europe.

Rumania. In 1883, King Carol of Rumania visited Germany. Bismarck sounded Austria "whether it would be desirable and possible to extended our League or peace with Italy to the East and thereby lead in firm paths the policy of Rumania and eventually also that of Serbia and the Porte." Austria agreed to the proposal and in October 1883 was signed a purely defensive treaty of alliance with Rumania. The treaty was to be secret and last for five years with an automatic extension for three years if not denounced by any of the parties.

England. Bismarck maintained friendly relations with England. A cardinal principle of his foreign policy was to "endeavour to avoid losing England's goodwill." England, like Germany, desired the maintenance of peace and was prepared to collaborate not only with Germany but also with other Powers. Bismarck rightly pointed out that there was no reason for a war between "a land rat and a water rat." He stated in 1885 that he could not see any reason for a war between the two countries "unless a Cabinet of inconceivable character should be in power in England, a Cabinet which neither exists nor which is ever likely to exist, and which criminally attacks us." Such a government never came to power in England. Bismarck appointed his son as German Ambassador in London and offered twice to enter into an alliance with England, but the offer was not accepted. With a view to avoid any conflict with England, Bismarck discouraged the growth of the German Navy and German Colonies.

Bismarck was an exceptionally skilful fisherman in troubled waters Anglo-Russian and Anglo-French rivalry often gave him weeks of excellent and profitable sport. At times, he poked up the over-smouldering embers of Anglo-Russian rivalry in Asia, but he did not allow the same to burst into a blaze as a war between England and Russia was bound to effect the other Powers and there was every likelihood of Germany and her allies being involved in the same. His system of alliances and counter-alliances might have collapsed under the strain. Consequently, he did not take the things to extremes. He also wanted the Anglo-French rivalry to continue and not to end in an **entente cordiale.** He was determined to maintain the balance of power. An alliance between England, France and Russia was bound to create a serious rival for the Triple Alliance.

In 1888, Bismarck declared, **"We Germans fear God and nothing else in the world."** However, that was not true. Bismarck himself admitted that he was haunted by the spectre of coalitions although he himself was responsible for the same. He had humiliated a high-spirited nation like France and with a view to check her from having her revenge, he transformed Europe into an armed camp. He ought to have known that force alone could not guarantee a settlement which was passionately resented by the people. It is true that Bismarck succeeded temporarily in isolating France but he neither conciliated her nor disarmed her. As a matter of fact, he built up a combination against her and that forced her to look for allies. The Franco-Russian Alliance of 1894 was the natural outcome of that policy.

The German-Austro-Russian triangle created by Bismarck was full of contradictions. The relations between Austria and Russia could never be cordial. That was particularly so after the Congress of Berlin which gave to Austria Bosnia, Herzegovina and the Sanjak of Novibazar and thus introduced her into the Balkans. Austro-Russian rivalry in the Balkans became intensified during the 1880's and reached its height on the occasion of the Bulgarian crisis. Bismarck had to face a very difficult situation on account of the differences between Austria and Russia on the question of Bulgaria. It is true that he backed Russia on the question of Bulgaria and thereby averted a clash between Austria and Russia, but the difficulty of reconciling Russia and Austria must have become evident to Bismarck. In 1888, Bismarck was forced to publish the Austria-German Treaty of 1879 which pledged Germany to help Austria against Russia. Thus it was that Russia came to know that she had been tricked by Bismarck and there is no doubt that even before 1890 when Bismarck resigned, Russia had already begun to drift towards France. A genius like Bismarck could make black look like white for some time, but not for ever. Austro-Russian collaboration was impossible and even a juggler like Bismarck could not make the two countries work together.

It is rightly pointed out that the foundations of the Triple Alliance were weak. There was no place in it for Great Britain. It is true that when Bismarck retired in 1890, the relations between England and Germany were cordial but England had already started feeling that it was dangerous to remain alone.

Critics point out that although Bismarck "had secured Russian neutrality in case of Austrian attack upon Germany, Austrian neutrality in case of Russian attack, Italian support against a French attack and Austro-Italian assistance against a combined Russian and French attack," yet the system was so very complicated that only Bismarck could work it out. He alone could throw five balls in the air and manage them skillfully. No wonder the system created by him collapsed after his disappearance from the scene. That was the tragedy of his foreign policy.

Critics point out that Bismarck was responsible for the war of 1914. He set the ball rolling and the process was completed in 1914. He created an alliance with Austria in 1879 and the same was transformed into the Triple Alliance in 1882 when Italy joined it. His alliances were bound to result in counter-alliances and ultimately that led to the division of Europe into two armed camps which was one of the important causes of the war of 1914. Moreover, by humiliating France in 1870-71 Bismarck also sowed the seeds of the war of 1914. The French were determined to get back Alsace and Lorraine and no wonder after Sedan, the Battle of Marne lay in the logic of history. Bismarck's policy of blood and iron was bound to result in a race for armaments among the European nations and militarism was one of the important causes of the war of 1914.

About the foreign policy of Bismarck, Taylor says that Bismarck's "system" was something of a conjuring trick, a piece of conscious virtuosity. Once started on the path of alliances, Bismarck treated them as the solution for every problem. He scattered promises so as not to carry them out. He promised to fight on the side of Austria-Hungary in order to make her friendly to Russia. He also promised to fight on the side of Italy in order to secure her neutrality. Perhaps the only promise he took seriously was that of diplomatic support for Russia against England at the Straits. His two great creations, the League of the Three Emperors' and the Triple Alliance were in direct contradiction. The League was based on Austro-Russian co-operation and the Alliance was in preparation for an Austro-Russian war. The League was an anti-British combination, its most practical clause designed to close the Straits against the British by common diplomatic action. The Alliance was specifically not directed against Great Britain and both Austria-Hungary and Italy hoped for her support in the long run. So far as the sympathies of Bismarck were concerned, the League was an affair of the heart and the Alliance was one of calculation. His deepest attachment was to the old Russo-Prussian friendship. He disliked the Austrians from his days at Frankfurt until his death. His view was that the British were concerned only "to get others to pull their chestnuts out of the fire." He preferred the sensible politicians of the French Republic such as Gambetta and Ferry to the restless and scheming Italians. His diplomacy was an insurance against the subversive forces in Russia and France and not against their official Governments. He is said to have observed thus about Russia, "The Emperor is himself well-intentioned....his ministers are prudent and inclined to a conservative policy. But will they have the strength to resist the pressure of popular passions if they are once unchained? The party of war is stronger in Russia than elsewhere." Bismarck claimed to be the apostle of stability and presented his system as "a League of peace." In fact, by the Triple Alliance, he associated Germany with the restless Powers and implicitly against the conservative ones. The choice of Austria-Hungary and Italy against Russia and France by Bismarck was, in large part, the repetition of the choice that he had made earlier in German affairs. He made foreign alliances in order to take his allies prisoner. He controlled his allies and did not co-operate with them. In international affairs, as in domestic policies, Bismarck disliked equals and sought for satellites. The system of Bismarck was a tyranny. It did not console others that it was a tyranny imposed for their good in favour of peace and social order.

Fall of Bismarck. From 1871 to 1890, Bismarck was supreme in the affairs of the State. The relations between Bismarck and William I were cordial throughout except on the question of an alliance between Germany and Austria in 1879. Bismarck took pride in the fact that he was the most faithful servant of William I. After the death of William I in March 1888, Emperor Frederick succeeded him. However, his reign did not last for more than three months and he was succeeded by William II the same year. Soon after his accession to the throne, the conflict between the Emperor and the Iron Chancellor started and resulted ultimately in the resignation of Bismarck in March 1890.

Many reasons have been given for the resignation of Bismarck. The new Emperor was a young man and was determined to do everything himself. He was not prepared to play second fiddle to anybody. Under the circumstances, he could not tolerate the complete control of Bismarck over the affairs of the State. To quote him, "I discovered that my ministers regarded themselves as Bismarck's officials." If this was the attitude of William II, Bismarck felt that he had the monopoly of power in the State and was not prepared to share the same with anybody. He considered himself the maker of Germany and felt insulted when William II tried to share the secrets of the State with the Chancellor. Bismarck had trained his son, Herbert Bismarck, in the affairs of State and the latter was working as Foreign Secretary since 1886. Bismarck himself thought that he would be succeeded by his son. Herbert Bismarck had capacity and considerable power of work and he tried to prove that **he was not only a chip of the old block, but the old block itself.** He tried to copy the brutality, coarseness and dictatorial insolence of his father. His manners were insufferable. People were prepared to put up with Bismarck but not with his son who had yet nothing to his credit. All that created bitterness.

During 1888 and 1889, Bismarck was away from Berlin for most of the time. He spent his time at the country-house and most of the business of the State was transacted from there. His absence from the capital was not due to his old age alone. His view was that his work could be carried on by his son as Foreign Secretary under his supervision and direction. Bismarck failed to realize the fact that it was absolutely essential to be near the young Emperor and that there was every possibility of differences arising between them on account of his absence. Bismarck lost touch with the personalities, ministers and the forces of politics and thereby was put at the great disadvantage. Criticism against the Chancellor began to grow and there was a demand for a change.

Before William II, the German Emperors left everything into the hands of Bismarck and they were prepared to hear from him whatever he considered fit to communicate to them. Beyond that, they did not bother themselves. However, William II was determined to play a different role. Instead of getting lessons from the Iron Chancellor, he was determined to see and learn everything for himself. He not only saw every part of Germany but also visited St. Petersburg, Vienna, London, Athens and Constantinople. His personal contact with foreign statesmen enabled him to think independently about the foreign policy of Germany. Bismarck resented the journeys of William II and expressed his disapproval of them. When William II came to know of it, he himself got bitter against him.

Bismarck had made many enemies during the tenure of his office. The Clericals, the Liberals, the Lu heran Conservatives, the industrialists, the anti-Semites and the soldiers "Demigods" were opposed to him. Waldersee, Moltke's successor as Chief of the General Staff, intrigued against him in high places. No wonder, Bismarck's opponents enjoyed his conflict with the young Emperor.

The real cause of the conflict between Bismarck and William II was that while the former was determined to maintain his control over the affairs of the State, the latter was determined to snatch away the same. According to the Grandduke of Baden. "The real question was whether Bismarck or the Hohenzollern dynasty should reign." To quote William II himself, "There is only one master in this country and I am he. I shall suffer no other beside me." Again, "I see in the people and the land which have descended to me a talent entrusted to me by God, which is my duty to increase. Those who will help me I heartily welcome; those who oppose me I shall dash to pieces."

Bismarck was pressed again and again to resign and ultimately he submitted his resignation on 20 March 1890. William II accepted with profound regret the request of the Iron Chancellor to be relieved of his offices. He referred to his "imperishable services" and conferred upon him the title of Duke of Lauenburg and Colonel-General with the rank of Field-Marshal in the army. The **Punch** summed up the matter in these words: "The Pilot who had steered the ship through so many storms and so many shoals was dropped."

Estimate of Bismarck. According to G.B. Smith, "As a statesman, Bismarck is one of the greatest figures in German history. Though imperious, he was yet prudent and he was accustomed to boast that he had opened up a new era in diplomacy by always telling the truth. He had great faults, however, being jealous towards rivals and vindictive and unscrupulous towards his foes. He was not an orator in the sense usually understood, but when the occasion was great, he could wield the mother tongue with vigour. By establishing the independence of Germany, he brought to maturity the fruits of the wars of liberation. The Chancellor wielded a personal power in Europe which was without precedent in the nineteenth century. In him was typified the Prussian race at its highest and strongest. In private life, he was a man of warm affection, his wife and children being always to him objects of tenderest devotion. His letters to his wife prove it....Without him, his country would have been a second-rate Power."

According to Prof. A. Phillips, "Bismarck was a statesman of the school of Machiavelli, sharing to the full his contempt for those brain-spun fogs of fancy which are apt to obscure the path of practical politics. Yet there is in his character none of the Italian suppleness. Its main trait was in fact rather brutal forthrightness, as though he could afford to be frank, his goal being so clear, and his power to reach it beyond dispute. And this impression he was able to produce, because he knew so well how to calculate the means to his end, to gauge the obstacles in his path; above all, when to keep silence and when to speak. Apart from Bismarck's character and his general sympathy with the King's ambitions for Prussia, his whole recent training had marked him out for the position he was now called upon to fill.... Bismarck had none of Metternich's shallow contempt for public opinion as a factor in politics. It was a blind and easily gullible monster, but strong and serviceable, if properly bridled and dangerous if unduly irritated. Nothing but 'urgent necessity' should make him flout German public opinion."

According to Sir J.A.R. Marriott, "In the history of the nineteenth century, Bismarck will always claim a foremost place; in the sphere of diplomacy no one except Cavour could dispute his claim to the first place. That he was a great patriot will be denied only by those to whom patriotism is an exploded superstition....Germany must be made not by the merging of Prussia in Germany, but by the merging of Germany in Prussia. That was Bismarck's supreme aim, and that was his remarkable achievement. The end was reached by methods which no plain man can approve, by diplomacy which was the masterpiece of bluff and duplicity and by overwhelming force unscrupulously applied."

According to Sarolea, "Bismarck was realistic and materialistic. He did not indulge like Talleyrand in visions of a distant future, in dreams of a German Oceana....Bismarck's ambition was to control the continent, to establish a Napoleonic Empire in Europe."

About Bismarck, David Thomson says that he ranks among the greatest heroes of German history and the most important statesman of the modern world. He was a massive man of stiff military bearing. He had a quick and sensitive mind. He possessed great personal charm, acute intelligence and indomitable will power. He was a man of action.

According to Seaman, "In considering Bismarck's aims and methods in Germany it has long been customary to compare with him Cavour; and it is certainly instructive to realize that they both sought to limit the Nationalism they claim to be fulfilling. Yet it is perhaps even more illuminating to compare him with Napoleon III. The constitution of the German Empire was much the same sort of transparent confidence trick as the constitution of the Second 'Empire' in 1852. There was first the lie involved in the word 'Empire'. Both France after 1852 and Germany after 1871 were called Empires to disguise the fact that they were not Empires. The Second Empire did not give France back her control of all Western Europe and the Bismarckian Empire did not give William I an Empire over all the Germans. The Second French Empire was nothing like the First French Empire. It was very little bigger than the French kingdom under the Bourbons or under Louis Philippe. In the same way to describe as 'the German Empire' a region which excluded of deliberate purpose all the Germans of Austria and Bohemia was just the sort of falsehood that Hitler might have had in mind when he said that the bigger a lie was the more likely people were to believe it. From 1871 to 1914 all the world's atlases solemnly described as 'The German Empire' what was in reality a Prussian Empire; and all the world's history books have gone on gravely describing as the 'unification' of Germany what was in reality the division of it.

"The unification of Germany was the one thing Bismarck was determined to prevent, because his whole purpose was the preservation of Prussian power against the rising tide of Liberalism and Radicalism. The demand for real German unity had been made clearly enough in 1848; but by the revolutionaries, and that in itself was enough to damn it. Bismarck was, therefore, fighting both Liberals and Radicals in Germany between 1862 and 1871, just as Napoleon III fought the same forces in France between 1848 and 1851. From 1862 till just after Sadowa the Liberals were opposed to him because he was acting in defiance of the Prussian Constitution. But just as, beneath the surface, the Liberals in the Second Republic wanted Louis Napoleon as their ally against the Reds, so in Prussia the Liberals wanted Bismarck as their ally against the rest of Germany. Many French Liberals forgave Louis Napoleon the **coup d'etat** in the interests of internal security. Most Prussian Liberals forgave Bismarck his illegal collection of taxes from 1862 to 1866 because he had created the North German Confederation, and won a decisive military victory for Prussia...

"In the final assessment, Bismarck's outstanding achievement is to have imposed his personality on half a century of history. The State he created, and the means he devised, for preserving it thereafter, were of his own unaided making. He had not collaborators; only agents, and willing and unwilling accessories. He had no spiritual or moral roots in the Europe in which he worked and triumphed. He destroyed the past, but feared the future which he built on its ruins; and for the deeper aspirations of his contemporaries he had nothing but contempt. This is perhaps most strikingly illustrated in his suggestion in 1890 that the Empire he had created should be dissolved and reconstituted without consulting anybody but the princes; and solely because he thought he could then govern it more autocratically than he was doing already. He stood, therefore, for no principles. His whole political existence was devoted to the task of putting Prussia into a position of predominance and of keeping it there, preserved inviolate against the possibility either of decline or advance. He created a Great Power and willed it not to behave like one because it would create problems he did not want to have to deal with. To give Prussia the mastery of Germany was in the end to make Prussia the agent of Germany as a power with world-wide ambitions: yet he held those ambitions in check throughout his career. Never before had the Germans possessed a State-machine capable of action against their hereditary Slav enemies. Bismarck gave them such a machine, and tried with inexhaustible ingenuity to prevent their using it for that purpose. In much the same way he created a Great Power and supposed it would not wish to assert itself by demanding oversea colonies, he yielded to the demand as if to the importunities of silly children."

About Bismarck, Ketelbey says that he was the greatest man of the nineteenth century. He was the greatest in the political manifestations of his powers and in the influence which his achievements have exercised on the history of the world. To the Prussian state, he gave an empire and colonies. To the Germans who "sailed the sea like pirates without a national flag," he gave an ensign which came to be as much respected as that of England or France. He shifted the political capital of Europe from Vienna or Paris to Berlin. He created the German Empire which was the most remarkable phenomenon of modern times.

SUGGESTED READINGS

Bismarck : **Reflections and Reminiscences.**

Bulow : **Imperial Germany.**

Clarke, C.W.: **Franz Joseph and Bismarck.**

Darmstaedter, F.: **Bismarck and the Creation of the Second Reich, 1948.**

Dawson, W.H.: **The German Empire (1867-1914).**

Eyck, E.: **Bismarck and the German Empire.**

Gooch, G.P.: **History of Modern Europe (1878-1919).**

Robertson, C.G.: **Bismarck.**

Taylor, A.J.P. : **Bismarck, The Man and the Statesman, 1955.**

Taylor, A.J.P.: **The Struggle for Mastery in Europe (1848-1918), 1954.**

CHAPTER

19 GERMANY FROM 1890 TO 1914

William II (1888-1918). The most important man in Germany in post Bismarckian era was William II. He came to the throne in 1888 after the short reign of his father Frederick III. At the time of his accession, he was a young man of 29. He had a lot of energy and possessed high ambitions. He was determined to make Germany one of the greatest Powers of the world. He believed in the policy of **"World Power or Downfall."** He was vain and impulsive. According to H.A.L. Fisher, "The new autocrat became at once a vital and disquieting force in European society. That he had some admirable and even brilliant qualities was at once apparent. His outlook on affairs was bold and spacious; his curiosity eager and comprehensive; his industry vast; his memory for detail powerful and exact. He was pious, dutiful, patriotic and sometimes, especially when he spoke of the sea, would rise to heights of moving eloquence. But with these shining qualities were mingled others of a baser alloy, an egregious vanity, an ungovernable temper, a love of theatrical ostentation which exposed hirm to ridicule, and a vein of malevolence which merited contempt. There was no flattery so base that he would not exploit it, no barbarity so extreme that he would not in a spasm of fury invest it with imperial authority. A nervous exaltability and impulsiveness, whether it gave a certain zest and charm to his companionship, always made him dangerous as a ruler, so that, after experience of many alarums and excursions, his ministers began to ask themselves in trepidation whether the headstrong and loquacious master of Germany was not in fact deranged in mind."

According to Grant and Temperley, "Had William II been a Frederick, the Great, he would have known, like him, how "to move millions with inhuman harmony." He could have forced their energies in almost any direction that he chose, and commanded their unquestioning allegiance. But harmony could only be secured if the purpose of the ruler was steady, unremitting, remorseless and fixed. Such a purpose was wholly lacking in the fickle, brilliant and easily swayed Kaiser. His religion, though sincere, led him towards absolutism. Yet he had much fear of the people, and assiduously courted them. At heart perhaps pacific, his reckless and impulsive public praise of his army and of war, his amazing private indiscretions to foreign diplomats, frequently produced the worst impressions and led to situations full of danger. He would always be a hero to himself and did not like contradiction or opposition in others. His admirers compared him (with his knowledge) to Siegfried or to Achilles, and his nostrils snuffed the incense of a truly Byzantine flattery. His nerves were unequal to a crisis as was shown in 1908, when the storm of wrath which arose against him for his **Daily Telegraph** indiscretion made him speak of abdicating and reduced him to a state of pitiable collapse."

Proclamations. On his accession to the throne in June 1888, William II issued proclamations to the army, the navy and the people. As regards the army, he declared: "These are days of sore trial and affliction in which. God's decree has placed me at the head of the army, and it is with deep emotions that I first address myself to my army. We belong to one another." In his address to the navy, he gave an assurance that he stood for its growth. He issued the proclamation to the people three days after. In his speech from the throne, William II declared, "As regards the foreign politics I am determined to keep peace with everyone, so far as it lies in my power. My love for the army will never lead me into the temptation to endanger the benefits which the country derives from peace. Germany is in no need of fresh military glory, nor does she require new conquests."

It has already been pointed out in the previous chapter how the new Emperor came into conflict with the Iron Chancellor and ultimately forced him to resign in 1890. After that, he became his own Chancellor and during the rest of his reign he had his own way and the ministers had merely to carry out his final decisions. However, reference may be made to the four Chancellors of his reign after 1890.

Chancellor Caprivi (1890-94). Bismarck was succeeded by Caprivi as Chancellor in 1890. Bismarck himself had referred to him as his successor in 1878 in these words: "I have often wondered who could be my successor; today I have seen him." In 1890, he himself suggested his name.

When Caprivi took office, he admitted his political inexperience. William II gave him the assurance in these words: "I will assume responsibilities for affairs." William II wrote thus to the Austrian Emperor about Caprivi: "He is the greatest German after Bismarck loyal to me and firm as a rock."

Caprivi was hated by the Prussian aristocracy and he himself was attracted towards businessmen. He was friendly inclined towards Great Britain. It was during his time that Heligoland was exchanged for Zanzibar in 1890. The German tariff system was put on the basis of reciprocity. The Reinsurance Treaty with Russia was allowed to lapse and it was during his period that the Franco-Russian alliance materialized. His dismissal was demanded by the Prussian conservatives and he resigned in 1894.

Chancellor Hohenlohe (1894-1900). Caprivi was succeeded by Hohenlohe. He was 75 at the time of his appointment and he was merely a figurehead in the affairs of the State. The actual conduct of the State affairs was in the hand of William II and Bulow (who was the Foreign Secretary at that time). Germany concentrated during this period on trade and investments overseas. William I declared thus in 1895 : The German Empire has become a world Empire."

In 1897, two German Christian missionaries were murdered in China. Germany took advantage of this and a lease for 90 years of about 202 square miles of territory in China. In 1899, Germany purchased from Spain the Caroline Islands in the Pacific. During 1899-1999, Germany got the two largest Islands of Samoa. In 1900, Germany participated in the action against the Boxer Rising in China. In 1899, German bankers got from the Sultan of Turkey some concessions for the building of railways up to Baghdad. German settlers were established in Brazil. German investments and trade in South Africa began to increase.

Germany began to take more interest in the growth of her navy. William II outlined the German policy in these words: "Germany's future lies upon the water." Again, "The ocean is essential to Germany's greatness." In 1898, the first law concerning the German navy was passed and in 1900 was passed the second. In this way, German navy went on growing. During all this period, William II was assisted by Tirpitz who was put in charge of the department of Navy in 1897 and who continued to occupy that position up to 1916.

Bulow (1900-09). After the retirement of Hohenlohe in 1900, Prince Bulow, who was already associated with William II, was appointed the Chancellor. It was during his regime that the British efforts to enter into an alliance with Germany failed. The Entente Cordiale between England and France was also made during his regime. The first and second Morocco arises of 1905-6 and 1908 also took place during his regime. He also sent William II to Tangier in 1905 to show that Germany was interested in Morocco and would not allow France to swallow the same. The Bosnian crisis of 1908-9 also took place during his regime. The German Navy continued to develop. German goods began to penetrate into every nook and corner of the world. Germany followed a world policy and she began to demand a "place in the sun."

It is stated that when Bulow became Chancellor, he offered the Foreign Office to Holstein who haughtily refused the same. This 'mystery-man' inspired a large number of articles in the press. He was responsible for countless diplomatic intrigues. His power was so great that he was sometimes able to overawe the Chancellor or the Foreign Office of the time. He did not care even for the Emperor and called him a mad man or a fool. The Emperor called him a 'mad hyena' in private but had not the courage to face him in public. He gave interviews to foreign ambassadors without the knowledge of the Chancellor or Foreign Minister. It is pointed out that most of the wrong decisions in foreign policy were due to him. This was particularly so when Germany refused to accept England's overtures in 1898 and 1901. The German attitude over Morocco in 1905 was also due to his influence.

He threatened many a time to resign his job in the German Foreign Office but neither the Emperor nor the Chancellor had the courage to accept the same on account of the fear that he would start a press campaign against them. However, they took courage in 1906 and he was relieved of his job.

Bethmann Hollweg (1909-17). Bulow was succeeded by Bethmann-Hollweg. It was during his regime that the third Morocco crisis took place in 1911. An honest attempt was made to come to an agreement with England on the question of naval competition but as William II backed Tirpitz, the Chancellor was helpless. No wonder, the Haldane mission failed in 1912. The Morocco question was amicably settled and Germany got some compensation in the form of some French territory in Africa.

Tension between Great Britain and Germany continued to increase and ultimately it resulted in the war of 1914.

SUGGESTED READINGS

Bulow: **Imperial Germany.**

Bulow: **Memoirs.**

Cambridge Modern History, Vol. XII.

Dawson, W.H.: **The German Empire (1887-1914), Vol. II.**

Gooch: **History of Our Times.**

Prothero: **German Policy before the War.**

Schmitt: **England and Germany.**

Tower, C.: **Germany of Today.**

CHAPTER

20

FRANCE FROM 1870 TO 1914

After the surrender of Napoleon III at Sedan in September 1870, the condition of France was deplorable. A republican government was set up in Paris and it was declared to fight the Germans. The cry was raised: "We will not yield an inch of French soil nor a stone of French fortresses." Metz with the army of Bazaine was still unconquered and the French felt that they could still defend Paris. While the Prussian armies marched towards the French capital, Thiers went on a tour of the capitals of Europe with a view to secure foreign help against Prussia. Paris was besieged by the Prussian troops and Gambetta went out of Paris in a balloon to arouse the countryside and thereby secure help for the Parisians against the Prussians. The result was that volunteers from all over France marched towards Paris to rescue the Parisians. Volunteers came also from abroad, including such persons as Garibaldi, his sons and Kitchener.

However, in spite of all the enthusiasm and the resistance, Metz fell and Bazaine also surrendered. After a siege of 4 months and the bombardment of four weeks, Paris also surrendered. Thiers tried to secure lenient terms from Bismarck and he left no stone unturned to achieve his objective. Regarding the interview between Thiers and Bismarck, Jules Favre wrote thus: "I still see him pale and agitated; now sitting, now springing to his feet; I hear his voice broken by grief, his words cut short, his tones suppliant and proud. I know nothing grander than the sublime passion of this noble heart bursting out in petitions, menaces, prayers, now caressing, now terrible, growing by degrees more angry in the face of the cruel refusal." Bismarck was in an uncompromising mood and addressed thus to Thiers: "We have no guarantees of permanence either from you or from any government that may come after you " The reply of Thiers was in these words: "Well, let it be as you will, these negotiations are a pretence. We appear to deliberate, we have only to pass under your yoke. We ask for a city absolutely French, you refuse it to us; it is to avow that you have resolved to wage against us a war of extremity. Do it. Ravish our provinces, burn our homes, cut the throats of our unoffending inhabitants —in a word, complete your work. We will fight to the last breath; we shall succumb at last, but we will not be dishonoured." The preliminaries of peace were signed at Versailles in February 1871 and were confirmed by the treaty of Frankfurt of May 1871. France had to surrender Alsace Lorraine including Metz and Strassburg but excluding Belfort. She also agreed to pay a war indemnity of £200,000,000 within three years and during that interval, a German army of occupation was to remain on the French soil and was to be supported by France.

The Paris Commune (1871). Although the war with Germany was ended, France was not destined to have peace and she had to face immediately a crisis at home. The trouble arose in the form of the revolt of the Paris Commune which is considered to be a great epoch in the history of socialism. It was an attempt to put into actual practice the ideas and ideals of Karl Marx with the help of military force.

It is to be observed that although a Republic was proclaimed in Paris, the same was not sanctioned by the country at large. A National Assembly was elected to ratify the terms of the Treaty with Germany and it chose Thiers as "Chief of the Executive" for the transitional period. The National Assembly was controlled by the Monarchists and there was a danger of the overthrow of the Republic and the restoration of monarchy. Paris which was republican in spirit and had returned republican candidates even in the time of Napoleon III, was not prepared to allow the Republic to be overthrown. Certain acts of the National Assembly added to the distrust. The National Assembly decided to shift the capital of France from Bordeaux to Versailles and not to Paris. This was insulting to the people of Paris who had suffered terribly at the hands of the Prussians to save the honour of the country. The prosperity of Paris was likely to be affected by the shifting of the capital to Versailles. No wonder, this move was resented by the property-owners, merchants and workmen. During the period of the siege of Paris, the payment of rents, debts and notes had been suspended by a decree of the government. There was a general demand to continue the suspension order as the economic condition of the people after the ending of the siege was miserable. They were not in a position to pay at once. There was a lot of unemployment. Unfortunately, the National Assembly refused to continue the suspension order and ordered the payment of all such debts to be made within 48 hours. As the people could not pay, more than 1½ lakhs of Parisians were exposed to legal prosecutions. This involved a lot of hardship to the business world.

A majority of the workmen were without employment and their only source of income was their remuneration as members of the National Guard. The National Assembly suppressed the National Guard except in the case of those who secured certificates of poverty. The National Guard included most of the able-bodied male population of Paris. It had defended Paris during the siege and the arms were left in the hands of the members after the conclusion of war. As soon as the siege was raised, the rich and well-to-do members of the National Guard left Paris in large numbers to rejoin their families. It is only the poor who continued to be the members of the National Guard and the National Assembly deprived them of their franc and a half a day. These people were armed, suspicious, discontented and wretched. They were inflamed by the rumours that the Republic was in danger.

Paris was also full of Anarchists, Jacobins and Socialists. The Socialist had a large following among the working classes. Among the restless, discontented and poverty-stricken masses of Paris, the Socialist leaders worked with great success. There arose out of the confusion of the time the idea of the Commune. It was proposed that in the future political set-up of the country, more emphasis should be put on the Communes. While they should be given more powers, the sphere of the State should be circumscribed. In other words it was a demand to decentralise the administration in a country which was completely centralised. It was felt that if the suggestion was accepted, many French cities or Communes which had republican sympathies, would be liberated from the control of the central government which was monarchist in spirit. There was every possibility of bringing about an economic and social revolution in the Communes.

The discontentment in Paris expressed itself through the National Guard which selected in February 1871 a committee of 60 members to regulate its activity. With a view to prevent any action being taken against Paris and the Republic by the National Assembly, the National Guard removed some cannon to one of the strongest points in the city of Paris. The National Assembly was not prepared to tolerate that and consequently tried to recapture the same on 18 March 1871. However, it failed in its objective. The authority of the government was defied by the members of the National Guard and the people at large. The spirit of revolt spread all over the city and it developed into a war between Paris on the one side and the National Assembly at Versailles on the other. Two of the generals of the Versailles government were captured and shot by the rebels. The government forces were withdrawn from Paris by Thiers and the city was left entirely in the hands of the rebels who secured complete control over the same.

On 26 March 1871, elections were held in Paris for the General Council of 90 members to serve as the government of the Commune. Ministers in charge of various departments were appointed. Republican calendar of the revolution and the red flag of the Socialists were adopted. All the Socialists did not subscribe to one ideology and many of them differed from one another. Paris denied the charge that it was trying to disrupt the unity of the country. It was maintained that it was merely trying to abolish the kind of unity "imposed on us up to this day by the Empire, the Monarchy and Parliamentarism," which was "despotic, unintelligent, arbitrary and onerous centralisation." The Paris Commune intended to abolish the old system of "militarism, exploitation, stockjobbing, monopolies and privileges to which the proletariat owes its servitude, and the fatherland, its misfortunes and its disasters." An appeal was made to the people of France to help them in their cause. "Let her be our ally in this conflict which can only end by the triumph of the communal idea or the ruin of Paris."

The Paris Commune could succeed only if it was able to overthrow the Versailles government. Troops were sent out from Paris to break up the National Assembly. They were unsuccessful in their attempt, and were captured and shot. In revenge, the Paris Commune ordered the arrest of many prominent men in Paris who were ordered to be kept as "hostages".

Men like Thiers were very unhappy at the prospect of a civil war in the country. It was humiliating to find Frenchmen fighting against Frenchmen, particularly before the eyes of the German soldiers who were still on the French soil. Thiers tried to remove the suspicion that any attempt was being made to destroy the Republic. A law was passed on 14 April 1871 by which the powers of the local bodies were enlarged. However, he made it clear that he was not prepared to weaken the authority of the government and the unity of the country and was also determined to crush the rebels of Paris. For a time, the work of Thiers was a difficult one. However, after some time, an army of 1½ lakhs of men was prepared to deal with the Paris Commune. A regular siege of Paris was started. There was a lot of bitterness and ferocity on both sides. The siege lasted from 2 April to 21 May 1871. After that, there was fighting in the streets of Paris for a week which is termed as "the bloody week." During these seven days, Paris suffered much more than she had suffered from the bombardment of the Germans for a week. There was wholesale burning and slaughter. According to Henotaux, "Everything was burning; there were explosions everywhere. A night of terror; the Porte Saint Martin, the Church of Saint Eustacha, the Rue Royale, the Rue de Rivole, the Tuileries, the Palais-Royal, the Hotel de Ville, the left bank from the Legion de Honneur to the Palais de Justice, and the police office were immense red braziers, and above all rose lofty blazing columns....from outside, all the forts were firing upon Paris....The gunners were cannonading one another across the town, and above the town. Shells fell in every direction. All the central quarters were a battlefield. It was a horrible chaos: bodies and souls in collision over a crumbling world." The Paris Commune shot its hostages. However, on 28 May 1871, the last of the rebels were shot down.

After the victory, the Versailles government had its revenge on the rebels. The latter were punished right and left. Many of them were shot on the spot. According to Hanotaux, "The number of men who perished in this horrible fray, without any other form of law, is estimated at 17,000. The cemeteries, the squares, private or public gardens saw trenches opened in which nameless corpses were deposited without register and without list, by thousands." Arrests and trials continued for years. Up to 1875, more than 43,000 persons were arrested and a large number were denounced. The prisoners were tried by courts-martial and given severe punishments. It was so late as 1879 that an amnesty was given as a result of the efforts of Gambetta. A lot of class-hatred was created in the country. Regarding the Paris Commune, Prof. Fyffe remarks: "When, after a siege of six weeks in which Paris suffered far more severely than it had suffered from the cannonade of the Germans, the troops of Versailles at length made their way into the capital, humanity and civilization seemed to have vanished in the orgies of devils. The defenders, as they fell back, murdered their hostages, and left behind them palaces, museums, the entire public inheritance of the nation in its capital, in flames. The conquerors during several days shot down all whom they took fighting, and in many cases put to death whole bands of prisoners without distinction. The temper of the army was such that the government, even if it had desired, could probably not have mitigated the terrors of this vengeance. But there was little sign anywhere of an inclination to mercy. Courts-martial and executions continued long after the heat of combat was over. A year passed, and the tribunals were still busy with their work. Above ten thousand persons were sentenced to transportation or imprisonment before public justice was satisfied."

Work of National Assembly (1871-75). The National Assembly which was elected in the beginning of 1871 to ratify the treaty of Germany continued to sit up to 31 December 1875. It not only ratified the Treaty of Frankfurt but also crushed the revolt of the Paris Commune. Having accomplished that, the National Assembly addressed itself to the work of national reconstruction. The problem of paying the war-indemnity was a very urgent one and consequently Thiers raised a large loan and thereby paid off the whole of war-indemnity in two years. The result was that the German troops were withdrawn from the French soil and Thiers came to be called "the Liberator of the Territory." The French army was reorganised on the model of the Prussian army. A law of 1872 provided for compulsory military service throughout the length and breadth of the country.

The National Assembly had to address itself to the task of framing a constitution for the country. Thiers was originally a believer in constitutional monarchy but he was not afraid of a republican government as well. With the passage of time, he came to believe that a Republic was the only possible form of government for his country. To quote him, **"There is only one throne and there are the claimants for seat on it."** "Those parties who want a monarchy do not want the same monarchy." As regards the republican form of government, **"it is the form of government which divides us least!"**

This fact is made clear if we refer to the various sections which advocated the cause of monarchy in France. Those sections were the Legitimists, the Orleanists and the Bonapartists. The Legitimists supported the cause of the Count of Chambord, the grandson of Charles X. The Orleanists supported the cause of the Count of Paris. The Bonapartists advocated the cause of Napoleon III or his son. Although the Monarchists had a majority in the National Assembly, they were not able to have their own way to set up a monarchy in the country on account of the differences among them. In 1873, Thiers was made to resign as he was showing a tendency towards republicanism.

Many efforts were made to write a monarchical constitution for France. The Count of Chambord had no children and it was decided that the Count of Paris should give up his claims in favour of the Count of Chambord who should succeed as Henry V of France. As the Count of Chambord had no children, Count of Paris was to succeed him. The compromise having been secured it seemed certain that monarchy would be restored in France and negotiations started for that purpose. Negotiations were successful on all points except on the question of the flag. The Count of Chambord openly declared that he was not prepared to accept the Tricolour flag of the revolution. To quote him, "Henry V could never abandon the white flag of Henry IV." His contention was that if he was to be the king of France, he must not sacrifice his principles and the flag. He was not prepared to be the king of the revolution. The negotiations failed on account of the stubbornness of the Count of Chambord.

In spite of this defeat, the Monarchists did not lose heart. Their view was that either the Count of Chambord would change his mind or he would die and be succeeded by the Count of Paris who was willing to accept the Tricolour flag of the revolution. Under the circumstances, the Monarchists started playing delaying tactics. Their object was to gain time so that they may be able to attack when the iron was hot. After the resignation of Thiers, Macmahon was made the President. The term of his office had not been fixed so far and the same was fixed for 7 years in 1873. The Monarchists hoped that within the next 7 years they would be able to carry their point.

As the National Assembly was following a policy of delay, it did not seriously address itself to the task of framing the constitution. In this way, months and years passed. However, during this period, Gambetta was carrying on a vigorous campaign in favour of republicanism in every nook and corner of the country. To meet the danger of republicanism, the National Assembly passed a law in 1875 by which the mayors of all the Communes in France were to be appointed directly or indirectly by the ministry and not by the local Council as before. This was intended to give the ministry control over the local affairs. Busts representing the Republic were removed from all public buildings. The name of Republic was omitted from all public documents. Republican newspapers were prosecuted and harassed. It is estimated that in one year, more than 200 Republican newspapers were suppressed. Instead of being disheartened, the Republicans continued their propaganda with more and more vigour.

At that stage, the Bonapartists became aggressive in the country and won a number of elections. The danger of a Bonapartist restoration changed completely the political situation in the country. A number of Orleanist members of the National Assembly were prepared to prefer Republicanism to Bonapartism. As their own chances were slender, they joined hands with the Republicans in the National Assembly. It was the combination of the Republicans and the Orleanists that enabled the National Assembly to frame a Republican constitution in France and the same was done in 1875. The Republican constitution was adopted by a majority of only one vote (353 to 352).

The Constitution (1875). The Constitution of 1875 used the word Republic only once. It provided for a President to be elected for 7 years. Provision was made for a Senate and a Chamber of Deputies. The Republicans were in favour of direct elections to the Senate, but as a result of a compromise, provision was made for indirect elections through an electoral college. The Chamber of Deputies could be dissolved by the President with the consent of the Senate. France was to have a parliamentary form of government. The ministers were to be jointly and severally responsible for the general policy of the government and individually for their personal acts.

The constitution of 1875 was a compromise between the opposing forces. The Monarchists in the National Assembly felt that they had introduced sufficient monarchical elements in the constitution to curb the aggressiveness of democracy and to facilitate the restoration of monarchy at some convenient time. The Republican accepted the constitution as there was no other alternative to it. Some radical Republicans condemned the constitution as a mockery. It was described as "a dose prepared for a convalescent country."

Dangers to Third Republic. Although a monarchist National Assembly was forced to write a Republican constitution on account of the curious circumstances, the Third Republic in France had to meet many dangers. It took many years before it could be said to be placed on a stable footing.

(1) Under the Constitution of 1875, elections were held in 1876. The Monarchists got a small majority in the Senate and the Republicans got a large majority in the Chamber of Deputies. President Macmahon appointed a Republican ministry but insisted that the departments of war, navy and foreign affairs were not under the control of the legislature. The Monarchists started a vigorous agitation against the Republicans and they were supported by the clergymen of France. The Republicans resented the interference of the clergymen in the politics of the country and Gambetta condemned that action in these words: "Clericalism—that is our enemy." The Roman Catholic Church came to be considered as the most dangerous enemy of the Republic. The enemies of the Republic persuaded Macmahon to believe that he was not found to follow the advice of the ministry and he could have a policy of his own. On 16 May 1877, Macmahon dismissed the Republican ministry which enjoyed the confidence of the Chamber of Deputies and appointed a new ministry which was largely composed of the Monarchists under the Duke of Broglie. The Senate agreed in the dissolution of the Chamber of Deputies and fresh elections were ordered. The Republicans were determined to oppose the moves of Macmahon. It was contended by them that the President had no right lo have a policy of his own. He could not dismiss a ministry which enjoyed the confidence of the legislature. Macmahon's contention was that he had that right and "if the Chamber did not approve, it remained for the people to decide between him and it." There was a bitter contest for political power between the President and the Senate on the one hand and the Chamber of Deputies on the other. The contest was won by the Chamber of Deputies.

When elections were held for the Chamber of Deputies, the Broglie ministry left no stone unturned against the Republicans under Gambetta. Republican officers were removed and reactionaries were appointed in their places. The machinery of the State was used to crush the Republican newspapers. Gambetta declared that after the people had given their verdict by means of a general election, President Macmahon must "either submit or resign." He was prosecuted and condemned to three months' imprisonment and a fine of 2,000 francs. Official candidates were put forward by the Monarchists and were supported by the officers and the ministry in power. The clergymen also helped the Monarchist cause. In spite of all this, the Republicans swept the polls. They secured a majority of over a hundred in the new Chamber of Deputies. President Macmahon "submitted" and appointed a Republican ministry.

When one-third of the members of the Senate were elected in 1878, the Republicans secured a majority in the Senate also. When both the Houses became Republican, the position of President Macmahon became very difficult. The legislature demanded the retirement of certain generals of the army on account of their anti-Republican leanings. Macmahon refused to do so on the ground that the army must be kept out of party politics. However, he himself resigned on 30 January 1879. Jules Grevy, a Republican of long standing, was elected the new President. Thus, for the first time since 1871, the Republicans came to have their control over the Senate, Chamber of Deputies and the President. As a token of Republican victories, the seat of the French Government was shifted from Versailles to Paris in 1880.

It is true that the Monarchists still continued to have some following but they did not count much on account of their dissensions. The Court of Chambord died in 1883 and the hopes of the Legitimists ended. The Count of Paris did not assert himself and the Bonapartists lost their incentive after the death of Napoleon III and his son.

However, if the danger from the Monarchists was over, the Third Republic in France had to face other difficulties.

(2) After the death of Gambetta in 1882, there was no commanding personality in French politics. The result was that ministerial changes took place very frequently. Politics seemed to be a game of getting offices and not pursuing mature politics of State. There was a lot of discontentment within the country. Many people did not approve of the policy of secularising education. There were others who did not approve of the colonial policy. The people felt that the parliamentary institutions in France had failed and only a dictator could handle the situation. A scandal was found in the household of President Grevy himself. Wilson, his son-in-law, was found to be using his influence for the purpose of trafficking in the bestowal of places in the Legion of Honour. President Grevy defended the action of his son-in-law and was ultimately forced to resign. Undoubtedly, this brought a bad name to the Republican regime.

(3) There was another scandal connected with the Directors of the Panama Canal Company. Some of the ministers and legislators were found guilty of corruption and the opponents of the Republic got another opportunity to attack the same.

(4) **Boulanger.** When such was the state of affairs in France, General Baulanger appeared on the scene. He was a dashing figure on horseback. He was an attractive speaker and he tried to exploit the public discontent to make himself a hero. In 1886, he was appointed the minister of war and he was able to win over soldiers by improving their conditions of life in the barracks and by advocating the reduction of the required term of service. He controlled many newspapers who tried to boost him up. He talked of France having revenge against Germany. He posed as the rescuer of the Republic and demanded a total revision of the constitution. His programme was vague but he aimed at the increase of the powers of the President and the decrease of the powers of the legislature. He advocated the direct election of the President.

For three years, the personality of Boulanger was a storm-centre. Discontented persons of all shades of opinion, whether they were monarchists, imperialists or clericals, flocked to him with a view to use him to overthrow the Republic. Various parties contributed funds towards the elections of

Boulanger and he became a candidate for Parliament from many vacancies. During the five months of 1888, Boulanger was elected a member of the Chamber of Deputies from six constituencies. In January 1889, he was elected from Paris itself by a majority of over 80,000.

Boulanger was at the height of his popularity and he could have struck. However, he let the opportunity slip. The Republicans also closed their ranks in the face of a common danger. The result was that the ministry summoned Boulanger to appear before the Senate sitting as a High Court of Justice to meet the charge of conspiring against the safety of the State. Instead of facing the charge, Boulanger ran away to Belgium and he was convicted in his absence. In his absence, his followers lost heart. Two years after, he committed suicide. The collapse of Boulanger strengthened the Republic, proved its vitality and discredited its opponents. The idea of a revision of the constitution was also discredited.

(5) **Dreyfus.** The Dreyfus affair also endangered the safety of the Republic for some time. Alfred Dreyfus was a Jew and a captain in the French army. He was arrested in October 1894 on a charge of betraying the military secrets of the country to a foreign power. He was tried by a court martial, found guilty and sentenced to imprisonment for life. In January 1895, he was publicly degraded in a most dramatic manner in the courtyard of the Military School before a large detachment of the army. His stripes were torn from his uniform. His sword was broken. In spite of all these humiliations, Dreyfus asserted his innocence and shouted **"Vive la France!"** He was deported to a small, barren and unhealthy island off French Guiana in South Africa called Devil's Island and kept there in solitary confinement. There was a general feeling that injustice had been done in this case.

Colonel Picquart was subsequently appointed the head of the Intelligence Department and he came to the conclusion that the document on the basis of which Dreyfus had been convicted was a forgery which was committed by Major Esterhazy. With a view to maintain the prestige of the army, the French Government tried to hush up the matter and Picquart was transferred. Colonel Henry was appointed in his place. However, there was a lot of agitation all over the country. Men like Emile Zola, Clemenceau and Anatole France took up the cause of Dreyfus which was opposed by the monarchists, the clericals and the army. The question was not merely the innocence or guilt of Dreyfus, but it involved bigger issues. The enemies of the Republic tried to discredit the Republic insisting on the guilt of Dreyfus.

The supporters of Dreyfus continued their agitation for his re-trial, but it was opposed by the vested interests. However, Colonel Henry admitted that one of the documents on the basis of which Dreyfus had been convicted, was forged by himself. After making that confession, Henry committed suicide in 1898. The confession of Henry strengthened the hands of the supporters of Dreyfus and the government was forced to order a re-trial. However, in the second trial also, Dreyfus was found guilty. His sentence of imprisonment was reduced to 10 years on account of the extenuating circumstances. President Loubet exercised his power of pardon in favour of Dreyfus and he was set at liberty.

In spite of this, the supporters of Dreyfus were not satisfied. In 1906, he was tried for the third time and on that occasion was declared to be completely innocent. As a result of that verdict, Dreyfus was promoted to a very high rank in the army and he became the symbol of the cause of-Republicanism.

According to Hazen, "The Dreyfus case, originally simply involving the fate of an alleged traitor, had soon acquired a far greater significance. Party and personal ambitions and interests sought to use it for purposes of their own and thus the question of legal right and wrong was woefully distorted and obscured. Those who hated the Jews used it to inflame people against that race, as Dreyfus was a Jew. The clericals joined them. Monarchists seized the occasion to declare that the Republic was an egregious failure breeding treason, and ought to be abolished. On the other hand there rallied to the defence of Dreyfus those who believed in his innocence, those who denounced the hatred of a race as a relic of barbarism, those who believed that the military should be subordinate to the civil authority and should not regard itself as above the law as these army officers were doing, those who believed that the whole episode was merely a hidden and dangerous attack upon the Republic, and all who believed that the clergy should keep out of politics.

"The chief result of this memorable struggle in the domain of politics was to unite more closely Republicans of every shade in a common programme, to make them resolve to reduce the political importance of the army and of the Church. The former was easily done by removal of monarchist officers. The attempt to solve the latter much more subtle and elusive problem led to the next great struggle in the recent history of France, the struggle with the Church."

According to Prof. Chapman, "As everyone knows who reads the history of France between 1870 and 1914, the Dreyfus case lies in his way, a vast and distracting maze, una selva oscura. It cannot be avoided. Unhappily much legend is attached to the Dreyfus affair. To accept the conventional reading of a clerico-military conspiracy is to swallow the propaganda of the Dreyfusards. No conspiracy existed in military circles, none in clerical. The arrest of Deroulede and his allies in August 1899 was no more than the spectacular method of a shaky and nervous government of rallying opinion to its side. This consideration led me back to a re-examination of the evidence from the beginning. It soon became apparent that much more is to be said for the War Office than has generally been admitted that anti-semitism played little, perhaps no part in the arrest of the unhappy victim or in his trial, that the accusations against the secular Church and, save the Assumptionists against the religious Orders have the flimsiest foundations. In short, the conventional story is overlaid with propaganda put out by partisans on the both sides." (**The Dreyfus Case**, p. 9).

It is to be observed that after the defeat of the anti-Dreyfusards, the position of the Third Republic became stabilized and it did not meet any danger from any other quarter.

Anti-church Policy (Ultramontanism). The anti-church policy of the Third Republic was due to many causes. The clericals had identified themselves with the royalist cause. When there was a struggle between the Monarchists and the Republicans, the Clericals joined hands with the Monarchists. Even on the occasion of the Dreyfus affair, the Clericals supported the anti-Dreyfusards. They also supported Boulanger, Gambetta, the popular leader of France, had pointed out the danger to the Third Republic from the church in these words: "Clericalism, there is the enemy." According to Combes, "Clericalism is, in fact, to be found at the bottom of every agitation and every intrigue from which Republican France has suffered during the last thirty-five years."

French politicians wanted to take away the control of the church over the educational system of the country. It was intended to inoculate with Republicanism every French boy and girl. Ferry, the French Minister of Public Instruction, passed many laws by which an attempt was made to remove the Catholic influence from education. Those laws prescribed compulsory attendance at some school for all children. Parents could still send their children to free schools run by the church, but if they did so, they had to support their schools out of their own funds. However, a complete system of public or national schools was established which was finalised and directed by the Republican Government. No religious instruction was given in those schools and only those laymen could teach in those schools who were accepted by the government. Gambetta's view was that the Prussian school master had won the last war and the French school master must win the next. Many Catholic clergymen condemned the public schools as Godless and atheistical. The government also hit back and ordered the dissolution of the Society of Jesus and its expulsion from France. All laws against the religious congregations of monks and nuns were revived. The government ordered the dissolution of those congregations which were not authorised by itself. Their members were also forbidden to run schools. It was also provided that all marriages were to be performed by civil ministries in order to give them validity. Another law empowered the civil courts to grant divorces and cancel marriages. The Catholics protested but submitted.

In October 1900, Premier Waldeck-Rousseau made a speech at Toulouse which resounded throughout France and foreshadowed a policy of great importance. According to him, the real danger confronting France arose from the growing power of the religious orders of monks and nuns. "In this country whose moral unity has for centuries constituted its strength and greatness, two classes of young people are growing up ignorant of each other until the day when they meet, so unlike as the risk not comprehending one another. Such a fact is explained only by the existence of a power which is no longer even occult, and by the constitution in the state of rival power." What he intended to say was that the youth of France was divided into two classes whose outlook upon life, whose mental processes, and whose opinions concerning politics and morals were so different from one another that the moral unity of the nation was destroyed. That was partly due to the astonishing and dangerous growth of religious orders of congregations whose influence was highly harmful. The orders were the rivals of the State. They had grown in wealth and numbers. Between 1877 and 1900, the number of nuns increased from 14,000 to 75,000 in unauthorised orders. The number of the monks was in the neighbourhood of 190,000. Their property was valued at about 50 million francs. The same property was worth more than a billion francs in 1900. The accumulation of wealth in the hands of the church was a source of great danger. There was opposition to teaching and preaching by the church. The church was declared the enemy of liberty.

In 1901, the **Law of Associations** was passed by which no religious order was to be allowed to exist in France without a definite authorisation by Parliament. The orders were to submit themselves to continuous regulation by the State. Although there were loud protests against the law, the same was vigorously enforced. The view of Combes was that "Clericalism is in fact to be found at the bottom of every agitation and every intrigue from which republican France has suffered during the last 35 years." Many refused to ask for authorisation from Parliament and there were others which were refused the authorisation even when they asked for the same. Thousands of monks and nuns were forced to leave their institutions and the latter had to be closed. Many of them left France and got shelter in Spain, Belgium, Great Britain and the U.S.A. Combes boasted that he not only exiled and silenced the critics of the Republic but also deprived the church schools of their best teachers.

Another law was passed in 1904 by which all teaching by religious orders, even by those authorised, was to cease within 10 years. The State was to have a monopoly of education of the young and consequently was to be in a position to teach them the principles of republicanism and liberalism. About 500 teaching, preaching and commercial orders were suppressed. Although Catholics condemned the law as the very negation of liberty, the same remained on the statute book.

The Republicans were not contented with this and were determined to go ahead with their programme against the church. For about a century, the relations between the church and the State in France were regulated by the Concordat of 1801. The Bishops and Archbishops were appointed by the State with the consent of the Pope. The Bishops appointed the priests with the consent of the State. The State paid the salaries of the priests and the bishops. The church recognised the confiscation of its property by the State. There were many Frenchmen who wanted to put an end to the Concordat of 1801. Their view was that religion was a private affair and the State had nothing to do with the same. The State had no right to tax people for the support of a church in which many had no belief or interest. It had no right to favour one denomination over another or over all others. It must be neutral towards all creeds and churches. Matters were precipitated when President Loubet of France paid an official visit to the King of Italy at Rome in April 1904. It was well known that such a visit was bound to offend the Pope who since 1870 had refused to recognise the King of Italy and had requested the Catholic sovereigns not to visit him. Pope Pius X protested to the Catholic powers of Europe against what he called "a grave offence to the Sovereign Pontiff." Jaures demanded "reprisals" for what he called foreign interference in the political affairs of France. The result was that Delcasse, the French Foreign Minister, recalled the French ambassador to the Vatican. Since June 1903, a preliminary committee had been studying the problem and trying to draft the measure which was intended to separate the church from the State. The law was finally passed on 9 December 1905. It abrogated the Concordat of 1801. The State was not to pay in future the salaries of the clergymen and was also to have no hand in their appointment. Clergymen who had served for many years, were to be given pensions. Young clergymen were to be given some compensation. The Church property which had been vested in the nation since 1789, was still to be at the free disposal of Roman Catholic church. However, the same was to be managed by Associations of Worship which were to vary in size according to the population of the community. Provision was made to prevent associations from amassing more than a given amount of wealth by legacies, gifts or otherwise.

The law was not universally condemned by the Catholics of France. There were many who believed that the church should adapt itself to the new circumstances. 74 Bishops decided to give it a trial if certain alterations were made in the character of the Associations of Worship.

However, a crisis was precipitated by the Pope who condemned the law of 1905 unreservedly. He declared that the fundamental principle of the separation of church and State was "an absolutely false thesis, a very pernicious error." He denounced the associations of worship as giving administrative control not "to the divinely instituted hierarchy, but to an association of laymen." That was a violation of the principles on which the church was based. The decision of the Pope was final and decisive for all Catholics and there was no scope for any compromise. There was the danger of all the Catholic churches in France being closed down and the government was not prepared to go to that extent. Briand decided to apply the law of 1881 which regulated the holding of public meetings. Although that law was concerned with secular meetings, the same was applied to religious meetings. It was announced that priests might make use of the churches after merely filing the usual application which covered the whole year. That compromise was also rejected by the Pope.

Another law was enforced in January 1907. By that law, most of the privileges guaranteed to the Roman Catholic Church by the law of 1905 were abrogated. As regards public worship in the churches, their use was to be gratuitous and regulated by contracts between the priests and prefects or mayors. Those contracts were to safeguard the civil ownership of the buildings, but worship was to go on in them as before.

According to Prof. Seignobos, "By this separation of church and State, France broke with the European tradition of Concordats by which the State officially recognised its religion; she adopted the American system which leaves the churches to be organised by the private initiative. This was a revolution in the ecclesiastical regime of France."

Labour Legislation. Some important labour legislation was enacted in France during the 1890's. The "great Act" of 1892 regulated the employment of women and forbade the employment of children under 13 years of age. It also laid down that workers were not to be made to work for more than 10 hours a day. There was to be a holiday once a week, preferably on Sundays. The interests of the minors were also safeguarded. Another Act of the same year provided for a machinery for voluntary arbitration in industrial disputes between employers and employees. Another Act was passed in 1893 which enabled the government to supervise the hygienic conditions in the factories. The government was also to see that measures were adopted for the safety of the workers in the industrial establishments. Another Act of the same year ensured free medical attendance for all workers and their families. An Act of 1898 laid down that employers were to pay compensation for personal injuries sustained by the employees.

Colonial Policy. France had already made some progress in the field of colonial development in the time of Louis Philippe and Napoleon III. During the regime of Jules Ferry, a vigorous colonial policy was pursued. In 1881, a protectorate was established over Tunis. Italy protested but had ultimately to keep quiet. In the tune of Napoleon III, France had occupied Cambodia and annexed

Cochin-China. Under Ferry, Tonkin was conquered and a protectorate was established over Annam. Ferry also laid the foundations of French Congo and sent an expedition to Madagascar. The work started by Ferry was continued by his successors. The result was that Madagascar was annexed in 1896 and Morocco was recognised as within the French sphere of influence in 1904. France also made acquisitions in Senegal, Guinea, Dahomey, Ivory Coast and the region of the Niger. It is true that Germany protested against French penetration into Morocco and precipitated the crises of 1905-6, 1908 and 1911, but Morocco was practically made a part of the French Empire by 1912. Germany was reconciled by the grant of some compensation to her elsewhere. Thus, France came to have a colonial Empire which was second in the world only to that of Great Britain.

Foreign Policy. From 1871 to 1890, France was diplomatically isolated. That was due to the deliberate policy of Bismarck who left no stone unturned to keep France isolated. Bismarck created the Three Emperors' League which continued to exist up to 1878. In 1879 he entered into an alliance with Austria-Hungary. By the entry of Italy in 1882, the same was transformed into the Triple Alliance. He revived the Three Emperors' League in 1881 and the same continued up to 1887. In 1887, he entered into the Reinsurance treaty with Russia and the same continued up to 1890. France could not have an alliance with England as there was going on a lot of colonial rivalry between the two countries. The relations were so much strained that on the occasion of the Fashoda incident of 1898, there was the possibility of a war between the two countries. Although Bismarck had succeeded in keeping Russia on his own side up to 1890, things changed after his resignation. The result was that France and Russia entered into a military alliance in 1893. The Dual Alliance continued up to 1914 although its importance became negligible during the Russo-Japanese War and the years that followed it. The Dual Alliance of 1893 ended the diplomatic isolation of France and enabled her to face the future with confidence and hope. There was no major change in foreign affairs till 1898 when Delcasse became the Foreign Minister of France. On account of the importance of his achievements, it is desirable to refer to his work at some length.

Delcasse (1898-1905). The foreign policy of Delcasse is associated with the reconciliation of France with England and Italy. When he entered the Quai D' Orsay in June 1898, there was bitterness between France and England and there was going on a great colonial competition between the two countries. When he left the Foreign Office in 1905, England and Italy were friends of France. That was due to the industry, patience and devotion of Delcasse.

Reconciliation with England. Captain Marchand had been sent by the French Government to forestall the English in the so-called Egyptian Sudan and thereby add to the French power. Even a change of government in France did not result in any change in the policy. The result was that Marchand reached Fashoda and hoisted the French flag. Kitchener met Marchand and asked him to retire from Fashoda as that was within the jurisdiction of Egypt. There was a lot of argument but all that was of no avail. Ultimately, the English flag was hoisted a few hundred yards away and Marchand was allowed to send a report to his government and get instructions from the same.

It is stated that when Delcasse became the Foreign Minister of France, he took steps in the direction of reconciliation of England. When Kitchener won the battle of Omdurman and entered Khartum, Delcasse offered his sincere congratulations on his victory "despite the differences about Egypt of the two governments." Delcasse also expressed his desire to settle all cases of differences between the two countries by discussion. However, he was informed by the British Government that there was nothing which could be discussed. Even on the day before the meeting of Kitchener and Marchand, an important interview took place between Delcasse and the British ambassador in Paris. During the interview, Delcasse told the British ambassador that the French Government had never recognised the British sphere of influence in the Upper Nile and as a matter of fact had protested against it. The Bahr-Ghazel has long been outside the influence of Egypt and France had as much a right at Fashoda as the English had at Khartum. The British ambassador told Delcasse that his government was not prepared to compromise and consequently the situation seemed to be serious. On another occasion, Delcasse told the British ambassador that he was prepared to discuss the question in the most conciliatory spirit, but he could not evacuate Fashoda without discussion or conditions. The stand taken by the French Government created a storm of opposition and resentment in England where the people demanded that France must be taught a lesson and England must not submit. Lord Rosebury announced that the British Government was not prepared to sacrifice anything and was prepared to fight out. The Chancellor of the Exchequer also spoke in a similar tone. Chamberlain announced the calling of the reserves. A cartoon in the Punch indicated the impatience of the man in the street in England. "What will you give me if I go away?" asked a Frenchman. "I will give you something if you don't", replied John Bull.

The British Government demanded an unconditional evacuation of Fashoda and Dr. Gooch is of the opinion that the British Government got it done by means of a threat of war. The French left Fashoda and the episode ended peacefully. The sagacity and moderation of Delcasse saved the situation. If Delcasse had been as violent as people on the other side of the Channel were, there would have been trouble. Such "a conflict would have involved sacrifices disproportionate to the object." France had already one enemy in Germany and she could not afford to have another. To quarrel with Great Britain was to play into the hands of Germany and thereby destroy all chances of recovering Alsace and Lorraine. The French fleet was weak and Great Britain could have taken possession of the whole of the colonial empire of France. It was this conviction that forced Delcasse to defy those Frenchmen who stood for a war with Great Britain.

According to Taylor, "Fashoda and its aftermath was for the French a crisis in political psychology, for the British not even that. They carried the day with the normal peace-time strength; the extra cost of Fashoda to the British admiralty was £13,600. The economy was, of course, illusory. The true 'battle for Egypt' had been fought in 1798, and the French never meant to renew it. Fashoda was a triumph for 'splendid isolation.' The British had become indifferent to the continent of Europe and the Balance of Power (or so they thought); therefore, they could build an invincible navy and dominate the Mediterranean. Fashoda, moreover, made 'splendid isolation' more secure. The British did not need the diplomatic support of other Powers in the Egyptian question, once they put it on a military basis; and with their troops close to the Suez canal they worried less than ever about a Russian occupation of a Constantinople. At any time after 1898 the British could say of the opening of the Straits what the Committee of Imperial Defence said in 1903 : 'it would not fundamentally alter the present strategic position in the Mediterranean.' Fashoda finished off what remained of the Mediterranean entente. Great Britain needed neither Italy nor Austria-Hungary. Italy, deprived of British protection, had to seek reconciliation with France. Austria-Hungary enjoyed an illusory security so long as Russian attention was concentrated on the Far East, once Russia turned back to the Balkans, Germany could no longer find a third party on whom to shoulder off the defence of Austria-Hungary, and a Russo-German conflict became well-nigh inevitable." (**The Struggle of Mastery in Europe,** pp. 382-83).

After the retirement of Marchand from Fashoda, negotiations started between the two countries and ultimately a settlement was made in 1899 regarding the respective spheres of France and England. By this, Great Britain recognised the right of France to expand from West Africa towards the Sahara and the interior. The settlement was the work of Delcasse and Salisbury who showed a lot of patience at the time of the crisis.[1]

---

1. It is pointed out that the Fashoda crisis paved the way towards a closer accord between England and France. Prince Bulow refers to a conversation between a French ambassador and an Italian colleague. The Italian asked the French ambassador, "What effect Fashoda would have on French relations with England ?" The French ambassador replied: "An excellent one. Once the difference about the Sudan is settled nothing stands in the way of a complete Entente with England." Bulow's own comment was in these terms: "There was disappointment in Paris because England would not, for the sake of French friendship, sacrifice any of her interests in the Sudan and on the Nile. But France was ready in any case, though with clenched teeth, to pay this price or even a higher one for England's friendship. The defeat in the Fashoda affair was set down in the debit account of the French policy of revenge, and finally resulted in renewed hatred of Germany rather than hostility towards England"."

When the crisis was over, Delcasse suggested through the French ambassador in London to settle the other outstanding points of dispute between the two countries. Lord Salisbury did not show any enthusiasm and said that they must wait and that waiting took four years (1899-1903).

According to Dr. Gooch, the idea of a rapprochement between England and France was born on the day of Delcasse's appointment as Minister for Foreign Affairs in June 1898. Though originally an Anglophobe, he informed the first visitor at the Quai D' Orsay of his intention to establish cordial relations with England. The decision to evacuate Fashoda cleared the ground. However, the Boer War created bitterness between the two countries on account of the anti-British attitude of the French newspapers and the public. In spite of the difficulties, the pioneers of reconciliation did not give up hope. In 1900, the British Chamber of Commerce expressed its desire to hold its meeting at Paris and Delcasse approved of the same. The English attended the meeting in large numbers. In 1903, King Edward visited France and he was welcomed by the French. The same year, Delcasse and President Loubet met of their respective claims. It was decided that while England was made a return visit to London. It was in this atmosphere of trust and friendship that negotiations started between the two countries of settlement of their respective claims. It was decided that while England was to have a free hand in Egypt, France was to have the same in Morocco. Likewise, the question of Newfoundland Fisheries was amicably settled. France gave up the right to the shores and she was given concessions in West Africa. The questions of Siam, Madagascar and the New Hebrides were also settled.

Both Lord Lansdowne and Delcasse were satisfied with the friendly settlement of the outstanding disputes between the two countries. Answering his critics, Delcasse maintained that in Newfoundland, France had abandoned privileges which were difficult to maintain and in no way necessary, while the essential right of fishing in territorial waters was preserved and the right of purchasing bait and drying nets was also not denied. In West Africa, the British concession's were of considerable importance. The Niger-Chad frontier was improved. To quote Delcasse, "Under our influence, Morocco would be a source of strength for our North African empire. If subject to a foreign Power, our North African possessions would be permanently menaced and paralysed." There was not much of sacrifice in the case of Egypt which had already been lost in 1882.

Italy. While Delcasse was busy in improving relations with Britain, he was also trying to conciliate Italy. In 1900, he secured the consent of Italy to the French exploitation of Morocco by telling Italy that she could develop her interests in Tripoli. In 1901, an Italian squadron visited Toulon. In 1902, the Italian Government assured the French Government that the Triple Alliance was not aimed at France and she gave a guarantee that she would not fight against France. In 1904, President Loubet visited Rome and the two countries were brought together.

Delcasse also took steps to settle things with Spain regarding Morocco.

A Franco-Spanish treaty was signed on 6 October 1904 by which Spain formally adhered to the Anglo-French Convention of April 1904 and thereby acknowledged the predominant interest of France in Morocco. She also accepted from France and England a guarantee of Moroccan independence.

Morocco. Having settled with Italy and Spain the question of Morocco, Delcasse sent a mission in December 1904 to the capital of Morocco. Morocco was to be developed under the auspices of France and the French were to help in the training of police, building of roads and telegraphs and the founding of a State Bank. The Sultan of Morocco accepted the suggestions of the French Government. Everything seemed to be progressing smoothly when all of a sudden a check came from Germany. Formerly, the attitude of the German Government was that she had only commercial interests in Morocco, but now the German Government changed its mind. William II went to Tangier and made a declaration that the German Government would not allow the subjection of the Sultan of Morocco of any Power. He also declared that the German Government was determined to defend the independence of the Sultan at all costs. Naturally, those declarations were resented in France.

The German regarded Delcasse as their enemy No. 1 and no wonder they wanted him to go. The German Government demanded that a conference of the powers concerned should be summoned to discuss the question of Morocco. Delcasse was not prepared to submit to this German demand. He felt that Germany was merely trying to vilify France by making unreasonable demands. He was supported by the President and Prime Minister of France. On the other hand, the German Government insisted that Delcasse must be dismissed and a conference must be called. The German press clamoured that it was not France which wanted to fight against Germany but it was the personal enmity of Delcasse which was responsible for the conflict. There were rumours of an ultimatum being given by Germany to France and the French feared that their army was not ready. Delcasse stated that Britain had made an offer of 100,000 men to support France. However, Dr. Gooch points out that the so-called "British Offer" existed only in the imagination of Delcasse. As a matter of fact the British Government had given no such guarantee. The British Government had merely given a warning that in case any unfriendly act was done. Great Britain was not to remain indifferent. Such a warning against aggression was different from a solemn undertaking to help France. Probably Delcasse's mistaken interpretation of the British official attitude was due to the statements of certain highly-placed Englishmen who expressed their individual convictions. The contention of the French Prime Minister was that even if the so-called British offer was accepted, that would mean war with Germany. At that stage, Bulow, the German Chancellor, informed the French Government that he was not going to have any dealings with Delcasse. It was this ultimatum which was responsible for the resignation of Delcasse and the French acceptance of a conference to deal with the question of Morocco.

During this period, one factor played a very important part. France used to depend upon her friendship with Russia on account of the Franco-Russian alliance. However, in 1905, Russia was very weak on account of her reverses in the Russo-Japanese War. Moreover, William II was making special efforts to win over Russia. So in the Russo-Japanese War, the Germans helped the Russians as much as they could. In 1905 was signed the Bjorko Pact by William II and Nicholas II. France submitted to the German demand for a conference because she could not trust her Russian ally and she was also not sure of any military help from England. The British Government also advised the French Government to accept the idea of a conference on Morocco. However, it cannot be denied that the French surrender cost her the services of a brilliant and selfless statesman who had done so much to enhance her prestige and strengthen her position in Europe. Lord Lansdowne wrote thus to a friend: "The fall of Delcasse is disgusting and has sent the Entente down a number of points in the market." It was the most humiliating incident that had occurred in France for many years. In spite of his fall, with the exception of Austria, all Powers voted against Germany in the Algeciras Conference in 1906. "Algeciras was a German defeat" and Delcasse had contributed not a little to it.

Even after retirement from the foreign office in 1905, Delcasse remained a prominent figure in French politics for a long time. He belonged to no party but was welcome because of his friends. When he became the Minister of the French Marine, he followed a policy of concentrating the French Fleet in the Mediterranean.

In 1914, he was sent as French ambassador to Russia. With his pro-Russian views, he was the most suitable person for bringing the two countries nearer each other. It is well-known that he had played an important part in 1904 on the occasion of the Dogger Mank incident. Without him, there might have been a clash between England and Russia.

The question has been asked as to how far Delcasse was responsible for the Entente Cordiale of 1904. It is true that it was the British Government which intimated in 1904 to the French Government that Edward VII would be happy to visit Paris on his way back from the Mediterranean, and the French Government responded favourably. It was the visit of the King and the welcome that was given to him that prepared the way. The same year Delcasse and President Loubet visited London. It was on that occasion that negotiations started between the two countries. It is maintained that it was Delcasse's sagacity and public spirit which led him to "grasp the hand which the British Government held out to him." It is true that in 1903, the British Government took the initiative, but Delcasse had already taken the initiative in that direction in 1899 after the settlement of the Fashoda incident. However, Lord Salisbury had replied thus to Cambon: "I have the greatest confidence in M. Delcasse and also in your present government. But in a few months time they will probably be overthrown and their successors will do exactly the contrary. No, we must wait a bit." It is clear that while the British Government rejected Delcasse's offer in 1899, the latter accepted the British offer in 1903, although he could have rejected likewise. The change in the British attitude was due to the fact that England had tried to win over Germany and had failed. After entering into an alliance with Japan in 1902, France was approached by the British Government with a similar objective.

It is stated that Lord Lansdowne was shocked to find in March 1904 that Delcasse had not communicated to the French Cabinet the negotiations that were going on between the two countries. That was due to the fact Delcasse was not sure of their effect on the colleagues of his Cabinet. When the negotiations reached the final stage, he communicated the same to the Cabinet. It shows that he worked secretly at his object till he became sure of his success. In spite of the many ministerial changes in France from 1898 to 1905, Delcasse managed to remain in the foreign office and consistently followed a policy of winning over England and Italy.

The Germans regarded Delcasse as their arch-enemy because it was contended that he aimed at the encirclement of Germany. However, there does not seem lo be any truth in the accusation. The fact is that Delcasse was a great patriot and he wanted to strengthen the position of his country by winning over England and Italy to her side. It was only in that way that France could hold her own against Germany. We may conclude with the following remarks of an eminent writer: "In spite of his limitations, he remains by general consent, the outstanding figure of the Third Republic in the field of foreign affairs."

Morocco Crisis of 1905. It was on three occasions that the question of Morocco came to the front and there was every likelihood of a war between Germany and France. On all these three occasions, England backed France and consequently Germany had to give way.

Reference has already been made to the first Morocco crisis of 1905-6. It has already been pointed out that after the **Entente Cordiale** of 1904, Delcasse sent a French mission to Morocco with a view to establish French control over the country. Although outwardly the object was merely to help the Sultan of Morocco to develop his country and improve his administration, the ultimate effect would have been the establishment of French control over the country. Although on previous occasions Germany had stated that she had no interest in Morocco, a change was visible in her attitude. The German Emperor went to Tangier and declared that Germany would not allow the establishment of French control over Morocco. Germany also demanded the dismissal of Delcasse and the summoning of a conference to deal with the question of Morocco. Delcasse was forced to resign in 1905 and the Algeciras Conference was held in 1906. Excepting Austria-Hungary, all other Powers including Italy voted with France and against Germany. The result was that Germany came out of the Conference empty-handed. It was recognised that while Germany had economic interests, France had political as well as economic interests. According to Dr. Gooch, the Conference of Algeciras did not improve the relations between Germany and France or the internal condition of Morocco. The kernel of the treaty was that power was given to France and Spain to provide police for 8 ports order a Swiss Inspector, but recruiting and instruction proceeded very slowly and was never fully carried out. Prince Bulow considered the results of the Algeciras Conference to be satisfactory although Germany did not get all that she desired. To quote Bulow, "We succeeded in preserving the sovereignty of the Sultan and in securing international control of the police organisation and the Morocco National Bank, thus ensuring the open door in Morocco for German economic interests as well as for those of all other countries....The decisions of the Algeciras Conference bolted the door against the attempts of France to compass the 'Unification' of Morocco. They also proved a bell we could ring at any time, should France show any similar tendencies again." However, according to impartial observers, the Algeciras Conference was a diplomatic rebuff for Germany. The Conference was held with the definite object of breaking the Entente between England and France. The actual result of the Conference was not the breaking but the strengthening of the Entente. Bulow himself admitted this fact in these words: "We have no thought of attempting to separate France and England. We have absolutely no idea of attempting to disturb the friendship of the Western Powers. Cordial relations between Germany and England are in perfect consonance with Entente, if the latter combination follows pacific purposes."

Casablanca Case (1908). The second Morocco crisis of 1908 was related to the Casablanca incident. On 25 September 1908, the German Consul at Casablanca tried to assist the deserters from the French Foreign Legions to escape. However, the deserters were captured and the German secretary and the soldiers who were escorting them, were roughly handled by French soldiers. The German Consul was blamed by the French authorities for the violation of international law by helping the deserters. On the other hand, the French authorities were blamed by Germany for having violated the rules of international law with regard to the privileges of the Consuls. There was a lot of excitement both in Germany and France. However, matters were not precipitated and both the countries agreed to submit the dispute to arbitration. The verdict of the arbitrators was that both sides were partly in the wrong. Both Powers were happy at the peaceful disposal of the dispute. The other European Powers were also happy as they were busy with the Turkish Revolution of 1908 and the Bosnian crisis of 1908-9. As there was the possibility of trouble in the Balkans, much importance was not attached to Morocco. Germany realised that it was not possible to check French control in Morocco without a war.

There were negotiations between Germany and France with regard to Morocco and the result was the Franco-German Agreement of February 1909. Germany was promised equality of economic opportunity in Morocco and she recognised the special interests of France and promised not to interfere with them.

Certain factors expedited the negotiations between the two countries. One of them was the possibility of a conflict between Austria and Serbia on the question of Bosnia and the other was the anxiety of Bulow to come to a settlement with England with regard to the naval programmes of the two countries. Bulow felt that negotiations with Germany could succeed only if the relations between France and Germany were not strained. The anxiety of England with regard to Morocco could be removed only if Germany and France shook hands on the question of Morocco. King Edward VII was to visit Berlin and Bulow decided to complete the negotiations before the arrival of Edward VII so that the credit of the success may not be given to the King. The Agreement of 1909 was enthusiastically supported in the French Press and Bulow was congratulated upon it. One important result was the establishment and maintenance of cordial relations between France and Germany for two years (1909-11).

The Agadir Crisis (1911). The Franco-German Agreement of 1909 established friendly relations between the two countries and for some time no difficulty arose with regard to Morocco. However, disorders in that country gave the French a pretext for a steady extension of their police and military control. The Sultan was forced by an ultimatum to accept a loan which brought him under the complete control of France. It was becoming clear that under the changed circumstances the independence of the Sultan could not be maintained and equal opportunities in the economic field could not be guaranteed to the Germans. The chieftains of Morocco did not like the French methods of control and consequently there was a revolt in Fez, the capital of Morocco. It was declared that lives of Europeans were in danger. Captain Marchand was murdered in Morocco and the French Government decided to send troops to Fez to save the lives of Europeans. It was declared that troops would be withdrawn as soon as order was restored in Fez.

Kiderlen, the German Foreign Minister, neither gave his approval nor put in any formal protest. His views on Morocco have been summarised in these words: "Three years have shown that the independence of Morocco, as contemplated in Algeciras Act, cannot be maintained in the face of native rebellion and imperialistic pressure from France and Spain. Sooner or later Morocco will inevitably be absorbed by these two neighbours. It is unlikely that a walled city like Fez can be captured by the natives and the revolt seems to be on the ebb. But the French fear for its safety and are preparing to send an expedition. This they have a right to do, and one must await the development of events. But if they march to Fez it is hardly likely that they will withdraw; even if French public opinion approved withdrawal, it would be regarded by the natives as a sign of weakness. This would lead to new uprisings and new French military expeditions. The course of events shows that the provisions of the Act of Algeciras cannot be carried out. A Sultan who can only assert his authority with the aid of French bayonets cannot maintain the independence which was the purpose of the Algeciras Act. Germany must recognize these facts and readjust her policy in accordance with them. After the French have been in Fez awhile, we shall ask in a friendly way when they expect to withdraw. When they say that they cannot withdraw we shall say that we understand this perfectly, but we can no longer regard the Sultan as a sovereign independent ruler as provided by the Act of Algeciras; and since this is a dead letter, the Signatory Powers regain their freedom of action. It will do no good to protest against the French absorption of Morocco. We must therefore secure an object which will make the French ready to give us Compensations. Just as the French protect their subjects in Fez, we can do the same for ours at Magador and Agadir by peacefully stationing ships there. We can then await developments and see if the French will offer us suitable compensation. If we get these, it will make up for past failures and have a good effect on the coming elections to the Reichstag."

The French Government informed the German Government that it was ready to negotiate on the question of compensation. Kiderlen desired to have the whole of French Congo. Cambon, the French Ambassador in Berlin, felt that no French Government could afford to give the whole of the Congo.

On 1 July 1911, the German gun-boat called the Panther entered the harbour of Agadir. Germany declared that she had sent the German gun-boat to protect the lives and property of the Germans in South Morocco. The warship was to be withdrawn as soon as order was restored in Morocco. It is pointed out that the real object of the Panther was to extort more concessions from France.

During all this interval, negotiations were continuing between Germany and France for a settlement of the question of compensation. The final impression of Kiderlen was that no satisfactory concession could be got from France without a war. However, the Kaiser was opposed to a war with France on the question of Morocco and gave directions to that effect to Kiderlen. The latter was prepared to resign but was persuaded to continue the negotiations with France.

It was at this stage that Great Britain intervened. Sir Edward Grey warned Germany on 4 July 1911 that "a new situation has been created by the despatch of a German ship to Agadir; future developments might affect British interests more directly than they had hitherto been affecting and, therefore, we could not recognise any new arrangement which was to come without us." Grey was prepared to accept a Franco-German settlement based on an exchange of French Congo territory for German African possessions provided Germany gave tip all claims to Morocco.

On 21 July 1911, Lloyd George, Chancellor of the Exchequer, made the following declaration in his famous Mansion House speech : "But I am also bound to say this that I believe it is essential in the highest interests, not merely of this country, but of the world, that Britain should at all hazards maintain her prestige amongst the Great Powers of the world. Her potent influence has many times been in the past, and may yet be in the future, invaluable to the cause of human liberty. It has more than once in the past redeemed continental nations, who are sometimes too apt to forget that service from overwhelming disaster, and even from national extinction. It would make great sacrifices to preserve peace. I conceive that nothing would justify a disturbance of international goodwill exceed questions of the gravest national moment. But if a situation were to be forced upon us in which peace could only be preserved by the surrender of the great and beneficent position Britain has won by centuries of heroism and achievement, by allowing Britain to be treated where her interests were vitally affected, as if she were of no account in the comity of nations, then I say emphatically that peace at that price would be a humiliation intolerable for a great country like ours to endure."

This speech had the desired result. There was a lot of indignation in Germany. It was interpreted as a threat to interfere in the Franco-German negotiations and it was felt that England had no business to do so. There was every possibility of a war and it was felt that the British Government was playing dangerously with fire. However, the actual result of the speech was that Germany informed England that she had no desire to establish herself on the Atlantic coast of Morocco. Germany also moderated her demands on France. After four months of negotiations, an agreement was signed in November 1911. According to that agreement, Germany agreed to the establishment of a French protectorate over Morocco. France gave 100,000 square miles of French Congo to Germany.

Although the Morocco crisis was over, the relations between England and Germany became all the more strained. England began to suspect the war-like inclinations of Germany. According to Grey, "The Agadir Crisis was intended to end either in the diplomatic humiliation of France or in war." Again, "The militarists in Germany were bitterly disappointed over Agadir, and when the next crisis came we found them with the reins in their hands." Grey's feelings are clear from his following remarks to the Russian Ambassador: "In the event of a war between Germany and France, England would have to participate. If this war should involve Russia, Austria would be dragged in too, for, although she has not the slightest desire to interfere in this matter, she will be compelled by force of circumstances to do so. There is no doubt that in such an event, the situation in Albania will become aggravated. Consequently, it would no longer be a duel between France and Germany—it would be a general war." According to Prince Bulow, "Like a damp squib, it started then amused the world, and ended by making us look ridiculous. After the leap of the Panther on Agadir, there was a fanfare which on Lloyd George's speech, died in the most inglorious charade." The Agadir Crisis tightened the bond between England and France. France was grateful to England for the Mansion House speech which helped to end the dispute. A day before the Mansion House speech, a conference took place between the French and English military staffs with a view "to determine the new conditions for the participation of English army in the operations of the French Armies in the North-East in case of war with Germany." Evidently, the crisis brought France and England nearers each other. Another effect of the Agadir Crisis was that Italy decided to capture Tripoli. This action of Italy so much weakened Turkey that the Balkan League was formed to finish the Turkish Empire in Europe. That led to the Balkan Wars of 1912-13 which ultimately led to the World War of 1914.

According to Grant and Temperley, "Agadir was a crisis infinitely more serious than Algeciras and undoubtedly more critical than the Bosnian one. The Triple Entente had been defeated over Bosnia and Russia humiliated. But their defeat and humiliation were perhaps less public and anyhow less recent than that of the Triple Alliance, and of Germany in particular, at Agadir. This time England had appeared 'in shining armour' at a grave moment to support her friend. An able publicist put his finger on the gravity of the new situation at once. He said that the bond of the Triple Entente is less close than that of the Triple Alliance, but for practical purposes Europe is divided by these two great combinations and the tenseness of the situation makes crises inevitably recur. Russia and the Entente accepted defeat without war in the crisis of 1909. Germany accepted defeat without war in that of 1911, neither would accept defeat without war in any future crisis. Both groups understood the danger, and both began to prepare. England had already been organising an expeditionary force of six divisions, new arrangements were made with the Admiralty to transport it rapidly overseas at need, *i.e.*, to co-operate with France. Preparations of all kinds lor press-censorship, for war legislation and the like were made. If a peace-loving country and government faced reality and made preparations like these, it is not surprising that military and naval activity developed elsewhere in a less liberal atmosphere. And the tensity of the situation was increased by military re-organisation everywhere and particularly by the designing and development of 'Russian strategic railways and of German strategic canals."

SUGGESTED READINGS

Bodley : **The Church in France.**

Bourgeois: **History of Modern France (Vols. I & II).**

Braco: **France under the Republic.**

Brogan, D.W.: **The Third Republic.**

Chapman, Guy: **The Drevfus Case, London, 1955.**

Galton: **The Church and State in France.**

Guerard: **French Civilisation in the Nineteenth Century.**

Seignobos, C.: **Political History of Europe since 1814.**

Seignobos, C.: **A History of the French People.**

Stannard, H.: **Gambetta.**

Taylor, A.J.P.: **The Struggle for Mastery in Europe (1848-1918), 1954.**

Visetelly: **Republican France.**

Wright: **History of the Third French Republic.**

Zola: **The Downfall.**

CHAPTER 21

ITALY FROM 1870 TO 1915

The unification of Italy was brought about by the efforts of men like Mazzini, Cavour, Garibaldi, Victor Emmanuel II, etc., and foreign help. According to Luigi Sturzo, "Italian unity was obtained too suddenly by a people for centuries divided and heterogeneous. Liberty, preserved as a torch in the little country of Piedmont, was rather given as a gift than won by the efforts of the people; and nationality, affirmed as self-determination and self-government by an elite, **did not find an equal echo in the popular consciousness."** No wonder, in spite of her unification, Italy did not play any important part in European politics, as was done by Germany. The people of Italy were backward. The country was still undeveloped and consequently her resources were small. The people were illiterate and did not take interest in the politics of the country. Regionalism also stood in the way of national progress. Political life of the country left much to be desired. There was corruption all round. Intrigues were the order of the day. The quarrel between the Pope and the Italian Government was not in the interests of the country. Italy was deprived of the services of those Italian Catholics who could not participate in politics on account of the imposition of the ban by the Pope. The net result was that Italy remained a third rate power. To quote Sturzo again, Italy "became a pawn in the various vicissitudes of the European political game, useful now to this Power, now to that, in a subtle contest of skill in which she seemed to derive benefits, but which earned her only pricks and disappointments. This was due partly to the inherent difficulties of her position, and partly to the lack of continuity in her foreign policy, so that time and again there slipped from the hands of her ministers those very cards which they had guarded with jealous care. In this way, Italy received no help from her allies and gave none."

"We have made Italy, we still have to make Italians." With a view to achieve that objective, many measures were adopted. The administrative and judicial systems, were reorganized and centralized. A system of local government was set up on the lines of France. The railways were nationalized. Compulsory military service was enforced in the country. Brigandage was suppressed. Secret societies like the Mafia of Sicily and the Camorra of Naples were exterminated. In 1897, the Compulsory Education Act was passed with a view to lessen illiteracy in the country. The measures was not successful on account of the lack of funds. The problem of property slowed the progress of the nation. The National Debt was very great and as the government had to spend a lot of money on many projects, the burden of taxes on the people was unbearable. The Italian Government was always on the verge of bankruptcy.

The population of Italy increased and the government did not know what to do with it. However, thousands of Italians migrated to North and South America.

The miserable condition of the people gave an opportunity to the socialists to fish in troubled waters. There were serious riots in Turin, Milan and Rome in 1889. Four years later, there was a serious labour trouble in Sicily. In 1898, there were serious riots all over the country especially in

Milan. In Southern and Central Italy, they took the form of "bread riots". There was so much of dissatisfaction in the country that King Humbert[1] was assassinated in 1900. He was succeeded by Victor Emmanuel III.

Internal Politics. A parliamentary system on the lines of Great Britain was adopted in Italy. However, the franchise was limited and only those were allowed to vote who had property and educational qualifications. The franchise was enlarged in 1882 when the number of voters was nearly quadrupled. In 1912, universal manhood suffrage was established in the country.

Italian politics was not a clean one. There was too much of jobbery, corruption and intrigues. The political life of the country was demoralized. The names of three persons are important in Italian politics during this period and those were Depretis, Crispi and Giolitti. Depretis was in power from 1876 to 1887. It was under him that Italy entered into the Triple Alliance in 1882. Elementary education was made compulsory. Railway system was completed. Franchise was extended. A new colonial policy was initiated. Depretis adopted corrupt methods to keep himself in power.

On the death of Depretis in 1887, Crispi became the head of the administration. He was a very powerful minister and he followed a vigorous colonial policy. It was during his regime that an Italian Protectorate was established over Somaliland. He fell from power in 1891 but came to power again after two years. From 1893 to 1896, he was practically a dictator. He fell on account of the defeat of Italy by Abyssinia in the Battle of Adowa in 1896. The name of Giolitti is prominently associated with the years before the World War I.

The state of affairs improved in Italy after the assassination of King Humbert in 1900 and the accession of Victor Emmanuel III. The new King was young, sympathetic and democratically minded. Industries began to develop in the North and vine culture was promoted in the South. Foreign capital began to flow into Italy and was utilized for the development of the country. The merchant marine was expanded. The Pope removed the ban on the Catholics with regard to their participation in politics. A new Social Insurance Act was passed. In 1904, a new Education Act was passed. For the first time, the budget of 1905 showed a surplus. Manhood suffrage was established in 1912. The use of hydroelectric power helped the industrial development of the country.

The Roman Question. The Pope had opposed the unification of Italy and in spite of that the same was completed in 1870. However, the entry of Italian troops into Rome in 1870 gave a blow to the position of the Pope. The Italian Government tried to reconcile the Pope and passed in 1871 the **Law of Papal Guarantees.** The new law gave to the Pope the government of the Vatican and Lateran palaces and grounds and villa of Castel Gandolfo. The Pope was also given the honours due to a reigning sovereign. He was given the right to communicate freely with governments and people abroad. He was given the use of Italian telegraphs, railways and mails. He was also given an annual subsidy of 3¼ million lire from the national treasury as compensation for the loss of temporal possessions. However, Pope Pius IX condemned the Law of Papal Guarantees. His acceptance of the law would have implied his recognition of the unjust entry of Italian troops into Rome in 1870. Moreover, he wanted the Papal Guarantees to be given not by a law of the Italian Parliament but an international treaty. Pius IX declared himself as a "prisoner" of the Vatican. He issued a circular letter called the Enyclical Non-expedit by which the Italian Catholics were forbidden to vote or hold offices under the royal government. The uncompromising attitude of the Pope was helpful to him in one way. So long as he was not on friendly terms with the government of Italy, he could not be suspected of being subservient to Italian interests. On account of his so-called "imprisonment", there was sympathy for him among the Catholics all over the world. However, it had a very unfortunate

1. He had succeeded Victor Emmanuel II in 1878. Over the tomb of the latter, the following was the inscription : "To the Father of the country."

effect on the fortunes of Italy. The country was deprived of the public services of many Italians who, obedient to the Pope, removed themselves from the politics of the country.

Pope Pius IX died in 1878, but his successor, Leo XIII, continued the policy of his predecessor. In 1905, the Encyclical Non-expedit was partially removed by Pius X. In 1919, it was completely repealed by Benedict XV. On his accession in 1922, Pius XI gave his blessings to the Italian troops.

Colonial Policy. Colonial expansion was a necessity for Italy on account of the very high rate at which her population was increasing. She tried to secure some concessions in China along with other European Powers, but she was the only European Power which failed to achieve anything. Great Britain proposed to Italy to annex Tunis and Tripoli but the latter failed to avail of the opportunity. However, in 1881, France established her protectorate over Tunis. That led to ill-feelings between the two countries and all chances of securing Tunis vanished once for all. However, it was in 1911 that Italy attacked Turkey and was able to secure in 1912 Tripoli and Cyrenaica. The new acquisition was given the name of Libya.

Having lost Tunis, Italy started seeking compensation somewhere else in Africa. In 1885, she occupied the Abyssinian port of Massowa. During the regime of Crispi, an Italian protectorate was established over Somaliland. The Italian settlements on the Red Sea were given the name of Eritrea and Italy began to expand towards Abyssinia. That led to a conflict between Italy and Abyssinia. However, she was defeated in 1896 in the Battle of Adowa. It was in the time of Mussolini that the Italians had their revenge for the defeat of Adowa and conquered and annexed the whole of Abyssinia.

Foreign Policy. To begin with, the Italian foreign policy was dominated by the Roman Question. As pointed out before, the Pope refused to co-operate with the Italian Government and called upon the heads of the Catholic States of Europe to take action against Italy. Thus, there was always the fear of French and Austrian intervention in the affairs of Italy. This fear was not an imaginary one but a real one.

Relations between Italy and France became very bad in 1881 when France established a protectorate over Tunis. There were anti-Italian demonstrations in France and many Italians were murdered. There was a possibility of French attack on Italy. It was under these circumstances that Italy joined Germany and Austria and thus the Triple Alliance came into existence in 1882. The Triple Alliance gave strength and prestige to Italy and thus the fear of French invasion was eliminated. Although Italy was the petitioner, she was able to secure very favourable terms. When the Triple Alliance was renewed in 1887, Italy was able to get still better terms. Her obligations were lessened but her previous security was maintained. Italy entered into another alliance with England in 1887. By that alliance, Great Britain and Italy agreed to maintain the *status quo* in the Mediterranean, Adriatic, Aegean and Black Seas. They also agreed to support each other in the Mediterranean if either Power went to war with another Power. Italy agreed to support the policy of Great Britain in Egypt. Great Britain agreed to support the policy of Italy in Northern Africa, particularly in Tripoli. After 1887, the relations between Italy and Britain became all the more cordial. In 1902, Italy gave an assurance to France that although she was a member of the Triple Alliance, she would not fight against her. On the occasion of the Algeciras Conference of 1906, Italy voted with England and France against Germany and Austria.

In 1909, Czar Nicholas II paid a visit to King Victor Emmanuel III. The two sovereigns agreed to do everything in their power to maintain the *status quo* in the Balkans. Russia agreed to maintain a benevolent attitude in reference to Italy's designs on Tripoli and Gyrenaica. Italy promised to reciprocate this attitude towards the ambitions of Russia and with regard to the Bosphorus and the Dardanelles.

It is to be observed that from the beginning of the 20th century, Italy had a foot in two camps. Although she was a member of the Triple Alliance, Austria and Germany did not put much trust on her help. She also betrayed them in 1906. On the occasion of the Bosnian crisis of 1908-9 also. Italy resented the fact that Austria had annexed Bosnia and Herzegovina without ever giving her a prior intimation. Otherwise also, the relations between Italy and Austria were not satisfactory. On account of the determination of the Italians to get back the Italian-speaking areas which were still within the Austrian Empire, even the highly-placed Italians helped the Irredentist movement. The plain fact was that in spite of the Triple Alliance, the relations between the two countries could not be cordial. The result was that when the World War I broke out in 1914, Italy did not declare war along with Germany and Austria. That may be partly due to the fact that she was still exhausted on account of her war with Turkey in 1911-12. However, a more important reason was that Italy was determined to get some concessions from Austria before she joined the Central Powers. Although Germany put pressure on Austria to give concessions to Italy, Austria was not generous in her concessions. Great Britain and France were also trying to woo Italy. As they were prepared to give Italy whatever she demanded, the Treaty of London was signed in 1915. After signing the Treaty, Italy precipitated matters with the Central Powers and declared war against Austria on 23 May 1915. Curiously enough, war against Germany was not declared till 27 August 1916.

Although Italy fought on the side of the Allies during the World War I, she was not happy at the Peace Settlement. She was not given what had been promised to her by the Treaty of London. The interests of Italy and Yugoslavia conflicted and as the Allies favoured Yugoslavia, Italy was discontented. There was, otherwise also a lot of unrest in Italy. Communist propaganda began to spread in the country, and consequently there were strikes everywhere. The peasants turned out their landlords and captured their property. There was chaos everywhere. There was every danger of the country becoming communist. It was at that time that Mussolini captured power in 1922.

SUGGESTED READINGS

Cambridge Modern History, Vol. XII.

King and Okey: **Italy Today.**

Underwood: **United Italy.**

Wallace: **Greater Italy.**

CHAPTER 22

RUSSIA FROM 1796 TO 1917

The year's not important,
    The place scarcely matters,
Where seven good peasants
    Once met on a high-road,
From Province "Hard-Battered,"
    From District "Most Wretched,"
From "Destitute" Parish,
    From neighbouring hamlets—
"Patched", "Barefoot", and "Shabby",
    "Bleak", "Burnt-out" and "Hungry",
From "Harvestless" also,
    They met and disputed
Of who can, in Russia,
    Be happy and free?

—NEKRASSOV

(*Who can be Happy and Free in Russia*?)

Although Russia had risen into prominence on account of the achievements of Czars like Peter the Great, and Catherine the Great, she was still a backward country as compared with other progressive States of Europe. She remained in that condition right up to the middle of the 19th century. It was only after that she abolished serfdom and started the industrialisation of the country, which brought liberal and revolutionary ideas in its wake. However, this does not mean that Russia did not play a prominent part in the foreign affairs of Europe. The fact remains that she was counted to be a great Power and her every move on the chess-board of international affairs was watched with interest, fear and anxiety.

Czar Paul I (1976-1801). Czar Paul I ascended the throne of Russia in 1796 after the death of Catherine II. Immediately after his coronation, many changes were made in the government of the country. An imperial edict declared that the order of succession to the Russian throne was to follow the principle of primogeniture. The costume, manners and occupations of the people were also changed. Military discipline was made strict. Favoured courtiers who formerly attended drill once a year and old officers who never smelt gun-powder, were called out for daily military parades. The dress and accoutrements of the Prussian army were adopted. Important changes were made in the personnel of administration. Efforts were made to remove corruption from the Russian finances. Czar Paul was a born despot and he possessed the old Russian sense of dignity. Court ceremonial was introduced and enforced with a rigour which made each day's attendance a dangerous ordeal for the trembling courtiers. The princes and ladies were compelled to come down from their vehicles into the snow to salute the passing imperial carriage. At the coronation at Moscow, the Poles saw their king relegated to a side-gallery and ordered to keep standing. A sort of a reign of terror was established in the country.

As regards foreign affairs, Czar Paul recalled Russian forces from Persia and Georgia. He released the distinguished Polish prisoners. He invited Stanislas to St. Petesburg and received him with royal honours. He went to the extent of telling the Polish leader that he did not approve of the partition of Poland. He declared a policy of peace with all. He felt that his country had been fighting since 1756 and consequently was exhausted and yearned for peace. He was prepared to be faithful to Russia's alliances and opposed by all possible means the French Republic and its Jacobinism. The Baltic policy of Catherine was continued and relations of close friendship were maintained with Denmark. Friendly relations were also established with Sweden. Paul was as good as his word : The Russian squadron was recalled and the design of despatching a Russian army of 60,000 men to the Rhine was given up. The oppressive system of recruiting was also replaced. However, there was no slackening of vigilance. Hostility to the French Revolution was a religion with him. When in later days he leaned towards Bonaparte, it was because he recognised in him the most powerful enemy of Jacobinism. Russian subjects were recalled forthwith from western travels. A strict censorship was imposed on the press and the theatre. Frenchmen entering Russia were required to produce passports attested by a Bourbon prince. In certain cases, Paul's anger against Parisian manners under the new regime was bizzare and even sank to the level of comedy High collars were denounced as symbols of liberalism. The unhappy wearer of a round-hat was chased by the police in the streets of the capital. Even an ambassador had to change his head-wear.

A ruler with Paul's bent of mental balance could not avoid trouble for long. His first diplomatic failure was with Sweden. He desired to be on good terms with that country, but met with a rebuff. Relations with France also remained unsatisfactory. In 1797, Paul patronised the Knights of St. John. There was a design to knit together all the nobility of Europe into an alliance of loyalty and honour against the invasion of those equalizing ideas which were attacking and undermining all the ranks of society. He was an 18th century crusader. While not sharing Catherine's pseudo-liberalism, he had all her willingness to shine in European politics. He was elected by the Knights of St. John to the Grand Mastership. Differences began to grow between Russia and England. The joint Anglo Russian expedition to Holland was a failure and the Russians suffered heavily. In 1799, Bonaparte handed over the Island of Malta to Russia as the Czar was the Grand Master of the Knights of St. John. The victory of Bonaparte over Austria at Marengo in Italy filled Paul with admiration for Napoleon Bonaparte. Bonaparte publicly recognised the interest taken by Paul in Sardinia, Naples and Rome and Paul must have felt gratified. Negotiations started with Bonaparte in 1800. Malta was captured by the British Government, but was not restored to Czar. Paul's anger found vent in the Second Armed Neutrality (1800). Russia, Prussia, Sweden and Denmark were brought together by means of treaties. It was agreed that every neutral vessel might navigate freely from port to port and on the coasts of the nations at war. Goods belonging to the subjects of belligerent powers with the exception of contraband of war, were to be free on neutral vessels. Neutral vessels were to be captured only for a just and sufficient cause and were to be adjudicated upon without delay. A uniform, prompt and legal procedure was to be followed. Bonaparte cooperated with the Czar. In 1801, Paul sent a messenger to Paris. He wrote to Bonaparte suggesting a French invasion of England and Napoleon Bonaparte agreed. He also asked Bonaparte to persuade Spain, Portugal and the United States to collaborate with him against Great Britain. He prepared a scheme for an invasion of India. A Russian army was to leave by way of Bokhara and Khiva. A French army was to move down the Danube. Another French army was to proceed by way of Herat and Kandhar. The Czar did not seem to care for the difficulties of the long journey through wild and hostile lands. No wonder, the British Government also hit back. In 1801, an embargo was placed on all Russian, Danish and Swedish vessels in British ports. A British fleet under Parker and Nelson was fitted out for the Baltic. The threatened powers prepared energetically for resistance. However, the Danes were defeated in the Battle of Copenhagen in 1801 but even before that, the Czar was already murdered.

It is pointed out that for many months before his murder, the Czar was showing signs of madness. He had fits of ungovernable and unreasoning rage. There was no consistency in his behaviour. People were promoted or demoted without any justification. Men of all ranks were persecuted on a mere shadow of suspicion. Officers of the guard were kicked and cuffed or confined for the most trivial offences. Ministers were exiled for a chance word. Scores of unfortunates were despatched to Siberia. One by one, he alienated all of his faithful servants. Many high officials were reprimanded, exiled or disgraced. Soldiers hated him because he treated their superiors badly. The atmosphere of suspense became unbearable. It was under these circumstances that a conspiracy was hatched and the Czar was brutally strangled in March 1801.

Alexander I (1801-25). Czar Paul was succeeded by Alexander I in 1801 and he continued to rule up to 1825. He was educated by a Swiss tutor and on account of his influence, the Czar came to have liberal ideas which dominated his mind up to 1820 when he came completely under the influence of Metternich. Alexander was an idealist and a visionary. The Holy Alliance was the outcome of his mysticism, idealism and despotism. His ideals were lofty and he sincerely believed that his mission was to apply the principles of the divine faith to the affairs of the states. He would like to play the roles of fathers to their subjects whom he considered as children. No wonder, he prevailed upon Louis XVIII of France to give a liberal charter in 1814 after his restoration. He himself gave a liberal constitution to the Polish territory under his control. A similar constitution was given to Finland which was secured by Russia at the Congress of Vienna.

After the Battle of Friedland in 1807, Alexander entered into the Treaty of Tilsit with Napoleon and agreed to cooperate with him in the enforcement of the Continental System. This state of affairs continued for some time. However, many factors combined to force Alexander to fall out with Napoleon. In 1812, Napoleon attacked Russia. After that Alexander co-operated with other European countries to bring about the fall of Napoleon. After his overthrow, Alexander was a dominating personality in the Congress of Vienna (1814-15). He had a huge army under his command and consequently was able to get his point of view accepted from the other powers. No wonder, Alexander was able to secure a lot for his country at the Congress of Vienna.

After the Congress of Vienna, the liberal ideas of Alexander began to change gradually. In 1818, he was willing to join hands with Austria and Prussia to guarantee the territorial *status quo* in Europe. In 1820, he was completely changed. At the Congress of Troppau in 1820, he made a public declaration of his conversion to Metternich and asked the latter to use him in any way he pleased to suppress the liberal forces in Europe. He was prepared to lead his troops to crush the revolts in Naples, Piedmont and Spain. Metternich cooled his enthusiasm as he was afraid of the strong military force of Russia. Alexander remained a reactionary for the rest of his life.

When the Greeks revolted against Turkey, there was every possibility of Russia going to their help. The temptation for Alexander was very great and pressure was also put on him for that purpose. However, Alexander was completely under the control of Metternich whose attitude was that the revolt should be allowed to burn itself out beyond the pale of civilisation. The result was that the revolt of Prince Ypsilanti was a complete failure. Alexander also did not help the Greeks when they raised the standard of revolt in the Island of Morea.

On the whole, Alexander I was a curious mixture of opposites. Mysticism, liberalism, despotism and imperialism were all combined in one and no wonder he was sometimes a liberal and sometimes a reactionary. Lord Byron wrote thus about him:

> "Now half dissolving to a liberal thaw,
> But hardened back whenever the morning's raw;
> With no objection to true liberty,
> Except that it would make the nations free."

The view of Ketelby is that Czar Alexander had neither the diplomatic astuteness nor the cynical persistence of Metternich. There was as little Napoleonic about his character as there was in his appearance, in his huge frame and round face, his irresolute mouth and dreamy eyes. To his contemporaries, he was a riddle. To Napoleon, he was "a shifty Byzantine" and the "Talma of the North." To Metternich, he was "a mad man to be humoured." By nature, Czar Alexander was unstable, impressionable, well-intentioned but infirm of purpose, imaginative egoist, and unpracticable and inconsistent idealist. He "erected incoherency into a system." His contemporaries saw him variously and intermittently incited by liberalism and despotism, mysticism and imperialism, and considered him unreliable and dangerous and often a deceiver and a hypocrite. From his Swiss tutor La Harpe, he imbibed the theories of Rousseau and the sentiments of French democracy. From his Russian governor, he acquired a taste for militarism and military display. The murder of his father in a conspiracy to which he himself was privy, bred in his sensitive mind a horror and remorse which later developed into a settled gloom and made him susceptible to the religious and pietistic influences of the age. In his liberal moods, he granted a constitution to Finland. He planned the regeneration of Poland. He emancipated the serfs of some of the northern Russian provinces. He supported the abolition of slavery and put forward proposals for a League of Nations. His imperialism led him to ambitious schemes for the territorial aggrandizement of Russia, to the conquest of Finland and to an alliance with Napoleon for the partition of Turkey and the subjugation of Asia. He became a prey to disillusionment and the fear of revolution and religious zeal confounded his liberalism. In the middle and last years of his life, the religious and visionary influences became dominant. As the defeat of his armies appeared to him to be a manifestation of the wrath of God, likewise, the retreat of Napoleon from Moscow was considered by him as a call to a heaven-sent mission. He began to feel that he was the divinely appointed instrument for the defeat of Napoleon. He thought of himself as the "man from the North," "from the rising of the Sun," spoken of by Isaiah, who should be summoned to the routing of Antichrist. Czar Alexander attained the height of his power in 1815. He was the conqueror of conquerors, the liberator of Europe, the soldier of God whose sword had been blessed by peoples and sanctified by the Lord.

Nicholas I (1825-55). Before his death, Alexander I appointed Nicholas I as his successor to the throne in preference to Constantine who was elder to Nicholas I. Nicholas I had a reputation as a reactionary and no wonder the liberals of Russia revolted in December 1825. Their slogan was: "Constantine and the Constitution." They demanded the rule of Constantine who was known for his liberal ideas, but the people were so ignorant that they mistook the Constitution for the wife of Constantine. Anyhow, the December revolt was put down with a heavy hand. Nicholas I ruled for 30 years. He was reactionary to the backbone. He was the very incarnation of absolutism. Autocracy reigned supreme over Russian affairs. Russia gave the appearance of absolute immobility. Liberal forces were ruthlessly suppressed. All popular manifestations were strictly controlled. Every avenue to freedom of thought and action was completely blocked. In 1826, he set up "The Third Section of the Imperial Chancery" for the detection and summary punishment of any one who advocated "political or social novelties." The record of the Third Section is one of the darkest pages in the history of Russia. The chief of police was the head of the Third Section and he was given unlimited power of arresting, imprisoning, deporting and making away with any one whom he pleased, without any restriction whatever. The Third Section "rivalled, if it did not exceed, the horrors of the Spanish Inquisition." Nicholas I tried to have his subjects from the infection of the liberal ideas of Western Europe. With that object in view, he put restrictions on foreign travel by the Russians. Foreign publications were not to be allowed to be admitted into Russia without a thorough scrutiny by the censors. Students were discouraged to join the universities. The teaching of philosophy was removed from the curriculum of the universities. Russian youngmen were not allowed to go to foreign countries for study. The press in Russia was put under censorship which was rigorously enforced. If anybody was found in possession of a forbidden book or he uttered an unguarded word, there was every likelihood of his being sent to some part of Siberia to live in exile. There was practically no trial or appeal.

After the third partition of Poland in 1795, there was no Polish state as such. All her former territory was annexed by the neighbours. But in spite of this, the national consciousness of Poland continued to be a vital factor in European politics. It was exploited by Napoleon and the subsequent enemies of Russia, Prussia and Austria. It was the inspiration of many Polish attempts to recover independence during the 19th century. Czar Alexander I granted a constitution to that part of the Russian empire which was inhabited by the Poles and himself opened the first Diet in March 1818. However, when he came under the influence of Metternich, his zeal for Polish liberties diminished. The Poles who were not satisfied with the constitution given to them, resented more and more its infringement and directed all their wrath and hostility against the Grand Duke Constantine, the brother of the Czar, who ruled the Polish territory with the powers of a Viceroy.

Czar Alexander died in 1825 and he was succeeded by Nicholas I. There was a rapid growth of secret agitation and conspiratorial societies. The Polish army was particularly infected. On hearing the news of the July Revolution in France in 1830, there was also a military revolt in Warsaw in November 1830. An attempt was made to murder the Grand Duke but it failed and he was able to escape with his life although he died later on. On 25 January 1831, the Polish revolutionaries declared the throne of Poland vacant. It was a declaration of war against Russia. On 5 February 1831, 200,000 Russians crossed the Polish frontier. It is true that the Poles fought with heroism but they were defeated on account of their disunion and lack of discipline. On 25 February 1831 they were beaten in the bloody battle of Grochow. The situation was made worse by the outbreak of cholera. In September 1831, the Polish resistance was completely broken. In February 1832, the Organic Statute was issued by Czar Nicholas I by which the constitution granted by Alexander I was abolished and Poland was incorporated into the Russian Empire though it was to have a separate government. The Organic Statute was followed by harsh disciplinary measures. An amnesty was granted but it was most unsatisfactory. The soldiers who had taken part in the revolt were drafted into remote Russian regiments. The male children of the rebels were carried off to Russia and brought up in Russian military schools. The Polish universities and schools were abolished. Even the national pictures were removed from the museums of Warsaw to Moscow and St. Petersburg. The Organic Statute which was not a liberal document at all remained a dead letter. All effective Government was conducted from the Russian capital. There were spasmodic risings in 1833 and they made the situation still worse. After the rising of 1846, the Organic Statute was revoked by the Government.

As regards his foreign policy, Nicholas I considered himself to be a champion of autocracy and the enemy of all progressive movements. In 1831, he was prevented by the Polish revolt from interfering in France on behalf of the Bourbon king. In 1833, he formed a close alliance with Austria and Prussia for mutual defence against revolutionary movements and to suppress liberalism. This triple alliance made Nicholas I the central figure in the European system and raised the prestige of Russia in Europe. In 1849, he sent his troops to fight against the Hungarians who had revolted against Austria and declared themselves an independent republic. They were also accused of oppressing the Croats, Slovaks and Rumanians. He threatened to interfere against the nationalist movement in Germany. It was his hostile attitude that was one of the important factors which forced Frederick William IV of Prussia to refuse the crown offered to him by the Frankfurt Parliament in 1849.

When he came to the throne, the Greek War of Independence was continuing. To begin with, he co-operated with England and France to help the Greeks against Turkey. The Russian fleet also participated in the naval battle of Navarino which completely destroyed the combined fleets of Turkey and Egypt. Although after the death of Canning, both England and France left the war, Nicholas continued to support the cause of the Greeks. The result was that in 1829, the independence of

Greece was recognised. The importance of the help given by Nicholas I to the Greek cause cannot be minimized.

Mehmet Ali had helped the Sultan of Turkey in the Greek War of Independence. After the war, he was given the island of Crete as a reward for his services. Mehmet Ali considered it to be inadequate and taking advantage of the weakness of the Sultan, he occupied Syria and Asia Minor. When he seemed to threaten Constantinople, the Sultan asked for Russian help. It was in these circumstances that the Treaty of Unkiar Skelessi was signed in 1833. Russia was to come to the help of Turkey and whenever she was at war, the Dardanelles was to be closed to the warships of other nations. This treaty made Russia the master of the Black Sea and protected her against invaders. It also opened the way into the Mediterranean for Russia.

In 1840, Russia co-operated with Great Britain, Austria and Prussia to maintain the integrity of Turkey. The four powers met in London and decided to help the Sultan. The Quadruple Alliance was considered to be an insult to France and there was every possibility of a war. However, Premier Thiers of France was dismissed by Louis Philippe. As a result of the concerted action of the European powers, Ibrahim, son of Mehmet Ali, was driven out from Syria and ultimately forced to surrender in 1841. By the Convention of the Straits of 1841, all the powers agreed to recognize the right of the Sultan to give a passage into the Black Sea through the Dardanelles and Bosphorus at will. Russia declared to treaty of 1833 as cancelled.

In 1844, Nicholas I visited London and proposed the partition of Turkey whose fall seemed to be inevitable to him. He proposed to allow England to have Egypt and Crete and himself would like to have control over the Balkans. He declared that he had no intention to occupy Constantinople. The offer was rejected by the British Government.

Finding Great Britain unwilling to interfere in Turkey, Nicholas I declared to act single-handed. He demanded the right of protecting the orthodox Christians in Turkey. As the demand was refused, Nicholas I ordered the occupation of the Danubian principalities in 1853. It was in these circumstances that the Crimean War started. Great Britain, France and Sardinia intervened to protect Turkey against Russian aggression. The Crimean War continued from 1854 to 1856. In the midst of the War, Nicholas I died in 1855.

It is clear from the above that Nicholas I followed a vigorous foreign policy and the influence of Russia was felt all over Europe.

About Nicholas I, Ketelbey says that his entire reign was spent in defence of autocracy. The Russian armies were lent abroad to support autocracy as in the case of Hungary. At home, all kinds of measures were adopted to exclude or suppress liberal ideas. "A stringent intellectual quarantine" was maintained on the western frontiers. All foreign literature of a political or philosophical nature was excluded. The Russian subjects were not allowed to go abroad. Censorship was imposed on the press in the country. Those writers who were not considered to be "well intentioned," were silenced. The humblest and the most powerful servants of the Emperor were protected from all kinds of criticism. Strict control was maintained on universities. The police was given arbitrary powers of "arresting, imprisoning, deporting and making away with" any one who was suspected by the chief of the police. Russian literature was encouraged so that the attention of the people might be diverted from politics. Russian nationalism was emphasized to counteract the influence of international liberalism. The people of Russia were treated as an army which was to be drilled in habits and thoughts. This was the condition when the Crimean War came. The Russians were defeated. The halo of autocracy was removed. The dishonesty and incompetency of Russian bureaucracy was exposed. The whole of the system was condemned. Russian autocracy was shamed and discontentment came into the open. Russian society was stirred by a violent movement. The condition of Russia was as that of France on the eve of the French Revolution.

We may conclude with the following comparison of Nicholas I with Philip II of Spain by Lipson: "Nicholas, like Philip, was an anachronism in the generation in which he lived. He was a 'Don Quixote of autocracy,' fanatically opposed to the spirit of his age, and fighting with unyielding tenacity for a worn-out ideal. Throughout Europe, he was the indomitable foe of democracy, just as the Spanish monarchy in the sixteenth century was the sworn enemy of the Reformation. Each employed similar instruments, the one the Inquisition, the other the Third Section; and they made their realms 'intellectual quarantines' in order to isolate them from the disintegrating influence of European thought. But the real strength of the monarchical structure in Russia, as in Spain, lay in the apathetic indifference and unquestioning loyalty of their subjects; and this was also the source of its weakness, for the structure was bound to crumble to pieces once the nation awakened to political consciousness. This awakening was delayed in Russia until 1855, when the Crimean War had the same effect upon her people which the destruction of the Spanish Armada had upon Spain, shattering their faith in the existing regime and in their own invincibility."

Alexander II (1855-81). Alexander II ascended the throne of Russia in 1885 in the midst of the Crimean War. It was he who had to negotiate and sign the humiliating Treaty of Paris of 1856. So far as the Black Sea was concerned, the Russian influence was completely liquidated for the next fourteen years.

After ending the Crimean War, Alexander II devoted his attention to domestic affairs. There was a lot of discontentment in the country. The people were bitter against the autocratic government which was considered to be responsible for their defeat in the Crimean War and the humiliating peace of 1856. Under the circumstances, it was considered to be desirable to give some concessions to the people with a view to appeasing them.

Abolition of Serfdom: The most important reform of Alexander II was the abolition of serfdom in 1861. There were about 45 million serfs in Russia, forming about half of their population. 23 million belonged to the Crown and the rest to private lords, the Church and other institutions. The condition of the serfs on the royal lands was better than those who were in private hands. The serfs from royal lands suffered from very heavy taxation, from forced labour and from various kinds of fiscal dues which were extorted from them. Restrictions were imposed on their movements and their right to acquire and dispose of property. However, they were grouped together in village communities known as Mirs and they enjoyed a certain measure of self-government through elected councils and village elders. The condition of other serfs in private hands varied with the character and views of their owners. They had practically no power of redress against any abuse on the part of their owners. There were very many cases of cruelty and oppression. The law of Russia gave the owner power "to impose upon his serfs every kind of labour, to exact money dues and personal services from them." An owner could sell a serf. He could send him to Siberia. He could hand him over as a recruit to the army. "They perished by hundreds in the factories established....to augment the incomes of these great landed proprietors. They were subjected to inhuman punishments, imprisoned, in underground cellars, kept in chains, or flogged to death with the knout....a whole series of such crimes were brought to light....on the properties of the highest dignitaries of state....men who enjoyed in St. Petersburg the reputation of statesmen and even of philanthropists." The serfs in Russia were more unfortunate than those in France before 1789. They were slaves in the real sense of the term.

Serfdom had its own effects on Russian society. It resulted in the moral degeneration of the owners. There was economic stagnation. There was the constant fear of insurrection. When the nobles were released from their obligation to military service in 1762, the serfs began to demand the abolition of serfdom. It was contended that serfdom was a corollary of compulsory military service among the nobles. There were many revolts during the reign of Nicholas I. Nicholas I himself thought of abolishing serfdom but he did not go beyond the appointment of commissions of enquiry. He died during the Crimean War. When the war was ended and the Treaty of Paris was signed. Alexander II decided to solve the problem of serfs.

Alexander II made definite proposals to the nobility. He addressed them in these words, "You know that the present system of serfs ownership cannot remain as it is; it is better that we should abolish it from above, than wait until it begins to abolish itself from below....Gentlemen, I beg you examine how this reform can be made." Outwardly, the nobility showed that they were in agreement with the King, but practically they did nothing to set their serfs free. The result was that the Government had to take the initiative in this matter. At the end of 1857, the nobles of the Lithuanian Province of the Russian Empire petitioned for a revision of the relations between the nobles and the serfs in their favour. Alexander II pretended that Lithuanian nobles wanted to emancipate their serfs and called upon the other provinces of Russia to follow the generous and patriotic example of Lithuania. The result was that Committees authorised by the Czar were formed "for ameliorating the conditions of the peasants." It was found that there was a conflict of interests and many problems had to be tackled in this connection. It was in 1861 that the edict of Emancipation was issued to abolish serfdom. About 35 million people were set free.

The edict of emancipation had both moral and economic importance. It was based on four main principles. The first principle was embodied in the concession of full civil rights to the emancipated serfs. Every serf became a free peasant and he was absolved from bondage to his masters. The second principle was that he was given not only freedom, but also some land and the noble lost thereby not only his labour, but also some of the property. This was done with a view to avoid the problem of the landless labourers which had been faced in other countries previously. The amount of land to be given to each emancipated peasant was to be fixed in each case by magistrates called Arbiters of the Peace who were to decide between the nobles and the peasants. It is true that the Arbiters in most cases were local proprietors, but experience shows that they did their job impartially. The third principle was that the land was not given to the peasants as personal property. It was given to the Mir or the village group and the peasant was attached to that land. The Mir held the land and it was collectively responsible for certain yearly payments which were to be given to the Lord in compensation. The fourth principle was that the Government was to give all the money to the Mirs required for payment to the landlords for the loss of their lands. The Government was to receive six per cent interest for a period of 49 years. Thus, the peasants were not only made free but were also given land for their subsistence. The collective ownership of the Mir was substituted for the private ownership of the lord and the entire peasant body became responsible for the collection of redemption dues.

So far as the effect of the abolition of serfdom on the land-owning classes was concerned, it varied in different parts of the country. Generally, it resulted in an enforced economy and a more scientific administration of their estates. The landowners were forced to rely upon whatever was left to them and consequently, they had to be very careful not only in spending, but also in finding out ways and means to produce more out of the balance of the land left to them. To quote one nobleman, "Formerly we kept no accounts and drank champagne. Now we keep accounts and content ourselves with beer." As regards the peasants, there was a lot of disappointment among them. Outwardly; the edict of emancipation seemed to be revolutionary, but in actual practice, it did not bring any great change in the condition of the peasants. After their emancipation they found themselves burdened with new taxes which were often more than the normal rent of their lands. They found the new taxes to be a very heavy drain on their scanty resources. The serfs had come to regard the land they occupied as their own, and consequently, they did not find any justification for making any payment to the landlords. Moreover, the authority of the Mirs was as much irritating to the peasants as that of their previous landlords. The general feeling among the peasants was that their emancipation was an illusion. The general feeling can be summed up in the following question : "What, then, is this liberty?" It is contended that the emancipation of the serfs was a great humanitarian act on the part of the Czar. If Russia was to be a progressive country, serfdom could not be allowed to continue. The abolition of serfdom freed a large number of persons who were later on employed in the factories of Russia. Thus indirectly the cause of industrialisation of the country was promoted. The area under cultivation increased and the total output of the country also began to rise. The value of land also began to increase. The state was able to get more taxes. There was an increase in export trade. The condition of the peasants also improved. However, the abolition of serfdom was not an unmixed blessing. Many peasants found themselves in a worse condition than before. The lands allotted to them were so small that it was difficult for them to have a comfortable living. The burden of installments which had to be paid to the state was very great. If the tyranny of the lords was ended, that of the Mir was imposed. The emancipated peasants were harassed by the tax collectors and police officials of the Central Government. The treatment of the state authorities was often harsh.

David Thomson maintains that the decree of emancipation gave the Russian peasants legal freedom and not economic freedom. They became the subjects of the Government. They were not required to pay dues to their former owner either in forced labour or in money. The control of the Mir replaced the old authority of the gentry. It was the Mir which paid the redemption money collectively, collected it under sanction of forced labour and other exactions and supervised the allocation and cultivation of the land by the members of the village community. Emancipation meant the abolition of personal servitude but the affirmation of communal responsibilities. The committees of nobles which were set up everywhere to carry out the reform were anxious to avoid the evils of the proletariat in the West. The peasant was to be given a stake in the soil and he was not left free to take up, try or migrate to towns. For that purpose, he required the permission of the Mir and that was not always given. The freedom of movement came when the Mir ceased to be collectively responsible for village dues and taxes and that happened only after 1905.

David Thomson is of the view that if emancipation was a mixed blessing for the peasants, it was usually a welcome arrangement for the landowners. The Russian nobility secured nearly half the arable lands. It was relieved of its responsibilities for the serfs. It received the redemption money in place of the serfs. The aristocracy was strengthened but not weakened by the change. Opposition to the measure came not from the aristocracy, gentry of Russia, but from the intellectuals.

The emancipation of the serfs did not bring about any marked change in the methods or output of agriculture. Whatever its object, the authority in the Mirs fell in the hands of ignorant and non-enterprising persons. For the next 40 years, the land was still mostly cultivated in strips. The traditional crops continued to be grown. The progressive and scientific methods of agriculture were not introduced. Each male child had a right to such land and the land of the Mir had to be divided periodically to provide for the new generation. The growing population made a decline in the size or the number of strips which each peasant held. The peasant had no incentive to improve his land which he was likely to lose at the next redistribution. He found it difficult to live on his holding. In certain cases, the peasants bought lands from the nobles. A few of them moved to the eastern frontier. As the productivity did not keep pace with the growth of population, famines became more frequent. Personal and family misfortunes ruined many peasants. Great inequalities arose and 80% of the redemption money was advanced by the state and repaid by the peasants in installments spread over many years. The redemptions were collected along with regular state taxes. The additional burden proved unbearable and by 1905, the outstanding arrears were cancelled.

Taking all these factors into consideration, David Thomson has come to the conclusion that the decree of emancipation did little to improve either the economic lot of most of the peasants or the economic prosperity of the country as a whole. It also did not make for a more stable and acceptable political system. Discontentment continued to grow and that provided an opportunity to the extreme Marxists and Anarchists to do their work in Russia. The Czar got neither credit, nor strength from these reforms. He was nearly assassinated in 1856, in 1873 and 1880 and finally killed by a bomb in 1881.

Judicial Reforms. Certain reforms were carried out in the judicial field in 1862. The trial of civil and criminal cases was transferred from the administrative officials to the courts of justices which were modelled after Western Europe. Provision was made for the election of the justices of the peace by the people. There were also to be district and circuit judges. The Senate was to act as the highest court of appeal. Instructions were given for the codification of the laws of the country. Prosecuting attorneys were appointed. Criminal cases were to be tried by means of jury. The trials were to be held in public and not in secret. The only exception was made in the case of the political offenders who could still be punished without any fair trial.

Zemstvos. A decree of 1864 provided that district of the 33 administrative provinces or governments into which Russia was divided, was to have a local assembly or Zemstvo. The Zemstvo was to consist of landlords and the representatives of the peasants and townsmen. It was to have control over public works, churches schools, prisons, poor relief and public health. It was also given the power of levying taxes. However, the provincial governor was given the power of veto over the action of the Zemstvos. Although their powers and functions were limited, the Zemstovs were to serve as the political training ground of the people. They were an important step in the direction of decentralization and self-government.

Polish Revolt (1863). The reforming zeal of the Czar got a setback after 1863. It was in that year that the people of Poland revolted against Russia. As in the case of Russia, Alexander II had followed a policy of moderation and liberalism towards his Polish subjects. The repressive system of Nicholas I was relaxed. The political exiles were allowed to return. The Polish Council of State was re-established, together with the Commission for the Regulation of Religious Affairs and Education which had been abolished in 1839. A considerable measure of self-Government was also given to the Poles. The Polish administration was separated from that of Russia. The civil and military departments were made separate and the former were put into the hands of the Poles. A system of local Government with elected councils was set up in Poland. Polish education was encouraged. The University of Warsaw was restored. The use of the Polish language was allowed in the schools. In brief, an honest effort was made to satisfy the nationalist aspirations of the Poles. However, this policy failed. The declaration of religious equality was welcomed by the Jews but was condemned by the Roman Catholics who considered it as a device to further the cause of the Orthodox Church. The political concessions were interpreted as a sign of weakness on the part of the Government. Encouraged by the emancipation of the Russian serfs, the extremists among the Poles increased their agitation and raised their claims. They demanded not only the complete independence of a new Polish Republic but also the re-establishment of the old "Great Poland" as it existed before its first partition in 1772. That would have involved a surrender of territories by Prussia and Austria also. Such demands were resented by the Russians and Alexander II himself decided to put an end to them. The Poles replied with intrigue, conspiracy and violence. The conciliatory or repressive measures of the Czar had no effect on the extremists among the Poles who were determined to have a revolution. In the spring of 1863, the Czar tried to put an end to the revolutionary agitation by enrolling a number of political suspects in Russian regiments scattered throughout the Russian Empire. The threatened men fled to the forests and raised the banner of insurrection. The extremists rose at once but the moderates hesitated. For even they joined the revolutionaries when they were given an assurance that Napoleon III of France would come to their help.

It is pointed out that the Polish insurrection of 1863 was not a war between organised armies as was the case in 1830. Trouble arose at one place while the same was being suppressed at another place. It was not a war of regular tactics and pitched battles but of raids and surprises. There was frightful brutality on both sides. There was heat and force but there were no chances of success of the Poles against the Russian army. The Poles were themselves divided. The nobles, gentry, townsfolk and the priesthood rose in revolt with enthusiasm but the peasants had their grievances against their lords and refused to join. Only foreign support could have helped the cause of the Poles. Prussia refused to help as she wanted to cultivate friendship with Russia. Bismarck is stated to have observed, "It is a matter of life and death to us also." He posted cordons of Prussian troops along the Polish frontier and thereby helped the Russians to crush the Poles. As regards France, Napoleon III took interest in the Polish cause. He was ready with his proposal of a European congress to help the Poles but England refused to oblige him as she suspected that Napoleon wanted to fish in troubled waters merely for his own advantage. Austria also refused to cooperate because Napoleon III raised the question of Poland along with that of Venetia and this was not liked by Austria. "The sorry result of weeks of negotiations was the presentation, first to Prussia and finally to Russia, of colourless protests which those Powers could afford to treat with contempt." The result was that the Poles were left to their fate.

The struggle in Poland was carried on by a self-constituted body, the secret national government at Warsaw. It terrorised and killed the Poles themselves. The Czar promised an amnesty and preservation and continuation of reforms but the Poles did not surrender. However, slowly and slowly the insurrection was suppressed by March 1864.

As a result of the revolt in 1863, Poland was deprived of all autonomy. The Polish kingdom was incorporated into the Russian Empire as the "Ten Governments of the Vistula." The Polish nobility was completely discredited and the Russian Government adopted the policy of winning over the peasants of Poland. A vast scheme of agrarian reform was undertaken in pursuance of that policy. All the peasants irrespective of the nature of their tenure, were turned into free holders. However, they were to continue to enjoy their right of access to the forests and pastures of their former landlords. The landlords received compensation, but they were compelled to take it in the form of treasury bonds so that they may continue to have interest in maintaining the credit of the Government. As a result of these decrees, a body of 1,340,000 peasant proprietors was created. More laws were passed to segregate the peasants from the rest of the community. The peasants were grouped in communes with an elected assembly taken wholly from the peasant class. The larger land-owners and the clergy were excluded. To the assembly was given the power of regulating all the affairs of the village community and the conduct of its relations with the Russian Government. The intention was to keep the happy peasant pure and undefiled by contact with the elements most hostile to Russia; the effect was to deliver him body and soul to the petty tyranny of the local representatives of Russian majesty." A policy of Russification was also deliberately followed in Poland. Every effort was made to remove or repress every stimulus to Polish nationalism and to effect complete organic incorporation of Poland with Russia. As the Roman Catholic Church was the backbone of Polish nationalism, it was deprived of its privileges and the ecclesiastical lands were confiscated and monasteries were suppressed. The Russian language was made the sole medium of public communication in the state and instruction in schools and universities. In course of time, the Poles were replaced by Russians in the courts of justice and other official posts. All those who had taken part in the revolt were banished. All movements towards independent political activity were suppressed. Every effort was made to keep people away from politics by keeping them well amused. The social life of Warsaw was encouraged in every way. Large sums were spent by the Russian Government on theatres and the opera. The result was that Warsaw rapidly developed into a cosmopolitan city of pleasure, the Paris of Eastern Europe.

It is pointed out that "on the ruins of the Polish revolution rose the work of Bismarck and the system of Russification in the Empire of the Cazars." This means that the Polish revolt enabled Bismarch to win over Russia. This he did by offering help to Russia against the Poles. It was this timely offer of help which enabled Bismarch to count upon the neutrality of Russia in 1866 and 1870 when he fought against Austria and France respectively. The Polish revolt also made the Czar the enemy of liberalism. He not only became a reactionary but also followed a policy of Russification of the minorities within the Russian Empire. The object was to crush the nationalist aspirations of the subjects and thereby absorb them into Russia.

Foreign Policy. As regards foreign policy, reference has already been made to the ending of the Crimean War. In 1865, Alexander II encouraged the Greeks of Crete to revolt against Turkey and demand their union with Greece. In 1870, he helped the Bulgars to establish a national Orthodox Church of their own, independent of the Greek patriarch at Constantinople. In 1870, he was able to repudiate the Black Sea clauses of the Treaty of Paris. He fortified Sebastopol and also maintained the Russian fleet in the Black Sea.

The rule of the Turks over the Christians of the Balkans was extremely oppressive. No wonder, there was a revolt in Bosnia and Herzegovina. There was also revolt of the Bulgars in 1875. The revolts were crushed with so much ferocity and ruthlessness that there was a demand to turn out the Turks bag and baggage from the Balkans. Although Great Britain did not come to the help of the Christians in the Balkans, Russia did come to their help and the result was the Russo-Turkish War of 1877-8. After some resistance, the Turks collapsed and Russia was able to impose the Treaty of San Stefano of 1878. A big Bulgaria was created. The Sultan was to carry out radical reforms in Bosnia and Herzegovina. He was to pull down all the fortifications along the Danube and open the Dardanelles and the Bosphorus to the free commerce of all nations. The Czar was to get a part of Armenia, a large war indemnity and a strip of Dobrudja.

The Treaty of San Stefano was not approved by other European powers and both Great Britain and Austria were prepared to go on war against Russia if the treaty was not submitted to a conference of European powers. As Russia was exhausted, she submitted. The result was that the Treaty of Berlin divided Bulgaria, into two parts and deprived Russia of all the gains which she had secured by the Treaty of San Stefano.

The liberals of Russia did not approve of the reactionary policies of Alexander II and consequently they continued their propaganda throughout the country. The result was that many secret and revolutionary societies came into existence. The industrialization of the country added to the discontentment of the people. The result was that Alexander himself was killed in 1881 by the explosion of a bomb hurled by the Nihilists.

Alexander III (1881-94). Alexander II was succeeded by his son. Alexander III, who ruled for 13 years. He was rough in body and mind and devoid of all polish and sentiments and he glorified in that fact. He was thoroughly devoted to the cause of the Slavs. He was sworn enemy of liberalism and believed whole-heartedly in autocracy. To quote him, "The voice of God orders us to stand firm at the held of government with faith in the strength and truth of the Autocratic power which we are called to consolidate and to preserve for the good of the people from every kind of encroachment." He had two energetic assistants who helped him in his policy and those were *Plehve and Pobedonostsev*. Plehve was put in charge of the police department and he organised the Russian police so efficiently that it could be used successfully to carry out the orders of the Czar. Pobedonostsev was a professor of law and a tutor of Alexander III. He was appointed as "Procurator of the Holy Synod" which controlled the Orthodox Church of Russia. In his new position, Pobedonostsev ordered the life and thought of the clergymen of Russia in such a way as was in line with the wishes of the Czar. Pobedonostsev's view was that the legislatures were the breeding places of the selfish, and ambitious persons. Freedom of the press was nothing more than the spread of falsehood. Secular education was immoral and dangerous. Trial by jury was "an invitation to the arts of casuistry." Limited monarchy was "a vain fancy." To quote him, "If all representatives of the people were saints, a parliamentary regime would be the very best kind of all, but as the morality of popular representatives is usually more than dubious, a parliamentary regime is the worst." His object was to quarantine the people of Russia from the infection of the liberal ideas of the West.

Persons who were in any way suspected to be associated with the murder of Alexander II were severely punished. Systematic efforts were made to crush liberalism and revolutionary ideas within the Russian Empire. The administration of the Mirs or village communities was put under the control of the landed proprietors who were appointed by the Central Government. The powers of the Zemstvos and Dumas were curtailed. Their constitutions were altered in such a way as to give more representation to the nobles and officials and exclude the professional classes altogether. The governors were given greater authority to use their powers of veto. Secular schools were discredited and the church schools were favoured. The State tried to control the curriculum and teaching staff of the universities. Censorship was imposed on all kinds of publication. Even private correspondence could be interfered with. Restrictions were imposed on associations and meetings. The police could arrest any person arbitrarily and also impose any punishment it pleased. Political offenders were liable to be exiled to Siberia or imprisoned in Russia.

Alexander III also followed a policy of Russification. No language other than the Russian and no religion other than the Orthodox, was to be tolerated within the Russian Empire. The minorities were to be crushed. They were required to give up their language, religion, customs and traditions and obey the Czar completely. Pobedonostsev persecuted all persons who did not belong to the Orthodox Church. The Czar issued decree after decree, goading on his officials to intensify their campaign of Russification. The Catholics of Poland were very harshly treated. The church was interfered with. Their schools were completely Russianised. Their literature and language were to be taught in Russian. They were excluded from all public offices in Poland. They were not allowed to sell their land to non-Russians. In White Russia and Lithuania, the Catholics were discriminated against. Their marriages and their children were treated as illegitimate. In the case of the Ukraine, the use of the Little Russian language was prohibited for printing, reciting or singing. In Latvia and Estonia, Russian was made the official language and the approval of the Procurator of the Holy Synod was required for making any new building for the Protestant Church. German language was not to be used in the university lectures or instruction in the schools. German place names were changed to Russian names. Local law-courts were suppressed. The Jews were also persecuted with great severity. In 1882, it was laid down that the Jews could not buy land. Restrictions were put on their admission to schools and universities. To begin with, their quota was fixed at 10 per cent but it was later on reduced to 3 per cent. It was laid down in 1890 that all Jews living in the interior of Russia were to migrate to the western provinces. If they did not do so, they were to get licences from the government. They were not allowed to own or lease land. They were put under the strict control and supervision of the government. Many Russian officials organised Pogroms or wholesale massacres of the Jews. The position of the Jews became intolerable and no wonder about three lakhs of them migrated from Russia in 1891 alone. Alexander III vigorously pursued a policy of imperialism. The conquest and occupation of Turkestan was vigorously pushed forward. A military regime was established throughout the Caucasus. Russian influence in Persia became supreme. He interfered in the affairs of Bulgaria and that resulted in a lot of tension. Prince Alexander of Bulgaria protested against Russian interference and ultimately abdicated. He was succeeded by Ferdinand. While he was supported by Austria and England, he was opposed by Russia and Germany. The stalemate continued but Bismarck managed to see that it did not result in an open clash between Russia and Austria. Alexander III encouraged the anti-Austrian feeling in Serbia and won over the tiny State of Montenegro. The Three Emperors' League was continued up to 1887. However, it could not be continued further on account of the Bulgarian crisis and the differences between Russia and Austria. Under these circumstances, the Reinsurance Treaty was made in 1887. This was also allowed to lapse in 1890 by William II after the resignation of Bismarck. Thus, the ground was prepared for a military alliance between Russia and France and it was concluded in 1893.

Nicholas II (1894-1917). Alexander III was succeeded by his son, Nicholas II. He was a weak man and he believed in mysticism and fatalism. He was obstinate. His wife had complete control over him. Unfortunately, she herself was under the influence of Rasputin. She considered him as a friend and divine counsellor. No important appointment could be made without his approval and it was true of any new policy. Rasputin was himself a thorough-going reactionary.

Nicholas II himself believed in autocratic principles and held the view that the lessening of his authority was "a senseless dream." He allowed Pobedonostsev to continue in his old job up to 1905. As regards Plehve, he was appointed in 1902 as the Minister of the Interior and given dictatorial powers. It was under these circumstances that the old policy of Russification, persecution and reaction was continued. The Armenian Church was interfered with. The Pogroms against the Jews became more and more frequent. Russian officials themselves were involved in them. Russian language was imposed on the Poles, Lithuanians, the Finns, Estonians, Latvians, etc. Plehve was appointed the Secretary of State for Finland to pursue vigorously the policy of Russification in that country.

The industrialisation of the country began to progress with great speed. Coal-fields and iron mines began to be extensively worked out, Oil wells began to be exploited. The factories made their appearance at various places. Shipping industry began to grow. The annual output of pig iron and coal increased tremendously. This wonderful progress was partly due to the flow of the French capital and partly to the cheap labour of the ex-serfs of Russia. Railway construction was pushed forward and that also helped the cause of industrialisation, trade and commerce. The building of the Trans-Siberian and Trans-Caspian Railways was bound to add to the wealth of the country. However, in spite of this development, Russia remained essentially an agricultural country.

Industrialisation in Russia had progressed under Count Serge Witte who was appointed the head of the department of railways in the ministry of finance of Alexander III. In 1892, he was appointed the minister of communications. Next year, he was made the minister of finance. Witte held that post for 10 years and during that period big business developed in Russia. Protection was given to the infant industries of Russia by a policy of protection. Foreign investments were encouraged. Bounties were given to the indigenous infant industries. Russian currency was stabilized and put on a gold basis. State banks were strengthened. Russian labour was made more efficient. This was done by making liquor business a state monopoly and reducing drunkenness among the workers. Workers were insured against accidents. The government started controlling the working of the factories and mines. The growth of industrialisation helped the cause of Russian imperialism.

There was a lot of opposition to the policies of Witte. Industrialisation strengthened the hands of the workers and thereby helped the cause of liberalism. No wonder, Plehve and Pobedonostsev pointed out the dangerous consequences of the policies of Witte. The landlords also opposed him as agriculture was ignored and prominence was given to industrialisation. It was under these circumstances that Witte retired in 1903. However, his policies were continued.

Russian imperialism brought her into conflict with Japan who was determined to check Russian influence and extend her own. In the Russo-Japanese War of 1904-5, Russia was defeated by Japan. The war was ended by the Treaty of Portsmouth in September 1905 by which Russia surrendered to Japan Port Arthur, Liaotung and a part of the Island of Sakhalin. Russia also agreed to leave Korea to Japan and Manchuria to China.

In 1907, Russia made up her differences with Japan and in the same year she made the Anglo-Russian Convention. It was agreed that neither England nor Russia was to interfere in the affairs of Tibet. Chinese sovereignty over Tibet was recognised. Russia was to deal with Afghanistan through the British Government. As regards Persia, Russia was to have her sphere of influence in the north and England in the south.

Nihilism in Russia. It is desirable at this stage to refer to the growth of Nihilism in Russia and the failure of the liberal experiment in that country. As regards Nihilism, the reactionary policies of Alexander II created feelings of disappointment and bitterness in the country. The feeling of bitterness passed through many stages. The first phase was the most pessimistic and the people started feeling that there was no room for liberal ideas in Russia. However, after reading the works of radical philosophers and scientists of Western Europe, the intellectuals of Russia became destructive critics and came to be known as the Nihilists. According to Stepniak, "The fundamental principle of Nihilism was absolute individualism. It was the negation in the name of individual liberty, of all the obligations imposed upon the individual by society, by family life, and by religion." Turgenieff defined a Nihilist as a "man who submits to no authority, and accepts not a single principle upon faith merely, however high such a principle may stand in the eyes of man." The Nihilists were extreme individualists who tested every human institution and custom by reason. As few Russian institutions stood the test, the Nihilists condemned them all. The Nihilists did not form a party of action, but their reckless criticism of the government, religion, marriage and ethics brought down upon them the displeasure of the authorities and the Nihilists either ran away to foreign countries or began to work in secret. While in exile they came into contact with other advanced radical schools of thought. One of those schools was represented by Bakunin who had managed to escape from Siberia and was living in London. Bakumin was an anarchist and believed in the immediate destruction of all existing institutions in the interests of human freedom so that "all these millions of poor human beings who are cheated, enslaved, overworked and exploited....may henceforth and for ever breathe in absolute freedom." On the ruins of the old society, a new one was to be constructed on socialistic lines.

Another movement was started in Russia after 1870. Its object was to send educated Russian young men and women to the countryside and to factories with a view to establishing their contacts with them and thereby awaken them from their lethargy and indifference to the state of affairs in the country. The members mixed with the people and tried "to found on the ruins of the present social organisation the Empire of the working classes." They worked under the most discouraging conditions with the heroism and self-sacrifice of the missionaries. A typical case was that of Sophie Berdine who got employment in a spinning factory and worked 15 hours a day only with the object of influencing the other workers in the factory. She was arrested for discussing a pamphlet before a group of workers and she admitted in the court that her aim "was to arouse in the conscience of the workers the ideals of a better organization more conformable to justice; to point out the vices of the present organization in order to prevent the return of the same errors." It is estimated that between 1872 and 1878, about two to three thousands of such missionaries were active in this work of propaganda. However, they did not succeed in their mission on account of the opposition of the police and the arbitrary methods of the government. Many of them were imprisoned or exiled to Siberia.

As peaceful propaganda was found to be impossible, violence was considered to be the only other alternative. It was felt that the only appropriate reply to the tyrannical rule of the Czar was the employment of terrorist methods. The terrorists were not bloodthirsty or cruel by nature. They simply believed that no progress was possible in Russia without getting rid of the unscrupulous and reactionary officials. They perfected their organization and entered upon a period of violence. Many high officials were disposed of in that way, but in return, many of the revolutionaries were also executed by the government. In the winter of 1878-79, nearly 2,000 arrests were made in St. Petersburg alone. The suspected persons were not given any fair trial and were summarily executed. Thousands of them were arrested and sent to Siberia by simple administrative decrees. Ultimately, the terrorists decided to kill the Czar himself. In April 1879, a school-master, Solovief by name, fired five shots at the Emperor but all of them were ineffective. In December of the same year, a train in which the Czar was supposed to be returning was wrecked, just as it reached Moscow, by a mine placed between the rails. However, the Czar was saved as he had already arrived by an earlier train. In February 1880, another attempt was made to kill the Czar while at dinner in St. Petersburg. The dynamite exploded and 10 soldiers were killed and 53 wounded. The floor of the dining room was torn up, but the Czar escaped as he did not go to dinner at the usual hour.

St. Petersburg was thoroughly terrorized. Czar Alexander II appointed Melikoff practically a dictator and the latter tried to follow a policy of moderation. He released hundreds of prisoners and commuted the death sentence in many cases. He urged the Czar to give the people some share in the government so that the Nihilist movement which was merely the violent expression of the discontentment of the people, might be weakened. His view was that concessions should be given without in any way undermining the authority of the Czar. After a lot of hesitation, the Czar ordered on 30 March 1881 the publication of the scheme of Melikoff in the official journal. However, on that very day, as he was returning from a drive, a bomb was thrown on his carriage. The carriage was wrecked and many of his escorts were injured, Alexander II escaped as if by miracle but a second bomb exploded near him as he was trying to help the injured. He was very badly, hurt and died within an hour. This was the end of the Czar Liberator. Although the hopes of the liberals in Russia were dashed, the Nihilist movement did not end. As Alexander III and Nicholas II followed a policy of ruthless repression, Nihilism was the only appropriate reply. Both Plehve and Pobedonostsev followed a policy of revenge. There was no peace in the country. There was terrorism everywhere. The liberals gave up all hopes and waited for better days to come.

Liberal Experiment in Russia. In the atmosphere of reaction and repression, certain new factors made their appearance. The Russian Czar encouraged the industrial development of the country with a view to having more armaments for imperialist purposes. However, with the advance of industrial revolution, their came to the front merchants, factory owners and bankers who made up their minds to put a check on the unrestricted powers of the Czar. Being affected by the Western ideas of liberalism, a group of these intellectuals began in 1902 the publication of a paper called *Liberation* at Stuttgart in Germany. In 1904, a liberal political party called the "Union of Liberators" was organized. At the same time, anarchist propaganda was making headway in the country. In 1904, Plehve was assassinated and Russian armies began to suffer defeats at the hands of the Japanese in the Russo-Japanese War. Both these factors had their effect on the Russian Government.

Nicholas II was in a mood to make a change in his policy and with that object he appointed Prince Mirski, a man of liberal tendencies, as Minister of Home Affairs in September 1904. The new minister declared that "though the Russian people are as yet unfit for constitutional government, the local representative institutions of the Empire, the Zemstvos, might be given greater freedom of action and larger opportunities without risk to the established system." He referred to the "sincere confidence in the people" as the basis of good government. The press was given greater freedom of expression. In November 1904, representatives from the Zemstvos were permitted to meet in St. Petersburg to discuss what they considered to be the needs of the country. Lawyers, learned societies, city councils and other professional and academic organizations pointed out the shortcomings in the existing system and also suggested remedies for it. Although there were differences in details, the people seemed to be unanimous with regard to the urgency of some of the problems. They demanded the freedom of conscience, speech, publication, public meetings and associations. They demanded that justice must be administered by judges. Fair trial should be given to all before any one was punished. The people must be given greater control over the affairs of local government. A parliament must be set up for the whole country and given the power to make laws and control the government. A demand for a national constituent assembly was also made.

The Czar was not prepared to oblige the people by giving the reforms demanded by them. The result was that discontentment continued. The Russian defeat in the Russo-Japanese War added to the discontentment among the people. Thousands of soldiers escaped to Germany and Austria. Many others were forced to proceed to Manchuria at the point of the bayonet. Many business enterprises failed on account of war and thousands of workers became idle and added to the ranks of the discontented persons. Harvests were bad. Officials were found to be enriching themselves at the expense of the country by selling the supplies for profits instead of sending them to the front. Even the funds of the

Red Cross Society were not spared. On 1 January 1905, Port Arthur surrendered after a long siege. The revolutionary agitation continued. The university students of Moscow and St. Petersburg paraded the streets and shouted the slogans of "Down with Autocracy" and "Stop the War." In December 1904, the Czar issued a decree in which he pointed out the reforms which were considered by him to be appropriate for the country. He ordered his ministers to prepare laws giving effect to those reforms. There was no mention of a National Assembly in those reforms and the people felt that although the Czar was willing to make a few insignificant concessions, he was not prepared to part with power and to admit the people to participate in the affairs. No wonder, the agitation continued in the country.

On 22 January 1905, there took place what is known as the slaughter of "Bloody Sunday." A large number of workers under the leadership of Father Gapon tried to approach the royal palace in St. Petersburg with a view to putting forward their grievances before the Emperor. Instead of listening to their grievances, they were attacked by the Cossacks and the regular troops and there was an enormous loss of human life. Throughout 1905, disturbances continued in various parts of the country. In February 1905, Prince Mirski was replaced by Buliguin and policy of repression was resumed. Deeds of violence and repression were answered by assassinations and bomb-throwing by the revolutionaries. Strikes were organized at various places. The houses of the nobles were burnt down by the peasants. There were mutinies in the army and navy. The Grand-Duke Surgus, the reactionary uncle of the Czar, was assassinated as he had the audacity to declare that "the people want the stick." Russia was on the verge of collapse.

It was under these circumstances that the Czar Nicholas II issued a manifesto in August 1905. In that document he declared that "while preserving the fundamental law regarding the autocratic power," he had resolved to call, not later than January 1906, the State Council or Duma, consisting of elected representatives from the whole of Russia. The manifesto did not satisfy the people as the Duma was going to be merely a consultative body and not a representative legislature having full authority to make laws. The workers and the professional classes were not given the right of vote. The sessions of the Duma were not to be public. An idea of the restricted franchise can be had from the fact that St. Petersburg with a population of more than 10½ million was to have only 9½ thousand voters.

As the concessions were considered to be inadequate and illusory, the revolutionary parties continued their agitation and made use of the weapon of strike. The beginning was made with the railway strike which spread all over the Russian Empire and cut off all communications both within and outside Russia. If any person wanted to travel, he had to use the ordinary highways or the water. Commerce was tied up. Merchants could neither ship nor receive goods. Similar strikes took place in other factories. Except the provision stores, all other shops were practically closed. In large towns, gas and electric companies stopped working. The druggists refused to sell medicines until reforms were given by the Czar. Students of the universities went on strike. Lawyers followed them and law-courts had to be closed. No newspaper could be printed. The whole of the national life seemed to be thrown out of gear.

It was under these circumstances that the Czar issued another manifesto on 30 October 1905. He granted "the immutable foundations of civic liberty" such as the freedom of speech, conscience and association. Franchise was liberalized. He declared "as an immutable rule that no law can come into force without the approval of the Duma, and that it shall be possible for the representatives of the people to participate effectively in the supervision of the legality of the acts of the public officials." Pobedonostsev was dismissed and Count Witte was appointed the Prime Minister.

The revolutionaries were not satisfied with the concessions and demanded the convocation of an assembly elected by universal suffrage to frame a constitution for Russia. As the Czar did not accept the demand, strikes continued throughout November 1905 and other classes such as letter-carriers and telegraph operators also joined. There were mutinies in the army and navy. There was a lot of fighting in the streets of Moscow and other places. The government refused to summon a constituent assembly and,ordered elections for the new Duma. Some concessions were given to Finland and the people of that country got some peace. However, there was no quiet in Russia where a kind of civil war was going on between the revolutionaries on one side and the reactionaries on the other. Repressive measures were continued in spite of the manifesto of October 1905. In January 1906 alone, 78 newspapers were suspended and 58 editors were arrested. Thousands of people were thrown into prisons or exiled to Siberia. Martial law was enforced in various parts of Russia.

Even before the meeting of the Duma, the Czar issued a decree which set up a Council of the Empire. The new body was largely to consist of the officials and was to act as the Upper Chamber of the legislature of which the Duma was to he the Lower Chamber. Laws had to be approved of by the Duma and the Council of the Empire before their submission to the Czar for approval. It is evident that the powers of the Duma were curtailed even before it met.

Elections to the Duma were held in March and April 1906 and a party called the "Cadets" came to have a majority. Witte resigned and he was succeeded by Goremykin. The first act of the new Prime Minister was to issue what were known as "Organic Laws" which could not be couched by the Duma.

First Duma (1906). The Duma was opened by Nicholas II on 10 May 1906. It had a short and stormy life. It expressed its desire to have a through reform of Russia along the lines of Western liberalism. However, it had to face opposition from the reactionary forces in the country who had failed to stop the summoning of the Duma but were determined to make it impotent. The Duma demanded an amnesty for all political offenders. "The first thought at the first assembly of the representatives of the Russian nation should be for those who have sacrificed their freedom for their country." In spite of its efforts, only a partial amnesty was declared. The Duma also demanded a change in the composition of the Council of the Empore which was completely under the thumb of the Czar. It also demanded the responsibility of the ministers to itself. The abolition of martial law was also demanded. It was also demanded that the lands belonging to the State, the Czar and the monasteries should be given to the peasants on long leases.

The first Duma lasted for only two months but the members showed a high degree of intelligence. The shortcomings of the government were criticised freely and scathingly. The attitude of the ministers was contemptuous and there was a lot of heat in the discussions of the Duma. It was opposed throughout by the Czar and the Council of the Empire. Ultimately, a deadlock took place on the question of the responsibility of the ministers to the Duma. The public was agitated and there were disorders in the country. A radical party among the peasants was in favour of giving the lands of the country to the peasants without any compensation. The Czar tried to resolve the deadlock by dissolving the Duma on 22 July 1906. He declared that he was "cruelly disappointed" and that the representatives of the nation, instead of applying themselves to productive legislation, had strayed into spheres beyond their competence, had enquired into the acts of local authorities established by himself, and commented upon the imperfections of the fundamental laws which could only be modified by his imperial will."

Second Duma (1970). 5 March 1907 was fixed as the date for the meeting of the second Duma. Stolypin was appointed the Prime Minister in place of Goremykin. Many members of the first Duma went to Viborg in Finland and issued a manifesto which was signed by 230 of them. In that manifesto, they protested against the dissolution of the first Duma and called upon the people to stand for the rights of the down-trodden for popular representation. They appealed to the people not to give the government either soldiers or money. All loans contracted without the approval of the Duma were declared to be invalid. The manifesto failed to create any effect among the people who were either indifferent or afraid of the terrorist regime of the Czar.

The second Duma met on 5 March, 1907 but there was no smooth working. From the very beginning, there was friction between the Duma and the ministry and it continued to increase with the passage of time. The government arrested 16 members of the Duma and indicted them for carrying on revolutionary propaganda. This action of the government was resented bitterly as an attack on constitutional liberties and while the Duma was preparing to measure swords with the Czar, it was dissolved on 16 June 1907. Orders were issued for the election of a new Duma in September 1907 and it was to meet in November. A manifesto was issued by the government by which the electoral law was radically changed. As a result of the change, most of the members of the new Duma were to be selected by about 130,000 landowners. While the people protested, the Czar maintained that "the right of abrogating the law and replacing it by a new law belongs only to the power which gave the first electoral law—the historic power of the Czar of Russia." The government was determined to maintain its autocratic control over the country. All kinds of illegalities were committed by the government officials and there was none to challenge them. Reaction was in full swing.

Third Duma (1907-14). It was in these circumstances that the third Duma was elected in September and met in November 1907. It was full of big landlords and reactionaries. No wonder, it proved to be a docile assembly. Although the reactionaries demanded the dissolution of the third Duma also, yet the Government did not accept their point of view. The Duma was allowed to continue but acted merely as a consultative body and not a legislative body. Its voice did not count much. This state of affairs continued up to 1914. It was in this way that the liberal experiment in Russia during the first two decades failed. The reactionaries came to power and the liberals were discredited.

The Russian Revolution of 1917. When the World War I broke out, there were many groups at work in Russia who were preparing to bring about a change in her institutions. The most moderate among them were the Octobrists who demanded that the Czar must carry out his proclamation of 30 October 1905 in which he had promised that no law would thereafter be considered binding without the consent of the Duma and to the people would be given "the power to exercise an effective supervision over the acts of the officials." The Octobrists consisted mainly of liberal nobles who were in favour of a Duma working in a subordinate position like the Landtag of Prussia. The Constitutional Democrats were definitely more liberal and were drawn chiefly from the professional classes, university men, capitalists and more progressive nobles. They demanded a wider franchise, more power for the Duma and ministerial responsibility like that in Great Britain. These two groups desired to take progressive steps towards constitutional rule but preferred to do so by peaceful means. They believed that the unifying influence of the Czar was necessary for the preservation of national unity.

The Social Democrats and the Socialist Revolutionaries were more radical in their aims. As regards the *Social Democrats*, they were mostly urban working men who had absolutely no real voice in the government and were oppressed by the industrial system in the country. They were a fertile field for socialist propaganda. They were dreaming of the time when all factories would be seized by them, capitalists turned out and they would get an opportunity to work under better conditions with shorter hours of work and more wages. They wanted to capture political power by overthrowing the Empire. In 1903, this party was split up into two parts known as Bolsheviki or "majority" and the Mensheviki or "minority". To begin with, their differences were only in matters of party organisation but later on fundamental differences arose between them on the question of party tactics also. The Bolsheviki were the extremists. They were opposed to any cooperation with the bourgeois parties and the policy of gradual reform. They stood for the establishment of the dictatorship of the Proletariat. The Mensheviki were moderates and they were willing to bring about a socialist regime gradually by educating the people and securing the cooperation of moderately liberal groups. To sum up, while the Bolsheviks were revolutionary, the Mensheviks were evolutionary. The Socialist Revolutionaries comprised the masses of the peasants under the leadership of a few radical intellectuals. Their main interest was in land and they wanted to transform the land from private property into "the property of the whole people." The lands in their possession were inadequate to support them. It is true that in 1914 about three-fourths of the land in Russia was in the hands of the peasants but they were eager to capture and divide among themselves the remaining estates of the Crown, the Church and the aristocracy. The revolutionaries demanded the destruction of the existing political and social regime in Russia in the interests of the peasants.

Before the outbreak of the World War I, there had been a persistent agitation in Russia against the abuses of the Russian administration. The country was simmering with discontent which manifested itself in many ways. Both constitutional and revolutionary methods had been tried to improve the state of affairs but all of them had failed. However, those failures had not disheartened the patriots of Russia who were full convinced that they would succeed in the long run. The Russian peasants had been clamouring for land and their land hunger had increased on account of an increase in the population of the country. They advocated terrorist methods to achieve their objectives. The Jews, the Poles, the Finns and other minorities were embittered by the policy of Russification and they were agitating for a change in the system of administration in the country. They were willing to join hands with any party which stood for the overthrow of the Czarist regime. Side by side with the industrial revolution in Russia had been going on a revolution in the realm of ideas. The Czars had tried to seal Russia hermetically against the liberal and radical ideas of the West, but in spite of that, the influence of Western thought and example had filtered into the country, and produced a movement which was determined to end the reactionary regime of the Czars. The great novels of Tolstoy, Turgenev and Dostoievsky had stirred the imagination of the youth of Russia. While the intelligentsia demanded political reforms on the western lines, the radicals who followed Marx, Bakunin and Kropotkin stood for socialism and anarchism. Nihilism aimed at destroying everything in the existing order of Russia. The failure of the liberal experiment in Russia convinced the people that the employment of peaceful methods was not going to bring about the necessary results. The Russo-Japanese War of 1904-5 had exposed the incompetence of the Czarist regime and the World War I completely destroyed it.

When the World War I broke out, there was a lot enthusiasm and a sense of unity among the people of Russia. That was partly due to the fact that the action of the Central Powers in attacking Serbia and Belgium was regarded by the Russians as unwarranted and flagrantly aggressive. Moreover, Russia's alliance with Great Britain and France was considered a happy augury for the future of the country. However, all hopes were falsified by the subsequent events and cooperation anticipated between the Government and the people did not materialise. As the war progressed, the entire machinery of Government disintegrated until it fell into a state of complete collapse. The general mobilization increased the size of the army to the staggering figure of 15 million strong. The Government was faced with the problem of equipping and provisioning those men. The national resources of the country had not been fully exploited to meet such an unprecedented situation and the acute shortage of labour due to mobilization made matters worse. The blockade of the Baltic Sea isolated Russia from the rest of the World and food supplies could not be imported into the country. Thus, starvation haunted the country in the midst of war. Profiteering and black-marketing flourished and no check was put on them. There was inefficiency and corruption both in the army and civil administration. The Government had also to face financial embarrassments. The Government adopted the stupid policy of prohibition in the country and suspended the operation of a state monopoly of liquor which ultimately brought to the exchequer more than a quarter of the state revenues. The policy of inflation created a vicious circle. Prices were soaring. Food shortages were common. The situation was made worse by the military reverses in the war.

When in 1915, the Russian armies were driven out of Galicia and Poland, the patriotic Russians condemned the incompetence of the military leaders and inefficiency and corruption in the Government. As defeat followed defeat and the number of the killed and wounded mounted to millions, the criticism of the Government became louder and angrier. There was demand that the inefficient commanders and officials must be punished and war must be prosecuted more vigorously. There were riots in the cities and strikes in the munition factories.

Only a sagacious rule could have saved the situation, but Czar Nicholas II "was far from being superhumanly clever and, with a few exceptions, the people who surrounded and influenced him, whether the ministers who passed in dreary succession across the political stage, the members of his immediate household, or hangers-on at the court were stupid, corrupt and revolutionary." The role of the Czarina was an unfortunate one. She was a neurotic and unbalanced woman and was under the influence of Rasputin, "an uneducated, coarse and licentious peasant." The Emperor had implicit faith in Rasputin and regarded him as the "man of God." The appointment and dismissal of the ministers and high officials of the Government rested with Rasputin. Under the influence of Rasputin, the Empress prompted the Czar to assume in person the command of the army. With the departure of the Czar at the end of August 1915 began the personal rule of the Empress and Rasputin. Everything in the Government depended upon the whims of Rasputin. There were frequent reshuffling of the permanent heads of the various Departments and that upset the whole of the administrative machinery. In 1916, Rasputin became the undisputed master of the country. Public resentment began to spread throughout the country and even the arch-reactionaries in the country warned the Czar of the impending catastrophe. The misfortune was that instead of profiting from the warnings given by the well-wishers, the Czar rebuked them. On 30 December 1916, Rasputin was assassinated by Prince Yusupov and other conservatives.

There was a general feeling in 1916 that victory in war was impossible so long as the methods of autocracy prevailed. In the fall of that year, preparations for a *coup d' etat* were begun in various circles which included military men of both Petrograd and Moscow and Duma members of as high standing as Rodzianko, its President and most of the plans involved the abdication of the Czar. The army was discouraged and discontented and tired of a futile war. By the winter of 1916-17, it was already in the process of dissolution. There was unwillingness to fight. There were desertions in the rear. There was a decline in discipline, distrust and suspicion of officers. By the spring of 1917, there was a discontent and unrest among the masses on account of the economic conditions created by the war. The cost of living had increased by leaps and bounds during the war. During the winter of 1916-17, there was a serious shortage of coal and many industries dosed down. The transportation system completely collapsed under the strain of the war. Passenger traffic had to be stopped for weeks at a time to enable military and supply trains to pass through to the front. Particularly in the larger towns and cities, there was an acute shortage of food. That was partly due to the fact that millions of peasants were recruited in the army to fight on the front and the demand for food increased to feed the fighting forces. The peasants working on the fields were not willing to part with the products for a currency which had practically no value. The collapse of the transport system added to the seriousness of the food situation. The result was short rations and bread lines in the cities and hungry people shouted for "bread."

On 8 March 1917, spontaneous riots took place in Petrograd. Crowds of people marched through the streets shouting for bread. On the same day, between 80 to 90 thousand workmen went on strike and joined the demonstrating masses in the streets. Red flags and revolutionary placards appeared on the scene. On 11 March 1917, one of the Companies of the Petrograd garrison mutinied when ordered to fire upon the people and had to be disarmed. The military Governor of Petrograd posted notices ordering the strikers to return to their work and the Duma was ordered to be prorogued. Instead of returning to work, the strikers established the Soviet of Workmen and Soldiers' Deputies and began to organise the masses and convert the soldiers to their cause. Even the Preobrashensky regiment which was the flower of the household troops mutinied and shot some of its officers. Many other regiments also mutinied and as many as 25,000 soldiers joined the workers. By the evening of 12 Match 1917, the revolutionary workers were in control of Petrograd.

On 14 March 1917, the Czar attempted to reach Petrograd, but his train was compelled to stop because workmen pulled up the tracks. Meanwhile, the Czar had sent an army under General Ivanov to take Petrograd but most of his troops went over to the revolutionaries. On 15 March 1917, the Czar decided to give way and grant a responsible ministry. Unfortunately, the concession came too late. There was a general demand that the Czar must abdicate and ultimately the Czar abdicated with a request that his throne should go directly to his brother Michael rather than to his young son Alexis. The Soviet of Petrograd was demanding a Re1public. A delegation of the Duma visited Michael and informed him that the popular demand was that he should surrender all his powers to the provisional Government until a Constituent Assembly could decide upon the future. The request was accepted by Michael and all power fell in the hands of the provisional Government which consisted of the Moderates representing the land-owning, capitalist, manufacturing and professional classes. The Czar was deposed and later on he along with the members of the royal family was put to death.

The provisional Government mentioned above was not acceptable to the Russian masses and following the example of the workmen of Petrograd, they set up throughout the country local Soviets, chosen in the town by the factory workers, in the rural districts by the peasant communes and in the army by military units. These Soviets were controlled by Socialist Revolutionaries and the Menshevik Social Democrats who were practically unrepresented in the provisional Government. Those who were controlling the Soviets stood for a thorough-going revolution in addition to a political change. They demanded the overthrow of the bourgeoisie. The peasants particularly demanded that all lands of the landlords must be confiscated without compensation. The workers demanded the expulsion of the capitalists and the establishment of their own control in the factories. All of them were sick of the war and would like to have peace as soon as possible. Early in April 1917, an "All-Russian Congress of Soviets" composed largely of Menshevik Social Democrats and moderate socialist revolutionaries met. The Congress demanded the abandonment of imperialism, acceptance of the principle of self-determination and conclusion of peace without annexations and indemnities. It voted to continue the war and support the provisional Government if its views were accepted. However, on 1 May 1917, Foreign Minister Miliukov sent a note to Allied Governments informing them about the determination of Russia to conclude no separate peace and to carry on the war to a "decisive victory" in conformity with her past agreements with the Allies. This was resented by the Petrograd Soviet and there were protest meetings in Petrograd and Moscow. There were hostile demonstrations in which the slogan was "Down with Miliukov." A number of regiments paraded with banners demanding the resignation of the War Minister and the result was that both the Foreign Minister and the War Minister resigned. Up to this time, the Menshevik leaders in the Petrograd Soviet had not taken any responsibility for the policies of the provisional Government and had refused to cooperate with it. In the reshuffling of the provisional Government, the Mensheviks and moderate Socialist Revolutionaries were given representation. Kerensky became Minister of War. One of the reasons why the Mensheviks and moderate Socialist Revolutionaries joined the provisional Government was the increasing activity of the Bolsheviks.

When the Revolution took place in Russia in 1917, Lenin, a revolutionary, was in Switzerland. He took advantage of the general pardon of political offenders proclaimed by the provisional Government of Russia and decided to come back to his country. He was not allowed to pass through the territories of the Allies but ultimately was able to secure permission from the Government of Germany to pass through her territory. Lenin reached Petrograd on 16 April 1917 and immediately began to work along with other Bolshevik leaders. With the freedom of the press, speech, assembly and organisation guaranteed by the provisional Government, the Bolsheviks got an opportunity to agitate for their programme and tactics. Lenin was able to exploit for his ends the food difficulties of the people, the protracted war and the delay in summoning the Constituent Assembly. He was able to collect around himself doctrinaire fanatics, masters of intrigue and propaganda, ambitious opportunists, sentimental visionaries, crazy degenerates and sincere idealists such as Trotsky, Zinoviev, Bukharin, Stalin, Rykov, Chicherin, Kamenev, etc. Lening occupied the first place and Trotsky the second. The Bolshevik leaders put before the masses a revolutionary programme including the immediate conclusion of a general peace, immediate confiscation of landed estates without compensation and without delay, possession and operation of factories by workmen, national control of production and distribution, substitution of Soviets of workmen, peasants and soldiers for all the existing agencies of Government and exclusion of the propertied classes from political rights.

War Minister Kerensky was doing everything in his power for a successful offensive against the Central Powers. His view was that a Russian victory would strengthen the hands of the provisional Government and raise the morale of both the soldiers and the civilians. The Russian advance began towards the end of June 1917 and for a few days all went well. Thousands of prisoners and vast quantities of war material were captured. An advance of some 20 miles was made. Wherever the Austrian lines were not strengthened by the Germans, they gave way. On 19 July a heavy concentration of German troops began a drive in the direction of Tarnopol. The Russians fell back under German pressure. Discipline and organisation broke down. Entire regiments shot their officers and refused to fight. The whole Russian line in Galicia took to flight and the Russian gains of 1916 were completely wiped out.

On 16 July, 1917, the Bolsheviks made their first serious attempt at an armed uprising in Petrograd. A part of the Petrograd Garrison revolted and paraded through the city with such banners as "Down with capitalist ministers," "Down with war," "All power to the Soviets", etc. Red flags appeared among the crowds. Speeches by men like Trotsky and Zinoviev were greeted with thunderous applause. From the front, Kerensky telegraphed demanding that the Government must take active steps to suppress the Bolsheviks and sent about 60,000 loyal soldiers for that work. After two days of fighting in the streets, both the disloyal troops and the Bolsheviks were defeated. As the strength of the Bolsheviks was weak in the army as a whole and on the countryside, Lenin gave up his programme of the immediate overthrow of the provisional Government and decided to make all possible efforts to win over the whole of the army on his side.

The provisional Government was in a very difficult position. There were defeats on the war fronts and there was a revolt at the capital. Kerensky took over as Prime Minister. Although he took steps to strengthen the Government, difficulties were created for him by the forces of reaction and militant monarchism. The Bolsheviks had demanded the dictatorhip of the Proletariat but the conservatives demanded the dictatorship of the military. In September 1917, under orders from General Kornilov, troops advanced from the front upon Petrograd. Kornilov gave an ultimatum to Kerensky demanding the proclamation of martial law in Petrograd and resignation of the provisional Government. Kerensky rejected the ultimatum and got Kornilov arrested. This created a favourable atmosphere for the Bolsheviks. There was a general belief among the people that the Czarist agents may not bring about the restoration of the old regime. It was given out that the sympathies of Kerensky were against the people. The Bolsheviks exploited the situation and within a few days the confidence of the people in the provisional Government was completely shaken. The Soviets became more revolutionary. Within a weak of the crushing of the Kornilov rebellion, the Bolsheviks gained control of the Executive Committee of the Petrograd Soviet for the first time. The moderates were fighting a losing game. There was practically chaos in the country. The military situation became more and more desperate. Desertions were on the increase. Most of the soldiers threatened to leave their trenchs. The Germans continued to advance. They captured Riga and threatened Petrograd. The provisional Government decided to move to Moscow. In the villages, the people were taking the law into their hands and forcibly taking possession of land. The finances and industry of Russia practically collapsed. Bolshevik propaganda, German propaganda and separatist propaganda were creating confusion in every direction. At this stage, the Bolsheviks raised the following slogans, "Peace to the army, land to the peasants, control of the factories to the workmen." This slogan had the desired result. The number of the Bolsheviks began to increase. The land-hungry peasants flocked under the Bolshevik banner. The same was the case with the workers who wanted to have complete control over industry. The soldiers who had been maltreated, betrayed, defeated in the war and compelled to undergo untold hardships, readily accepted the Bolshevik programme.

At this time Lenin decided to strike. In October 1917, he held a "Conspiratory Meeting" of the Central Committee of the Bolshevik Party and a decision was taken to have an armed revolt against the provisional Government. The occasion was the assembling of the All Russian Congress of Soviets which was scheduled to meet on 7 November 1917. A large majority of those who had been elected to this Congress were Bolsheviks and there was no doubt that the Congress would declare itself in favour of handing over power to the Soviets. On the evening of 6 November 1917, the Bolsheviks made the following declaration: "The counter revolution has raised its criminal head. The Kornilovists are mobilising forces in order to annihilate the All-Russian Congress of Soviets and the Constituent Assembly." During the night, all public buildings of Petrograd were occupied by the Bolshevik troops. They also brought under their control railway stations, telegraph and telephone offices, bridges, power plants and even the Bank of Russia. On the morning of 7 November 1917, it was announced by the Bolsheviks that the provisional Government had been overthrown. There were cries of "Long live the revolution of the workers, soldiers and peasants!" Kerensky escaped but all other members of the provisional Government were arrested and imprisoned. The same night the All-Russian Congress of Soviets approved the *coup d' etat* and passed a resolution taking over the Government. On 8 November 1917, the same Congress established a new provisional Government called the "Soviet of the Peoples' Commissars" of which Lenin was the Chairman and Trotsky, the Commissar for Foreign Affairs.

Trotsky sent to the foreign diplomats in Petrograd a note in which it was stated that the Soviet Government intended "to propose to all peoples and their respective Governments an immediate armistice on all fronts with the purpose of immediately opening pourparlers for the conclusion of a democratic peace." The note of Trotsky was ignored by all the Allied Powers but the Central Powers responded to it and negotiations were started for an armistice at Brest-Litovsk on 3 December 1917. The negotiations were protracted because both the parties tried to get the maximum. Ultimately the Treaty of Brest-Litovsk was signed on 3 March 1918. The Soviet Union agreed to give up Poland, Courland and Lithuania and to let Germany and Austria-Hungary determine the future status of these territories in agreement with their populations, to evacuate Livonia, Estonia, Finland, the Aaland Islands and the Ukraine and to recognise the treaties between the Ukrainian Peoples Republic and the Central Powers, to surrender to Turkey the districts of Ardahan, Kars and Batum and to discontinue all Bolshevik "propaganda in the territories of the Central Powers and in the territories ceded by the treaty. It is true that while signing this treaty, the Bolsheviks were able to secure peace for Russia, but her size was very much reduced. But this gave the Bolsheviks a free hand to try their experiment of the dictatorship of the Proletariat. The Allied Powers were involved in a life and death struggle with the Central Powers and had no time to intervene in the Soviet Union and the Central Powers were glad that they could withdraw their troops from the Russian front and utilise the same against the Allied Powers.

The Bolsheviks had to face many difficulties. There were many Russians known as White Russians who believed that Bolshevism was a passing phase and they hoped that by counter-revolutionary measures supported by the Allies, they would be able to overthrow the Bolshevik regime. The Allies were also not opposed to such an idea. Huge stores of military supplies had been landed at Murmansk, Archangel and Vladivostok for use against the Central Powers and the Allies would not like the same to fall into the hands of their enemies. France was particularly eager for the overthrow of the Bolshevik regime as billions of francs had been invested by the French people in Russia. The result was that after the signing of the Treaty of Brest-Litovsk, Allied Expeditionary Forces were despatched to Murmansk, Archangel and Vladivostok. In November 1918, French forces seized Odessa. British troops occupied the various trans-Caucasian republics. Each of the regions seized by the Allied armies served as a rallying ground for the anti-Bolshevik Russians who were plotting to overthrow the Soviet Government. With the White armies planning to advance from the East, from the South and from the West, it was hoped in anti-Bolshevik circles that the year 1919 would see the fall of the Soviet Government.

However, the Bolshevik leaders were able to face successfully the situation and for that purpose they depended chiefly upon two agencies, viz., Cheka and the Red Army. The Cheka had been organised immediately after the revolution of November 1917 in order to maintain law and order in the capital but it was later on transformed into an agency of terror which was used to force the population either into active support or passivity. The Cheka was given the power to arrest, try and shoot all those who were considered dangerous to the Government. In August 1918, an organised Red Terror started which was more bloody than the Reign of Terror of the French Revolution. Thousands of persons who were sympathisers of the old regime were murdered in cold blood. For some time, the Soviet Government had practically no army to face the situation. However, a voluntary Red Army was organised by Trotsky who was the Commissar for War. During the year 1918, it was developed into a well-equipped and well-trained force of more than 1,00,000 men.

In 1919 a simultaneous advance of the White armies began. Some of them actually reached near Leningrad which was a new name given to Petrograd by the Soviet Government on 22 April 1920. However, they were defeated and driven back. The defeat of the White armies was partly due to the fact that the Russian people, particularly the peasants, considered them as the agents of reaction who were trying to restore lands to the landlords and the old privileges to the aristocracy. The Russian peasants were not prepared to be liberated by the armies of the landlords. Moreover, wherever the White armies went, they resorted to looting. The masses of Russia came to believe that out of Bolshevism and extreme military reaction, the former was to be preferred as a lesser evil. Moreover, the conduct of the White armies and the bloody repressive measures of their leaders alienated popular sympathy in the Allied countries. The result was that by the close of 1919, all Allied forces were withdrawn from European Russia although the Japanese continued to occupy Vladivostok for some time more. The Bolshevik leaders had still to face another danger. The White forces of the South were actively supported by the French Government and during the early months of 1920, they moved northward in the Ukraine. At the same time, the Poles invaded the Soviet Union and in May 1920, they were able to occupy the city of Kiev. Once again, the people of the Soviet Union rallied to the support of their Government and the Poles were hurled back almost to Warsaw. It was the French help which saved them from a disaster. By the close of the year 1920, European Russia was cleared of active counter-revolutionary armies.

The Bolsheviks completely altered the political life of the people of Russia. In 1918, a new constitution was framed and that established the Russian Soviet Federated Soviet Republic with Moscow as the National Capital instead of Leningrad. Russia became a federal state in which all power belonged to the workers "united in urban and rural Soviets." The new Republic was declared to be a free socialist society of the working people of Russia.

The Russian revolution of 1917 was a great event in world history. It was the mightiest event of the World War I. It set up a novel type of state in which power rests in the Communist Party as representing the dictatorship of the proletariat. The Soviet Union is the dream of Marx given a practical shape. It is socialism in action. The Russian revolution is regarded with blind hatred or blind idolatry.

SUGGESTED READINGS

Beazley: **Russia from the Varangians to the Bolsheviks.**

Blackwell, A.S.: **The little Grandmother of the Russian Revolution.**

Blackwell, A.S.: **Cambridge Modern History, Vol. XII.**

Bunyan, J. & Fisher, H.H. (Eds.): **The Bolshevik Revolution, 1917-8, 1934.**

Chamberlin, W.H.: **The Russian Revolution, 1917-21, 1935.**

Carr, E.H.: **The Bolshevist Revolution, 1917-1923.**

Chernov, V.: **The Great Russian Revolution, 1936.**

Florinsky, M.T.: **The End of the Russian Empire, 1931.**

Hindus, M.G.: **The Russian Peasant and the Revolution, 1920.**

Judas, E.: **Rasputin, Neither Devil Nor Saint, 1942.**

Kerensky, A.F.: **The Catastrophe, 1927.**

Kerensky, A.F.: **The Prelude to Bolshevism, 1919.**

Kirby, L.P.: **The Russian Revolution, 1940.**

Kroff, S.A.: **Autocracy and Revolution in Russia.**

Meyendorff, Baron A.F.: **The Background of the Russian. Revolution, 1929.**

Miliukov, P.: **History of the Second Russian Revolution, 1920.**

Mazour, A.G.: **The First Russian Revolution (1825), 1937.**

Olgin : **Soul of the Russian Revolution.**

Rose: **Development of European Nations.**

Skrine : **Expansion of Russia.**

Trotsky, L.: **The History of the Russian Revolution, 1934.**

Wallace: **Russia.**

CHAPTER 23

MODERN SOCIALISM

The socialist movement started side by side with new industry and was intended to remove the social evils created in part by power machinery and the factory system. The word socialism is very commonly used but there is no clear and precise definition of it. Socialism has been described as a way of life, a class struggle, the obliteration of class hatreds and class distinctions, an attitude towards life, a form of society, practical Christianity, a science, the antithesis of capitalism, a programme of action, an opposite of individualism, etc. Critics describe socialism, as "a plan that people often enthusiastically advocate when poor, which automatically ceases to interest them when they become wealthy" and "an attempt to legislate unsuccessful men into success by legislating successful men out of it." Ramsay Muir writes, "Socialism is a chameleon-like creed. It changes its colour according to its environments. For the street corner and the club room, it wears the flaming scarlet of class war; for the intellectuals it is red shot with tawny; for the sentimentalists, it becomes a delicate rose pink, and in clerical circles it assumes a virgin white just touched with a faint flush of generous aspiration."

Inspite of it, there are certain things common to most of the socialists. All socialists aim at solving problems which are primarily economic. Socialism is primarily concerned with the production and distribution of wealth and all other considerations are secondary. Political power is desired by socialists only as a means of setting up an economic system. Every form of modern socialism is in one sense or another a protest against or a condemnation of the economic system called capitalism which has not only failed to effect a just distribution of wealth but has given rise to a conflict of interests between the employers and the employees. All modern socialists agree that capitalism must be replaced by a new economic order. It is true that there is no agreement among socialists regarding the precise form of the new order but they all agree that private property in land and industrial capital must be transformed into social or collective property. The idea of collective ownership is the core of socialism. Socialism stands for collective ownership and administration of land and industrial capital.

William Godwin

In his work entitled "Enquiry Concerning Political Justice" published in 1793, William Godwin (1756-1836) surveyed the evils of contemporary society, including the extreme inequality of wealth, the wretchedness of the poor and the oppression on the part of the rich. According to him, those, evils could be removed by abolishing private property. Godwin stood for a society on an individualistic basis, without a state organisation.

Babeuf

During the French Revolution, Babeuf (1760-1797) propounded a definite scheme for a socialist society and even attempted to establish it in 1796. He developed a plan according to which the state was to inherit all property until community of property was established.

Saint-Simon

Saint Simon (1760-1825) was by birth an aristocrat and even claimed descent from Charlemagne. He renounced his title during the French Revolution of 1789 and made a fortune through speculation in church lands. His life was spent in the quest for a new source of authority and faith in an industrial age. He preached the gospel of work. According to him, "Man must work". He insisted that property rights must depend on their social utility and not on any imprescriptible individual rights. He coined the slogan : "From each according to his capacity, to each according to his work."

Saint Simon was not a systematic thinker, but his speculations stimulated the minds of others. After his death, his disciples founded a school in which his doctrines were systematised and developed. For a time, the school attracted many artists, industrialists and men of letters but its success was short-lived.

Fourier

Charles Fourier (1772-1837) was a contemporary of Saint-Simon and Robert Owen. He was the son of a well-to-do draper who regarded commerce as the great enemy. He attacked all the ills of a commercial civilisation which made vice more profitable than virtue and set men in enmity with one another. The great sources of the evil were cut-throat competition, deceit, greed and inhumanity. In order to restore harmony to human life, there must be association and cooperation. In order to make work attractive, each worker must be given a share in the produce and be guaranteed a sufficient minimum to free him from anxiety. His suggestion was that the dirty and unattractive work of the community should be done by children who at a certain age are providentially endowed with a love of being dirty. They would be "passionately attracted" to scavenging and would be always on foot or riding on their ponies at 3 A.M. even in the depths of winter, repairing roads, killing vermin, attending to animals and working in the slaughter houses. Communities after the teachings of Fourier were set up during the 1840s in New Jersey, Wisconsin and Massachusetts.

Louis Blanc

The socialism of Saint Simon and Fourier was largely imaginative and Utopian. Louis Blanc (1811-1882) was the first to make use of the contemporary political machinery to achieve the ends of socialism. He was a journalist, author and politician. In 1840, he published his famous book entitled. "The Organisation of Labour". He denounced the existing competitive system. He advocated a political reform which would establish the state on a thoroughly democratic basis. Then, the state would provide social workshops—farms for agriculturists, factories for workmen and shops for tradesmen. The state was to provide the money for starting the workshops. During the February Revolution of 1848 in France, the ideas of Louis Blanc were put into practice and workshops were actually started but they failed.

Robert Owen

Robert Owen (1771-1858) was not only the patron saint of English socialism but also the father of the cooperative movement. He was a pioneer in advocating factory legislation and democratic education. He was also the originator of the nursery school. As early as 1800, he started the experiment of creating a model factory at New Lanark. He attracted international attention by showing that workers could be treated well, even generously, without the employer incurring any loss. His fellow mill-owners were impressed. In 1825, he made an experiment of "New Harmony" in Indiana in the United States. It was designed as a voluntary and freely self-governing cooperative community. Unfortunately, the experiment was a failure. Owen became a dreamer of dreams and his writings became more and more unrealistic and visionary. However, the core of his message was that the condition of men would improve if they replaced competition by cooperation as the mainspring of their economic activities and social life. If social conditions were bad, those could be changed. If the conditions were bad on account of human beings being bad, those persons can be changed. The great need was for education, social and moral. The minds of the people be changed and they should appreciate the advantages of cooperation.

Owen helped the growth of cooperative societies and the trade union movement. His name is closely connected with all the steps towards real progress, with all social reform movements and all legislation in the interests of the working classes.

Proudhon

Proudhon (1809-65) is generally known as "the father of anarchism". He was a printer, journalist and a member of the French Constituent Assembly of 1848. He was one of the greatest critics of Karl Marx. Communism, was his bug-bear. His view was that property is the exploitation of the weak by the strong and Communism is the exploitation of the strong by the weak. To quote him, "Communism is Utopian. Whenever an attempt is made to introduce Communism, it results in a caricature of property. I am opposed to Communism and I am now considered as being the least advanced of socialists, it is because I have left Utopia while the socialists are still in it." Proudhon regarded Communism as something incompatible with family. "It (Communism) is not science but annihilation of science. It is incapable of finding a formula of distribution and of organisation. It is eclectic, unintelligent and unintelligible. It is the religion of misery. It neither thinks nor does it reason. It does not know how to organise, produce and distribute; it suspects labour and is afraid of justice. It borrows its ideas from the most ancient, mystic, obsolete, vague and undefinable tradition. Communism means privation, everywhere and always."

Karl Marx (1818-1883)

Karl Marx was born in 1818 at Trier, in the Rhineland. His father was a legal official in the Prussian service. He was a Jewish convert to Christianity. His home was one of enlightenment. Marx studied at the Universities of Bonn and Berlin. He concentrated mainly on history, philosophy, jurisprudence and political economy. He came under the influence of Hegel from whom he imbibed the conception of history as a developing idea and an irresistible process that cannot be deflected. Marx became one of the keenest sympathisers of the revolutionary and democratic agitations of Germany. In 1841, he submitted a thesis for doctorate to the Jena University. He hoped to become a professor in the university but being unsuccessful, he became a journalist. He undertook the editorship of a liberal newspaper known as The Rheinische Zeitung but the same was suppressed in 1843. He moved to Paris where he came into contact with the French socialists. He also met there Friedrich Engels (1820-95) who became his life-long friend and co-worker. In 1845, Marx was expelled from Paris. He went to Brussels where he carried on his activities. He joined the League of the Just whose name was changed into the German Communist League in 1847. He was asked to draw a manifesto for the German Communist League and thus was published the Communist Manifesto in 1848, "the birth-cry of modern socialism." Marx paid a brief visit to Cologne and edited a socialist paper. In 1849, he went to London where he spent the rest of the 34 years of his life. He acted as he correspondent of the New York Tribune. He was instrumental in the formation of the First International in 1864.

Karl Marx died in London on 14 March 1883. The funeral address was read by Dr. Engels. To quote him, "His mission in life was to contribute in one way or another to the overthrow of capitalist society......to contribute to the liberation of the present day proletariat which was the first to make conscious of its own position and its needs of the conditions under which it could win its freedom. Fighting was his element. And he fought with passion, a tenacity and a success which few could rival.... and consequently was the best hated and most calumniated man of his time. He died, beloved, revered and mourned by millions of revolutionary fellow-workers from the mines of Siberia to the coasts of California, in all points of Europe and America. His name and his work will endure through the ages."

Karl Marx was a prolific writer. His writings are to be found in essays, tracts, correspondence and many complete works. Some of his important works are the Communist Manifesto, Das Kapital, Critique of Political Economy, The Holy Family, Value, Price and Profit, Poverty of Philosophy and the Civil War in France (1870-71).

The view of John Bowle is that the Communist Manifesto is "a masterpiece of propaganda. It is simple, authoritative, dogmatic, it struck home directly to the masses for which it was designed. It offered certainty, hope and revenge. Rousseau had written, 'man is born free but he is everywhere in chains'; now to Rousseau's heady phrases was added a sustained, apparently scientific, argument. Where Rousseau worked with gun-powder, here was dynamite." Berlin writes, "No summary can convey the quality of its opening or its closing pages. As an instrument of destructive propaganda, it has no equal anywhere; its effect upon succeeding generations is unparalleled outside religious history; had its author written nothing else, it would have ensured his lasting fame."

The style of Marx was bound to create on impression on the minds of the people who were suffering day after day with little hope of any improvement in their lives. A specimen of his style is the following passage with which the Communist Manifesto begins: "A spectre haunts Europe—the spectre of Communism. All the powers of old Europe have entered into a holy alliance in order to lay this spectre; Pope and Tzar, Metternich and Guizot: French Radicals and German Police spies. The Communists disdain to conceal their views and their aims. They openly declare that their ends can be attained only by the forcible overthrow of all existing social conditions. Let the ruling classes tremble at a communist revolution. The proletarians have nothing to lose, but their chains. They have a world to win. Working men of all countries unite!"

The Communist Manifesto presents all history as the story of class struggles. Technical advances in the methods of producing wealth change the nature and balance of social classes. Modern industry and commerce give power to the bourgeoisie, the industrial, commercial and financial capitalists who own the means of production and whose ruthless exploitation of the world's resources and of the labour of those who do not own the means of production, shapes contemporary history. The capitalists control the state and use it for exploiting and repressing the wage-earners. By the remorseless processes of history, the proletariat is destined to grow in size, misery and self-consciousness until it is able to overthrow the capitalists. To quote Marx, **"What the bourgeoisie produces, above all, are its own grave diggers. Its fall and the victory of the proletariat are equally inevitable."** Democracy is a sham. Parliamentary Government is only a mask for the class rule of the capitalists. The workers should have no national loyalties. They have common interests with the oppressed wage-earners of other countries but none at all with their own employers. The destined revolution by the proletariat will be a world revolution which will be triumphant and inaugurate a proletarian state called "dictatorship of the proletariat". Ultimately, a truly classless society will emerge.

Marxian Communism is primarily the offspring of German Hegelianism and French socialism. Its fundamental article is that of historical materialism. Marx followed Hegel in the interpretation of historical development on the basis of an irresistible, irreversible "dialectical" process. However, while Hegel found in this development the manifestation of the "Universal Spirit", Marx saw only economic forces. The economic impulse provides the mainspring of human aspirations and shapes consciously or unconsciously human actions, judgements institutions and society. Religion, art, and systems of philosophy are "ideological veils" which emanate from primary economic factors. The crises and transitions of history are economic in their real significance. Excepting the Hegelian doctrine that the historical process is dialectical which means the product of continual tension between "opposites" Marx saw the development of history through continuous conflict or tension between "opposing" economic classes. The view of Marx was that history was a perpetual class warfare. The historical progress was from ancient to medieval and from medieval to modern. It was the record of the destruction of the oppressor and the liberation of the oppressed. The next historical development must consist in a conflict of economic classes. Time was ripe for the final war between capitalists and the proletariat. The immediate programme was to bring about the class war, educate the proletariat in class-consciousness and the recognition of their capitalist enemy; to enlighten them as to their destiny and to prepare them for their "inevitable triumph and that of their disciples, to incite to revolution.

The Communists disdain to conceal their views and aims. They openly disclose that their ends can be attained only by the forcible overthrow of all existing social conditions. Let the ruling classes tremble at a communistic revolution."

Marx also developed the labour theory of value. The economic value of a commodity consists in "human labour crystalized."

The whole case of Marx rests mainly upon the assumption that capitalism and proletarianism are true "opposites" whose tension produces the next synthetic historical development. However, history shows that modern industrial development is producing out of capital and labour not opposites but ever-coalescing groups whose differences and tension are being reduced by state regulation, trade union action, philanthropic interests, a rising common standard of living and the growth of a wage-earning class with capitalistic investments. The result is that an inter-dependent labour-capitalist society is emerging which is an economic and financial organisation of wage-earners, shareholders and employers. Marx himself doubted the success of a proletarian revolution in England. Inspite of recurring economic agitation, the modern proletariat is not revolutionary according to the standard of Marx. The only countries where revolutionary Marxism has succeeded are Russia and China.

Many of the ideas of Marx have not stood the test of criticism. Some of his predictions have failed to materialise. Many socialist groups have discarded some of his teachings and modified others. Marx the theorist, the dogmatist, has been pushed into the background to some extent by Marx the leader and the tactician. What has been most effective is his general attitude, his hostility towards the capitalist system and his ability to envisage an alternative to this system. For multitude of workers, the general attitude was and still is, enough. Marx was a prophet who denounced in scathing terms the system that brought them only toil and poverty and also gave them hope for the future. He told them that their present condition was not permanent and a better state of things was inevitable because history was working in their favour. The workers were going to be the leaders and controllers. They were to carry on energetically and unceasingly the working class struggle and thereby hasten the coming of a new order. Marxism became for millions a gospel of salvation.

First International

The socialism of Marx was international. To quote him, "The Communists are further reproached with desiring to abolish countries and nationality. The working men have no country. We cannot take from them what they have not got." The proletariat was united in bonds of self-interest throughout the world. To promote that consciousness, Marx formed in 1864 the "International Working Men's Association" which is known in history as the First International. It consisted of delegates from most of the countries of Europe. Its rules and programme were drawn up by Marx himself. The congresses were held in different towns of Europe. From about 1868, the Marxian socialists were joined by anarchists headed by Bakunin. However, Marx and Bakunin quarrelled. During the Franco-Prussian War of 1870-71, Bakunin supported France and Marx supported Germany. In 1872, Marx was able to suppress the Bakunin faction and expelled it from the First International which died of inanition after the Congress at Geneva in 1874.

Second International

The Second International was founded in 1889 after the death of Marx. It was a loose federation of national parties rather than an international association in the true sense of the word. Besides the national differences, there was also a division of opinion in regard to the means to be employed and the ends to be achieved. While the Left Wing adhered to the idea of violent revolution and the dictatorship of the proletariat, the Right Wing revised the Marxian doctrine on those points. The members of the Right Wing were known as Revisionists and they were ready to compromise with the liberal democratic parties in order to gain legislation which could improve the condition of the working classes within the frame-work of existing institutions. This policy of reform led to rifts within the various national groups. When the World War I broke out in 1914, the Second International foundered on the rock of nationalism.

The Third International was formed in 1919. It was organised by the Russian Communists with headquarters in Moscow. It was definitely revolutionary in character. "Its chief purpose is to accelerate the development of events towards world revolution." It was dissolved in 1943. It was replaced by the Cominform (Communist Information), 1947-56.

Bakunin (1814-76)

Count Michael Bakunin was a Russian anarchist. He belonged to a noble family and started his career as an Artillery Officer. In 1835, he went to Moscow for the purpose of studying philosophy. In 1841, he went to Berlin. On account of the influence of A. Beug, Bakunin became a Communist. In 1843, he went to Paris and there he came into contact with Proudhon. However, four years after he was turned out from France on account of his criticism of the Russian Government. In 1849, he became one of the leaders of a revolt at Dresden. On three occasions, he was sentenced to death. However, he was not executed. He was transported to Siberia by the Russian Government, but he was able to escape. He went first to Japan, then to the U.S.A. and finally to London. He joined the International under the influence of Marx and Engels. In 1869, he founded the Social Democratic Alliance for the purpose of propagating his ideas among the people. He emphatically rejected all the institutions of political control. It did not make much difference even if those institutions were based on the principle of universal suffrage. Even the most democratic devices could not change the essential character of the State. The State had a demoralizing effect among the people. This applied both to the governors and the governed. The reason was obvious. The State did not act through persuasion and enlightenment. It acted through compulsion and force. It degraded the moral and intellectual level of the people. It made either tyrants or egoists.

Kropotkin (1842-1921)

Kropotkin was born in a noble family in Russia. In his boyhood, he became interested in liberalism. He got his education in a military school. He worked in the army for six years but resigned in disgust. Then he devoted his time to the study of physical geography. He did survey work and prepared maps, and became an authority on physical geography. In 1872, he visited Switzerland and got himself enrolled as a member of the International Workingmen's Association at Geneva. Finding the programme of the Association conservative, he left it and became an anarchist. When he went back to Russia, he took part in the Nihilist movement. He was arrested in 1874 and imprisoned. However, he managed to escape from jail in 1876. First he went to England and from there shifted to Switzerland. He also visited Paris in 1877 but returned to Switzerland. It was during his stay on the Swiss soil that he edited the revolutionary newspaper called Le Revolte. In 1881 he was turned out from Switzerland. Again, he went to England and from there to France. He was imprisoned in 1883 but released in 1886. He did a lot of writing work. The most important books written by him are the following :-

(1) The Conquest of Bread (1888).

(2) Anarchism: Its Philosophy and Ideal (1896).

(3) The State, its Part in History (1898).

(4) Fields, Factories and Workshops (1899).

(5) Mutual Aid, a Factor of Evolution (1902).

(6) Modern Science and Anarchism (1903).

He continued to live in London till 1917 when the Russian Revolution took place. Then he went to Russia, but was disappointed by the developments there and died in 1921. On his death the Russian Government made an offer of a State funeral for him but the members of his family declined the offer. Kropotkin was a man of gentle and attractive personality. He was respected by all who came into contact with him.

SUGGESTED READINGS

Beer, Max : **The Life and Teachings of Karl Marx,** 1918.
Berlin, Isiah : **Karl Marx, His Life and Environment,** 1948.
Bodin, Louis, B.: **Theoretical System of Karl Marx,** 1907.
Bober, M. M.: **Karl Marx's Interpretation of History,** 1927.
Burns, E.: **What is Marxism?**
Carr, E.H. : **Karl Marx: A Study in Fanaticism.** 1934.
Carr, E. H.: **Michael Bakunin,** 1937.
Chang, Sherman, H.: **The Marxian Theory of the State,** 1931.
Cole, G. D.H.: **A History of Socialist Thought,** 1953-60.
Cole, G. D.H.: **What Marx Really Meant,** 1934.
Cole, G. D. H.: **The Life of Robert Owen,** London, 1930.
Ebenstein, W.: **Great Political Thinkers,** 1965.
Gray, A.: **The Socialist Tradition.**
Hook, Sidney : **Towards the Understanding of Karl Marx,** 1933.
Hook, Sidney: **Marx and the Marxists,** 1955.
Hunt, R.N.C. : **Theory and Practice of Communism.**
Kirkup, Thomas: **A History of Socialism,** 1913.
Laidler, H.W.: **History of Socialist Thought,** 1927.
Laski, Harold J.: **Karl Marx,** 1922.
Laski, Harold J.: **Commentary on the Communist Manifesto.**
Laski, Harold J.: **Communism.**
Lenin : **The Materialistic Interpretation of History.**
Lenin : **Karl Marx.**
Leopold, R.W.: **Robert Dale Owen,** 1940.
Lightheim, George: **Marxism,** 1961.
Lindsay, A.D.: **Karl Marx's Capital, an Introductory Essay,** 1925.
MacCabe, J.: **Robert Owen,** London, 1920.
Manuel, Frank E.: **The New World of Henri Saint-Simon,** 1956.
Manuel, Frank E.: **The Prophets of Paris,** 1962.
Mehring, Franz: **Karl Marx,** 1936.
Popper, K.: **The Open Society and its Enemies,** 1945.
Possony, S.T. (Ed.): **The Communist Manifesto.**
Rae, J.: **Contemporary Socialism.**
Ruhle, Otto: **Karl Marx: His Life and Work,** 1929.
Russell, Betrand : **Roads to Freedom.**
Ryazanoff, D.: **Karl Marx and Friedrich Engels.**
Seligman, E.R.A.: **The Economic Interpretation of History,** 1924.
Spargo, J.: **Karl Marx: His Life and Work,** 1910.
Wolfe, Bertram : **Marxism: One Hundred Years in the Life of a Doctrine,** 1965

CHAPTER

24 THE EASTERN QUESTION

In the words of Miller, **the Eastern Question may be defined as the problem of filling up the vacuum created by the gradual disappearance of the Turkish Empire from Europe.** When the Turks were at the height of their power, they ruled over the Balkans, Asia Minor, Syria, Mesopotamia, Arabia, Egypt and almost the whole of the north coast of Africa. However, the Turkish Empire began to decline gradually. The peace of Karlowitz of 1699 has been justly described as "the first dismemberment of the Ottoman Empire." It was the initial step in the historical process which continued for more than two centuries. It is true that on certain occasions the Turks were able to gain some temporary advantage, but on the whole the process of disintegration continued and ultimately the Ottoman rule was practically ended from the Balkans and North Africa. So far as the Balkans were concerned, there were many Christian races, viz., the Serbs, the Bulgars, the Greeks and the Romanians. The Turkish rule was very oppressive and sometimes there was a wholesale massacre of the Christians in the Balkans. The subject people were encouraged to assert their independence partly on account of the decline of the military power of the Turks and partly on account of the growth of nationalism among them. They were also assisted by Russia and sometimes by other powers such as England and France. Lord Morley has described the Eastern Question as a **"shifting, intractable and interwoven tangle of conflicting interests, rival people and antagonistic faiths."** According to a Russian statesman, "The damned Eastern Question is like the gout. Sometimes it takes you in the leg, sometimes it nips your hand. One is lucky if it does not fly to the stomach." It came to the fore at various times during the 19th century and those can be called the various phases of the **Eastern Question.**

Two factors had delayed the dismemberment of Turkey in Europe. One was military and the other was geographical. Turkey never sank during the eighteenth century to the military weakness of Poland or Spain. She could offer considerable resistance to both Russia and Austria. As late as 1788, her armies defeated the Habsburg forces. On account of her geographical position, Turkey was away from the centre of political gravity. If she had been within the orbit of Western interests, she would probably have suffered a speedier political death. As it was, Europe was not primarily concerned with her. France alone realised the commercial opportunities of the Ottoman Empire. Austria-Hungary was concentrating her attention in the West. She seemed to be more concerned in Western than in Eastern issues. She was involved in rivalry with France and Prussia. She was worried about the defence of the Netherlands and the extension of her power in Germany. She was more interested in Bavaria than in the Balkans. Joseph II of Austria furthered the schemes of Catherine, the Great, in order to advance the Western interests of the Habsburgs. It is true that Russia also looked westwards and strove for position among the Western powers but she felt particularly interested in Turkey. She was bent upon the control of the Black Sea and the Straits in order to command a passage to the Mediterranean. She looked upon herself as the historical successor of that Byzantine-Empire which had once shared with Rome the rule of the civilized world. The Czar was the patron of the Greek Church to which most of the Christian subjects of the Porte belonged. It was the political mission of Russia to place the Cross upon St. Sophia. Russia wanted Constantinople to become great once again as Tsargrad. The ambitions of Russia in Turkey were a constant factor in the Eastern Question from the days of

Peter, the Great, to the World War I. However, the means differed from time to time. They alternated between the expulsion and dismemberment of Turkey on the one hand and the maintenance of a weak state over which she could assume lordship on the other. Russia made considerable progress in her ambitions in Turkey during the reign of Catherine, the Great. By the treaty of Kutchuk Kainardji of 1774 which ended the Six Years' war with Turkey, Russia got a firm hold on the north shore of the Black Sea and the control of the mouths of the Don and the Dnieper. Russia pushed Turkey back to the frontier of the Bug. She acquired trading rights in the Turkish waters in the Black Sea and the Danube. She got a permanent diplomatic footing in Constantinople. She got the right of placing consuls and vice-consuls wherever she wished. She was granted an ambiguous protectorate over the Greek Christians of the Ottoman Empire. She also acquired a vague but acknowledged right of interference in the internal affairs of Turkey so far as the government of the principalities of Wallachia and Moldavia was concerned. The treaty of 1774 was an important step towards territorial domination and religious and political control.

In alliance with Austria, Catherine, the Great, made war against Turkey in 1788. She manoeuvred to engage the Western Powers in war against Revolutionary France so that she may have a free hand for her own scheme. She had in her mind some scheme of partitioning Turkey but she was not successful. In 1791, Austria was forced to withdraw from the Turkish campaign. In 1792, Russia was also compelled to make peace with Turkey, but she managed to secure the Crimea and advanced her frontier to the Dniester. Catherine could boast, "I came to Russia a poor girl. Russia has dowered me richly, but I have paid her back with Azov, the Crimea and the Ukraine." For the next few years, Russia was occupied with the dismemberment of Poland and her participation in the second and third Coalitions against France. It was after the Treaty of Tilsit of 1807 that Czar Alexander I began to dream of partitioning Turkey with French help. However, Napoleon had no intention of furthering the ambitions of Alexander in the Balkans. On the eve of the Moscow campaign, Czar Alexander made in 1812 the peace of Bucharest with Turkey by which he got Bessarabia and thereby advanced Russian territory to the river Pruth. By 1815, the Russian Empire had reached the borders of the principalities of Wallachia and Moldavia. Many new factors arose to complicate what had so far been a simple issue between Russia and Turkey. As the various parts of Turkey rose in revolt during the nineteenth century, the other European powers such as Great Britain, France, Germany and Austria got involved in the fortunes of Turkey.

Serbia. The Serbs raised the standard of revolt against the Turkish rule. They began their struggle in 1804 under the leadership of Karageorge who was a man of peasant birth. The movement was supported by Russia up to 1812. However, the Czar was forced to make peace with Turkey in that year on account of the invasion of Russia by Napoleon. The Turks took advantage of the changed circumstances and were able to reestablish their hold over Serbia. However, the rising was renewed under Milosh Obrenovitch who was recognised by the Sultan in 1820 as "Prince of the Serbians". Backed by Russia, Obrenovitch continued to press for the independence of Serbia. By 1830, the connection of Serbia with Turkey became merely nominal. The country was ruled by the princes of the Obrenovitch family by hereditary right.

Greek War of Independence. The Greeks were the next to raise the standard of revolt against the Turks. They were subjected to heavy taxation and were otherwise treated with great severity. There was a revival of the Greek national spirit towards the end of the 18th century and the beginning of the 19th century. The ancient Greek literature was revived and an attempt was made to restore the classical Greek language in place of the corrupt dialect spoken by the people. The study of the glories of the past by their ancestors, gave them encouragement and hope and created a strong desire for independence. In 1814, a society called the Hetairia Philike was formed by some Greeks at Odessa. Its object was to drive out the Turks from Greece and establish the independence of the country. The society became popular and powerful in course of time.

The Greeks revolted in 1821 under the leadership of Prince Alexander Ypsilanti. Czar Alexander found himself in a difficult position. As the protector of the Greek Church, as the champion of oppressed nationalities, as the traditional friend of Turkey's enemies, he would naturally like to interfere on behalf of the Greeks. Alexander was also the sworn enemy of revolutionary principles wherever they were to be found. At the same time, Russia had her own quarrel with Turkey and she might like to take advantage of the Greek revolt to fulfil her own ambitions. However, the attitude of the Czar was decided by Metternich who had complete control over him. Metternich's own attitude was that the revolt should be allowed to burn itself out beyond the pale of civilization. No wonder, Czar Alexander did not show any sympathy for Ypsilanti and ordered him to return immediately to Russia. He also ordered the rebels to surrender themselves to the Sultan on pain of incurring his displeasure. The attitude of the Czar decided the fate of Ypsilanti who was defeated. He was arrested and had to spend the rest of his days in prison.

The Greeks also revolted in the Morea in 1821. Russia was excited by the execution of the Patriarch of Constantinople and the massacre of Greek Christians. It was feared that she might attack

Turkey at once. Both England and Austria took measures to avoid the danger of Russian intervention in Turkey. For some years, Canning and Metternich were in agreement in principle. The struggle between the Greeks and Turks was not the business of any other State and consequently it was the duty of the Great Powers to "hold the ring" and not to allow any power to interfere. Canning's view was that if Russia was allowed to interfere in Greece, she might "gobble Greece at one mouthful and Turkey at the next." Such was the situation between 1820 and 1825. Both the Greeks and the Turks were equally cruel and both of them were proving a match for each other. Both Castlereagh and Canning were friendly to the Greeks and their object was to induce Turkey to come to terms with them so that the Czar might not be able to fish in troubled waters. It is pointed out that the war in the Morea was literally a war of extermination. The Greek slogan was: "Turkey shall live no longer, neither in the Morea nor on the whole earth." There was a wholesale massacre of Christians in Thessaly, Macedonia, Asia Minor and Chios. There was a stage when the Czar gave an ultimatum to Turkey and war seemed imminent.

However a great change took place in the Greek War of Independence. When the Turkish Sultan risked for the help of Mehmet Ali Pasha of Egypt, the latter sent his son Ibrahim at the head of a great army and navy. He conquered and destroyed Crete in 1824 and landed in the Morea in 1825. Having secured Navarino as his base, Ibrahim advanced through the Morea "harrying, devastating and slaughtering in all directions." Missolonghi was captured and Lord Byron lost his life.

Things changed in Russia also. Czar Alexander who was too much under the influence of Metternich, died in 1825 and was succeeded by Nicholas I who was a man of a very different temperament and training. He was not under the influence of Metternich and consequently could afford to follow an independent policy. It is stated that although he did not care very much for the Greeks as such, he was also not disposed to allow the Sultan to play fast and loose with Russia.

At this time, Canning, Foreign Minister of England, sent the Duke of Wellington on a special mission to St. Petersburg. In April 1826, an agreement between Great Britain and Russia was reached and the two powers agreed to offer joint mediation to Turkey. According to the agreement, Greece was to pay tribute to the Sultan but otherwise she was to be practically independent.

Czar Nicholas had already despatched an ultimatum to the Sultan who submitted and signed a Convention. The Sultan agreed to evacuate the Principalities, make some concessions to Serbia and submit to the will of the Czar in all matters. However, there was no reference to Greece. The Sultan was not willing to accept any mediation unless it was backed by force. In July 1827, the Treaty of London was signed between Great Britain, Russia and France. It was agreed between the parties that if Turkey refused an immediate armistice, force was to be applied. The resistance of the Greeks was breaking down and there was every possibility of their collapse after the fall of Athens in June 1827. It was rumoured that Ibrahim intended to transport all the Greeks who fell into his hands to Asia and Africa. In August 1827, Greece accepted the mediation of the three powers. However, it was declined by Turkey as she considered herself to be strong.

Admiral Cordington received instructions to "intercept all ships freighted with men or arms destined to go against the Greeks" without "degenerating into hostilities." Ibrahim was informed by the English and French admirals that not a single ship would be allowed to harbour off Navarino, Ibrahim, in anger, tried to kill the wretched survivors in the Morea. The admirals remonstrated with Ibrahim and the Turks fired on the British. The Battle of Navarino began on 20 October, 1827. Before sunset, all the Turko-Egyptian ships "had disappeared, the Bay of Navarino was covered with their wrecks." The Battle of Navarino was the most decisive battle of the war and it ultimately secured the independence of the Greeks. However, the victors of Navarino did not get any praise for their achievement. Canning had already died in August 1827 and the Duke of Wellington who succeeded him, expressed regret for the "untoward event" of Navarino.

Great Britain left the war and France followed suit. The Turks felt happy and they decided to deal with the Greeks in their own way. No wonder, Czar Nicholas declared war against Turkey in April 1828. He crossed the Pruth and occupied the Principalities. The Russian fleet also entered the Dardanelles. The action of Russia seemed to destroy the work of Castlereagh and Canning who had tried to check the Russian influence in the Balkans. On the one hand, the Greeks were at the mercy of the Sultan and on the other the independence of Turkey was threatened by the Czar. The Turks put up a stiff resistance but they were no match for the Russians. In September 1829, peace was made between Russia and Turkey.

England and France successfully negotiated with Mehmet Ali and Ibrahim for the withdrawal of the Egyptian forces from the Morea, After their evacuation, the fortresses were occupied by the French. According to the terms of the Protocols signed in London, the Morea and Greece were placed under the protection of the two powers. Greece was to be an autonomous but tributary State under a prince selected by the powers. The frontiers of the new States were also defined. These arrangements were confirmed by the Treaty of Adrianople (1829). It was in this way that the independence of Greece was recognized.

France and England were afraid that Greece might become a vassal State of Russia. No wonder, Wellington proposed to divide her into halves so as to make her as small and weak as possible. Aberdeen went a step further and proposed to "trisect" her. However, Wellington and Aberdeen were turned out from office and Palmerston and Grey followed a different policy. In 1832, the boundaries of Greece were enlarged. She was declared independent and guaranteed a loan and a monarch. The independence of Greece was recognized by Russia, England and France, Greece was able to get rid of Russian influence also.

There was sympathy in France for the cause of the Greeks and the French helped them to some extent. As regards Austria, Metternich held the view that the Greeks were rebels and must be left to their fate. The Greek revolt was a disease and Austria should be saved from its contagion. Although Russia was checked in the beginning by Metternich, the Russians played their part and did the fighting single-handed after 1828. Prussia followed in the footsteps of Austria. As regards England, she sympathized wholeheartedly with the Greek cause. Every kind of help was given to the Greeks who were considered to be the givers of civilization to Europe. Canning was himself a Greek scholar. According to Fisher, "The gentry of England had no such apprehensions. English nationalism they enjoyed; Irish nationalism they had suppressed, Indian nationalism was in a distant future. Education made them Philhellenes, public life made them parliamentarians, their sympathies as sportsmen went out to a small nation struggling to be free. When Byron died at Missolonghi, a martyr to Hellenic liberty, the romantic enthusiasm of the English for the Greeks spread far and wide into the streets and taverns. No one stopped to ask how much of the ancient Hellas, which young men were taught to admire in the halls of Oxford and Cambridge, still survived in the herdsmen, the brigands and the sea-pirates of Greece and its islands. The name of Greece was a talisman. Though Turkey was still the official friend and make-weight against Russian designs in the East, the mass of England was behind George Canning when at last he was brought to recognize the Greek insurgents as belligerents and joined with France and Russia to save them from extinction."

Mehmet Ali and the Porte. Mehmet Ali, an Albanian adventurer, had through his efforts raised himself to the Governorship of Egypt. Although barbarous and uneducated, he had the ability to appreciate Western civilization. Under him, French experts were employed and Egypt became a prosperous and powerful State owing allegiance to the Porte only in name. Between 1824 and 1827, Mehmet Ali's Egyptian army nearly reconquered the whole of Greece. But for the intervention of Russia, Great Britain and France, the Greeks might have been finished once for all. However, after the Greek War of Independence, Mehmet Ali was given the island of Crete by Turkey as a reward for the services rendered by him. He considered the reward as inadequate. He had also come to know all the weaknesses of Turkey. No wonder, he thought of making himself independent of the Porte, and he found a pretext for it. In 1832, his son, Ibrahim, invaded Syria and advanced into Asia Minor. The Turks were defeated and the way to Constantinople was open for the invader.

Sultan Mahmud II turned to European powers for help. He appealed to Great Britain but she was busy in the Belgian question. He appealed to France, but public opinion in France wan sympathetic towards Mehmet Ali. In despair, the Sultan accepted the offer of help from Russia. The Sultan who had formerly declared that he would give Constantinople and his Empire to any one who would bring Mehmet's head, must have felt now that in accepting Russian help, he was making a similar bargain. The Russian Government was prepared to give help at once. The Russian squadron entered the Bosphorus. A Russian army encamped on the Asiatic shore. Five thousand Russian troops were landed at a place near Constantinople.

The French were afraid of Russian intervention from the moment Mehmet Ali started the war. France was keenly interested in Mehmet Ali and regarded him as her protege. The French Government had discouraged Mehmet Ali from declaring the war. Now that the war was declared, France sent a mission to Constantinople with a view to persuading Russia to withdraw from the conflict. She failed. Great Britain and Austria were successful. They were able to persuade the Sultan to give Syria and Adana to Mehmet Ali (1833). Thus, the "Egyptian affair" ended and Russia withdrew.

Treaty of Unkiar Skelessi. However, before Russia withdrew she had entered into a treaty with Turkey. The Treaty of Unkiar Skelessi of 1833 between Russia and Turkey was one of defence. It was made for 8 years. Russia promised to come to the help of Turkey whenever she was in danger. The treaty also laid down that if Russia went to war with any European power, the Porte would close the Dardanelles and make Russia impregnable on the side of the Black Sea. The Russian fleet was at liberty to pass through the Dardanelles to the Mediterranean and retire whenever she pleased to a place of security. The treaty implied the control of the foreign policy of the Turks by Russia. It converted Turkey into a sort of Russian protectorate. Nicholas I had given up the policy of conquest and partition in favour of that of penetration and control.

The Treaty of Unkiar Skelessi was more than what France and England could allow. The Czar managed to secure the consent of Austria and Prussia. Although Nicholas I assured Metternich that he would not invoke the treaty without first accepting the mediation of Austria, the treaty remained a danger to Europe. For months war appeared imminent. Great Britain was as much aggrieved with Turkey as with Russia, for the Porte's admission of Russian ships was contrary to the Anglo-Turkish treaty of 1809. Palmerston sent an official protest against the treaty. Public opinion in England was extremely agitated on this point. The British Government would have got plenty of support if she had resorted to a strong foreign policy. However, Palmerston moved very cautiously.

The cause of this caution was that Palmerston was not sure of the attitude which the French Government might adopt. She might have seen eye to eye with Great Britain in opposing Russia's designs on Turkey, but French and British policy tended to clash over the Carlist question in Spain and hence the uncertainty. Palmerston concluded a treaty with the Spanish and Portuguese Governments in 1834 and France also joined it. This Quadruple Alliance of April 22, 1834 was a great achievement and in the words of Palmerston, "this treaty was a capital hit in all my own doing." This famous alliance gave Palmerston whatever special confidence he might have needed to handle the Turco-Russian question firmly. Unfortunately, Melbourne's Government of which he was a member, fell in November 1834, but Palmerston's policy was carried on by the Duke of Wellington. In April 1835, Palmerston came to power once again. He thought that Russia would easily be beaten if there was a war. He wrote this to Temple : "The fact is that Russia is a humbug, and that if England were finally to go to war with her, we should throw her back half a century in one campaign." However, no one really wanted war. Since Russia showed no desire to assert her position at Constantinople, peace was maintained for four years and war was suspended.

In 1836, there was a change of ministry in France. Thiers became the First Minister. Although the Porte thought that Thiers was friendly towards England, the latter showed his inclination towards the central Powers. There was a proposal for marrying the Duke of Orleans to an Austrian princess. However, Thiers was dismissed by Louis Philippe on account of his militant policy and the new minister was Mole.

In the meanwhile, both Mehmet Ali and the Sultan were preparing for a final struggle. Mahmud II was westernising the army and Moltke was his military adviser.

Things were not going on smoothly in Egypt. In 1837, Mehmet Ali began to strengthen his position in Syria. In 1838, he told the British Consul at Alexandria that he was determined to be independent. Palmerston was astonished at this. He knew full well that Turkey would be defeated and Russia would have to get in owing to the provisions of the treaty of Unkiar Skelessi of 1833. There was also the danger of France supporting Mehmet Ali. Palmerston's policy had three objects in view, viz., to prevent any further disruption of the Turkish Empire by Mehmet Ali, to obtain the supersession of the treaty of Unkiar Skelessi and to prevent a combination of Russia and France. Palmerston handled the critical situation in a masterly manner. The Turkish and Egyptian forces were on a war footing and faced each other. Ponsonby said in 1839 that "nobody doubts of war".

There were certain factors which enabled peace to be preserved. The attitude of the Five Powers was one of peace. They recommended to the contending parties to come to a peaceful settlement, but as both the parties were irreconcilable, war started in June 1839. Mahmud's army was defeated and he died within a few days. The Turkish Admiral with his ships sailed off to join Mehmet Ali at Alexandria. "In three weeks, Turkey had lost her Sultan, her army and her fleet."

The news of the death of the Sultan and the battle of Nisibi convinced Palmerston of the necessity of decisive action. He wrongly took it for granted that France and England would co-operate with each other. He drafted orders that the British squadron should move on to Alexandria to bring pressure on Mehmet Ali. The French refused to co-operate on account of their pro-Mehmet Ali feelings. There was a possibility that Mehmet Ali might get whatever he wanted by bringing pressure on the Sultan. To avoid that contingency, the Powers advised the Porte not to enter into any treaty with Mehmet Ali.

When Palmerston found that France was not co-operating in exerting pressure on Mehmet Ali, he made up his mind to break off all connection with France and refer the matter to a Conference of Five Powers. The object of the Conference was to induce the powers to blockade Syria until Mehmet Ali should surrender the Turkish fleet. Palmerston was anxious to get the matter solved by a Conference because in that way there was the possibility of avoiding the combination of Russia and Turkey under the Treaty of 1833, Russia was also anxious to avoid a rupture. The Czar expressed his willingness to co-operate with the English to stop the advance of Ibrahim Pasha even if France stood aloof. Palmerston informed the French Government that the British Government would agree to act with Russia, Austria and Prussia "whether France joins or not; but that on every account we should deeply regret that France should not be a party to the proceedings."

Palmerston got the alarming news that the King of France had told some foreign minister that France was protecting Mehmet Ali because she would probably be at war with England in two years and would want the co-operation of Mehmet Ali's fleet in the Mediterranean. Palmerston described the King of France as "a man in whom no solid trust can be reposed." France complained that she was being isolated but in spite of that she persisted in supporting Mehmet Ali's pretensions in Syria. The French educated opinion was strongly in favour of Mehmet Ali and no French statesman could go against it. The French Government was under the delusion that the British and Russian Governments would not act in co-operation, but as matter of fact they had already agreed.

In March 1840, Thiers came to power in France. His policy was to maintain friendship with Great Britain, preserve for France her membership of the concert of Five Powers and yet to insist upon keeping Syria for Mehmet Ali. It was an impossible task for anybody to perform. Palmerston was determined to restrict the power of Mehmet Ali and Thiers would not agree to that. Thus arose the deadlock.

At this time, the Turkish Ambassador went to London and asked the Powers to redeem their promise of 1839 by which they had promised help. The Porte offered to give the Governorship of Egypt to Mehmet Ali if that could help matters. Thiers and his Government were indifferent to the negotiations at London. The reason was that while these deliberations were taking place at London, separate negotiations were going on at Constantinople through the mediation of the French Ambassador. When Palmerston heard of the negotiation at Constantinople, he got exasperated. A treaty was signed by the representatives of the Powers in London in 1840. The Turkish Ambassador also signed it. By this treaty, Mehmet Ali was to be made the hereditary Governor of Egypt. Acre and Southern Syria were to be given to him for life. The offer of Southern Syria was to hold good for 10 days. The offer of Egypt alone was to last for 20 days. The Four Powers also agreed to blockade Mehmet Ali to bring pressure on him. They also agreed to stop his advance on Constantinople by collective action. The Porte was to be under the protection of the Powers and the Treaty of 1833 between Russia and Turkey was superseded.

There was a storm of indignation at Paris. It was felt that France was insulted. For a few months, war seemed imminent between France and the rest of Europe. The French were in a mood to fight and Thiers was their mouthpiece. The only hesitation in the mind of Thiers was whether the attack should be directed against Russia or England. The patriotism of France was aroused. Palmerston told the French Government that "if France throws down the gauntlet, we shall not refuse to pick it up."

Things were moving very fast in Syria. Mehmet Ali rejected the terms of the Powers, and the latter decided to bring pressure on him. The blockade of the Syrian coast began. Napier bombarded Beirut and captured it. He won many other victories. The Sultan deposed Mehmet Ali. There was no possibility of peace. Louis Philippe, King of France, did not approve of the militant policy of Thiers. Palmerston wrote thus to the French Government in October 1840: "If France makes us a friendly communication tending to lead to amicable discussion of the present state of affairs, we shall receive it, and deal with it in the spirit in which it is made."

Fortunately, the peace party in Paris triumphed and Thiers was dismissed. The new government sent a conciliatory reply. By this time, Napier had captured Acre and Mehmet Ali had to retire from Syria. Napier proceeded to Alexandria and dictated the terms of peace. By this, Mehmet Ali was to retire from Syria on the condition of keeping Egypt in perpetuity. The Four Powers ratified the terms. In February 1841, the Sultan was induced to issue a Firman by which he cancelled the deposition of Mehmet Ali, and recognised him as the hereditary Governor of Egypt. The final settlement was made by a Conference at London in 1841 and the previous decisions were confirmed. The final solution of the crisis was universally regarded as a great triumph for Palmerston. The prestige of Great Britain was raised and the treaty of Unkiar Skelessi was cancelled without a war.

The Crimean War (1854-56). According to Sir J.A.R. Marriott, there are two conflicting views as to the origin of the difficulties which ultimately resulted in the Crimean War. Queen Victoria ascribed it to the "selfishness and ambition of one man (Nicholas I) and his servants." Kingslake held Napoleon III primarily responsible. However, neither of the two views can be accepted in entirety although there is a large element of truth in both the views. Napoleon III, if not the primary cause of war, was at least the immediate firebrand in the Eastern conflagration. By a treaty of 1740, France had obtained from Turkey the custody of several holy places in and near Jerusalem. The Latin monks became neglectful of their rights and the guardianship fell into the hands of the Greek monks. In 1850, Napoleon III was anxious to seek the support of the Clericals in France and asserted his right to place the Latin monks in possession of the holy places. He was supported by Austria-Hungary, Spain and other Roman Catholic Powers.

Seaman says, "It seems therefore proper to agree with those who argue that the Crimean War was as much a war about the European balance of power as it was about the Eastern Question. At any rate, the experience of the Greek and Syrian Questions suggested that if the Eastern Question was dealt with apart from and in disregard of the general clash of political theory normally dividing East from West it could be dealt with without war. Thus the principle that the Eastern question was international in character did not of itself cause the war. There had to be added to it the hostility of Liberal England and Napoleonic France to Russia on other grounds.

"Moreover, the Czar, though he did not think he was acting with the general agreement of Europe when he marched into Moldavia and Wallachia, certainly did think when he pressed his claims in the Balkans in 1853 that he would have English support. And once Russia had withdrawn from the Principalities, no further excuse for the war, except that of teaching the Czar a lesson, existed. Hence the diversion of the war from the Balkans, where it made sense in relation to the Turkish Empire, to the Crimean peninsula where it made very little sense at all. This diversion meant that a war supposedly planned for the defence of the Turkish Empire became, almost before a shot was fired, an act of aggression against Russia."

According to Prof. A.J.P. Taylor, "In one sense, it was predestined and had deep-seated causes. Neither Nicholas nor Napoleon nor the British Government could retreat in the conflict for prestige once it was launched. Nicholas needed a subservient Turkey for the sake of Russian security; Napoleon needed success for the sake of his domestic position; the British Government needed an independent Turkey for the security of the eastern Mediterranean. Yet none of the three had conscious plans of aggression, not even Napoleon, despite his welcome of disturbance for its own sake. The British fears that Russia planned the dismemberment of Turkey were as ill-founded as Russia's fears that the Western Powers threatened her security in the Black Sea. Mutual fear, not mutual aggression, caused the Crimean War. Nevertheless it was not a war without a purpose. At bottom, it followed from the events of 1848. British opinion would never have turned so harshly against Russia had it not been for Austria's victory in Italy and, still more, Russia's intervention in Hungary. The Crimean War was fought for the sake of Europe rather than for the Eastern Question; it was fought against Russia, not in favour of Turkey. But there was a deep-seated, unspoken disparity between the aims and outlook of the two western allies. Both resented the Russian preponderance which had, they thought, caused the failure of the revolutions of 1848; but only Napoleon III hoped to reverse the verdict. The British certainly wished for no new revolutions; they fought Russia out of resentment and supposed that her defeat would strengthen the European Balance of Power. Napoleon, on the other hand, thought that her defeat would destroy the balance. Hence, though the more ambitious, he was less bellicose. He was quite ready to call off the struggle once Russia abandoned interest in Central Europe.

"The real stake in the Crimean war was not Turkey. It was Central Europe, that is to say, Germany and Italy. The British hoped to substitute 'the Concert of Europe' for the hegemony of Russia; they failed. Napoleon III wished to substitute his own hegemony, and for a few years supposed that he had succeeded. As events turned out, the Central Powers evaded commitments; and for this reason the Crimean War was indecisive. This was in itself the decision. The Crimean War was fought to remake the European system. The old order of the Holy Alliance was destroyed; but no new system took its place—neither the liberal Concert of British ideal nor the revolutionary association of Napoleon's dreams. Instead there opened a period of European anarchy which lasted from the Crimean War until the next great struggle in the Near East." (**The Struggle for Mastery in Europe,** pp. 60-61).

According to Fyffe, the claims of the rival brotherhoods which related to doors, keys, stars and lamps could have been settled to the satisfaction of all the parties within a few hours by an experienced stage manager, but in the hands of "diplomatists bent on obtaining triumphs over one another they assumed dimensions that overshadowed the peace of Europe." Both the French and Russian ministers at Constantinople tormented the Porte for a decision. In 1852, the Porte granted similar rights to both the parties. In 1853, however, Turkey agreed to the claims of France and denied them to Russia.

Nicholas I treated the conduct of the Porte as an outrage upon himself. He would like to have revenge. In 1853, he addressed himself to Sir H. Seymour, British ambassador at St. Petersburg, in these words: "The sick man was in extremities; a time had come for clear understanding between England and Russia. The occupation of Constantinople by Russian troops might be necessary, but the Czar would not hold it permanently. He would not permit any other Power to establish itself at Bosphorus, neither would he permit the Ottoman Empire to be broken up to afford a refuge to the Mazzinis and the Kossuths of Europe. The Danubian Principalities were already independent States under Russian protection. The other possessions of the Sultan north of Balkans might be placed on a similar footing. England might annex Egypt and Greece. The British Government refused to enter into any understanding with the Czar. At this, Nicholas I sent Prince Menschikoff to Constantinople to demand from the Porte not only an immediate settlement of the questions relating to the Holy Places but also a treaty guaranteeing to the Greek Church the undisturbed enjoyment of all its ancient rights and benefit of all privileges that might be accorded by the Porte to any other Christian community.

The treaty which Menschikoff was instructed to demand would have placed the Sultan under the Czar and the position of contracting parties with regard to the entire body of rights and privileges enjoyed by the Sultan's subjects of the Greek faith would have made the violation of those rights in the case of any individual Christian a matter entitling Russia to interfere or to claim satisfaction. By the treaty of Kutchuk Kainardji of 1774, the Sultan had bound himself to protect the Christian religion and churches. However, this vague phrase did not create any matter for treaty obligation. If it had given to Russia any general right of interference on behalf of the members of the Greek Church, it would have given an identical right on behalf of the Roman Catholics and Protestants. However, the Czar had never claimed that the treaty of Kutchuk Kainardji had given him such a right. The treaty mentioned by name only one ecclesiastical building for whose priests the Porte did concede to Russia the right of addressing representations to the Sultan. That the Greek Church possessed by custom and by enactment privileges which it was the duty of the Sultan to respect no one contested. The novelty of the Russian claim was that the observation of those rights should be made a matter of treaty with Russia. The importance of the Russian demand was proved by the fact that Menschikoff forbade the Turkish ministers to reveal it to other Powers and Nicholas I caused the British Government to be informed that the mission was dispatched only to settle the question of the Holy Places. Regarding the Russian claim of a general protectorate over Greek Christians in Turkey, Lord Clarendon wrote thus: "No sovereign having a proper regard for his own dignity and independence could admit proposals so undefined as those of Prince Menschikoff and by treaty confer upon another and more powerful sovereign a right of protection over a large portion of his own subjects, however well-disguised it may be. While the fact is that under the vague language of the proposed Sanad a perpetual right of interference in the internal affairs of Turkey would be conferred upon Russia, for governed as the Greek subjects of the Porte are by their ecclesiastical authorities and looking as these latter would in all things do for protection to Russia, it follows that 14,000,000 Greeks would henceforth regard the Emperor as their supreme protector and their allegiance to the Sultan would be little more than nominal, while his own independence would dwindle into vassalage."

The Porte could not have stood the pressure of Russia, but the timely appearance of Lord Stratford De Radcliffe, the British Ambassador at Constantinople, on the scene changed the whole situation. Radcliffe was a master-mind and before him the Russian Prince was a mere child. The former had spent decades in service in the Balkans and his grasp of the situation was masterly. England was deeply interested in the Balkan affairs. Her anxiety to keep control over India forced her to keep a watchful eye on the advance of Russia in the Near East. The premature death of Canning had enabled Russia to reap the fruit all alone. The treaty of Adrianople of 1829 had increased Russian influence and prestige in the Balkans. The Treaty of Unkiar Skelessi of 1833 had also added to her strength. It was under the influence of Palmerston that the Russian influence diminished and the Treaty of Unkiar Skelessi was annulled in 1841. In 1844, Nicholas had paid a visit to London and discussed with Aberdeen, the British Foreign Minister, the problem of dividing the possessions of the sick man of Europe. However, he had received no encouragement from that quarter. The British Government once again refused to consider the Eastern Question with Russia in 1853. That shows that England was not prepared to allow Russia to increase her influence in the Balkans.

Lord Stratford played his part well. He persuaded Menschikoff to separate the question of the Holy Places from that of a general Russian protectorate over the Greek Christians. This important distinction having been secured, Stratford induced the Porte to give satisfaction to Russia on the former question. The problem of the Holy Places was thus solved. In spite of this, the situation did not improve. As the Porte became more conciliatory, Menschikoff became more and more menacing although his position was rather weak. He realised that he had been tricked by Stratford. The latter advised the Porte to refuse the protectorate claimed by Menschikoff and consequently the latter left Constantinople in May 1853. A week later, the Porte addressed a note to the Powers in which he announced the settlement of the question of Holy Places and the determination of Turkey to resist the control of Russia over her.

In July 1853, the Russian army crossed the Pruth and occupied the Principalities. Under normal circumstances, such an action would have been tantamount to a declaration of war. The Czar maintained that by occupying the Principalities, he had no intention of violating peace. The Turks were also advised to desist from war. Lord Aberdeen was the Prime Minister of England since December 1852. According to Fyffe, no man in England was more pacific in disposition or more anxious to remain on terms of honourable friendship with Russia than Aberdeen himself. The Czar had justly reckoned on Aberdeen's forbearance. However, he had not taken into consideration other forces which might force the hands of Aberdeen and his ministry to resist Russian advance. Palmerston was keen on action being taken against Russia. He believed that the only chance of convincing Russia that the English were in earnest was to order the combined fleets of England and France to move to the Bosphorus and, if necessary, into the Black Sea. In spite of this Aberdeen advised the Sultan not to resist Russian invasion by force "in order to exhaust all the resources of patience". Palmerston was convinced that it was already late in the day and Russia had been encouraged in her action by the apparent timidity of England.

In spite of the different views of Palmerston and Aberdeen, Stratford seems to have taken it for granted from the very beginning that in the event of a war between Russia and Turkey, Great Britain had to fight on the side of the Ottoman Empire. Stratford did not state this in express terms, but the communication which he made to the Sultan regarding his own instructions could have been merely intended to create such an impression. If the fleet was not to defend the Sultan, it was sheer treachery and bad faith to inform him that the Ambassador had powers to place it in readiness to sail. Such a deceit was alien to the character of Stratford. From the date of Stratford's visit to the palace, England stood committed in honour to fulfil the expectation which her envoy had held out.

An effort was made by the Central Powers to avert the danger of war. The representatives of England, France, Austria-Hungary and Prussia met at Vienna in July and agreed upon a Note which was intended to satisfy both Russia and Turkey. The Note was accepted by Russia, although not in the sense intended by the mediators. Turkey refused to accept it unless certain amendments were made in it. Turkey was not prepared to recognise the general right of Russia to interfere in her affairs.

Omar Pasha, the Turkish Commander-in-Chief, gave an ultimatum to Russia to evacuate the Principalities, but the latter refused point blank. The result was a declaration of war. The Turkish squadron at Sinope was destroyed in November 1853. The massacre of Sinope was the immediate prelude to the European war. Graham wrote thus: "I have been one of the most strenuous advocates of peace with Russia up to the last moment; but the Sinope attack and recent events have changed entirely the aspect of affairs. I am afraid that a rupture with Russia is inevitable."

The coalition nature of Aberdeen's ministry and the consequent want of harmony among its members, were largely responsible for the lack of a vigorous and consistent policy by Great Britain. Marriott says that if the Cabinet had been really homogeneous and Aberdeen had been in a position to impose his will on his ministers, war might have been averted. Stratford would not have returned to Constantinople. Turkey would never have depended upon the support of England and the Czar might possibly have been induced to modify his demands. Moreover, if Palmerston had been the Premier, the Czar would have thought twice before sending Menschikoff and provoking a quarrel in which Great Britain was sure to come in. Exasperated by the conduct of Napoleon III and Stratford, the Czar relied upon Aberdeen and the peace party in England to extricate himself from difficulties of his own creation. Even after the declaration of war, Aberdeen hoped to find out a suitable formula to maintain peace. Much against his wish, Aberdeen's ministry decided to order the fleet to enter the Black Sea. Even when that was done, Napoleon was permitted to write a letter to the Czar offering his good offices. However, there was only a savage snub. Although Austria and Prussia were co-operating with France and England to bring about diplomatic pressure upon Russia, yet they remained neutrals when Great Britain joined on behalf of Turkey.

Was the Crimean War Justified? According to J.A.R. Marriott, retrospective criticism has tended to show that war, if not a crime, was at least a blunder and that it ought to have been and might have been avoided. According to Seton-Watson, **"If ever a war was made by an ill-informed but ardent public opinion against better judgment, it was the Crimean War.** It is the classic disproof of the view that the people are always pacific and only the statesmen or financiers war-like." (**Britain in Europe,** p. 359).

The deliberate opinion of a great diplomat is that in the Crimean War "England put her money on the wrong horse." Others suggest that England was dragged into war in defence of a power notorious for her oppression and misgovernment, at the heels of a diplomat. The Duke of Argyll justified the war. Kingslake popularised the idea that England was an innocent tool in the hands of an unscrupulous adventurer, anxious to establish a throne unrighteously attained by a brilliant war causelessly provoked. It is true that Napoleon III was anxious to show that his rule was better than that of Louis Philippe, but, says Marriott, it is inaccurate to assert that Stratford or Aberdeen was the tool of his ambition. The truth is that thoughtful Englishmen were convinced that the ambitions of the Czar ought to be curbed. The bias of Russian policy during the last century and a half was unmistakable. From the Treaty of Azov to that of Belgrade, from Kainardji to Jassy, from Bucharest to Adrianople and from there to Unkiar Skelessi, the advance had been stealthy but continuous. Was the dissolution of the sick man to hastened to satisfy the impatient avarice of the heir-presumptive? Was the Czar to be allowed to convert the Black Sea into a Russian Lake and to establish an exclusive and dangerous domination in Eastern Mediterranean? It was not a question as to the goodness or badness of Turkish administration. The real question was whether Europe in general and England in particular, was prepared to allow Russia to force upon the Porte "a diplomatic engagement which would have made her the sole protector of the Christian subjects of the Porte and therefore the sole arbiter of the fate of Turkey." The Crimean War was the logical result of the conviction among the Englishmen that the Russian influence must be checked at all costs.

The war having been declared, the Allies sent their forces to Crimea. The important battles were those of Alma, Balaclava and Inkermann. The winter of 1854-55 was very severe. The Czar is said to have remarked, **"I have two generals who will not fail me,"** and those were "Generals January and February." The severity of the Crimean winter was very great. The camp of Sebastopol was six or seven miles from the port of Balaclava. After the storm, the roads became impassable. The horses were weakened for want of fodder and could not drag the wagons through the mud. Men and beasts perished from exposure. Although the stores were liberally supplied by the Home Government, those could not be transported to the soldiers in the camps. The trenches were half-frozen. The troops were inadequately clothed and fed. The result was that thousands of them died of fever, cholera, scurvy, etc. About 9,000 persons died and 13,000 were admitted into hospitals. The administration of the hospitals at Scutari (which was the base), was the worst.

The sufferings of the British soldiers in the Crimea aroused the public opinion in England. Appeals were made for help and there was a generous response. However, the people were indignant against the ministry for its mistakes of omission and commission. Mr. Roebuck gave a notice in 1855 that he intended to move for the appointment of a Select Committee to enquire into the condition of the English army before Sebastopol and the conduct of those departments of the government whose duty was to minister to the wants of that army. The result was that Russell resigned at once. His action was criticised by Palmerston, Gladstone and the Queen. On January 29, 1855, Roebuck's motion was carried by 305 votes to 148 and Aberdeen resigned. Lord Durby was invited to form the new ministry. However, his efforts failed. Russell also did not fare better. None was ready to serve under him. It was under these circumstances that Palmerston was asked to form the ministry and he did so successfully. Palmerston guided the destinies of the country during the rest of the Crimean War. He was backed in his work by a strong public opinion.

Palmerston reorganised the War Office at home. There was a lot of overlapping and confusion. "The soldier was fed by the Treasury and armed by the Ordnance Board, the Home Secretary was responsible for his movements in his native country, the Colonial Secretary superintended his movement abroad, the Secretary of War took care that he was paid and was responsible for the lawful administration of the flogging which was provided for him by the Commander-in-Chief." Palmerstone simplified the administration and concentrated practically all the powers in the hands of the War Office.

Although the siege of Sebastopol was progressing, there was no satisfactory progress. The ranks of the armies were being thinned by disease. The effects of the vigorous policy of Palmerston became visible after the lapse of some time.

Peace negotiations had been started in Vienna. The Allied Powers and Austria presented "Four Points" to the Russian Government on the basis of which peace negotiations could be carried on. Russia was to give up control over Moldavia, Wallachia and Serbia. The navigation of the Danube was to be free. Russian preponderance over the Black Sea was to be ended. Russia was to give up her claim to control the Christian subjects of the Porte. Palmerston sent Lord John to take part in the negotiations in Vienna.

In the meanwhile two important events took place. One was that Sardinia joined the Allies on 26 January 1855. Cavour did so with a view to winning friends who could help him to end the Austrian control in Italy. By April 1855, 18,000 Italian soldiers were on their way to the Crimea. The second event was the death of Nicholas I who was unquestionably the prime author of war. It was hoped that the accession of the new ruler might improve matters, but the behaviour of the new Czar was not helpful.

As regards the Paris Conference, Russia agreed to three points, but she was reluctant to accept the fourth point which would have weakened her influence in the Black Sea. Palmerston was determined to liquidate the influence of Russia in the Black Sea. Lord John, the French Ambassador and Austria did not see eye to eye with Palmerston. The insistence of Palmerston was responsible for the break-up of the Vienna Conference. Although peace was not made at Vienna, the end of the war was in sight. The Russians had been weakened and their loss was terrible. In spite of that, the war dragged on for a year. Sebastopol fell in September 1855 and Kars in November 1855. Peace negotiations started in Paris and the Treaty of Paris was signed in 1856. By this Treaty, the Black Sea was absolutely neutralised. It was opened to all nations for commercial purposes. Even Turkey and Russia could not keep their warships in the Black Sea. The Danube was internationalised. Russian Protectorate over the Danubian Principalities was abolished. These principalities were to be independent. However, they were to accept the nominal sovereignty of the Sultan. Turkey was included in the concert of the European Powers. The Turkish Sultan promised to treat the Christian subjects in a humane manner.

Results of the Crimean War. The Crimean War had far-reaching effects on the politics of Europe. A check was put on the Russian influence in the Balkans and the Black Sea. She was kept back from the Danube by the giving of Bessarabia to Moldavia. Her military strength in the Black Sea was completely finished for years to come. The creation of two autonomous States of Moldavia and Wallachia put a barrier between Russia and Turkey. Turkey was the greatest gainer by the war. She got a new lease of life under the protection of European Powers. Her territorial integrity was guaranteed and she was admitted into the concert of Europe from which she had been previously excluded. In this way, she got some prestige also. It appeared that the sick man of Europe was put on her legs again. However, experience showed that all the sacrifices made during the war were not worthwhile. Russia violated in 1870 the Black Sea clauses of the Treaty of Paris. By the Treaty of San Stefano of 1871, Russia was able to wipe out completely the humiliation of the Crimean War by recovering Bessarabia. All hopes of Turkey reforming herself had to be given up and the territorial integrity of Turkey became a diplomatic fiction. Turkey did not show any signs of improvement.

The Crimean War was an important chapter in the Eastern Question and the prelude to the most important political developments of the 19th century. The war had many important indirect effects. **"Out of the mud of Crimea, a new Italy was made and less obviously, a new Germany."** Cavour, the Prime Minister of Piedmont-Sardinia, had sent his troops to the Crimea and after the defeat of Russia, he was allowed to participate in the deliberations of the statesmen in the Congress of Paris in 1856. He raised the question of Austrian rule in Italy and thereby enlisted the sympathy of the Great Powers. He also won over Napoleon III to the cause of Italian independence. The Crimean War also affected the fortunes of Austria-Hungary—Russia and Austria had been friends for a long time and that was the cornerstone of the policy of Metternich. It was on account of that friendship that Russia came to the help of Austria in 1849 when the Hungarian revolt was crushed with the help of Russian troops. However, that friendship was ended by the Crimean War. Russia resented the hostile neutrality of Austria during the Crimean War and the old ties of friendship were broken. Bismarck took advantage of the cold relations between Russia and Austria and cultivated the friendship of Russia. Particularly on the occasion of the Polish revolt of 1863, Russia was won over by Bismarck by his positive help against the Poles. The result was that when the war broke out between Austria and Prussia in 1866, Russia remained neutral and Austria had to fight single-handed. Undoubtedly, this was an indirect effect of the Crimean War.

About the Treaty of Paris, A.J.P. Taylor says that it 'solved' the problem of the relations between Russia and Turkey in three ways. The Turks gave a voluntary promise to reform. The Black Sea was neutralized. The Danubian principalities were made independent of Russia. So far as the reforms in Turkey were concerned, it amounted to nothing. The Turks never fulfilled their promise. It is true that the neutralization of the Black Sea was a great achievement of 1856 and it seemed to provide a barrier against Russia without any effort on the part of the Western Powers. Like all disarmament clauses in a peace treaty, it was an attempt to perpetuate an existing balance of power when that balance should have changed. The Russians were required to behave for all time as if the British and French fleets were in the Black Sea although in fact they had gone away. There was no sanction for neutralization except the good faith of Russia. If good faith on the part of Russia could be relied upon, there was no necessity of neutralization. No such compulsory disarmament had been imposed upon a great power except by Napoleon I on Prussia in 1807. The Allies would not have imposed such terms on any power whom they considered to be European and it was done in case of Russia because she was considered to be a semi-Asiatic state which was not above the level of Turkey or China. The result was that the neutralization clause was very much resented by Russia, and its abolition became the principal object of her diplomacy after 1856 and the same was achieved in 1870 when France and Prussia were at war with each other. The real achievement of the Treaty of Paris was the freeing of the principalities of Moldavia and Wallachia. Their independence depended upon the jealousy between Russia and Austria. The Austrians had got the Russians out by threat of war in August 1854 but as they did not pay the price for western support by withdrawing from Lombardy and Venetia they did not get themselves in. The Russian troops occupying these principalities had to be withdrawn on the conclusion of peace. Ultimately, Rumania came into existence as a buffer state guaranteed by the rivalry between Russia and Austria and a barrier against either Russian invasion of the Balkans or an Austrian domination of the Danube. While the clauses neutralizing the Black Sea lasted for only 15 years, independent Rumania survived until 1941.

The view of Taylor is that the Congress of Paris was a disappointment to nearly all who attended it. The Prussians who came late and expected nothing, had their hopes fulfilled. The British Government knew that they had not got their way. It is contended that Cavour scored a victory at the Congress of Paris but Taylor does not agree with this view. Short of being excluded, Cavour could hardly have done worse. He got none of the concessions which he considered to be essential for taking part in the war. Nothing was changed in Italy. Austria was not estranged from the western Powers. Sardinia was not treated a great power and was not given even the chance of adhering to the treaty of guarantee of 15 April. It is true that Sardinia's military assistance had won British gratitude and during the Congress both Clarendon and Palmerston talked of supporting Sardinia in the coming war against Austria, but their enthusiasm did not last long. Soon after his coming back to England, Clarendon took offence at Cavour's relations with the members of the opposition. In April 1859, the British Government demanded that Cavour should lessen the tension in Italy by declaring his respect for the Settlement of 1815. It was not British policy but French policy which decided the future of Italy. Taylor maintains that there is no reason to support that Napoleon's latter attitude would have been different if Sardinia had remained neutral during the Crimean war. In 1856, the war of Italian liberation was still far away. If and when Napoleon III participated in the war of Italian liberation, he did not do so on account of Sardinia's contribution to the Crimean war. According to Taylor, the only defence for Cavour must be found in home policy. He prevented the war being fought by conservative Sardinian Government and thus kept open a door for the future. The Crimean War was not the moment when opportunity knocked so far as Italy was concerned.

The view of Taylor is that the Congress of Paris brought about no great change. In the words of Napoleon III, "what should have been a great political revolution had been reduced to a simple tournament." The Crimean war was a decisive defeat for Russia and the Congress of Paris was a setback without parallel. The result was that Russian policy after 1856 had a singleness of purpose, which was to get the Treaty of Paris revised. Before 1854 Russia had perhaps neglected her national interests for the sake of general European concerns but for coming 15 years, she neglected everything in Europe for the sake of her national interests or national honour. It is true that the Balkans offered very little to Russia as compared with what she could hope to get from Central Asia and the Far East but this fact was not appreciated by the Czar and the statesmen who had suffered the humiliation of the loss of territory and the compulsory neutralization of the Black Sea. The result was that Russian diplomacy was concentrated for a generation on getting the Black Sea clauses cancelled.

Seaman says, "The most important clauses of the Treaty of Paris were thus secret ones, unguessed at by the signatories. They provided free and unfettered opportunity for the destruction of Austrian power in Germany and Italy to those who had the courage to act upon them. Bismarck and Cavour were the chief beneficiaries of the Crimean War, and without it there might have been neither a Kingdom of Italy nor a German Empire. Not 1848, but the Peace of Paris, ends the Metternich era, for only with the Crimean War do those political unheavals become possible which Metternich had so long hoped to postpone."

Another indirect effect of the Crimean War was that Czar Alexander II was forced to carry out a large number of reforms in Russia with a view to winning over the people. The most important reform was the emancipation of the serfs. Moreover, as the Russian expansion was checked on the European side, its activity was transferred towards Central Asia and the result was that the Government of India had to face a headache on account of the growing influence of Russia.

Between 1856 and 1878, many violations of the settlement of 1856 took place from time to time. Moldavia and Wallachia were created into autonomous principalities by the Treaty of Paris. However, the people of these principalities came from the same stock and spoke the same language. Both of them called themselves Rumanians. There was a strong desire among them to be united under one government. In 1859, the people of both the principalities elected the same person as their ruler. England, Austria and Turkey opposed the union of Rumania as it was in violation of the Treaty of Paris. However, Napoleon III was sympathetic towards the nationalist aspirations of the Rumanians and he was able to persuade the Powers to allow the union of Wallachia and Moldavia. Thus, the kingdom of Rumania came into existence.

With the help of England and Austria, Serbia was able to secure in 1867 the evacuation of her fortresses by the Turkish garrisons. In this way, Serbia became practically independent of Turkey.

In 1865, Russia encouraged the people of Crete to revolt against Turkey. In 1870, she helped the people of Bulgaria to get ecclesiastical independence. When the war started between France and Prussia in 1870, Russia was encouraged by Prussia to repudiate the Black Sea clauses of the Treaty of Paris. Thus, she got in 1870 the right to refortify Sebastopol and maintain a Russian fleet in the Black Sea.

About the Crimean war, David Thomson observes that in the long term perspective, it was a strange combination of recurrent and unusual features in European history. In so far as it was a war between Russia and Turkey, it was but one of the long sequence of Russo-Turkish wars, roughly one every generation, stretching from 1768-74, 1787-92, 1806-12, 1828-29 and going on to 1877-78. They were the result of the persistent pressure imposed upon Turkey by the Russian desire to extend influence into the Black Sea and the Mediterranean. In so far as it involved a Western invasion of Russia, it was likewise one of a long historic sequence that included the invasions of Napoleon in 1812, of the Germans in 1916-18, the Western Allies in 1919-20 and Hitler in 1941-44. It was the first war of recent times in which Britain and France fought on the same side, the first in which women, led by Florence Nightingale, took an important part and the first in which the telegraph and press exerted any influence on the course of events. This mixture of familiar and novel features suggests its intermediate position in the history of modern Europe. It was fought not so much for Turkey as against Russia. Europe, in the decade after 1848, stood at the parting of the ways. The old concert was dying. The balance of power was beginning to shift and the new era of realism was dawning. The Crimean war was a token of a profound change in the place of Europe in a wider world. It was a fumbling war, probably unnecessary, largely futile, certainly extravagant but rich in unintended consequences. It broke the spell of peace. It removed the shadow of Russian power from central European affairs and cleared the way for the re-modelling of Germany and Italy by means of war.

According to Grant and Temperley, "The Crimean War occupies a peculiar place in the history of Europe in the nineteenth century. The military methods resemble rather those of the Napoleonic age than of the period soon to be opened by Moltke and the military system of Prussia. Steam vessels were used, but their full importance was not appreciated. The telegraph had been brought to Vienna, but Constantinople and the Crimea were still beyond its reach. All that concerned the feeding and the sanitation of the armies was almost medieval in character. It was the last war on a large scale to be fought without the help of the modern resources of science. And if its methods and instruments are strange to the modern student, its aims and its diplomacy seem still more so. Ecclesiastical questions that might belong to the time of the Crusades played a part in the causes of the war. The victors in the struggle gained little if anything from it. The integrity of Turkey was in fact not maintained. The advance of Russia was not permanently checked. In the Great War of 1914, France and Britain spent many thousands of lives and many millions of money in the effort to undo some of the consequences of their victory in the Crimean War, which had been won with so much loss of blood and treasure. Yet the war is in many ways very interesting. It provides us especially with a singularly instructive illustration of the way in which wars are brought about and the procedure of some of the actors in the story is seen without the concealment and the allegation of false motives behind which diplomatists have usually liked to work."

According to Prof. Taylor, "The Congress of Paris proved a disappointment to nearly all who attended it: only the Prussians, who came late and expected nothing, had their hopes fulfilled. The British were sharply aware that they had not got their way; in fact they exaggerated the case with which Russia would recover from her defeat. Cavour is often made out to have scored a triumph at the Congress; but short of being excluded, he could hardly have done worse. He got none of the concessions which even he had originally regarded as essential in return for taking part in the war. Nothing was changed in Italy. Austria was not, to all appearance, estranged from the Western Powers; Sardinia was not treated as a Great Power and was not even given the chance of adhering to the treaty of guarantee of 15 April. It is true that Sardinia's military assistance had won British gratitude; and during the Congress when the British were still full of fight, both Clarendon and Palmerston talked of supporting Sardinia in the coming war against Austria." (**The Struggle for Mastery in Europe,** p. 88).

Bulgarian Atrocities. There was a lot of restlessness and discontentment among the Christians of the Balkans. There was a strong Pan-Slav movement in the Balkans and that was encouraged by Russia. Austria-Hungary also began to aspire to expand to the Aegean Sea. A conflict between Russia and Austria became inevitable. The Sultan did not carry out his promises of reforms in the interests of his Christian subjects. Oppression of the Turks on their Christian subjects increased. The result was that in 1875, the people of Bosnia and Herzegovina revolted. They were helped by the people of Serbia and Montenegro. The movement began to spread and there was the danger of a general conflagration. With a view to localizing the conflict, the European Powers presented to the Sultan with what is known as the **Andrassy Note** in which the Turkish rule in the Balkans was condemned and its shortcomings were pointed out. The Sultan promised to make reforms. However, the Christian rebels of the Balkans did not attach any importance to the promises made by the Sultan and demanded some positive guarantee to carry out those promises. At this time, the people of Bulgaria also joined the struggle against Turkey. The situation became dangerous and consequently the Powers presented to the Sultan what is known as the **Berlin Memorandum.** The Sultan was asked to make certain definite concessions and was threatened with armed intervention if he failed to do so. The Sultan did not care for the protests of the European Powers on account of the indifferent attitude of Great Britain. The Turks tried to crush the rising of the Bulgarians by wholesale massacres. When the Baring Report of the atrocities committed by the Turks on the people of Bulgaria reached England, public opinion was aroused against the Turks. The eloquence of Gladstone added to their sympathy. Gladstone appealed to Disraeli, the Prime Minister of England at that time, to interfere in the Balkans and turn out the Turks "bag and baggage from the province they have desolated and profaned." However, Disraeli refused to act. He regarded the whole affair as a "coffee-house bubble." According to Crutwell, "No question of foreign policy has so aroused or bitterly divided the British public opinion within the living memory." Although Great Britain refused to intervene on behalf of the oppressed Christians of the Balkans, Russia came to their help. She could not sit quiet while her co-religionists were being persecuted. She declared war against Turkey in 1877 and she was assisted by Serbia, Montenegro,

Rumania and Bulgaria. The Turks put up a stiff resistance at Plevna which was defended by Osman Pasha with great heroism. However, after the fall of Plevna, Turkish resistance collapsed and Russia occupied Adrianople and marched on to Constantinople. Turkey submitted and signed the Treaty of San Stefano in 1878.

Treaty of San Stefano (1878). By the Treaty of San Stefano, the Sultan recognized the complete independence of Serbia, Montenegro and Rumania with increased territories. An autonomous tributary principality of Bulgaria was to be created, bounded by the Danube, the Black Sea, the Aegean and Albania. Sweeping reforms were to be carried out in Herzegovina and Bosnia in favour of the Christians. The straits of Bosphorus and Dardanelles were to be opened at all times to peaceful commerce. The Turkish forts along the Danube were to be destroyed. Russia was to get a part of Armenia, a strip of Dobrudja which she intended to exchange with Bessarabia from Rumania and Ardahani, Kars, Botoum and Bayazid. She was also to get a large war-indemnity. Certain reforms were also to be carried out by the Sultan in Armenia.

As was expected, the Treaty of San Stefano was opposed by Great Britain and Austria-Hungary. Austria-Hungary was determined to extend her influence to the Aegean Sea and occupy a dominating position in the Balkans. Likewise, Disraeli was determined to check, the spread of Russian influence in the Balkans. He was convinced that the security of the sea-route to India through the Mediterranean demanded a strong and friendly Turkey. Under the circumstances, there was correspondence between Great Britain and Austria-Hungary, and both of them agreed to present a united front to Russia. The ground having been prepared, Disraeli demanded from Russia that as the Treaty of San Stefano upset the settlement of 1856 which was made by European Powers, it must be submitted to a Congress of European statesmen. To begin with, Russia was not in a mood to submit and Disraeli ordered the Indian troops to proceed to Malta. The British fleet was ordered to be in readiness for action. There was talk of war everywhere. Queen Victoria could not understand the attitude of Disraeli who seemed to be very serious about war. The following song was sung everywhere in England.

"We do not want to fight,
But by Jingo if we do,
We've got the men, we've got the ships,
We've got the money too."

When Russia was convinced that a war was imminent, she agreed to the Austro-British proposal. The Congress met at Berlin under the presidentship of Bismarck who offered to play the role of an "honest broker". Disraeli and Salisbury represented Great Britain, Gortschakoff represented Russia, Wadington represented France, Andrassy represented Austria and Italy was represented by Corti.

Terms of the Berlin Settlement (1878). (1) In accordance with the preliminary agreement, Big Bulgaria was divided into two parts: Eastern Roumelia and Bulgaria. Eastern Roumelia was given back to Turkey, Russia gave up Bayazid but kept Kars, Ardahan and Batoum. Great Britain got Cyprus. Bulgaria lost 2,500,000 of her population and 30,000 square miles of her territory. She also lost an outlet to the Aegean. Bulgaria was to be administered by Russia for nine months and afterwards was to be an autonomous and tributary principality under the suzerainty of the Sultan. Its prince was to be elected by the people, confirmed by the Sultan and approved of by the Powers. No member of the reigning European family was to be elected as the ruler of Bulgaria.

(2) In Cyprus, Great Britain got "a place of arms" which was intended to enable her more easily to check Russian extension in Asia Minor and to defend the Suez Canal. Great Britain assumed moral responsibility for the protection and reforms of Armenia and Turkey promised to do the same.

(3) Austria got the right to occupy and administer Bosnia and Herzegovina which remained nominally under the suzerainty of Turkey and to maintain garrisons in the Sanjak of Novi-Bazar. It was in 1908 that both Bosnia and Herzegovina were annexed by Austria.

(4) The independence of Serbia was recognised. She got Nish and some Bulgarian territory and these additions represented a quarter of her former territory. She was unhappy because Austria was given control over the Sanjak of Novi-Bazar.

(5) The independence of Montenegro which she had enjoyed practically for many years, was formally recognised. She got a port on the Adriatic.

(6) Rumania was recognised as independent but she was compelled to give Southern Bessarabia to Russia in exchange for Dobruja. She also got some Bulgarian territory adjoining Dobruja. She promised to give political equality to her Jewish subjects.

(7) Greece asked for Crete, Epirus, Thessaly and Albania, but she got nothing. The Sultan did not care for a recommendation of the Congress that he should rectify the northern frontier of Greece.

(8) Turkey guaranteed full religious liberty to all her subjects. She promised to introduce reforms in Crete, Epirus, Thessaly, Macedonia and Albania.

Criticism of the Settlement. Critics point out that the Congress of Berlin was little more than a Court of Registration. It merely put in black and white the agreement which had already taken place before the meeting of the Congress at Berlin. However, the Congress of Berlin upset the settlement of the Treaty of San Stefano.

Russia lost important advantages which she had secured by the Treaty of San Stefano and her influence in the Balkans was weakened. After a costly war, Russia was deprived of the fruits of her victory by Great Britain and Austria with the connivance of Germany.

It was thought that a big Bulgaria would be under the influence of Russia and the separation of Eastern Roumelia and Macedonia would enable Turkey to defend easily the approaches to Adrianople and Constantinople.

Rumania bitterly resented the ingratitude of Russia and was driven to rely upon Austria and the Triple Alliance instead of Russia. Serbia complained that Russia had failed to support her in her attempt to maintain the Slav cause. That is why she made a secret treaty with Austria in 1881.

Beaconsfield, inflicted a serious check on Russia in Europe, but one of the defects of the Treaty of Berlin was that Russian activity was transferred from the Bosphorus to the frontiers of India and Afghanistan. That added to the worries of the Government of India and the British Government. Lord Salisbury's view was that in the Congress of Berlin, Great Britain "backed the wrong horse".

The conduct of Bismarck during the Congress of Berlin alienated Russia from Germany. The result was that there was a demand in Russia for a war with Germany. The bitter Russian propaganda against Bismarck was one of the important causes which forced Bismarck to enter into the Austro-German alliance of 1879. This created a vicious circle of alliances which was ultimately responsible for the division of Europe into two armed camps.

The Pan-Slav movement received a serious check. The occupation of Bosnia, Herzegovina and Novi-Bazar by Austria stood in the way of the union of Serbia, Bosnia and Montenegro. Austria became "the sentinel of the Balkans in the future."

Although Beaconsfield declared that he had brought peace with honour, it is pointed out that he brought neither peace to Europe nor honour to Great Britain. As a matter of fact, Cyprus did not prove to be of any military value to Great Britain and consequently was not developed. In 1886, Russia fortified Batoum. In 1896, there was a wholesale massacre of the people of Armenia. Great Britain could do nothing in spite of the fact that she had got a guarantee of reforms from Turkey. In 1885, Eastern Roumelia and Bulgaria were united as the people elected the same prince as their ruler.

The Turkish rule in Macedonia proved ineffective. That led to chronic unrest. In 1897, there took place a war between Turkey and Greece.

In spite of her promise, Rumania did not give political equality to the Jews.

Lord Salisbury made the following observations on the Treaty of Berlin : "Bulgaria is now confined to the river barrier of the Danube and consequently has not only ceased to possess a harbour on the Archipelago but is removed by more than a 100 miles from the neighbourhood of that sea. On the Euxine the important port of Bourgas has been restored to the Government of Turkey; and Bulgaria retains less than half the seaboard originally assigned to it and possesses no other port except the roadstead of Varna which can hardly be used for any but commercial purposes. The replacement under Turkish rule of Bourgas and the southern half of the sea-board on the Euxine, and the strictly commercial character assigned to Batoum, have largely obviated the menace to the liberty of the Black Sea. The political outposts of Russian power have been pushed back to the region beyond the Balkans; the Sultan's dominions have been provided with a defensible frontier."

The contention of the British Government was that while Russia had acquired a new dependency by the Treaty of San Stefano, Great Britain by the Treaty of Berlin, baffled that plan and restored to Turkey an effective military hold over all the countries south of the Balkans. However, according to Fyffe, "If history taught anything in the solution of the Eastern Question, it taught that the effort to reserve for the Sultan a military existence in countries which had passed from under his general control was futile, and that the best barrier against Russian influence was to be found not in the division but in the strengthening and consolidation of the States rescued from Ottoman dominions." Again, "Lord Beaconsfield's ideas, purposes and anticipations, in so far as they related to Eastern Europe, have hitherto been contradicted by events. What happened in Greece, Serbia and Rumania has happened in Bulgaria. Experience, thrown to the winds by English ministers in 1878, has justified those who listened to its voice. There exists no such thing as a Turkish fortress in the Balkans; Bourgas no more belongs to the Sultan than Athens or Belgrade; no Turkish soldier has been able to set foot within the territory whose very name. Eastern Roumelia, was to stamp it as Turkish dominion. National independence, a living force in Greece, in Serbia, in Rumania has proved its power in Bulgaria too. The efforts of Russia to establish its influence over a people liberated by its arms have been repelled with unexpected firmness. Like the divided members of Rumania, the divided members of Bulgaria have effected their union."

The enduring significance of the Treaty of Berlin is to be found in the new nations which were arising upon the ruins of the Turkish Empire. Pan-Slavism had failed to solve the problems of the Balkans, but nationalism which involved important modifications of the Treaty of Berlin proved more successful. "The history of the last 50 years in South-Eastern Europe is to a great extent the history of the disentanglement of the Slavonic races from the Greeks and Turks, and this is now succeeding the disentanglement of the Slavonic races from one another." Rumania became a kingdom in 1881 and Serbia in 1882. In 1908, Ferdinand was proclaimed the Czar of Bulgaria and in 1910 Nicholas became the first King of Montenegro. This proved the truth of Gladstone's assertion: "You want to place a living barrier between Russia and Turkey. There is no barrier like the breasts of free men."

According to Taylor, "The Congress of Berlin made a watershed in the history of Europe. It had been preceded by thirty years of conflict and upheaval; it was followed by thirty-four years of peace. No European frontier was changed until 1913, not a shot was fired in Europe until 1912, except in two trivial wars that miscarried. It would not do to attribute this great achievement solely, or even principally, to the skill of European statesmen. The decisive cause was, no doubt, economic. The secret that had made Great Britain great was a secret no longer. Coal and steel offered prosperity to all Europe and remade European civilization. The dream of Cobden seemed to have come true. Men were too busy growing rich to have time for war. Though protective tariffs remained everywhere except in Great Britain, international trade was otherwise free. There was no governmental interference, no danger of debts being repudiated. The gold standard was universal. Passports disappeared, except in Russia and Turkey. If a man in London decided at nine o'clock in the morning to go to Rome or Vienna, he could leave at 10 a.m. without either passport or travellers' cheques—merely with a purse of sovereigns in his pocket. Europe had never known such peace and unity since the age of the Antonines. The times of Metternich were nothing in comparison. Then men had lived in well-founded apprehension of war and revolution; now they came to believe that peace and security were 'normal', and anything else an accident and an aberration. For centuries to come men will look back at that age of bliss and will puzzle over the effortless case with which it was accomplished. They are not likely to discover the secret; they will certainly not be able to imitate it." (**The Struggle for Mastery in Europe,** pp. 255-56).

According to David Thomson, "The settlement reached at the Congress of Berlin had the remarkable outcome that it left each power dissatisfied and more anxious than before. It was a defeat for Russian prestige. Britain had sent a fleet through the Dardanelles in 1878 as a reminder of her interest in Turkey, and the crumbling of Turkey now left Russia face to face with Britain in the Near East. Austria-Hungary, too, had patently failed if her real interest lay in keeping the Ottoman Empire strong; as also had Disraeli, despite his boast of 'peace with honour' and the acquisition of Cyprus. In general Britain, however, had asserted and reinforced her naval supremacy in the eastern Mediterranean and the Straits, and France had opened new doors for her diplomacy of recovery and her future policy of colonialism. Territorial gains, such as Russia's recovery of Bessarabia and Austria's occupation of Bosnia and Herzegovina, were of little profit if the legacy of enflamed frustrated Balkan nationalism was to continue to embroil all the powers in further crises and wars. International tension was increased, not eased, by the events of these years. The new balance of power, now clearly centred on Germany, was destined to preserve the peace for another whole generation. But it was doomed to be a most uneasy and unstable peace, subject to recurrent crises and threats of war. The next general European Congress met forty years later not in Berlin but in Paris—and at it were to be no representatives of the Dreikaiserbund." (**Europe Since Napoleon,** pp. 432-3).

According to Sir J.A.R. Marriott, "Lord Beaconsfield's claim that he had brought back to England 'peace with honour', though conceded by the mass of his fellow-countrymen, evoked some derision among them. His statement that he had 'consolidated' the Ottoman Empire was received with polite scepticism both at home and abroad, a scepticism to some extent justified by the Cyprus Convention, to say nothing of the cession of Bosnia and Herzegovina. With some inconsistency, however, he was simultaneously assailed for having replaced under the withering tyranny of the Sultan a Christian population which Russia had emancipated. The charge is, on the face of it, difficult to rebut. But it does not lie in the mouths of the Philhellenists and Philo-Serbs to make it. Had the Treaty of San Stefano been permitted to stand, the ambitions both of Serbia and Greece would have been seriously circumscribed. It was not, indeed, of Serbia or Greece, still less of Rumania, that Lord Beaconsfield was thinking at Berlin. The motive of his policy was that which had inspired Lord Palmerston and Mr. Canning. He definitely repudiated the claim of Russia to dictate by her slow voice and in her own interests the solution of a secular problem."

According to Grant and Temperley, "The Congress was thus over and the Great Powers pacified. Queen Victoria offered Disraeli a Dukedom, and gave Garters both to him and to Salisbury, amid the enthusiasm which the careful stage management had evoked and which the phrase **'Peace with Honour'** embodied. It would be wrong to deny that Disraeli had shown great courage at the crises, but courage in diplomacy should be accompanied by knowledge, and in this Disraeli was poorly provided, and he did not try to obtain it from the more instructed Lord Salisbury. He seems to have had no belief in the strength of nascent nationality in the Balkan peninsula and no idea of resisting Russia except by military force. His belief in the virtues of Abdul Hamid and the Turkish desire to protect and ameliorate the condition of their Christian subjects whether in Europe or Asia was woefully mistaken. His policy in Asia speedily came to nought. The despatch of British military consuls to Armenia to arrange for its defence against Russia proved useless."

According to Seton-Watson, "The true significance of 1878 lies in the fact that, Bismarck made Andrassy his colleague and Disraeli his tool, and that he finally won and dominated Austria-Hungary without at the same time offending Russia". (**The Rise of Nationality in the Balkans,** p. 115).

Ketelbey says that although the policy of Disraeli at the Congress of Berlin was bold and to a point effective, yet out of it arose most of the causes of the Balkan Wars of 1912 and 1913 and the World War I. It is true that Turkey recovered 2½ million of people and 30,000 square miles of territory which she had lost by the Treaty of San Stefano, but her Empire was reduced by more than half its area and nearly half its population was mutilated beyond revival. All that Disraeli did was to prolong the process and multiply the pains of extinction. The restoration of Macedonia caused the Balkan War of 1912 and the curtailment of Bulgaria in the War of 1913. It is true that a check was put on Russia and victory was snatched from her hands and for a time, she retired from an active policy in the Balkans to active empire-making in Asia. However, 30 years after she returned again with ambitions renewed and in 1914 she set out to recover far more than she had lost in 1878. By holding back one foreign power from the Balkans, Disraeli merely let loose another. The introduction of Austria-Hungary into the Balkans by giving her Bosnia, Hersegovina and the Sanjak of Novi Bazar, created a new Balkan problem. From the Austria of 1878 to the Austria of 1914, and so to the World War I, there is a continuous development. Moreover, Turkey was bitter at the attitude of the self-styled friends who had forced themselves upon her in 1878 to save her and later on turned into robbers. The annexation of Cyprus and the extension of Austrian control in the Balkans were not natural moves on the part of the Powers who professed the doctrine of Turkish integrity. The boast of Disraeli that he had brought to England "peace with honour", needs to be translated into "peace together with the island of Cyprus and a check, in British interests, to the ambitions of Russia." If the settlement of Berlin actually lasted without serious disturbance for a generation, it is a tribute as much to the impotence and mutual rivalries of the powers and to the ineffectiveness of the Concert of Europe, as to the enduring nature of its terms. No human architect could have done better.

It is pointed out that out of Disraeli's policy at the Congress of Berlin arose most of the causes of the Balkan Wars of 1912-1913 and the World War I. Disraeli remarked with pride that "there is again a Turkey in Europe." He claimed credit for having saved Turkey from disintegration. However, it is pointed out that although Turkey recovered some territory and population which she had lost by the Treaty of San Stefano, yet she was mutilated beyond revival. All that Disraeli was able to accomplish was that he prolonged the process of the extinction of Turkey. The curtailment of Bulgaria cost the war of 1913 and the restoration of Macedonia cost the Balkan War of 1912.

It is also pointed out that by ousting Russia from the Balkans, Disraeli introduced Austria-Hungary into the same area. Austria-Hungary was given the right to occupy and administer Bosnia, Herzegovina and the Sanjak of Novi-Bazar. The result was that the ambitions of Austria-Hungary began to grow in the Balkans and she began to dream in terms of dominating the Adriatic Sea and the Aegean Sea. There started a bitter rivalry between Serbia and Russia on the one hand and Austria-Hungary on the other. That was hardly in the interests of peace in the Balkans and that was one of the important causes of the World War I.

Turkey was also satisfied with the settlement. She protested that her self-styled friends had become robbers. She did not like the proclamation of the independence of Serbia, Montenegro, Rumania and Bulgaria. She resented the giving of Bosnia, Herzegovina and the Sanjak of Novi Bazar to Austria-Hungary and Cyprus to England. It was pointed out that Disraeli's "peace with honour" should be read as "peace together with the Island of Cyprus and a check, in British interests, to the ambitions of Russia."

It cannot be denied that the Settlement of Berlin did not solve the Eastern Question. There were so many conflicting interests in the Balkans that it was out of the question to find a satisfactory solution for all of them. As a matter of fact, the Eastern Question was not tackled even when the World War I broke out in 1914.

The Eastern Question from 1878 to 1908. Reference may be made to this stage to the various developments which took place in the Balkans from 1878 to 1908. The countries concerned were Bulgaria, Armenia, Greece, Rumania, Montenegro, Serbia, Germany, and Turkey.

Bulgaria. The Bulgarian problem was created by the Congress of Berlin. While the Treaty of San Stefano had created a big Bulgaria, the Congress of Berlin separated Eastern Roumelia from Bulgaria and thereby the germs of future trouble were sown.

In 1879, Prince Alexander of Battenberg was elected the King of Bulgaria and he occupied that position up to 1886. "He was described as a wise statesman, a proved soldier and a remarkable man in every respect." He was only 21 at the time of his accession. He was pro-Russian and had fought in the Russo-Turkish war on the side of Russia. He was the choice of the Czar who was his uncle by marriage. He took his oath to the Constitution in the uniform of a Russian general. The Czar addressed thus to a deputation from Bulgaria: "Accept your prince from my hands, love him as I love him."

It is true that Prince Alexander was friendly inclined towards Russia, but the trouble arose when Russia tried to interfere too much in the affairs of Bulgaria which was turned into a Russian province. Things became worse after the death of Alexander II and the accession of Alexander III in 1881. Russian generals were appointed to the Departments of the Interior, War and Justice. Bulgaria was flooded with Russians. Prince Alexander did not like to hear from the Russian officials that they got their orders from the Czar and not from him. As he complained against Russian interference, the Czar began to hate the prince. This estrangement continued till 1885 when a crisis was precipitated.

To begin with, the attitude of Russia towards Eastern Roumelia was one of sympathy and she was in favour of her union with Bulgaria. The Czar sent a general to advise the people of Eastern Roumelia to submit to the separation for the time being. His message was in these words: "Russia had done what she could to help you. She is not responsible for your severance from Bulgaria. Accept these rifles, learn how to use them and later on help yourselves." However, this sympathetic attitude underwent a change after 1885.

Prince Alexander was invited by the Austrian Foreign Minister in 1885 to attend the military manoeuvres and on that occasion Giers, the Foreign Minister of Russia, was also invited. Prince Alexander met Giers and assured him that there would be no trouble with regard to Eastern Roumelia for some time to come and the status quo would be maintained. Unfortunately, without the knowledge of Prince Alexander a meeting of the patriots of Eastern Roumelia had already taken place and it was decided to unite Eastern Roumelia with Bulgaria. On his return from Austria, Prince Alexander was informed of the decision. Naturally, he hesitated. He did not like to go back on his promise to the Russian Foreign Minister that the status quo would be maintained in the Balkans. However, he was told that the country was tired of separation and either he should agree to the union or he would be set aside. The prince did not care for the threat. However, on the appointed day, a revolution did take place at Philippopolis, the capital of Eastern Roumelia. The people revolted and the Crown was offered to Prince Alexander. In spite of hesitation, he accepted the Crown under pressure.

Turkey might have been expected to take action against Bulgaria because Eastern Roumelia was a part of the Turkish Empire. However, Sultan Abdul Hamid hesitated to take action and kept quiet. But, in spite of its expression of goodwill and friendship, Russia did not approve of the action of Prince Alexander and she decided to oppose the union at all costs. The Russian officers were withdrawn from Bulgaria.

Queen Victoria had taken a fancy to Prince Alexander and she favoured the union. Lord Salisbury was also favourably inclined. The attitude of Austria was also sympathetic. However, Bismarck decided to support Russia on the question of Bulgaria. He declared, "In Bulgaria I am Russia," Bismarck's view was that the Congress of Berlin had earmarked Bulgaria as within the sphere of influence of Russia.

On February 1, 1886, Turkey recognised Prince Alexander as Governor-General of Eastern Roumelia for 5 years. However, Russia opposed it and she was supported by Bismarck. The result was that a change was made in the title of Prince Alexander and it was decided that "the Prince of Bulgaria was to be the Governor of Eastern Roumelia." Even this did not satisfy Russia. The Russian agents continued intrigues and some discontented officials entered the palace and kidnapped Prince Alexander. At this time, Queen Victoria wrote thus: "Words fail me to express my feelings. Your parents could hardly be more anxious. My indignation against your barbarian, Asiatic, tyrannical cousin is so great that I cannot trust myself to write about it." A provisional government was set up at Sofia under Stambolov, but it lasted only for 3 days. The Prince was requested to come back and he accepted the invitation. As soon as he reached the country he was informed by Russian Consul that Bulgaria's welfare could only be found in reconciliation with Russia. The Prince ought to have delayed a reply till he reached the capital. Unfortunately, he was tired of the hostility of the Czar and he committed the blunder of his life and sent the following telegram to the Czar: "Russia gave me my Crown and I am ready to return it into the hands of her sovereign." Russia and Germany were happy over the abdication but Queen Victoria and the Bulgarians were disappointed.

Although Prince Alexander was eliminated in 1886, the Bulgarian problem was not solved and the worst was till to come. The Great Powers were drawn into the controversy. On account of her alliance of 1879 with Germany, Austria felt that she was very near the country and consequently Germany was bound to help her on every issue. However, in the case of Bulgaria, the interest of Russia and Austria clashed as both the Powers wanted to increase their control and influence in the Balkans. The position of Bismarck became difficult as he had to keep friendly relations with both the powers. His position was described in these words by the German Emperor: "You are like a rider who tosses five balls in the air and catches them every time. Bismarck evolved a formula according to which he was ordinarily to help Austria but in the case of Bulgaria he was to support Russia. Bismarck was still convinced that the Eastern Question was not worth the bones of a Pomeranian grenadier and consequently was prepared to allow Russia a free hand in the Balkans. From the beginning of the crisis, Bismarck warned Austria not to do anything which was liable to provoke Russia and also to observe the letter and spirit of the Dreikaiserbund of 1881. He proposed that Austria and Russia should divide the Balkans into eastern and western zones of influence. The suggestion was accepted by Russia but rejected by Austria as the latter was determined to exclude Russia altogether from the Balkans. Austria was determined to offer resistance if Russia tried to occupy Bulgaria.

Austria did not seem to approve of the carte blanche given by Bismarck to Russia. The feeling in Austria was very strong on the question of Bulgaria. The view of Andrassy was that Russia should not be allowed to dominate Bulgaria from which she had been eliminated by the Congress of Berlin. He considered the Dual Alliance of 1879 as sufficient and was not in favour of continuing the Dreikaiserbund. (Three Emperors' League) of 1881. Other Austrian politicians also maintained that the alliance with Germany was useless if Austria had to yield to Russia. The result was that Bismarck informed Russia that although he would not oppose the occupation of Bulgaria by Russia, yet he advised her not to provoke Austria.

The throne of Bulgaria was offered to many princes but they all refused. Ultimately, in 1887 Prince Ferdinand of Saxe-Coburg Gotha was elected the King of Bulgaria and he continued to rule up to 1918. The Czar proposed to the Powers to eject the Prince and appoint a Russian general as the Governor of the two Bulgarias. Bismarck cut off diplomatic relations with Bulgaria. However, the British Government warned Russia that she would not like the intervention of Russia in Bulgaria. The British point of view was explained in these words by Lord Salisbury in December 1885: "A Bulgaria friendly to the Porte and jealous of foreign influence, would be a far surer bulwark against foreign aggression than two Bulgarias severed in administration but united in considering the Porte as the only obstacle to their national development." The attitude of the Italian Government was also sympathetic towards Bulgaria. Italy was prepared to recognise Ferdinand instead of ousting him as desired by Russia. Austria was prepared to go to the extent of fighting with Russia on the question of Bulgaria. There was a lot of excitement in both Russia and Austria and the presses in both the countries condemned each other. Even the Foreign Ministers of the two countries joined the chorus. Ultimately the Czar made a final attempt to solve the Bulgarian problem in a Russian way. He proposed that Ferdinand must withdraw, Bulgaria should choose another ruler and in that case Russia would not interfere. Russia was supported by Germany and France but she was opposed by Austria and the other Powers. At this time, Turkey declared the title of Ferdinand as illegal but in spite of this declaration neither Turkey nor Russia took any action against Bulgaria. The result was that Ferdinand continued on the throne of Bulgaria and although Russia was supported by Germany, yet she failed in Bulgaria. However, the one great achievement of Bismarck's support of Russia in Bulgaria was that a war between Austria and Russia was avoided. He was able to put a check on both the Powers and thereby was able to avoid a clash. That was no mean achievement.

A reference may be made in this connection to the question of the marriage of prince Alexander with the grand-daughter of Emperor William I. The princess who was the grand-daughter of Queen Victoria, had taken a fancy to Prince Alexander and the match was approved of by Queen Victoria and the father of the girl. However, Bismarck opposed the marriage on account of the possibility of Russia being annoyed. In 1884, he told the Prince bluntly: "The marriage is impossible and so long as I am Chancellor it will not take place. Germany has no interest in Bulgaria. Our interest is peace with Russia. Now you are Bulgarian, you must submit to Russia." The question of the marriage of Prince Alexander was revived once again in 1888 but even then Bismarck opposed it and was prepared to resign on that issue. He believed that there was still a possibility of the Prince being invited to return to Sofia and in any case the Czar might start distrusting Germany on account of the association of Prince Alexander with the royal family. He wrote thus to Emperor Frederick, the father of the girl: "The foreign policy of the German Empire since 1871 has been the maintenance of peace and the prevention of anti-German coalitions and the pivot of this policy is Russia." It may be pointed out that ultimately Prince Alexander married an opera singer, but died in 1893.

As regards Prince Ferdinand, he continued to rule up to 1918. He was young and ambitious but in spite of that he did not take an active part in the affairs of the Government which was carried on by Stambolov. In 1894, Stambolov resigned or was dismissed and Ferdinand became the real ruler of the country. He tried to establish friendly relations with Russia and his task was facilitated by the death of Alexander III in 1894 and the accession of Nicholas II. In 1896, Boris, the son and heir of Ferdinand, was baptized into the Orthodox faith. In 1898, both Ferdinand and his Queen went to Russia and thus the bitterness between the two countries was ended. Bulgaria continued to prosper under Ferdinand. In 1908 Prince Ferdinand declared himself as the King of Bulgaria. Bulgaria took part in the Balkan Wars of 1912-13.

The Armenian Question. The lot of the Christians of Armenia was unfortunate on account of the hostile attitude of the Turkish Government. By the Treaty of Berlin and the Cyprus Convention, the Sultan gave promises to the European Powers to give fair treatment to the Christians of Armenia. The promises were not fulfilled and the situation in Armenia deteriorated. On account of the interest of the European Powers in 1878, high hopes were raised among the Armenians and the Sultan was annoyed on account of the interest of the foreign powers in Armenia. The result was that Sultan Abdul Hamid decided to teach them a lesson. He knew full well that the European Powers were divided among themselves and would not be able to take action against him. The Sultan also detested the agitation among the Armenians and could not tolerate the idea of another independent State emerging out of the Turkish Empire. The policy towards the Armenians was described in these words by a Turkish statesman: "The only way to get rid of the Armenian question is to get rid of the Armenians." It was not difficult to find an excuse to crush the Armenians. In 1893, some Armenians offered resistance to the Turkish authorities and vengeance of the government started in 1894. Turkish soldiers were let loose on the Armenian Christians and horrible scenes were witnessed. This process continued throughout 1894 and 1895 and it is estimated that more than 50,000 Armenian Christians were disposed of. In August 1896, the Armenian Christians in Constantinople revolted and attacked the Turkish Bank in Galata. The result was that within 24 hours, more than 6,000 Armenians were murdered in the streets of Constantinople. The European Powers did not help the Armenians. As regards Russia, she did not like the revolutionary agitation among the Armenians and consequently did not help them. The Armenians were not Orthodox Christians and consequently Russia was not attracted towards them. There was no appeal of a common faith. Russia had also not forgotten the ingratitude of Bulgaria which had been liberated by her. She was not prepared to take the trouble of helping another State to become independent and then seeing her becoming ungrateful. Moreover, she was more busy in the Far East and was not in a mood to interfere in Turkey. Russia considered Armenia to be a hobby of England. As she was opposed to England, she did not help Armenia. Russian view was that as England had thwarted her in Bulgaria in 1878, she would thwart her in Armenia in 1896.

Germany also did not help Armenia as William II was following a policy of courting the friendship of Turkey. Austria-Hungary followed in the footsteps of Germany. France was angry with England on the question of Egypt, and consequently refused to join hands with her on the question of Armenia. The net result was that England alone was in earnest to help the people of Armenia. She protested. She threatened. However, Sultan Abdul Hamid ignored these protests and threats. Gladstone branded Abdul Hamid as "the Great Assassin". Sir William Watson described him as '"immortally, beyond all mortals damned." Although the people of England were indignant over the question of Armenia, Lord Salisbury was not prepared to provoke an European war on the question of Armenia. No wonder, the mutual jealousies of the Great Powers allowed the people of Armenia to be treated brutally. Lord Salisbury came to the conclusion that by helping Turkey, Great Britain had "put her money on the wrong horse."

Greece. After the recognition of the independence of Greece in 1829, the boundaries of the new kingdom were marked and in 1833 Prince Otto of Bavaria became the ruler of Greece. He continued to rule from 1833 to 1862. The country did not make much progress during his regime. There was administrative inefficiency, social disorder and financial bankruptcy. The condition of the people was so bad that there was a revolt in 1862 and the King was forced to abdicate.

A lot of difficulty had to be faced to secure another King for Greece. The throne was offered to Prince Alfred and Lord Stanley of England. Ultimately, it was accepted by Prince George of Denmark and he ruled as King George I from 1863 to 1913. In 1864, a new democratic constitutional government was established in the country. In spite of the difficulties in the way of the working of the parliamentary institutions in the country, the country made a lot of progress both materially and intellectually. Agriculture progressed and production of olive oil, currants, wine and grain was increased. One thousand miles of railways were constructed. One hundred factories were set up at Athens. The Greek ships captured a lot of the trade of the Eastern Mediterranean.

When the Kingdom of Greece was created, all the Greeks were not included into it. A large number of the Greeks lived in Epirus, Macedonia, Thrace, Ionian Islands, Crete, Constantinople, Smyrna and in the towns along the sea-coast of Asia Minor.

To begin with, the Government of Greece concentrated its attention to acquire Thessaly and Epirus. As both of these territories belonged to the Sultan, Greece had to fight against Turkey. During the Crimean War Greek troops attacked Thessaly but they were ordered to go back by the Great Powers. The king of Greece was forced to maintain neutrality. Greece got nothing even when the Congress of Paris took place in 1856. During the war between Russia and Turkey in 1877-78, Greek troops invaded Thessaly once again. They were again forced to withdraw and again got nothing by the Treaty of San Stefano or the Treaty of Berlin. The view of Disraeli was that "Greece is a country with future and can wait." However, through the efforts of Gladstone who was the Prime Minister of England at that time, Turkey was forced to give in 1881 about one-third of Epirus and the greater part of Thessaly to Greece. In 1864. Great Britain handed over to Greece the Ionian Islands which Great Britain had got in 1815. The people of those Islands were discontented and demanded union with Greece.

As regards the island of Crete, "the Greek island par excellence," the people were tired of the oppressive rule of the Sultan and were determined to be united with Greece. It is stated that there were as many as 14 revolts in Crete between 1830 and 1910. However, nothing was achieved before 1896 except mere promises of reform which were never fulfilled. The nationalist movement in Crete went on growing particularly after the union of Bulgaria and Eastern Roumelia in 1885. In 1894, the Greeks in Crete revolted. In 1897, Greece declared war against Turkey to help the Cretans. As the Greeks were not well prepared and the army of the Sultan had been reorganised by the Germans, the Greek troops were defeated. Greece was forced to give to Turkey a strategic advantage on the frontier of Thessaly. She was also made to pay a heavy war-indemnity. Although Greece failed to annex Crete, Turkey practically lost all control over it. Crete was given autonomy under the protection of the Four Great Powers—Russia, Great Britain, France and Italy. These Powers named a son of the Greek King as its Governor. The Cretan demand for closer union with Greece led to another insurrection in 1905. The Great Powers had to intervene once again. However, they insisted on retaining the fiction of the suzerainty of the Sultan over Crete, Greece was allowed to nominate its Governor. The Cretan militia was to be controlled and commanded by Greek army officers. Venizelos, a Cretan by birth, was a leader of the revolutionary movement for the union of Crete with Greece. He also played an important part in the administration of Crete from 1897 onwards. In 1910, he was made the Prime Minister of Greece. In his new position, Venizelos carried out a large number of reforms in the field of finance, the navy and the army. He played an important part in bringing into existence the Balkan League in 1912 which led to the Balkan Wars of 1912 and 1913. It was in 1913 that Greece got the island of Crete.

Rumania. The Treaty of Paris of 1856 granted autonomy to the provinces of Moldavia and Wallachia. In 1862, the two provinces were allowed to unite themselves under one prince and thus the kingdom of Rumania came into existence. In 1866, its native prince was deposed and in his place Prince Charles I of Germany became the ruler of Rumania. He ruled from 1866 to 1914. The Congress of Berlin recognized the complete independence of Rumania and in 1881, it was designated as a Kingdom. Prince Charles I became the King of Rumania.

Like Greece, a large number of Rumanians lived not only in Turkey but also in Bessarabia (under Russia) and Bukovina (under Austria). No wonder, the problem of the national unification of Rumania was much more complicated than that of Greece. Rumania had to face three Powers, viz., Russia, Austria-Hungary and Turkey.

The statesmen of Rumania were divided among themselves as to the policy to be followed for national unification. According to one school of thought, Rumania should forget about Bessarabia, and align herself with Russia and make a determined effort to secure Bukovina and Transylvania from Austria-Hungary. There were others who wanted Rumania to forget Bukovina and Transylvania and concentrate on getting Bessarabia from Russia. King Charles I was pro-German and hence pro-Austrian and the Rumanian effort was to get back Bessarabia from Russia. In 1883, Rumania entered into an alliance with Austria and for the next thirty years, the German influence was supreme in Rumania. Army was remodelled after Germany and it became the largest army in the Balkan States.

During this period, agriculture was developed by the adoption of the scientific methods of farming and the development of foreign markets. On account of her rich black soil Rumania became a great corn-growing country in the world. Foreign capital was employed to exploit the rich mineral resources of the country. A lot of coal and petroleum was found. Factories were constructed and railways were also built. However, the condition of the peasants of Rumania was deplorable and consequently there was a revolt in 1907 which was put down with great difficulty by the army.

Montenegro. The Serbs had two independent States of Montenegro and Serbia. Montenegro or Black Mountain was a very small State near the Adriatic Sea. It had been governed by the native princes for a long time but its complete independence was recognized by the Congress of Berlin. Nicholas I was its ruler from 1860 to 1918. He was a warrior king but was also a benevolent despot. He was a great admirer of Russia and consequently Montenegro had very cordial relations with that country. His ambition was to make Montenegro the leader of all the Serbs and unite them all under his rule. With that object in view, he sometimes intrigued with Serbia and sometimes against Serbia. In 1905, he guaranteed a democratic constitution. In 1910, he assumed the title of the King of Montenegro. In spite of the small size of the State, the fighting qualities of the people of Montenegro were such that they played a very important part in the Balkan Wars of 1912-13.

Serbia. The complete independence of Serbia was recognized by the Congress of Berlin. However, that country was torn by dissensions and rivalries between the Karageorge and Obrenovic families in Serbia. Karageorge was the original peasant leader of Serbia against Turkey. Obrenovic was the leader under whom Serbia actually secured her autonomy. The Obrenovic family was in power from 1817 to 1842 and from 1859 to 1903. During this period, there were many revolts of the Karageorge family and in 1868 and in 1903, there were two assassinations. The dynastic feuds created lawlessness in the country and made Serbia a kind of football in the game of international politics.

Milan Obrenovic was the ruler of Serbia during the war between Turkey and Russia in 1877-78. He was pro-Austrian and was specially annoyed with Russia as the latter cared more for Bulgaria than for Serbia in the Treaty of San Stefano and the Treaty of Berlin. No wonder, in 1881 he entered into a secret alliance with Austria-Hungary. In 1882, he transformed his principality into a kingdom. When Eastern Roumelia and Bulgaria were united in 1885, Serbia, declared war against Bulgaria but was miserably defeated. If Austria-Hungary had not intervened, Serbia might have been completely crushed. However, the result of Austrian intervention was that Serbia came completely under the control of Austria after 1885. This state of affairs continued up to 1903. In 1889, Milan Obrenovic granted a liberal and democratic constitution to his people. After two months he abdicated in favour of his son, Alexander II.

Revolution of 1903. Alexander II ruled from 1889 to 1903. He was a despot and wasted his energy on his favourites. He fell in love with a woman called Draga Masin. He not only married her but also showered favours on her relatives. This resulted in a lot of discontentment in the country. A conspiracy was hatched by a group of army officers belonging to a secret society known as the Black Hand with the object of assassinating the King, the Queen and their favourites. The result was that there took place in June 1903 the murder of King Alexander, Queen Draga and their ministers and attendants. This resulted in a dynastic revolution in Serbia and Peter I, a descendant of Karageorge, became the ruler of Serbia. He continued to rule from 1903 to 1921.

The importance of the **Revolution of 1903** cannot be over-emphasized. It was a turning point in the history of Serbia. It ended completely the Obrenovic dynasty and thus the disunity of the country was finished. It also ended the subordination of Serbia to Austria-Hungary. Henceforth Serbia began to collaborate with Russia for the realization of her dreams of uniting all the Serbs under her leadership. Peter I was a warrior-king and he sympathised with the aspirations of the people of Serbia. He restored the democratic constitution of 1889 and selected his ministers from the ultra-patriotic Radical Party whose leader was Nicholas Pasic. The king devoted all his energy to the reform of the army and Pasic reorganized the national finances and put them on a sound footing. He encouraged national propaganda abroad. He negotiated alliances with other Balkan States. Serbia began to prepare herself to bring under her control even those Serbs who were under Austria-Hungary. The annexation of Bosnia and Herzegovina by Austria in 1908 made the relations between Serbia and Austria-Hungary bitter and that was one of the causes of the war of 1914.

German Influence in Turkey. It is to be observed that for about a century, Great Britain was the supporter of Turkey. However, the relations between the two countries became strained after the Congress of Berlin. Lord Salisbury was particularly bitter against Turkey on the question of Armenia. As a result of the estrangement between Great Britain and Turkey, there was "a vacancy in the Ottoman Empire" and that vacancy was filled up by Germany. It is well known that Bismarck did not attach much importance to Turkey and he concentrated on maintaining friendly relations with Russia and Austria. However, after the dismissal of Bismarck, a new chapter was opened in the history of German foreign relations by William II. The new German Emperor paid his first visit to Turkey in 1889. The visit was repeated in 1899 and then he went on a pilgrimage of the Holy Land. At Damascus, William II declared that "His Majesty, the Sultan Abdul Hamid and the three hundred million Mohammedans who reverence him as Caliph, may rest assured that at all times the German Emperor will be their friend."

The Turkish Army was reorganized under the German officers. German traders and financiers also went to Turkey. A branch of the Deutsche Bank of Berlin was opened at Constantinople. The German Government also began to expand her influence in the Middle East. A very ambitious plan of building the Berlin-Baghdad railway was prepared. It was based on the concessions given by Turkey in 1899 to the German Company of Anatolian Railways. It was planned to construct a railway from the Bosphorus to Baghdad and from there to Basra. Its object was to prepare the way for the political and commercial penetration of Germany into the East.

The scheme was opposed by the Powers concerned. It threatened the security of the French Power in Syria and the British Empire in India. Russia also opposed it as a friend and ally of France. The German danger was a real one as Germany was consistently following a policy of expanding her influence in the East. German entered into an alliance with Austria Hungary in 1879. It was transformed into the Triple Alliance of 1882. A German Prince was put on the throne of Rumania in the person of Charles I. Another German Prince was put on the throne of Greece. Ferdinand of Bulgaria also was a German Prince.

Turkey. Sultan Abdul Hamid II had become the Sultan in 1876 and he continued to occupy that position up to 1909. He began his reign by giving a liberal constitution to the people of Turkey in 1876. However, there was a lot of opposition from the reactionary quarters in the country and the result was that the constitution was "suspended" for more than 39 years. It remained a dead letter. The efforts of Abdul Hamid to put down the insurrections of the Bosnians and the Bulgars by force resulted in a war between Turkey and Russia in 1877-78 and ultimately by the Treaty of Berlin, Turkey was deprived of a lot of her territory.

There were certain forces working against the very existence of the Ottoman Empire. There was the danger of aggression from the Great Powers, Russia, Great Britain and Austria-Hungary got territories from Turkey in 1878. The finances of the country were so much upset that Sultan Abdul Hamid had to agree in 1881 to put them under the direction of a commission of foreign bankers. The result was that the people were heavily taxed and that led do unrest in the country. Moreover, foreign capitalists, particularly those of Great Britain, Germany and France were able to secure profitable concessions and that strengthened the stranglehold of those countries over Turkey.

Another danger came from the nationalism of the Balkan peoples. In 1878, Turkey had to recognize the full independence of Rumania, Serbia, and Montenegro, the full autonomy of Bulgaria and the partial autonomy of Eastern Roumelia. None of these States were satisfied and consequently there was the propaganda of publications, army bands and secret societies. The Serbs, the Bulgarians and Greeks were incited to realize their national aspirations which could be done only at the cost of Turkey.

Another danger came from the rising nationalism among the Asiatic subjects of Turkey. The contagion spread to the Armenians, Albanians and the Arabs of Syria, Mesopotamia and Hedjaz. There was some discontentment even among Turks who were influenced by western ideas of nationalism.

Sultan Abdul Hamid was a clever man and he tried to handle the situation in his own way. He played off one Great Power against another and one Balkan State against another. To begin with he depended upon Great Britain to check Russia. Later on, he took advantage of the French jealousy of Britain and the Austrian fear of Russia. Ultimately, he began to depend on Germany which seemed to be less interested than other Powers in the internal affairs of Turkey. He welcomed the visits of William II in 1889 and 1899. German officers were employed to train the Turkish Army. German financial experts advised him. German bankers were given economic concessions. However, Abdul Hamid never put all his eggs in one basket. He sought German help for the development of Anatolia and Mesopotamia, French help in Syria and British help for the Persian Gulf. He tried to create jealousy and enmity among the Great Powers so that all of them might not be able to make a common cause against Turkey. The Sultan also used cruelty and trickery to strengthen his own influence. A large army of spies was employed to give him full information regarding the activities of the secret societies and to take timely action against them. Disloyal army officers and political opponents were dismissed and the administration was centralized. His policy of terrorism against the Christian subjects made them all the more fanatical for their cause and the Sultan was doing no service to his country by imposing cruel punishments on them.

Young Turk Revolution of 1908. The reactionary regime of the Sultan was hated by the progressive elements in the country. The latter were influenced by the western ideas of nationalism and democracy and were not prepared to put up with the autocratic and tyrannical rule of the Sultan. It is pointed out that Kiamil Pasha, a Turkish statesman, came to the conclusion that a liberal and constitutional government on the lines of Great Britain must be set up in Turkey. He had occupied important offices under the Sultan and was the Grand Vizier from 1881 to 1887 and again in 1896. He retired from his office to spread the liberal ideas and he was surrounded by a large number of enlightened "liberal" Turks. There were many young men in Turkey who were more radical than Kiamil Pasha and they formed secret societies and carried on propaganda in favour of establishing a national State in Turkey. These people were called Young Turks. Young Turks in exile had long planned and plotted for a Republic and a constitution. However, in 1905 the reform movement within the Ottoman Empire became independent of Paris and a network of committees was formed in European and Asiastic Turkey with their headquarters at Salonika. There was anarchy in Macedonia and the Great Powers were tempted to intervene. However, the Young Turks decided that the necessary reforms should be carried out by the Turks themselves and not by foreigners. Their programme was a strike of the troops at a critical moment and the Third Army Corps which was stationed in Macedonia was chosen for that purpose. From time to time, spies were able to find some traces of conspiracy and in March 1908, a commission was sent from Constantinople to collect evidence. Fearing discovery, the Committee of Union and Progress planned a rising for September 1908. However, the meeting between Edward VII and the Czar at Reval seemed to demand a quick action. On 3 July 1908 **Niazi** Bey raised the flag of revolt and he was joined by Enver Bey. On 6 July, the officers of the Monastir garrison deserted and volunteers poured in from Macedonia and Albania. On 22 July, **Niazi** entered Monastir and on 23 July the Constitution of 1876 was proclaimed. The Sultan was given the ultimatum of "surrender or we march on Stamboul." The result was that Sultan Abdul Hamid surrendered. He endorsed the restoration of the Constitution. He abolished the censorship of the press. He dismissed a large number of spies in his pay. He invited **Kiamil Pasha** to be the first Grand Vizier under the constitutional government. There was a little opposition but those who opposed were disposed of without much difficulty. In December 1908, a duly elected Parliament met at Constantinople and began to discuss the problem of reforms in the country.

Taking advantage of the Young Turk Revolution, Bulgaria declared herself independent and its ruler took up the title of the King. Austria-Hungary also annexed Bosnia and Herzegovina.

Differences arose between Kiamil Pasha and the Nationalists like Enver Bey. The Sultan tried to take advantage of the situation and removed **Kiamil Pasha.** He also started following a reactionary policy. The result was that in April 1908, Enver Bey and the Committee of Union and Progress carried out a second coup d'etat. As a result of it, Abdul Hamid was deposed and imprisoned. His brother was nominated the new Sultan with the tide of Mohommed V who ruled from 1909 to 1918.

From 1909 to 1918, Turkey was under the dictatorship of the Young Turks. The latter followed a policy of aggressive nationalism. Turkish was made the official language of the Empire. Turkish national schools were set up. The principle of compulsory military service for all citizens was enforced in the country. Attempts were made to Turkify the Ottoman Empire. It was an impossible task. Neither Christians of Europe nor the Arabs in Asia were prepared to accept the programme of the Young Turks. As there was resistance, the Young Turks resorted to repression. The greater the repression the greater became the resistance.

The Italo-Turkish War (1911-12). It was in these circumstances that Italy suddenly declared war against Turkey in 1911. For a long time she had an eye on Tripoli and Cyrenaica in North Africa. After the Young Turk Revolution, she began to fear that if she delayed very much, she might not be able to get Tripoli and Cyrenaica. The Young Turks might become too strong for her. In spite of the efforts of the Young Turks, Italy was successful. As the war was still going on, the Balkan League was formed in 1912 and as the danger from the Balkan League was much greater, Turkey made peace with Italy in October 1912 at Laussane. As a result of it, Italy got Tripoli. Hazen says, "The great significance of this war did not lie in the fact that Italy acquired a new colony. It lay in the fact that it began again the process, arrested since 1878, of the violent dismemberment of the Turkish Empire; that it revealed the military weakness of that Empire, powerless to preserve its integrity and, what is most important, that it contributed directly and greatly to a far more serious attack upon Turkey by the Balkan States, which, in turn, led to the European war. The tinder-box was lighted and a general European conflagration resulted. The Italian attack upon Tripoli was momentous in its consequences."

The Bosnian Crisis of 1908-9. By the Treaty of Berlin (1878), Austria-Hungary was given the right to occupy and administer Bosnia, Herzegovina and the Sanjak of Novi-bazar. For three decades, Austria continued to administer that territory without annexing it. However, in September 1908, a bargain was struck between Aehrenthal, Foreign Minister of Austria, and Izvolski, Foreign Minister of Russia. According to the so-called Buchlau bargain of September 1908, Izvolski agreed to the Austrian annexation of Bosnia and Herzegovina and Aehrenthal agreed to the opening of the Straits to Russian ships of war. Aehrenthal also promised to give up his project concerning the Sanjak railway and also all intentions of extending Austrian influence towards Salonica and to withdraw the Austrian military garrisons from the Sanjak of Novi-Bazar.

In spite of the bargain, Aehrenthal acted hurriedly and proclaimed the annexation of Bosnia and Herzegovina on 7 October 1908. Even Germany was not informed in time. The promise with regard to the opening of the Straits to Russian ships of war could not be carried out on account of the opposition of Great Britain and France. No wonder, Izvolski complained bitterly that Aehrenthal was "no gentleman" as he had "broken faith" in proceeding so quickly with the annexation.

But this was not all. The news of the annexation of Bosnia and Herzegovina by Austria caused great indignation and excitement in Serbia. Extraordinary editions of the newspapers condemned the violation of the Treaty of Berlin and demanded a war against Austria. The Minister of Serbia declared that war was inevitable and war preparations were ordered. The Prince of Serbia ran to Russia to get help from the Czar. Other Serbian Ministers went on a tour of the European capitals to secure help against Austria. The Serbians also demanded compensations.

Izvolski found himself in a very difficult position. He himself had made the Buchlau bargain but he was tricked by Aehrenthal. While he had got nothing, Austria had got her part of the bargain. He asked the Serbians to wait for some time so that he might be able to put the Straits in his pocket. He also demanded the calling of a conference of the Powers who had signed the Treaty of Berlin. Izvolski knew that he would have to admit a humiliating diplomatic defeat if he failed to get a conference of the Powers summoned. He began to pretend to the Serbians that he had never given his consent to the annexation of Bosnia and Herzegovina by Austria. "He condemned Austria-Hungary which had entirely lost the confidence of Russia and of the Western Powers; he expressed the conviction and hope that her action in this sphere would be avenged upon her in a sanguinary manner". However, he found that Germany was firm in supporting Austria in her refusal to submit the question of annexation to a conference of Powers unless its decisions were agreed upon beforehand. Izvolski felt that if he insisted upon a conference, there was a possibility of war and he knew full well that Russia was absolutely unprepared for war. She had not recovered completely from her defeats in the Russo-Japanese War (1904-5).

The position of Izvolski was a very awkward one. For months, he continued to encourage the Serbians with the hope that the question of annexation would be submitted to a conference of the Powers for revision and undoubtedly he did all that he could to achieve that objective, in spite of that, excitement and agitation continued to increase in Serbia, Bosnia and Croatia. Demonstrations were made against Austria. The result was that the Austrian Government resorted to a policy of repression and a large number of persons were arrested. All kinds of cases were fabricated against the agitators. The situation became so tense that Austria had to send troops on the Serbian frontier and there was every possibility of a conflict between Austria and Serbia. There was no guarantee that the local conflict might not spread to the whole of Europe. However, Russia was determined to avoid any armed conflict as she knew that she could not come to the help of Serbia. Moreover, Russia was not sure that she could be assisted by her ally, France, in a war in the Balkans. No wonder, Russia continued to beg the Serbians to submit for the present and to trust in the future. To quote, "When our armament programmes shall have been completely carried out, then we shall have our reckoning with Austria-Hungary; do not begin any war now, for this would be your suicide; conceal your purposes and make ready; the days of your joy will come." Again, "The situation is frightful, Russia is unprepared for war and a Russian defeat would be the ruin of Slavdom. The Czar has the feeling that a conflict with Germandom is inevitable in the future and that one must prepare for this."

It is often said that Germany instigated Aehrenthal to annex Bosnia and Herzegovina with a view to serving her own interest. Prof. Fay does not accept this view. According to him, such a view is absolutely unfounded. The truth is that Germany was not even informed in time and the Kaiser got the information only on the day when the annexation actually took place. He was indignant at the action of Austria which he considered as an attack on Turkey. Such an action on the part of Austria was damaging to the German influence at Constantinople and was liable to damage the project of the Berlin-Baghdad Railway. To quote the Kaiser, "Vienna will be charged with duplicity and not unjustly. She has duped us in a most unheard of fashion." Again, "My personal feelings as an ally have been most seriously wounded." The Kaiser's view was that if Germany did not oppose annexation, she would be held guilty of having approved of it. He was in favour of openly opposing the annexation even at the risk of breaking the alliance with Austria.

However, Chancellor Bulow differed from the Kaiser. He was not prepared to weaken the Triple Alliance and consequently was determined to support Austria in whatever she did. His view was that if Germany did not support Austria wholeheartedly, Austria might never forgive her. Germany might have a grievance against Austria as she was not informed in time, but when Austria had already annexed Bosnia and Herzegovina, it was not proper to protest after that. Ultimately, the Kaiser accepted the point of view of Bulot and the latter informed Vienna that "in case difficulties or complications arise, our ally can count upon us."

After the annexation of Bosnia and Herzegovina, Aehrenthal tried to buy off the Turks. Although the Turks were very indignant to begin with and wanted to wage a war against Austria, yet when they found that no European State was prepared to give them armed assistance, they agreed to accept the Austrian offer of a cash payment as a compensation for giving up their nominal sovereignty over Bosnia and Herzegovina.

The deal with the Turks made the Serbs all the more bitter. So far, the feeling was that all the Powers including Turkey would join to demand the submission of the question of annexation to a conference of the Powers and Serbia would be able to secure autonomy for the provinces and compensation for herself. After the deal with Turkey, all hopes were shattered and Austria stated in categorical terms that she was not prepared to make any concessions. The situation was obviously very serious.

It was at this stage that Germany came forward with a proposal to avoid a conflict. Germany was to request Austria to invite the Powers to give their formal sanction by an exchange of notes to the Austro-Turkish Agreement provided Russia promised beforehand to give her sanction when invited by Austria to do so. This German proposal of March 1909 had certain advantages. It was to give Austria what she wanted. It satisfied the Entente demand that no change in the Treaty of Berlin was to be made without the approval of the Powers concerned. It avoided the humiliation of Russia by not rejecting the idea of a conference directly. It was intended to help Izvolski to come out of the difficult situation into which he had placed himself. Izvolski appreciated the proposal and was inclined to accept it. He also knew that Russia was not at all prepared for a war and consequently was not in a position to help Serbia by force of arms. Izvolski also knew that by striking the Buchlau bargain, he had put himself in an inconsistent position and he was afraid of the consequences in case Aehrenthal published the documents concerning the Buchlau bargain.

Aehrenthal was willing to accept the German proposal if Serbia declared that she recognised the annexation of Bosnia and also promised to give up her attitude of opposition and protest.

It is, therefore, clear that it is wrong to maintain that Germany threatened Russia with an ultimatum and thereby brought about the surrender of Russia. Such a story was invented merely with a view to saving the face of Izvolski against his critics. The truth is that Germany did not give any ultimatum or exert pressure on Russia. All that she did was to avoid a conflict between Austria and Serbia which might have dragged Russia and given her a defeat. As a matter of fact, Russia gladly accepted the German proposal and on the invitation of Austria, all the Powers gave their approval to the annexation by an exchange of notes. Serbia also made the required declaration in these words: "Serbia recognizes that she has not been affected in her rights by the fait accomplish created in Bosnia, and that consequently she will conform to the decisions that the Powers may take in regard to Article 25 of the Treaty of Berlin. In defence to the advice of the Great Powers, Serbia undertakes to renounce the attitude of protest and opposition which she has adopted since last autumn with regard to the annexation. She undertakes, moreover, to modify the direction of her present policy towards Austria-Hungary, and to live in future on good neighbourly terms with the latter.

"In conformity with these declarations and with confidence in the peaceful intentions of Austria-Hungary, Serbia will replace her army, as far as it concerns its organization and the location and number of the troops, to the state in which it was in the spring of 1908. She will disarm and disband the volunteers and irregular forces and prevent the formation of new irregular corps on her territory." The result was that both Serbia and Austria demobilized their arms and the crisis was over.

A reference may be made to some of the consequences of the Bosnian crisis. It cannot be denied that Aehrenthal got in 1909 a diplomatic victory and Russia and Serbia felt that they were both humiliated. Although Aehrenthal got many congratulations and also got the title of Count, the action of Austria created a sort of distrust among the European Powers in the Austrian methods of diplomacy. It was felt that Austria had violated a solemn treaty without any justification. It was not proper to force from Serbia a humiliating declaration which could not be expected to be acted upon by any patriotic politician or statesman. The very object of strengthening the Austrian control over Bosnia and Herzegovina was defeated. Austria got temporary success but that created many difficulties for her in future. To quote Aehrenthal, "I hope our action will succeed; if not, I am naturally done for, but in that case at least, we shall have met defeat with honour; otherwise we should have continued to sink miserably step by step."

Germany also got her share of the bad name, on account of her association with Austria. Germany came to be distrusted in Serbia, Russia and England. Germany's efforts to find out a peaceful solution was twisted into a threat of force or an ultimatum. It was represented as a brutal German attempt to humiliate Russia and drive a wedge into the Triple Entente by forcing Russia to give up the Entente. It is possible that such an impression was created by the Kaiser's speech in 1910 that he stood by his ally "in shining armour."

The Bosnian crisis had an unfortunate effect on Italy. She was not consulted by Austria beforehand. She felt that her pride had been offended and her own ambitions in the Balkans thwarted by the Austrian action. Italy began to feel that the Triple Alliance was of absolutely no use to her and she was quite willing to sign with Russia a new agreement in 1909. The Triple Alliance got a shaking from the Bosnian crisis.

The crisis had also its effects on Russia. The propaganda against Germany was increased. It was declared that a war between Slavdom and Teutondom was inevitable. Russia began to reorganise and increase her army and navy so that she might be ready for the inevitable war with Germany and Austria. So far as Izvolski himself was concerned the Bosnian crisis was a great diplomatic defeat which made him very bitter and ultimately forced him to give up his job as Minister of Foreign Affairs in 1910.

The Balkan Wars (1912-13). The Balkan Wars of 1912-13 were the outcome of the Young Turk Revolution of 1908. As the Young Turks followed a policy of Turkification of the Christians under their control and carried out wholesale massacres, the Balkan States were frightened into a union. They made up their minds to unite themselves with a view to turning out the Turks bag and baggage from Europe before the latter could marshal all their forces against them.

When Turkey was busy in fighting against Italy in 1911-12 on the question of Tripoli, negotiations were started among the Balkan States and they ultimately resulted in the formation of the Balkan League. It was not easy to bring the Balkan States together on account of their mutual hatred based on historical, racial and sentimental grounds. However, their common dislike of the Turks on account of their sufferings, brought them together. The massacre of the Christians by the Young Turks inflamed the people and no wonder, they decided to sink their differences to fight against a common enemy. The creation of the Balkan League was a surprise for Turkey and the European Powers who could never dream of the Balkan States presenting a united front. The Balkan States were encouraged on account of the weakness and demoralization of Turkey as a result of her war with Italy.

In October 1912 the four Balkan States of Montenegro, Serbia, Bulgaria and Greece declared war against Turkey. The war was a brief one and resulted in an overwhelming victory for the Allies. Fighting started on 15 October 1912. The Greeks pushed into Macedonia and after three weeks were able to capture Salonica. The Serbians and Montenegrins were also successful. The Bulgarians also won victory after victory against Turkey. The result was that the military power of Turkey was completely smashed. By the middle of November, the Bulgarians had reached the Chataldja line of fortifications which extended from the Sea of Marmora to the Black Sea. Only twenty-five miles beyond them lay Constantinople.

The collapse of the Turkish power in Europe was nearly complete. Only Adrianople, Janina and Scutari had not fallen. This collapse came as a surprise to the Turks, to the Great Powers and to the

Balkan States. In December 1912, delegates from the various States met in London to settle the terms of peace. The talks were unsuccessful because Bulgaria insisted on getting Adrianople which the Turks refused to give. The result was that hostilities started once again in March 1913. Janina fell on 6 March, Adrianople on 26 March and Scutari on 23 April 1913. It was under these circumstances that Turkey accepted the terms of peace. On 30 May 1913, the Treaty of London was signed.

Treaty of London (1913). According to this Treaty, a line was drawn from the Enos on the Aegean Sea to Midia on the Black Sea and all Turkish territory west of the line was given to the Allies except the territory of Albania whose boundaries and status were to be determined by the Great Powers. Crete was given to the Great Powers and the latter were to decide as to who was to have the islands captured by Greece in the Aegean. In December 1913, Crete was given to Greece by the Great Powers. The dominions of the Sultan in Europe were reduced to a vanishing point. After five centuries of rule, the Sultan found himself almost expelled from Europe. This great achievement was the work of the four Balkan States who for once united in the common work of liberation. The Great Powers had done nothing. A great change had taken place in the map of Europe without involving the Great Powers in war.

However, the Treaty of London did not last long. After defeating Turkey, the Balkan States started quarrelling among themselves over the division of the spoils. The trouble arose on account of the determination of Austria and Italy to create a new independent State of Albania. The creation of the new State of Albania on the Adriatic coast prevented Serbia from realizing her ambition to have an outlet to the sea. It is to be noted that before the beginning of the war, Serbia and Bulgaria had defined their future spheres of influence in Macedonia. The larger part of Macedonia was to go to Bulgaria and Serbia was to get the coast-line on the Adriatic. The creation of Albania was to make Serbia a land-locked country. Austria was to go to Bulgaria and Serbia was to get the coast-line on the Adriatic State. She had always been opposed to the aggrandisement of Serbia, because she had millions of Slavs under her own rule who might be attracted to an independent Serbia, enlarged and with prestige heightened. Moreover, she believed that Serbia would be a tool of Russia, and she would not tolerate Russia's influence on her southern borders and along the Adriatic if she could help it. She did not propose to be less important in those waters than she had been in the past. Serbia must be excluded from the Adriatic. It was the blocking of Serbia's outlet to the sea that caused the second Balkan War between the Allies. Intense was the indignation of the Serbians, but they could do nothing. They, therefore, sought as partial compensation larger territories in Macedonia than their treaty with Bulgaria had assigned to them. But they encountered the stubborn opposition of Bulgaria which refused any concession along this line and insisted upon the strict observance of the treaty. Instantly the old, bitter hatred flared up again. The Serbians insisted that the expulsion of the Turks had been the work of all the allies, and that there should be a fair division of the territories acquired in the name of all. On the other hand, the Bulgarians argued that it had been they who had done the heavy fighting in the war, that they had furnished by far the larger number of troops, that it was their victories of Kirk Kilisse and Lule Burgas that had annihilated the power of the Turks in Europe, that they were entitled to annex territories in Macedonia which they declared were peopled by Bulgars. Other considerations also entered into the situation.

Bulgaria intended to have her way. Her army was elated by the recent astounding successes. She was rather contemptuous of the Serbians and Greeks and emphatically minimised the services rendered by them to the common cause. She thought that it could easily conquer both if necessary, and could take what territories it chose. It was Bulgaria, whose party had lost all sense of proportion, all sense of the rights of her former allies, that began the new struggle. She treacherously attacked Greece and Serbia at the end of June 1913. Fierce fighting ensued for several days.

Second Balkan War (1913). Bulgaria's action in plunging herself into the avoidable conflict was all the more foolhardy as her relations with her northern neighbour. Rumania, were unsettled and precarious. Rumania had demanded that Bulgaria should cede her a strip of territory in the north-east of Bulgaria, in order that the balance of power among the Balkan States might remain practically what it had been. Bulgaria had refused this so-called compensation. The result was that Rumania also now went to war with Bulgaria. The Turks, too, seeing a chance to recover some of the land they had recently lost, plunged into the melee.

Treaty of Bucharest (1913). Thus Bulgaria was confronted on all sides by enemies. She was at war with five States, not three, for Montenegro was also involved. By the middle of July she saw that her cause was hopeless and she consented to make peace. By the Treaty of Bucharest, signed on August 10, 1913, Serbia and Greece secured larger possessions than they had ever anticipated, and Rumania was given the territory she desired. Turkey also recovered a large area which she had lost earlier including the important city and fort of Adrianople. All this was at the expense of Bulgaria, who paid for her arrogance and unconciliatory temper by losing much territory which she would otherwise have secured. Bulgaria was deeply embittered and only waited for an opportunity to tear up the Treaty of Bucharest which she refused to consider as morally binding as a permanent settlement of the Balkans. The year 1913 remained a bitter memory in the minds of all Bulgarians.

Results of Balkan Wars (1912-13). In territory and population, Turkey was the only loser. Before the war, the European population was estimated to be 6,130,200 and her area 65,350 sq. miles. Of population, she lost 4,239,200 and she was left with only 882 sq. miles of territory. Greece was the largest gainer, increasing her population from 2,666,000 to 4,363,000 and her area from 25,014 sq. miles to 41,933 sq. miles. Serbia increased her population from just under three million to four and a half, and nearly doubled her territory, increasing it from 18,650 sq. miles to 33,891 sq. miles. Rumania added 286,000 to a population which was the largest in the Balkans, amounting to about seven and a half millions, and gained 2,687 sq. miles of territory entirely at the expense of Bulgaria. The net gains of Bulgaria were only 125,490 in population and 9,663 sq. miles; while Montenegro raised her population from 250,000 to 480,000 and her area from 3,474 to 5,603 sq. miles.

According to Grant and Temperley, "No single event influenced the outbreak of War in 1914 more than the Balkan War of 1912-13. Other incidents, as Algeciras, Bosnia or Agadir, disturbed the situation because they affected the Balance of Power in the future. But the overthrow of the Turks caused immediate danger, for it affected the Balance of Power in the present. Serbia, Bulgaria, Greece and Rumania were revealed as conquering military States. The Turkish army trained by Germany as a potential ally was utterly beaten. Serbia added a million to its population, erased the humiliations of the Bosnian annexation, and triumphantly asserted her prestige in an outburst of Pan-Serb and Yugo-Slav enthusiasm, which swept Dalmatia and Bosnia like a prairie-fire. Serbia, hitherto rebuffed and discredited, appeared armed, victorious and triumphant. As Italy had arisen from Piedmont so a united Yugoslavia was to arise from Serbia. The prestige gained by Greece and Rumania was only second to that of Serbia. All three States now looked forward to a time when each flag would cover all their kinsmen in the Balkans, a greater Greece, a greater Rumania, a greater Serbia. And their brethren beneath the Turkish or Hapsburg rule looked forward to the day when the arms of their free countrymen would break the hated yoke from off their necks. A perpetually increasing nationalistic agitation in Austria-Hungary and Turkey, where such agitation was so dangerous, was the direct result of the Balkan War."

David Thomson says that the Balkan Wars left the international scene more enigmatic than before. No belligerent believed that the decisions about the territory would last. Both Serbia and Montenegro regarded war against Austria-Hungary as inevitable. Bulgaria nursed plans for revenge against her neighbours and looked to Turkey and Austria-Hungary as possible allies. Russia decided to side with Serbia and Rumania against Bulgaria. Each state remained more warlike than ever before. The defiance of the great powers and the contempt for treaties deprived them of any expectation of gain or security by any means other than war. There was an atmosphere of war all-round.

Greece. The significance of changes effected in the map of "Turkey in Europe" cannot, however, be measured solely by statistics. The settlement made by the Treaty of Bucharest was neither satisfactory nor complete. Of the recent belligerents, Greece had most cause for satisfaction. To the north-east her territorial gains were not only enormous in extent but of the highest commercial and strategic importance. The acquisition of Salonika was in itself a veritable triumph for the Greek cause, and Greece would have been well advised to be content with it. The insistence upon Kavala, whatever her ethnographic claims might have been, is now recognised as a political blunder. On the north-west, Greece acquired the greater part of Epirus, including the great fortress of Janina, but she was still unsatisfied. For many months she continued to urge her claims to portions of southern Albania, assigned by the Powers to the new autonomous State. But to press them would have brought Greece into conflict with Italy. "Italy," said the Marquis di san Giuliano, "will even go the length of war to prevent Greece occupying Valona; on this point her decision is irrevocable." On that side, Greece remained unsatisfied. There remained the question of the islands. Crete was definitely assigned to Greece, and on December 14, 1913, it was formally taken over by King Constantine, accompanied by the Crown Prince and the Prime Minister M. Venizelos. The question of the rest of the islands was reserved to the Powers, who ultimately awarded to Greece all the islands of which the Porte could dispose, except Imbros and Tenedos, which were regarded as essential for the safeguarding of the entrance to the Dardanelles, and were left to Turkey. The Sporades, including Rhodes, remained in the occupation of Italy, Greece, therefore, had reason for profound dissatisfaction. Some 300,000 Greeks still remained under Bulgarian rule in Thrace and Eastern Macedonia, while in the Ottoman Empire Greece still claimed some 300,000 "unredeemed" co-nationals.

Rumania. As regards Rumania, in proportion to her sacrifices, her gains were considerable. However, for the satisfaction of her large claims, the Balkan Wars afforded no opportunity. The "unredeemed" Rumanians were the subjects either of Austria-Hungary or of Russia. Transylvania, Bukovina and Bessarabia were the provinces to which Rumania laid claims.

Bulgaria. Bulgaria's position in 1913 was less favourable, but her misfortunes was largely of her own making. When the Treaty of London was signed in May, fate seemed to hold for Bulgaria the promise of a brilliant future. Despite the hostility of the Greeks and the rivalry of the Latins, Bulgaria was the first favourite for the hegemony of the Balkans. The Bulgars lacked some of the cultural qualifications of their neighbours and they were the latest comers into Balkan society, but they had given proof of a virile and progressive temper, and were advancing rapidly in the arts of peace and war. Then suddenly they flung away in a short month the great position secured to them by the patient labours, of a generation. As it was, they got an area relatively circumscribed, with a wretched coastline. Above all, they lost the coveted districts of Ochrida and Monastir. The impartial judgment of history will probably incline to the view that in defining so narrowly the share of Bulgaria, Greece and Serbia showed short-sightedness and parsimony. Bulgaria ought at least to have been allowed a wider outlet on the Aegean littoral, with Kavala as a port. Nothing less could reconcile Bulgaria to the retention of Salonika by Greece.

Serbia. Serbia showed herself lacking in prudent generosity. The gains of Serbia were very considerable. The division of Novi-Bazar between herself and Montenegro brought her into immediate contact with the southern Slavs of the Black Mountain. The acquisition of Old Serbia and central Macedonia carried her territory southwards towards the Aegean. But Serbia's crucial problem was not solved. She was still a landlocked country and deprived of her natural access to the Aegean, and pushed into immediate conflict with the Bulgarians, perhaps into ultimate conflict with Greece. Disappointed for her dearest ambition, flushed with victory, duped by interested advice, Serbia can hardly be blamed for having inflicted humiliation upon Bulgaria, and for having yielded to the temptation of unexpected territorial acquisition.

Montenegro. Montenegro shared both the success and the disappointment of her kinsmen. King Nicholas's disappointment at being deprived of Scutari was acute, and was hardly compensated by the acquisition of the western half of Novi-Bazar. His position as regards sea-head was less desperate than that of Serbia, but he too had an account to settle with the European Concert.

Albania. The Powers were determined to secure autonomy for Albania. Such a solution offered obvious advantages. It might stifle the pretensions of Italy and Austria-Hungary. It might arrest the inconvenient claims of Greece upon the "Northern Empire". It might interpose a powerful barrier between the southern Slav and the Adriatic. It might repair the havoc which the formation of the Balkan alliance had wrought in German plans in regard to the Near East. Autonomy was given to Albania in November 1913, but disorders broke out in the country and its various parts were occupied by the various Powers.

Germany claimed special credit for the peace of Bucharest. William II sent congratulations to King of Rumania for his "wise and truly statesmanlike policy". To quote him, "I rejoice at our mutual co-operation in the cause of peace." The King of Greece was given a baton as Field Marshal in the Prussian Army.

It cannot be denied that Austria-Hungary tried its utmost to enlarge the area of war. Before the peace of Bucharest was concluded, Austria-Hungary communicated to Germany and Italy "her intention of taking action against Serbia, and defined such action as defensive." Both Italy and Germany put a check on Austria-Hungary and consequently the attack was postponed. However, the attack did come within a year in the form of the World War I. It was pointed out that Serbia had committed two unpardonable sins and therefore she must be annihilated. She had strengthened the barrier between Austria-Hungary and Salonika and also added to her prestige as the representative of the aspirations of the Slavs. However, Serbia was not alone, Rumania and Greece also seemed to be menacing Austria-Hungary. No wonder, Austria-Hungary took action in 1914 and Europe was involved in a great conflagration.

SUGGESTED READINGS

Anderson, M.S.: **The Eastern Question,** 1966.
Crawley, C.W.: **The Question of Greek Independence,** 1930.
Davis, W.S.: **Short History of the Near East.**
Forbes and Others: **The Balkans.**
Gooch, G.P.: **Modern Europe (1878-1919).**
Helmreich, E.C.: **The Diplomacy of the Balkan Wars** (1912-1913), 1938.
Henderson, G.B.: **Crimean War Diplomacy and Other Historical Essays,** 1947.
Marriott, J.A.R.: **The Eastern Question.**
Millard: **Democracy and the Eastern Question.**
Miller, W.: **The Ottomon Empire and its Successors,** 1934.
Miller, W.: **History of the Greek People.**
Rose : **Development of the European Nations.**
Schevill: **The Balkan Peninsula.**
Seton-Watson, R.W.: **The Rise of Nationality in the Balkans,** 1917.
Seton-Watson, R. W.: **Disraeli, Gladstone and the Eastern Question,** 1933.
Temperley, H.W.V.: **History of Serbia.**
Temperley, H.W.V.: **England and the Near East: The Crimea,** 1936.
Tolstoi: **Savastopol.**
Taylor, A.J.P.: **The Struggle for Mastery in Europe (1848-1918) 1954.**

CHAPTER 25

SCRAMBLE FOR AFRICA

Partitioning of Africa. From the 15th century onwards, many points on the African coast were occupied by the maritime nations of Europe. However, the scramble for power in Africa took place during the latter half of the 19th century. Up to that time, most of Africa was regarded as the "Dark Continent" and not much was known about it to the world at large. Explorers and missionaries opened the way and pointed out the potentialities of Africa. The names of Stanley, Livingstone, Baker, Burton, Grant and Speke are famous in this connection. These persons explored the courses of the four great rivers, viz., the Nile, the Niger, the Congo and the Zambezi. Christian missionaries carried on active propaganda in South Africa and on the Guinea Coast. The curiosity and interest of Europeans were aroused by the publication of the books of Stanley. His most important books were **How I Found Livingstone, Through the Dark Continent and In Darkest Africa.**

Leopold II, King of Belgium, took keen interest in African affairs. He summoned, in 1876, an International Conference of Geographers from all parts of the world to consider ways and means for the exploration and civilization of Africa. Suggestions were invited for opening the interior of Africa for industry and commerce. An International African Association was set up and its branches were also established in many countries. The voyages of Stanley directed the attention of the African Association to the Congo and it was decided to concentrate on its exploration. As the enterprise was financed by King Leopold himself as an individual, the Congo Free State became the personal monopoly of King Leopold himself. The gains of Leopold aroused the jealousy of others. Both Portugal and France also put forward their claims to the Congo. Many European nations sent their agents to the various parts of Africa to acquire concessions. Separate treaties were entered into with the native chiefs and thus spheres of influence were acquired. In 1884-85, a conference was held at Berlin and most of the agreements made with the native chiefs up to that time were recognised. Even after that, the process of penetration into Africa continued with the result that with the exception of Abyssinia and Liberia, practically the whole of Africa was acquired by the various European Powers.

Up to 1908, the Congo Free State continued to be the personal property of King Leopold II of Belgium. However, there was a lot of criticism against that arrangement, and consequently in that year the Government of Belgium took over the territory from the King. Portugal also established her hold over the province of Angola situated to the south of the Belgian Congo. She also established the colony of Mozambique or Portuguese East Africa. Italy secured Eritrea and Italian Somaliland. She tried to acquire Abyssinia but she was defeated in the battle of Adowa. Italy also intended to acquire Tunis, but as she delayed matters, France established her protectorate over it in 1881. However, Italy fought against Turkey in 1911-12 and secured Tripoli and Cyrenaica. Spain acquired a province on the north-west coast of Africa. In 1906, she acquired a sphere on the coast opposite to Gibraltar. Although Bismarck was reluctant to enter the colonial field, he was converted later on. Germany acquired the territories of South-West Africa, South-East Africa, the Cameroons and Togoland.

France had already established her control over Algeria in the time of Louis Philippe. The province was developed in the time of Napoleon III. In 1881, she established her protectorate over Tunis. Both France and Great Britain had dual control over Egypt, but in 1882 France refused to co-operate with

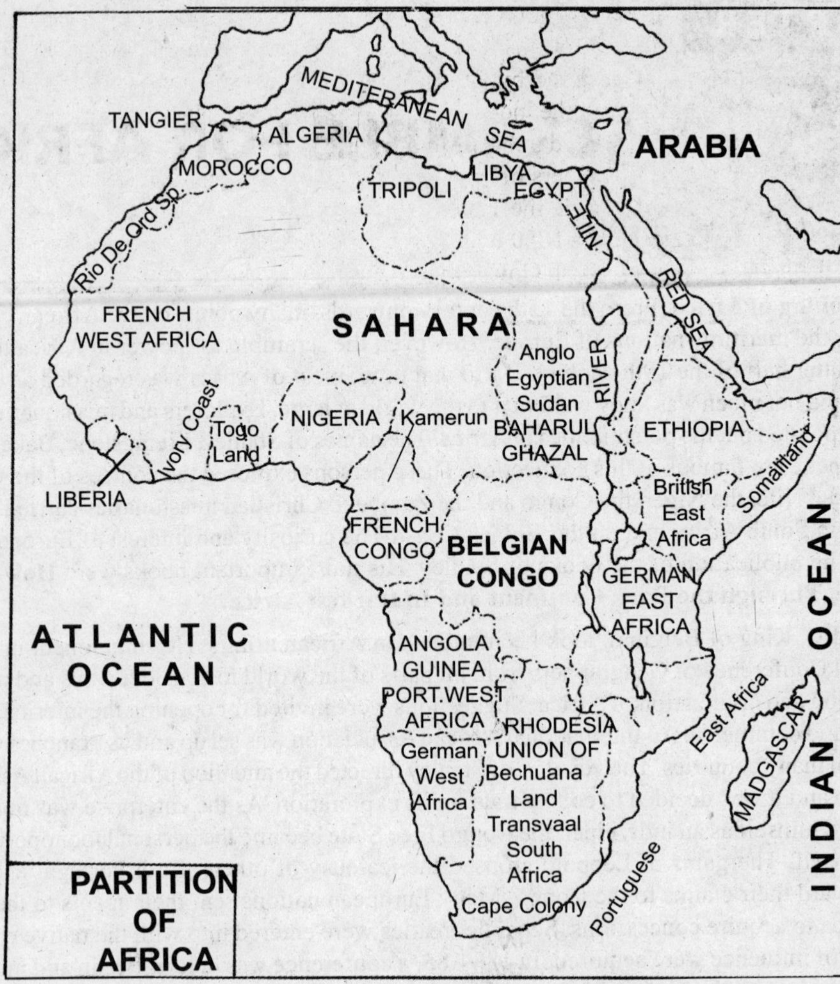

PARTITION OF AFRICA

Great Britain to put down the revolt of Arabi and the result was that from 1892 Great Britain came to have sole control over Egypt and France was ousted. France possessed a big colonial empire in North and West Africa and she intended to penetrate to the East of Africa. For that purpose, Marchand was sent by the French Government. In 1898, there occurred the famous Fashoda crisis. There was a possibility of war between England and France but it was avoided by Delcasse and Salisbury. The agreement of 1899 demarcated the spheres of influence of France and Great Britain. The Entente Cordiale of 1904 provided that England was to have a free hand in Egypt but she was to support France in Morocco. When France tried to establish her stranglehold over Morocco, three crises took place in 1905-6, 1908 and 1911. Ultimately, in 1912, Morocco became practically a protectorate of France. In 1896, France acquired the island of Madagascar. She had her control over the whole of the Sahara region. She also had her holdings on the Senegal, the Ivory Coast and the Congo.

South Africa. As regards South Africa, the Bushmen, Hottentots Kafirs, Zalus and other kindred races came into conflict with the Europeans. There was also competition between the Dutch and the British. The Dutch Boers were backward and cruel, but the British colonists, officials and soldiers were more advanced and were also supported by the British Government. There were frontier wars between the Kafirs and the Europeans. The Great Trek of 1836-40 resulted in the migration of more than 7,000 Dutch Boers from British South Africa to the valleys of the Orange and Vaal rivers. The

British policy towards the Boers was not a consistent one. For some time, they were allowed to be independent. However, in 1842, the British Government put forward its claim to Natal, and in 1848 the Orange River Colony was annexed by Great Britain. The Boers once again migrated into the Transvaal. Great Britain recognised the independence of the Transvaal and restored to the Boers the Orange River Colony. Disraeli wanted to bring about a union of all the States of South Africa under British control and he wanted the Boers of Transvaal to join the union. He commissioned Frere for that purpose, and after a lot of trouble the Transvaal was annexed. However, the Boers proclaimed their independence on 16 December 1880 under the leadership of Kruger. The war was a short one and was suddenly ended by the British Government after four disasters. The last disaster took place

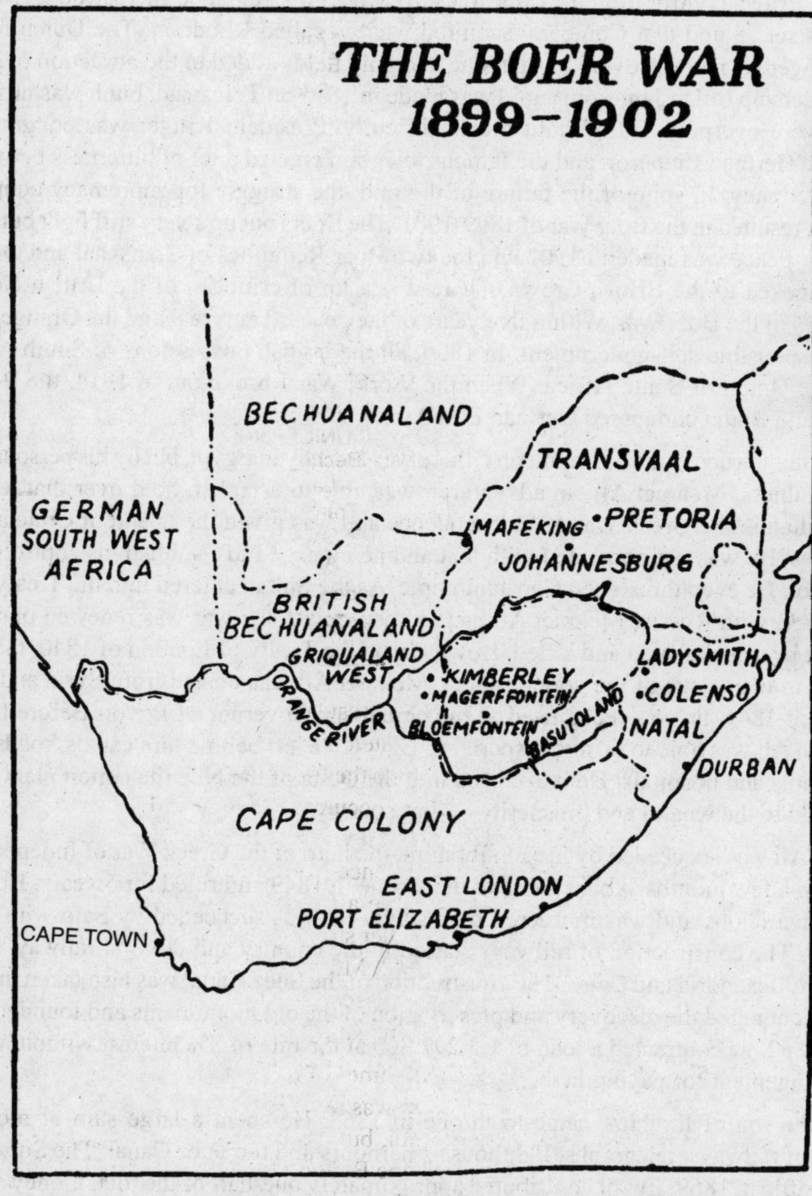

at Majuba Hill in February 1881. That defeat could easily have been repaired and General Roberts had already been sent to South Africa from India with an expeditionary force. However, the British

Government changed its mind and Gladstone came to the conclusion that the Boers were determined to have their independence and it was no use shedding blood by defeating them in the battlefields merely to restore the prestige of British arms. No power could change the determination of the Boers to be independent. Under the circumstances, a treaty was made with the Boers in March 1881. The Boers were given complete self-government under the suzerainty of the British Crown.

The conciliatory policy of Gladstone towards the Boers was interpreted by them as a sign of British weakness and a strong nationalist movement started among them under President Kruger. As a reaction, an equally strong nationalist movement was started among the British colonists as well and the leader of the movement was Cecil Rhodes. Rhodes was a great imperialist and he dreamt of expanding the British control from the Cape to Cairo. Under his guidance and patronage, a chartered Company was set up and that Company acquired what is called Rhodesia. The Dutch found their position endangered. The discovery of diamond and gold fields added to the attraction of Transvaal. Under the leadership of Dr. Jameson, a raid was made in 1895 on Transvaal, but it was unsuccessful. The raiders were overpowered without much difficulty. President Kruger was congratulated by William II, the German Emperor, and the famous telegram created a lot of bitterness between Great Britain and Germany. In spite of the failure of the raid, the struggle for supremacy continued and ultimately that resulted in the Boer War of 1899-1901. The Boers put up a very stiff fight but ultimately were defeated. Peace was made in 1902 and the two Boer Republics of Transvaal and Orange Free State were annexed to the British Crown. There was a lot of criticism of the British Government during the days of the Boer War. Within five years of the peace, Transvaal and the Orange Free State were given responsible self-government. In 1909, all the British possessions of South Africa were united into the Union of South Africa. When the World War I broke out in 1914, the Boer armies under Smuts and Botha conquered German East Africa.

Egypt. After the departure of Napoleon I, there was anarchy in Egypt, but by his personal initiative and resourcefulness, Mehmet Ali, an adventurer, was able to establish hold over that territory. He helped the Sultan in the Greek War of Independence and was given the Island of Crete as a reward for his services. He was not contented with that and he managed to establish his control over Syria and Asia Minor. He even threatened Constantinople. As the Sultan entered into the Treaty of Unkiar Skelessi in 1833 with Russia, Mehmet Ali had to keep quiet. The war was renewed once again by the Sultan but he was defeated and killed. However, by the Treaty of London of 1840, the European Powers came to the rescue of the young Sultan. Mehmet Ali was ousted from Syria and ultimately by the treaty of 1841, he was recognised as the hereditary Governor of Egypt. Before his death in 1847, Mehmet Ali was able to bring prosperity to Egypt. He left behind him canals, roads, factories, arsenals, schools and hospitals. He introduced into the Delta of the Nile the cotton plant which was destined to add to the wealth and prosperity of that country.

Mehmet Ali was succeeded by his son Ibrahim, the hero of the Greek War of Independence, but he died within a few months. Abbas came to the throne in 1849 and ruled for 5 years. He was cruel, sensual and avaricious and was murdered by a slave. He was succeeded by Said who ruled from 1854 to 1863. The construction of railways started in the country and the first railway was built in 1855 between Alexandria and Cairo. The construction of the Suez Canal was also taken up during his reign. Said encouraged the discovery and preservation of the old monuments and founded a museum at Cairo. In 1862, he contracted a loan of £ 3,292,800 at the rate of 8% interest without making any adequate arrangement for paying it.

Ismail, the son of Ibrahim, came to throne in 1863. He spent a large sum of money on the construction of railways, telegraphs, lighthouses, harbours and the Suez Canal. The Suez Canal was opened for traffic in 1869. Egypt contributed approximately one-half of the total money spent on the construction of the canal. Many rulers and statesmen of Europe were invited to Egypt on the occasion of the opening ceremony and a lot of money was spent on that occasion. A lot of money was also

wasted on the war in the Sudan. The construction of royal palaces involved a lot of expenditure. Ismail was careless about money matters and he kept no accounts. He was his own finance minister. Although he considered himself to be clever, he was tricked by others. Each loan cost the State more than 12%. The railway loan of 1866 actually cost the State 26.9%. The £32 million loan of 1873 pledged all the available securities of the State but the Egyptian treasury actually received the sum of £20,700,000 only. The financial position became so serious that on 8 April 1876, the payment of Treasury Bills was suspended.

On 2 May 1876, the Commission of Public Debt was set up by a decree of Ismail. France, Austria and Italy appointed their commissioners but the British Government refused to appoint their nominee. Ultimately, Dual Control was established over Egypt by Great Britain and France.

In 1879, Great Britain joined the French Government in demanding a full enquiry into the financial position of Egypt and Ismail had to submit. He was also forced to recognise the principle of ministerial responsibility in Egypt. The Dual Control was suspended and responsible ministers remained in power for 5 years. Most of the property of the Khedive was taken over by the State and a fresh loan was raised on that security.

Early in 1879, Ismail demanded the resignation of his ministers. This created a very difficult situation. Italy was friendly inclined towards the Khedive and Russia kept aloof. Turkey played a waiting game. England, France and Germany joined hands and demanded the deposition of Ismail by the Sultan. In June 1879, the Khedive was deposed by the Sultan and his son Tewfik was appointed in his place.

Tewfik. Tewfik Pasha succeeded to a bankrupt State and an undisciplined army and discontented people. On account of his youth and inexperience, he was unable to cope with the situation. An attempt was made by Turkey to tighten her hold over Egypt. The Anglo-French Dual Control was revived. Confidence was restored once again. Half the annual revenues of the State were earmarked for the creditors of the State. Things seemed to be improving when in 1881, Tewfik dismissed his War Minister on the demand of rebels.

About 1881 was started a movement with the slogan of "Egypt for the Egyptians". In September 1881, Arabi, an Egyptian officer, accompanied by 5,000 soldiers, surrounded the royal palace and demanded an increase of the army, a change of ministry and a national assembly. The government submitted and Arabi himself was promoted. Arabi became a national hero. However, the problem became complicated by the arrival of a Turkish mission.

Gambetta invited Great Britain to discuss matters for the security of Tewfik and proposed a joint assurance of sympathy and support to him. The note was accepted and communicated to Tewfik. The Anglo-French note of January 1882 was an unfortunate step. Tewfik was not grateful and everybody else was angry at the idea of foreign intervention. The National Party, the military and Chamber united in a common bond of opposition to England and France. According to Dr. Gooch the Anglo-French Note was a blunder of the first magnitude. It brought strength not to Tewfik but to

Arabi who became the hero of the nation. He was appointed the Minister of War and the power of the Controllers decreased. Lord Cromer says, "From the moment the joint note was issued, foreign intervention became an unavoidable necessity." After the note was communicated, Gambetta fell and he was succeeded by Freycinet. The Sultan opposed the intervention of the Powers in Egypt. Bismarck was the least concerned. He declared that Egypt was the Schleswig-Holstein of the two Western Powers and they would intervene together but quarrel over the spoils.

There were riots in Alexandria in June 1882 and many persons were killed. Freycinet began to think in terms of coming to terms with Arabi. However, the British Government decided to crash Arabi. As the Egyptians began to fortify Alexandria, the safety of the ships in that harbour was threatened. The British Squadron was instructed to destroy the earthworks if the erection of batteries was continued. France was asked to co-operate but she refused to do so and the French Fleet sailed away from Alexandria. Many reasons have been given to explain the withdrawal of the French Government. The proposed bombardment of Alexandria was an act of war and that could not be done without the consent of the Chamber of Deputies. France had established her protectorate over Tunis in 1881 and she found her hands too full. The French Government was also afraid that Bismarck might be laying a trap for her in Egypt. It was under these circumstances that England was left all alone in Egypt. England requested Italy to join but she also refused. It is stated that the British Foreign Minister was happy at the refusal. To quote him, "We have done the right thing. We have shown our readiness to admit others and we have not the inconvenience of a partner." In the case of a joint action there was every possibility of friction in the future. The Sultan offered to send troops but his conditions were not accepted England declared that the Suez Canal would be safeguarded.

General Wolseley sailed from Port Said and in September 1882 crushed Arabi in the Battle of Tel-el Kabir. Thus England became the master of the situation. Bismarck was delighted at the news of British victory and declared that "the friendship of the British Empire is much more important for us than the fate of Egypt." He did not oppose the annexation of Egypt by England but he was also not prepared to advise its annexation. France was offered the presidency of the Commission for debt, but it was declined on the ground that it was inconsistent with the dignity of France to accept the position of a cashier. There were some sharp diplomatic exchanges and after that France "resumed her liberty of action". The hostilities between the two countries on the question of Egypt continued up to 1904 when the Entente Cordiale gave England a free hand in Egypt and France a free hand in Morocco.

When Great Britain was consolidating her position in Egypt, there broke out in Sudan the fanatical rising of the Mahdi against the Egyptian rule. The Mahdi defeated the Egyptian Army. The British Government was in a fix and did not know what to do. After some delay, it was decided to withdraw from Sudan and General Gordon was sent for that purpose. Unfortunately, the General went beyond instructions and was besieged. Before help could reach him, he was caught and killed in Khartum. The Mahdi was able to set up a reign of terror and destruction. The British Government followed a policy of caution but ultimately Kitchener was sent to complete the conquest of Sudan. After its conquest, Sudan was put under the joint control of England and Egypt.

When England occupied Egypt in 1882, the Government of Gladstone declared that it would not stay there for long. Lord Granville "contemplated shortly commencing the withdrawal of the fresh troops from Egypt." Lord Dufferin was sent from Constantinople to Cairo on a special mission "to advise the government of Khedive in the arrangements which would have to be made for the re-establishment of His Highness's authority." Arabi Pasha was tried and sent to Ceylon to spend his days in exile. Lord Dufferin recommended that Egypt was to be governed neither from London nor by an irresponsible centralized bureaucracy but by the representative institutions of the people. The Legislative Council and the Assembly were to be created but they were to be merely consultative bodies. The army, police, the judicial system and the taxation system were to be overhauled and the help of foreigners was to be taken for that purpose. His recommendations were accepted by the British Government and carried out by stages. Granville declared that "His Majesty's Government are desirous of withdrawing as soon as the state of the country and the organization of proper means for the maintenance of the Khedive's authority will admit of it." The Suez Canal was to be neutral in times of war and open to all the Powers in times of peace.

Lord Northbrook visited Egypt in 1884 and submitted two reports to the British Government containing his recommendations. However, those were not accepted by the government. In 1888, the Suez Canal Treaty was made which was satisfactory to France. However, England reserved to herself the right to close the Canal in times of war.

Cromer in Egypt. The British Government appointed Mr. Baring in 1882 as agent and Consul-General and he continued his work up to 1907. Later on, he was called Lord Cromer. During his tenure of office, he accomplished a lot of work and added to the peace and prosperity of the country. Law and order was restored and maintained. The deficit budget was turned into a surplus budget. The police was reorganized on modern lines. Education was encouraged and public health was also promoted. Irrigation facilities were increased. The Egyptians were encouraged to go abroad and acquire higher education. These Egyptians brought from abroad the ideas of progress and nationalism. Corruption was removed from administration and inequitable taxes were abolished. The whole of the taxation system was put on a sound footing.

World War I. It was under these circumstances that World War I broke out in 1914. Nominally, Egypt was still under the Turkish rule. As Turkey was fighting against England, it was decided to put an end to the Turkish rule in Egypt. On 18 December 1914, the British Government declared that "in view of the state of war arising out of the action of Turkey, Egypt is placed under the protection of His Majesty and will henceforth constitute a British protectorate." The Khedive, Abbas Hilmi, who was then in Constantinople, was deposed and his uncle, Hussein Kiamil, was recognized as the future ruler and given the title of the Sultan. This action of Great Britain was resented by the nationalists of Egypt who felt that in spite of the repeated declarations of the British Government that they were determined to withdraw as soon as possible, the British stranglehold over the country was being strengthened. In spite of the resentment, there was quiet in Egypt during the period of war. Turkey and Germany made two attempts to get control of the Suez Canal and invaded Egypt, but both of those attempts were unsuccessful. In April and July 1915, attempts were made on the life of the Sultan.

However, there was serious trouble after the war when the Allies enunciated the principle of self-determination as the basis of their policy. Egypt felt that this principle should be applied to her and she should be allowed to decide her own future. The Egyptians demanded the complete independence of their country, neutralization of the Suez Canal and control over Sudan. However, the British Government was not prepared to give up its control over Egypt. Her Protectorate over Egypt was recognized by the Allies at Paris as well as by the Treaty of Sevres of 1920 between Turkey and the Allies.

Zaghlul. Zaghlul was the leader of the Egyptian nationalists. And he would not keep quiet, he was arrested in March 1919 and deported to the Island of Malta. But instead of crushing the nationalist movement, this action of the government added to the anti-British feeling in the country. Railroads were cut at many places. There were cases of arson and looting. British soldiers and civilians were attacked. Foreign quarters were besieged. Cairo was cut off from the rest of the country. Although the rebellion was crushed, yet it became clear to the British Government that it would not be an easy task to rule Egypt. It was decided to send a mission to Egypt under the chairmanship of Lord Milner "to enquire into the causes of the recent disorders and to report on the existing situation in the country and the form of the situation which, under the Protectorate, will be best calculated to promote its peace and prosperity, the progressive development of self-governing institutions and the protection of foreign interests." The mission was boycotted by the Egyptians. However, it made a liberal report and recommended the grant of a large measure of self-government to the people. Disorders continued in the country. General Allenby was sent to Egypt at the head of an army of 60,000 men. Although he crushed the revolt, his view was that Great Britain must either grant Egypt her independence or annex her by force. A treaty was made in 1921 by which it was declared that "Egypt is an independent, sovereign State." Sultan Ahmed Fuad was recognized as the King of Egypt. The treaty was rejected by leaders like Zaghlul and it had to be enforced by the British Government by a unilateral proclamation of February 1922. Zaghlul was ultimately released by the British Government and he became the Prime Minister of Egypt. Egypt proceeded to act as if she was independent and Great Britain continued to believe that Egypt was still a part of the British Empire.

Zaghlul died in 1927 but his programme was continued by his followers. During the reign of Fuad, British influence was very great in Egypt. In 1930, a new constitution was proclaimed.

In 1936, the **Anglo-Egyptian Treaty** was signed. At that time, the safety of Egypt was considered to be in danger on account of the action of Mussolini in Abyssinia. Egypt herself felt that her safety was in danger. The Treaty of 1936 pledged Great Britain to defend Egypt from external aggression. The defence of the Suez Canal zone was also taken over by the British Government. The treaty was to last for 20 years. During World War II, British troops were stationed in Egypt. Germany and Italy were busy in North Africa and no wonder Egypt once again felt that her security was threatened. Air attacks were made on the Canal Zone. However, the United Nations were able to push back the Germans and the Italians from their base in Egypt. Undoubtedly, Egypt played a very important part in the ultimate victory of the United Nations.

When the World War II ended in 1945, there was a demand for the cancellation of the Treaty of 1936. The treaty was regarded as a symbol of the slavery of the people of Egypt. The Wafd Government in October 1951 unilaterally repudiated the Anglo-Egyptian Treaty of 1936. King Farouk was declared to be the King of Egypt and Sudan. The British Government was asked to withdraw her troops from the Suez Canal zone. There was serious rioting all over Egypt. There were frequent changes of government in the country. By a coup d'etat, led by General Naguib and his colleagues, King Farouk was forced to abdicate and leave the country.

The people of Egypt were not prepared to tolerate the continuation of the British troops in the Suez Canal Zone. The British were also not willing to withdraw at once. As the Egyptian demand persisted, negotiations were started between the two countries and ultimately an agreement was signed on 27 July, 1954. The agreement provided that the British troops were to leave the Canal Zone within 20 months. However, they were to be allowed to return to the base in the event of an armed attack by an outside power on Turkey or on any Arab State. The base was to be maintained by a British civilian contracting firm. The duration of the new agreement was 7 years. This agreement recognised that the Suez Canal was a waterway of international importance and both the parties guaranteed the freedom of navigation through the Canal.

On 26 July 1956, President Nasser who had succeeded Naguib, declared the nationalisation of the Suez Canal and freezed the funds of the Suez Canal Company in Egypt. Great Britain freezed all Egyptian assets on 28 July 1956. The United States and France began to apply economic sanctions against Egypt from that date. Great Britain ordered general mobilization of her forces and despatched troops to an unknown destination. The United States and France stood behind her. Their object was to put pressure on Egypt and thereby get the decision reversed. Egypt, however, did not bother about the threats.

Great Britain invited 24 nations to attend a conference in London on 16 August, 1956 to discuss the question of the Suez Canal. Out of the 24 nations, 22 accepted the invitation. Egypt and Greece declined the invitation. The London Conference was held from 16 August to 23 August under the chairmanship of Selwyn Lloyd, Foreign Secretary of Great Britain. On the opening day, Mr. Dulles submitted a plan to solve the Suez Canal issue. According to his plan, the operation of the Suez Canal was to be made the responsibility of an international board. Egypt was to be represented on that board but there was to be no domination by any single power. There was to be no prejudice to any power. The right of Egypt to an equitable return was to be recognised. Fair compensation was to be paid to the Suez Canal Company. Dulles made it clear that while framing his plan he had taken into consideration four principles. The first principle was that the Canal should be operated efficiently and freely and in accordance with the Convention of Constantinople of 1888. The second principle was that the operation of the Canal must be divorced from national politics. The third principle was that the legitimate rights of Egypt should be recognised and she should be given a fair return. The fourth principle was that compensation should be paid to the company. The Soviet delegate put forward his own Plan.

The Dulles Plan was backed by 17 countries and the record of the London Conference was forwarded to Egypt. That plan was rejected by President Nasser. On 12 September 1956, British Prime Minister declared that the United States, Great Britain and France were setting up a Users' Association which was to be responsible for traffic through the Suez Canal. The matter was also referred to the Security Council by Great Britain and France. On 13 October 1956, the Security Council adopted a resolution which affirmed six principles providing a basis for further negotiations. Those principles provided that there should be free and open transit through the Canal without discrimination. The sovereignty of Egypt was to be respected. The operation of the Canal was to be separated from the politics of any country. The manner of fixing tolls and charges was to be decided by agreement between Egypt and the users. A fair proportion of the dues was to be allotted for purposes of development. All disputes were to be settled by arbitration with suitable provision for the payment of sums found to be due. Another resolution providing for international control of the Suez Canal was vetoed by the Soviet Union in the Security Council.

On 29 October 1956, the forces of Israel attacked the Egyptian positions in the Suez Canal area. On 31 October 1956, Great Britain and France also joined the attack on Egypt. A resolution was moved in the Security Council asking for the cessation of hostilities but that resolution was vetoed by Great Britain and France. On 2 November 1956 the General Assembly passed a resolution which expressed great concern at the British, French and Israeli military operations in the Suez Canal area and called upon the Powers concerned to order immediately a cease-fire. On 4 November 1956, the General Assembly adopted a resolution asking the Secretary-General of the United Nations to submit a Plan for an emergency United Nations force to secure and supervise the end of hostilities in Egypt. On 5 November 1956, the Soviet Union gave a warning to Great Britain and France that in case they did not stop fighting in Egypt, she would also join the war. The United States also put pressure on Great Britain and France, and thus the hostilities came to an end. A lot of damage had been done to the Suez Canal during the hostilities and a lot of money was spent by the United Nations for getting the same repaired and made suitable once again for navigation. All this was done by April 1957.

The Arab States were not prepared to put up with the very existence of Israel in their midst. Raids were organised on Israel by a Syrian terrorist organization known as Al Fateh or El Safa. On 7 January 1965, certain water installations were dynamited on the Israeli side of the Jordan border. These provocations continued off and on for nearly 18 months. Some of these came from Jordan, some from Lebanon, some from Syria and some from the United Arab Republic.

Major-General Rikhye, U.N. Secretary-General's Chief Military Observer, and another high U.N. official visited Jordan and held consultations with the two Governments on the means of avoiding further incidents. In spite of that, clashes continued to occur. The situation on the Syrian border took a turn for the worse in March 1965. There were repeated exchanges of fire. The Syrian claim that Israeli tractors were intruding into Syrian territory was rejected by the Israeli-Syrian Mixed Armistice Commission. Israeli reprisals for raids launched from Jordan and Syria in the summer of 1965 involved the destruction of 3 Syrian tanks and several Al Fateh bases and training camps. The incidents on both sides grew, in intensity from April 1966 onwards. However, a decisive development took place in November 1966. A joint defence pact was signed between the United Arab Republic and Syria. It provided that an attack on one would be regarded as an attack on the other. On 4 November 1966, Israel presented a complaint of "acts of aggression" by Syria to the Security Council. A resolution, co-sponsored by six countries and designed to promote a compromise solution, was vetoed by the Soviet Union. Israel launched on 13 November 1966 her biggest offensive against Jordan since the invasion of the Suez. A meeting of the Security Council was summoned and the State of Israel was condemned for the attack. The American Government declared on 22 December 1966 its decision to send defensive arms to Jordan to strengthen her security against Israel. On 7 April 1967, Israel got the opportunity to hit directly at Syria. A minor border incident over ploughing in the demilitarised zone south-east of the Sea of Galilee erupted into a near-war situation. Six Syria's most modern, M.I.G. fighters were shot down. Although the United Arab Republic was committed to intervene under the pact with Syria, she kept quiet. To bolster the morale of the Syrians, the number of roads on the frontier was increased. The American Sixth Fleet arrived in Arab waters. King Hussein of Jordan went to Teheran for a meeting with the Shah of Iran. King Faisal of Saudi Arabia went to London.

Heavy Egyptian troop movements were reported on 15 May 1967, President Nasser requested the Secretary-General of the United Nations to withdraw the United Nations Emergency Force which was a sort of barrier between the U.A.R. and Israel. The Secretary-General agreed and withdrew the Force. President Nasser then closed the Gulf of Aqaba to all Israeli ships. It was claimed that the waters of the Tirana Strait belonged to the United Arab Republic. The situation began to worsen and there was the imminent danger of a war. On 4 June 1967, Israel attacked the United Arab Republic and destroyed a large number of her aircrafts. Fighting started on many fronts. Although all the Muslim countries of the region declared war against Israel, most of the fighting was done by the United Arab Republic, Syria and Jordan. The war lasted for about a week and the Arabs were completely defeated. A cease-fire was declared in compliance with a resolution of the Security Council.

There was a lot of resentment as Israel refused to evacuate the territories captured by it. The Arabs were determined to have their revenge for the humiliation of 1967. On 27 May 1971, a treaty was concluded between the Soviet Union and Egypt by which both the parties agreed to cooperate with each other. The Soviet Union also agreed to help Egypt in every way. It was with the help of the Soviet Union that Egypt was successful in her attack against Israel on 6 October 1973. The Soviet Union played an important part in bringing about a cease-fire. However, there were violations on a large scale of the truce of 22 October 1973 by Israel and the result was that the Third Army of Egypt was encircled and the road between Cairo and Suez was cut off. When such was the situation, Brezhnev, the Soviet Chief, addressed a "brutal" note to President Nixon in which it was stated that Moscow would "be faced with the necessity urgently to consider the question of taking appropriate steps unilaterally" if the United States refused to join in sending forces to enforce the Arab-Israeli cease-fire. The result was that President Nixon ordered a world-wide alert of the U.S. forces and activated even the American nuclear weaponry. There was the possibility of a confrontation between the Super Powers of the magnitude of the Cuban crisis of 1962. However, the crisis was averted and the cease-fire was declared. In spite of that, war was continued by Syria.

In 1974, there were breaches of peace on the Suez and Syrian fronts. Efforts were made by the United States to bring about peace between Egypt and Israel. A conference, cosponsored by the United States and the Soviet Union, was attended by Egypt, Jordan and Israel but was boycotted by Syria. An agreement was reached on the dis-engagement of the forces on the Suez front and the same was carried out. An agreement was made on Syrian-Israeli dis-engagement later on. The U.N. dis-engagement forces were established on Syrian-Israeli front. In 1975, PLO was given a permanent observer status at the United Nations.

As a result of the restoration of friendly relations between President Sadat of Egypt and the United States, an agreement was arrived at by which Israel agreed to evacuate the Sinai territory, provided American observers were stationed on the spot to maintain peace between the two countries.

SUGGESTED READINGS

Allen: **Gordon and the Sudan.**

Cameron : **Egypt in the Nineteenth Century.**

Campbell, R.J.: **Livingstone.**

Colvin: **Making of Modern Egypt.**

Cory: **History of South Egypt.**

Cromer: **Modern Egypt.**

Doyle: **Great Boer War.**

Gibbons: **The New Map of Africa.**

Gliechen: **Anglo-Egyptian Sudan.**

Harris: **Intervention and Colonisation in Africa.**

Hopkins, H.L.: **European Imperialism in Africa.**

Hughes: **David Livingstone.**

Johnston, H.H.: **The Opening up of Africa.**

Johnston, H.H.: **The Colonisation of Africa.**

Keltie : **Partition of Africa.**

Lucas, C.: **The Partition and Colonisation of Africa.**

Stanley: **Autobiography.**

Theal: **History of South Africa.**

CHAPTER

26 THE FOREIGN POLICY OF JAPAN

Before 1867-68, Japan was a backward country, but in that year there took place a revolution which changed the very face of Japan. Feudalism was abolished. The Shogunate which controlled the Government was also came to an end. The people of Japan were infused into the soldiers. Japan adopted and assimilated European culture and institutions. She began to dream of becoming a Great Power in the world. Her population began to grow and she required raw materials for her factories and markets for the finished goods. She wanted vacant lands for her surplus population. She wanted to put an end to the unequal treaties which had been imposed on her by the European Powers in the past. All these factors demanded a vigorous foreign policy.

Sino-Japanese War (1894-95). The first important landmark in the foreign policy of Japan was the Sino-Japanese War of 1894-95. Japan had a quarrel with China over Korea. She was afraid that some European power might take advantage of the weakness of Korea and establish her control over it. She considered the independence of Korea essential to her own security because Korea in the hands of an enemy was "a dagger thrust at the heart of Japan." In 1894, Japan gave an ultimatum to the King of Korea to accept the Japanese programme of reforms. The King tried to avoid the issue and consequently Japan attached Korea and took her King as a prisoner. China entered the war on the side of Korea but was defeated. The Chinese were defeated because they were over-confident, ill-organized and inefficient. In less than a year, the Japanese overran the whole of Korea and Southern Manchuria and threatened Peking. In April 1895 was signed the Treaty of Shimonosheki.

By this treaty, China gave to Japan the Liao-tung Peninsula, Port Arthur and the Island of Formosa. China agreed to pay a huge war indemnity and make certain commercial concessions to Japan. She also recognized the independence of Korea and thereby gave a free hand to Japan. The result of Sino-Japanese War was that Japan was recognized as a Great Power and the European Powers began to fear what was called the "Yellow Peril". The extra-territorial rights of the foreign countries in Japan were ended.

However, Japan was not allowed to keep to herself the gains which she got by the Treaty of 1895. Russia, France and Germany presented a joint note to Japan offering their friendly advice that she should refrain from annexing any part of the Chinese mainland. Instead of risking a war, Japan took the advice and returned to China the Liao-tung Peninsula and Port Arthur. Japan found herself helpless before the three Powers, and felt humiliated.

The joint intervention of the three Powers was not out of any humanitarian consideration. They had their own axes to grind. The Russian imperialists felt that Korea and the Liao-tung Peninsula were of vital importance to their country. If Japan dominated Korea, she would be able to control both sides of the southern outlet of the Japan Sea on which was situated the Russian port of Vladivostok, the intended terminus of the Trans-Siberian Railway. If Japan annexed the Liao-tung Peninsula, there would be no possibility of Russia getting an ice-free port in the south. Under the circumstances, Russian interests demanded that Japan must be ousted from those regions. France joined hands with Russia as her faithful ally in world politics. William II, the German Emperor, was prepared to join

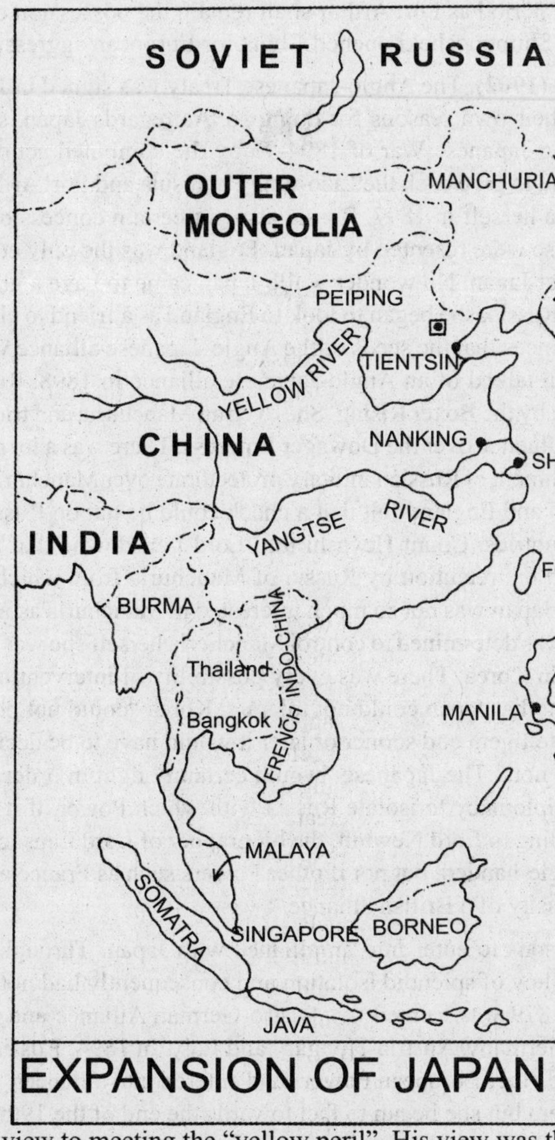

hands with a view to meeting the "yellow peril". His view was that Christendom must stand firmly against the pagan Orient. He wanted to cultivate good relations, with Russia and no wonder he tried to show himself more zealous than France as a friend of Russian imperialism. He wanted to weaken the Franco-Russian Alliance and rob it of its anti-German slant. The memoirs of William II and Tirpitz show that at that time Germany desired to have a naval base in the Far East. It is these considerations that brought Russia, France and Germany together.

Having deprived Japan of her spoils of victory, the three powers were most anxious to get whatever they could from the Chinese Government. France got control over all the mines in the three southern provinces adjoining French Indo-China. She also got the right to extend the French railway-line from Annam to China. Russia started her influence in China by the establishment of the Russo-Chinese Bank. She also got Port Arthur. Germany got the lease of the port and district of Kiao-Chow for 99 years and concessions for two railways in Shantung. Great Britain acquired the lease of Wei-hai-Wei "for as long a period as Port Arthur shall remain the possession of Russia." It cannot be denied that the Treaty of Shimonosheki opened China for European aggression.

The Anglo-Japanese Alliance (1902). The Anglo-Japanese Treaty was signed in January 1902 and both Japan and England had their own reasons for doing so. As regards Japan, she had been deprived of her gains from the Sino-Japanese War of 1894-95 by the combined action of Russia, France and Germany. She was forced to give back the Liao-tung Peninsula and Port Arthur to China. Port Arthur was occupied by Russia herself in 1897. Russia also got certain concessions regarding the Trans-Siberian Railway. All these were resented by Japan. England was the only country which did not join the other Powers against Japan. No wonder while Japan came to have a grudge against other European Powers, especially Russia, she began to look to England as a friend to check Russian ambitions. It was in these circumstances that the seeds of the Anglo-Japanese alliance were planted. It is stated that Joseph Chamberlain talked of an Anglo-Japanese alliance in 1898. Russia tried to exploit the situation created in China by the Boxer Rising. She overran Manchuria and tried to secure a recognition of her position by her influence over the Dowager Empress. There was a lot of opposition from the other Powers to the establishment of Russian military protectorate over Manchuria and Russia was forced to withdraw. Both Japan and England felt that a check could be put on Russian advance by an alliance between the two countries. Count Heyashi told Lord Lansdowne that the Japanese had "a strong sentimental dislike to the retention by Russia of Manchuria from which they had at one time been expelled." However, Japan was not so much interested in Manchuria as in Korea. The Russian attitude was that while she was determined to control Manchuria herself she was not prepared to allow Japan to have a free hand in Korea. There was every possibility of intervention by foreign Powers into the affairs of Korea and that Japan could not tolerate. Korea "could not possibly stand alone—its people were far too unintelligent and sooner or later it would have to be decided whether the country was to fall to Russia or not." The Japanese "would certainly fight in order to prevent it and it must be the object of their diplomacy to isolate Russia with which Power, if it stood alone, they were prepared to deal." According to Lord Newton, the biographer of Lord Lansdowne, "Japan was prepared to fight for Korea single-handed, but not if other Powers such as France and Germany were to intervene." Hence the necessity of a British alliance.

England also had her own reasons to enter into an alliance with Japan. Throughout the 19th century, England had followed a policy of splendid isolation and consequently had not entered into any alliance with any country. In 1879 was formed the Austro-German Alliance and in 1882 was made the Triple Alliance between Germany, Austria-Hungary and Italy. In 1894, Russia and France entered into an alliance. Thus, while other European Powers had entered into alliances, England had remained completely aloof from them but she began to feel towards the end of the 19th century that isolation was dangerous and not in the best interests of the country. A similar feeling was there on the occasion of the Fashoda incident of 1898. The attitude of the European Powers during the Boer War also made England feel that her policy of isolation was not a right one. She wanted to enter into an alliance with Germany but the attitude of William II was not helpful. All the efforts of men like Joseph Chamberlain to bring together Germany and England failed. The last effort was made in 1901 when William II came to England on the occasion of the death of Queen Victoria. When William II was approached for an alliance, his famous reply was: "The road to Berlin lies through Vienna." Chamberlain is reported to have stated that if the people in Germany had no sense, there was no help for that. It was under these circumstances that England decided to enter into an alliance with Japan and it was done in the beginning of January. There was another reason why England wanted to enter into an alliance with Japan. Both England and Japan were determined to check the further advance of Russia in the Far East and it was this community of interests that brought the two countries together.

Terms of the Treaty. (1) Both Japan and England declared that they had no idea of aggression in China or Korea. They also expressed their anxiety to maintain the status quo in both the countries.

(2) It was agreed between England and Japan that England had her interests in China and Japan had her interests both in China and Korea. It was agreed that it would be admissible for either of them to take such measures as might be indispensable in order to safeguard those interests if threatened either by the aggressive action of any other Power or by disturbances arising in China or Korea.

(3) If either England or Japan was involved in a war with another Power while safeguarding those interests, the other party was to maintain strict neutrality. It was also to do its utmost to prevent other Powers from joining hostilities against its ally.

(4) If any other Power or Powers should join in hostilities against that ally, the other party was to come to its assistance and conduct the war in common and make peace in mutual agreement with it.

(5) Both England and Japan agreed that neither of them was to enter into a separate arrangement with another Power to the prejudice of the interests of the other without consulting the other.

(6) Whenever, in the opinion of either England or Japan, the above interests were in danger, the two governments were to communicate with each other fully and frankly.

(7) The agreement was to come into force at once and was to remain in force for five years.

The Anglo-Japanese Treaty of 1902 was revised in 1905. According to the revised agreement, each country was to come to the help of the other if the latter were attacked even by a single Power and the scope of the alliance was also extended to embrace British India. The alliance was to last for 10 years. In 1911, the agreement was again revised in order to remove any danger of England being involved in a war between the United States and Japan. The alliance continued up to 1923.

Importance of the Treaty. The importance of the Anglo-Japanese alliance cannot be over-emphasized. It is rightly pointed out that there was no other treaty from which both the parties gained so much as did Japan and England from the treaty of 1902. Japan wanted an ally on whom she could depend to put a check to the further advance of Russia in the Far East. This she got in England. According to the treaty, if she was involved in a war with Russia, England was to do everything in her power to prevent other Powers from joining Russia against Japan. This was to enable Japan to deal effectively with Russia. Japan was not so much afraid of Russia alone as she was afraid of the help that Russia might get from some other Powers. Having secured herself by the Treaty of 1902, there is no wonder that Japan chose her own opportunity to begin the war with Russia in 1904, only two years after the Treaty.

Great Britain also gained a lot from this Treaty. She was as much interested in checking the further advance of Russia in the Far East as Japan herself. She would like to help Japan in every way so that the latter might be able to deal a blow to Russia. Moreover, England was getting worried over the naval programme of Germany. Germany was building her navy at a tremendous speed and that was liable to threaten the very existence of Great Britain. Under these circumstances, Great Britain wanted to withdraw her ships from the Pacific. This she could do after entering into an alliance with Japan which was a Great Power in the Pacific.

It is pointed out that this alliance was of very great importance to Japan from another point of view. It raised the status of Japan. She was admitted on terms of equality by the greatest of the world Empires.[1] Japanese ambitions to expand got an impetus.

According to Lansdowne, the treaty was concluded "purely as a measure of precaution." It did not threaten "the present or the legitimate interests of the other Powers." It was intended to make

1. It is pointed out that Great Britain did not feel it below its dignity to accept "the friendship of a barbarian Mongolian nation."

for the preservation of peace and if peace was unfortunately broken, it was to have the effect of restricting the area of hostilities.

The Treaty of 1902 gave Japan a free hand in the Far East. It was undoubtedly a great landmark in her history of expansion in the Far East. She could depend not only upon her own strength but also upon the help which she was to get under the amended Treaty of 1905 which required England to come to the help of Japan if Japan went to war even with one single Power.

According to Grant and Temperley, "This Treaty was of epoch-making importance in every direction. Its intention, so far as Japan was concerned, must remain a little mysterious. The English diplomats seem to have thought that they would be able to keep Japan in order and to prevent her aggression against Russia. It is easy to see now that this was an entire mistake. Japanese military and naval organisation would be complete by the end of 1903, and after that, England's alliance would (and did) enable them to attack Russia as soon as they found it convenient to do so. This was not the only British mistake. Her negotiators seem to have believed that the effect of this treaty would be confined to the local area of China. But the diplomacy of the Great Powers is world-wide in its action and extent, and an alliance affecting the Sea of Japan was bound to trouble the Mediterranean and the North Sea. England's situation, however, was not so perilous as it appeared. She was not indeed on friendly terms either with Russia or with France, but then neither was she with Germany. Even after the Japanese Alliance England could have joined either the Triple or the Dual Alliance. Germany seems still to have expected or hoped for the former."

According to Taylor, "The Anglo-Japanese agreement, signed on 30 January 1902, gave both parties what they wanted. The Japanese got recognition of their special interest in Korea, and the assurance that Great Britain would keep France neutral in case they went to war with Russia. The British prevented any Japanese combine with Russia and strengthened the barrier against any further Russian advance. The price they paid was small now that the Boer War was over; the British could easily spare the ships to counter France in the Far East; their only sacrifice was Korea, and that was only a sacrifice of principle. The gain, however, was not so great at the time as it was made by later unforeseen events. No one, not even the Japanese, supposed that they were capable of sustaining a serious war against Russia; both parties hoped to strike a bargain with Russia, nor to go to war with her. The agreement threaten Russia's position in Manchuria; at the most it made further Russian expansion more difficult. Again, the alliance did not mark the end of British isolation; rather it confirmed it. Isolation meant aloofness from the European Balance of Power; and this was now more possible than before. On the other hand, the alliance certainly did not imply any British estrangement from Germany. Rather the reverse. The British would no longer have to importune the Germans for help in the Far East; and, therefore, relations between them would be easier. The Germans had constantly suggested alliance with the Japanese to the British; and they were given advance notice of its conclusion. They believed that it would increase the tension between Great Britain and Russia, and welcome it much as Napoleon III had welcomed the Prussian alliance with Italy in the spring of 1866." (**The Struggle for Mastery in Europe,** p. 400).

According to Gottschalk and Lach, "Though the Americans feared the consequences of giving Japan a free hand in Korea, the possibility of Russo-Japanese cooperation in eastern Asia appeared an even greater danger. Secretary Hay was primarily concerned that, no matter what happens eventually in northern China and Manchuria, the United States shall not be placed in any worse position then while the country was under the unquestioned dominion of China. And President Roosevelt expressed the opinion: 'We cannot possibly interfere for the Koreans against Japan. They could not strike one blow in their own defence.' Thus the United States government, agreeing with Great Britain that the realities required the courting of Tokyo, was prepared to refrain from interference with Japan's obvious designs upon Korea.

"The end of England's diplomatic isolation and the conclusion of the Anglo-Japanese Alliance helped to crystallize the alliance systems of Europe. Great Britain's hostility to the Asiatic ambitions of Russia was viewed hopefully in Berlin, as presaging a conflict involving two of Germany's potential enemies. The Germans were also hopeful that the Anglo-Japanese Alliance might add to the hard feelings between France and England because of France's commitments to Russia against such an eventuality by providing for their neutrality in case of hostilities in the Far East limited to Russia and Japan alone. Under the terms of her alliance France was similarly protected from involvement on the side of Russia in an outbreak in eastern Asia. Neither the Anglo-Japanese nor the Franco-Russian treaty, therefore, put obstacles in the way of an entente of France and England regarding their common interests in Europe and Africa, and an Anglo-French entente was soon to become a reality."

The importance of this defensive and offensive alliance was realized at once. William II expressed his satisfaction over the Treaty. Both Austria and Italy sent congratulations. However, both Russia and France "made little attempt to conceal their disappointment."

The Anglo-Japanese alliance ended the British policy of isolation. After 1902, he entered into the Entenet Cordiale with France and in 1907, she made the Anglo-Russian Convention with Russia.

Russo-Japanese War (1904-5). Manchuria has been rightly called the granary of the Far East. In addition to her agricultural products, she is rich in timber and minerals and no wonder its importance to Japan was very great. In 1895, Japan reluctantly gave up her control over the Liao-tung Peninsula as she felt that she could not face the combination of Russia, France and Germany. However, Russia got for herself the lease of Port Arthur and the neighbouring harbour of Talien-Wan for 25 years. She also secured the right to carry the Trans-Siberian Railway across Manchuria to Vladivostok. Port Arthur was also linked up by the railway with the Trans-Siberian Railway. The Manchurian section of the Trans-Siberian Railway was known by the name of the Chinese Eastern Railway. It appeared to Japan that the Chinese Eastern Railway was as much a commercial project as a strategic railway. Thousands of Russian troops were garrisoned in Manchuria. Port Arthur was strengthened and a large fleet was stationed there. Japan dreaded that Russia would next pounce upon Korea. The situation was a serious one.

However, in 1902, a treaty was signed between China and Russia by which Russia undertook to respect the integrity of China and evacuate Manchuria. China agreed to be responsible for the safety of Russian subjects and Russian enterprises in that province. The evacuation was to be completed in three stages of 6 months each. At the end of each stage, a part of Manchuria defined in the treaty was to be restored to China. In October 1902, Russia fulfilled the terms of the treaty. However, in April 1903, the second section of Manchuria was still in the hands of Russian troops and the Russian Government informed China that any further evacuation was to be a conditional one. That was to take place only if China agreed to give certain concessions to Russia in Manchuria. This new demand of Russia was against the terms of the Treaty of April 1902. China was supported by Great Britain, the U.S.A. and Japan and consequently she refused to concede the Russian demand. At that time, Russian subjects were carrying on some activities in North Korea. Bezobrazoff, a Russian speculator, was engaged in extorting a concession from the Korean Government. That concession carried with it the right to cut timber on the Yalu river. Bezobrazoff had great influence on persons in the entourage of the Czar. Work was begun on the Yalu river in April 1903 and on that pretext Russian troops were moved towards the river. This was a direct violation of the agreement between Russia and Japan with regard to Korea. Japan had already spent a lot of money and taken great pains to develop her influence and control over Korea and consequently she was not prepared to allow Russia to have her own way. Japan made representations at St. Petersburg and protested that the activities of the Russian agents were not in accordance with the pledges made by the Russian Government. Japan was willing to enter into a new treaty by which Russian interests in Manchuria could be safeguarded but Japan's interests in Korea were also to be recognised and guaranteed. Russia gave her reply in

October 1903. While certain restrictions were to be put on Japan with regard to Korea, Russia was to have a free hand in Manchuria and on the Yalu river. Fruitless negotiations were continued between the two countries for many months. Russia took advantage of this interval and tried to strengthen her military position in the Far East. On 13 January 1904, Japan agreed to regard Manchuria as outside her sphere of influence but she also demanded that Russia should give a similar undertaking with regard to Korea. Japan asked for an early reply on account of the brisk movements of the Russian troops. As no reply was received, Japan decided to end the negotiations and on 5 February 1904 diplomatic relations with Russia were cut off.

In the beginning of February 1904, Russia had, east of Lake Baikal, about 80,000 field troops, 25,000 fortress troops and about 3,000 troops as frontier guards. Those forces were scattered over the immense area lying between Lake Baikal on the west, Vladivostok on the east, Nikolaievsk on the north and Port Arthur on the south. The distance between the two main groups was about 900 miles. The rate at which the resources of European Russia could be made available in the Far East was dependent upon the capacity of the Eastern Siberian Railway. Neither the permanent way of the Eastern Siberian Railway, nor the number and accommodations of stations and sidings. The quality of the rolling stock was such as to put up with the strain of heavy military traffic. However, the greatest headache was presented by Lake Baikal which created a gap of about 100 miles over which the railway had still to be constructed. On account of this gap, the passengers and goods had to be carried over an area of 30 miles of area. During a part of the winter season, the water was frozen and things had to be carried on the snow. However, when the snow melted, all traffic came to a standstill till such time as the water became navigable. That pointed to the difficulties in the way of the Russian Government while fighting against Japan. It was not possible to send sufficient reinforcements before the end of April. Japan was sure that she would have to deal with a very small army of Russia to begin with.

As compared with Russia, the position of Japan at the beginning of the war was that she had an active army of 1,80,000 men with a first reserve of 200,000 strong and 470,000 other trained men or about 850,000 trained men in all.

Japan was fully prepared for war. The huge indemnity which she had got from China was used profitably for the development of the army and the navy. "Her spies and secret agents had thoroughly familiarised themselves with the topography and resources of Korea and Manchuria; and her diplomatists had secured a clear ring for the fight by the Treaty of Alliance with Great Britain. Her soldiers had the opportunity of comparing themselves with the Russians in the Boxer campaign. The result had not discouraged them. Her credit in the great money markets was good, and her supply of ammunitions and stores was complete down to the last gaiter button. She threw down the gauntlet to one of the greatest Powers of Europe to the astonishment of the world—but with the most complete confidence in herself, a confidence that was shared by every unit in the Empire, from the Heaven-descended Emperor on the throne down to the humblest private in the ranks." (Longford).

The Russo-Japanese war was fought both on land and sea. The greatest battle of the war was that of Mukden, the capital of Manchuria. The fighting was so bitter that each side lost about 60,000 men in killed and wounded. The battle was won by Japan. However, as she was too much exhausted she could not follow up the victory. Russia sent her Baltic fleet to the Far East. When it entered the Straits of Tsushima between Korea and Japan, it was completely destroyed by Admiral Togo. The naval battle of Tsushima has been compared to the Battle of Trafalgar. It was a decisive battle. Japan got control of the Pacific.

Both parties were completely exhausted and peace was ultimately brought about through the good offices of President Theodore Roosevelt of the U.S.A. By the terms of the Treaty of Portsmouth which was signed in September 1905, Russia recognised Korea within the sphere of interest of Japan. She also transferred to Japan her lease of the Liao-tung Peninsula. She also gave the southern half of the Island of Sakhalin to Japan and agreed to evacuate Manchuria.

Its Effects. (1) The Russo-Japanese war had far-reaching effects. It affected the history not only of Russia and Japan, but also that of China, India,, the East in general and also the West. The Russian dreams of having a warm-water port in the Far East were shattered completely. As Russia got a setback in the Far East she began to concentrate more and more in the Near East and Middle East. The defeat of Russia also exposed the weakness of the autocratic regime of the Romanovs. The liberal and revolutionary forces in Russia became active and consequently the Czar was forced to make concessions in 1905. That led to the liberal experiment in that country for some time.

(2) Japan had been deprived of her gains in 1895 by Russia and her collaborators. By defeating Russia in 1904-5, Japan felt that she had got her revenge. She had suffered from a sense of frustration for some time, but after 1905, she felt that she could go ahead with her programme of expansion and conquest. Korea was completely at her mercy and she could annex it in 1910. Japan became a full-fledged imperialist country after 1905. She got a lead in the Far East and also entered into an open competition and rivalry with other European Powers in China. That process continued till the end of the Second World War.

(3) The Russo-Japanese war had its repercussions on European politics also. It was during this war that William II, the German Emperor, tried to win over Russia. Germany helped the refuelling of the Russian ships in the Baltic. Attempts were made to convince Russia that she could depend upon Germany in her hour of difficulty. Russia could not depend upon England as she was already in alliance with Japan. In July 1905, William II and Nicholas II met at Bjorko. Both the monarchs agreed that in the event of British attack on the Baltic, they were to safeguard their interests by occupying Denmark during the war. The Kaiser produced the draft of a treaty which was signed by the Czar in the presence of two witnesses. According to the draft treaty, if any European State should attack either Power, the other was to aid with all its forces and neither of the two was to conclude a separate peace treaty. The treaty was to come into force on the conclusion of peace with Japan and was to be cancelled only after a notice of a year. Russia was to make the terms of the treaty known to France and invite her to join it. The Kaiser was happy at his achievement. The alliance was to be of use to Russia as it was to create confidence in the minds of the people with regard to peace and was likely to encourage financial circles in foreign countries to invest money in Russian enterprises. That was likely to cool down the self-assertion and impertinence of William II. It was accepted that Holland, Belgium, Denmark, Sweden and Norway would be attracted to the new centre of gravity and revolve in the orbit of the great bloc of Powers. It appeared that the old dream of William II to create a combination of the continental Powers under the leadership of Germany was going to be realised.

However, the Czar did not seem to be enthusiastic about the Bjorko pact. After the conclusion of the war with Japan, he informed his Foreign Minister of what had transpired at Bjorko. It is stated that the Russian Foreign Minister "could not believe his eyes or ears." The Bjorko pact had to be denounced because France was opposed to it and the Russian Ministers also doubted its efficacy. The Czar also hesitated and repented. William II reminded Nicholas II of the moral obligations arising out of the Bjorko pact and asked Nicholas II to spend more time, labour and patience to induce France to join the pact. He reminded him of their joining these pacts before God and taking of the vows : "What is signed is signed; God is our testator." The pact could not make any headway. The Russian Ambassador at Paris informed the Czar that France was not prepared to join the German League on any condition. Nicholas II pointed out that the pact was not followed as it did not bear the signatures of the Foreign Ministers. It was under these circumstances that the Bjorko pact became a dead letter. It was treacherously extorted and quickly denounced and consequently did not affect the course of European politics.

(4) However, as a result of the efforts of France, Edward VII, Grey and Izvolski, the Anglo-Russian Convention was signed in 1907. This could be said to be an indirect effect of the Russo-Japanese War.

(5) The Russo-Japanese war shook China from her slumber. She felt humiliated at the thought that two foreign Powers made her territory as the battle-ground. The patriots of China would like to break with the past traditions and carry out revolutionary changes in their country with a view to putting their country on her feet. No wonder, the reform movement in China got an impetus from the war of 1904-5.

(6) The Russo-Japanese war profoundly influenced the imagination of the people of the East. It was for the first time in modern history that an Asiatic Power was able not only to face a Western power but also to defeat her completely. This gave encouragement to the nationalist forces in the East. It is pointed out that the Battle of Tsushima was more disastrous to the prestige of the West than the First Afghan War. To the East it held out fresh hopes and feelings of confidence. The victory of Japan profoundly affected the national agitation in India.

The World War I. When the First World War broke out in 1914, Japan also declared war against the Central Powers. She took full advantage of the preoccupation of the Great Powers in the European theatre of war. She captured Kiao-Chou and the other German concessions in Shantung. These possessions were guaranteed to Japan by the secret treaty with the allies. In January 1915, Japan presented the famous. "Twenty-one Demands" to China. An attempt was made to conceal the contents of those demands from other Powers, but they leaked out. Those demands related to Shantung, Manchuria, Eastern Inner Mongolia and coal and iron concessions. It was also demanded that China must not alienate any of her gulfs, harbours and coasts to any other Power. Its object was to close China to Europe and keep Asia for the Asiatics. It has been characterised as the "Asiatic Monroe Doctrine". Japan also demanded the appointment of a Japanese adviser, purchase of Japanese ammunition, control over the police and the right of carrying religious propaganda in China. Japan tried to put all kinds of pressure on China to get those demands accepted. The Chinese President Yuan Shih-kai was offered support for his own imperial schemes. He was also threatened with war. In May 1915, an ultimatum was presented to China and the latter had to accept most of the demands of Japan. It was pointed out that the treaty of 1915 between China and Japan "was the outcome of a Private deal between Yuan Shih-kai and Japan. From a legal point of view, it has never been passed by Parliament and therefore cannot be enforced from the practical point of view. Yuan Shih-kai had at this time already become a criminal traitor to the Chinese Republic and had no claim to represent the people who at that time regarded Japan with a universal and bitter hatred".

In 1917 Japan entered into the Lansing-Ishii agreement with the U.S.A. by which the latter recognised "that territorial propinquity creates special relations between countries" and Japan "has therefore special interests in China." In other words, the U.S.A. also accepted the special claims of Japan in China.

As both Japan and China fought on the side of the Allies, the Japanese and Chinese delegations at the Peace Conference presented opposing claims. However, the claims of Japan were accepted and those of China were rejected. Japan was given all the rights which Germany had in Kiao-Chou and the province of Shantung. She was also given the German islands north of the Equator. Obviously, China was disappointed by the peace settlement.

The Washington Conference (1921). The U.S.A. was not happy at the increase of the power of Japan and consequently she wanted to put some check on her power. Japan was the greatest naval Power in the Far East and the Americans could not put up with that fact. Consequently the American Government invited Japan, Great Britain, France, Italy, China, Portugal, Belgium and Holland "to participate in a conference on the limitation of armaments, in connection with which Pacific and Far Eastern questions would also be discussed." The Washington Conference was held in November 1921. Three treaties were signed at Washington, viz., Four-Power Treaty, Five-Power Treaty and Nine-Power Treaty. The Four-Power Treaty was made between Great Britain, Japan, France and the U.S.A. All the Powers agreed to respect the rights of one another in relation to their insular possessions in the Pacific. They were to consult one another if there was any dispute among them. They were also to consult one another if there was a threat of war from any other Power. The Five-Power Treaty provided for naval disarmament. It fixed the ratio of the navies of the various countries. There was to be naval parity between the U.S.A. and Great Britain. Japanese Navy was to be 60% of British or American Navy. The strength of the French and the Italian Navies was fixed at 35% of that of England or the U.S.A. These limitations related to the capital ships and did not apply to light cruisers, destroyers and submarines. The contracting parties were to maintain the status quo in the Pacific. By the Nine-Power Treaty, all the Powers assembled at Washington pledged themselves to respect the territorial integrity of China and "to refrain from taking advantage of the conditions in China to seek special rights or privileges which would abridge the rights of subjects and citizens or friendly States. At the Washington Conference Japan also agreed to return Kiao-Chou territory to China. It cannot be denied that the Washington Conference put a check on the growing power of Japan. She was given an inferior position with regard to her naval strength and was also forced to surrender the gains of the World War I. The Japanese patriots were not prepared to accept such terms for long and there was bound to be trouble in the future.

Manchuria. Japan was keenly interested in the affairs of Manchuria. Her population was increasing by leaps and bounds and she wanted additional territory for her surplus population. Her factories wanted not only raw materials but also new markets for the finished products. Japanese capital needed some area for investment. Manchuria was near Japan and her strategic importance was not unknown to the Japanese military strategists. She had already got control over the South Manchurian Railway. For the protection of that railway, she was entitled to keep 15,000 soldiers in Manchuria with their headquarters at Mukden. The terminus of the railway was at Darien which was under Japan and through that port passed more than half the foreign trade of Manchuria. The Japanese built towns along the railway and also executed modern projects which added substantially to the prosperity of the area. The foreign banking business of Manchuria was completely in the hands of the Japanese. By 1931, Japanese investment in Manchuria amounted to about one million dollars.

Japan had her eyes on Manchuria for a long time and she found that the year 1931 was the most appropriate one for the acquisition of that territory. Europe was busy with her own problems. World-wide depression confronted European statesmen. The latter had to face the problems of unemployment, debt moratoria, disarmament, tariff barriers, etc. Political situation in Germany and Italy was abnormal. China also was passing through a great crisis. After the death of Dr. Sun Yat Sen in 1925, many groups struggled to secure supremacy in China. Although General Chiang Kai-shek established his supremacy in the country he had still to face many rivals. There was no unity in the Chinese ranks. The hold of the central government over the outlying provinces was not secure. There was treachery in the dealings of the various parties. Famines and floods in the country added to the misery of the people. The local military chiefs were busy in their bandit activities. If Japan really intended to conquer Manchuria, there could not be any better opportunity for it.

On the night of 18-19 September 1931, a Japanese patrol claimed to discover a detachment of Chinese soldiers near Mukden trying to blow up the South Manchurian Railway. It was a good enough excuse for the Japanese. There was some fighting and about 10,000 Chinese soldiers in Mukden were either disarmed or dispersed. Within four days all the Chinese towns within a radius of 200 miles north of Mukden were occupied by the Japanese. The Chinese Government in Manchuria evacuated Mukden. By November 1931, practically the whole of North Manchuria was in the hands of the Japanese. By January 1932, the whole of the Manchuria was completely conquered by Japan.

The Chinese Government protested against the Japanese action in the League of Nations and appealed to the member-States in the name of collective security to intervene. The Japanese delegate in the League of Nations tried to remove the fears of the Powers by declaring that his government had no intention to annex Manchuria and the Japanese troops would be withdrawn as soon as the lives and property of the Japanese in Manchuria were secured. Japan characterised her action as merely a police action. In spite of the fact that Japan was the aggressor, the Council of the League of Nations decided not to take action against her and a resolution was passed unanimously on 30 September 1931, by which an opportunity was given to Japan to withdraw from Manchuria. The American Government also felt concerned over the Japanese attack. She would like to do all that lay in her power to maintain the territorial integrity of China. Although the U.S.A. was not a member of the League of Nations, she participated in the deliberations of the Council of the League of Nations and offered to co-operate if action was taken against Japan. While the League of Nations hesitated to take action against Japan, the attitude of Japan became all the more stiff. She resented the interference of other Powers in the affairs of Manchuria.

When it became clear that Japan was determined to persist in her course of action the League of Nations appointed the famous Lytton Commission to investigate, on the spot "any circumstances which affecting international relations, threaten to disturb peace between China and Japan." However, the Commission was instructed not "to interfere with the military arrangements of either party." After completing its work, the Lytton Commission submitted its report in November 1932. The report attempted to perform the impossible task of pleasing both the parties. Its recommendations were couched in a very guarded language. It recommended direct negotiations between the belligerents. China was asked to set up an autonomous government in Manchuria under her own suzerainty. It also made some recommendations with regard to the reorganization of railways, etc., in Manchuria. It recommended the employment of experts from outside for political and financial purposes. The report avoided to mention Japan as the aggressor. To quote, "The present case is not that of a country which has declared war on another country without previously exhausting the opportunities for conciliation provided in the Covenant of the League of Nations, neither is it a simple case of the violation of the frontier of one country by the armed forces of a neighbouring country," In spite of this, when the Lytton report was discussed by the Assembly of the League of Nations, the Japanese delegation left the hall and Japan gave a notice of terminating her membership of the League.

While Japan took a decisive action with regard to the League, the latter failed to take any effective action against Japan. That was partly due to the attitude of the various Powers. Sir John Simon, the British Foreign Minister, declared that his country was not prepared to go to war against Japan on the question of Manchuria. Mr. L.S. Amery, a leading Conservative statesman, declared thus in 1933 in the House of Commons: "I confess that we see no reason whatever that either in act or in word, or in sympathy, we should go individually or internationally against Japan in this matter. Japan has got a very powerful case based upon fundamental realities. When you look at the fact that Japan needs markets and that it is imperative for her, in the world in which she lives that there should be some sort of peace and order, then who is there among us to cast the first stone and to say that Japan ought not to have acted with the object of creating peace and order in Manchuria and defending herself against the continued aggression of vigorous Chinese nationalism? Our whole policy in India our whole policy in Egypt stands condemned if we condemn Japan."

As the League of Nations took no action, Japan was able to retain Manchuria under her control. The failure of the League was a great blow to the principle of collective security. It was bound to encourage persons like Mussolini and Hitler in their aggressive designs. Japan also felt that she could snatch away the other parts of China and no one would come to oppose her. No wonder, her imperialism got an impetus.

Regarding the conquest of Manchuria by Japan, Gathorne Hardy has made the following observation: "The shock, therefore, which the incident administered to the whole system of collective security was tremendous and well-nigh fatal and the only question on which opinion can be divided is as to whether the responsibility for this lies wholly at the door of Japan or whether it must be shared by those who planned a system which the world is incapable of working. There are, indeed, persons who think that the application of sanctions was practical, but the difficulties were so great and the prospect of plunging the world in war so formidable that the inaction of the members of the League must be considered pardonable if not wholly justified." According to Mackintosh, "Both Italy and Germany concluded that there was little risk in making treaties and carrying out aggressions, since the League Powers seemed loath to act in concert. Japan called the bluff of the League and proved to the world that even a slight danger of war was enough to cool the ardour of its supporters." It is also pointed out that the action of the League "struck a fatal blow at the collective system, killed any chance of disarmament and started the present drift towards a world war which, when it comes, will be infinitely most devastating to the present social and imperial order than anything that could have resulted from applying the Covenant to Japan."

The acquisition of Manchuria by Japan added to her hunger and Japanese patriots, industrialists and soldiers began to think in terms of bringing the whole of Eastern Asia under their control. The Japanese Government threatened other Powers with war if they tried to support the Chinese Government against Japan. "We oppose, therefore, any attempt on the part of China to avail herself of the influence of any other country in order to resist Japan; we also oppose any action taken by China calculated to play one Power against another Power. Any joint operation undertaken by foreign Powers even in the name of technical or financial assistance at this particular moment after the Manchurian and Shanghai incidents are bound to acquire political significance. While negotiations on normal questions of finance or trade would not be objected but supplying China with war aeroplanes, building aerodromes in China and detailing military instructors or military advisers to China or contracting a loan to provide funds for political uses, would obviously tend to alienate friendly relations between Japan, China and other countries and to disturb peace and order in Eastern Asia. Japan will oppose such projects." It is true that Great Britain and the U.S.A. repudiated the above claims of Japan, but in spite of that nothing was done to stop the further disintegration of China. Japan was determined to oppose tooth and nail every foreign attempt to help China. She also left no stone unturned to create dissensions among the Chinese. She decided to finish China once for all before the Chinese patriots were able to whip up the national enthusiasm to present a united front to the aggressor.

An attempt was made by Japan in 1935 to separate the northern province of China from the rest of the country. However, her efforts failed on account of the timely action of the Chinese. The local Japanese Military authority was able to set up a puppet government under the name of East Hopei autonomous government. Attempts were made by Japan to injure the Chinese finances by encouraging smuggling on a large scale. There was a lot of resentment against Japan in China, and in 1936 many Japanese were murdered in that country. In July 1937, there was a clash between Chinese troops and Japanese troops near Peking. There was no formal declaration of war but hostilities between the two countries assumed large dimensions. Like the Germans, the Japanese steamroller continued unchecked its work of conquering the whole of China. Peking was captured. Nanking fell into the hands of the Japanese. Although the Japanese attitude towards the Britishers in China was humiliating and even outrageous, Great Britain refused to be drawn up into the arena of war. The League of Nations contented itself by merely passing pious resolutions. Japan continued its work of conquest unhampered from any quarter. Hankow and Canton were also captured. Japan was able to establish her control over all the Chinese ports and the coastline. For some time, China got help from Russia, but that was lessened in course of time. In 1939, Japan was able to cut off the railway line to Indo-China. China was still getting her supplies through the Burma Road, but even that became superfluous after the conquest of Burma by Japan. On December 7, 1941, Japan attacked the Pearl Harbour and thus the U.S.A. entered the war. For some time, Japan was able to have her own way. Singapore fell into her hands. French Indo-China, Siam, Malaya and Burma were conquered by Japan. Even the security of Australia and India was threatened. Ultimately, as a result of the joint action of the United Nations, the Japanese were beaten back. The throwing of two atom bombs on Hiroshima and Nagasaki in 1945 brought about the surrender of Japan.

SUGGESTED READINGS

Allen : **The Hungry Guest.**

Asakawa: **Russo-Japanese Conflict.**

Causton: **Militarism, and Foreign Policy in Japan.**

Chamberlain : **Japan over Asia.**

Chang, C.F.: **The Anglo-Japanese Alliance.**

Colegrove : **Militarism in Japan.**

Douglas: **Europe and the Far East.**

Gibbons: New **Map of Asia.**

Hershey: **Modern Japan.**

Hornbeck: **Contemporary Politics in the Far** East.

Mellaren, W.W.: **A Political History of Japan.**

Saito : **Japan's Policies and Purposes.**

Treat: **Japan and the United** States.

Wildes: **Japan in Crisis,** 1934.

Whyte, Sir A.F.: **China and the Foreign Powers.**

Yen, E.T.: **The Open Door Policy.**

CHAPTER

27 AMERICAN FOREIGN POLICY

Mexico. The U.S.A. emerged as a Great Power after the Civil War of 1861-65 and she began to assert herself both in American and world politics. To begin with, she applied the Monroe Doctrine against France in Mexico. France under Napoleon III had intervened in Mexico when the government of that country repudiated her international debts. Napoleon sent a large army to conquer that country and having done so, he put Maximilian, the brother of the Austrian Emperor, on the throne of Mexico. France maintained her control over Mexico so long as the Civil War continued in the U.S.A. However, after peace was restored in the U.S.A. the American Government applied the Monroe Doctrine and demanded that France must leave Mexico. Napoleon III could not put up with the pressure and consequently decided to withdraw his army. As Maximilian delayed matters, he was shot dead. It was in this way that the American Government liberated the Mexican soil from the French troops.

'Alabama' Claims. The **Alabama** cruiser sailing from an English port had inflicted great losses on American commerce during the Civil War. Naturally, the U.S.A. demanded damages for the losses suffered by her. The situation was serious but ultimately both the governments agreed to submit the dispute to arbitration. After prolonged negotiations, between the two countries, the Treaty of Washington was signed in May 1871. It expressed "in a friendly spirit the regret felt by Her Majesty's Government for the escape, under whatever circumstances, of the Alabama and another vessel from British ports and for the depredation committed by these vessels." The treaty adjusted in minute details the outstanding disputes such as the fisheries between Canada and the U.S.A. It also referred the question of Vancouver boundary to the arbitration of the German Emperor who gave his award against Great Britain. New principles of international law involving greater diligence in preventing the equipment of ships in neutral harbours for use against friendly belligerents were accepted. It was agreed to refer the **Alabama Claims** to a tribunal of five persons nominated by Great Britain, the U.S.A., Italy, Switzerland and Brazil. As a result of the arbitration award, Great Britain had to pay £250,000 as damages to the U.S.A. Gladstone was primarily responsible for this arbitration and regarding the award, he expressed the opinion that "the sentence was harsh in its extent and unjust in its basis." Again, "I regard the fine imposed on this country as dust in the balance compared with the moral value of the example set when these two great nations of England and America, went in peace and concord before a judicial tribunal rather than resort to the arbitrament of the sword."

Venezuela Boundary Disputes. There was a dispute between Great Britain and Venezuela with regard to the boundary line between Venezuela and British Guiana. Many attempts were made to solve the difficulties but failed. In 1895, Mr. Olney, the Secretary of State under President Cleveland, demanded that Great Britain must submit the dispute to arbitration. The demand was startling and the terms in which it was made was nothing short of insolence. The American Government justified its interference on the basis of the Monroe Doctrine. The despatch of Olney contained the following passage: "That the distance of 3,000 miles of intervening ocean makes any permanent political union between an European and an American State unnatural and inexpedient will hardly be denied. The States of America, South as well as North, by geographical proximity, by natural sympathy, by similarity of governmental constitutions, are friends and allies, commercially and politically, of the

United States. Today the United States is practically sovereign on this continent, and its fiat is law upon the subjects to which it confines its interposition. There is, then, a Doctrine of American public law, well founded in principle and abundantly sanctioned by precedent, which entitles and requires the United States to treat as an injury to itself the forcible assumption by an European power of political control over an American State."

Although the despatch of Olney was highly provocative in tone, Lord Salisbury refused to be provoked. He politely questioned the applicability of the Monroe Doctrine to the particular dispute and insisted that the United States was not entitled to affirm "with reference to a number of states for whose conduct it assumes no responsibility, that its interests are necessarily concerned in whatever may befall those States, simply because, they are situated in the Western hemisphere." However, Lord Salisbury made it clear that he had no intention to allow Great Britain to be drawn into a serious quarrel with the U.S.A. In spite of the attitude of Lord Salisbury President Cleveland sent the following message to the American Congress on 7 December 1895: "If any European Power, by an extension of its boundaries, takes possession of the territory of our neighbouring republic against its will and in derogation of its rights, it is difficult to see why, to that extent, such European Power does not thereby attempt to extend its system of government to that portion of this continent which is thus taken. This is the precise action which President Monroe declared to be dangerous to our peace and safety." There was every possibility of a war between the two countries. However, "Lord Salisbury had a very good sense of humour and declined to take the matter too seriously." Both Great Britain and Venezuela agreed to submit their conflicting claims to a committee of investigation appointed by the United States. As a result of the arbitration, Great Britain got a lot of territory in dispute. However, by her action, the U.S.A. proved that she was the guardian of the Latin States of South America.

The American intervention in the dispute of Venezuela brought to end the period of American isolation in world politics. According to an American writer, "Cleveland's policy as to the Venezuelan boundary announced to the world with seismic suddenness and violence that the American democracy was of age." The U.S.A. could not retrace her steps from the position asserted by Cleveland and Olney. From the position taken up by the U.S.A. it followed that she could not avoid her responsibility for the doings of its neighbours and the general maintenance of order. Some of her neighbours were weak and turbulent and no wonder President Theodore Roosevelt declared in 1904 that "the adherence of the United States to the Monroe doctrine may force the United States, however reluctantly, in flagrant cases of wrong-doing or impotence, to the exercise of an international police power."

War with Spain (1898). On 21 April 1898, war broke out between Spain and the U.S.A. That was partly due to the unsatisfactory state of affairs in the Island of Cuba which was under Spain. The people of Cuba had revolted in 1868 and that state of affairs continued for practically 10 years. It is true that a compromise was arrived at in 1878, but the local Government was oppressive and corrupt and in 1895, a fresh revolt took place. General Weyler was sent to Cuba with powers to deal with the situation in any way he pleased. He employed barbarous methods to put down the revolt. The U.S.A. had intimate commercial relations with Cuba. The Americans had invested a lot of money in that island and consequently they suffered a great deal on account of the lawlessness in that country. In 1897, the United States offered its good offices to Spain but the latter did not avail of them. Meanwhile, there was great indignation in the U.S.A. against the atrocities of Weyler. A Cuban Relief Committee was set up in the U.S.A. President Cleveland threatened intervention. Matters came to a crisis in 1898 when the Maine, an American battleship in the harbour of Havana, was blown up. The Americans attributed the incident to the Spanish agency and clamoured for war. The American Congress and President Mckinley moved with the tide of popular feeling. Resolutions were passed demanding that Spain should grant independence to Cuba and give up all intention to annex it. Spain was provoked to declare war against the U.S.A. The naval supremacy of U.S.A. brought the war to a speedy end. The Spanish army and navy were both concentrated at Santiago where they were blockaded by the American forces. The Spanish Admiral was ordered to run the gauntlet of the blockade. The result was that the Spanish Admiral and his entire fleet were destroyed after fighting which lasted only a few hours. After a fortnight, the city of Santiago was also captured.

During this war, Porto Rico was acquired by the U.S.A. and Spain disappeared from the Caribbean Sea. Cuba was occupied for some time by the American troops, but later on it was declared independent. It was feared that the inclusion of Cuba into the U.S.A. would have complicated matters. However, the U.S.A. reserved to herself the right of interfering, whenever circumstances demanded.

The war between Spain and the U.S.A. was not confined to the Atlantic Sea alone. It extended to the Philippines also. The Spanish rule in the Philippines was oppressive, tyrannical and ineffective. The islands were ruled in the name of the King of Spain by the missionary friars. As there was chronic trouble, there was a demand for the expulsion of the missionary friars from the Philippines. A movement was also started for that purpose. In 1896, the people of the Philippines petitioned to the Emperor of Japan to annex the islands. Instead of accepting the offer, the ruler of Japan communicated the contents of the offer to the Spanish Government. The result was that a reign of terror started in the country. The people demanded a constitutional government, freedom of the press, equal laws and the expulsion of the friars.

Such was the state of affairs in the Philippines when the war started between Spain and the U.S.A. An American squadron under the command of Admiral Dewey appeared before Manila and within two hours destroyed the entire Spanish fleet. In July, Manila surrendered. When everything seemed to be lost, Spain made peace at Paris in December 1898. The Philippine islands were given to the U.S.A. and she paid to Spain a sum of 20,000,000 dollars as compensation for her losses. The Americans were not in a mood to restore the Philippine Islands on any condition. There was no possibility of their being declared independent. President Mckinley sent the following instructions to the American Peace Commission: "Without any original thought of complete or even partial acquisition, the presence and successes of our armies at Manila impose upon us obligations that we cannot disregard. The march of events rules and overrules human action. Avowing unreservedly the purpose which has animated all our efforts and still solicitous to adhere to it, we cannot be unmindful that without any desire or design on our part, the war has brought us new duties and responsibilities which we must meet and discharge as becomes a great nation on whose growth and career from the beginning the Ruler of Nations has plainly written the high command and pledge of civilisation."

The decision to annex the Philippines marked an important departure in the Pacific policy of the United States. "The Yellow Peril, the strategic and commercial advantages of the Philippines, and the active competition of the Germans for them helped to overcome idealism in Washington. In part, the switch over to imperialism can he accounted for by the rapid transition from agriculture to industry that was then taking pace in the United States with a consequently greater interest in foreign trade and empire. Besides, Protestant missionaries were eager for opportunities to penetrate untried areas. Finally, President Mckinley believed that the Filipinos were not yet ready for independence, and that to grant it would merely be to invite the Japanese or some European power to move in. The scramble for concessions in China, he believed, furnished an abject lesson as to what the future held in store for an oriental nation unable to protect itself from outside pressures."

Although the Philippines were given to the U.S.A. by the Treaty of Paris of 1898, peace could not be maintained. The insurgent leader, Aquinaldo by name, had been deported in 1897. In 1898, he was allowed to return to Manila. However, Aquinaldo proclaimed the independence of the Philippines and established a republican government with himself as President. This happened in February 1899 and the U.S.A. was forced to act once again. All organised resistance was smashed by the end of 1899. However, Aquinaldo was still at large and guerilla warfare continued for two more years. In April 1901, Aquinaldo was captured and in July the insurrection was finally declared to be at an end. When peace was restored the Philippines were handed over to a civil government with Judge Taft as its head. In 1902, a parliamentary form of government was set up there and the natives were given a large share in the administration of the country. President Theodore Roosevelt made the following declaration in a message to the Congress in 1904: "I firmly believe that you can help them (the Filipinos) to rise higher and higher in the scale of civilisation and of capacity for self-government, and I must earnestly hope that in the end they will be able to stand, if not entirely alone, yet in some such relation to the United States as Cuba now stands." By degrees, the Philippines were given more and more autonomy and ultimately given their independence after the World War II.

Sandwich Islands (1898). The U.S.A. had shown great interest in the future of the Sandwich Islands for more than a full half century. In 1854, she entered into a treaty with the native Government to annex the islands, but in spite of that, nothing was done to annex them. There were internal feuds among the chiefs and in 1887, King Kalakana accepted a form of government which involved control by the white settlers. In 1892, the native party reasserted itself and effected a coup d'etat. It was followed by a counter-revolutionary movement and a European Government was set up once again. A treaty of annexation was signed at Washington with the representatives of the Provisional

Government and sent to the Senate for approval. However, it was withdrawn by the President later on. In July 1898, the Sandwich Islands were finally annexed to the U.S.A. In 1909, they were constituted as a territory of Hawaii.

Samoa Islands. Germany showed a lot of activity in the Pacific for some time. In December 1885, friction arose between the German administrators and the natives. In January 1886, Mr. Bayard, Secretary of State at Washington, instructed the American Minister at Berlin "to express the expectation that nothing would be done to impair the rights of the United States under the existing treaty." The reply was in friendly terms and a conference was held in which Turkey, U.S.A. and Great Britain participated. In July 1886, Germany suddenly declared war on the reigning King of Samoa, deposed and deported him and set up her own nominee with a German commissioner as his adviser. In September 1888, the natives revolted against the German protege and his adviser and put another person on the throne. Thereupon the Germans landed a force of marines who were ambushed by the native forces and consequently suffered heavy losses. The Germans protested that the ambushing force was led by an American citizen and that led to unhappy relations between Germany and the U.S.A. However, Bismarck was anxious to maintain peace and another conference was held in Berlin in 1889. The result was that the Samoa Islands were placed under the joint control of Great Britain, Germany and the U.S.A. As the joint control did not work satisfactorily, the Samoa Islands were divided between Germany and the U.S.A. Great Britain got her compensation somewhere else.

Policy of open door in China. The U.S.A. followed a policy of open door in China. She believed in maintaining the territorial integrity of the Chinese Empire and along with all the nations to have an equal opportunity to trade with that country. Mr. John Hay, Secretary of State of the U.S.A., explained the open door-policy in these words: "We are of course opposed to the dismemberment of that Empire and we do not think that public opinion in the United States would justify this government in taking pan in the great game of spoliation now going on. At the same time, we are keenly alive to the importance of safeguarding our great commercial interests in that Empire and our representatives there have orders to search closely everything that may seem calculated to injure us, and to prevent it by energetic and timely representations. We do not consider our hands tied for future eventualities, but for the present we think our best policy is one of vigilant protection of our commercial interests, without formal alliances with other Powers interested." Great Britain accepted the open-door policy of the U.S.A. and other Powers also accepted it on account of their mutual jealousies. The co-operation between Great Britain and the U.S.A. was so great that there were rumours of an alliance between the two countries. However, an alliance was not possible without a ratification by the American Senate and no such alliance actually took place.

Hay's policy of open-door was nearly wrecked by the Boxer Rising of 1900. The Boxer movement was anti-foreign and it aimed at turning out the foreign devils and preserving China for the Chinese. It was partly due to the activities of the Christian missionaries in China and also to the rapacity of the Powers in seeking spheres of influence in China. The Empress and the Chinese Government were in secret sympathy with the Boxer leaders. The Boxers attacked the foreign legations in Peking and practically besieged them. For practically a month, no news reached the outside world. The situation was serious and there was every possibility of the surrender of the foreign legations on account of their insufficient resources and the lack of supplies. The U.S.A. joined other Powers in sending reinforcements to crush the Boxers. When the revolt was put down, the other Powers insisted on capturing the Chinese territory. However, Secretary Hay insisted on the withdrawal of the foreign troops and limited the demand on China to a war-indemnity. It is stated that he "held on like grim death to the Open Door." With the help of England and Japan, Hay was able to avert the immediate partition of China. The U.S.A. got her share of the war-indemnity but also later on, returned a part of it and that money was utilised for scholarships for Chinese students in American universities.

Blockade of Venezuela. Venezuela had many creditors and among them were England, Germany and Italy. As the creditors could not realise their claim by ordinary methods, Great Britain, Germany and Italy instituted a "pacific blockade" of the coast of Venezuela. In 1902, England and Germany cut off diplomatic relations with Venezuela. They also planned to bombard and occupy her ports. The U.S.A. protested and Great Britain expressed its willingness to withdraw. Germany refused to refer the debts to arbitration. Roosevelt cut the gordian knot by summoning the German Ambassador to the White House and informing him that Dewey had been given orders to take a squadron to Venezuela and prevent the seizure of any territory. If Germany withdrew, the whole matter would be kept secret and the Kaiser would be given credit for the generous deed. Germany found herself all alone and consequently the German fleet sailed away. The debts were referred to arbitration and being scaled down considerably, were finally paid. In this connection, Roosevelt referred to the policy of "speaking softly and carrying a big stick."

Panama Canal. The U.S.A. had the natural desire to cut a canal across one of the Isthmuses of Central America. However, the Treaty of 1850 was a great barrier in her way. By the Clayton-Bulwer Treaty of 1850, Great Britain and the U.S.A. had agreed that in the event of the construction of the Panama Canal, neither party should obtain exclusive control over it. However, on account of the acquisition of colonies in the Atlantic and Pacific Oceans, the U.S.A. felt that she must have the sole possession of the canal. President Theodore Roosevelt was able to persuade the British Government to give up its special position by cancelling the Treaty of 1850 and by substituting a new agreement for it. This was done by the Hay-Pauncefoote Treaty of 1901 by which the British Government recognised the right of the U.S.A. to construct and fortify a canal across the Isthmus of Panama under her own exclusive jurisdiction. The American Congress was divided between the advocates of Nicaragua and the Panama Isthmuses. However, the Congress authorised the President to build the canal through Panama if a satisfactory treaty could be made with the Republic of Columbia or otherwise through Nicaragua. Secretary Hay offered Columbia a lump sum of $25 million with an annual rental of a quarter of a million for the right of way. The offer was accepted by the Columbian Minister and a treaty was signed at Washington. However, there was a lot of opposition in Columbia itself and the result was that the Congress of Columbia almost unanimously rejected the Treaty. President Roosevelt took up the challenge and in a message to the American Congress, advocated the seizure of the Isthmus of Panama and the building of the Canal without waiting for further negotiations. He defended his high-handed action on the ground that such a step was necessary in the interests of civilization.

The people of Panama who had revolted more than once against the Central Government of Columbia, were disappointed at the rejection of the Treaty. The representatives of the French Company who had commenced the digging of the canal and who hoped to get compensation of 40 million dollars were also disappointed. However, there was a Treaty of 1846 between the U.S.A. and Columbia by which the U.S.A. had guaranteed the neutrality of Isthmus of Panama and the sovereignty of Columbia. The U.S.A. had intervened more than once to prevent insurrections in Columbia. However, the situation was completely changed and a new policy was made necessary. Roosevelt himself was in favour of the revolt of the people of Panama against Columbia. He wrote thus to a friend : "Privately, I freely say to you that I should be delighted if Panama were an independent State or if it made itself so at this moment; but for me to say so publicly would amount to an instigation of revolt and therefore I cannot say it." The rebel leaders of Panama were encouraged. An American battleship was sent to Colon with orders "to prevent the landing of any armed force, either Government or insurgent, at any point within 50 miles of Panama." As the only access to the Isthmus was by sea, the measure was intended to create a situation favourable to a revolution. The expected revolution did take place in

Panama and three days after, the Republic of Panama was recognised by the United States. A treaty was signed with the new Republic by which the U.S.A. secured, the required strip on very favourable terms. Undoubtedly, the whole of the Panama affair was a good thing for the people of Panama, the French stock-holders, the U.S.A. and the general interests of civilization itself. However, the people of Columbia bitterly resented it. Roosevelt acknowledged the part played by him in securing the Isthmus and defended his actions as wise and necessary. Later on, some compensation was paid to Columbia as well. The work of the construction of the Panama Canal was pushed forward with great energy and eagerness and the canal was completed in 1914 at a cost of 400 million dollars.

Boundary dispute with Canada. The U.S.A. purchased Alaska from Russia in 1867. For a long time, Alaska was neglected on account of its distance. However, the discovery of gold mines in 1897 brought her to limelight. The boundary between Alaska and Canada was defined as "lying 30 miles behind the windings of the coast." The Canadians claimed that the 30 miles were to be measured from the narrow bays and thus they were to have the right to deep water. The Americans regarded their claim as baseless. Theodore Roosevelt was not prepared to refer the matter to arbitration as he felt that arbitrators usually compromised and U.S.A. had a very good claim. He offered to refer the question to a joint commission but at the same time he made it known that in case the members of the joint commission failed to come to a conclusion, the matter would not be arbitrated upon and he would order the troops to Alaska to run to the line which he regarded as the correct one. In these circumstances, the joint commission was set up and the matter was decided in favour of the U.S.A. as a majority of the commissioners voted for it. Roosevelt was criticized in England and the U.S.A. for appointing on the commission those persons whose views on the controversy were already well known.

Santo Domingo. Santo Domingo was heavily in debt and Roosevelt appointed in 1905 an American Receiver of Customs in that island. The result was that a virtual protectorate was established over Domingo. The danger of foreign intervention to collect debt was removed by the Hague Conference of 1907 by accepting the Calvo doctrine. It provided that the creditor Power was not to collect debts by force until arbitration had been refused by the debtor State.

Russo-Japanese War. Theodore Roosevelt intervened in the Russo-Japanese war. It is pointed out that both Russia and Japan were exhausted by the war but neither Power was willing to talk of peace on account of prestige politics. Partly on humanitarian grounds and partly with a view to safeguarding the American interests, Roosevelt offered to mediate and bring about peace. The result was that the peace conference was held at Portsmouth (in Newhampshire) and Roosevelt remained in close touch with the deliberations. He was able to persuade Japan to give up the idea of a war-indemnity in the form of money. He also persuaded Russia to give to Japan the lower part of the Island of Sakhalin. It was in this way that the danger in the East was removed. However, Japan maintained that she was deprived of the legitimate fruits of her victory. The result was that there was a lot of tension between the two countries after 1905.

A large number of Japanese migrated to the western coast of the U.S.A. every year and there was a demand in the U.S.A. to stop their immigration. In 1906, matters were precipitated by the school authorities of San Francisco by closing the schools to Japanese children. After a lot of trouble, a compromise was arrived at and it was decided to exclude only those Japanese from the ordinary schools who were above 16 years of age. Secretary Root exchanged notes with the Japanese Ambassador at Washington by which Japan promised to prevent the immigration to America of coolie labourers and respect the status quo in China. This "gentleman's agreement" of 1908 was a diplomatic victory for the U.S.A.

President Roosevelt established a big fleet and ordered it to go on a voyage around the world.

While making that decision, he did not wait for the grant of funds by the Congress. He knew full well that if the fleet reached the Pacific the Congress would be forced to grant money to bring it back. The voyage of the American fleet was a great success.

President Roosevelt emphasized the new bonds of common interest between the U.S.A. and Great Britain in these words: "One practical problem of statesmanship must be to keep on good terms with the Japanese and their kinsmen on the mainland of Asia, and yet to keep the white men in America and Australia out of home contact with them. It is equally to the interest of the British Empire and of the United States that there should be no immigration in mass from Asia to Australia or to North America. It can be prevented, and an entirely friendly feeling between Japan and the English-speaking people preserved, if we act with sufficient courtesy and at the same time with sufficient resolution."

Algeciras Conference. The U.S.A. also participated in the Algeciras Conference of 1906. It is pointed out that the essential negotiations for the Conference were conducted in Washington and the plan finally adopted at the Algeciras Conference was signed by Secretary Root. The negotiations were helped by the close personal friendship between President Roosevelt and the Ambassadors of Germany and France at Washington. Roosevelt used all his powers of persuasion to prove to the German Ambassador the dangers of a war. The American delegate at the Conference refused to support the Austrian and German plan for a division of Morocco into virtual spheres of influence and proposed a plan of its own prepared by Secretary Root. That plan was adopted with minor alterations.

World War I. When the World War I broke out in 1914, the ex-President Roosevelt condemned the German invasion of Belgium and urged upon the American Government to intervene. However, President Wilson maintained for **a time an attitude of "watchful waiting".** In 1917, he declared war against Germany when the latter began an unrestricted submarine warfare which led to the loss of the Lusitania and American lives. The entry of the U.S.A. into the war on behalf of the Allies turned the scales against Germany. After the ending of the war in 1918, President Wilson played an important part in the peace settlement. It was on his insistence that the Covenant of the League of Nations was embodied in the Treaty of Versailles.

Washington Conference. In 1921 was held the Washington Conference to which were invited Great Britain, Japan, France, Italy, China, etc. Its object was to limit the armaments and also discuss the affairs of the Pacific and the Far East. Three treaties were signed at Washington. By one treaty, the U.S.A., Great Britain, France and Japan agreed to respect the rights of one another in the Pacific and also to consult one another in case of any dispute. Another treaty provided for naval parity between Great Britain and the U.S.A. The strength of the Japanese navy was fixed at 60% of the American and British navy. The strength of the French and Italian Navies was fixed at 35%. The parties also agreed to maintain the status quo in the Pacific. By the third treaty, all the nine Powers participating in the Washington Conference pledged themselves to respect the independence and integrity of China and not take advantage of her weak position. The main object of the Washington Conference was to put a check on the growing power of Japan. Although Japan submitted at that time, she had her own way later on.

Manchuria. In 1931, Japan attacked Manchuria and occupied it in due course of time. The U.S.A. was upset. She offered her services to stop the Japanese aggression. She took part in the proceedings of the League of Nations on the question of Manchuria. In spite of that, Japan had her own way in Manchuria and it was completely conquered. The U.S.A. could do nothing as the other Powers did not co-operate with her.

During the 1930's, the U.S.A. resorted to neutrality legislation by which she tried to keep out of the arena of the war. Even after the outbreak of the World War II in 1939 she did not formally enter the war but merely helped England, France and other countries. She was dragged into the war by the Japanese attack on Pearl Harbour in 1941. She was largely instrumental in the defeat of the Axis Powers in 1945.

SUGGESTED READINGS

Adams, J.T.: **The Epic of America.**

Adams, R.G.: **A History of the Foreign Policy of the United States.**

Bancroft, G.: **History of the United States.**

Beard, C.A.: **American Foreign Policy in the Making (1932-40).**

Bemis, Samuel F.: **The Latin American Policy of the United States,** 1949.

Brinton, Crane : **The United States and Britain,** 1948.

Buell, R.L.: **Washington Conference,** 1922.

Channing, E.: **History of the United States since** 1850.

Dulles, F.R.: **America's Rise to World Power, 1898-1954, Hamilton, London,** 1955.

Fairbank, J.K.: **The United States and China,** 1948.

Godshall, W.L.: **American Foreign Policy,** 1937.

Guerrant, E.O.: **Roosevelts Good Neighbour Policy,** 1950.

Kennan, George, F.: **American Diplomacy** (1900-1950), 1951.

Langer and Gleason: **The Undeclared War** (1940-1).

Langer and Gleason : **The Challenge to Isolation** (1937-40).

Lippmann, W.: **U.S. Foreign Policy,** 1943.

Morison, S.E.: **The Oxford History of the United States.**

Morley, F.: **The Foreign Policy of the United States,** 1951.

Perkins, D.: **The Monroe Doctrine.**

Rauch, B.: **Roosevelt: From Munich to Pearl Harbour, 1950.**

Reischauer, E.O.: **The United States and Japan,** 1950.

Rhodes, J.F.: **History of the United States since** 1850.

Schuman, F.L.: **American Policy towards Russia since** 1917.

Simonds, F.H: **American Foreign Policy in the Post-War Years, 1935.**

Wilson, Woodrow: **History of the American People.**

CHAPTER 28

BRITISH FOREIGN POLICY

Policy of Isolation. After the overthrow of Napoleon in the Battle of Waterloo in 1815, England followed a policy of aloofness from European politics. It is true that from 1815 to 1822, she co-operated with the other members of the Quadruple Alliance to maintain peace in Europe but after the death of Clastlereagh in 1822, Canning came to power. He was not enamoured of international co-operation, and consequently the era of Congresses ended after the Congress of Verona in 1822. In spite of this, Canning had to intervene in the Greek War of Independence. Palmerston also intervened in Belgium, Egypt and the Balkans. After the defeat of Russia in the Crimean war, England kept aloof from European politics for more than a decade. In 1877, the famous "Bulgarian atrocities" took place. Thousands of Christians were murdered by the Turks. Gladstone appealed to Disraeli to come to the help of the oppressed Christians, but the latter refused to do so. Russia came to the help of Bulgaria and declared war against Turkey. The latter was defeated and forced to sign the Treaty of San Stefano in 1878. By this treaty, Russia came to have a dominant position in the Balkans. This could not be tolerated by Great Britain and Austria. The result was that they asked her either to submit the Treaty of San Stefano to a Congress of European statesmen or take the consequences of non-compliance. When Russia found that Great Britain and Austria were making military preparations on a large scale and there was every likelihood of war being declared, she decided to submit. She was already exhausted and could not afford to fight against the fresh soldiers of Austria and Great Britain. At the Congress of Berlin, Great Britain was able to deprive Russia of her gains by the Treaty of San Stefano. She also got the Island of Cyprus. When Disraeli came back from Berlin to London, he declared that he had brought "peace with honour".

On the whole, Great Britain followed a policy of isolation towards European affairs. This policy was considered to be in the best interests of the country. There was no necessity of continuously interfering in European politics when the same purpose could be served by occasional interference. However, it became clear to the British statesmen towards the end of the 19th century that it was impossible to continue to follow a policy of splendid isolation. A more positive policy was made necessary by certain developments in European affairs since 1870.

Bismarck established the hegemony of Germany in Europe. Between 1871 and 1890, he was the most dominant personality in European politics. As he had injured the national pride of France in 1871 by taking away Alsace and Lorraine he feared a war of Revanche. He knew full well that France would try to get back Alsace and Lorraine and consequently he tried to isolate France in Europe. With that object in view, he formed the Three Emperors' League in 1873. It brought together the Emperors of Russia, Germany and Austria-Hungary. The League broke down in 1878 as a result of the differences between Austria-Hungary and Russia on the occasion of the Congress of Berlin. In 1878-79 the relations between Russia and Germany became very bitter and that led to the making of the Austro-German Alliance of 1879. By this alliance Germany and Austria-Hungary bound themselves to help each other in case of an invasion from Russia. Although this alliance was made for 5 years, it was renewed every time it fell due and continued to exist up to 1914. In 1882, Italy joined the Dual Alliance of 1879. Thus the Triple Alliance came into being in 1882.

When Bismarck was in power, he tried his utmost to isolate France and with that object in view maintained friendly relations with Russia. He was able to revive the Three Emperors' League in 1881 and it continued up to 1887. As the differences between Russia and Austria became very acute in 1887 on account of the Bulgarian question, Bismarck entered into the Reinsurance Treaty with Russia in 1887. This continued up to 1890 when Bismarck resigned. The Treaty of 1887 lapsed on account of the attitude of William II, the Kaiser of Germany. The mutual interests of Russia and France brought them together and the Franco-Russian Alliance was made in 1894. Germany, Austria-Hungary and Italy were on one side and France and Russia were on the other.

Taylor says that it is customary to speak of the last 20 or 30 years of the nineteenth century as the period of "splendid isolation" in British foreign policy, but this is true only in a limited sense. The British certainly ceased to concern themselves with the balance of power in Europe as they supposed that it was self-adjusting. However, they maintained close connection with the continental powers for the sake of affairs outside Europe, particularly in the Near East. The Mediterranean entente was a firmer combination against Russia than anything we had entered into earlier in the century. Until the autumn of 1893, the British still believed that they had "the liberal alliance" with France up their sleeve if they ever really needed it. However, everything was changed after the signing of the Franco-Russian alliance. Hitherto, they had assumed that they could pass the Straits in case of war with Russia and a squadron had been kept more or less permanently in the Aegean. After the alliance of 1893-4, the full resources of both the Mediterranean and Channel fleets were to be required to deal with the French and it was disputed whether they could do so or not. Chamberlain, is stated to have observed, "The British navy in the Mediterranean would have to cut and run—if it could run." Moreover, the Russian fleet was now supposed to be formidable and it was thought that the Russians would be able to reach Constantinople by sea avoiding the long land-route which put them at the mercy of Austria-Hungary. This demanded a change in the policy of England.

It was at this time that Great Britain felt that she was all alone in European politics. It was feared that in the event of a war, Great Britain might find herself in a difficult position. She thought of having allies and her first preference was for Germany. Queen Victoria was the maternal grandmother of William II. There was also a theory in those days that the English came from Germany. Moreover, the competition between France and England in Africa left her no other choice. However, there was no good response from the German side.

Fashoda Incident. On 2 September 1898, Kitchner won the battle of Omdurman in the Sudan and 4 days after he learnt that a French expedition under Captain Marchand had occupied Fashoda, higher up the Nile. The Anglo-French conflict over the Nile valley reached its decisive point. It was not a conflict between equals because the British had control of Egypt and the French wanted only some compensation for giving up their claim to Egypt. The French policy in the Upper Nile was a face-saving affair from the first to the last. Every sensible French politician knew that Egypt had been lost for good in 1882 and all that they asked for was something to satisfy the public opinion in France. Their ultimate object throughout was to restore "the liberal alliance" with Great Britain. Until March 1896 when the British Government decided to reconquer Sudan, the French policy had been reasonable. Even a token occupation of the Upper Nile would have strengthened their diplomatic position. Until the Italian defeat at Adowa they could hope for cooperation from Abyssinia. However, once the British put the question of the Upper Nile on a military basis, there was no place for diplomacy and the French were bound to lose unless they were prepared to fight and that was not possible for them in 1898. That was due to the fact that their navy had been neglected and the Dreyfus case had completely upset the internal politics of France. There was no desire in France to fight against Britain for Egypt. Delcasse had become the Foreign Minister of France in June 1898 and there seemed to be no difference of principle between him and his predecessor Hanotaux. Delcasse himself had helped to launch the Marchand expedition and Hanotaux had himself tried for an agreement with Great Britain. In June 1898, Delcasse had no clear-cut plan except to improve the diplomatic position of France.

Experience convinced them that Germany was not willing to come to any friendly understanding with France and hence Delcasse decided to reconcile Great Britain and Russia. The Fashoda crisis caught Delcasse unprepared. He knew that France could not go to war against Britain and his only hope was to put the question back on a basis of diplomacy. He offered "the liberal alliance" to the British Government provided he was given some reasonable compensation. At the same time, he sought diplomatic backing from Russia and even from Germany. Both of these policies failed. Lord Salisbury summed up his attitude in these words, "We claim the Sudan by right of conquest because that is the simplest and most effective". The British arguments were the Mediterranean fleet and Kitchener's army and their terms were unconditional withdrawal by Marchand. There was none to support France. Though the Russians welcomed Anglo-French conflict, they were not prepared to help France. Vague assurances of loyalty to the Franco-Russian alliance were of no avail. There were no prospect of any help from Germany. The latter was not prepared to offend the British as she wanted their support in the Far East. Germany had everything to gain from French humiliation and resentment. She wanted France to rely more and more on Russia in order to keep her away from Britain. Under these circumstances, Delcasse had no alternative but to surrender. In November 1898, Marchand left Fashoda. On 21 March 1899, Great Britain and France made an agreement by which France was excluded from the Valley of the Nile. That agreement did not settle the question of Egypt and the French attitude towards the British occupation remained unchanged. They continued to protest and hamper Cromer's schemes of financial reorganisation. Fashoda and its aftermath was for the French a crisis in political psychology and for the British not even that. They carried the day with normal peace-time strength. The extra cost of Fashoda to the British Admiralty was £13,600. Fashoda finished off what remained of the Mediterranean entente. Great Britain needed neither Italy nor Austria-Hungary. Italy had to seek reconciliation with France. In October 1898, while Marchand was still at Fashoda, William II paid a second visit to the Ottoman Empire.

Britain Approaches Germany. At this time, efforts were being made by men like Chamberlain to win over Germany. When Victoria died in 1901, William II went to England and stayed there for many days. He expressed feelings of profound sorrow at the death of Queen Victoria. People were impressed by it. He boasted of Germany's links with Great Britain. He took pride in the fact that he had been associated with the British navy. The result was that great honours were showered on him. The British statesmen thought that that was the most opportune time for entering into an agreement with Germany. The offer was duly made, but unfortunately there was no friendly response. The reply of William II was that "the road to Berlin lies through Vienna." The reply had a damping effect on those enthusiasts who were clamouring for an alliance with Germany. The result was that all attempts to win over Germany were given up and Great Britain thought of finding allies in some other direction.

Anglo-Japanese Alliance (1902). The first breach in the policy of splendid isolation was made in 1902 when Great Britain entered into a Treaty of Alliance with Japan. The treaty declared that Great Britain and Japan were actuated "solely by a desire to maintain the status quo and general peace in the extreme East." Their object was to uphold "the independence and territorial integrity of the Empire of China and the Empire of Korea." Equal opportunities for commerce and industry were to be guaranteed to all nations. England was stated to have special interests in China, and Japan both in China and Korea. It was provided that if either Japan or England was involved in a war with any other power in defence of her interests, the other country was to remain neutral. If Japan or England was involved in a war with two or more Powers, the other country was to join the war. The result of this treaty was that Japan got the protection of British sea-power against the hostile intervention of France or Germany or both in the case of a Russo-Japanese war. The story of 1895 was not to be repeated again when Japan was deprived of her gains in the war against China. By this treaty, Great Britain was able to withdraw her navy from the Pacific Ocean and thereby concentrate herself in the North Sea where she was apprehending danger from Germany.

The Entente Cordial (1904). England was not satisfied with an alliance with Japan alone. As the menace from Germany began to grow, her search for friends increased. In 1903 Edward VII visited France and he was cordially received everywhere in that country. It left a very good impression on his mind. Edward VII personally hated William II who called him by the name of old peacock. This created a congenial atmosphere in which the two countries could come near each other. After the visit of Edward VII, President Loubet of France and Delcasse visited England. There was an exchange of views among the statesmen of England and France with regard to the outstanding disputes between the two countries. The ultimate effect of all this was the **Entente Cordiale** was signed on 8 April 1904. The Entente was not an alliance but it certainly removed the caused of friction between, the two countries and thereby made it possible for them to co-operate more and more with each other. By the Entente, France recognised the special interests of England in Egypt and Great Britain agreed to back the special interests of France in Morocco. As regards the Newfoundland fisheries, it was agreed that France was to give up her claims to the coastline and Great Britain was to give all facilities to French fishermen on the coastline of Newfoundland. The other outstanding conflicts were also resolved by mutual negotiations.

Taylor says that the Entente Cordiale appeared to contain, a gross inequality because the British gains in Egypt operated immediately and the French gains in Morocco depended on their future exertions. However, the inequality was apparent and not real. The British were already established in Egypt beyond all challenge and their gain was merely a free hand for Cromer and his financial schemes. On the other hand, the French were at liberty to add the finest part of North Africa to their Empire. When Delcasse gave up Egypt, he renounced a cause which ranked second to the lost provinces. When Lord Lansdowne gave up Morocco, he wrote off a country unknown to all except a few traders and experts in strategy. Both British and French opinion believed that France had paid the higher price. The result was that the Entente was on trial in France as it was not in Great Britain. The Entente was essential for France but it was merely an advantage for the British. But the French had paid cash down and the British with a promissory note. British good faith was on trial. They had to back the French in Morocco when international difficulties arose. All that the Entente did for the British was slightly to lessen their naval needs in the Mediterranean and to give Cromer a field-day in Egypt. Paul Cambon wrote thus on the conclusion of the Entente, "Without the war in the Transvaal which bled Great Britain and made her wise, without the war in the Far East which made for reflection on both sides of the Channel and inspired in all a desire to limit the conflict, our agreements would not have been possible." Taylor does not accept this view. The British yielded nothing of the demands they had made in 1890's before the Boer war. The only change was perhaps their loss of faith in the ability of independent Morocco to keep going. The great change was on the French side. The Far East and the Far East alone caused the Anglo-French entente.

As time went on, the **Entente Cordiale** became stronger and stronger. There were certain factors which forced Great. Britain and France to come nearer each other. The defeat of Russia in the Russo-Japanese War (1904-5) forced France to depend more and more on England. The growing strength of the German navy compelled Great Britain to concentrate all her naval forces in the North Sea. The result was that she had to withdraw her naval forces from the Mediterranean. That could be done safely only if the French navy took over the defence of the Mediterranean Sea. This forced England to depend more and more on France.

The attitude of Great Britain on the occasion of the three Morocco crises showed that she was coming nearer and nearer to France. When France tried to establish a foothold in Morocco in 1905, William II went to Tangier and declared that Germany would not tolerate the establishment of French control in Morocco. Germany also demanded the dismissal of Delcasse and the summoning of a conference on Morocco. Both of these demands were accepted and preparations were made for the Algeciras Conference in 1906. On the eve of the Conference, military and naval staff talks were held between French and England. At the Conference itself, England backed France and Germany found herself practically all alone. Likewise in 1908 and 1911, Great Britain backed France against Germany. When Lord Haldane went to Berlin in 1912, the British Foreign Minister declared that England would not sacrifice France for any price. Thus the ties between England and France kept on strengthening with the passage of time.

Anglo-Russian Convention (1907). It was in the interests, of France that a reconciliation should be brought about between England and Russia. Delcasse had done his best to achieve that. Even after his dismissal, efforts continued in that direction. The result was that in 1907 was made the famous Anglo-Russian Convention. As a result of this agreement, a solution was found for the settlement of the disputes between England and Russia with regard to Afghanistan, Tibet and Persia. As regards Afghanistan, it was agreed that Russia would not interfere in the internal affairs of Afghanistan and deal with that country only through the British Government. The agreement was disliked by the Government of Afghanistan because she was not consulted with regard to its terms. As regards Tibet, both England and Russia agreed not to interfere in the internal affairs of that country. Both the countries accepted the suzerainty of China over Tibet. As regards Persia, its northern portion was recognised as within the sphere of influence of Russia and its southern part was recognised as the British sphere of influence. Central Persia was left under the control of the native government of that country. The Anglo-Russian Convention, treated what is known as the Triple Entente.

It is clear from above that at the beginning of the 20th century, Great Britain gave up her policy of splendid isolation and entered into those alliances which resulted in the war of 1914.

Sir Edward Grey (1905-16). After the resignation of Lord Lansdowne, Sir Edward Grey became Foreign Minister of England in December 1905. He was England's Foreign Minister at a time when she was passing through a very critical period. It goes to the credit of Sir Edward Grey that he handled the situation in a masterly manner and did all those things which enabled England to win the World War I.

If one were to ask the question as to what exactly was the policy which determined Grey's attitude at the Foreign Office, one cannot do better than quote Grey himself. According to him, "If all secrets were known, it would probably be found that British Foreign Ministers have been guided by what seemed to them the immediate interests of this country when making elaborate calculations for the future." If that was the statement which he made about the British Foreign Ministers in general, he himself was no exception to the general rule. He was never opposed to the Triple Alliance, but would like to have reconciliation between the Triple Alliance and the Triple Entente. There was one definite object which could be seen in all his actions. He was determined to find allies for England. He was not a follower of the policy of isolation. He did not want war, but his policy was to see that if war came, England was not all alone. He directed his foreign policy with that objective in view.

Grey and Morocco Crises. Grey's attitude in 1905-6, 1908 and 1911 with regard to the problem of Morocco shows that he was determined to fight against Germany, and not willing to allow her to crush France. There was a definite commitment on the part of the British Government to allow France to have a free hand in Morocco. As France had agreed to British control over Egypt, there was no justification on the part of England to hesitate from fulfilling her part of the bargain. Germany demanded the dismissal of Delcasse and that was done. She also demanded that the Morocco question should be referred to a conference and France also gave way on that point. France had to submit before Germany because she was not sure of any definite help from England.

So far, the attitude of England might have created some doubt in the minds of the French. But when the French Ambassador, Cambon, put before Grey the possibility of an unprovoked attack by Germany, Grey, with the consent of the British Prime Minister, allowed the holding of "military conversations" between the French and British staffs. Prof. Trevelyan approves of this. According to him, "To contemplate a contingent possibility of British intervention and yet have no war plan ready would have been madness, for while Britannia was fumbling with her sword, the Germans might be in Paris in a month. The military conversations of 1906 were amply justified, as events of August 1914 were to show." However, this action of Grey was criticised by his opponents. It was contended that the "Staff Talks" paved the way for a military alliance. It was further maintained that although Grey professed to give no guarantee of help to France, yet by his actions, he committed England to come to the help of France if the latter was attacked by Germany. Grey declared that neither government was bound by the "Staff Talks" to any particular policy. England was not committed to any policy from which she could not deviate if her interests so demanded.

The "Staff Talks" took place in January 1906. When the Conference met at Algeciras to decide the Morocco question, Grey stood by France. The importance of Grey's attitude on the occasion of the Conference has been put in these words by Trevelyan : "Germany had resented Lansdowne's settlement of Anglo-French quarrels in 1904 and wished to show France that she could not depend on England : Grey showed her that she could. It was the testing of the **Entente.**" Although England supported France, she tried to impress that she was not bound. However, the impression created on Germany was that France would be helped by England at the time of her difficulty.

In the Casablanca case of 1908, Grey supported France against Germany and the latter had to keep quiet. In 1911, Germany objected to the interference of France in Morocco. The Sultan of Morocco was afraid of his safety on account of the rise of a pretender. On the pretext of protecting the Europeans in Fez, the French sent their troops to the capital of Morocco. The Foreign Minister of Germany did not approve of this move of France. While putting pressure on Paris, he ordered the German gunboat, the **Panther,** to proceed to Agadir. Germany refused to withdraw her ship unless her own interests were safeguarded. Sir Edward Grey was shocked at the German attitude. He regarded the voyage of the **Panther** as an unprovoked attack on the status quo and made the following declaration: "We were of opinion that a new situation had been created by the despatch of the German ship to Agadir. Future developments might affect British interests more directly than they had hitherto been affected. We could not recognise any new arrangements that might be come to without us." He told the French Ambassador that "the British Government deems a discussion necessary between France, Germany. Spain and England." Although the attitude of Germany was rather provocative, the Mansion House speech of Lloyd George in 1911 made it clear to Germany that England would fight if her honour and interests were attacked. It was under these circumstances that Germany came to her senses and adopted a reasonable attitude.

Anglo-Russian Convention (1907). Sir Edward Grey tried to bring England and Russia together by removing the causes of friction between the two countries. It was in the interests of the **Entente Cordiale** that friendly relations should be established between Russia and England. Russia was a friend of France. In the event of a war between Russia and England, France was bound to suffer. Through the efforts of the Government of France and Sir Edward Grey, the Anglo-Russian Convention was made in 1907. By this Convention, the two countries settled their differences with regard to Afghanistan, Tibet and Persia. Both of them recognised the suzerainty of China in Tibet and pledged themselves not to interfere in her internal affairs. Russia agreed to deal with Afghanistan through the British Government. She also agreed to give up her right to deal directly with the Government of Afghanistan. Likewise, Russia was given Northern Persia as her sphere of influence and she recognised the interests of England in Southern Persia. As a result of the efforts of Grey the **Entente Cordiale** of 1904 was converted into the Triple Entente of 1907. Although the Anglo-Russian Convention was attacked on the ground that England sacrificed her interests in Persia and gave very favourable terms to Russia, Trevelyan is of the opinion that the Convention "was the only possible course consistent with our own safety."

A.J.P. Taylor says that the Triple Entente was essentially a settlement of differences and not a disguised alliance. Its two great weaknesses sprang from causes inside Great Britain and Russia and not from any German threat. On the one side, the Russians found it difficult to moderate their ambitions for long. They soon slipped back into assuming that Russia was the greatest or even the only power in the world. The temptation to cheat in Persia was increased by the fact that the capital of Persia was in the Russian zone. Whatever the Foreign Ministry said in St. Petersburg, the Russians at Teheran constantly encroached upon the independence of Persia. On the British side, the Triple **Entente** stirred up imperialist and radical opposition. Russia was the most reactionary power in Europe and hence the Entente seemed an unprincipled act of "power politics". This was particularly so because the Russians worked against the Parliament in Persia. Radical feeling turned even against France. Her association with Russia, instead of making Russia respectable, made France appear reactionary and militaristic. French ambitions in Morocco were blamed for the crisis of 1905 and Germany was presented as a pacific power threatened by French longings for Alsace and Lorraine and by Russian designs in the Balkans and at the Straits. If the Germans had kept quiet, the Triple Entente might have dissolved but the German actions turned it into a reality. In August 1907 when the Entente was concluded, both the British and Russians supposed that they had no quarrel with Germany except in regard to France. The Russians were pledged to defend French independence and the British were committed over Morocco but neither appeared a dangerous issue. The Germans were no longer attempting to bring France into subordination and the French were feeling their way towards a bargain with Germany over Morocco by which they would get political supremacy in exchange for sharing the economic advantages.

Grey's attitude towards Russia and France requires elucidation and appreciation. Both the countries complained that although England professed to be their friend, she was reluctant to commit herself to come to their help whenever they were attacked by any other Power. However, Grey's policy had a great advantage and was calculated to maintain the peace of Europe. While he kept the hands of England free to follow any policy she considered necessary for her own safety, it had a very healthy influence on the attitude of France and Russia. If Grey had committed England to help Russia and France whenever they were attacked, that would have encouraged them to pick up a quarrel with Germany and Austria-Hungary. This is clear from the events of 1914. At first, France and Russia hesitated, but when it became clear to them that England would come to their help, Russia at once declared herself on the side of Serbia and thus the Great War of 1914 started. However, the hesitant and indefinite attitude of Grey served a purpose. In the absence of such an attitude, war would have come earlier.

Grey and Germany. It was wrong to say that Grey was in any way inimical to Germany. He was not an enemy of Germany as such. His cry of August 3, 1914, in the House of Commons, "I hate war, I hate war," gives a peep into his mind. Grey had no intention to fight against Germany. He was always ready to do all that lay in his power to remove the causes of friction between the two countries. Grey's policy towards Germany can best be explained in the following words of Lichnowsky, German Ambassador from 1912 to 1914: "It was not his object to isolate us, but to the best of his power to make us partners in the existing association...Without interfering with England's existing friendship with France and Russia, a friendship which had no aggressive aims...he wished to arrive at a friendly rapprochement and understanding with Germany in order to bring the two groups nearer." Grey's policy was to bridge the guilf between the Franco-Russian Aliance and the Triple Alliance. It was unfortunate that William II consistently rejected the opinions and advice of his ambassadors and followed that of his military and naval experts.

Grey made every effort after 1906 to remove all causes of friction between Germany and England. He did his best to tackle the problem of Anglo-German naval rivalry. He made it very clear to the German Government that Britain's naval supremacy would be maintained at all costs, but she was prepared to come to a settlement with Germany to have a proportionate reduction in the navies of the two countries. Unfortunately, William II treated every British offer as a sign of weakness. The policy of Tirpitz was to keep peace by frightening his rivals. He believed in the "exaggerated estimation of fear as an instrument of negotiation." Germany believed that she could terrify England into submission, but she was sadly mistaken. No doubt England was in favour of maintaining peace, but it is wrong to maintain that she was prepared to do so at the cost of her safety and self-respect.

William II refused to make any naval concessions unless Britain undertook to remain neutral in the event of a Franco-German war. Without such a guarantee, the Kaiser was not prepared to reduce his navy. His contention was that he "did not wish good relations at the expense of the fleet." It was under these circumstances that the negotiations broke down in 1912. Grey was not prepared to sacrifice France in order to maintain good relations with Germany.

The failure of the naval negotiations in 1912 did not discourage Sir Edward Grey. He continued his efforts to bring about an understanding between England and Germany. By June 1914, an agreement was reached with regard to the Berlin-Baghdad Railway, and the fate of the Portuguese colonies in case Portugal abandoned them. The friendly settlement averted a quarrel and brought the two countries nearer.

On the occasion of the Bosnian crisis of 1908-09, there was every likelihood of a war. However, Grey used his good offices to avert the crisis and Europe was saved from a catastrophe.

Grey and the Balkan Wars (1912-13). Reference may be made to the attitude of Sir Edward Grey towards the Balkan Wars of 1912-13. He did his level best to localize the trouble in the Balkans. A conference was held in London under his presidentship and he was very much impressed by the success of the experiment in international co-operation. But for his tactful handling of the delicate situation, there is reason to believe that the trouble might have spread to various parts of Europe and that was not in the interests of Europe which at that time was a powder magazine.

When Archduke Francis Ferdinand, the heir to the throne of Austria Hungary, was murdered in 1914 at Sorajevo, Grey suggested a conference for the settlement of the dispute. If William II, instead of giving carte blanche to Berchtold, had agreed to the suggestion of Grey, there is reason to believe that the Great War might have been avoided.

It goes without saying that Grey's foreign policy strengthened the position of England in the international field. She had allies on which she could depend. She was not all alone in Europe. Grey's policy was responsible for postponing the war for some time. Unfortunately, on account of the working of powerful adverse forces, war broke out in 1914 and England was also dragged into it.

Anglo-German Relations (1890-1914). During the latter half of the 19th century, the relations between Germany and England were friendly, Germany was not suspected as a rival by Great Britain. On the occasion of the Franco-Prussian War, public opinion in England regarded Napoleon III as a danger and not Bismarck. The Iron Chancellor made it a cardinal principle of his policy to keep on good terms with the British Government. He was not prepared to do anything which might result in the alienation of Great Britain. That was one of the reasons why he refused to develop the navy and acquire colonies for his country. He know full well that Great Britain would not tolerate the building up of a strong navy by Germany as that was liable to threaten the very existence of that country. On more than one occasion, Bismarck suggested to Disraeli and Salisbury the formation of an alliance between the two countries. He remarked thus in 1889: "The peace of Europe can be secured by the conclusion of a treaty between Germany and England." However, Salisbury refused to enter into an alliance with Germany. Bismarck appointed his son, Herbert, as the German ambassador in England. Frederick, the son of William I, was married to the daughter of Queen Victoria and this brought the two countries together. In England, a theory was prevalent at that time that the ancestors of the English came from the north of Germany. All these factors brought the two countries together.

Exchange of Zanzibar for Heligoland (1890). Chamberlain, the Colonial Secretary of Great Britain, proposed to Herbert Bismarck the transfer of the Island of Heligoland to Germany with a view to strengthen the friendly relations between the two countries and in 1890, a treaty was signed by which Germany recognised the British protectorate over Zanzibar and the basin of the Upper Nile up to the border of Egypt as within the British sphere of influence. Great Britain promised to urge the Sultan to sell the coastal strip to Germany. Germany also got the Island of Heligoland which was very near to her and could be developed for naval fortification. The deal was criticised, in both the countries but Salisbury and Caprivi defended it. The contention of Salisbury was that Heligoland was of no strategic value to Great Britain. It could be captured by Germany at any time in the event of a war with that country. To quote him, "We have made an agreement which removes all dangers of conflict and strengthens the good relations of nations, who by their sympathies, interests and origin, will always be good friends." Zanzibar was to be the key of an empire in Eastern Africa. According to Stanley, Great Britain exchanged a trouser-button for a suit of clothes. The contention of Caprivi was that Germany could not surrender Zanzibar as she had never owned it. Moreover, there was no possibility of acquiring it as the British position was stronger there than that of Germany. To quote him, "We must ask ourselves how much colonising strength we possess, how far the available money and human resources will go. Germany has too many irons in the fire. It is no use having her hands full of things of which she cannot make use. The worst thing that could happen to us would be to give us the whole of Africa, for we have got quite enough as it is." William II approved of the deal in these words: "Without a battle, without the shedding of a tear, this beautiful island has passed into my possession. We have acquired it by treaty, freely concluded with a country to which we are indebted for the transfer." However, Bismarck criticized the deal on the ground that Germany would have got the island without paying the price she actually paid.

William II professed feelings of great friendship for Great Britain from time to time. When the Prince of Wales visited Berlin in 1890, the Kaiser put on the uniform of an English Admiral and referred to the brotherhood of arms at the battle of Waterloo (1815) and expressed the hope that the British Navy and the German army would keep the peace of the world. During his visit to England in 1891, William II remarked thus: "I have always felt at home in this lovely country, being the grandson of a queen whose name will ever be remembered as a noble character and a lady great in the wisdom of her counsels. Moreover, the same blood runs in the English and the German veins. I shall always, so far as it is in my power, maintain the historic friendship between our nations. My aim is above all the maintenance of peace. Only in peace can we bestov our earnest thoughts on the great problems, the solution of which I consider is the most prominent duty of our time."

Friendly relations between the two countries were thus maintained. William II crossed to Cowes every summer and the members of the English royal family were always welcomed in Berlin. The German Chancellor declared thus in 1893 : "I fully agree that the aim of our policy is gradually to win England for an official adhesion to the Triple Alliance." Towards the end of the same year, agreements relating to the delimitation of the Kilimanjaro district and the hinterland of the Cameroons were also amicably settled. The boundaries of Togoland were also amicably fixed.

However, according to Dr. Gooch, "The sky began to darken in 1894 and Anglo-German relations were never to regain the confidence and intimacy of the opening years of the reign of William II." Bad blood between the two countries was created by the partitioning of Africa. A treaty of 1894 between Great Britain and the Congo Free State leased the Sahr-e-Ghazel district to King Leopold of Belgium for life. In return, Great Britain got a strip of territory west of Tanganyika for the proposed Cape to Cairo Railway and telegraph line. The British Government had no right to give Bahr-el-Ghazel to Leopold and the British acquisition of the territory west of Tanganyika was opposed to the terms of the Congo-German Treaty of 1884. Germany protested and Great Britain gave up that strip of territory. However, the incident left an unpleasant memory.

On the occasion of the opening of Kiel Canal, William II invited all the Great Powers. According to Gooch, "The host had a friendly welcome for all his guests but his warmest words were reserved for Great Britain." He observed thus on that occasion: "Ever since our fleet was established we have tried to form our ideas in accordance with yours and in every way to learn from you. The history of the British Navy is as familiar to our officers and the seamen as to yourselves. I am not only an Admiral of the Fleet but the grandson of the mighty Queen. I hope you will express our heartfelt thanks to Her Majesty for her graciousness in sending you here."

At this stage, a change was noticed in the manners of William II. His behaviour became objectionable. He tried to dominate. He called his uncle "an old peacock". Besides this personal factor, many other factors complicated the situation. A section of the British Press began to criticise William II and advised him to be considerate like his grandmother. Lord Salisbury was not friendly towards Germany. His views on the question of Armenia were different from those of Germany. He was convinced that Turkey could not be reformed and, consequently, he stood for its partition. However, the policy of William II was one of maintaining the integrity of Turkey and establishing the most friendly relations with that country.

The situation in Africa also complicated the position. President Kruger of Transvaal had visited Germany in 1885 and asked for help from Bismarck, but the latter had refused it. However, things changed after the resignation of Bismarck. Germany began to take more and more interest in South Africa and Kruger could hope to get help from Germany. In 1894, two German warships were sent to Delagoa Bay as a demonstration against British interference. The German consul in Pretoria declared in January 1895 that Germany was determined to support the Transvaal in its efforts to maintain political equilibrium. Naturally, Great Britain protested, but Germany maintained that she was doing only that which was necessary to safeguard her own interests. The British Government was asked to put a check on the activities of Jameson and Rhodes.

Kruger Telegram. Both Great Britain and Germany were in opposite camps in South Africa and were trying to put a check on each other. There could be a clash at any time between the two countries. On 30 December 1895, Jameson's troops crossed Mafeking. The German ambassador informed the British Government that the attack on the Transvaal could not be tolerated. The raid failed and Jameson and his companions were arrested. When William II heard the news of the failure of the raid, he sent the following telegram to President Kruger: "I heartily congratulate you on the fact that you and your people, without appealing to the aid of friendly Powers, have succeeded in your unaided efforts in restoring peace and preserving the independence of the country against the armed bands which broke into your land." The President sent the following reply: "I express to Your Majesty my deepest gratitude for Your Majesty's congratulations." William II wrote thus to Nicholas II: "I hope all will come right, but come what may, I will never allow the British to stamp out the Transvaal." The Kruger telegram had a very unfortunate effect on the Anglo-German relations. The Morning Post wrote: "The nation will never forget this telegram and it will always bear it in mind in the future orientation of its policy." Lord Salisbury observed thus in 1899: **"The raid was a folly, but the telegram was even more foolish."**

In spite of this, the relations between the two countries were friendly for a brief period and that was due to certain circumstances. Great Britain was opposed to Russia and France, both in Asia and Africa. In 1898, England and France were on the verge of a war on the question of Fashoda. Great Britain was also opposed to Russian penetration into China and was determined to check it. The Triple Alliance Powers supported Great Britain against Russia and France and that brought the two countries together. William II sent a telegram of congratulations to the British Government on the occasion of the victory of Atbara. In 1898 the Duke of Devonshire and Chamberlain arranged an interview with the German Ambassador in London and a proposal for an Anglo-German alliance was put forward. However, there was no response from other side in spite of the fact that the offer was made thrice. William II seemed to be more interested in maintaining friendly relations with Russia than in entering into an alliance with England. His feeling was that Great Britain was trying to find "a constitutional army to fight for their interests." Much could not be expected in these circumstances.

However in October 1898, Great Britain and Germany entered into a secret treaty by which they divided the Portuguese colonies into spheres of influence. But nothing came out of it as Portugal recovered from her financial difficulties. Mr. Rhodes visited Berlin in 1899 and William II extended to him a hearty welcome. Germany promised to allow Rhodes to carry the telegraphic wires through German East Africa. Rhodes was so much pleased with the interview that he referred to William II as "a big man, a broad-minded man." He asked William II to send a number of Rhodes' scholars to the Oxford University every year. According to Dr. Gooch, "This visit was one of the factors in the Kaiser's friendliness to Great Britain during the Boer War."

When the Boer War started in 1899, the world opinion seemed to be on the side of the Boers and Great Britain was considered to be the bully. In 1900, Russia and France proposed intervention in the Boer War, but William II refused to do so. He also refused to meet Kruger when the latter ran away from the Transvaal, although he was warmly greeted in Paris. In 1899, William II paid a visit to England and he was given a hearty welcome. Chamberlain availed of this opportunity to discuss the possibility of an Anglo-German reconciliation and cooperation. He referred to the "natural alliance" between the two countries. To quote him, "At bottom, the character of the Teutonic race differs very slightly indeed from the character of the Anglo-Saxon race." Emperor Francis Joseph of Austria declared thus: "**In this war, I am on the side of England**." When Queen Victoria died in 1901, William II went to England and shared the grief of the royal family. Englishmen were very much impressed by his attitude on that occasion. It appeared as if there was a possibility of bringing the two countries together. Both Great Britain and Germany cooperated with each other on the occasion of the Boxer Rising in January. Waldersee, a German, was selected the Commander of the Peking Legation as a result of the backing of Salisbury. Germany also promised to support England in her efforts to check the Russian influence in China.

In 1901, Chamberlain proposed to discuss with the German Government all the outstanding disputes between the two countries and thereby, prepare the ground for an alliance with that country. Although William II was favourably inclined, Bulow refused. The British Government asked Germany to collaborate with her to oppose the fortification of the settlement of Tientsin in China by Russia, but the latter refused to do so. In March, 1901, Germany proposed that if she guaranteed the British Empire, the latter should join the Triple Alliance and also bring Japan with her. However, the negotiations were to take place at Vienna. Lord Lansdowne, the British Foreign Minister, refused to do so. The view of William II was that Great Britain wanted to use the German sword against Russia. The same was the view of Waldersee. William II referred to the Ministers of King Edward VII as "unmitigated noodles". Such an atmosphere was not congenial to an alliance between the two countries and no wonder Chamberlain gave up all hopes by June 1901. To quote him, "If the people in Berlin are short-sighted, there is no help." It was in these circumstances that Great Britain entered into an alliance with Japan in 1902.

In 1902, it appeared that the relations between the two countries were going to improve, Lord Roberts and Brodrick accepted an invitation to attend the manoeuvres of the German army. William II also refused to meet the Boer generals who came to Germany to collect funds. He also visited England. In 1903, Germany and England cooperated in the blockade of Venezuela. However, there was again a set-back on account of the question of the Berlin-Baghdad Railway. Public opinion in England demanded that under no condition should the British Government agree to cooperate with Germany. That was bound lo endanger the very safety of the British Empire in India. In 1904, Great Britain made the Entente Cordiale with France. She also supported France on the occasion of the Algeciras Conference in 1906. The Anglo-Russian Convention of 1907 created misgivings in the mind of William II as he began to feel that the Triple Alliance was not a match for the Triple Entente. Great Britain also supported France on the occasion of the Morocco crises in 1908 and 1911. There was also going on a naval competition between the two countries. Germany under William II and Tirpitz was determined to defeat England in the field of naval development. The British Government was not prepared to allow itself to be beaten. The result was that the relations between the two countries became strained to the maximum.

Lord Haldane, British Minister of War, was sent on a mission to Berlin with a view to arrive at some settlement with the German Government. The main object of the mission was to lessen the tension between the two countries arising out of naval competition. Unfortunately, his mission was a failure. William II was not prepared to give up naval programme of his country. Germany was determined to beat Great Britain in the field of naval strength and thus the British Government was not prepared to concede. No wonder, his mission was a failure.

There was no ground for reconciliation between Great Britain and Germany. Great Britain was not prepared to allow William II to make Germany the strongest power in the world. The simple problem was who was stronger out of the two and that could be decided only by a war which was fought to the finish. It was under these circumstances that the war of 1914 became inevitable. No wonder, when Germany backed Austria-Hungary on the question of Serbia, Great Britain took up the cause against Germany and supported France and Russia who in turn supported Serbia.

SUGGESTED READINGS

Grey: **Twenty-Five Years.**

Montageles: **British Foreign Policy Under Sir Edward Grey.**

Trevelyan, G.M.: **Grey of Fallodon.**

Woodward: **Great Britain and the German Navy.**

CHAPTER

29 INTERNATIONAL RELATIONS (1871-1914)

The period between the ending of the Franco-Prussian War and the beginning of World War I witnessed revolutionary changes in the alignment of the Great Powers in Europe. There seemed to be comparative calm in 1871, but in 1914, Europe was divided into two armed camps. It is both interesting and instructive to describe the grouping of the European States during this period.

Three Emperors' League. Between 1871 and 1890, there was the hegemony of Germany in European affairs. Bismarck, the Chancellor of Germany, seemed to be the arbiter of European politics. After 1871, Germany was a saturated country and as such had no desire to add to her territories. However, as Bismarck had wounded the pride of France and therefore feared an attack from that country, his main concern in foreign affairs was to isolate France so that she might not be able to have revenge against Germany. With that object in view, Bismarck created the Three Emperors' League or the **Dreikaiserbund** in 1873. The rulers of Germany, Austria-Hungary and Russia agreed to co-operate with one another for the preservation of peace and to consult one another "in order to determine a common course of action" in case of a threat of war. This League continued up to 1878 when it was broken on account of the Congress of Berlin. Germany and Austria co-operated and Russia felt that she was betrayed by Germany. The relations between Germany and Russia were positively hostile between 1879 and 1881. However, Bismarck was able to renew the Three Emperors' League in 1881. According to the new agreement, the three Powers mutually promised benevolent neutrality in case any of them was involved in a war with a fourth Power. This arrangement was made for three years and was renewed in 1884 for another period of three years. It is to be observed that the Three Emperors' League was not a strong union from the very beginning. Bismarck gave an undertaking to Austria that in the event of any difficulty between Austria and Russia, Germany would back Austria against Russia, and the understanding of 1881 would not stand in her way. Moreover, Germany followed a policy of protection which was partly against the import of Russian grain into Germany. As the rivalry between Austria-Hungary and Russia began to grow after 1878 in the Balkans, the relations between the two countries became bitter and consequently these two countries could not pull on together. The bitterness between these two countries weakened the Three Emperors' League.

About the Three Emperors League of 1881 Taylor says that this treaty was a practical agreement about the Near East. Its only general principle was a pact of neutrality if one of the three Emperors was involved in a war with a fourth Power. As there was no immediate likelihood of a war between Germany and France, this was a straight gain for Russia. It was a promise that Germany and Austria-Hungary would not join England. The only limitation was with regard to Turkey. Neutrality was to apply if there had been agreement beforehand. The view of Taylor is that this was an unnecessary precaution because the Russians had no intention of going to war with Turkey. Moreover, the three Powers recognised "the European and mutually obligatory character" of the rule of the Straits and would insist that Turkey enforce it. This was the essential security against a British expedition to the Black Sea which the Russians had been seeking all along. As a Russian garrison at the Straits was impossible, this was the next best thing. The Russians gained still more. The Austrians promised not to oppose the union of the two Bulgarias although the British Government considered the division of Bulgaria as an essential achievement of 1878. In return, the Russians recognised the right of Austria-Hungary to annex Bosnia and Herzegovina. The League of 1881 was a victory for the Russians and perhaps for Bismarck. Germany was freed from having to choose between Russia and Austria-Hungary in the Balkans. Russia got security in the Black Sea in exchange for a promise of peaceful behaviour which her internal weakness compelled her to keep in any case. Austria-Hungary committed herself to an eventual breach with England although she owed her Balkan position to the co-operation with England in 1878. She got in exchange merely Russian promises which she regarded as worthless. The League of the Three Emperors which was a pact of friendship with Russia, led in a round-about way to the Triple Alliance.

Reinsurance Treaty. The Three Emperors' League broke down in 1887. Russia and Austria were in opposite camps on the question of Bulgaria and no wonder they failed to pull on together. Bismarck had already bound Germany with Austria in 1879, but he could not afford to lose the goodwill of Russia. There was every possibility of Russia joining France if she was left alone. Moreover, there was every likelihood of a war between Austria and Russia if the latter joined another camp. No wonder, Bismarck entered into the Russo-German Reinsurance Treaty in 1887. The Treaty was to last for three years. According to it, if one Power found itself at war with a fourth Power, the others were to observe benevolent neutrality and try to localise the conflict. Russia, in agreement with Germany, declared her firm resolution to respect the interests of Austria arising from the Treaty of Berlin. Any modification in the territorial status quo of Turkey in Europe was to be accomplished by means of an agreement among the parties. They recognised the principle of the closing of the Straits. They were to see that Turkey did not make any exception in favour of any Power. If Turkey did so, the three Powers were to regard Turkey as putting herself in a state of war. It is rightly pointed out **"that new friendship of Germany and Russia prevented an Austro-Russian War and a Franco-Russian Coalition."**

Seaman says, "Signed in June 1887, it reaffirmed Bismarck's recognition of Russia's rights in Bulgaria. Before the end of August 1887 Russia was asking Bismarck to support her in ejecting Ferdinand of Saxe-Coburg from Bulgaria, and Bismarck was again failing to fulfil his obligations. So far apart had Russia and Germany become, indeed, that as his career was closing, Bismarck was toying with the idea of bringing in England to help him prop up the Habsburgs. The English were not interested; and an alliance between England and the two German powers would almost certainly have produced the war against Russia that Bismarck so anxiously wished to avoid.

"Arguments as to how far the Reinsurance Treaty was incompatible with the Dual Alliance of 1879 are largely academic. The important fact about it is that it did not appreciably slow down the steady movement of Russia towards France. Indeed, by driving Russian bonds off the Berlin stock market at the end of 1887, Bismarck did as much as anybody to increase those financial links between France and Russia which preceded the closer military and diplomatic links."

About the Reinsurance Treaty of 1887, Taylor says that the two parties, Russia and Germany, promised neutrality of a meaningless kind. Russia was to remain neutral unless Germany attacked France and Germany was to remain neutral unless Russia attacked Austria-Hungary. Germany renewed the promises of diplomatic support for Russia in Bulgaria and at the Straits which she had made in 1881 at the time of the Three Emperors' League. She added new promises against Alexander of Batterberg and moral support in case Russia seized the Straits herself. In later years, the Reinsurance Treaty acquired an exaggerated importance although in reality it did not amount to much. Perhaps it put Alexander III in a better temper with Germany. The Reinsurance Treaty did not prevent a Franco-Russian alliance. That alliance was retarded, though not finally prevented, solely by the French reluctance to give Russia a free hand in the Near East. Russia announced her intention of supporting France in 1887 and not in 1891. The Reinsurance Treaty demonstrated the approaching failure of Bismarck's policy. Bismarck had hoped that the prospect of Constantinople would make the Russians abandon France and by the Reinsurance Treaty, he offered them Constantinople. He had always refused to support Austria-Hungary in the Balkans and had hoped that this would be enough to preserve Russo-German friendship. The Russians now showed that they would be satisfied with nothing short of German neutrality in an Austro-Russian war. Failing that, they kept themselves free to support France. As a matter of fact, the treaty set it down in black and white that Germany would one day face war on two fronts unless she abandoned the Habsburg monarchy. The Austro-German alliance had imprisoned Germany and Bismarck would like to escape from it. The Reinsurance Treaty was, at best, an expedient for postponing the catastrophe of war on two fronts which Bismarck's diplomacy had made inevitable. It is often said that estrangement with Russia was forced on Bismarck by economic developments. Once the pillars of Russo-German friendship, the land-owners of Prussia now wanted tariffs against the cheap grains from Russia. There was something in this change of sentiment. The view of Taylor is that friendship would have continued if Bismarck had been able to promise neutrality in an Austro-Russian war. Much has been made of Bismarck's dishonesty in making the Reinsurance Treaty but Taylor contends that there was certainly no dishonesty towards the Austrians. He had always insisted that he could not support them in Bulgaria nor at the Straits. He had taken the same line with the British Government. Taylor maintains that the Reinsurance Treaty was a fraud on the Russians, more particularly on Alexander III in which Giers and the Shuvalovs took part with their eyes open.

The Austro-German Alliance (1879). The immediate cause of the dual alliance between Germany and Austria was the Congress of Berlin. The policy of Bismarck since 1871 was one of maintaining friendship with Austria and Russia and thereby keeping France isolated. This he achieved by the **Dreikaiserbund** which he started in 1873 and which lasted till 1878. The interests of Austria and Russia conflicted in the Balkans. It was very difficult for Bismarck to keep them together. He managed it till 1878. But on the occasion of the Congress of Berlin, it became evident that they could not pull on together. Russia had established her hold over the Balkans by the Treaty of San Stefano. But Austria was not prepared to allow Russia to retain all that she had got. Austria had won over England to her side and on the occasion of the Congress these two powers acted together. The result was that Russia found herself alone before a combination of England and Austria. Bismarck who called himself the "honest broker" had to make a decision as to whether he would side with Austria or Russia. The choice had to be made as Russia and Austria were not prepared to pull on together. Ultimately, he decided to side with Austria. "The outstanding result," says Dr. Gooch, "of the Congress of Berlin in the realm of high politics was the estrangement of Russia from Germany."

The Russians felt bitter about the attitude of Germany. They were utterly disappointed at what they had got. It appeared to them that Bessarabia, Batoum, Kars and Ardahan were no compensation for the amount of money that they had spent and the amount of blood they had shed. Aksakoff remarked: "The Congress is a conspiracy against the Russian people in which the Russian representatives have taken a part. The diplomacy of St. Petersburg is more dangerous than Nihilism. It is a disgraceful treachery to the historic mission of Russia and has lost for ever the respect and affection of the Slavs. Russia has been crucified by her own statesmen. A fool's cap and bells have been set upon her head." Katkoff proclaimed that Germany had left Russia in the lurch. Milutin, the War Minister of Russia, worked openly for a French alliance. Schuvaloff who was the chief Russian plenipotentiary at the Congress was recalled from London and disgraced. Gortchakoff, the Foreign Minister of Russia, was hostile towards Bismarck and would like to have nothing to do with him. The Czar also was very bitter. He spoke bitterly of the European coalition under Bismarck's leadership.

Another factor increased the bitterness of Russia. The German representatives on the international commission appointed to carry out the delimitations supported the Austrians against the Russians. Russia thought that it was being done intentionally. But the fact is that the German agents had got the instructions that they should side with the majority. Since Austria was supported by England and

Russia was all alone, the German agents also supported Austria. It is wrong to say that they had special instructions to go against Russia. However, the fact remains that the siding of the German agents with the Austrians annoyed the Russians. The bitterness was so great that in 1879, Italy was approached as to whether she could co-operate in a war against Austria. Similarly, the French Government was also approached regarding her attitude. But these soundings brought no result. The Russian troops were mobilized and concentrated on the German and Austrian frontiers. In June 1879, the Czar cancelled a visit to Berlin for the golden jubilee wedding of his uncle. The Czar was heard to say: "If Germany wished the friendship of a hundred years to continue, she must alter her ways." He wrote a letter to the Kaiser in which he complained of the German attitude. He reminded the Kaiser of his services in 1870, "which you said you would never forget" and added that the consequences would be disastrous for both the countries. The Kaiser was pained by the violence of the letter and asked Bismarck to draft a reply. If the Kaiser had replied in a similar tone, there would certainly have been a war. Germany was not prepared to kneel before Russia. The Kaiser merely denied the charge.

But after this incident, Bismarck chalked out a new policy. He flared up at the conduct of Russia. The press campaign in that country annoyed him. He was denounced everywhere. He regarded this as the height of ingratitude on the part of Russia. In 1888, he wrote thus: "I conceived my role almost as if I were a third Russian delegate. No Russian wish reached me which I did not adopt and fulfil. I behaved in such a manner that at the end of the Congress I thought to myself, 'If I did not already possess the highest Russian order in brilliance, I ought to receive it now.' I had the feeling that I had performed a service for a foreign power which a minister is seldom in a position to render. The campaign therefore surprised me."

Bismarck had to make a choice. He had already sided with Austria on the occasion of the Congress of Berlin. He thought over once again. It is true that from the material point of view, Russia would have been more advantageous. But he preferred Austria because it had a large population of Germans and consequently they would be more favourably inclined towards Germany.

Another event forced him to hurry up. He heard the news that Andrassy, the Foreign Minister of Austria, was going to resign. Andrassy was the man whom he had favoured in the Congress of Berlin. Before he resigned, Bismarck made up his mind to enter into an alliance with Austria. Andrassy was also anxious to insure against Russia. Both the statesmen were anxious for an alliance. There was to be no delay. The statesmen met at Gastein. They discussed the problem and the danger of Russia. They parted to meet again and in the meanwhile to consult their masters. Andrassy wrote back saying that Francis Joseph was willing to allow Austria to join with Germany. But the Kaiser protested. He told the Iron Chancellor that he could not agree to it. The Kaiser refused to enter into an alliance with Austria against Russia whose ruler was his cousin. He had an interview with the Czar in September. The Czar apologized for the letter and told the Kaiser that he would like his country to remain a friend of Germany. The Kaiser was satisfied that the Czar had no ill-will. Next day, he met Giers and Milutin and assured himself that they also were not in any way against Germany. The result was that the Kaiser came back satisfied.

He refused to allow Bismarck to enter into an alliance with Austria against Russia. He refused to change the old traditional policy of Germany towards Russia. "Put yourself in my place for a moment. I am in the presence of a personal friend, a near relative and an ally, in order to come to an understanding to some hasty and indeed misunderstood passages in the letter, and our interview also leads to a satisfactory result. I will not absolutely deny that the danger set forth in your memorandum may arise one day, particularly on a change of rulers; but I am utterly unable to see that there is any imminent danger. It is against my political convictions and my conscience to bind my hands for the sake of a possible eventuality, but I do not authorise you to conclude a convention, to say nothing of a treaty I cannot tell you how painful this episode has been to me, when it seemed, for the first time in 17 years, as if we do not agree."

In spite of what the Kaiser said, Bismarck was determined to bring about an alliance with Austria. He pointed out that there was no idea of attacking Russia. If Austria were attacked and in danger, Germany would be compelled by self-interest to support her, alliance or no alliance, since Germany's position, confronted by a victorious Russia, a defeated Austria and a hostile France, would be untenable. The Czar was only friendly till he could win France or Austria or both. The Chancellor persisted in his attitude. He won over the King of Bavaria to his side. He brought influence from all quarters on the Kaiser and tried to convert him. The Kaiser was virtually besieged. The Prince who was deputed to win over the Kaiser complained that while on the one side Bismarck threatened to resign, on the other the Kaiser threatened to abdicate. The Kaiser was heard to remark: "Rather abdication than perfidy." But Bismarck was determined to get it done. The Kaiser hesitated but ultimately had to give way on 5 October 1879. The treaty was signed in Vienna and ratified by both the Governments the same month.

Terms of the Alliance. By the dual alliance, the two countries were bound together and the following were its important provisions :—

1. Should, contrary to their hopes and desires, one of the two was attacked by Russia, the other was bound to assist and to conclude peace only in common.

2. Should any of the two be attacked by another Power supported by Russia, the other Power would assist. If any Power attacked either Austria or Germany and was not helped by Russia, the other party was to keep neutral.

3. The treaty was to remain secret.

4. The treaty was to last for five years and was to be prolonged for three years, unless the parties wanted to stop it.

It is said that both Andrassy and Bismarck were happy at the completion of the negotiations. The Chancellor was overjoyed. He said: "The fear of war has everywhere given place to confidence in peace." "It is the completion of my work of 1866," said Bismarck with pride. Andrassy had secured for Austria exactly what he wanted. He was proud of his handiwork. Next month, Bismarck remarked to the French ambassador: "Six weeks ago, Russia was dreaming of fire and flame. My deal with Austria has brought her to reason. A week after it was notified in St. Petersburg, the Detente began. The press campaign against Germany and Austria has been wholly stopped, and the heir to the throne is coming to pay his respects to the Kaiser."

Dr. Rose says that to the end of his days Bismarck maintained that the Austro-German alliance did not imply the lapse of the Three Emperors' League, but that the new compact by making a Russian attack on Austria highly dangerous, if not impossible, helped to prolong the life of the old alliance. Obviously, however, the League was a mere "loud-sounding nothing" when two of its members had to unite to guard the weakest of the trio against the most aggressive. Dr. Rose maintains that the old Triple Alliance slowly dissolved under the influence of new atmospheric conditions. The three Emperors met for friendly intercourse in 1881, 1884 and 1885, and at or after the meeting of 1887, a Russo-German agreement was formed by which the two Powers promised to observe a friendly neutrality in case either was attacked by a third Power. Probably the Afghan question and Nihilism brought Russia to accept Bismarck's advances; but when the fear of an Anglo-Russian war passed away, and the revolutionists were curbed, this agreement fell to the ground; and after the fall of Bismarck the compact was not renewed.

It might be contended that the immediate effect of the Austro-German alliance was not the estrangement of Russia: Bismarck was able to repair in 1881 the wire to St. Petersburg and continued friendly relations till 1890, but none can deny that it was this alliance which brought the two countries into the battlefield in 1914. Russia regarded this treaty as a blow if not a meance. "Russia lost Austria after San Stefano, and now she has lost Germany." But the King of Italy was satisfied and Waddington of France described it as a pledge of peace. Lord Salisbury remarked in October, "The papers say a defensive alliance of Germany and Austria has been concluded. If true, it is good tidings of great joy."

Whatever might be the reactions of the various powers on the conclusion of this treaty, it started a game which when followed by every country, was the most dangerous. Italy joined the Dual Alliance in 1882. In 1893-94, Russia and France entered into an alliance of a similar nature. No one can deny that the disease started in 1879 and it made almost all the European nations its victims. It was to a large extent responsible for World War I and Bismarck cannot be excused for starting the nightmare of alliances.

According to Prof. Fay, "The Austro-German alliance consolidated the Central Empires and became henceforth, until their collapse in November 1918, the very foundation-rock of German policy. It indicated a political course from which neither Bismarck nor his successors ever seriously swerved. In its origin, and as long as Bismarck remained at the helm, it was essentially defensive in purpose and fact. Germany and Austria mutually protected each other against the rising tide of Pan-Slavism; and Germany, if attacked by an outbreak of French revanche, could count upon Austria's neutrality, just as Austria could count on that of Germany in case of an outbreak of Italian Irredentism. Contemporary opinion regarded Bismarck's establishment of this Alliance as a masterstroke."

The Triple Alliance (1882). The Austro-German Alliance of 1879 was transformed into the Triple Alliance in 1882 with the accession of Italy to the Dual Alliance. Even before that year, Italy had tried to come to an understanding with Austria and Germany. Bismarck in 1877 had told Crispi: "If Italy is attacked by France, we should join and we will make a treaty for this purpose. But I do not expect such an attack unless France returns to monarchy, *i.e.*, to clericalism. I could not, however, consider the possibility of Austrian hostility. I am your friend, but I will not break with Austria. If she takes Bosmia, you can take Albania."

In 1879, Bismarck was prepared to welcome Italy as a third partner in the Austro-German alliance but the Italian Government did not accept the offer. However, the establishment of a French protectorate over Tunis by the Treaty of Bardo in 1881 brought about a change in Italian attitude. Italy had an eye on Tunis as it was near that country and was also considered to be a good place for Italian colonization. The establishment of French control over Tunis created a lot of indignation in Italy. The pride of the Italian patriots was wounded and they decided to do something against France. It was feared that Tunis might be a prelude to Tripoli. France might "encircle her with a ring of iron." There was some trouble at Marseilles. Many Italians were killed and many others left the city. There were anti-French demonstrations in Italy. It was felt that isolation was tantamount to annihilation. Italy would have loved to enter into a treaty with Great Britain as she was the strongest naval power in the Mediterranean, but Great Britain declined.

It was in these circumstances that the King of Italy, accompanied by his Prime Minister and the Foreign Minister, visited Vienna. The alliance was not proposed by the hosts and the guests avoided the risk of a rebuff. However, a friendly welcome and a general discussion of the situation prepared the way. Bismarck informed the Austrian Foreign Minister that any agreement with Italy would be one-sided and Italy was not a trustworthy ally. He referred to the jackal policy of Italy and hinted that the inclusion of Italy might not be of much value. However, the Italians were very anxious to have an alliance and were determined to have it at any cost. It is true that the negotiations were not easy but ultimately they came out successful and the Triple Alliance was made in 1882.

Prof. Fay points out that the view that Bismarck was responsible for the Triple Alliance is not a correct one. It is true that Bismarck encouraged France to **pluck the ripe Tunisian** fruit and also helped her in colonial adventures, but this does not mean that he felt that France would forget her humiliation of 1870-71 and keep peace with Germany. The fact is that the Triple Alliance originated with Italy.

The Triple Alliance treaty was signed on 20 May 1882 between Italy, Germany and Austria-Hungary. It was to last for five years and its contents and existence were to be kept secret. By this treaty, Germany and Austria-Hungary bound themselves to assist Italy with their whole military strength if she was attacked by France without provocation. Italy bound herself to render reciprocal aid to Germany under similar circumstances. In the case of an unprovoked attack by Russia alone upon Germany or Austria, Italy was bound only to benevolent neutrality. If the attack was made by two or more Great Powers, her assistance was to be active. Italy was not informed of the contents of the secret alliance between Germany and Austria-Hungary by which Germany was pledged to help Austria against Russia. Italy wanted to bring Great Britain into the Triple Alliance. Austria was also in favour of it but Bismarck negatived the suggestion. However, declarations were made that the Triple Alliance was not "in any case to be regarded as directed against England."

Dr. Gooch rightly points out that "though Italy was the petitioner, she obtained greater advantages than Austria." Although Austria was bound to help Italy against a French attack, Italy was not pledged to help Austria against a Russian attack. Moreover, on account of the treaty, Italy was protected against an Austrian attack. Although Italy had played a minor part in the Congress of Berlin of 1878, she came to be recognised as a Great Power after 1882. Though she failed to secure the guarantee of her capital, her hold over it was strengthened. The treaty also brought solid advantages to the Central Powers. Bismarck was not only freed from the remote fear that Italy might join France in an attack, but secured an ally in resisting such an attack. Austria was no longer to fear a stab in the back if she was engaged in a life-and-death struggle against Russia. She could also count upon Italian assistance in repelling a Franco-Russian attack. Italy gained much, but she lost in one respect. The treaty closed the doors on her ambitions in the Adriatic and the Balkans.

The Triple Alliance fitted Bismarck's purposes. He was able to kill "two birds with one stone. (1) The pact with Italy further isolated France, since, in case of war, the French would have to fight not only the Germans and Austrians but the Italians as well. (2) It strengthened Germany's alliance system, since the pact diminished the ill-will between his two allies, making it impossible for Italy (or so it seemed) to clamour for the "unredeemed" Italian-inhabited Austrian districts of Southern Tyrol and Trieste, while at the same time impending the Austrian Government's interest in restoring the secular power of the Pope. Thus, the mutually resented ambitions of both Italy and Austria-Hungary were checked, and a double danger to the peace of Europe was neutralized."

According to Prof. Fay, "The Triple Alliance in its wording and in its origin was essentially defensive in character and designed primarily to preserve the peace of Europe. This is now clear from the detailed negotiations concerning its formation, which have been revealed by Pribram from the Austrian archives, and by the extensive German documents in **Die** Crosse Politik. Its defensive character is now admitted even by French historians who are by no means friendly to Bismarck. Bismarck himself, in a private despatch which he never expected would be made public, referred to it as 'our League of Peace.' Its peaceful and defensive intent was especially marked in the case of Germany. But it became less so in the case of Italy and Austria, who later wished to use it to support their aggressive intentions. It was in fact not long before Italy sought to make use of her new alliance to promote her ambitions in North Africa and elsewhere."

According to Prof. Taylor, "The Triple Alliance looked formidable and elaborate; its real aims were modest. Ostensibly it welded Central Europe together and recreated the Holy Roman empire at its most grandiose so far as foreign affairs were concerned. In practice it merely propped up the Italian monarchy and secured Italian neutrality in an Austro-Hungarian war against Russia. The Austrians paid little in return. Kalnoky would not allow the Italians any say in the Balkans and therefore did not ask their aid against Russia. The sole price for Austria-Hungary was a vague approval of the Italian monarchy and therewith an indirect repudiation of that support for the papacy which had been traditional to the house of Habsburg. The price was paid by Germany; she promised to defend Italy against France, since Italian assistance was worthless and it got nothing in return. In plain terms, Bismarck undertook to defend Italy in order to meet the Austro-Hungarian complaints against the League of the Three Emperors: even this was better in his eyes than pledging support to Austria-Hungary in the Balkans. Besides, he knew that the French were not intending to attack Italy, and therefore he did not regard the obligation as onerous. The Italians knew this also; recognition as a Great Power, not protection from France, was their real need. The Triple Alliance gave them this; it bolstered up the myth of Italian greatness, and therefore staved off internal discontent for almost a generation. There was one striking omission in the original Alliance. Though humiliation over Tunis played only a secondary part in driving Italy over to the Central Powers, the Italian politicians certainly wanted backing for their imperialist designs in the Mediterranean. In 1882 they did not get it. But just as the Austrians thought that the Austro-German alliance would gradually draw Germany into supporting their Balkan plans, so the Italian counted that the Triple Alliance would gradually involve Germany in their Mediterranean schemes. So long as Russia was peaceful and Italian neutrality therefore of academic interest, their hopes were thwarted; once the peace of the Balkans was disturbed, Italy had something of value to sell and then Germany had to pay a real price." (**The Struggle for Mastery in Europe,** pp. 275-76.)

The Triple Alliance was renewed in 1887 and certain changes were made in favour of Italy. In 1882, Italy was the suiter, but in 1887, Austria was in fear of a Russian and Germany of a French attack, and consequently Italy could demand her own price. Austria was compelled to recognise Italy's interests in the Balkans and her claim to compensation if Turkey was partitioned. Italy refused to promise support if Austria was attacked. Germany undertook to take part in an offensive war if Italy's ambitions in North Africa demanded it. Austria was to allow Italian troops to cross her territory on their way to the western front.

How and why Italy left Triple Alliance. It is true that the Triple Alliance brought the three Powers together but there was not much of intimacy with Italy as it was between Austria and Germany. That was due to a feeling that Italy was following a crooked policy and consequently could not be trusted. To quote Bismarck, "Insatiable Italy with furtive glances, roves restlessly hither and thither, instinctively drawn on by odour of corruption and calamity and always ready to attack any one from the rear and make off with a bit of plunder......"

There was another difficulty and that was due to the presence of certain Austrian territories in the north of Italy which were inhabited by the Italians. The Irredentist movement aimed at conquering those territories from Austria and consequently there was always bad blood between Austria and Italy. In spite of friendship and co-operation, there was rivalry and hostility.

While Italy outwardly maintained friendly relations with the Central Powers, she went on improving her relations with the other countries. After the fall of Bismarck, her relations with France improved. The Italians started feeling that they had more in common with democratic France than with autocratic Germany. In 1896, Italy recognised the French protectorate over Tunis. In 1898 ended the tariff war between the two countries. In December 1901 an agreement was made with France defining the interests of both the countries in the Mediterranean. France recognised the right of Italy to extend her influence in Tripoli. In June 1902, a few days before the renewal of the Triple Alliance, Italy assured France that it did not bind her to take part in a war of aggression against France. In November of the same year, France and Italy agreed that if one were attacked the other should remain neutral. A cordial welcome was extended to King Victor Emmanuel and his Queen in Paris (1903), and to President Loubet in Rome (1904). The rupture between France and the Vatican which followed the visit of the French President to Rome tended to increase the cordiality between France and Italy. The **Entente Cordiale** of 1904 between England and France helped to bring Italy and France together in the same way as it improved the relations between Great Britain and Russia. The Algeciras Conference of 1906 demonstrated the growing solidarity of England and France and the cooling of warmth between Italy and her partners in the Triple Alliance.

The Bosnian crisis of 1908-9 showed that the continuance of the Triple Alliance was a diplomatic mockery. Italy was perturbed by the annexation of Bosnia and Herzegovina by Austria. "The only State," declared a deputy in the Italian Chamber, "which really threatens us with war is in alliance with us." There were Italian politicians who demanded that Italy should break with the Central Powers and join the Triple **Entente.** But Tittoni, her Foreign Minister, emphatically refused to choose between alliance and friendship or to give up either the one or the other. "Our alliance with Germany and Austria-Hungary to which we remain true, must not to my mind be an obstacle to our traditional friendship with England, to our renewed friendship with France, and to the recent understanding with Russia." For some months after the annexations were announced, Tittoni earnestly strove to bring about an agreement between Italy, Austria-Hungary and Russia, but in vain.

The growing estrangement between Italy and the Central Empires was further emphasized by the visit paid by the Czar Nicholas II to King Victor Emmanuel at Racconigi (1909). The two sovereigns agreed to do everything in their power to maintain the status quo in the Balkans. If that was found impossible, they were to encourage the development of the national States to the exclusion of both Austria and Italy. Russia agreed to maintain a benevolent attitude with regard to Italy's designs on Tripoli and Cyrenaica. Italy promised to reciprocate this attitude towards Russian ambitions with regard to the Dardanelles and the Bosphorus. France and England agreed to adhere to the Racconigi Agreement. The Agreement marked the further progress of Italy from the Triple Alliance towards the Triple Entente. In spite of that, the Triple Alliance remained formally intact.

In 1887, Great Britain and Italy entered into an agreement by which both the parties agreed to maintain, if possible, the status quo in the Mediterranean, Adriatic, Aegean and Black Sea. They agreed to support each other in the Mediterranean if either of them went to war with another power. Italy agreed to support the policy of Great Britain in Egypt and Great Britain agreed to support Italy in Northern Africa and particularly in Tripoli. The relations between the two countries became more and more cordial with the passage of time, and in 1906, Italy voted with England against Germany on the occasion of the Algeciras Conference.

In addition to the Irredentist movement, there were other factors which strained the relations between Italy and Austria. Austria resented the desire of Italy to secure Albania and Italy was opposed to Austria having control over Albania and Valona. Although both the countries agreed to maintain the status quo in Albania, each tried to strengthen her influence by more or less underhand means. Anti-Austrian riots broke out in Italy. The Austrian attempt to construct a railway through the Sanjak of Novi-Bazar added to the ill-feelings between the two countries.

Germany found great difficulty in maintaining friendly relations with Italy. German policy was to win over Turkey and she was doing her best to achieve that objective. However, Italy declared war against Turkey in 1911 and occupied Tripoli. During the period of the war, Germany found her position very awkward as she could not avert a war between the two allies.

From 1902 to 1914, Italy had a foot in two camps and she was finding it difficult to reconcile her obligations under the Triple Alliance with her inclination and promises towards the Triple Entente.

It was in these circumstances that the World War I broke out in 1914. In spite of the Triple Alliance, she did not join the war. She asked for compensation and hinted at Trentino. The suggestion was dismissed by Austria. The policy of Italy was to get whatever she could possibly get. "What is needed is a freedom from all pre-conceptions and prejudices, from every sentiment except that of sacred egotism." Italy was not in a hurry to join the war as she had not recovered from her exhaustion in the Tripolian War. Germany put pressure on Austria to give something to Italy, but Austria refused. The Austrian policy was not changed even after the dismissal of Berchtold. Instead of accepting the demands of Italy at once and winning her over, the Austrian Government slowly and slowly went on raising the offer. Italy also went on raising its demands. Ultimately, the Italian Government demanded in April 1915 the whole of south Tyrol, Gorizia, Gradisca and Trieste, several islands off the Dalmatian coast, Italian sovereignty over Valona and Austrian disinterestedness in Albania.

It was natural that Italy's price of intervention should be higher than that for neutrality. It was equally natural that the **Entente** Powers should be more generous in their promises to Italy than Austria herself. France and Great Britain were willing to pay a higher price and consequently negotiations started in London. Italy's demands were considered exorbitant by Russia and France. Russia opposed Italian designs on the eastern coast of the Adriatic to which Serbia had a better claim. However, the military situation was in favour of Italy and the Allies badly needed the help of Italy. It was in these circumstances that the Treaty of London was signed in 1915.

By the Treaty of London, Italy was to get Trentino, the Southern Tyrol up to Brenner Pass, the city and district of Trieste, the country of Grandisca, North Dalmatia, Istria, etc. She was also to get the twelve islands. In Libya, she was to enjoy all rights and privileges. Italy was to be allowed to expand in Somaliland, Eritrea and Libya. Great Britain was to help her to raise a loan and she was also to have a share in war-indemnity. The Treaty was to be kept secret and the new ally was to begin hostilities within a month. It cannot be denied that the Treaty of London increased the material strength of the Allied Powers, but it undoubtedly took away from their moral prestige. The Serbs were furious at the prospect of the Adriatic Sea becoming an Italian lake.

Even after the signing of the Treaty of London, Italy continued negotiations with Austria with a view to finding out an excuse to attack the country. On 21 April 1916, Italy declared that the differences between the two countries were so wide that it was impossible to bridge them. On 3 May, Italy denounced the Triple Alliance. The Austrian Government tried to make concessions to win over Italy, but it was too late. Italy declared war against Austria on 23 May 1916. Curiously enough, war against Germany was not declared till 27 May 1916. **It is clear from this as to how Italy joined the Triple Alliance in 1882 and left it in 1915.** On both these occasions, Italy was actuated by her personal interests.

Franco-Russian Alliance (1893). It is to be observed that while the Austro-German Alliance was concluded within a very short period, the Franco-Russian Alliance was discussed in public and private for many years before official negotiations started, and even then it took many years before it was finally concluded. The delay was due to many causes. Between 1871 and 1890, Bismarck consistently followed a policy of isolating France and consequently he would not allow Russia to be aligned with France. He brought into existence the Three Emperors' League which continued from 1873 to 1878. Although the relations between Germany and Russia were strained from 1879 to 1881 and there was a possibility of an alliance between France and Russia during that period, Bismarck was able to avoid the eventuality by following a pro-French policy during that period. On the occasion of the Bulgarian crisis, Bismarck supported Russia against Austria. In 1881, he renewed the Three Emperors' League which continued up to 1887. He was able to keep Russia with Germany up to 1890 by entering into the Reinsurance Treaty with her in 1887.

Another cause was that the French ministries changed very often and the negotiations started by one ministry could not be successfully concluded by another. The Czar wanted to enter into a secret alliance and he felt that the secrecy of the alliance could not be maintained on account of the frequency of changes in French ministries. Russia was an autocratic country and France had a democratic government and it was felt that an alliance between democracy and autocracy was not a happy one. The Czar was hesitant to enter into an alliance with a democratic country which was the refuge of the revolutionaries. Giers, the Foreign Minister of Russia, had very bad health and consequently the negotiations had to be delayed to suit his convenience. Even the Czar himself changed his mind very often, and on certain occasions, refused to carry on negotiations for an alliance with France. However, in spite of these difficulties the alliance between the two countries was concluded in the long run on account of the community of interests.

In 1873, the French Government enquired from the Russian Government whether the latter would help her if she was attacked. The Russian Government did not make any promise but stated that she desired to see France a Great Power.

On the occasion of the war scare of 1875, Russia gave a proof of her practical sympathy for France. Germany wanted to attack France and crush her before she became sufficiently strong to challenge her. On that occasion, the Czar and Gortchakoff, the Russian Foreign Minister, went to Berlin and pacified the Germans. Russia told Germany frankly that she should not count upon her neutrality in the event of a German attack on France. To the French the Russian action appeared as a harbinger of more intimate relations with that country in the future.

In 1877, Waddington came to power in France. He was in favour of maintaining good relations with Germany. Although during the tension that followed the Congress of Berlin the Russian Government offered to enter into an alliance with France, the French Government refused Waddington remarked thus: "I think Russia is inclined to a rapprochement, but Bismarck has his eyes on us. If a treaty were on the anvil, he might reply with war." Even Gambetta, who was otherwise an enemy of Germany, was in favour of maintaining good relations with Bismarck. To quote him, "France must play a secondary role in Europe and be very reserved till we have got a very strong army and then I shall like you to be a partisan of a Russian alliance." Bismarck remarked in 1881 that he would like to go "hand in hand" with France. Such was the cordiality of the relations between Germany and France and the French indifference towards Russia that in 1880, Freycinet refused the extradition of Hartmanns who was charged with planning a bomb attack on the Czar. The Czar was so angry that he recalled the Russian Ambassador from France. In 1885, the French Government annoyed the Russian Government by the release of Kropotkin from a French prison before the expiry of his sentence and the recall of the French ambassador to whom the Czar, was greatly attached. In anger the Czar refused to welcome the new French ambassador.

The possibility of a Franco-Russian Alliance existed during the Bulgarian crisis, and a campaign was started in the two countries for that purpose. Katkoff wrote thus: "If Germany stands so big, is it not because she has climbed on Russia's shoulders? If Russia was to resume her liberty of action, the phantom of German omnipotence would vanish. We are not asking for a Franco-Russian alliance. We wish that Russia should remain in free and friendly relations with Germany, but also that similar relations should be established with the other nations, and above all with France who occupies in an increasing degree a situation in Europe worthy of her power. What have we to quarrel about, and what are her domestic concerns to us?" Again, "I hate France, for she has been and is a school of revolutionary propaganda. But now when Russia is threatened by Austria and Germany, an alliance is imposed upon her by an ineluctable necessity." However, when a formal offer for an alliance was made to France in 1886, the latter refused.

In 1887, a new Government came to power in France. The new Foreign Minister was friendly towards Russia and he advised the Bulgarians to come to a settlement with Russia and not to quarrel. According to Dr. Gooch, "At a time when every European statesman except Bismarck was a critic of Russia's high-handed conduct in Bulgaria, the support of the French Government caused pleasure and gratitude in Petrograd."

In the same year, the Boulanger crisis took place. The Russian Government intervened to pacify the Germans. As the tension was still persisting, there was every likelihood of a conflict between France and Germany. Bismarck enquired from the Russian Government what her attitude would be in the event of a war. The reply of the Czar was in these words: "Russia was neutral in the three wars though it would have been her plain interest to abandon neutrality. Today Russia must consult her own interests in a greater degree and cannot constantly aid Prussia, who is besides the ally of the Emperor Francis Joseph." The Czar refused to promise neutrality as the annihilation of France was bound to upset the balance of power in Europe. He wanted to keep his hands free. He also assured France that she could count upon her moral support.

In 1883, the Grand Duke of Russia visited Paris and he expressed a wish to inspect the new French rifles. The request was granted after some hesitation. In 1889, Russia asked France to manufacture 500,000 rifles. The French Government agreed to do so in case "they will not fire at Frenchmen." The manufacture of rifles started in 1890, but in the meanwhile the Russian officers studied the system of mobilisation, transport and supply from the French. A French engineer was sent to Russia to organise the manufacture of munitions.

In 1888, the Russian Government tried to raise a loan in France and it was over-subscribed. Russia was obliged to France. A similar loan was raised next year. These loans brought the two countries together.

The French ministry of Freycinet was inclined towards Russia. The fall of Bismarck in 1890 and the lapse of the Reinsurance Treaty with Russia removed a great obstacle from the way of Franco-Russian collaboration. In 1890 the Grand Duke visited Paris again and remarked thus: "If I have any voice in the matter, the two will be one in time of war. And that, if it were known, would prevent war, for no one would care to challenge France and Russia". His parting words were: "In me, France has a friend."

In 1890, the French Chief of the Staff, General Boisdeffre, went to Russia to expedite an alliance with that country. However, nothing came out of it as the Czar was not convinced of the utility of an alliance. But the French were clamouring for an alliance. According to the Belgian minister, "The dream obsesses every one at Paris. It comes from the very natural desire to lean on a great nation in resisting attack from the Central Powers: but it has become also a matter of sentiment. The infatuation for Russia has gained upon all classes. This Power is as popular today as Poland under the Second Empire. Many are convinced of the existence of a sort of Entente—secret engagements, if not a treaty. Thus the arrival of any official personage acquires the proportions of an event, and the Grand Dukes can no longer travel in France without political significance being attached to the visits of courtesy which they pay to the authorities. A new journal, **L'Union Franco-Russe,** has just appeared, and reproduces the dithyrambs of the Paris press in honour of the Russian alliance. The contrast between the institutions of the two countries is not felt in Paris."

In 1891, Empress Frederick, mother of William II, visited France. When she went to Versailles and St. Cloud, there were hostile demonstrations. William II made it clear that if his mother was insulted in any way he would declare war on France. However, the danger was averted by the departure of the train an hour before the specified time. The Russians stood by the side of France on this occasion also. The Grand Cross of St. Andrew was presented to Carnot, the President of France. In spite of all this, Russia was still reluctant to enter into an alliance with republican France. There was a French exhibition at Moscow. The Czar openly opposed it and also ordered his brother who was the Governor of Moscow, not to appear and take part in the banquet. The exhibition was a complete failure.

However, the momentary tension between Russia and France was ended by the renewal of the Triple Alliance. Great Britain appeared to be sympathetic towards the Triple Alliance. Russia found herself alone and no wonder she felt the necessity of an ally. It was this fact which forced the Russian Government to invite the French Fleet to Russia. The Cronstadt visit took place in 1891 and the French were given a rousing welcome in Russia. The Czar ordered the naval band to play the Marseillaise, the French national anthem. According to Freycinet, "When the fleet weighed anchor, the **rapprochement** was made. It merely remained to translate it into official language. The Czar had committed himself." The visit of the French fleet created a profound impression in Europe. It was felt that an alliance between Russia and France was in the offing.

Giers informed the French Government that the Russian Government would be willing to discuss matters common to both the countries. In 1891, a political agreement was made between the two countries. It was declared by the two governments that they would confer with each other on every question which threatened peace and take consolidated action to meet the danger, whether actual or potential.

In 1891, the Russian Government raised in France another loan at 3% for a million bonds of 500 francs each and it was over-subscribed eight times. The Russian Government moved slowly in the matter and when Giers visited Paris the same year, he refused to commit himself for a military alliance. In spite of that, Russia had been completely won over. In 1891, Russia and France co-operated with each other in Turkey and the Sultan was informed that both the countries would act together with regard to the Mediterranean.

Although a military convention was being discussed, the French were impatient of delay. The sickness of Giers was delaying matters. The Czar was worried about the secrecy of the terms of the alliance. It was not till October 1893 that a Russian squadron visited Toulon and thereby returned the visit of the French fleet in 1891. Both men and women in Paris ran with the carriages carrying the Russians and kissed or touched their hands as a token of their affection. They were compelled very often to appear on their balconies. Sometimes they cut their gloves into pieces for distribution among the crowds. A similar reception was given to the Russian officers at Marseilles and Lyons.

We do not know what brought Alexander III to his final conclusion to enter into a military convention with France. He had kept the French waiting for long and perhaps it was his conviction that they would not drag him into a war of revenge. On 16 December 1893, Alexander III is stated to have told Montebello, the French ambassador, "You would not be good patriots, you would not be Frenchmen if you did not hold to the thought that the day will come when you can recover possession of your lost provinces; but there is a great distance between this natural feeling and the idea of provocation to realise it, of revenge in a word; and you have often shown that you want peace above everything and that you know how to wait with dignity." On 27 December 1893, Giers informed Montebello that Alexander III had approved the military convention and the same was signed between Russia and France on 31 December 1893. On 4 January 1894, the French Government gave their approval and thus the alliance formally came into existence. The convention was of a defensive nature. If France was attacked by Germany or by Italy supported by Germany, Russia was to employ all her resources to attack Germany. If Russia was attacked by Germany or by Austria supported by Germany. France was to employ all her forces to fight Germany. Both France and Russia were to employ a certain number of troops against the enemy. The Staffs of the Armies of the two countries were to co-operate at all times in preparing and facilitating the execution of the measures above-mentioned. They were to communicate to each other all information regarding the armies of the Triple Alliance. The two countries were not to conclude separate treaties. The clauses of the treaty were to be kept secret and the treaty was to last as long as the Triple Alliance lasted.

The existence of the Dual Alliance between Russia and France was revealed to the world in January 1895, when Premier Ribot declared: "France has associated her interests with those of another nation in the interest of peace and European equilibrium. This alliance which was ratified by the universal sentiment of the country, constitutes today our dignity and our strength." Regarding the alliance, William II wrote thus to Czar Nicholas II in September 1895: "I perfectly know that you do not dream of attacking us, but you cannot be astonished that the Powers get alarmed seeing how the presence of your officers and high officials in an official way in France fans inflammable Frenchmen into a white-heat passion and strengthens the cause of chauvinism and revanche. If you are allied for better or worse with the French, well then, keep those damned rascals in order and make them sit still." Again, "It is not the friendship of France and Russia that makes me uneasy, but the danger to our principle of monarchism through the lifting up of the Republic on a pedestal. The constant appearance of princes, Grand Dukes, etc. at Reviews, Burials, Dinners, Races, with the head of the Republic makes Republicans believe that they are quite honest, excellent people, with whom princes can consort and feel at home."

According to Dr. Gooch, "The conclusion of the Dual Alliance was an event of capital importance not only for France and Russia, but for Europe. That a first-class Power should desire an alliance with France was an emphatic recognition that she had recovered from her catastrophic defeat. The glaring differences of political institutions and ideas were forgotten in the satisfaction of procuring a powerful France and the secrecy of its terms enabled eager patriots to hope that it might perhaps contain same assurance with regard to the recovery of the Rhine provinces. On the side of Russia, who had less cause to fret about prestige, the alliance was hailed as good business. Her plans of Far Eastern expansion, among them the Siberian Railway, required unlimited capital, which thrifty France was ready and indeed eager to supply at a moderate rate. From the standpoint of European politics, the conclusion of the alliance was a sign that the reign of Bismarck was over."

According to Prof. Fay, the Franco-Russian alliance was defensive in its origin but in the time of Delcasse, Izvolsky and Poincare, it was transformed into an offensive alliance. The defeat of Germany was the first and principal objective of the alliance in case of German aggression. To begin with Germany was not alarmed because she felt that the Triple Alliance was equal in strength to the Dual Alliance. She also believed that England would not join the Dual Alliance and consequently the balance of power would be maintained. However, it cannot be denied that the existence of the Dual Alliance forced Germany to show due respect to both Russia and France. In a way, the Dual Alliance tended at first to secure the peace of Europe in the same way as "one sword holds another in its sheath." The isolation of France was ended and France could afford to take a stiff attitude towards Great Britain and Germany. On many occasions, William II proposed to merge the Triple Alliance and the Dual Alliance into a grand "Continental League." His view was that such a combination would maintain peace and put an end to the domination of England in colonial affairs. To quote Fay, "Thus the first years of the Franco-Russian Alliance tended to strengthen rather than endanger the peace of Europe. It established a healthy counterpoise to the Triple Alliance. Neither group was so greatly superior as to be able safely to attack the other, or even to seek to dominate it by threats of force. But during the decade from 1894 to 1904, two changes occurred which tended ultimately to destroy this equilibrium. They are of the greatest importance in the development of the system of secret alliance—England's exchange of splendid isolation for an Entente Cordiale with France, and Italy's dubious loyalty towards her Allies."

The Entente Cordiale (1904). The year 1898 is a great landmark in the history of Anglo-French relations. In that year, Anglo-French rivalry reached its high water-mark and there was every possibility of a clash between the two countries. Great Britain and France had been rivals for a long time. During the later half of the 19th century, the scramble for Africa had made them keen rivals. The Anglo-French African settlement of 1890 had solved some of the thorny problems and France was allowed to establish a protectorate over the Island of Madagascar, French influence was recognised as supreme in the Sahara. In spite of that, the rivalry between the two countries continued. That was due to the fact that the French wanted to penetrate from the west of Africa to the east of Africa and dominate the Sudan. The British Government was equally determined not to allow France to do so as she was determined to link up her possession in North and South Africa. The British Government regarded Anglo-Egyptian Sudan as their own preserve although it had not been conquered.

In 1897, Captain Marchand, a French soldier and explorer who was a passionate opponent of English colonialism, started his march across dark Africa, taking with him in pieces the Steamer **Faidherbe** which he could reassemble when he reached the Nile. Its boiler was rolled on logs for hundreds of miles through the tropical forest. After more than a year, Marchand reached Fashoda on July 16, 1898. He restored the fort, made a treaty with the local chief who put his territory under the French rule and hoisted the French flag on the fort.

After a fortnight, Kitchener arrived on the scene with a much stronger force than that of Marchand. There was every likelihood of trouble. When Marchand undertook the expedition, he had been assured of his Government's help by the then French Foreign Minister in these words: "You are going to fire a pistol shot on the Nile; we accept all its consequences."

However, both Kitchener and Marchand behaved with dignity and gallantry and the situation was saved. There was the following conversation between the two. Kitchener said: "I must hoist the Egyptian flag here." The reply of Marchand was: "Why, I myself will help you to hoist it—over the village." Kitchener added: "Over the fort." Marchand replied: "No, that I shall resist." Kitchener said: "Do you know, Major, that this affair may set France and England at war?" Marchand records that to that question he bowed without replying. Ultimately they agreed that Kitchener should hoist the Egyptian flag over an outlying part of the fort and the French flag should remain over the fort itself. They also agreed to refer the dispute to their respective home governments.

At this time, a new ministry was formed and Delcasse became the Foreign Minister of France. The latter brought a new approach to the whole problem. His view was that France could not afford to fight against England. That was due to the fact that if France was to get back Alsace and Lorraine from Germany, the only way to do so was by getting help from England. Under the circumstances a fight with England was suicidal, and no wonder Delcasse decided to retire from Fashoda and sent orders accordingly. Negotiations started between the two countries with regard to the territory claimed by France but on account of the stiff attitude of England, Delcasse had to give way. An Anglo-French convention of March 1899 fixed a line beyond which Great Britain was not to seek territory or influence westwards and France eastwards. Although Delcasse asked the British Government to settle the other outstanding disputes between the two countries and thereby bring them together, the British Government declined the offer. That was partly due to the fact that England was more favourably inclined towards Germany than towards France. Moreover, the British Government had no faith in the stability of the French ministries. The matter had to be dropped for the time being.

The settlement of 1899 between France and England was not popular in France. It was maintained by the French patriots that Delcasse had surrendered before Great Britain. In spite of the best efforts made by Delcasse to make Frenchmen understand his point of view, the feeling remained. When the Boer War started the relations between England and France became bitter once again. The French supported the Boers in their fight against the British Government. On the other hand, Germany supported the British stand. No wonder, there was too much of anti-French feeling in England. The visit of William II to London on the occasion of the death of Queen Victoria and his attitude there brought England and Germany together and nobody thought of France. However, events took a different turn when William II was approached to enter into an alliance with England and he tried to put off by saying that the road to Berlin lay through Vienna. It was then that statesmen like Chabmerlain who stood for an Anglo-German collaboration, felt disgusted with the German attitude and decided to seek friends elsewhere. It was in that spirit that Great Britain decided to enter into an offensive and defensive alliance with Japan in 1902.[1]

Negotiations were started with France in 1902 when Chamberlain made a formal proposal to Cambon, the French Ambassador in London. The scope of those proposals was colonial and their object was to solve the Anglo-French disputes in the colonial field.

The Anglo-French differences fell into two classes. In the first category fell a long string of local colonial disputes. The French claims rested on treaties and were more detrimental to Britain than of advantage to her. Their main value was a bargaining counter. France could be persuaded to surrender them only by giving her compensation elsewhere. Although it was a tedious job, yet it was not so hopeless. To the second category belonged two questions of high policy and those were Morocco and Egypt. France had not forgotten how in 1882 she was deprived of her interests in Egypt as a result of the unilateral action of Great Britain. The bitterness against Great Britain on that score was very great and it was difficult to reconcile her, French interest in Egypt had been long and intimate, dating back to the time of Napoleon I. At the same time, the Sultanate of Morocco was falling to pieces and could link the North and West African possessions of France. Moreover, the control of Morocco by any other rival power would have endangered French position. If this was the French view, the British Admiralty was not inclined to allow the falling of the southern shore of the straits of Gibraltar into the hands of France. Most of Morocco's small trade was done by British merchants and they were not prepared to lose it so easily. However, a bargain was struck between the two countries. Great Britain was to have a free hand in Egypt and France was to have a free hand in Morocco and both of them were to support each other. The problem of the straits was solved by a non-fortification clause and by reserving a northern strip to satisfy the historic claim of Spain. It was also provided that equal liberty of commerce was to be given to England for thirty years.

The ratification of the treaty needed a feeling of friendship in France towards Great Britain. However, that feeling was lacking for some time. The French newspapers were most bitter against England. However, President Loubet and Foreign Minister Delcasse sent friendly messages to Edward VII on his accession to the throne. The King was greatly impressed by them. Moreover, Edward VII had an inborn hatred for the Germans and their king who had insulted him many a time. He was extremely popular with the people of Paris whom he visited often. In 1903 when Edward VII visited France he was given a hearty welcome everywhere. The people ran after his carriage and cheered him. The visit was a grand success. In the same year, President Loubet and Delcasse went to London on a return visit and were warmly received. The result was that an Anglo-French Arbitration Treaty was signed in October 1903. However, the main treaty was signed in April 1904 and it dealt with Egypt, Morocco, Newfoundland, West Africa, Madagascar, Siam and New Hebrides. The Treaty was ratified both by Great Britain and France. The question of Newfoundland fisheries was amicably settled. France gave up her claim to the shores of Newfoundland where she had the right of fishing and drying her nets, but she was guaranteed the right of fishing as before. She got concessions in West Africa. She got 14,000 square miles of territory and uninterrupted access from her territories on the Niger to those in Lake Chad. The difficulties with regard to Siam, Madagascar and New Hebrides were also solved.

Both Lord Lansdowne and Delcasse were satisfied at the friendly settlement of the outstanding disputes between England and France. Answering the critics, Delcasse maintained that in Newfoundland France had only abandoned privileges which were difficult to maintain and in no way necessary, while the essential right of fishing in territorial waters was preserved. In West Africa the British concessions were of considerable importance. The Niger-Chad frontier was improved. To quote him, "Under our influence, Morocco would be a source of strength for our North African

1. A full discussion of this alliance is to be found in the chapter in the Foreign Policy of Japan.

empire. If subject to a foreign Power, our North African possessions would be permanently menaced and paralysed." The sacrifice in Egypt was small. No change was made in the political status and all necessary guarantees for French financial interests were obtained. Great Britain also agreed to abide by the terms of the Suez Canal Convention of 1888.

It is wrong to think that the **Entente Cordiale** of 1904 was in any way a military alliance between Great Britain and France. It was nothing of the kind. It was merely a settlement of the outstanding disputes between the two countries. However, the settlement of the disputes created an atmosphere of cordiality and friendship between the two countries. There was every possibility of strengthening the Entente in the future.

Although the **Entente** of 1904 did not commit the two countries to help each other, certain circumstances brought them together. There was the alarming growth of the German navy and it was feared in England that if Great Britain was to maintain her naval supremacy in the world, she must build more ships than the Germans did. The British Government also decided to withdraw her navy from the Pacific and concentrate all the British navy in the North Sea. That could be done only if Great Britain withdrew her navy from the Mediterranean also. That could be done only if a friendly power took over the control of the Mediterranean. It was the question of the withdrawal of the British navy from the Mediterranean that forced England to depend more and more on France whose navy could be entrusted with the command of the Mediterranean.

The **Entente** was tested in 1905-6, 1908 and 1911 on three occasions of the Morocco crises. On all these three occasions, Great Britain backed France. The testing of the Entente made it grow stronger. As a matter of fact, it was the community of interests between England and France that solidified the Entente and brought them nearer each other. Anglo-French collaboration had reached such a stage that on the occasion of Haldane's mission to Berlin in 1912 Grey declared that England would not sacrifice France for the sake of friendship with Germany.

It is desirable to refer to the views of Bulow and Dr. Gooch on the **Entente Cordiale.** According to Bulow, "I can only say that we have no reason to suppose that this agreement is directed against any power whatever. It seems to be an attempt to eliminate the points of difference between France and Great Britain by means of an amicable understanding. From the point of view of German interests we have nothing to complain of for we do not wish to see strained relations between Great Britain and France, if only because such a state of affairs would imperil the peace of the world, the maintenance of which we sincerely desire. Concerning Morocco, which constitutes the essential point of the agreement, we are interested in this country, as in fact in the rest of the Mediterranean, principally from the economic point of view...We must protect our commercial interests in Morocco, and we shall protect them." According to Dr. Gooch. "It is regrettable that the British Cabinet did not perceive—or at any rate did not help France to perceive—the wisdom of securing German consent by a solatium. Though the Secret Treaties of 1904 reserved no share for Great Britain in the contingent partition of Morocco and though it has been argued it was reasonable for the contracting parties to make alternative arrangements in the event of Morocco collapsing from internal weakness, our share in the transaction which suggested double-dealing involves the British Government in partial responsibility for the crises of 1905 and 1911."

According to Tayor, "The agreement, signed on 8th April 1904, therefore appeared to contain a gross inequality: the British gains in Egypt operated immediately; the French gains in Morocco depended on their future exertions. The inequality was apparent, not real. The British were already established in Egypt beyond all challenge; their gain was merely a free hand for Cromer and his financial schemes—gratifying, no doubt, but irrelevant to their imperial strength. The French, on the other hand, were at liberty to add the finest part of North Africa to their empire. But in politics it is the apparent which counts. When Delcasse gave up Egypt, he renounced a cause which ranked, however mistakenly, second only to the lost provinces; when Lansdowne gave up Morocco, he wrote off a country unknown to all except a few traders and experts in strategy. Both British and French opinion believed that France had paid the higher price. Because of the sentimental weight of Egypt, the entente was on trial in France as it was not in Great Britain. The entente was essential for France; it was merely an advantage for the British. But the French had paid cash down, the British with a promissory note. Hence the French could take an independent line—could try to go back in their bargain towards Spain and could flirt with Germany. British good faith was on trial; they had to back the French up in Morocco when international difficulties arose. Yet all the entente did for the British was slightly to lessen their naval needs in the Mediterranean and to give Cromer a field day in Egypt; for the French the situation in the Far East made it a matter of life and death." (**The Struggle for Mastery in Europe,** pp. 415-17).

Anglo-French Military and Naval Talks. It is desirable to refer to the military and naval talks between England and France from 1905 to 1914. The **Entente Cordiale** of 1904 bound England merely to give diplomatic support to France on the question of Morocco. However, after the visit of William II to Tangier, the British Government and the public opinion in England felt that Germany was trying to break up the entente by bullying France. It was also felt that France was being threatened merely on account of her friendship with England. There was also political and commercial rivalry between England and Germany. The rapid growth of the German navy was also worrying British statesmen. It was found that on the question of Morocco, the English press was "more French than the French." It was hinted that in the event of a war on the question of Morocco, "England will stand unconditionally and actively on the French side and will go against Germany, even with enthusiasm."

It was in the atmosphere that talks started between Lord Lansdowne, the British Foreign Minister, and Cambon, the French Ambassador in London. Great Britain was prepared to "take a step further" and offer to France more than mere diplomatic support. Negotiations had reached the final stage when Delcasse fell in 1905.

In December 1905, Sir Edward Grey became the Foreign Minister of England. It was the eve of the Algeciras Conference and Germany was adopting a threatening attitude towards France and consequently the French Government was feeling very nervous. It was in these circumstances that in January 1906, Cambon asked Grey whether the British Government would be prepared to render France armed assistance in the case of German aggression and whether it would sanction the continuation of military and naval talks. The reply of Grey was that although he could not give a definite reply without consulting his colleagues, his personal view was that if France was attacked by Germany on the question of Morocco, public opinion in England would be strongly moved in favour of France. The naval talks had already been done by Sir John Fisher himself and Grey assured Cambon that even military talks would take place on a satisfactory basis and it was actually done. While Grey encouraged the French to expect British help in the case of necessity, he reserved to himself the liberty of action.

Cambon quoted Grey that "in the event of an attack by Germany upon France, no British Government could remain neutral," but Grey pointed out that "a personal opinion was not a thing upon which, in so serious a matter, a policy could be founded." Much was to depend upon the manner in which a war broke out between France and Germany. While England was not prepared to fight against Germany to put France in possession of Morocco, the English public opinion would be in favour of helping France if she were attacked by Germany. To quote Grey, "Events might change, but as things are at present, I do not think it necessary to press the question of a defensive alliance."

It is true that Grey was favourably inclinel towards France but he was not prepared to enter into any formal agreement with France which might bind England to go to war. Such an agreement had to be sanctioned by Parliament and the latter might not be willing to do so. Moreover, such an agreement was bound to add to the hostility between France and Germany. The whole of the British

Cabinet might not approve of his view. Consequently, Grey left the whole thing in the melting pot and approved the holding of military and naval conversations between the military staffs of both the countries. These talks continued up to 1914 and the military preparations in both the countries were linked up with each other. The British and French officers thoroughly surveyed the grounds upon which their armies were to fight in Belgium and France. Sir Henry Wilson, Director of Military Operations, spent his holidays cycling on the ground where the war was likely to be fought. The whole wall of his London office was covered by a big map of Belgium. Ways and means were found out for putting the English armies on the French soil within as short a period as possible. The estimate was that within 12 days of declaration of war, English troops would be fighting in Europe.

Prof. Fay has condemned Grey for concealing the military and naval talks from the Cabinet for years. It was in 1912 that the British Cabinet came to know of them. The British Parliament and the public came to know of them in 1914. It is pointed out that that was not an honest way of doing things. Grey ought to have placed the whole matter before the Cabinet and not taken action in consultation with the Prime Minister alone. It is also maintained that the naval military talks committed England to come to the help of France although there was no definite pact to that effect between the two countries. The only justification of Grey was that he did everything in the best interests of his country and there was absolutely no dishonesty about what he did.

The Anglo-Russian Entente of 1907. During the 19th century, England followed a policy of splendid isolation and refused to commit herself in spite of the efforts made by Bismarck. However, by the end of the 19th century she came to realise that the policy of splendid isolation was not in her best interests and was another name for annihilation. It was this realisation that was responsible for the Anglo-Japanese alliance of 1902. It was with the same objective that the **Entente Cordiale** of 1904 was made with France and all the outstanding disputes between the two countries were amicably settled. Although the Entente of 1904 was not a military alliance, both the countries came nearer each other by the force of circumstances, and England backed France in 1906, 1908 and 1911 on the question of Morocco.

It is rightly pointed out that the Anglo-Russian Entente was a complement of die Anglo-French Entente. When Delcasse was in office, he did his utmost to bring Russia and England together. He felt that in the event of a war between England and Russia, French position would be very much weakened and even the utility of the Franco-Russian alliance of 1893 and the Entente Cordiale of 1904 would be very much lessened. France would be put in a very awkward position if her two partners quarrelled among themselves. No wonder when the Dogger Bank accident took place, Delcasse worked hard to bring about a settlement between Russia and Great Britain. In spite of the tense atmosphere prevailing in England against Russia, the matter was hushed up and the possibility of a war between England and Russia was avoided, Delcasse felt that in the event of a war between England and Russia, the latter might join Germany and thereby endanger the very existence of France. Russia had been weakened very much in the Russo-Japanese War and there was every possibility of a conflict between Russia and Japan in the future. Russia needed peace for a long time to put herself on her feet and that was possible only if England, the friend of Japan, "could be won over."

According to Taylor, "The Dogger Bank affair marked, indeed, the end of an epoch in European history—the epoch in which an Anglo-Russian conflict seemed the most likely outcome of international relations. This conflict had been expected in the Near East for fifty years, in Central Asia for twenty, and in the Far East, with the greatest likelihood of all for ten. After November 1904 the conflict was indefinitely postponed. The British has settled their differences with France: they had escaped war with Russia, Their security, and therewith their isolation from continental affairs, seemed at its height." (The Struggle for Mastery in Europe, p. 425).

It appears that during the Russo-Japanese War, Edward VII and Izvolski, who later became the Foreign Minister of Russia, discussed the question of Anglo-Russian relations and the possibility of rapprochement between the two countries. Both of them seem to have approved of the idea of an **Entente** between the two countries. It was felt by Russia that if she could end her disputes with Great Britain, she could pursue an active forward policy in the Balkans and also in the Far East. If there was an Anglo-Russians Entente and reconciliation with Japan; there could come into existence a quadruplicate combination stronger than that of the triplicate.

Both Edward VII and Sir Edward Grey were in favour of an understanding with Russia. The first Morocco crisis (1905-6) and the growing naval strength of Germany created a lot of anxiety in England and there was a genuine desire to come to an understanding with Russia so that in the event of a war with Germany, British position might not be weakened. Sir Charles Hardinge who had worked as British ambassador in Russia, was also a strong advocate of a friendly settlement with Russia. He exerted a lot of influence on Sir Edward Grey in favour of Russia. Sir Arthur Nicholson, the new British ambassador in Russia, also played an important part.

Negotiations started soon after Izvolski became Russia's Foreign Minister in May 1906. He admitted in October 1908 that such negotiations were going on. To begin with Russia was opposed to the partition of Persia into spheres of influence, but on account of the insistence in London, she had to give way. In March 1907, a Russian fleet visited Portsmouth. On the invitation of the British Government a deputation of Russian officers and sailors visited London and they were entertained as guests at the Admiralty. After the banquet, there was a gala performance which was attended by Sir John Fisher, First Lord of the Admiralty and Sir Edward Grey. This was an unusual thing.

The progress of negotiations was hampered by certain difficulties. It was difficult to reconcile English liberalism and Russian autocracy. Both the Czar and the Russian reactionaries and militarists were opposed to an understanding with England and Izvolski had to face great difficulties. The Liberal press of England condemned Russian pogroms and the reactionary and oppressive character of the Czarist regime. In spite of this, difficulties were overcome on account of the sincere efforts on both sides.

Another cause of delay was the British desire to bring Russia and Japan together. It was felt that there must be a satisfactory reconciliation between Japan and Russia on the question of China. An Anglo-Russian Entente was of no use if the two friends of Great Britain were to fight with each other. So great was the interest taken by the British Government with regard to the Russia-Japanese negotiations that they were actually concluded before an Anglo-Russian agreement was made on 31 August 1907.

The Anglo-Russian Convention of 1907 dealt with Tibet, Afghanistan and Persia. As regards **Tibet**, both England and Russia recognised the sovereignty of China and agreed not to interfere in her internal affairs or get any concessions there. The land of the Lamas was to remain a barrier between the Russian bears and the British lions.

As regards **Afghanistan,** Great Britain promised not to annex it and Russia pledged herself not to interfere with the affairs of Afghanistan. Russia declared Afghanistan outside the sphere of her influence. She withdrew her diplomatic agents from Herat. She agreed to deal with Afghanistan only through the British authorities. There were to be no more intrigues in Afghanistan either by England or by Russia.

As regards **Persia,** both England and Russia agreed to respect the territorial integrity and independence of Persia, but at the same time the country was divided into three regions. In the North, Russia was to have her own sphere of influence and in the South Great Britain was to have her own sphere of influence. Between these two spheres of influence, a central new region was created in which neither England nor Russia was to get any concession. It is to be noted that the King of Persia was not consulted with regard to the settlement concerning Persia and the treatment of the King of Persia was the subject of a cartoon in the Punch in which the British lion and the Russian bear were shown mauling between them an unhappy Persian cat. The lion said to the bear: "Look here. You can play with his head and I can play with his tail and we can both strike the small of his back." The cat merely said: "I don't remember having been consulted about this."

According to Grey, England made a better bargain than Russia. To quote him, "What we gained by it was real—what was gained by Russia was apparent." However, Prof. Fay does not agree with this view. His view is that Russia was the gainer while England was not. Although England gained peace of mind with regard to her Indian frontiers, she otherwise lost a lot. She lost independent action in Persia and although Grey protested on many occasions, he could not check Russia. On one occasion, he was prepared even to resign. The Russians took advantage of the British fear of Germany and consequent reliance on Russia. The Russian attitude was put in a nutshell by Sazonov in these words: "The London Cabinet looks upon the Anglo-Russian Convention of 1907 as being important for the Asiatic interests of England, but this Convention possesses a still greater importance for England from the viewpoint of the policy which is being pursued by England in Europe....... The English, engaged in the pursuit of political aims of vital importance in Europe, may, in case of necessity, be prepared to sacrifice certain interests in Asia in order to keep a Convention alive which is of such importance to them. This is a circumstance which we can, of course, exploit for ourselves, as, for instance, in Persian affairs."

According to Professor Fay, "Though Izvolski hoped that the Triple Entente would give him greater freedom of action in the Near East and Middle East, and though the French counted on it in the same way in Morocco, so far as England was concerned it aimed at the preservation of peace through the establishment of a balance of power. It was insurance against the supposed danger of possible German aggression and not for any aggression against Germany's existing position in Europe and in the commercial world. But to German eyes, it had a more ominous and irritating appearance."

Although all the terms of the Anglo-Russian convention were made public and there was no military obligation of any kind between the parties, both Russia and England came nearer each other with the passage of time. It was felt that the danger of Germany was so great that they must forget their minor differences. It was this Entente which brought England and Russia on the side of France in the war of 1914-18.

Ketelbey says that the Anglo-Russian Convention completed the entente of Great Britain with the Dual Alliance. In the words of Lord Oxford, "It put an end once and for all to the Russian 'menace to India' which had haunted the minds of British statesmen and diplomats—even of those who used the largest maps—for generations." There could be no objection to the composing of the long-standing quarrels between England and France and England and Russia, but opinion is seriously divided on the question how far Great Britain was wise to abandon her diplomatic isolation. No military alliance was involved in the Anglo-Russian Convention, no menace was implied to Germany and it could only be regarded as a defensive combination against the Central Powers. It gave the greatest security to France. It heartened her chauvinists. It encouraged her revanche policy. The people of France looked to the recovery of Alsace-Lorraine with eagerness and the Convention created new hopes in that direction. Although Russia could not with certainty count on British support, the understanding gave her greater security. Checked in Asia, Russia was awakened again to her interests in the Balkans and her rivalry there with Austria. It strengthened Great Britain in her bitter naval competition with Germany. Germany was very much upset by this Convention. In that country there was something like a scare which produced a sort of hysteria among the Pan-Germans, Navy-Leaguers and Prussian Generals. It is not that Germany feared Great Britain although she began to hate her for her successful imperialism and her "traditional policy of opposing whatever Continental Power was for the time being the strongest." What she feared was the effect of Britain's support upon France in Alsace-Lorrain and upon Russia in the Balkans. To quote Bethmann Hollweg, "England was well aware that the eyes of France were steadfastly fixed upon Alsace-Lorraine and could hear the deep notes of the revanche motif sounding, evening through the harmonies of the Russo-French fraternization." Again, "The general tension throughout the world originated, indeed, in the certainty of English support enjoyed by a Franco-Russian policy through whose ultimate objects we were endangered." Ketelbey maintains that it was from this time that Germany began to bring forward against Great Britain and particularly against King Edward VII, the repeated charge of "encirclement", a deliberate policy of surrounding Germany with a combine of hostile nations—France, Russia, Great Britain, Japan by affiliation, and Italy by seduction from the Triple Alliance.

The Haldane Mission, 1912. Lord Haldane, British Minister of War, went on a mission to Berlin with a view to arriving at some settlement with the German Government. The main object of the mission was to lessen the tension between the two countries arising out of naval competition. The relations between the two countries were so much strained that it was felt that unless something was done at once, the two countries might be dragged into a war against each other. Count Metternich, the German Ambassador in England, was unhappy at the mutual misunderstandings and recriminations between the two countries. English public opinion demanded that the British Government must insist upon the "Two-Power Standard." This meant that the English Navy was to be as strong as the combined navies of any other two Powers. The view of Metternich was that the fundamental cause of the alarm and agitation was the enormous growth of the German Navy and there was the necessity and desirability of slowing down the German programme of construction of her ships. Bulow himself was in favour of arriving at some understanding on the question of the navy, but Admiral Tirpitz, German Navy Minister, was not prepared to arrive at any settlement which aimed at reducing the German Navy or retarding its growth.

Mr. McKenna, First Lord of the Admiralty, also proposed that England would build six Dreadnoughts a year against the four Dreadnoughts of Germany. There was a strong feeling in England that Germany was trying to steal a march over England and consequently there was a demand that eight Dreadnoughts should be built instead of six as proposed by McKenna. The popular cry was: "We want eight and we won't wait."

As the situation was deteriorating, two persons played an important part to bring together the two countries and remove the points of conflict. Those persons were Ballin and Cassel. Ballin was the head of the Hamburg-American Line, and his view was that the main cause of Anglo-German animosity was the rapid growth of the German Navy. Ballin had friendly relations with William II, the German Chaneellor and Tirpitz. Sir Ernest Cassel was a London banker who was born in Germany. He had great influence with Edward VII and the big business of England. In 1909, Ballin and Cassel met to find our ways and means of bringing about an understanding between the two countries. In the winter of 1911-2, Ballin met Cassel and the latter met Sir Edward Grey. In January 1912, Cassel went to Berlin with a memorandum which had been approved by the important members of the British Cabinet. That memorandum was to serve as the basis of the negotiations and its text was as follows:—

"1. Fundamental. Naval superiority recognized as essential to Great Britain. Present German naval programme and expenditure not to be increased, but if possible retarded and reduced."

"2. England sincerely desires not to interfere with German colonial expansion. To give effect to this she is prepared forthwith to discuss whatever the German aspirations in that direction may be. England will be glad to know that there is a field or special points where she can help Germany."

"3. Proposals for reciprocal assurance debarring either Power from joining in aggressive designs or combinations against the other would be welcomed."

Cassel met the German Chancellor and showed him the memorandum. The view of the German Chancellor was that it would be best if Sir Edward Grey visited Berlin to conduct the negotiations. Cassel returned to England and communicated what had transpired.

Sir Edward Grey was not willing to go to Berlin and he had his own reasons for it. His view was that his visit to Berlin was bound to create distrust and suspicions in France and thereby weaken the **Entente** which the British Government was not prepared to do. This was particularly so because the British Government had decided to withdraw the British ships from the Mediterranean and replace them by the French ships. Grey also believed that if the negotiations failed, there was every possibility of the German Government putting all the blame on him. His fear was that the whole plan might be "one of those petty unofficial manoeuvres that could be avowed or disavowed at Berlin as best might suit German convenience." His feeling was that nothing would come out of the talks because the German Government had already decided to increase her navy and the public opinion in England would not tolerate a deal with Germany particularly when the British Government was to spend more and more on the development of her navy. To quote Grey, "The mutual arrest or decrease of naval expenditure is the test of whether an understanding is worth anything."

Ultimately, it was decided to send Lord Haldane to Berlin. His visit was to be private and informal so that if nothing came out of it, there might be no sensation or disappointment among the public. Haldane was required "to find out whether Germany's recent overture was serious or not. He was also to attempt to gather information about the Baghdad Railway. But there is no question of entering upon negotiations. We desire only to learn the intention of the German Government and to enquire about its plan for naval programme." This points out to the restricted scope of the mission.

On the day of the arrival of Haldane in Berlin, William II declared that projects for the increase of the German Navy and Army would be introduced in the next session of the Reichstag. Mr. Churchill's reply was in these words: "The British Navy is to us a necessity and, from some points of view, the German Navy is to them more in the nature of luxury......We shall make it clear that other naval Powers instead of overtaking us by additional efforts will only be more outdistanced in consequence of the measure which we ourselves shall take." The speeches of William II and Churchill were not favourable to the success of Haldane's mission.

Lord Haldane was given a good welcome in Berlin. He felt that the German Chancellor was very sincere to avoid a war. He told William II and Tirpitz that England was determined to build two ships for every ship built by Germany. As the question of the Navy seemed to be difficult William II suggested that other questions like colonies might be settled first and then the question of navy might be tackled. Bethmann, the German Chancellor, was asked by William II to prepare a formal draft for a settlement between the two countries. The formal draft prepared by the German Chancellor read as follows :—

I. "The High Contracting Powers assure each other mutually of their desire of peace and friendship.

II. "They will not, either of them, make any combination, or join in any combination, which is directed against the other. They expressly declare that they are not bound by any such combination.

III. "If either of the High Contracting Parties becomes entangled in a war with one or more other Powers, the other of the High Contracting Parties will at least observe towards the Power so entangled a benevolent neutrality, and use its utmost endeavour for the localisation of the conflict.

IV. "The duty of neutrality which arises from the preceding Article has no application in so far as it may not be reconcilable with existing agreements which the High Contracting Powers have already made. The making of new agreements which make it impossible for either of the Contracting Parties to observe neutrality towards the other beyond what is provided by the preceding limitation is excluded in conformity with the provision contained in Article II."

Lord Haldane proposed the following modifications in Articles II and III of the draft :—

II. "They will not either of them make or prepare to make any unprovoked attack upon the other, or join in any combination or design against the other for purposes of aggression, or become party to any plan or naval or military enterprise alone or in combination with any other power directed to such an end."

III. "If either of the High Contracting Parties becomes entangled in a war with one or more other Powers, in which it cannot be said to be the aggressor, the other of the High Contracting Parties will at least observe towards the Power so entangled a benevolent neutrality and use its utmost endeavour for the localisation of the conflict."

Lord Haldane came back to England with a draft of the proposed German Navy Law. The same was handed over to the Admiralty Department, and after a thorough study and discussion the British Government forwarded a memorandum to Berlin. Germany did not approve of the British memorandum and was indignant that the British Government was putting forward very unreasonable proposals. William II did not like the attitude of the British Government, but both the German Chancellor and the Foreign Minister persisted that another effort should be made to arrive at a settlement with England. William II overruled the Chancellor and directed the German Ambassador in London to inform the British Government that he was determined to get his Navy Law passed through the legislature. He warned the British Government that if it withdrew its ships from the Mediterranean and concentrated them in the North Sea, that was to be considered as a threat of war. Although the German Chancellor resigned, yet he was persuaded by William II to continue in office. Tirpitz was able ultimately to carry his point by a threat of resignation. The net result was that William II agreed to act according to the advice of Tirpitz and not that of the Chancellor.

Seeing the attitude of the German Government, Churchill placed before the British Parliament the British Navy Estimates which provided for two keels to every additional German keel. The negotiations were abandoned as hopeless on 29 March 1912. The German Navy law was passed by the Reichstag on 14 May 1912. Thus ended the Haldane mission to Germany.

According to Prof. Fay, two causes were responsible for the failure of the Haldane mission. One cause was that the British Government was not prepared to let down the French Government in case France was attacked by Germany. Grey was prepared to go to any length to remove the fear of France that she may not be helped in the event of a German attack. He was prepared to wreck the talks with Germany rather than create any doubt in the minds of the French statesmen. If such was the attitude of the British Government, the German Government insisted that Great Britain must declare that she would not help France and remain neutral. Another cause of the failure of the mission was that the German Government was not prepared to compromise on the question of the German Navy. While Germany was determined to increase her navy, Great Britain was equally determined to maintain her naval superiority. Under the circumstances, there was no scope for any compromise and no wonder the mission failed in spite of the sincere efforts of certain persons.

Encirclement of Germany. A reference may be made to the so-called encirclement of Germany by the **Entente** Powers. It is well known that in the time of Bismarck, Germany was the arbiter of Europe, but things changed after his resignation in 1890. There was a stage when England was anxious to enter into an alliance with Germany. However, that stage was over in 1901 when William II gave an evasive reply to a definite British proposal for an alliance between the two countries. It was then that Great Britain entered into an alliance with Japan in 1902. In 1904, the Entente Cordiale was made with France. The Anglo-Russian Convention of 1907 brought Russia and England together. At the same time, the differences between Russia and Japan were amicably settled through the good offices of the British Government.

Germany was faced with a new situation and she felt that Great Britain had strengthened her position to such an extent that her position had become comparatively weak. Although outwardly she did not show any signs of nervousness, she felt at heart that the Triple **Entente** was stronger than the Triple Alliance both in economic resources and military and naval strength. Germany felt that her progress was checked in every quarter by the **Entente** Powers. On subjects like Alsace-Lorraine, Morocco, naval competition, the Berlin-Baghdad Railway, etc., one or the other **Entente** Power was opposed to Germany. Even in the case of the Balkans, there was a conflict between Russia and Austria for domination and if Austria was involved in a war, Germany was likely to be dragged into the same. In such an eventuality, Germany was either to surrender or fight and neither of the two alternatives was a happy one. Although both Russia and England protested that the Anglo-Russian Convention of 1907 was not aimed against Germany, the latter was not satisfied. It appeared to Germany that all the **Entente** Powers were opposed to her and she was actually being encircled by them.

The bitterness was intensified on the question of the Berlin-Baghdad Railway. Russia was opposed to the project for political, economic and strategic reasons. Delcasse was opposed to the project on account of the French alliance with Russia. He went to the extent of disallowing the bonds of the Baghdad Railway to be quoted on the Pairs Bourse. The British Government opposed the project as that was likely to affect adversely the British interests in Mesopotamia and the Persian Gulf and also endanger the safety of the British Empire in India. The Germans completed a part of the railway in 1904 but they found their further progress blocked on account of the opposition of the Entente Powers. Germany was prepared to give up her claims in Morocco if France supported the Berlin-Baghdad railway project. This France refused to do. The British Government demanded either the internationalisation of the whole of the project or British control over the Railway from Baghdad to the Persian Gulf. Germany felt that she could not oblige England up to that extent and the bitterness continued to increase. The naval competition between Germany and England forced Sir John Fisher to follow a "ruthless and remorseless" policy. Great Britain was determined to maintain her naval supremacy and William II was equally determined to beat England on that point. There was no possibility of a compromise and that is amply proved by the following statement of William II: "Count Metternich must be informed that good relations with England at the price of the building of German Navy are not desired by him. If England intends graciously to extend us her hand only with the intimation that we must limit our fleet, this is a groundless impertinence which involves a heavy insult to the German people and their Kaiser, which must be rejected in limine by the Ambassador. France and Russia might with equal reason then demand a limitation of our land armaments. The German fleet is not built against any one and not against England, but according to our need. This is stated quite clearly in the Navy Law and for 11 years has remained unchanged. This Law will be carried out to the last iota; whether it suits the British or not, is no matter. If they want war, they can begin it; we do not fear it." In a speech to the German officers, William II gave expression to his inner feeling in these words: "A strong navy, a strong army and powder dry."

William II was himself determined to make Germany the strongest power in the world. That could be done only if he was able to defeat Great Britain and her allies. William II believed in a policy **"World Power or Downfall"** and was prepared to go to any extent to achieve that objective. If he himself was prepared to defeat everybody, he ought not to have grumbled when his potential victims joined hands to offer joint resistance. There was no encirclement of Germany as such. What actually happened was that William II felt that the realisation of his ambitions was blocked on account of the combined opposition of the **Entente** Powers. Prof. Fay made the following observations on this point: "The effect on Germany of England's opposition to the Baghdad Railway, of her efforts to limit the German Navy, entry of England into a Triple Entente was to produce a conviction that Germany was being encircled. Germans believed that this encirclement was Edward VII's personal work and that it aimed at strangling German commercial and colonial expansion, and even at crushing Germany's political and military position. There is no substantial evidence that there was any deliberate encirclement with such aims on the part of King Edward or the British Government. Such notions were the product of German imagination, fear and suspicion."

Rivalry between Triple Alliance and Triple Entente. Between 1907 and 1914, there was a keen rivalry between the Triple **Entente** and the Triple Alliance. While Germany tried to strengthen the Triple Alliance, Poincare tried to tighten and strengthen the Triple **Entente** and the latter was more successful than the former. Although the Triple Alliance was renewed in 1907 and 1912, it became weaker and weaker on account of many causes. There were troubles within Austria herself. She was also too much entangled in the Balkan politics. There was distrust between Austria and Italy on account of "unredeemed Italy". The Italians were determined to get back the Italian-speaking territories under the control of Austria. As Austria was not prepared to oblige Italy, there was no genuine co-operation between them. Moreover, both Austria and Italy were rivals in the Balkans and both of them were determined to control the Adriatic Sea. All these factors weakened the effectiveness of the Triple Alliance. Italy entered into an agreement with France in 1902 and with Russia in 1909. She voted with France against Germany on the occasion of the Algeciras Conference.

On the other hand, the Triple **Entente** was positively much stronger. The conflicting interests among the Powers were reconciled. Moreover, they were prepared to ignore petty differences for the sake of higher objects. The naval and military staff talks between England and France and Russia and France pooled together the resources of the **Entente** Powers. The **Entente** Powers were cautious to avoid any doubt or suspicion among the partners, Grey was prepared to allow the Haldane mission to fail rather than create any suspicion in France. He supported France wholeheartedly on the question of Morocco and was prepared even to risk a war with Germany.

Europe was divided into armed camps, one represented by the Triple Entente and the other by the Triple Alliance. Every effort was made to lessen friction and suspicion and increase harmony, solidarity, and security of the camp. Sometimes, "blank cheques" were given by one ally to another. Sometimes, assurances of "complete fulfilment of the obligations of the alliance" were given. Regarding his interview in 1913 with William II, Berchtold, the Austrian Foreign Minister, observed thus: "As often as opportunity offered during one hour and a quarter's talk to touch upon our relations as Allies, His Majesty ostentatiously used the occasion to assure me that we could count absolutely and completely upon him. This was the red thread that ran through the utterances of the illustrious sovereign. His Majesty did me the honour to say that whatever came from the Vienna Foreign Office was a command for him." The allies were coming to rely more and more on the support of one another. There was feverish activity for the growth of military and **naval armaments**. That led to suspicious and fears and that in turn gave an impetus to the race **of armaments. According** to Prof. Schmitt, **"In 1907 the Triple Alliance and the Triple Entente had stood side by side; in 1914 they stood face to face."** According to Grant and Temperley, "This remarkable arrangement of international checks and balances for a long time preserved peace among the peoples, but by the very fact of its existence ultimately engendered strife. For the system was one of competing alliances, not of a universal league. It was a Balance, not a Concert, of Power. As one combination strengthened or developed its growth alarmed other States outside its orbit and mechanically produced a counter-combination. Competing alliances produced competing armaments, and the rivalry of hatred and of fear ended in the two opposed groups carrying their competition to the battlefield." According to J.A. Spender, "The stage which Europe had reached was that of a semi-internationalism which organised the nations into two groups but provided no bridge between them. There could scarcely have been worse conditions for either peace or war. The equilibrium was so delicate that a puff of wind might destroy it..." According to Lord Oxford, "We were often conscious that we were skating on the thinnest of ice and that the peace of Europe was at the mercy of a chapter of unforeseen and unforeseeable accidents." That accident took place on 28 June 1914 when Archduke Francis Ferdinand was murdered by the Serbians and that led to World War I.

SUGGESTED READINGS

Albrecht-Carrie, R.: **A Diplomatic History of Europe since the Congress of Vienna,** 1958.

Brandenberg: **From Bismarck to the World War,** 1927.

Coolidge, A.G. : **The Origins of the Triple Alliance.**

Dickinson, G. Lowes: **The International Anarchy (1904-14), 1926.**

Fay: **Origins of the World War.**

Gooch, G.P.: **Franco-German Relations, 1871-1914.**

Gooch, G.P.: **History of Modern Europe (1878-1919).**

Gooch, G.P.: **Recent Revelations on European Diplomacy.**

Grey, Lord : **Twenty-Five Years.**

Langer, W.L.: **Diplomacy of Imperialism (1890-1902).**

Langer, W.L.: **The Franco-Russian Alliance.**

Lippmann : **Stakes of Diplomacy.**

Mansergh, N.: **The Coming of the First World War (1871-1914), 1949.**

Michon, G.: **The Franco-Russian Alliance (1891-1917), 1929.**

Renouvin, P.: **The Immediate Origins of the War, 1928.**

Rohrbach: **Germany's Isolation, 1915.**

Seton-Watson, R.W.: **Britain in Europe, 1789-1914, 1937.**

Sontag, R.J.: **European Diplomatic History (1871-1932), 1933.**

Spender, J.A.: **Fifty Years of Europe, 1936.**

Taylor, A.J.P.: **The Struggle for Mastery in Europe (1848-1918),** 1954.

CHAPTER 30

THE WORLD WAR - I (1914-18)

Causes of the War. (1) The World War I was due to many causes and the most important cause was the system of secret alliances. Before 1914, Europe was divided into two armed camps. In 1879, Germany had entered into an alliance with Austria-Hungary. In 1882, Italy joined the Austro-German Alliance and thus came into existence what is known as the Triple Alliance. As a result of the efforts of Bismarck, France and Russia had not been able to come together. However, after his dismissal in 1890, Germany did not care for Russia and consequently, Russia began to lean towards France. Many other factors also brought the two countries together. Thus in 1894 was made the Franco-Russian Alliance. Things remained in this condition for some time.

Although England had followed a policy of splendid isolation during the 19th century, she began to feel that she was all alone. She began to fear the consequences of being alone in the world. To begin with, she tried to enter into an alliance with Germany. When she failed to do so, she entered into an alliance with Japan in 1902. In 1904 was made the **Entente Cordiale** between England and France. When in 1907 England signed the Anglo-Russian Convention with Russia, there came into existence what is known as the Triple **Entente.** Germany won over Turkey to her own side. Thus, Europe was divided into two camps. In one camp were England, France, Russia and Japan. In the other camp were Germany, Austria-Hungary, Turkey and Italy. There was not only jealousy but also enmity between the two camps. It was the mutual hatred created by the system of secret alliances which ultimately brought about the War of 1914. The importance of the secret alliances in bringing about the War can be explained thus: It all came from this D—D system of alliances, which was the curse of modern times."

(2) Another cause of the war was militarism. This means the dangerous and burdensome mechanism of great standing armies and large navies along with an espionage system. It also means the existence of a powerful class of military and naval officers headed by the General Staff. It is these people who dominated the affairs of the countries particularly at the time of crises. The military and naval armaments of all the Great Powers began to grow year after year. These armaments were alleged to be for defence and in the interests of peace. They were intended to produce a sense of security. However, their actual result was that there was universal fear, suspicion and hatred among the various nations. This is amply proved by the naval competition between Germany and England. Both countries entered into a race of naval armaments. For every ship built by Germany, two ships were built by England. Such a race could end only in a war. Moreover, militarism put too much of power into the lands of the General Staff of every country. That was not conducive to the maintenance of peace.

(3) Another cause of war was narrow nationalism or competitive patriotism. The love of one's country demanded the hatred of the other. Love of Germany demanded the hatred of France and vice versa. It was, intense nationalism in Serbia which created bitterness between Serbia and Austria-Hungary. That was also responsible for the murder of Archduke Francis Ferdinand, the heir to the throne of Austria-Hungary, in 1914.

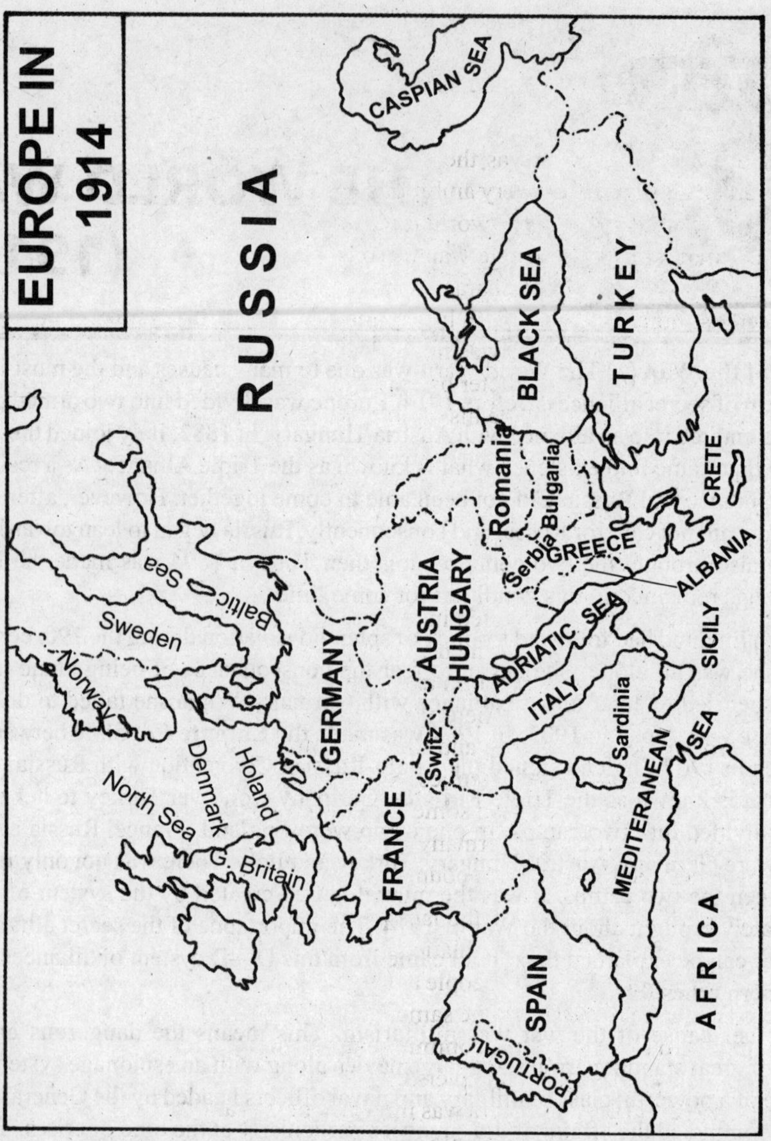

(4) Economic imperialism was also responsible for the war. Economic imperialism led to international rivalries. Every country tried to capture markets in every nook and corner of the world. That led to bitterness and heart-burning. The efforts to establish protectorates and spheres of influence in various parts of the world also resulted in bad blood among nations. When Germany tried to capture markets which were already in the hands of the English, that led to bitterness between the two countries. Great Britain was not prepared to give up her colonies, protectorates, spheres of influences and markets to humour Germany. As Germany was bent upon getting them at any cost, war followed. There were also tariff wars between the various countries. That also resulted in the worsening of the relations.

(5) Another cause of the war was the poisoning of the public opinion by the newspapers. Very often, newspapers in all countries tried to inflame nationalist feeling by misrepresenting the situation in other countries. Ambassadors and Cabinet ministers frequently admitted the senseless attitude of the leading newspapers in their own countries. They offered apologies and promised to put restraint on them if the other governments would do likewise. The newspapers of two countries often took

up some point of dispute, exaggerated it, and made attacks and counter-attacks until a regular newspaper war was created. According to Bismarck, "Every country is held at some time to account for the windows broken by its press; the bill is presented some day or other, in the shape of hostile sentiments in the other country."

(6) Another cause of the war was the character of William II, Emperor of Germany. He was very arrogant and haughty. He was very ambitious. He wanted Germany to be the strongest Power in the world. He believed in a policy of "world power or downfall." He was not prepared to make any compromise in international affairs. He wanted to have his own way in every case. He had formed a very poor opinion of the English character. His view was that Englishmen would accept all his demands rather than fight against him. In his estimate of the English nation, he was sadly mistaken. The British desire to maintain peace was not an indication of her cowardice or weakness. It was a misunderstanding of the British character by William II that was responsible for his attitude towards England and that mistake proved to be his undoing.

(7) Another cause of the war was the desire of the people of France to get back Alsace-Lorraine which had been snatched away from them in 1871 by Germany. The Government of the Third Republic in France left no stone unturned to keep alive the spirit of revenge and the hope for the restoration of the two provinces. The statue of Strasbourg in the Place de la Concorde in Paris reminded the Frenchmen of their lost territories "La derniere class" of Daudet brought forth tears from the eyes of the school children of France and created in them the spirit of revenge. Likewise, the songs of Paul Deroulede inculcated among the young men a feeling of revenge. There was also the economic motive for getting back Alsace-Lorraine. The iron and steel magnates of France felt that they could not do without the iron mines of Lorraine. There was a feeling that the industrial prosperity of Germany was due to the iron mines of Lorraine and the Frenchmen must have burnt their blood when they found the same in the hands of their enemies. It is pointed out that if Germany had not interfered in Morocco, Frenchmen might have found some material compensation for the loss of Alsace-Lorraine and forgotten their revenge against Germany but the German interference in the affairs of Morocco added to the bitterness between the two countries.

(8) Another cause of the war was the lack of any machinery to control international relations. There was anarchy in the international relations of the various countries. Everything was secret and nothing was known about them to the people at large. It was found that the secrets of diplomacy were not known even to all the members of the same ministry. Even the legislatures were kept completely in the dark with regard to international commitments. Although Sir Edward Grey allowed in January 1906 the holding of naval and military conversations between France and England, the Cabinet came to know of them in 1912 and the Parliament was informed of the same in 1914. Secret diplomacy created a lot of confusion in the minds of the people and thus the issues and responsibilities were beclouded. Hysteria took the place of sobriety and sincerity. Forgery, theft, lying, bribery and corruption existed in every Foreign Office and Chancellory throughout Europe.

(9) Although there was a "code of international law and morality", there was no power to enforce the same. Many resolutions were passed at the Hague Conferences of 1899 and 1907 but those were observed by the various States according to their convenience. Every State considered itself to be sovereign and did not regard itself to be bound by its international commitments. Although Italy was a member of the Triple Alliance, she entered into separate agreements with France in 1902 and Russia in 1909. She was prepared to have an extra dance with the members of the opposite camp.

(10) Another cause of the war was the permeation of Germany by the Prussian spirit. According to that spirit. "He who succeeds is never in the wrong." Victory was identified with morality. The Prussians were taught that war was the most logical thing in the world. According to Mirabeau, "War is the national industry of Prussia." According to Treitschke, the State is power. "The care for

its power is the highest moral duty of the State. Of all political weaknesses that of feebleness is the most abominable and despicable; it is the sin against the Holy Spirit of politics." To quote Nietzsche, "Ye say, a good cause will hallow even war. I say unto you...A good war hallows every cause. War and courage have accomplished greater things than love of their neighbour." The younger generation of Germany was indoctrinated with such a practical philosophy. Eminent historians like Dahlmann, Droyden, Sybel and Treitschke devoted their energy and learning to the task of justifying to the Germans the ways of Prussia. A similar effort was made by Bernhardi in his writings. To Bernhardi, "All which other nations attained in centuries of natural development—political union, colonial possessions, naval power, international trade—was denied to our nation only—quite recently. What we now wish to attain must be fought for and won, against a superior force of hostile interests and powers." According to Prof. Lamprecht, "After bloody victories the world will be heated by being Germanised." To quote Treitschke again. "Just as the greatness of Germany is to be found in the governance of Germany by Prussia, so the greatness and good of the world is to be found in the predominance of all German culture, of the German mind—in a word, of the German character."

(11) Another cause of the war was the desire of the people of Italy to recover the Trentino and the area around the port of Trieste which were inhabited by Italians but were still a part and parcel of Austria-Hungary. There was frequently heard the cry of **Italia Irredent**a or "unredeemed Italy" and even the Italian ministers participated in those demonstrations. Such cries were those of war and were not likely to maintain peace in Europe. Italy also entered into a competition with Austria to control the Adriatic Sea. As Austria was not prepared to put up with that competition, there was bound to be bitterness in the relations of the two countries.

(12) Another cause of the war was the "Near-Eastern Problem". Many factors complicated the situation in the Balkans. The misrule of Turkey resulted in discontentment. There was a rivalry between Greece, Serbia and Bulgaria for the control of Macedonia which had a mixed population. Russia was keenly interested in the Balkan politics and she backed Serbia on the occasion of the Bosnian crisis of 1908-9 and could be expected to do the same in future. The forces of Pan-Slavism added another factor into an otherwise complicated situation. The Austro-German **Drang nach Osten** or "Urge towards the East" made matters worse.

(13) The provinces of Bosnia and Herzegovina created another "Alsace-Lorraine" in the Balkans. These two provinces were given to Austria-Hungary by the Congress of Berlin of 1878. However, she was given the right merely to occupy and govern them and not to annex them. The sovereignty of the Sultan was maintained over them. However, Austria-Hungary annexed them in 1908 by her unilateral action. This brought forth bitter protests from Serbia. A strong agitation was started in Serbia to separate these provinces from Austria-Hungary and unite them with Serbia. The people of Bosnia and Herzegovina were more anxious for their independence from Austria-Hungary than for their union with Serbia. However, they were willing to accept help from Serbia in their efforts to become independent. After 1909, the rivalry between Austria-Hungary and Serbia in the Balkans became very keen and by 1914 it burst into a war.

(14) The immediate cause of the war was the murder of Archduke Ferdinand who was the heir to the Austrian throne. What actually happened was that there was going on rivalry between Austria-Hungary and Serbia in the Balkans. Its intensity increased after 1909. The Balkan Wars of 1912-13 added to the territory, population and resources of Serbia. She was flushed with victory. She had not forgotten her humiliation of 1909. Many secret societies had been set up to bring about the union of all the Slavs. The **"Black Hand"** or **"Union or Death"** Society planned to kill Oskar Potiorek, the Governor of Bosnia. The seal of the society showed a skull and cross-bones, a dagger, a bomb and bottle of poison. However, it came to be known at that time that Archduke Ferdinand was coming to Bosnia. Highly placed persons in the Serbian Government supplied weapons, munitions and instructors to the persons who were actually to carry out the murder. According to the plans, the Archduke and

his wife paid a visit to Sarajevo, a city of Bosnia, on 28 June 1914. Unfortunately, that was a day of mourning in Serbia as it commemorated the battle of Kossovo of 1389 in which the Serbians were defeated by the Turks and they lost their independence. When the official party was on the way to the Town Hall, one of the conspirators threw a bomb on the automobile of the Archduke. Somehow, the Archduke escaped and others were injured. The accused was captured and the official party reached the Town Hall. After finishing the ceremonies at the Town Hall, the party proceeded to visit the City Museum. Unfortunately, the automobile of the Archduke went into a wrong street and the driver had to back it. This gave an opportunity to another member of the gang who had come to kill the royal party. He came forward from the crowd and fired two shots point blank. The result was that both the Archduke and his wife were killed.

Austria-Hungary was already sick of Serbia and she decided to take advantage of the new situation to crush her. Germany promised to support Austria-Hungary. She did not give her any advice but merely gave her a blank cheque. The following passage occurs in the German White Book published on August 1, 1914: "It was clear to Austria that it was not compatible with the dignity and the spirit of self-preservation of the monarchy to view idly any longer this (Serbian) agitation across the border. The imperial and Royal Government apprised Germany of this conception and asked for our opinion. With all our heart we were able to agree with our ally's estimate of the situation, and assure him that any action considered necessary to end the movement in Serbia directed against the conservation of the monarchy would meet with our approval.

"We were perfectly aware that a possible warlike attitude of Austria-Hungary against Serbia might bring Russia upon the field and that it might therefore involve us in a war, in accordance with our duty as allies. We could not, however, in these vital interests of Austria-Hungary, which were at stake, advise our ally to take a yielding attitude not compatible with his dignity, nor deny him our assistance in these trying days. We could do this all the less as our own interests were menaced through the continued Serb agitation. If the Serbs continued with the aid of Russia and France to menace the existence of Austria-Hungary, the gradual collapse of Austria and the subjection of all the Slavs under one Russian sceptre would be the consequence, thus making untenable the position of the Teutonic race in Central Europe. A morally weakened Austria under the pressure of Russian pan-Slavism would be no longer an ally on whom we could count and in whom we could have confidence, as we must be able to have, in view of the ever more menacing attitude of our easterly and westerly neighbours. **We, therefore, permitted Austria a completely free hand in her action towards Serbia,** but have not participated in her preparations."

To begin with, Austria was in favour of having a local war but as time passed on the situation became all the more grave. If Austria wanted to finish Serbia, the same was the attitude of Serbia towards Austria. The attitude and utterances of Serbian officials and newspapers were "downright intolerable". Austria gave an ultimatum to Serbia. The Russian Foreign Minister, Sazonov, told the Serbian Ambassador in Russia that **"Russia would in no circumstances permit Austrian aggression against Serbia."** This gave encouragement to Serbia and she refused to accept in full the Austrian demands.

In most of the countries, the reply of Serbia was considered to be reasonable. Even William II felt that the reply removed "every reason for war." Austria was asked to try mediation but instead of doing so, she declared war on Serbia on 28 July, 1914. Serbia herself welcomed war and even before sending her reply had already ordered general mobilization.

Great Britain and Germany tried to localize the war but it was soon found that matters had gone out of their hands. President Poincare of France visited Russia from 20 July to 23 July 1914 and promised French help to Russia against Austria. To quote him, "Serbia has very warm friends in the Russian people and Russia has an ally, France."

When Russia ordered general mobilization on 23 July 1914, Germany sent an ultimatum demanding demobilization within 12 hours. As Russia refused to accept that ultimatum, Germany declared war on Russia. According to Prof. Fay, "It was primarily Russia's general mobilization when Germany was trying to bring Austria to a settlement, which precipitated the final catastrophe, causing Germany to mobilize and declare war."

It is pointed out that although Sir Edward Grey tried to maintain peace, he did not follow the right course to achieve the same. He might have prevented the war by frankly telling Germany that if she attacked France or Russia, Great Britain would fight against her. A similar result might have been secured if he had told France and Russia that if they insisted on war, Great Britain would remain neutral. However, Grey did not adopt either of the two courses. On account of differences in the British Cabinet, he did not support Russia and France whole-heartedly. Although Grey maintained that England was not committed to help any country, he was not telling the whole truth because the military conversations between England and France had committed the two countries to each other. Grey may not have been in favour of joining war but if a war was actually to come, he was ready to join hands with Russia and France. The public in England was opposed to the participation of Great Britain in a war which was over a Balkan question. However, Germany ordered her troops to march into Belgium. That was in violation of the International Treaty of 1839 by which Belgium had been guaranteed neutrality and England was one of the signatories to that Treaty. The King of Belgium resisted and Great Britain also came to his help. Thus Great Britain also joined the World War I in August 1914.

In the war that followed, Serbia was supported by Russia and France and France was supported by England. Japan also joined them. Although Italy was a member of the Triple Alliance, she did not declare war on the side of Austria-Hungary and Germany. She remained neutral for a year and then she declared war against Austria and Germany. Turkey declared war against the Allies and fought on the side of the Central Powers.

Course of War. Although England joined the war on the plea that Germany had violated the neutrality of Belgium, the latter could not be saved. The German steam roller was able to smash the resistance of the people of Belgium. Then came the turn of France. There was bitter fighting on the French soil. The Battle of Marne is a memorable one for trench warfare. The Battle of Verdun decided the fortunes of the war in favour of the Allies. Germany started submarine warfare on a large scale and nothing was spared on the seas. All laws relating to naval warfare were thrown to the winds. Only the principle of victory at any price was pursued.

Russia fought on the side of the Allies up to 1917 when a revolution took place in that country. The Czarist regime was overthrown and power was ultimately captured by Lenin and his followers. The Bolshevist regime in Russia wanted peace and consequently it came to terms with Germany and thus the Treaty of Brest Litvosk was signed between Germany and Russia.

After the defection of Russia in 1917, the position of Germany became very strong. The drives of Hindenburg and Ludendorff carried everything before them. It appeared as if the Allies were going to lose. However, the U.S.A. came to their help. The **Lusitania,** an American ship, was torpedoed by a German submarine and consequently many Americans lost their lives. There was a lot of resentment in the U.S.A. and that enabled President Wilson to declare war against Germany.[1] Fresh troops began to pour into Europe from the U.S.A. In spite of her best efforts, Germany could not stand and ultimately she surrendered in November 1918.

---

1. Regarding the aims of the United States in fighting the war, President Wilson declared thus : "We shall fight for the things which we have always carried nearest to our hearts—for democracy, for the right of those who submit to authority to have a voice in their own government, for the rights and liberties of small nations, for a universal domination of right by such a concert of free peoples as shall bring peace and safety to all nations and make the world itself at last free."

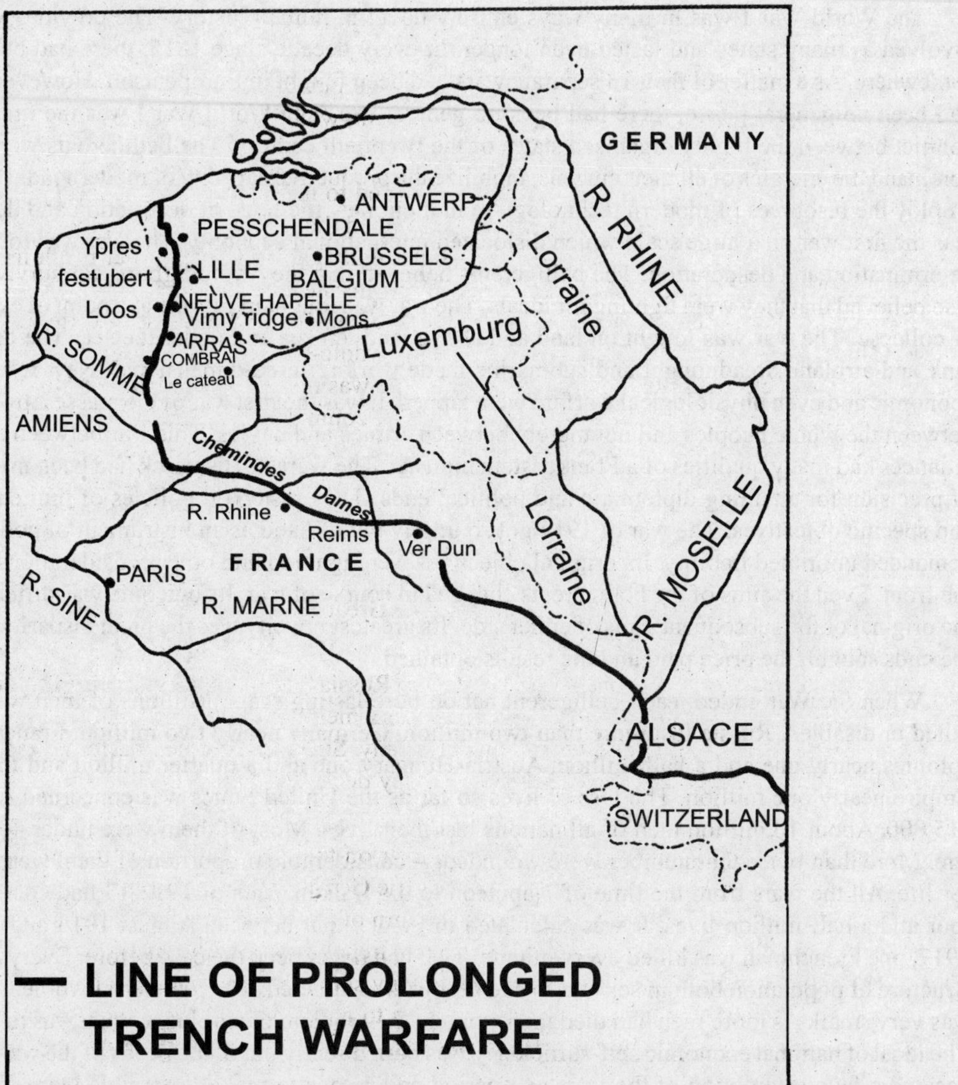

Turkey also fought on the side of the Central Powers. It is true that she had initial success and the Allies met with reverses particularly in Mesopotamia and Gallipoli, but ultimately Turkey was defeated and she also had to surrender.

Japan declared war against the Central Powers in 1914 and she was able to capture the province of Kai-Chow and the German concessions in the province of Shantung. Although China also joined the Allies, she was presented with 21 demands by Japan. The European Powers were entangled in a life and death struggle and consequently Japan was able to have her own way. Most of her demands were conceded and China virtually came under the control of Japan. It is true that there was bitterness in China, but the position of Japan was vindicated even at the Paris Conference in 1919.

The spirit in which the war was fought, is described thus:—

There is but one task for all
One life for each to give.
What stands if Freedom falls?
Who dies if England lives?

The World War I was in many ways entirely novel in human history. The previous wars had involved as many states and lasted even longer. In every decade since 1815, there had been a war somewhere. As a matter of fact, 13 separate wars had been fought in Europe itself. However, if there had been no general peace, there had been no general war. The World War I was the first general conflict between the highly organised states of the twentieth century. The belligerents were able to command the energies of all their citizens, mobilize the productive capacity of modern industries, and employ the resources of modern technology to find out new methods of destruction and defence. It was the first war on a large scale which dislocated international economy. The war was fought with determination and desperation. The belligerents believed that they were fighting for survival. They also believed that they were fighting for ideals. The war was fought in Europe to a point of exhaustion or collapse. The war was fought on land and above land, on sea and under the sea. The coming of tank and airplane dreadnought and submarine made warfare three-dimensional. New resources of economic and even physiological warfare were tapped. It was the first war of the masses. It was a war between the whole peoples and not merely between armies and navies. This war between the grand alliances had many qualities of a Frankenstein monster. The wars of Bismarck had been instruments of precision for attaining diplomatic and political ends. They rested on policies of limited liability and specific objectives. The war of 1914 got so utterly out of hand as an instrument of policy that it demanded unlimited liability. Its original objectives were ignored and other considerations came to the front. Even the aims of the belligerents changed in course of war. Its outcome was different from the original or the subsequent aims of either side. Its greatest novelty was the great disparity between the ends sought, the price paid and the results obtained.

When the War ended, each belligerent nation bore lasting scars. Millions of men were either killed or disabled. Russia lost more than two million, Germany nearly two million, France and her colonies nearly one and a half million, Austria-Hungary one and a quarter million and the British Empire nearly one million. The loss of lives so far as the United States was concerned was about 115,000. About 10 million men of all nations lost their lives. Most of them were under 40 years of age. More than twice that number were wounded. A considerable proportion of them were maimed for life. All the wars from the time of Napoleon to the Balkan Wars of 1912-13 had cost less than four and a half million lives. It was calculated in France that between August 1914 and February 1917, one Frenchman was killed every minute. That had never been the case before. Everywhere the structure of population both in sex and in age groups was affected. The number of women who died was very small. As more men had died than women, the problem of surplus women was to be faced. The ideal of national economic self-sufficiency was born directly out of the needs of the war. Autarky became a favourite notion of the inter-war period and means to make it possible were discovered during the war. To make explosives, Fritz Haber perfected the process of extracting nitrogen from the air because nitrates could no longer be imported from Chile, Cellulose was invented in the laboratory as a substitute for cotton. Further research in that direction resulted in a series of new industries making rayons and plastics and synthetic materials. The occupied territories of Europe suffered very much. As Belgium was a battlefield, there was great destruction there. The economy of the country was wrecked. Its cities were ruined. Many of its people became refugees or deportees or prisoners of war. When the Russians were driven out of Polish territory, the Germans behaved as liberators. Many Poles preferred German rule to Russian rule.

Peace Settlement (1919-20). After the overthrow of Germany, Austria-Hungary and Turkey, the Allied statesmen met at Paris to decide the future map of Europe. The choice of Paris as the venue of the Conference was not a happy one. That was due to the fact that a lot of fighting and destruction had taken place in the neighbourhood of Paris and unhappy memories and associations were bound to have their effect on the conclusions of the Conference. It would have been better if some other suitable place in Switzerland had been chosen for that purpose. However, the Conference met at

Paris and President Wilson, Lloyd George, Glemenceau and Orlando played a very important part in the deliberations of the Conference. The work of negotiation was not an easy one. Germany had surrendered on the basis of Fourteen Points of President Wilson, but those could not be made the basis of the settlement. They had to be adjusted to fit in with the secret treaties among the Allies regarding the distribution of the possessions of the enemies. The force of circumstances compelled President Wilson to compromise on many points. No wonder, the Settlement of Paris was unsatisfactory in many ways.

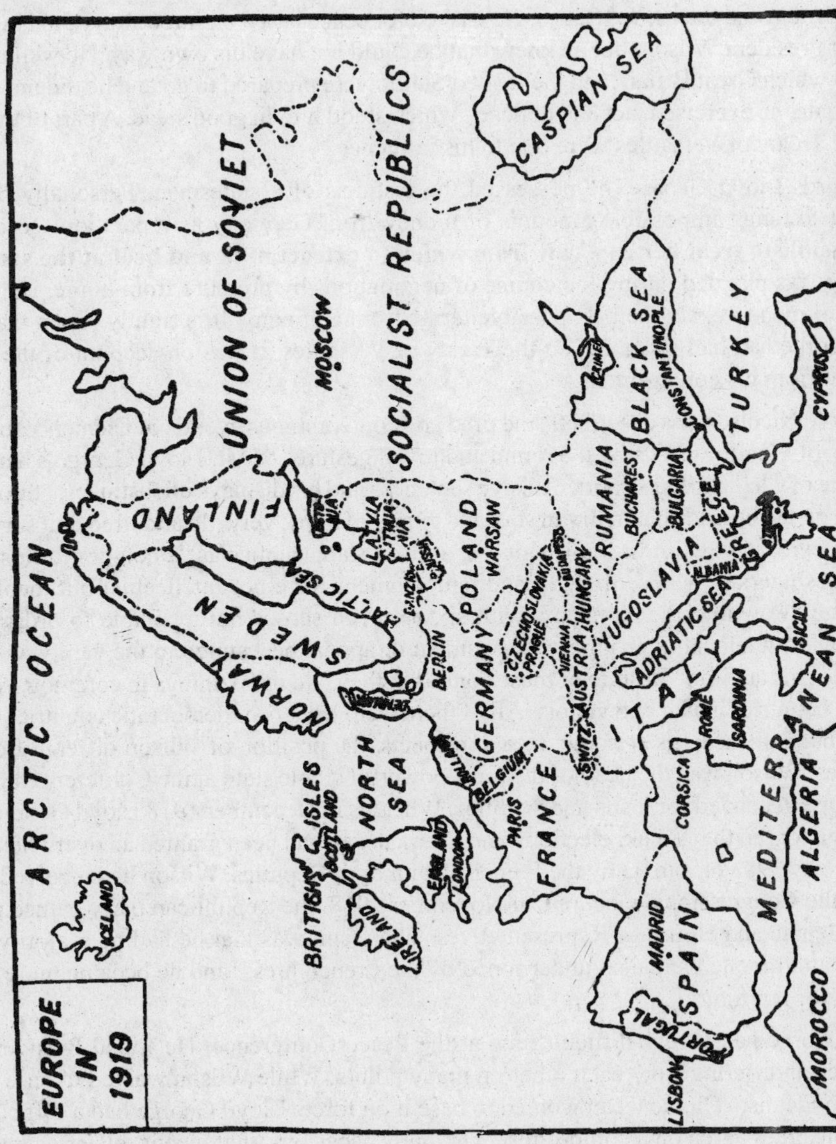

A few words may be said about Wilson, Clemenceau and Lloyd George. As regards Wilson, he was resolute and formidable. He could break and not bend. His stiffness was both a virtue and a defeat. Sometimes, it was responsible for wrong decisions and unwise concessions. He was a great orator but he had no precision of mind. He was not an expert in readiness in debate and conversation. He lost himself in details. By the weight of his character, Wilson exercised a power which could neither be understood nor resisted. It was his persistence which was responsible for the inclusion of the Covenant of the League of Nations into the Treaty of Versailles. He was no match for Clemenceau and Lloyd George in their cleverness. No wonder, they were able to get things done from him which he would not have voluntarily approved of.

Clemenceau was the Prime Minister of France. He has been rightly called the "Tiger". Short in size, he looked like some grave oriental sage. At times he was satirical and cynical. At other times, he showed a literary and artistic insight. He knew when and where to change his moods. He treated the smaller powers with indifference but understood that he could not have his own way while dealing with Great Britain and the United States. He wished for peace based on force alone and laughed at the 14 Points of President Wilson, but he knew that he could not have his own way. He well understood the limits to which Great Britain and the United States were prepared to go and he did not go beyond them. In debate, he exercised tact and delicacy which stood him in good stead. A part of the unhappy terms of the Treaty of Versailles were due to his influence.

As regards Lloyd George, he possessed the instincts of a statesman. Personally he was not in favour of exacting impossible amounts of money from Germany as reparation. To quote him, **"Was it sensible to treat her as a cow from which to extract milk and beef at the same time?"** However, he was plagued during the course of negotiations by pressure from home. He was asked by his countrymen to exact the best possible terms from Germany. It is rightly stated that in so far as Lloyd George had had influence on the Treaty of Versailles, it was on account of the telegrams which he got from his countrymen.

Sir Harold Nicolson has described "the tired and contemptuous eyelids of Clemenceau, the black button-boots of Woodrow Wilson, the round and jovial gestures of Mr. Lloyd George's hands". Lord Keynes wrote of Clemenceau's short, decisive sentences and his displays of obstinacy, "throned, in his gray gloves, on the brocade chair, dry in soul and empty of hope, very old and tired, but surveying the scene with a cynical and almost impish air", of Wilson's appearance as "a non-conformist minister, perhaps a Presbyterian" whose thought and temperament were not intellectual but theological, of Lloyd George "watching the company, with six or seven senses not available to ordinary men... compounding with telepathic instinct the argument or appeal best suited to the vanity, weakness or self-interest of his auditor." In spite of these contrasts, they had many things in common. All of them had led their countries in war and victory. All of them were leaders of democratic countries and hence sensitive to national feelings at home. In two respects, the position of Wilson differed from that of his colleagues. Wilson was the head of the most powerful single state at the Conference upon which most of Europe depended for loans and supplies. Whereas in December 1918 Lloyd George had won resounding victory in the "Khaki election" and Clemenceau had been granted an overwhelming vote of confidence by 398 votes to 93 by the French Chamber of Deputies, Wilson had received a setback at home. In the Congressional elections of November 1918, the Republican party gained majorities both in the Senate and House of Representatives. The result was that he had no majority at home. His position and morale were also undermined by the French press, and he became more and more a lonely and forlorn figure.

Lloyd George had a very difficult time at the Peace Conference. He found President Wilson and Clemenceau differing from each other on many points. While Wilson wanted to base the peace settlement on idealism Clemenceau wonted to base it on force. Lloyd George had a difficult time to make his colleagues agree on a compromise. On many occasions, that meant self-effacement on his part. It cannot be said that he neglected any purely British interests. However, it cannot be denied that while doing so he included many nobler and universal interests.

Treaty of Versailles (1919). The signing of the Treaty of Versailles between the Allies and Germany on 28 June, 1919 was not an easy affair. When the draft of the Treaty was ready, Germany was asked to send her delegates. She decided to send some subordinate officials to bring the document to Berlin for consideration. This was interpreted as an insult to the Allies and Germany was told that she must send a full-fledged diplomatic delegation to receive the document or there would be trouble. Ultimately, a German delegation led by its Foreign Minister went to Versailles. Unfortunately, the movements of the members of the delegation were strictly watched and they were not given the liberty of going about. They were kept in a hotel behind barbed wires. They were not allowed to communicate with anybody. On 7 May 1919, the peace terms were handed over to the German delegation. It is pointed out that on that occasion when the Allied and American delegations came to the spot, they were saluted by a Guard of Honour but the same was withdrawn when the German delegation arrived. Clemenceau, the French Premier, addressed the German delegation in these words: "You have before you the accredited plenipotentiaries of all the small and great Powers united to fight together in the war that has been so cruelly imposed upon them. The time has come when we must settle our accounts. You have asked for peace. We are ready to give you peace." The German Foreign Minister replied to Clemenceau while sitting. He confessed that the Germans "were under no illusion as to the extent of their defeat and the degree of their helplessness," but he denied the charge that Germany was responsible for the war. He declared that Germany was friendless, yet she had justice on her side. The German delegation was informed that they must send their reply within three weeks and all communications by them must be addressed in writing.

We are informed that the publication of the peace terms sent a wave of bitterness all over Germany. The Allies were condemned for their treachery and deceit. The German Government submitted a detailed memorandum on the Treaty. While the terms of the Treaty covered 230 printed pages, the German Memorandum consisted of 443 pages. A few minor alterations were made in the original treaty on the suggestion of Lloyd George and the revised treaty was given to the Germans and they were given 5 days to accept the same and were warned that if they failed to do so, their country would be invaded. The terms of the treaty were so unjust that there were many Germans who were prepared to wreck their country while fighting against the Allies rather than accept the terms of the Treaty. However, Field-Marshal Hindenburg made it clear that it was impossible to fight successfully against the Allies. Germany was in the throes of a famine and the German Assembly at Weimar decided to accept the terms of the treaty but objected to the provisions relating to war-guilt and the demand for the surrender of the war criminals. The Allies demanded unconditional acceptance and when the Germans found no other alternative, they submitted. It was contended by the German representative that his country was submitting to "overwhelming force, but without on that account abandoning her views in regard to the unheard of injustice of the conditions of peace." It was difficult to find some prominent German to go to Versailles to sign the Treaty. Ultimately, the German Foreign Minister headed the delegation. For the second time, the German delegates were treated like prisoners during their stay in Paris. When the German delegates left Paris for Versailles where the ceremony of signing the Treaty was to be held in the Hall of Mirrors, the Parisian mob threw stones at them and also hurled abuses on them. It was in these circumstances that the German delegates signed the Treaty of Versailles on 28 June, the 5th anniversary of the murder of Archduke Ferdinand.

Provisions of the Treaty. The documents containing the terms of the Treaty of Versailles consisted of 15 parts and had 440 articles and a score of annexes.

(1) Germany had to give Alsace-Lorraine to France, Eupen and Malmedy to Belgium, Memel to Lithuania and a large part of Posen and Western Prussia to Poland. She agreed to give Upper Silesia and the southern part of East Prussia to Poland if the people concerned were in favour of joining it and their wish was to be ascertained by means of a plebiscite. When the plebiscite was actually held, the returns showed that more than 700,000 persons voted for Germany and 480,000 for Poland. When that happened, Poland demanded that he must be given those areas which had Polish majorities. The contention of Germany was that the entire region was an indivisible economic unit and could not be divided. There was a deadlock for some time and ultimately it was decided to partition Silesia in

such a way as to leave more than half of its people and the land area to Germany, but Poland was given more of economic resources. The latter got 53 out of 67 coal mines. She also got all the zinc and lead foundries and about three-fourths of the coal producing area. She also secured 11 out of 16 zinc and lead mines.

(2) Danzig was taken away from Germany and set up as a Free City under the League of Nations. Poland was given special rights in the city of Danzig.

(3) The Rhineland was demilitarised. Germany was forbidden to "maintain or construct any fortifications either on the left bank of the Rhine or on the right bank to the west of a line drawn 50 kilometres to the east of the Rhine." The existing fortifications were to be destroyed. No military force was to be maintained in that area. No manoeuvres of the army were to be held in the Rhineland.

(4) "As the compensation for the destruction of the coal mines in the north of France and as part payment toward the total reparation demand from Germany for the damages resulting from the war," Germany had to give the coal mines of the Saar Valley "in full and absolute possession, with exclusive rights of exploitation." The Saar Valley was put under the League of Nations for 15 years and then a plebiscite was to be held to decide as to whether the Saar Valley was to remain under the League of Nations or go to Germany or France. When the plebiscite was actually held, the people of the Saar Valley voted for Germany.

(5) It was provided that the fortifications and the harbours of the Islands of Heligoland and Dune were to be destroyed. Germany promised to acknowledge and respect the independence of Austria.

(6) Germany was forced to give up all her rights and titles over her overseas possessions to the Allies and those were divided among themselves by Great Britain, France, Japan, Austria, New Zealand, Union of South Africa and Belgium. Japan got the lease of Kiao-Chow and other German concessions in the province of Shantung. New Zealand got the German portion of the Island of Somoa. England got the German West Africa, England and France divided among themselves the Kameroons and Togoland.

(7) The complete independence and full sovereignty of Belgium, Poland and Czechoslovakia were recognised by Germany. She also agreed to cancel the treaties of Brest-Litovsk and Bucharest.

(8) Germany gave up her special rights and privileges in China, Thailand, Egypt, Morocco and Liberia. The Allies also reserved to themselves the right to retain and liquidate all property, rights and interests of the German nationals or companies abroad and the German Government was required to pay compensation to them. The property and concessions enjoyed by Germany in Bulgaria and Turkey were forfeited.

(9) An attempt was made to cripple once for all the military strength of Germany. The German General Staff was abolished. The total strength of the German army was fixed at one lakh. The German army was to be maintained only for the maintenance of law and order within the country and the protection of her frontiers. It was specifically provided that the number of the customs officials, coast guards and forest guards was not to exceed the figure of 1,913. The police force was to be increased only in proportion to the increase in the population. Restrictions were put on the manufacture of armaments, munitions and other war materials by Germany. Both the import or export of war materials was banned. She was neither to make nor to purchase from outside tanks, armoured cars and poison gases. There was to be conscription in Germany. The German soldiers and officers were not to be retired prematurely and frequently to add to the effective military strength of the country. "Educational establishments, the universities, societies of discharged soldiers, shooting or touring clubs and generally speaking associations of every description, whatever be the age of their members, must not occupy themselves with any military matters."

(10) The German Navy also met with a step-motherly treatment. Germany was allowed to have only 6 battleships, 6 light cruisers, 12 destroyers and 12 torpedo boats. No submarines were to be allowed. Submarine cables were to be surrendered. A new warship could be built only to replace on old one and not otherwise. The navy was not to have more than 15,000 men including officers. The members of the German merchant marine were not to get naval training. All the surplus war vessels were to be destroyed or converted into merchant ships or handed over to the Allies. Germany was not to have any military, naval or air force. She had to surrender all aeronautical war materials. The Allies reserved to themselves the right to appoint commissioners to find out whether the above military provisions were being carried out faithfully by Germany or not.

(11) William II, the German Emperor, was charged with "the supreme offence against international morality and the sanctity of treaties." He was to be tried by a tribunal. This provision became infructuous because the Government of the Netherlands refused to hand over the German Emperor to the Allies. Germany also agreed to surrender other persons "accused of having committed acts in violation of the laws and customs of war." However, only a dozen unimportant German war criminals were tried by the tribunal and given light punishments.

(12) Germany had to admit that she was responsible for the war of 1914-18. To quote Article 231, "The Allied and Associated Government affirm and Germany accepts the responsibility of Germany and her allies for causing all the loss and damage to which the Allied and Associated Governments and their nationals have been subjected as a consequence of the war imposed upon them by the aggression of Germany and her allies." However, it was realised that Germany could not pay for all losses and damages and she was allowed "to make compensation for all damage done to the civilian population of the Allied and Associated Powers to their property, by land, by sea and from the air, and in general all damage as defined in Annexure I..." There were 10 categories of losses and damages in the Annexure. Germany was to compensate Belgium for all the money borrowed by the latter during the war. She was also to pay interest at the rate of 5%.

(13) Provision was made for the appointment of a Reparations Commission to determine the total amount of reparations to be paid by Germany and the methods by which the same was to be done. However, up to May 1921, Germany was required to pay about 500 million dollars. The economic resources of Germany were to be employed for the physical restoration of the invaded areas. Germany agreed to deliver specified quantities of coal to France, Belgium, Italy and Luxembourg. France was also to receive certain quantities of benzal, ammonium sulphate and coal-tar.

(14) Germany was required to return the trophies, works of art and flags taken from France in the Franco-Prussian War of 1870-71. She was to compensate the University of Louvain for the destruction of her manuscripts and documents. She was to restore the original Koran of the Caliph Othman to the King of Hedjaz. She was to restore to England the skull of the Sultan Mkwawa.

(15) The Elbe, Danube, Oder and Niemen rivers were internationalised. The River Rhine was put under the control of an international commission. The Kiel Canal and its approaches were opened to all nations. Germany was to give on lease free zones to Czechoslovakia for 99 years in the ports of Hamburg and Stettin. The Allied goods were to be given a favourable treatment on the German railways.

(16) Provision was also made for the enforcement of the above clauses. The German territory west of the Rhine, together with the bridgeheads, was to be occupied by the Allied troops for a period of 15 years. If Germany carried out her obligations faithfully, the bridgehead at Cologne was to be evacuated after 5 years, that at Coblenz after 10 years and that at Mainz after 15 years. If Germany misbehaved, the occupation was liable to be prolonged. As a matter of fact, all the troops were withdrawn by 1930.

The Reparations Commission was duly appointed and ultimately it fixed the war-indemnity at 54 billion dollars.

Treaty of St. Germaine (1919). This treaty was made between Austria-Hungary, and the Allies. Austria recognised the complete independence of Hungary, Czechoslovakia, Poland and Yugoslavia. She gave up many territories which formerly were included in Austria-Hungary. The result of this treaty was that Austria was reduced to a small Republic with an area and population smaller than those of Portugal. She was deprived of her sea-ports. Her army was reduced to 30,000 men. The International Reparations Commission was to fix the war-indemnity to be paid by Austria.

According to Grant and Temperley, "The Treaty of St. Germaine reduced Austria to less than half her old population. She surrendered seven and a half million Slavs in Galicia to the new Poland, and over a million other non-Germans. She gave up also nearly four million Germans, of whom three and a half millions went to Czechoslovakia. Austria's new boundaries confined her to the Austrian Archduchies, Styria and the Tyrol, with a population of about eight millions odd, nearly all of pure German race. The once proud Austria, which had ruled over twenty million subjects and fifteen different races, was reduced to less than half of her former size, and lost a third of her purely German population. She became miserably poor and dragged out a pathetic existence from this time, and was annexed by Germany in 1938."

Treaty of Neuilly (1919). This treaty was signed on 27 November 1919 between Bulgaria and the Allies. Bulgaria gave up most of those territories which she had got during the Balkan Wars of 1912-13 and the World War I. She gave up a part of Macedonia to Yugoslavia and the whole of Dobrudja to Rumania. She gave the Thracian Coast to the Allies and the latter gave the same to Greece. Bulgaria was to pay a war-indemnity of about half a million dollars. Her army was reduced to 33,000 men.

Treaty of Trianon (1920). This treaty was signed on 4 June 1920 between Hungary on the one hand and the Allies on the other. By this treaty, Hungary gave up the non-Magyar population. While Slovak provinces were given to Czechoslovakia, Transylvania was given to Rumania and Croatia was given to Yugoslavia. Banat was divided between Yugoslavia and Rumania. The Hungarian army was reduced to 35,000 men. The population of the new State of Hungary was eight million and area about 35,000 sq. miles.

Treaty of Sevres (1920). Turkey had fought on the side of the Central Powers and she too was defeated along with them. The Treaty of Sevres was signed on 10 August 1920 between Turkey and the Allies. By this treaty the Arab State of Hedjaz was nominally freed and put under British control. Armenia was created into a Christian Republic and she was put under an international guarantee. Mesopotamia, Trans-Jordan, Syria and Palestine were taken away from Turkey, Syria was given to France under the Mandate of the League of Nations. Palestine, Mesopotamia and Trans-Jordan were given to England under the Mandate system. Galicia was recognised as a French sphere of influence, Southern Anatolia was recognised as an Italian sphere of influence. Adrianople, Gallipoli, the Islands of Ambros and Tenedos, Smyrna, and the territory on the coast of Asia Minor were given to Greece. Greece also got the Dodecanese Islands with the exception of two islands. The Dardanelles and the Bosphorus were internationalised. Turkey was to pay a huge war-indemnity.

The treaty with Turkey was a harsh one and was extremely unpopular. This led to the rise of Mustafa Kamal in Turkey. The Turks resisted the Treaty of Sevres under his leadership. There was a lot of confusion and ultimately, a war broke out between Greece and Turkey. Nobody joined on any side and consequently, the war dragged on. Ultimately, the Treaty of Lausanne was signed on 9 July 1923 with Turkey. By this treaty, Turkey got very favourable terms. However, he agreed to give up Trans-Jordan, Palestine, Mesopotamia, Syria and Hedjaz. She was allowed to retain the whole of Anatolia, Armenia, Adrianople, Eastern Thrace, Smyrna, Galicia, Adalia, etc. The Dardanelles and the Bosphorus were internationalised.

Poland. The three partitions of Poland in the 18th century had effaced the name of Poland from the map but the Poles put up a heroic struggle for freedom during the 19th century. During the World War I, as Russia, Austria-Hungary and Germany suffered defeats, they relaxed their hold over Poland. The Poles took full advantage of that opportunity and became a free nation before the War actually ended in November 1918. When the Peace Conference recognised the independence of Poland, it merely acknowledged an accomplished fact.

The Great Powers fixed a boundary line for Poland which represented the eastern limit of purely a Polish territory. This was known as the Curzon Line which ran from Punsk in the North to Grodow-Vlodava, north of Kholm and from there to the boundary of Eastern Galicia. This was not acceptable to Poland and she occupied East Galicia and Vilna. She fought against Soviet Russia and by the treaty of Riga (1920) she got a population and territory about double of that recommended by the Curzon Line. There were some 27 million people in all Poland in which the Ruthenians and Lithuanians were aliens.

Criticism of Peace Settlement. The Treaty of Versailles was assailed by the Germans as "Carthagian peace", a dictated peace, a shame and an outrage, an unheard of robbery of the German people, fraudulent, selfish and even vulgar. It was a dictated peace because it was dictated to a mortified foe and because throughout the three and half months spent in drawing up the first draft, the Germans were not consulted at all. The armistice was periodically reviewed and with every renewal, the threat of invasion, was given to a blockaded Germany and more concessions were extorted. The following statement of Lloyd George shows the spirit in which the Treaty of Versailles was imposed on the people of Germany : "These terms are written in the blood of fallen heroes. We must carry out the edict of Providence and see that the people who inflicted this War shall never be in a position to do so again. The Germans say they will not sign. Their newspapers say they will not sign. If you don't do so in Versailles, you shall do so in Berlin." The German representatives signed the Treaty at the point of bayonet. They were threatened with the invasion of their country if they did not sign. E.H. Carr says that nearly every treaty which brings a war to an end is in one sense a dictated peace but in the Treaty of Versailles, the element of dictation was more apparent than in any treaty of modern times.

The peace settlement was made in a spirit of revenge. The principle underlying the settlement was: "To the victors belong the spoils and the Allies are the victors." Lloyd George won the famous Khaki election with the following slogan: "We shall hang Kaiser and make Germany pay to the last penny." The peace-makers of 1919-20 ought to have known that a lenient treatment of Germany was more likely to maintain peace in Europe. William II, the real author of the War, had run away from Germany and a Republican Government had been set up. The victors ought to have treated with leniency the newly created German Republic. As they failed to do so, the Republican forces in Germany were weakened from the very beginning. The harsh treatment of Germany by the Treaty of Versailles and the subsequent behaviour of the Allies, particularly France, towards Germany, destroyed all chances of the Republican regime in Germany. That facilitated the rise of Hitler to power in 1933. The Allies who made the Peace Settlement of 1919-20, paved the way for the World War II. If the treatment of France by Bismarck in 1870-71 led to the War of 1914, the Treaty of Versailles of 1919 was partly responsible for the War of 1939. The terms of the Treaty were resented by all the patriots of Germany. The humiliation was so great that it was not possible to put up with the same.

The Treaty of Versailles was the peace of the statesmen and not of the people. John Smuts writes, "The promise of the new life, the victory of the great human ideals, for which the peoples have shed their blood and their treasure without stint, the fulfilment of their aspirations towards a new international order and a fairer, better world, are not written in this treaty. There are guarantees laid down which we all hope will soon be found out of harmony with the new peaceful temper....There are punishments foreshadowed over most of which a calmer mood may yet prefer to pass the sponge of oblivion. There are indemnities stipulated which cannot be exacted without grave injury to the industrial revival of Europe and which it will be in the interests of all to render more tolerable and moderate......The real peace of the peoples ought to follow, and amend the peace of the statesmen."

The Treaty of Versailles was based on transitory passions and not on permanent wisdom. It embodied the momentary hatred, bitterness and resentment and not balanced judgement, sagacity and justice. To quote Lord Bryce, "Peace can come only with content. If the result of these treaties is to make nations discontented, you are preparing for revolts and wars."

The reparations demanded from Germany dislocated the economy both of the giver and the taker. To quote Churchill, "History will characterise all these transactions as insane. They helped to breed the martial curse and the economic blizzard. Germany now borrowed in all directions, swallowing greedily every credit which was lavishly offered to her. This is a sad story of complicated idiocy in the making of which much toil and virtue was consumed."

The Treaty of Versailles was "harsh in the wrong places and lenient in the wrong ways." It was not realistic to insist on German acceptance of the war guilt clause. To quote David Thompson, "A sense of moral responsibility could not be created by including a statement of it in a document which German representatives were compelled to sign." The demand for reparations was fixed in astronomical figures which could not be paid by Germany. The 15-year administration of the Saar by the League of Nations and its return to Germany in 1935 was hardly justified. The Allied occupation of the Rhineland proved illusory as it implied the Allied withdrawal just after the interval of a period which Germany required to regain her military power.

Since reciprocity was not observed in the disarmament, transportation and economic clauses of the treaty, Germany virtually signed away her sovereignty and put herself into the hands of the receivers. All the ideals upon which the Treaty of Versailles was based were forced upon Germany alone and completely disregarded by the Allies. With reciprocity in all matters where it would have been for the common good, the treaty would have been a peace of justice. Without reciprocity, it was a peace of force and its terms were possible of execution only so long as the force that caused Germany to sign it, continued to make them execute it.

So far as the terms of the Peace Settlement deviated from the Fourteen Points of Wilson, they constituted a breach of faith. The attempt of France to get the Rhine frontier, of Italy to get Dalmatia and of Poland to secure the Whole of Upper Silesia could not be justified on grounds of nationality. Although a compromise was reached on the above points, the very desire of the victorious Powers for such aggrandisement was not consistent with their loyalty to the Fourteen Points.

The Peace Settlement fragmented Europe. Before 1914, Europe comprised of 19 States and after 1919, there were 26 States. Many of those States were so small that from an economic point of view they could not sustain themselves and economics played an even more important role after 1919 than it had before the opening of the War. When those small States were seized by a tariff psychosis, their policies seriously interfered with the flow of goods from one part of Europe to another.

Self-determination had been heralded as one of the corner-stones of new Europe but that principle was not applied universally. After the treaty had been put into effect, millions of Europeans still lived beyond their national homes. Several of the new States carved from Austria-Hungary were only smaller replicas of the Empire whose abuses had stimulated their own nationalistic demands for independence.

The Peace Conference was not a Conference at all but a tribunal before which the Central Powers were summoned to hear their doom. In spite of the claim of Clemenceau that the Conference "called in all parties interested" and "all who had anything to say were heard," the Treaty of 1919 was imposed. As Germany did not participate in drafting the Treaty, the Conference was deprived of energetic opposition and no voice of prudence warned the negotiators against extremism. As no Germans were consulted in drafting the Treaty, it was almost impossible to mobilise any opinion in Germany in support of it. The framers of the Treaty of Versailles should have kept in view the following dictum of Castlereagh when he went to the Congress of Vienna (1815) : "We have assembled here not to bring back trophies of victory but to restore Europe to the paths of peace."

The Treaty of Versailles was the work of parliamentarians and not of diplomats. It was full of explanatory clauses which were open to rebuttal and debate. That weakness in the formulation of the Treaty was important in paving the way to War in 1939.

Certain failures of the Conference were immediately discernible. Two important objectives of erecting safeguards against a revived Germany and drawing boundary lines to achieve ethnic unity, were incompatible. Czechoslovakia was set up to include 30,000,000 Germans and more than a million outsiders. Austria was denied the right to join Germany which it wished to do and which self-determination required. One-third of the population of Poland belonged, by racial test, to other States, but were assigned to Poland to strengthen her against Germany and to give her economic viability and access to the sea. In spite of drastic revision of boundaries, national minorities persisted in the States of Eastern and South-Eastern Europe, totalling more than one-fifth of the population.

The Allies were condemned for their attitude towards the Christians of Armenia who had suffered terribly under Turkish rule as a result of wholesale massacres from time to time. During the War, Britain declared that the Armenians would be liberated from Turkish yoke, but when the final settlement was made with Turkey at Lausanne, the promise was not kept. The unfortunate Armenians were left entirely at the mercy of the Turks to suffer terribly later on.

Not only Germany, even her allies were given a shabby treatment. Austria-Hungary was reduced to a tiny state. Her Empire, dynasty and army disappeared in the whirlwind. The Hungarians declared themselves independent. The Czechs and Slovaks broke away. The Serbs also took advantage of their victory and a big Yugoslavia was created partly at the cost of Austria-Hungary. Ultimately, a small Republic of six million souls was all that was allowed to remain out of the mighty Empire of Austria-Hungary which once dominated the politics of Europe in the time of Metternich. She became an insignificant state in Europe. The same was the case with Hungary. She was deprived of her non-Magyar population. Slovakia was given to the Czechs. Transylvania was captured by Roumania. Croatia was annexed by Serbia. About six lacs of men and women of Magyar race and 45 lacs of her former subjects were put under alien domination. That was a great humiliation for the Magyars.

The Treaty of Versailles contained a series of bargains and compromises between the high-minded but often unrealistic desire of President Wilson, the nationalistic and realistic demands of Clemenceau and the somewhat unstable and opportunistic aims of Lloyd George. The pledges of the Secret Treaties were preferred to the vague slogans of democracy and self-determination. Many frontiers were drawn in violation of the principle of self-determination. The inclusion of South Tyrol in Italy was a concession to Italian claims for a strategic frontier. Likewise, the Polish Corridor was in defiance of national considerations.

The Treaty of Versailles inaugurated a new stage in the struggle of European nations for world power. Upto 1919, international law made a distinction between the property of a Government and that of its nationals and private property was not seized. According to the Treaty of Versailles, a belligerent country, within its own dominion or those of its allies, could confiscate property of any nature belonging to the subjects of an enemy country and if victorious at the end of the war, could compel the Government of the defeated country to agree to indemnify its own nationals for the property thus confiscated. That created a new precedent for the future.

About the Peace Settlement of 1919-20, J.I. Carvin writes that Europe was balkanised, *i.e.*, broken into many fragments, jarred by violent antipathies of the irrendentist problems like Alsace-Lorraine, more were created than were solved. The new States were as protectionist as military. The Fourteen Points of Wilson became Fourteen Disappointments. General Smuts observed, "I have signed the Treaty, not because I consider it a satisfactory document, but because it is imperatively necessary to close the War." A day after the signing of the Treaty of Versailles Colonel House wrote thus in his diary : "I should have preferred a different peace." No wonder, the Senate of the United States refused to ratify it. The Peace Settlement was described by some critics as "Clemenceau peace" for no map of Europe, save that drawn by Napoleon I, had ever been more clearly marked "Made in France." President Wilson was outwitted by Clemenceau, Lloyd George and Orlando.

The Peace Treaties of 1919-20 have their defenders, apologists and critics. While signing the Peace Settlement, we must not forget the conflicting difficulties and the complicated problems facing the peace-makers in Paris. Moreover, they had before them the treaties of Brest-Litovsk and Bucharest, imposed by Germany herself on the defeated states and the peace-makers in Paris were undoubtedly, affected by their contents.

Wilsonian Peace. In January 1918, President Wilson appealed to the world to back the Allies as they were fighting for certain fundamental principles and he described those fundamental principles in his famous Fourteen Points. These Fourteen Points provided for the following:—

(1) Open covenants of peace, openly arrived at and not secret diplomacy.

(2) Absolute freedom of navigation upon seas, outside the territorial waters, both in times of peace and war.

(3) Removal of all barriers to international trade.

(4) Reduction of national armaments.

(5) Impartial adjustment of all colonial claims. The interests and sentiments of the subject peoples were also to be considered and not only the claims of the colonial powers.

(6) Evacuation of Russian territory. Russia was to be given full opportunity to decide her future course of action.

(7) Evacuation and restoration of Belgium.

(8) Evacuation and restoration of French territory and the righting of the wrong done to France in 1871 in the matter of Alsace-Lorraine.

(9) Readjustment of Italian frontiers along her recognizable lines of nationality.

(10) Autonomous development for peoples of Austria-Hungary.

(11) Evacuation and restoration of Serbia, Montenegro, Rumania and an outlet to the sea for Serbia.

(12) Securing of sovereignty for the Turkish portion of Ottoman Empire, with autonomy for other portions and freedom of shipping through the Straits.

(13) Establishment of an independent Poland with access to the sea.

(14) The creation of an international organisation to guarantee independence and territorial integrity to small and big States of the world.

President Wilson elaborated and extended his general principles of peace-making in a number of speeches between February and September 1918. However, the specific points were never modified. His most important additions to the general principles were two. "Each Part of the final settlement must be based upon the essential justice of that particular case and upon such adjustments as are most likely to bring a peace that will be permanent." "The impartial justice meted out must involve no discrimination between those to whom we wish to be just and those to whom we do not wish to be just." This concept of absolute justice gave a lot of headache at the time of the peace settlement. No arrangement conceivable in modern Europe could be expected to reach the ideal of absolute justice. The peace aims of Wilson were broadly endorsed by the Allied Governments and were made the basis on which the German Government accepted the armistice in November 1918. However, the Allied Governments made it clear that they wished to reserve judgement about the exact meaning of the "freedom of the seas" and what "restoration" of invaded territories meant for them. They also made it clear to Germany that compensation will be made by Germany for all damage done to the civilian population of the Allies and their property by the aggression of Germany by land, by sea and from the air." These principles, aims and interpretations were all communicated to the Germans before they agreed to end hostilities.

It cannot be denied that although the Fourteen Points of Wilson had to be compromised in many ways with a view to adjust them to the mutual commitments of the Allies, yet many of them were put into the Peace Settlement of 1919-20. As regards the creation of an international organisation, it is rightly pointed out that without the whole-hearted support of President Wilson, the Covenant of the League would not have been drafted then and placed within the framework of the treaties. The idea of a League of Nations was not original with Wilson. It was an Anglo-Saxon conception which germinated during the course of the World War I in the minds of peace-loving people. Those ideas were given the shape of definite proposals and most important of them were drafted by General Smuts and Lord Phillimore. Wilson took over the drafts of Smuts and Phillimore and put them in the forefront of the discussions of the statesmen who had assembled at Paris. He himself presided over a commission which drafted the Covenant of the League of Nations. It was his great authority that helped him to bring the work to a successful conclusion. President Wilson was prepared to compromise on any other point but he was absolutely determined to embody the Covenant of the League of Nations into the peace treaties. Thus, the League of Nations came into being.

The Peace Settlement also acted upon the principle of self-determination. The Poles, Croats, Czechs, Letts, Finns, Alsatians, etc., were released from subjection to alien rule. It is rightly pointed out that in no previous settlement so much of attention was paid to the principle of nationality. Plebiscites were held in some cases and thus the people were given an opportunity to express their own wishes. No other treaty ever "emancipated" so many peoples living under alien yokes as the Peace Settlement of 1919-20 did. In 1914, there were 40 million people living under alien rule, but in 1919 their number was reduced to 16 millions. The calculation of Herbert Fisher was that only 3 per cent of the whole population of Europe was left under alien rule. It goes without saying that in actual practice, ethnic anomalies ran never be eliminated completely and the territorial adjustment can completely solve the problem of minorities, but an attempt was made to do everything that could possibly be done. Special provisions were made for the protection of the minorities. They were to be protected in matters of religion, language and citizenship.

The creation of the independent States of Yugoslavia, Poland and Czechoslovakia and the restoration of Alsace-Lorraine to France were in accordance with the Fourteen Points of Wilson. The peace-makers did not hesitate to create even small petty States in accordance with the principle of "one nation, one State."

Rejection of Treaty of Versailles by the U.S.A. Although President Wilson was the prime-mover in the Peace Settlement of 1919-20, the U.S.A. did not ratify the Treaty of Versailles. Particularly, the Covenant of the League of Nations was the main target. While the Democrats supported the Peace Settlement, the Republicans condemned the same. The American constitution demands that a treaty must be ratified by a two-thirds majority of the Senate. Many amendments were proposed by the Senate but they were rejected by the Democratic majority. However, when the vote was taken on 18 November 1919, there were 55 votes in favour and 39 against it. Thus, there was no requisite majority. The Treaty was brought before the Senate once again in March 1920. Although 57 voted in favour of it and 37 against, the Treaty was not ratified as required by law. During the Presidential election of 1920, the question of the ratification of the treaty was very prominent and that was one of the important causes of the rout of the Democratic Party. However, the new administration entered into separate treaties with Germany, Austria and Hungary and those treaties were ratified by the Senate in October 1921.

According to Gottschalk and Lach, "A striking result of the war was the shift of the centre of gravity, political, military, and economic (but not yet cultural), from Europe to America. Before the war six great powers had manoeuvred for advantage in Europe. When the war was over, Austria-Hungary had ceased to exist, Russia was in the turmoils of civil war, intervention, and revolution; Germany was in a state of chaos; only Great Britain, France, and Italy were left as Europe's great powers, all three in a state of exhaustion. The might of two non-European powers, the United States and Japan, had correspondingly increased. The United States had provided the Allies with guns, ammunition, and other military equipment long before it had entered the war. The Allies became heavily indebted to the United States largely because of loans made by the Washington Government. A transfer of capital from Europe to America had taken place as European corporations and investors liquidated their holdings to meet the demands for money arising from increased taxes and the expansion of war industries at home. For the first time American loans and investments abroad were greater than foreign loans and investments in the United States. The United States was transformed from a debtor country into a creditor country. The stock exchange of New York became the world's foremost stock market, replacing London in that role. Europe was weary, damaged, and impoverished, and the United States was still fresh. Europeans felt that Americans had suffered little and profited much, from the war. Americans believed that without their timely aid Europe might have been crushed by the heel of Prussian militarism."

Lloyd George on Peace Settlement. It may be interesting to refer to the view of Lloyd George on the Peace Settlement. He declared in the House of Commons in 1919: "I do not think any one can claim the terms imposed constitute injustice to Germany unless he believes justice in the war was on the side of Germany." He pointed out that some of the terms of settlement were terrible because the deeds of the Germans were also terrible. "The world is rocking and reeling under the blow that failed. If the blow had succeeded, the liberty of Europe would have vanished.". Referring to the restoration of Alsace-Lorraine, Schleswig and Poland, he remarked that "they are all territories which ought not to belong to Germany." To quote him again, it was not vengeance "to take every possible precaution against a recurrence of the war and make such an example of Germany as will discourage ambitious rulers and peoples from ever again attempting to repeat this infamy. The German people approved the war, and, therefore, it was essential in the terms to show if nations entered into unprovoked wars of aggression against their neighbours, what lies in store for them." Again, "Having regard to the uses Germany made of her army, there is no injustice in scattering and disarming it. If the Allies had restored the colonies to Germany after the evidence of the ill-treatment of the natives and the part the natives have taken in their own liberation, it would have been a base betrayal. Then take the trial of those responsible for the war. If wars of this kind are to be prevented, those personally responsible for them, who have taken part in plotting and planning them, should be held personally responsible. Therefore, the Entente decided that the man who undoubtedly had the primary responsibility, in the judgment, at any rate of the Allies, should be tried for the offences he committed in breaking treaties he was bound to honour, and by that means bringing on the war. It was an exceptional course, and it is a pity it was, because if it had been done before there would have been fewer wars."

Again, "These terms are written in the blood of fallen heroes.... We must carry out the Edict of Providence and see that the people who inflicted this (war) shall never be in a position to do so again.

The Germans say they will not sign. Their newspapers say, they will not sign. The politicians say the same. We say, 'Gentlemen, you must sign, if you don't do so in Versailles, you shall do so in Berlin'."

According to Seaman, "The Peace Treaties of 1919 have a clear justification as an attempt to contain the German Reich by the liberation of the Slavs, and the peasants of Transylvania. The cause both of peace and justice was served in eastern Europe by the treaties; and better, served than they had been for centuries. It was not the Versailles system but the success of the Germans in wrecking it in 1938 and 1939 that caused the Second World War. The real German grievance against the settlement was not that it was a 'diktat' or that they had been cheated by President Wilson. It was chiefly that it prevented them from dominating and exploiting the valleys of the Vistula and the Danube and kept them away from the approaches to Asia Minor and the Ukraine, and because it emphatically asserted that in south-eastern Europe the Slavs had as much, right to an independent existence as the Germans and Magyars."

Responsibility for the War. When, the First World War was over, Article 23 of the Peace Treaty forced Germany to accept "responsibility for all the loss and damage to which the Allied and Associated Governments and their nationals have been subjected as a consequence of the war imposed upon them by the aggression of Germany and her allies." However, this forced acceptance of responsibility by Germany did not settle the issue and the question of responsibility for the war has agitated the minds of politicians, journalists and historians of the world. The present view is that it was not Germany alone that was responsible for the war but all the great powers had their share of responsibility, although some had a lesser share than that of others.

Serbia. So for as Serba was concerned, she cannot avoid a certain share of the war guilt. It cannot be denied that the Serbian officials were accessories to the assassination of the Archduke Francis Fredinand. The Serbian Government did not discourage the nationalist and Irredentist Serbian societies. It ought to have taken action against those societies which had their headquarters in Serbia and which were responsible for the murder. However, it cannot be denied that after the commission of the crime, when Austria-Hungary made certain demands on Serbia, the latter was willing to make honourable amends, although she was not prepared to accept dishonourable conditions. All the European Governments, including that of Germany, thought that Austria should be satisfied with the reply of Serbia. War could have been avoided if Austria had shown satisfaction with the reply and not insisted on impossible demands. It is true that Serbia was the first country to begin mobilisation but that was principally meant for defensive purposes.

Austria-Hungary. So far as the responsibility of Austria-Hungary was concerned, it cannot be denied that she was very bitter and was determined to blot out of existence her enemy, Sarbia. Austria-Hungary hoped that she would be able to finish Serbia before any great power could come to her help. However, she was sadly mistaken. Russia at once showed her willingness to come to the help of Serbia. It is pointed out that it was the action of Austria that forced Russia to mobilise. It cannot be denied that the Austrian Government was guilty of aggression against Serbia and provocation of Russia.

Russia. As regards the responsibility of Russia, it cannot be denied that she was the first big power to decide mobilisation. She was not prepared to allow Austria-Hungary to have the upper hand and was determined to keep her out of Eastern Europe. The provocation of Russia was great and that forced other countries also to mobilise at once. After mobilization by Russia, it became impossible to localise the war. The Russians must be held guilty of taking the first steps that moved the issue from the realm of big power diplomacy into the realm of big power military strategy. The result was that the major decisions were withdrawn from statesmen and were left to be decided by soldiers. It is pointed out that if Russia had not mobilised, it was possible that the controversy might have been settled by a quid pro quo arrangement short of war.

Germany. As regards the responsibility of Germany, it cannot be denied that she was guilty of having given a carte blanche to Austria from the very beginning. Germany realised the gravity of the situation and tried to put a check on Austria but by the time she did so, the situation had already gone out of control. Moreover, the German Government was guilty of many miscalculations. Germany thought that she will be able to have a quick victory over her enemies. Experience showed that their calculations were wrong. They actually failed to achieve what they thought of achieving. If Germany had not begun the shooting among the big powers, Russian mobilisation might not have led to war with Austria as Austro-Russian negotiations had in fact begun and the Allies of Russia were anxious to submit the whole controversy to pacific international consideration.

The war guilt of Germany was great but she was not the only culprit. France and Great Britain were also guilty for having encouraged Russia in her aggressive action. Both the governments had given Russia an understanding that they would come to her help against Austria-Hungary and Germany. We must not ignore the fact of French passion for revanche, her commercial competition with Germany and the bitterness between France and Germany created by the Berlin-Baghdad Railway, the Morocco Crises, etc. If the French Government had not supported Russia whole-heartedly, the situation would not have become so dangerous. A similar charge can be brought against Great Britain. It is true that Great Britain and France were not so aggressive in their actions, but it cannot be denied that they did not put a check on their allies in time, and hence were dragged into the war.

The real culprit in 1914 was not a man or a government or a people. It was an international system which was responsible for the war of 1914-18. Europe was divided into two armed camps and each camp was determined to defeat the other and under the circumstances war was inevitable.

SUGGESTED READINGS

Adam: **Clemenceau.**

Bakeless, J.: **Economic Causes of Modern War.**

Baker: **What Wilson did at Paris?**

Baker: **Wilson and World Settlement.**

Barnes, H.E.: **The Genesis of the World War,** 1926.

Bethmann-Hollweg: **Reflections on the World War.**

Birdsall: **Versailles Twenty Years After,** 1941.

Carey and Scott: **An Outline History of the War.**

Churchill. W.: **The World Crisis.**

Churchill, W.: **The Aftermath.**

Chitwood, O.P.: **The Immediate Causes of the Great War.**

Crutwell, C.R.M.: **A History of the Great War,** 1934.

Davis, W.S.: **Roots of the War.**

Halevy, E.: **The World Crisis of 1914-18.**

Hart, B.H.L.: **The Real War, 1914-18.**

Harris : **The Peace in the Making.**

Hayes: **Brief History of the Great War.**

House and Seymour: **What really happened in Paris?**

Keynes : **Economic Consequences of the Peace.**

Keynes : **A Revision of the Treaty.**

Lawrence, T.E.: **Revolt in the Desert.**

Lee : **Ten years, The World on the Way to War.**

Lloyd George : **Memoirs of the Peace Conference.**

Mckinley, A.E.: **Collected Materials for the Study of the War.**

Newbolt, Sir Henry: **A Naval History of the War,** 1914-18.

Nicolson, H.: **Peace-Making,** 1919.

Pollard: **Short History of the Great War.**

Ramsay Muir: **Political Consequences of the Great War.**

Riddle : **Treaty of Versailles.**

Rose : **Origins of the War.**

Scott, A.P.: **Introduction to Peace Treaties.**

Seton Watson, R.W.: **Sarajevo,** 1926.

Simonds, F.H.: **The World War.**

Stieve: **Izvolsky and the World War.**

Schmitt, B.E.: **The Coming of the War,** 1914 (2 Vols).

Temperley (Ed.): **History of the Peace Conference of Paris** (5 Vols.).

Wolff: **The Eve of 1914.**

CHAPTER

31 THE LEAGUE OF NATIONS

Origins. It is wrong to say that President Wilson alone was the author of the League of Nations. Private initiative also played an important part in this connection. During the World War I many suggestions were made from time to time for the creation of an international organisation which could check wars in the future. Popular interests in the possibility of such a league began to manifest itself in the United States after the outbreak of the World War I and grew rapidly during the period of American neutrality. A "League to Enforce Peace" was established by a group of public leaders, including many outstanding Republicans headed by Taft. The organisation held a Conference in June 1915 and adopted a Four Point Programme which received wide publicity. It called for the submission of all justiciable international disputes to arbitration, the submission of all disputes to a Council of Conciliation, the application of economic and military force by all states against any state resorting to war without submitting its disputes to pacific settlement and convocation of periodical congresses to codify international law. At another conference held in May 1916, President Wilson declared that the United States was willing to become a partner in any association of nations formed to check aggression. In January 1917, he addressed the American Senate on a "World League for Peace." When the United States entered the War, President Wilson insisted in his war message that peace in future can never be maintained except by a world-wide partnership of democratic nations. One of the 14 points of Wilson was an Association of Nations formed for the purpose of affording mutual guarantees of political independence and territorial integrity to all States, whether small or big. In 1915 was published a draft known as "Proposals for the Avoidance of War" to which a Preface was written by Lord Bryce. "The League of Nations Society" was set up in 1915 and "The League of Free Nations Associations" was started in 1918. Later on both the Associations were amalgamated into, the "League of Nations Union." In March 1918, a Committee of the British Foreign Office with Phillimore as Chairman, prepared a draft convention. In July 1918, President Wilson prepared his first draft. In December 1918, General Smuts prepared a plan containing the germs of the Council and the Mandate System. President Wilson prepared a second draft on 10 January 1919, and a third draft 10 days after. The third draft was submitted to Hurst and Miller for revision and the composite draft prepared by them was used by the League of Nations Commission of the Peace Conference as a basis for discussion. A Commission of 19 members was set up under the Chairmanship of President Wilson and on 14 February 1919, the tentative draft was presented to the Peace Conference for its consideration. On 28 April 1919, the revised draft was adopted unanimously and the Covenant of the League of Nations was incorporated into the Treaty of Versailles which was signed by the German Delegation on 28 June 1919. On 10 January 1920, the League of Nations officially came into existence and its headquarters were fixed at Geneva in Switzerland.

Membership. There were two kinds of members of the League, original and non-original members. The original members were those states and dominions who had signed the Treaty of Peace and who were invited to accede to the Covenant and actually did so before 20 March 1920. Provision was made for the admission of other states into the League of Nations.

The Assembly. The main organs of the League were the Assembly, the Council and the Secretariat. The Assembly was the supreme body and consisted of the representatives of the various states which were members of the League. Every member-state was given the right of one vote in the Assembly and all its decisions were required to be unanimous. The Assembly held deliberations on international, political and economic matters which were likely to endanger the peace of the world. It was to advise the members to reconsider the question of amendment of the Treaties which had become inapplicable on account of the lapse of time and change of circumstances. It was to revise the budget prepared by the Secretariat. It was to supervise the work of the Council.

Council. The Council was the executive of the League and it consisted of permanent members, non-permanent members and *ad hoc* representatives. Only the Great Powers were the permanent members of the Council but additional permanent members could be admitted with the approval of the Assembly and the Council. There were as many as elevent non-permanent members of the Council. The Council was to meet at least once a year. It was required to deal with any matter within the sphere of the action of the League or affecting the peace of the world. It was required to formulate plans for the reduction of armaments by the various states. It was required to suggest ways and means to avoid the evil effects of the manufacture of munitions and implements of war by private enterprises. It was to make suggestions regarding the methods by which the territorial, integrity of the states could be ensured. If a dispute among the states was likely to lead to a conflict, the Council was required to enquire into the matter and submit a report within six months of the submission of the dispute to it. If any member of the League resorted to war, the Council was required to recommend to the other governments the effective military, naval or air force to be contributed by the various members of the League of Nations with a view to protect the aggrieved party. If there was a dispute between a member state and a non-member state, or among the non-member states alone, the Council was required to go into the matter and make its recommendations for the settlement of the dispute.

Secretariat. The Secretariat of the League consisted of the Secretary-General who was appointed by the Council with the approval of the Assembly and of such other staff as were required for its work. The Secretariat was located at Geneva and the staff was appointed by the Secretary General in consultation with the Council. The member states had to pay towards the expenses of the Secretariat in certain proportions. While the meetings of the Council and the Assembly were held from time to time, the Secretariat continued to work throughout the year. The officials of the League enjoyed certain privileges and immunities while engaged in the work of the League.

Permanent Court of International Justice. The Permanent Court of International Justice was opened on 15 February 1922 and it continued to work till October 1945. Its Judges were elected by the Council and the Assembly and the League of Nations had no power to remove them. The budget of the Court was under the control of the Assembly. The jurisdiction of the Court comprised all cases which the parties referred to it and all matters specifically provided for in the Treaties and Conventions in force. The Council and the Assembly were given the powers to ask for the advisory opinion of the Court. The decisions of the Court were binding only on the parties in dispute and in respect to the particular case alone. There was no provision for appeal although the Court could review its own judgement in the light of the facts brought before it.

International Labour Organisation. The International Labour Organisation was also attached to the League of Nations. Its object was to improve the labour conditions in various parts of the world. Its governing body consisted of the representatives of the governments, employers and workers. Important decisions were taken on the occasion of its annual meetings.

Many international unions and organisations were put under the direction of the League and some of them were the International Hydro-graphic Bureau, Central International Office for the Control of Liquor Traffic in Africa, International Bureau for Information and Enquiries regarding Relief to

Foreigners, International Commission for Air Navigation, Nansen International Office for Refugees, International Exhibitions Bureau, International Institute of Intellectual Cooperation, International Institute for the Unification of Private Law, International Centre for the Study of Leprosy, International Educational Cinematographic Institute, etc.

Its Functions. The main function of the League of Nations was to avoid wars and maintain peace in the world, and it was required to do all that lay in its power to achieve that ideal. A check was to be put on armaments. The size of the army was to be reduced to such an extent that it was just sufficient for the maintenance of law and order and defence from foreign aggression. The members of the League were required not to go to war without exhausting all the pacific means for the settlement of disputes. The Assembly, the Council and the Permanent Court of International Justice were to help in the matter of maintaining peace. Provision was made for collective action against a state which dared to violate the provisions of the Covenant of the Leaue. Coerecive action could be taken against the rebellious states. Provision was also made for the enforcement of economic sanctions against an aggressor country.

Mandate System. Provision was made for the Mandate System under the League of Nations. The territories captured from the Central Powers and Turkey were not to be restored to them and were also not to be given to any victorious country in full sovereignty. The administration of those countries was to be given to the various powers under the supervision of the League of Nations. While appointing the Mandatory powers, their resources, experience and geographical position were taken into consideration. The mandatory territories were considered to be inhabited by backward communities and were to be regarded as a sacred trust of civilization. The mandate was not a form of annexation and a mandated territory could not be annexed or ceded without the consent of the League of Nations.

The mandated territories were divided into three classes. Class A mandated territories were those which formerly belonged to the Turkish Empire and had reached a stage of development where their existence as independent nations could be provisionally recognised, but they were to get administrative advice and assistance by the mandatory power. The mandate for Iraq and Palestine was given to Great Britain. Syria and Labanon were put under the mandate of France. Class B Mandatory territories were those in respect of which the mandatory power was to be responsible for its administration. She was required to guarantee freedom of conscience and religion, stop such abuses as slave trade, arms and liquor traffic, prevent the establishment of fortifications, or military and naval bases and secure equal opportunities for the trade and commerce of other members of the League. Under this category Great Britain was given the mandate for British Cameroon, British Togoland and Tanganyika. France was given mandate for French Cameroon and French Togoland. Belgium was given mandate for Ruanda Urundi. Class C Mandatory Territories were those which on account of their small size, sparseness of population, remoteness from centres of civilization and their geographical contiguity to the territory of the mandatory power could best be administered under the laws of the mandatory state as an integral part of that state. Under the category, South-West Africa was put under the mandate of the Union of South Africa, Samoa under New Zealand, Nauru under Great Britain and Australia and New Zealand and the Pacific Islands, North of Equator under Japan and those south of the Equator under Australia.

The mandatory powers were required to administer the mandatory territory in such a way as to help the political, social and economic development of that territory. They were required to submit every year a report on the working of the mandate. The League could send its own nominees to see how much progress was made by the territories under the mandate system.

It is true that the mandate system suffered from certain shortcomings, but it cannot be denied that it represented an important adventure in international supervision over backward areas. The very feeling that those who were entrusted with the mandates owed some responsibility towards the civilized world, was distinct improvement in colonial administration. In 1932, Iraq was granted independence and she became a member of the League. The Mandates' Section of the League collected information and focussed the world public opinion upon the deeds or misdeeds of the mandatory powers.

Work of the League

It is true that the League of Nations was called a League of notions, a league of robbers and a league of procrastinators. It was also said that the League could only bark and did not bite. However, in spite of it, it did a lot of useful work during its existence for about twenty years. The League was called upon to examine about forty disputes. As a rule, the cases were handled by the Council, but a few of them were referred to the Assembly, the Council of Ambassadors or the Permanent Court of International Justice. Some of the earlier disputes such as that of 1923 between Italy and Greece over the murder of several Italians on Greek soil were serious threats to world peace. Disputes such as that of 1921-22 between Finland and Soviet Russia over the treatment of inhabitants of Eastern Karelia were of lesser importance. There were also some disputes which the League was not able to settle at all. On the whole, the League was able to assert its political mission more successfully where small nations were involved. The larger nations were more likely to regard investigations by the League as an infringement of their sovereign rights. They were also in a position to bring pressure on their behalf.

(1) **The Aaland Island.** One of the first disputes brought to the attention of the Council of the League concerned the Aaland Islands which lie between Sweden and Finland. Both Finland and the Islands once belonged to Sweden, but those were acquired in 1809 by Russia. In 1917 Finland declared her independence which was recognised by Sweden in January 1918 without making any reservation with regard to the Aaland islands. This was so, in spite of the fact that the inhabitants of the islands were chiefly of Swedish stock and spoke the Swedish language.

The inhabitants of the islands began to agitate for their union with Sweden, The Government of Sweden kept aloof from the movement, but her people sympathised with the agitators who were arrested by the Government of Finland. The people of Sweden demanded that their government must send help to the Islanders and there was every possibility of a war. In June 1920, Great Britain directed the attention of the League to the happenings in the Islands. A meeting of the Council was held in London and both the parties represented their case. The matter was referred to a Committee of Jurists. The Council gave its decision in June 1921. Finland was to have sovereignty over the Islands whose people were guaranteed autonomy and protection of their political rights. The rights of private property and the use of the Swedish language in schools were to be preserved. The area was to be neutralised and unfortified. In April 1922, an international convention was made which guaranteed the neutrality of the Islands and also gave them the requisite international protection.

(2) **Mosul Boundary Dispute.** According to the Treaty of Laussanne of 1923, the frontier separating Turkey from Iraq was to be drawn in a friendly manner by Turkey and Great Britain and if no agreement was arrived at within 9 months, the matter was to be referred to the Council of the League. Both failed to agree on a mutually acceptable boundary line as they both claimed the Mosul Vilayat which was rich in oil. The matter was referred to the League in 1924. The situation was very grave. There occurred a number of frontier incidents. An emergency session of the League Council was called at Brussels. A provisional boundary line was drawn pending the final judgement. Turkey was to maintain order north of the Brussels line and Great Britain was to maintain order to the south of that line. A neutral Commission of Enquiry heard both the parties to the dispute and submitted its report to the League Council in September 1925. The report established the sovereignty of Turkey over the Vilayat and explained that neither Great Britain nor Iraq had a right to claim it by conquest. Certain points were referred to the Permanent Court of International Justice, but the dispute was not solved. Ultimately, the League Council gave its final judgement on the subject. The Brussels line was to be the permanent boundary line between Turkey and Iraq. Great Britain was to take steps to secure the extension of her control over Iraq for a further period of 25 years. The Kurdish minority

in Mosul was to be guaranteed the appointment of Kurdish local officials and the use of Kurdish language in its schools. Great Britain and Iraq accepted the award but Turkey refused. As Turkey began to lean more on the Soviet Union, Great Britain entered into a compromise. In June 1926 a Treaty was made between Turkey and Great Britain by which a small part of the Vilayat was given to Turkey. Some royalties from the Mosul oil fields, were also given to Turkey.

(3) **Dispute between Bolivia and Uruguay.** In December 1928, an armed clash took place between Bolivia and Paraguay. The matter was taken up by the League Council and a telegram was sent by it expressing its full conviction that the two States would resolve their differences through peaceful means. Both the states agreed to accept the good offices of the Pan-American Conference on Arbitration and Conciliation. The result was that the immediate quarrel was resolved, but the underlying causes of the dispute remained. Fresh trouble occurred in May 1929. The representatives of the two states met in Washington to conclude a non-aggression pact and hostilities were suspended. There was trouble again in 1932. Efforts were made by the neighbouring states to stop the war, but with no success. Bloody conflict continued. The League of Nations appointed a Commission of Enquiry which reported that the struggle was inhuman and criminal. When attempts to restore peace failed, it was decided to put an embargo on arms shipment to Bolivia and Paraguay. Some states cooperated while others did not. As Paraguay had the upper hand, she refused to accept a compromise formula. Paraguay also gave a notice to resign from the membership of the League. The League did not take any interest in the matter after March 1935. However, as a result of the efforts of Argentine, Brazil, Chile, Peru and the United States, the Foreign Ministers of Bolivia and Paraguay signed in June 1935 a protocol outlining the machinery for the negotiation of peace. It was in July 1938 that a Peace Treaty was signed. It is obvious that the League did not succeed in the dispute between Bolivia and Paraguay.

(4) **Eupen and Malmedy.** In 1920 and 1921, Germany addressed to the League Council a series of protests against the giving of Eupen and Malmedy to Belgium. The League Council discussed the matter in September 1920 and wrote to the German Government, that its decision regarding the transfer of Eupen and Malmedy to Belgium was final.

(5) **The Corfu Incident.** In August 1923, an Italian General, two officers and one chauffeur were murdered on Greek soil. The Italian Government demanded apologies and full reparation for the crime. As Greece refused to accept all demands of Italy, the latter occupied the island of Corfu. In September 1923, Greece referred the matter to the League Council. It was notified by the President of the League Council that a communication had been received from the Conference of Ambassadors announcing the settlement of the dispute as a result of diplomatic negotiations undertaken by the Conference.

(6) **The Gorfu Incident.** In August 1923, an Italian General, two arose a dispute between France and Great Britain over the nationality decrees in Tunis and Morocco. The decrees issued by France in Tunis and Morocco provided that any person born in France or on the territory of French colonies would be a French citizen. These decrees conflicted with the British nationality laws. The British Government asked the French Government to refer the matter to arbitration but the contention of France was that it was a purely domestic affair. Ultimately, it was decided by the Permanent Court of International Justice that the matter was not purely one of domestic jurisdiction. The dispute was finally decided by mutual negotiations between the foreign ministers of the two countries.

(7) **Dispute between Greece and Bulgaria.** There was some trouble on the frontier between Greece and Bulgaria on account of the activity of Macedonian brigands. In October 1925, the commander of a Greek frontier post and one of his men were killed. By way of reprisal, a Greek army marched into Bulgaria. The latter appealed to the League. The League Council met and asked the Greek Government to withdraw its troops. The Governments of Great Britain, France and Italy were asked to send military officers to the spot to see what was happening. These measures had a deterrent effect on the Greek Government. The Greek forces were withdrawn and Greece was asked to pay compensation to Bulgaria for the violation of her territory on a scale to be fixed by a League Commission.

The League also did a lot of non-political work. A Slavery convention was set up at Geneva in 1925. In 1932, it was decided to set up a Permanent Slavery Commission.

The Financial Committee of the League advised the Council on financial matters in general, on financial assistance to Governments and on financial problems which could be solved by international co-operation. It helped to tackle the problem of counterfeiting, falsification of commercial documents, double taxation and fluctuating value of gold. The Financial Committee was responsible for the issue and supervision of various League loans for Austria, Hungary, Greece, etc. A general finance conference was held in Brussels in 1920. The Economic Committee of the League did the preliminary work for the World Economic Conference of 1927 and the Monetary and Economic Conference of 1933.

In order to implement the provisions of Article 23 of the Covenant of the League, the autonomous Communications and Transit Organisation was set up in 1920. This Organisation co-operated with river commissions, labour unions, railway agencies, air traffic associations, etc.

The League also set up in 1923 the Health Organisation with a Health Committee and a secretariat. It performed a lot of useful work in organising action against malaria, small-pox, leprosy, rabies, cancer, tuberculosis, syphilis, heart disease, etc. It helped researches in medicine. It helped the nations to improve national health. It organised technical conferences. It co-operated with governments in reporting epidemics and their spread. The League helped to fight typhus and prevented cholera and plague from the East. It brought home from Russia 4,27,000 prisoners of war. It co-operated with China to organise relief work in flood areas. It helped the Greek Government to settle 15 lakhs of refugees. Dr. Nansen played an important part in the work of the settlement of refugees under the aegis of the League.

In 1922, the League appointed an International Committee on Intellectual Co-operation. In 1926 was established the International Institute of Intellectual Co-operation at Paris. It tried to co-ordinate "international collaboration with a view to promoting the progress of general civilisation and human knowledge and notably the development and diffusion of science, letters and arts."

The League did a lot of useful work in the field of the control of traffic in dangerous drugs, prohibition of traffic in women, suppression of trade in obscene literature, promotion of child welfare, etc. It was responsible for drawing up a large number of very valuable international agreements and conventions. An attempt was made to codify the law regarding nationality, territorial waters and state responsibility. When Austria was on the verge of economic collapse in 1921-22, the League arranged an international loan to put the country back on her feet. Similar help was given to Hungary, Greece and Bulgaria. The League gave valuable financial advice at the international conference in Brussels in 1920, in Geneva in 1927 and in London in 1933. It established international conventions regarding customs, export of certain commodities, suppression of counterfeit currency, etc. It tried to simplify administrative formalities with a view to facilitate passenger and goods traffic. In 1920, a model passport for general use was adopted and it was recommended that stringent passport and visa regulations should be removed. Conventions were drawn up with regard to transport in international rivers, maritime signals, the lighting of coasts and road traffic. Expert help was given to the Polish Government to settle certain inland shipping questions and the Chinese Government for road development and improvement of certain waterways. Cordell Hull says, "The League of Nations has been responsible for more humanitarian and scientific endeavour than any other organisation in history."

Collective Security and the League

The Covenant of the League provided for a system of collective security so that peace could be maintained in the world. Members of the League undertook to respect and preserve as against external aggression the territorial integrity and existing political independence of all the members. In the event of an aggression or threat or danger of aggression, the Council of the League was required to decide what measures were necessary to meet the situation. In case an emergency arose, the Secretary General of the League was required to summon at once a meeting of the Council on the request of any member of the League. It was the right of every member of the League to bring to the notice of the Council or the Assembly any circumstances which could threaten or disturb international peace. The members of the League agreed among themselves that if there was a dispute among them which could lead to war, they would submit the same either to arbitration or judicial settlement or enquiry by the Council. They agreed not to resort to war until three months after the award of the arbitrators or the judicial decision or the report of the Council. Certain disputes were declared to be among those which were generally to be submitted to arbitration or judicial settlement and those were to be referred to the Permanent Court of International Justice, or any Tribunal agreed upon by the parties to the dispute. The members of the League also agreed to abide by the decision or award that might be given. They undertook not to resort to war against a member of the League which complied with the award or decision. If there arose between the members of the League any dispute likely to lead to a rupture which was not submitted to arbitration or judicial settlement, the members of the League were required to submit the same to the Council which was to give full consideration to the same. If any member of the League resorted to war in disregard of the provisions of the Covenant, it was deemed to have committed an act of war against all other members of the League and the lattre were required to subject that member state to the severance of all trade, financial, commercial or personal intercourse between nationals of the Covenant-breaking state and the nationals of any other state, whether a member of the League or 'not.' It was the duty of the Council in such a case to recommend what effective measures could be taken to meet the situation. The members of the League agreed that they would mutually support one another in the financial and economic measures which were taken in order to minimise the loss or inconvenience resulting from the above measures. They also agreed mutually to support one another in resisting any special measures aimed at one of the members of the Covenant-breaking state. They also undertook to take necessary steps to afford the passage through their territories to the forces of those members of the League who were cooperating to protect the Covenant of the League. Any member of the League who violated the Covenant was to be removed from the membership of the League. If any dispute involved a state which was not a member of the League, that state was to be invited to accept the obligations of the members of the League for the purposes of that dispute alone, and if the invitation was accepted, the Council was required to institute immediately an enquiry into the circumstances of the dispute and recommend measures which were considered to be effective. If a non-member rejected the invitation, all members of the League were required to take collective action against that state.

As regards the working of the system of collective security as established under the League, some Italian Commissioners were murdered in 1923 by the bandits on Greek territory near the Albanian frontier. The contention of Greece was that the murderers were Albanians and the Albanians blamed Greece. Italy held Greece responsible and bombarded and besieged the island of Corfu. Greece appealed to the League of Nations but Italy refused to accept the invitation of the League and the result was that the League took no action against Italy.

In 1925, there was a border dispute between the soldiers of Greece and Bulgaria and the Greek army marched into Bulgaria. When Bulgaria appealed to the League, the latter asked the Greek Government to withdraw its troops. The Governments of Great Britain, France and Italy were directed to send military officers to the spot and the result was that the Greek forces were withdrawn and Greece agreed to pay compensation to Bulgaria for the violation of her territory.

There were armed clashes between Bolivia and Paraguay in 1928. The matter was taken to the Council of the League and the parties were requested to act in accordance with the pledges given by them as members of the League. The matter was settled through the good offices of the Pan-American

Conference on Arbitration and Conciliation. There was trouble again in 1932 and the neighbouring states failed to stop the war between the two countries. A Commission of Enquiry appointed by the League of Nations reported that the war between the two states was inhuman and criminal. As the efforts to stop the war failed, it was decided to put as embargo on the shipment of arms to both Bolivia and Paraguay. Some states cooperated, while the others did not. As Paraguay had the upper hand, she refused to accept the suggested compromise and threatened to give up her membership of the League of Nations. The result was that the League did not take any further interest in the matter.

Japan had an eye on Manchuria for a long time and she took action in 1931. Within four days, all the Chinese towns within a radius of 200 miles north of Mukden were captured by the Japanese. By November 1931, practically the whole of North Manchuria was in the hands of Japan. China appealed to the League of Nations which after waste of a lot of time, appointed the Lytton Commission to go to the spot and make a report. The report was submitted in 1932. Its recommendations were couched in a very guarded language. The report avoided to mention Japan as the aggressor. When the Lytton Report was discussed by the Assembly of the League of Nations, the Japanese delegation left the hall and Japan gave a notice giving up her membership of the League. The result was that the members of the League did not take any action against Japan and the whole of Manchuria was occupied and annexed by Japan.

The system of collective security was tested again in Abyssinia and there also it failed. There were clashes between the troops of Abyssinia and Italy in 1934-35. Italy put forward unreasonable claims for compensation and subsequently conquered the whole of Abyssinia in spite of the fact that sanctions were enforced by the League of Nations against Italy. The result was that the system of collective security was completely discredited and every state felt that it could do what it pleased without any fear of collective action against her.

When the German troops marched into the Rhineland in March 1936 in violation of the provisions of the Treaty of Versailles, no action was taken against Germany although the safety of both France and Belgium was endangered. When the civil war broke out in Spain in 1936, General Franco was backed by Hitler and Mussolini and was given all possible assistance but countries like Great Britain and France did nothing to help the Republican regime. When Hitler annexed Austria in 1938, no action was taken by the League. When there was a crisis in Czechoslovakia, nobody came to her help and Germany was allowed to dismember her in October 1938. No action was taken by the League when the rest of Czechoslovakia was merged into Germany in March 1939. Within six months the World War II started in which practically all the states of the world were involved at one stage or the other and the system of collective security collapsed completely.

Many reasons have been given for the failure of the system of collective security under the League. One reason was that the interests of all the states were not identical and in many cases clashed with one another. Each state was determined to follow that policy which was in her own interests and such an attitude was not congenial to any collective action. The result was that each state was left to defend herself and there was no question of the other states coming to her help. Experience shows that a country was prepared to support another country if it was friendly towards her even if she was guilty of aggression. Such an attitude was fatal to the success of the system of collective security. Experience also showed that every state was afraid of being involved in a war for the sake of another state. In every war heavy losses are certain and nobody is sure about the final outcome of the war and hence all states tried to avoid war instead of joining hands to stop the aggressor. They were not prepared to pay the price involved in defending others although they could expect a similar treatment for themselves in future. The League had a very effective weapon in the form of economic sanctions but the same were not applied strictly. Their effectiveness was tested in 1931, 1955-56, but they failed. As regards diplomatic sanctions, they were merely an expression of disapproval but as a means of coercion, they were merely a slap on the wrist. The world was rent as under by conflicting ideologies and many states were trying for global dominance and in such circumstances, the system of collective security could not work.

Causes of failure of League. There were many causes which were responsible for the failure of the League of Nations. The Covenant of the League was made a part and parcel of the peace settlement. It would have been better if it had been kept separate. There were many states which considered the Treaty of Versailles as a treaty of a revenge and were not prepared to ratify the same. By not ratifying the Treaty, they could not be members of the League. The absence of the great Powers from the international organisation weakened her from the very beginning and that was partly responsible for its ultimate failure. Japan, Germany and Italy left the League and that certainly weakened it. The League was dominated by England and France and consequently, the other states began to lose their confidence in that organisation. The League was intended to perform a miracle by doing the impossible task of maintaining the *status quo* in the world. That would have been possible if the peace settlement of 1919-20 had been based on justice and fairplay. Further, as countries like Germany were completely humiliated by that settlement, there were no chances of peace. Germany was bound to defy the provisions of the Treaty of Versailles and that she actually did under Hitler. The rise of dictatorship in Italy, Japan and Germany weakened the chances of success of the League. Japan was determined to acquire fresh territories and as the League criticised her on the question of Manchuria, Japan left the League. Germany was not prepared to honour her commitments under the Treaty of Versailles with regard to her armaments, and consequently she decided to leave the League. The states continued to be the members of the League so long as their national interests were not in any way endangered or sacrificed. They preferred to pursue and achieve their national aspirations than to care for the strengthening and perpetuation of the international organisation which was the only hope of the world. Small nations lost their faith in the effectiveness of the League to save them from any aggression. The examples of Manchuria, Abyssinia, Austria and Czechoslovakia could be cited as examples in this connection. The League was given an effective weapon in the form of economic sanctions, but that weapon was not used effectively to produce good results. The economic sanctions against Italy were applied in a halting manner. The League failed because it was an organisation of the governmental authorities and the people of the various states had no say in its deliberations. There was no popular backing or enthusiasm. While Great Britain and France joined the League, they did not change their attitude. Great Britain looked upon the League as a means to perpetuate the balance of power. France looked upon the League as a means to encircle Germany. She did not transform French security into collective security. The League failed because it was based on the principle of equality. The idea of one nation, one vote led to Liberia being as important as the United Kingdom or France or the Soviet Union. That was not a sound basis on which to found an international organisation. The League though conceived as universal was in fact never universal. The narrow nationalism prevailing in the world was also responsible for the failure of the League. If the nations of the world were not prepared to sacrifice their national interests for the sake of the League or world interests, the League was bound to fail.

SUGGESTED READINGS

Allen, D.: **The Fight for Peace,** 1930.

Baker, P.J.N.: **The League of Nations at Work,** 1926.

Bartlett: **The League to Enforce,** 1944.

Bassett, J.S. : **The League of Nations, London,** 1928.

Beer, M.: **The League on Trial,** 1933.

Burton, M.E.: **The. Assembly of the League of Nations,** 1941.

Cecil, R.: **A Great Experiment,** 1941.

Chowdhuri, R.N.: **International Mandates and Trusteeship System,** 1955.

Eppstein, J.: **Ten Years' Life of the League of Nations,** 1929.

Gibbert, Kathleen : **The League in our Time.**

Howard, Ellis C.: **The Origin, Structure and Working of the League of Nations,** 1928.

Jones, R. and Shermann, S.S.: **The League of Nations: From Idea to Reality,** 1929.

Knudson, J.I. : **A History of the League of Nations,** 1938.

League of Nations: **Ten Year of World Co-operation,** 1930.

Low, David : **Years of Wrath: A Cartoon History,** 1946.

Marburg, T.: **Development of the League of Nations Idea,** 1932.

Miller. D.H.: **The Drafting of the Covenant.**

Pollock, F.: **The League of Nations.**

Rappard, W.: **The Geneva Experiment,** 1932.

Shotwell: **On the Rim of the Abyss,** 1936.

Walters, F.P. : **A History of the League of Nations,** 1952.

Wild, P.S.: **Sanctions and Treaty Enforcement,** 1934.

Wilson, F.: **The Origins of the League Covenant,** 1928.

Wright, Q.: **Mandates under the League of Nations,** 1930.

York, E.: **League of Nations: Ancient, Medieval and Modern,** 1928

Zimmern, A.: **The League of Nations and the Rule of Law.**

CHAPTER

32 GERMANY BETWEEN THE WARS

Although Germany had started the World War I, she was defeated and surrendered before the Allies on 11 November 1918. William II, the German Emperor, ran away to Holand. A Provisional Government under Friedrich Ebert, a saddler and leader of the Social Democrats, as Chancellor was proclaimed at Munich. In February 1919, a Democratic National Assembly was elected to prepare a democratic constitution. The constitution framed by the National Assembly is known as the Weimar Constitution of 1919. It provided for a republican form of Government and Ebert became the first President of the German Republic. He continued to occupy that office till 1925.

The first task of the new German Republic was to negotiate the treaty with the Allies. The terms offered by the Allies were so harsh that it was difficult to accept them. However, when the Allies gave an ultimatum, the German Republic had to submit and ultimately on 28 June 1919 was signed the Treaty of Versailles by the representatives of Germany. It is rightly maintained that the victors of 1918 did not show much wisdom when they imposed very severe terms on the new Republican regime in Germany. They ought to have imposed very lenient terms on Germany and thereby helped the new democratic regime in that country to take roots into the soil. The harshness of the terms weakened the foundations of the newly-born democracy in Germany and thereby facilitated the establishment of dictatorship under Hitler. Germany had traditions of autocracy but that autocracy was defeated in 1918. If the Allied statesmen desired the establishment of democratic traditions in Germany, they ought to have treated her leniently in 1919. Another mistake made was that Germany was obliged "to accept the responsibility of Germany and her Allies for causing all the loss and damage to which the Allied and Associated Governments and their nationals have been subjected as a consequence of the War imposed on them by the aggression of Germany and her Allies." The German representatives were forced to sign the treaty containing the war-guilt under a threat of renewal of war and thus the war-guilt clause lacked moral binding. It was a blunder to incorporate such a clause in the treaty. While it brought no material advantage to the victors, it created bitter resentment in Germany. The futility of the clause becomes obvious when it is remembered that not only Germany but other countries were responsible for the World War I.

Another mistake committed by the Allies was that they publicly arraigned "William II of Hohenzollern, former German Emperor for a Supreme offence against international morality and the sanctity of treaties". William II was to be tried by a court of five judges to fix the punishment. The Allied Governments requested the Government of Holland to hand over William II to them but the latter refused on the ground that it was contrary to international usage to surrender a political refugee. If the Dutch Government had accepted the request and handed over William II to the Allied Governments, that would have complicated matters. The trial of William II would have raised his prestige in Germany and made him a national hero and martyr. The attitude of the Dutch Government was a blessing in disguise. By another article of the Treaty of Versailles. Germany had agreed to hand over to the Allied military courts for trial any persons in Germany accused by the Allies of having "committed acts in violation of the laws and customs of war". The list prepared by the Allies included a large number of German personalities, *e.g.*, Crown Prince of Germany, Field Marshal Hindenberg, Lundendorff etc. The Germans refused to hand over the persons included in the list. Ultimately, a compromise was arrived at by which the German Government agreed to bring 12 of the accused before the Supreme Court at Leipzig. The trial took place in 1921 in which the Allied Governments acted as the prosecutors. Six of the accused were convicted and sentenced to various terms of imprisonment.

The new republic of Germany was threatened from the Right and the Left. On 13 March 1920, Dr. Kapp and General Luttwitz unsuccessfully attempted to overthrow the German Republic. Ebert's Government was successful in crushing the monarchist movement. The Communists and Independent Socialists clashed in 1920 with the Government troops and there were as many as 10,000 casualties. They were ruthlessly suppressed. In November 1923, Adolf Hitler proclaimed the overthrow of the Republic and announced himself as the president of Germany. The rebels paraded the streets of Munich but the revolt was crushed.

The Treaty of Versailles had provided that the Rhineland was to be permanently demilitarised and occupied by the Allied troops for 15 years. Although the United States did not ratify the Treaty of Versailles, the American troops remained in the Rhineland up to 1923. The attitude of the Allied troops belonging to the various powers occupying the Rhineland was not the same. While English troops established very friendly relations with the German people, the French troops tried to dominate them and put on airs of conquerors in a hostile land. The French troops had also a detachment of coloured soldiers and this was very much resented by the Germans who described it as the "black shame."

The treaty of Versailles had provided that if Germany voluntarily defaulted in her obligations, the Allied Powers could undertake definite reprisals against her. Raymond Poincare, a native of Lorraine, bitterly hated the Germans. In 1923, he became Prime Minister of France. He examined the records of payments which were required to be made by Germany and found that Germany had defaulted in timber, telegraph poles, coal, cattle, etc. That information was sent to the Reparation Commission for necessary action. The German Government maintained that the default was temporary and unvoluntary, but that did not satisfy France and Belgium. In spite of the protests of the British representative, it was decided to take action against Germany and consequently French and Belgian troops entered the Ruhr valley. The Ruhr valley was the very heart of German Industry as it produced about 80 per cent of the coal, iron and steel of the country and was responsible for about 70 per cent of its commercial railway traffic. Its occupation was bound to result in the economic dislocation of Germany. However, the Germans were helpless and they resorted to a policy of passive resistance. They refused to cooperate with the foreign invaders and the result was that factories and mines were deserted. The essential services of the State came to a standstill. Local officials refused to carry out the orders of the invaders. The newspapers refused to publish the commands of the Commanders. The Germans were cruelly treated but that did not help the invaders to secure their cooperation. Germany refused to pay reparation. It is rightly contended that "two men have united German people—Bismarck in 1870 and Poincare in 1923." The occupation was disastrous both for France and Germany. France lost the goodwill and cooperation of Great Britain. The occupation created a lasting bitterness in the minds of the German people towards France. It completed the economic collapse of Germany. Thousands of Germans were thrown out of employment and many of them died of starvation. The French troops were withdrawn in 1924 when Harriot came to power in France after the fall of Poincare. Gustav Stresemann, the Chancellor of Germany from 1923 to 1929, also helped to bring about a compromise between the two countries.

An attempt was made by the French Government to set up a separatist state in the Rhineland called the "Revolver Republic." The discontented workers and radicals, released convicts and rowdies from all over Germany were imported into the Rhineland and encouraged to proclaim the region independent. This move of the French Government was very much resented by the British

Government and ultimately the French Government was forced to withdraw her support from it. As the whole movement was fictitious and had no popular support, it soon collapsed.

Germany had to face a great financial crisis. The value of the German Mark began to fall. By the middle of 1920, it fell from its normal value of 20 Marks to the pound sterling to about 250 to the pound. By November 1921, it reached the figure of 1,000 to the pound. In the summer of 1922, it fell to 3,500 Marks to the pound. There were many causes for this abnormal inflation. The most important cause was the unsound financing of the World of the World War I. The German Government was so much confident of its victory in the war that it collected only four per cent of the total war cost of 171,000 million Marks by taxation and the rest was raised by inflation. A large amount of paper currency without gold backing was printed and this process was continued. Another cause was the reduction in Germany's gold supply. Whatever purchases were made from the neighbouring countries during the War, had to be paid for in gold and that resulted in the exodus of gold to the tune of 12,000 million Marks. The cost of maintaining the armies of occupation also necessitated inflation. The German view was that reparation payments were responsible for inflation. Until 1923, the transfers of money were not enough to affect the monetary situation, but the occupation of the Ruhr valley drove the currency situation out of control. During this period, Germany printed vast quantities of paper money. As the presses of the Government were not able to satisfy the demand, the Government had to get the help of additional presses to print paper currency. Inflation was also due to the deliberate plan of the great industrialists to cancel their own indebtedness and evade reparation payments.

The depreciation of the Mark was not without effects. It produced a false sense of prosperity. There was lot of industrial activity. A large number of factories were set up and there was no unemployment. However, after some time those who possessed real wealth refused to exchange it for paper Marks. The merchants and farmers refused to sell their things. Millions of people were threatened with starvation. The depreciation of the Mark also produced a deficit in the national trade. There was a general liquidation of loans and savings. Debtors pursued their creditors and paid off their debts in the worthless paper currency. The clever speculators and industrialists gained.

The financial chaos demanded drastic measures. The German Government issued new "rentenmark" with an exchange value of 23.8 cents. The Rentenbank was established. Provision was made for the surrender of old paper currency at the rate of one billion old paper Marks for one rentenmark.

Dawes Plan

It was under these circumstances that the Dawes Committee was appointed to examine the question of payment of reparations by Germany. After a detailed examination of the question, the Committee made its recommendations. Full economic and fiscal sovereignty was to be restored to Germany and the Ruhr Valley was to be evacuated. A Central Bank of Issue was to be established for the payment of reparations. The Bank was to have a monopoly for the issue of paper currency for fifty years. The amount of annual payments to be made by Germany was also fixed. It was to vary according to the index of prosperity of that country. Germany was to be given a foreign loan of 800 million gold Marks. A foreigner was to act as an Agent-General to supervise the execution of the Dawes Plan and he was to be assisted by a Transfer Committee. Gilbert was appointed the Agent-General.

The Dawes Plan had many merits. It fixed the amounts which Germany could pay in favourable circumstances. It separated the question of payments from the question of transfers. It gave the creditors security of certain specified revenues. It removed the question of reparation from politics. It was to be treated as an ordinary commercial debt. The question of reparations was taken away from the hands of the Reparation Commission and was handed over to an impartial agent for reparation payments. However, the Plan had certain shortcomings. Although it fixed the annual payments to be made by Germany, it did not fix the number of years for which the payments were to be made.

That did not give the Germans an incentive to save. It gave Germany the money with which she could make the reparation payments. Germany borrowed money from the United States and paid to her creditors. The result was that she cleared off one debt and created another. The prosperity which was created by the Dawes Plan was an artificial one. In the words of Gilbert, "As time goes on and practical experience accumulates, it becomes clearer that neither the reparation problem, nor the other problems depending upon it will be finally solved until Germany had been given a definite task to perform on her own responsibility without foreign supervision, and without transfer protection."

The Young Plan

The Dawes Plan was supported by the Young Plan in 1929. According to it Germany was to make 37 annual payments, at the rate of £ 100 million a year. In addition to that, she was to pay 22 smaller annual payments. By the final reduction and fixation of the German debts, by the establishment of progressive scale of annuities and by the facilities which the new Bank afforded for lessening disturbance in the payment of annuities, the Young Plan set the seal on the conclusion of German debts in the list of international settlements. It involved an appreciable reduction of payments to the creditor-countries on what might have been expected under the Dawes Plan and were equally inimical to the interests of the debtor and to the creditors by substituting a definite settlement under which the debtor knew the exact amount of his obligations. The Allied Troops were completely withdrawn from the German soil soon after the coming into force of the Young Plan in 1930.

With Sir Austen Chamberlain, the British Foreign Secretary and Briand, the Foreign Minister of France, Stresemann drew up treaties of Locarno in 1925. The Franco-German Treaty declared the frontier between the two countries to be permanent. It pledged both the states to resort to arbitration instead of war for the settlement of any future dispute. Similar treaties were concluded between Germany and Czechoslovakia, and Germany and Poland. The Treaty between Germany and France was guaranteed by Great Britain and Italy. The signing of the Locarno Treaties was followed in 1926 by the admission of Germany to the League of Nations and a seat on its Council.

In 1926, Briand and Stresemann met at Thoiry near Geneva. Stresemann begged for the immediate evacuation of the Rhineland and return of the Saar to Germany, offering in return concession in the form of reparation payments. The French Government was not prepared for this drastic extension of the time limits fixed by the Treaty of Versailles. Stresemann's offer of a large capital payment of reparation amounts was financially impracticable. No wonder, nothing came out of these conversations.

President Ebert died in 1925 and he was succeeded by Field Marshal Hindenburg. He was a hero of the World War I and was nearly 80 years old. He was a soldier, and unlike many German politicians of that time, a man of honour. He remained faithful to the republic which gained in stability during his Presidency. Under Hindenburg and Stresemann, Germany maintained the reparation payments due under the Dawes Plan. As the Dawes Plan was not working well, it was succeeded by Young Plan. From the autumn of 1929, the world was faced with an economic crisis and Germany was also adversely affected by the same. During the year 1932, Hinderberg first made Von Papen the Vice Chancellor and then allowed General Schleicher to overthrow him and succeed him as Chancellor. Early in 1933 Von Papen made an alliance with Hitler with a view to overthrow Schleicher, and urged Hindenberg to choose Hitler as his next Chancellor, hoping that he would be a mere tool. Hitler actually became Chancellor on 30 January 1933. It was the end of Von Papen and beginning of Hitler's triumphs.

Rise of Hitler

President Hindenberg who was opposed to Hitler and had given the following assurance to Gergor Strasser: "I gave my word of honour that Bohemian Corporal will never be Chancellor...... I will make him Postmaster and he can lick my face hundred times a day." In spite of that, Hitler was appointed the Chancellor by Hindenberg and that was due to many causes.

Germany was badly humiliated by the Peace Settlement of 1919. It was impossible for a proud nation like Germany to forget the loss of her colonies and other concessions in various parts of the world. Her military strength was completely crushed. Her navy was practically wiped out. She was saddled with such a huge war indemnity that it was practically impossible for her to pay. The Allied troops continued to be stationed on the German soil up to 1930 and they had to be provided for by Germany. The unhappy behaviour of the French troops who put on airs of conquerors, created a lot of bitterness. All this created an atmosphere which was exploited by Hitler to come to power.

Hitler's own character also helped him to come to power. He was a politician who possessed great resourcefulness. He was a great orator who could control and influence audiences of millions of people. His technique of propaganda helped him to carry the audience with him. He thundered. He asked for blood. He infused politics with a religious fervour. He was a fanatic in his views and was able to hypnotise all those who came to hear his speeches. The result was that his followers began to swell and ultimately he was led to power.

The character of the German nation also helped him. Most of the people of Germany were not democratic at heart. They cared more for that party which could give them security and glory than for freedom as such. They were sick of the treachery and cowardice of the Republican politicians who had brought the country to ruin. The Germans wanted a strong man who could take them out of the mess which had been created by the politicians since 1919. Hitler promised them and they flocked to him.

The declining fervour of Protestantism in Germany indirectly led to the rise of Hitler. Having lost their enthusiasm in religion, they were in search of some other job of devotion. The Republican regime in Germany was not able to win over their devotion and they found the job in the National Socialism of Hitler. That added to the strength of Hitler's party and his followers. Hitler gave to German nationalism a new life which had been eclipsed by the defeat of 1918. The Germans felt humiliated after the events of 1918 and they wanted a strong man who could raise them in the eyes of the world. Such an assurance was given by Hitler and he was accepted by the people.

Hitler was most vocal about the injustices of the treaty of Versailles. He denounced its provisions in the strongest possible terms. The more he did so, the greater became his popularity with the people who wanted somebody who could interpret their inner feelings to the world. They found in Hitler the man they wanted and that helped him to come to power.

Hitler gave to the Germans a high-sounding programme of 25 points which was a catalogue of promises and promised something to every group of the German nation. He promised protection of property from the communists. He promised protection of labourers against exploitation. He promised protection to consumers against producers. He promised protection to small business men against corporations. As he promised something to everybody, he was able to secure the support of a large number of people.

The miserable economic condition of the country also helped the rise of Hitler. Both the Dawes Plan and the Young Plan failed to solve the economic problems of Germany. In 1919 there started the world-wide economic depression and Germany was also affected. Chancellor Bruning failed to tackle the problems of the country and his Government was styled as "the starvation government." The number of the unemployed began to increase. There was a lot of economic distress in the country which was exploited by Hitler. In the words of F.L. Schuman, "The disaster begot 6,000,000 unemployed and general bankruptcy and impoverishment. Jobless workers flocked to the Communist Party, desperate burghers and peasants joined the NSDAP or Nazis, whose hysterical. Further promised prosperity, pride and power through the overthrow of the Weimar Jew Republic and the establishment of glorious Third Reich to be based upon anti-Marxism and Semitism and anti-capitalism and misty National Socialism. Industrialists and Junkers subsidised the brown-shirted Nazi Storm Troopers hoping to make use of them against Communists, Socialists, the trade unions and other threats, real or imaginary, to property and privilege."

The above factors were exploited to the maximum by Hitler and his followers began to multiply. With that, his strength and popularity also grew in the country. This is proved by the increasing number of seats captured by the Nazi party from 1924 onwards. In December 1924, the Nazi party won only 14 seats. In 1930 Hitler polled 6,000,000 votes and secured 107 seats. In July 1932, he more than doubled the number of votes and the seats, securing nearly 14 million votes and 230 seats. In March 1933, he won 288 seats.

President Hindenburg dismissed Bruning from Chancellorship and appointed Von Papen as Chancellor. When Von Papen found that he could not maintain law and order in the country he resigned. He was succeeded by General Schleicher. Early in 1933 Von Papen made an alliance with Hitler to overthrow Schleicher and urged Hindenberg to appoint Hitler as the Chancellor. Hitler actually became Chancellor on 30 January 1933. On the death of Hindenberg in 1934, he got himself elected the President of Germany and thus combined in himself the offices of the Chancellor and the President till his death in 1945. He abrogated the Weimar Constitution and himself became the Dictator of Germany.

From 1933 until his death in 1945, Hitler was supreme in Germany. The first half of this period was spent in preparing for war and war itself occupied the second half. His internal policy was authoritarian and totalitarian in every sense. Both economics and finance were controlled by the state. Rigorous and ruthless measures were adopted to improve the industrial situation. Unemployment was met by turning the unemployed into labour corps and by an enormous programme of armaments. In the political sphere, all organised opposition soon disappeared. The Jews who were the first object of persecution proved incapable of resistance in Germany and were expelled, deprived of their rights and cowed into silence or submission. However, Hitler met with subborn opposition both from the Protestants and Catholic churches. The most uncompromising opposition came from the Protestant Pastors. To begin with, the Roman Catholic Bishops were inclined to support Hitler in his fight against Bolshevism. However, both the churches stood firm against Nazi attempts to coerce them into approving the new racial theories as defined in the "Nuremberg laws" of September 1935. Those decrees deprived the Jews of all citizen rights, forbade their marriages with Aryans and virtually excluded them from the official, political and cultural life of Germany. In 1937, the Church was deprived of the control of its finances. All action on the part of the Protestant opposition was forbidden. Participation in the church affairs was made illegal. During the summer, a large number of Protestant Pastors were arrested and sent to concentration camps. Prominent among them was Pastor Niemboller who was arrested and imprisoned on a charge of "misuse of pulpit and incitement to disregard the laws of the German Government." In spite of protests from outside Germany, the persecution of both Catholics and Protestants continued, but did not succeed in exterminating either of them. As a matter of fact, the moral authority of both churches increased in Germany.

The position of the Jews in Germany further deteriorated. In April 1938, a decree was issued by which all Jews in Germany were ordered to declare their property in excess of 5,000 Reichmarks (£ 250 approximately). Towards the end of October 1938, the first mass expulsion of the Polish Jews began. The murder of Von Rath, a member of the German Embassy in Paris, by a young polish Jew gave Hitler an excuse for barbarous attacks on Jews throughout Germany. The Times wrote on 11 November 1938, "No foreign propagandist bent upon blackening Germany before the world could outdo the tale of burnings and beatings of black-guardly assaults upon defenceless and innocent people which disgraced that country yesterday." The indignation in the United States was so great that President Roosevelt recalled the American ambassador to Washington to report." All this had no effect on Hitler. Further measures against the Jews were decreed and they were deprived of all their movable and immovable property. It was made impossible for them to resort to any economic activity. It was contended that the object of those measures was to impoverish them and turn them into a criminal class and then to "extirpate them with fire and sword" as criminals.

A secret police organisation called the Gestapo was formed to deal promptly and severely with the slightest indication of opposition to or even criticism of the Government. Liberty disappeared completely. Newspapers were censored or suppressed. The teaching in schools and universities was made to conform with the views of the Nazi officials. Broadcasting was controlled in the interests of the Nazi party. The people were expected to spy and inform against one another. The workmen were to inform against employers, neighbours against neighbours, brothers against brothers and children against parents. The Nazi view was that the supreme duty of every individual was to the state and not any other individual or organisation.

Hitler proclaimed the superiority of the German race over all others. People with non-Aryan blood were deprived of the rights of citizenship and were excluded from all professions and the public service.

Hitler withdrew Germany from the Disarmament Conference in October 1933 and from that time onwards, the programme of rearmament was pressed on. In March 1935, conscription was introduced. The German Air Force was revived and it increased rapidly. Submarines, destroyers, cruisers and battleships were built for the German navy. Likewise, aeroplanes, guns, tanks, shells and all kinds of equipment were pressed on. After the re-occupation of the Rhineland in March 1936, the Siegfried Line of fortifications was constructed on the German side of the Franco-German frontier opposite to and parallel with the Maginot Line on the French side.

Foreign Policy of Hitler

The rise of Hitler to power shocked the people of Europe who had not forgotten his utterances from time to time and also what he had stated in a Bible of the Nazi party. The real objective of his foreign policy lay in the South and East of Europe. It was there that German nationalism hoped to fulfil her objective. It was felt that Germany had a growing population and it was only that region which could give her more space to accommodate that population. That region was thinly populated by races which could not make full use of the potentialities of that region. It was also maintained that that region was economically complementary to Germany. It was rich in coal, oil and wheat which Germany required for her development. As things were, it was not possible to exploit fully the resources of that region. While Austria had coal, she did not have grain. Hungary had grains, but no factories. Rumania had ores and oil but she had no markets. The best results could be achieved only after one political power was established in the whole region and that role was intended to be played by Germany under Hitler.

The pursuit of such a foreign policy soon after his coming to power in Germany would have created trouble. All the enemies of Germany could have joined hands and all prospects of success would be doomed once for all. To avoid such an eventuality, Hitler decided to follow a policy of caution. He would like to do all that lay in his power to remove the suspicions of his neighbours. He declared in unequivocal terms that Germany was determined to follow a policy of peace. Even if she would like to get the treaty of Versailles revised, that was to be done by peaceful means. Hitler decided to consolidate his position at home and make friends among the neighbours. To quote him, "The German Government and the German people are united in the will to pursue a policy of peace, reconciliation and understanding as the foundation of all decisions and all negotiations." In January 1934,, Germany entered into a non-aggression pact with Poland for 10 years. So far as the motives of Germany in making that pact were concerned, it was felt that such a pact would be a good conclusive proof of the peaceful intentions of Germany. Hitler had shocked and antagonised Western Europe and he feared the isolation of his country. If Germany wanted to advance Southwards, she must make peace with her Eastern neighbour. Polish friendship was purchased by giving her a guarantee for

10 years. Hitler felt that he could not win over the Soviet Union on account of his persecution of the Communists and the Jews. Austria was also hostile as she feared her own security from the Nazis. Czechoslovakia was considered to be too small to be bothered about. No wonder, Hitler decided to enter into a friendly pact with Poland. Poland had also her own reasons to join the pact. She had an uneasy time from 1919 to 1934. The German minorities had proved too much of a headache for her. It was felt that a treaty with Germany would silence the German minorities and Poland would be safe from the perpetual nuisance. Moreover, Poland had become suspicious of France whose ally she had been for the last many years. It was felt in Poland that there was a tendency on the part of France to subordinate the interests of Poland with a view to guarantee her own security. The attitude adopted by France on the occasion of the Locarno Pact of 1925 and the Four Power Pact of 1933 could be pointed out to prove their contention. As both the parties hoped to gain by the pact, the same was signed. However, as the events of 1939 show, it was merely a stop-gap arrangement so far as Germany was concerned. She had no intention of permanently guaranteeing the frontiers of Poland and to be on friendly terms with her. As a matter of fact, the World War II started on the question of Poland.

Austria

Hitler was an Austrian by birth and that partly explains his interest in the affairs of Austria. The Austrians were also Germans and they had been kept separate from Germany by the Treaty of Versailles as the Allies did not want to create a very strong and powerful Germany which could be a perpetual source of danger to the peace and security of Europe. However, Germany would like to annex Austria and with that objective in view. Hitler encouraged the Nazi agitators in Austria to capture the Government. No wonder, their agitation increased day by day. There was a wholesale condemnation of the Austrian Government by the broadcasts issued from Germany. Leaflets were distributed in large numbers throughout the length and breadth of Austria. Money and arms were also smuggled into Austria. The Austrian Government could not be expected to remain idle in the face of these provocations. No wonder, the Nazi party in Austria was suppressed in June 1933 by the orders of the Government. The Government of Austria remained firm against German pressure on account of the backing of Mussolini and other powers. Both Great Britain and France were determined to maintain the independence of Austria and they joined hands with Mussolini to make representations to the German Government. The Italian Government also subsidised the Heimwehr which was considered to be bulwark of the independence of Austria. In spite of this, the Nazis in Austria revolted in July 1934, occupied the Federal Chancery and were successful in fatally wounding Dollfuss, the Austrian Chancellor. Their chances of success were not many as they were not supported by the people of Vienna. When the revolt failed, Hitler, declared that the he had absolutely no hand in the whole affair.

Saar Plebiscite (1935)

With a view to compensatite France for the losses suffered by her during World War I, she had been given by the Treaty of Versailles the right to occupy and exploit the Saar for 15 years. However, it was provided that after the lapse of that period, a plebiscite would be held under the auspices of the League of Nations with a view to allow the people of the Saar to decide for themselves whether they would like to go back to Germany or not. Such a plebiscite was arranged in January 1935. About 5 lakhs of people cast their votes and more than 90 per cent of them voted for Germany. Hence the Saar was handed over to Germany on 1 March 1935. The recovery of the Saar added to the resources of Germany. It also proved the effectiveness of the Nazi techniques of propaganda.

German Re-militarisation

On 16 March 1935, Hitler declared that Germany was not bound by the military clauses of the Treaty of Versailles and the peace strength of the German army would be 36 Divisions or 5½ lakhs of men. The German army was to be raised by conscription which was also against the provisions of the treaty of Versailles. In April 1935, there was an agreement at Stresa among Great Britain, France and Italy to form a "united front" against German aggression.

Anglo-German Naval Agreement (1935)

In June 1935, Hitler entered into a Naval Agreement with Great Britain by which Germany agreed to limit the size of her Navy to 35 per cent of the strength of the British Navy. By this agreement, Hitler was able to remove the suspicions of Great Britain and win her to his side. However, this agreement was against the provisions of the Treaty of Versailles which required Germany to maintain a much smaller naval force than that allowed by the Anglo-German Naval Agreement. This agreement was a master-stroke of Hitler's diplomacy.

Re-militarisation of the Rhineland

The Treaty of Versailles had demilitarised the Rhineland. It had been specifically provided that no German troops were to be stationed in that region. These provisions were considered to be essential for the safety and security of France and Belgium. However, in March 1936, Hitler denounced the Locarno Treaties and German troops marched into the Rhineland. While this action of Hitler was condemned by all, his own defence was that France herself was to be blamed for it. It was she who had entered into a military pact with Soviet Russia in May 1935 and as Germany regarded that alliance to be directed against her, she was justified in occupying the Rhineland. However, it cannot be denied that after the German occupation of the Rhineland, France became exposed to German attack. The same was the case with Belgium. At the time of the occupation of the Rhineland, Hitler made many offers to the Western Powers for a compromise. He offered to demilitarise the German territory on the German side of the border to the same extent to which Belgium and France were prepared to demilitarise on their side of the border. He also offered to enter into another Locarno Pact. He also expressed his willingness to enter into a non-aggression pact with his Eastern neighbours. However, nothing came out of those offers. Hitler was absolutely insincere in all that he was doing. His only object was to keep the people busy at a time when he had shocked them by his action. The result was that Hitler was able to have his way and no action was taken against him.

Spain

A Civil War broke out in Spain in 1936. The Republican Government of Spain was helped by the Soviet Union and General Franco and his followers were held by Hitler and Mussolini. They got a large number of volunteers from Germany and also a lot of war material with which they were able to overthrow successfully the Republican Government. Great Britain and France followed a policy of neutrality and that helped both Hitler and Mussolini.

Berlin-Rome-Tokyo Axis

In 1936, Germany entered into an anti-Comintern Pact with Japan. In 1937, Italy also joined the pact and thus the Berlin-Rome-Tokyo Axis came into being. Germany and Japan came together as both of them were opposed to Communism. Japan had left the League of Nations on account of her condemnation by the League of Nations on the issue of conquest of Manchuria. So far as Mussolini was concerned, he opposed Hitler in 1934 on the question of Austria. However, things changed after Italian intervention in Abyssinia. It was during the Abyssinian war that Mussolini was condemned by the Western Democracies. They also enforced economic sanctions against Italy. Hitler adopted a friendly attitude towards Italy on the question of Abyssinia. It was this friendly act which brought Mussolini to the side of Hitler. Not only the two dictators agreed to cooperate with each other, Mussolini also agreed to give Hitler a free hand in Austria.

Annexation of Austria (1938)

Having removed the Italian hurdle from his way. Hitler decided to annex Austria. After the Nazi failure in 1934 in Austria, Hitler had changed his tactics in his dealings with Austria. The latter was made to understand that the former had absolutely no designs against her. The result was that by 1936, a favourable climate was created in Austria for Germany. In July 1986, Hitler entered into a pact with Austria. A sort of Italo-German condominium was established over Austria and the relations between Austria and Germany became cordial. In spite of all this, violent demonstrations were made by the Nazis in Austria in 1938. Those were inspired and helped by the German Government. On 12 February 1938, Hitler sent for Schuschnigg, the Austrian Chancellor, to meet him at his personal residence at Berchtesgaden. The Austrian Chancellor was threatened with an invasion of his country and thereby forced to grant amnesty and full freedom of action to the Nazis of Germany. He also agreed to take the Nazi leaders of Austria into his cabinet. The Austrian Chancellor appointed Arthur Seyss. Inquart, the Austrian Nazi leader, as his Minister of the Interior. He also agreed to appoint other Nazi leaders as Ministers of Justice and Foreign Affairs. It was announced on 9 March 1938 that a plebiscite would be held on 13 March 1938 to decide whether Austria would like to remain independent or merge herself with Germany. The Nazi leaders were not willing to have the plebiscite on 13 March as that did not give them enough time for propaganda. Consequently, on 11 March 1938, Arthur Seyss Inquart presented the Austrian Chancellor with an ultimatum demanding his resignation and the postponement of the plebiscite. He was told that in case he failed to do so, the German troops would enter Austria. The result was that the Austrian Chancellor not only cancelled the plebiscite but also resigned. Arthur Seyss Inquart himself became the Chancellor and in his new position, he invited Hitler to come and save Austria from internal chaos. The German army and air force rushed into Austria. On 14 March 1938, Hitler himself went to Vienna. The Western Democracies did practically nothing. Their attitude can be compared to sincere widows who moaned and shouted but otherwise did nothing. The annexation of Austria was of great importance to Germany. The Austrian National Bank brought to the German Treasury 20 million pounds of additional gold and foreign exchange. Germany came into direct contact with Italy at the Brenner Pass. She also came into contact with Hungary and Yugoslavia. In the words of Churchill, "Mastery of Vienna gives to Nazi Germany military and economic control of the whole of communications of South-Eastern Europe, by road, by river and by rail." Czechoslovakia was isolated and she became absolutely at the mercy of Germany who could deal with her as she pleased.

Munich Crisis (1938)

The State of Czechoslovakia had been created by the Peace Settlement of 1919-20. Her greatest weakness was that she had many minorities in her population and the most important among them was the Sudeten Germans. Although they were nicely treated, they never forgot their separate German nationality in Czechoslovakia. They had been given seats in the Cabinet and were pretty well off. After five years of Hitler's propaganda, the Sudeten Germans began to look up to Germany for their absorption into that country.

Hitler had a special reason to intervene on behalf of the Sudeten Germans. The Sudetenland was important from the strategic point of view. Its Northern frontier had a mountain range which blocked off German expansion to the South. If this territory were to come under Hitler's control, it would become easy for him to penetrate into South Europe. This area was also full of factories and its occupation was to add to the industrial output of Germany. However, there were certain difficulties in the way. Czechoslovakia had a large number of forts in the Sudetenland and consequently it was difficult to conquer that region. By a treaty of 1925, France was bound to help Czechoslovakia in case she was attacked by any foreign power. A similar guarantee had been given by the Soviet Union to Czechoslovakia. However, the advantages of capturing the Sudetenland were so great that the difficulties seemed to be insignificant. Moreover, the manner in which the western democracies had acted in Manchuria, Abyssinia and Spain showed that they would not lie willing to save Czechoslovakia from Hitler. So far as the Soviet Union was concerned, even if she would like to help her, she could not accomplish much on account of the barrier policy of Poland and Rumania. The latter were not prepared to allow the Soviet forces to march through their territories. Hitler thus felt sure that he could deal with Czechoslovakia as he pleased.

The Sudeten Germans were encouraged to stage demonstrations against their government. They demanded the right to join Germany. The government of Czechoslovakia headed by Dr. Benes tried to meet their demands in every possible way. However, no reconciliation was possible as the

Germans instigated them not to do so. The situation began to deteriorate. On 12 September 1938, Hitler demanded the right of self-determination for the Sudeten Germans. He declared that if the latter could not defend themselves, they would be helped by Germany.

The Soviet Union proposed a conference with Great Britain, France and the United States and expressed her willingness to take part in any collective action that might be taken to defend Czechoslovakia against Germany. However, the proposal was not accepted. The British Government asked Premier Hodza to accept an Adviser. Lord Runciman was sent as an adviser and was accepted by the Government of Czechoslovakia. A plan was prepared which granted practically everything to the Sudeten Germans except their incorporation into Germany. That offer did not satisfy the Sudeten Germans who were backed by Hitler. The Western democracies were in a very difficult position and they did not know what to do. If they supported Czechoslovakia, there was the certainty of a war in which every one was likely to be involved. If they did not support her, she could not be expected to resist German pressure single-handed and in this war of nerves Hitler won.

Chamberlain, Prime Minister of Great Britain, decided to prevent war by following a policy of appeasement. He met Hitler on 15 September 1938 and he was frankly told that nothing could stop the war unless the Sudeten Germans were given the rights of self-determination. Chamberlain went back and conferred with the French Government. It was agreed that the only way to stop the war was to give to the Sudeten Germans the right of self-determination. On 19 September 1938, both Great Britain and France asked Czechoslovakia to agree to the immediate transfer to Germany of the areas inhabited by a population of more than 50% Germans. The Government of Czechoslovakia agreed to the proposal under pressure. However, at this stage, Hitler increased his demands which were considered by Chamberlain as unreasonable and he refused to do more than refer them to the Government of Czechoslovakia. It was decided that if Germany immediately attacked Czechoslovakia, the latter would be supported by Great Britain and France. War preparations were ordered. It was declared that the Soviet Union and Great Britain would stand by France if the latter helped Chamberlain against Germany. At this stage, President Roosevelt made a "Peace by conference" proposal to Hitler to settle the matter amicably. On 27 September 1938, Chamberlain declared: "We cannot in all circumstances undertake to involve the whole British Empire in war simply on her (Czechoslovakia) account." On 28 September 1938 Chamberlain told Hitler, "You can get the essentials without war and without delay." On the same day, Mussolini asked Hitler to settle the matter amicably instead of going to war. On 29 September 1938, Chamberlain. Daladier and Mussolini went to Munich to meet Hitler. There was no Czech or Russian representative present at the conference. After prolonged discussions, the Munich Pact was signed on the night of 29-30 September 1938. Czechoslovakia was to evacuate all the territory occupied by the Sudeten Germans and this was to be completed before 10 October 1938 without any existing installations being destroyed. The Government of Czechoslovakia was to be held responsible if any damage was done to those installations. The territory to be evacuated by Czechoslovakia was to be occupied by the German troops. An international commission was to be set up to decide in which territories the plebiscite was to he held and those territories were to be occupied by international bodies until the plebiscite was completed. The same commission was to fix the conditions in which the plebiscite was to be held, taking as a basis the conditions of the Sarr plebiscite. The date to be fixed by the commission was not to be later than the end of November 1938. The final determination of the frontiers was to be carried out by the international commission. Within a period of four weeks from the date of the agreement, the Government of Czechoslovakia was to release from their military and police force any Sudeten German who may wish to be released. She was also to release the Sudeten German prisoners who were serving terms of imprisonment for political offences.

It is rightly said that the heart of the lamb of Czechoslovakia was butchered in the darkness in the midnight by a knife supplied by Chamberlain. Dr. Benes, President of Czechoslovakia, declared that "He had been forced to yield to pressure to which there was no precedent in history and all that was due to the presence of Chamberlain and Daladier." Ribbentrop, Foreign Minister of Germany, remarked, "The old man (Chamberlain) has signed his death warrant and now it is for us to fill the date." Sir John Simon observed, "It can only be for history to decide hereafter whether the things that were done at Munich the day lead, as well as all of us everywhere in this House hope they will, to better things, or whether the prognostications or increasing evil will prove, to be justified." Winston Churchill described the situation after Munich as "a disaster of the first magnitude." His prophecy was in these words : "I think you will find that in a period of time which may not be measured by years, but may be measured only by months, Czechoslovakia will be engulfed in the Nazi regime." According to L.S. Amery, the Munich settlement represented the triumph of sheer naked force. It was "the greatest and cheapest victory ever won by aggressive militarism." F.L. Schuman says, "The Munich Pact was the culmination of appeasement and warrant of death for the Western democracies. It was a symbol of the collapse of collective security."

The question has been asked why the Western democracies submitted to the dictates of Hitler. One reason is that Hitler assured Chamberlain that in case his demands on Czechoslovakia were met, he would like to follow a policy of peace and he had no further aggressive designs. To quote Hitler, "I have assured Mr. Chamberlain and I emphasise it now, that when this problem is solved, Germany has no more territorial problems in Europe. I shall not be interested in the Czechoslovakian state any more and I can guarantee it. We do not want any Czechs any more." It is rightly pointed out that fault lay not in the intentions of Chamberlain, "but in his willingness to believe the words of Hitler. He ought to have known the German dictator better. His words were intended to suit merely the occasion and he was not going to keep them as the future events showed. Another reason given for the attitude of Chamberlain is that there was a strong longing for peace in Western Europe. It would take some time before the people were converted to fight against Germany. However, in case Germany attacked at once, there was every possibility of their facing disaster on account of the preparedness of the German armed forces. There was a wrong belief in Great Britain and France that after having got everything in Czechoslovakia, the attention of Hitler would be diverted towards Soviet Russia, the two dictatorships would get involved in a life and death struggle and thereby exhaust themselves. The Western democracies were likely to gain under those circumstances. Hence they allowed Hitler to have his way at Munich. Chamberlain also believed that the appetite of Hitler was limited. His view was that Germany and Italy had certain grievances and if those were redressed, peace could be maintained in Europe. That is the reason why he persisted in the policy of appeasement in spite of warning from Winston Churchill. Chamberlain believed in the good faith of Hitler. When Hitler introduced conscription and violated the provisions of Treaty of Versailles, he promised to adhere to the Locarno treaty. When he violated that also, he promised that he had no other territorial claims. Then there was the Anschlus and Munich. All that showed that the basic calculation of Chamberlain was wrong. Another reason why the policy of appeasement was followed was that Great Britain and France were not prepared to enter into an alliance with Soviet Russia on account of ideological differences. Chamberlain is said to have observed, "I must confess to the most profound distrust of Russia." The only alternative was to come to terms with Hitler as Great Britain and France were not ready for war.

Critics of Chamberlain point out that if he had decided to fight in September 1938, the Soviet Union would have joined the war against Germany. Moreover, in September 1938, there were thirty to forty well-trained Divisions of the Czech army which would have fought against Hitler. All that was not there when Chamberlain ultimately decided to fight against Hitler in September 1939. All the resources of Czechoslovakia also fell into the hands of Hitler and he fought with more resources in September 1939 than he would have done in September 1938 if the war had been declared then. The British armies were not in a better position in September 1939 than they were in September 1938 when Chamberlain made a humiliating peace with Hitler.

After the Munich Pact, the Poles and Hungarians made their demands on Czechoslovakia. Poland demanded and got the Teschen area with its important coal mines. Hungary demanded that area in which there were about a million Magyars and got the same.

Annexation of Czechoslovakia (1939)

In spite of giving his word of honour in September 1938 regarding the rest of Czechoslovakia, Hitler began to make preparations to annex the same. On 14 March 1939, the Governments of Slovakia and Ruthenia declared their independence after holding a conference with Hitler. On the same day, Hitler asked Dr. Hacha, the successor of President Benes, to meet him in Berlin. When Dr. Hacha went to Berlin, he was made virtually a prisoner. He was surrounded by the associates of Hitler and was asked to sign a document which was to put the fate of the Czech people into the hands of Hitler. General Goering told him that in case he refused to sign the document, his country would be attacked by the German Air Force and completely destroyed. No wonder, Dr. Hacha fainted and he was brought to his senses after administering injections to him. Finding himself helpless, Dr. Hacha singed the aforesaid document at 4.30 P.M. on 14 March 1939. On the morning of 15 March Czechoslovakia was occupied by the Nazi troops. On 16 March 1939, Hitler declared that henceforth Czechoslovakia would be known as "Protectorate of Bohemia and Moravia." Hitler was also invited to become the Protector of Slovakia. The invitation was gladly accepted and Czechoslovakia ceased to exist.

The annexation of the whole of Czechoslovakia had very unfortunate results. The Soviet Union was completely disgusted with the attitude of the Western Powers. She felt that the Western Powers were trying to help and instigate Germany against her. Under the circumstances, she felt that her alliance with France was not binding on her. The system of collective security completely broke down. States like Yugoslavia and Rumania began to realise the uselessness and futility of their alliances with France, It was felt that the security of every state was in danger.

Chamberlain was shocked. On 17 March 1939, he observed, "Public opinion in the world has received a sharper shock than has ever yet been administered to it, even by the present regime in Germany. Hitler had violated his own declared principles by including in the Reich a people of non-German race. He had manifestly departed both from the assurances at Munich, as to the extent and nature of his claims and from his undertaking to deal with any further questions in consultation with great Britain." Chamberlain promised British resistance "to the utmost of its power to any power which attempted to dominate the world by force." The joint Anglo-French protest against Germany was followed by the simultaneous withdrawal of their ambassadors from Berlin. On 23 March 1939, Chamberlain was forced to make the following admission, "The possible aim of the German Government is the domination of the whole of Europe." The policy of Great Britain and France underwent a radical change. Instead of trying to appease Hitler, it was decided to resist him in the future. On 31 March 1939, Great Britain and France declared that "in the event of any action which clearly threatened Polish independence and which the Polish Government accordingly considered it vital to resist with their national forces, they would at once lend Poland all support in their power." On 6 April 1939, Poland agreed to regard the British guarantee as a mutual obligation. Similar guarantees were given to Greece on 6 April and to Rumania on 13 April 1939. On 19 April Chamberlain indicated British intention to extend the guarantee of independence to Denmark, the Netherlands and Switzerland. On 26 April 1939, the British Government announced its decision to enforce military conscription in the country. On 12 May 1939, Great Britain gave a guarantee to Turkey. In his Albert Hall address on 12 May 1939, Chamberlain declared, "No more deadly mistake could be made than to assume that Britain and France were not in earnest and could not be relied on to carry out their promises."

Mamel (1939)

After the dismemberment of Czechoslovakia, Lithuania was given an ultimatum by Hitler. The latter demanded the surrender of Memel and the surrounding districts. The German forces occupied this region on 21 March 1939. The port of Memel was remilitarised.

Poland (1939)

Just as in September 1938, Hitler had declared his intentions on Czech independence, so in January 1939 he spoke warmly of the friendship existing between Germany and Poland. That was merely a preliminary to his making claims on Poland. With the passage of time, the attitude of Hitler towards Poland began to change. It was given out that the German minorities in Poland were being oppressed. Poland was asked to give back Danzig to Germany. She was also asked to give a strip of territory to connect East Prussia with the rest of Germany. The Polish Government was not prepared to accept the demands of Germany. Poland was backed by Great Britain and France. Germany not only abrogated her Non-aggression Pact with Poland of 1934, but also repudiated her Anglo-German Naval Agreement of 1935. Hitler protested that Great Britain was going back on the Munich Pact which was "symbolical of the desire of both people never again to wage war on one another." Hitler accused Great Britain of following a policy of encirclement. However, before taking the final step against Poland, Hitler decided to ensure himself against a possible attack from the Soviet Union. Ribbentrop went to Moscow and on 23 August 1939 was signed the Non-Aggression Pact between Germany and the Soviet Union. This master-stroke of Germany weakened the defences of Poland, Great Britain and France.

Having neutralised the Soviet Union, Hitler was ready and on 1 September 1939, German troops invaded Poland. The war which started between Germany and Poland developed into a global war. The hunger of Hitler was not satisfied even after the defeat and annexation of Poland. He also conquered Belgium, Holland and Denmark. In June 1940, France also fell.

The problem of Hitler in the middle of 1940 was either to conquer or to make peace with Great Britain. He put out feelers in June 1940, asking only the return of German colonies and British acceptance of his control over Western Europe. However, there was no response. The idea of compromise and British approbation to a German attack on the Soviet Union was long in dying. In May 1941, Hess flew to Scotland in what was considered to be a peace mission. The problem of preparing an invasion of England proved difficult as the German sea power was not strong enough and General Goering's Air Force was not able to snatch control of the air from the Royal Air Force. Elaborate preparations were made, but the battle of Britain was lost in September 1940 and the invasion of England had to be postponed indefinitely.

The decision to crush the Soviet Union before attacking Britain was reached in secret in August 1940. Plans of invasion in the autumn were given up for logistic reasons. However, preparations were pushed forward energetically throughout winter and spring with a view to assault in May 1941. The invasion had to be postponed to June 1941 because of the invasion and conquest of Yugoslavia and Greece in April 1941. Ribbentrop's invitation to Molotov was no more than a device to remove suspicion and gain time. The German invasion of the Soviet Union turned out to be a blunder. In spite of the initial success made by the German armies in Soviet Russia, the Germans were ultimately beaten and driven out of the Russian soil. That was partly due to the bravery of the Russian people and partly to the enormous help which was given to her by the United States. In 1945 Germany fell before the combined attacks of the United Nations. Too much greed of Hitler brought ruin to Germany. He himself committed suicide before Berlin fell and his associates were tried by a Military Tribunal and put to death.

SUGGESTED READINGS

Abel, T.: **Why Hitler Came to Power,** 1938.

Banse, E.: **Germany Prepares for War,** 1941.

Brady, R.A.: **The Spirit and Structure of German Fascism,** 1937.

Braunthal, J.: **The Tragedy of Austria,** 1948.

Bullock, A.L.C.: **Hitler: A Study in Tyranny,** 1953.

Dean, V.M.: **Europe in Retreat,** 1939.

Fraser, L.: **Germany between Two Wars.**

Fuchs, M.: **A Pact with Hitler,** 1939.

Handley, W.W.: **Munich Before and After,** 1944.

Hitler, A.: **Mein Kampf,** 1939.

Jarman, T.L.: **The Rise and Fall of Nazi Germany,** 1956.

Olden, R.: **Stresemann,** 1930.

Pollock, J.K. & Thomas: **Germany in Power and Eclipse,** 1952.

Robert, S.H.: **The House that Hitler Built,** 1937.

Robertson, E.M.: **Hitler's Pre-War Policy and Military Plans** (1933-9).

Schuman, F.L.: **Germany since** 1918-19.

Schuman, F.L.: **The Nazi Dictatorship,** 1936.

Sheele, G.: **The Weimar Republic.**

Shirer, W.L.: **The Rise and Fall of the Third Reich.**

Vallet, N.: **Stresemann,** 1951.

Wheeler-Bannett, J.W.: **Munich, Prologue to Tragedy,** 1952.

CHAPTER

33 FRANCE BETWEEN THE WARS

France came out victorious in the World War I but she was exhausted. Both in the East and North-East France was devastated. Her casualties in the war were more than those of the other Allied nations. One-tenth of the country was in ruins. Towns had been reduced to rubble. Factories and mines had been destroyed. Farms had been turned in the wilderness. All this demanded a determination on the part of the people of France to put their country on pre-war footing and the work was done with remarkable speed. The expectation that a lot of money will come to France as reparations from Germany also encouraged them in their task.

Unfortunately, the people of France suffered throughout the period between the two wars from the defects in their political system. There were too many political parties or groups and the result was that their ministries were unstable. Intrigues were common. There was corruption all round. This state of affairs continued in France even after Hitler came to power in Germany in 1933 and began to arm his country. The leaders of the various political parties continued to fight and failed to prepare the country for a war against Germany.

Raymond Poincare was the President of the French Republic throughout the World War I and Clemenceau was Prime Minister. When the term of office of Poincare expired in 1920, Clemenceau offered himself as a candidate for the Presidency but he was not elected. In 1922, Poincare became Prime Minister. He stood for strong action against Germany and it was during his tenure of office that France occupied the Ruhr valley. Poincare fell in 1924. In 1926, Poincare again became Prime Minister and held office until 1929. Formerly an opponent of Poincare, Briand became his Foreign Minister. His view was that any effort to keep Germany low was bound to fail and, therefore, it was in the interest of both the countries to come to an understanding. It was during his term of office that the Locarno Treaties were signed in 1925 and Germany became a member of the League of Nations in 1926. It was also during his time that the Kellogg-Briand Pact was signed and the Allied armies of occupation withdrew from Germany.

The French Governments were not able to balance their budgets and that led to a decline in the value of the France. The unstable ministries in France and not the courage and determination to balance the budget by imposing more taxes. The Punch commented on the situation in France in these words :

> We will not pay our foreign debt
> But we will change our Cabinet.

When the World was faced with economic depression in 1929-32 President Hoover suggested a moratorium in the payment of reparations by Germany and all war debts by other countries, but the suggestion was not welcomed in France. It is true that the moratorium was for one year but the people of France feared that payments would never be resumed again and as a matter of fact they were discontinued completely in 1932.

France constructed a system of fortifications known as the Maginot line on the frontier between France and Germany. Experience showed that the same was useless. Germany had attacked France in 1914 through Belgium and she did the same in 1940 reducing the Maginot line useless. It appears that the military strategists of France had learnt nothing from history.

From 1932 to 1934, there was a succession of Ministries in France. Ultimately, Gaston Doumergue who had been President of France from 1924 to 1931, became Prime Minister in 1934. He tried to introduce certain constitutional changes but his proposals were rejected. He was succeeded in 1935 by Pierre Laval. He had to resign on account of the premature disclosures of the Hoare-Laval negotiations. Laval was succeeded by Leon Blum, a Socialist and a Jew, as Prime Minister. Blum was Prime Minister for a year. He also resigned in 1937. Daladier was the Prime Minister of France at the time of the Munich Pact of September 1938.

In spite of their victory in the war, the main consideration before the French representatives at the Peace Conference was one of security for France. It is true that Germany was defeated but the French feared the potential danger from Germany in the future. The French knew that while there were only 42 million Frenchmen, there were 67 million Germans. The disparity in numbers was increased by an even greater disparity between German and French industrial development. In machine power even more than in man-power, French inferiority was to great that they could not hope to get any victory in Germany. No wonder, the French were conscious of the problem of their security and put the same in the forefront.

From Clemenceau to Laval, French politicians put the greatest emphasis on the security of their country. In moments of crisis, even Harrot spoke the language of Tardieu. For all Frenchmen of the Left and of the Right, there was only one question and that was the security of France. There was only one enemy and that was Germany. There was only one policy and that was security. The French policy can be understood only if we understand the psychology of the French. While in Germany it was the Treaty of Versailles which created a lot of resentment, in France it was the Treaty of Frankfurt of 1871 which had imposed a humiliating peace on that country which was remembered. By that Treaty Alsace and Lorraine had been snatched away from France and a huge war indemnity was exacted from her. Even during the World War I, the German statesmen frequently and openly declared that in the event of their victory, they would annex the Briery district of France to Germany and also take away Belfort and Verdun. The French had also fresh in their memory their sufferings in 1870-71 and 1914. The result was that when victory was won in 1918, the thing that was foremost in the minds of the French was their security in the future. They did not want approximate, relative or reasonable security, but absolute security.

The French representatives at the Peace Conference demanded that the Rhineland be given to France so that they may be in a stronger position to defend herself against Germany. However, they were persuaded by President Wilson and Lloyd George to give up that demand on the condition that both the United States and Great Britain would guarantee France against any possible German attack. Unfortunately, in spite of the best efforts of President Wilson, the Treaty of Versailles was rejected by the American Senate and consequently, the American guarantee became ineffective. Great Britain also backed out from her pledge on the ground that in the absence of the United States, she was not bound to honour the pledge. In the word of President Poincare, "It was in this respect that we suffered our greatest disillusionment after the signing of the Treaty of Versailles. President Wilson and Mr. Lloyd George before leaving Paris, had signed guarantee pacts which promises France the aid of the United States and England in case of an attack by Germany. However, these pacts were never ratified. France remained alone in the presence of Germany."

Left to themselves, the French started their search for security and the ways and means to achieve the same. The French Government entered into a large number of alliance with a view to strengthen her own hands against Germany. Belgium was as much exposed to Germany as France, and consequently, military conversation between the two countries resulted in the signing of a military convention on 7 September 1920. The new state of Poland had been created at the expense of Germany, and consequently, she was afraid of her. The danger from a common source brought Poland and France together and on 19 February 1921 was signed the Franco-Polish treaty of Alliance. Thus in the event of an attack from Germany, France could count upon help from Poland in the East and Belgium in the West. In 1924, a Treaty of Alliance was made between France and Czechoslovakia. In 1926, a Treaty of Friendship was signed between France and Rumania, by which both countries promised to consult each other in all matters which might threaten their external security. A similar treaty was entered into between France and Yugoslavia in 1927.

In 1925 was signed the Locarno Pact by which Great Britain and Italy guaranteed the Western frontiers of Germany with Belgium and France. This pact started the so-called Truce of Locarno and there prevailed comparative peace in Europe for the next two years. Before the World War II, writers frequently referred to the Locarno era as the "years of hope", but now there is a tendency to regard them as "years of illusion." Locarno never led to a permanent settlement of the Franco-German difficulties or established the basis of a lasting reconciliation. Locarno left many Germans and Frenchmen dissatisfied. Moreover, Locarno meant that France was to subordinate herself to Great Britain. By yielding to the British demand to evacuate the Ruhr Valley and by bringing in the Britishers as the guarantors of the Franco-German frontier, France completely gave up any hope of a policy independent of Great Britain. Immediately after Locarno, both the British and Americans began to put pressure on France to agree to disarmament conferences. It was argued by the British Government that as the French had got the guarantee of security asked for, they were in a position to start disarmament. It was contended that after the signing of Locarno Pact, the French lost a part of their nerve and felt themselves helpless to act alone without the British Government. They followed closely behind the British Lion whose roar was frequently not very loud. The foreign policy of France became a prisoner of British foreign policy. It was the first, but an important, step on the road to Munich.

There were differences of views between the French and the British Governments. Britain's idea of French security stopped with the Rhine and she did not seem to be concerned with what happened in Central and Eastern Europe. However, France being a continental power, was very much interested in the happenings in those parts of Europe. France very much relied upon the military alliances into which she had entered with the states of Central and Eastern Europe. The French foreign policy throughout the 1920's was caught on the horns of a dilemma for which there was no simple solution and for which most probably there was none at all. That dilemma was that while it was impossible for France to enlist Great Britain as an ally in the East, it was impossible for France to get along without her. To follow Britain implied that her ties with Central Europe were worthless and to rely on continental allies without Britain was to have no real strength at all.

Britain did not see eye to eye with France on the question of Germany. She wanted to treat the Germans leniently. She did not want France to insist on recovering from Germany all the war indemnity. She wanted France to revise the Treaty of Versailles in such a way as to strike off all its obnoxious clauses. However, France was not willing to follow such a course. She was terribly afraid of her security and she realised the consequences of leniency towards Germany. It was contended by France that if Germany was allowed to rearm herself, she would one day be able to have union with Austria by force. After that Czechoslovakia would be helpless. She would be surrounded by German territory and the presence of a German minority would add to her troubles. After Czechoslovakia. Germany would be able to bring Bucharest and Belgrade under her control. Poland would be deprived of the Polish Corridor. If once the principle of the revision of treaties were accepted, there would be no end to the same and the old tragedies of 1866 and 1870 would be repeated.

Nobody could doubt the logic of French foreign policy. At the same time, nobody could deny the defects inherent in that policy. It cannot be denied that the humiliating treatment meted out to Germany for 14 years from 1919 to 1933 was partly responsible for the rise of Hitler in Germany.

When that happened, the Englishmen pointed out to the failure of the foreign policy of France towards Germany. The French policy of repression ultimately failed to give France the security she was seeking so earnestly. When Hitler came to power in January 1933, the whole system of French security proved ineffective.

France found herself in a very weak position after 1933. In January 1934, Poland entered into a non-aggression pact with Germany and thereby weakened the position of France vis-a-vis Germany. In 1936, Belgium also terminated her military alliance with France. Germany was also able to win over Yugoslavia to her own side. Many other states were drawn into the German economic sphere. Germany introduced conscription in the country and began to rearm herself. In 1935, Germany entered into a naval agreement with Great Britain.

Barthou, Foreign Minister of France, went on a tour of many countries of Europe with a view to win over friends for France. Unfortunately, on 9 October 1934, both Barthou and King Alexander of Yugoslavia were assassinated at Marseilles by a terrorist. It not only made France weak, but also deprived her of a very able Foreign Minister.

In May 1935, France entered into a Treaty of Mutual Assistance with Soviet Russia. That Treaty provided that in the event of France or Soviet Russia being threatened with or in danger of aggression on the part of any European state, the Soviet Union and France would both proceed to immediate consultation in regard to the measures to be taken. In the event of France or the Soviet Union being subjected to unprovoked aggression on the part of any European State, both France and Soviet Union were immediately to come to each other's aid and assistance. In consideration of the fact that any member of the League and recourse to war, she was to be considered as having committed an act of war against all other members of the League. Both France and the Soviet Union agreed in the event of one of them being subjected to unprovoked aggression on the part of any European state to lend each other aid and assistance. Nothing in that treaty was to be interpreted as restricting the duty of the latter to take proper measures to safeguard peace in the world. The Treaty was to last for five years after its ratification. While France entered into an alliance with Soviet Russia in 1935, she did nothing to implement the same and the treaty remained a dead letter from the very beginning. The various French Ministers who came to power did not show any interest in the matter. No wonder, the Soviet Union complained of the indifferent attitude of the French Government. Moreover, from the practical point of the view, this alliance was not of much help as the Polish Government was not prepared to allow the Russian troops to pass through her territory.

The year 1935 was a bad one for French diplomacy. In the words of a French Diplomat, "If France commits herself definitely to Russia, Germany will reply by occupying the left bank of the Rhine; if Italy emerges weakened from her current difficulties in Abyssinia, that means Anschluss; if there is war between Britain and Italy in the Mediterranean and we come in, Germany is prepared to move against us. Only the closest understanding between France and Britain can keep the peace from now on."

Instead of meeting the foreign dangers as a united nation, France was involved in domestic troubles from May 1936 to April 1938. In its eagerness to achieve an ambitious programme of social reforms, the Popular Front did not bother about the development abroad although those were affecting the security of the country. At a time when Germany was feverishly turning out arms day and night, the industrial plant of France was thrown out of grear on account of labour disputes, strikes, the flight of capital, the decline of France and the general instability arising out of "reform politics." The new 40-hour week imposed on the employer did not allow the French to compete with Germany and Italy who were working their factories overtime. In the autumn of 1937, the series of outrages revealed the existence of a "Secret Committee of Revolutionary Action" who were getting arms and money from Germany and Italy to set up a Fascist Government in France. The exposure of the plot was hushed up as too many persons in the army and high finance were involved in it.

The French Government did not help the Republican Government of Spain against General Franco and his colleagues. In the name of peace and non-intervention, all arms shipments to Spain were forbidden. Prime Minister Blum appealed to the Powers to adopt common rules of non-intervention. The farcical London Non-Intervention Committee was set up. The followers of Blum protested and asked for the despatch of planes to Spain, but Blum was not moved at all. The decision was fatal. The victory of Franco drove more nails into the coffin of the Eastern alliances of France and left France discredited and weakened. It also strengthened the hands of pro-Fascist elements in France whose slogan was "Better Hitler than Blum."

Daladier became the Prime Minister of France in April 1938 and he continued to occupy that position up to March 1940. By that time, the people had come to realise the gravity of the situation and Daladier was given the right to rule by decrees so far as the finances of France were concerned. He managed to restore confidence in the national economic structure by settling the strikes, balancing the budget and removing unemployment. An atmosphere of confidence was restored.

On 29 April 1938, the Franco-British alliance was concluded. It was the most sweeping engagement of its kind since World War I. It provided not only for diplomatic cooperation but also for the establishment of an unitary command of the British and French Military, Naval and Air Force. The King and Queen of England visited Paris in the middle of July 1938. In the succeeding weeks, tension in Europe continued to increase. The Germans worked day and night and completed the construction of the Siegfried Line, along their Western frontier. On 5 September 1938, Daladier cancelled all leave for the army and air force and ordered all the reservists to occupy the Maginot Line. On 10 September 1938, France had 12 lakhs of soldiers under mobilisation. The British Navy concentrated its principal contingents in the North Sea. In spite of these preparations, France made an abject surrender at Munich.

The views of Great Britain and France on the defence of Czechoslovakia differed. The Foreign Minister of France told the German ambassador in unequivocal terms that German aggression against Czechoslovakia would mean war with France. He also tried to win over the British Government to his point of view. However, Lord Halifax, Foreign Minister of England, replied that the British would honour their commitments to France under Locarno but could not "see their way clear to adding to them." While the French Government urged a firm stand against Germany, Lord Halifax counselled pressure on the Czechs. In the Anglo-French conversations at the end of April 1938, the French were not able to get a definite commitment from Great Britain for the defence of Czechoslovakia and consequently the French began the process of surrender to Britain by agreeing to put pressure on the Czechs to make the maximum concessions. On 21 May 1938, Bonnet, Foreign Minister of France, re-affirmed in a Press Conference that France would stand by Czechoslovakia in case that country was invaded by Germany. Lord Halifax at once instructed in these words the British ambassador in Paris to dispel any illusions on the part of Bonnet: "If French Government were to assume that His Majesty's Government would at once take joint military action with them to preserve Czechoslovakia against German aggression, it is only fair to warn them that our statements do not warrant any such assumptions." The view of Halifax was that the military situation was such that the conquest of Czechoslovakia could not be prevented "even with such assistance as might be expected from Russia." By the night of 22 May 1938 Bonnet was a chastened man and he told the British ambassador in Paris that "he would not dream of taking action....without ample consultation" with Great Britain. If the Government of Czechoslovakia was not reasonable in its attitude, France "might well declare herself released from her bond." On the same evening, Daladier was seen weeping on the soldiers of the German ambassador begging the Reich not to compel him to come to war for an alliance which he "had not made and was certainly not happy about."

During the months of August and September 1938, several plans were worked out by the Czech Government to solve the Sudeten problem. Many concessions were made by the Government, consistent with the preservation of the Czech nation. However, all those plans were rejected by the Sudeten Germans, In September 1938, Russia declared that if France gave military help to Czechoslovakia, she would also do the same. However, the French Foreign Minister was not enthusiastic about collaboration with the Soviet Union.

On 15 September 1938, Prime Minister Chamberlain went to Berchtesgaden to see Hitler. On 18 September 1938, there was a joint meeting of the British and French Ministers in London to discuss the demands of Hitler. On 19 September 1938, the Government of Czechoslovakia was informed of the joint decision of the British and French Governments that the Sudeten area should be surrendered to Germany. The Government of Czechoslovakia tried to postpone the decision. On 21 September 1938, the French and British Ministers in Prague met Dr. Benes, President of Czechoslovakia, and told him that if the terms were not accepted unconditionally, Czechoslovakia would be held responsible for the war and would not receive any help either from Great Britain or from France. Under these circumstances, President Benes decided to accept the advice given by Great Britain and France. On 22 September 1938, Chamberlain went to Germany to see Hitler and informed him personally that the German demands had been accepted by Czechoslovakia. Chamberlain was surprised to find that Hitler had increased his demands. On 29 and 30 September 1938, Hitler, Mussolini, Chamberlain and Daladier met at Munich where an agreement was arrived at regarding the area to be handed over by Czechoslovakia to Germany. On his return from Munich, Daladier feared that the crowd at the Airport might denounce him for betraying France, but to his astonishment he found that the crowd had come to cheer him as "the saviour of peace." He was joined by Bonnet and Gamelin, Chief of the General Staff of France. They were all praised as heroes. Gamelin remained silent when a visitor remarked, "General, you have lost 35 divisions." Daladier declared, "I accept my popularity with the modesty that is only one of the forms my duty takes." Blum was also happy that "peace was saved." However, it cannot be denied that the Munich Agreement was one of the greatest defeats of French diplomacy. She had lost not only the defence advantage of 35 well-equipped divisions in Czechoslovakia, but also her alliance and prestige in Eastern Europe. Winston Churchill is said to have observed, "France and Great Britain had to choose between war and dishonour. They chose dishonour. They will have war."

On 30 November 1938, the speech of Count Ciano, Foreign Minister of Italy, was greeted in the Italian Chamber with a demonstration of Deputies during which shouts of Tunis, Nice and Corsica were raised. On 6 September 1938, Bonnet signed with Ribbentrop a declaration of "pacific and good neighbourly relations." In spite of this declaration of friendship between France and Germany, Italy notified to France on 22 December 1938 that she regarded the treaty of 7 January 1935 by which the conflicting colonial and naval claims between Italy and France had been settled as null and void. Under these circumstances, Daladier went on a tour of inspection of the defence establishments in Corsica and the African colonies on 1 January 1939. On his return, Daladier declared on 26 January 1939, "Not an inch of territory would be ceded." The budget of 1939 provided for an expenditure of 40 million francs on defence alone. That was the largest peace-time budget of its kind in French history.

The German seizure of the rest of Czechoslovakia and Memel, the final victory of Franco in Spain, the signing of a trade agreement between Germany and Rumania, the capture of Hsinan and Spratly Islands and the ever increasing demands of the Axis Powers for colonial concessions gave a severe blow to the security and prestige of France. However, this shock had a good effect also. The French were awakened to a sense of responsibility. The result was that on 19 March 1939, sweeping powers were given to the Government to rule by decree wherever necessary to meet any emergency endangering the safety of France. There was also a psychological and material change in France. Munich was a shock, it was also an education. France in 1939 was united. Entrenched behind the Maginot Line, the people of France knew that they had the most powerful army in Europe. If war could be postponed till the winter of 1940, the balance in air power would also shift in favour of the

Democratic Front. It was under these circumstances that the World War II began. The opportunity of winning over Soviet Russia was lost as both Great Britain and France were not prepared to pay the price demanded by Stalin for an alliance against Germany.

Even after the beginning of the war between Germany and Poland, France made an attempt to arrange another Munich. On 1 and 2 September 1939, Bonnet accepted Italian proposals for peace through conference with German troops reminding where they were on the Polish soil. However, Lord Halifax insisted that there could be no conference without the cessation of hostilities and the evacuation of Poland and the French Government had to accept the British line. The reply of Count Ciano was that as Hitler was unwilling to accept the condition, no further action could be taken. At 5 P.M. on 3 September 1939, war began between Germany and France.

Daladier was able to put some enthusiasm among the people of France. On 26 September 1939, he ordered the dissolution of the Communist party. When war broke out between Soviet Russia and Finland, Daladier Camelin and Wevgaud prepared plans for a war not against Germany but against Soviet Russia. Daladier resigned in March 1940 as Prime Minister but came back as Defence Minister in the new Ministry of Reynaud. During the Nazi conquest of the Netherlands and the Low Countries, Reynaud and Daladier quarreled violently. Camelin had no plan for holding the Blitzkrieg. His only slogan was "Win or die." All his calculations were based on the belief that the Maginot Line was impregnable. On 19 May 1940, Reynaud dismissed Gamelin and appointed General Weygand as the Commander-in-Chief. There were practically no prospects of defending France against Germany. The French Cabinet ran away from Paris, first to Tours and then to Bordeaux. Reynaud appealed for immediate American help but without success. Ultimately, he resigned and was succeeded by Marshal Petain who made peace with Germany.

SUGGESTED READINGS

Brogan, D.W.: **France under the Republic,** 1940.

Camerson, E.R.: **Prologue to Appeasement,** 1942.

Carr, E.H.: **Twenty Years' Crisis.**

Carr, E.H.: **International Relations between the two World Wars,** 1947.

Daladier, E.: **In Defence of France,** 1939.

Gathorne Hardy, G.M.: **A Short History of International Affairs** (1920-1939).

Goguel, F.: **France under the Fourth Republic,** 1952.

Langsam, W.C.: **The World Since** 1914.

Lazareff, P.: Deadline: **The Behind the Scene Story of the last decade in France,** 1940.

Maillaud, P.: **France,** 1943.

Moore, W.G.: **France and Germany.**

Ormesson, W.d': **France,** 1939.

Schuman, F.L.: **War and Diplomacy in the French Republic,** 1931.

Simon, Y.: **The Road to Vichy,** 1918-38, 1942.

Street, C.J.: **The Treachery of France,** 1924.

Thompson, V.: **Briand, Man of Peace,** 1930.

Vaucher, P.: **Post-War France,** 1934.

Werth, A.: **The Twilight of France,** 1942.

Werth, Alexander: **France and Munich,** 1939.

Weyer, E.: **The Decline of French Democracy: The Beginning of National Disintegration.**

Wolfers, A.: **Britain and France between two Wars,** 1940.

CHAPTER

34 GREAT BRITAIN BETWEEN THE WARS

When the World War I ended in November 1918, George V was the King of England and he continued to rule up to 1936. He was succeeded by Edward VIII who ruled from January 1936 to December 1936. Unfortunately, he was faced with a crisis when he tried to marry one Mrs. Simpson, an American lady. The Ministry did not approve of the marriage and the Dominions also opposed it. As the King insisted on marrying the woman he loved, he abdicated on 10 December 1936. Edward VIII was succeeded by his brother George VI who continued to rule up to 1952. In spite of his handicaps, he was able to win the affection of the people.

When the war ended, Lloyd George was the Prime Minister of England and he continued to occupy that position up to 1922. Soon after the surrender of Germany, general elections were held and Lloyd George was able to win a victory and formed a Coalition Ministry. He resigned in 1922 because he lost the confidence of the people. The Bonar Law Ministry remained in power from 1922 to 1923. It resigned on the tariff issue. Stanley Baldwin was the Prime Minister of England from 1923 to 1924. He tried to change the tariff system of the country with a view to tackle the problem of unemployment. Ramsay Macdonald formed the first Labour Ministry in 1924. As his party did not possess an absolute majority in the House of Commons, he was forced to resign after a few months. After his fall, Baldwin formed his second Ministry in 1924 and he remained in power up to 1929 when he was defeated in the general elections, Ramsay Macdonald formed his second ministry in 1929 and he continued in office up to 1931. He resigned on account of the economic crisis which was facing not only England but the whole world. After his resignation as the head of the Labour Ministry, he agreed to form a Nationalist Government. The new ministry consisted of Conservatives, Labourites and Liberals. Every effort was made to tackle the problem of economic depression. England went off the gold standard. The policy of free trade was given up. The Imperial Economic Conference was held at Ottawa in 1932. Efforts were made to tackle the problem of unemployment. In 1931 was passed the Statute of Westminster which gave complete equality of status to all the Dominions. When elections were held in 1935, Ramsay Macdonald lost the confidence of the country and the Conservatives under Baldwin came to power. Baldwin played an important part in the abdication of Edward VIII. In 1937, he was succeeded by Neville Chamberlain. The new ministry stood for peace and reconciliation. However, a policy of rearmament had to be followed on account of the threat from Hitler. Chamberlain remained in office up to June 1940, when he was succeeded by Winston Churchill who headed the Coalition Ministry during the World War II.

France. As regards the foreign policy of Great Britain between the two Wars, although both Great Britain and France had fought together during World War I there arose differences between them after 1920. President Wilson on behalf of the United States and Lloyd George on behalf of Great Britain had agreed to guarantee the security of France against possible German aggression and thereby persuaded France to give up her claim to the Rhineland. Unfortunately, the United States backed out as the American Senate refused to ratify the Treaty of Versailles. The British Government felt that she alone was not in a position to give that guarantee and consequently, she also backed out of her commitment to France. It was natural for France to feel aggrieved and no wonder, the relations between the two countries got strained. Moreover, Great Britain and France held different attitudes towards Germany. The view of Lloyd George was that a free and prosperous Germany was essential to civilization. Before the war, Germany was a good customer of British goods and Britain would like to restore Germany to normal conditions and thereby revive the old trade with her. There was also a realisation in the British circles that it was beyond the capacity of Germany to pay all the costs of the war. On account of the French attitude, Lloyd George proposed to leave the question of reparations to a commission. His calculation was that the United States and Great Britain would have the controlling influence in that commission and would be able to fix a reasonable amount as reparations which was within the capacity of Germany to pay. As the United States did not approve of the Treaty of Versailles and hence did not take part in the proceedings of the Reparation Commission, France was able to fix a figure which was beyond the capacity of Germany to pay. The Treaty of Versailles put in the hands of France the power to postpone war or even to prevent German recovery by insisting that reparation defaults which were inevitable should be punished by infliction of penalties. When the French and Belgian troops occupied the Ruhr Valley in 1923, Great Britain did not approve of that action. As a result of the Locarno Treaties of 1925, Great Britain guaranteed the Franco-German and Belgo-German frontier. Great Britain agreed to become a party to the Kellogg-Briand Pact of 1928 on the condition that she was allowed to reserve to herself the liberty of action in certain regions of the world, "the welfare and integrity which constitute a special and vital interest for her peace and safety."

The peace of Locarno was broken by the British Government in 1929. That was partly due to the fact that public opinion in Britain was becoming restive over the subordination of Great Britain to France. The Englishmen did not like the prestige enjoyed by France in the League of Nations. They were not prepared to play the part of "Shining second" to France. The only part they were willing to play was one of an impartial arbiter between France and Germany. The demand of the British Government was that she should henceforth occupy the centre of the "teeter" and not always sit on the French end. Lord Snowden, Chancellor of the Exchequer, attacked the French Government in 1929 at the Hague and thereby the truce of Locarno came to an end. In the Naval Conference of 1930 held in London, France blocked the way to any Five-Power Treaty whatsoever and even made a Three-Power Agreement conditional. France also attacked the Labour Government for having broken the truce of Locarno.

In spite of the growing menace from Germany under Hitler, the old policy of isolation was continued by Great Britain. It is true that Great Britain joined France and Italy at the Stresa Conference in April 1935 to denounce the Nazi rearmament and the implied threat to peace in Europe, but two months after, Sir John Simon went to Berlin and entered into the Anglo-German Naval Agreement by which Germany agreed to limit the size of her Navy to thirty-five per cent of the strength of the British Navy. By this agreement, Hitler was able to remove the suspicions of Great Britain and thereby win her over to his own side. This agreement was against the provisions of the Treaty of Versailles which required Germany to maintain a much smaller Naval force than that allowed by the agreement. No doubt, the agreement was considered to be a master-stroke of Hitler's diplomacy.

In spite of the differences between Britain and France on different issues, both Chamberlain and Daladier acted together in September 1938 on the occasion of the Munich crisis. Both the countries gave a joint undertaking to Poland, Greece and Rumania. France began to lean more and more on Britain and both the countries declared war against Germany on the question of Danzig.

Germany. As regards the British attitude towards Germany after World War I, it was one of sympathy. It was felt that unless the new regime in Germany was given a fair trial, there was every possibility of a violent reaction in that country. Great Britain tried to bring Germany into the League of Nations and the same was actually done in 1926. Great Britain did not make any secret of her disapproval of the French occupation of the Ruhr Valley and this attitude continued up to the rise of Hitler in 1933.

To begin with, the attitude of the British Government towards Hitler was not one of hostility. Great Britain regarded the dictatorship as an insurance against Communism. Hitler represented himself an open enemy of Communism and it was felt that it was more in the interest of Britain to enter into friendly relations with Germany than with the Soviet Union. That partly explains the agreement of 1935 between Britain and Germany. A policy of Anglo-German collaboration or appeasement was advocated by many prominent men in Britain. The view of L.S. Amery was that Germany's armaments were her own affair and it was no business of others to interfere with them. The time had come for a revision of the Covenant of the League of Nations. Similar views were expressed by the Marquess of Londonderry. He wanted the British Government to make common cause with Germany against the Soviet Union.

When Hitler scrapped in March 1936 the provisions of the Treaty of Versailles and ordered the occupation of the Rhineland by German troops, Great Britain kept quiet although it was a clear violation of the Locarno pact. In the same year, the civil war started in Spain. General Franco and his followers were helped by Hitler and Mussolini, but Great Britain and France followed a policy of neutrality and the result was that Franco was successful. When Hitler annexed Austria in 1938, Britain did nothing. It is ironically stated that both Britain and France, like sincere widows, moaned and shouted, but otherwise did nothing.

A very difficult situation was created in Czechoslovakia where the Sudeten Germans formed an important minority. Every effort to reconcile them had failed. After the rise of Hitler in 1933, the Sudeten Germans began to look up to Germany for their absorption into that country. They were encouraged to stage demonstrations and demand the right to join Germany. On 12 September 1938, Hitler demanded the right of self-determination for the Sudeten Germans. He declared that if the latter could not defend themselves, they would be helped by Germany. Allegation of torture and repression were levelled against the Government of Czechoslovakia. The Soviet Union proposed a conference with Great Britain, France and the United States and expressed her willingness to take part in any collective action that might be taken to defend Czechoslovakia against Germany. However, the proposal was not accepted. The British Government asked the Government of Czechoslovakia to accept an Adviser and Lord Runciman was sent as an Adviser and accepted by the Government of Czechoslovakia. A plan was prepared which guaranteed practically everything to Sudeten Germans except their incorporation into Germany. The offer was rejected. Great Britain and France found themselves in a very difficult position. If they supported Czechoslovakia, there was the certainty of a war in which everyone was likely to be involved. If they did not support her, she could not be expected to resist German pressure single-handed. In this war of nerves, Hitler won. Chamberlain decided to prevent war by following a policy of appeasement. He met Hitler on 15 September 1938 and was frankly told that nothing could stop the war unless the Sudeten Germans were given the right of self-determination. He came back and conferred with the French Government. It was agreed that the only way to stop the war was to give the Sudeten Germans the right of self-determination. On 19 September 1938, Great Britain and France asked Czechoslovakia to agree to the immediate transfer to Germany of the areas inhabited by a population of more than 50 per cent Germans. The Government of Czechoslovakia agreed to the proposal under pressure. At this moment, Hitler increased his demands which were considered unreasonable by Chamberlain and he refused to do more than merely refer them to the Government of Czechoslovakia. It was decided that if Germany immediately attacked Czechoslovakia, the latter would be supported by Great Britain and France. War preparations were ordered. British Navy was alerted. It was declared that the Soviet Union and Great Britain would stand by France if the latter helped Czechoslovakia against Germany. On 27 September 1938, Chamberlain declared, "We cannot in all circumstances undertake to involve the whole British Empire in war simply on her (Czechoslovakia) account." On 28 September 1938, Chamberlain told Hitler that he could have the essentials without war. On 29 September 1938, Chamberlain, Daladier and Mussolini went to Munich to meet Hitler. After prolonged discussions, the Munich Pact was signed on the night of 29-30 September 1938. Although Chamberlain declared that he had brought peace with honour, his boast was an empty one. It was a defeat of British diplomacy.

Many reasons have been given in support of the policy of appeasement followed by Chamberlain. He was deceived to believe in the assurances of Hitler that he had no further ambition beyond Czechoslovakia. Chamberlain could have learnt from the experience of the past and should not have relied upon the word of Hitler. He ought to have known that Hitler did not mean what he said. Chamberlain also knew that his country was not ready for war and he wanted time. It is possible that if Britain had been involved in war in September 1938, she might have met with disaster. The Germans had been making preparations for war since 1933. The seriousness of the situation had not been appreciated in Britain and nothing had been done to meet the danger. Probably it was wisdom to delay and thereby have some breathing time for making the necessary preparations before going to war. There was also a longing for peace both in Britain and France and hence September 1938 was not the opportune time to start the war. It is true that there was the possibility of the Soviet Union joining the war in September 1938 on the side of Britain and France, but the British Government did not trust the Soviet Union. They were more afraid of the danger from Communism than from Hitler and no wonder Chamberlain preferred to come to terms with Hitler than accept the offer of Soviet help and cooperation.

When the rest of Czechoslovakia was annexed in March 1939, Chamberlain was shocked. He was not prepared for such an action by Hitler, particularly because the new area annexed contained people of non-German race. There was a joint Anglo-French protest against Germany. Both the countries recalled their ambassadors from Berlin. The policy of Great Britain and France underwent a radical change. Instead of trying to appease Hitler, it was decided to resist him in the future. On 31 March 1939," both Great Britain and France pledged themselves to help Poland in every possible manner. Similar guarantees were given to Greece and Rumania. Prime Minister Chamberlain indicated his intention to extend the guarantee of independence to Denmark, the Netherlands and Switzerland. On 26 April 1939, the British Government announced its decision to enforce conscription in the country. On 12 May 1939, Great Britain gave a guarantee to Turkey. The guarantee given to Poland was transformed into a reciprocal treaty of mutual assistance between the United Kingdom and Poland and it came into force on 25 August 1939. On 22 August 1939, Chamberlain wrote to Hitler making it clear that Great Britain would stand by her commitments. Hitler sent a reply to the very next day in which he declared his determination to fight for the honour of his country. On 23 August 1939, Germany entered into a non-aggression pact with the Soviet Union. This was considered to be a failure of British policy. It is contended that Chamberlain did not realise the importance of entering into an alliance with the Soviet Union, which alone could help him to fight against Germany. It is true that anti-Soviet attitudes of Poland and Rumania was also responsible for Chamberlain's failure to come to a definite understanding with the Soviet Union, but Chamberlain's personal responsibility for that failure cannot be denied. He ought to have given all the concessions demanded by the Soviet Union in view of the dangers facing the world. Unfortunately, he could not give up his prejudice against the Soviet Union. To the end, he continued to hope that he would be able to come to an understanding with Germany instead of the Soviet Union. As a matter of fact, even during the negotiations between Britain and the Soviet Union, Chamberlain tried to return to his appeasement policy by offering to Germany a political partnership.

Soviet Russia. As regards the relations of Great Britain with Soviet Russia, the two countries had entered the World War I as Allies and fought together. However, things changed after the Bolshevik Revolution of 1917. In 1919-20, the British forces fought in North Russia. British forces were despatched to help the state of Estonia against Russian attacks. As the danger of invasion of Poland by Russia became imminent, Lloyd George declared that Great Britain would protect

Poland with all the means at her disposal. However, when Russia attacked Poland, Great Britain did nothing to defend her. Lloyd George entered into a trade agreement with Russia in 1921 on the express understanding that Russia would stop all propaganda against Britain. However, the Soviet Union did not keep her word. The policy of the Third International was inimical to British interests. In 1924, de jure, recognition was given to Soviet Russia by Great Britain. In spite of that, there was a lot of resentment in England against Russia in 1926. That was due to the fact that the Soviet Union gave encouragement to the general strike in England. Soviet intervention in the internal affairs of Britain was resented. When the Labour Party came to power in 1929, Great Britain entered into a commercial treaty with Soviet Russia and granted diplomatic status to the Soviet trade allegation. The Soviet Union joined the League of Nations. However, Stalin detested the attitude of the British Government on the question of Czechoslovakia.

After the annexation of the rest of Czechoslovakia in March 1939, the Soviet Union was drawn more and more to the side of Great Britain and France. All the three countries joined in the denunciation of the German annexation of Czechoslovakia. The same was the case when Germany made territorial demands on Poland and also assumed a hostile attitude towards Rumania. There was the urgent necessity of an immediate agreement between Great Britain and France on the one hand and the Soviet Union on the other for collective action against Germany and negotiations were started for that purpose. However, it was found that there were certain difficulties in the way which it might not be possible to overcome. The view of the Governments of Great Britain and France differed fundamentally from those of the Soviet Union. Britain and France proposed a Three-Power declaration in which the signatories were to announce their readiness to help one another if one or more of them were compelled to fight against Germany as a result of German attack on Poland or Rumania. The Soviet Union stood for a binding alliance whereby the three Powers were to guarantee the integrity not only of Poland and Rumania but also of all other States on the Western border of Russia from the Black Sea to the Baltic Sea. The Soviet Union demanded a commitment on the part of each power to help the other if they went on war with Germany and also a specific outline of the nature of the Military assistance to be given in the event of such a war. The British Government was not prepared to accept such a proposal and the French Government followed the lead of the British Government. Neither Britain nor France was prepared to commit herself to war in defence of Finland, Estonia and Latvia. This was not to the liking of the Soviet Union. Molotov, the new Foreign Minister of the Soviet Union, declared that Moscow would not make any pact on the basis of reciprocity and equality. The result was that negotiations dragged on without any result. Both Great Britain and France did not send any important person to negotiate with the Soviet Union and this was not liked by the Soviet Union. While the Soviet Union was carrying on negotiations with Britain and France, she was at the same time carrying on negotiations with Germany. As the negotiations with Britain and France were dragging on, the Soviet Union entered into a non-aggression pact with Germany on 23 August, 1939. There was a lot of criticism of the British Government with regard to the negotiations with the Soviet Union. To quote Lloyd George, "Negotiations have been going on for four months with Russia and no one knows how things stand today....you are dealing with the greatest military power in the world; you are asking them to come to your help; you are not negotiating terms with an enemy, but with a friendly power whose aid you want. Mr. Chamberlain negotiated directly with Hitler; he went to Berlin to see him; he and Lord Halifax made visits to Rome, but whom they have sent to Russia? They have not sent even the lowest in rank of a Cabinet Minister. They have sent a clerk in the Foreign Office. It is an insult. Yet the Government want the help of their gigantic army and air force."

For full two years, the relations between Britain and the Soviet Union remained cold. However, things changed after the German attack on the Soviet Union in June 1941. Then it was that the two countries became partners in a common war against Germany and the friendly relations continued between the two countries during the World War II.

Italy. As regards the relations of England with Italy, those were cordial to begin with. Both England and Italy became the guarantors of the provisions of the Locarno Pact of 1925. In April 1935, Italy and Great Britain met at the Stresa Conference to denounce the German re-armament. However, Mussolini resented the British condemnation of his country on the question of Abyssinia and that drove him into the arms of Hitler. Although many efforts were made by Britain to win over Italy, there was no success. Certain agreements were made between the two countries in January 1937 and April 1938, but there was no material change in the relations between the two countries. The mission of Chamberlain and Lord Halifax to Rome in January 1939 was a failure.

Turkey. As regards relations of Great Britain with Turkey, the Sultan of Turkey did not ratify the Treaty of Sevres and the Allies allowed him to keep Constantinople to himself. Both France and Great Britain authorised Greece to take possession of Thrace, the town of Smyrna and the adjoining country of Ionia. The Turks revolted under Kemal Pasha. There was every possibility of a war between Greece and Turkey, but as a result of the restraint shown by Kemal Pasha and the British Government, and armistice was signed in 1922. The Independence of Egypt was recognised. Great Britain and Turkey agreed to settle the frontiers of Iraq mutually. In May 1939, an announcement was made of the official acceptance of the treaty of guarantee between Britain and Turkey by which the Government of Ankara promised that the Dardanelles would at all times be open to the British fleet for entrance into the Black Sea for the defence of Rumania in return for the British promise of the naval defence of Turkey and particularly against Italian aggression in the Eastern Mediterranean.

Disarmament. Between 1919 and 1939, Great Britain sincerely followed a policy of disarmament. She not only summoned, but also participated in the deliberations of the Disarmament Conference. She took an active part in making it a success. However, she failed on account of the militarism in Germany and Italy and the non-committal attitude of France and other countries. By the Kellog-Briand Pact of 1927, Great Britain agreed to outlaw war. She was also one of the signatories to the four-Power Pact of 1933. It was on account of the influence of Great Britain that the Allies evacuated the Rhineland in 1930 in advance of the stipulated period.

League of Nations. Great Britain did not take an active part in the work of the League of Nations. That was partly due to the fact that after 1919, she disarmed herself and followed a policy of isolation from European blocs as far as possible. As the League of Nations was dominated by France and her satellites, Great Britain was not in a position to carry her point of view in the League and hence became indifferent.

When Manchuria was occupied by Japan in 1931, Great Britain did nothing to stop the Japanese aggression. The British view was that Japan had a right to Manchuria. Moreover, she was not prepared to fight for the sake of others. The same was the attitude of Britain on the question of the conquest of Abyssinia by Mussolini. It is true that the British Government was prepared to run the risk of enforcing sanctions against Italy, but as there was no cooperation from others, she could do practically nothing.

SUGGESTED READINGS

Armstrong: **"We or they"**, 1936.

Cameron: **Prologue to Appeasement,** 1942.

Carr, E.H.: **Britain: A Study of Foreign Policy from the Versailles Treaty to the Outbreak of the War,** 1939.

Coates & Zeldak: **A History of Anglo-Soviet Relations.**

Eden, A.: **Foreign Affairs,** 1939.

Foot, M.R.D.: **British Foreign Policy since 1898.**

Franks, O.S.: **Britain and the Tide of World Affairs.**

Gedye, G.E.R.: **Betrayal in Central Europe.**

Gooch. G.P.: **British Foreign Policy since the War,** 1936.

Grigg, E.: **British Foreign Policy.**

Hartmann, F.L.: **The Relations of Nations.**

Henderson, Sir Nevile: **Failure of a Mission,** 1940.

Jerrold, D : **Britain and Europe,** 1900-1940, 1941.

Kenney, J.F.: **Why England Slept,** 1940.

Langford. R.V.: **British Foreign Policy: Its Formulation in Recent Years,** 1942.

Medlicott, W.N.: **British Foreign Policy since Versailles,** 1940.

Namier, L.B.: **Diplomatic Prelude,** 1938-9, 1948.

Northedge, F.S.: **The Troubled Giant: Britain Among the Great Powers,** 1916-1939, 1956.

Pelling, H.: **Modern Britain** (1885-1955), 1960.

Ray, J.: **History of Britain,** 1900-1939, 1967.

Rayner, Robert & Airey: **Britain and World Affairs,** 1783-1946.

Seton-Watson, R.W.: **Britain and the Dictators: A Survey of Post-War British Policy,** 1938.

Sharp & Grayson : **Contemporary International Politics.**

Sipple, C.E.: **British Foreign Policy since the World War,** 1932.

Strang, Lord: **Britain in World Affairs,** 1961.

Taylor, A.J.P.: **English History,** 1914-15, 1965.

Wheeler-Bennett, J.W.: **Munich,** 1948.

Wheeler-Bennett, J.W.: **King George VI, His Life and Reign,** 1958.

Willert, Sir A.: **Aspects of British Foreign Policy,** 1928.

Wolfers, Arnold: **Britain and France between Two Wars,** 1940.

Young, G.M.: **Stanley Baldwin,** 1952.

CHAPTER

35 ITALY BETWEEN THE WARS

Although Italy had fought on the side of the Allies during the World War I, she was not happy at the peace settlement. During the actual negotiations the people of Italy overthrew Orlando and Sonnino and substituted Nitti and Tittoni for them. In spite of that, Italy did not get what had been promised to her by the Treaty of London of 1915. The interests of Italy and Yugoslavia conflicted and as the Allies favoured Yugoslavia, Italy was discontented. In September 1919, D'Annunzio captured Fiume with a number of Italian soldiers and induced the occupying French and British troops to leave at short notice. D'Annunzio held the town as an independent free-lance and the Italian Government, whom he condemned, had not the courage to take action against him. The Government was neither strong nor bold enough to subdue him. There was chaos in Italian politics. There was no morality among the politicians of Italy. They changed sides unmindful of the consequences to the country. Rioting and street fighting were of daily occurrence in large towns and strikes were numerous and violent. The Socialists and Fascists fought with each other in all the big towns. The Ministers allowed these disturbances to go on unchecked and nothing was done to punish the instigators. It was this negligence on the part of the Government which gave the Fascists their opportunity. Their better organisation and leadership enabled them to triumph over the Socialists and encouraged them to capture power. The Ministers were impotent and timid. Bold leadership could have saved the situation, but that was not forthcoming. Giolitti, who, had resigned in June 1921, hoped that the Socialists and Fascists would destroy one another and he would be able to step in and dictate peace. A foreign traveller in Italy at that time observed that the combinations of politicians in Italy were so delicate and so carefully adjusted that the existing Premier had already arranged not only who was to succeed him, but who was to succeed his successor. Giolitti was the brain behind these arrangements and he hoped to be the next Prime Minister but one. J.H. Jackson says, "Italians felt themselves disgraced in the eyes of the world, swindled by their own politicians. War had cost Italy dear draining her of money, saddling her with a budget deficit of over 12,000 million Lire, forcing up the cost of living. The political party in power in 1919 was pacifist, its leaders old and cynical. It is little wonder that Italians turned to violence." (**The Post-War World,** p. 80).

At the end of September 1922, Mussolini declared that he favoured a constitutional monarchy. On 24 October 1922, while addressing a gathering of the Fascists at Naples, he made far-reaching demands of the Government. Facta, Prime Minister of Italy, resigned on 27 October 1922. Mussolini decided to march on Rome with his followers. He met with practically, no resistance on the way and arrived at Rome on 30 October 1932. He was appointed the Prime Minister by the King of Italy. Mussolini secured the army by giving the War Office to General Diaz. The existing political situation in Italy had excited the contempt of most of the serious Italians and they all agreed that radical changes were necessary. It is not correct to say that the people of Italy welcomed the advent of Mussolini to power. But there seemed to be no other alternative. The attitude of the people towards Mussolini can be expressed in these words. "He is not all that we wish, they (those whom he had expelled) are all that we hate."

Mussolini had a varied career. At different times he had been a teacher, a soldier, a pacifist, a journalist and a socialist agitator. Soon after the War, he gave up his socialism and formed in Milan the Fascist Party, recruited from ex-soldiers, students and many people of the middle class. The Fascists claimed to be not a party, but an organisation. They were supported by the people who were sick of the industrial disorder on the one hand and gross profiteering on the other. They earned reputation by intervening in strikes and putting them down by force. They grew in numbers in Milan and gradually spread to other towns in the north of Italy. They wore black shirts and carried sticks. Mussolini was ambitious, vain and self-centred. He believed that he was giving to his countrymen what they needed most. He restored law and order in the country. He gave them glory. The people supported him and he continued to remain in power till his death in 1945. It is true that constitutionally speaking, he was merely the Prime Minister of Italy, but actually he was a dictator. Sumner Wells says, "The members of what was politely termed the Italian Government were no more than Mussolini's lackeys. The will of the Duce however perverse, however ignorant and however blindly mistaken the Fascist leaders knew him to be, was law. For no one in Italy, from the King to his Ministers, from the generals to the industrial magnates, dared to oppose him."

Under Mussolini, the efficiency in administration increased. Colonies were planted in what had been malarial swamps. Industry made progress and trade increased. Vast public works were undertaken. New roads were constructed. The Pontine Marshes were drained and buildings were erected. Wages and hours of work were regulated. A scheme of national insurance was started. Attention was given to education and the number of illiterates in the country fell. Brigandage in Naples and Sicily was suppressed. Although strikes were banned, no solution was found of agricultural and industrial unrest. Little was done to solve the problem of distribution of land.

There was also the dark side of the picture. There was no freedom of opinion in the country. Parliamentary Government disappeared. The Fascist Party became the state and all opposition parties were destroyed. The result was that in 1929, the Parliament contained only Fascist members. The people were subjected to the rule of the corrupt officials and there was no scope for any relief so long as the Fascist regime lasted.

The most notable achievement of Mussolini was the reconciliation of the Kingdom of Italy with the Roman Catholic Church. On 11 February 1929, a solemn Concord was signed between the Pope's representatives and Mussolini. Before 1870, the Pope was the Vicar of Christ and as such, the earthly head of the Roman Catholic Church. He was also the sovereign, prince of the Papal States. After the entry of Victor Emmanuel into Rome in October 1870, the things underwent a violent change. Victor Emmanuel's decree of 9 October 1870 declared Rome and the Roman Provinces to be an integral part of the Kingdom of Italy. Thus, the King deprived the Pope of his power as a temporal sovereign, although he left him in unmolested possession of the Vatican. Bismarck recognised the Pope as an arbitrator in territorial disputes. However, the Hague Conference refused to admit his representatives in 1889 and the League of Nations declined to accept the Pope as a member. There was a great increase in the prestige of the Pope during and after the World War I. His appeal for peace was considered seriously by the parties to the war. In 1928, France established a regular Legation to the Holy See. Negotiations took place between Mussolini and the highly placed officials of the Vatican and those resulted in the Lateran Treaty of 1929. Italy recognised the Vatican as a state with access to the sea and the Pope as an international person. Considerable rights and privileges were granted to the Church throughout Italy. The Pope got reconciled to the Kingdom of Italy. It is maintained that the survival of Mussolini's dictatorship for more than 21 years was due partly to his reconciliation with the Pope. Mussolini is said to have observed, "One could finally be both a good Italian which is synonymous with Fascist and a good Catholic."

Mussolini put before his countrymen a new programme which included the protection of private property, exaltation of the state and the acquisition of new territories by a vigorous foreign policy. Mussolini followed an aggressive foreign policy. That was partly due to the fact that he was determined to raise the prestige of Italy in the eyes of other powers and that was possible only if he was able to show that Italy had strength enough not only to protect herself, but also to conquer other territories. Mussolini glorified in the past of Italy and would like to revive the glories of the Roman Empire. Being himself a dictator, he would like to divert the attention of the people from home politics and that was possible only if he kept his country busy in one foreign adventure or the other. The people of Italy had not forgotten their defeat by the Abyssinians at Adowa in 1896. They also had not forgotten the humiliations to which they were subjected after the World War I. Italy was in need of colonies to provide an outlet for hundreds of thousands of her children deprived of work in the fatherland and no longer able to emigrate abroad on account of the limitations imposed on immigration by foreign countries. To quote Mussolini, "We are hungry for land because we are prolific and intend to remain so." Again, "We are becoming and shall become so increasingly because this is our desire—a military nation. A militarist nation, I will add, since we are not afraid of words—the whole life of the nation, political, economic and spiritual, must be systematically directed towards our military requirements. War has been described as the court of appeal between nations."

To begin with, Mussolini had to concentrate in south-east Europe. That was due to the fact that while on the West there were national states which had taken definitive form, that was not the case with eastern Europe. It was this fact which enabled Mussolini to have some gains for his country there. In 1920, Italy had surrendered the Dodacanese Islands to Greece but she got them back by the Treaty of Laussane in 1923. In the same year, the Italians bombarded the Island of Corfu. Mussolini also made peace with Yugoslavia by the Treaty of Rome signed on 27 January 1924. Fiume was divided between Italy and Yugoslavia. Fiume proper was given to Italy while the neighbouring town of Porto Baros was given to Yugoslavia. In 1926, Mussolini concluded the Treaty of Tirana with Albania. By that Treaty, Albania became practically a dependency of Italy. It was in 1939 that Albania was annexed to Italy. An internal revolt was planned against Zogu's regime by the distribution of money among the leaders of the opposition. Count Ciano himself supervised the military preparations for the enterprise. There was not much of opposition. In 1928, Great Britain, France and Spain invited Italy to have a share in the international government of the Free City of Tangier on the west coast of Morocco. At the London Naval Conference held in 1930, Mussolini demanded naval parity with France and got the same. In 1931, he advocated the revision of the Peace Treaties. It is obvious that Mussolini was successful "in strengthening Italian hold on the Adriatic, in increasing her prestige in the Mediterrenan and in expanding her diplomatic and commercial influence in South-Eastern Europe."

Conquest of Abyssinia

Many factors were responsible for the conquest of Abyssinia by Italy. The population of Italy was on the increase and there was the necessity of acquiring some territory for the surplus population. Italy wanted raw materials for her industries and markets for finished products. The dictatorship of Mussolini in Italy deprived the people of their liberties and it was necessary that they must be given some compensation. It was also necessary to divert the attention of the people from their miserable economic condition at home. It is true that economic depression had affected every state of Europe, but the condition of Italy was most unhappy. The Italian currency had depreciated. Unemployment had increased and the wages of those employed were cut down. It was found difficult to adjust the budget. Italy had an adverse balance of trade. A war against Abyssinia could arouse the patriotic spirit of the Italians, who had been defeated and humiliated by Abyssinia in 1896. The conquest of Abyssinia would put minerals into the hands of Italy. Abyssinia was also of great strategic value to Italy. It could link the Italian possessions in Somaliland, Eritrea and South-East Africa. From Abyssinia, Italy could afford to attack the British position in the Sudan. It could also help Italy to make the

Mediterrenan an Italian lake. Mussolini started the Abyssinian war at a time which he considered to be the most appropriate. From the attitude of the League of Nations and the Great Powers towards the conquest of Manchuria by Japan, Mussolini had come to the conclusion that in spite of the principle of collective security, nobody was going to stop him from conquering Abyssinia. Resolutions might be passed condemning his action, but no solid help would be given to the ruler and the people of Abyssinia. Moreover, the world had not yet recovered from the effects of economic depression. The economic problems were giving a headache to all the statesmen of Europe. The rise of Hitler to power in Germany and the pursuit of an aggressive policy by him, were occupying the attention of the European statesmen. As Italy was considered to be a lesser evil, it was possible that the other powers may not like to interfere while she was busy conquering Abyssinia. They may care more to maintain the peace of Europe than to prevent Italy from conquering Abyssinia.

Mussolini took a lot of time to make preparations for an attack on Abyssinia. In 1932, a high-ranking Italian official was sent to Abyssinia to spy out the land and report on the possible chances of success. His report was that "the political conditions in Abyssinia are deplorable and it should not be a difficult task to effect the disintegration of the Empire if we work it on political lines and it could be regarded as certain after a military victory on our part." A lot of money was spent by Italy to create dissensions among the people of Abyssinia and preparations for the war. Italy merely wanted an excuse to start the war against Abyssinia and that came in December 1934, when there was a clash between the troops of Abyssinia and Italy near the village of Walwal in which a few Italians were killed. Although the Italians put forward unreasonable claims for indemnity, they refused to submit the dispute to arbitration. After having made preparations in 1935, the Italian troops crossed the frontier and entered Abyssinia in October 1935.

The matter was taken to the League of Nations by the Emperor of Abyssinia. The Italian delegate in the League opposed the discussion on the Walwal incident on the ground that he "did not regard it as likely to affect the peaceful relations between the two countries." The Council of the League agreed to postpone the matter as the Italian delegate offered to settle the dispute by peaceful means. In spite of the pledge, the Italian Government did not appoint an arbitrator. When Abyssinia protested again, the Italian representative informed the League that Italy was ready to proceed with the work of arbitration. The arbitrators were appointed and their unanimous decision was that neither Abyssinia nor Italy was responsible for the Walwal incident.

Great Britain was anxious to avoid a clash and a formal proposal was made to Mussolini according to which Great Britain was to give the Port of Zeila to Abyssinia who was to give the southern province of Ogaden to Italy. The offer was rejected by Mussolini. Delegates of Great Britain, France and Italy met in Paris in August 1935 and it was decided that Abyssinia should be invited to apply to the League for collaboration in promoting "the economic development and administrative reorganisation of the country." This offer was also rejected by Mussolini. In September 1935 Sir Samuel Hoare declared in the League that Great Britain was willing to carry out her obligations under the Covenant of the League. The League was busy with the proposals for the adjustment of boundaries between Italy and Abyssinia, but, at that stage, the Italian invasion of Abyssinia started in October 1935. This forced the League to move in the matter. On 7 October 1935, the Council of the League declared that Italy had "resorted to war in disregard of its covenants under Article 12 of the Covenant." Two days after, the Assembly of the League recommended the appointment of a Committee for the purpose of coordinating the work. The Coordination Committee asked the members of the League to prohibit all loans or credits to Italy and place an embargo on exports to Italy. Excepting Austria, Hungary and Albania, those measures were backed by the other European states. Economic sanctions were enforced in November 1935 but France was not happy on account of her fear that Mussolini might not plunge the whole of Europe into a war. In the words of Laval, "Sanctions were imposed in order not to break with Great Britain and the League of Nations and they were applied in moderation in order not to break with Italy and to prevent war." The people of Abyssinia could not stand against the Italian troops who were thoroughly mechanised and fully equipped in every way. The Abyssinians had practically no modern weapons of warfare. Their resources were scanty. The result was that the Italian armies penetrated far into Abyssinia.

Sir Samuel Hoare and Laval conferred with each other and offered to Mussolini more territory in Abyssinia than what Italy was occupying at that time. However, the proposals leaked out and nothing came out of them. Sir Samuel Hoare was forced to resign. After the failure of the Hoare-Laval Plan, Italy took in earnest the conquest of Abyssinia and before the end of April 1936, the Italian army was near the capital of Abyssinia. The Emperor of Abyssinia left his country on 1 May 1936 and with him all resistance ended. Abyssinia was occupied and the King of Italy was proclaimed the Emperor of Abyssinia.

The conquest of Abyssinia by Italy was a flagrant violation of the Covenant of the League of Nations and the League was completely discredited. Hitler got encouragement in his aggressive designs. He was fully convinced that the League of Nations was an impotent institution and its members were not prepared to risk a war to save any state from any aggressor. The League was practically dead and after 1936 continued to exist merely in name. The view of G.M. Gathorne Hardy is that the conquest of Abyssinia "Marks a crucial turning point in post-war history. The triumph of Italian aggression naked and unashamed, affected the whole world with fundamental consequences. To England it meant the virtual destruction of the institution which successive governments of different parties had proclaimed to be the keystone of their foreign policy. To France...it meant that the enemy or whom she stood most in terror was encouraged to fresh audacity and rescued from his previous isolation and finally to the Italian transgressor by an act of poetic justice, it was destined to mean the extinction of his influence on the Danube, and the arrival of German forces on the Brenner."

Austria. Mussolini was opposed to the union of Austria with Germany. That was due to the fact that such a thing would bring the military frontier of the Reich to the Brenner Pass and the hinterland of Trieste and might also prove the preface to the construction of a Mittel-Europe which would automatically put a stop to Italian influence in Europe. In 1931 Chancellor Bruning had tried to achieve an Austro-German tariff union, but the same was opposed by Mussolini. In 1934, the Nazis revolted in Austria, occupied the federal Chancery and fatally wounded the Austrian Chancellor. Mussolini ordered Italian mobilisation to help Austria against Germany and thus Austria was saved from annexation by Germany. However, things changed after the conquest of Abyssinia by Italy. Hitler recognised Italian sovereignty over Abyssinia while the democratic countries were criticising Italy on the issue of Abyssinia. That changed the attitude of Mussolini towards Hitler. The result was that when Hitler annexed Austria in 1938, there was no protest from Mussolini.

France. Italian interests demanded the destruction of French political influence in the Danubian area by the dissolution of Little Entente and substitution of a combination directed from Rome. Mussolini joined Germany against French plans for reconstruction in the Danubian region. In the matter of disarmament, Italy supported Germany against France. The view of Mussolini was that parity between Germany and France would give to the Italian army the balance of power on the continent. When Germany rearmed herself to the French level, Italian expectations were realised and Italy was able to defy Great Britain and France on the issue of Abyssinia. In June 1934 Hitler and Mussolini met at Venice. The two dictators found that their points of view were different and it was practically impossible to agree for the time being. When the Nazis intervened in Austria, Mussolini gave up hopes of cooperation from Germany, and he decided to win over France. On 7 January 1935 was signed the Rome Pact by which France met the main demands of Italy in Africa in return for concessions by Italy in Central and Eastern Europe. Both the countries agreed to consult each other in case of a future threat to Austrian independence. It was agreed that there was the necessity of a multilateral understanding in which Germany, Italy, Austria, Czechoslovakia, Hungary and Yugoslavia should undertake to respect their mutual frontiers and abstain from meddling in the internal affairs of each other. Both Italy and France agreed to oppose any unilateral revision of the treaty. France gave to Italy 44,500 sq. miles of territory bordering on the Anglo-Egyptian, Sudan and a strip of French Somaliland giving Eritrea an outlet to the Gulf of Aden. France recognised Italian sovereignty over the Island of Doumerrah in the Red Sea. France gave to Italy a share in the ownership and management of the Addis-Ababa-Jibuti Railway in Abyssinia. France agreed to continue for 30 years the old concessions enjoyed by a lac of Italians living in the French protectorate of Tunisia. She also granted some new concessions for a long period. France agreed to give Italy a free hand in Ethiopia. She also agreed to press Great Britain and the League to do the same. However as France participated in the economic sanctions enforced against Italy, the friendly relations between France and Italy disappeared. Mussolini declared that so long as the French Government maintained towards Italy the present attitude, the Italians were bound to do the same.

Britain. Mussolini had to make a choice between Great Britain and Germany and the choice was not an easy one. Great Britain was a Mediterranean power and it was difficult for Italy to be on unfriendly terms with her. Her long coast-line exposed her to an attack from the sea at any moment. At the Stresa Conference in 1934, Italy had aligned herself with France and Great Britain against Germany. Vigorous efforts were also made by Great Britain to remove the points of dispute between the two countries. However, the progress of the negotiations was not satisfactory. In January, 1937, both Great Britain and Italy issued a joint declaration that they agreed to preserve the status quo in the Mediterranean. The utility of such a declaration became negative on account of Italian help to Franco's Governments in Spain. Another agreement was made in April 1938 between Great Britain and Italy. It resolved a number of issues in the Mediterranean and Near Eastern area connected with Italy's conquest of Abyssinia. Great Britain recognised Italy's African Empire and Mussolini agreed to withdraw a substantial number of volunteers from Spain. In January 1939, Prime Minister Chamberlain and Foreign Minister Halifax went to Rome but the mission was not a success.

Germany. If the attitude of Italy towards Great Britain and France was one of hesitation and reserve, her advance towards friendship with Germany at this stage seemed to be smooth and steady. Germany was quick in recognising Italy's African Empire. In October 1936, Count Ciano, son-in-law of Mussolini and Foreign Minister of Italy, visited Germany and met Hitler. On 1 November 1936, Mussolini coined the famous phrase that the Berlin-Rome line represented "an Axis". Both Germany and Italy acted together in the London Non-intervention Committee. A large number of Nazis visited Italy. In September 1937, Mussolini went to Germany and Hitler paid a return visit to Rome in May 1938. Mussolini acquiesced in the Nazi annexation of Austria in March 1938. In 1936, the Anti-Comintern Pact was signed between Germany and Japan. In 1937, Italy joined the pact, and thus the Berlin-Rome-Tokyo Axis came into being. Hitler referred to the Axis as a "great world political triangle" which "consists not of three powerless images, but of three states which are prepared and determined to protect decisively their rights and vital interests".

In the spring of 1936, Spanish military Generals made several visits to Rome and Berlin and placed before Mussolini and Hitler their plans for a revolt. Their plans were approved and they revolted in July 1936. General Franco started and organised the war against the Democratic Republican Government of Spain. A large number of volunteers were sent by Mussolini to Spain to help General Franco and his Government was recognised in November 1936. The success of Italian intervention in Spain in spite of opposition from the Soviet Union, brought prestige to Mussolini.

The view of Wiskemann is that superficially the Munich agreement of September 1938 might be counted as a triumph of Mussolini. He had shown that he did not fear war and he had proved to be a saviour of peace. He returned to Italy perhaps more popular than he had ever been before. The

King paid a tribute to his success. He came from his estate to meet him at Florence on the journey back to Rome. For two years, the Italians had felt themselves slipping down a slope into the sea of vassalage to Hitler. But now it seemed that Mussolini alone in the world could stop the war. The British recognition of Victor Emmanuel as Emperor of Ethiopia on 16 November 1938 crowned Mussolini's success at Munich in September 1938.

Count Ciano did not like the attitude of Germany with regard to her determination to attack Poland at any cost and it took him a lot of time to win over Mussolini to his point of view that Italy must not join the war at once when Germany attacked Poland. The result was that when the World War II started in September 1939, Italy remained neutral. She decided "to attack when the Allies were almost exhausted by the ravages of war, but had not yet capitulated, for that would save Italy from the destruction of war and would entitle her to a share in the spoils of victory". Such an hour came in June 1940, when France was on the point of collapse. It was then that Italy declared war on Great Britain and France on 10 June 1940. When Roosevelt heard of it, he observed, "The hand that held the dagger had struck it into the back of its neighbour". France fell and she signed an armistice with Germany on 22 June 1940 and with Italy on 24 June 1940. On 27 September 1940, Mussolini joined the Triple Alliance with Germany and Japan. Italy opened war with Great Britain by invading Greece, Egypt, Somaliland, the Sudan and Kenya. The Italian troops made some progress and were able to occupy British Somaliland. However, the British troops recovered their position and inflicted crushing defeats upon the Italians on almost every front. In June 1941, Italy declared war against Soviet Russia and in December 1941 against the United States. When the Allied Forces invaded Sicily in 1943, King Victor Emmanuel dismissed Mussolini and ordered his arrest. Mussolini was imprisoned and Marshal Badoglio was appointed the Prime Minister. The new Prime Minister followed a double policy. On the one hand, he declared that war would go on and asked Germany to defend the whole of Italy and on the other started negotiations with the United Nations for an Armistice. The Germans were able to recover their position in Italy. They released Mussolini from jail and put him in power. The King and Badoglio ran away to the South. Victor Emmanuel and Badoglio declared war on Germany in October 1943 and were declared as co-belligerants by the United Nations. Mussolini was captured and murdered by Italian partisans.

SUGGESTED READINGS

Alfieri, D.: **Dictators Face to Face,** 1955.

Badoglio, B.: **The War in Abyssinia,** 1937.

Binchy, D.A.: **Church and State in Fascist Italy,** 1942.

Bonomi, I: **From Socialism to Fascism,** 1924.

Borgese, G.A.: **The March of Fascism,** 1937.

Currey, M.: **Italian Foreign Policy,** 1918-1932, 1932.

Dombrowski, R.: **Mussolini: Twilight and Fall,** 1956.

Ebenstein, W.: **Fascist Italy,** 1939.

Elwin, W.: **Fascism at Work** 1934.

Farratt, Geoffrey T.: **Mussolini's Roman Empire.**

Finer, H. **Mussolini's Italy,** 1935.

Hullinger, E.W.: **The New Fascist State,** 1928.

Kemechy, L.: **"II Duce" : The Life and Work of Benito Mussolini,** 1930.

King, B.: **Fascism in Italy,** 1931.

Macartney, M.H.H. and Cremona, P.: **Italy's Foreign and Colonial Policies,** 1914-37, 1938.

McClellan, G.B.: **Modern Italy,** 1933.

Matthews, H.L.: **The Fruits of Fascism,** 1943.

Nenni, P.: **Ten Years of Tyranny in Italy,** 1932.

Pini, G.: **The Official Life of Benito Mussolini,** 1939.

Potter, P.B.: **Wal Wal Arbitration,** 1938.

Salvemini, G.: **The Fascist Dictatorship in Italy,** 1927.

Sarfatti, M.C.: **The Life of Benito Mussolini,** 1925.

Schmidt, C.T.: **The Corporate State in Action: Italy under Fascism,** 1939.

Schneider, H.W.: **Making the Fascist State,** 1928.

Villari, L.: **Italian Foreign Policy Under Mussolini,** 1956.

Villari, L.: **The Expansion of Italy,** 1930.

Wiskemann: **The Rome-Berlin Axis,** 1949.

Work, E.: **Ethiopia : A Pawn in European Diplomacy,** 1935.

CHAPTER

36 RUSSIA BETWEEN THE WARS

Lenin. Lenin and his followers were able to capture power in 1917, but they had many problems to face. Land was given to the peasants who were expected to cultivate the same, but they were not given full control over the produce of their labours, the whole of which belonged to the state. The peasants were allowed to retain as much as was needed by them, but the surplus was taken over by the state at a price fixed by itself. The result was that the peasants did not grow more than what was sufficient to sustain themselves. As there was no surplus, famine appeared in the towns. The result was that the government had to change its policy and allow the farmers to sell their surplus produce in the open market.

The Russian Government had a two-fold problem—one was to establish communism in Russia and the other was to spread the same throughout the world. There were many idealists among the Bolsheviks who were of the opinion that communism and capitalism could not live side by side and if communism was to survive in Russia, capitalism in other parts of the world must be overthrown. The leader of this group was Trotsky who was the right hand man of Lenin. Zinoviev was closely associated with him and his duty was to organise communist propaganda in Western Europe. There were many practical men among the Bolsheviks who were of the opinion that they should concentrate all their energy in Russia and make their country so great that the other countries were made to feel jealous of their progress. The leader of this section was Stalin. The struggle between the two groups continued.

Stalin. Lenin died in 1924 having put communism on a stable basis in his country. His death was followed by a struggle for supremacy between Stalin and Trotsky. It was both a struggle of personalities and ideologies. Both of them were determined to make themselves supreme in the country. Ultimately Stalin won in 1927. Trotsky was turned out first from the Communist Party and then from Russia itself. He ran away to Mexico where he was murdered in August 1940.

The Government of Russia under Lenin and Stalin was essentially a dictatorship where the political opponents had to place. It is true that elections were held but there was only one candidate from each constituency. The very existence of the other parties was not allowed. There was jealousy and suspicion among the members of the Communist Party itself. The result was that one tried to oust the other. Occasionally there were purges in the Communist Party. Those who did not see eye to eye with the Communist Party were put in labour camps. As Communism was opposed to Christianity, the Orthodox Church suffered in Russia. The Ogpu or the secret police organisation was always busy to trace out every sign of disaffection or disloyalty to the new Communist state in Russia.

If the people in Russia had no liberty as such, they made progress in many ways. Education spread in the country. Both children and adults learned to read and write. Education spread even among the peasants. There was no unemployment as the state found work for all. The working conditions were improved. Medical and dental treatment was given to all those who were in need of it. Homes were built for the aged. Large blocks of flats were erected in many towns. The general standard of living improved. But the price for all this was to be paid and that was the worker had to be completely subordinate to the state.

After having established his supremacy in the country, Stalin prepared a Five-Year Plan for the development of agriculture and industry in the country. In place of the small peasant farms, very large farms were established in the country and the most modern agricultural machinery was installed to produce the maximum. Those who opposed the change were imprisoned and put in labour camps. Some of them were even murdered. But the result was increased production. The important industries, such as mines, railways, steel and textiles were entirely under the control of the state. It was for the state to decide what material was to be used, what quantity was to be produced and what wages were to be paid to the workers. In 1932, it was declared that the plan had achieved in four years what was expected to be achieved in five years. A second Five-Year Plan was announced for the period 1933-38. Stalin continued to rule till 1953. He led his country to victory in World War II.

Foreign Policy. Up to 1917, the Russian foreign policy had many objectives, viz., security against Japan in the Far-East including ports in Manchuria and trade outlets into Asia, the Russianizing of or acquisition of full rights over the Bosphorus and the entrance to the Mediterranean Sea, Pan-Slavism with Russia as a leading member of the Slav family of nations, a belt of subject-nationalities in the West to act as a buffer against the larger nations of Europe. Then came the Revolution of 1917. The Communists were forced to start negotiations and in March 1918, an armistice was signed with Germany and Austria-Hungary at Brest Litovsk. The war was brought to an end in Eastern Europe, but Russia had to surrender vast territories to the Central Powers. She agreed to pay three hundred million gold Roubles as war indemnity. She undertook to set up independent Finland, Estonia and Lithuania.

The Communists in Russia had to fight against the interventionists from various countries of Western Europe and the United States who seemed to be determined to uproot the Communist regime in Russia. The old aristocracy in Russia also tried to stage a counter revolution and considerable forces were raised by General Denikin in South Russia and Admiral Kolchak in the North. Great Britain and France also sent assistance to these "White" leaders. People of Russia were asked by the Communist Government to fight what they called a patriotic war against the capitalist countries and it took about three years to drive out the foreigners from the Russian soil. Trotsky played an important part in driving out foreigners from the Russian soil with the help of the Red Army.

To begin with, Russia was regarded as the pariah of Europe and consequently no country would like to deal with her. However, the situation began to change gradually. In 1921 Great Britain entered into a trade agreement with Russia and thereby recognised the new regime in Russia. In the same year, Russia entered into a treaty of friendship with Germany. This repudiated all previous agreements between the two countries. Both parties agreed to refrain from entering into any hostile agreement against each other. Similar agreements were made with Turkey, Afghanistan and Outer Mongolia. In 1922, Russia and Germany entered into the Treaty of Rapallo by which both the countries gave up all financial claims including war indemnities arising out of the World War I. Diplomatic and consular relationships were started. The principle of the most favourable nation was adopted in the treaty which made a tremendous sensation in the world. However, it had not any lasting effect. The fact that Germany had made a bargain with Russia, damaged her case in the United States and Great Britain. There was close cooperation between the German Generals and the Red Army after Rapallo and consequently many alarmist reports were started. In 1922 the Soviet Union was invited to the World Economic Conference at Geneva. The Soviet delegation proposed the consideration of that Article of the Treaty of Versailles which had prescribed general disarmament and also recommended that efforts should be made to implement proposals regarding general disarmament. As her suggestions were not accepted, she herself summoned a disarmament conference of the states bordering on her frontiers. She also recognised the independence of Finland, Lithuania, Estonia, Latvia and Poland.

The Peace Settlement had fixed the Polish Eastern frontier on a line suggested by Lord Curzon and known as the Curzon Line. That included in Poland territories with a mainly Polish population, but left to Russia lands farther east that were inhabited by Russian-speaking people. The Poles were dissatisfied and in 1920, they made war on Russia. They were defeated and driven back almost to

Warsaw. French assistance was sent to the Poles under General Weygand and the tide turned again. The Russians were defeated in the battle of Vistula and driven back into their own country. By the Treaty of Riga, signed in March 1921, Poland got extensive lands to the east of Curzon Line.

In 1924, Russia entered into an agreement with China regarding the Chinese Eastern Railway. In 1924, de jure recognition was accorded to the Soviet Union by Great Britain and she was followed by Italy and France. The United States granted recognition in 1933.

To begin with, the Communists of Russia believed in spreading Communism in every nook and corner of the world and were prepared to adopt any measures to achieve their objective. The Comintern was started in 1919 for that purpose. However, there was a change in Russia under Stalin. To quote Stalin, "The goal is to consolidate the dictatorship of imperialism in all countries." After 1927, the Soviet Union entered into the Proletariat in one country, using it as a base for the overthrow of a series of non-aggression pacts with many countries. She not only signed the Pact of Paris, but also saw to it that the countries under her influence did the same. She was in favour of the Pact coming into force at once.

The Soviet Union proposed to Poland and Germany the conclusion of a Baltic Pact including the Baltic States for guaranteeing mutual aid and assistance in the event of any signatory state being attacked, but those proposals were not accepted either by Germany or by Poland. The Soviet Union proposed to Germany the conclusion of an eastern Locarno in which the principles of the Locarno Pact of 1925 were to be applied, but the suggestion was rejected by Germany. Another attempt was made by the Soviet Union to enter into a tripartite mutual assistance pact with Germany and France. However, she was not successful in her attempt. It was under these circumstances that the Soviet Union entered into a Treaty of Friendship with France alone in 1935.

.. **The League.** To begin with, the Soviet Union Condemned the League of Nations as "a Holy Alliance of the bourgeoisie for the suppression of the proletarian revolution" and this continued to be her attitude throughout the 1920's. In 1928, a manifesto of the Sixth Congress of the Comintern declared, "The League of Nations, the product of Versailles, the most shameless robber treaty of the last decade, cloaks the war-like work of its members by working out projects for disarmament". However, as the danger from Nazi Germany began to increase, there was a change in her attitude towards the League. In 1933, both Molotov and Litvinov spoke favourably of the League and gave a hint that the Soviet Union would be willing to join it. The initiative was taken by France and the Soviet Union joined the League of Nations in 1934. Litvinov, the Soviet representative in the League, was very enthusiastic about the work of the League. He wanted the League to play an important part in world politics. He was particularly emphatic about collective security. His view was that peace was indivisible and he criticised those members of the League who were not prepared to take action against the aggressors. He condemned the attitude of the members of the League on the question of Abyssinia.

Spain. When the Civil War broke out in Spain, France and Great Britain followed a policy of non-intervention and refused to support the Russian efforts to save the Republican regime in Spain. The result was that General Franco and his colleagues were successful in overthrowing the Republican Government in Spain. That was a great defeat for the Soviet Union.

Germany. The Soviet Union expected trouble from Hitler and consequently she left no stone unturned to make her defences as strong as possible. It is estimated that in 1936, the Red Army had 13 lacs of troops, 6,000 tanks and 7,000 aeroplanes. Every effort was made to increase the output of mechanised armaments.

France. As both the Soviet Union and France were afraid of Hitler's designs, they entered into a Treaty of Mutal Assistance in May 1935. This treaty was linked up with an agreement to be signed with Germany, Poland, Czechoslovakia and the Baltic states. As the second part was not realised, the treaty between France and the Soviet Union remained practically ineffective. There is no comparison between this treaty and the Franco-Russian Alliance of 1894 which brought the two countries together into the World War I in 1914.

Czechoslovakia. On the occasion of the Munich crisis, over Czechoslovakia, the Soviet Union offered to help Czechoslovakia against Germany but nobody bothered about the offer. The things were taken to such extremes that no representative of the Soviet Union was invited to take part in the negotiations with Hitler regarding Czechoslovakia. This was resented by the Soviet Union. It is possible that this treatment might have forced the Soviet Union to come to an understanding with Germany directly and that could be the possible basis of the non-aggression pact of August 1939.

Anglo-Soviet Negotiations. After the annexation of the rest of Czechoslovakia by Hitler in March, 1939, the Soviet Union was drawn once more to the side of Great Britain and France. All the three countries joined in the denunciation of the German annexation of Czechoslovakia. The same was the case when Germany began to make territorial demands on Poland and also assumed a hostile attitude towards Rumania. There was the urgent necessity of an immediate agreement between Great Britain and France on the one hand and the Soviet Union on the other for collective action against Germany and negotiations were started for that purpose. However, there were certain difficulties in the way which were not possible to overcome. The views of the French and the British Governments differed fundamentally from those of the Soviet Union. Great Britain and France proposed a Three-Power Declaration in which the signatories were to announce their readiness to help one another if one or more of them were compelled to fight against Germany, as a result of German attack on Poland or Rumania, but the Soviet Union stood for a binding alliance. The Great Britain was not willing to do because she still hoped to have some peaceful settlement with Germany. Such an alliance was bound to offend Poland which feared Soviet help as much as the German attack. Moreover, neither Great Britain nor France was prepared to commit herself to war in defence of Finland, Estonia and Latvia. The result was that the negotiations dragged on and nothing came out of them.

Non-Aggression Pact

On 23 August 1939, the non-aggression pact between Germany and the Soviet Union was signed in Moscow. There was a secret additional protocol added to the pact in which the parties agreed to divide the territory of Poland among themselves. The pact was a bargain between enemies, each of whom gained by it. Germany gained through the assurance that she would not face a Soviet attack from the East and she paid for that assurance by granting concessions to a power whom she expected ultimately to fight. However, she was confident that she could choose the time of the conflict and Russia was too weak to begin an offensive war. Russia felt that she was making the best of a bad bargain. She was not sure of the attitude of Great Britain and France, and the agreement with Germany freed her for the time being from the fear of involvement in a war and increased her prestige in Eastern Europe. There was the possibility of a war between Germany on the one hand and Great Britain and France on the other over Poland and all three could exhaust themselves and the Soviet Union could gain thereby. The pact was a gamble which the Soviet leaders were compelled to do. All hopes of Great Britain and France for Three-Power action were ended. For two years from August 1939 to June 1941, there was collaboration between the Soviet Union and Germany, but on 22 June 1941, the German forces invaded Russia and that brought her near Great Britain, France and the United States.

China. As regards the relations between Russia and China, the Chinese Government broke off relations with Russia after the Bolshevik Revolution. She took part in the Allied expedition to Siberia. She tried to extend her hold on the border areas, notably Outer Mongolia and Sinkiang. It took over the management of the Chinese Eastern Railway in Manchuria. The situation in China seemed to be favourable for the spread of Communist propaganda and hundreds of Communist agents were sent to China. In 1923 Dr. Sun Yat-Sen asked for Russian help to bring about law and order in his country. Borodin, one of the top organizers of the Comintern, went to China along with advisers. He helped Dr. Sun Yat-Sen in re-organising and building the influence of the Kuomintang. In January 1924, the Communists were admitted into the Kuomintang. The Communists hoped to overthrow the Government in China and take possession of the same. General Chiang Kai-Shek did not like the Communist influence in China and in 1927, he was successful in turning them out from the country. They were not only expelled from the Kuomintang but hundreds of them were killed and many saved their lives by hiding themselves.

After the Japanese invasion of Manchuria in 1931, tension between the Soviet Union and Japan increased. In order to meet the Japanese danger, the Soviet leaders strengthened their defences in the Far East and tried to improve relations with China. Diplomatic relations with China were resumed in 1932. In 1935, the Chinese Communists offered to join the Kuomintang in order to resist Japanese aggression in China. From 1935 to 1945, the relations between the Soviet Union and China were technically all right. In August 1937, China and the Soviet Union signed a non-aggression pact. For two years, Russia gave China diplomatic support and considerable war material. After Nazi attack on Russia, the relations between the Soviet Union and China improved again.

Japan. As regards the relations of Russia with Japan, Stalin had a horror of war on two fronts. He was eager to avert war in the Far East so that he could fight effectively in the West. In order to maintain peace in the Far East, Stalin sold the Chinese Eastern Rail Road which had cost Russia 225 million dollars to Japan for 30 million dollars only. He also negotiated fishery treaties on terms favourable to Japan. Stalin would not like to follow a policy which could be taken for cowardice. Consequently, when Japanese troops, in an effort to test Soviet strength, attacked Russian troops in an undeclared war, along the Outer Mongolian frontier, the Soviet Army under "General Blucher" routed the Japanese forces. The Japanese invasion of Manchuria in 1931 was considered by the Soviet Union as a direct threat and she condemned it in the strongest possible terms. Between 1933 and 1941, the Soviet Union and Japan were engaged in what is called a semi-war which had all the qualities of a cold war warmed up to the boiling point. The border clashes at Changkufeng in 1935 and at Namonhan in 1939 were full-scale battles and in both cases Japan was defeated. In 1936, Japan entered into the anti-Comintern pact with Germany against Russia. This pact was treated with contempt by the Soviet Union. In 1941, the Soviet Union entered into a non-aggression pact with Japan. In April, 1942, when Japan renewed the anti-Comintern pact, the Soviet Union protested and cancelled the Japanese oil and coal concessions in Northern Sakhalin. The Soviet Union did not declare war against Japan throughout World War II.

SUGGESTED READINGS

Carr, E.H.: **German-Soviet Relations between the two World Wars** 1919, 1939.
Carr, E.H.: **The Soviet Impact on the Western World.**
Carr, E.H.: **The Bolshevik Revolution** 1917-1923.
Coates: W.P.: and Zelda, K.: **A History of Anglo-Soviet Relations.**
Dallin,. D.J.: **The New Soviet Empire** 1951.
Dallin, D.J.: **The Rise of Russia in Asia,** 1949.
Dean, V. N.: **The United States and Russia,** 1947.
Deutcher, Isaac : **Stalin : A Political Biography,** 1949.
Laserson. Max H.: **The Development of Soviet Foreign Policy in Europe,** 1917-42.
Laserson, Max H.: **Russia and the Western World.**
Lederer, I. (ed.) : **Russia's Foreign Policy,** 1962.
Ludwing, Emil : **Stalin.**
Ross, M.: **A History of Soviet Foreign Policy,** 1940.
Schuman, F.L.: **Soviet Politics at Home and Abroad,** 1946.
Schuman, F.L.: **Russia since 1917; Four Decades of Soviet Politics, 1957.**
Taracouzio, T.A.: **War and Peace in Soviet Diplomacy,** 1940.
Warth, R.D.: **Soviet Russia in World Politics,** 1963.
Yakhontoff, V.A.: **U.S.S.R. Foreign Policy,** 1945.

CHAPTER

37 MODERN TURKEY

Turkey had fought the World War I on the side of Germany and Austria-Hungary. Like her Allies, she was also defeated and the Treaty of Sevres of 1920 was imposed on her. By this Treaty the Arab State of Hedjaz was nominally freed but put under British control. Armenia was created into a Christian Republic and put under an international guarantee. Mesopotamia, Trans-Jordan, Syria and Palestine were taken away from Turkey. Syria was given to France under the Mandate of the League of Nations. Palestine, Mesopotamia and Trans-Jordan were given to Britain under the Mandate System. Galicia was recognised as a French sphere of influence. Southern Anatolia was recognised as an Italian sphere of influence. Adrianople, Gallipoli, the Islands of Ambros and Tenedos, Smyrna and the territory on the coast of Asia-Minor were given to Greece which also got the Dodecanese Islands with the exception of two Islands. Dardenelles and the Bosphorus were internationalised. Turkey was required to pay huge war indemnity.

Ominous signs began to appear soon after the signing of the Treaty of Sevres. The United States, Yugoslavia and the Arab King of Hedjaz refused to sign at all. Turkey had signed under protest. But Turkish army in Asia-Minor began to look dangerous. There was no one to execute the Treaty. Venizelos, Prime Minister of Greece, undertook to do so. The Greeks defeated the Turks and captured Brusa. Soon after, Venizelos fell from power in Greece and ran away from the country. The Ex-King Constantine came back to Greece and took charge of the affairs of the country. However, the fall of Venizelos deprived Greece of the favour of the Allies.

At this time, Mustafa Kemal appeared on the scene. He had all the patriotic Turks behind him. The people of Turkey had not approved of the signing of the Treaty of Sevres by the Sultan of Turkey who lived at Constantinople beneath the guns of the British fleet. The presence of the Greeks at Smyrna aroused the feelings of the patriotic Turks against the Treaty of Sevres. Mustafa Kemal took advantage of the situation in the country and openly revolted. In 1920, he had been defeated in the first round by Venizelos and driven into the interior. However, early in 1921, he summoned a National Assembly at Angora which was later on named Anakra, and drew up the Angora Pact, which demanded complete independence for the Sultan and Constantinople and the union under Turkish sovereignty of all parts of the Ottoman Empire inhabited by an Ottoman Muslim majority. The manifesto amounted to a defiance of the Treaty of Sevres. It was a declaration that Mustafa Kemal and his followers would conquer by force any part of Turkey that they could.

King Constantine decided to crush Mustafa Kemal and his followers. His plan was to penetrate to Ankara and dictate peace in the highlands of Asia-Minor. It is true that Constantine was himself a distinguished general, but his project was declared impossible by the best military experts including Sir Henry Wilson and Field Marshal Foch. In spite of this, Constantine decided to attempt the impossible. Mustafa Kemal was confident of his victory. He is stated to have declared that the Greeks might beat him but he did not mean to be rounded up. He would retire to regions where the Greeks could not get at him and would continue the war until the Greeks gave in. In 1921, the Greek offensive began. In spite of all gallantry shown by the Greek soldiers, they were not able to penetrate into the stony and waterless plateau around Ankara. The Greeks found themselves in a very difficult position. They could not go forward for geographical reasons and they dared not go back on grounds of prestige and the end was inevitable. In August 1922, Mustafa Kemal attacked the Greeks and penetrated into the Greek lines and routed them. It was a complete and colossal disaster. In September 1922, Smyrna fell and was given to the flames. Mustafa Kemal expelled not only all the Greek soldiers but every Greek inhabitant of that territory.

After that, Mustafa Kemal led his troops towards the Straits which were held by British, French and Italian troops. The British troops still garrisoned Constantinople and British warships were in the Sea of Marmora. The French and Italian troops withdrew but not the British. Prime Minister Lloyd George thought he would defend the "Freedom of the Straits" and prevent Mustafa Kemal from crossing into Europe. Mustafa Kemal wisely did not attack the British forces and thereby did not involve himself in a war with Great Britain. Instead, he entered into negotiations which led to the Treaty of Lausanne which was signed on 24 July 1923. Turkish sovereignty in Asia-Minor was recognised. The boundary of European Turkey as it existed after the Treaty of Bucharest, 1913 was restored. Greece had to give up Eastern Thrace and Adrianople. The Dardanelles remained under Turkish control, but the same was not to be fortified without the consent of the League of Nations. Mustafa Kemal refused to submit to any limitation of his armaments. Turkey was the only ex-enemy power which was not restricted in the manufacture or use of armaments or in the number of her troops. The Treaty of Laussane was humiliating to the great Powers of Europe. In everything except demilitarising the Straits, Mustafa Kemal was strong enough to defy them. He shifted his capital from Constantinople to Ankara which was difficult to reach.

Mustafa Kemal was a man of great courage and determination. He introduced sweeping reforms in his country. He completely overhauled the administrative machinery of the country. He introduced and enforced new legal codes. He improved the means of communication and transport. He improved agricultural and industrial methods. He emancipated women. There was to be no **purda** for women. Women got not only the right of vote but also became members of the Assembly. The Sultanate was abolished and Turkey became a Republic with Mustafa Kemal as its President. Islam was not to be the State religion and all religions were to be equally tolerated. He Europeanised the dress of the people. He introduced the Latin characters in place of old Turkish script. Polygamy was prohibited. A national system of education was introduced. The calendar which was in use in Western Europe was adopted. A law of 1934 compelled all Turks to adopt a surname and Mustafa Kemal himself took up the name of Ataturk or father of the Turks.

Ataturk was ruthless in the suppression of all opposition. This was particularly so in the early days of his regime. His methods were those of a dictator. In 1932, he is said to have observed, "Let the people leave politics alone for the present. Let them interest themselves in agriculture and commerce. For ten or fifteen years more I must rule. After that perhaps I may be able to let them speak openly."

Although Ataturk was a dictator, he was not aggressive. He was very scrupulous in observing international obligations. In 1936 he wanted to refortify the Dardanelles and he applied to the League of Nations for permission and actually got the same. He was on very good term with other states. Although there had been fighting between Turkey and Greece in 1921-2, the relations between the two countries became cordial. There was great friendliness between Turkey and Great Britain and the two countries entered into a treaty of alliance in 1939.

Ataturk died in November 1938 but before his death he had built up a Turkish state which gave to his citizens, both men and women, greater freedom and security than any of their forefather had enjoyed. He had transformed Turkey into an independent sovereign state free from foreign interference.

Ataturk was succeeded by Ismet Inonu. He was also a dictator. Turkey remained neutral during the World War II.

SUGGESTED READINGS

Allen. H.F.: **The Turkish Transformation** (1935).
Armstrong. H.E. : **The Gray Wolf.**
Ataturk. K.: **A Speech Delivered by Ghazi Mustapha Kemal, October,** 1927 (1929).
Bisbee. Eleanor : **The New Turks: Pioneers of the Republic,** 1920-1950: (1951).
Ekrem, S.: **Turkey, Old and New,** 1947.
Froembgen, H.: **Kemal Ataturk** (1937).
Ikbal Ali Shah: **Kemal: Maker of Modern Turkey** (1934).
Mikusch, D. Von : **Mustapha Kemal: Between Europe and Asia** (1931)
Paneth, P.: **Turkey-Decadence and Rebirth** (1943).
Parker. J., & C. Smith : **Modern Turkey** (1940).
Tobin, C.M.: **Turkey-Key to the East** (1944).
Ward, B.: **Turkey** (1942).
Webster, D.E.: **The Turkey of Ataturk-Social Process in the Turkish. Reformation** (1930).
Wortham, H.E.: **Mustapha Kemal of Turkey** (1931).

CHAPTER

38 SPAIN

Spain is one of the few countries in Europe which remained neutral during the two World Wars. That is partly due to her geography as Spain is walled off from the rest of Europe by the Pyrenees and is cut off by mountain ranges into different provinces.

Alfonso XIII, the King of Spain, came to the throne at his birth in 1886. When he was still a minor, Spain had to fight against the United States and she lost not only Cuba, but all other remnants of the once vast Spanish colonial empire. This saved the country from the colonial embarrassments and wars. Some material progress was made but that was not much. The King was an autocrat and he believed in the divine right of kings to rule. The nobility was very strong in the country and the army was under his control because most of the military officers came from the nobility. Spain had a Cortes or Parliament, but the people were illiterate and could not make much use of it. They were indolent. Their agriculture was backward. Industry and trade were practically stagnant. There was corruption everywhere in the government. The Roman Catholic Church exercised great influence throughout the country. The Jesuits owned vast trading concerns and estates. In this atmosphere, the Communists, Anarchists, Socialists and Fascists made their appearance.

In 1923, General Primo de Rivera asked King Alfonso to dismiss his ministers and appoint him as a dictator. The king was so weak that he could not resist the demand and the result was that for seven years, General Primo de Rivera was the real ruler of Spain. The rule of the General was unpopular. Many plots were hatched against him and ultimately he resigned in 1930. The discontentment prevailing in the country did not end with the resignation of the General but the same was now directed against the King who had resumed full authority in the state.

When General Elections were held in April 1931, the popular slogan was, "Your vote must be an arrow into the heart of Monarchy". The Republicans won the elections and King Alfonso abdicated and ran away to Paris. The Parliament met in July 1931 and the new Constitution declared Spain a Democratic Republic of Workers of all Classes. A large number of reforms were carried out by the Republican Government and those created a lot of trouble. The situation in the country became unstable. The vested interests which were attacked by the Republican regime became its enemies. While the friends of the new regime had not learnt the necessity of loyalty to it, its enemies gained in strength. In the new elections held in November 1933, the landlords and the clericals scored a victory. The new Government tried to nullify most of the legislations which had been enacted previously. The Church got back once again the annuities from the state. The Priests were reinstated as instructors in state schools and private institutions. The Army officers who had been dismissed were reinstated. Catalonia began to be afraid of her autonomy. There was a lot of unrest in the country. There were conflicts between the Clericals and anti-Clericals, the peasants and the landlords and the Socialist and Conservative Republicans.

When such was the condition in the country, General Franco revolted on 17 July 1936 and crossed into Spain from Morocco. The military garrisons in Spain also revolted. In order to paralyse the rebellion, the Leftist forces staged a general strike throughout the area occupied by Rightists.

Although President Azana was not an effective war leader, he improvised armies out of labourers, untrained in military tactics. He was short of officers and half of the fleet went over to the side of Franco. In spite of that, the Republican Government held Madrid, Barcelona and other big cities. The Republican Government had a definite superiority in planes and tanks. When the struggle between General Franco and his followers on the one hand and the Republican Government on the other started, the latter seemed to be in a stronger position. In spite of that, General Franco came out successful in the Civil War which lasted for three years.

The Civil War ran its full course and entailed intervention on both sides. The people of Spain were in a real sense the first victims of the World War II. What prolonged the struggle was the remarkably even balance of resources between the two sides. The Navy was divided and the lack of naval supremacy told against the rebel forces, which, to begin with, operated from Morocco. Of the two battleships of the Navy, one was seized by each side and the other vessels were almost equally shared. If the officers were nationalists, the sailors were Republicans. On the Republican side, there were a few army officers such as General Miaja and General Rojo, a mass of workers and peasants trained in military service, large sections of urban workers and most of the Basques and Catalans. They also held important economic resources in the industrial areas of Madrid, Barcelona and Asturias. By the end of 1936, the Nationalists under General Franco held rather more than half of Spain mostly in the south, west and north-west and the Balearic Islands. General Franco installed himself at Burgos as "Chief of the Spanish State". 30 Junker transport planes provided by Germany were ferrying troops to Spain from Morocco. The Republican Government was led by Largo Caballero and it held all eastern and south-eastern Spain, Madrid and most of the northern coast-line belt.

The Republican forces recovered from the first shock and were able to organise resistance. The war was ferocious because the extremists on both sides indulged in great barbarities. In November 1936, Germany and Italy officially recognised the Government of Franco. In 1937, General Miaja organised the defence of Madrid and among the strong reinforcements sent to him was the first International Brigade which was recruited from the Left-Wing opponents of Fascism in several European countries, including France and Great Britain. The Soviet Union also sent fighter planes to the Republican Government of Spain. In March 1937 came the first trial of strength between the major international contingents. The Italian troops launched an attack on Guadalajara with a view to capture Madrid. The attack was met and repulsed by the International Brigade. Franco attacked the northern zone of the Basque Provinces and Asturias and captured the key port of Bilbao. The Republican forces launched attacks from Madrid and Aragon. In May 1937, Largo Caballero was replaced by Don Juan Negrin who by the end of the year commanded an army of about 800,000 men. In October 1937, the Republican Government moved to Barcelona and in December 1937, it defeated the Nationalists at Teruel. By the end of 1937, there was a stalemate in the country and each side had consolidated its defensive positions.

Salazar, the new dictator of Portugal, showed all sympathy for Franco and gave him all possible help. The sympathies of Leon Blum of France were with the Republican Government of Spain, but he had to show moderation on account of the internal politics of his country where he did not want to annoy the Rightist elements in the country. In Britain, the Labour Oppositions sympathised with the Spanish Government but the Conservative Government of Britain under Baldwin was not prepared to annoy General Franco who was expected to come out successful. The British Government also did not want to annoy Italy whom it wanted to keep apart from Germany. It was under these circumstances that the British Government welcomed and backed the proposal of Blum to establish a Non-intervention Committee whose purpose was to prevent other powers from becoming involved in the Civil War in Spain and to withhold military aid from both sides. Such a Committee was actually set up in September 1936. In spite of that, Franco got his supplies from Portugal and the Republican Government from France. In December 1936, the Council of the League resolved that all other states were under an obligation not to intervene. President Roosevelt got the neutrality laws of his country amended to prevent the sale of American arms to either side. In spite of all these measures, volunteers came to join the sides. General Franco got both troops and equipment from Italy and Germany. A critical examination of the circumstances shows that the working of the Non-intervention Committee was in favour of General Franco and against the Republican Government of Spain. That was due to the fact that General Franco continued to get illegal help from Portugal, Germany and Italy, while the sources of the Republican Government in Spain dried up. All attempts by the Non-intervention Committee to check the flow of supplies by naval blockade and frontier supervision broke down.

In the spring of 1938, General Franco, who was backed by 100,000 Italian troops and efficient German equipment, was strong enough to renew his advances. The Government forces were torn by internal dissensions. In February 1938, the rebels retook Teruel and they were also able to cut the Government territory in half. There was stubborn fighting to occupy more and more territories. General Franco resorted to indiscriminate bombing of civilian population. But in spite of that, Barcelona and Madrid held out until early in 1939. Barcelona fell at the end of January 1939 and Madrid at the end of March 1939. Thousands of Spaniards fled to France to escape reprisals at the hands of General Franco. The Non-intervention Committee was dissolved. The Italian and German Legions were withdrawn. The Civil War probably cost Spain a million in dead or exile. Many cities were destroyed. The countryside was laid waste. General Franco set up a Fascist state in Spain. Communism, Anarchism, Socialism and Liberalism were either destroyed or driven underground. However, the chief beneficiary of the war was not Mussolini, but Hitler. While Mussolini was busy in Spain, Hitler extended his influence in the Balkans at the expense of Italy. Italy had been used as Germany's cat's paw.

The victory of General Franco was due to many causes. He got a lot of help both from Italy and Germany. A week after the opening of the struggle, Italian planes were flown to Spanish Morocco at the request of General Franco. In September 1936, hundreds of German planes bombarded Republican cities. From December 1936 to April 1937, more than one lac of Italians were sent to Spain. About 40,000 more Italians were sent later on. The Italian planes raided the Republican cities and dropped thousands of tons of explosives. Italian warships managed to send Franco large quantities of tanks, trucks, automobiles, cannon and ammunition. The Republican coast was blockaded by Italian ships. Thousands of Italians were killed and wounded. Three days after the break-out of the civil war, Marshal Goering of Germany started recruiting an air force to help General Franco. On 31 July 1936, 85 aviators disguised as tourists sailed from Hamburg. Before the ending of the Civil War, the Condon Legion consisting of more than 15,000 aviators and ground crewmen had fought practically on all the fronts. They also set up air training schools and worked in different capacities. The German navy played an important part in blockading the Spanish coast. More than one thousand Germans lost their lives in the civil war in Spain.

Another cause of the victory of General Franco was the working of the Non-intervention Committee. This Committee was not able to stop the flow of help to General Franco from Italy, and Germany but put a great strain on the Republican regime in Spain. She could not get her requirements from anywhere. It is true that the Soviet Union gave some help to the Republican Government, but that was not enough. Under these circumstances, the success of General Franco was merely a matter of time.

It cannot be denied that the Civil War in Spain solidified and strengthened the position of the Fascists in Europe and weakened that of the democratic states of Great Britain and France. Their successful intervention in Spain convinced them that the democracies were so much scared of communism that they would not take any action against them. Under these circumstances, the system of Collective Security completely collapsed.

As regards the attitude of the various powers towards the civil war in Spain, the French Government was headed by Blum and Daladier and the British Government by Baldwin and Chamberlain. Both the Governments were determined to avoid war at any cost. They wanted the war to be localised and not to spread to the whole of Europe. That is why they stood for a policy of non-intervention. Great Britain was very much interested in the defence of Gibraltar and consequently she wanted to be on friendly terms with General Franco who was expected to win. The Englishmen were so much afraid of the bogey of communism that they would like to help the dictators to become stronger so that they could become an effective bulwark against communism. That is why they allowed Franco to strangle the Republican regime in Spain without any help from any quarter. France was merely following the lead given by Great Britain. She was also following the policy of winning over Italy against Germany. As Italy was helping General Franco, France had to follow a policy of Non-intervention. Mussolini intervened in Spain as he thought that by doing so he would be able to eliminate completely the British and French control from Western Mediterranean. Franco also promised to give Mussolini bases in Africa, Spain and the Canaries Islands. It was the lust for gains that made Italy energetic in her help of General Franco. Germany helped Franco as his regime in Spain was bound to help Germany against France. Moreover, Hitler wanted to test his new weapons and military tactics in Spain. The Soviet Union made a serious effort to help the Republican Government in Spain but stopped doing so after some time. She also became a member of the Non-intervention Committee. The United States also followed a policy of non-intervention. It is stated that when four members of the House of Representatives requested the Secretary of State on 2 June 1937 to apply the Neutrality Act to Germany and Italy, he is stated to have given the following reply : "This is not our war. We must be cautious, We must be quiet".

After his victory in the Civil war, General Franco ruled Spain from 1939 to 1976. Spain under him remained neutral during the World War II. It is true that his autocratic regime was criticised from many quarters but the circumstances forced the United States to come to an understanding with him. Spain became a member of the NATO.

SUGGESTED READINGS

Alvarez Del Voyo, J.: **Freedom's Battle** (1940).

Brandt, J.A.: **Toward the New Spain** (1933).

Brenan, G.: **The Spanish Labyrinth** (1943).

Dundas, L.: **Behind the Spanish Mask** (1943).

George, R.E.G.: **Spain's Ordeal** (1940).

Last, J.: **The Spanish Tragedy** (1939).

Madariaga, S.: **Spain** (1942).

Manual, F.E.: **The Politics of Modern Spain** (1938).

Padelford, N.J.: **International Law and Diplomacy in Spain** (1939).

Peers, E.A.: **The Spanish Tragedy,** 1930-1936 (1936).

Regler, G.: **The Great Crusade** (1940).

Robles, G.: **Spain in Chains** (1937).

Sender, R.: **Counter-Attack in Spain** (1937).

Thomas, Hugh: **The Spanish Civil War, New York,** 1963.

Villalba, A.M.M.: **The Martyrdom of Spain.**

Whyle, G.F.: **A Century of Spain and Portugal.**

CHAPTER

39 INTERNATIONAL RELATIONS BETWEEN TWO WARS

On 7 September 1920, a Military Convention was signed between Belgium and France. On 19 February 1921, the Franco-Polish Treaty of Alliance was signed. It was provided that in the event of an attack from Germany, France could count upon help from Poland in the East and Belgium in the West. In 1924, a Treaty of Alliance was made between France and Czechoslovakia. In 1926, a Treaty of Friendship was signed between France and Rumania by which both the countries promised to consult each other in all matters which might threaten their external security. A similar Treaty was entered into between France and Yugoslavia in 1927.

Locarno Pact. The Locarno Pact of 1925 was an expression of the common weariness of the French, British and German people on account of the struggles which had continued without interruption from the time of the Peace Settlement to the occupation of the Ruhr Valley. During that period, Great Britain had tried to restore a balance of power. French policy had tried to hold Germany within the limits of the Treaty of Versailles until such time as Great Britain was prepared to guarantee her security. During the same period, German statesmen had tried to exploit, the Anglo-French differences in order to escape from the chains of the Treaty of Versailles. In this triangular struggle, France came, out successful and British policy proved to be a failure. The occupation of the Ruhr Valley brought about the economic ruin of Germany. However, German resistance proved that although France had the upper hand she had gained nothing substantially. By 1924, the French found themselves dangerously isolated. The value of franc began to fall. It was found that the occupation of the Ruhr Valley had brought nothing but a harvest of hatred. Germany was also completely exhausted. Great Britain felt that unless she was prepared to make war against France, she had to meet the legitimate demand of France for security. Thus there was a move for a compromise for the first time since 1919. The Labour Government in Britain was also inclined towards a settlement between France and Germany. The coming to power of Briand in France also facilitated the task. He was favourably inclined towards Germany. Stressemann was the greatest supporter of Franco-German collaboration. Great Britain offered to safeguard the Franco-German frontier against aggression by Germany or by France. When negotiations started in the summer of 1925, it was agreed to put the frontier between Germany and Belgium on the same footing as between Germany and France. The guarantee was to apply to the Rhineland as well. Italy offered to guarantee the frontier along with Great Britain. As a part of the settlement. Germany was to join the League of Nations and get a permanent seat on the Council of the League.

It was in this atmosphere that delegates from Germany, France, Great Britain, Italy, Czechoslovakia, Poland and Belgium met at Locarno from 5 October to 16 October 1925 and seven treaties were signed there. There was a Treaty of Mutual Guarantee of Franco-German and Belgo-German frontiers between Germany, Belgium, France, Great Britain and Italy. There were arbitration conventions between Germany and Belgium and Germany and France. There were arbitration Treaties between Germany and Poland, and Germany and Czechoslovakia. There were also Franco-Polish and Franco-Czechoslovakian Treaties for mutual assistance in case of aggression by Germany.

The major treaty referred to the western frontier of Germany with France and Belgium and secured the same. It was provided that the powers "collectively and severally", guaranteed both "the maintenance of territorial status quo resulting from the frontiers between Germany and Belgium and Germany and France" as fixed by the Treaty of Versailles. The de-militarisation of the German territory west of a line drawn 50 kilometres east of the Rhine, as stipulated in the Treaty of Versailles, was also guaranteed. Germany, Belgium and France agreed that they would, in no case, attack or invade each other or resort to war against each other, except in legitimate defence in case of flagrant breach of the demilitarisation formula, in fulfilment of the sanctions of Article 16 of the Covenant of the League of Nations or as a result of the action of the League against a state which was the first to attack a member of that body. They also undertook to settle by peaceful means, "all questions of every kind which may arise between them and which it may not be possible to settle by the normal methods of diplomacy." All the signatories to the Treaty pledged themselves to help that state which was the victim of aggression. If the question of the violation of the Treaty was a doubtful one, the matter was to be referred to the Council of the League for final disposal. The Treaty was to come into force only after the entry of Germany into the League of Nations and was to remain in force till such time as the Council of the League by a two-thirds majority might decide that the League "ensures sufficient protection to the High Contracting Parties."

The four arbitration treaties and conventions provided that all disputes between Germany and other signatories "which it may not be possible to settle amicably by the normal methods of diplomacy, shall be submitted for decision either to an arbitration tribunal, or to the Permanent Court of International Justice". However, this provision was not to apply "to disputes arising out of the events prior to the present convention and belonging to the past", and it was not binding in the case of the problems which arose out of the Peace Settlement. The Franco-Polish and France-Czechoslovak Treaties provided that if the signatories to the main treaties were made to suffer from a failure to observe the undertakings of Locarno, they would "lend each other immediate aid and assistance if such a failure is carried by an unprovoked recourse to arms."

The Locarno Pact made a distinction between the German frontier on the west and the German frontier on the east. While the western frontier of Germany was guaranteed to be sacred and both Great Britain and Italy came forward to guarantee the same, that was not true of the eastern frontier of Germany with Poland and Czechoslovakia. It was implicitly conceded that the eastern frontier of Germany was not based on justice and Germany would be justified in asking for its revision. However, she was not to resort to war to get the same changed and was to follow the method of arbitration to achieve her objective. Obviously, that led to the grading of the frontiers of Germany. The Locarno Treaties were a violation of the Treaty of Versailles and were a recognition of the fact that the Peace Settlement of 1919-1920 was not based on justice. However, it cannot be denied that the Locarno Treaties lessened the tension between France and Germany for some time to come. The Locarno Pact was violated in 1936 when Hitler ordered the German troops to occupy the Rhineland.

The Locarno Pact gave satisfaction to France as the frontier between France and Germany was accepted by Germany. France would have liked to have similar guarantees regarding the eastern frontier of Germany as that involved the security of the states who were the members of the Little Entente. Great Britain and Italy were not prepared to give such a guarantee with regard to Eastern Europe and that left scope for German aggression on her eastern borders. Germany was prepared to put up with the loss of Alsace, Lorraine, Eupen and Malmedy, but the loss of Danzig, the Polish Corridor and Upper Silesia remained what Schuman called a '"festering wound in the hearts of all patriots and none could abandon the hope of recovering these territories in future. Their recovery however demanded a new dismemberment of resurrected Poland and behind Poland stood France and the Little Entente, firmly resolved to maintain frontiers as they were." What Germany agreed at Locarno was that she would not resort to force for the revision of her eastern frontier and nothing more.

The states in Eastern Europe highly disapproved of the differentiation between the Rhine and the Vistula frontiers made by the Great Powers. The Soviet Union looked upon the Locarno agreements with suspicion and distrust. The unwillingness of Great Britain and the refusal of Germany to guarantee the eastern frontiers was an eye-opener to the Soviet diplomats. Four days before the signing of the Locarno Pact a new trade agreement was signed between Germany and the Soviet Union. This was described as the anti-Locarno Pact by the western democracies. In April 1926 a non-aggression pact was signed between Germany and the Soviet Union.

Briand referred to the importance of the Locarno Pact in these words: "Peace for Germany and for France; that means, that we have done with the long series of terrible and sanguinary conflicts which have stained the pages of history. We have done with black veils of mourning for suffering that can never be appeased, done with war, done with brutal and sanguinary methods of settling our disputes. True, differences between us still exist but henceforth, it will be for the judge to declare the law. Away with rifles, machine-guns, cannons, clear the way for conciliation, arbitration and peace!"

Gathorne Hardy says that the immediate effect on international relations in Europe was most unfavourable. The sense of improved security which the British guarantee implanted in the minds of Frenchmen and Germans had great importance. "Locarno Pact was a most effective and formidable-looking scare-crow," which went far to justify the opinion of its creator, Mr. Austen Chamberlain, that "its erection marked the real dividing line between the years of war and the years of peace." The view of E.H. Carr is that in the long run, the Locarno Treaty was destructive both of the Versailles Treaty and of the Covenant of the League. It encouraged both the view that the Versailles Treaty, unless confirmed by other engagement of a voluntary character, lacked binding force and the view that Governments could not be expected to take military action in defence of frontiers in which they themselves were not directly interested. Ten years later, nearly all Governments appeared to be acting on these assumptions. L.A. Mander says that the Locarno agreements were of limited value because the general diplomatic situation might so develop as to reduce the Rhineland problem to a secondary factor. The view of Simonds and Emeny is that the importance of the Locarno episode lies in the fact that it clearly demonstrated the value of the League machinery for a worth which actually desires to employ it and is ready to endure the existing territorial conditions. According to Langsam, the Locarno achievements were widely hailed as precursors of a new era in world history, but neither the Pacts nor the spirit of Locarno were actual guarantees of peace. The problem of the eastern frontiers of Germany remained unsolved and there was no guarantee that the same would be solved peaceably. The spirit of friendliness was evident only sporadically in international affairs after 1925. It seemed to have been entirely forgotten in the very next year when Germany's application for membership of the League was under consideration.

David Thomson says that in the favourable atmosphere of 1925, the Locarno treaties undoubtedly contributed to the general pacification of Europe. They were the first successful attempt to recognise impartially the needs of both France and Germany. Germany was brought back into the circle of Great Powers. Yet the implications of Locarno were sinister as well as re-assuring. The implicit grading of frontiers implied that the Settlement of 1919 was followed in so far as it had later been voluntarily endorsed by Germany. The distinction made by Britain between frontiers that she would guarantee and those which she would not guarantee, undermined the general obligations of the Covenant of the League. If the Versailles Settlement lacked binding force unless it was voluntarily reinforced in this way, it was precarious as a whole. France had over-burdened herself by special obligations in Eastern Europe without partnership in Britain. If the members of the League were to distinguish between those parts of the Settlement in which they were intimately interested and were prepared to guarantee and the other parts in which they were less interested and were not prepared to uphold by military action, general security suffered from Locarno. There were technical absurdities in the notion of planning in any military cooperation between the General Staffs of Britain and France against possible German attacks, if the British Staff were at the same moment supposed to be concerting similar action with the Germans against a possible French attack. These realistic problems were not considered at that time and were smothered by the prevailing mood of optimism and goodwill. The view of Grant and Temperley is that the agreement of Locarno was not useless though it was short-sighted. It did not fulfil the prediction of Austen Chamberlain that it marked the real dividing point between the years of war and the years of peace. It did produce an atmosphere of goodwill and a period of appeasement which was actually of importance and might have been decisive. Austen Chamberlain and Briand worked hard for cooperation with Germany and the same was true of Stressemann. However, the future depended on the League being able to negotiate a general disarmament all round. The limitation of armaments had been promised at Versailles and that promise was now repeated and its observance would have made Locarno a real treaty but the same was not done.

Kellogg-Briand Pact (1928)

The object of the Kellogg-Briand pact was to outlaw war as an instrument of national policy and the settlement or international disputes. After the establishment of the League of Nations, many efforts had been made to avoid the necessity of war. Cecil-Requin Draft Treaty of Mutual Assistance of 1923 had declared that aggressive war was an international crime. The Preamble of the Geneva Protocol of 1924 declared that "a war of aggression constitutes a violation of the solidarity of the members of the international community and an international crime." The signatories were to agree "in no case to resort to war" except in resistance to aggression or with the consent of the Council or the Assembly of the League. They were also to agree to "abstain from any act which might constitute a threat of aggression against a foreign state". However, nothing came out of the Geneva Protocol on account of opposition from Great Britain.

The negotiations which ultimately resulted in the Kellog-Briand Pact in 1928 were initiated in June 1927 when Briand made a proposal to Mr. Kellogg, Secretary of State of the United States, for a bilateral pact between France and the United States by which war was to be given up as an instrument of national policy. The proposal was not of much importance in its original form as there were not many points of dispute between the United States and France. However, Mr. Kellogg suggested to Briand to make the pact multilateral instead of bilateral. After a lot of hesitation, Briand accepted the suggestion and the draft of the multilateral treaty was prepared. On 24 September 1927, the Assembly of the League of Nations unanimously adopted a Polish Resolution by which all wars of aggression were prohibited and it was declared that pacific means must be employed in all cases to settle international disputes. A similar resolution was moved and passed by the Sixth Pan-American Conference held in February 1928.

As regards the negotiations concerning the Kellogg-Briand Pact, Great Britain agreed to become a party to the Pact on the condition that she was allowed to reserve to herself the liberty of action in certain regions of the world, the welfare and integrity of which constitute a "special and vital interest for our peace and safety". The Monroe Doctrine of the United States was accepted. The Pact was signed at Qaid' Orsay on 27 August 1928 by the representatives of 15 States. By the end of 1930, it had been accepted by 61 States. The Soviet Union was the first to ratify the Pact although its provisions were criticised on grounds of indefiniteness and irrelevance. The Soviet Minister in Poland proposed on 29 December 1928 that Poland and Russia, along with Lithuania, should sign a Protocol known as the Litvinov Protocol by which the Kellog-Briand Pact was to be made effective between them at once without waiting for the general exchange of ratifications. Certain objections were raised by Poland, but those were met by Russia, Russia, also, persuaded Latvia and Estonia to ratify the Pact. The result was that on 9 February 1929, the Litvinov Protocol was signed at Moscow by the representatives of Russia, Poland, Rumania, Latvia and Estonia. Lithuania and Turkey joined it on 1 April 1929, Danzig on 30 April 1929 and Persia on 4 July 1929. On 24 July 1929, President However declared that the Kellogg-Briand pact was in force.

In the United States, it was understood that the Kellogg-Briand Pact did not interfere with the right to enforce the Monroe Doctrine in the name of self-defence. It was agreed by all the parties that the Pact forbade only wars of aggression and did not apply to a defensive war or a war against a state which violated its obligations under the agreement, or a war required by the Covenant of the League, the Locarno Pact or other agreements of neutrality or alliance.

The Preamble to the Pact contained the following declaration, "Deeply sensible of their solemn duty to promote the welfare of mankind, persuaded that the time has come when a frank renunciation of war as an instrument of national policy should be made to the end that the peaceful and friendly relations now existing between their people should be perpetuated and all changes in their relations with one another should be sought only by pacific means—thus uniting civilised nations of the world in a common renunciation of war as an instrument of their national policy...." As regards the provisions of the Pact, the signatories solemnly declared "in the names of their respective peoples that they condemn recourse to war for the solution of international controversies, and renounce it as an instrument of national policy in their relations with one another". They also agreed that "the settlement or solution of all disputes or conflicts of whatever nature or whatever origin they may be, which may arise among them, shall never be sought except by pacific means." The pact was to be ratified by the high contracting parties in accordance with their respective constitutional requirements and was to take effect as between them since the instruments of ratification were deposited at Washington.

The Kellogg-Briand Pact differed from the Covenant of the Nations. The League Covenant was a political treaty but the Kellogg-Briand Pact was a moral obligation based on the general sense of sinfulness of war. While the League Covenant allowed some wars and prohibited others and provided for the punishment of those wars which were prohibited, the Kellogg-Briand Pact condemned all wars but punished none.

Regarding the legal effect of the pact, the Nuremberg International Military Tribunal observed that the solemn renunciation of war as an instrument of national policy necessarily involved the proposition that such a war was illegal in international law and those who planned and waged such a war were committing a crime in doing so. Stimson, Secretary of State of the United States, observed in 1932 that war between nations was renounced by the signatories of the Kellogg-Briand pact and it became throughout practically the entire world an illegal thing. Hereafter, when nations engaged in armed conflict, either one or both of them must be termed violators of the treaty.

The view of Gathorne Hardy is that as a historical event, the almost universal repudiation of war as an instrument of policy seemed to have an unique importance. As a gesture indicative of a new ethical attitude to war, it was undeniably impressive. It was particularly important in that it created a basis upon which the great nations outside the League could take a direct interest in the collective organisation of peace. However, actually the Kellogg-Briand Pact did not carry the outlawry of war any further than the Polish Resolution of September 1927. It served at the moment as a magnificent advertisement of the pacific disposition of the world and might have been thought to constitute a great step forward on the road to international security. However, it depended merely on the good faith of the signatory nations and imposed no sanctions upon those who disregarded its pledges. The view of Ball and Killough is that the value of the Kellogg-Briand Pact was psychological and its effect was short-lived. While it lasted, it gave rise to a host of bilateral and multilateral agreements for non-aggression and mutual assistance. E.H. Carr says that although the Pact of Paris or the Kellogg-Briand Pact was imperfect, it was a considerable landmark. It was the first political agreement in history of almost universal scope. Barring a few exceptions, every other state hastened to accede to it. However, the pact of Paris was a moral declaration based on a general sense of the sinfulness of war. The pact condemned all wars but punished none. The Covenant of the League allowed some wars and prohibited others, but the prohibited wars it punished. The view of Schuman is that the pact lacked any effective means of enforcement. It was understood that if one signatory violated the pact, others were released from it. The pact was not stronger than its weakest link. Langsam says that the efficacy of this pact was considerably lessened by the qualifications and interpretations placed upon the text by a number of signatories. In effect war was outlawed except when resorted to in self-defence, in the execution of obligations assumed under previous treaties or in fulfilment of the responsibilities incurred through the signing of the League Covenant or the Locarno agreements. The pact was founded on the hope that public opinion might be strong and influential enough, even in time of emergency, to restrain any particular nation from violating what were simply moral obligations. Nevertheless, the general acceptance of the pact appeared as a step in advance towards world cooperation as an ideal and a goal.

The pact of Paris was a "tiger without teeth". Although it had laid down certain principles, it provided no machinery to implement them. It was "a high sounding nothing". No doubt, it has been called an "instrument of international confusion".

The Little Entente

In August 1920, Czechoslovakia entered into a bilateral convention with Yugoslavia. Its object was the maintenance of the Treaty of Trianon and mutual defence against Hungarian aggression. On 23 April 1921, an agreement was also made between Czechoslovakia and Rumania. On 7 June 1921, an agreement was signed between Rumania and Yugoslavia. This treaty was aimed not only against Hungarian aggression, but also against Bulgarian aggression. Thus, Czechoslovakia, Yugoslavia and Rumania became members of the Little **Entente.** The main purpose of the Little Entente was protection against Hungary which was the only country mentioned by name in the treaties. It was only in the case of Yugoslavia that the name of Bulgaria was also mentioned. The interests of Yugoslavia differed from the other partners. She was jealous of the position of Italy in the Adriatic. Italy had got far more Slav territories than she was entitled to and that was the cause of the tension between Yugoslavia and Italy. The Little **Entente** was closely bound to France by financial and treaty obligations. Both France and Little Entente Powers worked in close collaboration from the very outset. Between 1924 and 1927, France also entered into treaties with all the Little Entente Powers. She also supplied them with war materials. She guaranteed them protection against Hungary. She also undertook to help Yugoslavia against Italy. The Little Entente Powers became the satellites of France. They food for status quo as provided by the peace treaties and they were opposed to the revision of the treaties. They prevented the union of Austria with Germany.

In October 1921, the three Powers along with France asked the Government of Hungary to pass a law by which the Hapsburg dynasty was to be ended and the desired law was passed by Hungary. Encouraged by this, the Little Entente Powers began to hold periodic conferences with a view to keep an eye on the settlement in Eastern Europe. The Little Entente was fairly successful till the rise of Hitler in Germany.

The Statute of the Little Entente was signed on 16 February 1933 by the Kings of Yugoslavia and Rumania and President of Czechoslovakia. It was stated in the Preamble that the three countries were desirous of maintaining and organising peace and were firmly determined to strengthen economic relations with all countries without distinction and in particular with the states of Central Europe. They were also anxious to see peace safeguarded in all circumstances, to assure the progress of Central Europe towards a condition of definite stability and to secure a proper regard for the common interests of the three countries. They had resolved to give to the relations of friendship and alliance already existing between them an organic and stable basis. They were convinced of the necessity of bringing about stability on the one hand by the complete unification of their general policy and by creating a body which was to direct that policy common to them.

The Statute of the Little Entente created a Permanent Council of the three states consisting of their Foreign Ministers and delegates specially appointed for that purpose. The decisions of the Permanent Council were required to be unanimous. In addition to regular intercourse through diplomatic channels, the Permanent Council was put under an obligation to meet at least three times a year. One of the obligatory meetings each year was required to take place in each of the three states in turn. Others were to be held at Geneva. The President of the Permanent Council was to be the Minister of Foreign Affairs of the state where the annual obligatory meeting was to be held. It was the duty of that President to fix the date and place of the meeting and also prepare the agenda. He was to remain President for one year only. In all questions discussed and in all decisions taken, the principle of absolute equality between three states had to be rigorously respected. Every political treaty of each state of the Little Entente, every unilateral act changing the actual political situation of one of the states of the Little Entente in regard to an outside state and every economic agreement involving important political consequences, was to require in advance unanimous consent of the Permanent Council of the Little Entente. The existing political treaties of each state of the Little Entente with outside states, were required to be made progressively and as far as possible uniform. An Economic Council of the states of the Little Entente for the progressive coordination of the economic interests of the three states was to be set up. The Permanent Council was empowered to appoint other stable bodies, commissions or committees for the purpose of studying problems. Provision was made for the Secretariat of the Permanent Council. Its seat was to be at the same place where the Capital of the President of the Permanent Council was. One section of the Secretariat was to be permanently located at Geneva. It was specifically provided that the treaties of alliance between Rumania and Czechoslovakia and Rumania and Yugoslavia were renewed for an indefinite period.

Four Power Pact

The final text of the proposed Four Power Treaty was signed at Rome on 16 July 1933 by Germany, France, Great Britain and Italy. It was stated in the Preamble that Germany, Great Britain, France and Italy were conscious of the special responsibilities placed on them as possessing permanent representation on the Council of the League. They were also conscious of their responsibilities resulting from their signatures of the Locarno Agreements. They were convinced that a state of disquiet which obtained throughout the world could only be dissipated by reinforcing their solidarity in such a way as to strengthen confidence in peace in Europe. They also declared their faithfulness to their obligations under the Covenant of the League of Nations. The proposed Treaty provided that the four Governments mentioned in it were to consult jointly as regards all questions relating to them. They undertook to make every effort to pursue within the framework of the League of Nations a policy of effective cooperation among all the powers with a view to the maintenance of peace. They decided to examine among themselves and without prejudice the decisions which could only be taken by the regular organs of the League of Nations, all proposals relating to the methods of procedure calculated to give effect to Articles 10, 16 and 19 of the Covenant of the League. They undertook to make every effort to ensure the success of the Disarmament Conference. In case of its failure, they were to re-examine those questions among themselves with a view to ensure their solution through appropriate channels. They affirmed their desire to consult each other as regards all economic questions which had a common interest for Europe and particularly for its economic restoration. The agreement was to be concluded for a period of ten years and a notice of two years was required for terminating the same. The agreement was to come into force as soon as all the ratifications were deposited in Rome, but that never happened as France and Germany did not ratify it.

Looked at from one point of view, the Four Power Pact was practically useless. It was never acted upon. However, it had far-reaching effects. It created estrangement between France and her allies who felt that France had not bothered about them and was more worried about her relations with Germany, Italy and England. It was contended by them that while their vital interests were attacked by Italy, France did not support them enthusiastically. Poland bitterly resented the success of Italy. She felt very much her exclusion while Italy was included in the discussions. The Pact had the unfortunate effect of loosening the bonds between France and her allies.

German-Polish Declaration of 1934

On 26 January 1934, a joint declaration was made by the Governments of Germany and Poland. It was stated therein that time had come to begin a new era in the relations between the two countries through direct contacts between them. They agreed through the present declaration to establish the basis for the future development of their relations. Both Governments asserted that the peaceful development of their mutual relations was not to impair any international obligation which they had already undertaken in respect of other states prior to the making of this declaration. They also affirmed that this declaration did not repudiate those obligations but left them undisturbed. Both the Government announced their intention to communicate directly with each other on all questions which might arise pertaining to their mutual interests. In case disputes arose and the settlement was not attained by direct negotiations, the two Governments agreed to seek solution through some other peaceful means and by common understanding so that the possibility of such settlement might not be disturbed. In case of necessity, they agreed to employ those measures which had already been fixed by them to arrive at future accord. They agreed under no circumstances to use force to settle those disputes. The guarantee of peace was to facilitate the task of the two countries in finding solutions of their political, economic and cultural problems. It was declared that both the Governments were convinced that the relations between them would develop fruitfully and lead to the establishment of a good-neighbourly intercourse. The agreement was to remain in force for ten years from the date of its ratification. However, it could be terminated by any party by giving a notice of six months.

The Balkan Pact of 1934

Rumania, Greece, Turkey and Yugoslavia entered into the Balkan Pact or Balkan Entente on 9 February 1934. The Pact provided that Rumania, Greece, Turkey and Yugoslavia guaranteed mutually the security of their Balkan frontiers. They undertook to consult one another regarding the measures to be taken in the face of eventualities capable of affecting their interests as defined in the agreement. They undertook not to embark on any political action against any other Balkan country which had not signed the present agreement without mutual discussion. They were not to assume any political obligation towards any other Balkan state without the consent of the other contracting parties. This agreement was to come into force immediately after the signatures of all the contracting powers. It was to be ratified as soon as possible. The Balkan Pact was welcomed by France but criticised by Italy. Without Bulgaria and Albania, the Pact failed to stabilise the affairs of the Balkans. It was a very weak structure. The interests of the States joining the Pact were not identical. While Yugoslavia wanted to have help against Italy, Greece was not prepared to give such help. That led to the straining of relations between them. The relations between Bulgaria and Yugoslavia improved and consequently Yugoslavia came nearer to Bulgaria than to Greece. In 1938 an agreement was made by which Bulgaria was also brought into the Pact. She was released from the military restrictions of the Treaty of Neuilly.

Rome Protocols of 1934

On 7 March 1934 were signed the Rome Protocols by Italy, Austria and Hungary. It was stated that the three Governments understood to concert together on all problems which particularly interested them and also on those of a general character with the aim of developing a concordant policy which was to be directed towards effective collaboration between the European States and particularly between Italy, Austria and Hungary. The three Governments undertook to extend the scope of the accord already in force by increasing the facilities for reciprocal export and thus exploiting the complementary nature of the respective national economies. They resolved to take the necessary measures to overcome the difficulties felt by Hungary from the fall in the prices of grain. They agreed to facilitate and develop the transits traffic through the Adriatic ports and conclude agreements for that purpose. They agreed to set up a permanent committee of three experts to follow the course of economic relations and to frame proposals for their development. It was agreed between Italy and Austria that they would institute negotiations for the conclusion of a new agreement to widen the scope of the existing economic agreement between the two countries. The new agreement was to set up a preferential system for as large a number of products as possible.

The Baltic Pact

The Baltic Pact of 1934 brought Latvia, Lithuania and Estonia together. It was agreed by the three countries that their Foreign Ministers would consult one another at more or less regular intervals to develop a common foreign policy. On 12 June 1938, these countries decided to follow a common neutrality policy. In spite of that, the Soviet Union demanded from them naval and military bases and also occupied them.

The Stresa Declaration of 1935

When Hitler declared on 16 March 1935 that Germany "no longer considered herself bound by the military clauses of the Versailles Treaty, that the peace strength of his army would in future be fixed at 36 Divisions and that it would be raised by conscription", Mussolini invited the Prime Ministers and Foreign Ministers of Great Britain and France to meet him at Stresa in Switzerland. In April 1935, Great Britain, France and Italy issued a declaration condemning the German action in the most solemn and outspoken terms. The Stresa Declaration was followed immediately by signing of an alliance between the Soviet Union and France. Like Locarno, Stresa is a landmark in the history of the 20 years between the two Wars. Locarno was an attempt to bring Germany back to her proper place as a colleague and a collaborator in the peaceful development of Europe. Locarno failed and Hitler came to power. Stresa was an attempt to convince Germany that the non-German Powers were not prepared to tolerate the Nazi lawlessness. If necessary, they were prepared to take collective action to crush her. However, the Stresa front failed because within six months of the declaration, Italy started the Abyssinian War. She was criticised whole-heartedly by Great Britain and half-heartedly by France and the result was that Italy got inclined towards Germany and thus the Stresa Front broke down.

Laval-Mussolini Pact

The Laval-Mussolini Pact of 1935 was signed at Rome. Some French territory and railway rights in Africa were given to Italy. Certain privileges enjoyed by Italian citizens in French-owned Tunisia were to be continued till 1945. It was also agreed that if the independence of Austria was threatened in any way, both France and Italy were to consult each other.

Franco-Russian Alliance (1955)

In 1935, Russia and France entered into a joint pact of non-aggression and mutual assistance. The two countries agreed to consult each other if there was a danger of aggression. They were also to help each other in case of unprovoked aggression. The pact was to last for five years. It was declared that all the countries of North-Eastern Europe were to be invited to join the Pact. There is no comparison between the Franco-Russian Alliance of 1935 and the Franco-Russian Alliance of 1894. While the former was practically not acted upon and not much weight was given to it by either party, the latter was responsible for France and Russia fighting together in the World War I.

Naval Agreement between Germany and Britain

In June 1935, Hitler entered into a naval agreement with Great Britain by which Germany agreed to limit the size of her Navy to 35 per cent of the naval strength of Great Britain. This agreement was considered to be a master-stroke of Hitler's diplomacy as it was opposed to the provisions of the Treaty of Versailles.

Berlin-Rome-Tokyo Axis

Japan was not satisfied with the Washington Settlement of 1921 which fixed her naval strength at 60 per cent of that of Great Britain and the United States. She considered that as a symbol of the "moral superiority of the United States and Great Britain and her own humiliation". In 1934, the representatives of the United States, Great Britain and Japan met and discussed the question of naval limitations. Japan demanded parity with her neighbours but that was refused. The result was that Japan gave in December 1934 the required two years' notice of the termination of the naval agreement. The notice was to expire in 1936. Hitler was outspoken in the denunciation of communism and Russia. Japan also was opposed lo Russia. In November 1936, Hitler entered into an Anti-Comintern Pact with Japan by which the contracting parties agreed "to keep each other informed concerning the activities of the Third International, to consult upon the necessary defence measures and to execute these measures in close cooperation with each other." The two governments agreed to invite jointly the third parties whose domestic peace was endangered by the disruptive activities of the Communist International to embark upon measures for warding them off in accordance with the spirit of this agreement. The Pact was to remain in force for five years. After the expiry of that period, the two governments agreed to arrive at an understanding with each other concerning the form that cooperation was to take. In a supplementary Protocol it was provided that the competent authorities of both the Governments would cooperate most closely in connection with the exchange of information concerning the activities of the Communist International, as well as in connection with publicity and defence measures against the Communist International. Those authorities were to take strong measures against those who at home or abroad, directly or indirectly, were active in the service of Communist International or gave helping hand to its disruptive work. With a view to facilitate the cooperation of the competent authorities of both the Governments, a permanent commission was to be created and in that commission, further defensive measures necessary for combating the disruptive work of the Communist International were to be considered and deliberated upon.

When the anti-Comintern Pact was signed, there was not much support for it in Japan. In his speech delivered on 23 December, 1936, Matsuoka attacked the lukewarm and apologetic attitude shown towards the Pact by the government and the press in these words: "The historical significance of the Pact can be understood only if it is regarded as an alliance by which Japan, for the first time since 1922, entered upon an active foreign policy. And this alliance cannot be close enough; it must mean going together through thick and thin and it must be based on complete loyalty and mutual self-sacrifice as these find expression in Japanese Shinju".

It took a lot of time before a formal alliance between Germany and Japan could be concluded. When Japan started her invasion of China in 1937, Germany resisted attempts to represent her as supporting the Japanese action. However, in January 1938, Ribbentrop recommended to Hitler that an alliance with Japan be sought. In October 1938, Ribbentrop disclosed the plan to Mussolini who gave his consent in January 1939. There was a lot of opposition in Japan and the Japanese Cabinet remained in a state of virtual paralysis over that issue until Germany announced in August 1939 the signing of a non-aggression pact with Soviet Russia. The outbreak of the War in Europe in September 1939 confronted the Japanese government with new opportunities and difficult choice. The Nazi conquest of France enabled Japan to impose a Protectorate over Indo-China. Prince Konoye became Prime Minister in July 1940 with Matsuoka as Foreign Minister. Washington was giving aid to China and preparing to give aid to Britain. It was under these circumstances that Japan yielded to Nazi pleas for a full alliance. On 27 September 1940, Japan signed with Germany and Italy a 10-year treaty of cooperation by which the three Axis Powers reciprocally recognised and respected one another's leadership in establishing "new order in Europe and a new order in Greater East Asia". They also agreed to assist one another with all political, economic and military means when one of the three contracting parties was attacked by a power at present not involved in the European war or in the Chinese-Japanese conflict. Japan was given an assurance that whether or not a contracting party was to be considered to have been attacked within the meaning of the Pact, was to be considered upon consultation among the three contracting parties.

In the minds of Hitler and Ribbentrop the Pact was prompted largely by the immediate concern to restrain the United States and the Soviet Union from intervening to defraud them of their anticipated early victory over Britain. It was a manoeuvre of Nazi diplomacy and its value was to be considered primarily in terms of its immediate propaganda impact. However, so far as Japan was concerned, her immediate concern was to accommodate herself as quickly as possible to the prospects of a British defeat. She was to get an assurance that the vacuum which was to be created as a result of the collapse of the British Empire in the Far East was to be filled by Japan and not by any other power including Germany. If the object of the Pact was to check the American intervention in the Far East, that object was not going to be realised. As a matter of fact, the pact accelerated the process of American involvement and widened the area of contest. In the American minds, the problem of peace or war with Japan became inseparable from the problem of peace or war with Germany.

It still remains to be seen how Italy joined Germany and Japan in the formation of the Axis. It is true that although Italy was not satisfied with the Peace Settlement of 1919-20, she continued to cooperate with the Western Democracies. As a matter of fact, she was one of the guarantors of the Western frontiers of Germany with Belgium and France under the Locarno pact. She opposed the annexation of Austria by Germany. When Hitler tried to establish his control over Austria in 1934, Mussolini was the foremost in the denunciation of Germany. He induced France and Great Britain to subscribe to a declaration that the three Powers took "a common view regarding the necessity of maintaining Austria's independence in accordance with the relevant treaties". However, all this was changed by the Abyssinian war. Mussolini did not like the attitude of the Democratic States towards Italy on the question of Abyssinia. He resented very much the enforcement of the economic sanctions against Italy. He also resented the action of the League of Nations against his country. Moreover, the Abyssinia war weakened Italian military strength available for service in Europe. Real Politik demanded an alliance with Germany as the only way out of the difficulty. Italy had become so very weak that Mussolini had to accept Hitler's terms for friendship. In July 1936, a treaty was made between Germany and Austria by which the Nazis were given the green light in Austria. This treaty was made with the knowledge and approval of Mussolini. In October 1936, Hitler and Mussolini agreed to work together to preserve Western civilisation, to cooperate in the Danubian area, to reconstruct Spain with the recognition of General Franco and to support a new Locarno Pact for Western Europe. Italy made some economic concessions to Germany in Abyssinia. The agreement provided for a common defence against communism. It was in November 1937 that Italy joined the Anti-Comintern Pact which had already been signed in November 1936 between Germany and Japan. The agreement of 1937 between Hitler and Mussolini created what was described by Mussolini as Rome-Berlin Axis. Mussolini referred to it as "An Axis around which all European states animated by the desire for peace might collaborate". He also declared that "the struggle between the two worlds (Axis and non-Axis) can permit no compromise. Either we or they". Hitler described the Axis as a "great world political triangle" which "consists not of three powerless images but of three states which are prepared and determined to protect decisively their rights and vital interests". The Axis continued throughout the World War II and was smashed in 1945 after the overthrow of Italy, Germany and Japan.

The Steel Pact

On 22 May 1939 was signed in Berlin what is known as the German-Italian Pact of Steel. That Pact had a Preamble, seven Articles and a secret Protocol. The Preamble provided that the time had come when the close relationship of friendship and affinity which existed between Germany and Italy should be strengthened through a solemn Pact. Since a safe bridge for mutual help and support had been created by the common frontier between Germany and Italy which had been fixed for all times, the two Governments acknowledged once again a policy which in its basis and objects had already been agreed upon by them and which had proved itself successful. Closely bound together through internal relationships of ideologies and solidarity of interests, the German and Italian peoples had decided in the future to stand up for the securing of their sphere of living and maintenance of peace. Germany and Italy desired to devote themselves to the task of securing the foundations of European culture. It was provided in the Pact that the parties would remain permanently in contact with each other in order to agree on all questions affecting their interests or the European situation as a whole. If their common interests were endangered through international events of any sort, they would immediately enter into consultation with each other in order to take measures to protect those interests. If the security or other vital interests of one party were threatened from outside, the other party would afford the threatened party its full political and diplomatic support in order to remove that threat. If one of the parties get involved in war-like complications with another power or powers, the other party would come to its aid as an ally and will support it with all its military forces of land, sea and air. The Governments of the two countries would further intensify their cooperation in the military sphere and would keep each other permanently informed about the measures necessary for the practical execution of the provisions of the Pact. They were to set up a Permanent Commission which was to be subject to the direction of the Foreign Ministers of the two countries. In the case of a jointly waged war, the parties were to conclude an armistice and peace only in full concord with each other. The Pact was to come into force immediately upon being signed. It was to last in the first instance for ten years, but the same could be extended by the parties.

The Secret Protocol attached to the Treaty provided that the Foreign Ministers of the two countries were to come to an agreement as quickly as possible regarding the organisation, seat and methods of work of the Commissions on military questions and questions of war economy. They were to arrange the necessary measures conforming to the spirit and aims of the Pact in matters of the press, the news services and propaganda. Each of the two Foreign Ministers was to assign to the Embassy of his country in the respective capital one or several specially well-experienced specialists for constant discussion in direct close co-operation with the respective Ministry of Foreign Affairs of the suitable steps to be taken in the matter of the press, the news services and the propaganda for the promotion of the policy of Axis and as a counter-measure against the policy of the enemy powers.

Non-Aggression Pact

On 23 August 1939 was signed in Moscow the Nazi-Soviet Non-Aggression Pact which provided that both the parties obligated themselves to desist from any act of violence, any aggressive action and any attack on each other either individually or jointly with other powers. If one of the parties became the object of belligerent action by a third power, the other party was not to lend its support to the third power in any manner. The Governments of Germany and Russia were to maintain constant contact with each other for the purpose of consultation in order to exchange information on problems affecting their common interests, Neither of the two parties was to participate in any grouping of powers whatsoever, which was directly or indirectly aimed at the other party. If any dispute arose between the parties, they were to settle the same exclusively through friendly exchange of opinion or, if necessary, through the establishment of arbitration commissions. The Treaty was to last for ten years, and if the same was not determined within that period, it was to be extended automatically for another period of five years.

A secret additional protocol was added to the Treaty by which both Germany and the Soviet Union laid down the boundaries of their respective spheres of influence in eastern Europe. It was laid down that in the event of a territorial and political rearrangement in the areas belonging to the Baltic States of Finland, Estonia, Latvia and Lithuania, the northern boundary of Lithuania was to represent the boundary of spheres of influence of Germany and the Soviet Union. In that connection, the Interests of Lithuania in the Vilna area was recognised by each party. In the event of a territorial and political rearrangement of the areas belonging to the Polish state, the spheres of influence of Germany and the Soviet Union were to be bounded approximately by the line of the rivers Narew, Vistula and San. The question whether the interests of both parties made desirable the maintenance of an independent Polish state and how such a state should be bounded could only be definitely determined in the light of further political developments. In any event, both the Governments were to resolve that question by means of a friendly agreement. With regard to south-eastern Europe, attention was called by the Soviet Union to her interests in Bessarabia and Germany declared its complete disinterestedness in those areas. The Protocol was to be treated by both the parties as strictly secret.

The Non-Aggression Pact was a bargain between two enemies and both of them gained from it. Germany gained through the assurances that she would not have to fight on two fronts and she paid the price for it to the Soviet Union. Germany was confident that she could choose the time of her attack on Russia as the latter was too weak to start an offensive war. Russia felt that she was making the best of a bad bargain as she was not sure of the attitude of Great Britain and France towards Germany. Germany was to be strengthened by the extension of her control over western Poland. There was also the possibility that Great Britain and France would fight against Germany over Poland and thereby exhaust Germany and in that case, the Soviet Union would have the upper hand. The Pact was a gamble and the Soviet leaders were forced to play the same. It gave the Soviet Union practically two years of respite. In spite of this Pact, Germany attacked the Soviet Union on 22 June 1941.

Pact between United Kingdom and Poland

A reciprocal Treaty of mutual assistance between the United Kingdom and Poland was signed and came into force on 25 August 1939. It was provided in that treaty that if one of the parties became or get engaged in hostilities with an European power in consequence of aggression by the latter against that party, the other party was to give at once all the support; and assistance in its power. These provisions were also to apply in the event of a war by an European power which clearly threatened directly or indirectly the independence of one of the parties and was of such a nature that the party in question considered it vital to resist it with its armed forces. If one of the parties got engaged in hostilities with an European power in consequence of action by that power which threatened the independence or neutrality of another European state in such a way as to constitute a clear menace to the security of that party, the provisions of Article I will apply. If an European power attempts to undermine the independence of one of the parties by processes of economic penetration or in any other way, the contracting parties will support each other in resistance to such attempts. If the European power concerned embarks on hostilities against one of the parties, Article I will apply. The parties were to communicate to each other the terms of any undertakings of assistance against aggression which they had already given or may give in future to other states. If the parties were engaged in hostilities as a result of the application of this agreement, they were not to conclude an armistice or treaty of peace except by mutual agreement. Within a week of the coming into force of this Treaty, Poland was attacked by Germany and thus the World War II started.

SUGGESTED READINGS

Armstrong, G.G.: **Why another World War? How we missed Collective Security,** 1941.

Beloff, M.: **The Foreign Policy of Soviet Russia,** 1921-41.

Birdsall, P.: **Versailles Twenty Years After,** 1941.

Butler, H.: **The Lost Peace,** 1942.

Cameron, E.R.: **Prologue to Appeasement,** 1942.

Carr, Edward H.: **German-Soviet Relations between the two World War** 1919-1939. **Baltimore,** 1951.

Coates, W.P. & Z.K.: **A History of Anglo-Soviet Relations.**

Daladier, E.: **In Defence of France,** 1939.

Foot, M.: **Armistice,** 1919-39, 1940.

Graham, H.: **From War to War,** 1917-49.

Haines and Hoffmann: **The Origins and Background of the Second World War,** 1943.

Jordan, W.M.: **Great Britain and the German Problem,** 1918-1939, 1944.

Kain, R.S.: Europe : **Versailles to Warsaw.**

Langford, R.V.: **British Foreign Policy,** 1942.

Medlicot, W.N.: **British Foreign Policy Since Versailles,** 1940.

Mowat, R.B.: **A History of European Diplomacy,** 1914-25.

Orton, W.A.: **Twenty Years' Armistice,** 1918-39.

Rayner, R.M.: **The Twenty Years' Truce,** 1943.

Ross, M.: **A History of Soviet Foreign Policy,** 1940.

Schuman, F.L.: **Design for Power: The Struggle for the World,** 1941.

Seton-Watson, R.W.: **Britain and the Dictators: A Survey of Post-War British Policy,** 1938.

Spender, J.A.: **Between two Wars,** 1943.

Taylor, A.J.P.: **The Origins of the Second World War. London,** 1963.

Werth, A.: **France and Munich: Before and After the Surrender,** 1939.

Wiskemann, E.: **The Rome-Berlin-Axis, London,** 1949.

Wolfers, A.: **Britain and France Between two Wars: Conflicting Strategy of Peace Since Versailles,** 1940.

CHAPTER

40 THE WORLD WAR II AND PEACE SETTLEMENT

Causes

In his book entitled "The Second World War", Cyril Falls says that the World War II was essentially a war revenge initiated by Germany. German National Socialism stood first and foremost for revenge. The other aims, the 'living room' to be obtained by the subjugation of neighbouring states, the absorption of all Teutonic or so-called Teutonic population, the colonisation of agricultural districts like the Ukraine, the control of all major industries in Europe, were either the means of consolidating the revenge once achieved, or the expression of purely predatory instinct such as had always flourished in Prussia and were later on diffused all over Germany. Hitler stood for rearmament and revenge and then for loot and German domination.

(1) The Treaty of Versailles had in itself the germs of the war of 1939. Germany was very badly treated. She was forced to sign the Treaty at the point of bayonet and the Treaty itself was based on the spirit of revenge. Germany was deprived of her colonies and concessions abroad. She was deprived of her territories in Europe. She was cut into two parts by the establishment of the Polish Corridor. Her navy was completely destroyed. Her army was reduced to an insignificant position. She was deprived of her coal and steel resources and was burdened with reparations which it was impossible for her to pay. Her soil was occupied by the foreign troops to enforce the provisions of the Treaty. The Allied Troops stationed on the German soil did not behave properly towards the people and created unhappy memories. The French occupation of the Ruhr Valley added insult to injury. The result was that the problems facing the newly created Republic of Germany were so big that it was impossible for her statesmen to cope with them. The democratic states of Western Europe did nothing to help the Weimar Republic to strengthen her hold over the people and she had to meet opposition, often armed, of the extremists from the Right and the Left. On account of its own nationalistic outlook and reliance on the army, the German Republic was more severe with the Radicals than with the reactionaries. The foundations of democracy in Germany remained as weak as they could be. The political extremists enjoyed legal protection under the Weimar constitution although they themselves did not bother about the legal niceties. The introduction of proportional representation multiplied the number of political parties in the country and made the ministries unstable. The people of Germany demanded a revision of the Treaty but there was no possibility of getting it done on account of opposition of France which considered the Peace Settlement of 1919-20 as the only tangible guarantee of security. France felt that any concession given to Germany would weaken the whole structure, and hence refused a revision of the Treaty which alone could satisfy the Germans. The Weimar Republic struggled hard to cope with the situation; but ultimately it lost the fight. It was under these circumstances that the Nazi Party began to gain ground on the German soil and in January 1933 Hitler, its leader, was appointed the Chancellor. To begin with the Nazis followed a very cautious policy and tried to silence the suspicions of the other powers with regard to their future programme of action. Hitler took pains to emphasise that he stood for peace and to prove his bona fides, he entered into a Treaty with Poland in 1934 and with England in 1935. When there was a revolt in Austria in 1934, Hitler denied that he had any hand in it. The Saar Plebiscite held in 1935 went in favour of Germany.

However, after having consolidated their position at home and strengthened their military resources, the Nazis began to unfold their inner aims and objects. The Rhineland was occupied in March 1936. Austria was annexed in 1938. The Sudeten Germans in Czechoslovakia were encouraged to demand their union with Germany and Hitler openly backed their demands. As Great Britain had already guaranteed military support to Czechoslovakia there was every possibility of a war. However, Chamberlain went personally to Germany and ultimately by the Munich Pact, Czechoslovakia was forced to submit to the demands of Germany. War was avoided at the cost of the dismemberment of Czechoslovakia although Chamberlain claimed that he had brought "peace with honour." Although there was some relief at the idea that war had been averted, many agreed with the view of Churchill that the Munich Agreement was "a total unmitigated defeat" for Great Britain. The peace which followed the surrender at Munich lasted hardly for 11 months. In defence of policy of appeasement of Chamberlain it was contended that Great Britain was not at all ready for war. After 1919, she had reduced her military strength to a dangerous point in the name of economy. The British army was short of tanks. Although the Royal Air Force was efficient, it was no match for the German Air Force. There was no conscription in the country. The training of the second line of national defence, the Territorial Army, was hopelessly inadequate. British statesmen, British publicists and the British nation as a whole, were responsible for the sad state of affairs. No British Government, no political party and no organ of public opinion had demanded that the military defence of the country must be put on a war footing. The voice of Churchill was the solitary voice in the wilderness. The British public opinion and her statesmen ought to have stopped Hitler when he ordered the German troops to march into the Rhineland in March 1936. They ought to have intervened on the occasion of Japanese occupation of Manchuria and the Italian conquest of Abyssinia. They ought not to have allowed Hitler to annex Austria without risking a war. Even in the case of Czechoslovakia, the British Government ought to have adopted a policy of "no surrender". As it was, Hitler and his other partners in the Berlin-Rome-Tokyo Axis were allowed to have their conquests without any let or hindrance. Such an attitude was bound to create an unfortunate impression in the minds of the dictators and encourage them in their aggressive designs. As success followed success, with little more than verbal interference, they became bolder and bolder. They saw no point in stopping when it was so easy to go on.

After the annexation of the rest of Czechoslovakia on 15 March 1939, Hitler concentrated his attention on Danzig and the Polish Corridor. He followed the old technique of press campaign in which the atrocities of the Poles over the Germans were condemned. On 31 March 1939, Chamberlain declared that Great Britain and France would help Poland if she was attacked by Germany. However, Hitler defied the warning and threatened the Poles with dire consequences if they continued to be obstinate. In April 1939, Great Britain and France guaranteed the independence of Greece and Rumania. Mussolini annexed Albania in April 1939. President Roosevelt appealed on 15 April 1939 to both Hitler and Mussolini to help the cause of peace by giving a 10-year pledge of non-aggression against certain states, but his request was rejected. On 28 April 1939, Germany denounced her naval agreement of 1935 with Great Britain. She also denounced the non-aggression Pact of 1934 with Poland and demanded the return of Danzig and the right to construct and maintain a rail and motor road across the Polish Corridor to East Prussia. Poland rejected those demands on 5 May 1939. On 22 May 1939, Ribbentrop, Foreign Minister of Germany, and Ciano, Foreign Minister of Italy, signed a 10-year alliance at Berlin which provided for diplomatic cooperation and consultation, collaboration in the field of war economy and immediate military aid in case any of the two powers was involved in a war. Germany also signed non-aggression pacts with Denmark, Estonia and Latvia. On 23 August 1939, Soviet Russia and Germany entered into a non-aggression Pact by which they agreed not to resort to war against each other. They were not to support any third power in the event of a war in which one of the signatory powers was involved. Both the states were to consult each other on all matters of common interest and refrain from associating with any group or powers aimed at the other. This pact was a master-stroke of German diplomacy, as thereby Germany was able to avoid a war on two fronts. Soviet Russia agreed to sign the pact because she was disgusted with the attitude of Great Britain and France, and she herself was not so strong as to stand alone against Germany.

After the signing of non-aggression pact between Germany and Soviet Russia, events began to move rapidly. The German and Polish newspapers were already publishing stories of atrocities committed by each other. Hitler bewailed that his "racial comrades" in Poland were being brutally treated. Military preparations were given the final touches. Stories of atrocities were multiplied and boosted. Hitler began to thunder against Poland with greater and greater vehemence. The world was passing through breathless days.

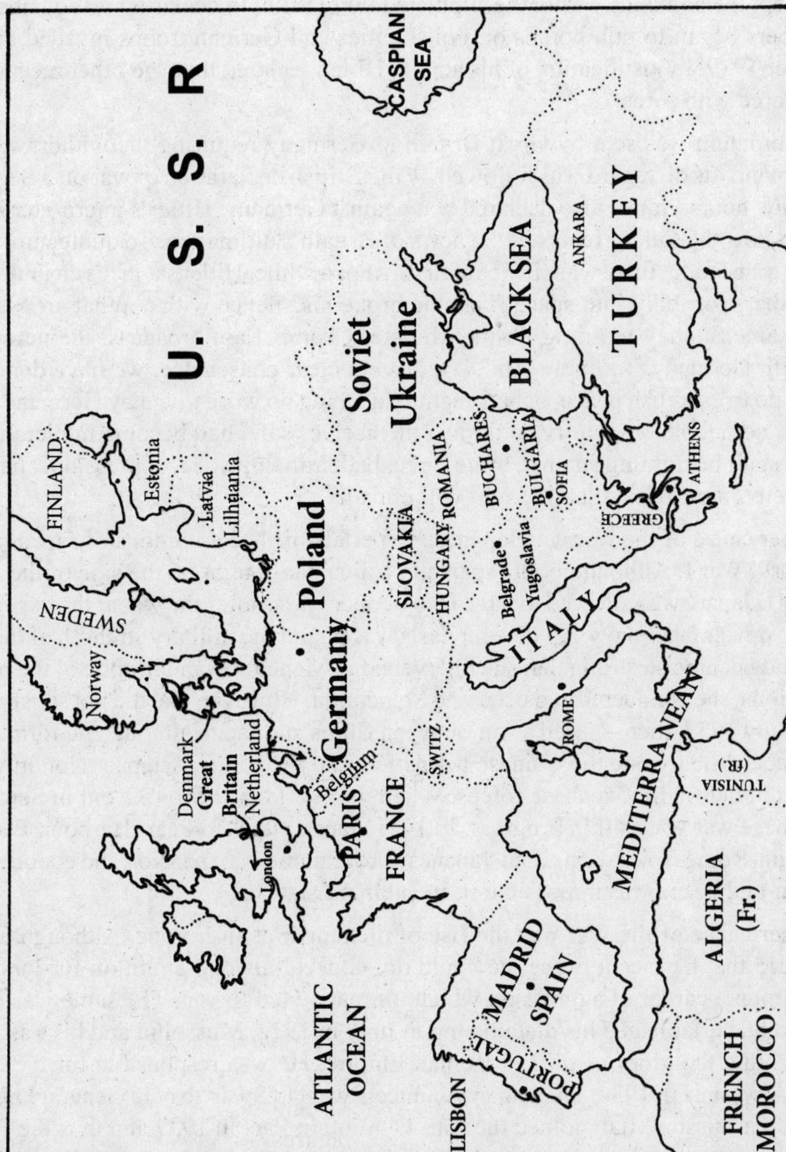

It was in this atmosphere that Germany asked Great Britain on 29 August 1939 that she must arrange to have a Polish delegate with full powers to negotiate in Berlin on the next day. The reply of Great Britain was that the demand was unreasonable and impracticable and the time was not sufficient for that purpose. Germany was asked to submit her demand on Poland through the Polish ambassador. When Ribbentrop got this reply from the British Ambassador at midnight, he is stated to have read out at top speed in German language his 16 demands whose acceptance alone could avoid the war. Sir Neville Henderson, the British Ambassador in Berlin, asked for a copy of those demands and the reply of Ribbentrop was that "it was now too late as Polish representative had not arrived in Berlin by midnight". On 31 August 1939, the German Government broadcast her 16 demands. However, when the Polish ambassador in Berlin tried to communicate those demands to his country, he could not do so as all communications between Poland and Germany were cut off. The German Government declared that the Polish Government had failed to send their representative and also refused to accept the demands within the stipulated time. Without declaring war against Poland, the German bombers began to rain bombs on Polish cities and German troops invaded the Polish soil on 1 September 1939. In justification of his action, Hitler declared that "no other means is left to me than to meet force with force."

(1) An ultimatum was sent by Great Britain to Germany requiring the withdrawal of German forces from Poland. Its disregard was followed by the British declaration of war on 3 September 1939 and within a few hours France also declared war against Germany. Hitler's interpreter Paul Schmidt later described how the Fuhrer received the news of Britain's ultimatum. To quote him, "When I had completed my translation, there was silence at first.....For a while, Hitler sat in his chair deep in thought and started rather worriedly into space. Then he broke his silence with...'What are we going to do now'?" That same Sunday morning, Prime Minister Chamberlain broadcast the news that Britain was at war with Germany. To quote him, "We have a clear conscience, we have done all that any country could do to establish peace, but a situation in which no word given by Germany's ruler could be trusted, and no people or country could feel themselves safe, had become intolerable.....For it is evil things we shall be fighting against, brute force, bad faith, injustice, oppression, and persecution. But against them I am certain that the right will prevail."

(2) Another cause of the war was Japanese imperialism. The ambitions of Japan had increased during the World War I. Although both Japan and China had fought on the side of the Allies during the World War I, Japan, was allowed to have many concessions after the war at the expense of China. Japan began to develop her navy. All the emphasis was put on the military strength of the country. By 1931, Japan had become so strong that she intervened in Manchuria and in spite of the protests in the League of Nations, she conquered and occupied Manchuria. However, that did not satisfy the Japanese ambitions. In July 1937, there started a war between China and Japan although no formal declaration of war was made. One by one the Chinese towns fell into the hands of Japan. Not only Peking, but Nanking also fell before the Japanese forces. When the World War II broke out in September 1939, the Sino-Japanese war was still in progress. In 1941, Japan attacked Pearl Harbour. Earlier, she had joined the Berlin-Rome-Tokyo Axis. Pan-Japanese programme of expansion and conquest was bound to result in war and peace was impossible in such circumstances.

(3) Another cause of the War was the rise of dictatorships in Europe. Although Hitler tried to assure the world that he meant peace, he could not conceal his real ambition for long. Very soon, he embarked upon a career of aggression which ultimately led to war. The same was the case with Mussolini who had established his dictatorship in Italy in 1922. Mussolini and his Fascist followers boasted of reviving the glory of the old Roman Empire. He was responsible for the conquest and annexation of Abyssinia in 1936. The Italian volunteers went to Spain to help General Franco and were successful in their mission. Italy joined the Anti-Comintern Pact in 1937 and thus the Berlin-Rome-Tokyo Axis came into existence. In May 1939 Italy entered into a 10-year alliance with Germany. In the presence of Axis Powers there could be no peace in the world and no wonder the war came.

(4) There was also a conflict of ideologies between dictatorships on the one hand and democracies on the other. Countries like Germany, Italy and Japan represented one kind of ideology and Great

Britain, France and the United States represented another. Mussolini described the conflict between the two ideologies thus, "The struggle between the two worlds can permit no compromise. Either we or they". Basically the distinction between the two ideologies lay in their different attitude towards the individual in the State. In the case of democracy, the individual was regarded as the creator and the beneficiary of all the state activities. He could be interfered with only when his acts were prejudicial to the interests of other individuals. Under a totalitarian regime, the individual did not figure anywhere. He was to be merged in the state and sacrificed for the sake of the state. The two ideologies also differed in spiritual, territorial and economic matters. The democratic states stood for the maintenance of the status quo in political and territorial matters and were designated as the "Haves". They had no immediate expansionist aims. On the other hand, the Axis states were called the "Have-nots". On grounds of prestige and strategy, they demanded additional territories. Japan was land-hungry and she was determined to establish her supremacy in the Far East. She was not prepared to accept any compromise and was willing to fight with any country which dared to intervene in her sphere of influence. The same was the case with Germany and Italy. Hitler not only demanded the return of the colonies which had been snatched away from Germany after the World War I, but he also asked for more territories so that Germany could stand on the same footing as the colonial powers like Great Britain and France. The Germans under Hitler could not understand why Great Britain and France should have great colonial empires and they should have nothing. They considered themselves to be a 'Master Race' and were not prepared to put up with the limitations placed on them and no wonder they were willing to risk a war to achieve their objectives. On the eve of the War in 1939, the world was divided into two armed camps viz., the Axis world and the non-Axis world. Co-existence was impossible between the two camps and one of them had to go tinder. A conflict was absolutely inevitable under the circumstances.

(5) Another cause of the war was the weakness of the democratic states and a sense of over-confidence" in their strength among the Axis powers. Soon after the Peace Settlement of 1919-20, Great Britain and France began to drift apart from each other. Great Britain began to follow a policy of aloofness from European politics and refused to accept any commitment for the preservation of peace. She was bothered more about her business and trade than about the foreign affairs of Europe. She thought that she was more to gain from the economic recovery of Germany than by quarrelling over the question of reparations, war debts, occupation of the Rhineland, armaments, etc. However, that was not the case with France. After winning victory over Germany, France began to dread Germany. She felt that while the German population was increasing, her own population was declining. Under the circumstances, in the event of a future war, Germany was bound to have the upper hand. There was also the possibility of Germany having her revenge for her humiliation of 1919. France asked for guarantees from Great Britain and the United States and when she failed to get them, she entered into military alliances with countries like Poland, Czechoslovakia, Belgium, etc. Unfortunately, her alliances were more of liabilities than assets and no wonder she did not enjoy a sense of security. Under the circumstances, she continued to oppose every effort to revise the Peace Settlement in any way. In 1935, she entered into an alliance with Soviet Russia and made an agreement with Italy but in spite of that, she did not find herself safe and ultimately decided to throw in her lot with Great Britain. Great Britain herself was not ready for war and consequently up to 1938, nothing could be done to stop the aggressors. If the democratic states had been ready for a war when the Axis powers launched upon a career of aggression, there is reason to believe that a check could have been put on them. However, that was not to be. The weakness of their military strength and the division in the ranks of the democratic states encouraged the Axis Powers. It was too late in the day for them to retrace their steps in 1939 even when they found that the democratic states also meant business and were determined to resist further aggression. The policy of appeasement also contributed towards war. The various concessions made to Hitler and Mussolini from time to time convinced them that Great Britain and France would never fight whatever the provocation. It was this feeling which encouraged

them on the war path. They could not believe that Great Britain could come to the help of Poland when the latter was attacked by Germany.

(6) It was realised by the statesmen of Europe that militarism was one of the important causes of the World War I. It was with that idea in their minds that the League of Nations was established with the primary object of maintaining peace in the world and lessening the causes of tension. The Treaty of Versailles disarmed Germany and it was expected that the other powers would follow suit. As a matter of fact, Great Britain began to disarm herself gradually and she followed that policy to a dangerous point of national security. France was asked to do likewise but she refused to do so on the ground of national security. The same was the case with the other countries of Europe. Disarmament Conferences were summoned and very earnest attempts were made to arrive at some workable arrangement, but those efforts were not crowned with success. The result was that when Hitler came to power in Germany he decided to scrap those clauses of the Treaty of Versailles which put limitations on German armaments. The German air force began to grow and came to be recognised as one of the strongest air forces in Europe. In 1935, conscription was introduced in Germany. The Rhineland was occupied by the German troops in March 1936. All these steps were on the road to militarism. The same was the case in Japan and Italy. The military preparations of the Axis Powers forced the democratic states to arm themselves. That was particularly so after the Munich surrender in September 1938. Militarism in both the camps was bound to result ultimately in an armed conflict.

(7) Unfortunately, when hostility was growing between the two camps there was no effective international organisation which could bring the leaders of the two camps on a common platform and bring about a reconciliation between them. The League of Nations was practically dead. It had ceased to exist as an effective force after her failure on the question of Manchuria and Abyssinia. Both big and small states lost their confidence in that international organisation and the only alternative left was that the parties should have a trial of strength by an armed conflict. It was unfortunate that the very people who could have worked for the success of the League were not honest and sincere in their actions. They all tried to use the League to serve their personal ends. Prime Minister Lloyd George tried to utilise the League as an "alternative to Bolshevism". In the words of Clemenceau, the best use of the League was as "Instrument for perpetuating the Peace Settlement". To Germany, the League was a "grouping of the victorious imperialist powers and all secondary states assembled to preserve the fruits of their victory and to maintain the status quo." To Soviet Russia, the League was "a forum of the imperialists assembled to thwart her new civilisation". Gaetano Salvemini says, "The history of the League of Nations between World War I and the World War II was a history of the devices, ruses, deceptions, frauds, tricks and trappings by means of which the very diplomats who were pledged to operate the Covenant of the League managed to circumvent and stultify it. They were its most effective foes since they were undermining it from within, while nationalists, militarists and Fascists were attacking it openly from without in all lands".

(8) Another cause of the war was the economic needs and material interests of the European powers. It was a struggle for raw materials, markets for exports and colonies for increasing population which had partly brought about the war of 1914 and that struggle did not end then but continued and became even more acute. Both Germany and Italy were struggling hard to acquire colonies for raw materials and markets for surplus goods. Both of them were equally dissatisfied after the war. Germany was deprived of all that she had and Italy felt that she was not given at the Peace Conference what had been promised to her by the secret Treaty of London of 1915. The same was true of Japan. Germany, Italy and Japan were the poorest in natural resources. The bulk of undeveloped and underdeveloped regions of the world had been occupied by Great Britain, France, Portugal, Belgium, the Netherlands and the United States. Out of the 25 essential raw materials and minerals, there were in British Empire adequate supplies of 18 while Germany possessed only 4. The condition of Italy was still worse. She had virtually no coal, little oil and only small iron resources. Japan had no resources in oil,

insufficient coal and iron and no surplus land for her ever-increasing population. During the period of pacification from 1925 to 1929, these countries found markets for their finished goods and also got raw materials. However, the situation was radically changed as a result of the economic crisis. Almost all the countries resorted to a policy of protection to save their own industries. Everywhere the cry raised was "Buy at home". International trade came to a standstill. Germany, Italy and Japan suffered terribly. High tariff walls, quotas and embargoes caused wide-spread distress, particularly in the countries which did not possess the raw materials required for their industries. A feeling of economic suffocation was created on account of the non-availability of raw materials and the absence of markets for manufactured goods. It is these circumstances that brought Germany, Italy and Japan together and they embarked upon a course of aggression. Japan invaded Manchuria, Italy occupied Abyssinia and Germany started a long course of aggression which ultimately led to the World War II.

(9) Another cause of the World War was the dissatisfaction of the national minorities. It is true that the Allied Powers had committed themselves to the principle of self-determination, but in actual practice that principle was not always applied. In the words of Robert Engang, "Its application was conditioned by such factors as economic necessity, military defence; religious and political traditions and punishment of the defeated nations." In some areas of Central Europe, the principle could be applied as the national minorities were intermixed in such a way that the drawing of clear-cut frontiers was not possible. The result was that the members of one nationality were included in the boundaries of other states in which they were in a minority. It is these minority groups which became the hot-beds of discontent and dissatisfaction. They were encouraged by propaganda from the countries in which the people of their own nationality lived and they demanded their reunion with their mother country or full autonomy. They asked, "If it is true that World War I was fought for the self-determination of nationalities, why was Austria forbidden to unite with Germany? Why were a large part of Germany put under foreign rule?" Germany under Hitler raised the cry that the Germans were being mercilessly persecuted, and she had every right to liberate them. That served as a convenient pretext for annexing Austria, the sudetenland and subsequently Poland which led to World War II.

(10) Another cause of the war was the failure of the disarmament efforts. The Peace Settlement of 1919-20 had completely disarmed Germany and the Allied Powers pledged themselves "to apply the same measure to themselves and to open negotiations immediately with a view to adopt eventually a scheme of general reduction." Many conferences were held inside and outside the League of Nations to achieve the ideal of disarmament, but practically nothing came out of them. The German Government called upon the Allied Powers to disarm themselves in the same way as she had been disarmed, but the attitude of France was: "Security first; disarmament afterwards." Security could not be had on account of the conflicting interests of Great Britain and France and hence disarmament was not possible. Lloyd George conceded in 1927, "The nations which had pledged themselves to disarmament had not reduced their armaments by a single division, flight of aeroplanes or battery of guns." The refusal of the Great Powers to disarm themselves gave Hitler a handle to arouse the indignation of his countrymen and assert that "rearmament was the only road to power and national achievement." It was the German rearmament under Hitler which directly led to the war of 1939.

(11) Another cause of the war was the strong feelings of nationalism prevailing in various countries. The Peace Settlement of 1919-20 was made primarily along national lines. The victorious nations were guided solely by their national interests. They ridiculed internationalism as "sickly and wishy-washy". In many cases, nationalism at this time was more intolerant than before. In Germany, Italy and Japan, the state was worshipped by the people and was considered to be an end in itself. Their only motive was the extension of the frontiers of their states. In several cases, the dictators rode to power on a wave of popular nationalist enthusiasm. To retain themselves in power, it was necessary that enthusiasm must be sustained and to do this, they resorted to aggression against other countries. The people in the dependencies and colonies also made common cause with one or the

other of the big powers and helped precipitate the war which they thought would weaken the big powers and help them in obtaining their own independence.

Course of the War

The World War I was in a sense the last major traditional war. It was fundamentally fought by foot soldiers and with guns. Tanks and aircrafts were ancillary to the fighting which was essentially static. After weeks of battle, the front would have advanced or receded only a few kilometres. The majority of the civilians were still outside the battle area. The World War II was utterly a new kind of war. It was a mobile war fought by men enclosed in armoured cars, tanks and aircrafts in which the battleline might move 50 or 100 kilometres in a day. Millions of civilians were involved as tanks crashed through their towns and dive-bombers dropped bombs containing from ½ to 10 tonnes of TNT equivalent on them. Only six European countries remained neutral viz., Ireland, Portugal, Spain, Sweden, Switzerland and Turkey. Britain escaped invasion in 1940 by a hair's breadth. Every other European country with the partial exception of Russia was either occupied or controlled by the Germans and most of them experienced bitter fighting on their soil.

The refusal of Poland to surrender resulted in the German invasion of Poland in September 1939. In spite of stiff resistance put up by the Poles, they were completely defeated. When the Germans were smashing the Polish resistance, the Russians also invaded Poland from the East. The result was that after its conquest, Poland was divided between Germany and Russia. In the autumn of 1939, Russia attacked Finland. She demanded a part of Finnish territory on the ground that its possession was necessary for the safety of Leningrad. Russia had no faith in German professions of peace and friendship and consequently was trying to take all the necessary precautions. It was feared that Germany might conquer Finland and thereby endanger the safety of Russia. The Russians conquered the regions they wanted and ultimately made peace with Finland. Russia also annexed the Baltic States of Latvia, Estonia and Lithuania. In April 1940, German troops occupied Denmark. Norway was also occupied after some resistance. In May 1940, Holland and Belgium were attacked and conquered. France was attacked by Germany from the side of Belgium and when Great Britain feared that her army might be entrapped, she evacuated her troops. After the evacuation of the British troops from Dunkirk, France could not stand against the might of Germany and she surrendered in June 1940. After the collapse of France, Italy also joined the War. Mussolini demanded Nice, Savoy and Corsica. After the entry of Italy into the war, the conflict started between Italy and British forces in North Africa. Mussolini attacked Greece, but the attack was a failure. When the Germans joined the Italians, Greece was conquered. Yugoslavia and Crete were occupied by the Germans.

After the fall of Dunkirk, Great Britain was left all alone in Europe. Her Air Force was the finest in Europe in quality, but not in quantity. Hitler could have attacked England in June 1940 when she was still weak but he missed that opportunity. Under the dynamic leadership of Churchill, Great Britain was able to pull herself up. Churchill promised nothing to his countrymen, but "blood and toil and tears and sweat". In this historic speech, he made the following declaration, "We shall fight on the seas and oceans, we shall fight with growing strength in the air, we shall defend our island whatever the cost may be, we shall fight on the beaches, we shall fight on the landing grounds, we shall fight on the fields and in the streets, we shall fight in the hills, we shall never surrender." The people of England responded to the call of their leader. The slogans of "Who wins if England loses", and "We are not interested in the possibility of defeat; it does not exist" were raised. The Germans started their attack of Great Britain in right earnest in the autumn of 1940. The technique they intended to adopt was first to destroy the Royal Air Force and then to invade the country. A large number of aircrafts were sent to England for that purpose, but the Royal Air Force was not beaten. The Battle of Britain proved to be the determining point of the war. A large number of enemy aircrafts were destroyed and ultimately, the German attack began to slow down. Churchill could rightly boast that "Never in the history of mankind did so many owe so much to so few." The Germans started the bombardment at night of London and other great cities. A lot of property was destroyed and many Englishmen lost their lives. However, after some time, the Britishers learned the technique of protecting themselves from air raids and after the construction of air-raid shelters, and widespread use of anti-aircraft guns, the losses became less and less. The Royal Air Force also started attacking the ships and docks in the Channel ports of France and Belgium, Holland and Norway, so that the German preparations for the invasion of England might be frustrated.

To begin with, the American view was that the fall of Great Britain was merely a question of time and hence they did not bother themselves about the same. However, in June 1940, a large number of French ships at Oran were destroyed by the British fleet with a view to avoid their being captured by Germany. The result was that the Vichy Government of France cut off all diplomatic relations with Great Britain, but the battle of Oran impressed the Americans and they began to feel that the boast of Churchill that he wanted to fight the war to the bitter end was not an empty one. Moreover, it began to be realised that it was not wise to ignore the fate of Great Britain as after her conquest the turn of United States was bound to come. President Roosevelt was moving cautiously on account of the public opinion in the United States, but when he found a change in that attitude in favour of Great Britain, he transferred 50 Destroyers from the American Navy to the British Navy in lieu of the lease of naval and air bases. In March 1941, the American Congress passed the Lease-Lend Act by which the United States undertook to help those countries which were fighting against Axis Powers. In August 1941, President Roosevelt and Premier Churchill met on board a British battleship in the Atlantic and drafted a document known as the Atlantic Charter in which the war aims were enunciated.

When Russia was attacked by Germany in June 1941, the mission of Cripps to Russia became successful and an agreement was signed between the two countries in July 1941. The United States sent all the necessary war materials to Great Britain and the Soviet Union to fight against Hitler.

In December 1941, Japan attacked Pearl Harbour and that brought the United States into the war. General MacArthur was made the Supreme Commander in the Pacific and Lord Mountbatten was given the command of South-East Asia with his headquarters at Delhi. Lord Mountbatten drove out the Japanese from Burma and the Philippines were captured by General MacArthur. There was a lot of fighting in Africa between 1941 and 1943. Abyssinia was conquered by the United Nations. The Italian Somaliland was also conquered. The British forces advanced into Libya up to Benghazi, but were forced to withdraw. In November 1942, the "Desert Rats" of General Montgomery turned out the Germans and Italians from Libya. Montgomery also conquered Tripoli and advanced into Tunisia. An Italian squadron was defeated by a British fleet in the battle of Cape Matapan near the Greek coast. Many a time, the Island of Malta was attacked by the Italians but it managed to hold its own against the enemy to the end and never surrendered. In November 1942, American and British troops occupied the French colony of Algeria. North Africa was cleared of Italian and German troops in 1943. In the summer of 1943, the Island of Sicily was captured by English and American troops. The mainland of Italy was attacked. There was a revolt in Italy and Mussolini was arrested, but he managed to escape. In September 1943, Italy surrendered unconditionally. Mussolini was captured in 1945 and was shot by the Italians themselves.

In the winter of 1943-44, preparations were made in England under General Eisenhower for the invasion of the continent. He was assisted by General Montgomery and Air Chief Marshal Tedder. A large number of artificial harbours known as "mulberry" were constructed to be towed across the English Channel to the coast of France. For the supply of petrol to the invading armies, the Pluto or "Pipe Line Under the Ocean" was constructed. By this time, the Royal Air Force had become very strong. It had thousands of well-trained pilots. Both the British and American pilots attacked day and night the war targets in Germany and succeeded in paralysing completely the war industries of

Germany. The bombing of military targets of Germany struck terror in the hearts of the people and everything was dislocated in Germany.

The Germans expected an invasion of the continent. But could not make out as to where the invasion was to come. Consequently, they tried to protect the whole of the coast-line facing Great Britain. In June 1944, Normandy was attacked. In spite of hard fighting, the troops of the United Nations were able to make a landing on the mainland. After getting reinforcements, the United Nations were able to capture Paris and also succeeded in driving out the Germans from the French soil. After completing the conquest of Italy, the army of General Alexander invaded France from the South-East and then the South of France was also cleared of the enemy. The army of General Alexander joined that of Eisenhower on the Rhine. There was a German counter-attack in December 1944 under Rundstedt, but after some success, the same was repulsed. When the armies under General Eisenhower crossed the Rhine and moved towards the Elbe, the Russians also invaded Germany from the East. The Germans could not fight on two fronts and Hitler, Goebbels and Himmler committed suicide and their successors surrendered unconditionally on 7 May 1945.

After the fall of Germany, the United States and Great Britain concentrated their forces against Japan. On 6 August 1945, an atom bomb was thrown on the city of Hiroshima and it is estimated that more than one lac of persons were destroyed by one single bomb. Japan was asked to surrender and when she refused, another bomb was thrown on 9 August on the city of Nagasaki. On 14 August, 1945, Japan surrendered unconditionally.

The World War II was over. It had brought about the death of over 50 million people, including 15 million Russians, 6 million Jews, 3,700,000 Germans, 2 million non-Jewish Poles, 1,600,000 Yugoslavs, 1,200,000 Japanese, nearly one million Italians, 600,000 British, 500,000 Rumanians, 300,000 Frenchmen, 292,000 Americans and 22 million Chinese. At the end of the War, some 13 million Europeans had been killed in battle and 17 million civilians had died as a result of the fighting. Houses, factories and communications had been shattered on a large scale. Nearly all the major German cities were in ruins and 25 million Russians were rendered homeless. Agriculture was disrupted. Food rationing was everywhere. The Allied troops in Germany were forbidden to give away their rations. In the Don region of Russia, people were eating cats, dogs and grass. Fuel was scarce and millions spent the first two post-war winters in un-heated homes.

Peace Settlement

It is not possible to appreciate the post-war peace treaties without a reference to the conferences, declarations and decisions arrived at by the statesmen of the United Nations during and after the World War II. It was in August 1941 that Roosevelt and Churchill met and issued what is known as the Atlantic Charter. They pledged themselves to seek no aggrandizement from the War, to respect the rights of all peoples to self-determination, to promote the enjoyment by all of free access to markets and raw materials of the world, to persist in the destruction of Nazi tyranny and seek universal disarmament and peace. On 1 January 1942 was issued the United Nations declaration by which the United States, the United Kingdom, Russia and China pledged themselves to employ all their resources for the destruction of the Axis Powers and their satellites. In January 1943, Roosevelts, Churchill and their military staffs met at Casablanca. In October, 1943 was held a meeting of the Foreign Ministers of the United States, Great Britain and Soviet Russia. In November 1943, Roosevelt, Churchill and Chiang Kai-shek met at Cairo to plan the defeat of Japan. The Teheran Conference was attended by Roosevelt, Churchill and Stalin. It was there that the final plans for victory over Germany were prepared by them along with their Chiefs of Military Staffs and a communique was issued on 1 December 1943. In February 1945, Roosevelt, Churchill and Stalin met at Yalta in Crimea and they made decisions regarding Germany, Poland and Japan. After the fall of Germany, the Berlin or Potsdam Conference was held from 17 July to 2 August 1945. It was attended by Stalin, President Truman and Prime

Minister Attlee. It was decided to set up a Council of Foreign Ministers to do the preparatory work for the Peace Settlement. The Council was to draw up treaties of peace with Italy, Rumania, Bulgaria, Hungary and Finland. After about 15 months of preparatory work, the peace treaties were given a final shape by the 21 participating countries and they were signed on 10 February 1947, in Paris by the representatives of the five enemy states and the Allied Powers.

Italy

As regards Italy, she was to give to France small districts in the regions of Little St. Bernard, Mont Thabor, Chaberton, Mont Ceins, Tenda and Briga. She was to give Zara, Pelagosa, Lagosta and other islands along the Dalmatian coast to Yugoslavia. The Istrian Peninsula and most of the remainder of the province of Venetia, Giulia, with Trieste were to become a "Free Territory" to be governed under a statute approved by the Security Council. For 9 years, the city was a focal point of tension between the Communists and the Western Powers and in 1954, the Soviet Union and Yugoslavia agreed that Trieste could return to Italy. Italy was to give to Greece the Rhodes and other Dodecanese Islands. She was to give up her sovereignty over her African colonies and recognise the independence of Albania and Ethiopia. She was to submit to the demilitarisation of frontiers with France and Yugoslavia. She was not to have atomic weapons, guided missiles and guns with range over 30 Kms. She was not to have mines, torpedoes, aircraft-carriers, submarines, etc. She was not to have more than 200 heavy medium tanks. Her navy was reduced to two battleships, 25,000 officers and men. Her army was reduced to 250,000. Her Air Force was reduced to 200 fighters, and reconnaissance and transport aircraft to 150. She was to pay the Soviet Union 100 million dollars in 7 years. She was to pay 5 million dollars to Albania during the same period.

Bulgaria

As regards Hungary, her frontiers of 1 January 1938 with Austria. Her army was limited to 55,000, anti-aircraft artillery to 1,800 men, Navy to 3,500 men, air force to 5,200 men and 90 air planes. Bulgaria was to pay 45 million dollars to Greece and 25 million dollars to Yugoslavia in kind in 8 years.

Hungary

As regards Hungary, her frontiers of 1 January, 1938 with Austria and Yugoslavia were restored. She was to give to Yugoslavia three villages west of the Danube. The Vienna award of November 1938 was cancelled. The result was that Transylvania went to Rumania. The army of Hungary was limited to 65,000, air force to 5,000 and air planes to 90. Hungary was to pay 200 million dollars to the Soviet Union and 50 million dollars each to Yugoslavia and Czechoslovakia.

Rumania

As regards Bulgaria, her frontiers of 1 January, 1945, were restored. Her army was limited to 120,000, anti-aircraft artillery to 5,000, navy to 5,000 men and 1,500 tons. Her air force was reduced to 8,000 men and 150 air planes. She was to pay 303 million dollars to the Soviet Union in kind in 8 years.

Finland

As regards Rumania, her frontiers of 1 January, 1947 were restored, province of Petsamo was given to the Soviet Union. The Soviet-Finnish peace treaty of March 1940 was restored. The Soviet Union gave up leasehold of Hango and acquired 50 years' lease of Porkkala-Udd area for a naval base. The Finnish army was limited to 34,400, navy to 4,800 men and 10,000 tons, and air force to 3,000 men and 60 air planes. She was to pay 300 million dollars to the Soviet Union in kind in 8 years.

Austria

Austria and Vienna were divided into four zones of occupation but in contrast to the treatment of Germany, Austria was allowed to form a national Government in 1945. Although it was decided at Potsdam not to exact reparations from Austria in order to avoid the economic collapse which had occurred after the World War I, the Russians took oil and equipment from their zone. Until 1955, Austria remained an occupied country because the Russians refused to consider its future apart from that of Germany. Then Khrushchev suddenly agreed to a peace treaty on the understanding that the country should be neutral, joining no political or military alliance an having no foreign troops stationed on its sail.

Germany

As regards Germany, she was occupied by the Big Four. After its fall in May 1945, it was divided into four zones, each of which was administered separately by one of the occupying Powers. Berlin came under joint occupation and each occupying Power was assigned a sector of the city. An Inter-Allied body was charged with the function of governing the city as a whole. With a view to bring about a coordination of their policies as a whole, an Allied Control Authority was set up for the whole of Germany. In 1947, Great Britain and the United States established economic unity of their two zones. Their invitation to join them was accepted by France but rejected by the Soviet Union. In June 1948, a new currency was put into circulation in West Germany. In 1948, delegates were chosen from American, British and French zones and from the non-Russian sectors of Berlin to constitute the Constituent Assembly and the Bonn Constitution of 1949 was adopted. The Russians also framed a constitution for their own zone. Germany was caught in the cold war. In June 1948, the Soviet Union cut off all communications by land and water between the Western zone of Germany and Berlin. The Western Powers resorted to what is known as the Berlin-Airlift which lasted for 10 months. Ultimately the Russians were forced to lift the blockade. In May 1952, the Western states entered into an agreement with West Germany, by which the Federal Republic of Germany got virtual autonomy in foreign and domestic affairs. West Germany was also put under the protection of the NATO. In 1955, she became a member of the NATO.

Japan

As regards Japan, a peace treaty was signed with her at San Francisco in 1951. Japan recognised the independence of Korea and gave up all claims on Korean territory including the islands of Quelpart, Port Hamilton and Dagelet. Japan renounced all rights to Formosa and the Pescadores, the Kurile islands, that part of Sakhalin which belonged to Japan since 1905, the Pacific territories governed by Japan under the mandate of the League of Nations, the Antarctic area and the Spratly and Paracel Islands. All Allied occupation forces were to be withdrawn from Japan within 90 days of coming into force of the treaty. Japan recognised all treaties concluded by the Allies for ending the World War II. She gave up all special rights and interests in China. She agreed to enter into stable and friendly trading and maritime relations with all signatories of the treaty. It was agreed in principle that Japan was to repair damage and suffering caused by her during the last war. Japan undertook to indemnify those members of the Allied armed forces who had suffered undue hardships as prisoners of war of Japan. Japan recognised her pre-war debts. Soviet Russia did not sign the peace treaty at San Francisco and India entered into a separate peace treaty in 1952.

SUGGESTED READINGS

Churchill, W.S.: **Blood, Sweat and Tears,** 1941.

Churchill, W.S.: **The Second World War, Vols. I to V.**

Churchill, W.S.: **The Second World War (Abridged version with Epilogue),** 1959.

Collier, B.: **The History of the Second World War : The Defence of the United Kingdom,** 1957.

Collier B.: **The Battle of Britain,** 1962.

Commager, H.S. (Ed.): **The Story of the Second World War,** 1945.

Ehrman, John : **The History of the Second World War,** 1956.

Falls, Cyril: **The Second World War: A Short History.**

Fuller, J.F.E.: **The Second World War,** 1949.

Grunberger, R.: **Germany,** 1918-1945 (1964).

Haines and Holffmann : **Origins and Background of the Second World War.**

Holt, E.: **The World at War,** 1939-1945. **Putnam,** 1956.

Lee, D.E.: **Ten Years: World on the Way to War,** 1930-40, 1940.

Millis, Why Europe Fights, 1940.

Opie, Redvers and others: **The Search for Peace Settlement,** 1951.

Schuman, F.L.: **Night over Europe,** 1941.

Schuman, F.L.: **Europe on the Eve,** 1939.

Sellman, R.R.: **The Second World War, Methuen,** 1964.

Shugg and Deweerd : **The World War II,** 1949.

Smith, N.D. : **The Battle of Britain, Faber,** 1962.

Taylor, A.J.P. : **British History,** 1914-1945. **Oxford,** 1965.

Taylor, A.J.P.: **Origin of the Second World War.**

Turner, E.S.: **The Phoney War on the Home Front,** 1961.

Wheeler-Bennett: **Munich: Prologue to Tragedy,** 1952.

Woodward, Sir Llewellyn: **History of the Second World War,** 1962.

CHAPTER

41 THE UNITED NATIONS

The World War II ended in Europe on 7 May 1945, and the Charter of the United Nations was signed at San Francisco in June 1945. The United Nations with its headquarters in New York was created for the maintenance of international peace and security, development of friendly relations among nations, achievement of international cooperation in solving international problems of economic, social or humanitarian character and the promotion and encouragement of respect for human rights and fundamental freedoms for all without distinction of race, sex, language or religion.

There are two kinds of members of the United Nations. Some of them are original members but new members can be admitted by a certain procedure. The membership is open to all peace-loving states who accept the obligations contained in the Charter and who in the judgement of the organisation, are able and willing to carry out their obligations. The Security Council plays the most important part in admitting or refusing admission to any State. On the recommendation of the Security Council, the membership of a State can be suspended or the State can be out-lawed by the General Assembly.

The General Assembly

The important organs of the United Nations are the General Assembly, the Security Council, the Economic and Social Council, the Trusteeship Council, the International Court of Justice and the Secretariat. As regards the General Assembly, every member-state of the United Nations is a member of this Assembly. As a rule, the Assembly meets once a year but there can be a special session under certain circumstances. The General Assembly has been given powers of discussion, review, supervision and criticism of the work of the United Nations as a whole. It can discuss and recommend measures for the maintenance of international peace and security. It directs and supervises international, economic and social cooperation. It supervises the working of the trusteeship system. It controls the finances of the organisation. It admits suspends and expels members. It adopts international conventions. It initiates, studies and makes recommendations for the encouragement of progressive development of international law. It appoints a large number of members of the various organs of the United Nations. It can debate amendments to the Charter of the United Nations Organisation.

Security Council

The Security Council meets more often than the General Assembly. It consists of some permanent members and the others selected for two years by the General Assembly by a system of rotation. Regional considerations are taken into account at the time of electing the members. Each member of the Security Council has one vote and the approval of all the permanent members is essential in every case. Every permanent member of the Security Council has the power of veto. To begin with, the Soviet Union exercised the veto power on very many occasions and the same is being done now by the United States. The veto power has been criticised but it appears that the Big Powers would not like to be members of the United Nations without the veto power. They would not like anything to be done by the United Nations simply because small states who may be in majority in the United Nations may decide to do something which is not approved of by the Big Powers.

As regards the functions of the Security Council, its primary duty is to maintain international peace and security. It has to submit annual or special Reports to the General Assembly. It can submit plans to the General Assembly for the regulation of armaments among the member-states. While doing so, it can avail of the help of the Military Staff Committee. The Security Council has to establish regional agencies. It has to supervise and control Trust Territories, which are under the charge of the various states. It has to use its good offices to resolve international disputes through peaceful methods. Whenever it considers necessary, it can call upon the parties to a dispute to settle the same by negotiations, inquiry, mediation, conciliation, arbitration, judicial settlement, action by regional agencies or under regional arrangements or other peaceful means.

Economic and Social Council

The Economic and Social Council consists of members who are elected lor three years by the General Assembly. However, one-third of them retire every year. Its main function is to make or initiate studies and reports with respect to international, economic, social, cultural, educational, health and other related matters. It can prepare draft conventions on the same subjects and submit them to the General Assembly. It can coordinate the activities of the specialised agencies and also regulate the flow of the reports from those agencies at regular intervals. It has to perform those functions which are given to it by the General Assembly and also those for which request has been made by the member-states and the specialised agencies.

Trusteeship Council

The Trusteeship System is an improvement on the Mandate System provided in the Covenant of the League of Nations. The Trusteeship Council is to be incharge of this work. It has to consider reports submitted to it by the administering authority. It has to examine the petitions in consultation with the administering authority. It has to visit the territories under the Trusteeship System to see how their administration is going on. The Trusteeship Council can send a questionnaire to the states concerned with the object of getting information regarding the political, economic, social and educational progress of the mandated territories.

International Court of Justice

The International Court of Justice is an improvement on the Permanent Court of International Justice. It consists of 15 members who are elected by the General Assembly. It exercises two kinds of jurisdiction. It decides those cases which are the subject of dispute between two or more states. It has also been given advisory jurisdiction.

Secretariat

As regards the Secretariat, the Secretary General is the chief administrative officer. He is assisted by a large number of subordinates who have to look to the details concerning the various aspects of the activities of the United Nations. The headquarters of the Secretariat are in New York. The member-states have to foot the bill for the maintenance of the Secretariat.

Collective Security under United Nations

Article I of the United Nations Charter calls for "effective collective measures for the prevention and removal of threats to the peace and for the suppression of acts of aggression or other breaches of the peace." Chapter VII of the Charter points out in deal what those "effective collective measures" can be. It is provided that the Security Council shall determine the existence of any threat to the peace, breach of the peace or act of aggression and shall make recommendations or decide what measures shall be taken to maintain or restore international peace and security. In order to prevent aggravation of the situation, the Security Council may call upon the parties concerned to comply with such provisional measures as it considers necessary or desirable. Such provisional measures will be without prejudice to the rights, claims or position of the parties concerned. The Security Council shall duly take action in case of failure to comply with the provisional measures. It must decide what measures, not involving the use of armed forces, are to be employed to give effect to its decisions and may call upon the members of the United Nations to apply such measures. These may include complete or partial interruption of economic relations and of rail, sea, air, postal, telegraphic radio and other means of communication and the severance of diplomatic relations. If these measures are considered to be inadequate by the Security Council, it may take such action by air, sea or land forces as may be necessary to maintain or restore international peace and security. Such action may include demonstrations, blockade and other operations by air sea or land forces of the members of the United Nations. All members of the United Nations, in order to contribute to international peace and security, have undertaken to make available to the Security Council, on its call and in accordance with a special agreement or agreements, armed forces, assistance and facilities including the right of passage, necessary for the purpose of maintaining international peace and security. Such agreement or agreements shall govern the members and types of forces, their degree of readiness and general location and the nature of facilities and assistance to be provided. The agreement or agreements shall be negotiated as soon as possible on the initiative of the Security Council. They shall be concluded between the Security Council and the members or between the Security Council and groups of members and shall be subject to ratification by the signatory states in accordance with their respective constitutional process.

When the Security Council has decided to use force, it shall, before calling upon a member not represented on it to provide armed forces, invite that member to participate in the decisions of the Security Council concerning the employment of contingents of the armed forces of the member. In order to enable the United Nations to take urgent military measures, the members shall make immediately available national air force contingents for combined international enforcement action. The strength and degree of readiness of these contingents and plans for their combined action shall be determined by the Security Council with the assistance of the Military Staff Committee. Plans for the application of armed forces shall be made by the Security Council with the assistance of the Military Staff Committee.

The action required to carry out the decisions of the Security Council for the maintenance of international peace and security shall be taken by all the members of the United Nations or by some of them as the Security Council may determine. Such decisions shall be carried out by the members of the United Nations directly and through their action in the appropriate international agency of which they are members. The members of the United Nations shall join in affording mutual assistance in carrying out the measures decided upon by the Security Council. If preventive or enforcement measures against any state are taken by the Security Council, any other State, whether a member of the United Nations or not, which finds itself confronted with special economic problems arising from the carrying out of those measures, shall have the right to consult the Security Council with regard to a solution of those problems.

Article 51 provides that nothing in the Charter shall impair the inherent right of individual or collective self-defence if an armed attack occurs against a member of the United Nations, until the Security Council has taken the measures necessary to maintain international peace and security. Measures taken by the members in the exercise of the right of self-defence shall be immediately reported to the Security Council and shall not in any way affect the authority and responsibility of the Security Council to take at any time such action as it deems necessary in order to maintain or restore international peace and security.

Experience shows that the system of collective security as provided in the United Nations Charter has failed to achieve its objective. In spite of the salutary provisions, there has been plenty of aggression in all parts of the world and the members of the United Nations have failed to come together to meet the danger.

Work of the United Nations. The United Nations has done a lot of useful work in the political field. In January 1946, Iran formally charged the Soviet Union with interference in her internal affairs and asked the Security Council to investigate and effect a settlement. The Security Council asked the two Governments to settle their differences by direct negotiations. On 23 May 1946, Moscow and Tehran announced that the Soviet troops had evacuated from Iran.

After the World War II, the people of Indonesia proclaimed the Republic of Indonesia and declared their independence. Holland refused to accept her independence and there were armed clashes. The matter was brought before the Security Council which directed the parties to stop hostilities and issued cease-fire orders. It offered its good offices to settle the dispute and appointed a Good Offices Committee for that purpose. In spite of many ups and downs, the United Nations played an important part in the recognition of the independence of Indonesia.

In January 1946, the Soviet Union complained that the stationing of British troops in Greece and British interference in the internal affairs of Greece endangered peace and security in that region. The view of the Security Council was that British troops were called into Greece by her own Government. In August 1946, Ukraine alleged that the policy of Greece was threatening peace in the Balkans. The allegation of Greece was that Yugoslavia, Albania and Bulgaria were provoking Communist guerillas against her. The Security Council appointed a Special Investigation Commission which reported that Yugoslavia, Albania and Bulgaria were actually aiding the pro-Communist revolutionaries of Greece. The General Assembly also appointed a Sub-Committee on the Balkans which reported that the Northern neighbours of Greece were giving large-scale aid to Greek guerillas. In December 1950, the General Assembly set up a Standing Committee to go into the matter.

Supported and incited by the Government of Pakistan, the tribals launched raids upon Kashmir in October 1947. On 1 January 1948, India lodged a complaint with the Security Council that the Government of Pakistan was assisting the raiders who were attacking the State of Jammu and Kashmir. The Security Council set up a United Nations Commission on India and Pakistan. The Commission asked the two Governments to stop fighting, withdraw their troops from the State of Jammu and Kashmir and to plebiscite be held to determine the future of the State. India and Pakistan agreed to those proposals and cease-fire became effective from 1 January 1949. The United Nations appointed Admiral Nimitz, Sir Owen Dixon and Dr. Frank Graham to mediate between the two countries. The Security Council also discussed the Kashmir issue on many occasions but nothing has come out of that. When there was a war between India and Pakistan in 1965, the Security Council issued several calls for an immediate cease-fire and withdrawal of armed forces. The efforts of the Security Council succeeded in bringing about a cease-fire between the two countries. When Pakistan attacked India in 1971, the Security Council asked both the parties to stop fighting. In spite of all the help given by the United Nations, the question of Kashmir remains unresolved.

When Britain announced her intention to terminate her mandate of Palestine, the General Assembly appointed a Sub-Committee on Palestine. The United Nations also appointed a mediator for Palestine. It also appointed a Truce Commission in April 1948. When Israel was attacked by the Arab States, a cease-fire was ordered by the Security Council and a truce was brought about. The United Nations appointed Count Bernadotte and Dr. Ralph Bunche to act as mediators. The General Assembly appointed a Conciliation Commission. It also established the United Nations Relief and Works Agency for Palestine refugees which has done a lot of useful work.

In 1946, India complained to the General Assembly against the discriminatory policies of the Government of South Africa which violated the principles enshrined in the United Nations Charter. The General Assembly took up the issue. Many resolutions have been passed by the United Nations against the Government of South Africa. It has also recommended mandatory sanctions against South Africa.

In June 1950, North Korea attacked South Korea. The matter was brought before the Security Council which directed North Korea to withdraw her troops. North Korea refused to withdraw. The Security Council branded North Korea as the aggressor. The United Nations appointed General MacArthur as the Supreme Commander of the forces sent to fight against North Korea. The offensive of North Korea was halted. The United Nations took keen interest in bringing about peace. In July 1953, a truce agreement was signed and hostilities ended.

In 1948, a complaint was made that a serious situation had arisen as a result of the unilateral imposition of restrictions by the Soviet Union on transport and communication between Western Zones of occupation and Berlin. The President of the Security Council played an important part in the lifting of the Berlin blockade.

The United Nations played an important role in diffusing the situation created by the nationalisation of the Suez Canal in 1956. The General Assembly called upon France, Britain and Israel to withdraw their troops from the Egyptian territory. Ultimately, a cease-fire was arranged. Egypt agreed to the stationing of a United Nations force on her territory. The General Assembly authorised the Secretary-General of the United Nations to go ahead with the plan to clear the Canal area under the auspices of the United Nations and make the Canal ready for navigation. The United Nations played an effective role in the Suez crisis of 1956.

When the Soviet Union sent her troops to Hungary in 1956, there was criticism of her action. The Soviet Union continued in Hungary in spite of protests from many countries.

The General Assembly called upon the member states to recall their ambassadors and ministers from Franco's Spain. In spite of that, the United States entered into a treaty with Franco's Government on account of the strategic position of Spain in the world.

When there was trouble in the Congo after her independence in June 1960, the Secretary-General of the United Nations organised a United Nations operation in the Congo. The Congo question was referred to the General Assembly after its veto by the Soviet Union. The General Assembly directed the Secretary-General to continue his efforts "to assist the Central Government of the Congo" and created a Conciliation Commission of Asian and African representatives. A nominee of the Secretary-General of the United Nations visited the Congo. Dag Hammarskjoeld was killed while bringing about peace in the Congo.

The General Assembly authorised the establishment of the United Nations temporary executive authority under the ultimate authority of the Secretary-General to take over West Irian and hand over the same to Indonesia.

On the occasion of the Cuban crisis in 1962, U Thant, the Acting Secretary-General of the United Nations, took the initiative and ultimately succeeded in diffusing the situation.

Both the Security Council and the General Assembly took keen interest in maintaining peace in Cyprus after her independence.

In December 1966, the Security Council applied selective mandatory economic sanctions against Southern Rhodesia. In May 1968, the Security Council imposed comprehensive military sanctions and also set up a Sanctions Committee to enforce them. The Security Council condemned the Government of Southern Rhodesia when it declared herself a Republic in 1970. It also called upon its members to cut off all diplomatic, consular, trade, military and other relations with the Republic of Southern Rhodesia.

When Egypt closed the Straits of Tiran and the Gulf of Aqaba to Israeli shipping, Israel asserted her right of free navigation in those waters. The Security Council held an urgent meeting to consider the situation and was in almost continuous session for many days. It unanimously adopted a resolution calling for an immediate cease-fire. Similar resolutions were passed again. The Security Council also adopted a resolution asking Israel to "ensure the safety, welfare and security of the inhabitants of the area where military hostilities have taken place and to facilitate the return of the Arab civilians in the areas occupied by her." The United Nations played its part in the crisis of 1967.

The Soviet Union intervened in Czechoslovakia first in 1948 and then in 1968. On 22 August 1968, the Security Council met to consider the situation arising out of Soviet intervention in Czechoslovakia. A resolution condemning the Soviet Union was introduced in the Security Council but was vetoed by the Soviet Union.

When there was a war between Israel and the Arab countries in 1973, the Security Council called upon the parties to stop hostilities.

The Soviet Union sent her troops into Afghanistan in December 1979. She vetoed a resolution of the Security Council calling for an immediate and unconditional withdrawal of foreign troops from Afghanistan. In spite of its efforts, the Security Council failed to prevail upon the Soviet Union to withdraw from Afghanistan.

The Security Council adopted a resolution on 18 August 1982 for maintaining an international peace force in Lebanon.

In September 1980, a war started between Iraq and Iran and the same is continuing even now. The United Nations has not succeeded in stopping it.

The United Nations is concerned not only with the maintenance of peace but also with promoting the conditions under which genuine peace is possible. In the words of Philip E. Jacob, "In the long run, the United Nations leadership in the struggle for world welfare holds the chief promise of creating the underlying conditions of social stability and human satisfaction essential to a lasting peace." The Charter specifically provides that the United Nations shall promote "higher standards of living, full employment and conditions of economic and social progress and development." The responsibility for implementing these goals rests on the General Assembly and the Economic and Social Council. All functional and regional commissions and specialised agencies and committees are seeking in various ways to carry out the mandate of the Charter in economic and social fields.

The United Nations is supplying vital information to various countries. It publishes annual reports on world economic conditions. Many agencies and commissions of the United Nations have prepared important studies in the field of technical assistance and economic development. The United Nations also provides funds and loans through the International Bank and the International Development Association. These loans are of great help to developing countries. The Food and Agriculture Organisation has done a lot to meet the world food crisis. The International Labour Organisation has drafted scores of conventions and recommendations, collectively designated as the international labour code. The United Nations is concerned with the furtherance of human welfare, social justice and aspirations of men for a better lot in life. It provides advisory and social welfare services such as public welfare administration, child welfare, social insurance, etc. The United Nations is giving help to the physically handicapped. The World Health Organisation is the central directing and coordinating authority in international health work. It provides advisory and public health services to the member states. It administers health and sanitary regulations, maintains a medical library and an international centre for the compilation and analysis of medical and health statistics from all countries.

A large number of persons who have been uprooted in various parts of the world have benefited from High Commissioner for Refugees. The UNESCO seeks to stimulate a world-wide attack on illiteracy and raises educational standards. It promotes international understanding. The Commission on Human Rights gives considerable attention to the right of self-determination. The United Nations has been successful in securing equality for women.

It is true, the United Nations has failed in tackling successfully the problem of collective security in the world, but that is a problem which is difficult to be tackled by any international organisation. Every state, whether big or small, seems to be determined to do all that it can to promote its own interests, regardless of the interests of other states or mankind as a whole. In an atmosphere where there is violence all over the world and each state is spending recklessly to add to its armaments, regardless of its costs and repercussions on its own economy or that of the world, peace in the world is a dream which no international organisation can achieve. All that can be done is to lessen the prevailing tension in the world and undoubtedly the United Nations has played its part. It is true that the United Nations is not a perfect organisation but its utility cannot be denied. Donald J. Puchala writes, "Despite the paralysis of the Security Council and the often times vitriolic clamour of the General Assembly, the UNO has acted to diffuse international tensions surrounding a number of disputes. It has even played a modest part in Super-Power disputes. Moreover, it has acted to impose non-military sanctions pursuant to the enforcement of its decisions." (*International Politics Today*, p. 343).

SUGGESTED READINGS

Asher, Robert E.: **The United Nations and Promotion of the General Welfare, Washington,** 1957.

Bailey, Sydney D.: **The United Nations, New York,** 1963.

Claude, Inis L.: **Changing United Nations, New York,** 1967.

Elchelberger, Clark M.: **U.N.: The First Ten Years, New York,** 1955.

Feller, A.H.: **United Nations and the World Community, Boston,** 1952.

Goodrich, Leland M.: **The United Nations, London,** 1960.

Green, J.F.: **The United Nations and Human Rights, Washington,** 1956.

Nicholas, H.G.: **The United Nations as a Political Institution, New York,** 1959.

Vandenbosch and Hogan: **The United Nations, New York,** 1952.

CHAPTER

42 EUROPE SINCE 1945

The Cold War

It is true that Great Britain and the United States cooperated with the Soviet Union during the World War II for the overthrow of Hitler, but as soon as the War was over, the former allies began to drift in opposite directions. There steadily developed a state of tension among them which came to be known by the name of the Cold War. The Anglo-American bloc was not prepared to allow the Soviet Union to extend her sphere of influence beyond what she had already achieved up to the beginning of 1947. The United States started with the Truman Doctrine and followed it up with the Marshall Plan, NATO, SEATO, Baghdad Pact, etc.

Truman Doctrine

The Truman Doctrine came to be enunciated under the following circumstances. After the cessation of hostilities in 1945, the Communists selected Italy, France, Greece, and Turkey as their main targets. They strengthened their position in France and Italy by taking advantage of the chaotic conditions prevailing in those countries after the War. They resorted to acts of sabotage and made the working of administration practically impossible. However, the situation in Greece and Turkey was more critical. The Greeks were in danger of even losing their independence. The danger came from 13,000 Communist led guerillas who received equipment, arms and refuge from Greece's Northern Communist neighbours viz., Yugoslavia, Bulgaria and Albania. Most of the guerillas were Greeks, but they could not keep a civil war going on for two years without active and substantial help from outside. In December 1946, Greece complained to the Security Council against the violation of her territorial integrity by her neighbours. A Commission was sent by the Security Council to make a report. In January 1947, the United States sent an Economic Mission to Greece to find out what could be done for that country to save her from collapse. It was at that time that the British Government decided to withdraw her troops from Greece. The United Nations Relief Agency was also due to wind up its business on 31 March 1947.

The situation in Turkey was also alarming. In 1945, the Soviet Union refused to renew the old treaty of friendship with Turkey. It also demanded that Turkey must share with the Soviet Union her control and defence of the Dardanelles. An old claim to the two large provinces of Eastern Turkey was also revived by the Soviet Union and a propaganda campaign was started against the Turkish Government which was described as Fascist and reactionary. The people of Turkey were urged to revolt against their Government. It was under these circumstances that the Turkish Government asked the United States to help her against the Soviet menace.

On 12 March 1947, President Truman addressed a joint session of the American Congress and accounted what came to be known as the Truman Doctrine. To quote Truman, "The very existence of the Greek State is today threatened by the terrorist activities of several thousand armed men led by Communists who defy the Government's authority...Greece must have assistance if it is to become a self-supporting and self-respecting democracy. Turkey has sought financial assistance from Great Britain and the United States for the purpose of effecting that modernisation necessary for the maintenance of its national integrity. That integrity is essential for the preservation of order in the Middle East. We shall not realise our objectives unless we are willing to help free people to maintain their free institutions and their national integrity against aggressive movements that seek to impose upon them totalitarian regimes. This is no more than a frank recognition that totalitarian regimes imposed on free peoples by direct or indirect aggressions undermine the foundations of international peace and hence the security of the United States. The United States has made frequent protests against coercion and intimidation in violation of the Yalta agreement, in Poland, Rumania and Bulgaria.......I believe that it must be the policy of the United States to support free peoples who are resisting attempted subjugation by armed minorities or by outside pressures. We must take immediate and resolute action. The free peoples of the world look to us for support in maintaining their freedom. If we falther in our leadership we may endanger the peace of the world, and we shall surely endanger the welfare of our own nation". President Truman asked the Congress to sanction 400 million dollars by June 1948 to help Greece and Turkey.

The Truman Doctrine was a proposal to send military and economic aid to Greece and Turkey. In May 1947, the American Congress authorised aid to Greece and Turkey. By 1950, it was found that the American policy had completely changed the state of affairs in Greece and Turkey. The guerillas were completely eliminated from the Greek scene. Peace was restored in the country. Railways began to operate normally. Traffic on roads became safe. Bridges were restored. Thousands of new houses were built. Agricultural production surpassed the pre-War level. There was more land under cultivation than ever before. The same was the case in Turkey. Peace was restored in that country. Fresh elections were held. The one party government in Turkey disappeared after 27 years.

Marshall Plan

On 5 June 1947, Secretary of State Marshall delivered his famous speech at Harvard which initiated the European Recovery Programme. In that speech, he declared, "The truth of the matter is that Europe's requirements for the next three or four years of foreign food and other essential products—principally from America—are so much greater than her present ability to pay, that she must have substantial additional help or face economic, social and physical deterioration of a very grave character. It is logical that the United States should do whatever it is able to do to assist in the return of normal economic health in the world without which there can be no political stability and no assured peace." Again, "Initiative, I think, must come from Europe. The role of this country should consist of friendly aid in the drafting of an European Programme and of later support of such a programme as far as it may be practicable for us to do so. The programme should be a joint one, agreed to by a number of, if not all, European nations."

The Marshall Plan was an extension of the principle underlined in the Truman Doctrine. The Plan dealt with Europe in general and not with any particular state or states, as was the case with the Truman Doctrine. It was essentially an economic plan. It represented an elaborate programme as it was to last for four years. The plan showed an anxiety on the part of the United States to avert the economic crisis which was apprehended as a result of the World War II. The plan also underlined the American anxiety and determination to fight out Communism. President Truman had already dismissed Henry Wallace in September 1946 on account of his pro-Soviet views. The situation in France and Italy was a source of great anxiety to the American administration. The Communist Parties of France and Italy were gaining in strength and it was being impressed upon the American Government that in order to put a check on the Communist influence, the United States must come to the help of France and Italy. While the political objective of the Marshall Plan cannot be denied, its humanitarian aspect cannot be ignored. The Marshall Plan strengthened the movement for European unity. As the Truman doctrine bypassed the United Nations, the same was true of the Marshall Plan.

As regards the reactions to the Marshall Plan, it was welcomed in the United States as it was directed against the Soviet Union. In Europe, "the Marshall offer was like Manna from Heaven and it did not require much imagination to grasp it with fervour." As was to be expected the Marshall Plan was attacked by the Soviet Union which described it as an intervention in the internal affairs of other states. It was interpreted as a symbol of American imperialism and betrayal of the United Nations. The tension between the United States and the Soviet Union increased and the relations between the two countries further deteriorated. The countries of Eastern Europe, under the Soviet influence, kept away from the Marshall Plan.

On 15 December 1947, the American Congress passed the Interim Foreign Aid Bill authorising $522 million as interim aid to meet the crisis in France, Italy and Austria until March 1948. This amount was increased to $577 million in March 1948. On 19 December 1947, Truman sent the European Recovery Programme Bill to the Congress in which he asked for a sum of $17,000 million over a period of four years. The Foreign Assistance Act was passed by the American Congress and it received the assent of the President on 3 April, 1948. Bilateral agreements were signed between the United States and Great Britain, Italy, France etc. The Economic Cooperation Administration was established to give help to Europe.

In spite of opposition from the Soviet Union, the Marshall Plan achieved a great measure of success. During the years of its operation (1947 to 1951), the United States gave $11 billion in aid and thereby helped to protect Europe from economic collapse and Communist domination.

Point Four Programme

On 20 January 1949, President Truman enunciated what is known as the Point Four Programme. The four points emphasised by the American President were unfaltering support to the United Nations, continuation of their programmes for forward economic recovery, strengthening of freedom-loving nations against the dangers of aggression and a bold programme of technical assistance to the under-developed areas. The American Congress passed the necessary legislation and provided funds to implement the Point Four Programme.

Rio Pact of 1947

The Rio Treaty or Pact or the Inter-American Treaty of Reciprocal Assistance was signed at Rio de Janeiro in 1947 at the Inter-American Conference for the maintenance of continental peace and security. Its Preamble states that the Treaty has been concluded in order to assure peace through adequate means to provide for reciprocal assistance to meet armed attacks against any American State and to deal with threats of aggression against any of them. The Treaty has 26 clauses. The parties to the Treaty condemn war and undertake not to resort to the threat or use of force in any manner inconsistent with the provisions of the Charter of the United Nations. They also undertake to submit any controversy which may arise between them to methods of peaceful settlement and to settle any such controversy by means of the procedure in force in the Inter-American system before referring the matter to the United Nations. It is agreed that an armed attack by any state against an American state is to be considered as an attack against all the American States and consequently, every party to the Treaty undertakes to assist in meeting the attack in the exercise of the inherent right of the individual or collective self-defence recognised by the Charter. Measures of self-defence are to be taken until the Security Council takes measures necessary to maintain international peace and security. If the integrity of the territory or sovereignty or political independence of any American state is affected by an aggression which is not an armed attack, or by an extra-continental or intra-continental conflict, or by any other fact or situation that may endanger the peace of America, the Organ of Consultation has to meet immediately in order to agree on the measures to be taken in case of aggression to assist the victim of aggression or the measures to be taken for common defence and maintenance of peace and security of the continent. In the case of a conflict between two or more American States, the contracting parties are required to call upon the contending states to suspend hostilities and take all necessary measures to re-establish or maintain Inter-American peace and security and the solution of the conflict by peaceful means. The measures on which the Organ of Consultation may agree consist one or more of the following: recall of chiefs of diplomatic missions, breaking of diplomatic relations, partial or complete interruption of economic relations, or of rail, sea, postal, telegraphic, telephonic and radio-telephonic or radio-telegraphic communications and use of armed force. The Treaty was made for an indefinite period, but any state can leave it by a notification in writing to the Pan-American Union.

The view of Secretary of State Duties was that the Rio Pact was a significant development in American foreign policy. It was based on the principle of one for all and all for one. The Pact set a precedent from which the United States went on to develop the even more significant North Atlantic Pact. The Monroe Doctrine was "continentalized" by the Rio Treaty.

North-Atlantic Treaty Organisation (NATO) of 1949

The North Atlantic Treaty was signed in Washington on 4 April 1949 by the United States, Canada, Belgium, Denmark, France, Iceland, Italy, Luxembourg, the Netherlands, Norway, Portugal and the United Kingdom. Greece and Turkey became its members in February 1952. The Federal Republic of Germany joined the NATO in May 1955.

As regards the circumstances leading to the establishment of the NATO, it was due to the war-like policy followed by the Soviet Union in the post-war period. She put pressure on Iran for the maintenance of Soviet forces in the North of Iran. She made territorial demands on Turkey including claims to the bases in the Straits. She helped guerilla warfare in Greece and also the Communists who stirred up a civil war. She captured control of eastern Europe, culminating in the *coup d'etat* in Czechoslovakia in 1948. She rejected the Marshall Plan and left no stone unturned to cripple the economic recovery of the West. She reorganised the Cominform. She violated the terms of the Potsdam agreement of 1946. She resorted to the Berlin blockade in 1948 and continued the same for more than ten months. She refused to ratify the peace treaties with the former enemy countries. She abused the Veto power in the United Nations. She counted upon its chances of setting up Communist regimes in countries where there was economic distress as a result of World War II. She also encouraged subversion, sabotage and unrest in all those countries.

Many efforts were made to persuade the Soviet Union to agree to a peaceful settlement of the differences and to cooperate in a universal approach to peace, security and progress under the United Nations. However, all those efforts were unsuccessful. It appeared that the Soviet Union was determined to exploit any situation that might help her to realise her goal of a world empire. Under these circumstances, the United States could not keep quiet. She gave military and economic aid to Greece and Turkey. The Marshall Plan helped the nations of Western Europe to rebuild their shattered economies. However, it was felt that all that was not enough. In 1948, Belgium, France, Luxembourg, the Netherlands and the United Kingdom signed the Brussels Treaty under which each pledged herself to assist the others in case of a military attack. The American Government welcomed the Treaty. Shortly thereafter, Senator Vandenberg proposed a resolution which called for "the association of the United States, by constitutional process, with such regional and other collective arrangements as are based on continuous and effective self-help and mutual aid, and as affect its national security." The resolution was adopted by the Senate in June 1948. After that the American President began negotiations with other countries in the North Atlantic area. Those led to the development of the North Atlantic Treaty.

The North Atlantic Treaty has a Preamble and 14 Articles. The Preamble states that the parties to the Treaty reaffirm their faith in the purposes and principles of the Charter of the United Nations and their desire to live in peace with all peoples and all Governments. They are determined to safeguard the freedom, common heritage and civilization of their peoples founded on the principles of democracy, individual liberty and the rule of law. They are resolved to unite their efforts for collective defence and the preservation of peace and security in the North Atlantic area.

Article 1 provides that the parties undertake to settle any international disputes in which they may be involved by peaceful means in such a manner that international peace and security and justice are not endangered and to refrain in their own international relations from the threat or use of force in any manner inconsistent with the purpose of the United Nations. Article 2 provides that the parties will contribute towards the further development of peaceful and friendly international relations by strengthening their free institutions, by bringing about a better understanding of the principles upon which those institutions are founded and by permitting conditions of stability and well-being. They will seek to eliminate conflict in their international economic policies and encourage economic collaboration between any or all of them. Article 3 provides that in order more effectively to achieve the objectives of this Treaty the parties separately and jointly by means of continuous and effective self-help and mutual aid, will maintain and develop their individual and collective capacity to resist armed attack. Article 4 provides that the parties will consult one another whenever in the opinion of any of them, the territorial integrity, political independence or security of any of the parties is threatened. Article 5 provides that parties agree that an armed attack against one or more of them in Europe or North America shall be considered as an attack against all of them. They agree that if such an armed attack occurs, each of them in the exercise of the right of individual or collective self-defence, will assist the party or parties so attacked by taking forthwith, individually and in concert with the other parties, such action as it deems necessary, including the use of armed force, to restore and maintain the security of the North Atlantic area. Any such armed attack and all measures taken as a result thereof, shall immediately be reported to the Security Council. Such measures shall be terminated when the Security Council has taken the measures necessary to restore and maintain international peace and security. Article 6 provides that armed attack on one or more of the parties is deemed to include an armed attack on the territory of any of the parties in Europe or North America, on the Algerian departments of France, on the occupation forces of any party in Europe, on the islands under the jurisdiction of any party in the North Atlantic area, north of the Tropic of Cancer, or on the vessels or aircraft in these areas of any of the parties.

Article 7 provides that this treaty does not affect the rights and obligations under the Charter of the parties which are members of the United Nations or the primary responsibility of the Security Council for the maintenance of international peace and security. Article 8 provides that each party declares that none of the international engagements now in force between it and any other of the parties or any third state is in conflict with the provisions of this treaty and undertakes not to enter into any international engagements in conflict with this treaty. Article 10 provides that the parties may, by unanimous agreement, invite any other European State in a position to further the principles of this treaty and to contribute to the security of the North Atlantic area, to accede to this treaty. Article 12 provides that after the treaty has been in force for 10 years or at any time thereafter, the parties shall, if any one of them so requests, consult together for the purpose of reviewing the treaty having regard for the factors then affecting peace and security in the North Atlantic area including the development of universal as well as regional arrangements for the maintenance of international peace and security. Article 13 provides that after the treaty has been in force for 20 years, any party may cease to be a party one year after its notice of denunciation has been given to the Government of the United States which shall inform the other parties concerned.

The NATO was intended to strengthen the morale of Western Europe. The association of the United States with the other NATO powers was bound to halt the Soviet expansion westwards. Since the stand taken by the United States, was definite and clear, the Soviet leaders were not expected to take any risk in Western Europe. The advocates of the NATO point out to a large number of its achievements during the period of its existence. It is emphasized that there has been no war in Western Europe since the NATO came into existence. This fact alone testifies to the effectiveness of the NATO as an instrument of peace. The Communists made no territorial gains anywhere in Europe or in the Atlantic area since 1949. The NATO forces are always ready to meet any challenge. The NATO air power has increased tremendously and the same is true of its naval force. There has been a vast improvement in the effectiveness of ground, air and naval forces since 1949. This has been accomplished through better training and equipment. NATO forces are equipped with the most modern weapons. Organisational arrangements have been developed to assure effective coordination in the use of forces and other military resources. Indirectly, the NATO has contributed to the development of closer practical unity among European Nations and lessened their rivalries and antagonisms. The Paris agreements of October 1954 restored to West Germany its sovereignty, created a Western European Union and tied Germany to the west through her membership of the NATO and the Western European Union.

The critics of the NATO point out that as a result of the NATO, the rivalry between the United States and the Soviet Union increased and international tension became more and more acute. There was always the possibility of a war as the NATO powers were determined to stop Soviet expansion at all places in the Atlantic area. In spite of the criticism, the NATO is very strong even today. Its members feel that their security is linked up with that of the United States. They feel that they cannot defend themselves alone against the Soviet Union and her satellites. They are alarmed by the spectacular expansion of the Soviet navy in the Baltic and the Mediterranean and the increasing evidence of its activity in the Atlantic, the Caribbean, the Red Sea, the Persian Gulf and the Indian Ocean. The Europeans are convinced that the American nuclear deterrent will be used as their shield only so long as American troops are stationed in Europe. That is the reason why the European members have accepted the American demand that the burden of the alliance should be shared more equally. President Nixon once declared that American forces in Europe would be reduced in size in 1971 and the fear of American withdrawal brought home to the European members the situation in which they will be placed when that happened. No wonder, they are willing to cooperate with the United States in her efforts to put a check to Soviet expansion. If the United States requires the help of the NATO partners, the latter also require her help. It is in the mutual interests of all concerned that the NATO remains strong in spite of the lapse of more than a quarter of a century.

Western European Union

On 27 May 1952, a treaty was signed at Paris to establish the European Defence Community. It contained provisions for common political institutions, armed forces, budget and arms programme. The single integrated army was given the name of European Defence Forces and plans were prepared for political institutions to supervise the European Defence Forces and act as the governing body of the Community. The Assembly of the Coal and Steel Community was to act for the European Defence Community. The Netherlands and West Germany were the first to ratify the treaty but France refused to do so. Consequently, a conference was held in London from 28 September to 3 October 1954 with a view to work out a compromise. The Conference devised a system which provided for Western Unity within the framework of the Brussels Treaty of 1948. The newly formed Western European Union had the same members as the European Defence Community except the addition of the United Kingdom. The Council of the Western European Union was given broad authority with the power to act in a number of important measures by majority vote thereby replacing national with international control. It was also decided that Western Germany was to be restored her sovereignty. The Allied High Commissioners gave up the exercise of most of their occupation rights. Provision was made for West Germany to join the NATO and make her contribution to the defence of the West.

Anzus Pact of 1951

A treaty was entered into between the Governments of Australia, New Zealand and the United States in 1951 for the purpose of coordinating, their efforts for collective defence and preservation of peace in the Pacific area. Article 1 of the Pact provides that the parties undertook to settle any international dispute in which they may be involved by peaceful meant in such a manner that international peace and security are not endangered. They also undertook to refrain in their international relations from the threat or use of force in any manner inconsistent for the purposes of the United Nations. Article 2 provides that in order to achieve more effectively the obligations of this treaty, the parties separately and jointly, by means of continuous and effective self-help and mutual aid, will maintain and develop their individual and collective capacity to resist armed attack. Article 3 provides that the parties shall consult one another whenever in the opinion of any of them the territorial integrity, political independence or security of any of the parties is threatened in the Pacific. Article 4 provides that each party recognises that an armed attack in the Pacific area on any of the parties will be dangerous to its own peace and safety. Each party declares that it will meet the common danger in accordance with its constitutional processes. Any armed attack will be immediately reported to the Security Council for necessary action. Article 5 provides that an armed attack is deemed to include an attack on the metropolitan territory of any of the parties or the island territories under its jurisdiction in the Pacific or on its armed forces, public vessels or aircraft in the Pacific. Article 6 provides that this treaty does not affect and shall not be interpreted as affecting in any way the rights and obligations of the parties under the Charter of the United Nations or the responsibility of the United Nations for the maintenance of international peace and security. Article 7 provides that the parties shall establish a council consisting of their Foreign Ministers or their deputies to consider the methods concerning the implementation of this treaty. The Council is to be so organised as to be able to meet at any time. According to Article 10, this treaty is to remain in force for an indefinite period but any country can leave after giving a notice of one year. However, none has done so far.

SEATO or Manila Pact of 1954

Plans for the defence of South-East Asia had been canvassed ever since the emergence of Communist China as a major factor in Asian and world politics after 1949. Countries like the Philippines, Siam and South Korea which considered themselves to be menaced by the Communists made suggestions from time to time for the setting up of a defensive organisation. However, nothing substantial came out of those suggestions. In 1951, a Conference was held between the Far East Military Commands of Great Britain, the United States and France. On that occasion, it was contended by France that her struggle in Indo-China was really a fight for the preservation of South-East Asia from communism and it was the duty of other states to help her. The outbreak of the Korean war and the help given to North Korea by Communist China and the Soviet Union frightened the Anzus powers. The Chinese Government helped Dr. Ho Chi Minh. The possibility of a Chinese thrust to the Pacific was feared. The talks which started in Singapore were continued in Washington in 1952 and Canada, New Zealand and Australia joined the deliberations. However, no definite action was taken. In 1953, Prime Minister Churchill proposed to the American Government that the principles of the NATO should be extended to South-East Asia but he did not get any favourable reply. It was in April 1954 that Secretary of State Dulles flew to London and asked the British Government to examine the possibility of establishing a collective defence system for South-East Asia and the neighbouring Pacific regions. Mr. Dulles wanted to set up the defensive organisation without the Colombo Powers but Sir Anthony Eden insisted on including them because "without their understanding and support no permanent South-East Asia Defence Organisation would be fully effective." The American Government wanted the British Government to sign the military pact at once and discuss its details later on. The object of the American Government was to strengthen her hands before going to the Geneva Conference of 1954, but the British Government did not agree. However, within a few weeks of the Geneva Agreement, an Indo-China Conference was summoned to meet in the Philippines on 6 September 1954. Invitations were sent to the United States, Great Britain, France, Australia, New Zealand, Thailand and the Philippines. It was left to Sir Anthony Eden to approach the Colombo Powers. Invitations were sent to all of them, but with the exception of Pakistan all others declined to participate. As India refused the invitation, Pakistan accepted it.

On 8 September 1954, the United States, Great Britain, France, Australia, New Zealand, Pakistan, Thailand and the Philippines signed a Treaty known as the SEATO, or Treaty of Collective Defence of South-East Asia at Manila. The Contracting Parties recognised the sovereign equality of all its members. They reiterated their faith in the purposes and principles set forth in the Charter of the United Nations and their desire to live in peace with all peoples and all Governments. They reaffirmed the principles of equal rights and self-determination of peoples. They declared that they would earnestly strive by every peaceful means to promote self-government and to secure independence of all countries. They declared publicly their sense of unity so that any potential aggressor would appreciate that the parties stood together in the area. It was declared that the contracting parties desired to co-ordinate their efforts for collective defence for the preservation of peace and security.

Under the Treaty, the contracting parties undertook to settle any international disputes in which they might be involved by peaceful means in such a manner that international peace and security and justice were not in danger. They undertook to refrain in their international relations from the threat or use of force in any manner inconsistent with the purposes of the United Nations. It was agreed that the parties separately and jointly, by means of continuous and effective self-help and mutual aid, would maintain and develop their individual and collective capacity to resist armed attack, and to prevent and counter subversive activities directed from without against their territorial integrity and political stability. The parties undertook to strengthen their free institutions and cooperate with one another in the further development of economic measures, including technical assistance, designed both to promote economic progress and social well-being and to further the individual and collective efforts of the Governments towards those aims. Each party recognised that aggression by means of an armed attack in the "treaty area" against any of the parties, or against any state or territory, which the parties by unanimous agreement might designate, would endanger its own peace and safety. Each party agreed that it would act to meet the common danger in accordance with its constitutional processes. The measures taken were to be immediately reported to the Security Council of the United Nations. If in the opinion of any of the parties, the inviolability or the integrity of the territory or the sovereignty or political independence of any party in the "treaty area," or any other state or territory, was threatened in any way other than by armed attack, or was affected or threatened by any fact or circumstances, which might threaten the peace of any area, the parties were to consult immediately in order to agree on the measures which should be taken for common defence. No action on the territory of any state was to be taken except on the invitation or with the consent of the Government concerned.

Provision was made for the establishment of a Council on which each of the contracting parties was to be represented. The Council was to consider matters concerning the implementation of the Treaty. It was also to provide for consultation with regard to military or any other planning as the situation obtaining in the "treaty area" might from time to time require. The Council was to be so organised as to be able to meet at any time. It was declared that the Treaty did not affect in any way the rights and obligations of any of the parties under the Charter of the United Nations, or the responsibility of the United Nations for the maintenance of international peace and security. Each party declared that none of the international engagements then in force between it and any other country was in conflict with the provisions of the Treaty. Each party undertook not to enter into any international engagements in conflict with this Treaty. Any other state in a position to further the objectives of this Treaty and to contribute to the security of the area could be invited to accede to this Treaty by the unanimous agreement of the parties. The "treaty area" mentioned in the Treaty was the general area of South-East Asia, including the entire territories of the Asian parties and the general area of the South-West Pacific, not including the Pacific area north of 21 degrees North Latitude. The parties were given the authority to include any other area in the Treaty area. The Treaty was to remain in force for an indefinite period. However, any party could cease to be a member after giving notice of one year.

While signing the Treaty, it was made clear on behalf of the American delegation that its main object was to stop Communist aggression. The effectiveness of this Treaty was tested during the Vietnam War. Although there were many members of the SEATO, the main burden of fighting the Vietnam War fell on the United States. After a protracted war, North Vietnam won a victory over South Vietnam in 1975. The prestige of the United States fell and the Treaty was dissolved in the same year.

The Baghdad Pact or CENTO (1955)

The Baghdad Pact consists of a Preamble and eight Articles. The Preamble states that the friendly and brotherly relations existing between Iraq and Turkey are in constant progress and it is desirable to implement the contents of the Treaty of friendship and good-neighbourliness concluded between Iraq and Turkey on 29 March 1946, which recognised the fact that peace and security between the two countries was an integral part of the peace and security of all the nations of the world and in particular the nations of the Middle East and was the basis of their foreign policies. Both Iraq and Turkey realised the great responsibilities borne by them in their capacity as members of the United Nations concerned with the maintenance of peace and security in the Middle East region. Both the countries were completely convinced of the necessity of concluding a pact fulfilling those aims. It was under the above-mentioned circumstances that the Baghdad Pact was signed in 1955.

Article 1 of the Pact provides that the contracting parties will cooperate for their security and defence. Such measures as they agreed to take to give effect to this co-operation may form the subject of special agreements with each other. Article 2 provides that in order to ensure co-operation, the competent, authorities of the contracting parties will determine the measures to be taken as soon as the Pact comes into force. Those measures will become operative as soon as they are approved of by the parties. According to Article 3, the parties undertook to refrain from any interference whatsoever in the internal affairs of each other and settle any dispute between themselves in a peaceful manner in accordance with the United Nations Charter. Article 4 provides that the parties declared that the provisions of the present Pact are not in contradiction with any of the international obligations contracted by either of them with any third state or states. They do not derogate from and cannot be interpreted as derogating from the said international obligations incompatible with the present Pact. Article 5 provides that this Pact shall be open for accession to any particular state of the Arab League or any other state actively concerned with the security and peace in this region and which is fully recognised by both the parties. Accession shall come into effect from the date when the instrument of accession is deposited with the Ministry of Foreign Affairs of Iraq. Any acceding state may conclude special agreements with one or more states parties to the present Pact. The competent authority of any acceding state may determine measures in accordance with Article 2. Article 6 provides that a Permanent Council at ministerial level will be set up to function within the framework of the purposes of this Pact when at least four powers become parties to the Pact. The Council will adopt its own rules of procedure. Article 7 provides that the Pact shall remain in force for a period of five years, renewable for other five-year periods. Any contracting party may withdraw from the Pact by notifying to the other parties in writing its desire to do so.

The Baghdad Pact was declared to be open for accession to any member state of the Arab League or any other state which is actively concerned with the peace and security of this region. It was under this clause that Britain joined the Baghdad Pact in April 1955. A special agreement was concluded between Britain and Iraq by which Britain became a member of the Baghdad Pact and also undertook to co-operate in the sphere of planning and combined training of Iraq's armed forces for the defence of Iraq. Britain pledged herself to help Iraq in creating and maintaining an effective Iraqi Air Force, efficient airfields and an efficient system of warning against air attacks. Provision was made for British technical personnel to be made available to Iraq. It was also provided that "in the event of an armed attack against Iraq or threat of an armed attack, which in the opinion of the two contracting governments endanger the security of Iraq, the Government of the United Kingdom, at the request of the Government of Iraq, shall make available assistance including, if necessary, armed forces, to help the defence of Iraq." In July 1955, Pakistan acceded to the Baghdad Pact. In November 1955, Iran joined the Pact. In the same month, the United States guaranteed the territorial integrity of the Baghdad Pact countries. The United States joined the Baghdad Pact in its economic sphere in May 1956 and joined the same in military sphere in 1958 to combat international communism. Iraq announced her withdrawal from the Baghdad Pact in March 1959 and the Pact was renamed as Central Treaty Organisation.

The Baghdad Pact was directed not only against the Soviet Union, but also against the non-aligned Arab states. In order to strengthen its position on the Kashmir issue, Pakistan exploited the Pact against India. The Baghdad Pact divided the Arab World. Through its membership of that Pact, Pakistan was responsible for contributing to that division. By destroying Arab unity, the Baghdad Pact also increased instability in the region. In the war between Pakistan and India, Iran and Turkey supplied arms to Pakistan, though Britain and the United States were neutral. In February 1968, President Nasser condemned the Baghdad Pact as representing foreign domination in the region. The Baghdad Pact did not add to the security or confidence of the people in the Middle East. It created panic and fear. It encouraged a race for armaments which was not conducive to peace. It is doubtful if the professed objectives of the Baghdad Pact have been actually realised. There is no unity of objectives of the members of the Pact. The main aim of the Western Powers was to secure control over the oil-rich Middle East and to secure bases in the name of fighting international communism. At the Ankara meeting held in January 1958, the Prime Minister of Pakistan frankly admitted that communism posed no real threat to his country and the real threat was from the neutralists. The Iraqi delegate told the Council that communism was no problem in the Middle East and the real problem was that of Israel. Although the professed object of the Western sponsorers of the Baghdad Pact is to combat international communism, the Asian partners have been using the alliance only to strengthen their position. The Pact has failed to achieve the unity of the Arab powers. If the objective of the Pact was to keep off the Soviet Union from the Middle East, it has been a total failure.

The Warsaw Pact (1955)

If the Western powers were able to set up military alliances against the Soviet Union and her camp followers, the latter could not be expected to lag behind. In December 1954 a conference of eight European states viz., Albania, Bulgaria, Hungary, Czechoslovakia, East Germany, Poland, Rumania and the Soviet Union, with an observer from Communist China, was held in Moscow to consider their attitude towards the Paris Peace Treaties. The conference opposed the ratification of the treaties and declared that in the event of their ratification, the participating countries would adopt joint measures of defence. It was further declared that they would meet again to consider concrete measures for a joint defence command. As the Paris Treaties were ratified in spite of the above declaration, the eight countries mentioned above met in Warsaw for four days from 11 May to 14 May 1955. After long discussions, they concluded the Treaty of Friendship, Cooperation and Mutual Assistance known as the Warsaw Pact.

Under this Pact, it was decided to set up a joint command of the armed forces of the signatory states with its headquarters in Moscow. The unified command was to be headed by Konier, Marshal of the Soviet Union. The Defence Ministers or other military leaders of the signatory countries were appointed Deputy Commanders-in-Chief and given command of the armed forces assigned to the unified armed forces by each respective signatory country. The contracting parties confirmed their striving for the creation of a system of collective security in Europe based on the participation of all European states in respect of their social or state structure which would make it possible to unite their efforts in the interests of ensuring peace in Europe. They also took into consideration the situation which had arisen in Europe as a result of the ratification of the Paris Agreements envisaging the formation of a new military alignment in the form of West European Union with the participation of West Germany. That created a threat to the national security of the peace-loving states and it was necessary for them to take measures necessary to safeguard their security. It was declared that the contracting parties were guided by the aims and principles of the United Nations Charter.

The Treaty provided that the contracting parties undertook to abstain in their international relations from threats of violence or its use and settle international disputes by peaceful means. They declared their readiness to cooperate in all international actions for the purpose of assuring international peace and security. They were to strive to reach agreement with the states desiring to cooperate in that cause and take measures to reduce armaments, and the ban of atomic, hydrogen and other kinds of weapons of mass destruction. The contracting parties were to consult each other on all important international problems affecting their common interests. They were to consult each other immediately in the event of a threat of armed attack against one or other states, signatories to the Pact, in the interests of their ensuring mutual defence and maintaining peace and security. In case of an armed aggression in Europe against one or several states parties to the treaty by a state or group of states, each state member of the treaty in order to put into practice the right to individual or collective self-defence was to afford to the state or the states which was the object of such an aggression, immediate assistance, individually and in agreement with other states, who were parties to the treaty, with all means which appear necessary including the use of armed forces. The parties were required to take immediate joint measures necessary to establish and preserve international peace and security. The measures taken by the states were to be stopped as soon as the Security Council took steps for establishing and preserving international peace and security.

The parties agreed to set up a joint command of their armed forces to be allotted by agreement between the parties, at the disposal of this command and used on the basis of jointly established principles. They were also required to take other agreed measures necessary to strengthen their defences in order to protect the peaceful toil of their people guaranteeing the integrity of their frontiers and territories and ensure their defence against possible aggression. With the object of carrying out consultations provided by the present Treaty among the states participating in the Treaty and for the examination of questions arising in connection with the fulfilment of the Treaty, a Political Consultative Committee was to be set up in each state participating in the Treaty. The Committee was authorised to set up any auxiliary organs it considered to be necessary. The contracting parties undertook not to enter into any coalition or union and not to enter into any agreements whose aims were contrary to the terms of the Treaty. They declared that they would act in a spirit of friendship and cooperation in order further to develop economic and cultural ties between them and would be guided by the principles of mutual respect and would not interfere in the internal affairs of one another. The Treaty was to remain in force for twenty years. Those states which did not give notice of abrogation one year before the Treaty expired, were to remain bound by it for a further period of ten years. In the event of a system of collective security, being set up in Europe and a Pact to that effect being signed, the present Treaty was to lapse from the date on which a collective security treaty came into force.

The Warsaw Pact, in its essentials, is a carbon copy of the NATO. However, there are certain differences between the two. The Warsaw Pact is open to any state whereas unanimity is required to extend the membership of the NATO. The Warsaw Pact is provisional in the sense that it is to remain in force only until a European collective security system comes into existence. This is in keeping with the expressed objective of the Pact which is to preserve world peace threatened by the admission of Germany to the NATO. It is true that all the members of the Warsaw Pact are equal in theory but actually that is not so. The freedom enjoyed by the member states varies. In spite of the dominant position of the United States in the NATO, she does not over-balance the others so overwhelmingly as is the case of the Soviet Union in the Warsaw Pact. Very little, if anything of importance, is added by the Warsaw Pact that is not included in the bilateral treaties between the Soviet Union and five of its members. Even in the absence of the Warsaw Pact, the relations between the Soviet Union and the other member states would not have differed.

It is well known that the Warsaw Pact powers intervened in Hungary in 1956 when there was a revolt in that country. Likewise, they intervened in Czechoslovakia in 1968 when that country started following liberal policies. Rumania is a member of the Warsaw Pact, but the Soviet Union is having a lot of trouble from Mr. Ceausescu who is the Secretary General of the Communist Party in Rumania. The Rumanians are virtually against everything the Russians want to see accomplished in the Warsaw Pact. They want the Warsaw Pact and all other similar military alliances to go. The view of Ceausescu is that the military pacts are an "anachronism" incompatible with the national independence and sovereignty of every country. Rumania strongly opposes the Soviet schemes of integration of member forces in the alliance and refuses to place her army, air and naval forces under the direct command of the Warsaw Pact Powers. The attitude of Rumania is not liked by the Soviet Union, but she is helpless in the matter. Albania has left the Warsaw Pact and joined hands with Communist China, which at present is the enemy of the Soviet Union.

Revolt in Hungary (1956)

In 1956, there was a revolt in Hungary. In order to put it down, the Government of Hungary asked the Soviet Union to send her troops. Her request was accepted by the Soviet Union who sent her troops to Hungary and law and order was restored. The Soviet forces left the Hungarian capital soon after. However, trouble started once again and there was a lot of bloodshed. Many persons were murdered. Many leaders were hanged at lamp posts in the streets of Budapest. The rebels burnt the national museum in Budapest. They became stronger and stronger every day. They smashed the nationalised enterprises and state-owned establishments. There was a general demand for the return of Mr. Nagy who had been arrested earlier. On 30 October 1956, Mr. Nagy declared that they would set up a coalition government of all democratic parties and free elections on the lines of Western democracies would be held. Mr. Nagy was deserted by Mr. Kadar and his other colleagues and a new Hungarian Revolutionary Workers' and Peasants' Government was established. The new Government declared that it would safeguard the democratic achievements of the Hungarian people and defend the people's democratic system. Kadar's Government requested the Soviet Union for assistance in putting down the rebellions in the country. The Soviet Union sent her forces to Hungary and the rebels were hunted out and suppressed. Great atrocities were committed on that occasion. On 4 November 1958, it was declared that the rebels had been completely crushed. Mr. Nagy and many other members of his government were arrested by the Soviet troops. The new Government in Hungary was headed by Kadar who was the first Secretary of the Communist Party. On 4 November 1956, a resolution was moved by the American Government in the Security Council that the Soviet Union must withdraw her troops from Hungary and not interfere in the internal affairs of that country. That resolution was vetoed by the Soviet Union. An emergency session of the General Assembly was called and a resolution was passed calling upon the Soviet Union to withdraw her troops from Hungary so that free elections could be held under the auspices of the United Nations. Another resolution was passed by the General Assembly censuring the Soviet Union for her violation of the Charter by depriving Hungary of her liberty and independence and the Hungarian people of their fundamental rights and the Soviet Union was requested to withdraw her troops. However, all those resolutions were ignored by the Soviet Union.

There are two different views with regard to the real nature of the Hungarian revolt of 1956. The Soviet view is that the persons who revolted were Fascists and they were backed by outsiders. The Hungarian Government of Kadar was within its right in putting them down with a heavy hand. The Soviet Union performed its obligations under the Warsaw Pact when it sent its troops to Hungary. The Western view is that the people of Hungary were fed up with the Communist regime which put all kinds of restrictions on their lives and consequently they revolted. The revolt was a spontaneous rising of the people against the tyranny of the Communist regime, and had the backing of most of the people. If the Soviet troops had not gone to Hungary to crush the revolt, the rebels would have been successful in setting up a government of their own choice. The continuation of the Soviet troops in Hungary was also condemned.

Soviet Occupation of Czechoslovakia (1968)

There was a Communist Government in power in Czechoslovakia since 1948. From the end of 1967, there was the emergence of a wave of regenerative process in the country. In January 1968, Alexander Dubcek was elected the First Secretary of the Communist Party of Czechoslovakia. It was the beginning of a process of liberalisation away from the "Democratic centralism" of the Stalin era. On 22 March 1968, President Novotny resigned and General Ludvik Svoboda took over as President on 30 March 1968. Liberalising forces began to operate in the country. The press was given a lot of freedom. Censorship was abandoned in the practice. The Central Office for Publication was abolished. Respect for minority views within the Communist Party was guaranteed and the members were given the right to criticise official policies at party meetings and also in the press.

The Soviet Union and other members of the Warsaw Pact did not approve of the changes in Czechoslovakia and consequently their relations were strained. A meeting was held in Warsaw in July 1968 in which the situation in Czechoslovakia was described as "completely unacceptable". Certain demands were made on Czechoslovakia, but those were rejected. Two meetings were held between the Soviet and Czech leaders at Cierna and Bratislava. After the meeting at Cierna, President Svoboda declared, "We will not leave the path we have started out. We shall continue along the road." On 28 July 1968, the Pravada warned Czechoslovakia that "time does not wait". The Warsaw powers addressed a joint letter to the Communist Party of Czechoslovakia in which they condemned the new policies being followed by it. The allegations were denied. Ulbricht, the East German Communist leader, visited Czechoslovakia on 12 August 1968 and had long discussions with Mr. Dubcek. On 16 August 1968, the Pravada accused the anti-Socialist reactionaries of stepping up subversive activities in Czechoslovakia. On 20 August 1968, a special meeting of the Central Committee of the Soviet Union was held at the Kremlin and the same night Czechoslovakia was invaded by the Soviet, Polish, Hungarian, Bulgarian and East German troops and Prague and other Czechoslovak cities were occupied within a few hours.

Many reasons are given for Soviet intervention in Czechoslovakia. Within the East European defence system, Czechoslovakia is the most vulnerable because she has a boundary along West Germany and Austria which in the event of an East-West conflict, leaves her open to a direct attack from the West. If the Western forces occupy Czechoslovakia, that splits the East European defence system into two and provides a direct corridor to Russian soil. That makes Czechoslovakia the most vital spot for both sides in an East-West war. That is the reason why the Russians feel that they cannot allow any reforms which would lead to a possible weakening of Czechoslovakia's military relationship with the other members of the Soviet bloc. The fact that Czechoslovakia borders on two democratic countries, viz., Austria and the German Federal Republic, leaves her exposed to the infiltration of Western influences. Apart from military reasons, the action taken by the Soviet Union was intended to serve as an example of what will happen to other members of the East European Communist States if they pressed for a more democratic system of government. The rapid changes in Czechoslovakia coupled with open demand for an equal voice in Warsaw Pact organisations convinced the Soviet Union of a danger to communism in Czechoslovakia.

On 22 August 1968, the Security Council met to consider the situation arising out of the Soviet intervention in Czechoslovakia. A resolution condemning the Soviet Union and the Warsaw Pact allies was introduced, but the same was vetoed by the Soviet Union. The Peking Radio condemned the Soviet Union and her allies for their intervention in Czechoslovakia. The view of Castro of Cuba was that while the military action of the Soviet Union and her allies was a flagrant violation of Czech sovereignty, it was politically right. Rumania demanded an immediate end of the military intervention in Czechoslovakia. Yugoslavia also condemned the military intervention in Czechoslovakia. The attitude of the Soviet Union and her allies was expressed by Gomulka in these words : "Socialist ethics and the principles of inter-nationalism cannot be reduced to sitting back with folded arms when the socialist system is being abolished in a fraternal country". In spite of criticism from various quarters, more occupation forces were flown to Prague on 25 August 1968 and according to one estimate, their total number was about 5 lacs. The Soviet Union and her allies were determined to crush all liberal forces in Czechoslovakia. By and by Mr. Dubcek and his friends were removed from their posts and power was put in the hands of those who were prepared to toe the Soviet line. Censorship of the press was reimposed. Czechoslovakia entered into a treaty, with the Soviet Union by which she agreed to the stationing of Soviet troops within her territory. The treaty is silent regarding the number of troops to be stationed in Czechoslovakia and the period of their stay. The events in Czechoslovakia disturbed the relations between the East and the West. The NATO powers were profoundly disturbed on account of their failure to obtain information about Soviet intervention before it actually took place. The NATO powers warned the Soviet Union against the recurrence of any such action to upset the balance of power in Europe.

U-2 Incident (1960)

On 1 May 1960, an American aircraft called U-2, while operating from bases in Pakistan and Turkey crossed into the Soviet territory and penetrated more than 2,000 kilometres. It was shot down by the Soviet Union. That led to a lot of bitterness between the United States and the Soviet Union. The American Government could justify her action on the ground of self-preservation and the extensive Soviet espionage activities and the Soviet Union was justified in shooting down the U-2 and in proceeding against its pilot under criminal law.

Cuban Crisis

It was reported in 1962 that Soviet military equipment had arrived in Cuba along with a large number of technicians and other military personnel. There was a widespread demand in the United States for the establishment of a unilateral Pacific blockade of Cuba. Some demanded the application of the blockade to Russian and other foreign vessels. A conference of the American Foreign Ministers was held in the beginning of October 1962 in Washington. It was decided to adopt economic and security measures to cope with the Cuban armament build-up. A request was made to the non-Communist states to tighten their control over ships, flying their flags and carrying Soviet goods to Cuba. The United States closed its ports to all ships carrying arms to Cuba. It also closed its ports to ships sailing between a Communist bloc port and Cuba. It prohibited all vessels registered in the United States from engaging in any manner in Cuban trade. The West German, Norwegian, Turkish and Japanese lines ordered their ships off the Cuba run. The Council of the Organisation of American States initiated work on further steps designed to isolate Cuba from the rest of the Western Hemisphere.

It was found from aerial survey that medium range ballistic missiles had been installed in Cuba. It was also found that sites for intermediate range missiles had been constructed in Cuba. That led to a crisis. On 22 October 1962, President Kennedy declared the adoption of seven measures. There was to be a strict "quarantine" on all offensive military equipment bound for Cuba. All ships so bound from whatever nation or port, were to be turned back by the American navy if found to be carrying offensive weapons. There was to be a continued and increased aerial surveillance of Cuba. If the offensive build-up continued, other steps were to be taken and the armed forces were directed by the American President to prepare for any eventuality. It was declared by the American Government that it regarded "any nuclear missile launched from Cuba against any nation in the Western Hemisphere as an attack by the Soviet Union on the United States requiring a full retaliatory response upon the Soviet Union". The American Government ordered re-enforcement of the garrison of the U.S. naval base at Guantanamo in Cuba from which the American dependants had been evacuated. An urgent meeting of the Organ of Consultation under the Organisation of American States to consider the Cuban situation was ordered. A request was made for summoning an emergency meeting of the Security Council "to take action against this latest Soviet threat to world peace". Khrushchev was asked to "halt and eliminate this clandestine, reckless and provocative threat".

On 23 October 1962, the Organisation of American States decided to take all measures necessary to end the threat to the peace and security of the Western Hemisphere resulting from the military build-up in Cuba. The decision was conveyed to the United Nations. At the same time, the American President issued the Quarantine Proclamation and on 24 October 1962, the same went into effect. It was first to be implemented by the Naval and Air Force units of the United States. The American Navy actually stopped the Soviet ships which were later on diverted from the Cuba run. U Thant tried to prevail upon the United States to suspend the blockade of Cuba and also asked Khrushchev to halt shipments to Cuba. The Soviet Union proposed to withdraw offensive weapons from Cuba if the American Government withdrew its rockets from Turkey. The proposal was rejected. Ultimately the Soviet Union agreed to dismantle the Cuban missile sites and transport the missiles back to the Soviet Union and the same was actually done. Aerial surveillance of Cuba continued even after the blockade was lifted.

It must be admitted that there was an imminent danger of a world war on the occasion of the Cuban crisis and the same was averted on account of the enormous restraint shown by Khrushchev at that critical juncture. He withdrew from the conflict in spite of criticism from Communist China.

Partial Nuclear Test Ban Treaty (1963)

The Nuclear Test Ban Treaty Conference met at Geneva from October 1958 to April 1961 and Great Britain, the United States and the Soviet Union took part in its discussions. It was agreed that all tests in the earth's atmosphere, in outer space, in ocean and underground should be stopped except those producing signals of less than 4.75 seismic intensity as it was difficult to detect them. The annual inspections were to be limited to three in future, though originally the United States insisted on 20 inspections in a year. The treaty was to be enforced by a worldwide detective system operated by a single neutral administrator and an international staff. Control ports were to be set up on land and ships at sea to detect illegal tests by their sound and light, radio waves, nuclear radiation, radio-active debris or earth shocks. Unfortunately, certain differences arose and negotiations came to an abrupt end.

The Three-Power Partial Nuclear Test Ban Treaty was initialled on 25 July 1963 in Moscow and formally signed on 5 August 1963. It provided for a limited ban on nuclear tests in the atmosphere, beyond its limits, including outer space or underwater, including territorial waters or high seas. It covered all tests except those underground as no fool-proof method had yet been evolved for detecting underground tests. The treaty was to be open to all states for signatures. Each party was given the right to withdraw from the treaty after giving a notice of three months. The treaty was welcomed by all the nations of the world as it was likely to reduce tension. It was the first agreement between the East and the West and India was the first to sign it. France refused to sign it because that was likely to halt her nuclear programme. Communist China also refused to sign the treaty and condemned the

Soviet Union for entering into an anti-Chinese alliance with the United States and selling out the interests of its own people and other Communist countries.

Nuclear Non-Proliferation Treaty (1968)

On 12 June 1968, the General Assembly passed a resolution by which it recommended the adoption of the Nuclear Non-Proliferation Treaty. Certain members of the United Nations abstained from voting while certain others voted for the resolution with reservations. President Johnson of the United States appeared before the General Assembly and personally urged the members to adopt the Treaty. He asserted that the Treaty in question went far to prevent the spread of nuclear weapons and committed the Nuclear Powers to redouble their efforts to end the nuclear arms race. It also ensured the use of nuclear energy for peaceful purposes.

Under the Nuclear Non-Proliferation Treaty, the nuclear powers agreed not to transfer their nuclear weapons or control over them to any non-nuclear power or to provide assistance in producing weapons. Under the Treaty, the nuclear powers will have full liberty to develop and multiply their nuclear weapons. Restriction was only on the non-nuclear powers. However, the nuclear powers could give their nuclear know-how to non-nuclear powers for the use of nuclear energy for peaceful purposes. Steps were to be taken to prevent the diversion of peaceful nuclear establishments to military use. No provision was made for the control and inspection of nuclear establishments.

After the passing of the resolution by the General Assembly, a demand was made that the United States, the Soviet Union and Great Britain should make a declaration that they would protect the aggrieved party in the event of an attack by nuclear power. The result was that a declaration to that effect was made by these powers on 17 June 1968. It was declared that "Any state which commits aggression accompanied by the use of nuclear weapons or which threatens such aggression, must be aware that these actions are to be countered effectively by measures to be taken in accordance with the United Nations Charter, to suppress the aggression or to remove the threat of aggression." On 19 June 1968, a resolution to that effect was also adopted by the Security Council.

France and Communist China refused to associate themselves with the Treaty. France was going on with her nuclear programme and the same was the case with China. Peking described the Treaty as "a fraud jointly hatched by the United States and the Soviet Union as an anti-Chinese plot." It described the assurances against aggression as a means of turning other countries into docile "protectorates" and promoting "encirclement" of China, by providing India with a "nuclear umbrella". Chen Yi, Foreign Minister of China, condemned the Treaty as "out and out unequal treaty", a tactics of "power politics being played by big nations", and a "serious plot" all calculated to protect "Big Powers' nuclear monopoly". The Treaty had given nuclear powers the surest way to blackmail. Non-proliferation without nuclear disarmament would help technologically advanced nations to fight others under far more favourable conditions. India also refused to sign the Treaty.

Strategic Arms Limitation Treaty (1972)

On 26 May 1972, two agreements were signed in Moscow by President Nixon and Communist Party Chief Brezhnev. Those agreements were the Treaty on Limitation of Anti-Ballistic Missile Systems and the "Interim Agreement on Certain Measures with respect to the Limitation of Strategic Offensive Arms." The Treaty on the limitation of Anti-Ballistic Missile System is of unlimited duration, but the Interim Agreement is for five years. The ABM Treaty limits the United States and the Soviet Union to two sites for ballistic missile defences, one to protect their national capital areas and the other to protect a field of ICBMs. Article III lays down in detail the dimensions of the two ABM systems the two countries can have. Limited to a deployment area of 150 km radius, each one of the systems will have no more than 100 ABM launchers and no more than 100 ABM interceptor missiles at launch sites. The national capital area complex will have no more than six ABM-radar complexes, each with a diameter not exceeding 3 km. The complex around the missile launching force will have no more than 18 ABM radars, and two large-phased array ABM radars. Under the Treaty, the United States will be able to continue the construction of the safeguard complex at Grant Forks, ND and will start development on an ABM system for Washington. The Soviet Union will enlarge its 64 missile Galosh system now defending Moscow and add a protective shield to one of their missile sites. Under Article V, both parties have undertaken not to develop, test or deploy the ABM systems or components which are sea-based, air-based, space-based or mobile land-based. They have also undertaken neither to deploy ABM launchers which will launch more than one interceptor missile at a time for each launcher, nor to provide already developed launchers with a capability. Development, testing or deployment of automatic, semi-automatic or other similar systems for rapid reload of ABM launchers is also prohibited. Article VI stipulates prohibition on giving other air defence systems, anti-ballistic missile intercepting capability. However, modernisation and replacement of ABM systems or their components is allowed, subject to the quantitative ceiling provided for in Article VII of the Treaty.

The Interim Agreement is a complex accord covering both land-based ICBMs and submarine launched ballistic missiles. For the construction of fixed land-based ICBMs, the cut-off date is 1 July 1972. It means a numerical freeze on ICBMs in the Soviet inventory on 1,618 and the American inventory at 1,054. Article 11 provides that the parties "undertake not to convert land-based launchers for light ICBMs or for ICBMs of older types deployed prior to 1964 into land-based launchers for heavy ICBMs of types deployed after that time." With regard to the submarine launched ballistic missile launchers and modern ballistic missile submarines, the Agreement stipulates a freeze on the numbers in operation and under construction as on 28 May 1972. The agreement does not forbid modernisation and replacement within these stipulated numerical limits of strategic offensive weapons. The two countries are allowed to improve the accuracy, size and penetration capabilities of their warheads as well as to increase the total number of warheads through MIRV-ing. Both countries have agreed with regard to the procedure to be followed for verification. It is for the first time that the freedom of spy satellites to move about the skies of another country has been guaranteed and the parties have agreed neither to interfere with the means of verification of each other nor to undertake deliberate measures of concealment which hinder verification.

To consider the questions which arise concerning compliance with the agreements, there is a provision for the establishment of a Standing Consultative Commission. It is also to be used to promote the objectives and implementation of the provisions of the Interim Agreement. It will not only provide a forum for the voluntary exchange of information between the parties to assure confidence, but will also consider possible changes in the strategic situation and discuss appropriate proposals for further measures aimed at limiting strategic arms. There is also an undertaking between the two countries to continue active negotiations for limitations on strategic offensive arms.

Washington Agreements (1973)

President Nixon had visited Moscow in 1972 and Brezhnev paid a return visit in June 1973. The talks between the two leaders started on 18 June 1973 in Washington. At the very outset they both pledged themselves to work for a lasting world peace and to speed up negotiations to end the nuclear arms race between the two countries. They also pledged themselves to work in earnestness to reach an agreement on all matters in their Summit talks. Brezhnev declared that the result of the first Soviet-American Summit talks in Moscow "laid a good and sound base for peaceful relations between our countries".

President Nixon and Brezhnev signed on 21 June 1973 an agreement committing their countries to negotiate before the end of the next year a treaty calling for reduction of nuclear weapons. They also signed an agreement calling for intensified Soviet-American cooperation in nuclear power research with the objective of ultimately harnessing the power of H-Bomb to produce badly needed electricity. The accord on the basic principles concerning the SALT negotiations aimed at speeding up the second phase of the talks dealing with qualitative limitations on offensive nuclear weapons.

On 22 June 1973, the two leaders signed an agreement undertaking to do everything possible to avoid nuclear war not only between the two countries but also with third nations. In the 8-point agreement, the United States and the Soviet Union undertook to hold urgent consultations any time a risk of nuclear war arose in the world so as to eliminate the risk. President Nixon was invited to visit Moscow in 1974 and he accepted the invitation. The next year's Summit was to provide a forum for the signing of a treaty permanently limiting the offensive nuclear arsenals of the two countries under guidelines. The two nations agreed as a matter of principle that efforts by one or the other to obtain a nuclear advantage would be inconsistent with the goal of strengthening peaceful relations. The agreement was intended to expedite the negotiations going on at Geneva between the two countries. The arms limitation envisaged by the end of the next year included not only the numbers but also the quality of the missiles themselves. The two leaders agreed that limitation on strategic offensive arms must be subject to "adequate verification". Both nations were to be free to modernise and replace weapons only under conditions to be agreed upon at Geneva. The two leaders also signed a 10-year pact to expand cooperation between the two countries on peaceful uses of atomic energy. The major areas of the joint arms effort included controlling thermo-nuclear fusion, research on "fast-feeder" reactors which create more fuel than consumed and research in the fundamental properties of physical matters. At the end of the Summit talks, a joint communique was issued on 25 June 1973.

Moscow Summit (1974)

During his visit to the Soviet Union in June-July 1974, President Nixon agreed with Brezhnev to limit underground testing for 5 years, but the restriction was to go into effect in 1976. The two countries agreed to restrict themselves to a single anti-ballistic missile system instead of two. They also agreed that the existing ban on some offensive weapons will be followed by a new agreement between them and that agreement should cover the period until 1985 and "deal with both quantitative and qualitative limitations". It was agreed that such an agreement should be completed at the earliest possible date. The new agreement was to try to limit both newer lines of weapons including missiles with multiple warheads and the numbers being deployed. The two countries also signed two protocols which regulate replacement, dismantling or the destruction of strategic armaments if these questions arise in the course of the implementation of the treaty limiting missile system and the interim agreement limiting offensive nuclear weapons.

Vladivostok Summit (November 1974)

As President Nixon had to resign on account of the Watergate Scandal, President Ford and Brezhnev met at Vladivostok in November 1974 and a U.S.-Soviet Agreement on guidelines for a 10-year "cap on the arms race" was reached. The two leaders agreed on a limit on the number of such offensive nuclear weapons as missiles launched from land, sea and air, bombers and multiple war-head missiles. The new agreement enabled the two countries to begin work not only on limiting nuclear arms, but also on reducing them. Both sides were allowed to have a certain agreed number of strategic delivery vehicles. They also agreed to have a certain aggregate number of ICBMs and SLBMs (submarines launched ballistic missiles) equipped with multiple independently targetable war-heads.

A Peace Conference on security and cooperation in Europe was held at Helsinki and the representatives of 32 European countries and the United States and Canada participated in it. That conference ended in June 1973 after a "Collective Agreement" on an agenda for the coming Conference on Security and Cooperation in Europe. The Collective Agreement on the agenda was considered to be the first step in the transformation of Europe by the establishment of cooperative co-existence between the European Communists and the West and meaningful collaboration in economic, scientific and cultural fields. The agreement on the agenda laid the foundation for the substantial negotiations that were to come.

The Conference on Security and Cooperation in Europe began at Helsinki on 3 July 1973. It was attended by the representatives of 35 countries. There was a spirit of peaceful cooperation between the East and the West. Without dissent the Foreign Ministers adopted an Agenda that eventually would expand "human contacts" within the Warsaw Pact nations. The main task of the Conference was to approve the agenda drawn after six months of negotiations and appoint Committees to work out the agreement on the four items—security, scientific, economic, environmental and technological cooperation, including freer human contacts and dissemination of information and follow-up measures.

Helsinki Conference (1975)

The 35-Nations Summit Conference on Security and Cooperation in Europe opened on 30 July 1975 at Helsinki and concluded on 1 August 1975. It was attended by President Ford, Brezhnev, Prime Minister Wilson and others. Towards the end of the Conference, a Charter was signed by the participating States. The signatories agreed to "respect each other's right freely to choose and develop its political, social, economic and agricultural systems as well as its right to determine its laws and regulations". There are two parts of the Charter. One governs the conduct of the countries in their intercourse with other countries and the other deals with their relations with their own citizens. While undertaking to respect the sovereign equality and rights of other nations, the signatories also pledged themselves to respect human rights. They re-affirmed their "objective of promoting better relations among themselves and ensuring conditions in which their people can live in true and lasting peace." They guaranteed the inviolability of their frontiers and "right of peoples to equality and self-determination". The other highlights of the agreements were peaceful settlement of disputes by refraining from threat or use of force, non-intervention in internal affairs, cooperation among them and fulfilment in good faith of obligations under international law. The signatories agreed to notify all other States of major military manoeuvres deploying more than 15,000 troops. They recognised the interest of all of them "in efforts aimed at lessening military confrontation and promoting disarmament which are designed to complement political detente in Europe and to strengthen their security". They agreed to hold meetings in Belgrade and other places. The meeting was held at Belgrade between October 1977 & March 1978 but there was no further progress in the matter except the reaffirmation of the agreement of Helsinki.

On 18 May 1977, a Convention on Prohibition of Military or other Hostile Use of Environmental Modification Techniques was signed at Geneva. It aimed at consolidation of peace and halting of arms race with a view to bring about general and complete disarmament under strict and effective international control.

SALT-1 was valid for five years and it expired in October 1977. The Super Powers engaged themselves in coming to terms with SALT-2. President Jimmy Carter of the United States and President Brezhnev met at Vienna in June 1979 to put their signatures on a comprehensive SALT-2 treaty. However, that treaty was never ratified by the United States as President Reagan refused to endorse it on the ground that it conferred extra advantages on the Soviet Union and did not fully safeguard the interests of the United States. In 1982, President Reagan suggested the commencement of a new set of consultations called "START" (Strategic Arms Reduction Talks).

The Intermediate-Range Nuclear Force talks were broken off by the Russians on 23 November 1983 just after NATO installed the first of its new medium-range cruise and Pershing-2 missiles in Europe. Those warhead NATO missiles were a reply to the Russian triple warhead SS-22 which they started deploying in 1977. The Russians came back to the negotiating table in January 1985.

On 25 April 1985 the Soviet Union decided to suspend the deployment of its intermediate range nuclear missiles in Europe and implementation of other measures in reply to the NATO deployment of cruise and Pershing-2 missiles, but the United States did not reverse the process of missile deployment in Europe which she was able to initiate after great difficulty.

The Super Powers began their talks about nuclear arms control again in early 1985 after a pause of 14 months. The leaders of the two delegations were the soul of courtesy but they admitted that the talks would be extremely difficult and protracted.

There was a two-day Summit at Geneva on 19 and 20 November 1985 between US President Reagan and Soviet leader Gorbachev. In a joint statement issued after the end of negotiations, the two leaders acknowledged that serious differences persisted between them on vital issues. However, they affirmed that "any conflict between the USSR and the USA would have catastrophic consequences." They said that they would not seek to achieve military superiority and emphasized the importance of preventing any war between them. The two leaders agreed to accelerate nuclear arms control negotiations and to meet again "in the nearest future." Gorbachev accepted an invitation from President Reagan to visit the United States and President Reagan agreed to visit the Soviet Union.

A summit meeting between Gorbachev and Reagan was held at Reykjavik on 12 and 13 October 1986. The United States and the Soviet Union were close to a major agreement on nuclear disarmament when the summit broke down over the US refusal to yield on its Star War research. Gorbachev stated that the two sides were about to agree on a plan to cut strategic weapons by 50% in five years, eliminate medium-range missiles in Europe and reduce the number of warheads on Soviet medium-range missiles in Asia to 100. While Gorbachev demanded that those cuts be linked to a ban on Star War research outside the laboratory, Reagan rejected it outright. Both sides blamed each other for the failure of the summit.

The Schuman Plan

Originally proposed by the French Foreign Ministry, the Schuman Plan was intended to create a single market for coal and steel for all European countries willing to participate and accept the principle of supra-national control. Only five countries responded. Negotiations continued and ultimately on 18 April 1951, a convention setting up the European Coal and Steel Community was signed by Belgium, the Netherlands, Luxembourg, France, Italy and West Germany. The convention was ratified in 1952 and the single market was opened in 1953. The object of the European Coal and Steel Community was to contribute to economic expansion and development of employment and improvement of the standard of living in the participating countries through the establishment of a Common Market. Article 4 prohibited and abolished within the community import and export duties, charges on the movement of coal and steel, measures or practices discriminating among purchasers, buyers and consumers regarding prices, etc., subsidies or state assistance in any form whatsoever and restrictive trade practices tending towards division of markets or exploitation of markets. The institutions of the Community were the High Authority, the Consultative Committee, the Common Assembly, a Special Council and a Court of Justice. The Schuman Plan was a bold, far-reaching and in many ways an original attempt to overcome the dilemma of balancing the necessity of closer economic and political integration of Western Europe against the impossibility of introducing at one stroke a supra-national government. The plan provided for a careful delicate balance between international authority and national sovereignty. The economic and social provisions of the Treaty show a very complex and delicate balance between the conflicting pulls. One of the most progressive provisions of the Treaty is the unqualified prohibition of national discrimination regarding employment in the coal and steel industries. The object is to guarantee a free flow of workers among the member-states which means a revolution in traditional immigration policies. The Plan is an epoch-making experiment in international relations.

European Common Market

The tremendous success of the European Coal and Steel Community prompted the six states to link themselves still further economically. In 1955, they decided on the formation of the European Economic Community. On 25 March 1957, the Treaty of Rome was signed, and it was decided to form a European Common Market which came into being on 1 January 1958. It is a further step towards the economic and political integration of Europe.

The main objectives of the European Common Market were the abolition of tariff restrictions on imports and exports, the adoption of a common customs tariff and trade policy, elimination of all barriers to the free circulation of persons, services and capital and the creation of a European Investment Fund to facilitate the economic development of the Community. A common customs tariff and a common commercial policy was to be followed towards the non-member countries. It was expected that the European Economic Community would lead to the political integration of Europe and ultimately the United States of Europe would be born.

The European Common Market functions through the Council of Ministers, the Parliamentary Assembly, Court of Justice and the Executive Commission. Great Britain hesitated to join the European Common Market and that was due to the fact that she had not suffered the same disillusionment and political convulsion before and during the War as the states of continental Europe. There was also the aversion of the British to any written Constitution and particularly one which was likely to disturb the unwritten Constitution of their own country. There was also the belief that the true interests of Great Britain lay more with the Commonwealth countries and the United States than with continental Europe. There was also a psychological distrust of the dilettante politics of those European enthusiasts who wished to transform Europe with mere speeches in the Parliamentary assemblies.

As a matter of fact, Great Britain formed another organisation known as the European Free Trade Association consisting of Great Britain, Austria, Denmark, Norway, Portugal, Sweden and Switzerland. All these countries agreed upon a plan at Stockholm in November 1959. Unfortunately, this organisation was not a success. Great Britain was very much impressed by the record of the achievements of the European Common Market, whose members had made more progress than those of the European Free Trade Association. The result was that Great Britain applied for the membership of the European Common Market, but the same was refused on account of opposition from General de Gaulle of France, who was not prepared to allow his position to be challenged by Great Britain in Europe. There was disappointment in Great Britain. However, she persisted in her efforts to join the European Common Market and ultimately she joined the same in January 1973.

The Soviet Union and China

In 1949, the Communists were also to drive out Chiang Kai-shek and his government from the mainland of China and a Communist Government was set up with Peking as its headquarters. To begin with, the Soviet Union gave a lot of economic and military help to Communist China. On 14 February 1950 was signed a "Treaty regarding Friendship, Alliance and Mutual Aid between the Soviet Socialist Republics and Chinese People's Republic." In that Treaty the two countries declared their readiness in the spirit of sincere cooperation to participate in all international actions aimed at securing peace and security throughout the world. The Treaty bound the parties to prevent "the resumption of aggression and violation of peace on the part of Japan or any other power which would unite with Japan directly or in any other form in acts of aggression." Any power that would use Japanese territory as a base of operation against the Soviet Union or China would logically come within the purview of the Treaty obligation. Article 5 of the Treaty guaranteed the sovereignty of each state from any interference from each other in the execution of any undertaking covered by the Treaty. It was declared that all actions under the Treaty had to be performed in the spirit of friendship and co-operation in conformity with the principles of equality, mutual interest and also mutual respect for state sovereignty and territorial integrity, and non-interference in the internal affairs of the other party." The two countries agreed to cooperate with each other in all important international questions and to develop and strengthen economic and cultural ties between them. The Soviet Union has also made a number of concessions to China in the Far East. She promised a loan over a period of five years to the tune of $300 million.

Under this Treaty, not less than 141 enterprises were set up in China under the joint boards of management, half Russian and half Chinese. Thousands of Chinese students attended the universities in the Soviet Union to get their training. The Chinese army was modernised and expanded with Soviet help. On 31 December 1953, the Soviet Union agreed to give up her property rights in Manchurian Railways. The Soviet Union also agreed to leave Port Arthur by a Treaty negotiated in October 1954. This Treaty also provided for a Russian credit amounting to about a billion roubles. The Soviet Union also agreed to give up its shares in the mixed companies.

However, friendship between the Soviet Union and Communist China did not last long and differences arose between the two countries. Admittedly, the Soviet Union is a Euro-Asian Power and China only an Asian Power and the interests of the two are bound to be different and there was always the possibility of a clash. Communist China would not like the Soviet Union to dominate South-East Asia and such a proposition would not be acceptable to the Soviet Union. There are also certain ideological differences between the two countries. When Khrushchev came to power, he initiated a new policy of peaceful co-existence between capitalism and socialism. He believed that the Communists could beat the capitalists in competition. He was not prepared to risk a nuclear war. This new policy of Khrushchev was condemned by Communist China under Mao Tse-tung and Chou-En-lai. The Chinese leaders believed in a policy of revolution and fight to the finish against capitalism. They believed in the complete destruction of capitalism. No wonder, the new Soviet policy was not acceptable to the Chinese and they accused Khrushchev of cowardice and revisionism.

The differences between the two countries came to the fore in 1958 and by 1959, the Chinese began to attack the Soviet policy indirectly. Two important meetings were held in 1961, one at Bucharest and the other in Moscow. In the Twenty-second Party Congress held in Moscow in 1961, Khrushchev attacked the Albanian Communist Party which was receiving support from the Chinese Government. When Khrushchev started his drive against Stalinism, the same was not approved of by the Chinese Government. Communist China condemned Khruschev in 1962 on the occasion of the Cuban crisis and the virtual surrender of the Soviet Union before the United States. The pro-India policy of the Soviet Union was also condemned by China. The result of all these things was that Russia withdrew all support from Communist China and both the countries became open enemies.

When in October 1964, Khrushchev was removed, it was hoped that the relations between the two countries might improve. As a matter of fact, many conciliatory moves were made by Kosygin to win over Communist China but without any result. The relations between the two countries were further strained when Vietnam intervened in Kampuchea in January 1979 and Russia intervened in Afghanistan in December 1979. However, President Brezhnev declared in 1981 that the Soviet Union was ready to negotiate an all-round improvement in her relations with China. In March 1982, Moscow sent feelers and Beijing reciprocated. The process of reconciliation was continued by Yuri Andropove, Chernenko and Gorbachev. The change in China's foreign policy after the death of Chou En-lai and Mao Tse-tung in 1976 has also helped the process of reconciliation.

The United States and Communist China

In spite of American help, Chiang Khai-shek was driven out from the Chinese mainland in 1949 and he took shelter in Formosa (Taiwan). The Communists would have liked to complete their victory by capturing Formosa also, but the United States stood in their way. In July 1950, the Chinese

Communists seemed to be getting ready to attack Formosa. For two days, their shore batteries shelled the Quemoy Island which is three miles off the mainland of Amoy. However, President Truman neutralised Formosa by posting the Seventh Fleet in between so that neither Formosa was attacked by the Chinese Communists nor the Chinese Communists under Chiang Khai-shek attacked the Chinese mainland. This state of affairs continued up to January 1953 when President Eisenhower cancelled the order of President Truman and issued instructions that the Seventh Fleet would no longer be employed to shield Communist China. Nationalist China was thus given freedom to attack the Chinese mainland and Chinese Communists were allowed to attack, if they pleased, Formosa. The plea of Eisenhower was that the American Navy could not be allowed to be used to serve as a defensive system of Communist China. Chou En-lai, the Chinese Premier, gave a challenge to the American Government that the Communist were going to liberate Formosa in spite of American help. The challenge was accepted by President Eisenhower. On many occasions, attempts were made by the Chinese Communists to bomb the Islands in the neighbourhood of Formosa, but they did not dare to attack the Islands of Formosa. The United States entered into a military pact with the Government of Chiang Kai-shek and pledged herself to come to her help if the Island of Formosa was attacked. The Chinese Communists knew full well that an attack on Formosa would mean a war with the United States. It was such a high stake that both Communist China and the Soviet Union, in spite of their repeated declarations, were not prepared to take the risk.

When the Korean War started in June 1950, the United States at once came to the help of South Korea. A resolution was passed by the United Nations branding North Korea as the aggressor. North Korea was helped openly by Communist China and indirectly by the Soviet Union. Communist China sent lakhs of volunteers to help the people of North Korea. There was every possibility of a war between the United Nations on the one hand and Communist China on the other. However, General MacArthur was not allowed to cross the 38th Parallel and he himself was removed from the United Nations Command. The part played by the United States in the Korean War was bound to embitter the relations, between Communist China and the United States.

In 1962 Communist China attacked India. The Government of India requested the American Government to help her and President Kennedy openly came forward to help India against Communist China. It was partly due to American help to India which forced Communist China to stay her hands and declare unilateral cease-fire in November 1962. The American Government helped India to prepare herself against the Chinese attack in the future and this alienated Communist China against the United States. Communist China helped North Vietnam against South Vietnam which was backed by the United States. That also embittered the relations between the two countries. For more than two decades, the United States opposed the entry of Communist China into the United Nations. She also refused to recognise her. There was bitterness between the two countries. It is true that earlier also, efforts had been made by the United States to establish contacts with Communist China, but not much had come out of them. It was in 1971 that Dr. Kissinger paid a secret visit to Peking via Pakistan. It was after that visit that it was declared that President Nixon would pay a visit to Communist China. China was admitted into the United Nations on 26 October 1971 with American help. Elaborate preparations were made and ultimately President Nixon actually went to Communist China in February 1972. At the end of his visit, a joint communique was issued in which it was stated that President Nixon had a serious and frank exchange of views on Sino-U.S. relations and world a flairs. Extensive, earnest and frank discussions were held between President Nixon and Premier Chou En-lai on the normalisation of relations between the two countries as well as other matters of interest common to both sides. In the communique both states stated their separate points of view with regard to Indo-China, Korea, Japan, India, Pakistan, Vietnam, Loas and Cambodia. The American Government accepted the contention of China that the liberation of Taiwan was an internal affair of China in which no other country had a right to interfere and all U.S. forces and military installations must be withdrawn from

Taiwan. The United States admitted that there was but one China and Taiwan was a part of China. The United States also admitted that a peaceful settlement of the Taiwan question was to be made by the Chinese themselves and the United States would withdraw all her forces and military installations from Taiwan in the long run. The two countries agreed to facilitate the progressive development of trade between the two countries. They also agreed to maintain contacts through various channels.

In February 1973, Dr. Kissinger visited Peking to explore further avenues of mutual cooperation. In March 1973, David Bruce was sent to Peking. In August 1977, Mr. Cyrus Vance, the US Secretary of State, visited China. President Carter agreed to derecognise Taiwan and bury the two-China theory. This led to the abrogation of the US-Taiwan Treaty of 1955 in 1979. This was very much appreciated by China. Deng Xiao-ping paid an official visit to the United States in January 1979. President Reagan visited China in 1984. On 23 July 1985, the United States and China signed a nuclear pact.

The Jewish state of Israel was proclaimed at Tel Aviv on 15 May 1948 and was recognised simultaneously by the United States and the Soviet Union. However, this was not liked by the Arab states and they joined hands to attack the new-born state. In spite of their superiority in numbers, the Jews were able to beat back the Arabs. After many efforts, some kind of truce was established on all the fronts by July 1949.

When Egypt nationalised the Suez Canal in 1956, Great Britain and France joined hands with Israel to attack Egypt. There was bitter fighting and ultimately the war was brought to a close on account of a threat of intervention held out by the Soviet Union.

The relations between Israel and the Arab States were most unsatisfactory. There was bitterness on both sides. In January 1965, certain water installations were dynamited on the Israel side of the Jordan border. Many raids were organised by Al-Fateh against Israel. That state of affairs continued for about two years. A joint defence pact was signed between Egypt and Syria by which it was provided that an attack on one would be considered as an attack on the other. In November 1966, Israel presented a complaint of "acts of aggression" by Syria to the Security Council. In the same month, Israel launched her biggest offensive against Jordan. A meeting of the Security Council was summoned on the complaint of Jordan and the state of Israel was condemned for her attack. In April 1967, Israel attacked Syria and did a lot of damage. In May 1967, heavy Egyptian troop movements were reported out of Cairo. President Nasser requested the Secretary-General of the United Nations to withdraw the United Nations Emergency Force which was a sort of barrier between Egypt and Israel. The Secretary-General withdrew the Emergency Force. After that, President Nasser closed the Gulf of Aqaba to all Israeli ships. It was proclaimed that the waters of the Tirana Strait belonged to Egypt. War seemed to be imminent. It was under these circumstances that Israel attacked Egypt on 4 June 1967, and destroyed a large number of her aircraft. Although many Muslim states declared war against Israel, the main strain of war was on Egypt, Syria and Jordan. War lasted for about a week and the Arabs were completely defeated. Cease-fire was declared in compliance with a resolution of the Security Council.

Many years passed away and there was no peace. Both parties were determined to fight it out. Israel was not prepared to evacuate the territories conquered and occupied by her during the war of 1967. There was a lot of violence due to the activities of the Arab guerillas. There was a marked change in the situation on account of the new Soviet policy towards the Arab states. The Soviet Union agreed to give and eventually gave Egypt what she required to fight against Israel. The result was that the Egyptians made thorough preparations for a war against Israel and also succeeded in getting solid support from the other Arab countries. Israel was attacked all of a sudden in October 1973 by Egypt. Syria also joined the war. There was a lot of destruction and ultimately through, the good offices of the United States, a cease-fire was declared. That cease-fire proved ineffective and war started again. There was another cease-fire and a negotiated peace settlement between Egypt and Israel. Israel agreed to evacuate the Sinai territory provided American observers were stationed on the spot to maintain peace between the two countries.

The Congo Crisis

The Congo was formerly a dependency of Belgium. When it was declared independent on 30 June 1960, it was absolutely unprepared to shoulder the responsibilities which independence brought in its wake. The former government had done nothing to train the people of Congo in the field of administration. There were not more than a dozen graduates in the whole of the country. Not a single Congolese was holding any senior administrative post in the country. Medical services were entirely under the control of Belgian doctors. Education was a monopoly of the Catholic Church. Trade and business were in the hands of Belgian capitalists and their European and American collaborators. Congolese army was officered by Belgians. Even before the grant of independence to the people of Congo in June 1960, an Economic Conference had been held at Brussels in April 1960, and it was attended by the representatives of both Belgium and the Congo. Unfortunately, the delegation from Congo did not include the important political personalities of that country, and hence the recommendations of the Conference were rejected by the Government of Congo after her independence. Elections were held in May 1960 to the Chamber of Representatives, the Lower House of the future Congolese Parliament. Elections were also held in the six Provincial Legislatures at the same time. Provincial Legislatures elected the members of the National Senate. Even before the holding of elections, there was disorder and violence in various parts of the country, and the same state of affairs continued after the elections. A state of emergency was declared, from time to time, to meet the situation. In the Katanga Province, powerful Belgian business houses and the Catholic Church interfered in the elections on the side of those personalities and political parties which were favourably inclined towards Belgium.

When the elections were over, it was found that no political party had an absolute majority. However, the Congolese National Movement led by Patrice Lumumba emerged as the strongest single party in the Chamber of Representatives, having secured 41 seats out of 137 seats. This party had also seats in all the Provincial Legislatures. It dominated Parliament in Eastern province and controlled one-third of total seats in Kasai.

The Congokat Party of Katanga led by Tshombe was not able to get even one seat in the Parliament. The Abako Party of Katanga was able to secure 12 seats. Lumumba's party was not the strongest single party in the Senate. It is true that Lumumba had no absolute majority in the Legislatures, but he was able to form a coalition with other parties and thereby formed the Ministry.

On 2 June 1960, Mr. Lumumba declared at a Press Conference that the Belgian officers were trying to stand in the way of his becoming Premier and he demanded the immediate withdrawal of all Belgian troops from the Congo. There were difficulties both at the Centre and in the provinces to form ministries. Efforts were made to separate Lumumba and Kasavubu and make them fight against each other. However, as a result of a compromise Lumumba formed his Cabinet on 28 June 1960 and Kasavubu was elected President of the Republic of Congo. Fresh difficulties arose from the side of Kalonji and Tshombe. Kalonji demanded three seats in the Ministry and when his demand was not accepted, he declared himself at the King of Independent South Kasai State. On being instigated by the Belgian Government and the local foreign businessmen, Tshombe also declared himself President of the Free Katanga State. To make matters worse, the Belgian Government sent her troops to the Congo. The Government of Belgium did not care for the protests of the Congo government. Southern Rhodesia also helped Tshombe. Lumumba appealed to the United Nations for help and also requested the Belgian Government to withdraw her troops immediately. On 13 July 1960, the Soviet Union declared that Belgium and other Western powers were trying to exploit the Congo and that would lead to disastrous consequences. An emergency session of the Security Council was called but it failed to take any decision. Lumumba threatened to invite Russian troops to turn out the Belgians from the Congo and also put an end to the secession of Katanga. The Security Council met again and a resolution was passed calling upon the Belgian Government to withdraw all her troops. A promise was made to Congo for military assistance to maintain law and order. The Secretary General visited Congo and Katanga but refused to use the troops of the United Nations to suppress the Katangan secession.

In the meanwhile, President Kasavubu and Prime Minister Lumumba quarrelled with each other. Kasavubu dismissed Lumumba and Lumumba dismissed Kasavubu. However, the Congolese Senate cancelled both the orders. Col. Mobutu took advantage of the situation and seized power in September 1960. In alliance with Kasavubu, Mobutu placed Lumumba under house arrest. On 2 December 1960, Lumumba was captured by Mobutu's troops while attempting to escape to Stanleyville. Kasavubu and his aides handed over Lumumba to Tshombe and Lumumba was cruelly murdered on 1 February 1961.

To resolve the problem of Katanga UN Secretary-General Dag Hammarskjold flew to Northern Rhodesia for peace talks, but he was killed in an aircrash on 18 September 1961. U Thant, the new Secretary-General, took firm action against Tshombe which resulted in his surrender and thus the secession of Katanga ended. In July 1964, Tshombe became Prime Minister of the Congo, but later on he was dismissed in 1965. In November 1965, Kasavubu was overthrown by Mobutu in a bloodless coup. Mobutu resorted to forceful methods to curb tribalism and personal political rivalries.

Southern Rhodesia

Great Britain granted independence to Northern Rhodesia but not to Southern Rhodesia as there were a large number of Whites of British origin. On 11 November 1965, the White minority in Southern Rhodesia declared its independence unilaterally. It was a serious challenge to British authority and the declaration of independence was declared illegal by the British Government. Both the General Assembly and the Security Council condemned Southern Rhodesia for her action. In January 1966, a meeting of the Commonwealth countries wars held at Lagos, capital of Nigeria, to decide upon the steps to be taken against the government of Southern Rhodesia headed by Ian Smith. In December 1966, the Security Council applied selective mandatory economic sanctions against Southern Rhodesia. In May 1968, the Security Council imposed comprehensive mandatory sanctions and also set up a Sanctions Committee to see to their enforcement. In 1969, it was reported that in spite of the sanctions there was going on a lot of trade between Southern Rhodesia on the one hand and Portugal and South Africa on the other. An attempt was made in June 1969 to censure Portugal and South Africa, but it failed. Southern Rhodesia declared herself a Republic in 1970. On that occasion, the Security Council passed a resolution condemning the Government of Southern Rhodesia and also called upon the member states to cut off all diplomatic, consular, trade, military and other relations with the Republic of Southern Rhodesia. Many attempts were made by Prime Minister Wilson to come to a settlement with Ian Smith, but nothing came out of them and the deadlock continued. In 1971, Sir Alec Douglas-Home, Foreign Minister of England, and Ian Smith entered into a constitutional arrangement by which the majority rule was to be restored in the distant future. In order to find out the reactions of the people, the Pearce Commission was appointed and it submitted its report in May 1972. The proposals were rejected by the Africans and the stalemate continued. There was a lot of tension on the question of Southern Rhodesia. The African States made it clear that they would leave no stone unturned to overthrow the government of Ian Smith even by force. The American Government made it clear that it would not help Southern Rhodesia against the African States. The British Government also advised Ian Smith to come to a settlement.

Negotiations continued in an atmosphere of great tension. Dr. Kissinger played an important part in bringing about a compromise. On 24 September 1976, Prime Minister Ian Smith announced at Salisbury that his White minority Government would surrender power to the black majority within two years. That announcement was made by Smith under pressure from the United States and the British Government. It was made clear to him that he would get no help unless he accepted the solution arrived at. A Conference was held at Geneva to finalise the matter. There was a wide divergence of views with regard to the date on which the transfer of power was to take place. Ultimately, on 15 November 1976, 1 March 1978 was fixed as the deadline for the transfer of power.

During the September 1979 Prime Ministers' Conference, Tanzania, Zambia, Botswana, Mozambique and Angola prevailed upon British Prime Minister Mrs. Thatcher to convene a meeting of the parties to resolve the crisis amicably. Shortly afterwards, Southern Rhodesia became once again a British colony and talks on a peace settlement started in the Lancaster House, London. The historic Peace Settlement was a tribute to the genius of Lord Carrington, British Foreign Secretary and the willingness of the African leaders to avoid any further bloodshed. Elections were held in Southern Rhodesia in February 1980 when Robert Mugabe secured a majority at the polls by winning 57 out of 80 black seats. Southern Rhodesia became independent in April 1980 under the new name of Zimbabwe.

Vietnam

After the World War II, France had to wage a bloody war in French Indo-China to defend her empire in that region. The Viet Minh Communists were led by Dr. Ho Chi Minh and helped by Communist China and the Soviet Union. In spite of American help, the French position became critical in the beginning of 1954. After protracted negotiations, an agreement was arrived at the Geneva Conference and hostilities were ended. The French Colonial empire in that region was liquidated Cambodia and Laos were declared independent States. The State of Britain was divided into North Vietnam and South Vietnam and was made independent. A Communist government was recognised in North Vietnam under Dr. Ho Chi Minh. Provision was made for the holding of elections in 1956 to decide the future of Vietnam.

In spite of the Geneva Settlement of 1954, there was no peace in Vietnam. The United States did everything in her power to help South Vietnam against North Vietnam supported by Communist China and the Soviet Union. There was a wholesale bombing of the targets in the North Vietnam but there was no end of the war. President Johnson declared on 31 March 1968 that the United States would stop air and sea attacks on North Vietnam with a view to bring peace in that region. North Vietnam responded to the move of President Johnson and suggested that talks between the two countries regarding the future of Vietnam should be held in Paris. It was in this atmosphere that talks between the two countries started in May 1968. Years passed away and nothing came out of those talks. Each side was determined to put forward its own point of view with vehemence and refused to compromise.

In spite of American participation in the war in South Vietnam, the same did not end. As a matter of fact, it appeared that the forces of North Vietnam were making headway against South Vietnam in the beginning of 1972. As the United States was not prepared for such an eventuality, American bombing on North Vietnam was intensified. Not only military objectives were bombed, even bridges, rail-tracks, electric installations, factories, etc. were bombed and wrecked. The American government spread mines in the harbours and rivers of North Vietnam. Efforts were made to bring about peace in the region. President Podgorny of the Soviet Union went to Hanoi to advise the government of North Vietnam to come to trans with the American government. Dr. Kissinger also visited Peking for a similar purpose. China also put pressure on North Vietnam. The result was that in January 1973, a peace agreement was made between Hanoi and Washington. In pursuance of that agreement, fighting ended in Vietnam. The Paris Conference on Vietnam was also held. Although the war ended in Vietnam, complete peace did not come back to that area. There were many set-backs. Consequently a new peace accord on Vietnam was signed on 13 June 1973 in Paris between the United States, North Vietnam. South Vietnam and the Provisional Revolutionary government of South Vietnam, in spite of these accords, peace did not come to Vietnam. North Vietnam continued to make preparations for a war and was ultimately successful in conquering South Vietnam in April 1975. The American influence was liquidated from Vietnam, Cambodia and Laos.

Cambodia (Khmer)

Cambodia had declared her independence in March 1945. After the collapse of Japan, the French were able to re-establish their authority in the country. A movement was started for the complete independence of the country and the same was actually achieved in July 1954. Prince Norodom Sihanouk became the head of the State. He was a shrewd politician and he managed to keep Cambodia out of the Vietnam war. On 18 March 1970, he was deposed by the National Assembly while he was on a State visit to the Soviet Union and real power fell into the hands of Prime Minister Lon Nol backed by the United States. The new regime of Lon Nol was anti-communist and its first task was to get rid of the communists in Cambodia, who had taken shelter in the sanctuaries. There were more than 40,000 Vietcong guerrillas in Cambodia. In spite of all the help from the United States, Lon Nol was not able to crush the Communists. A sort of civil war was continued in the country by the Khmer Rouge the communist insurrectionaries who were occupying about 30% of the total area of Cambodia.

When Prince Norodom Sihanouk was ousted, he retired to Communist Chink. On 4 May 1970, the Royal Government of National Union of Cambodia was established in Peking and was recognised by Communist China the next day. An understanding was arrived at between Prince Sihanouk and the Khmer Rouge by which it was agreed that the real power or leadership in Cambodia would rest in the hands of the Khmer Rouge. The civil war continued and on 17 April 1975, Cambodia surrendered to the Khmer Rouge. After a lot of hesitation, Prince Sihanouk returned to Cambodia but later on resigned as the Head of the State and a representative of the Khmer Rouge also became the Head of the State.

The world is passing through a great crisis. It is true that there is the United Nations which is surviving for peace in the world, but there are very many forces all over the world which stand in the way of the establishment of peace. The Soviet Union and Communist China are deadly enemies and there seem to be no prospects of a solution of the points of conflict between the two countries. If Communist China insists on getting back her territories from the Soviet Union, there can be no peace between the two countries as the Soviet Union with all her strength will not surrender them. For very many years, the cold war continued between the United States and the Soviet Union and the world had no peace. It is true that some sort of a Detente between the two countries prevails and every effort are made by the leaders of the two countries to avoid open conflicts, but it cannot be denied that tension between the two countries exists. This is clearly proved by the attitude of the two countries on the question of Angola. Although the United States helped one of the parties contesting for power in Angola, the party backed by the Soviet Union came out successful and the United States had to eat the humble pie. Cuba sent her army. It is the horrors of a nuclear war that are putting a check on the Super Powers. It is well-understood that in the event of a war, there will be no victors. All will perish.

SUGGESTED READINGS

Alting, Von Gensan, F.A.M.: **NATO and Security in the seventies,** 1971.

Arnold, G.L.: **The Pattern of World Conflict,** 1955.

Barnett, D.: **Communist China and Asia,** 1963.

Belloff, Max: **The United States and the Unity of Europe,** 1963.

Blackmer, H.M.: **United States Policy and the Inter-American Peace System, Geneva,** 1952.

Boorman, H.L.: **Moscow-Peking Axis,** 1957.

Boyd, Endrew, K.H.: **Atlantic Pact, Commonwealth and United Nations, London,** 1949.

Granshaw, Edward : **The New Cold War—Moscow v. Peking.**

Dutta, Vidya Prakash : **Chinese Foreign Policy.**

Fifield, Russel H.: **Diplomacy of South-East Asia,** 1945-1958, 1958.

Fleming, D.S.: **The Cold War and its Origins.**

Freymond, Jacques: **Western Europe since the War,** 1964.

Gaitskell. H.: **The Challenge of Co-existence,** 1957.

Griffith, William E.: **The Sino-Soviet Rift,** 1964.

Horowitz, David: **From Yalta to Vietnam.**

Ingram, A.: **The History of the Cold War,** 1955.

Lancaster, Donald: **The Emancipation of French Indo-China,** 1961.

Lippmann, Walter: **The Cold War,** 1947.

Low, Sir Francis: **Struggle for Asia.**

Luard, Evan (Ed.): **The Cold War, London,** 1964.

Moore Ben, T.: **NATO and the Future of Europe,** 1958.

Patterson, T.S.: **Soviet-American Confrontation: Post-War Reconstruction and the Origins of the Cold War,** 1973.

Price, H.B.: **Marshall Plan and its Meaning,** 1955.

Schwartz, B.I.: **Chinese Communism and the Rise of Mao,** 1951.

Zagoria, Donald : **The Sino-Soviet Conflict,** 1956-61, 1962.

CHAPTER

43 THE COMMUNIST REGIME IN RUSSIA (1917-1939)

The Bolsheviks seized power on 7 November 1917. The Congress of the Soviets declared itself to be the repository of all power and established a government called Council of People's Commissars, composed solely of Bolsheviks, headed by Lenin. Its most important members were Rykov, Trotsky, Stalin and Lunacharsky. Immediately on coming to power, they renamed themselves Communists. They also shifted the seat of Government from Petrograd to Moscow.

The Congress of the Soviets adopted the Decrees on Peace and Land. The Decree of Land envisaged the immediate, abolition of landed estates, including crown, monastery and church lands, without any compensation and their transfer to the Soviets of Peasants' Deputies. Private ownership of land was abolished. Land and its material wealth were proclaimed the property of the whole people. Another step of great importance was the publication of the Declaration of the Rights of the people of Russia. Those rights included the right to national self-determination and an eight-hour working day and insurance against unemployment and sickness benefits.

A strict censorship was imposed on the press. Only the Bolshevik papers were allowed to appear. Public meetings were prohibited and only the Bolsheviks were allowed to spread their doctrine. Lenin tried to control elections to the Constituent Assembly which was to meet in January 1918. When he found that the Constituent Assembly was controlled by the Socialist Revolutionaries, he sent a contingent of sailors to disperse it by armed forces and he was successful in doing so.

After the dissolution of the Constituent Assembly, Lenin and Trotsky organised a reign of terror with the help of the Cheka which was the secret police. Its powers were unlimited. A large number of aristocrats, members of the middle classes and peasants were killed and among them were the Czar and the members of his family. Hundreds of thousands of Russians, whether they were reactionaries, liberals, or moderate socialists sought shelter in exile. It is rightly said that the year 1918 was one of carnage and general misery. There was so much of food shortage that the Government had to resort to a system of strict rationing. The people were divided into categories for rationing purposes. "While the manual workers were able to get a skinny lion's share, the hated middle class were lucky indeed if they got some crumbs. But the terror prevented even the desperate from rising in their own defence."

With the help of Trotsky, Lenin was able to raise a large army known as Red Army which fought successfully the civil war in Russia, enforced the reign of terror and helped the establishment of the dictatorship of the proletariat.

Constitution of 1918

The people of Russia were given a new Constitution in 1918. The declared object of the new Constitution was to establish the dictatorship of the proletariat and uproot the exploiters. The capitalists, clergymen, members of the imperial dynasty. Kulaks, persons living on unearned incomes and certain categories of officials of the old Czarist regime were not given the right of vote. The church was separated from the state and no religious instruction was to be allowed in schools. A provision was made for an all-Russian Congress of Soviets. Representatives to this body were to come both from the urban and rural areas but more representation was given to urban areas as the Communists had greater hold over the cities than on the countryside

Constitution of 1924

In 1922, the Union of Soviet Socialist Republics (USSR) came into being. In July 1923, the Central Executive Committee drafted the new Constitution for the USSR which came into force in January 1924. Provision was made for an all-Union Congress of Soviets in which once again weightage was given to the people living in the urban areas and the capitalists, clergymen, criminals and certain categories of officials of the Czarist regime were not given the right to vote. The Central Executive Committee was to have two Houses, viz., Union of Soviets and Soviet of Nationalities. Provision was also made for the Presidium consisting of 27 members.

The Central Executive Committee was also to appoint the Council of People's Commissars whose members were to be the heads of the various departments of the Federal Government. Lenin, was the first Chairman of the Council of People's Commissars. This Constitution lasted up to 1936.

War Communism (1918-21)

The period from the middle of 1918 until the spring of 1921 is described in the Soviet history as the period of War Communism. This was done to meet the challenge of imperialist intervention and the civil war in Russia. To concentrate all industrial production in the hands of the State, the Government nationalised not only large-scale industries but also middle-sized and relatively small enterprises also. On 20 November 1920, a decree was issued by which all enterprises employing more than 10 workers as well as all shops with a mechanical engine and five or more workers were nationalised. This action of the Government certainly weakened the hands of the counter-revolutionaries in Russia and placed enough of material resources in the hands of the Government to fight against the counter-revolutionaries. The food policy of the Government provided for the requisitioning of food. The Government took no foodstuffs from the poor peasants. The middle peasants were required to give a moderate part of their surpluses. The rich peasants were required to surrender the greater part of their surplus stock. The Government curtailed the market activities. The workers were paid in kind. They were supplied with necessaries of life and also free services like public utilities, transport facilities, education, medical treatment, etc. The Communist Government introduced universal labour conscription. He who did not work was not to eat. A system of barter of goods like grain, floor, salt, sugar, cloth, etc., was introduced. Banks and credit institutions were temporarily closed.

Under the policy of War Communism, the State acquired full control of foreign trade, heavy industries, banking corporations, railways, forests and rivers.

In 1921, Lenin wrote thus: "The peculiarity of War Communism consisted in the fact that we really took from the peasants all their surpluses, and sometimes even what was not surplus but part of what was necessary to feed the peasants. We took it to cover the costs of the army and to maintain workers." Again, "It was the war and the ruin that forced us into War Communism. It was not and could not be a policy that corresponded to the economic tasks of the proletariat. It was a make-shift. Though this policy involved a retreat to capitalism but it was necessary as the Soviet Government wanted to grasp the forces and then resume the offensive."

It is contended that the immediate effect of the strategy of War Communism was disastrous to Russian economy. In some provinces, the confiscation of grain drove the peasants into rebellion. They hid their own corn and their cattle. Crops were not sown and the livestock was killed and eaten. With workers starving, factories ceased to produce and by 1920, famine stalked the land.

In March 1921, Lenin admitted that "tens and hundreds of thousands of disbanded soldiers" were turning to banditry and there were violent peasant risings.

Lenin's New Economic Policy (NEP), 1921-1925

Lenin was a realist and he abandoned the policy of War Communism in 1921 and started a new economic policy which practically amounted to the abandonment of the programme of pure communism and adoption of a new economic policy which combined state socialism, state capitalism and private enterprise. The principal purpose of NEP was to consolidate the economic and political alliance between the working class and the peasants, to rehabilitate the ruined economy of Russia by the efforts of the labouring classes and build a socialist economy. The farmers were given freedom to use their economic resources. The system of requisitioning surplus was substituted by a tax in kind. The Government gave up its monopoly in grain and introduced free trade in all agricultural products. The Government helped private capital to speed up the rehabilitation of industry. Private capital was allowed to operate in the sphere of trade under certain restrictions. Efforts were also made to revive and improve the system of money circulation. Incentive of private profit was provided to boost production. However, private capital was not allowed to enter large-scale industry, transport, foreign trade and the banking system. Experts were imported for responsible positions. Foreign capital was welcomed to increase production. It is rightly pointed out that the New Economic Policy was a compromise with capitalism.

It is true that the adoption of the New Economic Policy implied the admission of capitalist elements into the socialist economy and could be regarded as a retreat, but it is pointed out that this retreat was planned, orderly and short-lived. The revolutionary policy of collectivization was temporarily halted but it was "a setback in order to move two steps forward later." The Government kept a watch over the socialist and capitalist elements, ensuring the growth of the former and restricting and ultimately liquidating the latter.

The State General Planning Commission was set up in February 1921 and the work of planning, control and management was placed in its hands. During the rehabilitation period, there was a substantial and rapid development of the Soviet economy. A great effort was made to supply agriculture with farm machines and implements. Through the Central Agricultural Bank, credit was given to the peasants. It is pointed out that during 1923-25, the total sum of loans granted to the peasants by the Central Agricultural Bank increased 81 times over from 8.1 million to 657.6 million roubles. Both agricultural production and productivity of labour in agriculture increased.

The Government put great emphasis on the development of industries. Key industries and big enterprises were rehabilitated. Small and medium-sized enterprises were either temporarily closed or leased. The leases and concessions given to foreign capital paved the way for state capitalism. There was an unprecedented growth of production. It is estimated that the average annual increase in industrial output during the period 1921-25 was about 41 per cent. Much of the rise in production could be attributed to the enthusiasm of the working people who felt that they were working for themselves and their socialist state. There was not only rise in production but also in wages. It is estimated that in 1925-26, wages were 34 per cent above those in 1913. The workers also gained on account of Government expenditure on social and agricultural requirements, medical services, annual paid holidays, etc. There was a rise in the level of material and agricultural advancement of the people.

The work of economic rehabilitation is said to have been completed towards the end of 1925. In spite of that, the Soviet Union had a backward economy. There was the necessity of following a policy of wholesale industrialisation. The Soviet Union had to equip its army with guns, tanks, planes and other modern weapons. Without a stable industrial base, the development of transport, light and food industries and even agriculture was not possible. In order to achieve a high degree of industrialisation, the Government was forced to concentrate on building heavy industries and deliberately restricting the production of many essential consumers' goods.

The Soviet Union took full advantage of industrialisation under conditions of public ownership of means of production. Hundreds of new enterprises were built. Many old enterprises were reconstructed. Many new coal mines were opened. It is estimated that in 1926, the gross output of heavy industry increased by 43.2% as compared with the previous year. In 1927 it increased by 14%. In 1928, it increased by about 25%. In 1928, industry accounted for 45.2% of country's gross output as against 42.1% in 1913. There was a rise in labour productivity in industry by 10% on an average and a drop in production costs on an average of 6%. The rise in production helped the Government to improve the living standards of the people. Wages were increased and unemployment was reduced.

There was a crisis in the procurement of grain. All surplus grain was in the hands of Kulaks. During 1927-28, they refused to sell grain to the state. The result was that in December 1927 the Communist Party decided to follow the policy of collectivization of agriculture. Small individual peasant farms were turned into large-scale collective farms.

Estimate of Lenin (1870-1924)

Lenin ruled Russia for about 6 years and died on 21 January, 1924. He virtually transformed the life and institutions of the people of Russia. He had a genius for organisation. He believed in his own capacity to win and not to be defeated. To quote Gorky, "Lenin speaks with an iron tongue, with the logic of an axe. His speech is a hammer which smashes relentlessly all obstacles." Lenin believed in the ultimate triumph of his cause although he knew that the vested interests would not surrender without a major fight. He was confident that the change could not be brought about by constitutional methods and there was bound to be confrontation.

Lenin was selfless. He had an abnormally powerful and unquestioned belief in himself and his destiny. He was certain of his rightness in every controversy. He believed that he was the best and virtually the only true master and exponent of Marxism. To quote him, "Out of every hundred Bolsheviks, seventy are fools, twenty-nine rogues and only one a real socialist." He wrote for his own eyes, "After a half century not a single Marxist has understood Marx." It is estimated that he was probably the most influential man in history from the time of Julius Caesar. He was the hammerer of world revolution. His embalmed body was placed in a mausoleum outside the Kremlin. "Devout pilgrims to Moscow even today defile in an unending cortege before the embalmed corpse of the great revolutionary figure, once so violent and rugged, who lies there in the peace of death, while his will and mind continue to fashion the ideals of the Russian state."

Joseph Stalin (1879-1953)

After the death of Lenin in January 1924, there was a struggle for power. Among those who aspired to succeed Lenin was Trotsky (1877-1940). Trotsky was a brilliant Jew. He had participated in the revolution of 1905 and was exiled for a long period. He joined Lenin in 1917. He was a gifted orator and a powerful writer who with "the flame of fire" aroused the people to revolutionary fervour. He was a fine organiser. He was the organiser of the Red Army and was rightly called the Russian Carnot.

Joseph Stalin was the son of a cobbler. He was a Bolshevik since 1903. He fought the Czarist tyranny and was exiled to Siberia. He became a member of the Political Bureau of the Communist Party. In 1919, he became the General Secretary of the Central Party Committee. The main difference between Stalin and Trotsky was that while Stalin stood for "socialism in a single country", Trotsky stood for a "permanent" world revolution. In the historic contest, Stalin was successful and Trotsky was expelled from the Communist Party in 1927 and exiled. On 20 August 1940, Trotsky was murdered in Mexico.

Stalin ruled the Soviet Union with an iron hand up to 1953. He led the Soviet forces to victory in the Second World War. Until 1942, Stalin did not hold any office in the Government. He was merely the Secretary General of the Communist Party and a dominant member of the Politbureau.

The Stalin Constitution (1936)

In 1936, Stalin gave to the people of the Soviet Union a new Constitution known as the Stalin Constitution. In that Constitution, the principle of democratic centralism was the guiding principle of the state and party organisation. The largest measure of democratic freedom was given to the people. Provision was made for universal adult franchise and secret voting. Every citizen of the USSR who had reached the age of 23 was eligible for election to the Supreme Soviet of USSR. Every citizen was given one vote and all citizens participated in the elections on an equal footing. Women were given the right to elect and be elected on equal terms with men. In spite of this democracy, there was central control by the Communist Party. Nothing could be done against the views of the Communist Party and the Central Government which was controlled by the members of the Communist Party. The Communist Party controlled the affairs of both the Central Government and the Union Republics.

The USSR was described as a socialist state of workers and peasants. The political foundation of the USSR was the Soviets of Working People's Deputies. All power in the USSR belonged to the working people of the towns and countryside. The economic foundation of the USSR was the socialist system of economy and the socialist ownership of instruments and means of production. Work in the USSR was a duty and a matter of honour.

The Constitution of 1936 provided for fundamental rights and duties of citizens. The citizens were given the right to work, that is, the right to guaranteed employment and payment for their work in accordance with its quality and quantity. The citizens were given the right to rest and leisure. They had the right to maintenance in old age and also in case of sickness or disability. The right to education was ensured by universal compulsory elementary education, by a system of state stipends for students of higher educational establishments who excelled in their studies. Women were given equal rights with men irrespective of their nationality or race, in all spheres of economic, government, cultural and other public activity. Freedom of religious worship and freedom of anti-religious propaganda was recognised for all citizens. They were guaranteed freedom of speech, freedom of press, freedom of assembly and freedom of street processions and demonstrations. They were given the right to unite in public organisations.

They were also required to perform certain duties. It was the duty of every citizen to abide by the Constitution, to observe the laws, to maintain labour discipline, honestly to perform public duties and respect the rules of socialist intercourse. It was the duty of every citizen to safeguard and fortify public, socialist property as the source of wealth and might of the country and the prosperity and culture of all working people. Persons committing offences against public or socialist property were the enemies of the people. Universal military service was law. Military service in the armed forces of the USSR was an honourable duty of the citizens of the USSR. To defend the country was a sacred duty of every citizen. Treason to the Motherland was punishable with all its severity of the law as the most heinous of crimes.

The Constitution set up a cabinet form of Government and the Council of Ministers was made responsible and accountable to the Supreme Soviet of the USSR. It also provided for the Presidium of the Supreme Soviet of the USSR.

The Constitution described the Communist Party of the Soviet Union as "the vanguard of the working people in their struggle to strengthen and develop the socialist system." The Communist Party was "the leading core of all organisations of the working people, both public and state." The courts in the Soviet Union were made the organs of the Soviet Socialist State of Workers and Peasants and their duty was "to fight the enemies of the Soviet Government and secondly to fight for the consolidation of the new Soviet system to firmly anchor the new socialist discipline among the working people." The Stalin Constitution remained in force for 41 years and was replaced by the Brezhnev Constitution of 1977.

Purges of 1935-38

During the years 1935-38, there were a series of sensational trials in Russia. Most of the old guard of the Bolshevik Party and some Generals of the Red Army were accused of high treason, tried and disposed of. In January 1935, Zinoviev, the organiser and head of the Third International and Kamenev, Vice-President of the Union Council of People's Commissars, were arrested and charged with the offence of conspiring to murder Stalin with the help of the German secret police. Zinoviev was sentenced to ten years' imprisonment and Kamenev to five years' imprisonment. In August 1936, they were re-tried before the Supreme Military Tribunal and sentenced to be shot. In January 1937, charges of conspiracy to assist foreign aggressors in an attack on the Soviet Union were brought against Radek, a former leader of the Third International, Sokolnikov, former Soviet Ambassador in London and Piatakov. In June 1937, Marshal Tukhachevsky and seven Red Army Generals were convicted and sentenced to death. In the same year, thousands of persons in all walks of life were arrested and punished. Many famous Bolsheviks who were the heroes of the Revolution like Borodin and Bela Kun, were imprisoned or deported or deposed. Even the military judges themselves were eventually liquidated. Six out of the eight military judges who tried the Red Army Generals in 1937 were degraded by the end of 1938. In March 1938, the remaining "old Bolsheviks" were tried and purged. Rykov, Bukharin, Rakovsky and Yagoda were among them. Trotsky who was in exile in Mexico, was murdered in August 1940.

It is contended that the above-mentioned purges were the outcome of the determination of Stalin and his close associates to concentrate all power in their own hands at all costs. "If this is true, the purges take their place in the physiological history of single party totalitarian dictatorship as further evidence that the nemesis of monolithic parties is self-destruction and the price of absolute power is absolute corruption. Only when the entire old guard had been destroyed would Stalin feel secure." Isaac Deutscher, the biographer of Stalin, writes that the chief motive of Stalin was "to destroy the men who represented the potentiality of alternative Government, perhaps not of one but of several alternative Governments. With the long story of Trotskite opposition in mind, Stalin took no chances. His enemies had to die as traitors not martyrs; hence the grossly exaggerated charges and the insatiable thirst for confession."

First Five Year Plan (1928-32)

Planned economic development of the Soviet Union was considered essential for the growth of the country. The development of all branches of the economy had to be coordinated. With the aid of the economic data available at that time, the first Five Year Plan was prepared. It was an extensive programme for the socialist reconstruction of the national economy. The Plan conformed to the general policy of industrialising the country, reconstructing the countryside on socialist lines, overcoming the capitalist forces and strengthening the socialist elements in the economy of the country and boosting the defence capacity of the country. The targets of the Plan were to build a modern highly developed heavy industry and make it possible to begin the reconstruction of the entire national economy, to lay the foundations for the economic independence of the country and to strengthen its defence capacity. The Plan was intended to reorganise the small individual peasant economy into a large-scale collective economy capable of supplying the country with the necessary food and industry with agricultural raw materials. Another object of the Plan was to oust capitalist elements from all branches of the economy and abolish the exploiter class. To fulfil these tasks, the Government planned to invest 64,600 million roubles in five years. The bulk of the investments were channelised into industries producing the means of production. It was planned to increase the gross industrial output by 180% and production of the means of production by 230%. The value of agricultural production was to increase from 16,600 million roubles to 25,800 million roubles.

It is worthy of notice that the people of the Soviet Union launched a mass movement for the fulfilment and over-fulfilment of the Plan under the slogan of "The Five Year Plan in four years". There was a lot of enthusiasm in the country and an important part was played by the young Communist League. The result was that the target of the Five Year Plan was fulfilled in four years and three months. By the close of 1932, all the key target figures of the plan were reached and even surpassed. More than 1500 large industrial enterprises were built. In 1932, the volume of heavy industrial output was more than twice as high as in 1928. Each year the output of the industries producing the means of production increased by more than 28%. The output of consumers' goods industries increased every year by 11.7%. The Plan had provided for the investments of 18,800 million roubles in industry but actually 23,300 million roubles were invested. The share of industry in the gross output increased from 48% in 1927-28 to 70% in 1932. Priority was given to the development of key industries such as engineering, power and iron and steel. The light and food industries did not expand as quickly as the heavy industries. On account of the shortage of raw materials, the textile industry was not able to reach the target. However, the food industry surpassed the plan target.

During the Plan period, the middle peasants began to join the collective farms in large numbers. Collectivisation became a mass movement. Complete collectivisation made it possible to liquidate the Kulaks. Collective farms were supplied with trained personnel, farm machinery, credits, etc. Twenty-five thousand members of the Communist Party and foremost workers were sent to help the implementation of the Party's programme of collectivisation of farms. Many mistakes were committed and Kulaks tried to take advantage of them. The result was that on 1 February 1930, the laws sanctioning the lease of land and employment of hired labour by private households in areas of total collectivisation were repealed. The Kulaks were turned out by the peasants themselves. It is pointed out that the success of the collective farms was a revolutionary change in agriculture which uprooted capitalism on the countryside. Private ownership of means of production was supplanted by socialist property.

In 1932, private trade was abolished. The State built thousands of shops, warehouses and commercial bases and trained a large number of trade workers. On account of the shortage of consumer's goods rationing was introduced in that area. The Soviet Union exported grain, butter, oil products, ore, timber, etc., and imported machines, plants and industrial raw materials. Capital goods formed 93% of the total imports.

It was during the first Five Year Plan that illiteracy was completely wiped out from the country. A system of universal primary education was introduced. A large number of technical schools and institutions of higher learning were set up. The circulation of newspapers and magazines increased tremendously. Radio stations, cinemas, reading rooms, theatres, etc., were constructed in various parts of the country.

As regards the achievements of the first Five Year Plan, industrial production went up by 70% of that in 1928. The number of workers was doubled. Seven-hour day was enforced in the country. Real wages went up by 50%. Unemployment disappeared.

Second Five Year Plan (1933-1938)

The main objective of the Second Five Year Plan was to remove the remaining capitalist elements and make the socialist mode of production the only mode of production in the country. The entire economy was to be re-equipped and built on a new technical basis resting on the heavy industry. The collective farms were to be further consolidated. The defence capacity of the country was also to be increased. The Second Five Year Plan allocated 1,33,400 million roubles for capital construction. Industrial output was to increase by over 100%. Attention was focussed on machine building electrical engineering, metallurgy and other branches of heavy industry. Chemical industry was also to be developed. New techniques and new industries were expected to increase the productivity of labour by 63%. All transport facilities, particularly the railways, were to be radically improved.

As in the case of the First Five Year Plan, the targets of the Second Five Year Plan were fulfilled by 1 April, 1937, that is, in four years and three months only. The fixed production assets of the engineering and metal working industries were increased by 200%. Gross output in these industries rose to 283%. The output of steel surpassed that of pig iron. The power industry expanded rapidly. Railway transport was improved immensely. The light and food industries made good progress. The rates of agricultural development were lower than those in industry. Collectivisation of farms was completed. Once a land of small individual peasants, the Soviet Union became a country of world's biggest collective agriculture. The ranks of the working class intelligentsia were increased by six million. Unemployment was wiped out. Wages of factory and office workers were doubled. The income of workers on collective farms rose by 170%. The output of sugar rose by 100%. All commerce and trade came in the hands of the state and co-operatives. Rationing was abolished in 1935.

Third Five Year Plan

The Third Five Year Plan was started in 1938. It was under way when the Soviet Union was attacked by Germany on 22 June 1941. When the War started, the Plan was converted into a war munition plan to meet the enemy.

Estimate

It cannot be denied that the Soviet Union made a lot of progress under the Communists. Production was enormously increased in every field. From a backward economy, the Soviet Union came to have a forward-looking economy. As a result of industrialisation and development of heavy industries, the country came to have its own base for further development. By 1941, she had become so strong that she was able to withstand the onslaughts of the German hordes. Illiteracy was practically wiped out. The Russians got security of their jobs. The State looked after them in many ways. They had nothing to fear from old age, sickness or unemployment. The administration of justice, excepting the political offences, was made humane. Much was done to improve the health of the people. A lot of progress was made in the field of sanitation and the death rate was lowered. Equality was attained for men and women in all spheres. The lot of the ordinary people improved. They found more interest in their lives. The Communist leaders were always, anxious to improve the lot of the common people. The communist regime gave the people of Russia a new outlook. They could look to the future with confidence. The Communists made Russia a great Power.

For achieving all this, the people of Russia had to pay a price. They had to do what their leaders said. Any disagreement was to be seriously dealt with. There was always the possibility of losing one's life. There was more of equality but less of liberty. The people of Russia sacrificed their liberty to make their country strong and great.

SUGGESTED READINGS

Becker, C.: **Modern History,** 1939.
Benns, F.L.: **Europe Since** 1914.
Benns, F.L.: **European History Since** 1870.
Brunn, G.: **The World in the Twentieth Century,** 1952.
Chamberlain, W. H.: **Soviet Russia.**
Ergang, Robert: **Europe in Our Time,** 1953.
Ergang, Robert : **Europe Since Waterloo,** 1954.
Florinsky, M.T.: **Russia, A History and an Interpretation,** 1953.
Grant, A.J. and Temperly H.: **Europe in the 19th and 20th Centuries.**
Hall, P.H. and Davis, S.D.: **The Course of Europe Since Waterloo,** 1951.
Hayes, C.J.H.: **A Political and Cultural History of Modern Europe.**
Hazen, C.D.: **Modern European History.**
Kulski, W.W.: **The Soviet Regime,** 1954.
Ogg, F.A. and Zink, H.: **Modern Foreign Governments.**
Pares, B.: **History of Russia.**
Riker, T.W.: **History of Modern Europe,** 1948.
Ross, E.A.: **Russia in Upheaval.**
Schapiro, J.P.: **Modern and Contemporary European History.**
Schevill, F.: **A History of Europe from the Reformation to the Present Day.**

CHAPTER

44 THE INDUSTRIAL REVOLUTION

The term "Industrial Revolution" was coined by Auguste Blanqui, a French economist, in 1837 to denote the economic and social changes arising out of the transition from industries carried in the homes with simple instruments, to industries in factories with power-driven machinery in Britain, but it came into vogue when Arnold Toynbee, the great historian, used it in 1882. However, historians question the appropriateness of the term on the ground that the Industrial Revolution covers a period far too long to justify a single label. The period is from about 1740 to about 1850 in Britain and from 1815 to the end of the nineteenth century in Europe. Moreover, the term "Revolution" is misleading for describing a complicated series of forces, processes and discoveries which worked very slowly but gradually and created a new economic organisation. It is contended that it is better to call it evolution and not revolution. It is also suggested that instead of calling it the Industrial Revolution, it should be called "The Transition of Industrialism". In spite of these objections, the term industrial Revolution is preferred and is in common usage.

Upto the middle of eighteenth century, European society was mainly agricultural. Whatever industries there were, were confined to the "domestic" sphere. There was no machinery or water-power or steam to work those industries. Manual labour was the chief source of power. Each village was practically self-sufficient. There was not much of inter-village trade. Roads were in a very bad condition and travelling was extremely risky and inconvenient. Practically, each villager took to some small industry to supplement his income. There was no large-scale corporate industry. The individual worker worked as a single unit.

The Industrial Revolution brought a series of changes in the methods of manufacture, production and distribution and drastically affected the economic and social life of the people. It transformed an overwhelmingly agricultural society into an industrial society. This revolution was not a revolution in the normal sense of the word. Revolutions are generally associated with suddenness, violence and bloodshed. However, the Industrial Revolution was free from all these characteristics. It was a long, slow process of change, beginning obscurely, we cannot say precisely when, and only ending recently, if indeed it has ended yet.

Why its beginning in England?

Political and economic conditions in England in the latter half of the eighteenth century were the most suitable for the beginning of the Industrial Revolution in that country. It enriched her and gave her a lead over all other European countries. It spread to the main Continent of Europe and further abroad almost fifty years later. It influenced Belgium, France and the United States only after the fall of Napoleon in 1815. Germany was affected still later and the East European countries continued to be mostly agricultural right upto the end of the nineteenth century.

The Industrial Revolution was preceded by Agrarian Revolution in England. Jethro Tull (1674-1741) invented a drill which deposited the seeds in straight furrows with adequate space in between to help luxuriant growth. Tull is rightly called the father of scientific agriculture. Viscount Townshend

(1674-1738) turned his lands into an agricultural laboratory. He is called the founder of the innovation commonly known as the rotation of crops. In the past, every piece of cultivable land was left fallow for a year after two years of consecutive cultivation to recuperate itself which meant that every year one-third of arable area grew no crops. Through his experiments, Townshend showed that the existing method was wasteful and suggested that if root crops and artificial grasses were alternately grown on the same piece of land in successive season with grain, depletion in the mineral salts required for healthy growth of plants would be minimal. He recommended a system of four-year rotation which means wheat in the first year followed by turnips in the second, barley in the third and cloves in the fourth. By this system of rotation of crops, Townshend doubled his income. As he popularised the growth of a new plant called turnip, Townshend got the nickname of "Turnip" Townshend. In the field of cattle-breeding, Robert Backwell tried in 1750 a novel method of mating the finest specimens with a certain breed and then making their offsprings mate with offsprings of better breeds of species. The result was that more meat was available for human consumption at cheaper rates. At the end of the eighteenth century, iron ploughs drawn by horses began to displace wooden ploughs drawn by oxen. A new threshing machine displaced the existing threshing implement. In 1834, McCormick developed a new reaper which revolutionized the process of harvesting. Increased agricultural output was achieved by the new trend of *enclosures*. In the past, agricultural areas had no fences. Cultivation was in strips and no cultivator had all his strips located at one place. Much land was wasted because pathways had to be made to enable a cultivator to go from one strip of his own to another. Enterprising landlords started enclosing the common land, reclaiming marshland, consolidating their strips into "unified fenced off fields" by brow-beating or intimidatory tactics. They also got passed through Parliament Enclosure Acts which enabled the landlords to add millions of acres of land to their estates. It caused hardship to the poorer classes but land came increasingly under the strict control of private ownership and management. This encouraged greater investment by landowners and higher production was the result. Food supply increased substantially as new methods of cattle-breeding meant fatter cattle yielding more meat and also more cereals. England virtually became the "granary of Europe". Those persons who were forced to leave their lands on the countryside, came to cities and thus labour was available in England for the new factories which came into existence as a result of the Industrial Revolution. It is rightly said that agricultural revolution in England paved the way for Industrial Revolution. The latter would not have been possible without the former. With abundant food, surplus labour, requisite managerial skill, forward-looking entrepreneurs and willing bankers, the ground for Industrial Revolution was well prepared in England.

Ship-building was an old and popular industry in England. England had a powerful navy which had defeated all her rivals like the Dutch and the French. She was the undisputed mistress of the seas. This enabled her to build up an enormous and lucrative trade. Her ships sailed to many parts of the world and brought raw material, tobacco, tea, sugar, spices and cotton in large quantities. England acquired a number of colonies and founded a few settlements. British expansion beyond the seas opened up new vistas of foreign trade. Her expanding foreign trade made it necessary that her exports should keep pace with imports. It was necessary to step up domestic industries to meet the increased demands. If England was to become the richest country of the world, more and more goods for export must be manufactured to capture foreign markets. That required great effort. Stakes were high and the prize was worth attaining. The English capitalists and inventors rose to the occasion. There was a strong urge among the people to improve production and that prompted the people to make a number of inventions.

Nature was specially kind to England. She had given England vast stores of iron and coal which are the life-blood of industry. They were found in abundance in close proximity to each other in Lancashire and Yorkshire. Both of these minerals were needed in the manufacture of machines and production of steam. Moreover, the moist climate of England was ideally suited to the manufacture of cotton textiles.

The Bank of England which was started in 1694 and the National Debt were institutions of great importance. They were brought into existence to provide ready money to finance the war against Louis XIV Loans were made available to the state on the security of the taxes. In peaceful times, that money was available for economic and industrial development at a nominal rate of interest. "The engines of the Industrial Revolution which made England so rich and powerful that she was able to stand the strain of Napoleonic wars, were moved by the oil of finance, and at the heart of the English financial system stood the Bank."

Political condition in England was also favourable for Industrial Revolution. England was a free country. Her parliamentary system of Government had become stable and there were no political upheavals to disturb, domestic peace, unlike France and other European countries. Peaceful political conditions provided a suitable environment for the growth and development of commerce and industry. The capitalists of England felt secure in investing money in them and were not afraid of a change of Government.

Englishmen had established wide contacts with different countries of the world. Their spirit of adventure which was confined to maritime activity, was now turned to other spheres. A large number of talented English workers applied their energy and knowledge to industrial development and invented a large number of machines.

No other country in Europe had so many potentialities for industrial development. Forces were favourable for a change in England. The Industrial Revolution provided England with money for her wars against Revolutionary France and Napoleon. As a matter of fact, those wars gave a further fillip to the English Industrial Revolution and encouraged greater production. "Napoleon's career enabled the Industrial Revolution to go forward in England and the Industrial Revolution enabled England to overthrow Napoleon."

Cotton Industry. The Industrial Revolution was mainly confined to developments in the fields of cotton industry, mining and transport. As regards cotton industry, the urge to increase production of cotton cloth led men to apply their knowledge and energy to invent machines and a number of weaving and spinning machines were invented. In 1733, John Kay invented what was known as "The Flying Shuttle". This doubled the speed of weaving and saved labour considerably. This invention enabled the weavers to turn out greater output. It made possible the weaving of broad cloth by one man. In 1765, James Hargreaves invented a machine known as "The Spinning Jenny". The new machine had 8 spindles and consequently one spinner was able to do the work of 8 spinners. The Spinning Jenny was a simple wooden frame on which 8 spindles moved by the turning of a wheel.

In 1769, Richard Arkwright (1732-1792) invented "Waterframe". This machine consisted of a series of rollers and was run by water power or horse power. It helped the manufacture of hard and firm yarn suitable for weaving. The rollers could not work in small places and consequently the water-frame of Arkwright ushered in the factory system. That is why he has been called the "parent of the factory system."

In 1779, Samuel Crompton (1763-1827) invented a machine known as "The Mule". The new machine combined the advantages of the Spinning Jenny of Hargreaves and water-frame of Arkwright. It made the production of fine muslin possible.

In 1785, Edmund Cartwright invented what was called "The Power Loom". Although the Power Loom was clumsy in shape, it helped the work of weaving to be done with great speed.

In 1793, Whitney invented a machine by which seeds could be separated from the cotton fibres. Previously, this was done with the help of hand and that was a slow process.

In 1785, cylinder printing was invented. A roller with a design engraved upon it ran over the paper. In 1800, a speedy method of bleaching with the help of chemicals was found. The result was that it was not necessary to expose cloth to the sun for weeks for drying it. Likewise, the help of industrial chemistry was taken for dyeing purposes.

Mining and Metallurgy. As regards mining and metallurgy, wood was used for smelting iron in old days. That process was long and tedious. There was also the danger of denuding the country of her forests. It was found that coal was a much better substitute for wood. Coal was available in abundance but the problem was how to take it out of the mines which got flooded with water. Inventors began to pay attention to the problem of pumping out water.

Thomas Newcomen (1663-1729) invented a steam engine which helped the miners in pumping out water quickly. There were many defects in the engine. It wasted a good deal of heat and fuel and sometimes it did not start. Its defects were removed by the invention of James Watt. Abraham Derby used coke successfully for smelting iron but its quality was crude. In 1784, Henry Cort (1740-1800) discovered better processes to improve the quality.

The steam engine revolutionized industry and mining. As motive power, steam had a distinct advantage over water power. It was not necessary now to set up factories near waterfalls. Steam could be produced anywhere and everywhere. James Watt (1736-1819) studied the steam engine of Newcomen and removed its defects and invented a new engine with a separate condenser. The new engine was called Beelzebub. It was first employed in mines. Later on, the invention of the rotary motion brought the steam engine into cotton factories also. Steam replaced horse and water power in the textile industry also.

There was a great demand for steam engines. With the financial assistance of Boulton, James Watt began to produce steam engines for industrial purposes. "The union of machinery with steam force multiplied tremendously the resources of mankind".

On account of the lack of precision tools, James Watt had great difficulty in making the steam engine. Maudslay's "Slide-Rest" was a great invention which helped considerably in the making of such tools.

Transport. As regards transport, the old roads were in a very bad condition. Navigation by sea and river was very slow. There were yet no railways or aeroplanes. There was the necessity of improving the means of transport.

John Metcalf, Thomas Telford and John Macadam (1756-1836) made tremendous improvements in the art of road construction. Gravel, stone and tar were used in making pucca roads and a network of roads was laid all over the country. Travelling by coach became more comfortable and transport quicker. According to a distinguished British historian, "Macadamising was not only, in its liberal sense, a practical work of great public utility; it became a symbol of all progress and was metaphorically used in common, parlance for any aspect of a new age where improved and uniform scientific methods were in demand."

As heavy goods could not be carried to distant places by means of roads, it was decided to use water for transport purposes. The Duke of Bridgewater (1736-1803) employed Brindley (1716-1772) to design the Bridgewater Canal from Worsely to Manchester. After that, Mersey and Calder canals were dug.

George Stephenson (1781-1848) is called the father of steam locomotive. He invented the first locomotive for hauling coal over iron rails. It moved at a speed of 3 miles an hour. Gradually, it was improved. By 1823, a locomotive factory was established at Newcastle. At the opening of the Liverpool-Manchester Railway in 1830, the locomotive moved at the speed of 30 miles an hour. The invention of locomotives and introduction of railways were a great boon to mankind. It became possible to transport goods more speedily and cheaply from one part of the country to another.

The motive power of steam was also applied to transport by sea. In 1807, a steamboat constructed by Robert Fulton sailed from New York to Albany, a distance of 150 miles in 32 hours. The first regular steamboat service in Great Britain was inaugurated in 1812 on the Clyde between Glasgow and Greenock by a boat called the Comet. In 1819, the first steamship, the Savannah, crossed the Atlantic from the United States to England in 29 days with the help of sails. In 1838, two steamers crossed the Atlantic without sails in 18 and 15 days respectively. Until about 1870, sailing vessels competed successfully with steamships. After 1878, steamships demonstrated their superiority. Early steamships were made of wood. In 1843 the first iron steamship crossed the Atlantic.

Communication. A lot of improvement was made in the means of communication. In the middle of the nineteenth century, Charles Wheat-stone with the collaboration of two Americans Samuel Morse (1791-1872) and Alfred Vail produced the electric telegraph. It was due to the joint efforts of Sir Charles Bright and Cyrus Field that the first Atlantic telegraphic communication across water was laid in 1866. Telephone owes its origin to Philip Reis, a German inventor.

Michael Faraday (1791-1867) invented electro-magnetic induction in 1831. In 1839, Louis Daguerre (1789-1851) devised a method of photography by mercury vapour development of silver iodite exposed on a copper plate. In 1836, John Ericsson (1803-1889), a naval engineer, built the Monitor, the screw-propeller. In 1844, Charles Goodyear (1800-1860) invented rubber vulcanisation. In 1856, Sir Henry Bessemer (1813-1898) invented the so-called "Bessemer process" of making steel direct from cast-iron, for rails, ship plates, etc. by forcing a blast of air through the molten metal in order to burn out the impurities. Then came the "open-hearth process" of making use of a shallow hearth of reverberating type for the large-scale manufacture of steel.

As the Industrial Revolution progressed machinery became more and more complicated and expensive. It was beyond the financial resources of single individual to instal factories. Hence arose the necessity for co-operative effort. There sprang up Corporations and limited companies in which thousands of people invested their money in the hope of gaining good dividends. The system of individual industrial proprietorship yielded place to joint stock companies and managing directorships. There also arose the demand for the services of engineers to man the new machines and to invent new ones to keep pace with the demand for greater production. By 1828, the Civil Engineers Society was founded in London. Specialisation in industry required a variety of engineers such as mechanical, mining, road, marine, electrical engineers. They built up new industries and improved the old ones. England became the workshop of the world. English industrial capital and English engineers sought new avenues of investment and work in foreign countries and companies with English capital and English technicians were floated in many foreign countries. Thus, the benefits of the English Industrial Revolution were spread far and wide.

More and more complicated industrial machinery could thrive on the inventions and discoveries of scientists. Progress in industrial inventions benefited the development of the Industrial Revolution proportionately.

The Safety Lamp of Davy was a boon to miners. Faraday's invention of electroplating of iron plates with nickel stopped rusting and increased the life of machines. Siemen's dynamo supplemented steam power. Bunsen's electric lighting made life more cheerful. Kelvin enabled submarine cables to be laid between America and England. Clement's planing machine, Nasmyth's steam hammer and machine for cutting grooves in metal, Robert's drilling machine and Bessemer and Siemen processes for large-scale conversion of iron into steel revolutionized and expanded industry. The cotton and wool industries became more and more mechanised. The expansion of steam navigation was phenomenal. The steamships could now cross the Atlantic and other seas without fear. Steamship companies like the Cunard Lines were inaugurated.

A variety of other industries like building, furniture making, laundering, brewing and shoe-making also made tremendous progress. Food preservation, canning industry, gas-lighting and heating and a number of electrical appliances gave more amenities to the people. The invention of the telegraph made transmission of news from one place to another quicker and cheaper and that enabled the newspapers to publish news of the world.

Rubber and petroleum industries expanded tremendously. Rubber pipes, tyres and washers were available in large quantities. Petroleum products proved of great value to men and industry. Weapons of warfare were also improved. The old flint-lock muskets were substituted by breech-loading grooved rifles whose striking power was several times greater. Richard Gatling, an American, invented the first machinegun which could fire 350 shots a minute.

Industrial Development in England. The period between 1830 and 1848 was the heroic age of railway building. To begin with, rail-roads were resisted by the existing interests of roads and canals. There were people who had advanced money for making and repairing the turnpike roads and canals. There were people who were making a living as coach-makers, harness-makers, horse-dealers, inn-keepers, etc. The first attempt to get through Parliament a bill permitting the making of the rail-road between Liverpool and Manchester, failed. It cost £ 70,000 to secure parliamentary permission in 1826 even before starting the capital outlay needed to buy the land and construct the line. British railroad builders were pioneers and they incurred the costs and burdens of all pioneers and paid the price for technical experiments and mistakes. The opening of the Liverpool and Manchester Railway in 1830 inaugurated the new era. By 1838, there were 490 miles of railroad in England and Wales and 50 in Scotland. Their construction cost more than £ 13 million. By the end of 1850, there were 6,621 miles of rail-road in operation. The two boom periods of building came in 1836 and in the years 1844-47. In spite of wild speculations and financial disasters in 1847, there was considerable consolidation of lines which had been built piecemeal. George Hudson, the British "Railway king", devoted his business and administrative skill to bring about extensive amalgamations and improvements in their general running.

The revolution in transport through railways brought with it new demands for coal and iron and stimulated a revolution in heavy industries, especially mining and metallurgy. Britain's coal output which was about 16 million tons in 1815, rose to 30 million tons by 1835 and 50 million tons by 1848. Her output of iron doubled from one million tons in 1835 to two million tons in 1848. By 1850, about half the whole world's production of pig iron took place in Great Britain. Engineering proper and the industries devoted to making machines, were still small-scale in 1848. The main progress in engineering techniques came after 1848. The railroads encouraged the rise of big contractors. They offered employment to thousands. A great new industry was born in little more than 20 years and the fears of unemployment proved to be unfounded. There was a general stimulus to the whole economic system.

Above all other commodities, cotton was linked with the expansion of British overseas trade. In 1830, three-quarters of the new cotton came from the United States. In 1849, the total import was as high as 346,000 tons, worth about £ 15 million. By the middle of the nineteenth century, more than half a million people were engaged in cotton industry alone. Textiles as a whole employed more than one million. Textile manufacture was the industry which was most representative of the age of machinery and power. Although mechanization was slow, cotton set the pace in factory production.

Cotton trade boosted shipping. Between 1827 and 1848, the total tonnage of British shipping, both sail and steam, rose from 2½ to 4 million tons. At the middle of the 19th century, 60 per cent of the world's ocean-going tonnage was British. The tonnage of all shipping entered and cleared from ports in the United Kingdom rose from 6 million tons in 1834 to more than 14 million tons in 1847. By 1850, the United Kingdom had established herself as not only "the workshop of the world" but also as the shipper, trader and to a great extent the banker of the world.

Belgium. Industrial development in Belgium was facilitated because important coal fields were discovered there. The Government in that country played a notable part when its funds were channelled into shipbuilding and manufactures.

Belgium set the pace in rail-road building. Her rich supplies of coal and the spirit of national enterprise, released particularly after her independence in 1830, made possible an Industrial Revolution comparable in intensity, if not in scale, with that of Great Britain. The line from Brussels to Malines was opened in 1835. It carried in its first year more than half a million passengers. This was more than the passengers carried by all the British lines in 1835. Belgium was ahead of Britain in having a railway policy and in planning rail-road construction as a national concern to serve national needs. The railway lines were designed to take full advantages of the geographical and economic position of Belgium as a land of passage. The lines were planned to link up England, France, Germany and Holland and make Belgium the commercial entrepot of Western Europe. The plan began in 1834 and was completed within ten years. Throughout that period, Belgium produced more coal than France. Liege and Southern Hainault were the first developed coal-mining areas of the Continent of Europe. The Liege district was a well established metallurgical centre. Belgium sent machinery all over Holland, Germany and even Russia. Her spirit of national enterprise and traditions of craftsmanship, her urban society and her network of railways gave her an economic lead in Europe second only to Great Britain.

After her independence in 1830, the Government gave financial help for the construction of railways and by 1850, about 900 kilometres of rail were laid. Private entrepreneurs were also encouraged to invest. During the 1850s and 1860s the Government virtually withdrew from the field and private investors were allowed to develop private lines rapidly which rose from 150 kilometres in 1850 to 2,100 kilometres in 1870. Thereafter, the state again entered the field competing with private lines. The output of coal, iron and textiles went up steeply. Upto 1870, Belgium was self-sufficient in its entire requirements of food. After that, she was able even to export its agricultural products which between 1840 and 1900 touched high figure of 50 per cent.

France. On the eye of the French Revolution, the textile mills of Abbevilla employed 12,000 workers. The Anzin Mining Company employed about 4,000 workers. In Paris, there were about 50 "manufactories" and they employed between 700 and 800 workers. The workers were subjected to quasi-military type of discipline. Napoleon took keen interest in the matter. Many French industrialists and technicians visited England, purchased English machines and even hired English workers. All this was under the patronage of the Government. Between 1788 and 1812, the number of looms in France increased from 7,000 to 17,000 and workers from 76,000 to 131,000. There were 452 mines with 43,305 workers, 41 iron works with 1,202 workers, 1,219 forges with 7,120 workers and 98 sugar refineries with 585 workers. It has been estimated that French industry reached by 1815 the level of mechanization of England in 1780.

After the French Revolution, the pace of mechanization did not pick up because the ruling elite in France was not mechanically minded. The landed proprietors were also not interested in mechanization. In 1832, horse power of French industry was under 1,000. By 1848, it increased seven times. In England, even in 1820s, six times more horse power was used. French coal production in 1790 was about one-twentieth of that of England. During the July Monarchy (1830-1848), the increase was three times which was inadequate to meet her requirements. The output of iron ore went up only two times. It took long before modern methods of smelting were adopted in France. The use of charcoal in furnaces continued in France till the World War I (1914-18). The development of roads and railways in France was faster but there was the difficulty of adequate funds at the beginning. However, the Government of Louis Philippe gave sufficient funds for that purpose. A law was passed in 1836 for the construction and upkeep of local roads. From 1830 to 1848, the length of canals was doubled. Railway construction was slow in France on account of a controversy. The governing elite opposed the investment of funds on railway construction. Even a man like Thiers (1797-1877) resisted it. Private capitalists were not coming forward for the construction of railways. Ultimately, a law was passed in 1842 which provided that capital for railway construction was to be jointly contributed by public authorities and private interests. The authorities were responsible for providing the "infrastructure" such as land, track, bridges and tunnels. They were also asked to provide much of "super-structure" such as stations, rails, equipment, etc. The state was given representation on the boards of management and also retained the right to nationalise the lines after the expiry of the prescribed concession period. From 1844 to 1846, France was in the grip of its first railway mania. By 1846, France had railway lines approximately 1,800 kilometres. However, many small local lines went bankrupt in 1847. In 1848, the length of French railways was only 1,921 kilometres. The boom revived under Napoleon III (1852-1870). Private initiative was encouraged by guaranteeing assured interest on investment. The result was that while railways in 1851 were under 4,000 kilometres, they went upto 7,000 in 1857 and 17,000 in 1870.

The construction of railways boosted the production of coal and iron. The consumption of coal was trebled between 1851 and 1871. In the same period, the use of horse power in industry went up five times. The average price of steel was almost cut by half. The greatest iron works at Le Creusot which produced 5,000 tons in 1,836 was able to produce 18,000 tons in 1847. Iron output increased from 35,000 tons in 1855 to 133,000 tons in 1867. During the same period, foreign commerce increased three times.

By 1846, there were hardly more than a million workers employed in large-scale industries in France. They were congested into a few big towns and industrial areas—the cotton textile areas of Alsace, Normandy and the Nord, the metallurgical areas of Lorraine and the basin of the Loire and the silk area around Lyon. This means an abnormal growth of a few towns. In the ten years from 1831 to 1841, Saint Etienne grew from a population of 16,000 to 54,000 and Roubaix from 8,000 to 34,000. The unregulated employment of women and children for long hours in bad factory conditions exposed the industrial workers not only to insanitary living conditions and hardships but also to widespread tuberculosis and epidemics of cholera which ravaged France in 1831-32 and 1847-48. It was found in 1840 that out of every 10,000 youngmen drafted for military service in France, 9,000 had to be rejected as medically unfit.

Germany. The mechanization of industry came comparatively late in Germany. In 1815, the German states as a whole were far more rural in character than France. There were a few trading towns of some size like Hamburg and Frankfurt but there was no city comparable to Paris. The largest city was Berlin with a population of about 150,000. Of the 1,016 towns, only 18 had more than 10,000 inhabitants. 73.5 per cent population of Germany was definitely rural. The unit of production was the small shop. In most industries, guilds still played an important role. It is true that their power had been broken but in many states the guild regulations continued in force. Methods of trade were backward. As a rule, craftsmen sold their goods directly to the consumers at the weekly markets and fairs. Economically, most of the Germans were living in the Middle Ages.

There were many reasons for this state of affairs. The political division of Germany was an obstacle to commerce and industry. Each of the 39 states into which Germany was divided was a law unto itself in economic matters. Trade was obstructed by tariff barriers and differences in the systems of coinage, weights and measures. Each state, whether small or big, had its own laws. So long as the states remained as separate units, no industrial development could be expected. German markets were not sufficiently large to absorb the products of large-scale production. German manufacturers had no outlets for their products. The home market in Germany was limited by the difficulties of transportation. Germany as a whole was ill-provided with roads. After the Napoleonic Wars, the roads in Germany were so bad that it was difficult and at times impossible, to move even food supplies except in dry seasons. German manufacturers were hampered by the lack of free capital. Germany had not reaped the advantages of a profitable foreign trade. As a matter of fact, it had suffered from the devastating effects of the Napoleonic Wars. It was a poor country in every sense of the term. There was no surplus capital which could be used in industrial enterprises. Banking and credit facilities were lacking. The so-called banks of Germany were only places for money changing. Credit facilities were in an elementary stage. During the first decade and a half after the Napoleonic Wars, there was practically no progress. Sombart writes, "I believe it will not be amiss to assume that the economic condition of the people was worse in 1830 than in 1802."

After 1830, a movement began which gained momentum after 1850. In that development, Prussia took the lead. The Prussian Government had freed the serfs in the first decade of the nineteenth century and thereby created a supply of free labour. During the same period, it abolished the guild restrictions and thereby established industrial freedom which permitted each person to choose his own trade. Power machinery was introduced there slowly. In 1846, less than four per cent of the cotton looms of Prussia were driven by power. Industrial development along factory lines made headway after the middle of the nineteenth century. Upto 1850, coke smelting furnaces were rare. After that, improved methods were introduced rapidly. The railway era was inaugurated by the Prussian state in 1848 when work began on the railway running from Berlin towards the Russian border.

The state of Prussia took an important step towards the economic unification of Germany by establishing the Zollverein or the Customs Union. When it was started on 1 January, 1834, the Zollverein included 18 states. During the subsequent period, its membership was extended until it included most of the German states. Within the framework of the Zollverein, traffic among the states was made free from customs barriers of every kind. The aim of the Union included the establishment of uniform coinage, weights and measures.

The Zollverein proved to be a stimulant to industrial development after 1850. The consumption of raw cotton in Germany arose from about 28,000 tons in 1851 to about 50,000 tons in 1865. The annual consumption of silk increased from 300 tons in 1840 to 950 tons in 1870. A beginning was made in the systematic exploitation of the natural resources of coal and iron. The production of iron ore quadrupled during the two decades from 1850 to 1870. The production of coal increased from three million tons in 1846 to 18½ million tons in 1867 and nearly 30 million tons by 1871. During that period, the modern credit banks appeared. Rail-roads were extended until Germany had 11,501 miles of rail-roads by 1870.

By the time of the establishment of the German Empire in 1871, she got rich lands of Alsace and Lorraine from France in 1871. From 1871 to 1914, Germany became the most powerful state in Europe. She already produced more coal than France in 1850. Both countries almost doubled their coal production from 1850 to 1860. Between 1850 and 1880, France multiplied her production by a little more than four and Germany by nearly ten. Coal production in Germany was dependent on the building of railways which in their turn needed greater coal production. The use of the steam engine to accelerate transport on land and sea was important for Germany.

Italy. Like Germany, Italy was divided into many states. The pace of industrial development in Italy was fitful and varied from state to state. There came into existence many industrial complexes mostly located in Northern Italy. The industrialisation of Italy picked up real momentum after the completion of her unification in 1870.

The Austrian Empire. Although Maria Theresa (1717-1780) adopted a policy of selective industrialisation, its pace was slow. There were many conflicting ethnic, political and economic issues which stood in the way of her progress.

Russia. In mid-eighteenth century, Russia produced more cast iron than England and France and twice as much as Germany. However, her production of cast iron was surpassed by Britain in 1805, by France in 1828 and Germany and Austria in 1855. It seems curious that while Russian diplomatic prestige and influence was at its highest in Central and Western Europe from 1815 to 1854, her economic life was primitive. Before the Crimean War (1854-1856), the great majority of Russians never handled money but gave services and received payments in kind. At the village markets, trade was mostly carried on by barter. A money economy developed in Russia after the Crimean War partly because of emancipation of serfs, partly because of the export of wheat abroad and partly because of the building of railways. Until the 1860s, industries remained merely unimportant supplements to agriculture. Industrial workers often worked in factories only in winter and returned to land in summer.

Russia was handicapped by the location of her mineral wealth. The iron ore of the Urals was far from the areas of dense population and from the coal needed for smelting iron ore. To take the products of the Urals to Moscow and St. Petersburg, canals and rivers had to be used. That could be done only when the weather conditions were favourable. The iron ore of the Krivoi Rog region and the coal of the Donetz region were equally remote from Moscow and St. Petersburg and the great rivers flowed in the wrong direction. Hence, the building of railways was of vital importance for the economy of Russia. Unlike the countries of Western Europe, Russia began to acquire a railway network before industrialisation had started. In 1843, the Government built a line from Warsaw to the Polish-Austrian frontier, on the way to Vienna. In 1851, the line from St. Petersburg to Moscow was completed. By 1855, there were only 660 miles of railway track in Russia. Under Alexander II, encouragement was given to investment in the railways by Reutern, the Minister of Finance. By 1861, there were a thousand miles of railway trade. In 1880, there were 14,000 miles of railway track.

From a completely unindustrialised society in 1860, production of coal and iron was building up in the period to 1880. From 1860 to 1876, coal production multiplied itself by 16 and steel production by ten. Russian industry was born fully grown. A few large factories, rather than many small ones, was the pattern. In 1879, about 40 per cent of the industrial workers were in factories employing more than a thousand men. That was partly due to the role played by the state in the Industrial Revolution in Russia. In 1860, the State Bank, was founded. Capital was made available for industry and industrial enterprises were run by the Government. In 1857, the Russian Government founded a railway by decree.

In economic terms, Poland was the most modern part of the Russian Empire. Polish industry developed quickly from small beginnings in the 1870s. The textile industry was the first to be modernised. Poland began training her own engineers and technicians. Coal and iron industries were developed in the South-West.

The Balkans. Most of the Balkan states were under the Ottoman Empire and they remained insulated from European industrialisation.

Industrial Expansion After 1870. If the forty years from 1830 to 1870 saw a veritable "Industrial Revolution" in Great Britain and the preparatory stage in Western and Central Europe and in Eastern North America, the next forty years from 1870 to 1910 were marked by a progressive output of industries already largely mechanised, a rapid evolution of novel industries and a transformation of agricultural into industrial population. These developments applied equally to Britain, European states and the United States. During this period, the number of engineers and scientists, physicists and chemists multiplied and they allied themselves to machine industry. A large number of polytechnic schools and schools of applied sciences were set up in all countries which aspired to be civilised and progressive. Tools of precision were multiplied.

Coal Iron and Steel. The production of coal and iron was speeded up during this period. British production of coal increased from 100 million tons in 1870 to 265 million tons in 1910. Likewise, production of pig iron increased from six to nine million tons. In Germany, the output of coal increased from 37½ million tons to 222 million tons. It increased in France from sixteen to forty million tons. In the United States, it increased from 35 to 415 million tons. The output of pig iron in Germany increased from two million tons to about 15 million tons. In France, it increased from 1½ million tons to five million tons. In the United States, it increased from 1-2/3 to 27-1/3 million tons. There was an improvement in the Bessemer and Siemens processes for the manufacture of steel. The steam locomotives were improved. There was further expansion of railways not only in Europe but also in the United States, Canada, Australia, Latin America, Asia and Africa. By 1905, Trans-Siberian railway linked Moscow and Western Europe with Vladivostok on the Pacific Ocean. The steamships increased in numbers, size and speed. Regular services were multiplied for passengers and goods from London and Liverpool, Hamburg and Bremen, Le Havre and Marseilles, Antwerp and Rotterdam, Genoa and Trieste, New York and Montreal, Yokohama and Shanghai, Bombay and Melbourne, Cape Town and Buenos Aires.

Textile Industry. The textile industry kept on growing during this period. In Britain, the number of spindles increased from 36,700,000 in 1870 to 53,500,000 in 1910. The number of power looms increased from 475,000 to 700,000. In 1870, Britain possessed more spindles, and power looms than all the rest of the world put together, but in 1910, it had only about 40 per cent of the spindles and 30 per cent of power looms. In 1910, there were 37,200,000 spindles on the Continent of Europe, 27,800,000 in the United States and 10,000,000 in other parts of the world. There were similar improvements in the other textile industries of wool and linen. The silk industry of France and Italy was mechanized and expanded. Search of artificial silk led to rayon. There was a steady progress in applying chemistry to the dyeing of fabrics. A large number of chemical dyes were derived from coal tar. With the improvement of machines, enlargement of factories and increase in markets, there was a mounting output of cutlery, porcelain, tinware, boots and shoes, paper, furniture, tools, fire-arms and other implements of war. The machinegun was improved and made automatic in 1889 by Sir Hiram Maxim, an American. In 1908, he also invented the "Maxim Silencer". His brother Hudson Maxim perfected a smokeless powder. Rifles were improved in quality. Alfred Nobel, a Swedish chemist and engineer, introduced dynamite in 1867. In 1875, John Holland invented the first practical submarine.

Many new industries were set up. One of them was the rayon industry. There was an increase in the knowledge and exploitation of electricity.

Electricity. After 1870, the use of electricity became popular and common. Side by side with the steam engine, there developed a wide range and great variety of electrical devices. Electrical dynamos and motors were improved and multiplied. Lighting by gas or kerosene was largely supplanted by lighting. Thomas Edison invented the incandescent electric light in 1878. Bell invented the telephone in 1876. By the end of the 1880s, most cities of Europe and America were being provided with systems of electrically-powered street railways. Later on, electric railways were also introduced. In 1895, Marconi, a youthful Italian, devised a practical system of wireless telegraphy. In 1898, wireless telegraphic communication was established across the English Channel and in 1901 across the Atlantic. The application of electricity became more and more popular. People came to have electric lights and telephones and small electric motors for vacuum cleaners, for sewing machines and for washing machines. There was rapid progress in electroplating, in electro-typing and in the use of electric furnaces for making steel.

Many other things for personal comforts were invented. Artificial heating was provided by a variety of furnaces. The first sewing machine was designed and patented by an American, Elias Howe, in 1846. The first commercial exploitation of it was undertaken in the 1850s. In 1863, the Singer Manufacturing Company was established. The electric sewing machine was patented in 1889. The first really successful typewriter was made in 1867-1872. Its commercial manufacture was started in 1874 by Remington and Sons. Other firms also started making typewriters in America and in Europe. The manufacture of bicycle developed after 1870. Ball bearings were introduced in 1877. Pneumatic rubber tyres were added in 1889. By the 1890s, the bicycle was widely used in Europe and America.

One form of cellulose called celluloid was first made in the United States in 1869. Other forms came to be employed for new artificial silk, for explosives, for photographic films and for print paper. The extensive manufacture of cheap wood-pulp paper was of great importance in the evolution of journalism.

Photography made great progress after 1870. In 1884, the film-roll was invented. In 1885, George Eastman laid the foundations of his great photographic industry at Rochester, New York, by patenting a machine for the manufacture of films. In 1888, the Eastman Company marketed the first Kodak, a small portable roll-film camera. By 1900, photography was an important and widespread industry.

A lot of progress was made in the direction of moving pictures. In 1891, Thomas Edison patented a peep-show device. In 1895, two Frenchmen patented the cinematograph, a mobile machine, combining a camera, a film-printing device and a projector. This marked the real beginning of the motion picture industry. After 1900, the display of motion pictures became a regular feature of life. In 1905, the first exclusively motion picture theatre was opened at Pittsburg.

The internal combustion engines were applied to motor cars, motor-boats and aviation. The utilization of the principle of the turbine for a steam engine was an invention of Sir Charles Parsons who patented his steam turbine in 1884. In 1889, he established at Newcastle a large factory for the manufacture of steam turbines. The diesel engine was patented in 1892 and publicly demonstrated for the first time in 1898. By 1910, it was being employed in electrical works, ocean-liners and locomotives.

In 1885-1886, a small portable internal combustion engine, fuelled with light oil and capable of propelling vehicles and boats was made. This was the gasoline engine. Daimler applied the gasoline engine to a bicycle in 1886 and to a wagon in 1887.

Aviation was rendered practicable by the gasoline engine. In the 1890s Daimler's engine was utilised for airships. The first Zeppelin was constructed in 1900 and the first successful flight was made in 1906. Many mechanics and engineers devised motor airplanes (heavier than air). In 1903, a gasoline engine was set up in a glider. In 1909, Bleriot, a French aviator, flew across the English Channel from Calais to Dover.

Petroleum and Rubber. There was a great demand for petroleum products on account of their rapidly extending utilization for motor parts, motor-boats, airplanes, etc. The output of crude oil throughout the world increased from half a million barrels in 1860 to 325 million barrels in 1910. To begin with, most of the petroleum came from the United States but later on it came from Russia, Rumania, Mexico, South America, Persia and the Dutch East Indies also. It was a big undertaking to refine the crude oil and transport it to the places where it was required for consumption.

There was also the development of rubber industry. More and more of rubber was required for making tyres for motor-cars. The production of crude rubber rose from 10,000 tons in 1870 to 75,000 tons in 1910. To begin with, rubber was got from Brazil but later on most of it started coming from rubber plantations in the Dutch East Indies, Ceylon, Borneo, French Indo-China and various regions of tropical Africa.

Lime cement had been made in the eighteenth century. About 1825, good cement was invented in Great Britain and named Portland cement as it resembled in colour to Portland limestone. Portland cement was manufactured in Britain and France in the 1850s. After 1870, cement came to be manufactured on a large scale in many other countries.

After 1870, there was a steady mechanizing and industrialisation of agriculture. Farm machinery continued to be improved and multiplied. To bigger and better drills, seeders, cultivators and harvesters were, now hitched gasoline engines. There was a better knowledge and use of chemical fertilizers.

There had already been industrialisation in Britain and Belgium between 1830 and 1870 and from 1870 to 1910, Germany and the United States were industrialised. France was also industrialised but not to the same degree. In lesser and varying degree, Italy, Austria, Bohemia, Holland, Sweden, Spain, Russia, Canada, Australia, New Zealand and Japan were also industrialised. In 1870, England and Belgium were the only countries in the world where more people were engaged in manufacture and mining than in agriculture. However, in 1910, Germany and the United States could be ranked with England and Belgium in that respect. Even in other countries, more people were now engaged in manufacture and mining.

The so-called Industrial Revolution was not halted by the World War I. As a matter of fact, it reached a new stage of achievement in the next thirty years. The output of previously mechanised industries was increased by technological improvements. At the same time, new machine industries sprang up and expanded with great speed. Industrialisation was intensified not only in the so-called capitalist countries but also in a Communist country like the Soviet Union and also in Turkey and Mexico. The whole of Europe was mechanised. As a matter of fact, industrialisation spread to all parts of the world.

The production of coal and iron was almost doubled throughout the world between 1910 and 1940. There was a slight decline in Great Britain but it was more than offset by gains in the United States, in Russia and in Japan. By 1940, Russia was mining almost as much coal and iron as Germany, and Japan almost as much as France. There was also a large-scale production of coal in China and South Africa.

The same was the case with industries dealing with textiles. The production of cotton increased slightly, but that of wool increased by more than a third and production of natural silk was more than doubled and that of artificial silk or rayon was multiplied four hundredfold. Rayon development was one of the great achievements of industrialisation. From the very start, it was a thoroughly mechanised industry. Not only the raw material was made by machinery, but its whole manufacture of thread and cloth was also done by machinery. It became suddenly important all over the world.

Alongwith textile industries, many other industries were established, *i.e.*, leather, pottery and porcelain, paper and printing, typewriters, cutlery, fire-arms, furniture, tinware, tools, canning and refrigeration and electric goods. Electrical industries developed at a very high speed. Electric power was substituted more and more for steam power. Hydro-electric power plants were multiplied. Electric lighting was improved by the use of the tungsten filament lamps.

There was further improvement in the means of communication and transport. The existing network of railways was extended to Asia, Africa and South America. Rail locomotives carried a very large number of persons and large quantities of goods from one place to another. Over the whole earth, messages were carried fay telegraph and telephone wires. The existing network of steamship lines was expanded. The total tonnage of the world's merchant shipping rose from 40 millions in 1910 to 59 millions in 1935. Great Britain kept a large merchant fleet than any other nation. The tonnage of the United States, Italy and the Netherlands doubled between 1910 and 1939 and that of Japan tripled. The number of motorcars, motor-trucks, airplanes, motion pictures and radios increased immensely. Their production assumed colossal proportions. Production of motorcars and trucks developed rapidly in the United States. Gradually, increasing number of cars were produced in Great Britain, France, Germany, Spain, Italy, Canada and Japan. By 1939, the number of registered motor vehicles throughout the world exceeded 43 millions.

Aviation also developed rapidly and was used for commerical carrying of mails and passengers. Regular airplane services were inaugurated between Paris and London, Paris and Alexandria and on to Baghdad and India, from Paris to Brazil and from New York to Mexico and Central and South America. In 1929, a Zeppelin aeroplane circumnavigated the world from Germany via Tokyo and Los Angeles and New York back to Germany, in 20 days. In 1927, Lindberg, an American aviator, flew his airplane alone and without a stop from New York to Paris. Admiral Richard Byrd explored the Arctic Ocean and visited the North Pole in 1927. In 1929, he explored the Antarctic Continent and flew over the South Pole. By 1939, commercial airlines were being operated by every major nation and were carrying mail, merchandise and passengers over all the oceans and Continents of the world.

The fuelling of gasoline engines gave an impetus to petroleum industry. Between 1910 and 1939, the world output of petroleum increased over sixfold, from 325 million barrels to 2,000 million barrels.

Rubber industry also made great progress. Its consumption rose from 75,000 tons in 1910 to more than a million tons in 1939. Most of the rubber came from the Dutch East Indies, the Malaya Peninsula and Ceylon. There was a beginning in the production of synthetic rubber.

There was a widespread use of concrete. Concrete roads paralleled railways or provided a substitute for them. Concrete was also used for public buildings, industrial plants, garages, hangars, piers, bridges and even ship-building.

In the post-war period, motion pictures became popular all over the world. They were perfected and popularised during the World War I and more particularly after 1920. In 1928, talking movies were first made and very shortly afterwards, they were heard and seen all over the world. A large number of films were made in the United States. A beginning was made in other countries also.

There was also the development of radio. In 1920, the first permanent radio broadcasting station was put into operation by the Westinghouse Company of the United States. Private homes began to be equipped with radio receiving sets. There was rapid progress in the production and use of radios. Within 15 years, every nation in the world had broadcasting stations. Everywhere there were enough receiving sets to enable most of the people of the world to receive practically simultaneous news of what was happening in different parts of the world, particularly the metropolitan cities. In the United States alone, there were 51 million radio sets in use in 1940. In 1928 began the transmission of pictures across the Atlantic and in colour.

There was also an increase in the output of foodstuffs in the world. Agriculture continued to be industrialised and mechanised more and more. The result was that there were more vegetables, fruits, grain and meat. The output of wheat in the world increased from 3,250 million bushels in 1920 to 4,600 million bushels in 1938. Industrialisation promised to provide humankind with an ample supply of food and clothing, quicker means of communication and more and more of comforts.

Results of the Industrial Revolution : Economic Effects. The Industrial Revolution had its effects in various fields. As regards its economic effects, it resulted in the factory system. A variety of articles and goods began to be manufactured in large quantities in big factories. The factory system led to the division of labour and mass production through standardisation of processes and parts. Before the Industrial Revolution, industry was the hand-maid of commerce. After the Industrial Revolution, industry became a big field for investment. It was industry that furnished commerce with an ever-increasing supply of saleable commodities and extended enormously its range. Commerce grew by leaps and bounds. There was a rapid rise in the producer's goods industries as distinguished from consumer's good industries.

The Industrial Revolution created surplus wealth which came to be owned by the capitalists. With the progress of the Industrial Revolution, the power and influence of the captains of industry grew more and more. They shaped the course of further industrialisation by reinvesting their gains in new enterprises. There was so much of increase in production by machines that in spite of lavish personal expenditures on non-productive display, only a small fraction of the total increase in wealth was immediately consumed. The growth of the joint stock companies with limited liability facilitated the investment of surplus capital and the progress of new industries.

Machines produced much more than what was necessary for the domestic markets and hence arose the necessity of foreign markets for the disposal of the surplus goods. That ultimately led to imperialistic expansion and spheres of influence in the undeveloped countries of the world. The Industrial Revolution introduced the new phenomena of large-scale booms and depressions after intervals. Industrial Revolution led to international economic dependence. The cotton spindles of Britain depended upon a steady supply of raw cotton from the United States. As urbanization progressed in Britain and Europe, less food was grown in these countries which became heavy importers of wheat, meat and tropical food products. Europe exported manufactured goods in exchange for food. "The entire world became a market place. Dislocation of industry in any part of the world often has important repercussions in countries thousands of miles away."

Industrial Revolution led to the expansion of trade all over the world. There was expansion of trade, both inland and overseas. Articles made in one country found their way into foreign countries and brought in a good deal of wealth to the producers.

Before the Industrial Revolution, there was a great strain on manual labour. The rate of production was slow. The output was small and the finished products were costly. The new machines worked by steam power or by oil worked faster and saved time and labour. They produced much more and more cheaply too.

The Industrial Revolution was directly responsible for the construction of tarred roads, the introduction of steam engines, railways and steamships and the expansion of the canal system. Industrial centres were linked with business centres by sea, by road and by rail. The new highways, railways and steamboats carried goods safely and quickly from one part of the world to another and also provided comfortable travelling to the people. As more and more factories and mills were constructed, the demand for workers went up and expanded industries absorbed millions of people as workers, labourers, technicians, managers, salesmen, etc.

The Industrial Revolution had its impact on agriculture also as some of the inventions included agricultural machines. Mechanical ploughs, cultivators, drills, threshers, etc., reduced the labour and time of farmers and performed their work better. The result was larger production, more food and greater prosperity.

Social Results. As regards social results of Industrial Revolution, there was a migration of workers on a vast scale from small agricultural villages to cities. Thousands of agricultural workers who were without work on account of the Agrarian Revolution and the "Enclosure" movement in England left their homes in the agricultural South for the industrial North in the hope of finding employment in factories. That caused untold miseries and hardships. Those workers found that the living conditions in the industrial towns were absolutely unfit for human beings. No attention was paid to sanitation and the workers had to live in slums with foul smell. The employers found it more profitable to employ women and children in their factories because they were easier to control than men and they could be employed on lower wages. The result was that while men were unemployed, their wives and children worked in factories. The children and women were mercilessly exploited. Children of pauper parents were farmed out to factory owners on terms which amounted to slavery. They were literally worked to death. They were given something as trifling wage, sometimes only board and lodging. They were forced to work for very long hours till they dropped from sheer exhaustion. Not infrequently, they fell into the machinery to be killed or maimed for life. The brutality with which they were treated was simply unbelievable. The food given to them was bad and insufficient. Many of the factories were entirely without ventilation. Not infrequently, workers were victims of certain diseases traceable to the character of their work. Schapiro writes, "Early every morning the pauper children sent to factories by the overseers of the poor were awakened and taken to the mill where, in stench, in heated rooms and constant whirling of a thousand wheels, idle fingers and little feet were kept in ceaseless action, forced into unnatural activity by blows from the heavy hands and feet of the merciless overlookers and the infliction of bodily pain by instruments invented by the sharpened ingenuity of insatiable selfishness. If they were suspected of a desire to run away in order to escape from their unbearable misery, they were regarded as criminals, mercilessly chained to the machines which they operated."

Dance observes, "Most of the factories were cramped, dirty, unhealthy places merely to work in and often causing the working people to catch diseases of various kinds. Often too, they were badly built so that they collapsed under the weight of their machines and injured the workmen. Hardly were any of these machines protected by railings and it was quite common for those incharge to be caught in the wheels and get either injured or killed. It was not at all unusual for men to be kept at work from six in the morning till ten at night, sixteen hours of work, often without a break, even for meals. In the cotton factories in Lancashire, it was worse still. In many cotton mills, the air had to be kept very warm and very damp, or the cotton was spoilt. This warm, damp atmosphere was very bad for the workers and in the old days of 16 hours' work, many of them got fearful coughs, consumption and rheumatism so that before long they either died or became crippled. Worst of all, the women and children suffered from all this just as much as the men who could stand it better. Their hours were as long as the men's, they were kept in the same unhealthy rooms and the children were especially given dullest work to do since they were not old enough to do the more difficult work. Boys and girls of six had to work even for 12 or 16 hours and remained without attention. There were no proper arrangements for latrines as well as for recreation after hard labour."

Industrial Revolution led to insecurity of work. The number of workers who went to industrial towns was considerably more than the total number of jobs available in factories. The result was that many of them remained unemployed. That led to the practice of underselling themselves in order to get employment. The problem of unemployment of men was aggravated by the employment of women and children on lower wages. If a worker employed on daily wages became unwell or otherwise he could not attend the factory on a particular day, he lost his wages. There was no provision for old age or insurance against unemployment. The workers did not know what was in store for them in future.

When industry was in the domestic stage, there was a variety of work for a worker. He completed all the processes of manufacture himself. A change from one process to another provided recreation for him. A shoemaker would cure and tan the skin and would cut the "upper" and the sole and finish the entire job of making the shoe himself. Under the factory system, there was specialization and day after day, the worker had to handle the same machine. Consequently, the work became monotonous and uninteresting and the worker felt bored.

Although under the Industrial Revolution, the factory-owners and big industrialists made fortunes and lived in luxury, the workers remained miserably poor. Their wages were small. They were forced to live in abominable conditions. The disparity between the living standards of the capitalists and workers was very great. The factory workers launched the Chartist movement claiming better conditions of work and higher wages. That resulted in a perennial strife between capital and labour.

There was insecurity and mass unemployment as a result of Industrial Revolution. There was also the danger of large-scale shut-down as a result of business depressions. Mass unemployment became one of the gravest social problems arising from Industrial Revolution.

As a result of the Industrial Revolution, the old personal relationship between the employers and the employees disappeared. There occurred a sharp cleavage between the employers and the employees. Under the domestic system, the employers brought raw materials to the worker to be turned into finished products and those were returned to the employer. The workers themselves often possessed the spindles and looms. Under the factory system, the employer seldom saw his workers and much of the capital invested in the factory was owned by the people who never saw the factory. Although their interests were common, there was an unbridgeable gulf between the industrial masters and their men.

Under the factory system, labour became more and more impersonal. For example, the man who made a shoe was himself concerned with the making of every part of it. There was a chance to display individual skill. Things changed after the Industrial Revolution. The worker performed only a fraction in the process of making a shoe. That function was purely mechanical. He was merely a hand. Work was changed by the Industrial Revolution into a monotonous and deadening affair. The unskilled labourer largely replaced the skilled labourer.

Political Results. As regards the political results of the Industrial Revolution, there was a strengthening of the middle class. A large number of villages became rotten boroughs. While the rotten boroughs were sending two members each to British Parliament, very many new industrial towns were completely unrepresented. The result was that Parliament passed a bill to remove discrepancies in the teeth of bitter opposition from the big landlords who constituted a large majority of the Conservative Party. There was the necessity of disenfranchising the rotten boroughs and giving representation to the newly founded industrial towns. Parliament passed laws to remove this anomaly. The Reform Act of 1832 redistributed seats in Parliament to give representation to the new industrial centres. The bourgeoisie were successful in putting down the Chartist agitation which aimed at the extension of political power to the working classes. The position of the bourgeoisie in France was strengthened by the July Revolution of 1830 which put Louis Philippe on the throne of France.

In the long run, labour became a great political force. As democracy progressed, the labouring classes became stronger politically and ultimately were able to make their influence felt at the time of elections. Many radical movements were started as the Government failed to take prompt action to improve the lot of the workers. Society came to be divided into two parts, the haves and have-nots.

As a result of the Industrial Revolution, the military superiority of a country became dependent upon the extent of industrialisation in that country. Industrialised countries, alone could produce modern military weapons. The Northern States succeeded in the Civil War (1861-1865) because they were more industrialised than the Southern states.

The Industrial Revolution also had intellectual and cultural results. In his book entitled "Wealth of Nations," Adam Smith (1723-1790) forcefully expressed himself against interference by government with business. His view was that each man is the best judge of his own economic affairs. The free play of competition and universal desire for enrichment would result in the maximum increase in total wealth. Though individuals may be selfish and unconcerned with the common good, their collective activity would automatically tend to the economic welfare of all. He supported the economic doctrine of Laissez faire. The function of government was merely to be an omnipresent policeman protecting property and compelling the performance of contracts. Laissez faire implied two things : unfettered relations between seller and buyer and between employer and employee. It was the social and economic changes brought about by the Industrial Revolution which stimulated the growth of economics or political economy.

The ideas of Adam Smith were developed and elaborated by the classical economists such as Thomas Malthus (1766-1834) and David Ricardo (1777-1823). In 1798, Malthus asserted that any improvement in the economic condition of the poor would be counter-balanced by an increase in population, as population tends to increase to the limit of the means of subsistence. Grinding poverty and high death rate from starvation, disease and war must for ever be the lot of the mass of mankind. The only alternative was the limitation of population by moral restraint. Ricardo enunciated the "iron law of wages" which means that wages must inevitably tend to an amount just capable of maintaining life, such as "the coal fed into a steam engine was just capable of maintaining the fire under the boiler". The socialists rejected this thesis. Robert Owen (1771-1858) set up a model factory where he put emphasis on good working conditions, fair wages, public schools, good homes and cooperative stores. Saint Simon (1760-1825) was in favour of an industrial state organised and directed by scientists and engineers. Charles Fourier (1772-1837) proposed to abolish the state and substitute phalansteries or working cells. Louis Blanc (1811-1882) tried to improve working conditions by setting up national workshops through which he hoped to eliminate unemployment and relieve the pressure of competition. Proudhon (1809-1865) expressed the view that property is theft.

Industrial Revolution also encouraged scientific investigation. The necessity of experts was felt as manufacturing techniques became, more complex. The profession of engineers became an integral part of the industrial civilization. A lot of money was spent on laboratories carrying out research in various technological problems.

Industrial Revolution secularised interest. "The mass-circulation newspaper, the automobile, the motion picture and the radio—all products of the Industrial Revolution—have supplied men with a whole new set of interests and far more than the arguments of philosophical agnosticism have brought about the secularisation of viewpoint and widespread religious indifferentism that is characteristic of contemporary life."

It has rightly been said that "the immediate economic effects of the Industrial Revolution were on the one hand, to add enormously to English wealth and capital and on the other hand to degrade the English masses, enlarging the urban proletariat and holding it to poverty as a permanent condition".

Industrial Revolution was all-pervasive and comprehensive. It radically altered the face of Europe. Its impact was on every phase of European life. However, it was not an unmixed blessing. It had both its merits and demerits. It raised the standard of living of Europeans but made them psychologically shaky. It opened new vistas of unusual potentialities but also aggravated the rat race which tended to dehumanise them. If there were numerous pockets of affluence, there were more segments of poverty and starvation. There were more slums than the sky-scrapers. The rich became richer and the poor poorer. Urbanization spoiled the beauty and serenity of the natural landscape. Population increase upset the ecological balance. Life expectancy of men went up but alongwith it insecurity has increased. Spiritualism has been thrown in the background. Industrialisation reinforced by rapid scientific progress has made man arrogant and belligerent and he is fast losing his balance and sobriety. Man has lost his sense of direction. Moral values are being obscured. There is a craze for more material possessions. Industrialisation has many more boons to offer provided man is prepared to tame it for the welfare of humanity at large.

SUGGESTED READINGS

Ashley, W.J.: **The Economic Organisation of England,** 1914.

Ashton, T.S.: **The Industrial Revolution (1760-1830),** 1948.

Ashworth, W.: **A Short History of the International Economy, 1850-1950,** London, 1951.

Beales, H.L.: **The Industrial Revolution (1750-1850),** 1928.

Buer, M.C.: **Health, Wealth and Population in the Early Days of the Industrial Revolution,** 1926.

Cameron, R.R: **France and the Economic Development of Europe, 1800-1914,** 1961.

Clapham, Sir John H.: **An Economic History of Modern Britain, Vol. I, 1820-1850,** 1930.

Clapham, Sir John H. : **Economic Development of France and Germany, 1815-1914, Cambridge,** 1936.

Dunham, A.L.: **The Industrial Revolution in France, 1815-1848, New York,** 1955.

Fay, C.R: **Great Britain from Adam Smith to the Present Day,** 1928.

Gzeggy, Pauline : **A Social and Economic History of Great Britain.**

Habakkuk, H.G. and M. Postan (Eds.) : **The Industrial Revolution and After, Cambridge,** 1965.

Hamilton, H.: **The Industrial Revolution in Scotland,** 1932.

Heaton, H.: **An Economic History of Europe, London,** 1948.

Henderson, W.O.: **Britain and Industrial Europe, 1750-1850, Liverpool,** 1954.

Henderson, W.O.: **The Industrial Revolution on the Continent, London,** 1960.

Henderson, W.O.: **The State and the Industrial Revolution in Prussia, 1740-1870, Liverpool,** 1958.

Knowles, L.C.A.: **The Industrial and Commercial Revolution in Great Britain during the Nineteenth Century,** 1921.

Lipson, E.: **The Economic History of England, Vol. II,** 1931.

Mantoux. P.: **The Industrial Revolution in the Eighteenth Century,** 1928.

Pinchbeck, I.: **Women Workers and the Industrial Revolution,** (1750-1850).

Reford, A.: **Labour Migration in England, 1800-1850,** 1926.

Toynbee, Arnold: **The Industrial Revolution in England,** 1884.

CHAPTER

45 EUROPE IN 1815

The view of Dr. David Thomson is that the Continent of Europe in 1815 was not a mere geographical expression. It was also not a community of peoples with enough in common to justify our regarding Europe as an organic entity, sharing a culture, an economy, a complex of traditions which made it in a real sense one. Neither of the two views is accurate. Each view, is flat and distorted. Just as nineteenth century diplomats thought of a balance of power in Europe which, by holding a certain equilibrium between the largest states, allowed all states to co-exist peacefully, similarly we may picture the cohesion of Europe as being compatible with its great diversities by a sort of internal balance of forces. In some important respects, it was one. In other equally important respects, it was many things. From the tensions between these two contrary qualities came much of that inherent impetus to development, change and greatness which made Europe the most important and dynamic Continent in the world during the nineteenth century. There existed within Europe tension between the forces of continuity and forces of change. The former included the institutions of monarchy, church, land-owing aristocracy and a widespread desire for peace and stability. The latter included the rapid growth of population, spread of industrialism and urban life, the ferment of nationalism and political ideas disseminated throughout Europe by the French Revolution and the conquests of Napoleon. (Europe since Napoleon, p. 81) .

The Roman Catholic church emerged in 1815 as a militant and powerful force transcending state frontiers. The Pope claimed the loyalty of millions of men and women in every European state. The landed aristocracy cherished their feudal rights of administering justice and exacting dues from their vassals in Austria and Russia. They clamoured for the restoration of those rights in France and Germany. The economy of every European country still rested on the labours of peasants in the fields. The peasantry were the mass of the population. Except in parts of North-Western Europe, they worked the land using methods and tools not different from those used by their medieval ancestors. Much of the political history of the nineteenth century is concerned with the activities of the non-peasant section of the population. In Western Europe, some peasants were now rapidly improving their social and legal status. They were improving their economic status by new methods of farming. Peasants in Eastern Europe made very little advance during the nineteenth century.

Behind the patchwork political map, there existed a general monarchical dynastic system which reduced conflicts between states to simple categories of rivalries between a few large families. The Bourbons of France and the Habsburgs of Austria provided most of the states of Europe with their ruling monarchs. This "cousinhood of kings" remained an important factor in European diplomacy even in 1815. There were no dynastic wars, but there were dynastic alliances, marriages, disputes and wars. In Eastern Europe were the Habsburg Empire, the Russian Empire and the Ottoman Empire. The United Kingdom had her link with Hanover till 1837. It is said that when Queen Victoria celebrated the fiftieth year of her reign, most of the rulers of Europe who attended the Golden Jubilee were related to her.

From the time of Louis XIV, French had replaced Latin as the normal language of diplomacy. Likewise, the rationalism of French thought conquered the minds of Europe. Englishmen such as Gibbon, the great historian and Bentham wrote and spoke in French as readily as in English. The enlightened despots of eighteenth century Europe like Frederick the Great of Prussia and Catherine the Great of Russia, adopted French writers and artists. Members of the aristocracy all over the Continent were familiar with the writings and ideas of the French. Europe was united in its Frenchness. During the days of Napoleon. French laws, institutions, administrative methods and systems of weights and measures spread throughout Western and Central Europe. Much of the material and cultural unity of Europe fame from France.

The degree of cohesion and unity in Europe can be measured not only in terms of internal conditions but also in terms of the relations between European states as a whole and other parts of the world. In 1815, no Western European power held any part of North Africa. The Mediterranean was the frontier between Europe and Islam. Overseas connections were restricted to Great Britain, France, Spain, Portugal and the Netherlands. Great Britain lost her control over the American colonies but consolidated her position in Canada. She had her Empire in India. The Netherlands had an overseas Empire in the Dutch East Indies.

Geography has broken up the Continent of Europe into many regions. The regional differences were profound on account of the absence of railways, good roads and old-fashioned means of transport and communication.

Forces of Continuity : Monarchy. In 1815, there were certain forces of continuity and among them the most important was the institution of monarchy. It is pointed out that even the French revolutionaries of 1789 had no intention of overthrowing monarchy but they took the daring step only in 1792 when they decided to set up a Republic in France. The only Republics in Europe were Switzerland, Venice and Genoa. They seemed to be exceptions that proved the rule. The traditions of dynastic absolutism were deep-rooted and well-tested. It is not correct to think that the *Ancien regime* was totally destroyed by the French Revolution and the conquests of Napoleon. Not only the ideas and institutions of old monarchies survived throughout the upheavals of the period from 1789 to 1815, they enjoyed a new popularity and struck fresh roots in the generation after Waterloo.

The basic idea of monarchy was the hereditary title to political power. The functions of the Government in those days were very much restricted. They were mainly the functions of organising security for the whole of the kingdom at home and abroad. The people were to be saved from foreign invasions or subjection to foreign powers. Law and order were to be maintained within the kingdom. These were big responsibilities in those days. Monarchy at that time was the most natural form of Government in the world.

The rulers of Europe believed in absolutism. The pattern of absolute monarchy was set by Louis XIV of France (1660-1715). He inherited a throne that was strong because the nobles were quarrelling among themselves and there were religious factions in France. Louis XIV made the nobles weak by living at the costly court of Versailles. He subordinated the church to his control. He took away from the Huguenots the rights and liberties formerly enjoyed by them. Many of the monarchs all over Europe tried to imitate his methods during the eighteenth century. They adopted French culture and even French language. They also claimed for themselves absolute powers. This applied to Frederick the Great of Prussia, Catherine the Great of Russia and Maria Theresa of Austria. They centralised Government in their own hands as against local and feudal privileges and thus acquired absolute authority in the state. The rulers who wanted to be absolute, had to be more efficient. They had to seek popular support against nobles and church. That support they tried to get by experiments in popular reform and enlightened Government. Hence, absolute monarchy became "enlightened" monarchy or "benevolent despotism". Those rulers justified their existence by fostering material progress and adopting more enlightened methods of Government. During the French Revolution, the king was executed and a republic was established in France. The property of the Church was taken away. The revolutionaries of France threatened to spread revolution throughout Europe. Absolutism was bound to react violently against it.

The traditions of dynastic monarchy were so strong that even Napoleon got himself married in the royal family of Austria-Hungary. He was not opposed to the institution of monarchy. He himself aimed at becoming the head of a new dynasty. He made Joseph, his elder brother, the King of Spain. He made Louis, his younger brother, the King of Holland. He appointed Jerome, his youngest brother, the King of Westphalia. Even after the overthrow of Napoleon, the principle of legitimism was adopted for claiming political authority. The statesmen who assembled at the Vienna Congress in 1815, accepted the principle of legitimism. The result was that the Vienna Settlement gave a new lease of life throughout Europe to the ideas and institutions of hereditary monarchy. The scene was dominated by the rulers of the Governments that were not overthrown by the French Revolution or Napoleon and had weathered the storm. Among them the prominent were Tsar Alexander I of Russia, Frederick William III of Prussia and Francis I, the Emperor of Austria. The King of England was represented first by Lord Castlereagh and later on by George Canning. The triumph of monarchy and all that it stood for, seemed complete. The defeat of Napoleon was a victory for the allied monarchical Governments acting in a grand alliance. The Battle of Waterloo was not won by popular uprising or guerrilla fighters, but by the tough soldiers of the British and Prussian armies.

In addition to the above monarchs, there were many more smaller kings in Europe at that time. It is true that the Holy Roman Empire which was abolished in 1806, was not revived in Germany. However, 39 states emerged in Germany in 1815. Those states were formed into a loose confederation. Each state had its own monarch or prince. Those monarchs came out of the old aristocracy. They were assertive of their social privileges and political rights. Ferdinand VII was restored to the throne of Spain. He annulled the Spanish Constitution of 1812 and resumed all the prerogatives of absolute monarchy. A similar thing happened in Italy. Lombardy and Venetia were ruled by the Emperor of Austria directly from Vienna. The King of Sardinia was his cousin. Francis IV, the Duke of Modena, was also his cousin. Archduke Ferdinand III, his brother, became the Duke of Tuscany. His aunt became the Queen of Naples. Ferdinand I, king of Naples and Sicily behaved in a reactionary manner. The administration of the Papal States was among the worst in Italy. The kingdom of Piedmont was ruled by Victor Emmanuel I. This state was destined to play the same role in Italy which was played by Prussia in Germany.

It is true that there was almost universal restoration of monarchy, but the fact remains that the tradition of kingship had been badly shaken. Most of the magic of monarchy had gone. The rulers of Europe were defeated by the revolutionary armies of France. Many of the kings who were restored in 1814, suffered from the disadvantage that they were put on their thrones by the allied armies. The manner in which Louis XVIII of France was restored in 1814 and then turned out by Napoleon during the Hundred Days, shows that royal authority had become fragile. Legitimism alone was not a sufficient basis for Government. However, there were other factors which helped the monarchs of Europe.

The Church. There was not only the restoration of monarchy in 1815, but also of the Church. A close alliance between the throne and altar was traditional in Europe. The Roman Catholic Church in France suffered from the excesses of the French Revolution. The Civil Constitution of the Clergy of 1790, reduced the Church in France to the position of a department of state. Many high clergymen joined the aristocratic and royal emigres in exile abroad. Things did not improve even after the Concordat between Napoleon and Pope in 1802. Napoleon still enjoyed considerable control over the clergy in France. With the growth of state universities and schools, the Roman Catholic Church lost most of its former grip over education.

The Roman Catholic Church gained from the violence and extremism of the French Revolution. There was a strong reaction in favour of the Church on account of its sufferings. In 1815, the Roman Catholic Church in France regained a highly privileged position. However, it was not possible to restore to it all the lands and property which had been taken away from the Church during the French Revolution. However, the Government gave generous grants to the Church which resumed its control over education. Even the Protestant Powers of Prussia and Britain were willing to support the revival of Papal power in Europe. They were backed by Russia in this matter. Pope Pius VII enjoyed personal sympathy on account of his humiliation by Napoleon. He entered Rome in 1814 as if he was a victor. The Jesuit Order got official favour at the Vatican. The Pope re-established the Index and the Inquisition. However, there was opposition to the Jesuit Order. The Jesuits organised societies of Catholic laymen, particularly in France, Spain and Italy. Laws were passed in France also to restrict the activities of the Jesuits. The Tsar of Russia expelled the Jesuits.

The Anglican Church in England enjoyed a highly privileged position. However, its influence was predominantly conservative. Until 1828, Protestant dissenters remained subject to many disabilities. They were excluded from all important civil and military offices and also from teaching in the universities. Churchmen did not support the movements for reform. They did not advocate such humanitarian reforms as the reform of prisons and the penal code. They belonged to the forces of established order. Sydney Smith suffered on account of his liberal views.

There was also the revival of religious faith. Rationalist ideas of natural rights and secularist doctrines of state power were not favoured. Many of the greatest intellects of Europe supported the dogmas of Christianity and old religious beliefs. The case for traditionalism and reverence for established institutions as advocated by Burke in "Reflections on the Revolution in France", was accepted. Joseph de Maistre and Vicomte de Bonald supported legitimist monarchy and power of the Pope. They seemed to demolish the ideas and arguments of liberalism and their influence spread outside France to Italy and Germany. Their ideas were further popularised by Lamennais.

Before 1800, most of the intellectuals stood for rationalism, democratic ideas and anti-clericalism. At least for a decade after 1815, forces of conservatism enjoyed more positive prestige and power than before.

The Landed Aristocracy. Land was still the most important form of property and it carried with it the right to social importance and political power. The events in France between 1789 and 1815 brought an unprecedented transference of landed property from the great landowners and corporations (particularly the church), to a number of small property owners. Large estates, alongwith those of the Church, were declared national property and were either put up for sale or exchange for the paper bonds like Assignats. Many people such as lawyers, financiers, millers and brewers, made fortunes by speculating in the Assignats. When Napoleon came to power, there were still large stocks of land which had neither been sold nor granted to anybody. Napoleon created a new aristocracy which was given those lands.

As land was possessed by a few, political rights were also enjoyed by a few. The equation between land and political power remained intact. It was only the old aristocracy, the wealthy bourgeoisie and the peasant proprietors who gained from the redistribution of land. The bulk of land in France was still owned by a small number of persons. Political power was in the hands of these persons. The right to vote for the Chamber of Deputies in France was given only to those citizens who were 30 years of age or more and paid at least 300 francs a year in direct taxation. To be a Deputy, a man had to be over 40 and pay at least 1,000 francs a year in direct taxation. The rights of landed wealth were deeply entrenched in the new monarchy. This was a guarantee that its whole policy would be conservative. The ministers of the king were drawn mainly from the aristocracy. Duc de Richelieu and the Comte Decazes were the Chief Ministers of France and they were reactionaries. Between 1814 and 1830, the restored monarchy rested on a balance between the powers of the old aristocracy and the power of the new business oligarchy which was rapidly growing in power. The aristocracy became more an office-holding class than a land-owing class. It shared power with the wealthy bourgoisie who possessed landed property. There was a balance and a compromise between aristocracy and oligarchy. The Chamber of Deputies had a permanent majority on the right and a permanent minority on the left. There was no party system. There was occasional criticism. The Government remained exclusively the job of the king and his ministers.

In England of the eighteenth century, the landed aristocracy virtually monopolised state power. The House of Lords reserved its control over legislation. The electorate was a small one. There were property qualifications for the voters and Members of Parliament. The right of vote was enjoyed by about 400,000 men. On account of the system of patronage, corruption and intimidation, the sons of the nobility were returned to Parliament. The Landed Property Qualifications Acts provided that the Members of Parliament for the counties must have a landed estate of at least £ 600 a year and for the boroughs, a landed estate of £ 300 a year. The predominance of the landed and agricultural interests in 1815 is proved by the passing of the Corn Law in 1815. It gave farmers protection by prohibiting the import of corn from abroad until the prices at home had reached the level of 80 shillings a quarter. The Game Laws made it illegal for anyone who was not a squire or a squire's eldest son to kill the game and for anyone to buy and sell game.

Great Britain and France were among the most advanced and liberal countries in Europe, both politically and economically. In Germany, Italy, Spain and Austria, the landed aristocracy enjoyed their landed property. The Prussian Junkers were enterprising and progressive in their methods. They tended to expropriate the peasants and build up larger estates. Unlike English landowners, the Junkers did not let out the land to be cultivated by tenants but organised its use under their own supervision. The peasantry was emancipated in Prussia from heavy feudal obligations but the work of emancipation proceeded slowly. It often resulted in the economic subjection of peasants and surrender of large portions of their land to the junkers as compensation. There was a concentration of landed wealth in the hands of the Junkers who provided Prussia with money, administrators and officers.

The power of the land-owning aristocracy remained intact in Poland and Russia in 1815. They were not opposed to the emancipation of serfs who provided labour on their lands. The peasants were opposed to personal emancipation from serfdom at the cost of losing land. The common saying was: "We are yours, but the land is ours." The peasants were willing to adopt progressive methods of cultivation and husbandry.

Popularity of Peace. Another force of conservatism in Europe in 1815 was a longing for peace and weariness of war. Almost every country had known more than two decades of recurrent war. The French wars had imposed unusual strains on all the combatants. The Continental system had affected the standards of living throughout Europe. Britain also had endured heavy burdens and strains. France was exhausted after the invasion of Russia in 1812. The war had done a lot of destruction in Prussia, Austria and Russia. People wanted peace and freedom to live their own lives and that was possible only if there was peace in Europe. People welcomed monarchy because that gave them hopes of peace. The prevailing mood in Europe favoured the forces of conservatism. That is why the conservative Governments were able to get measures of repression passed by their Parliaments which would not have been possible before 1789. The Tory Government of Britain suspended the Habeas Corpus Act in 1817. In 1819, it passed Sidmouth's Six Acts which were designed to prevent large public meetings, undermine the whole movement for radical reform and kill or at least control the radical press. It is true that there were protests against those measures but those were passed through Parliament without much difficulty. Likewise, in France the Chamber of Deputies passed a series of Acts in 1815 which gave the King of France the power to suspend liberties of the individual and freedom of the press guaranteed by the Charter of 1814 granted by Louis XVIII at the time of his restoration to the throne of France. It authorised laws of proscription which sent many eminent Frenchmen into exile. Metternich, the Chancellor of Austria, established his system which was designed to keep public order by a network of spies and secret police. The Carlsbad Decrees of 1819 applied to the whole of Germany and let loose a reign of repression. In every country, Governments relied on informers and *agents provocateurs*, on secret police and military repression. In Naples and Sicily, the poor were mobilised against the middle class liberals. In other places, the fears of the propertied classes were exploited to justify repression of popular disturbances.

The years between 1815 and 1854 were an era of revolutions but they were not an era of wars. As compared with the period after 1854, there was no large-scale fighting in Europe between 1815 and 1854. Between 1854 and 1878, there were six important wars in which the major powers took part. Those wars were the Crimean War (1854-56) which involved Turkey, Britain, France and Russia, the War of 1859 which involved France and Austria, the War waged by Prussia and Austria against Denmark in 1864, the Austro-Prussian War of 1866, the Franco-Prussian War of 1870 and the Russo-Turkish War of 1877 which turned into a general European conflict. It is suggested that revolutions before 1854 served as a kind of substitute for war. In other words, international peace after 1815 was an endemic civil war that produced the revolutions of 1830 and 1848 and a host of intermediate revolts. Peace was popular because Governments were aware of their own weaknesses and were also exhausted by the wars of the French Revolution and the Napoleonic period. Another reason, was that enemies at home seemed to be a more important challenge than enemies abroad. Civil war absorbed belligerent spirits which were diverted into the cause of militant nationalism.

Forces of Change : Growth of Population. If the years after Waterloo were marked by the forces of continuity, order and resistance to change, Europe entered upon an era of rapid and fundamental changes. One of those forces was the growth of population in Europe. It is pointed that the population of Europe as a whole began to increase since about the middle of the eighteenth century. If the population was 140 millions in 1750, it was 180 millions in 1800, 266 millions in 1850, 401 millions in 1900 and 540 millions in 1950. This shows that there was nearly four-fold increase in population in about two centuries. The speed of this growth was completely a new phenomenon. No social and political orders could remain unaffected by this abnormal increase of population. The events of the nineteenth century cannot be understood intelligently without keeping this growth of population in mind. This enormous growth of population changed the course of world history. Between 1815 and 1914, about 40 million Europeans migrated to other Continents. The United States, Canada, Australia and many other parts of the globe were populated mainly from the overflow of Europe. In 1815, the whole of the population of Europe was only 200 millions. By 1914, that number of people of European birth or stock existed outside Europe, while the population of Europe itself rose to 460 millions. European civilisation was spread throughout the world.

Many reasons have been put forward for the abnormal growth of population. It was certainly due more to a decrease in death rates than to an increase in birth rates. Populations grew not because more people were born but because more people survived and more people stayed alive longer. The causes of lower death rates were improvements in public order and security, ending of civil and religious wars, destruction of brigandage and violence and also relief from famine, plague and destitution. Another cause was the progress made by medical science in the eighteenth century. Infant death rates fell. Fewer mothers died at the time of child birth and more people lived to an advanced age. Diseases which affected cattle and crops were conquered. Food supplies were improved. Better transport, first by road and canal and then by railway and steamship made it possible to end localised famine and shortages. There took place agricultural revolution which increased food production and made possible the feeding of an increasing number of mouths. Where all the best land available was already under cultivation, greater supplies of food could be obtained by more intensive cultivation or importation of foodstuffs. Both of these methods were adopted by Europeans. By the use of winter root crops such as turnips and beetroot and green crops like clover and alfalfa, the old three-field rotation system was replaced by four-course rotation. The result was that all the land could be used every year for cultivation. It also gave enough cattle food to keep larger stocks of cattle alive during winter. The increase in the number of cattle gave more meat and milk for human consumption and also manure to keep land fertile. The improvement in the methods of transport helped the import of food from the United States and Canada to Europe.

The pace of growth of population varied from country to country according to the circumstances. The pace was set by the United Kingdom. Its population was about 18½ millions in 1811 and more than double that figure in 1891. France had a population of more than 29 millions in 1806 and 38½ millions in 1896. Germany increased her population from 25 millions in 1815 to about 50 million in 1890. Belgium had a population of 3¾ millions in 1831 and 7½ millions in 1910. Italy and Spain grew less rapidly though in the end they also doubled their population between 1815 and 1920. Russia nearly doubled her population during the first half of the nineteenth century and again doubled it during the second half. This explains why there was great Russian expansion towards Asia.

Industrialism and Urbanism. It was during the nineteenth century that Industrial Revolution made progress in various states of Europe. Industrial Revolution changed the very face of Europe. Large factories employing thousands of workers came into existence. As big machines were set up at certain places, they led to urbanism. Factories were required for coal, iron and steel production. The concentration of large population at the industrial centres created many problems like that of sanitation, regulation of hours of work, safety and recreation of workers, payment of adequate wages and limitation of hours of work, etc.

Industrialism and urbanism revolutionized the whole meaning and function of Government and politics. Instead of being concerned only with general matters of public health and national unity, Governments had to deal with the problems of social and economic life. The old dynastic conception of ruler and ruled, was replaced by the conception of a state and its citizens. This notion of Government and society is mutually inter-dependent. It was incompatible with the old order and the sharp dynastic distinctions between ruler and subjects. It was the common basis of all the great movements of the nineteenth century such as nationalism, liberalism, democracy and socialism.

Nationalism. European nationalism in its modern sense is mainly a product of the nineteenth century. It was launched by the French Revolution and the Napoleonic Empire. The Jacobin doctrine of sovereignty of the people asserted the claims of the nation as a whole against its monarch and the right of a people to determine its own form of government and to control the conduct of that government. Government should be the voice of the people and not merely of a people. Nationalism proclaimed the rights of all citizens to have an equal voice in the decisions of politics. The conquests of Napoleon in Europe strengthened the ideas and sentiments of nationalism. By 1815, nationalism was a great force in Europe.

Germany and Italy were the two countries where the nationalist feelings were very strong, although the imperialism of Napoleon had similar effects in Spain, Poland, Russia and Belgium. To begin with, nationalism was a spirit of resistance against domination of foreigners and was therefore anti-French. New value was attached to local institutions, native customs, traditional culture and national language.

Germany at that time was having a great cultural Renaissance. It was famous for her musicians, men of letters and philosophers. It was the age of Beethoven, Goethe, Schiller, Kant and Hegel. This helped Germany to oust France from the cultural domination which she had in the eighteenth century. Herder and Fichte taught the Germans to cherish and reverence the Volksgeist or peculiar national character which they presented as the foundation of all good culture and civilisation. After her defeat by Napoleon in the Battle of Jena in 1806, Prussia drastically reorganised her army under the guidance of Gneisenau and Scharnhorst. Her machinery of Government was overhauled by Stein and Hardenberg. After 1815, Prussia emerged as the chief focus of German nationalist hopes. The chief intellectual support for the regeneration of Prussia and growth of nationalism of Germany came from the new University of Berlin where Hegel expounded a new philosophy of authority and state power which captivated many German, Italian and even English thinkers during the nineteenth century. Much of the reorganisation of the Prussian state was an imitation of French revolutionary reforms. Hardenberg wrote to the Prussian King in 1807, "We must do from above what the French have done from below". He praised the success of Carnot's *Levee En Masse*, the conscription of the whole of French manhood and its inspiration with a sense of national mission. The reforms of Prussia were struck by "what endless forces not developed and not utilised slumber in the bosom of a nation". They valued most the creative and irresistible energy which could be generated by a people in arms. They set about building a strong central authority, a truly national army and a system of national education designed to infuse a common spirit into the whole people, a patriotic reverence for the German heritage and a devotion to the cause of German nationalism.

Napoleon paved the way for the unification of Germany by his destruction of the Holy Roman Empire in 1806, by his assembling Bavaria, Wurthemberg, Baden, Hesse-Darmstadt, Saxony and 12 other German states into the Confederation of the Rhine and by his introduction into all Western Germany the Code Napoleon to replace the old laws and judicial procedures. German nationalism was further aroused by the Prussian victory at Leipzig in 1813. It was interpreted as the fruit and justification of all that the nationalists had been preaching and reformers doing to regenerate Prussia. It became a patriotic legend. It forced Napoleon out of most of Germany and even freed the left bank of the Rhine. The victory gave consolation to German national pride. It heartened German patriots. It gave a total fillip to the ideas of total liberation.

Napoleon aroused the nationalist spirit in Italy also. His regime in Italy lasted from 1796 to 1814. Italian sentiment was less anti-French than was German or Spanish. The middle classes in towns welcomed the greater efficiency and weakening of the clerical influence which came with the demolition of the power of petty princes and of the Pope. The reduction of the states to three in Italy by Napoleon encouraged the ideas of ultimate unification of Italy. While he was the ruler of Naples, Murat conceived the idea of uniting the whole of Italy in his own hands and proclaimed the union of Italy in 1815. It is true that he was defeated and shot but his action was not forgotten by Italian patriots.

Both in Germany and Italy, the effect of French rule was to stimulate directly a new spirit of nationalist pride and hope. The unification of these two countries loomed large in European affairs between 1850 and 1870.

As regards Spain, two French divisions surrendered to Spanish forces at the Battle of Baylen in July 1808. Spanish guerrilla bands played an important part in French defeats in the Peninsular War. These achievements were glorified as expressions of Spanish national spirit. As a matter of fact, the forces in Spain which were most actively hostile to Napoleon were the royalist and clerical elements in the country. The rebellious juntas which were organised for local resistance, were mostly run by nobles and priests who were enraged by the treatment of monarchy by Napoleon and the efforts of the French to secularise church property. Popular resistance was led by lower clergy and the monks. It was not at all typical of nationalist uprisings. Without the military genius of Wellington and efficiency of the British infantry, the Spanish guerrillas would have collapsed before the French forces. The strongest stimulus to a real nationalist spirit was the savagery of the fighting in the Peninsular War.

Poland was the centre of aggrieved nationalism in Eastern Europe. Her territory was partitioned among the Empires of Russia, Prussia and Austria between 1772 and 1795. When Napoleon set up the Grand Duchy of Warsaw in 1807 with a new constitution, it was welcomed by the Poles as a step towards restoration and independence. However, Napoleon kept Poland subservient to himself. It became clear that Napoleon was interested in Poland only as a pawn in his relations with Russia. When Napoleon started his Russian campaign in 1812, he gave the Poles vague promises of future independence. The victory of 1814 again obliterated Poland as a state. However, the Code Napoleon and the ideas of the French Revolution were introduced into Poland by Napoleon. The result was that even disappointment added fuel to the burning resolve of Polish patriots to regain national unity and independence which was achieved in 1919.

As regards Russia, the heroic resistance that led to the burning of Smolensk and Moscow and the retreat of the Grand Army of Napoleon through the snows of Russia made a national legend. The pillaging and devastations of the French troops consolidated the resistance of all classes in Russia against Napoleon and the Tsar could not dare to negotiate with Napoleon as there was great hatred against Napoleon among nobles and peasants alike. Just as Germany made a patriotic legend out of the Bathe of Leipzig, the same was done by the Russian patriots from the Moscow campaign. However, these events had little immediate effect on nationalism in Russia.

It is pointed out that in his relations with Europe, Napoleon had no coherent policy. His only desire was to make the conquered countries the satellites of France and adjuncts of his own dynastic ambitions. He followed no consistent policy of arousing nationalities against their Governments. He worked out no principles for organising his Empire. Whatever he did was done in view of the military needs of the moment. The results of his conquests varied according to the conditions of each country. He did not bring about any uniformity among the European states. During the interlude of the Hundred Days in 1815 he declared that he had liberal and constitutional aims and he stated in the Bonapartist legend that he had interests of national independence at heart. That was not correct. His greatest contributions to the growth of nationalism were unwitting. They were more the outcome of revolt against his Empire than the deliberate intention of it.

Liberalism. Another force of change was liberalism. The view of the Liberals was that there should be a more organic and complete relationship between the government and the community and between state and society than it existed during the eighteenth century. European Liberals believed that Governments existed to secure individual rights and derived their just powers from the consent of the governed. The obstacles to these ideas were the privileges of the aristocracy and the church and lack of privileges of merchants, businessmen and manufacturing classes. The spearhead of the liberal attack against feudal rights and the rights of the church was the middle and professional classes. These classes were the central driving force of the French Revolution.

The European Liberals stood for rule of law, parliamentary government, social reform and safeguards against absolutist governments. Liberalism differed from democracy as it stood for the sovereignty of Parliament and not the sovereignty of the people. It advocated the grant of the right of vote to all men of property but not to those who were without property. Liberalism put more emphasis on liberty than equality. To Liberals, the French Revolution had condemned itself by its excesses such as the Reign of Terror, mob democracy and military dictatorship. The Liberals stood for a constitutional monarchy which guaranteed certain rights equally to all citizens or a parliamentary republic which upheld the equality of all before law but a restricted franchise. The Liberals criticised the Vienna Settlement of 1815 on the ground that it had restored absolutism and threatened to restore the privileges of the aristocracy and the church.

Democracy. Another force of change was democracy. Democracy was like liberalism but it was more radical. It stood for the sovereignty of the people and not of a representative parliamentary assembly. It favoured male suffrage. It subordinated the Parliament to the will of the people as a whole. It even advocated the devices of direct democracy such as plebiscite or referendum. It stood for equality of political and civil rights. In extreme forms, it demanded greater social and economic equality. It not only demanded equality of all before law but also equality of opportunity for all. The liberals wanted to secure these rights even at the cost of greater economic levelling. That is why democracy was considered more revolutionary than liberalism. The conservative Governments between 1815 and 1848 were afraid of radical democracy. To meet this danger, Liberals joined hands with conservatives to crush popular movements and uprisings that favoured democratic ideals. More than liberalism, democracy was a central cause of change and revolution after Waterloo.

Socialism. Another force of change was socialism. Until after 1848 socialism was connected in the minds of the people with harmless cranks or with the multitude of pietist Christian communities which fled to the United States in order to lead a simple community life which was free from the complexities of European life. Robert Owen (1771-1858) put into practice many of his utopian theories in his new Lanark Mills. He also set up his cooperative colony of "New Harmony" in North America. He also helped in the growth of cooperative societies and the trade unions. He stood for legislation in the interests of the working classes. Charles Fourier (1772-1837) supported the cooperative movement in France and denounced the economic, social, political and moral disorders from which the society suffered. Those disorders were concerned with poverty, social inequality, war and failure of family life. He stood for the reorganization of society into independent groups called Phalanx. Each person was to do the work he could enjoy best. There was to be no government at all. He had a tendency towards anarchism. Proudhon (1809-65) is generally known as the father of anarchism. According to him, all property is theft. Saint Simon (1760-1825) was not a systematic thinker, but his speculations stimulated the minds of others. He stood for an industrialist state directed by science. In that state, the right of inheritance was to be abolished because it transmitted social privileges from one generation to another without consideration of merit. He did not believe in the natural equality of man. According to him, each man was to be employed according to his ability and rewarded according to his capacity. Louis Blanc (1811-1882) published his famous book "The Organization of Labour" in 1840 in which he denounced the existing competitive system and proposed measures for getting rid of it. He advocated a political reform which would establish the state on a thoroughly democratic basis. The state was to provide farms for agriculturists, factories for workmen and shops for tradesmen. His experiment was tried during the Revolution of 1848 in France.

Socialist ideas were derived from the doctrines of Rousseau and the ideals of the French Revolution. Just as liberals put great emphasis on the ideals of liberty and democrats on the ideals of equality, the socialists put emphasis on the ideal of fraternity. Their contention was that men were good by nature and if they were not influenced by social inequality and poverty, they would behave as brothers towards others. The socialists put emphasis on cooperation rather than competition. They protested against industrialism as a new cause of poverty and inequality.

It is contended that there was enough common ground among liberals, democrats and socialists and they joined hands on the barricades in 1848 and 1871. All of them had the common desire to make Government an organ and agency of society. However, none of the three could depend upon a reliable alliance with the forces of nationalism. Upto 1848, the liberals and nationalists worked together. In order to achieve national unity and independence, patriots felt that they needed the support of all classes which liberalism and democracy would secure. Things changed after 1848. After some time, the socialists felt that they had more to gain from an alliance with authoritarian nationalist governments and undemocratic regimes. Ferdinand Lassalle, the socialist leader of Germany, was prepared to come to terms with Bismarck. When the World War I started in 1914, the socialists in all countries supported their national governments. There was a combination of nationalism and communism in Russia in the form of Bolshevism.

SUGGESTED READINGS

Artz, F.B.: **Reaction and Revolution, 1814 : 1832,** 1934.

Artz, F.B.: **France under the Bourborn Restoration, 1814-1830,** 1931.

Dickinson, G. Lowes : **Revolution and Reaction in Modern France,** 1927.

Elton, G.: **The Revolutionary Idea in France, 1789-1871,** 1923.

Ergang, R.E.: **Herder and Foundations of German Nationalism,** 1931.

Fisher, H.A.L.: **Napoleonic Statesmanship in Germany,** 1903.

Ford, G.S.: **Stein and the Era of Reform in Prussia, 1807-1815,** 1922.

Goodwin, A.: **The European Nobility in the Eighteenth Century.**

Hudson, N.E.: **Ultra-Royalism and the French Restoration,** 1936.

Johnson, D.: **Guizot,** 1963.

Langsam, W.C.: **The Napoleonic Wars German Nationalism in Austria,** 1930.

Phillips, C.S.: **The Church in France, 1789-1848; A Study in Revival,** 1929.

Plamenatz, J.: **The Revolutionary Movement in France, 1815-1871,** 1952.

Shanahan, W.O.: **Prussian Military Reform, 1786-1813,** 1945.

Thomson, David : **Europe Since Napoleon, London,** 1983.

Woodward, E.L.: **Three Studies in European Conservatism,** 1923.

Woodward, E.L. : **French Revolutions,** 1934.

CHAPTER

46 THE ROMANTIC MOVEMENT

If the eighteenth century is called the age of rationalism, the first halt of the nineteenth century is often called the Age of Romanticism. It is true that there were other powerful influences at work, but romanticism was the dominant one, at least in literature and fine arts.

In a broad sense, romanticism was a reaction against the forms and conventions of the eighteenth century. Enlightenment told the people how exactly to think, feel and behave. Neo-classicism set down hard and fast rules which the poet, playwright or artist must observe if he wanted to produce a perfect composition. The result was that rules, formulas and conventions reigned supreme in literature, in fine arts and in society generally. Romanticism was a revolt against classical restraint, intellectual discipline and artificial standards. Romanticism did not oppose everything for which the past stood as literary romanticism proceeded from neo-classicism. A writer or an artist is neither exclusively classical nor romantic. Wordsworth was not entirely free of classicism. Pope was not wholly unromantic.

While enlightenment and neo-classicism put emphasis on reason, romanticism put emphasis on feelings and imagination. During the age of reason, both feeling and imagination were kept under the restraint of taste and decorum. A cultured person was expected to check his feelings and imagination as "something plebian and uncultured." Lord Chesterfield told his son that he had not laughed since he had the use of his reason. Fontenelle never laughed, ran or wept. The restraint which was exercised in polite society was expected to be maintained in literature and fine arts. Only those sentiments were allowed to be expressed which could be suitably displayed in a drawing room.

The Romanticists asserted the rights of feelings and imagination. According to them, feeling was more important than reason. Novalis wrote, "The heart is the key to the world." Goethe maintained that "feeling is everything." Madame de Stael asserted that feeling far surpasses reason as a means of arriving at the truth. The view of Lamartine is that man is really himself only "under the stress of powerful feeling." Man must discard artificial standards in the expression of feelings and follow the prompting of the heart. Imagination must be free from its shackles. The romanticists believed that there should be no check on genius and hence men must follow their imagination. If a work of literature or art shows the sovereignty of reason, with measure, harmony and sympathy in representation, it may be called classical. If it is characterised by the dominance of feeling and imagination, it can be called romantic.

As feelings and imagination differ in each person, romanticism involves the accentuation of the personal or individual. Hence, some of the writers styled romanticism as "the liberation of personality" or "the Emancipation or the ego." During the age of reason, there was standardization which avoided local variations and individual diversities. The individual was subordinated to the general or universal. The rules of neo-classics demanded that the subject-matter of literature must be limited to that which is universal in human experience. As opposed to this, romanticism emphasized the particular and the personal. It was not contrary to good taste to exploit one's own personality.

Accentuation of the person accounts for the diversity of subjects treated in romantic literature and art. The various romanticists led their imagination roam far and wide. What was interesting to them was the primitive, the grotesque, the supernatural, the infinite, the exotic, the medieval, the pastoral, the startling and anything which was novel.

The origins of romanticism cannot be traced to one figure or to one specific movement. There were stirrings in various religious movements of the late seventeenth and early eighteenth centuries. In the church, religion had given way to mere acceptance of certain dogmas and obedience to the authority of the church. Gradually, religion became as cold in its formality as the literature of that time. In Germany, the reaction against dogmatism appeared in the form of Pietism which put emphasis on the inner spirit and emotions and not outward conformity. It considered reason as presumptuous and misleading. It asserted the value and dignity of the individual human soul, with emphasis on God's love for the individual. The Quakers, Baptists and Methodists in England protested against the age of reason. The Methodist movement rekindled once again a sense of religious ardour and enthusiasm in England. It brought feelings once more into repute. Methodist preachers proclaimed their message with fervent enthusiasms. Their hymns were full of emotions. They sounded a deep personal note by putting emphasis on God's interest in every human being. They stressed supreme value of the individual soul and its preciousness in the sight of God. The opening line of a hymn of Charles Wesley was : "Jesus, Lover of my soul."

There was a reaction in the Roman Catholic Church against reason when the goddess of reason was enthroned in the cathedral of Notre Dame in 1793. Chateaubriand published in 1802 in four volumes his book entitled "The Spirit of Christianity" and that book heralded the advent of a sentimental Catholicism. He did not consider religion merely a collection of theological dogmas but a living creed, an aesthetic force. Voltaire had declared Christianity to be ridiculous but Chateaubriand tried to show that Christianity was sublime. He asked his readers to admire the sublimity of Christianity and seek in it satisfaction for their religious emotions. Madame Hamelin wrote, "What! Is that Christianity! Christianity is perfectly delightful."

Romanticism did not leave any area of life untouched, but it found its widest expression in literature. Neo-classicists had shown preference for city life as contrasted with life in the country. To quote Dr. Johnson, "when a man is tired of London, he is tired of life." Life in the country without society, without coffee houses, without news was considered as dreary and monotonous. In Dryden's "The Wild Gallant," Isabella expressed the general sentiment in these words: "I cannot abide to be in the country like a wild beast in the wilderness." However, a feeling arose that man had gone too far from nature and hence a movement started which asked people to go back to nature. The love of nature shown by the romanticists was for the wild and the primitive. They were interested in the spiritual potencies of nature. They transformed the primitive man into the good child of nature who was supremely happy because he obeyed only the pure impulses implanted in him by nature. The romanticists praised the native instincts and emotional qualities of primitive man. They idealized the American Indians, the natives of Africa and the South Sea Islanders. While depicting primitive life in glowing colours, the romanticists relied upon reports of the various expeditions such as that of Captain Cook to Australia and New Zealand. In those reports, there were many accounts of the happy and carefree life of splendid races of savages. Lord Edward FitzGerald reported from New Brunswick in 1788, "Savages have all the real happiness of life, without any of those inconveniences or ridiculous obstacles to it which custom has introduced among us. I have seen human nature under almost all its forms, but the wilder it is, the more virtuous." The romanticists made the most of those reports. In the play entitled "The Indians" which appeared in 1790, an Indian chieftain said, "Away with your culture and refinement! Enjoy the freedom and simplicity of nature. Be guileless! Be an Indian!"

The advocates of reason regarded the masses as inferior to the cultured classes because they were led by their emotions. Voltaire referred to the common people as the "vile canaille." Prevost regarded the common people as too stupid to be depicted in literature. On the other hand, the romanticists considered the lowly classes like primitive man, a repository of goodness because they had been far less exposed to the corruptions of culture and civilisation than the other classes.

Some romanticists regarded folk poetry as the only true poetry because it was the spontaneous expression of the natural impulses of man. They also held legends and myths in high regard. Numerous poets were inspired to write in the manner of the folk song. Collections of folk poetry, folk tales and fairy tales were published. Among them were Percy's Reliques of Ancient English poetry (1765) and Herder's Volkslieder (1778-1779). The Grimm brothers published in 1812 their collection of folk and fairy tales.

The rationalists of the eighteenth century regarded the medieval period of history as a period of barbarism and superstition. They called them the dark ages. Hume treated the Middle Ages with contempt. Moliere Racine and Corneille simply ignored the Middle Ages. Voltaire compared the study of the Middle Ages with a study of the doings of wolves and bears. However, the romanticists considered the Middle Ages as the Golden Age. They found in that period more justice, more happiness, more variety, more colour, more romance and more adventure. Novalis, another German romanticist, praised the Middle Ages as the age of spiritual unity, profound humanitarianism and joy in poverty. In a series of Waverly novels, Sir Walter Scott revived interest in the Middle Ages in Britain. His novels were widely read in Europe. In France medievalism became almost a mania. Young men wore their hair long and grew beards like the people of the Middle Ages. The ladies of France copied the medieval style in their head dresses and jewellery. Masked balls were staged in medieval dress. Plays, operas and novels were built around medieval subjects.

Literary Romanticism. Herder (1744-1803) was the father of German romanticism. He had a high opinion of the irrational, the spontaneous, the natural and the individual of the Middle Ages. He regarded folk poetry as "the true expression of feeling." The other romantic writers of Germany were Goethe, Schlegel, Fichte and Schleiermacher. They praised feudalism, chivalry, the crusades and the medieval folk songs.

As regards France, "The Spirit of Christianity" by Chateaubriand (1768-1848) revived interest not only in Christianity but also idealized the Middle Ages. In his other writings, Chateaubriand glorified nature and pictured the American Indian as a "noble savage." Victor Hugo (1802-1885) carried the romantic tradition of Chateaubriand to its loftiest heights. In his drama entitled "Cromwell" published in 1827, Hugo repudiated the traditions of neo-classicism and embraced all the romantic ideas and aspirations which had been current since the beginning of the century and he became the leader of the romantic movement. He published his famous drama entitled "Hernani" in 1830 and that book made romanticism the vogue for years to come. He published in 1831 his novel called "The Hunchback of Notre Dame" which is considered to be the most successful single work of the period. It stirred men's hearts to the depths.

English romanticism was neither so intense nor so comprehensive as that in Germany and France. It was largely restricted to poetry. Sir Walter Scott is the outstanding figure in novel. English romanticism was an expression of the desire for freedom from the restraining forces of reason and the assertion of the rights of feeling and imagination. The beginning of the age of romanticism in England is usually dated from the publication in 1798 of *Lyrical Ballads*, a collection of poems of Wordsworth (1770-1850) and Coleridge (1772-1834). In his preface to the second edition published in 1800, Wordsworth set forth his ideas of poetry. As regards the subject, his purpose was "to choose incidents and situations from common life." To quote him, "Humble and rustic life was generally chosen because in that condition the essential passions of the heart find a better soil in which they can attain their maturity, are under less restraint and speak a plainer and more emphatic language." As regards style, Wordsworth declared that the language of poetry should be "the language really used by men." The poem entitled "The Rime of the Ancient Mariner" by Coleridge thrills with its images of horror and supernatural beauty. The turbulent soul of Lord Byron (1788-1824) found relief in the wilder aspects of nature, more particularly in mountain peaks and the sea. Byron won fame as the author of the first two cantos of Childe Harold published in 1812. His Don Juan published in 1819 is considered one of the great satirical poems in the English language. He died in Greece while he was fighting for the independence of the Greeks. As regards Shelley (1792-1822), two passions, those for nature and humanity, characterized almost everything he wrote. For him, nature was the incarnation of the divine. Some of the best examples of his poetry of nature are "The Cloud," "To a Skylark" and "Ode to the West Wind." As regards John Keats (1795-1821), the keynote of his work is to be found in the opening line of Endymion (1818), "A Thing of Beauty is a Joy for ever." His odes are among the imperishable things of English verse. Of these, "To a Nightingale" is considered as his masterpiece. Mathew Arnold writes, "No one else in English poetry save Shakespeare has in expression quite the fascinating felicity of Keats, his perfection of loveliness."

As regards Spain, romanticism revived her past. The only genuine romanticist in Russia was Lermontov (1814-1841). Next to Pushkin, he was the greatest Russian poet of the nineteenth century. His most important poetical work was "The Demon" published in 1838. He also published his novel entitled "A Hero of Our Times" in 1839. As regards Italy, Manzone (1785-1873) was a poet, novelist and dramatist. He was a representative of the romantic movement. Like Chateaubriand, he stressed the sublimity of Christianity. His "Sacred Hymns" are among the most beautiful lyrics ever offered to Christianity. His "The Betrothed" is considered the best prose work of Italian romanticism.

Architecture. As regards architecture, the romantic tendency manifested itself in a revival of the Gothic style. Previously, the term "Gothic" was considered to be one of disparagement and even of contempt. It was used as a synonym for "barbarous." However, gradually the term "Gothic" ceased to be one of reproach and became one of admiration. In England, Horace Walpole heralded the revival by his *Castle of Otranto* and *Strawberry Hill.* In Germany, Goethe hailed in Von deutscher Baukunst (1773) Gothic architecture as the glory and peculiar expression of the Germanic spirit. Schlegel and Chateaubriand sang the beauties of Gothic architecture. In France, the new enthusiasm expressed itself not so much in the erection of new buildings as in the restoration of medieval structures. In Germany, there was considerable restoration and reconstruction. The new buildings in a pure Gothic style were limited to a few churches. However, the Gothic revival had the greatest effect in England. The group of parliamentary buildings in London, constructed after the burning of the Old Westminster Palace in 1834 were after the Gothic style. In the succeeding period, the Victorian Gothic became supreme. Not only churches and houses but also railway stations and hotels were built in Gothic style.

Painting. The spirit of romanticism also asserted itself in the field of painting. In romantic paintings, more emphasis was put on spontaneity rather than restraint. For a romantic painter, beauty was not in the subject-matter, harmony or unity but in the depth of feeling. He demanded freedom not only in his choice of subject but also in his way of treating it. He expressed his own personality in his art. Goya (1746-1828), the Spanish artist, depicted Spanish life in all its picturesque diversity, with each individual work reflecting a personal reaction. The leadership in romantic painting fell to two Frenchmen, Gericault (1791-1824) and Delacroix (1799-1863). The work of Gericault is the expression of his personal feelings. His important pictures were painted in 1812 and the succeeding years and they recorded various phases of the end of the Napoleonic era. Some of those pictures are "Wounded Soldiers in a Cart" and "The Return from Russia." His best historical work is "The Raft of the Medusa" (1818). This picture is considered to be "a masterpiece of dramatic vigour and vivid characterization of wide and deep human interest." Delacroix was the greatest painter of the romantic school. He freed himself completely from the conventional rules and types of painting. While choosing his subjects, he allowed his imagination to roam up and down the vistas of history. He was particularly fascinated by the Middle Ages. This is clear from his "Entrance of the Crusaders into Constantinople" and "Templars Carrying Off Rowena." He tried to depict the spirit of his age, particularly its passion for liberty. His "Liberty Leading the People" was inspired by the Revolution of 1830. He has been called "the painter of the soul of his age." The picture which caused the greatest sensation was his "Massacre of Scio" (1824) which is an episode in the Greek struggle for freedom from Turkish rule.

Music. In classical music beauty of form was the primary aim and everything else was secondary. Emotional content was subordinated to form. In romantic music, emotional content comes first and form is subordinate to emotion. Untrammeled self-expression became the primary interest of the romantic composers. Each one tried to express himself in a unique manner. In some of his works, Beethoven showed how music could be the language of personal feeling and individual passion. In his "Pastoral Symphony", Beethoven depicted rustic dances, songs of shepherds and notes of birds of the countryside. Franz Schubert (1797-1828) has rightly been called "the father of the song." His fund of melodies was so great that he could hardly find enough verses to set to music. The number of recorded titles is nearly 500 and he wrote not less than 144 of the melodies in 1815 alone, eight of them on one day. No other composer worked with so much ease as Schubert did. At the time of his death at the age of 31, he left more than 1100 compositions. All his music is characterised by a persistent lyricism. The view of Liszt was that when listening to the music of Schubert, one was bound to exclaim, "How poetical, how beautiful, how intensely Schubert."

Robert Schumann (1810-1856) promoted romantic conceptions not only as a composer but also as a critic. In 1834, he assisted in founding a journal which had as its principal aim the advancement of romanticism in music. To him, music was the language in which he expressed his moods, his sympathies and his literary devotions. Music, was also the medium for making characterizations and portraits of his friends. His symphonies are regarded by some, as the most notable contributions to music.

The compositions of Frederic Chopin (1809-1849), the Polish pianist and composer, have a characteristic finesse, grace and tenderness. In them, he expressed all the ills of his soul. Most of his work is marked by a national spirit, voicing the grievances of the people of Poland. A critic writes about his music, "Like the fugues of Bach, the symphonies of Beethoven, the songs of Schubert and the music dramas of Wagner, Chopin's piano pieces touch the high water-mark in their kind." Schumann called Chopin "the boldest and proudest poetic spirit of the time."

Felix Mendelssohn (1809-1847) ranks high among the composers of music in a happy vein. His two completed oratories. Saint Paul and Elijah, awakened a new interest in this form of music. His other important compositions are "Hymns of Praise" and "Songs without Words," particularly the Spring Song and the Spinning Song.

The two important exponents of programme music were Hector Berlioz (1803-1869), the French composer and Franz Liszt (1811-1886), the Hungarian pianist and composer. Berlioz founded the programme school of music with his "Symphonie Fantastique and the Cantata," "The Death of Sardanapalus." Both of these compositions are distinguished by the concreteness of their imagery, wealth of detail and descriptive literalness. Berlioz is acknowledged as one of the fathers of modern orchestration. Liszt was a prolific composer. He wrote symphonies, songs, piano-forte pieces, masses, psalms and oratorios. As the music of Schumann represents the soul of Germany and the music of Chopin the soul of Poland, the music of Liszt typified the spirit of the Magyars. His influence on pianoforte music was great. His largest works are his *Dante* and *Faust* symphonies.

About the romantic movement Dr. David Thomson writes that as a whole, it corroded the cosmopolitan and non-nationalist outlook on which absolutism has prospered. The romantic writers promoted nationalist sentiments. As the Germany of Goethe, Novalis and Schlegel replaced France as the focus of cultural and intellectual interest, likewise emphasis shifted to pride in nationalism and Volksgeist, the particular genius of a people. The romantic movement, in all its cultural forms, emphasized emotion and sentiment rather than reason and intellect. By turning attention to a misty past, it stirred pride in folk tales and past heroisms. By its very traditionalism, it appealed to sentiments of separatism. It reminded man of all that was special, individual and personal. By its emphasis on creative and original genius, it made human personality more important than society. It condemned restrictions on individual freedom of expression. In its search for the creative genius of an age or of a people, it nourished belief in the supreme value of popular traditions and national development. It made it easy to abandon rationalism for nationalism. The people saw in romanticism the literature of emancipation. Lord Byron declared; "I have simplified my politics into a detestation of all existing Government." Lord Byron became a great personal influence throughout Europe in support of nationalist and liberal causes. Victor Hugo observed. "Romanticism is liberalism in literature." Alexander Pushkin, the Russian poet and dramatist, wrote his greatest works, Boris Godunov and Eugen Onegin in the 1820s. In 1828, Adam Mickiewicz produced his great epic of the Polish nation named Conrad Wallenrod. Czech, Magyar and Serbian poets revived popular interest in the folk legends and wistful memories of their past glories. The Greek War for independence aroused every impulse behind the romantic movement. It recalled the Crusades in its heroism and in its struggle between Cross and Crescent. It sufficiently evoked the old sense of the unity of Christendom. Both Louis XVIII of France and the Pope contributed money to the cause of the Greek War of Independence. As committees in nearly every country raised funds to help the Greeks, the romantic writers threw their influence into the struggle. Chateaubriand and Hugo in France and Shelley and Byron in England sponsored the cause of the Greeks. Shelley declared, "We are all Greeks." Lord Byron died in 1824 in Greece while actually taking part in the Greek War of Independence. By doing so, he became the symbol of the new spirit. Philhellenism created a new current of European opinion in favour of nationalism and liberalism which was against the policies and practices of most of the existing Governments. It won its greatest triumph when it compelled the Governments of Britain, France and Russia to intervene on behalf of the Greeks against the Turkish Government in 1827. (Europe since Napoleon, pp. 142-143).

SUGGESTED READINGS

Anderson A. E.: **Romanticism and the Gothic Revival.**

Barzun, J.: **Classic, Romantic and Modern,** 1961.

Beers, H.A.: **A History of English Romanticism in the Eighteenth Century,** 1932.

Beers, H.A.: **A History of English Romanticism in the Nineteenth Century,** 1929.

Bernbaun, E.: **Guide Through the Romantic Movement,** 1949.

Bowra, C.M.: **The Romantic Imagination,** 1949.

Breul, K.H.: **The Romantic Movement in Literature,** 1927.

Brion, Marcel: **Schumann and the Romantic Age,** 1956.

Brion, Marcel: **Romantic Art,** 1960.

Cippico, A.: **The Romantic Age in Italian Literature,** 1918.

Clark, Kenneth: **The Gothic Revival,** 1928.

Clement, N.H.: **Romanticism in France,** 1939.

Comfort, A.: **Art and Social Responsibility,** 1946.

Comfort, W.W.: (Ed.): **French Romantic Plays,** 1933.

Einstein, A.: **Music in the Romantic Era,** 1947.

Elwin, Malcolm: **The First Romantics,** 1948.

Finch, M.B. and E.A. Pears: **The Origins of French Romanticism,** 1920.

Hough, G.G.: **The Last Romantics,** 1950.

Locke, A.W.: **Music and the Romantic Movement in France,** 1921.

Lucas, F.L.: **The Decline and Fall of the Romantic Ideal,** 1936.

Mason, D.G.: **The Romantic Composers,** 1926.

Mowat, R.B.: **The Romantic Age : Europe in the Early Nineteenth Century.**

Peers, E.A.: **A History of the Romantic Movement in Spain,** 1940.

Porterfield, A.W.: **An Outline of German Romanticism, 1766-1866,** 1914.

Stewart, H.F. and A. Tilley (Ed.): **The French Romanticists,** 1931.

Talmon, J.L.: Political Messianism : **The Romantic Phase,** 1960.

Welby, T.E.: **The Victorian Romantics, 1850-1870,** 1929.

Willoughby, I.A.: **The Romantic Movement in Germany,** 1930.

CHAPTER

47 SPAIN DURING THE NINETEENTH CENTURY

Charles IV

When the French Revolution started in 1789, Spain was being ruled by Charles IV (1788-1808). He was boorish, foolish and easily duped. His Queen was a coarse sensuous woman "with a tongue like a fishwife's." Their heir was Prince Ferdinand who was a conceited, irresponsible young braggart in his early twenties. The true ruler of Spain was Godoy, a vain adventurer who was loved by the Queen, shielded by the king and envied by Prince Ferdinand. From 1795 to 1808, Spain was a vassal of France. No wonder, Napoleon was able in 1807 to secure the approval of the king of Spain to the partition of Portugal of which a liberal share was promised to Godoy. The French troops were allowed to pass through Spain in October 1807 to invade Portugal. On 1 December 1807, Lisbon was occupied and the continental system was proclaimed in force.

Joseph Bonaparte becomes King of Spain

In spite of that, French troops continued to cross the Pyrenees and possess themselves the whole of the Iberian peninsula. Public opinion in Spain blamed the king and Godoy for the invasion of their country. Prince Ferdinand supported the people. There were riots in Spain. In order to save Godoy, the king abdicated and announced the succession of Prince Ferdinand as Ferdinand VII on 17 March 1808. On the pretext of mediating between the rival factions in Spain, Napoleon lured King Charles IV, Ferdinand and Godoy to Bavonne on the French frontier. By threats and cajolery, Napoleon persuaded both Charles and Ferdinand to resign all of their claims to the throne of Spain. Charles retired to Rome on a pension from Napoleon. Ferdinand was kept for six years under strict military guard in France. The Bourbons ceased to reign in Spain. Napoleon appointed his brother Joseph Bonaparte the king of Spain. In July 1808, Joseph Bonaparte was crowned King of Spain at Madrid. Soon after his accession to the throne, Joseph granted to the people of Spain the favours of the Napoleonic regime. He decreed equality before the law, individual liberties, abolition of feudalism and serfdom, educational reforms, suppression of the Inquisition, diminution of monasteries, confiscation of church property and public improvements.

Spanish Resistance

It is true that Napoleon was able to put his brother on the throne of Spain without much difficulty, but he had now to face opposition from the people of Spain. The Spanish people hated their late king for his weakness and treachery. They hated Joseph Bonaparte as a foreigner and an upstart. They were devoted to the cause of Spain. Priests and nobles made common cause with the common people. They were all agreed that they would not allow a foreigner to rule over them. Spain blazed forth in angry insurrection. Revolutionary committees were set up in the provinces. People were recruited to fight for their country. A nationalist reaction was in full swing. By August 1808, Joseph Bonaparte was forced to run away from Madrid and the French troops were in retreat towards the Pyrenees.

British help

It was at this time that George Canning, the Foreign Minister of England, promised help to the people of Spain. He declared, "We shall proceed upon the principle that any nation of Europe which starts up to oppose a power which, whether professing insidious peace or declaring open war, is the common enemy of all nations, becomes instantly our ally." In August 1808, a British army under the command of Sir Arthur Wellesley (later Duke of Wellington) landed in Portugal and proceeded to cooperate with the Portuguese and the Spaniards against the French. It was the beginning of the Peninsular War which was to last until 1813 and spell disaster for Napoleon.

Joseph Bonaparte driven from Spain

Within three weeks after their landing, the British were in possession of Portugal. Realising the gravity of the situation, Napoleon assumed personal command of the French forces in the Peninsula. So great was his vigour and resourcefulness that Napoleon was able to reinstate his brother Joseph in Madrid in December 1808 and drove the main British army out of Spain. Early in 1809, Napoleon had to go away from Spain on account of developments in another part of Europe. The Marshals whom Napoleon left behind quarrelled with one another and they were not able to put up a united front against the people of Spain who were being helped by the people of Great Britain. The French troops had to face many difficulties in Spain. The nature of the country created many obstacles. Farms were poor, Settlements were sparse and provisions were scarce. The French armies were not able to support themselves at the cost of the people of Spain. There were sudden alternations of heat and cold in Northern Spain. There were insanitary conditions in many towns in Spain. The result was that disease spread among the French soldiers. The succession of fairly high and steep mountain ranges in Spain prevented any campaigning on a large scale to which the soldiers and generals of Napoleon were accustomed. The result was that the French troops were not able to meet the Spaniards who were adepts in irregular guerrilla fighting. The fierce patriotic determination of the people of Spain to drive out the foreigners was an additional advantage for them. They were also helped by England with arms and trained commanders. The warfare in Spain dragged on. In 1812, Wellington, with his allied British and Spanish troops, won a great victory at Salamanca. He captured Madrid and drove Joseph Bonaparte and the French to Valencia.

The Spanish Constitution of 1812

In 1812, radical groups of Spaniards who had learnt revolutionary doctrines from the French, assembled at Cadiz and drafted a constitution for their country. This Spanish Constitution of 1812 served for long as a model for liberal constitutions throughout Southern Europe. The Constitution proclaimed the basic principle of the French Revolution : "Sovereignty is vested essentially in the nation and accordingly it is to the nation exclusively that the right of making its fundamental laws belongs." The legislative power was to be exercised by the Cortes, a single chamber Parliament elected for two years by indirect suffrage. The executive power was to be exercised by the king through his ministers. He was to have only a suspensive veto on the acts of the Cortes. The Constitution proclaimed the principles of individual liberty and legal equality and sought to abolish the old regime completely. Provision was made for a thorough reorganisation of courts, local administration, taxation, the army and public education. The Constitution provided that "the religion of the Spanish nation is and always will be the Apostolic Church of Rome, the only true Church." However, the Inquisition was suppressed and ecclesiastical property was secularised.

In 1813, Wellington started from Portugal for Spain and drove the French before him. In the Battle of Vittoria, Joseph Bonaparte lost all his artillery and stores. Wellington's campaign of 1814 began in the South of France but by that time the Battle of Nations was going on and Napoleon himself was overthrown in 1814.

Restoration of Ferdinand

After the downfall of Napoleon, Ferdinand VII was restored to the throne of Spain in 1814. Not through any efforts on his part but rather through the efforts of Wellington and the British and his own patriotic subjects, he found a robust sense of nationalism and constitutional Government in the country. The Constitution of 1812 which was largely the work of middle class persons, scholars, theorists and army officers was in force. It had been tolerated by most Spaniards so long as it seemed necessary for the whole nation to present a united front against the French. However, as soon as peace was restored and national independence of the country was assured, the nobles and the clergy protested against the Constitution. Ferdinand VII who has been described by one historian as "cowardly in adversity and in prosperity tyrannical," declared the Constitution of 1812 null and void and abolished the Cortes. Ferdinand surrounded himself with advisers drawn exclusively from officials of the old regime, and instituted a thoroughly reactionary policy. He was not prepared to compromise with revolutionary principles. He restored the old system of absolute Government with all its inequalities and injustices. The privileges of the clergy and nobility, including exemption from taxation, were restored. The Inquisition was reestablished. Individual liberties were taken away. The press was placed under strict censorship. The Liberals who had assisted in making the royal restoration possible, were arbitrarily arrested. They were banished from the country or thrown into prison. It is true that there was not much bloodshed but that was due to the role of Wellington.

Reactionary Policy of Ferdinand

Ferdinand was unscrupulous. He was vindictive and not gifted with prudence and foresight. Instead of following a middle path between the extremists and those seeking to consolidate the whole nation, he threw all his weight on the side of reactionaries. He took so strong action against the liberals that even Metternich advised him to be moderate. Instead of trying to repair the injuries inflicted on his country by the Peninsular War, he hampered trade and industry. He squandered enormous sums of money upon himself and his favourites. Instead of adopting a policy of conciliation towards the Spanish colonies in America, he neglected them at the beginning and when it was too late, tried to subjugate them by force of arms. The result was that within five years of his restoration, Spain was hopelessly divided into two camps of conservatives and liberals. There were grave scandals and abuses in administration. The Spanish army was honeycombed with disaffection. The treasury was bankrupt. The Spanish colonies in America were in open revolt. The liberals started agitation against the king. As there was no right of public meeting and there was no freedom of the press, the agitators gradually were attracted to such secret societies as the Carbonari and Freemasons. The lodges were centres of revolutionary propaganda. The liberals also carried on their propaganda throughout the country by means of signs and grips and mysterious passwords. They were able to communicate to the people of Spain the teachings of liberty, equality and fraternity. Spain was faced with a civil war.

Surrender of Ferdinand to Liberals

In 1819, Ferdinand assembled at Cadiz an army for the subjugation of the Spanish colonies in America. There was a mutiny in that army. It was a signal for a general insurrection in the country. There was trouble in Seville, Barcelona, Saragossa and the Asturias. Instead of facing the revolt, Ferdinand surrendered in March 1820. He took an oath to support the Spanish Constitution of 1812 and appealed to the Liberals in these words: "Let us advance frankly, myself leading the way along the constitutional path." The rebels believed in him and laid down their arms.

Although Ferdinand surrendered in 1820, he had no intention of keeping his pledge. For two years (1820-1822), he ruled the country in accordance with the statutes of the newly convened Cortes and under the direction of his liberal ministers. However, during that time, he kept on strengthening reactionary forces in the country. He also wrote letters to the great Powers, especially the ruler of France to help him. The liberals in Spain started quarrelling among themselves. The clergy and the nobles resisted the execution of reform legislation. The Catholics in Spain treated as sacrilege and blasphemy the anti-clerical tendencies of the new Parliament. In many districts, there were riots. There was anarchy in the country.

The reactionary powers of Europe considered the situation in Spain to be grave and decided to interfere. Tsar Alexander I offered to lead a Russian army across Europe to reinstate Ferdinand VII to absolutism. Both Metternich and the King of France were opposed to that proposal. At the Congress of Verona held in 1822, it was proposed that a French army, acting on a general European mandate, should intervene in Spain. The advantage in the proposal was that France would be spared the humiliation of seeing foreign troops cross her borders. Ferdinand VII, a Bourbon king, would be restored in absolutism. The cause of reaction would be successful in Spain. The monarchy of France would get the credit and hence would be strengthened. The proposal was accepted by Metternich but objected to by Britain.

French Intervention in Spain

Early in 1823, the Governments of France, Austria-Hungary, Russia and Prussia presented separate notes to the liberal ministry of Spain and demanded the abolition of the Constitution of 1812 and liberation of Ferdinand VII from the restraints which had been put on him. The liberals of Spain protested against unwarranted interference in their domestics affairs. However, the French army under the Duke of Angouleme, a nephew of Louis XVIII crossed the Pyrenees. In May, 1823, Angouleme was in possession of Madrid. The liberal ministry and Cortes fled to Cadiz and took away along with them Ferdinand VII as a hostage. From June to October 1823, Cadiz was closely besieged by the French. On 1 October 1823, the liberals released the king on the understanding that he would grant a general pardon and set up a "moderate Government." Ferdinand promised and Cadiz immediately capitulated. The liberals laid down their arms.

As soon as Ferdinand VII found himself safe within the French lines, he repudiated all his promises and pronounced sentence of death upon all "constitutionalists." Angouleme asked Ferdinand VII to be moderate and conciliatory. The representatives of Metternich, Tsar Alexander and Frederick William III of Prussia urged vigour to the royal arm. Ferdinand VII could always, be vigorous. In 1824, there was a reaction throughout Spain. The recent liberal measures were abrogated. The revolutionaries and the sympathizers with constitutional Government were hunted out with cleverness. Hundreds were put to death arbitrarily. Hundreds more were exiled and jailed. By the time the French army withdrew from the country, Ferdinand VII had broken the back of liberalism in Spain.

Revolt of Spanish Colonies in America

There was a sort of revolution in Spanish colonies for about two decades from 1810 to 1830. There were many reasons for that. Some of the upper-class Spanish colonists had become infected with the enlightened political philosophy of the eighteenth century. They were also inspired by the successful revolt of the English colonies in North America in the latter half of the eighteenth century. They were influenced by the French Revolution to become independent of Spain. The conditions prevailing in Spain during the Napoleonic era and the fighting between the French and the English, gave rise to disputes concerning the authority of the Spanish Governors in America and enabled Spanish colonial leaders to direct their affairs in Mexico, New Granada, Peru and Buenos Aires without any reference to Madrid. Moreover, the Spanish colonies who were accustomed to free trade with Great Britain during the Napoleonic era, were not willing to return to the mercantilist system of Spain and exclude British goods from their ports. They were encouraged by British traders and even by the British Government to disobey Spanish Government.

In 1806, colonial patriots of Argentina expelled from Beunos Aires an invading British expedition. In Venezuela, Francisco Miranda who had served under Washington in the War of American Independence and under Dumouriez in the Wars of French Revolution, undertook to overthrow Spanish rule and set up a republic with the help of Britain. By 1810, there were widespread unrest and revolts throughout Spanish America. In Mexico, Miguel Hidalgo led thousands of peasants in an uprising against colonial landlords and the Spanish Government. In Argentina, the Spanish colonists set up a local committee as a provisional government and adopted a blue and white national flag. In Chile, a similar revolutionary committee was set up, including Bernardo O'Higgins, an able military leader. In Venezuela and Mexico Miranda resumed his seditious efforts with the cooperation of Bolivar who had taken an oath to "liberate" all Spanish America.

To begin with, the revolutionary disturbances were repressed by royalists and reactionaries among the Spanish colonists in America. Hidalgo was captured, tried and put to death in Mexico in 1811. Morelos, another priest who had incited a similar insurrection, was put to death in 1815. Miranda was taken prisoner in 1812 and he died four years after. The revolutionary committee or Junta of Chile was overthrown in 1814. O'Higgins ran away to Argentina. In the same year, Bolivar ran away and took refuge in Haiti.

In 1812, San Martin, a selfless colonial patriotic leader, came to the help of the Junta at Buenos Aires. Under his guidance, Argentina was cleared of royalist opposition and was proclaimed an independent republic in 1816. After that, San Martin carried the struggle against Spain into Chile and Peru. The independence of Chile was secured in 1818. Lima was captured by San Martin and the independence of Peru was declared in 1821. In the meantime, Paraguay had asserted its independence in 1811 and had entrusted dictatorial powers in Jose Francia.

In 1817, Bolivar returned to Venezuela. He was instrumental in the creation in 1819 of the independent republic of Colombia embracing New Granada, Panama, Venezuela and Equador, in the completion of the work of San Martin and freeing Peru in 1824 and in the erection of upper Peru into another independent republic named Bolivia in 1825. There were quarrels amongst his lieutenants and the people whom he had liberated. When he died in 1830, Colombia was already breaking up into three separate republics of Colombia, Venezuela and Equador. However, his achievements against Spanish rule in America were lasting and his tomb is a shrine for all Spanish Americans.

Florida was ceded to the United States in 1819. Santo Domingo rebelled against Spain in 1821 and was conquered by the Negro republic of Haiti in 1822. In Mexico, the conservative Spanish colonists took matters in their own hands and established in 1821 an empire with Iturbide as Emperor. The Spanish colony of Guatemala revolted and was incorporated in the Mexican empire. In 1823, there was a revolution in Mexico. Iturbide was overthrown and executed. Central America seceded and formed an independent union of its own. Mexico adopted a republican constitution.

When all this was happening, Ferdinand VII of Spain could not do anything to re-establish his authority in the new world. He wished to do so and Metternich and Tsar Alexander encouraged him to do so. In 1819, he assembled an army at Cadiz for the subjugation of the American colonies, but there was a mutiny in the army and that precipitated the revolutionary regime of 1820-23 in Spain. By the time Ferdinand VII was restored to absolutism in 1823 by the French forces, the way to intervention and restoration in Spanish America was barred by Great Britain and the United States.

Monroe Doctrine

So far as Great Britain was concerned, British traders and manufacturers were carrying on flourishing business with Spanish America during the French Revolution and the Napoleonic era. They were opposed to the restoration of Spanish control in Spanish America as that was against their economic interests. Great Britain was motivated by commercial considerations. However, the fear of the United States was that she did not want Metternich's policy of intervention to be extended to Spanish America. Whatever the differences in the aims of the two countries, they stood for the liberation of the Spanish colonies and prevention of foreign intervention in their internal affairs. With the backing of the British Government, the United States formally recognised in 1822 the independence of Colombia, Chile, Argentina and Mexico. In December 1823, President Monroe enunciated the famous Monroe doctrine in these words : "In the wars of the Europeon powers, in matters relating to themselves, we have never taken any part, nor does it comport with our policy so to do. It is only when our rights are invaded or seriously menaced that we resent injuries or make preparations for our defence. With the movements in this hemisphere we are of necessity more immediately connected, and by causes which must be obvious to all enlightened and impartial observers. The political system of the allied powers (Austria, Russia and Prussia), is essentially different in this respect from that of America....We owe it, therefore, to candor, and to the amicable relations existing between the United States and those powers, to declare that we should consider any attempt on their part to extend their system to any portion of this hemisphere as dangerous to our peace and safety. With the existing colonies and dependencies of any European power we have not interfered and shall not interfere. But with the Governments who have declared their independence and maintained it and whose independence we have on great consideration and on just principles acknowledged, we could not view any interposition for the purpose of oppressing them or controlling in any other manner their destiny by any European power in any other light than as the manifestation of an unfriendly disposition towards the United States."

In 1824, Great Britain formally recognised the independence of Mexico and Colombia. Her recognition of the independence of other Spanish colonies was temporarily withheld. Metternich gave up all hope of using the concert of Europe for the suppression of liberalism beyond the seas. Spain also made no efforts to subdue her colonies in America although she delayed for a long time the recognition of their independence.

Isabella (1833-68.) Ferdinand VII died in 1833. He had only one daughter at the time of his death. However, before his death, he annulled the Salic law which restricted the succession only to the male line. He summoned the great officers of the state, the grandees of Spain and the members of the Cortes to take a solemn oath of allegiance to his daughter as the future ruler of Spain. The result was that after his death, his daughter was proclaimed Queen as Isabella II with her mother Maria Christina as regent. This was resented by Don Carlos, the younger brother of Ferdinand VII, who wanted to become the king of Spain after the death of his brother in 1823. His claim was supported by the church and the great nobles while the claim of Isabella was upheld by a large part of the army, by the Cortes and by most of the middle class. This led to a civil war which lasted for 7 years. There was a lot of ferocity during this civil war but ultimately Isabella II won.

In 1843, Isabella attained the age of 13 and was declared of age. She continued to occupy the throne for the next 25 years. As a Queen, Isabella was foolish and frivolous. She was impulsive and impatient of restraint. At the age of 16, she was married to Don Francisco, a cousin. When the marriage proved unhappy, she threw away all restraint and moved from one affair to another. She shocked Europe with the scandals of her private life. On account of increasing financial difficulties and endless changes of ministries, there was a revolt against Isabella in 1868 and she was driven into exile.

In 1869, a constitution based on popular sovereignty was promulgated. It was decided to offer the crown of Spain to some prince other than Alfonso, the son of Isabella in whose favour she had abdicated. However, the choice of finding a suitable ruler for Spain was found to be very difficult. In the words of Prim, the Minister of War, "Finding a democratic king on earth is like looking for an atheistic king in Heaven." The crown was offered to a number of persons including Prince Leopold of Hohenzollern, whose candidature was the immediate cause of the Franco-Prussian war in 1870. Finally, Amadeo, the second son of Victor Emmanuel II, accepted the crown and he has proclaimed King in 1871. However, he realised soon that the throne was not a bed of roses. He tried to placate all factions but failed. His highest disqualification was that he was a foreigner. He resigned and a republic was proclaimed in Spain. However, the people were not willing to have a republic and that led to the restoration of the Bourbons in the person of Alfonso XII, the son of Isabella.

Alfonso XII (1874-1885). During his reign, Spain attained some degree of stability. A constitution was drawn up by the Cortes in 1876 which limited the powers of the king, provided for a ministry responsible to the lower house of the Cortes and granted individual liberty. This constitution remained in force until after World War I. The Senate was partly appointive and partly elective. The members of the House of Representatives were elected for 5 years. In spite of the new constitution, there were disorders in the administration. Spain made some recovery during his reign. He died in 1885 at the age of 28.

Alfonso XIII (1886-1931). A few months after the death of Alfonso, a son was born to his wife, Maria Christina of Austria. The mother acted as regent during his childhood. It was during this period that Spain lost her remaining colonies. The important colonies of Spain were Cuba, Puerto Rico and the Philippines. Cuba had risen in revolt in 1868. Fighting ceased after a decade but there was no peace. In 1895, rebellion broke out on a large Scale in Cuba. When the Government resorted to savage repression, the Americans grew indignant over the treatment of the Cubans. The American battleship *Maine* was blown up in Havana harbour. Public opinion in the United States demanded the evacuation of the Spaniards from Cuba. War was declared in 1898. Admiral Dewey won the Battle of Manila and Admiral Sampson destroyed the Spanish fleet. The Spaniards gave up the fight. By the provisions of the peace treaty, Spain gave up her sovereignty not only over Cuba, but also over Puerto Rico and the Philippines. A little later Spain sold most of the scattered remnants she still held.

In 1902, the regency came to an end and the young Prince took his place among the monarchs of Europe as Alfonso XIII. As a youngman, he excelled in polo, tennis, hunting and yachting. As a King he insisted upon playing a vigorous role in the solution of the problems of his country. No less than ten attempts were made to assassinate him but he remained unhurt. He gave peace to his country which for decades was torn by dynastic, religious, personal, economic and regional hatreds. Spain made steady progress in the development of her industries, in the expansion of her foreign trade, in removing illiteracy and other respects.

There was an increase in enterprises of every kind—banks, financial establishments, industries and mines. 15,000 kilometres of rail roads stretched across Spain in 1920. Spanish trade increased considerably. Her credit recovered as a result of a vigorous reorganisation of finance and budgets.

However, the condition of the masses left much to be desired. The agricultural labourers lived just above the subsistence level. Agriculture suffered from the systems of land tenure. The proprietors of the large estates were mostly absentee landlords. Total production was very low. The condition of the industrial worker was a little better. Laws were passed to protect the workers against accidents. Old age pensions were established. The hours of Work in the mines were limited. In these conditions, socialism began to make progress. Most of the recruits of socialism were workmen. The Socialist Labour Party of Spain had one member elected to the Cortes in 1910.

In general, there was considerable friction between the church and the state in Spain. The view of Madariaga is that "the history of the nineteenth century in Spain would have been much quieter and much richer in results had the evolution of the Spanish people taken place in the absence of clericalism and militarism" (Spain, p. 220). The power of the Roman Catholic Church in Spain was very great and the Church interfered in the administration in every way. In 1913, there were about 3,800 religious orders in Spain with some fifty-five thousand members, almost three-quarters of them being women. There were many causes of friction between the clericals and anti-clericals. Some of the liberals were frankly anti-clerical. There was a lot of resentment as religious orders were allowed to engage in trade without being taxed. The reactionary attitude of the orders in the field of education created much opposition. Many Spaniards, particularly the working classes, were enemies of the monastic orders. In 1910, the Government passed the Congregations Act which provided that no new congregations could establish houses without authorisation from the Government and orders engaged in trade or manufacture of any kind must pay taxes and submit to inspection like other individuals. All orders were forbidden to own any property which was not absolutely necessary for the purpose to which the association was devoted.

SUGGESTED READINGS

Altamira, R.: **History of Spain from the Beginning to the Present Day,** 1949.

Angell, Hildegarde: **Simon Bolivar South American Liberator,** 1930.

Hasbrouck, Alfred: **Foreign Legionaries in the Liberation of Spanish South America,** 1928.

Hennessy, C.A.M.: **The Federal Republic in Spain,** 1962.

Humboldt, Alexander Von: **Political Essays in the Kingdom of New Spain.**

Madariaga: **The Fall of the Spanish American Empire,** 1948.

Mitre, Bartolme: **Emancipation of South America,** 1893.

Moses, Bernard: **Spain's Declining Power in South America, 1730-1806,** 1919.

Oliveira, A.R.: **Politics, Economics and Men of Modern Spain, 1808-1946,** 1946.

Peter de Poland: **A Queen of Spain, Isbella II,** 1962.

Robertson, W.S.: **Rise of the Spanish American Republics,** 1918.

Robertson, W.S.: **Life of Miranda,** 1929.

Sencourt, R.E.: **The Spanish Crown, 1808-1931,** 1932.

Trend, J.B.: **The Origins of Modern Spain,** 1934.

CHAPTER 48

EUROPE AND THE WORLD

Even before the nineteenth century, the Europeans had expanded in various parts of the world. Spain and Portugal were foremost in this matter. They had not only trade in various parts of the world but also had established their colonies. Portugal acquired a foothold in India in the beginning of the sixteenth century and established her control over Goa and other places. She also had her colony in Brazil in South America Spain had a big colonial empire in Central and South America. The Dutch set up their colonies in the Far East. The French set up their colonies in North America and also acquired some territory in India. In the straggle for supremacy, the French were defeated by the British in India. The French colonies in North America were conquered by Britain in the Seven Years' War. Britain lost the American colonies during the last quarter of the eighteenth century. Spain also lost her colonies in Central and South America during the first quarter of the nineteenth century. In 1882, Portugal lost Brazil.

European Expansion during Nineteenth Century

During the second half of the eighteenth century, the Physiocrats preached in France the doctrine of freedom from restrictions. They made the old French colonial system with its monopoly regulations their target. In England, Adam Smith asserted in his book entitled "The Wealth of Nations" (1776) that the burdens of the British colonial system were undeniable but the benefits were purely imaginary. Bentham advocated the emancipation of the colonies. There was an aggressive and vocal opinion in England against colonies. One group known as "Little Englanders" of which Gladstone was a member, even believed that time was not far distant when the British Empire would dissolve completely. In 1852, Disraeli wrote to the British Foreign Secretary, "These wretched colonies will all be independent in a few years and are millstones around our necks". There was a similar sentiment in France. Most of the French statesmen of that period believed that colonies were an unjustifiable luxury. It is true that during the period from 1815 to 1870 France had more than doubled her possessions outside Europe by securing footholds in Algeria, Senegal and Indo-China, but those ventures were launched by a small group and were not a part of a wider policy. In 1861, the French Government expressed its idea of empire by throwing open the trade of her colonies to all nations. In Germany, neither the Government nor public opinion showed much interest in colonies before the 1880s. Bismarck observed thus in 1868 : "All the advantages claimed for the mother country are for the most part illusory. England is abandoning her colonial policy; she finds it too costly."

Revival of Imperialism

However, during the last decades of the nineteenth century, the pendulum swung in the other direction. Books and pamphlets were written to show that colonies were a necessity and not a burden. Colonial societies were organised to stimulate interest in imperialism. Britain gave up her policy of free trade and set up protective tariffs. Disraeli himself announced his conversion to imperialism in 1872. In France, the movement in that direction was led by a number of prominent statesmen including Gambetta and Jules Ferry. Ferry was the arch-champion of French imperialism. To quote him, "Every fragment of our colonial domain, every tiny morsel should be sacred to us.....It is not a question of tomorrow's future, but the future of fifty or a hundred years from now." In 1882, Leroy-Beaulieu, the economist, asserted that "colonial expansion must occupy me first place in our national consciousness" because it "is for France a question of life or death; either France will become a great African state or she will be in a century or two but a second rate power". In Germany, imperialist sentiments became fashionable in the early eighties. In 1882, a colonial society was set up in Germany and it enrolled more than 10,000 members within three years.

There were many factors which were responsible for the revival of imperialism. Some of them were political ambition, military adventure and missionary enterprise. The argument of over-population in Europe was also given but it was pointed out that actual over-population in Europe did not exist in any serious degree until near the end of the nineteenth century. Another factor was national prestige. There was a belief that the acquisition of colonies reflected the glory of the mother country. Some defenders of imperialism attributed true altruism as the cause of imperialism. Their contention was that European imperialism bestowed on "backward" nations the blessing of civilisation, law and order and Europeans should be ready to sacrifice their ease and comfort to bring those blessings to the backward people. This theory was called "The White Man's Burden". Rudyard Kipling was one of the advocates of this theory and he wrote thus :

> Take up the White Man's burden,
> Send forth the best ye breed,
> Go bind your sons to exile,
> To serve your captive's need.

Regarding White Man's Burden, Lord Oliver wrote, "No nation has ever colonized, annexed or established a sphere of influence from motives of disinterested philanthropy towards a native people". It is rightly pointed out that the assertion of high principles by statesmen and imperialists was a pretext for acquiring colonies. Sentimental, moral and altruistic considerations were convenient justifications of imperialism. Of themselves, they could not have set imperialism in motion.

As regards the actual motives behind this imperialism, J.A. Hobson, a famous British economist, attributed the colonial expansion of this period to special new economic forces at work in the most industrialised nations of Western and Central Europe. Whatever political, religious or idealistic excuses might be made, the real impulse was always one of capitalistic greed for cheap raw materials, advantageous markets, good investments and fresh field of exploitation. The argument is that what Hobson called "the economic taproot of imperialism" was "excessive capital in search of investment" and that excessive capital came from the savings made possible by the unequal distribution of wealth. Hobson maintained that the remedy was internal social reform and a more equal distribution of wealth. To quote him, "If the consuming public in this country raised its standard of consumption to keep pace with every rise of productive powers, there could be no excess of goods or capital clamorous to use imperialism in order to find markets." It cannot be denied that the search for lucrative and secure overseas investment played a very, great part in the European urge to acquire colonies at the end of the nineteenth century.

In his pamphlet on "Imperialism, the Highest Stage of Capitalism" (1916), Lenin elaborated the argument to emphasize the importance of finance capital rather than industrial capital, and the priority of the desire to find new outlets for investment rather than new markets. His thesis was that imperialism was "a direct continuation of the fundamental properties of capitalism in general" and that "the War of 1914 was on both sides imperialist."

The view of Dr. David Thomson is that imperialism was not entirely or even basically an economic phenomenon. Howsoever important the economic forces were, they cannot explain why France, one of the least fully industrialised countries of Western Europe, was the one which had already set the pace of expansion by more than doubling her colonial possessions between 1815 and 1870 when she got firm footholds in Algeria, Senegal and Indo-China. It is not mere thirst for exporting surplus capital which can explain the new shape given to the British Empire by the grant of Dominion status to Canada, Australia, New Zealand and the Union of South Africa. This also does not explain the increase in British commercial and capitalist interests in the United States after her independence or the migration of Englishmen to the United States or British interest in the construction of railways in Argentina as compared with the construction of railways in India. German economic penetration of Eastern Europe, the Balkans and the Ottoman Empire was without any of these territories becoming German colonies. This new imperialism spread mainly in Africa and Asia. Those areas of Africa and of Asia had not been brought under European influence before 1870. This expansion took place at a time when the European nations were competing with one another.

Among the economic forces behind it, the urge to find new outlets for the "glut of capital" and fresh markets for industrial output were more important than the quest for raw materials or the factor of overpopulation. Africa and Asia offered many of the raw materials needed by the multiplying factories of Europe such as cotton, silk, rubber, vegetable oils and rare minerals. Many of those raw materials could be and were, got by trading without political control. The pressure of population in Europe was becoming great by the early twentieth century, but it still found free outlet in migration to the United States, Australia and New Zealand. Neither Africa nor Asia offered climatic or economic conditions strong enough to attract large-scale white settlements and the pressure of population within Japan, China and India was so great that there was hardly any scope for immigration. The main impediments to European migration came only after 1918.

The search for markets to sell manufactured goods was an important factor, but here also the political factor was not less important than the purely economic factor. Upto 1870, British manufacturers of textiles, machinery and hardware found good markets in other European countries. After 1870, Germany, France, Belgium and other nations were able to satisfy their own home markets which they began to protect against imports from Britain by tariff barriers. They even produced a surplus for which they wanted markets abroad. With increasing saturation of European markets, all started looking for more open markets overseas. They found their Governments responsive to national needs to undertake the political conquest of undeveloped territories. The vast undeveloped areas of Africa and Asia offered the most inviting opportunities provided they could be made safe for investment by conquering them. The ports of Africa and the Far East were valuable as naval bases and ports of call and also for trade and investment. The international anarchy prevailing at that time gave an impetus to the general race for colonies. Normally, the co-existence of economic interests with political aims made a country imperialistic. In some countries like Russia and Italy, political considerations predominated. Neither Italy nor Russia had a surplus of manufactures or capital to export, yet both of them joined in the race for colonies. Although Norway had a large merchant fleet, she did not join the race. The Dutch were active in colonialism before the more industrialised people of Belgium. What determined whether a country became imperialistic or not, depended more upon the activity of small groups of people, often intellectuals, economists or patriotic publicists or politicians who were anxious to ensure national security and self-sufficiency, than the economic conditions of the country itself. Moreover, nations that had traditions of colonialism were more prompt to seek colonies than those nations which had no such traditions.

In addition to the above, there were many other considerations which created the desire for colonies. One of them was the activities of the explorers and adventurers. The names of Du Chaillu and De Brazza are associated with explorations in equatorial Africa. The name of Stanley is associated with explorations in the Congo basin, and of Karl Peters in East Africa. Men of initiative and energetic enterprise who wanted money and power also played their part. Such was the role of Cecil Rhodes in South Africa.

Christian missionaries also played their part in the spread of colonialism. The most famous among them was David Livingstone. He was originally sent to Africa by the London Missionary Society. Later on, he returned to Africa under Government auspices as an explorer "to open a path for commerce and Christianity". When he disappeared for some years in search of the source of the Nile, Stanley was sent to find him and he met him in 1872 on the shores of Lake Tanganyika. When Livingstone died in Africa in 1873, his body was taken to London under naval escort to be buried in Westminister Abbey as a great national hero. France also sent many missions to Africa to convert the natives of Africa to Christianity. The Catholic missions of France were exceptionally active. They were spread all over the world, including the Near and Far East. In 1869, Cardinal Lavigerie founded the Society of African Missionaries who came to be known as "White Fathers". By 1875, they spread from Algeria into Tunisia and set up a religions protectorate that preceded the political protectorate. Gambetta said of Cardinal Lavigerie that "his presence in Tunisia is worth an army for France". There were other French missions which penetrated into all the parts of Africa. They set up schools and medical services in Africa for the benefit of the natives. Belgian missionaries were active in the Congo.

Another element responsible for the growth of imperialism was the administrator and soldier who was not a missionary but welcomed an opportunity to bring order and efficient administration in the new colonies. To this category belonged Lord Cromer in Egypt, Lord Lugard in Nigeria, Lord Milner at the Cape, Marshal Lyautey in Morocco, and Karl Peters in German East Africa. Without their help, it would not have been possible to consolidate European control over Africa.

The sources and nature of the urge to imperialism were many and they varied considerably from one country to another. Sometimes trade followed the flag. Sometimes the flag accompanied the botanist and buccaneer, the Bible and the bureaucrat, the banker and the businessman. The unexplored and unexploited parts of the world offered temptations which could not be resisted in the modern world of competition. Those opportunities were availed of by the Europeans.

The acquisition of colonies was not connected with any one political party. The colonies of Belgium were mostly the personal achievement of the King of Belgium. In Germany and Britain, colonies were mainly the work of conservative Governments. However, former radicals like Joseph Chamberlain and Liberals like Lord Rosebery supported them. In France, they were the work of radical Europeans like Jules Ferry and Gambetta. In Italy, colonies were the work of Liberals like Depretis. In Russia, colonization was mainly the work of official military class and bureaucracy. The beneficiaries of imperialism were not always those who initiated the same, although King Leopold of Belgium, Cecil Rhodes and many other empire-builders made fortunes and got power. Men like Jules Ferry in France and Crispi in Italy earned a bad name for themselves for their achievements. In Great Britain, Disraeli committed the Conservative Party to a general policy of imperialism in 1872. He bought the shares of the Suez Canal in 1875 and conferred the title of "Empress of India" upon Queen Victoria in 1877. In 1882, a colonial society was formed in Germany. In 1883 was set up a Society for German Colonisation. The Primrose League was set up in 1883 by the Conservatives in England. The Liberals also founded the Imperial Federation League. The British League was set up in 1894. The German Flottenverein was set up in 1898.

European Expansion in Asia

There was a considerable power vacuum in Asia at the beginning of the nineteenth century and into that vacuum the energetic Europeans were bound to expand. Russia was the European power nearest to Asia and the Russians annexed vast areas of Asia. The Russians had been on the offensive in Asia since the sixteenth century. They had reached the Ural mountains and the Caspian Sea before the end of the seventeenth century. The region in which they made the advances now was Central Asia. This region was occupied partly by primitive but settled agricultural people. Most numerous of the nomadic peoples were the Kazakhs who were Muslims. The Kirgiz were the close relatives of the Kazakhs. The Turkmen were settled farmers.

Fresh advances were made in the reign of Nicholas I. In 1839, the Russians attacked the independent Muslims principality of Khiva. In the 1840s and 1850s, the Russians built forts deep in country outside the original Russian borders in that region. Russian expansion in Central Asia continued unnoticed arid without protest. Only the British were alarmed at the advance of Russian forces towards India. In the reign of Alexander II, the Russian advance continued more rapidly. The Czar and his Chancellor, Gorchakov, were anxious not to antagonize Britain but they were unable to control those elements in Russia who were eager for expansion. There were active local Governors like Muraviev (who was the Governor of Eastern Siberia from 1847 to 1861) and active military officers. The army realised the ease with which vast new territories could be secured in Central Asia. The result was that while expansion was not the determined policy of the Russian Government, the officers on the spot could not be restrained from the kind of energetic action which was rewarded subsequently by promotion and military honours. The Department dealing with Asia in the Foreign Ministry was also reluctant to be restrained by the Chancellor. Businessmen were anxious to secure concessions for exploiting the mineral wealth of Central Asia.

In the Far East, the forward policy of Muraviev secured the founding of Vladivostok in 1860. The policy of Ignatyev carved the Russian Maritime province out of the Chinese empire in the regions of the rivers Amur and Ussuri. For this acquisition, the approval of Alexander II had been obtained. The same was the case with the conquest of the Caucasus region from 1857 to 1864. Gorchakov was opposed to Russian advance southwards, along the Eastern shore of the Caspian Sea, towards Persia. However, he could not prevent the establishment of a Trans-Caspian military district in 1874. Work was started on a Trans-Caspian railway in 1879. Farther to the East, earlier advances had been made. The capture of Tashkent in 1865 was the work of a mere army colonel named Cherniaev who had no real authority from the Czar. In. 1866-67, the Governor-Generalship of Turkestan was formed from the conquests of the previous twenty years. The new post of the Governor-General was given to General Kaufman. It was under Kaufman that Russian expansion continued. Bokhara and Samarkand fell in Russian hands in 1868.

Russian imperial expansion in Turkistan East of the Capsian Sea brought her into contact with Afghanistan and Persia, just as her earlier spread southwards to the West of the Caspian had led to encroachment upon Persia. Britain was afraid of Russian designs upon India and she supported the Afghans and Persians as buffers against such pressure. In 1885, they settled by arbitration details of the Russo-Afghan frontier in the Pendjeh area. By 1894, they reached an agreement about the frontiers between the Russian and Indian empires in the Pamir mountains.

In 1890, the Persian Government was given a loan by Britain. Ten years later, Persia got a similar loan from Russia. In 1907, Britain and Russia signed a convention defining their spheres of influence and erecting neutral zones between them. The northern part of Persia, adjoining the Caspian Sea and the Caucasus, became a Russian sphere of influence. The south-eastern part of Persia, adjacent of Afghanistan and India, became a British sphere of influence. Central Persia, including the Persian Gulf was to be a neutral zone. Russia renounced direct contact with Afghanistan. Tibet was made a neutral buffer state. In spite of that, the relations between Britain and Russia were strained till 1915 when Russia agreed to British control over the original neutral zone.

In the Sino-Japanese War of 1894-95, China was defeated and forced to sign the Treaty of Shimonosheki in 1895. By that treaty, China gave to Japan the Liao-Tung Peninsula, Port Arthur and the Island of Formosa. However, Russia, France and Germany forced Japan to return to China the Liao-Tung Peninsula and Port Arthur. The Russian imperialists felt that Korea and Liao-Tung Peninsula were of vital importance to their country. If Japan dominated Korea, she would be able to control both sides of the Southern outlets of the Japan Sea on which was situated the Russian Port of Vladivostok, the intended terminus of the Trans-Siberian railway. If Japan annexed the Liao-Tung Peninsula, there would be no possibility of Russia getting an ice-free port in the South. Hence, Russian interests demanded that Japan must be ousted from those regions. Having deprived Japan of her spoils of victory, Russia started her influence in China by the establishment of the Russo-Chinese Bank. She also got Port Arthur from China.

Japan did not forgive Russia for the part played by her against her. Japan attacked Russia in 1904 and defeated her in 1905. By the Treaty of Portsmouth of 1905, Russia agreed to transfer to Japan the lease on the Liao-Tung Peninsula and Port Arthur and to cede to Japan the southern half of Sakhalin Island. Shortly afterwards, Japan and Russia agreed to delimit "spheres of influence" between themselves. Japan annexed Korea in 1910 and acquired railway concessions in Manchuria. In 1913, Russia established a virtual protectorate over Outer Mongolia.

China

China was being ruled by the Manchu dynasty in the nineteenth century. However, the authority of the Manchu Emperors was somewhat shadowy. For all purposes of administration, the heads of the 18 provinces into which China was divided were largely independent. She was not only disunited but also militarily weak. The Chinese hated the foreigners. To keep the foreigners out of their country, the Chinese Government had restricted foreign trade to the port of Canton. However, the Government lacked the military force to resist foreign encroachments. They were forced to open more and more ports to foreign trade.

The first ports were opened as a result of the Opium War (1840-1842). In addition to cotton, the British East India Company was selling in Canton considerable quantities of opium produced in India. For some years, the Chinese took no action. However, when the opium trade grew to such proportions that it caused widespread demoralisation, the Chinese officials tried to stop the import of opium into China. When other measures failed, the Chinese Imperial Commissioner in 1839 confiscated the opium held by some British merchants who at once called on the British Government to avenge the insult to the British flag. The British fleet smashed the forts at the entrance to the Canton River. British troops took possession of Canton and other maritime cities. The first Opium War was concluded by the Treaty of Nanking in 1842 by which the Chinese Government agreed to pay the British a large indemnity, cede the Island of Hongkong to them and open four additional ports of Amoy, Fuchow, Ningpo and Shanghai to foreign trade. France, Spain, Belgium, the Netherlands and the United States also signed similar treaties giving them the same commercial rights.

These concessions did not satisfy the European nations and the United States for long. In 1843, the British signed a commercial treaty which extended their privileges by setting land aside for their residence. Similar advantages were secured by France and the United States from China. These treaties marked the beginning of "the right of extra-territoriality", *i.e.*, the right which gave foreigners immunity from Chinese jurisdiction. Thereafter, a provision was incorporated in the treaties which all the Western nations signed with China. The result was that no foreigner residing in China was subject to Chinese law as regards his person or property. Any charge or claim against him had to be presented before the Consul of his own country and was judged according to the law of his nation.

The Treaty of Nanking which ended the first Opium War did not settle the opium question. During the succeeding period, its sale was extended to other ports. When the Chinese authorities in 1857 seized a small Chinese boat engaged in opium smuggling which was flying the British flag, the second Opium War broke out. By the Treaty of Tientsin (1858), the Chinese Government agreed to open 14 additional ports to British trade, to open the Yangtse River to British ships, to allow British subjects to travel freely in China and to permit trade in opium. Other nations also succeeded in getting the same privileges from China.

Upto now, European efforts were restricted to obtaining commercial and extra-territorial rights. During the succeeding decades, many European powers proceeded to establish their domination over large sections of Chinese territory. Through the conquest of Cochin China, Cambodia, Tonking and Annam, France virtually laid claim to Southerns China. The British also compelled China to recognise British sovereignty, over Burma in 1886. Japan forced China in 1895 to give her the Liaotung Peninsula together with Port Arthur, acknowledge the independence of Korea and surrender to Japan the Island of Formosa. With the support of France and England, Russia forced Japan to give up her gains. Russia got from China Port Arthur. She also got permission to run a branch line of the Trans-Siberian railway (which had been built in 1892 with French help) through Manchuria. The British got a lease on the harbour of the Weihaiwei. France got several rail-road concessions and the control of the Bay of Qwang-Chow-Wan. Using the murder of two German missionaries as an excuse, Germany got a lease of Kiaochow Bay for 99 years.

The result was that by the end of the nineteenth century, the Chinese found that their best ports were leased to foreign nations and their coastal and inland trade was controlled by foreigners. Almost two-thirds of Chinese territory was marked out in "spheres of influence". In 14 of her important ports, foreign settlements were established which were not subject to Chinese law. All this created a feeling of humiliation and resentment among the Chinese. Kuanghsu, the Chinese Emperor, issued a series of reform edicts for the introduction of Western methods of education. He encouraged the building of rail-roads, the establishment of a bureau of mines and the translation of foreign technical and scientific literature into the Chinese language. These measures created an alarm among the reactionaries in China. Tzu-hsi, the Dowager Empress, led the reactionaries, seized the reins of Government, dismissed the members of the reforms cabinet, revoked most of the reform edicts, suppressed the Chinese newspapers and persecuted all the progressive people. She encouraged the formation of societies whose object was to oppose the foreigners and everything foreign. The most important of those societies was called Iho-chaun which is translated as "Righteous Harmony Fists", popularly known as "Boxers". Their aim was to exterminate all foreigners and destroy all traces of Western civilisation. Their main targets were the missionaries, churches and mission stations. There were instances of looting, arson and murder in the spring of 1899. Bands of Boxers made widespread raids in which foreigners were murdered and their homes were looted and burnt. Many missionaries and thousands of Chinese Christians were killed. In Peking and other cities, the Boxers laid siege to the foreign legations. A relief expedition consisting of British, French, German, Russian, Japanese and U.S. troops was sent to China. The besieged foreign legations were rescued. The Boxer movement was stamped out with cruelty. By a treaty of 1901, China agreed to pay an indemnity of 325 million dollars, to punish the leaders of the Boxer rising and grant further commercial advantages to the foreign powers.

Japan

Upto 1853, Japan was sealed against all foreign influences. However, in that year a squadron of US ships under Commodore Perry sailed into Yeddo Bay. The Commodore presented to the Japanese Government a friendly letter from the American President alongwith certain demands, one of which was that Japan be opened to foreign trade. The Japanese authorities accepted the demand and a treaty was signed in March 1854 which terminated the Japanese policy of exclusion. Similar treaties were made with Great Britain, Russia and France.

Upto 1867, the real power in Japan was in the hands of the Shagun, a great feudal lord. In that year, the Shogun was forced to resign and all power came into the hands of the Emperor of Japan. In 1871, feudalism was abolished in Japan. In 1889, the Emperor promulgated a constitution providing for a Parliament or an Imperial Diet of two Houses. That constitution was a gift from the Emperor to his people and did not limit full sovereignty in any way. Cabinet ministers were responsible only to him.

After 1868, changes were introduced in every phase of Japanese life. The laws of the country were revised on the basis of the Code Napoleon. A new educational system was introduced for all levels from elementary school to the university. Rail-road construction was started in 1870 and by 1900, there were more than 4,000 miles of rail-roads in operation in Japan. By 1901, Japan had more than 5000 vessels built on the European pattern. French officers were called in 1866 to give military training. German officers replaced them after the Franco-Prussian war. The Japanese army was based on a combination of French and German tactics. A navy was also built and British experts were invited to organise it. Heavy industries were set up in the country. The Japanese imitated the European nations in the matter of imperialism. In 1894, Japan attacked China and defeated her. By the treaty of 1895, China had to acknowledge the independence of Korea. She was to give Formosa to Japan and transfer to Japanese control the Liaotung Peninsula together with Port Arthur.

The Japanese were not prepared to forget that they were forced to give up their gains by Russia. Japan entered into an agreement with Britain in 1902. Japan launched a surprise attack on the Russian fleet at Port Arthur in February 1904 and inflicted heavy losses. The Russian fleet was destroyed bit by bit whenever Russian ships ventured out into the open. On land also, the Japanese were successful against the Russian troops. The war ended in Russian defeat. By the treaty of 1905, Russia agreed to transfer to Japan the lease on the Liaotung Peninsula and Port Arthur and to cede to Japan the Southern half of Sakhalin Island. Japan annexed Korea in 1910. In 1931, she annexed Manchuria.

French Expansion

France already possessed Pondicherry, Mahe and Chandranagar in India. She now extended her sphere of influence in China and South-East Asia. In 1844, she acquired the right to intervene on behalf of the Christian people in China. In 1858, France virtually got a protectorate over the Chinese Catholic converts. In 1862, she completed the conquest of Indo-China. In 1867, she annexed Cambodia and conquered Annam. In 1885, the Chinese Government went to war in a vain effort to retain Tonking and was compelled to make a formal cession of both Tonking and Annam. The population of Indo-China was not very great but its area exceeded that of France. In 1893, when the French tried to extend their influence from Indo-China to Siam, Britain objected to a French naval blockade of Bangkok and the result was an agreement which preserved the integrity of Siam.

Expansion in Africa

For a long time, Africa was regarded as the Dark Continent and not much was known about its people and natural resources. However, recent explorations revealed the unlimited industrial potentialities that lay hidden and buried in Africa. The Industrial Revolution demanded their exploitation and hence a scramble for colonies in that Continent.

At the beginning of the nineteenth century, there were only a few European settlements in Africa. There were some English, French and Dutch trading stations on the North coast. In the South, England owned the Cape Colony and Natal.

It was the cherished desire of traders and statesmen to connect the Mediterranean with the Red Sea by means of a canal so that the sea route to the East might be cut down by several thousand miles. That desire was realised by Ferdinand de Lesseps, a French engineer, who conceived the plan of constructing a canal in 1854 and got concessions from the Khedive of Egypt. In 1859, a company was floated for that purpose. The Suez Canal was completed by Lesseps in 1869. France scored a victory over the other European powers. It was realised that the country which controlled the Suez Canal would also control the new sea route to India. Prime Minister Disraeli realised the importance of the Suez Canal and wanted to have a share in its control. The Khedive Ismail Pasha owned 176,000 shares of the Suez Company. He was heavily in debt and hence was eager to sell his shares. In spite of opposition from the Foreign Minister and the Chancellor of the Exchequer, Disraeli bought all

Leopold paid back all the contributions the Association had received from non-Belgians. By 1890, all the important officials of the new state were Belgians. Although the promoters had promised at Berlin to look after the moral and material well-being of the natives, they were treated mercilessly and with great difficulty, their condition improved. The new state was put under full Belgian sovereignty in 1908.

German Expansion

To begin with, Bismarck was against any colonial enterprise. After the Industrial Revolution in Germany, Germany began to feel the need of raw materials and foreign markets and suitable settlements for her increasing population. Germany felt "too cribbed, cabined and confined" and demanded "a place in the Sun." Bismarck now followed a forward colonial policy. As expansion in America was not possible on account of the Monroe Doctrine, he turned his attention to Africa.

Von der Decken, a German, had already explored East Africa and suggested to the German Government the desirability of establishing a German colony there. In 1882, the German Colonial Union was formed. Within two years (1884-85), Germany established her protectorate over German South-West Africa, Togoland, Cameroon and Tanganyika. These were very profitable possessions acquired "without a fleet and without moving a soldier". The British did not oppose German expansion in Africa. As a matter of fact, Gladstone welcomed it.

When after the Entente Cordiale of 1904 between France and Britain, France tried to penetrate into Morocco, Germany resisted it. William II went to Tangier in 1905 to show that Germany was interested in Morocco and would not allow France to swallow the same. The dispute was referred to the Algeciras Conference in 1906. Britain supported France against Germany. In the Casablanca case of 1908, Britain again supported France against Germany and the latter had to keep quiet. In 1911, the Panther, the German gunboat, was sent to Agadir and Germany refused to withdraw the ship unless her own interests were safeguarded. Britain again supported France against Germany and the latter had to give way. Later on, a Franco-German agreement provided for German consent to the occupation of Morocco by France and Spain in return for a section of the French Congo.

Italian Expansion in Africa

The ambitions of Italy were thwarted in Tunisia by France and she felt frustrated. However, she also had her share of the scramble in Africa. In 1882, she occupied Assab which finally led to her acquisition of Eritrea in 1885.

By the Treaty of Ucciali of 1889, the Emperor of Abyssinia was believed to have recognised an Italian protectorate over his country. However, Italian forces were defeated by Abyssinia at Adowa in 1896.

In 1911, Italy began the process of dismembering the Turkish Empire. Many Italians felt that the territories of North Africa which touched the Mediterranean rightfully belonged to Italy since they had been a part of the old Roman Empire. However, the other European powers had taken all the North-African territories except Tripoli. For some years, there was a gradual occupation of Tripoli by Italians. When Italy found chaos in Turkey in 1911, she decided that time had come to occupy the province. Italian troops occupied the coastal towns, but their hold on the interior was precarious on account of native opposition instigated by Turkish agents. In order to compel the Turkish Government to release its hold on the province, the Italian force seized the Dodecanese in the Aegean Sea. Harassed by internal troubles, Turkey was forced to open peace negotiations with Italy. On 15 October 1912, a treaty was signed by which Turkey gave Tripoli to Italy.

It is clear from above that Britain got the lion's share in Africa, she got all the principal areas which were climatically suitable for White settlers. She nearly completed her all-British route from

Cairo to the Cape Colony. Except for Dakar, she held each of the key points for the strategic control of Africa from Gibraltar to Simonstown, from Alexandria, to Durban. She bestrode three out of the four great African rivers on which the share of trade and civilisation largely depended. However, the French share was the largest in area, though not in population. It included a portion of the fourth river basin, the Congo and Madagascar, the third largest Island in the world. In the North, her African colonies were ideally situated for the French colonial policy of assimilation. The experience of the Germans in Africa was disappointing. Not one of their colonies there ever paid its way. None of them proved attractive to German emigrants who were flocking to America. In 1914, there were more Germans earning their livelihood in Paris than in all the German colonies put together. Serious native wars cost money and damaged prestige. The Germans were rightly accused of cruel treatment of the native population. As a market for German goods, the German colonies proved negligible. However, in 1914, the Germans were just turning over their colonies to an alternative use as plantations which could supply all the needs of German industry for rubber, oilseeds, cotton and other raw materials. In 1911, the acquisition of two considerable portions of the French Congo, which might have paved the way for larger acquisitions from Belgium, made those schemes feasible.

The opening of Africa to European influences was one of the most important enterprises in European history. Four of the six Great Powers took part in it. Considerable shares were also allotted to Belgium and Holland. They worked in rivalry with each other but accepted common rules of procedure and a system of peaceful bargaining within the general framework of the Concert of Europe. It was indeed an important achievement for Europe to divide the entire Continent of Africa without a European war.

Australia

Australia was discovered in 1606 by Captain Jansz, a Dutchman. In 1788, the British made their first settlement in Australia. At that time, Australia was inhabited by about 200,000 natives whose way of life had probably not changed for thousands of years. The civilization which, was built up in Australia in the nineteenth century was simply the result of strange geographical conditions playing upon an English community. The first settlement in 1788 was of 717 convicts at Port Jackson where the city of Sydney was built later on. Over the years, some 60,000 or 70,000 more convicts were transported to Australia from Britain until the practice was ended in 1840. By 1840, the convicts were already a small minority of the population. Six separate colonies were founded by settlers in Australia between 1825 and 1859. It was almost certain that the whole of Australia would become British. During the succeeding years, there was rapid development of sheep-breeding and corn-growing. In 1851, gold was struck in Australia, and that attracted many settlers.

By 1859, there were six states in Australia and each state had a Government like that of Britain. The advancement of a federal Australia came slowly. In 1881, the project was temporarily laid aside. However, negotiations were resumed. In 1897, an agreement was reached on a plan which the British Government embodied in the Australian Commonwealth Act of 1900.

New Zealand

New Zealand was discovered by Captain Cook in 1770. After that, the Island was left to sealers, whalers and traders of various kinds. There were rumours of French designs on New Zealand and that moved the British Government to sign an agreement in 1840 with the Maoris, the natives of New Zealand. That agreement put New Zealand under British protection. British settlers began to migrate to New Zealand. In 1867, self-Government was given to New Zealand. In 1907, New Zealand became a Dominion. She also became a separate nation of the British Empire.

The Pacific Islands

The Dutch Empire of the East Indies had been founded as early as the seventeenth century. New Guinea was added in 1828. Under the harsh regime of the Dutch Governors, the East Indies were exploited with ruthlessness for the economic advantage of Holland.

The ownership of Ceylon, the coastal regions of Burma and the Straits Settlements of Singapore, Malacca and Penang put Britain in a strong position for further expansion. The French had been established in Tahiti since 1843 and had recently taken possession of New Caledonia. To Germany, the impulse to expand in the Pacific came in 1884.

In 1874, the British annexed the Fiji Islands. In 1884, the Germans took North-Eastern New Guinea. There was opposition from Australia but without any result. The Germans also secured the Offshore Islands which they named after Bismarck and within two years the neighbouring Solomon Islands and the Marshall group Islands.

In 1888, Britain set up a protectorate over North Borneo where a chartered British North Borneo Company had been active since 1881 and where in Sarawak, Rajah Brooke had established a remarkable personal power as an independent sovereign. By the end of the century, Britain also took the South Solomon, Tonga and Gilbert Islands. France occupied the Marquesas, the Society Islands and other small groups adjoining Tahiti which she had held since 1843. After her war with Spain, the United States annexed Puerto Rico and set up a protectorate over Cuba in the Caribbean Sea and also took the Philippines and the Hawaiian Islands.

American trade interests required the maintenance at least of coaling stations. That brought the Americans to Samoa. In 1889, a hurricane dispersed the warships of the three Great Powers. Friction continued. After the defeat of Spain in 1899, the United States divided Samoa with Germany and Britain. The Philippines was put under direct American control. The United States also annexed Guam. The rest of the Marianas and the Caroline Islands were sold by Spain to Germany. In 1899, Hawaii was annexed by the United States.

South and Central America

In the first quarter of the nineteenth century, the mixed people of the Spanish and Portuguese Empire in Central and South America secured their independence. By 1825, only the small colonies of British, French and Dutch Guiana were being ruled from Europe. By the end of 1830, revolutions against Spain and against the heirs of Spain had transformed Spanish America into 11 independent states. These states were Colombia, Ecuador, Venezuela, Peru, Bolivia, Paraguay, Uruguay, Chile and the United Provinces of La Plata (which became Argentina) in South America, and Mexico and the United Provinces of Central America. From Colombia Panama seceded in 1903. In the 1840s, Central America broke up into the five separate republics of Guatemala, Honduras, Nicaragua, Salvador and Costa Rica. Santo Domingo became a state distinct from Haiti. Cuba became an independent republic in 1899.

Brazil

The largest and the most important state of South America was Portuguese-speaking Brazil. Its area exceeded that of the United States. Its economic resources and development were remarkable. By 1914, it was furnishing almost three-fourth of the world's coffee, exporting large amounts of timber, minerals and meat and producing manufactured goods worth half a billion dollars. Monarchy was set up in Brazil in 1822 by a branch of the Portuguese royal family. There was a movement against Pedro I of Brazil and he was forced to abdicate in 1831 in favour of his five-year old son, Pedro II. Pedro II ruled from 1831 to 1889. He was proclaimed of age in 1840. He was an enlightened prince and inveterate reformer. The slave trade was abolished in 1853. Negro slavery was ended in 1888. The link between Brazil and Europe in the reign of Pedro II was mainly an economic one. British investors, in particular, preferred Brazil to the other South American states, partly because of its comparatively stable regime. The Rothschilds of London provided considerable sums for the development of Brazil, especially for the building of the railways. However, Pedro II was overthrown in 1889 by influential landlords who resented the loss of their slaves and army officers who did not approve of the subordinate position in which they were kept by Pedro II. Marshal Fonseca proclaimed republic in Brazil in November 1889. Pedro II offered no resistance and he and his family were exiled.

Marshal Fonseca was a military dictator. He was accused of corruption and overthrown in 1891 by Marshal Peixoto. Peixoto retired in 1894 and the republic passed into civilian hands and gradually gained stability and respect.

Argentina

During the first half of the nineteenth century, Argentina was a prey to civil war and military dictatorship, but from 1862, under a more orderly republican Government, it gained in population and material well-being. In 1829, Juan Manuel de Rosas became the Governor of Buenos Aires and in 1835 seized power as dictator of Argentina. He remained dictator until 1852. His bad treatment of French subjects in Buenos Aires led to a blockade of the city by the French in 1838. The French were allied with Uruguay which Rosas had tried to annex. The British also sympathised with Uruguay and joined the blockade in 1845. The French and British were persuaded to lift the blockade without toppling Rosas from power. However, he fell in 1852 as a result of internal rebellion rather than external pressure. Rosas went into exile in England where he spent the rest of his life.

After the fall of Rosas, the constitution for the Argentine confederation was drawn up and finally accepted by the whole country in 1861. The constitution followed the pattern of the United States. Argentina enjoyed considerable economic development in the 1860s. The railways were built and immigration from Europe started. British investment played an important role in the development of Argentina.

Paraguay

Francisco Solano Lopez was the dictator of Paraguay. He made war on a triple alliance of Argentina, Brazil and Uruguay. In the six years of bitter fighting from 1864 to 1870, more than half of the population of Paraguay and some nine-tenths of her men, were exterminated. From this war of mass slaughter and destruction, the European states kept aloof. Napoleon III was busy in Mexico and the rest of Europe was fully occupied by the German Question.

Chile

Chile had greater political stability than her neighbours. She had close trade links with Britain. The rich nitrate industry depended heavily on British capital. Chile received immigrants from Europe, particularly from Germany. Peru and Bolivia, with their acute poverty, corrupt Government and political instability, did not attract European immigrants or capital. As a result of a war with Bolivia and Peru in 1879-1883 Chilean rule was extended northward over the provinces of Tacna and Africa, with their rich nitrate deposits.

Mexico

Mexico was the most populous of all the Spanish American states. Though exceeded in area by Argentina, it had twice its population. Mexico was relatively backward. Most of the country's basic agriculture was conducted on extensive plantations. The condition of the lower classes was deplorable.

Before the intervention of Napoleon III in Mexico in the 1860s, Mexico had been the battlefield for a struggle between the forces of the church and the landowners on one hand and the anti-clericals and the working class on the other. The civil war was won in 1860 by the radical leader, Benito Juarez, who as President inherited a land disorganised and hopelessly impoverished by the fighting. In 1861, he suspended payments on foreign loans. France, Britain and Spain signed a treaty in London by which they agreed to combine efforts for an intervention in Mexico for the specific and only object of securing the financial interests of their subjects. Napoleon III had more ambitious plans than the Governments of Britain and Spain. A group of Mexican exiles in Europe hoped to establish a monarchy in Mexico.

In order to please the French Catholics, Napoleon III decided that the civil war in the United States provided an opportunity for a major French intervention in Mexico. If a liberal Catholic prince could be put on the throne of Mexico, the spread of "Anglo-American barbarism" in North America could be halted. Napoleon did not want to colonise Mexico for France, but merely wanted to create a zone of political influence as a base for economic exploitation. The Anglo-France-Spanish expedition arrived in Mexico and occupied Vera Cruz in December 1861. When Napoleon tried to restore monarchy in Mexico, the Governments of Britain and Spain protested and they withdrew their forces in April 1862. Napoleon III was left alone in the field. He decided to put Archduke Maximilian, brother of Francis Joseph, Emperor of Austria-Hungary, on the throne of Mexico. As the Governor of Lombardy, Maximilian had acquired a reputation as a liberal and effective administrator. In June 1865, the French army entered Mexico city. An assembly of notables was called to prepare the way for monarchy. In 1864, Maximilian assumed the title of Emperor of Mexico. For two years, he reigned in Mexico city while Juarez maintained his authority both to the North and to the South. As soon as the Civil War ended in the United States in 1865, the Government of the United States demanded the evacuation of the French army whose presence in Mexico was against the Monroe Doctrine. In 1866, Napoleon began to withdraw his troops from Mexico. By the spring of 1867, the last of Napoleon's troops left Mexico and Maximilian found himself without support. Napoleon advised Maximilian to escape back to Europe, but Maximilian resisted to the end. He was taken a prisoner and was executed by a firing squad on 19 June 1867. Juarez again became the President of the republic of Mexico and for the remaining five years of his life stayed at the head of a reforming Government.

Both the United States and Britain were interested in the construction of a canal which connected the Atlantic and Pacific Oceans. Besides her West Indian colonies, Britain had for some years claimed a protectorate over the Indians of the so-called Mosquito Coast of Nicaragua and Honduras. In 1841, the British occupied the Bay Islands, off the coast of Honduras and established a naval base at Belize. During the war between the United States and Mexico from 1846 to 1848, the British occupied the Port of San Juan and renamed it Greytown. This shows that Great Britain did not care for the Monroe Doctrine in the 1840s. However, as soon as the United States freed herself from the Mexican war, she followed a policy of strong diplomatic pressure to prevent Britain from dominating the potential canal routes.

The United States and Britain signed the Clayton-Bulwer treaty in 1350 by which both powers agreed that any future canal would be free from the exclusive control of either of them and would be a neutral waterway, without fortifications on its banks and neither power would in future extend her sovereignty into Central America. By the Treaty of 1901, Great Britain surrendered her rights in favour of the United States. The Panama Canal was to be constructed, maintained and protected by the United States but to be opened to the vessels of all nations. The Canal was eventually constructed and opened in 1914.

The United States

From the time of her getting independence, the United States was becoming more and more powerful. The famous Monroe Doctrine of 1823 was an assertion of the right of a strong nation which was prepared to go to war to save America from intervention of European powers. By the 1850s, the United States had become a force to be reckoned with throughout the American Continent.

The long and terrible Civil War from 1861 to 1865 weakened her. When the Federal Union of the North established a naval blockade of the Confederate states of the South, it became clear that the war would have grave economic effects in Europe, particularly in England. The cotton industries of Europe depended very heavily for their raw cotton on the Southern states of the United States. By far the largest cotton industry in the world was in Lancashire. By 1860, 72 per cent of the cotton required in Lancashire came from the Southern States of the United States. The blockade of the South led to an acute cotton famine in Lancashire with the resulting slump, unemployment and widespread suffering. French cotton industries also suffered, particularly those in Normandy. The Confederacy of the South hoped for European intervention in the form of pressure to stop the blockade and also in the form of friendly mediation. They hoped that the European powers would at least grant them recognition as an independent country. The Confederacy assumed that Britain and France were bound to come to their aid on account of cotton famine and for that reason, the South was inclined to withhold cotton even when it was possible to break the blockade. When Englishmen first heard of the differences between North and South in the United States, they interpreted them as simply a defence of the institution of slavery by the Southern states and its rejection by the Northern states. Palmerston, the Prime Minister of England from 1859 to 1865, was inclined to sympathise with the struggle of the Confederacy as one of national independence. He had an ulterior motive as the split between North and South would become permanent and would for ever weaken a growing rival to British power. However, he had no intention of intervening unless forced to do so by some issue of British prestige. Mainly because of the condition of Lancashire, Gladstone tended to sympathise more overtly with the South. Disraeli made no secret of his sympathy for the North. However, all Englishmen were concerned about the defence of Canada.

Both Britain and France followed a policy of neutrality, but they were reluctant to recognise the South or even to protest at the blockade. In November 1861, the Confederate states of the South sent two agents, Mason and Slidell, aboard a British steamer, the Trent, across the Atlantic to negotiate with Britain and France. A warship of the United States intercepted the Trent and removed Mason and Slidell. The British Government protested strongly and seemed to threaten war against the North. President Lincoln and his Secretary of State had not authorised the removal of Mason and Slidell from the Trent. The result was that the Federal Government released Mason and Slidell. By the spring of 1862, the French Government was more willing to intervene in favour of the South either by breaking the blockade or at least giving diplomatic support to the South by mediation. Palmerston was reluctant to abandon neutrality and Napoleon would not act without Britain. In January 1863, the French Government offered its good offices to both sides but the same were rejected by President Lincoln.

During the nineteenth century, all those who were in trouble in Europe migrated to the United States. Most of them were from Western and Central Europe. The largest number of emigrants came from Ireland. Many came from Germany, England, France, Switzerland, Scandinavia and the Low Countries. Many of the emigrants from the mainland of Europe were Jews. A few Italians also went to the United States. There was a lot of work in America in the ambitious projects of canal, road and railway-building.

Canada

After the conquest of Canada by the British, an irresponsible Government was set up in Canada by the Act of 1791. The British colonists had a majority in Upper Canada and the French colonists had a majority in Lower Canada. Led by a young Frenchman named Louis J. Papineau, the French party in Lower Canada raised the standard of revolt in 1837. A party in Upper Canada led by William Lyon Mackenzie followed suit. The rebellion was more violent in Upper Canada than in Quebec. The risings were put down. In 1838, Lord Durham, a distinguished member of the Whig cabinet, was sent to Canada as the Governor of the whole of Canada. He remained in Canada for about five months. He resigned on account of his criticism in the British Parliament. He was the victim of party and personal politics of England. On his return to England, he submitted his famous report to the Parliament known as Durham Report. The Report "arrested men's attention throughout the Empire in 1839 and has kept its pages fresh and influential to the present day". The Report contained a full description of the situation in Canada and the proposed sweeping changes in colonial policy. Examining the history of six provinces of Canada, Lord Durham declared that "the natural state of Government in all these colonies is that of collision between the Executive and the representative body." He declared that the situation in Canada "was the unavoidable result of a system which stinted the unpopular branch of the legislature of necessary privileges of a representative body." The Assembly in Lower Canada had been conducting "a constant warfare with the executive for the purpose of obtaining the powers inherent in the representative body by the very nature of representative Government." Durham recommended complete home rule by an elected and responsible government, with the imperial Government retaining control only over the drawing up of the constitution, foreign affairs, the regulation of trade and disposal of land. Upper and Lower Canada were to be integrated into a single colonial state.

The Durham Report has been called "the Magna Carta of the colonies", "the most valuable document in the English language on the subject of colonial policy", and the "textbook of every advocate of colonial freedom in all parts of the globe". The Report is asserted to have "broadened, once for all, the lines of constructive statesmanship in all that relates to the colonial policy of England."

The Union Act of 1840 incorporated much of the Durham Report, but did not introduce responsible Government in the sense intended by Durham. The Governor-General was still to remain responsible to the Government in London and not to the Assembly in Canada. Full responsible Government was achieved in the time of Lord Elgin, the son-in-law of Lord Durham who was the Governor-General of Canada from 1847 to 1853. The two provinces of Nova Scotia and New Brunswick were granted responsible Government in 1847. The British North America Act was passed in 1867. It created a Confederation of Canada out of the two parts of united Canada (Quebec and Ontario), Nova Scotia and Brunswick. The westward expansion of Canada over the Rocky Mountains led to the establishment of the colony of British Columbia in 1858. The province of Manitoba was founded in 1870. The British North America Act of 1867 continued to be in force till 1982 when it was replaced by a new constitution of Canada.

Contraction of Europe

If there was expansion of Europe during the nineteenth century, it contracted during the twentieth century. There were many factors which were responsible for this. Colonial ambitions and rivalries played little or no part in the policy of Hitler who was pre-eminently continental and racialist in outlook. He concentrated upon power in Europe. He thought of the Balkans and South-Western Russia as a richer field of colonial gains than overseas territories. Though he never gave up German claims to overseas colonies, he was prepared to subordinate them to conquests in Europe. Colonial issues became prominent only after the entry of Italy and Japan into the War. The reverses of the Western powers, particularly those of the Netherlands, Belgium, France and Britain exposed to revolutionary forces the overseas possessions of those powers in Africa and Asia, the Near East and the Far East. A few years of Japanese invasion and occupation of parts of Indo-China, Malaya, Burma and Indonesia transformed those countries into more self-conscious, neutralistic and psychologically detached people. Both the Soviet Union and the United States after the World War II were in sentiment and in policy hostile to colonialism. The predominance of left wing sentiment throughout Europe after 1945, whether socialist or Catholic democrat, militated against the old-fashioned spirit of imperialism. Public opinion in Western Europe was now more responsive to the principle that colonial peoples should be encouraged to seek independence and helped to win rights of self-determination.

This change was not a sudden by-product of the World War I. Its roots lay deeper. Upto 1914, the relationship between the colonies and the colony-owners was that of political dependence, racial inequality and economic subservience. Politically, the colonies were governed by decisions taken in London or Paris, Brussels or Berlin, Lisbon or Amsterdam. Socially, the members of the imperial power resident in the colonies established for themselves a position of racial superiority and influence. They were mostly concerned in administering, developing and generally running the country. They acquired much of the best land, the best houses and social amenities of a ruling group. Economically, the main functions of the colonies were to supply raw materials for use in the manufactures of the governing country, to provide markets for its manufactured goods and to be secure places of investment for commercial enterprise and surplus capital. The relationship varied from one empire to another. Even in 1914, it was modified here and there by limited participation of the native inhabitants in running their own affairs or by the development of certain native industries and enterprises. Such a policy was followed by Britain in Nigeria.

The colonial revolution of the twentieth century was much more than a colonial revolt. One of its roots was the growth of population, wealth, literacy and national awareness among the peoples of the colonial territories. There was a demand for ending political dependence, racial inequality and economic subservience. The demand grew with the spread of Westernization itself. It was nourished by the liberal ideals of freedom, equality and industrialism within the colonies. The demand was greatly accelerated and intensified by the two World Wars. There was also a change in the policies, attitudes, circumstances and needs of the colonial powers. They were too weak to preserve colonial relationships of the old pattern. They were compelled to discover new relationship as tutors, trustees, partners or allies and not conquerors, rulers, administrators, or exploiters. This important change took place mainly after 1919.

The Mandate System

The World War I produced the first major change. The extent of colonial empires was not diminished in any way. The British, French, Belgian, Dutch and Portuguese empires lost none of their territories. Italy gained by additions to Libya and Somaliland. Japan gained more than Italy. Germany alone lost all her overseas possessions. Those were administered after 1918 by the powers which had seized possession of them during the World War I. However, they were administered under the new principle of Mandates, whereby the administering powers undertook specific obligations towards the inhabitants of those territories. For the fulfilment of those obligations, they became accountable to the Permanent Mandates Commission and had to report annually to the Council of the League of Nations. This acceptance of a code of behaviour by the colonial powers was an important event. Great Britain was appointed the mandatory power for Iraq and Palestine. Iraq became in 1937 an independent sovereign state. She also became a member of the League of Nations. Syria and Lebanon were put under the mandate of France. During World War II, France agreed to recognise their independence on certain conditions. Those countries were recognised as independent states and became the original members of the United Nations. Great Britain was given class B mandate with regard to British Cameroon, the British Togoland and Tanganyika. France was given Class B mandate with regard to French Cameroon and French Togoland. Belgium was appointed mandatory for Ruanda-Urundi. South-West Africa was put under Class C mandate of the Union of South Africa, Samoa under New Zealand, Nauru under Great Britain, Australia and New Zealand and the Pacific Islands and north of the Equator under Japan and those South of the Equator under Australia.

British Empire

Important changes took place within the British Empire and the Commonwealth. They set a new standard of principles and aims in colonial administration. The autonomy and independence of the Dominions was formally recognised in the Statute of Westminster. Separate representation was given to Canada, Australia, New Zealand, the Union of South Africa and India at the Paris Conference in 1919. They were also made members of the League of Nations.

As regards India, the Government of India Act was passed in 1919. It introduced dyarchy in the provinces. Many other changes were made giving more scope for participation in the Government by the Indians. As the reforms of 1919 did not satisfy the Indians, a new Government of India Act was passed by the British Parliament in 1935. It granted provincial autonomy and also provided for a sort of dyarchy in the Federal Government. The Act separated Burma from India.

As a result of the Anglo-Irish Treaty of 1921, the Irish Free State was set up in 1922 with the status of a British dominion. The six northern provinces of Ulster were to remain separate as Northern Ireland which was to send representatives to the British parliament at Westminster. In 1932, de Valera came to power as the Head of a new party called the Fianna Fail (Soldiers of Destiny). Bit by bit, he demolished the provisions of the Anglo-Irish Treaty of 1921 and promulgated a new constitution in 1937. He severed all formal links with the United Kingdom and made the Irish Free State (Eire) an independent sovereign state. Between 1939 and 1945, Eire remained neutral.

French Empire

There was a tendency in the British Empire to concede increasing measures of independence and responsibility for self-Government. However, such a tendency was less conspicuous in France, Belgium, the Netherlands and Portugal. In France, the theory of colonial rule shifted officially from that predominant before 1914 of assimilation, spreading French culture and civilisation throughout her territories and making Africans not better Africans but better Frenchmen. It changed officially to the theory of association, greater respect for native traditions and ways of life, but a strengthening of their economic and political links with France. However, the change in French policy by 1939 was more apparent than real, more theoretical than substantial. Strong economic interests linked France with her overseas territories. By 1939, France was drawing nearly one-third of her imports from her own colonies and sending nearly one-third of her exports to them. Those economic links strengthened the tendencies to assimilation. The general distinction between French citizens and French subjects was also maintained. Most of the French colonies were economically subservient. Madagascar was obliged to have the same high tariff walls as France although the free import of cheap textiles would have helped the people of Madagascar.

Belgian Empire

The Belgian Congo, together with the mandatory territory of Ruanda-Urundi, was more than 78 times larger than Belgium. The Netherlands East Indies were 54 times bigger in area than the Netherlands. Portuguese West Africa was 23 times larger than Portugal. Each power had its own policy towards her colonies. The Belgian Government adopted a paternalist policy of progressive social and economic development. There was no question of any partnership in responsibility or attainment of self-Government in the long run. The economic growth of the Congo was shaped according to the needs of Belgium. By 1939, the Congo was shipping more than 80 per cent of its exports to Belgium and got from Belgium nearly half of its imports. The Congo administration concentrated on improving conditions in agriculture, transport, education and public health. It treated its colonial dependants as primitive and backward. Nothing was done to allow the participation of the people in the administration of their country. The result was that when the Congo was granted independence in 1960, it was absolutely unprepared for it.

Dutch Empire

Dutch colonial policy was traditionally firm and paternalistic. There was a growth of Indonesian nationalist movement beginning in 1908. Various concessions were made to the people for their participation in politics and public life. There was also a tendency towards assimilation. In 1922, the constitution of the Netherlands was amended to make Indonesia a part of the Dutch Kingdom. The people of Indonesia complained of racial discrimination and gross economic inequality. There was virtually no middle-class in Indonesia.

Portugal

As regards Portugal, the Colonial Act of 1933 centralised colonial Government in Lisbon. It aimed at strengthening the economic and political inter-dependence of Portugal and her colonial empire. Portuguese colonies had their trade mostly with Portugal. The tendency towards integration continued uninterrupted. In 1921, the Portuguese colonies were made "oversea provinces".

Colonies during World War II

During the World War II, French Indo-China, Dutch Indonesia, British Malaya and Italian East Africa were conquered and occupied by the enemy. The result was that they were virtually cut off from contact with their normal governors. The African possessions of Belgium and Britain and most of the French colonies were found very valuable in the war against the Axis Powers. The French colonial empire was divided between those areas like French Equatorial Africa which became the mainstay of the Gaullist Free French movement and those areas like French North Africa and West Africa or Madagascar that remained under the rule of Vichy. In the territories occupied by Japan during the World War II, there was great political tension. Opportunities were offered for every sort of separatist agitation and intrigues. The necessities of the War obliged every power to encourage economic development and industrialisation in its colonies. The combination of political upheaval with economic expansion strengthened both the demand for national independence and concession of greater self-Government in colonial relationships.

During the last years of the World War II, ideals opposed to the restoration of old imperialism were spreading throughout the world. At Brazzaville was held in January 1944 the first imperial conference of free France presided over by General de Gaulle. It recommended the development of local assemblies to voice colonial opinion, employment of natives in the public services and direct representation of all the colonial peoples of France in the French Parliament. In May 1946, the French Constituent Assembly proclaimed unanimously that "from 1 June, 1946 all subjects of overseas territories, including Algeria, possess the quality of citizens with the same rights as French citizens in the home country and in the overseas territories". Thus the distinction between citizens and subjects was ended in France. The International Labour Organization met at Philadelphia in 1944. It was attended by delegations from 41 member countries. The meeting adopted a declaration of its purposes and principles which included universal equality of rights and status. French representatives fully endorsed the Philadelphia Charter.

Trusteeship System

The United Nations Charter adopted in 1945 created a system of colonial trusteeship which replaced the system of mandates. The Trusteeship Council was put incharge of the trusteeship system. The Council was to consider reports submitted to it by the administering authority. It was to examine the petitions in consultation with the administering authority. It was to visit the territory under the trusteeship system to see how the administration was going on. It could send a questionnaire to the states concerned with the object of getting information regarding the political, economic, social and educational progress of the mandated territories. The trusteeship system is not the "old wine in new bottles". It is better than the mandate system. It is considerably broader in scope and involves a more extensive international supervision of the territories given to countries under the trusteeship system. The nations with colonies such as Great Britain, France, Belgium, the Netherlands and others have agreed "to recognise the principle that the interests of the inhabitants of those territories are paramount and accept as a sacred trust the obligation to promote to the utmost, within the system of international peace and security established by the present Charter, the well-being of the inhabitants of these territories."

The Pacific Islands formerly mandated to Japan, were put under the trusteeship of the United States. Italy held Italian Somaliland under trusteeship for 10 years as from 1950. The Union of South Africa refused to accept the trusteeship system and continued to administer South-West Africa under the old class C mandate. Provision was made for states voluntarily to place any of their own colonial territories under the new trusteeship system, but none showed its willingness to do so.

India

As regards the contraction of Europe, it is rightly pointed out that when the San Francisco Conference was held in 1945 to shape the United Nations, some 600 million people in the world were not self-governing, but by the end of 1963, the peoples who had not attained full national equality and sovereignty were merely a handful. In this connection, the most important event was the independence of India in August 1947 and the creation of two independent states of India and Pakistan. The Indian National Congress was not satisfied with the Government of India Act, 1935. In August 1942, it started the Quit India movement. All the Congress leaders were arrested and they remained in jails upto 1945. In 1946, the Cabinet Mission submitted its scheme for the solution of the Indian problem but the same did not work. In June, 1947, Lord Mountbatten got his scheme accepted both from the Congress and the Muslim League and the same was given effect to by the Indian Independence Act passed in July 1947 and on 15 August 1947 India achieved independence.

Burma

Burma was separated from India in 1937. It was the scene of bitter fighting between the Allies and the Japanese during World War II. The Japanese set up a puppet Government in Burma and proclaimed it an independent state. After the surrender of the Japanese, the British tried to re-establish their rule but the independence movement continued to assert itself. There were lengthy negotiations which resulted in British recognition of "a free and independent Burma whether within or without the British Empire". For a year, Burma was to remain a member of the British Commonwealth of Nations and at the end of that period, she was to be free to withdraw if it so desired. The Burmese decided to become an independent country outside the British Commonwealth. The new order took effect on 4 January 1948.

Ceylon (Sri Lanka)

In 1927, the Donoughmore Commission prepared a constitution for Ceylon which came into effect in 1931. In 1943, Britain promised to grant Ceylon a considerable degree of constitutional reforms and "full internal civil administration". The Soulbury Commission of 1945 provided for limited self-Government. In December 1947 the Ceylon Independence Act was passed. In February 1948, Ceylon became a free Dominion. She is a member of the Commonwealth of Nations.

Ireland

In December 1948, the Dail of the Eire passed the Republic of Ireland Act which cut the last link with the British Crown and the Commonwealth of Nations.

South Africa

General Smuts was defeated in the elections of May 1948. The new Nationalist Government of Dr. Malan pursued a racialist policy and showed its determination to leave the Commonwealth. When Malan resigned in 1954, he was succeeded by J.C. Strijdom as the Head of the Nationalist Party. After 1958, Dr. H.F. Verwoerd pursued the policy of apartheid (racial segregation) with more vigour and ruthlessness. In 1960, a referendum was held which resulted in a small majority for declaring South Africa a republic. South Africa left the Commonwealth of Nations in May 1961.

British Colonies

During the 1950s, many British colonies got independence. In 1951, the Gold Coast and Nigeria got new constitutions. In March 1957, the Gold Coast and the trustee territory of Togoland joined to establish the independent state of Ghana. Dr. K. Nkrumah, Prime Minister of Ghana, had an ambition to make Ghana the nucleus of a future African federation and to this end, combined with the former French colony of Guinea in 1958. The people of Nigeria clamoured for independence. The Federation of Nigeria developed regional self-government and in 1960 attained complete independence as a dominion.

The Fereration of Rhodesia and Nyasaland was formed in 1953. The main object of the Federation was to retain the supremacy of the Whites over the Blacks. However, the Federation did not enjoy the confidence of the Africans. In March 1963, it was decided to give independence to Northern Rhodesia and Nyasaland on 31 December 1963. It was decided not to give independence to Southern Rhodesia. In spite of that, Southern Rhodesia declared herself independent on 11 November 1965 and refused to owe any allegiance to the British Government. There was a demand on the part of the African states that Great Britain should take military action against Southern Rhodesia. There was a stalemate for many years. In February 1980, elections were held in Southern Rhodesia and in April 1980, Southern Rhodesia became independent as Zimbabwe.

Tanganyika was formerly a Trust territory. She won her independence in December 1961. Uganda got her independence in 1962. Kenya became independent in December 1963. The people of Kenya had to pay a very heavy price for their freedom. They suffered terribly under the leadership of Jomo Kenyatta. Kenyatta became the first Prime Minister of Kenya. Mauritius attained independence in 1968. Cyprus became an independent sovereign state in August 1960. The constitution of Malta set up in 1947, proved unable to reconcile the interests of United Kingdom in the Island as a defence base, with the interests of the people of Malta. In 1958, attempts to improve the arrangements failed. Self-Government had to be temporarily replaced by the interim constitution of April 1959. In Malaya, with its plural society of Chinese, Malayas, Indians and Europeans, there appeared terrorist organisations led by the Malayan Communist groups. Guerrilla fighting and acts of terrorism continued after federation in 1948 until full independence in 1957. In Cyprus, independence was preceded by a decade of civil war between the Greeks and Turks.

Palestine

England was caught between Zionist demands that the Jews persecuted in Europe should be free to immigrate into Palestine and Muslim Arab insistence upon protecting the economic rights of the Arabs in Palestine. Britain tried to devise a scheme of self-Government for Palestine which she held under "A" mandate. Her proposal in 1937 to partition Palestine into an Arab state and a Jewish state was rejected by the Arabs. Another proposal of 1939 was rejected by both sides. The matter remained in suspense until 1947. In February 1947, the British Government declared that as it had become impossible for her to carry on the mandate, she was going to place the issue before the United Nations. In August 1947, a special Commission of the United Nations on Palestine submitted its report. A majority of its members recommended the partition of Palestine. The partition plan was accepted by the General Assembly in November 1947. The plan provided for separate Jewish and Arab states in Palestine. It was accepted by the Jews, Soviet Union and the United States but opposed by the Arabs. In the midst of confusion and chaos prevailing in Palestine and the parties not coming to any mutual agreement, the British Government declared its intention of withdrawing completely from Palestine on 15 May 1948. It was on the night between 14 May and 15 May 1948 that the Jewish state of Israel was proclaimed with Dr. Weizmann as its first President. The new State was recognised both by the Soviet Union and the United States.

Iraq

After the World War I, Iraq was put under the mandate of Great Britain. The latter invited Feisal to assume the Crown of Iraq and entered into a number of treaties with that country. The Treaty of 1922 gave England control over the army and foreign affairs of Iraq. In 1930, Great Britain signed another treaty of alliance and announced the termination of the British mandate from the date Iraq became a member of the League of Nations. In October 1932, Iraq became a member of the League of Nations.

Egypt

In 1936, the Anglo-Egyptian treaty was signed. It pledged Great Britain to defend Egypt from external aggression. The defence of the Suez Canal Zone was also taken over by the British Government. The treaty was to last for 20 years. During the World War II, British troops were stationed in Egypt. Germany and Italy were busy in North Africa and Egypt felt that her security was threatened. Air attacks were made on the Canal Zone. However, the United Nations were able to push back the Germans and the Italians from their bases in Egypt. When the World War II ended in 1945, there was a demand for the cancellation of the Treaty of 1936 which was considered as a symbol of the slavery of the people of Egypt. The British Government was asked to withdraw her troops from the Suez Canal Zone. There was rioting all over Egypt. By a coup d' etat General Naguib and his colleagues like Colonel Nasser seized power in Egypt. The people of Egypt were not prepared to tolerate the continuation of British troops in the Suez Canal Zone and the British were not willing to withdraw. On 26 July 1956, President Nasser declared the nationalisation of the Suez Canal and froze the funds of the Suez Canal Company. The United States and France applied economic sanctions against Egypt. Great Britain ordered general mobilisation of her forces and despatched troops to an unknown destination. The United States and France stood behind her. A conference was held in London to solve the problem. On 29 October 1956, the forces of Israel attacked the Egyptian positions in the Suez Canal Zone. On 31 October, 1956, Great Britain and France joined the attack on Egypt. Fighting was stopped only when the Soviet Union gave a warning to Great Britain and France that in case they did not stop fighting in Egypt, she would also join the war.

The Sudan was governed jointly by Great Britain and Egypt from 1899 to 1 January, 1956 when she became a sovereign independent republic.

Morocco

Morocco was a dependency of France. There was a vigorous agitation for the liberation of Morocco from foreign yoke. Ultimately, an agreement was reached and Sidi Mohammed returned to Morocco in November 1955 and was recognised as the Sultan of Morocco. In April 1956, the Spanish regime in Morocco was also ended. In May 1956, an agreement giving Morocco the right of full diplomatic representation as a sovereign state was signed in Paris. In December 1956, Morocco became a member of the United Nations.

Tunisia

Tunisia was a dependency of France. The French treated the people of Tunisia with contempt and indifference and hence there was a vigorous agitation against foreign rule. There was a lot of violence. Ultimately, the French Government was forced to come to terms with the people of Tunisia. By a Joint Protocol signed in Paris on 20 March 1956, France recognised the independence of Tunisia and she became a member of the United Nations the same year.

Algeria

Algeria was also a dependency of France. There was also agitation for the liberation of their country from foreign yoke. The problem was complicated because a large number of Frenchmen had settled in Algeria and considered Algeria as their motherland. They opposed the demand for Algerian independence. Algeria won independence in 1961 after a lot of trouble.

Portuguese Colonies

The Portuguese colonies in Africa consisted of Angola, Mozambique, Cape Verde Islands, Portuguese Guinea, Sao Tome and Principle. President Salazar of Portugal treated the African colonies as the provinces of Portugal and refused to give them freedom. For years, Portugal used Angola as the source of the supply of three million slaves to run the Portuguese coffee plantations of Brazil. The Portuguese exchequer was enriched with diamonds and uranium from Angola. In March 1961, the people of Angola started their guerrilla campaign against Portugal who retaliated by airlifting more than 20,000 troops to Angola. The revolt was mercilessly crushed and more than 50,000 Africans were killed. In 1962, the Angolans were successful in getting the support of Congolese Premier Adoula. Military training camps were set up. The General Assembly called upon Portugal to grant the right of self-determination to her colonies. Ultimately, the Portuguese withdrew from Angola on 11 November 1975 unilaterally without setting up a successor Government. Traditional Portuguese ties with Angola were snapped. The result was internal disorder which gave an opportunity for outside intervention. Both the Soviet Union and the United States tried to have a Government of their choice in Angola. However, the Soviet Union came out successful in that race.

Belgian Congo

The Belgian Congo was a dependency of Belgium. It was abruptly given independence and a new constitution on 30 June 1960. A Round Table Conference of the representatives of Belgium and the Congo had been held in Brussels at the beginning of 1960. It accelerated the process of granting independence although Belgium had done nothing to prepare the people of Congo for independence. Elections were held and Joseph Kasavubu was made President of the Republic of the Congo and Patrice Lumumba became Prime Minister. There was a mutiny and intervention by Belgian troops. The Congolese Government appealed to the United Nations which sent an international force to maintain order. Katanga province declared its independence and welcomed Belgian troops. The Soviet Union supported Lumumba and the Western powers supported President Kasavubu. There were massacres and outrages. The Secretary-General of the United Nations and Lumumba were killed. It took a lot of time to restore law and order in the country.

End of Italian Empire

When Mussolini joined the World War II in 1940, Italy had an overseas empire of a million and a quarter square miles with a population of more than 14 millions. In 1941, British and Allied forces overran Eritrea. Ethiopia and Italian Somaliland and during the next two years also occupied Libya. This left Albania and the Italian Aegian Islands, both of which were occupied by either Allied troops or German troops. The result was that when the War ended in 1945, Italy was without an empire. The Communists and socialists opposed the restoration of any colonies as the colonies had always been a serious drain on Italian economy.

By the terms of the peace treaty signed in 1947, Italy was obliged to renounce her sovereignty over her former colonies. Independence had already been restored to Ethiopia and the ties which bound Albania with Italy had already been cut. The General Assembly of the United Nations decided in November 1949 that Libya comprising Cyrenaica, Tripolitania and the Fezzan be given independence not later than 1 January 1952. The General Assembly also decided that Italian Somaliland be given independence at the end of 10 years. Italy was to be the administering authority for that period. The General Assembly also decided in December 1950 that after an interim period, Eritrea be federated with Ethiopia.

Syria

Before the World War I, Syria was a part of the Turkish Empire. After the War, she was placed under the mandate of France. There were clashes between the nationalists of Syria and French authorities. In 1936, France agreed to give freedom to Syria after three years. The time-table was upset due to the outbreak of the World War II in 1939. When France fell in 1940, the danger from the Axis Powers became very great. In July 1941, the Allied forces occupied Syria and Lebanon. In 1945, France tried to reoccupy Syria but Great Britain intervened. In 1946, all French troops were withdrawn from Syria.

Lebanon

Lebanon was placed under the mandate of France alongwith Syria and she won her independence alongwith Syria in 1946.

Jordan

In 1923, Trans-Jordan was put under the control of Abdullah who was granted a large measure of autonomy. Full independence was given to her in 1946 and Abdullah assumed the title of King.

Indonesia

Indonesia is a country of about 80 million people covering an area of about 57,600 sq. miles. For more than 300 years, it was under the Dutch rule. It was in December 1949 that it became independent.

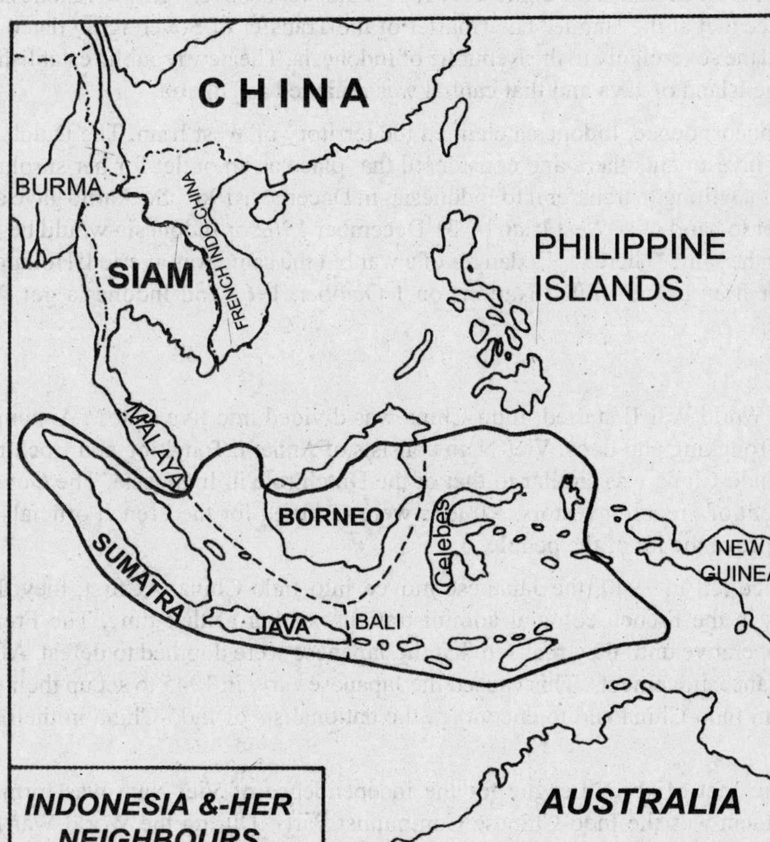

The people of Indonesia had to struggle very hard to win their freedom. In 1910, they started a party known as Sarekat Islam. It stood for political and social reforms. In 1920 was started the Indonesian

Communist Party. In 1927 was started the National Indonesian Party whose founder was Soekarno who later on became the first President of Indonesia. In 1939, the first all Indonesian Congress was held in Batavia. Its object was to bring all the nationalist groups on one platform.

In 1940, Holland was defeated by Germany. The Dutch authority in the Dutch East Indies also collapsed. The Japanese established their control over the Dutch East Indies. During the five years of Japanese rule, the Indonesian leaders played a double game. They accepted offices under the Japanese with a view to moderate the policies of the Japanese towards the native people. At the same time, they kept themselves in constant touch with underground movements of resistance. During the War and particularly when they saw that defeat was inevitable, the Japanese encouraged the nationalist movement in every way. They even supplied weapons to the Indonesians. Only two days after the Japanese surrender, a group of nationalists led by Soekarno declared their determination not to revert to a colonial or semi-colonial status. Insurgents in Java, Sumatra and other Islands of the Dutch East Indies organised a union, proclaimed the Republic of Indonesia and adopted a national flag.

The leaders and people of Indonesia had to fight very hard against the Dutch Government which tried to re-establish its authority. In March 1947, the Dutch Government extended de facto recognition to the Republic of Indonesia. In spite of that, there were periods of truce or armed hostilities or police action. One such truce agreement was made in January 1948 and broken in December of the same year. In January 1949, the Security Council asked the parties to stop hostilities. On the request of the government of the Netherlands, the Security Council asked the Commission of the United Nations to make arrangements for a round table conference for the transfer of sovereignty to Indonesia. The Round Table Conference met at the Hague. The Charter of the Transfer of Sovereignty dated 2 November 1949 transferred the sovereignty to the Republic of Indonesia. The new republic established its capital at Batavia on the Island of Java and that capital was renamed as Djkarta.

After her independence, Indonesia claimed the territory of West Irian. The Dutch Government had made huge investments there and considered that place as an outlet for her surplus population and hence was not willing to transfer it to Indonesia. In December 1961, Soekarno gave an ultimatum to Holland either to hand over West Irian by 31 December 1962 or Indonesia would be forced to use force to recover the same. There was a danger of a war but the same was averted. Holland transferred her control over Irian to the United Nations on 1 October, 1962 and Indonesia got West Irian on 1 May, 1963.

Indo-China

Before the World War II started, Indo-China was divided into five states : Annam, Cambodia, Cochin-China, Tongking and Laos. Viet-Nam consists of Annam. Tongking and Cochin-China. The French rule in Indo-China was similar to that of the Dutch rule in Indonesia. The Government was run for the benefit of French investors. All jobs were reserved for the French officials and nothing was done to improve the lot of the people.

When France fell in 1940, the Japanese moved into Indo-China. At first, they did not make radical changes in the French colonial administration existing at that time. The French in Indo-China were cooperative until they realised that the Japanese were doomed to defeat. After that, they organised resistance movements. This caused the Japanese early in 1945 to set up their own colonial administration in Indo-China and to encourage the nationalists of Indo-China in their demands for independence.

In 1941, the Viet-Minh or League for the independence of Viet-Nam was formed in China. Its main constituent was the Indo-Chinese Communist Party. During the World War II, the Vichy Government of France headed by Marshal Petain had allowed Japan to occupy Indo-China. When after the liberation of France in 1945, de Gaulle came to power, the Japanese deposed the French

Governor-General of Indo-China, disarmed the French troops and interned all the French civilians. This happened on 9 March, 1945. When the Japanese found that their defeat was approaching, they established closer contacts with the Viet-Minh. Just before the surrender of Japan, the Viet-Minh ordered a general revolt in the country and no attempt was made by the Japanese to suppress it. The result was that the rebels were able to capture Hanoi. On 20 August, 1945, the Republic of Viet-Nam was declared. The Viet Minh formed a Government for the whole of Viet-Nam on 28 August 1946. Dr. Ho Chi-Minh became the first President of the Republic of Viet-Nam.

Under the Potsdam Agreement, the Japanese troops in the North of Indo-China were to surrender to China and those in the South to Great Britain. The French Government was to take over the administration from China and Great Britain. That led to a lot of trouble. The people of Viet-Nam were not prepared to go back to pre-1939 days. There were demonstrations in Saigon long before the arrival of French troops. Lawlessness prevailed all over Indo-China. The Japanese had helped in the creation of lawlessness by selling arms to the Viet-Minh. A cease-fire agreement was signed in October 1945 but it was difficult to enforce it. The Viet-Minh was firmly entrenched in North Viet-Nam. By the agreement of March 1946, Viet-Nam was recognised as an autonomous unit in an Indo-Chinese Federation. In spite of that, peace was not restored. On 19 December 1946, Dr. Ho Chi Minh revolted openly against the French and fighting broke out at many places.

During the first two years, fighting was done on the lines of guerrilla warfare. The position of Dr. Ho Chi Minh became very strong after the establishment of the Communist regime in China in 1949. Communist China supported Dr. Ho Chi Minh and the United States supported the French Government in her war in Indo-China. In the beginning of 1954, the situation became critical. The Viet Minh forces besieged the fortress of Dien Bien Phu which surrendered on 7 May, 1954. There was the possibility of an open war between the United States and Communist China. To avoid such a situation, arrangements were made for a conference on Indo-China at Geneva. The Geneva Settlement provided for the partition of Viet Nam roughly along the 17 Parallel. The Viet Nam People's Army was to have control over the Northern and the French Union forces were to have control over the Southern zone of Viet Nam. Viet Nam was partitioned but that partition was to be provisional as provision was made for general elections for the unification of Viet Nam.

Even after the Geneva settlement, there was no peace in Viet Nam and fighting continued. In 1968, hostilities were stopped and peace talks started at Paris in May 1968. An agreement was made in January 1973 but that proved to be merely a truce. Another accord was made in June 1973 but in spite of that, there was no peace in Viet Nam. North Viet Nam and her allies continued the war and they won victory after victory over South Viet Nam. The capital of South Viet Nam fell in their hands in April 1975 and the war ended in Viet Nam. The whole of Viet Nam was unified. Both Laos and Cambodia had achieved their independence in 1954.

Although there has been contraction of Europe in the world, a reference may be made to certain new tendencies. One is a greater concentration of colonial policy on economic development and social welfare based on large-scale investment and technical assistance. Under the Colonial Development and Welfare Act of 1945, Britain made available the sum of £ 120 million to be spent in and on the colonies. The amount was increased in 1950 by another 20 millions. This money was spent mainly on developing agriculture and transport system and extending medical and educational services. In 1948, the Colonial Development Corporation was set up "to develop the resources and trade of, and to expand the production of, foodstuffs and raw materials in colonial territories". Another tendency is the growth of new forms of relationship between all states which cut right across the old political relationships. Nations and states came together not in terms of colonialism or dependency but on functional cooperation within specialised agencies for promoting mutual interests. Within the Colombo Plan of 1950, the United Kingdom, Australia, Canada, Ceylon, India, Pakistan and New Zealand came together with Indo-China. Thailand and the colonial territories of South and South-East Asia, to plan a six-year economic development scheme for India, Pakistan, Ceylon, Malaya, Singapore, British North Borneo, Brunei and Sarawak. Its aims were similar to those of the Colonial Development and Welfare Act at Great Britain. The Food and Agriculture Organisation, the World Health Organisation, UNESCO and other functional agencies of the United Nations had a similar influence.

Dr. David Thomson rightly points out that "the shrinkage in area of the Empires of particular European powers did not mean a contraction of the ambit of European civilisation in general. On the contrary, Asia ought to use its new independence to adopt more fully the techniques of industrialism and modern science and even the education and technical advice of Europeans. Communist China borrowed from Russia what Russia had borrowed from Europe. Never had the impact of European civilisation been more truly world-wide than when the range of Europe's political power was being most rapidly contracted. Economic westernization advanced even while political westernization was in retreat." (Europe Since Napoleon, p. 874).

SUGGESTED READINGS

Allen, H.C.: **Great Britain and the United States** (1783-1952).
Attlee; Clement: **Empire Into Commonwealth,** 1961.
Barnard, Marjorie : **A History of Australia,** 1963.
Beasley, W.G.: **The Modern History of Japan, London,** 1963.
Bemis, S.F.: **A Diplomatic History of the United States, New York,** 1947.
Brebner, J. Bartlet: **Canada, A Modern History,** 1960.
Cady, John F.: **The Roots of French Imperialism in Eastern Asia,** 1954.
Cameron, William J.: **New Zealand,** 1951.
Carrington, C.E.: **The British Overseas,** 1950.
Clark, G.M.H.: **A History of Australia,** 1962.
Clubb, O. Edmund: **Twentieth Century China,** 1964.
Cole. T. and J.H.
Hallowell (Eds.): **Postwar Governments in the Far East,** 1947.
Costin, W.C. **Great Britain and China,** 1833-1860, **Oxford,** 1937.
Coupland, R.: **The Exploitation of East Africa,** 1856-1890, 1939.
Cowen, Zelman: **The British Commonwealth of Nations in a Changing World,** 1964.
Craig, Gerald M.: **Upper Canada; The Formative Years,** 1784-1841, 1963.
Elton, Lord: **The Imperial Commonwealth,** 1946.
Emerson, Rupert: **From Empire to Nation,** 1960.
Fage, D.: **Introduction to the History of West Africa, Cambridge,** 1919.
Fishel, W.R.: **The End of Extraterritoriality in China,** 1952.
Hall, H.D.: **Mandates, Dependencies and Trusteeship,** 1948.
Harris, N.D.: **Europe and the East,** 1926.
Hearder. H.: **Europe In the Nineteenth Century,** 1830-1880, **Longman,** 1966.
Hobson, J.A.: **Imperialism, Third Edition,** 1938.
Hughes, E.R.: **The Invasion of China by the Western World,** 1938.
Hyndman, H.M.: **The Awakening of Asia,** 1919.
Johnston, Sir H.H.: **A History of the Colonization of Africa by Alien Races,** 1930.
Kiernan, E.V.G.: **British Diplomacy in China,** 1880-1885, 1939.
Kimble, David: **A Political History of Ghana,** 1850-1928, **Oxford,** 1963.
Kirk., G.E.: **Short History of the Middle East,** 1949.
Knaplund, Paul: **The British Empire,** 1815-1939, 1941.
Knight, M.M.: **Morocco As a French Economic Venture,** 1937.
Knowles, L.C.A.: **Economic Development of the British Overseas Empire.**

Koebner, Richard and Helmut D. Schmidt: **Imperialism,** 1840-1960, 1964.
Langer, William L.: **The Diplomacy of Imperialism,** Second Edition, 1951.
Lenin, V.I.: **Imperialism, the Highest Stage of Capitalism,** 1937.
Lovell, R.I.: **The Struggle for Africa**, 1875-1899, 1934.
Lucas, C.P.: **The Partition and Colonization of Africa,** 1922.
Manning, Helen Taft: **The Revolt of French Canada,** 1800-1835, 1962.
Masani, R.P.: **Britain in India,** 1960.
Michael Franz H. and George E. Taylor: **The Far East in the Modern World, London,** 1956.
Middleton, L.: **The Rape of Africa,** 1936.
Moon, Penderel: **Divide and Quit,** 1962.
Moon, P.T.: **Imperialism and World Politics,** 1926.
Morton, W.L.: **The Critical Years: The Union of British North America,** 1964.
Mosley, Leonard: **The Last Days of the British Raj,** 1962.
Muir, Ramsay: **The Expansion of Europe,** Sixth Edition, 1939.
Murphy, Agnes: **The Ideology of French Imperialism,** 1871-1881, 1948.
Norman, E.H.: **Japan's Emergence as a Modern State,** 1940.
Palmer, Leslie H.: **Indonesia and the Dutch,** 1962.
Panikkar, K.M.: **Asia and Western Dominance, London,** 1959.
Pierce, Richard A.: **Russia and Central Asia,** 1867-1917, California, 1960
Power, T.F.: **Jules Ferry and the Renaissance of French Imperialism,** 1944.
Pratt, J.T.: **The Expansion of Europe into the Far East,** 1947.
Purcell, Victor: **The Boxer Uprising,** 1963.
Reischauer, E.O.: **Japan, Past and Present,** 1946.
Robinson, Ronald: **Africa and the Victorians: The Climax of Imperialism in the Dark Continent,** 1961.
Rudin, Harry R.: **The Germans in the Cameroons,** 1938.
Sanderson, G.D.: **India and British Imperialism,** 1951.
Sansom, G.B.: **The Western World and Japan,** 1950.
Shepperson, W.S.: **British Emigration to North America,** Oxford, 1957.
Simmons, Jack: **Livingstone and Africa,** London, 1955.
Slade, Ruth: **King Leopold's Congo,** 1962.
Spear, Percival : **India, a Modern History,** 1961.
Spender, J.A.: **The Changing East** 1926.
Strachey, John : **The End of Empire,** 1960.
Tan, Chester : **The Boxer Catastrophe,** 1955.
Taylor, A.J.P.: **Germany's First Bid for Colonies,** 1884-1885, 1938.
Taylor, Don : **The Years of Challenge,** 1960.
Townsend, Mary E.: **Origins of Modern German Colonialism,** 1871-1885, 1921.
Toussaint. C.E.: **The Trusteeship System of the United Nations,** 1956.
Wehl, D.: **The Birth of Indonesia,** 1928.
Wiedner, D.L.: **A History of Africa South of the Sahara,** London, 1963.
Wieschoff, H.A.: **Colonial Policies in Africa,** 1944.
Williamson, J.A.: **A Short History of British Expansion,** 1930.
Winks, Robin: **British Imperialism,** 1964.
Yanaga C.: **Japan Since Perry,** 1949.

CHAPTER

49 THE POLICY OF APPEASEMENT

Great Britain, France and the United States had the power and resources to check the aggressive actions of Germany, Italy and Japan during the 1930s but they failed to do so on account of the policy of appeasement followed by them towards the Axis Powers. Their policy of appeasement reflected their desire for peace, an attempt on their part to recover their bearings and to re-assert their self-respect and "exasperation with any one who would try to probe that mass of emotional pretence and questionable reasoning."

POLICY OF APPEASEMENT BY GREAT BRITAIN

British policy of appeasement during the inter-War period rested on five bases. The first basis was that Britain had intense fear of Communist Russia and Communism. There was a clash of interests between Britain and Russia in the Middle East, China and Europe. On account of the activities of the Comintern, there was an apprehension of Communist uprising in Britain. There existed a sort of panic among the propertied classes in Britain caused by the mere mention of Communism. The result was that Great Britain hated the Soviet Union and was willing to assist any country which was opposed to the Soviet Union. Germany, Italy and Japan took advantage of the Russophobia in Britain and carried on their aggressive activities successfully. They covered their aggression with the thin guise of anti-Communism. The long drawn-out negotiations between Britain and the Soviet Union during 1939 can be understood only in this background.

Another aim of British policy of appeasement was to maintain the balance of power in international politics although ultimately it ended in a complete destruction of that balance. Britain expected that Germany, the Soviet Union and Japan would check and exhaust each other by their mutual conflicts and that will allow Britain to maintain her isolation. If Germany and her partners invaded the Soviet Union and liquidated her, the danger from world revolutionary Communism would disappear. If they failed, the Fascist danger would be automatically eliminated. If there was a chance of the Soviet Union winning a victory over Germany; Britain was to help Germany with full force to avert that eventuality. It was with this reasoning that Britain allowed Germany to re-arm herself and to infringe the Treaty of Versailles and the Locarno Pact. Britain did not put up any resistance against German aggression in Austria and Czechoslovakia and indirectly even supported Japan in occupying Manchuria. Britain encouraged Italy to conquer and occupy Abyssinia. The tragedy of this policy was that with every concession given to the Axis Powers, Britain allowed the destruction of the balance of power. The policy of appeasement could be successful only if there was a sound balance of power without which appeasement degenerates into servility.

Another reason for British appeasement was the differences between Britain and France on the issues of collective security, reparations, disarmament and German recovery. The view of Britain was that a disarmed and weak Germany was "a vast centre of economic depression" which was not at all desirable. A weak Germany would be an open invitation to Communist expansion. A strong Germany could act as a bulwark against the Soviet Union and also counter-act the hegemony of France in Europe. The harshness of the clauses of the Treaty of Versailles created sympathy for Germany in England. The result was that Britain was in favour of relaxing the provisions of the Treaty of Versailles and making concessions on reparations. She was also willing to allow the gradual re-armament of Germany and the revision of her frontiers. She was not in favour of stiffening the provisions of the Covenant of the League of Nations. She preferred regional security to world-wide collective security. She was not in favour of entering into military alliances or commitments in Eastern Europe. She refused to make any commitments in Eastern Europe in 1925. France differed from Britain in all these respects. From 1919 to 1933, the policies of France prevailed and that contributed to the rise of Hitler. From 1933 onwards, British policies prevailed over those of France and that led to the War of 1939-1945. Hitler paralysed all possible opposition by playing upon the Western fear of Communism. He also exploited the differences between Britain and France. Germany tried to isolate the Soviet Union with the help of Britain and France. Likewise, she isolated France through the goodwill of Britain. Upto one stage, Britain appeased Germany out of sympathy. In 1935, the policy of appeasement was justified on the basis of expediency. When Britain concluded the Anglo-German Naval Treaty on 18 June 1935, Paris protested. The reply of Britain was that "it was better to get Germany voluntarily to limit herself to reasonable level of armaments than to adopt a high moral attitude towards treaty violation." In 1936, the policy of appeasement was justified on the plea of self-determination. When Germany denounced the Locarno Pact and France protested, the reply of Britain was that German troops were marching in their own territory. Even after 1937, Britain continued her policy of appeasement towards Germany on the pretext of gaining time for war preparations. It has rightly been said that in every case, "with delicate feelings and consciences, the appeasers threw their victims to the wolves and pleaded a higher righteousness in order to give them a beautifully eliminated safe conduct."

Another cause of British policy of appeasement was the internal weakness of Britain after the World War I. Appeasement was "almost predetermined by the precarious state of her economy, her own indecision in policy and by sundry embarrassments within the Empire." It was her economic condition which created the imaginary fear of Communism. The same weakness led her to emphasize the necessity of German economic recovery for her own recovery. Her economic condition forced her to follow a policy of peace which alone could give her time to put her house in order.

Another cause of British policy of appeasement was the inability of the ruling circles in England to understand correctly the character and ambitions of the Axis Powers. Chamberlain, the architect of British policy of appeasement, believed that Hitler meant business and would honour his word if the injustice done to Germany was removed. It was only when Britain declared war on 3 September 1939 that he realised the hollowness of his belief. Addressing the nation on 3 September 1939, Chamberlain admitted, "This is a sad day for all of us and to none is it sadder than to me. Everything that I have worked for, everything that I have hoped for, everything that I have believed in during my public life, has crashed into ruins."

Appeasement towards Germany

Since 1919, Britain was in favour of a lenient treatment. Germany was able to reduce the amount of reparations in her favour. Foreign troops were removed from the Ruhr. Britain continued to follow a policy of sympathetic treatment towards Germany even after the infringement of the Treaty of Versailles and the Locarno Pact by Hitler. On the pretext of saving Spain from the influence of Russia, Germany and Italy jointly intervened in 1936 the Civil War in Spain. Both Italy and Germany sent their technicians, aircraft and pilots and divisions of regular ground forces. In support of their action in Spain, Germany and Italy declared that their chief aim was to liberate Spain from the influence of Communist Russia. Under the spell of her Russophobia, Britain believed in the pretext of Germany and Italy. The Spanish Government appealed to the League of Nations. The first appeal in November 1936 was sidetracked at the instance of Britain and France. The second appeal in May 1937 was lost. The third appeal in August 1937 led to the Nyon Conference in September 1937 where an agreement was reached that naval patrols should be organised in the Mediterranean to stop piracy, but the resolution sponsored in the Assembly of the League of Nations was lost. The Committee of Non-intervention was set up in London in September 1936 under British Chairmanship to preserve peace in Europe and ensure neutrality. The Non-intervention Committee created a lot of confusion. It merely prevented the Spanish Government from getting the required arms from foreign countries. Under the name of non-intervention, General Franco got the whole army corps in the disguise of volunteers. The Non-intervention Committee was reduced to a farce. The Soviet Union suggested the withdrawal of all foreign volunteers from Spain but the proposal was not supported by Britain. The British Government concluded the Anglo-Italian Agreement on 16 April 1938 by which the Italian force were to remain in Spain until the end of the Civil War.

In 1938 Hitler decided to occupy Austria and Czechoslovakia. On 13 January 1938, President Roosevelt proposed a conference of neutral states to prepare a set of principles that should govern international relations and achieve an equitable distribution of raw materials. The acceptance of this proposal would have revived, with American participation, collective security against Germany and Italy and halted Chamberlain's policy of appeasement but the proposal was opposed by Chamberlain. About this matter, Sir Winston Churchill writes, "Mr. Chamberlain with his limited outlook and inexperience of the European scene should have possessed the self-sufficiency to wave away the preferred hand stretched out across the Atlantic, leaves one, even at this date, breathless with amazement". (The Gathering Storm, p. 199).

On 4 February 1938, Ribbentrop who was against Britain, was appointed his Foreign Minister by Hitler. On 20 February 1938, Anthony Eden who was against the Axis Powers, was made to resign as Foreign Minister. This was done to appease the Axis Powers.

On 3 March 1938, Henderson had an interview with Hitler in which he discussed the prospects of disarmament, the question of Austria and the German demand for colonies.

Schuschnigg, the Chancellor of Austria, appealed for help to Britain against Germany. The reply of Britain was that she could not take any "responsibility of advising the Chancellor to take any course of action which, might expose his country to dangers against which His Majesty's Government are unable to guarantee protection." In the words of Amery, the Austrian crisis "found our Government straddled between the abandoned policy of collective security and an unachieved settlement with Italy. All that Chamberlain could do was to make a show of virtuous indignation and to submit to an insolent rejoinder that this was an internal affair of the of the German people and no concern of his." On 16 April 1938, the Anglo-Italian Agreement was signed between Italy and Britain.

As regards Czechoslovakia, she had an alliance of mutual assistance with France and the Soviet Union. The Soviet Union proposed to call a conference of the Western states against Hitler but Chamberlain did not agree. His policy was to put pressure on Germany to moderate the Sudeten German demands so that the Government of Czechoslovakia could accept them. He put pressure on Czechoslovakia not to be recalcitrant and accept the Sudeten demand so that Germany may not attack Czechoslovakia. He put pressure on France to agree to his policy so that Czechoslovakia may not be tempted to offer any resistance. France wanted to adopt a stiffer attitude towards Germany but Chamberlain made it clear to Daladier and Bonnet that England was not prepared for war. In July 1938, Chamberlain sent Lord Runciman to mediate between the Czechs and the Sudetens. On 13 September 1938, Daladier suggested to Chamberlain that they should meet Hitler together but Chamberlain rejected the suggestion and decided to meet Hitler alone. On 15 September 1938, Chamberlain went to Munich and had a meeting with Hitler who proposed self-determination for the Sudetens. Chamberlain returned to London where Daladier and Bonnet meet him on 18 September 1938. Chamberlain insisted that self-determination for the Sudetens was the only way to avoid war. France had to yield to the pressure of Britain. It was agreed that after the cession of the Sudetenland to

Germany, the rest of Czechoslovakia would be given an international guarantee. However, it is pointed out that the idea of such a guarantee was fantastic after stripping Czechoslovakia of her strategic frontier and powerful fortifications. Czechoslovakia refused to accept the plan. However, when she was warned by Britain and France that if she did not accept the plan and Germany attacked her, they would not help her, Czechoslovakia surrendered. When the plan was put before Hitler, he refused to give international guarantee for the rest of Czechoslovakia. Hitler also made further demands which were rejected by Czechoslovakia. There was mobilization in Czechoslovakia. It was declared that if Czechoslovakia was invaded, France would honour the obligations of an alliance and Britain and Russia would support France. Chamberlain agreed to mobilization of the British fleet. When Hitler gave an ultimatum that Czechoslovakia must accept his terms by 1 October 1938 or face the consequences, the British Government requested Mussolini to persuade Hitler to accept the idea of a conference. The Conference was held on 29 September and the Munich Pact was signed on 30 September 1938. Chamberlain surrendered to Hitler on the ground that Czechoslovia could not be defended even with the help of the Soviet Union as both Poland and Rumania had refused to allow Soviet troops to pass through their territories. Public opinion was opposed to war and the Munich Settlement averted the war. The offer of the Soviet Union for collective resistance to Hitler was refused on the ground that the Russian army was inefficient and was disintegrating. That was not correct. Amery writes, "Only sheer infatuation with appeasement at almost any price can explain the cold shouldering of Russian offers of help when things were already on the eve of war, even if that help had amounted to no more than sending aeroplanes to help the Czechs and holding back the Poles."

On 11 January 1939, Chamberlain went to Rome and met Mussolini. He discussed with him the question of disarmament. On 10 March 1939, Chamberlain stated that the international outlook was improving. On 15 March 1939, the German troops occupied Czechoslovakia. On 31 March 1939, Britain gave a guarantee to Poland. Italy occupied Albania on 7 April 1939. On 13 April 1939, a British guarantee was given to Greece and Rumania. Negotiations were started with Turkey. On 26 April 1939, Chamberlain announced compulsory training for six months. Negotiations were continued with the Soviet Union but on account of prejudices, miscalculations and suspicions on both sides, nothing came out of them. The view of the British Government was that Poland was a better ally than the Soviet Union and the price which the Soviet Union demanded for a pact with Britain was too high. The refusal of the Soviet Union to endorse the British guarantees to Poland, Greece and Rumania indicated that the Soviet Union had designs on those states. It is pointed out that as Chamberlain did not make any serious effort to come to an understanding with the Soviet Union, Germany concluded on 24 August 1939 a Non-Aggression Pact with the Soviet Union. L.B. Namier writes, "It had been a mistake on the part of the British Government, so quick, unstinting and easy about terms when handing out guarantees to second and third rate powers, to have treated Soviet Russia like a suppliant, and to have started off with suggestions which were both ludicrous and humiliating; it was a further mistake to have gone on haggling about every concession which rendered it ungracious and unconvincing; it was a third mistake to have sent a junior official to negotiate with Russia and later on servicemen of less standing than were sent, for instance, to Poland or Turkey. Behind it all was a deep, inseparable aversion to Bolshevist Russia such as was not shown in dealings with Hitler or Mussolini; and whether it was justified or not, it certainly was not conducive to success in the very difficult negotiations" (Diplomatic Prelude, 1938-39, pp. 187-8).

As late as July 1939, Chamberlain tried to enter into a defensive alliance with Germany for 25 years. He also offered a large loan to Germany. He also offered to return the German colonies in case Hitler undertook not to invade Poland.

However, all that failed. The policy of appeasement followed by Chamberlain ultimately failed. The very object for which the policy of appeasement was advocated, was defeated. Instead of peace, Chamberlain had to face a war. Being unfit to carry on war he had to resign in 1940 in disgust.

British Appeasement towards Italy

British policy towards Italy was not consistent. It varied from time to time. On the whole, it aimed at cooperation with Italy against Germany.

When Mussolini came to power in Italy in 1922, business circles in Britain welcomed it as a bulwark against the growth of leftism in the country and also as a powerful counter-force to the menace of Communism. Although the existence of a dictatorship in Italy did not fit in with the principles of democracy and constitutionalism as practised in Britain, the two countries did not quarrel with each other. After the Peace Conference of 1919, Italy demanded rewards in accordance with the terms of the secret Treaty of London of 1915 and Britain tried to honour the moral commitment whenever possible. The imperialistic tone of foreign policy was also a cementing factor.

As the conquest of Abyssinia by Italy would have threatened Britain economically, strategically and diplomatically, the British Government followed a muddle-headed policy of appeasement. Britain took a firm stand against Italy in January 1935. Sir Anthony Eden, the British delegate in the League of Nations, denounced the action of Italy in harsh terms and managed to influence the Council of the League with the decision of imposing sanctions against Italy. One may say that such an action amounted to the abandonment of the policy of appeasement, but later developments showed that as France was reluctant to implement the decision of sanctions against Italy, Britain also decided to do likewise. The decision of the Council regarding sanctions was not carried out. The Hoare-Laval Deal of December 1935 showed that both Britain and France were not willing to take action against Italy. They were determined not to apply sanctions against Italy on account of the fear that those may not result in the defeat of Mussolini. There was a fear that his defeat may result in a revolution in Italy which was likely to have incalculable repercussions on the social order throughout Central Europe and might have started insurrections in the whole of the colonial world.

On 2 January 1937, Britain signed a "Gentleman's Agreement" with Italy whereby both agreed that "freedom of entry into, exit from, and transit through the Mediterranean is a vital interest both to the different parts of the British Empire and to Italy, and that those interests are in no way inconsistent with each other." By this agreement, both Italy any Britain disclaimed "any desire to modify, or so far they are concerned, to see modified the status quo as regards national sovereignty of territories in the Mediterranean area." Mussolini was forced to strengthen Italian relations with Britain after Hitler annexed Austria in March 1938. It strengthened the position of Germany to a great extent. In order to counteract it, Italy signed a new Agreement with Britain on 16 April 1938 which went beyond the vague terms of the Agreement of 1937. In January 1939, Chamberlain and Lord Halifax went to Rome to win over Mussolini.

When both Germany and Italy interfered in the Civil War in Spain, Britain did not help the legitimate Government of Madrid or denounce the role of General Franco, Mussolini and Hitler. As a matter of fact, Chamberlain adopted a policy of non-intervention in Spain. The role of the Non-intervention Committee formed in London under the Chairmanship of Lord Plymouth indirectly strengthened the hands of Mussolini and Hitler. Chamberlain did nothing to stop the rise of Fascism in Spain inspite of the fact that he admitted that "a considerable number of regular Italian troops had been in Spain since the early days of the war."

It has to be admitted that the British policy of appeasement towards Italy did not bring about the desired result. As a matter of fact, instead of appeasing Italy, it aroused her suspicion and pushed her more and more into the arms of Germany. Italy might have remained attached to the anti-German camp if Britain and France had not proposed any action against Italy in the League of Nations. "Mussolini, bitter at Britain's treachery, fearful of the consequences of his action, triumphant in his victory and contemptuous of the fifty nations led by one whom he had successfully defied—Mussolini could never again be content in friendship with the West, and his eyes had now been turned towards the road that was to end in a public square in Milan."

Appeasement Towards Japan

Britain also followed a policy of appeasement towards Japan. There was a belief in Britain that Soviet influence and dominance would be strengthened in Inner Mongolia, Manchuria and China if Japan was weak, Japan would concentrate her attention on South-East Asia if China put up resistance to the advance of Japan and that would adversely affect British interests. The cooperation of Japan was considered necessary for the preservation of the interests of foreign nationals in China where the nationalist movement had been growing steadily. There was a feeling in Britain that she would suffer a great loss in the Far East if any kind of military action was taken against Japan. To quote Bruce, "The task of checking by force a Great Power like Japan at the other side of the world, was an experiment and a risk that Britain would, very properly have hesitated to undertake, even if she had been at the height of her military and economic security."

On account of these factors, Britain did not take any action to stop Japanese aggression in Manchuria in 1931. This was so inspite of the fact that the Lytton Committee appointed by the League of Nations to investigate the matter by going to Manchuria declared Japan as an aggressor and the League Assembly without dissent indicted Japan of aggression. Ultimately, Britain recognised the conquest of Manchuria by Japan. An official mission under the leadership of Sir Fredrick Lieth-Ross was sent to Tokyo to conciliate Japan. A mission of the Federation of British Industries, was also sent to Japan. The business circles appreciated the role of Sir John Simon in the League Assembly whose "wise and moderate" affirmations ruled out the possibility of putting an embargo on shipment of arms to Japan as that would have amounted to interference with British industry. L.S. Amery wrote, "It would be no concern of ours to prevent Japanese expansion in Eastern Siberia." The Morning Post of 30 January 1932 observed, "Japan, broadly speaking, is the only element making for order and good Government in the Far East." The Daily Mail wrote on 5 November 1931 that the presence of Japan in Manchuria "has been a benefit to the world." The same newspaper wrote on 10 December 1932 that Japan was "rendering good service to the civilisation by restoring law and order in Manchuria".

The rulers of Japan took full advantage of the weakness of the British Government and the Japanese invasion of China continued although British subjects and traders were humiliated in China. In August 1937, the Japanese inflicted physical injuries on the person of Sir Hughe Montgomery Knatchbull-Hughesson, the British Ambassador but the British Government did not take any action. The invasion of the Yangtse Valley extinguished British trade hegemony in that region but still Britain did nothing. After the surrender at Munich in 1938, Japan's army overran the Canton Delta and her navy seized the Spratly Islands off French Indo-China, but Britain took no action. Gross insults were inflicted on Europeans by the Japanese occupation forces in Tientsin, Amoy and Shanghai. The official motor car of the Ambassador was machine-gunned near Nanking but still Britain took no action.

In 1934, Japan warned all European powers to keep their hands off from China. Britain merely enacted the drama of the Conference at Brussels in November 1937 where it was decided to ask the Soviet Union to stop Japanese aggression in China. However, Stalin refused to oblige.

It was wrong on the part of Britain to assume that Japan would act as her watch-dog in the Far East and amicably settle the division of China with her. Britain openly backed Japan "as the champion against the Soviet Union and even against the United States."

POLICY OF APPEASEMENT BY FRANCE

From 1920 to 1924, France followed the policy of vindictive fulfilment of the terms of the Treaty of Versailles. From 1924 to 1932, she attempted conciliation with Germany. From 1933 to 1936, she pursued the policy of appeasement on "principle." This helped Germany to repudiate the Treaty of Versailles and the Treaty of Locarno. From 1936 to 1938, she followed the policy of appeasement based on "necessity" and abdicated French leadership to Britain. From 1938 onwards, she ceased to be a major force in European diplomacy and merely followed Britain.

It is true that France was victorious in the World War I, but even then her statesmen were terribly afraid of Germany which lay prostrate and exhausted. The question which dominated France at the Paris Peace Conference was how the settlement could serve the permanent interests of French security. The programme pursued was "restitution, reparation, guarantee". Restitution implied the recovery of Alsace and Lorraine. Reparation implied that Germany should compensate for the losses and damages done to France and contribute, to the reconstruction of the French areas destroyed during the war. Guarantee implied that Germany should fulfil her obligations and the Allies should give guarantees for French security. The Peace Settlement did not satisfy the French. The Rhineland was not separated from Germany. Only the left bank of the Rhine along with a zone about 30 miles East of the Rhine was demilitarised. The military occupation of the Rhineland was to last for only 15 years. Instead of an indefinite occupation of German territory, France was given a joint Anglo-American guarantee against unprovoked German aggression. However, this guarantee also remained merely on paper. Germany was to pay reparations only for the damage done to the civilians and their property and not the entire cost of the war. The coal mines of the Saar were given to France only for 15 years at the end of which a plebiscite was to be held and when it was actually held, the Saar went to Germany. France suffered from a sense of insecurity. In the matter of population, France did not find herself in a position to match with Germany. In 1919, France had a population of about 40 millions while Germany had a population of 70 millions. The birth rate in France was falling and that was a cause of worry for French statesmen.

In order to strengthen her position against Germany, France entered into a large number of alliances. In September 1920, France and Belgium entered into a military alliance against Germany. In February 1921 was signed the Franco-Polish Treaty of Alliance. Thus, in the event of an attack from Germany, France could count upon help from Poland in the East and Belgium in the West. In 1924, a Treaty of Alliance was made between France and Czechoslovakia. In 1926, a Treaty of Friendship was signed between France and Rumania. A similar treaty was made in 1927 between France and Yugoslavia. With Britain, no success could be achieved and there was no formal agreement between France, and Britain under which either party was to help the other. France pursued the policy of supporting the League of Nations and making it a strong international organisation so that it could serve as a regulator of German power in Europe.

From 1924 to 1932, France attempted reconciliation with Germany. The Ruhr was evacuated. The Treaties of Locarno were signed in 1925. Germany entered the League of Nations. The Allied military control of Germany was ended. The Rhineland was evacuated in 1930, five years in advance. At the instance of the French Foreign Minister, the Pact of Paris was signed. The questions of reparations and inter-Allied debts were settled. However, the economic depression of 1930 led to the development of aggressive forces which destroyed French confidence and prepared the ground for a policy of appeasement which was followed by France after 1932.

The economic depression wiped out reparations. Even the truncated payments from Germany stopped. Political developments at home in the form of cabinet crises added to the weakness of France. There was a gradual disintegration of her security. After Hitler came to power in 1933, the French leaders found themselves helpless. In the international sphere, the power of the League of Nations was seriously weakened by the resignation of Japan and the prospective withdrawal of Germany. Under these conditions, a new and disastrous epoch was inaugurated in French diplomacy which has been described as the "physiology of paralysis" by Prof. F.L. Schuman. To quote him, "As German truculence increased and German military power grew. French willingness to resort to force to maintain the status quo diminished. French opinion was so firmly attached to peace that it would no longer approve recourse to preventive violence to meet the menace of the new militarism now dominant in the Reich. The great issue before the Republic was no longer that of keeping a weak Germany in subjection but that of preserving the remnants of security and checkmating a strong, re-armed and defiant Reich." (International Politics, p. 739).

Political developments at home also weakened France. On 9 October 1934, French Foreign Minister Barthou and King Alexander of Yugoslavia were murdered at Marseilles. The result was that France lost a very capable Foreign Minister and also a reliable friend in the Balkans. Laval was the successor of Barthou and he proved himself to be a misfit. Peter II was the successor of Alexander and he was just a boy who had no strong position in the Balkans. On 22 November 1934, Philippe Berthelot who had served as the Secretary-General of the Quai d' Orsay for a long time, died. In him, France lost an able diplomat. Inspired by the wave of Fascism in Italy, a section of the French politicians staged riots in the country on 6 February 1934 and that weakened the socialist and Communist forces in the country. The liberals and the radical socialists became anti-Fascists. A Papular Front came into existence. It swept the polls of April-May 1936. The result was that Blum became the Prime Minister and Laval the Foreign Minister. The Blum Government did not take strong action to face the challenge posed by Fascism at home and abroad. A Treaty of Friendship had already been signed with the Soviet Union in 1935. The new Government looked forward to Poland for the same purpose. In August 1936, General Gamelin, Chief of the French General Staff, visited Poland. In return, General Edward Rydz-Smigly visited Paris. The fear of Germany brought France and Poland together. In 1936, German troops occupied the Rhineland. France merely protested although the German action was a clear violation of the Treaty of Versailles and the Locarno Pact.

The morale of the French army was not high. The material at the disposal of the French soldiers was insufficient. The productive capacity of French factories in the 1930's was about a third of the capacity of the German factories. Between 1934 and 1938, Germany spent four times as much as France on national defence. France did not keep her armed forces fully prepared for war. She ignored tanks and aviation. The French generals were suffering from outmoded military theories. The French people were suffering from a sort of schism. Political parties were not united. Social classes were opposed to each other. Fascism was gaining popularity in France. The number of fifth columnists had increased to such an extent that they were endangering the security of the country. French democracy and French political institutions had thoroughly degenerated. The French Parliament reflected a gulf between a Liberal and democratic France and France of the Restoration and the Empire. There was acute ministerial instability. Between 1929 and 1936, there were as many as 20 ministerial crises. Between 1920 and 1940, 80% of the ministerial crises were due to the differences between the Chamber of Deputies and the Senate on financial matters. Big business dominated the Third Republic.

Another phenomenon which developed in France at this time was the horror of war among the French. France had lost more men, in the World War I than any other country. A horror of war was created by the sad and disabled fathers or miserable widowed mothers. The new psychology which developed among the Frenchmen was that "the worst international agreement was better than the best of wars." France had a diminishing and ageing population. The memory of the bloodshed of World War I was still fresh. The French had failed to secure themselves against Germany. There was a confession of military inferiority vis-a-vis Germany among the French. The French opinion was so firmly attached to peace that it was not prepared to fight a war to stop aggression by Germany, Italy or Japan.

Another cause of the policy of appeasement was the tremendous fear of Communism and the Soviet Union. Both Daladier and Bonnet wanted to save France from Bolshevism. To quote Bonnet, "It is the struggle against Bolshevism which is essentially at the basis of the common German and

Italian political conception." On account of their dread of Communism, Frenchmen were prepared to appease both Germany and Italy to divert them against the Soviet Union and save their own privileges. This effort continued even after the second World War had begun after the invasion of Poland by Germany.

Another source of French appeasement was the French desire to have Italian friendship at any cost. After the coming to power of Hitler in Germany in 1933, Mussolini proposed the Italo-Anglo-Franco-German Combine. Daladier agreed to it and by doing so, France lost Poland. In January 1935, the Franco-Italian Agreement was signed. That gave Mussolini a free hand in Abyssinia. France tried to humour Mussolini against Germany in the Civil War in Spain. The result was that one by one, the bases of French security were destroyed by 1936. The Little Entente was in ruins. The German menace was growing. The United States was keeping aloof. France disintegrated under the Popular Front Ministry. When Daladier signed the Munich Pact on 30 September 1938, he alienated the Soviet Union and made the invasion of Poland by Germany a certainty. On 6 December 1938, Bonnet signed with Ribbentrop the Franco-German Declaration of Friendship. In 1939, Germany and the Soviet Union invaded Poland. In 1940, Germany and Italy invaded France.

The result of all this was that France became more and more dependent on Britain and merely followed her lead. French Governments abdicated their leadership to the British Government. France did whatever was decided by Chamberlain. When Britain gave guarantees to Poland, France followed. When Britain declared war against Germany on 3 September 1939, France did likewise although much against her wish. When Germany invaded France in 1940, France collapsed like a house of cards and her leaders joined hands with Hitler.

At the time of the Abyssinian crisis, France followed a policy of appeasement towards Italy. When the matter was taken up by the League of Nations, the conservative statement of Britain preferred the survival of a Fascist system in Italy as they were afraid of the consequences arising out of the failure of Mussolini. Under the circumstances, Britain decided to apply limited economic sanctions against Italy. Outwardly, Sir Samuel Hoare took up a bold stand in the Assembly of the League of Nations but secretly he entered into negotiations with Laval of France to prepare a plan to appease the dictator of Italy. That plan showed the willingness of Britain and France to give approximately two-thirds Abyssinia to Italy. This was so at a time when Italy had been indicted as aggressor by the League of Nations and she was being subjected to economic sanctions. On 25 June 1939, Laval stated that economic sanctions were imposed because "we did not want to break with Britain and the League of Nations and they were implemented in moderation because we did not want to annoy Italy."

The role of France in the Abyssinian crisis shows that she was following a policy of appeasement of choice. It was the first important occasion when her statesmen could have stuck to the right side of the problem. They could have helped the Emperor of Abyssinia and thereby proved that they were the defenders of the peace of the world. What actually happened was that while Sir Samuel Hoare resigned after the publicity of the plan regarding Abyssinia, Laval continued to remain in office. That convinced Mussolini that in no case France would stand in his way in Abyssinia. Mussolini rightly came to the conclusion that if French interests "were no bar to his plans, Ethiopian interests were not a matter in which France would be greatly concerned."

France played a similar role during the Civil War in Spain. When Mussolini and Hitler interfered in Spain in a big way, France did not help the democratic Government of Spain against General Franco. Along with Britain, France followed a policy of non-intervention in Spain. A Non-intervention Committee was set up in London with 27 states and an embargo was put on the export of arms to Spain. That was positively helpful to General Franco who with the help of Hitler and Mussolini went ahead confidently in the face of appeasement shown by France and Britain. On 6 September 1936,

Blum observed, "But should we undertake a competition of armaments on Spanish soil? If certain powers furnish arms and planes to the rebels, should France furnish them to the Popular Front?... No." At Geneva, the Spanish delegate was dissuaded from making specific accusations against Italy and Germany because France wanted to shield the guilt of Mussolini and Britain wanted to shield the guilt of Hitler. France and Britain got their policy of non-intervention approved, by the Council of the League of Nations.

The guilt of defending an aggressor at the expense of an aggrieved party was shared by both France and Britain. The French policy resulted in frustration abroad. There was a feeling of moral guilt that France had let down Spain and helped the dictators. That "broke Blum's heart and the heart of the Front Populaire, hastening its end and leaving the Republic more divided and poisoned by hatred than it had been."

The role of the French Government in the Civil War in Spain showed that in the steadily deteriorating international situation, France "made it the first axiom of its foreign policy not to become separated from Britain." By failing to stress that France was as important to Britain as Britain was to France, France tended to surrender to an unnecessary degree the guidance of her policy into British hands.

While dealing with Germany under Hitler after 1936, the policy of appeasement was a matter of compulsion for France. When Mussolini supported Hitler on the question of Austria, France had no option. In 1933-34. France had opposed the move of Hitler to annex Austria as on that occasion Mussolini also opposed Hitler on that issue. In 1938, Mussolini sided with Hitler on the question of the annexation of Austria and France acted like a silent and horrified spectator. There was an obsession in France for maintaining friendship with Italy. On 13 March 1938, German troops marched into Austria and Blum did nothing to oppose it. He resigned on 8 April 1938 and Daladier, his successor, also did nothing in the matter. Graham H. Stuart writes, "The culmination of Anglo-French impotence seemed to have been reached on March 13, 1938 when Chancellor Hitler marched his Nazi troops into Austria and consummated the Anschluss, while neither democracy dared more than protest verbally."

It is true that after the annexation of Austria by Hitler in March 1938, France took a very serious view of the real designs of Hitler, but she was helpless because she was firmly tied to the apron-strings of Britain. The policy of appeasement became a matter of compulsion for her. In the talks in London on 28-29 April 1938, Prime Minister Daladier and his Foreign Minister Bonnet emphasized that the real design of Hitler was not to gain concessions for the Sudeten Germans but "to use their grievances as a pretext to destroy Czechoslovakia and eventually to secure a domination of the Continent in comparison with which the ambitions of Napoleon were feeble." Daladier is said to have observed, "Today it is the turn of Czechoslovakia. Tomorrow it will be the turn of Poland and Rumania. When Germany has obtained the oil and wheat, she will turn on the West. Certainly we must multiply our efforts to avoid war. But that will not be obtained unless Great Britain and France stick together, intervening in Prague Great Britain and France stick together, intervening in Prague for new concessions but declaring at the same time that they will safeguard the independence of Czechoslovakia. If, on the contrary, the Western powers capitulated again, they will only precipitate the war they wish to avoid." Inspite of this warning, British statesmen stuck to the policy of appeasing Hitler in the hope that ultimately he would collide with the Soviet Union without moving his face to the West. The reaction of the British Government was made clear by Lord Halifax, the Foreign Minister of Britain. He stated that Britain had given the most serious warnings to Germany but it would be highly dangerous if the French Government read more into those warnings than was justified by their terms. Britain will always honour her pledge to come to the help of France if, she was attacked by Germany. However, if the French Government assumed that Britain would at once take joint military action to preserve Czechoslovakia against German aggression, our statements did not warrant any such assumption. The view of the British Government was that the military situation was such that France and England, even with the help of the Soviet Union, were not in a position to prevent Germany overrunning Czechoslovakia. The only result would be a European war the outcome of which was doubtful. In the face of this attitude of the British Government, France had to yield before Hitler. It is rightly said that at Munich, Daladier supplied the knife with which Chamberlain butchered the lamb of Czechoslovakia. Daladier threatened Czechoslovakia that if she did not accept the decision of France and Britain with Hitler, the consequences would be the most serious. To quote Daladier, "France in agreement with England has set forth the only procedure which it judges in the actual circumstances can prevent the Germans from marching into Czechoslovakia. In rejecting the Franco-British proposal, the Czech Government assumes the responsibility for Germany resorting to force. It thus ruptures the Franco-British solidarity which has just been established and by doing so, it removes any practical effectiveness of assistance from France. Czechoslovakia thus assumes the risk which we believe to have been removed. She must herself understand the conclusions which France has the right to draw if the Czechoslovakia Government does not accept immediately the Franco-British proposal."

It has rightly been said that Munich represented the climax of the policy of appeasement. Bonnet publicly pledged support to Czechoslovakia but "privately worked for an Entente with Hitler at Prague's expense." Schumann writes that both Daladier and Bonnet "were destined to bring France and the Republic to destruction. Munich was the symbol of their folly. They made the Quai d' Orsay completely subservient to Chamberlain's designs." As the Munich decision was taken without consulting the Soviet Union, she was alienated. The stand taken by Daladier was that the Munich decision was taken to save the country from Bolshevism. On 6 December 1938, Bonnet signed with Ribbentrop a declaration of pacific and good neighbourly relations. He supported his action in these words, "It is the struggle against Bolshevism which is essentially at the basis of the common German and Italian political conception and without saying so formally, Ribbentrop perhaps wished to give us to understand that there is no other objective to be attributed to it."

When Germany attacked Poland on 1 September 1939, the French Foreign Minister tried to make an effort to satisfy the hunger of Hitler by arranging another Munich on the Polish question. He accepted the Italian proposal for peace through a conference with German troops remaining where they were on the Polish soil. He was so particular about his move that he did not join Lord Halifax in issuing a common warning to Hitler. When Lord Halifax said that there could be no conference with Hitler without the withdrawal of German troops from Poland, the French Foreign Minister insisted upon a separate course of action. Daladier also vacillated but he told the Parliament on 2 September 1939 that France would not abandon Britain. It was only then that the French Foreign Minister accepted it, although with reluctance. It was at this stage that the French policy of appeasement towards Germany ended and France entered into the war against Germany on 3 September 1939. That shows that the policy of appeasement ultimately failed. "France and Britain had to choose between war and dishonour. They chose dishonour. They will have war."

POLICY OF APPEASEMENT BY THE UNITED STATES

When the World War I ended in November 1918, the United States emerged virtually as the dominant leader of the world. She played a dominant role in the deliberations of the Peace Conference at Paris. However, the American Senate refused to ratify the Treaty of Versailles and hence the United States did not become a member of the League of Nations. A separate peace was signed with Germany by the United States in August 1921. The United States joined the other Allies in their efforts to interfere in Russia after the Russian Revolution of 1917 and refused to recognise the Soviet Government until 1934. As regards Europe, the United States continued to take interest in disarmament, reparations and inter-Allied debts. She also took part in the conferences and committees. She sponsored the

Pact of Paris in 1928. However, her main area of interest was the Pacific. She called a Conference at Washington in 1921 to strike a balance of power in the Far East. From these beginnings, the United States followed the policy of appeasement till she joined the second World War in December 1941.

There were many reasons why the United States followed a policy of appeasement. There was a similarity between the economic systems of the United States and the Fascist states. Their main object was to protect their own capitalists and industrialists against the competition of foreign states. Such a policy was opposed to the economic policy of the Soviet Union. Hence there could be no cooperation between the United States and the Soviet Union. The United States had sympathy for the Fascist states and did not hesitate to utilise them against the Soviet Union. The Roman Catholic Church in the United States also helped in following the policy of appeasement. That Church was opposed to all progressive reforms in the internal sphere. As regards external affairs, it was opposed to Communism in general and the Soviet Union in particular. A very large number of Americans are the followers of the Roman Catholic Church and they play an important role in the politics of their country. Hence, the sympathy of the United States towards the Fascist States could be presumed.

Another reason why the United Slates followed a policy of appeasement was that the industrialists of that country were terribly afraid of Communism and were willing to support Hitler and Mussolini so that the progress of Communism could be checked in the world. The American Government considered the progress of Russia and Communism as a threat to the prevailing social and economic systems of the United States. It was for this reason that after 1922, the United States continued to support the Fascist Governments of Japan, Italy and Germany.

Even before the Manchurian crisis of 1931, the United States encouraged Japan to occupy the Russian outposts in Siberia from 1917 to 1920. It is true that President Wilson opposed Japanese ambitions at the peace Conference at Paris but that was due to the fact that Japan threatened the American commercial interests in the Far East. The United States put pressure upon Britain to abandon the Anglo-Japanese Alliance of 1902. This was done not due to American aversion to Japan but to deprive Japan of the naval help from Britain. Apart from that, the United States continued to support Japan directly or indirectly in every adventure of Japan.

When Japan attacked Manchuria in 1931, the United States refused to cooperate with the Western countries to resist Japan. She also refused to use her naval power against Japan as she was more interested in preserving her trade and commerce with both Japan and China. Charles Dawes, the American Special representative at Geneva, was friendly towards Japan and was strongly opposed to any action being taken against Japan. On the question of sanctions to be applied against Japan, the stand of the United States was that both the Pact of Paris and the Nine Power Treaty were based on the sanction of public opinion only. By this attitude, the United States killed all possibility of an active resistance to Japanese aggression. The year 1932 was a Presidential election year in the United States and hence the American administration was not in a mood to adopt a stiffer course of action against Japan that might result in the deepening of the economic crisis. After making a show of participating in the proceedings of the League of Nations, the United States ultimately refused to take any concrete step against Japan.

In the following years, the American appeasement towards Japan was consistently expressed in the Neutrality Legislation of 1935. Under that legislation, the American Government ordered all her citizens to leave China.

In the Brussels Conference of November 1937, President Roosevelt and his Secretary Hull refused to give any promise of an effective action against Japan who had started a fresh offensive in China in July 1937 as a result of the Marco Polo Bridge incident. The Conference ended in a fiasco. From 1937 onwards, both the United states and Britain did not move against Japan although the Japanese hurled insults and losses on the United States and Britain and bombed the American oil tankers and gunboats on the Yangtse river. It is true that in July 1939 Hull denounced the American-Japanese Commerce Treaty of 1911, but the Japanese were allowed to purchase 70% of their imported oil, 65% of lorries, 75% of their aircraft and 90% of their steel, iron and copper from the United States. It was only when Japan attacked the Pearl Harbour in December 1941 that the United States was awakened to the danger and declared war on Japan.

When Italy invaded Abyssinia, the Neutrality Legislation of 1935 was enacted to prohibit the sale of war materials and banning of loans to the warring States. By that law, the United States treated both the aggressor and the aggrieved on the same footing. The Neutrality Legislation of 1935 was amended in 1937. The old law was replaced by a permanent Neutrality Act under which the ban on the shipment of munitions and loans was retained. The cash and carry provision required that the non-embargoed goods purchased in the United States by belligerent nations had to be fully paid for before leaving the country and could not be transported in American ships. The United States gave up its claim to respect natural shipping and to a right of travel for neutral citizens. In the case of Italian aggression in Abyssinia, the American President declared that a state of war existed between Italy and Abyssinia and the export of American arms and amunitions to both Italy and Abyssinia was illegal and the Americans would in future travel on belligerent ships at their own risk. The arms embargo turned out to be beneficial to Italy. The American traders started exporting to Italy all commodities other than arms. Between 1934 and 1936, the crude oil export to Italy went up. "Mussolini floated to victory on a sea of oil, much of which came from the United States." In July 1935, the Emperor of Abyssinia appealed to President Roosevelt for help, but the American President expressed the pious hope that the dispute would be settled amicably.

A similar policy was followed in Spain. There was a Civil War in that country. General Franco raised the standard of revolt against the legitimate Government of Spain. He was helped by Hitler and Mussolini with war materials and soldiers. President Roosevelt did not help the Republican Government of Spain and followed a policy of non-intervention like that of Britain and France. He got the Neutrality Legislation amended and applied the same to civil strifes also. One reason why the United States followed a policy of appeasement towards General Franco was that the Republican Government of Spain was supposed to be in sympathy with Communism. The Roman Catholics of the United States were inclined towards General Franco who was also a Roman Catholic. Roosevelt was not willing to alienate the Catholic votes in the United States for the democratic candidates in the Congressional elections of 1938. The Americans also did not want the enlargement of the Civil War in Spain into a general war in Europe.

The United States had the power to stop further aggression by Hitler but it decided to follow a policy of neutrality. Hull, the Secretary of State of the United States, circulated his famous "Eight Pillars of peace". The result was quite the opposite. Hitler and Mussolini came to the conclusion that the United States would continue her policy of non-intervention in European affairs. A few days before the signing of the Munich Pact in September 1938, President Roosevelt advised the Governments of Germany, Czechoslovakia, Britain and France to resolve the European problem by peaceful means. He reminded them of their responsibility under the Pact of Paris. He separately sent to Hitler and Mussolini an appeal for peace. The only reply of Hitler was that he occupied Prague and Memel in March 1939. Although war seemed to be imminent, President Roosevelt proposed to Hitler and Mussolini disarmament and a trade conference with a view to reduce international tension. However, his suggestion was rejected. When the Non-Aggression Pact was signed between the Soviet Union and Germany, President Roosevelt requested Hitler to make a settlement with Poland. Poland accepted the proposal but the same was rejected by Hitler. On 1 September 1939, Germany invaded Poland. On 3 September 1939, Britain and France declared war on Germany. The same day Roosevelt declared America's neutrality in the European war. To quote Roosevelt, "This nation will remain a neutral nation, but I cannot ask every American to remain neutral in thought as well. I hope the United

States will keep out of this war. I believe that it will. And I give you assurance and re-assurance that every effort of your Government will be directed towards that end. As long as it remains within my power to prevent it, there will be no black-out of peace in the United States." However, gradually but steadily, the United States was pushed in the World War II in defence of democracy against the Axis Powers. The policy of appeasement failed and the autocratic Governments of Germany, Italy and Japan continued their aggressive activities.

SUGGESTED READINGS

Amery, L.S.: **My Political Life,** London, 1955.

Brogan, D.W.: **The French Nation: From Napoleon to Petain (1814-1940), London,** 1960.

Brown, Hodges and Roucek (Eds.): **Contemporary World Politics: An Introduction to the Study of International Relations,** New York, 1939.

Bruce, M.: **British Foreign Policy : Isolation and Intervention, London,** 1938.

Carr, E.H.: **International Relations Between the Two World Wars, 1919-1939, London,** 1952.

Claude, I.: **Power and International Relations, New York,** 1963.

Friedmann, W.: **An Introduction to World Politics, London,** 1965.

Gathorne-Hardy: **A Short History of International Affairs, 1920-1939, London,** 1964.

Grant and Temperley: **Europe in the Nineteenth and Twentieth Centuries, London,** 1985.

Hannah, I.C.: **British Foreign Policy, London,** 1938.

Hill, Norman: **Contemporary World Politics, New York,** 1954.

Langsam, W.C.: **The World Since 1919, Delhi,** 1981.

Palmer and Perkins : **International Relations: The World Community in Transition, Calcutta,** 1965.

Schleicher, C.P.: **International Relations, New Delhi,** 1963.

Schuman, F.I..: **International Politics, New York,** 1948.

Seton-Watson, R.W.: **From Munich to Danzig, London,** 1939.

Sharp and Kirk: **Contemporary International Politics, New York,** 1943.

Shirer, W.L.: **The Collapse of the Third Republic.**

Simonds and Emeny : **The Great Powers in World Politics, New York,** 1939.

Thomson, David : **Europe Since Napoleon, London,** 1978.

CHAPTER 50

THE COLD WAR

Definition

The term "Cold War" had an American origin and was used for the first time by Bernard Baruch who observed thus on 16 April 1947. "Let us not be deceived today. We are in the midst of a Cold War." The term was picked up by Walter Lippmann who through his book on the Cold War, popularised it. After that, the term Cold War was used to describe the relations between the Soviet Union and the Western Powers after the World War II. Cold War has been defined by R.K. Garthoff as "the conflict between the Communist Powers and the rest of the world waged by means short of overt major war."

Prof. Young Hum Kim writes, "Though the term Cold War defies precise definition, it may be described as the international environment characterised by persistent tensions and conflicts between the free world and the Communist camp in general and between the United States and the Soviet Union in particular. This new war of cold realities in international politics has been waged in every conceivable field of international life, especially in national defence, economic growth, diplomacy and ideology."

Cold War was not a state of armed struggle but a state in which the rivals while maintaining their peace-time diplomatic relations, continued their hostility. They used all means other than war to weaken each other. The Cold War was an ideological war or a propaganda war or a diplomatic war. It was neither a condition of war nor a condition of peace. It was a state of uneasy peace. R. Barnet calls it "hot peace." Kennedy describes it as "hard and bitter peace."

Its origin

There is a difference of views regarding the origin of Cold War. One view is that its beginning can be traced back to the time of the Bolshevik Revolution of 1917 when the Communists openly declared their intention to control and dominate the world. Some writers find the genesis of the Cold War in the period of the Grand Alliance of World War II. Although the Western Powers and the Soviet Union cooperated during the War, there were sharp differences among them particularly over the treatment of anti-Nazi resistance forces in Poland and Yugoslavia, the establishment of the Second Front, coordination of military strategy and post-War reconstruction. Still another view is that the Cold War actually crystallized only in 1947 when the Soviet Union and the Western Powers intensified and formalised the differences in the interpretation of the provisions of the Yalta and Potsdam Agreements. The delay in opening the Second Front, the secrecy over the atom bomb and refusal to invite the Polish provisional Government to San-Francisco made Russia suspicious of Anglo-American designs. Likewise, the Western Powers were agitated over the occupation of considerable portions of territory in the Far East by Russia by declaring war against Japan at the last moment. Prof. Young Hum Kim writes, "At the war's end, the basic incompatibility between Soviet Communism and Western democracy in terms of ideology and security took a new turn towards higher intensity as Stalin reverted from the policy of war-time expediency (alliance with the West) to the policy of pre-War orthodoxy (hardlined dogmatism)". The view of some scholars is that the first signal for the development of Cold War was given by Winston Churchill in his Fulton speech in which he observed, "If the Western democracies stand together in strict adherence to the principle of United Nations Charter, their influence for furthering those principles will be immense and no one is likely to molest them. If, however, they become divided or falter in their duty and if these all important years are allowed to slip away, then indeed catastrophe may overwhelm us all".

Reasons for Cold War

Many reasons have been given for the Cold War. Though the Soviet Union and the Western Powers cooperated with each other during the World War II, there did not develop a spirit of real cooperation among them. Towards the end of the war, tension increased tremendously. The opposite stands taken by the Soviet Union and the Western Powers on various matters failed to arouse a spirit of cooperation and friendship. The actions of both the parties showed that mutual distrust existed among them. Another cause of the Cold War was the existence of ideological differences between the Soviet Union and Western democracies. The Western Powers considered the Soviet Union a greater enemy than Hitler and Mussolini. They followed a policy of appeasement towards Hitler and Mussolini because they felt that Communism was a greater danger than Fascism and Nazism. Narrow national interests after the end of the World War II also contributed to the Cold War. In spite of protests from the Western Powers, the Soviet Union continued her plans to increase her influence in Eastern Europe. After consolidating her position there, she started penetrating into the Middle East which was resented by the Western Powers.

Its beginning

The view of Possony is that "the Cold War began while the hot war was still raging." Even before the end of the World War II, the Soviet Union imposed Communist regimes in the East European countries of Poland, Bulgaria, Rumania, Hungary and Yugoslavia. After putting Eastern Europe behind the iron curtain, the Soviet Union turned her attention towards western Europe. She also put pressure on Turkey and Iran to get concessions. She engineered a Communist revolution against Greece and expanded her influence in Italy. These moves of the Soviet Union were viewed with great concern by the Western countries. When Britain expressed her inability to check Soviet expansion, the United States took up the responsibility of containing the onward march of Communism. The Truman Doctrine and the Marshall Plan were the steps to save the European Continent from further Communist influence. The Soviet Union also initiated the Molotov Plan and established the Council of Mutual Economic Assistance. These moves and counter-moves constituted the beginning of the Cold War.

Truman Doctrine

On 12 March 1947, President Truman addressed a joint session of the American Congress and enunciated what came to be known as the Truman Doctrine. Truman asked the Congress to sanction 400 million Dollars by June 1948 to help Greece and Turkey. In May 1947, the American Congress authorised aid to Greece and Turkey. It was found in 1950 that American policy had completely changed the state of affairs in Greece and Turkey. The guerillas were completely eliminated from the Greek soil and peace was restored. The same was the case in Turkey. The danger from Communism was successfully checked by American action.

The Marshall Plan (1947)

The Marshall Plan was an extension of the principle underlying the Truman Doctrine. It dealt with Europe in general and not with any particular state or states as was the case with the Truman Doctrine. It was essentially an economic plan. It represented an elaborate programme which was to last for four years. It showed an anxiety on the part of the United States to avert the economic crisis which was apprehended as a result of the World War II. It also underlined American determination to fight against Communism. The situation in France and Italy was a source of great anxiety to the United States. The Communist parties of France and Italy were gaining in strength. It was felt that in order to put a check on Communist influence, the United States must come to their help. The Marshall Plan was welcomed in the United States as it was directed against the Soviet Union. By the time the programme was completed, its object was achieved and the danger from Communism was successfully met.

The Soviet Union and the Communist and non-Communist countries of Eastern Europe were invited to accept the Marshall Plan but the offer was rejected. It was contended that under the cover of the Plan, the United States aimed at creating an economic empire by taking advantage of the conditions in Europe. The negative attitude of the Soviet Union towards the Plan led to the continuance of the struggle between Eastern and Western Europe.

Brussels Treaty (1948)

The Marshall Plan stiffened the Cold War between Eastern and Western Europe instead of bringing about a *rapproachment* between the two. The Soviet Union had already branded the Truman Doctrine as imperialistic. In order to check Russian supremacy and influence, Britain, France, Belgium, The Netherlands, Luxemburg, etc. signed the Treaty of Brussels in March 1948. The signatories to the treaty expressed their complete reliance on the Charter of the United Nations and pledged mutual military, economic and political cooperation. This treaty played a vital role in strengthening the unity and security of the Western countries

NATO (1949)

The North Atlantic Treaty was signed on 4 April 1949 by the United States, Canada, Belgium, Denmark, France, Iceland, Italy, Luxemburg, the Netherlands, Norway, Portugal and the United Kingdom. Greece and Turkey became its members in February 1952. West Germany joined it in May 1955. The NATO was a defensive organisation. After the signing of the Brussels Treaty and particularly when the conflict between Eastern and Western Europe over the German problem assumed serious proportions, the United States decided to establish a Mutual Military Assistance Organisation with the Western countries and the NATO was the result. The NATO was intended to strengthen the morale of Western Europe. The association of the United States with the other NATO Powers was bound to halt Soviet expansion Westwards. As the stand taken by the United States was definite and clear, the Soviet leaders were not prepared to take any risk in Western Europe. The result was that the Communists made no territorial gains in Europe or the Atlantic area after April 1949.

Germany

After the World War II, there was a conflict of interests between Eastern and Western blocs over Germany. The defeat of Germany and her occupation by the Soviet Union and the Western Powers gave rise to complications in the field of European and international politics. The United States, Russia, Britain and France partitioned Germany among themselves into four zones. In January 1947, British and American zones were unified. The French zone was also merged into it in the same year. The three zones came to be known as West Germany. East Germany came into existence under Russian control. As a result of the Cold War, Germany became the centre of dispute between Eastern and Western blocs and that continued for years.

When the Soviet Union proceeded to collect reparations from Eastern Germany, disputes and tension began to develop between the Soviet Union and the Western Powers. In 1948, the Western Powers introduced currency reforms in West Germany. In reply to that, the Soviet Union blockaded the city of Berlin by closing down all her entrances. However, the Western Powers managed to supply the necessary foodstuffs to the citizens of Berlin by airlift from June 1948 to September 1949. The representatives of the Western Powers met in Bonn and drafted the Bonn Constitution. The Federal

Republic of West Germany was born and elections were held in 1949. The Soviet Union proclaimed the German Democratic Republic in East Germany under her control. West Germany joined the Anglo-American bloc and East Germany joined the Soviet bloc. Tension between the two blocs continued over the question of Germany.

China

The United States refused to recognise the new Communist Government of China set up in 1949, and continued to recognise the Nationalist Government of Formosa under Chiang Kai-shek. The result was that the Nationalist Government of Formosa continued to be a permanent member of the Security Council till October 1971 when there was a reconciliation between Communist China and the United States. If the United States backed Formosa, the Soviet Union backed Communist China and the cold war continued.

Korea

By 1949, the territorial limits of the cold war in Europe were more or less established. By 1950, the theatre of the cold war shifted from Europe to East Asia. Under the impact of the cold war, Korea was divided into North Korea and South Korea. In North Korea, a Communist government supported by the Soviet Union was set up. In South Korea, an American-sponsored Government was set up. On 25 June 1950, North Korea attacked South Korea. The Security Council declared North Korea as the aggressor and authorised the creation of command under the Flag of the United Nations to repel the aggressor. The Korean War was virtually a conflict between the Soviet bloc and the Western bloc. If North Korea was fighting with Soviet weapons and Chinese troops, the United States was fighting on behalf of South Korea under the Flag of the United Nations. The result was that the Cold War was turned into a hot war. After the death of Stalin in 1953, an armistice was signed on 27 July 1953.

Anzus Pact (1951)

When the Communist success in China and the Korea war creased an atmosphere of uneasiness in the Pacific region, the United States signed a treaty with Australia and New Zealand in 1951 known as the Anzus Pact. It was to remain in force for an indefinite period. This Pacific security system was an endeavour of the Western Powers to meet the Communist challenge.

Indo-China

After the fall of Japan in 1945, Britain and China occupied Southern and Northern parts of Indo-China respectively. France regained her lost hold over the whole of Indo-China in 1946. The Vietminh refused to acknowledge the authority of France. Supported by Communist China, the Vietminh attacked the Red River Valley in 1949. As Communist China helped the Vietminh, the United States helped France with money and arms. The Soviet Union also helped the Vietminh. The result was that a clash between the Soviet Union and the United States became almost inevitable. The fall of Dien Bien Phu in 1954 brought the final collapse of France in Indo-China. At the Geneva Conference in July 1954, Vietnam was partitioned between North Vietnam and South Vietnam. In spite of the Geneva Settlement, there was no peace in Vietnam. The United States did everything in her power to help South Vietnam against North Vietnam which was supported by Communist China and the Soviet Union. In spite of strong action by the United States, there was no end of the war. Negotiations started in Paris in 1968 but without any settlement. The forces of North Vietnam made headway against South Vietnam in the beginning of 1972 and the United States intensified the bombing of North Vietnam. Mines were spread in the harbours and rivers of South Vietnam. On many occasions, negotiations were started for peace but without any result. North Vietnam backed by the Soviet Union continued to fight till the fall of South Vietnam in April 1975. Thus the Cold War was fought in Indo-China between the Soviet Union and the United States and the Soviet Union was the victor.

SEATO

Like the NATO, the SEATO (1954) was born out of Communist fear. Its object was to put a stop to the further spread of Communist influence in South-East Asia. The United States was not happy over the establishment of a Communist regime on the mainland of China in 1949. She was also not happy over the events in Indo-China where French power was being liquidated. The decisions taken in Geneva in 1954 were not to her liking. Hence the SEATO was set up by the United States, in collaboration with Britain, France, Australia, Thailand, The Philippines and Pakistan, to stop the further infiltration of Communist influence in that area. The signatories to the treaty agreed to consider enemy attack upon any one of them as an attack upon all of them and to cooperate with one another against the enemy. In the long run, the SEATO failed in its objectives and had to be wound up but it served its purpose for the time being.

The Baghdad Pact

Another centre of the Cold War between the Eastern and Western blocs was the Middle East. Some of the countries of that region were associated with the Soviet Union and some with the American bloc. The Baghdad Pact was an attempt by the Western Powers to form an anti-Soviet bloc in the Middle East. This Pact was signed in 1955 between Turkey and Iraq. Later on, Britain, Pakistan and Iran joined it. The United States guaranteed the territorial integrity of the Baghdad Pact countries. She joined the Baghdad Pact in the economic sphere in May 1956 and in the military sphere in 1958 to combat international Communism. When Iraq withdrew from the Pact in March 1959, it was renamed Central Treaty Organisation.

The Warsaw Pact (1955)

The Soviet Union was alarmed at the aggressive attitude of the Western Powers when the NATO was formed, but for a few years she was not able to set up a rival organisation. She strongly protested against the entry of West Germany into NATO. On 4 May 1955, the Soviet Union, Poland, Hungary, Czechoslovakia, Bulgaria, Albania and East Germany signed the Warsaw Pact. The signatory states agreed to resist the attacks of the imperialists and capitalist states upon any member state. The Warsaw Pact, in its essential features, was a carbon copy of the NATO. Its only object was to meet the challenge from the NATO Powers.

Between 1955 and 1958, West Asia became the centre of the Cold War. This fact is proved by the signing of the Baghdad Pact with a view to exclude the Soviet Union from that region.

Austria (1955)

No treaty had been concluded with Austria in spite of the lapse of many years after the ending of the World War in 1945. That was due to the differences between the Soviet Union and the Western Powers over the terms of the peace treaty. However, at the Summit Conference of July 1955, the Austrian Peace Treaty was signed and Presidents Eisenhower and Bulganin exchanged assurances that neither of them will start a nuclear war. Both of them undertook not to seek political or economic union of Austria with Germany, directly or indirectly. Austria was not to join the NATO and remain neutral. Friedmann writes, "The Austrian Peace Treaty is the first major international treaty on which the four erstwhile allies have been able to agree after years of an unbroken record of dissension and tension, sometimes threatening to lead to the brink of war."

On the Suez Canal crisis of 1956, both the Super Powers stood on the same side and thus a major crisis was averted.

Eisenhower Doctrine (1957)

The United States proclaimed the Eisenhower Doctrine on 5 March 1957 by which the Truman Doctrine was extended to the Middle East. Its object was to check the possibility of Communist aggression, direct or indirect, in that region. The United States was to give military assistance and protect any state whose territorial integrity and political independence was threatened.

Hungary

There was a revolt in Hungary in 1956 and the Soviet Union sent her troops to suppress it. The Soviet action was condemned by the countries belonging to the American bloc. A demand was made that the Soviet Union must withdraw her troops but she refused.

Germany

There was a tussle between the Soviet Union and the Western Powers in 1956 over the issue of elections in Berlin. As the Social Democratic party won the elections by defeating the Communist party, the Soviet Union abrogated that election by applying her veto power. That led to tension between the Soviet Union and the Western Powers.

In November 1958, Khrushchev stated that the imperialists wanted to make Germany a chronic problem and were disturbing the peace of East Germany, Poland and other socialist states. He warned that any march towards East Germany would lead to disastrous consequences. He handed over notes to Western Powers asking them to withdraw from West Berlin within six months. The reply of West Germany was that if the Soviet Union renounced unilaterally her international treaties, political tension would increase and the Soviet Union would be held responsible for violating international law. The Western Powers showed their determination to defend their rights.

During 1959, there were negotiations between the Soviet Union and the Western Powers regarding the unification of Germany. In September 1959, Khrushchev met Eisenhower at Camp David and agreed to resume talks on the Berlin question at the proposed Summit Conference to be held in May 1960 in Paris.

On 25 April 1960, Khrushchev warned the Western Powers that if they did not sign a peace treaty with East Germany, their right of access to West Berlin would cease and the Soviet Union would conclude a separate peace treaty with East Germany. He also declared that as the city of Berlin was situated within East Germany, the latter would have complete control over the whole of Berlin. The Western Powers protested and maintained that their right over West Berlin was not due to any concession from the Soviet Union but was based on their conquest of Germany. They also contended that the Soviet Union could not revoke unilaterally all the treaties regarding Germany and Berlin. When Khrushchev met President Kennedy in Vienna in June 1961, he declared that the Camp David formula was dead.

A serious situation was created in Germany as a result of the influx of refugees from East Germany to West Germany in large numbers. On 13 August 1961, East Germany sealed her border between East Berlin and West Berlin and 25-mile long Berlin Wall was erected between two Berlins. There was great tension. After lengthy negotiations, the pass system was introduced between the two cities in September 1963.

There was another crisis in 1969 when the West German government decided to hold Presidential elections on 5 March 1969 in West Berlin. East Germany protested and reimposed restrictions on land routes to prevent the members of the Electoral College from reaching West Berlin. The West German Government managed to send the members of the Electoral College and other officials to West Berlin by air. President Nixon threatened action if the Soviet Union resisted and the result was that the Soviet Union kept quiet.

In September 1971, the Soviet Union, the United States, France and Britain signed the Berlin Accord. In November 1972, the Basic Treaty was signed between East Germany and West Germany. In September 1973, both East and West Germany became members of the United Nations and thus the Cold War ended in Germany.

Cuban Crisis (1962)

The Cold War was at its height at the time of the Cuban crisis in 1962. The Soviet Union sent military equipment to Cuba alongwith a larger number of technicians and other military personnel. The United States opposed the Soviet move and declared her intention to use all possible means to end the Soviet presence in Cuba. There was every danger of a war between the Soviet Union and the United States. However, U Thant, Secretary-General of the United Nations, prevailed upon the United States to suspend the blockade of Cuba and asked Khrushchev to halt shipments to Cuba and also withdraw the offensive weapons from Cuba. The Soviet Union agreed to dismantle the Cuban missile sites and transport the missiles back to the Soviet Union. It was in this way that a great catastrophe was avoided.

The Congo

In the Congo, Soviet activity was of the most Cold War kind. The sending of vehicles, aircrafts, transport aircrafts, provisions and equipment in the summer 1960 was an act of intervention. Khrushchev sent a telegram to Kasavubu and Lumumba in July 1960 in which he declared that "if the hand of the aggressor is raised against the Congo, then the Soviet Union declares that the necessity will arise of taking more effective measures". The Soviet Union continued to help the Congo in order to balance her influence against that of the Western Powers.

Detente

After the Berlin crisis and the Cuban crisis, the stage was set for a thaw in the Cold War. It was realised by both sides that any nuclear war between them would lead to mutual destruction. That realisation pointed to the necessity of peaceful coexistence. The result was the signing of the Nuclear Test Ban Treaty on 5 August 1963 between the Soviet Union, the United States and Britain. It provided for a limited ban on nuclear tests in the atmosphere including outer space or under water. A Hot Line Agreement was signed between the Super Powers.

The Nuclear Non-Proliferation Treaty was signed in 1968 between the Soviet Union and the United States. On 25 May 1972, two agreements were signed in Moscow by President Nixon and Communist Party Chief Brezhnev. Those agreements were the Treaty on Limitation of Anti-Ballistic Missile System and the Interim Agreement on certain measures with respect to the Limitation of Strategic Offensive Arms. Brezhnev visited Washington in June 1973. He signed with President Nixon an agreement by which they committed their countries to negotiate before the end of the next year a treaty calling for the reduction of nuclear weapons.

In June-July 1974, President Nixon visited the Soviet Union and agreed with Brezhnev to limit underground testing for five years. In November 1974, President Ford (successor of President Nixon) and Brezhnev met at Vladivostok and a US-Soviet agreement on guidelines for 10-year "cap on the arms race" was reached. The 35-Nation Summit Conference on Security and Cooperation in Europe opened on 30 July 1975 at Helsinki and concluded on 1 August 1975. It was attended by President Ford, Brezhnev, Prime Minister Wilson and others.

The Treaty on the Limitation of Strategic Offensive Arms signed in 1972 between the United States and the Soviet Union lapsed in October 1977 but both sides tried to preserve its main provisions. The Ford administration made little efforts for negotiations on a new agreement. However, after prolonged negotiations, a treaty was signed between the United States and the Soviet Union in Vienna on 18 June 1979 on the limitation of strategic offensive arms. This treaty is popularly known as SALT-II.

It is true that President Carter signed the SALT-II treaty but he began to have doubts about it even before he returned to Washington. The United States discovered the presence of a Soviet brigade in Cuba and demanded its withdrawal but the Soviet Union refused to oblige. In 1979, the Shah of

Iran was overthrown and the United States made a bid to secure base facilities in Kenya, Somalia and Oman to protect American interests in the Indian Ocean and the Persian Gulf region. The NATO decided to deploy American-made cruise missiles and advance medium-range Pershing II missiles in Western Europe from 1983. When such was the situation, Soviet armed intervention in Afghanistan in December 1979 aggravated the situation. The American Government arranged secret supply of arms to Afghan rebels to pressurise the Soviet Union to negotiate but that did not happen. When the United States intervened in El Salvador, the Soviet Union and her allies supplied arms to insurgents and also gave them training. President Reagan projected the issue of El Salvador as an international confrontation between the West and the Soviet Union.

There are certain differences between the old and new cold wars. Unlike the cold war of 1950's, the alliance partners are not actively involved in the new cold war. China, Japan and even Western European countries are lukewarm in their support and the war persists mainly between the two Super Powers. In the old cold war, nuclear armaments build-up was not an issue and the main stress was on quantitative build-up of conventional arms. In the new cold war, there is a nuclear arms race between the two Super Powers and they are trying to achieve greater sophistication in conventional, weaponry. The new cold war is more threatening than the old cold war.

However, efforts are being made to stop the nuclear arms race. Talks on the limitation of missiles began in Geneva on 1 December 1981. The Soviets walked out in 1982 but the talks were resumed in 1985. There was a two-day summit at Geneva on 19 and 20 November 1985 between President Reagan and Soviet leader Gorbachev. In a joint statement issued after the end of negotiations, the two leaders acknowledged that there were differences between them on vital issues but they affirmed that any confrontation between the two countries would have catastrophic consequences. They emphasized the importance of preventing any war between them. They agreed to accelerate nuclear arms control negotiations and to meet again "in the near future". Gorbachev accepted an invitation from President Reagan to visit the United States and President Reagan agreed to visit the Soviet Union.

A summit meeting was held at Reykjavik on 12 and 13 October 1986. However, the negotiations broke down over the US refusal to yield on its Star War research.

On 8 December 1987 the Intermediate Range Nuclear Forces Treaty for the destruction of Europe-based missiles was signed between the United States and the Soviet Union. For the United States, the treaty meant scrapping of Pershing missiles stationed in West Germany and Tomahawak cruise missiles in Britain, West Germany, Italy and Belgium. The Soviet Union was to eliminate Silo-based SS-4 rockets, SS-20. SS-22 and SS-23 missiles. On 1 June 1988, that treaty was ratified in Moscow by President Reagan and Soviet leader Gorbachev.

On 14 April 1988, Pakistan and Afghanistan formally signed a US and Soviet Union guaranteed Accord at Geneva by which the Soviet Union agreed to pull out all Soviet troops from Afghanistan within a maximum period of nine months from 15 May 1988. Half of those troops were to be withdrawn by 15 August 1988. This Accord was the result of the pressure exercised by the Soviet Union on Afghanistan and the United States on Pakistan.

In August 1988, South Africa, Angola and Cuba announced a cease-fire as agreed upon during the negotiations in Geneva. This was the result of Moscow's pressure on Angola and Cuba and that of Washington on South Africa. In the same month, Iran and Iraq ended the war which was going on for many years.

SUGGESTED READINGS

Abel, Elie : **The Missile Crisis,** 1966.

Fleming, D.S.: **The Cold War and its Origins.**

Ingram, A.: **The History of the Cold War,** 1955.

Keller, John W.: **Germany, the Wall and Berlin,** 1964.

Larson, David L.: **The Cuban Crisis of 1962, 1963.**

Lippmann. Walter : **The Cold War,** 1947.

Luard, Evan (Ed.) : **The Cold War, London,** 1964.

Lukacs, John A.: **A History of the Cold War,** 1961.

Q' Conor, John F.: **Cold War and Liberation,** 1961.

Patterson, T.S.: **Soviet-American Confrontation : Post-War Reconstruction and the Origins of the Cold War,** 1973.

Price, H. B.: **Marshall Plan and its Meaning,** 1955.

Roberts, H.L.: **Russia and America : Dangers and Prospect,** 1955.

Seton-Watson, H.: **Neither War nor Peace : The Struggle for Power in the Post-War World,** 1960.

CHAPTER

51 GERMANY AFTER WORLD WAR II

The defeat of Germany in the World War II and her occupation by the Soviet Union and the Western Powers gave rise to complications in the field of European and international politics. Those complications related to the problems of German unity and the future of Berlin.

PROBLEM OF GERMAN UNITY

It was decided at the Potsdam Conference in 1945 that Germany would be divided into four occupation zones as a temporary measure. The British zone lay in the North-West, the American in the South, the French in South-West and the Soviet zone extended from Oder-Neisse line to the Elbe. Berlin was also divided into four zones among the Big Four. The Four-Power Allied Control Council was set up to make decisions for Germany as a whole. The Council was to follow a joint policy and the whole of Germany was to be treated as a single economic unit.

In January 1947, British and American zones were unified. In the same year, the French zone was merged into it. The three zones together came to be known as West Germany. The Western Powers introduced a currency reform in the three Western zones in June 1948 which proved extremely successful. The Soviet Union protested and imposed a blockade on Berlin which became fully effective upon the introduction of the new currency into the Western sector of the city. The contention of the Soviet Union was that her action was intended to safeguard the currency of their own zone and by adopting the above-mentioned measures in their own zones, the Western powers had forfeited the right to participate in the administration of Berlin which was a part of the Russian zone. The Western Powers organised a massive airlift to send supplies to two million residents of West Berlin and kept open communication with West Berlin. The Berlin blockade lasted from June 1948 to September 1949. The Western powers earned the gratitude of the German people. The representatives of the three Western powers met in Bonn and drafted a Federal Constitution for West Germany which came to be known as the Bonn Constitution. According to the new Constitution, elections were held to the Federal Parliament in August 1949 and Dr. Adenauer was elected as the Chancellor of the Federal Republic of West Germany.

The German Federal Republic became a member of the O.P.E.C. in 1949 and of the Council of Europe in 1951. She became one of the three major partners of the European Coal and Steel Community in 1952. She also joined the European Economic Community. On 16 May 1952, the United States, Great Britain and France concluded peace agreements with West Germany in Bonn. Nearly complete independence was restored to West Germany. Protocols signed in Paris on 28 October 1954 by West Germany and 14 other Western nations gave West Germany virtual sovereignty and opened the way for it to enter NATO and the Brussels Treaty Organisation (Western European Union). West Germany became officially independent on 5 May, 1955 and progressed both politically and economically. She rebuilt her shattered cities as well as industries and became a leading exporter of finished industrial products in the world market.

The Soviet Union set up on 7 October 1949 a Provisional Peoples' Chamber and declared the German Democratic Republic with Otto Grotewohl as Prime Minister. Thus, there were two

Germanies. The G.D.R. (German Democratic Republic) became progressively Stalinized. It concluded treaties of friendship with other nations in Eastern Europe belonging to the Soviet Sphere. She also entered into a treaty with Poland and fixed Poland's boundary on the Oder-Niesse line. The German Democratic Republic set up a zone along her 600-mile border with West Germany. Berlin's telephone system was separated into two sections. The Soviet Union proclaimed Eastern Germany as a sovereign state on 26 March 1954 and declared that Soviet troops would remain temporarily in connection with the security and the Potsdam agreement.

The Foreign Ministers of the Big Four Powers met at Berlin from 25 January to 18 February 1954 and discussed the problem of the unification of Germany. The Western Powers proposed re-unification through the process of free elections and freedom for the new and unified state to join one bloc or the other. Molotov, the Foreign Minister of the Soviet Union, proposed that a provisional all-German Government should be formed from the two existing zones to frame a constitution. The new Government should negotiate a peace treaty but must not join any alliance in the Cold War. The Western powers knew full well that free elections would lead to a United Germany aligned to the West and a member of the North Atlantic Treaty Organisation. The Russians also knew that Germany would choose the policies of Federal Republic.

On 5 May 1955, the Western powers terminated their 10-year old occupation of West Germany. The Soviet Union also restored sovereignty to East Germany and got her associated with the Warsaw Treaty Organisation. West Germany joined the O.P.E.C. East Germany became associated with COMECON.

Views on German Unification

The view of the Western Powers was that the German problem should be settled on the basis of the right of self-determination. They wanted free elections to be held in the whole of Germany and the new state was to conclude a peace treaty. East Germany was not to be recognised as that might perpetuate the partition of Germany. West Germany claimed that she was the sole successor of the old German state. She opposed the neutralisation of Germany.

The Soviet view was that the peace treaty should be concluded with both the German states separately. Her contention was that the question of peace treaty was different from the issue of recognition. If the Soviet Union could recognise West Germany, there was no reason why the Western powers could not recognise East Germany. As the whole of Berlin lies in the territorial limits of East Germany, the Western powers had no right to have their presence in Berlin. As Germany surrendered under pressure from Soviet forces, the Soviet Union alone had the right to keep her forces in Berlin. Objection was raised to the military bases in West Berlin. The Soviet Union wanted Germany's neutrality as the price of German unification. She was not prepared to accept a rearmed Germany aligned with the West.

The German question came up for discussion when the Big Four Foreign Ministers met at Berlin but nothing came out of it. Another attempt at unification was made in July 1955 at the Summit Conference of Big Four at Geneva but again nothing came out of it. A ministerial level meeting was held at Geneva from 27 October to 16 November 1955. The West again took its stand upon uniting Germany through free all-German elections if there could concurrently be established a European Security Pact. The Russians proposed a European collective security treaty which was to replace the North Atlantic Treaty Organisation, the West European Union and the Warsaw Treaty Organisation. The two German Governments should join the treaty and establish an all-German Council composed of representatives of both. There was a deadlock.

On 8 September 1955, Chancellor Adenauer visited Moscow and pleaded for the release of German prisoners of war and Russian cooperation in achieving the unification of Germany.

West Germany declared in December 1955 that she would break off diplomatic relations with those states which recognised the Government of Eastern Germany. This came to be known as the Hallstein Doctrine. It was named after Walter Hallstein of the Bonn Foreign Office. The object of this doctrine was to boycott the German Democratic Republic in the international arena and prevent its consolidation. Sanctions were directed against those states which set up normal relations with the German Democratic Republic. At first, the Bonn Government used this policy only in the area of diplomatic relations but later on it was extended to trade and cultural relations. The Bonn Government claimed that it was the successor to the German Reich and its sole successor. It was supported by Britain, the United States and France. The view of the Soviet Union was that there were two Germanies with equal status and she exchanged Ambassadors with both West Germany and East Germany.

When the United States decided to supply nuclear weapons to NATO forces, the Soviet Union warned West Germany not to keep them in her territory. The prospects of nuclear arms at NATO bases led Poland to suggest a nuclear-free zone in Central Europe. The Soviet Union suggested another Summit Conference but Dulles was not ready for it unless the Soviet Union accepted Western terms.

On 10 November 1958, Khrushchev stated that the imperialists wanted to make Germany a chronic problem and were disturbing the peace of German Democratic Republic, Poland and the socialist states. He warned any march towards East Germany would mean disaster for West Germany. If West Germany really wanted unification, she would have talked with East Germany. Any settlement could be on the basis of liquidation of Fascism, German militarism and demilitarisation. Likewise, the problem of Berlin could be discussed by West and East Germany. Khrushchev handed over notes to the Western Powers requesting them to withdraw from West Berlin within six months. He offered West Berlin the status of a free city. He cancelled the agreement of the Soviet Union with the United States and Britain of 12 September 1944 (delineating zones of occupation of Germany and providing for joint administration of Berlin) and the agreement of 1 May 1945 between the Big Three and France establishing the control machinery for the occupation of Germany and Berlin. He also declared his intention to hand over to East Germany the functions hitherto performed by the Soviet authorities.

In reply, the West German Government issued a statement to the effect that if the Soviet Union unilaterally renounced the international treaties concluded by the Four Powers regarding Berlin, political tension in Europe would increase, Soviet-German relations would deteriorate and Soviet Russia would be accused of violating international law. While the Western Powers were determined to defend their rights, they were also ready to negotiate. The Soviet Union proposed a draft treaty which provided that Germany was to accept the frontiers of 1 January 1959, recognise Austrian neutrality and renounce Sudetenland. Other articles prohibited the Nazi party, militarization and propaganda against peace. The Western powers did not accept the draft treaty and suggested a meeting of Foreign Ministers.

The Foreign Ministers of the United States, the Soviet Union, Britain and France met at a Conference in Geneva on 11 May 1959 on the issues of reunification of Germany and the future of Berlin. On behalf of the Western Powers, Herter placed before the Conference a plan for the settlement of all the problems. That plan is known as the Western Peace Plan. It provided for the unification of Germany by accomplishing the reunification of Berlin through free elections as the first step towards German Unity. The Four powers were to guarantee the independence of united Berlin. A commission of 35 representatives (25 from West Germany and 10 from East Germany) was to prepare the electoral laws on the basis of which a legislative assembly for the whole of Germany was to be elected. The United German Government was to enjoy the full right of joining either NATO or the Warsaw Pact. Peace treaty would be concluded with the all-German Government.

On 25 May 1959, Gromyko, the Foreign Minister of the Soviet Union, produced a counter proposal which provided that separate peace treaties were to be concluded with both the German states and the task of German reunification was to be left to them. West Berlin was to remain independent and free from foreign armies until the reunification of Germany. The NATO members were to withdraw their forces from Germany and dismantle their military base. The Soviet Union was also to remove her armies from Germany, Poland and Hungary.

Both Herter and Gromyko rejected each other's peace proposals. Gromyko then placed before the Conference fresh proposals which provided that within one year the Western Powers should agree to the abolition of the occupation regime in West Berlin, to reduce the number of their armies in Germany and refrain from engaging themselves in any kind of hostile activity or propaganda against East Germany. The Western Powers rejected that proposal also. On 20 June 1959, the Western Foreign Ministers proposed a Four-Power treaty which would guarantee the West unrestricted access to West Berlin. Gromyko refused to accept the proposal. There was a deadlock and thus the Conference ended.

In September 1959, Khrushchev met President Eisenhower at Camp David and agreed to resume talks on the Berlin question at the proposed Summit Conference in May 1960 in Paris. However, on account of U-2 incident, Khrushchev decided to boycott the Summit.

On 25 April 1960, Khrushchev warned the Western powers that in case they refused to sign a peace treaty with East Germany, their right of access to West Berlin would cease and the Soviet Union would conclude a peace treaty with East Germany unilaterally. He also declared that as the city of Berlin was situated within East Germany, with the signing of the peace treaty with East Germany, the sovereign right of the latter would be established upon the whole of East Germany. The Western powers protested and argued that they had a right over West Berlin as a result of conquest of Germany and not as a concession from the Soviet Union. Moreover, the Soviet Union could not revoke unilaterally all the treaties concluded earlier with regard to Germany and Berlin.

Khrushchev met President Kennedy at Vienna in June 1961 and on 21 June, he declared that Camp David formula was dead.

On 11 August 1961, the Soviet Union announced protective measures to check West German subversive acts in East Berlin. On 12 August 1961, the Government of East Germany introduced permit system for East Germans who went to West Berlin. On the morning of 13 August, the Government of East Germany sealed East Berlin borders with West Berlin. In the next few days, cement and concrete walls were erected. Thus the Berlin Wall came into existence. The United States ordered the calling up of 76,500 reserves and there was great tension. After long negotiations, the Pass Agreement was signed on 17 September 1963 which allowed Berliners of the two sides to meet one another.

In 1970, the coalition Government of West Germany led by Chancellor Willy Brandt inaugurated a new approach towards East Germany known as Ostpolitik. He wanted to start new relations with East Germany and agreed to the idea of two German states in one German nation. The result was that on 12 August 1970 was signed the Non-Aggression Treaty between Moscow and Bonn. The treaty recognised the Post-War map of Central Europe. It recognised *status quo* in Eastern Europe. Both West Germany and the Soviet Union agreed to recognise the Post-War frontiers of Poland, Czechoslovakia and the frontier between East and West Germany. They agreed not to challenge those frontiers in the future. They agreed to support the entry of the two German states into the United Nations. The treaty enabled West Germany to establish diplomatic and cultural relations with the East European countries and went a long way to lessen the East-West tension.

On 8 November, 1972, the representatives of East and West Germany met in Bonn and signed a treaty concerning the relations on a formal basis. The two states agreed to recognise the sovereignty and territorial integrity of each other and accepted the right of self-determination. Both claimed to be admitted to the United Nations. The treaty pledged normal, good neighbourly relations, sovereign equality, promotion of European security and cooperation in economic, social and scientific exchanges. Bonn renounced the Hallstein Doctrine without abandoning the notion of a common nationhood, with East Germany as second German state within German territory. This treaty, also known as the Basic Treaty, made it possible for the two German states to be admitted to the United Nations as members in September 1973. The admission of two Germanies to the United Nations was the result of a series of treaties signed between West Germany and Poland, West Germany and the Soviet Union, East Germany and West Germany and the Soviet Union, France, Britain and the United States in regard to Germany. The admission of two Germanies as sovereign and equal states marked the end of the Cold War and the new territorial arrangements following the defeat of Germany in 1945. However, the dream of German unity does not appear to be in sight even in the distant future. It seems that two German states have come to stay. Each German Government is interested in perpetuating the Post-War division of Germany.

THE BERLIN PROBLEM

Geographically, the city of Berlin is situated within the territory of East Germany. It is inside East German territory, 100 miles away from the frontiers of West Germany.

The story of the Post-War arrangements on Berlin began in October 1943 when the Foreign Ministers of the United States, Britain and the Soviet Union met in Moscow and agreed in principle on joint responsibility for and joint occupation of defeated-Germany. They established the European Advisory Commission and gave it the task of working out the necessary arrangements. Out of their lengthy deliberations emerged the protocol of 12 September, 1944 which ran as follows: "Germany, within her frontiers as they were on 31 October, 1937, will, for the purpose of occupation, be divided into three zones, one of which will be allotted to each of the three powers and a special Berlin zone which will be under the joint occupation of the three powers." On 14 November, 1944, the European Advisory Commission reached an agreement on the establishment of an Allied Control Council which was to function as the Government of Germany for the interim period till an indigenous German Government could be established.

The Yalta Conference of the Big Three in February 1945 confirmed the arrangements reached in London and implemented them by giving France a separate zone of occupation together with a sector of Berlin and by making France a member of the Allied Control Council. The Yalta Accord was followed by the agreement of the European Advisory Commission on 1 May, 1945 regarding control mechanism in Germany.

On 8 May, 1945, the United States' forces were deep in the territory designated as the Russian zone, while Russians were in possession of the whole of Berlin. The Russians would not permit Allied entry into Berlin unless the Allies withdrew to their respective zones. When the four Commanders issued their proclamations of 5 June, 1945 assuming supreme authority over Germany, they decided to honour the mutual obligations undertaken by their respective Governments. The Potsdam Agreement of 2 August, 1945 to which France was not a party, continued the antecedent agreements of the four Allied Commanders and assigned to the Allied Control Council specific functions of denazification, democratization, demilitarisation and deconcentration. The Potsdam Agreement made no mention of Four Power regime to be established in Berlin.

First Berlin Crisis (1948-9)

The problem of the access of the Western Allies to West Berlin was left to the Allied Commanders. On 29 June, 1945, General Clay, as representative of General Eisenhower, met General Zhukov in Berlin. He agreed, "as a temporary arrangement," to the allocation of one main highway and one rail line, as well as two air corridors for the purpose of the Western Powers' access to Berlin. The agreement was not put to writing. However, the omission was subsequently rectified by the decision of the Allied Control Council on 30 November 1945 which granted the West three air corridors to be used without advance notice. In 1948, the Soviet Union blockaded the land routes and the Allies overcame the difficulty by organising the Berlin airlift for about 10 months till the Soviet Union lifted the blockade. On 4 May 1949, an agreement was reached by which the Soviet. Union agreed to end the blockade of Berlin and the Western Powers agreed to lift their restrictions on communications with Eastern Germany which they had imposed as reprisal for the blockade.

The Nine-Power Agreement on Germany and European Defence of 3 August, 1954, concluded in Paris between the Western Powers and West Germany, which ended Allied occupation and restored full sovereignty to West Germany, reserved to the Allies "the existing rights and responsibilities relating to Berlin." In an agreement with East Germany on 20 September, 1955, the Soviet Union recognised the sovereignty of the German Democratic Republic (East Germany) and resolved for herself the control of traffic-both personnel and freight—destined for Berlin.

Second Berlin Crisis (1958)

In December 1958, the NATO Council decided to equip West Germany with atomic weapons and rockets. That provoked the Soviet Union and precipitated a second Berlin crisis. The Soviet Union sent the following notes to the Western Powers :—

(1) The whole of Berlin formed geographically a part of East Germany and therefore the Western Powers had no legal right over Berlin.

(2) The Western Powers should withdraw from West Berlin within six months.

(3) West Berlin would be declared a demilitarized free city.

(4) The Soviet Union gave six months' ultimatum to resolve the Berlin problem failing which Western access rights would end and any Western violation would immediately cause appropriate retaliation.

(5) The Soviet Union declared her intention to entrust to East Germany control over communications which meant that Western Powers were to take the permission of East Germany to reach West Berlin.

On 31 December, 1958, the United States along with the other Western Powers rejected the Soviet proposal. They claimed their right in Berlin from the conquest of Germany and not on the basis of Potsdam Agreement. They refused to be bowed down by threats or ultimatums. On 11 May, 1959, the Foreign Ministers Conference of Big Four Powers met in Geneva but could not arrive at any agreement. A new Summit was arranged for 16 May, 1960 but it did not meet on account of the U-2 incident. The Berlin crisis was over but the problem was not solved.

Third Berlin Crisis (1961)

When Khrushchev met President Kennedy in June 1961, he fixed a deadline for a separate treaty with Germany by the end of 1961. The United States was willing to negotiate on the question of Germany but was not willing to accept the Soviet view on Berlin. The result was that both the leaders exchanged threatening notes on the question of Berlin. A serious situation was created in Germany as a result of the influx of refugees from East Germany. Doctors, engineers and skilled workers defected to West Germany on a large scale and caused brain drain in East Germany. On 13 August, 1961, East Germany sealed her border between East Berlin and West Berlin and a 25-mile-long Berlin wall was erected between two Berlins. There was great tension. A Pass Agreement was concluded in 1963 which allowed people on both sides of Berlin to meet each other.

Fourth Berlin Crisis (1969)

There was another Berlin crisis in 1969. The West German Government decided to hold presidential elections on 5 March, 1969 in West Berlin in order to reassert her claim over West Berlin. East Germany opposed and re-imposed restrictions on land routes to prevent the members of the electoral college from reaching West Berlin. The West German Government sent the members of the electoral college and other officials to West Berlin by air. On that occasion, President Nixon of the United States gave the following warning: "Let there be no miscalculation. No unilateral move, no illegal act, no form of pressure from any source will shake the resolve of Western nations to defend their rightful status as protectors of the people of free Berlin." The result was that the Soviet Union did not take any action and the situation was saved.

Berlin Agreement (1971)

After prolonged negotiations lasting for 18 months, the United States, Britain, France and the Soviet Union concluded an agreement over Berlin on 23 August, 1971. The restrictions on movement between East and West Berlin were removed. The Western powers and West Germany recognised the separate authority of East Germany. The West German Government and the Berlin Administration were urged to have direct dealings with East Germany. The Four Big Powers accepted that West Berlin did not form an integral part of West Germany which means that West Berlin was not under West Germany but under the three Western Powers. In other words, the authority of West Berlin was separated from that of West Germany. The Western Powers assumed directly the responsibility for the security of West Berlin. East Berlin was accepted as an integral part of East Germany. The Four Big powers understood not to change the *status quo* by force unilaterally. The agreement put a temporary end to years of tension. The problem of Berlin is intimately connected with the unification of Germany and can be finally solved only when Germany is reunified.

SUGGESTED READINGS

Balfour, M. and Mair, J.: **Four Power Control in Germany and Austria,** 1956.

Bolling, K.: **The Republic in Suspense,** 1963.

Brandt, W.: **My Road to Berlin,** 1960.

Clay, L.D.: **Decision in Germany,** 1950

Crowley, D.: **The Background to Current Affairs.**

Davidson, E.: **The Death and Life of Germany,** 1959.

Erhard, L.: **Germany's Comeback in the World Market,** 1954

Freund, G.: **Germany Between Two World Wars,** 1961.

Friedmann, W.: **An Introduction to World Politics.**

Friedrich, C.J.: **The Soviet Zone of Germany,** 1956.

Golay, J.F.: **The Founding of the Federal Republic of Germany,** 1958.

Gottlieb, M.: **The German Peace Settlement and the Berlin Crisis,** 1960.

Grosser, A.: **The Colossus Again,** 1955.

Hautmann, Fredrick H.: **The Relations of Nations.**

Hiscocks, R.: **Democracy in Western Germany,** 1957.

Hiscocks, R.: **The Adenauer Era,** 1967.

Kissinger, Henry: **The White House Years, New Delhi,** 1979.

Mander, J.: **Berlin: Hostage for the West,** 1962.

McInnis, E.: **The Shaping of Postwar Germany,** 1960.

Merkl, P.H. : **Germany: Yesterday and Tomorrow,** 1965.

Merkl, P.H.: **The Origin of the West German Republic,** 1963.

Nettle, J.P.: **The Eastern Zone and Soviet Policy on Germany,** 1945-50, 1951.

Prittie, T.: **Germany Divided,** 1960.

Schleicher, Charles P.: **International Relations, Cooperation and Conflict.**

Schleicher, Charles P.: **Introduction to International Relations.**

Smith, Gorden Connell: **Pattern of the Post-World War.**

Srivastava, L.W. and V.P. Joshi: **International Relations, Meerut,** 1979-80.

Stahl, W. (Ed.): **The Politics of Post-War Germany,** 1963.

Wallich, H.C.: **Mainsprings of the German Revival,** 1955.

Weymar, p.: **Adenauer: His Authorized Biography,** 1957.

CHAPTER

52 GERMANY REVOLUTION AND THE WEIMAR REPUBLIC (1918-1933)

It is true that Party Truce had been proclaimed on 4 August 1914 in Germany, but the same could not be maintained throughout the duration of the World War I. The munition strikes took place in June 1916, April 1917 and January 1918. The extreme Left after 1 January 1916 known as the Spartacists led by Karl Liebknecht and Rosa Luxemburg rejected the Party Truce and were too ready to use illegal means to promote the Revolution. They were wholly anti-war, anti-parliamentarian and were ready to receive money and support, after 1917, from Soviet Russia. Liebknecht and Rosa Luxemburg were feared and respected, the former on account of his courage and integrity and the latter on account of her intellectual ruthlessness. On 30 December 1918, the Spartacist League reconstituted itself as the German Communist Party.

On 19 July 1917, Reichstag passed the peace resolution moved by Erzberger, the leader of the Catholic Centre Party and supported by the Progressive People's Party and some National Liberals. As a result of the passage of that resolution, Bethmann Hollweg resigned as Chancellor of Germany. After that, it became impossible to control the distress and discontent consequent upon economic collapse. This was particularly so because it was accompanied by a political movement arising from a revival of the pre-War protest against the Prussian franchise and the absence of a Reich Ministry responsible to the Reichstag. The economic collapse came in 1917-18 partly as a result of the blockade which confined Germany to her own resources or those of the conquered territory for her food supply and partly because her highly cartelised and centralised economy could not be adapted to the changed situation. Urban hunger, peasant hoarding, the black market, pilfering and profiteering created conditions of hostility in society and despair among the people. Rations were reduced. There were shortages of coal, leather and textiles. The work capacity and the morale of the people went down. There were industrial strikes in Berlin, Magdeburg, Halle, Brunswick and Leipzig. There had been demands for constitutional reforms but those were not satisfied by Bethmann Hollweg and that had created bitterness. The new Chancellors were not able to handle the situation. In September 1918, Prince Maximilian became Chancellor. He hoped to save the throne for the Hohenzollerns by rushing through a number of reforms which converted Germany into a constitutional monarchy. On 20 September, 1918, Ludendorf told the German Emperor that there was no prospect of victory in the war and that fact was confirmed by Hindenburg on 1 October 1918. On 27 October, the Reichstag resolved that the Chancellor must henceforth possess the confidence of the Reichstag and that resolution was approved by the German Emperor. On 29 October, the Emperor fled from Berlin to the headquarters of the army at spa in the hope of defending himself with the help of the army.

Prince Maximilian was negotiating with President Wilson for an armistice based on the Fourteen Points. He emphasized that the new German administration was a government "of the people, in whose hands rested both actually and constitutionally the authority to make decisions". However, President Wilson insisted that as long as William II was the Emperor, he would not negotiate. On 23 October, a demand was made in the Reichstag that the Emperor must abdicate. The demand was supported by the newspapers. On 29 October, Philipp Scheidemann, as leader of the Majority Socialists, requested Prince Maximilian to secure the abdication of William II.

Meanwhile, at the Kiel naval base, the rumour spread that armistice negotiations would probably result in a surrender of the German fleet. The reaction of the German naval officers was that they would prefer to have an honourable death by an unexpected attack on the blockading British fleet than to surrender to the Allies. However, about 80,000 sailors involved in it refused to commit suicide in that manner and mutinied. The spirit of the revolt spread to the workers of Kiel where revolutionary councils demanded the abdication of William II and amnesty for the leaders of earlier mutinies. Their movement spread and the great ports of Hamburg, Bremen and Cuxhaven were in the hands of Workers' and Sailors' Councils on 8 November 1918.

At a demonstration in Munich on 7 November 1918, an Independent Socialist Editor, Kurt Eisner, demanded the overthrow of the Bavarian dynasty. The Wittelsbach family fled and a "democracy and social republic" was set up in Bavaria with Eisner as its head.

Inspired by the success of the Bolshevik Revolution, the Spartacists tried to establish a Communist Government. Karl Liebknecht and Rosa Luxemburg addressed gatherings in Berlin and other industrial centres and called upon the proletariat to rise up and establish "a free socialist republic". On 9 November 1918, a group of Spartacists seized the royal palace and police headquarters in Berlin. However, they lacked public support and were crushed by the government.

On 10 November, Prince Maximilian announced the abdication of William II and named Ebert, the leader of the Majority Socialists, as the new Chancellor. The same day, William II fled to Holland and Phillipp Scheidemann, the Foreign Secretary, proclaimed the German Republic. Ebert as Chancellor formed a Government of the Social Democrats and the Independent Socialists but left out the Spartacists. That Government was recognised by Hindenburg, the Chief of the General Staff. The Workers' and Soldiers' Councils of Berlin also supported Ebert's Government which was pledged "to save Germany, not to save revolution". On the evening of 10 November, Ebert formed an alliance with General Groner, the successor of Ludendorff. Ebert would have the support of the army to keep order and to keep the Communist revolution at bay. On 11 November, armistice was signed and that robbed the Revolution of its mass appeal.

Two meetings from all Germany were held. The first assembled the Prime Ministers from all the German states on 25 November 1918. This meeting supported the call for the Constituent Assembly. In the second meeting were assembled representatives from the Workers' and Soldiers' Councils from all over Germany and it lasted from 16 to 21 December, 1918. Its deliberations showed that most Germans wished to live in a parliamentary state, that they wished for a greater degree of demilitarization than what the armistice demanded and that though there was widespread support for a socialist programme of industrial nationalisation, the restoration of the economy was their aim and not further revolution. The Spartacists, led by Liebknecht and Rosa Luxemburg demanded a people's government. They shouted, "whoever votes for the Constituent Assembly, votes for the rape of the working class." However, Ebert succeeded in getting a resolution passed on 19 December that elections for the Constituent Assemblies be held on 19 January 1919. The Spartacists occupied the Chancellery and took Ebert himself a prisoner. He was rescued on 24 December by the German troops who had been sent to Berlin by General Groner. On 29 December, the three Independent Socialists resigned from Ebert's cabinet in protest against his counter-revolutionary policies. That strengthened Ebert who appointed Gustav Noske, a Majority Socialist, as Governor of Berlin on 4 January 1919. Noske organised a volunteer corps, to crush the revolution and "to play the blood hound". On 5 January 1919, the Spartacists declared at a mass meeting Ebert's Government deposed. By 15 January, they created revolutionary conditions by seizing barracks, railway stations and printing offices. On 9 January, Noske entered the field with about 20,000 men and supported by machine guns and howitzers, ruthlessly crushed the revolution and took hundreds of prisoners who were mercilessly executed. On 15 January, Rosa Luxemburg and Liebknecht were brutally murdered. Thus, the Spartacists revolution was crushed.

Critics point out that the German Revolution of 1918 can hardly be called a revolution. The change did not go beyond the change of Government. After the departure of William II for Holland, 25 sovereigns of individual states resigned and Germany was proclaimed a republic, but the entire social and economic organisation in the country remained the same as it was before. Practically all the imperial officials remained at their posts and continued to administer the routine of their Bureaus. The attempts of the Spartacists to set up a Communist government failed.

The German Revolution of 1918 cannot be compared with the French Revolution of 1789. It was no outgrowth of active, sustained and bitter criticism of the existing institutions and no indignant protest against a long-continued denial of political liberty. It had no background of preparation. It was a storm that had suddenly blown up, not the explosion of a slowly gathering hurricane. Yet this brief and sudden crisis, born of military disaster, swept away the supposedly strongest monarchy in Europe, set up a republic in its stead and greatly changed the face of Germany. Not only did the Emperor disappear from the scene which he had dominated for 30 years, but the Bundesrat, the organ of the princes, vanished when the princes vanished, and the Reichstag, in the whole affair, gave no sign of life. The conservative political parties which had controlled the Reichstag since the founding of the Empire, collapsed with the collapse of the royal power. The former radical parties, particularly the Socialists, occupied the centre of the scene.

The establishment of the Republic in Germany was not due to the victory of a German republican party over the monarchists as the Germans did not fight for liberty and democracy. As a matter of fact, there was little demand for a change of government. It was only when President Wilson insisted that he would not deal with the Government which was responsible for the war, did the demand for the abdication of William II arise. Germans were ready to sacrifice their Emperor only because they believed that they would obtain better peace terms by doing so. Thus, in a way, the Republic was imposed on the people of Germany. There was little real enthusiasm for it. To those who were not in favour of it, the republic was the result of defeat in the war and foreign intrusion into German affairs. It was considered by many as the symbol of national humiliation.

With the revolution thus crushed, elections to the National Assembly which was to draft the Constitution of the new Republic, took place on 19 January 1919. The elections were boycotted by the Spartacists. Although the Majority Socialists (Social Democrats) polled more votes than all the other parties put together, the seats won by them were 163 out of 399. The Independent Socialists won 22 seats. The rest were captured by the Centrists, Democrats, People's Party, Nationalists and others. After the elections, Ebert decided that the Assembly should meet in a quiet town and not in Berlin in which there was a lot of unrest. The place chosen was Weimar which is associated with Goethe, Schiller, Herder, Bach and Liszt.

Before taking up the task of drafting a permanent Constitution, the National Assembly drew up a provisional Republican Constitution and elected Friedrich Ebert as President. While assuming the office of the President, Ebert said, "I desire and intend to act as the authorised representative of the entire German people, not as leader of a single party." He also observed that he had "grown up in the world of ideas according to socialism". However, he was quite moderate in his outlook as the President of the Republic. He was not an extraordinary man but he was an unflinching supporter of parliamentary democracy.

The Majority Socialists who were the single largest party in the National Assembly, made a coalition government with the bourgeois parties, the Democrats and the Centre Party Philipp Scheidemann became the Chancellor. The first task was to sign the terms of the peace offered by the Allies. Sheidemann refused to sign so humiliating a document, saying, "Let the hand that signs it wither". Bauer, his successor, signed the treaty of peace under duress on 28 June 1919 and the National Assembly ratified the same.

The Weimar Constitution (1919)

The National Assembly started its work on 6 February 1919. After several months of deliberations, a Constitution was adopted on 31 July 1919 and it came into force on 11 August 1919. Under that Constitution, the former name of the German national state, Deutsches Reich, was preserved, but that state was declared a Republic based on the sovereignty of the people. The national flag was changed from the black-white-red tricolour of the Empire to black-red-gold. It was provided that every state of Germany must have a republican Constitution. The old states were preserved so that Germany could become a federal Republic like that of the United States and not a unitary one like that of France and Britain. A proposal was urged in the National Assembly that the large states like Prussia be split up into a number of small states and a number of petty states be united into larger units so that every state might have about two or three million people and all states may be approximately equal, but that proposal was rejected. The executive head of the state was to be a President chosen by the whole German people, men as well as women. He was to be elected for seven years but he could be re-elected. He could be deposed before the expiration of his term by a referendum, but if the referendum resulted in his favour, that was to be counted as a new election of the President. The President had a powerful position which he could abuse. He appointed the Chancellor, the head of the Government and the latter made his Ministry which was to have the confidence of the Reichstag. The President's choice of the Chancellor played an important part in the events of 1930-33. The President had the power to dissolve the Reichstag so that he could appeal to the electorate over the heads of the Reich Ministry and against it. That too was a power which could be abused. The President was given emergency powers which allowed him to dispense with the Reichstag altogether.

The Reichstag was chosen by universal and secret suffrage according to the principle of proportional representation. It was elected for four years. The Chancellor and the Ministers were made responsible to it. The Reichsrat was the Upper House which represented the states. It could hold up but could not veto, most laws passed by the Reichstag. However, its consent was necessary for the passage of any measure affecting the states as such. To prevent Prussia's securing a preponderant influence, the Constitution provided that no state could have more than two-fifths of the total representation.

Provision was made for a Bill of Rights in the Constitution. A Supreme Court was instituted at Leipzig.

The Weimar Republic was not a socialist but a liberal democracy. The Socialists did not stand by their commitment to nationalise industry. As they were a party in government, their duty was to govern and restore confidence to industrialists who were afraid of expropriation and to have nationalised industries in 1918-20 would, have loaded the state with debt. A commission was appointed to enquire which industries were ripe for nationalisation but its recommendations were ignored and the arguments of the Minister of Finance for its postponement were adopted.

The Constitution contained a Section on the economy. It formulated the principle of social justice, but guaranteed the economic freedom of the individual. It gave power to the Reich to take economic enterprises by legal enactment into the possession of the community. However, it was not provided that it must be done. The state was to have the oversight of the economy but not its direction. No provision was made in the Constitution for the Councils of Workers and Soldiers. However, provision was made for eight-hour working day and unemployment relief.

Critics point out that the will to work the Weimar Constitution was weak. The Weimar Republic had no positive friends and too many enemies. The Socialists virtually deserted it. They lost seats in the general elections of June 1920. They were not a part of the coalition government between 1920 and 1922. After the assassination of Eisner on 21 February 1919 and a brief Communist interlude, a government without Socialist participation was installed in Bavaria in May 1920. Only in Prussia a Socialist Government survived. The Liberal Parties should have been the source of strength of the Republic but they lost heavily in the general elections. Moreover, Liberal Parties were middle class parties and the middle classes were seriously disabled by the economic crisis and their loss of wealth. Positive action on behalf of the Republic was not in their power. The civil service of Germany which included the judiciary, was either hostile to the Republic or failed to understand the importance of active goodwill. The Constitution safeguarded the position of civil servants. They had been appointed under monarchy and were either monarchists or only nominally loyal to the new Republic. The judiciary was so hostile that there was a state of war between the judiciary and the people. The schools were strongholds of monarchical and nationalist feelings. The churches were also not friendly towards the Republic. There was violence in the country and there was no republican army to deal with it effectively.

Challenges to Weimar Republic

The Republic had to face many challenges and dangers. While the Government was busy in suppressing the Communists, the rightist diehards took advantage of it to form strong ultra-nationalist organisations such as the Stahlhelm (Steel Helmet). These organisations had a long list of grievances against republicans. It was rumoured that cowardly republicans had made defeat inevitable by undermining the military power of the Empire during the last months of the War. The National Assembly at Weimar was attacked for accepting the "Versailles Dictate" and for permitting the Allied Commissions to "overrun" the country. Some individuals feared that the German authorities might surrender "war criminals" to the Allies for trial.

In March 1920, a rightist *Putsch* was attempted. It was planned by Dr. Wolfgang Kapp who had gained notoriety during the World War I for a fierce attack upon the policies of the then Chancellor, Bethmann Hollweg. On 11 March 1920, a detachment of German crack troops disbanded by the Allies marched into Berlin under Captain Ehrhardt. They were in alliance with the Commander of Berlin, General Luttwitz. The Republic was dissolved and a provisional Government headed by Dr. W. Kapp and Luttwitz was formed. Noske had only 2000 men to oppose and hence the Government took shelter first at Dresden and then at Stutgart. President Ebert reacted by calling a general strike. Workmen throughout the country responded and Berlin's public utilities and communications were tied up. The strike was a success. The conspirators fell out among themselves, gave up the attempt and fled. Thus, the attempted counter-revolution was checked not by any vigorous action taken by the government but due to the opposition of the workers. Even after the failure of the *coup*, the government did not take strong measures to punish the offenders. General Seeckt who had refused to open fire on the insurgent officers was appointed Chief of the German army in place of Luttwitz. Dr. Kapp who had fled to Sweden, returned to Germany and surrendered himself to the authorities. However, he died in prison in 1922 while awaiting trial.

The Kapp affair did not end the attempt of reactionaries to avenge the "betrayal" of the Fatherland. They instituted a reign of terror against the persons connected with the signing of the Treaty of Versailles in June 1919, persons who gave aid to the Allied Commissions in Germany and individuals prominently identified with socialism. Erzberger, the Centrist leader who had urged peace without annexations in 1917, was killed in 1921. Walther Rathenau, an industrialist, political philosopher and efficient cabinet Officer was assassinated in 1922. Attempts were also made on the lives of Ebert and Scheidemann.

In January 1919, the German Workers' Party was created. In March 1920 it was given the name of National Socialist German Workers' Party after Adolf Hitler joined it. That party was backed by the reactionaries, Junkers and militarists including General Ludendorff. It was vehemently anti-

Communist and against the Jews. In November 1923, an attempt was made by this group in Munich to overthrow the Government. It is known as Ludendorff-Hitler *Putsch.* However, the army remained loyal to the Government and the plan of the conspirators clashed with another group of Bavarian conspirators. It ended in a fiasco and Hitler found himself in jail.

It is true that the Republic was saved, but its position was shaky. This is proved by the fact that in the first Reichstag elections in June 1923 under the new Constitution, the vote of the parties which openly accepted the republican government was much smaller while the parties with monarchist tendencies gained three million votes. Monarchist sympathy was not confined to the old generation. Education in the high schools and Universities in Germany was almost completely in the hands of the reactionaries who instilled monarchist ideas in the minds of the young. The result was that the Republic in Germany had a precarious existence.

HISTORY OF THE WEIMAR REPUBLIC

First Period (1919-23)

The history of the Weimar Republic can be divided into three periods : from 1919 to 1923, 1924-29 and 1929-1933. During the first period, the Weimar Republic signed the Treaty of Versailles in June 1919. The Weimar Constitution was adopted on 31 July 1919 and it came into force on 11 August 1919. Dr. Kapp's Putsch was foiled. In 1923, Ludendorff-Hitler Putsch failed.

The most serious problem of the new Republic was economy. That was due to the fact that Germany was required to turn over to the Allies large quantities of materials. The transfer of Alsace-Lorraine to France with its iron ore and potash deposits, the temporary loss of the highly industrialised Saar District and the giving of Upper Silesia with its coal mines to Poland, dealt a severe blow to German industry. Germany was also required to surrender to the Allies all merchant ships exceeding 1600 gross tons, half of the merchant ships between 1000 and 1600 gross tons, one-quarter of the fishing fleet, 5000 locomotives and 1,50,000 motor trucks. All German investments in the Allied countries were seized or surrendered. The credit of Germany in the capital markets of the world was seriously undermined. The result was that Germany was not in a position to pay the reparations to be imposed on her.

The task of fixing the amount of reparations was given to the Reparation Commission which was to make its report by 1 May 1921. Prior to that date, Germany was to pay 5000 million dollars to the Allies. An agreement was made at the Spa Conference in July 1920 by which out of the money paid by Germany, France was to have 52%, Britain 22%, Italy 10%, Belgium 8% and others 8%. In 1921, the Allied statesmen met at Paris to settle the question of allowing Germany to pay a lump-sum in settlement of her entire liability. The Germans made a counter proposal which was not acceptable to the Allies who occupied three German towns of Ruhrort, Duisburg and Dusseldorf on 8 March 1921. Germany appealed to the League of Nations and the United States but by that time the Reparation Commission announced on 27 April 1921 that they had assessed the German liability at 132 billion gold marks equivalent to 32 billion dollars or £ 6600 millions. On 2 May 1921, the Supreme Council directed the Reparation Commission to forward to Germany a scheme prescribing the time and manner of discharging her obligations. That was done on 5 May 1921, accompanied by an ultimatum by the Allied Powers. A demand was made that £ 50 million must be paid by the end of May 1921 failing which the Ruhr valley would be occupied by the Allied troops. As there was no alternative, the schedule was accepted by Germany who paid the first instalment by August 1921. Additional payments were made early in 1922. In June 1922, Germany was forced to request a moratorium on reparation payments for two years as economic situation had deteriorated. Since the announcement of the reparation debt, the mark had declined steadily. In May 1921, the mark was worth 62 to the US dollar (4.2 to the dollar was par). After the announcement of the Reparation Commission, the mark declined to 105 in September 1921 and 270 by the end of November 1921.

Britain was ready to agree to a moratorium, but the French view was that the German request was a trick to evade payment. In December 1922, Germany having failed by a small margin to fulfil her commitments of deliveries in kind, the Reparation Commission declared Germany in voluntary default. Both France and Belgium declared that on account of default by Germany, a Mission of Control would be sent into the Ruhr and that Mission would be accompanied by an adequate number of troops. On the next day, the Mission settled at Essen. The occupation of the Ruhr in January 1923 was opposed by Britain. It was a blunder for France and disaster for Germany. France lost the goodwill and cooperation of Britain. Her action created a lasting bitterness in the minds of the German people towards France. There was so much of bitterness in Germany that its inhabitants resorted to the policy of "passive resistance" in which representatives of all classes participated. The people were asked not to pay customs duties, local taxes or other demands made from them. Thousands of men in the Ruhr were thrown out of employment and food became scarce. Millions of people suffered. The telephone, telegraph and railway service came to a standstill. Mines and factories were closed. Newspapers refused to publish the decrees issued by the Governments of Belgium and France. Local officials disobeyed foreign commands. However, the population of the Ruhr numbering about 5 millions had to be fed and supported. For that purpose, the Government had to issue more and more marks. German presses worked at top speed day and night to supply the demand. The effect on the value of the mark was catastrophic. By the middle of June 1923, it fell to 100,000 for a dollar, by 8 August to 5 millions, by the middle of September to 10 millions, by 9 October to more than 1,000,000 millions and by November 1923 to 4,200,000 millions.

Inflation

The financial crisis was a very serious one. The unprecedented inflation was due to many reasons. It was caused partly by the financial policies of all the German governments since 1914. The World War I was financed by borrowing and not by high taxation. In August 1914, the restriction placed upon the printing of notes beyond the sum covered by the gold reserves of the banks was removed and the organisation of Loan Banks, to afford credit on securities which did not qualify as securities under the existing regulations, was provided for. By 1918, the mark had already declined to about half its value in gold. After the War, international trade was resumed. There was a general loss of confidence in the mark which caused further depreciation. At that stage, Germany had large gold reserves and could have stabilised her currency by following the right policy but it continued to increase the money supply. Another cause of inflation was the magnitude of the financial and economic burdens imposed upon Germany by the Allied Powers. The Reparation Commission assessed the German liability at 132 billion gold marks. The notification demanded not only the acceptance of that figure but also the payment of a billion gold marks within 25 days. Germany paid by selling newly printed paper currency on the foreign currency exchanges. The result was that the mark fell during 1921 from 60 to the American dollar to 310. By October, Chancellor Wirth, with Rathenau's assistance, got a revision of the arrangements which lessened the amount to be paid in money and increased that to be paid in commodities. Cuno was then made Chancellor in the hope that his place in the business world would enable him to contrive means for Germany to pay. At the end of 1922, the Reparation Commission declared Germany in default. On 12 January 1923, French and Belgian troops marched into the Ruhr Basin.

Inflation was at its worst from March to November 1923. One of its effects was the complication of all business affairs. Rates at first were increased every week, then each day and finally workmen were paid several times a day in order to enable them to change the marks into anything that had inherent value before they became worthless. Shop-keepers had to increase the selling price of their commodities from hour to hour. In the rural districts, peasants refused to accept marks and would exchange goods only for other goods. Inflation reduced to poverty many families of established wealth and position. Fortunes which had taken so long to make, disappeared overnight. The lower middle class was hit the hardest. Inflation wiped out pensions, savings and insurance. This class never recovered from the blow and many of its members became the bitterest enemies of the Republic. Those who could manipulate credit, made enormous profits. The debts of the borrowers were wiped out. There were moderate difficulties for wage earners, greater difficulties for civil servants and professional people who relied on fees and salaries. There was complete ruin for those who depended upon income from invested capital. Small businessmen, shopkeepers and self-employed artisans were almost as badly hit as the professional classes. The farmers and land-owners fared better. The year 1923 closed with the revelation of General Seeckt's plan to resurrect the German army with Soviet help. By 1924, inflation was over. Before his fall in November 1923, Chancellor Gustav Stresemann had made the arrangements which enabled production to start again in the Ruhr Basin and with the assistance of Schacht and his Finance Minister, Hans Luther, had taken steps which stabilised the currency on the basis of a new mark, Rentenmark which was first issued in November 1923.

Second Period (1924-29)

The second period of the Weimar Republic began in stability. This period was essentially the period of Stresemann. It is rightly called the Stresemann era. When he assumed power in the summer of 1923, Germany was almost out of leaders. Public sentiment had turned against the Social Democrats whose attitude towards the country's late enemies did not seem to be sufficiently patriotic. Matthias Erzberger and Walther Rathenau had perished at the hands of nationalist fanatics. Stresemann's three months of power as Chancellor marked the turning point for the republican regime. It ended the era of constant uncertainty in which the people scarcely knew from month to month under what sort of authority they were going to live. Through a resort to martial law and firm action against both types of extremists that were threatening the state—the Communists in Saxony and Hitler's National Socialists in Bavaria—Stresemann, like Poincare three years later, proved the seriousness of his intentions and his resolve that middle class democracy in Germany should become a reality and that actually happened. When in November 1923, Stresemann retired as Chancellor, the Weimar Constitution had come to function in an approximately "normal fashion". Stresemann continued to be Foreign Minister of Germany upto October 1929 when he died.

By a determined effort on the part of the government and the people to rescue their Fatherland from ruin and a foreign loan to the extent of 800 million marks under the Dawes Plan, Germany was saved. German recovery was also due to the scheme of rationalisation under which labour savings were effected. For instance, a bank that worked in 1914 with 334 persons carried on the same volume of work in 1929 with only 284 persons. Such economy and labour-saving devices were applied also in agriculture, industry and other departments of economic life. However, its drawback was that thousands of persons became unemployed, but for the time being the scheme worked for the recovery of German business and economic life. German recovery was also visible in the development of coal, chemistry and cartels. The development of coal industry was effected by the improvement of techniques and also by the replacement of black coal by brown coal. The growing demand of the steel industry was met by the development in coal mining which reached nearly pre-War level. German chemists invented synthetic quinine, camphor, indigo, menthol, nitrate, rubber, gasoline, artificial silk and other chemical products. Those products minimised the dependence of Germany upon the outside world for raw materials. The cartels or trusts had become very powerful in Germany and they abused their power by controlling prices and sales. By a law of 1923, the Government tried to curb their activities but in spite of that, international cartels made great progress in steel, rail and potash industries. The development of German merchant marine received Government patronage. German shipping occupied the twelfth place among world's commercial fleet, but by 1930, the German merchant marine made so much progress that it came to occupy the third place, next only to the United Kingdom and the United States. In motor industry, Germany received aid and cooperation from American firms which opened branches in Germany. Berlin, with its skyscrapers, appeared to be more influenced by Americanism than any other city of Europe. Germany came to have new factories, new industries, and new techniques of production. In 1929, the Young Committee granted Germany a further loan of 300 million dollars. In the Laussane Conference of 1932, reparation payments virtually stopped. However, there were certain drawbacks in this economic prosperity. The problem of securing foreign loans and making reparation payments presented increasing difficulty. Rationalization added to unemployment. German attempt to decrease consumption in rye and potatoes increased the economic crisis of the agriculturists. Increasing foreign tariff enhanced the problem of marketing German goods in foreign markets. The withdrawal of government patronage from munition industries caused loss for business in military and naval supplies. The loss of the Russian market caused serious damage to German trade and industry. The result was mounting unemployment. The Government had undertaken welfare projects and kept per capita taxation at lower rate than even the rate of taxation in Britain and France. That was done notwithstanding heavy reparation obligations. Germany's economic prosperity entirely depended upon foreign loans and it collapsed as soon as foreign loans stopped. During these years, the United States was the creditor country which helped Germany to reconstruct her industry and make reparation payments. The money ultimately came back to the United States through the payment of inter-Allied debts. However, it did not contribute to the actual flow of goods in international trade. The result was a pressure on world's economy which resulted in the economic crash of 1929. The Great Depression had first affected the economy of the United States but it had its repercussions on European economy also. It had a shattering effect on Germany. Foreign investors started withdrawing their investments and consequently there was contraction of trade and commerce. Banks and factories closed down. Thousands of persons were thrown out of employment.

The formation of Stresemann Government signified the introduction of a new element in the foreign policy of Germany. It was the policy of national reconciliation and reconstruction through international cooperation. Instead of merely crying for the defence of the down-trodden or sticking to the destructive course of passive resistance, or repeatedly yielding to external pressures, Stresemann and his associates regarded international cooperation as a positive method and goal though well-tied to the task of national reconstruction. On one occasion, he declared, "International cooperation for national reconstruction....If you try to find a general formula for Germany's foreign policy, you must discover it in the international agreements in which we are and must be involved. The task before us is to devote all our strength to the maintenance of peace in Europe. The road ahead of us is clear; we must strengthen our own national life by the advancement of peaceful understanding."

When Stresemann became the Chancellor and later on the Foreign Minister of Germany, there was a lot of bitterness between Germany and France. In spite of that, Stresemann had the courage to declare that only a policy of reconciliation and cooperation with France could help his country and not confrontation. At that time, the French Ministry was headed by Herriot who was also prepared to cooperate with Germany. The result was that there was an agreement between the two countries in November 1923 whereby the Ruhr industrialists promised to deliver commodities to the Allies. That eventually led to the withdrawal of French forces from the Ruhr in summer of 1925. In November 1923, the Government of Stresemann was able to stabilise the mark through the issuance of Rentenmark which had little intrinsic value but was supported by public confidence. The public was happy to accept it @ of one Retenmark for a trillion old paper marks. The Rentenmark was replaced in 1924 by Reichsmark, based on gold and so usable in international trade.

Britain had opposed the occupation of the Ruhr by France and Belgium. She played an important role in the adoption of the Dawes Plan in 1924 that put Germany back on the road to economic recovery. Shortly thereafter, Britain and France advanced loan to Germany whose result was that instead of remaining a debtor, Germany became a creditor country.

Stresemann conducted his foreign policy as a coordinated whole. He cooperated with the West and confirmed Germany's alliance with Russia in the East. The three men, Stresemann, Briand and Austen Chamberlain, understood one another in the West. The Rapallo Treaty of 1922 with Russia had given Germany an ally in the East. Stresemann made a proposal to Britain for the guarantee of existing boundaries between Germany, Belgium and France combined with treaties of friendship and cooperation with Britain and Italy. That paved the way for the Locarno Treaties which were initialled in October and signed in London on 1 December 1925. By these treaties, the states bordering on the Rhine abjured the use of force in their relations with one another and together with Britain and Italy, mutually guaranteed their existing boundaries. In addition, Germany and France signed the Rhineland Pact by which Germany reaffirmed her acceptance of the demilitarised zone in the Rhineland. Germany was promised admission to the League of Nations with a permanent seat on the Council. Britain and France failed to get a guarantee from Germany with regard to her Eastern frontier as permanent. All they obtained was Germany's signature of arbitration treaties with Poland and Czechoslovakia. The entry of Germany into the League did not take place, as intended, in March 1926, but she was admitted in September 1926. On 24 April 1926, Stresemann signed the Treaty of Berlin with Russia.

There was an appreciable improvement in the status of Germany after her becoming a member of the League of Nations. In 1927, the last of the Allied Commissions were withdrawn from Germany. The report of the Young Committee on the reparation problem was published on 27 June 1929. That eased the reparation problem of Germany. As a result of the acceptance of the Young Plan, Stresemann was able to persuade the Allied Powers to start evacuation of the occupation troops from the Rhineland five years ahead of the schedule. That evacuation was completed in June 1930. That was the final fruit of Stresemann's policy.

Grant and Temperley observe that the balance sheet for Stresemann was not bad. On the credit side, Germany had been freed from most of the restrictions placed on her sovereignty by the Treaty of Versailles. She had been accepted as one among the Great Powers. On the debit side, she had not regained military parity with the other European powers. She had not regulated her relations with Austria. She had not rectified her Eastern frontier. Perhaps, Stresemann had simply postponed internal problems. They could not all be solved by being exported. The primacy of foreign policy can never be absolute. (*Europe in the Nineteenth and Twentieth Centuries*, Seventh Edition, Volume II, pp. 150-51).

In 1925, President Ebert died. Whatever his limitations, he was a firm supporter of the Republic. There were many candidates for that office and ultimately Field Marshal Hindenburg, "the hero of Tannenberg", was elected as the new President. The report of his victory caused consternation among the ardent supporters of the Republic and jubilation in the ranks of the reactionaries. It is true that Hindenburg was a conservative but he kept his oath to the Constitution.

Third Period (1929-1933)

The third period of the history of the Weimar Republic was from 1929 to 1933. During this period, Bruning, Papen and Schleicher were in turn Chancellor. They presided over the struggle of the Republic against Hitler and his followers.

It is true that at the beginning of 1929, there was a large measure of contentment among the people of Germany and that was good for the long life of Republic. Through the efforts of Stresemann, the foreign relations of Germany, particularly with France, had improved considerably. There was economic prosperity in the country. However things began to change very rapidly. Two events were responsible for the change. The first was the death of Stresemann in October 1929. As a result of his death, the ship of the state began to founder. The reactionaries openly turned against the Republic. The relations between Germany and France also got strained. However, the economic depression hit the German Republic the hardest. The economic blizzard which had started in the United States in October 1929 also hit Germany whose economy and prosperity during 1924-29 was largely based on foreign loans. When that source dried up and the loans already made were called in, Germany started cracking under the crushing weight of contracting trade and production, fall in prices and wages, closing of factories and business, unemployment and bankruptcy and the forced sale of property and farms. Many Germans got frightened and they withdrew their deposits either to hoard them or invest them in, other countries where they could be more safe. The result was that a large number of banks had to close their shutters. The lack of working capital forced industry to curtail its output. The number of the unemployed rose from 1,320,000 in September 1929 to 3,000,000 in September 1930, 4,350,000 in September 1931, 5,102,000 in September 1932 and 6,000,000 in February 1933. There were millions standing frustrated and forlorn in the street corners of every industrial centre in Germany, without food, fuel and clothes. There were lacs of young boys and girls leaving schools with no prospects of a job. There were thousands of clerks shopkeepers, small businessmen, young lawyers and doctors and pensioners who were threatened with the loss of their savings and their respectability. There was no provision for unemployment insurance. In the towns and villages, shopkeepers and white collared classes, business and agriculture suffered alike. Unable to get fair return for the work put into raising crops or stock, the peasants were hard-pressed to pay the interest on mortgages and loans or be turned out of their homes. Wages were reduced by 17% in 1931 and still more in 1932. As the purchasing power of the workers went down, home markets collapsed. The amount of taxes realised also fell. The number of bankruptcies rose. There were more than 17,000 bankruptcies in 1931 and the number was still higher in 1932. Nothing tilted against the Weimar Republic so much and nothing shifted the weight of advantage to the side of Hitler so much as the Great Depression of 1929. Uniforms became more prominent in the streets—the Stahlhelm (Steel helmets), the Reichshanner, the Free Corps, the Red Front and the S.A. (Sturmabteilung—storm troopers) took the Republic towards extinction. The world was astounded and perturbed when in the elections of 1930 the Nazis increased their votes from 810,000 to 6,401,000.

The tragedy could have been averted if there had been a stable party system and an honest, scrupulous and non-political army in Germany. In the elections of 1930, ten parties polled more than a million votes each. That ruled out the possibility of a majority Government. There were unscrupulous and manoeuvring leaders wedded to sectional economic interests. There were coalition cabinets moving like jigsaw puzzles and ensuring weak, corrupt and inefficient governments. President Hindenburg was aging fast and virtually losing all political judgment and failing to bring the antagonistic political elements to a common bond of agreement in national distress. There was a complete disruption of bourgeois values which could have controlled the elemental national resurgence roused by Hitler's demagogic appeal to nationalist sentiments. In defeat, the Germans could not smile through their tears. National disasters made them morbid. From 13 February 1919 to 28 January 1933, 19 Ministries were formed and since 28 June 1928 five Chancellors had come and gone.

It is pointed out that a creeping paralysis and decay began to affect the parties most intimately associated with the Weimar Republic. First the Democrats started losing votes. In the election of 1928, this party made a poor showing from which it never recovered. Then the Centre Party lost its democratic moorings. Since the death of Erzberger, it had lacked decisive leadership and it gradually drifted into a situation of ideological confusion. As a Catholic Party, it appealed to all types of voters from socialist-minded trade unionists to conservative land-owners and businessmen. Its central situation in the ideological spectrum made it an indispensable partner in all coalitions, whether of the Right or of the Left. No Government ever lacked Centre Ministers and the Centre provided the Chancellor more frequently than any other party. However, this political bigamy was bad for the Centre. No clear policy line was possible for the Centre when the same Ministers served first in a Government of the Right and then in one of the Left. The confusion was further compounded when the Centre was simultaneously participating in a Right coalition for the Reich and a Left coalition for Prussia. If such was the condition of the Centre, the other great party on which the regime rested, Social Democrats, was succumbing to weariness and ossification. The Social Democrats and the trade unionists were hard hit by the inflation of 1923. In subsequent years, they reknit their cadres and tried to carry on as before. But the life seemed to have gone out of them. Both the party and the unions found their leadership aging and becoming more bureaucratized and the young people less and less interested in their activities. In the election of 1928, the Social Democrats made a surprising recovery but they did not know how to devise and carry out an imaginative social programme. The same election produced other and more threatening symptoms of approaching change. Two million voters cast their ballots for small parties and independent candidates that appealed to discontents and resentments of all sorts, more particularly of the peasantry. Still worse, the Nationalists came under new leadership. The industrialist and super-propagandist Alfred Hugenberg became the head of this party. He entered into an alliance with Hitler.

By 1928, the forces of nationalism and reaction began to come to life again. Only on the surface and in great cities Germany had changed. However, throughout the countryside, the old imperial mentality lingered on. With the passage of time, the superficiality and incompleteness of the Revolution of 1918 became apparent. What the builders of German democracy had left undone, began to plague them. They had not broken up the great estates of the Prussian nobility. They had not purged the judiciary and the civil service. They had not altered the composition and prestige of the officers' corps. In all these places, reaction remained entrenched. Land-owners concealed the veterans of extremist bands as farm workers. Judges acquitted nationalist terrorists and gave them ridiculously short sentences. The civil servants sabotaged the reforming measures of the Republic. By the restrictions imposed in the Treaty of Versailles, the German army became still more aristocratic and tight-knit. It pursued with impunity its goal of clandestine rearmament. It reported not to the Chancellor but to President Hindenburg himself who cast a cloak of respectability over its illicit activities.

As the economic situation began to worsen in Germany, criticism of the German Republic also increased. In the minds of many Nationalists, the Weimar Republic and the Treaty of Versailles were almost interchangeable. The same Assembly which drafted the Weimar Constitution also accepted the humiliation of the Treaty of Versailles. The two documents betrayed the irremediable taint of anti-patriotism. The reconciliation of 1925-1928 was transitory and largely unreal. The irreconcilables in Germany never actually abandoned their nostalgia for the past glory of Germany before 1914.

Criticism of the Republic came from all directions. The lower middle classes had no love for the German Republic which was held responsible for the inflation of 1923 which brought about their ruin. The workers also joined the ranks of the critics of the Republic. The number of the unemployed persons began to mount and many of them blamed the republican system of government for the existing conditions in Germany. The result was that all discontented persons listened to the speeches and writings of those who were trying to overthrow the Republic in Germany. Many Germans joined the Communist Party. Many more joined the National Socialists whose leader was Hitler. There was a trend towards extremism. That was clear from the general election of September 1930. On the previous occasion, the Communists had got 3.25 millions of votes. Their number increased to 4.5 millions in 1930. In 1928, only 12 Nazis were elected to the Reichstag which had more than 600 members. However, in 1930, the Nazis won 107 seats. The result was that only the Moderate Socialists continued to support the German Republic.

There were other factors also which weakened the foundations of the German Republic. The Weimar Constitution contained Article 48 which gave the President of Germany the right to issue emergency legislation. That power enabled him to suspend many Articles of the Constitution itself. The fathers of the Weimar Constitution intended the use of Article 48 only on rare occasions at the time of a real emergency such as an armed revolt. However, Dr. Bruning, the new Chancellor of Germany, began to use it as a regular instrument of government. After the election of 1930, the National Socialists and the Nationalists had about 150 Deputies in the Reichstag. The Marxists had 220 members. Chancellor Bruning had the support of about 200 members only. The result was that his government was a minority government. It did not enjoy the confidence of a majority in the Reichstag. As he had no majority in the legislature, he was forced to rule by means of decrees issued by the President. The Reichstag did not figure in the matter of making laws. The continuance of the Government of Bruning depended upon the discretion of the President of Germany. That development was not congenial for the long life of the German Republic.

In 1932, there was an election for President of Germany and Hitler was one of the candidates. President Hindenburg secured about 19 million votes against 13 million secured by Hitler. In May 1932, Chancellor Bruning was dismissed by President Hindenburg. After his dismissal, Franz von Papen, a reactionary, was summoned by President Hindenburg to form the Ministry. He had no support in the Reichstag. Even the dissolution of the Reichstag and a new election failed to improve his position. Hindenburg offered Hitler a post in the cabinet of von Papen but he refused. General Schleicher was appointed the Chancellor. He tried to check the Nazis but failed. At that time, Hitler entered into a coalition with von Papen who convinced Hindenburg that the appointment of Hitler as Chancellor was the only solution to the political crisis facing the country. Hindenburg did not accept the advice for many months but ultimately appointed Hitler as the Chancellor of Germany on 30 January 1933.

The question has been asked why Hindenburg who knew full well that the Nazis were the sworn enemies of the Republic, invited them to form the government. One View is that his action was a treachery to the Republic. He was devoid of any sympathy for republicanism and he was always on look out for an opportunity to destroy it. Another view is that his appointment of Hitler was not a rational act. It was sheer senility. He was already 85 years of age. His mind was so clouded that he did not know the import of the decree he was signing. One of the jokes of contemporary Germany relates that Hindenburg's secretary had to discard promptly miscellaneous scraps of papers, including sandwich wrappers, lest the venerable gentleman may not put his signatures on them. Others advance the theory that Hindenburg was tricked into signing the decree. A plausible explanation is that President Hindenburg was sick of having on his hands a succession of coalition governments who were always asking for the issuing of decrees by him and he appointed Hitler as Chancellor as his party was the largest single party in the Reichstag and he could be expected to have an absolute majority in the near future. It was on the initiative of Hitler himself that fresh elections were held in March 1933 and he won an absolute majority in the Reichstag. Between 5 March and 12 March 1933, the transfer of power was effected. Between 12 March and 7 April 1933, the leaders, parties and institutions of republican Germany were put to rout or ruin. By a vote of 441 to 94, the Reichstag passed on 22 March 1933 the Enabling Act by which it practically signed away the Weimar Constitution and then adjourned indefinitely. Hitler gave a new name to Germany, the Third Reich.

Field Marshal Hindenburg was a good President still his extreme old age rendered him helpless in the hands of his advisers. Like most soldiers, he was a good judge of men, but a bad judge of political tendencies. His position as President under the Weimar Constitution was a difficult one and it was hard to observe the Constitution and yet maintain efficiency and order. His very presence as President ensured continuity of government in Germany. "He remained sphinx-like and impassive while a succession of embarrassed and transient Ministries passed like shadows before him."

Causes of Downfall of Weimar Republic

The downfall of the Weimar Republic was due to many reasons. It "had a hard hoe to row" in foreign and internal affairs. From the very beginning, the Republic had to face tremendous difficulties.

The Revolution of 1918 was a superficial one. It is true that the German Emperor and 25 princelings of Germany were driven out, but the bureaucratic structure of the state and the socio-economic base of the Republic remained the same. The democratic form of government established through the Weimar Constitution was a super-imposition with which Germany was not familiar. German unification itself was the work of the authoritarian statesman Bismarck and the same tradition was continued even after his fall in 1890. When a democratic form of government was established in Germany in 1919, the people of Germany were not familiar with a democratic tradition and hence the Weimar Republic had to work in an hostile atmosphere and surroundings and no wonder it failed.

From the very outset, the Weimar Republic was associated in the minds of the people of Germany with the hated Treaty of Versailles. The stringent and harsh terms of the Treaty of Versailles, the imposition of the War guilt clause and the humiliations associated with it were criticised by the enemies of the Weimar Republic which was held responsible for accepting those terms. The Social Democrats and Republicans were branded as betrayers of German cause and were held responsible for the defeat and degradation of Germany. The militarists and malcontents, the Nazis and Junkers sought to discredit the Democrats as the architects of Germany's misfortune in the World War I. The Reichswehr undermined the authority of the Weimar Republic. Disbanded soldiers, hungry, unemployed and disillusioned youth and discontented industrialists and businessmen lost confidence in the high-sounding phrases used by the Parliamentarians. The opportunists and supporters of the Nazi Party took advantages of the smouldering fire of discontent to create the myth that Germany's salvation lay in the abolition of the Weimar Constitution and establishment of a strong government. The working of the democratic system of government in Germany left much to be desired. Between 1919 and 1933, as many as 19 Ministries rose and fell. The result was that parliamentary system did not inspire confidence among the majority of the people of Germany who prayed for the return of the good old times and the rise of a saviour which they found in Hitler.

Some writers do not agree with this view. They point out that the rise of Hitler was not due to the terms of the Treaty of Versailles. There was a lapse of fourteen years between the Treaty of Versailles in June 1919 and the coming to power of Hitler in January 1933. Immediately after the World War, the Nazi revolution did not assume any concrete shape. The Nazi Party came to power ten years after the recovery of Germany's lost prestige as is evident from the entry of Germany into the League of Nations and the signing of the Locarno Pact. By 1930, the Allied troops were withdrawn from different parts of Germany. In 1931, the reparation problem of Germany came to an end. In 1932, the equality of Germany with other states in respect of armaments was recognised. Hence it is clear that the Nazi Party captured power when Germany had freed herself from the fetters of the Treaty of Versailles. Hence, the Treaty of Versailles may be said to be the partial cause of the success of the Nazi Party. On the pretext of the Treaty of Versailles, the Nazis branded themselves as patriots and each of the German governments as traitors.

The crisis in confidence in the Weimar Republic was also psychological and the National Socialists took full advantage of it. This psychological factor was strengthened by the attitude taken up by the Allies towards Germany. The French occupation of the Ruhr and the opposition that Germany faced on the question of her admission to a permanent seat in the Council of the League of Nations were few among many other developments in the international field which hurt German feeling and pride. The men of Weimar discarded old German symbols and heroes. Many in Germany including young war veterans, University students, conservative peasants and aristocrats yearned for the good old days of pomp and glory of colour and triumph. The result was a loss of credit for the Republic. The most significant book produced during those years was Spengler's "The Decline of the West". In that book, he appealed to the German intellectuals already full of Schopenhauer, Nietzsche and Wagner and to German youth in revolt against the reason of mechanisation, technology and science and to Europeans everywhere. He presented a pessimistic future for the West, but prophecised with confidence a revival of the West by Caesarism. A pessimistic atmosphere was created by Egon Fridell in "Cultural History of Modern Europe", by Count Hermann Keyserling in "Troubled Diary of a Philosopher" and by Erich Maria Remarque in "All Quiet on the Western Front". Increasingly, the German people felt the need of a strong man who could salvage Germany from the predicament in which she found herself in the post-Versailles period due to the bungling of her democratic statesmen.

Hitler came to power not by using force but by using constitutional means. He banked upon the desire of the German people to secure for themselves a place in the Sun. The failure of the Weimar Republic to restore the prestige of Germany was one of the chief causes of its downfall. Hitler merely voiced that desire. The anti-semetic policy of the Nazis also found easy response among the Junkers, militarists and industrialists of Germany. The Nazi theory of race-superiority appealed to the German mind.

The leaders of the German Republic did not exert themselves to nip the Nazi Movement in the bud. They were not willing to shed blood. They were men without faith who could not inspire or organise. They were theorists, elderly arm-chair doctrinaires who allowed power to slip from their hands into those of the Nazis. It has rightly been said that Germany under them was a Republic without republicans. Although they had in their hands all the instruments of popular propaganda such as the radio, the press and the platform, they did not make use of them to educate the people to have faith in democracy and in Republic. The workers of Germany did not rise in support of the Republic as they were themselves suffering from acute unemployment. From the very beginning, the German Republic worked under many handicaps. By accepting the Treaty of Versailles, the republican leaders were condemned as the "authors" of the national humiliation and thus lost all popular respect and sympathy. The Allied Powers were also responsible for the fall of the German Republic as they treated the German Republic in a very shabby manner. They imposed very harsh terms on defeated Germany. They occupied the Ruhr which humiliated the Germans. They made the German Republic appear in the eyes of the German masses as totally unworthy of being vested with ruling power. The Nazis took full advantage of the existing circumstances. They joined the masses in condemning the German Republic and promised everything to everybody. They used all the symbols of mass appeal—the Swastika badge, the uniform of brown and black shirts, the acclamation (Heil Hitler) and the salute. Millions of Germans secretly sympathised with the campaign of violence and terrorism resorted to by the Nazis. Theirs was the only programme which seemed to offer a solution to the many problems facing Germany. The Nazis successfully befooled the people of Germany in believing that they alone were their saviours. The big land-owners and capitalists contributed huge funds to the Nazi Party. The middle classes ranged themselves behind the Swastika banner. The people of Germany who worshipped power and authority, were ready and willing to be ruled by a party which professed to improve the intolerable living conditions in which the people of republican Germany were at that time. The Weimar Constitution was worked by old civilians who were authoritarian in spirit and gave only lip-deep loyalty to the Republic. The failure of the workers of Germany against the Nazis is attributed to a fatal split in their ranks of which the Soviet Union was responsible. The Communist Party of Germany undermined the solidarity of the working classes. It seduced younger members and sowed dissensions between the leaders and their followers. When one German Communist leader realised the needs of the situation in Germany, he was replaced by Stalin by another who was more orthodox in Communist theories. The result was that the workers failed to do anything to save the German Republic.

The character of Hitler himself helped him to come to power. He possessed great resourcefulness. He was a great orator who could control and influence audiences of millions of people. His technique of propaganda helped him to carry the audience with him. He thundered. He asked for blood. He infused politics with religious fervour. He was a fanatic in his views who was able to hypnotise all those who came to hear his speeches. The result was that the number of his followers began to rise and ultimately he became Chancellor.

The character of the people of Germany also helped Hitler. Most of the people of Germany cared more for that party which could give them security and glory rather than freedom as such. They were sick of the treachery and cowardice of the republican politicians. They wanted a strong man who could take them out of the mess created by the republican politicians.

The declining fervour of Protestantism in Germany indirectly led to the rise of Hitler. Having lost their enthusiasm in religion, they were in search of some other object of devotion. The Republic in Germany was not able to win over their devotion and they found their object in the national socialism of Hitler. That added to the strength of Hitler's party and his followers.

Hitler was most vocal about the injustice of the Treaty of Versailles. He denounced its provisions in the strongest possible terms. The more he did so, the greater became his popularity with the people who wanted somebody who could interpret their inner feelings to the world. They found in Hitler the man they wanted and that helped him to come to power.

Hitler gave to the Germans a high-sounding programme of 25 Points which was a catalogue of promises and promised something to every group of the German nation. He promised protection of property from the Communists. He promised protection to labourers against their exploitation. He promised protection to the consumers against producers. He promised protection to small businessmen against corporations. As he promised something to everybody, he was able to secure an overwhelming support from the Germans.

Another cause of failure of the German Republic was that the army and the civil service were still supreme. Although the social superiority of the aristocracy, the army and the officials was no longer aggressively proclaimed and there was less "ceremonious bowing and heel-clicking", Germany never experienced that uprising of a great democratic majority which was the solid guarantee of the survival of democracy. During the terms of the successive governments from 1919 to 1933, the army was slowly laying fresh foundation of military power. The Free Corps and the Reichswehr became a real power against which the civil authorities were helpless. "There is indeed little doubt that the army was almost as responsible for the second counter-revolution under Hitler as it was for the first counterrevolution under Noske fourteen years earlier". Side by side with the army stood intact the structure of the bureaucracy, authoritative and authoritarian in temper, having utter contempt for democratic processes and pining for the old Prussian absolutist regime. Thus, the rule of law always remained in Germany spasmodic and precarious.

The German tradition facilitated the rise of Hitler and fall of the Republic.

Achievements of the Weimar Republic

It is true that the Weimar Republic failed but it bridged the years between the Hohenzollerns and Nazis. Although the Republic was threatened since its inception both by the extreme Right and the extreme Left, it had some outstanding achievements to its credit. With the introduction of the Dawes Plan in 1924, there came an unprecedented prosperity in Germany. Industrial production crossed the pre-War figures. American investors lent huge amounts of foreign money to Germany. The re-establishment of the currency and the enormous foreign sale of the paper money added about 2000 million dollars to the real wealth of Germany. The industrial and business life of Germany was rationalized and that tended to standardize products and materials and introduce scientific management and planning. The formation of vertical trusts and combines prevented ruinous competition. The establishment of the branches of foreign firms in Germany such as the General Motors, Ford, Chrysler and Eastman Kodak brought foreign capital, provided employment to German labour and utilised German raw materials.

On 20 March 1921, a plebiscite was held in Upper Silesia which resulted in a majority voting for Germany which claimed the whole of Upper Silesia. The matter was referred to the League of Nations which, in its Award of 20 October divided the province, giving two-thirds of the area to Germany but leaving the coal mines, the principal industrial areas and a sizeable German minority on the Polish side.

On 16 April 1922, Germany signed a treaty of friendship with the Soviet Union at Rapallo under which both sides established normal diplomatic relations with each other, waived their respective reparation claims and agreed to promote mutual trade. The Soviet Union undertook to allow German officers and units to acquire experience with the Red Army and to provide opportunities for experiments in forbidden weapons. This treaty irritated the West, particularly France which decided to have its revenge and occupied the Ruhr in January 1923.

With the adoption of the Dawes Plan, the Republic started sailing smoothly. By 1925, order was restored, currency was stabilised and reparation problem was somewhat settled. The Ruhr was evacuated. In 1925, the Weimar Republic signed the Locarno treaty. The relations with France improved. Germany entered the League of Nations on 8 September 1926 as a permanent member of the Council on the understanding that her relations with the Soviet Union would not be affected.

In April 1926, Germany signed the Treaty of Berlin with the Soviet Union. At the end of January 1927, the Allied Military Control Commission was withdrawn. In 1928, Germany signed the Pact of Paris on equal terms with other powers. On 7 June 1929, the Young Committee report was made public which substantially reduced reparation claims of the Allies and removed all international controls from German economy. At the Hague Conference in August 1929, Stresemann persuaded the French to agree that the withdrawal of the occupying forces should begin in September 1929, five years ahead of the time and be completed by the end of June 1930. On 13 March 1930, the Young Plan laws were passed by the German Government, but by that time Germany was fully encircled in the whirlpool of the Great Depression.

SUGGESTED READINGS

Abel, T.: **Why Hitler Came into Power,** 1938.

Allen, W.S.: **The Nazi Seizure of Power: Experience of a Single German Town,** 1920-1935, 1965.

Angell, J. W.: **The Recovery of Germany.**

Angress, W.T.: **Stillborn Revolution: The Communist Bid for Power in Germany,** 1921-1923, 1963.

Bretton, H.L.: **Stresemann and the Revision of the Versailles Theaty,** 1955.

Bruck, W.F.: **Social and Economic History of Germany from William II to Hitler, 1888-1938: A Comparative Study,** 1938.

Carsten, F.L.: **The Reichswehr and Politics,** 1918-1933, 1966.

Clark, R.T.: **The Fall of the German Republic,** 1935.

Daniels, H.G.: **The Rise of the German Republic,** 1928.

Dorpalen, A.: **Hindenburg and the Weimar Republic,** 1964.

Eyck, E.: **History of the Weimar Republic,** 2 Vols.

Fraser, L.: **Germany between two Wars.**

Fraser, C.M.: **British Policy on War Debts and Reparations.**

Fridell, Egon: **Cultural History of Modern Europe.**

Gatzke, H.: **Stresemann and the Rearmament of Germany,** 1954.

Gooch, G.P.: **Germany,** 1925.

Gordon, H.J.: **The Reichswehr and the German Republic, 1919-1926,** 1957.

Halperin : **Germany Tried Democracy,** 1946.

Heiden, K.: **Hitler,** 1936.

Hitler, A.: **Mein Kampf,** 1939.

Holborn, H.: **History of Modern Germany,** 1947.

Hunt, R.N.: **German Social Democracy, 1918-1933,** 1964.

Kaufmann, W.: **Monarchism in the Weimar Republic,** 1953.

Keyserling, Count Hermann : **Troubled Diary of a Philosopher.**

Kraus, H.: **Germany in Transition,** 1924.

Kuczynski, R.R. : **American Loans to Germany,** 1927.

Lipson, E.: **Europe (1914-1939).**

Luehr, E.: **The New German Republic,** 1929.

Lutz, R.H. : **The German Revolution, 1918-1919,** 1922.

Manthey-Zorn : **Germany in Travail,** 1922.

Moore, W.G.: **France and Germany,** 1932.

Nicholls, A.J.: **Weimar and the Rise of Hitler,** 1968.

Olden, R.: **Stresemann,** 1930.

Padover, S.K.: **Experiment in Germany,** 1946.

Remarque, Erich Maria : **All Quiet on the Western Front.**

Ryder, A.J.: **The German Revolution of 1918,** 1967.

Schuman, F.L.: **Germany Since 1918-19.**

Shot well, J.T.: **What Germany Forgot.**

Spengler, Oswald: **Decline of the West.**

Stamp, J.C. : **The Financial Aftermath of the War.**

Stresemann, G.: **Essays and Speeches on Various Subjects,** 1930.

Thompson, David: **Europe Since Napoleon.**

Turner, H.A.: **Stresemann and the Politics of the Weimar Republic,** 1963.

Vallet, N.: **Stresemann,** 1931.

RULERS OF EUROPEAN STATES (1789-1945)

Great Britain

1760-1820	:	Reign of George III.
1820-30	:	Reign of George IV.
1830-37	:	Reign of William IV.
1837-1901	:	Reign of Queen Victoria.
1901-1910	:	Reign of Edward VII.
1910-36	:	Reign of George V.
1936	:	Reign of Edward VIII.
1936-52	:	Reign of George VI.
1952	:	Reign of Queen Elizabeth II.

France

1774-92	:	Reign of Louis XVI.
1792-99	:	The First French Republic.
1799-1804	:	The Consulate.
1804-14	:	Napoleon Bonaparte as Emperor of France.
1814-24	:	Reign of Louis VIII.
1824-30	:	Reign of Charles X.
1830-48	:	Reign of Louis Philippe.
1848-52	:	The Second French Republic.
1852-70	:	Napoleon as Emperor of France.
1870-1940	:	The Third French Republic.
1940-45	:	The Vichy Government under Marshal Petain.
1945	:	The Fourth French Republic.

Prussia and the German Empire

1740-86	:	Frederick, the Great, Ruler of Prussia.
1786-97	:	Reign of Frederick William II.
1797-1840	:	Reign of Frederick William III.
1840-61	:	Reign of Fredericy William IV.
1861-70	:	William I as King of Prussia.
1871-88	:	William I as Emperor of Germany.
1888	:	Reign of Frederick III.
1888-1918	:	Reign of Emperor William II.
1918-34	:	The Weimar Republic.
1919-25	:	Frederick Elbert as President of the German Republic.
1925-34	:	Hindenburg as President of the German Republic.
1934-45	:	Dictatorship of Adolf Hitler.

Russia

1762-96	:	Reign of Catherine, the Great.
1796-1801	:	Reign of Paul I.

1801-25 : Reign of Alexander I.
1825-55 : Reign of Nicholas I.
1855-81 : Reign of Alexander II. He was assassinated.
1881-94 : Reign of Alexander III.
1894-1917 : Nicholas II. He was murdered.
1917-24 : Lenin as Dictator of Russia.
1924-53 : Stalin as Dictator of Russia.

Austria-Hungary

1780-90 : Reign of Joseph II.
1790-92 : Reign of Leopold II.
1792-1835 : Reign of Francis II.
1835-48 : Reign of Ferdinand I.
1848-1916 : Reign of Francis Joseph, Emperor of Austria-Hungary.
1916-18 : Reign of Charles I.
1938-45 : Annexation of Austria by Germany under Hitler.
1945 : Republic of Austria.

Turkey

1789-1807 : Reign of Selim III.
1807-8 : Reign of Mastapha IV.
1808-39 : Reign of Mahmud II.
1839-61 : Reign of Abdul Majid.
1861-76 : Reign of Abdul Aziz.
1876-1909 : Reign of Abdul Hamid II.
1909-18 : Reign of Muhammed V.
1918-22 : Reign of Muhammed VI.
1923-38 : Kamel Ataturk as President of the Turkish Republic.
1938-50 : General Ismet Inonu as President of the Turkish Republic.

Sardinia and Italy

1773-96 : Victor Amadeous III as King of Sardinia.
1796-1802 : Charles Emmanuel IV as Ring of Sardinia.
1802-21 : Victor Emmanuel I as King of Sardinia.
1821-31 : Charles Felix as King of Sardinia.
1831-49 : Charles Albert as King of Sardinia.
1849-61 : Victor Emmanuel II as King of Sardinia.
1861-78 : Victor Emmanuel as King of Italy.
1878-1900 : Humbert I as King of Italy.
1900-1946 : Victor Emmanuel III was King of Italy but he abdicated in 1946.
1922-43 : Dictatorship of Mussolini.

Spain

1788-1808 : Reign of Charles IV.
1808-14 : Rule of Joseph Bonaparte.
1814-33 : Reign of Ferdinand VII.
1833-68 : Reign of Isabella II.
1868-70 : Provisional Government in Spain.
1870-73 : Reign of Amadeo I.
1873-74 : Republic in Spain.

1874-85 : Reign of Alfonso XII.
1885-86 : Reign of Queen Maria.
1886-1931 : Reign of Alfonso VIII.
1931-39 : Republic of Spain.
1931-36 : Niceto Zamora as President of Spanish Republic.
1936-39 : Manuel Azana as President of Spanish Republic.
1939-76 : General Franco as Dictator of Spain.

Portugal

1777-99 : Maria I as Ruler of Portugal.
1799-1816 : Prince John as Regent.
1816-26 : Rule of John.
1826 : Abdication of Pedro IV.
1826-28 : Rule of Maria II.
1828-33 : Rule of Don Miguel.
1838-53 : Rule of Maria II.
1853-61 : Rule of Pedro V.
1861-89 : Rule of Louis I.
1889-1908 : Rule of Carlos I.
1908-10 : Rule of Manuel II.
1910 : Republic of Portugal.

Serbia

1842-58 : Rule of Prince Alexander.
1858-60 : Rule of Milosh.
1860-68 : Rule of Michael.
1868-89 : Rule of Milan.
1889-1903 : Rule of Alexander who was murdered in 1903.
1903-21 : Rule of Peter I.
1921-34 : Rule of Alexander I.
1934-46 : Rule of Peter II.

CHRONOLOGICAL TABLE

1740-86	Reign of Frederick, the Great, of Prussia.
1740-80	Reign of Maria Theresa.
1762-96	Reign of Catherine, the Great, of Russia.
1765	Joseph II became Holy Roman Emperor.
1768	War started between Russia and Turkey.
1769	Birth of Napoleon on 15 August.
1772	First Partition of Poland.
1774-93	Reign of Louis XVI.
1774-6	Turgot as Controller of Finance of France.
1774	Treaty of Kutchuk-Kainardji between Russia and Turkey.
1776-81	Necker as Controller of Finance of France.
1780	Joseph II inherited the territories of Austria-Hungary on the death of his mother, Maria Theresa.
1783	Pitt, the Younger, became Prime Minister of England in December.
1787	Louis XVI summoned Assembly of the Notables.
1788	Louis XVI decided in July to summon the Estates-General.
1789	The French Revolution started.
	The Estates-General summoned on 5 May after the lapse of 175 years.
	The Third Estate of Estates-General declared itself as National Assembly on 17 June.
	Tennis Court Oath taken by members of National Assembly on 20 June.
	Louis XVI ordered on 27 June that all the three Estates would sit as one body.
	Necker and his colleagues dismissed on 11 July.
	Fall of the Bastille on 14 July.
	Special Privileges abolished on 4 August by National Assembly.
	Declaration of the Rights of Man issued.
	Church property confiscated in France in November.
1790	Leopold II ascended the throne of Austria-Hungary.
	Monasteries and other religious communities suppressed in February.
	Religious toleration proclaimed in April.
	The Civil Constitution of the Clergy enacted in July.
	A decree passed by which all Catholic clergymen were required to take oath of allegiance to the Civil Constitution.
1791	Death of Mirabeau.
	Flight of Louis XVI from France in June.
	The National Assembly finished its work on 30 September and was dissolved.
1791-92	Legislative Assembly.
	France gave an ultimatum to Austria and war declared in April.
	Parisian mob attacked residence of Louis XVI on 20 June.
	Revolt in Paris in August.
	Louis XVI suspended on 10 August.
	Allies defeated in the battle of Valmy on 20 September.
	Massacres of September.

1792-5	The National Convention.
	National Convention met on 21 September.
1793-4	Reign of Terror in France.
1793	Second Partition of Poland.
	Louis XVI guillotined on 21 January.
	Compulsory levy ordered in February.
	Revolutionary Tribunal set up on 9 March.
	The Girondists attacked Marat in April.
	The First Coalition consisting of England, Prussia, Russia, Austria, Spain, Holland and Sardinia formed and continued up to 1797.
	Every Frenchman between ages of 18 and 25 ordered in August to render military service.
	Marie Antoinette executed in October.
	Madame Roland executed on 10 November.
	"Religion of Reason" inaugurated in November.
	Napoleon captured Toulon in December.
1794	Death of Danton in April.
	Fall of Robespierre on 28 July.
1795-99	The Directory.
1795	Treaty of Basle by which Prussia and Spain left the First Coalition.
1796-1801	Reign of Czar. Paul I.
1796-7	Italian Campaign of Napoleon lasted from April 1796 to April 1797.
1796	The Babeuf Plot.
	Battle of Areola fought from 15 to 17 November.
1797-1840	Reign of Frederick William II of Prussia.
1797	Napoleon inflicted a crushing defeat upon the Austrians on 13-14 January.
	Napoleon appointed General of the army which was to attack England.
	Battle of Cape St. Vincent in which the Spanish fleet was defeated.
	Treaty of Campo Formio signed on 17 October.
1798	Battle of the Nile in which Nelson defeated Napoleon.
	The Second Coalition consisting of England, Russia, Austria.
	Turkey and Naples formed and continued up to 1801.
1799	Bonaparte handed over Island of Mallta to Russia.
	Napoleon over-threw the Directory on 9 November.
	Constitution of France prepared in December.
	Napoleon became First Consul and continued as such up to 1804.
1800	Napoleon appointed a Committee in August to draw up a Civil Code.
	Battle of Marengo.
	Armed Neutrality consisting of Russia, Prussia, Sweden and Denmark created against England.
1801-25	Reign of Alexander I.
1801	Czar Paul-I suggested to Napoleon to attack England.
	Treaty of Luneville.
1802	Concordat concluded in August and it governed relations between Church and State in France for 103 years.
	Legion of Honour created.
	Peace of Amiens made between England and France.
1803	Napoleon sold Louisiana to the United States.
	War broke out again between England and France.

1804	Napoleon became Emperor.
	Pope came to Paris on 2 December to invest Napoleon with the sword and sceptre of the Empire.
1805	The Third Coalition consisting of Prussia, Austria, Sweden, and England formed.
	Battle of Trafalgar in which Nelson defeated the French fleet. Defeat of Austria in the battle of Ulm.
	Defeat of Russia and Austria in the battle of Austerlitz in December.
1806	Treaty of Pressburg.
	Battle of Jena in which Prussia was defeated by Napoleon.
	Continental System started.
	Berlin Decree issued by Napoleon.
	Holy Roman Empire came to an end on 6 August.
1807	Battle of Friedland in which Czar was defeated.
	Treaty of Tilsit between Napoleon and Czar.
	Warsaw Decree issued.
	Milan Decree issued.
	Copenhagen bombarded and Danish fleet destroyed.
	Rome occupied and Papal States became French territory.
	Code of Criminal Procedure issued.
	Metternich as Chancellor of Austria.
	Battle of Talavera in Spain.
	Rome added to the French Empire in May.
	Pope ex-communicated Napoleon in June.
	Pope arrested and put in prison.
	Napoleon appointed Ecclesiastical Commission for France in November.
1810	Ecclesiastical Commission superseded in January.
	Penal Code issued.
	Fontainebleau Decree issued.
1812-22	Castlereagh.
1812	Napoleon's invasion of Russia.
	Pope brought to France in June.
1813	Pope made a new Concordat with Napoleon in January.
	The Fourth Coalition.
	Battle of Vittoria in Spain.
1814-24	Reign of Louis XVIII of France.
1814	Pope released by Napoleon.
	Overthrow of Napoleon after the Battle of the Nations.
	Wellington defeated the French at Toulouse.
	Treaty of Chaumont entered into between Great Britain, Russia, Prussia and Austria in March.
	Louis XVIII issued a Liberal Charter on 4 June 1814.
	The Hetairia Philike society formed by the Greeks.
1815	Birth of Bismarck on 1 April.
	Wellington defeated Napoleon in the battle of Waterloo.
	The Vienna Settlement.
	The Holy Alliance.
	Quadruple Alliance made in November between Great Britain, Austria, Prussia and Russia.

1815	The Battle of Waterloo.
	Congress of Vienna and Vinenna Settlement.
	The Quadruple Alliance.
	The Holy Alliance.
	German Confederation set up.
1815-30	Union of Holland and Belgium.
1815-48	The Metternich System.
1817	Spain sold Florida to the United States.
1818	Congress of Aix-la-Chapelle.
	Allied army of Occupation withdrawn from French soil.
	Congress of Axis-la-Chapelle.
	Zollverein or the Customs Union set up by Prussia.
1819	The Carlsbad Decrees enacted in Germany.
	Kotzebue, a Russian spy in Germany, assassinated by Karl Sand.
1820	Murder of Due de Berry in February by Louvel.
	Revolt in Spain.
	Revolt in Naples and request for help.
	Congress of Troppau.
	Czar Alexander came under the influence and control of Metternich.
1820-21	Ministry of Richelieu in France.
1821	Revolt in Piedmont in March.
	Congress of Laibach.
	Austria suppressed revolts in Naples and Piedmont.
	The Greeks revolted under Alexander Ypsilanti.
1821-27	Ministry of Villele in France.
1822-27	George Canning.
1822	Congress of Verona.
	Censorship of press made more rigorous in France.
1823	French troops sent to Spain to restore Bourbons to absolute power.
	Canning appointed Consuls to Spanish Colonies for protection of British Trade.
	President Monroe enunciated Monroe Doctrine in December.
1824-30	Reign of Charles X.
1824	Ibrahim, son of Mehmet Ali of Egypt, conquered and destroyed Crete.
1825-55	Reign of Czar Nicholas I.
1825	Revolt of the Liberals of Russia in December.
	Ibrahim landed in Morea and destroyed everything.
	Law passed in France to indemnity emigres for loss of their lands during French Revolution.
1826	King of Portugal died.
	Agreement between Great Britain and Russia in April to mediate in Greece.
1827	The National Guard disbanded in France.
	Treaty of London signed in July between Great Britain, Russia and France to intervene in Greece.
	Battle of Navarino on 20 October 1827.
1828	Russia declared war against Turkey in April.
	A Customs Union set up in the South under the leadership of Bavaria and Wurtemburg.
1828-9	Ministry of Martignac in France.
1829-30	Ministry of Poignac in France.

1829	Treaty of Adrianople.
	Peace made between Russia and Turkey in September.
	Treaty of Adrianople regarding Greece.
1830	Charles X issued four ordinances on 25 July.
	Charles X abdicated in July.
1830-48	Reign of Louis Philippe of France.
	Revolt in Belgium.
	Revolutions in France, Belgium and Poland.
1831	Organisation known as "Young Italy" started by Mazzini.
	Hesse Cassel joined the Zollverein.
1832-39	Guizot, Minister of Instruction, in France.
1832	Independence of Greece recognised.
	France sent an army to occupy Ancona.
	Ibrahim invaded Syria and advanced into Asia Minor.
1833	Treaty of Unkiar Skelessi between Russia and Turkey.
	Nicholas I entered into an alliance with Austria and Prussia for mutual defence against revolutionary movements.
1834	Bavaria joined Zollverein for 8 years.
1836	Louis Napoleon asserted his claim for the first time to the throne of France.
1839	Louis Napoleon wrote a book called "Napoleonic Ideas."
	Treaty of London recognised neutrality of Belgium.
1840-61	Reign of Frederick William IV of Prussia.
1840-48	Guizot as Chief Minister of France.
1840	Danger of war between England and France on the question of Mehmet Ali.
1842	Treaty of London.
1844	Czar Nicholas I paid a visit to London to discuss the future of Turkey in Europe.
1846	Louis Napoleon managed to escape from the fortress of Ham and reached London.
	Pius IX became Pope.
1848	Revolution broke out in Palermo in January.
	Revolutions in France, Germany, Austria and Italy.
	Expulsion of Louis Philippe.
	Republic declared in France on 26 February.
	Bitter fighting in Paris from 24 to 26 June.
	National Assembly framed a Republican Constitution for France in October.
	Louis Napoleon elected President of French Republic in December and he continued as President up to 1852.
	Demons rations in Vienna in March and Metternich ran away to England.
	Revolt in Berlin in March.
	50 German leaders met at Heidelberg on 5 March and issued invitations.
	Frankfurt Parliament met on 31 March to draft a Constitution for United Germany.
	Republic declared in Rome by Mazzini.
	Charles Albert, ruler of Piedmont, declared war against Austria in March.
	Charles Albert defeated by Austria in the battle of Custozza in July.
	Piedmont and Tuscany got Liberal Constitutions.
	Karl Marx published the Communist Manifesto.
1819	Louis Napoleon sent French troops to Rome to restore the Pope.
	Charles Albert declared war but was defeated by Austria in the battle of Novara.
	A new Constitution for the Habsburg Empire announced in March.
	Kossuth elected President of the Hungarian Republic in April.

	Venice captured by the Austrians in August.
	Frankfurt Parliament offered throne of Germany to Frederick William IV of Prussia on 28 March but he rejected the offer on 3 April.
	Nicholas I sent Russian troops to fight against the Hungarians who had revolted against Austria.
1850	Convention of Olmutz.
	German Parliament met at Erfurt in March.
	King of Prussia gave a new Constitution to his people.
1851	Louis Napoleon gave an ultimatum to the Assembly in November.
1852	Louis Napoleon promulgated a new Constitution for France on 14 January.
	Plebiscite held in France in November.
	Treaty of London by which Denmark was forbidden from in corporating Schleswig-Holstein into her territory.
1852-70	Napoleon III as Emperor.
1852-61	Cavour as Prime Minister of Sardinia and Piedmont.
1853	Treaty made between Zollverein and Austria-Hungary.
	The Danubian principalities of Moldavia and Wallachia occupied by Russia.
1854-6	The Crimean War.
1855	Sardinia joined the Crimean on 20 January on the side of France and Great Britain.
	Fall of Sebastopal in September.
1855-81	Reign of Car Alexander II.
1856	Moldavia and Wallachia given autonomy.
	Treaty of Paris which ended the Crimean war.
1858	Attempt made on life of Napoleon III by Orsini.
	Agreement between Napoleon III and Cavour at Plombieres.
1859	The Austrian Government gave an ultimatum to Sardinia in April.
	Battle of Magenta.
	Battle of Solferino.
	Armistice of Villafranca between Napoleon III and Austria.
	Treaty of Zurich.
	Bismarck appointed Prussian Ambassador to Russia.
	Revolt in Sicily.
1860	Expedition of the Thousand.
	Abraham Lincoln elected President of the United States.
	Treaty of Turin signed in March.
1861-88	Reign of William I of Germany.
1861	Abolition of Serfdom in Russia in March.
	Death of Cavour.
1862	Napoleon III sent French troops to Mexico.
	Bismarck appointed Prussian Ambassador to France.
	Bismarck became Minister President of Prussia.
	Judicial reforms carried out in Russia.
1863	Schleswig incorporated into Denmark.
	Revolt of the Poles against Russia.
	Polish Revolt suppressed.
1864	Schleswig Holstein War.
	Treaty of Vienna by which King of Denmark surrendered Schleswig and Holstein to Austria and Prussia.
	Pope Pius IX issued the "Syllabus of Errors."

	Zemstvos set up in Russia.
	Great Britain handed over the Ionian Islands to Greece.
1865	Bismarck had an interview with Napoleon III at Biarritz in October.
	Italy entered into an alliance with Prussia to fight against Austria.
1866	Austro-Prussian War.
	Battle of Sadowa and defeat of Austria by Prussia.
	Treaty of Prague between Austria and Prussia.
	Annexation of Venetia to Italy.
1867	Ausgleich or Dual Monarchy of Austria-Hungary.
	The United States purchased Alaska from Russia.
1868	Law of Nationalities attempted to solve the problem of Non-Magyar races in Hungary.
	Austria summoned a Congress of German Princes to consider reform of the German Confederation.
1869	The Suez Canal was opened for traffic.
	Proclamation of the Third Republic in France in September.
1870-1	Franco-Prussian War.
1870	Battles of Weissenburg, Spicheren, Worth, Gravelotte and Sedan.
	Surrender of Napoleon III.
	Third Republic in France proclaimed in September.
	Rome added to Italy.
	Pope Pius IX propounded doctrine of Papal Infallibility.
	Russia repudiated the Black Sea clauses of Treaty of Paris.
1871-75	National Assembly of France.
1871	Birth of the German Empire at Versailles.
	France offered to Bismarck some French colonies instead of Alsace-Lorraine.
	Treaty of Frankfurt signed in May between Germany and France.
	The Paris Commune.
	Law of Papal Guarantees passed by which the Pope was given a special status in Italy.
	Treaty of Washington signed in May and it settled the Alabama claims.
1872	Jesuits expelled from Germany.
	Compulsory military service provided for everybody in France.
1873	Law passed against Roman Catholics in May in Germany.
	Three Emperors League consisting of Austria, Russia and Germany set up by Bismarck.
	President Thiers resigned as President of the French Republic.
1874	Law passed against Roman Catholics in May in Germany.
1875-1940	The Third French Republic.
1875	All religious orders dissolved in Germany.
	Social Democratic Party founded in Germany.
	The Constitution of the Third Republic in France came into force.
	Bulgarian atrocities.
1877	President Macmahon dismissed Republican Ministry on 16 May. Russia declared war against Turkey.
1878	Treaty of San-Stefano between Russia and Turkey.
	Congress of Berlin and Treaty of Berlin.
	Turkey recognised full independence of Serbia, Rumania and Montenegro, full autonomy of Bulgaria and partial autonomy of Eastern Roumelia.
	Attempt made on life of Emperor William I.
1879	Dual Alliance between Germany and Austria-Hungary.
	High tariff walls created in Germany to protect indigenous industries.

	A German Trading Company got some privileges in the Island of Samoa.
	President Macmahon resigned on 30 January.
	Prince Alexander of Battenberg of Germany elected King of Bulgaria and he occupied that position up to 1886.
1880	French capital shifted from Versailles to Paris.
	The Boers proclaimed their independence on 16 December under the leadership of Kruger.
1881	Dreikaiserbund or the New Three Emperors League between Russia, Germany and Austria set up.
	France established her protectorate over Tunis.
	British defeat at Majuba Hill at the hands of the Boers in February.
1882	Triple Alliance between Germany, Austria-Hungary and Italy. German Colonial Union formed.
	Death of Gambetta.
	Battle of Tel-el-Kabir in September in which Arabi was defeated by General Wolseley.
1883	Law passed in Germany to insure workers against sickness.
	Rumania entered into an alliance with Austria-Hungary.
1884	Law passed in Germany to insure employees against accidents.
1884-85	Protectorate established over German commercial out-posts.
1885	Italy occupied Abyssinian port of Massowa.
1886	Laws against Roman Catholic Church repealed.
	The German Government gave subsidies to German steamers plying between Germany and her Protectorates.
	General Boulanger appointed Minister of War of France.
	Russia fortified Batum.
1887	Law passed in Germany regulating the employment of women, children, working hours, etc.
	Re-insurance Treaty between Germany and Russia signed. Italy entered into an alliance with Britain.
1888-1918	Reign of William II.
1888	Proclamations issued by William II in June.
1889	Provision made in Germany for insurance of workers against old age and invalidity.
	General Boulanger elected member of Chamber of Deputies. First visit of the German Emperor William II to Turkey.
1890	William II accepted resignation of Bismarck on 20 March.
	Treaty between Germany and Britain by which Germany recognised British Protectorate over Zanzibar and got Island of Heligoland from Britain.
1890-94	Chancellor Caprivi.
1893	Military Alliance signed between Russia and France.
	Witte appointed Minister of Finance of Russia.
1894-1917	Reign of Nicholas II.
1894	Armenian Massacres.
	Dual Alliance between France and Russia.
1894-1900	Chancellor Hohenlohe.
1894	Treaty between Great Britain and the Congo Free State by which Bahre-el-Ghazel was given to King Leopold of Belgium for life.
	Dreyfus arrested in October on charge of betraying military secrets.
1894-5	The Sino-Japanese War.
1895	Opening of Kiel Canal.
	Dreyfus publicly degraded in January.

	Treaty of Shimonosheki signed in April between China and Japan.
	The United States interfered in the Venezuela boundary dispute between Great Britain and Venezuela.
	Dr. Jameson's raid on the Transvaal on 30 December.
1896	Madagascar annexed to France.
	Battle of Adowa in which Italy was defeated by Abyssinia.
1897	Tirpitz put incharge of German Navy.
	Greece declared war against Turkey to help the Cretans.
1898-1905	Delcasse an Foreign Minister of France.
1896	The first law concerning German Navy passed.
	The Fashoda incident and possibility of war between Britain and France.
	War broke out between Spain and the United States on 21 April.
	Treaty of Paris between the United States and .Spain by which the Philippines were given to the United States by Spain.
	The Sandwich Islands annexed to the United States in July and in 1909 they were made a part of the territory of Hawaii.
1899-1901	The Boer War.
1899	First Peace Conference at The Hague.
	Cecil Rhodes visited Berlin.
	Second visit of the German Emperor William II to Turkey.
1900-1909	Chancellor Bulow.
1900	The second law concerning German Navy passed.
	Russia and France proposed intervention in the Boer war but Germany refused.
1901	German proposal in March that if Germany guaranteed British Empire, Britain should join Triple Alliance and also bring Japan with her.
	Law of Associations passed by which no religious order was to exist in France without permission of Government.
	An Italian squadron visited Toulon.
1902	Italy gave an assurance to France that she would not fight against her although she was a member of Triple Alliance.
	The Anglo-Japanese alliance signed on 30 January.
1903	Revolution in Serbia and a dynasty inimical to Austria came to power in Serbia.
	Germany and England co-operated in the blockade of Venezuela.
1904	The Entente Cordiale.
	All teaching by religious orders to be stopped within 10 years in France.
	President Loubet of France visited Rome.
	A treaty signed between France and Spain on 6 October by which Spain acknowledged predominant interest of France in Morocco.
	Decasse sent a mission in December to Morocco.
1904-5	The Russo-Japanese War in which Russia was defeated.
1904	Plehve assassinated.
1905	Union between Sweden and Norway made in 1815 was dissolved.
	An Act of 9 December abrogated Concordat of 1801 in France.
	Bjorko Pact signed by William II and Nicholas II.
	First Morocco crisis.
	Treaty of Portamouth signed in September between Russia and Japan.
	Bloody Sundary on 22 January in Russia.
	Sir Edward Grey became Foreign Minister of England on December and continued as such up to 1916.

1906	The Algeciras Conference on Morocco.
	Dreyfus tried for the third time and declared innocent.
	Italy voted with England and France and against Germany and Austria-Hungary at the Algeciras Conference.
	The first Duma of Russia.
	Staff Talks between Britain and France in January.
1907	Law passed in January by which privileges granted to Roman Catholic Church in 1905 were withdrawn in France.
	The Second Duma of Russia.
	The Anglo-Russian Convention signed on 31st August.
1907-14	The third Duma.
1908	Young Turk Revolution in Turkey.
	Casablanca case or second Morocco crisis.
	The Bosnian Crisis.
	Austria annexed Bosnia and Herzegovina on 7 October.
1909-17	Chancellor Bethmann-Hollweg.
1909	Franco-German agreement signed in February.
	Czar Nicholas II paid a visit to Italy.
	Union of South Africa was created.
1911	The Panther, the German Gunboat, entered Harbour of Agadir on 1 July.
	Sir Edward Grey, Foreign Minister of England, warned Germany about the consequences of the Panther.
	Lloyd George, Chancellor of the Exchequer, made a declaration on 21 July in his famous "Mansion House" speech in which he pledged British support to France against Germany on the question of Morocco.
	Italy attacked Turkey and was able to get in 1912 Tripoli and Cyrenaica which were given the name of Libya.
1911-12	The Italo-Turkish War.
1912	The Chinese Revolution.
	Haldane Mission to Berlin failed.
	Montenegro, Serbia, Bulgaria and Greece declared war against Turkey in October. First Balkan War.
1913	The Panama Canal completed by the United States.
	Greece got the Island of Crete.
	Treaty of London ending the first Balkan war signed on 30 May. The second Balkan War.
	Treaty of Bucharist ending second Balkan War signed on 10 August.
1914	Construction of the Panama Canal by the United States completed.
	The Serbians murdered Archduke Francis Ferdinand of Austria Hungary at Serajevo, capital of Bosnia, on 28 June.
	Austria-Hungary declared war against Serbia on 28 July 1914.
	Russia ordered general mobilisation on 23 July.
	Great Britain declared war.
1914-18	The First World War.
1915	Treaty of London by which Italy agreed to declare war against the Central Powers.
	Italy declared war against Austria-Hungary on 23 May.
1916	Italy declared war against Germany on 27 August.
1917	The Russian Revolution.
	Union made between Russia and Finland dissolved.

	Japan entered into an agreement with the United States by which the latter accepted the special claims of Japan in China.
1918	William II of Germany abdicated and signing of the Armistice on 11 November.
1919	Treaty of Versailles signed on 28 June.
	Treaty of Trianon between Hungary and the Allies on 4 June.
1920	Treaty of Sevres signed on 10 August.
	France entered into a military alliance with Belgium.
1921	The Washington Conference.
	France entered into an alliance with Poland.
1922	Mussolini came to power in Italy.
1923	The French troops occupied the Ruhr Valley.
	Treaty of Lausanne between Turkey and the Allies signed on 9 July.
1925	Locarno Pact or Treaties signed in October.
1927	The Kellogg-Briand Pact to outlaw war signed.
1931	Conquest of Manchuria by Japan.
1933	Hitler appointed Chancellor of Germany in January.
	The Four-Power Pact between Germany, Great Britain, Italy & France.
1934	The Soviet Union became a member of League of Nations. Hitler elected President of Germany.
1935	France entered into an alliance with Russia.
1936	The Rhineland occupied by Germany in March.
	Conquest of Abyssinia by Italy.
	The Anti-Comintern Pact signed between Germany and Japan. The Anglo-Egyptian Treaty signed but it was repudiated in October 1951 by Egypt.
1937	Italy joined the Anti-Comintern Pact and thus the Berlin-Rome-Tokyo Axis came into existence.
	War started again by Japan against China in July.
1938	Hitler annexed Austria.
	The Munich Pact.
1939	Ribbentrop and Ciano signed on 22 May 10-year Alliance in Berlin between Germany and Italy.
	The German armies marched into Poland in September.
	France declared war against Germany in September.
	The Soviet Union attacked Finland in November.
1940	German troops occupied Denmark in April.
	Germany occupied Holland and Belgium in May.
	France surrendered in June to Germany.
	The Soviet Union occupied in June the States of Lithuania, Latvia and Estonia.
1941	Germany attacked the Soviet Union in June.
	The Soviet Union came to an understanding with Britain.
	President Roosevelt sent greetings to the Soviet Union in November.
	Japan attacked the Pearl Harbour in December.
1943	Roosevelt, Churchill and their military staffs met at Casablanca in North Africa in January.
	Roosevelt, Churchill and Chiang Kai-shek met at Cairo in November to plan the defeat of Japan.
	The Tehran Conference attended by Roosevelt, Churchill and Stalin.
1944	The United Nations forces landed in Normandy in France in June.
1945	Hitler committed suicide in April.
	Germany made unconditional surrender in May.

Charter of the United Nations signed in June at San Francisco.
Roosevelt, Churchill and Stalin met at Yalta in Crimea in February.
Berlin or Potsdam Conference held from 17 July to 2 August and attended by Stalin, President Truman and Prime Minister Attlee.

1947 Five treaties signed in Paris on 10 February by representatives of Italy, Bulgaria, Hungary, Rumania and Finland with the Allied States.
Truman Doctrine announced in March.
The American Congress authorised aid to Greece and Turkey in May.
Marshall Plan enunciated.
The Inter-American Treaty of Reciprocal Assistance signed at Rio for maintenance of continental peace and security.

1948 The Russians cut off in June communications by land and water between Western Zones of Germany and Berlin and this blockade continued for 10 months.
The Brussels Treaty.
The Jewish State of Israel proclaimed at Tel-Aviv on 15 May.

1949 The North Atlantic. Treaty Organisation signed in Washington on 4 April by the United States, Canada, Belgium, Denmark, France, Iceland, Italy, Luxembourg, the Netherlands, Norway, Portugal and the United Kingdom.
Chiang Kai-shek driven out from the Chinese mainland in October and he took shelter in Formosa or Taiwan.
Indonesia became independent under Soekarno.

1950 The Korean War started in June.

1951 Peace treaty signed with Japan in September.
A separate treaty signed between the United States and Japan, Anzus Pact entered into between Australia, New Zealand and the United States.

1952 The Western States entered into an agreement with Western Germany by which she was given virtual autonomy in foreign and diplomatic affairs.
Greece and Turkey became members of the NATO in February.
A treaty signed at Paris on 27 May to establish the European Defence Community.

1954 The Western European Union set up in October.
The United States, Great Britain, France, Australia, New Zealand, Pakistan, Thailand and the Philippines signed a treaty known as the SEATO or Treaty of Collective Defence of South-East Asia at Manila on 8 September.
Prime Ministers of Iraq and Turkey entered into a Pact on 24 February known as the Baghdad Pact which was later on changed into the Central Treaty Organisation or CENTO.

1955 Peace Treaty with Austria on 5 May.
West Germany became a member of the NATO.
Treaty of Friendship, Co-operation, Mutual Assistance known as the Warsaw Pact signed in May at Warsaw between the Soviet Union, Poland, East Germany, Czechoslovakia, Hungary, Bulgaria, Rumania and Albania.
The Bandung Conference held.

1956 Revolt in Hungary.

1960 U-2 Incident on 1 May.
The Congo got independence.

1962 The Cuban Crisis in October.
Communist China attacked India in October.

1963 Three-Power Partial Nuclear Test-Ban Treaty signed on 5 August in Moscow.
Malaysia came into existence as an independent State on 16 September.

1965	China gave an ultimatum to India on the occasion of the war between India and Pakistan.
	Singapore left Malaysia and became independent.
	The White Minority in Southern Rhodesia declared itself independent unilaterally.
1967	Israel attacked the United Arab Republic on 4 June.
1968	Soviet intervention in Czechoslovakia.
	The Nuclear Non-Proliferation Treaty signed in June.
1970	Southern Rhodesia declared herself a Republic.
1971	Treaty of Peace, Friendship and Co-operation signed on 9 August between India and the Soviet Union.
	Pakistan attacked India in December.
1972	The Simla Summit held from 28 June to 2 July 1972.
	President Nixon went to Peking in February.
	President Nixon went to Moscow in May.
	The Strategic Arms Limitation Treaty signed on 26 May 1972 between the United States and Russia.
	Great Britain joined the European Economic Community in January.
1973	Brezhnev went to Washington in June to establish cordial relations with the United States.
	War between Egypt and Israel.
1974	Vladivostok summit in November between President Ford and Brezhnev.
1975	South Vietnam conquered by North Vietnam in April.
	Cambodia surrendered to the Khmer Rouge in April.
	Summit Conference on Security and Cooperation in Europe opened at Helsinki on 30 July and concluded on 1 August.
	Portugal withdrew from Angola on 11 November.
1976	Death of Chou En-lai in February.
	Death of Mao Tse-tung on 9 September.
1977	General Zia overthrew Bhutto in July.
1978	Pact of Friendship signed between China and Japan in August.
	Camp David Accord signed on 17 September between Egypt and Israel.
1979	Diplomatic relations established on ambassarodial level between the United States and China on 1 January.
	Shah of Iran left Iran in January.
	Ayatollah Khomeini come back to Iran on 1 February.
	China attacked Vietnam in February.
	Treaty between Egypt and Israel signed on 26 March.
	Bhutto executed in April.
	Iran declared an Islamic Republic.
	Soviet troops landed at Kabul on 25 December.
1980	Zimbabwe declared independent in April.
	Olympic games opened in Moscow on 19 July.
	Iraq attacked Iran on 21-22 September.
	Ronald Reagan elected President of the United States in November.
1981	Reagan took over as President on 20 January.
	Release of American hostages in Iran on 20 January.
	President Zia-ur-Rehman of Bangladesh assassinated on 30 May.
	President Sadat of Egypt assassinated on 6 October.
1982	Special session of United Nations on Disarmament held in New York.
	Israel attacked Lebanon in June.

1983	35-Nation Conference on Security and Cooperation met at Madrid. Non-Aligned Conference held in New Delhi. Martial law lifted in Poland.
1984	President Reagan visited China. Prime Minister P.W. Botha of South Africa became President in September. Assassination of Mrs. Indira Gandhi on 31 October. 20th Summit of Organisation of African Unity held in Adis Ababa in November.
1985	President Reagan re-elected. Prime Minister of New Zealand refused entry of American Destroyer with nuclear arms. Summit meeting of seven richest countries of the world held in Bonn in May. The United States and China signed a nuclear pact on 23 July.
1985	Two-day summit at Geneva on 19 and 20 November, between Reagan and Gorbachev on nuclear disarmament.
1986	Two-day summit at Reykjavik on 12 and 13 October between Reagan and Gorbacheov on nuclear disarmament.
1987	On 8 December, Intermediate Range Nuclear Forces Treaty signed between the Soviet Union and the United States.
1988	On 14 April, Pakistan and Afghanistan signed a U.S. and Soviet Union guaranteed Accord at Geneva by which the Soviet Union agreed to pull out all Soviet troops from Afghanistan.
1988	In August, South Africa, Angola and Cuba announced a cease-fire. In the same month, the war between Iran and Iraq ended.

INDEX

A

B

J

K

L

M

N

O

P

Q

R

S

T

U

V

W

Y

Z